TOY CAR
COLLECTOR'S GUIDE

IDENTIFICATION AND VALUES FOR
- DIECAST
- WHITE METAL
- OTHER AUTOMOTIVE TOYS & MODELS

DANA JOHNSON

BMT 216A

COLLECTOR BOOKS
A Division of Schroeder Publishing Co., Inc.

On the front cover:
Majorette AC Cobra, 1:24 scale, $15.00 –20.00.
Corgi Bedford Pantechnicon, $35.00 –40.00.
Hot Wheels Talbot Lago Darracq, $8.00 –10.00.

On the back cover:
Maisto 1:18 scale Volkswagen, $35.00 – 40.00.
Matchbox Corvette T-top by White Rose, $5.00 – 10.00.
Rhino Mini-Cooper with pullback action, $3.00 – 5.00.

Cover design: Terri Hunter
Book design: Karen Smith

Collector Books
P.O. Box 3009
Paducah, Kentucky 42002-3009

www.collectorbooks.com

Copyright © 2002 by Dana Johnson

The current values of this book should be used only as a guide. They are not intended to set prices, which can vary from one section of the country to another. Auction prices as well as dealer prices vary and are affected by condition as well as demand. Neither the author nor the publisher assumes any responsibility for any losses that might be incurred as a result of consulting this guide.

Searching for a Publisher?

We are always looking for people knowledgeable within their fields. If you feel that there is a real need for a book on your collectible subject and have a large comprehensive collection, contact Collector Books.

ABOUT THE AUTHOR

Mr. Dana Johnson was seven and living in Lansing, Michigan, when he first started collecting toy cars. That was in 1962. His first ones were Matchbox cars. When Hot Wheels blazed on the scene in 1968, he remained unimpressed. At the time, he thought the colors were unrealistic and the wheel wells were too big (...and they were missing their hoods!).

By the 1970s, he had put his toys aside to pursue other interests — girls. It wasn't until 1985, when he discovered a Hatfield's department store in Madras, Oregon, that stocked a large number of Majorette toys from France, that his interest was rekindled. He has amassed a large collection of many brands of toy cars since then, incorporating models, mostly diecast, from all over the world.

ACKKNOWLEDGMENTS

The list of people to whom I am indebted is growing constantly... and, thanks to the Internet, now it includes collectors from all over the world. Appreciation goes to all whose books, lists, letters, catalogs, and samples have contributed to the completeness of this book. Special thanks to Jeff Bray Jr.'s Diecast Miniatures for his list of 200+ brands of toys and models; to Toys for Collectors for their exquisite Auto Miniatures catalog; to Alger Podewil, Joe Altieri, Ron Gold, and Ivan Fedorkew for their information on Majorettes and other variations; to Bob Blum for his invaluable information on Tomicas; to Boyd Dunson and Alex Antonov for their information on Russian models. Thanks to Dario "Dino" Vidovic for filling in the gaps on Mikansue models. Thanks to Russell Alameda, Dr. Craig S. Campbell, Bill Cross, John Dean, Harvey Goranson, Tjeng-Bo Lie, Henri Mueller, Aaron Robinson, Jarek Skonieczny, Robert Speerbrecher, Larry Stitt, and Brian Willoughby for various contributions. Thanks to Ian Cousins of New Zealand, Staffan Kjellin and Crister Skoglund in Sweden, Wiebe Buising in Holland, Dr. Alexander V. Barmasov of St. Petersburg, Russia, and Werner Legrand in Belgium for filling in details on various lesser known brands. Thanks to Jeff Koch for his photos of models otherwise missing from this book, and to many others for providing price lists, variation lists, and mounds of other information used in this book. Special thanks to Claudia Valiquet for encouraging me to collaborate with Collector Books in the first place.

Thanks especially to Lisa Stroup, editor of Collector Books, and Bill Schroeder, publisher, for their continuing enthusiastic support of all my book projects, and to Sharon and Bob Huxford for their book *Schroeder's Collectible Toys*.

Appreciation also goes to Richard O'Brien and Elizabeth Stephan for information provided in *O'Brien's Collecting Toy Cars & Trucks* series of books, Markus R. Karalash for his contributions on the various brands of DeTomaso Pantera models, and Stephen Demosthenes who has provided the most comprehensive list of Porsche models I've ever seen, contributing greatly to models listed in this book.

BRAND NAMES

Over 800 brands and manufacturers of diecast, white metal and related automotive toys and models are listed below, all of which are represented in this book. While some 95 percent of those named below represent diecast toys and models, a few represent brands made of white metal, cast iron, aluminum, plastic, and other materials.

A-Line
Aardvark
A.B.C. Brianza
Abraham, L. D.
A. C. Williams
Academy Minicraft
ACB (also see Le Phoenix)
Accucast
Acme (also see Thomas Toys)
Action Performance
Action Products
ADJ
Advanced Products Company
Agat (also see Radon)
AGM
Agritec (also see Ros, Ross)
Aguti-toys
AHC (also see AutoPilen, Pilen)
Ahi
AHL (see American Highway Legends)
Albedo
Alezan
ALJ
All-American
All American Toy Company

Allied
All-Nu
Alloy Forms, Inc.
Alterscale
American Highway Legends (also see Hartoy)
American National
American Precision Models (APM)
Ampersand
AMR–Century (also see Andre-Marie Ruf)
AMT
Andre-Marie Ruf (also see AMR)
Anguplas Mini Cars
Anker
Anso (see Anson)
Anson
Antex
APM (see American Precision Models)
Aquli
A.R.
Arbur
Arcade
Archer
Argo

Armour (also see Detail Cars)
Arnold
Arnold, Bruce (see Bruce Arnold Models)
Arpra
ARS
Art Model
Asahi Model Pet
Ashton
Auburn Rubber Company
Aurora Cigar Box
Authenticast (see Comet–Authenticast)
AutoArt (also see Gateway Global)
Auto Buff
Autocraft (also see Hongwell)
Autohobby
Auto Pilen (also see AHC, Pilen)
Auto Replicas
Autoreplica
Aviva (also see Hasbro)
BAM (see Boutique Auto Moto, Bruce Auto Model)
Bandai (also see Dapper)
Bandi

Bandii
Bang
Banner
Banthrico (see also National Products)
Bapro
Barclay
Barlux
Basteltip
Bayshore Repli-Cars
BBR
Bburago (also see Martoy)
Beaut
Beckman Collection
Belgium Trucks
Benbros
Benson Brothers (see Benbros)
Best
Best-Box of Holland (also see Efsi/Holland-Oto)
Best Model of Italy
Best Toy Co., Ltd.
Best Toys of Kansas
Betal
Big River Models (also see Milestone Brüder Mini Models)

Bijou (see Modelauto)
Bing
Bison
Bitsi-Toys (see Lehigh Bitsi-Toys)
Blue Box
Boley (also see High Speed Smart Toys)
Bonux (also see Cle)
Boss
Bossat Dermov
Bourbon
Boutique Auto Moto (BAM)
Box Model (also see Art Model, Bang, Best)
Brand S
Bren L Toys
Breslin
Brianza (see A.B.C. Brianza)
Brimtoy Pocket Toys
Britains
British Motoring Classics
Brookfield Collectors Guild
Brooklins
Bruce Arnold Models (BAM)
Brüder Spielwaren
Brüder Mini
Brumm

Buby (also see Collector's Classics)
Buccaneer
Budgie (also see Morestone)
Bugattiana (see Modelauto)
Burago (see Bburago)
Busch/Praliné
Bush
Cam-Cast
Carette, Georges
Carlo Brianza (see A.B.C. Brianza)
Carmania
Carousel 1
Castle Art (also see Gaiety)
C. A. W. Novelty Company
C.B.Car
C.B.G. Mignot (see Mignot, C.B.G.)
CCC
C.D.
CDC (see Detail Cars)
Century (see AMR–Century)
Chad Valley
Champion
Champion Hardware Co.
Champs of the Road (also see Universal)
Charbens
Charmerz (also see Playart)
Chein
Cherryca Phenix (also see Taiseiya, Micro Pet)
Chico (see Tekno/Chico)
Chrono
Ciba
Cigar Box (see Aurora Cigar Box)
C.I.J.
Circle N Toys
City (See Vitesse)
CKO
Classic Construction Models
Classic Metal Works
Classy Chassies (see Mega-Movers)
Clau-Mar
Cle (also see Bonus)
Clover (also see New Clover)
CMA (also see Creative Masters)
CMC
Code 3 Collectibles
Cofalu
Cofradis
Collector Case
Collector's Classics (also see Buby)
Collector Mint
Collectoy
Comet – Authenticast
Comet Miniatures (also see Simba)
Con-Cor
Conquest
Conrad (also see Gescha)
COPy Cars
Cor-Cor
Corgi (also see Original Omnibus Co., Oriental Omnibus Co., Race Image, Husky, Detail Cars)
Cougar (see Solido)
Courtland
CPM
Craftoys
Cragstan (also see (Gamda Koor, Sabra)
Creative Master (also see Creative Masters)

Creative Masters (also see Creative Master)
Crescent Toys (also see D.C.M.T.)
Cristian
Crossway Models
Crown Premiums
C-Scale
Cursor
Custom Miniatures
Dale Model Company
Dale Jr./Dale Sr. Models (also see Revell)
Dalia (also see Tekno Solido)
Danbury Mint
Danhausen (also see Paul's Mode Art)
Dapper (also see Bandai)
Darda
David Deanstyne
Day, John (see John Day Models)
Days Gone (see Lledo)
D.C.M.T. (also see Cresent Toys, Impy, Lincoln, Lone Star, River, and Roadmaster)
DDR
Deanstyne, David (see David Deanstyne)
Dehanes
Deles
Del Prado
Dent Hardware Company
Deoma Micromodels of Italy
Design Studio (see Motor City USA)
Desormeaux
Detail Cars (also see Corgi, Armour)
DG
DG Productions
Diamond
Diapet
Dicascale
Dimension 4 (also see Hot Pursuit)
Dimestore Dreams
Dinkum
Dinky
DMP Studios
Doepke
Doorkey
Dragon Wings
Druge Brothers
Dugu
Duravit
Durham Classics
Dust & Glory (see Great American Dreamcar)
Duvi
Dux
Dyna-Mo
Dyna-Model (see Dyna-Mo)
Dynamic
Eagle Collectibles
Eagle's Race (see Eagle Collectibles)
Ebbro
Edil
Edocar (also see Zee Toys/Zylmex)
EFE (see Exclusive First Editions)
Efsi/Holland-Oto (also see Best-Box)
E.G.M.
EiDAI (also see Grip Zechin)
E J Enterprises
Eko

Elegance
Eligor
Elysee
Emek
Empire (see Zaugg)
Enchanted (see Enchantment Land Coach Builders)
Enchantment Land Coach Builders
Enco
Enstone Emergency Models
EPI Sports Collectibles
Epoch (also see MTech)
Equipe Gallois
Eria
Erie
Ertl
Esci (see C.B. Car)
Escuderia Pilen (see Auto Pilen)
Esdo
Eska
Espewe
Estetyka
Evrat 87 – LP Creations
Excel
Excite (also see Magic)
Exclusive First Editions (EFC)
Exem
Exemples
Exoto (also see Progetto K)
F & F
Faie
Fairfield Mint
Faller
Faracars
Fastwheel (see Yat Ming)
Feeling43
Feil
Fidart
Fimcar
Fine Art Models
Fine Model
Finoko
First Choice
First Gear
Fisher-Price
Fletcher, Barnhardt & White
Fly
Forma
43rd Avenue/Gems 'N' Cobwebs
Fournier Enterprises
Framberg, H. L. (also see Dale Model Company)
France Jouets
Franklin Mint
Freeway Flyers (see Playart)
Freewheels
Frobly
Fun Ho! (also see Streamlux)
Funmate
Funrise (see Code 3 Collectibles)
FYP
Gabriel
Gad (see Great American Dreamcar)
Gaffe
Gaia
Gaiety (also see Castle Art)
Galgo
Galoob (see Micro Machines)
Gama
Gamda Koor (also see Crescent, D.C.M.T., limpy, Lone Star, Cragstan, Sabra)
Gasqui (or Gasquy)
Gate (also see Gateway Global)

Gateway Global (also see AutoArt Gate)
Gaz (see Volga)
Gearbox
Gege
Gemini Jets
Gems 'N Cobwebs
Generic
Georges Carette (see Carette, Georges)
Gescha (also see Conrad)
Gingell
Giodi
Gloor
Golden Classics (see Golden Wheel)
Golden Wheel (also see Ja-Ru)
Goldvarg
Gonio
Goodee
Govorski (also see Russian Models)
Gran Toros (also see Hot Wheels, Mebetoys, Johnny Lightning)
Grand Prix
Great American Dreamcar
Grip Zechin (also see EiDAI)
GTS (see Le Mans Miniatures)
Guiloy
Guisval
Gulliver
H. L. Framberg (see Framberg, H. L.)
Hallmark (also see Kiddie Car Classics)
Hartoy (also see American Highway Legends, Precision Engineered Models)
Hasbro (also see Aviva, Kenner, Playskool)
Hasegawa
Herpa
Hess
High Speed
Highway Travelers
Holland-Oto (see Efsi)
Hongwell (see Autocraft)
Horsman
Hot Pursuit (also see Dimension 4)
Hot Wheels
HP Toys
Hubley
Husky (also see Corgi)
Icibi
Igra
IHC (see International Hobby Corp.)
Ilario
Imperial Diecast
Impy (also see Crescent, D.C.M.T., Lone Star)
Imra (or IMRA)
Integral
Intercar (see Nacoral)
International Hobby Corp. (IHC)
Intex (see Zee Toys/Zylmex)
Irwin
Ites
J43 Kawabatakikaku (see Kawabatakikaku)
Jaco
Jane Francis Toys
Ja-Ru (also see Golden Wheel)
Je Toys
Jemini
JEP (see Jouets de Paris)

Jet/Jet Wheels
JNG
Joal
John Day Models (also see Precision Autos)
John Smith (see Smith Family Toys)
Johnny Lightning (also see Topper Toys)
Jolly Roger
Jouef
Jouets de Paris (JEP)
Joustra
JPS
JRD
JRI (see Road Champs)
JRL Collectibles
JTE
Juguinsa
Jupiter
Jurgens
K&M
K&O
K&R
K-Line
Kaden
Kado
Kansas Toy & Novelty Company
Kawabatakikaku (or J43 Kawabatakikaka)
Kawada
Kazan
Kemlows
Kenna
Kenner
Kenton
Kibri
Kidco
Kiddie Car Classics
Kiddietoy (see Hubley)
Kiko (Corgi)
Kilgore
Kim Classics
King K (also see Xonex)
King of the Road (see Horsman)
Kingsbury
King Star
Kinsmart (see Kintoy)
Kintoy
Kirby
Kirk
Kookaburra
Kyosho
Lacquer & Leather (Lack & Ledder)
Lada
Lansdowne (see Brooklins)
Lansing Slik-Toys
L D Abraham (see Abraham, L. D.)
L'Eau Rouge
Lee Toys
Le Jouet Mecanique
Legends of Racing, Inc.
Lehigh Bitsi-Toys
Leksakshust
Le Mans Miniatures
Lemeco
Le Phoenix
Lesney (see Matchbox)
Les Rouliers
Les Routiers
Liberty Classics (also see SpecCast)
Lincoln (see Lincoln Industries, Lincoln International, Lincoln Toys, Lincoln White Metal)
Lincoln Industries
Lincoln International

Lincoln Toys
Lincoln White Metal Works
Lindberg
Line Mar
Lintoy
Lion Car (see Lion Toys)
Lion Toys
Lion Models
Lionel
Lit'l Toy (Mercury Industries U.S.A.)
Litan
Lixin
LJN (also see Hallmark)
Lledo
Loden Aquli
Lomo
Londontoy
Lone Star (also see Crescent, D.C.M.T., Impy, Roadmaster)
LP Creations (also see Evrat 87)
Lucky Plan (see Dimension 4)
Luso
M C Toys (see Maisto)
Ma Collection
Madison
Madmax (see Grip Zechin)
MAFMA
Magic (also see Excite)
Magnason Models
Maisto
Majorette
Mandarin
Mangalick
Manoil
Mark One Collectibles (see Dimension 4)
Märklin
Marque
Mars, Inc.
Marsh
Martino Models
Martoys (also see Bburago)
Marusan
Marushin
Marx
Mascot
Master Models
Masterpieces in Miniature
Master Toys (see Maisto)
Masudaya
Matchbox
Mattel (also see Hot Wheels, Matchbox, Fisher-Price, Tyco, Sesame Street)
Max Models (see Paul's Model Art)
Maxwell Mini Auto Toys (Matchbox of India)
May Cheong (see Maisto)
May Tat (also see Maisto)
McGregor (also see Politoys)
Mebetoys
Meboto (see Maisto)
Meccano (see Dinky)
MegaMovers
Megatoys (see MegaMovers)
Mego
Mercury
Mercury Industries USA (see Lit'l Toy)
Message Models (also see Fun Ho!)
Metalcar
Metal Cast Products Company
Metal Masters
Metal Miniatures
Metosul
Mettoy (also see Corgi)

Miber
Micro Machines
Micro Models
Micromodels (see Deoma)
Micro Pet (also see Taiseiya, Cherryca Phenix)
Microtoys (see Deoma)
Midgetoy
Midget Toys
Midwestern Home Products, Inc.
Mignon
Mignot, C.B.G.
Mikansue
Milano
Milestone Miniatures
Milestone Models (also see Big River Models)
Milton
Minialuxe
Miniature Auto Emporium
Miniature Pet
Miniature Vehicle Castings Inc. (MVC)
Miniautotoys (see Dugu)
Minic (see Tri-Ang)
Minichamps (see Paul's Model Art)
Minicraft (see Academy Minicraft)
Minimac
Mini Marque 43
Mini Metals (see Simba and Comet Miniatures)
Mini Power (see Shinsei)
Mini Racing
Miniroute
Mira
Mitrecraft
MK Models
Moboto (or Meboto)
Modelauto/Sun Moto Company, Bugattiana, Rapide, Bijou
ModelCast
Model Pet (see Asahi)
Model Planning Co. Ltd. (also see Toyo Kogyo)
Model Power
Model Products Corporation (MPC)
Model Toys (see Doepke)
Models of Yesteryear (see Matchbox)
Moko (also see Matchbox)
Montego
Moose Mountain Toymakers, Ltd.
Morestone (also see Budgie)
Moskovich
Motor City Classics
Motor City USA (also see USA Models)
Motomax (see Redbox)
Mountain Service International (see Pole Position Collectibles)
MPC (see Model Products Corporation)
MR
MRE
MTC
MTech
Muky (also see Hot Wheels)
MVC (see Miniature Vehicle Castings)
Nacoral Intercars
National Products (also see Banthrico)
National Toys

Nevco
Nevins International, Ltd.
New Clover (also see Clover)
New-Ray
New Trax (see Top Gear Trax)
Nicky Toys (also see Dinky)
Nigam
N.J. International
Norev
Norscot
Nostalgic
Novacar
NSG Marketing Corp. (also see Traffic Stoppers, Summer)
Nutmeg Collectibles
NuToyz
NZG
Oddzon
Off 43
OGDI Toys of Yesterday
Old Cars
Omega
Onyx (see Vitesse)
Oriental Omnibus Company (also see Corgi)
Original Omnibus Company (also see Corgi)
Oto
Oxford Die-Cast Limited
Papillon Toys
Paradise Garage
Paragon Models & Art
Parker White Metal (see Erie)
Past-Time Hobbies (see PTH Models)
Pathfinder Models
Paul's Model Art/Minichamps
Paya
Peachstate Muscle Car™ Collectors Club
PEM (see Precision Engineered Models)
Penjoy
Penny (also see Politoys / Polistil)
Pepe
Piccolino
Piccolo (see Schuco)
Pilen (also see AHC, Auto Pilen)
Pioneer
Piranha
Plan 43X
Platypus
Playart
Playing Mantis (see Johnny Lightnings)
Play Power
Playskool
Playtoy
Playtrucks
PM
Pocher
Poclain
Pocketcars (see Tomica)
Pocketoys (see Brimtoy Pocketoys)
Pole Position Collectibles
Polistil (see Politoys)
Politoys/Polistil (also see Penny)
Poll
PP Models
Praliné (see Busch/Praliné)
Prämeta
Precision Autos (also see John Day Models)
Precision Engineered Models (also see Hartoy)

Precision Miniatures
Pride Lines (also see Manoil)
Process
Profil 24
Progetto K (also see Exoto, Inc.)
Protar
Provénce Moulâge
PTH Models
Qualitoys (see Benbros)
Quarter Mile (see Great American Dreamcar)
Quartzo (also see Vitesse)
Quiralu
R&M
R. W. (see Ziss)
Race Image Collectibles (see Corgi, Dimension 4)
Raceway Replicars
Racing Champions
Racing Collectables Club of America, Inc. (RCCA)
Racing Collectables, Inc. (RCI) (see Action Performance)
Radar
Radon (also see Agat)
R.A.E.
Raf
Ralstoy
Rami
Rapide (see Modelauto)
Rapitoy
Ra-Ro
Rasant
RCCA (see Racing Collectables Club of America, Inc.)
RCI (see Action Performance)
Reader's Digest
Real Cars (see Esci)
Real Wheels (see Ja-Ru)
Realistic
Realtoy
Record
Redbox (also see Zee Toys/Zylmex)
Reen Replica
Rei
Remco
Renaissance
Renwal
Replex
Repli-Cars (see Bayshore Repli-Cars)
Replicars
Replicast
Reuhl Products, Inc.
Revell
Revival
Rex/Rextoys
RHI
Rhino
Richmond
Rio
Rivarossi
River Series
Road Legends (see Yat Ming)
Road Machine
Roadmaster (also see D.C.M.T., Impy, Lone Star)
Roadmates
Road Rovers (see Hallmark, LJN)
Road Runners (see MegaMovers)
Road Tough (see Yat Ming)
Robeddie (see Brooklins)
Roberts
Roco
Rolux

ROS (also see Agritec, Ross)
Ross (also see Agritec, ROS)
Rosso
Rozkvet Mini Models
RS Toys
Ruehl (see Reuhl)
Ruestes
Rullero
Russ
Russian models (also see Agat, Lada, Litan, Lomo, Moskovich, Radon, Saratov, Vaz, Volga)
RW (see Ziss)
Sablon
Sabra (also see Cragstan, Gamda Koor)
Safar
Safir
St. Louis
Saico
Sako
Sakura
Salza
Sam Toys
Saratov
Savoye Pewter Toy Company
Scale Models (also see Ertl, Scamold)
Scaleworks
Scamold
Schabak
Schuco (also see Spiel-Nutz)
Schwung
Schylling
SCM
Scorchers (Hot Wheels)
Scottoys
Septoy
Sesame Street (see Fisher-Price)
Shackleton
Shinsei
Sibur
Sieperwerke (see Siku)
Siku
Silhouette
Silver Pet
Simba
Singfund
Sizzlers
Sky
Skyline
Slik-Toys (see Lansing Slik-Toys)
SM
Small Wheels (also see Western Models)
Smart Toys
Smer
Smith Family Toys
Smith-Miller
SMTS (Scale Model Technical Services)
Solido
Somerville
South Eastern Finecast
Spa Croft Models
Spec-Cast
Specialty Diecast (see Race Image, Dimension 4)
Speed Wheels
Speedway Collection (also see Dimension 4)
Speedy Power (also see Toymark)
Speedy Racer (see Speedy Power, Toymark)
Spiel-Nutz
Spot-On (also see Tri-Ang, Minic)

Stahlberg (or Stallberg)
Starter
Streamlux
Strombecker (see Tootsietoys)
Stylish Cars
Summer
Sun Motor Company (see Modelauto)
Sun Star
Sunnyside (also see Superior)
Sunshine Toys
Super Champion (see Champion)
Supercar Collectibles
Superior (also see Sunnyside)
SVP
Swan Hill
Tai Cheong Toys
Taiseiya (also see Micro Pet, Cherryca Phenix)
Takara
Tak-A-Toy (also see Welly)
Tamiya
Tbilisi
TD
Team Caliber
Techno Giodi (see Giodi)
Tekno/Chico (also see Dalia)

Tenariv
TfC (see Toys for Collectors)
Thomas Toys
Timpo Toys
Tin Wizard (also see Skyline, Zaugg)
Tins Toys (also see Simba)
Tintoys
Tip Top Toy Co.
Togi
Tomica
Tomy (also see Tomica)
Tonka
Tonkin
Tootsietoys
Top Gear Trax
Top Marques
Top Model Collection
Topper Toys (also see Johnny Lightnings)
Toy Collector Club of America (see First Gear)
Toymark (also see Speedy Power)
Toyo Kogyo (also see Model Planning Co. Ltd.)
Toys for Collectors

Toys of Yesterday (see OGDI Toys of Yesterday)
Traffic Stoppers
Trax (see Top Gear)
Tri-Ang
Trident
Troféu
Tron
True Dimensions
Tru-Scale
Tucker Box (also see Lincoln)
Tuff Ones (see Remco)
Turtle Creek Scale Models, Inc.
Tyco (see Matchbox, Mattel, Fisher-Price)
Tyco Preschool (see Fisher-Price)
Uaz
Unique Industries, Inc.
Universal (also see Matchbox)
Universal Hobbies Ltd., Inc. (also see Eagle's Collectibles)
U.S.A. Models (also see Motor City U.S.A.)
U.S. Model Mint (also see SMTS)

UT
Vanguard (see Lledo)
Vanbo
Vanke (see Vanbo)
Vaz (see Lada)
Verem
VF-Modelautomobile Germany
Victoria (see Vitesse)
Victory Models
Viking
Vilmer
Vintage Casting
Vitesse (also see Quartzo)
Vivid Imaginations (Tyco Canada)
Voiturette (see SMTS)
Volga
Walker Model Service
Walldorf
Welly
Western Models (also see Small Wheels)
Wheeler
White Rose Collectibles
Wiking
Williams, A. C. (see A. C. Williams)

Winross
World Zechin (see Grip Zechin)
Xonex
Yat Ming
Yatming (see Yat Ming)
Yaxon (also see Forma, Giodi)
Yidalux
Yoder
Yonezawa (see Diapet)
Yorkshire
Yot
Zaugg (also see Tin Wizard)
Zax
Zebra Toys (see Benbros)
Zee Toys/Zylmax (also see Redbox)
Zil
Zinoki
Ziss
Zschopau
Zyll (see Zee Toys)
Zylmex (see Zee Toys)
Zowees (see Hot Wheels)

INTRODUCTION

The Purpose of this Book

There are just a few books on the market that cover the most popular brands of diecast, white metal, and related automotive toys and scale models — Corgi, Dinky, Hot Wheels, Lledo, Matchbox, Solido, Tootsietoys. Many lesser known brands meanwhile have been essentially ignored — Bburago, Dugu, Joal, Maisto, Majorette, Oto, Pocher, Siku, Tomica, Yatming, Zylmex, just to name a few. The intent of this book therefore is to present the most comprehensive guide to toy cars ever published.

The main reasons for producing this book are to provide a comprehensive reference to the lesser known brands, encourage more people to collect toy and model cars, show collectors how affordable toy car collecting can be as a hobby, demonstrate the value of collecting new models well as old ones, showcase current and obsolete models, and demonstrate to collectors everywhere that they are not alone in their fascination for these diminutive cars and trucks.

Arrangement of this Book

This book is arranged alphabetically by brand name. Whenever applicable, manufacturer model numbers are included, along with description, scale, color, distinguishing marks, and value. The author has attempted to provide a brief profile of each brand represented when any background information is available.

Values

Regardless of the values indicated in this or any price guide, you can often purchase items for far below book value, and I encourage you to seek the lowest price for a particular acquisition. You will most often need to sell for far less than book value as well, especially when you intend to sell an entire collection. So what good are values if not for buying and selling? Stated book values establish a basis for personal evaluation of your collection, for insurance purposes, speculation, auctions and estate sales, and for your own future purchases, because ultimately you or another avid collector may agree to pay full book value for an item if it is considered desirable and worth the asking price. Consider the values indicated in this book to be only a guide, not a bible.

In order to establish a standard for grading diecast toys, the following is offered as a generally accepted grading system. Note the popular word "mint" has been replaced by the word "new," since it has been argued that "mint condition" indicates something in perfect, unflawed and untouched condition. "New condition," on the other hand, represents a fairer classification of toys that could show wear even within the sealed package, whether from friction with the package itself, or from flaws and defects overlooked at the factory. Condition is abbreviated "C" or "c" in most books, with a C10 being the best, and C1 being the worst. All grading systems are arbitrary and somewhat flexible, but

---

CONDITION RATING CHART

C10, 100% – New condition with original container

C9, 80–99% – New condition without container

C8, 60–79% – Near new condition, close inspection reveals minor wear

C7, 40–59% – Excellent condition, visible minor wear

C6, 20–39% – Very good condition, visible wear, all parts intact

C5, 10–19% – Good condition, excessive wear, paint chipped, or heavily worn

C4, 4–9% – Fair condition, parts broken or missing

C1-3, 2–3% – Poor condition, paint worn off, parts broken or missing

C0, .5–1% – Salvage for parts only

are relatively similar for grading most toys. In addition, some collectors base a part of the condition rating on the condition of the package. So here is a guide to help determine the condition of a particular model.

Rule #1: There is no such thing as "mint condition except for..." or "new condition except for...." It is either mint/new, or it isn't. When someone offers something with "a few paint chips, otherwise mint," it is not "otherwise mint," but considerably less than mint, and should be offered that way.

Brands and Models Represented

While this book attempts to represent every known brand and manufacturer of automotive toys and models, it is impossible to represent every model and variation ever produced by each manufacturer. A separate book could be written for each of the 800+ brands represented in this book. But the small market for such books would be understandably cost-prohibitive to the consumer as well as the publisher. So, as with most things in life, a compromise is reached by presenting a sampling of each brand of toys produced over nearly a century.

Of course, for every rule, there is an exception. Several brands, such as Tomica, Majorette, Siku, and others, represent a major force in the diecast toy collector market. Many requests have come to me for a book on Tomicas, Majorettes, and selected other brands. So, I have made a special effort to present these brands as comprehensively as possible.

The First Automotive Toys

The earliest commercially produced automotive toys were made of cast iron, tin plate, zinc alloy, or lead. Cast-iron models from A. C. Williams, Arcade, and Kenton are the best known. Tootsietoys were the first to offer diecast toys. Tin-plate toys were produced mostly in Germany at first, then later in Japan beginning in the 1950s.

Origin of Diecast Toys

The process of diecasting was first introduced to the world at the Columbian Exposition of 1893, when Charles Dowst observed a new machine known as the Line-O-Type. Mr. Dowst applied the process to the manufacture of various items, eventually producing the first diecast toys in 1910. These toys soon after became known as Tootsie Toys. (Later the name was changed to Tootsietoys.)

The Diecasting Process
(and a Short Spelling Lesson)

Diecasting is an injection mold process using a zinc alloy commonly known as "zamak," or less commonly "zamac" (96% zinc, 4% aluminum, trace magnesium) to produce accurately formed metal components. ("Mazak" is reportedly a similar alloy that contains slightly more magnesium.) The diecast

process itself is very inexpensive, but the dies must be made of a very hard metal and are therefore very expensive to produce. But once a die is produced, it can continue to be used for nearly a million castings before showing signs of fatigue. Even then, dies have often been sold to other companies to produce still more models. One example is that Eligor of France has used old Norev dies to produce some of their current models. Many other toy companies have also done this.

Some early metal cast toys used a lead alloy process known as "slushmold," but it was eventually replaced by comparatively non-toxic zamak. The manufacturing of a die for diecasting is very expensive, so production of large numbers of items from one die is necessary to offset the initial cost.

On the matter of spelling, "diecast" is most commonly two separate words without a hyphen. The *Software Toolworks Multimedia Encyclopedia* places a hyphen between the two words. While the diecast Car Collectors Club separates the two words as well, the Diecast Toy Collectors Association and this author chooses, for brevity and convenience, to merge the two words together to form a single word. In comparison, Asheville DieCast opts for a customized spelling as a company trademark. While all forms are acceptable, the combined form "diecast" is used in this book for standardization.

White Metal

White metal is a softer alloy with a lower melting temperature than zamak, and so can be cast using less expensive techniques. Brands such as Brooklin, Goldvarg, Western, and Durham are just a few examples of models produced using white metal.

The process generally used to produce white metal models includes a mold made of inexpensive vulcanized rubber rather than expensive hard metal dies. The result is that less models can be made before the mold wears out, but more variety is possible due to the inexpensive die. Such models are more expensive than diecast due to their low production numbers. If diecast models were made in such low quantities, the cost would increase dramatically.

Plastic, Resin, Cast Iron, and Other Materials

Although this book is devoted mostly to diecast toys, many plastic, resin, and cast-iron toys are included in this book due to their historical significance or because of their accuracy, scale, detail, or other distinguishing characteristics. Since plastic is now used in addition to metal alloys in most modern diecast toys, the result is a blurring of the line between diecast and non-diecast toys.

A few early toys were even made of flour-base paste. These toys are rare and valuable if found in mint or near-mint condition, because of the tendency for them to crumble or discolor with age and handling.

Safety Factor

Cast-iron toys, while popular at the turn of the century, are heavy and would occasionally become destructive weapons when wielded by a rambunctious child bent on rendering them airborne. Beyond that, shipping of cast-iron toys was, and still is, expensive due to their weight.

Later, the manufacture of lead alloy toys (pot metal or slush mold) in the twenties, thirties, and forties, especially toy soldiers, was eventually stopped when it was discovered that small children were suffering from lead poisoning from putting such things in their mouths.

Safety and lighter weight, therefore, have been major factors in the growth and popularity of diecast toys made of zamak, the name given to the zinc alloy that defines diecast toys.

Toys Versus Scale Model Miniatures

Many automotive toys demonstrate such precise detail that they can no longer be called toys, but qualify as precision scale models. References to precision models as toys is for simplicity and not for condescension. Whether a toy or a model, they are all represented in this book with apologies to collectors of the latter.

Scale:
O, HO, N, S & Z Gauge, and Other Scales

The purpose of all this scale talk is to acquaint you with the relative size of a model based on its scale, and to expose collectors to the many different sizes of models available on the market.

With the rising popularity of model railroads in the early part of the twentieth century, it was important to establish a standard track size so that various manufacturers could make model railroad cars that fit on each others tracks. O gauge was arbitrarily established as the standard, based on the odd ratio of 7 mm to the foot, with rails approximately 1¼" apart. This results in a scale of 1:43 (actually closer to 1:43.5). It seemed a convenient size at the time for most economically producing the electrical systems inside the locomotive that drove the whole system. Automobile models of 1:43 scale typically measure about 4 to 4½ inches long. Later, U.S. model makers rounded the 7 mm to a quarter inch to the foot, making it 1:48 scale.

Later, HO, or Half O, gauge, representing a ratio of 3.5 mm to the foot, was introduced with rails about ⅝ inches apart. HO translates to roughly 1:87 scale, allowing for a more elaborate layout in less space. Miniature automobiles of this scale are generally about 1½" long and many are made of plastic rather than diecast metal.

The more recent introduction of N gauge model railroads is due to the advance in technology that allowed smaller and smaller electric motors and mechanical parts to be produced, giving rise to what was, until recently, the smallest gauge railway system produced, with rails just 9 millimeters apart. This scale is so small that few, if any, diecast car models are made for this scale, opting instead for diminutive plastic models.

Even smaller than N gauge is Z gauge. The fact that electric motors and tracks can be manufactured to fit such a small scale is incredible on its own. Accompanying vehicles are obviously extremely small and almost invariably one piece plastic models, measuring barely a half-inch long.

Going in the other direction in relation to scale, L gauge has been established for what are referred to as lawn trains, a scale of about 1:24, which for a toy train is quite large.

In addition, double O, or OO, gauge was developed for smaller models of around 1:76 scale with Dinky Dublo models having set the precedent. Why the designation "double O" when size is closer to "HO" remains a mystery to this author, since double O gauge represents 4 mm to the foot.

While O scale (1:43) and HO scale (1:87) have been adopted for manufacturers of diecast model vehicles intended for model railroads, other scales were established for diecast models that were popular enough on their own. Siku of Germany established the popular 1:55 scale, in which most of their diecast toys are produced, and which many other manufacturers have adopted.

Manufacturers of heavy equipment miniatures meanwhile lean toward producing 1:50 scale models. Conrad and NZG in particular have concentrated on this scale, although they have produced a few models in other scales.

Another popular scale for miniatures is 1:64, and it is the scale to which Matchbox, Hot Wheels, and others are referred, even though their actual scale varies greatly from one model to the next. In fact, most current diecast miniature

cars of the 3 inch long variety hover around 1:55 to 1:60 scale, while trucks of the same length tend to fall closer to the 1:87 scale down to 1:100 or smaller scale. Ertl is one of few companies that produces a line of specifically 1:64 scale models, particularly farm tractors.

Becoming more popular recently are 1:24 and 1:18 scale models, with a few 1:12 scale models reaching the market as well. Very expensive models, such as Pochers, are even made to 1:8 scale, but their price begins at..$500 each for new models of such scale.

Racing Collectibles

Some collectors specialize in racing collectibles. Action Performance, Racing Champions, Quartzo, and Hasbro Kenner Winners Circle are primary examples of companies that specialize in producing diecast models specifically for these collectors, but it is hardly the only one. While an entire book could be written on racing diecast, this book will necessarily present just a survey.

Racing is a dangerous sport, and the potential for serious injury or death is an accepted risk for the drivers. The best known and best loved driver in auto racing history is NASCAR champion Dale Earnhardt. His death in February 2001 serves as a tragic reminder of how dangerous auto racing is. Regardless, NASCAR, the Winston Cup, the Indianapolis 500, and other world famous races will continue undaunted by his loss, but fans around the world will not soon forget how much Dale Earnhardt gave to the sport.

Livery

Livery, as it relates to toy cars, refers to the various product brands and company logos rep-

resented on various toys. Many diecast toys are produced specifically with licensed trademarks, logos, promotion, and advertising on them, such as Coca-Cola, Campbell's, Kodak, and so on. Livery is often the primary attraction for collectors, hence its significance.

Details, Details...

A process many manufacturers use in applying printing to diecast toys in particular is called "tampo" or "tempa." This has been the most common technique of applying logos, trim colors, and accents since the early seventies. Before that time, decals, labels, and hand painting were the main methods of applying detail to models. The tampo process is now the prevalent form of applying details, particularly on inexpensive toys. Occasionally, other types of detailing are mentioned in this book to illustrate a variation to the tampo version of a particular model.

A new process just introduced for 2000 is a heat-applied decal that allows for a more efficient and cost-effective application of colors, details, and gradients. The first to use them is Mattel on their Hot Wheels toys.

Customizing and Restoration

Much debate continues between purists — those people who feel that any altering, such as repainting or detailing, of production models renders a model worthless — and hobbyists — those who believe they can make a model better by customizing it. Depending on the original value and condition of a model and the degree of skill involved in making such alterations, a model can in fact be rendered worthless or more valuable. One man, Dan Coviello, a retired New York City policeman now living in North Carolina, makes a living customizing pro-

COMMON SCALES USED IN TOY AND MODEL MANUFACTURING

Scale	Equivalent	Comments
1:8	1½ inches or 38.1 mm to the foot	Used for the most expensive precision models such as Pocher
1:12	1 inch or 25.4 mm to the foot	The largest models available from Maisto, Ertl, Solido, et. al.
1:18	⅓ inch or 16.9 mm to the foot	The newest standard for precision diecast models
1:24	½ inch or 12.7 mm to the foot	L Gauge, the common scale for Franklin and Danbury Mints
1:32	⅜ inch or 9.53 mm to the foot	I Gauge
1:43	0.28 inch or 7 mm to the foot	O Gauge, actually closer to 1:43.5
1:48	¼ inch or 6.35 mm to the foot	Scale adopted by SpotOn (Tri-Ang)
1:50	0.24 inch or 6.1 mm to the foot	Common scale for construction models
1:55	0.22 inch or 5.5 mm to the foot	Most Siku toys are in this scale
1:64	0.19 inch or 4.75 mm to the foot	S Gauge, actually closer to 1:64.2
1:76	0.16 inch or 4 mm to the foot	Double O or OO Gauge, actually closer to 1:76.2
1:87	0.14 inch or 3.5 mm to the foot	Half O or HO Gauge, actually closer to 1:87.1
1:100	0.12 inch or 3.1 mm to the foot	
1:144	1⁄12 inch or 2.1 mm to the foot	
1:152	0.079 inch or 2 mm to the foot	Triple O or OOO Gauge, actually closer to 1:152.4
1:160	0.08 inch or 1.9 mm to the foot	N Gauge
1:220	0.06 inch or 1.4 mm to the foot	Z Gauge
1:250	0.04 inch or 0.3 mm to the foot	Larger scale for airplanes from Herpa, Schabak, and others
1:500	0.02 inch or 0.6 mm to the foot	Commonly used for airplane models from Herpa and Schabak

duction model police cars and others to suit whatever state, county, or municipality the buyer wishes to have represented.

Restoring toys is a different matter. Old, rare toys such as Dinkys or Tootsietoys are now being restored by skilled artisans to return at least some of their value in lieu of finding such models still in new condition. Resulting value is usually 50–60 percent of such a model in original unretouched mint condition.

Second Market

Retail chains such as K-Mart, Shopko, Target, Toys R Us, Wal-Mart, as well as specialty dealers such as EWA, Exoticar, Toys for Collectors, Toys Plus, Asheville DieCast, and others provide the primary sources for many currently available models.

But much of the collector market is supported by what is known as the "second market," consisting of individuals and dealers who buy selected models in smaller quantities, frequently from private individuals or auctions, but often new from retail stores. Because second market dealers sometimes purchase whole collections, they usually try to buy at well below book value. They then resell to individual collectors, whether through hobby shops, collectibles stores, swap meets, mail order price lists, classified ads in popular magazines, or on the Internet.

It is these second market sources that often drive the market of certain models far above current retail prices. Such tactics have received mixed receptions from diehard diecast collectors. Some accept the high price to fill the gaps in their collections. Others complain of artificially inflated price gouging from people out to make a fast buck. The debate continues.

Auctions are another driving factor in the growing value of diecast toys. Auctioneers such as Bill Bertoia, Lloyd Ralston, and Noel Barrett who specialize in toy auctions contribute greatly to establishing values for antique and collectible toys. Now Internet auction sites such as eBay provide a huge marketplace for items of every conceivable kind, which drives prices even higher on antiques and collectibles.

The Toy Car Collectors Association

Their are many collector clubs devoted to one brand or another of diecast toys, such as Corgi, Ertl, Hot Wheels, and Matchbox, but there is one club that represents a broader appeal, the Toy Car Collectors Association (TCCA). Benefits include 12 issues per year of *Toy Car Collector*, the official monthly magazine of the TCCA, discounts on books and toys, and a comprehensive website at www.toynutz.com. Through its monthly magazine, *Toy Car Collector*, members receive information on new models and old favorites representing many of the manufacturers listed in this book. TCCA membership rates are as indicated below:

1 year – $29.95 to USA, $34.95 to Canada, $39.95 international

2 years – $54.95 to USA, $64.95 to Canada, $74.95 international

3 years – $79.95 to USA, $94.95 to Canada, $109.95 international

To enroll, send check or money order (U.S. funds, please) payable to:

Dana Johnson Enterprises
P O Box 1824
Bend, OR 97709-1824 USA
e-mail: toynutz@earthlink.net
or online at www.toynutz.com/TCCA.html

TOY CARS A to Z

A-LINE

Most of A-Line's product line is devoted to freight cars, motors, and parts for HO gauge train sets. Their Fruehauf "Z" Van series features a miniature version of the prototype 40 foot Fruehauf "Z" Van commonly seen on piggyback trains and highways. These Fruehauf semi trailer kits are molded in aluminum and black styrene with separate tires, spoked wheel hubs, mud flaps, door bars, and other details. Each kit includes two undecorated trailers with complete instructions and a list of correct decals. Kits sell for $11–12.

AARDVARK

Aardvark of St. Paul, Minnesota, was at one time a small manufacturer of precision handcrafted models, of which only one model is known.
241B 1961 Maserati Type 61, 1:24 scale $330–350

A. B. C. BRIANZA
Mailing Address:
A.B.C. Brianza
C.P.40
21049 Tradate
VA Italy

Showroom:
via Mazzini 23
22070 Locate Varesino
CO Italy

According to Exoto Tifosi January–March 1995 catalog, "A Brianza is more than a model, it's a work of art, an investment. Each 1:14 scale replica is a limited and numbered edition, all hand formed and assembled using genuine Ferrari paint for the finish, leatherette and carpeting for the interior." Suggested retail for the 1:14 scale models is $2,450. A. B. Carlo Brianza is the founder of the company, hence the "ABC" commonly associated with the brand name.

It is not clear which ABC Brianza models are diecast and which are plastic or resin. Several brands are actually offered under the Brianza umbrella. Carlo Brianza models are 1:14 scale masterpieces limited to 1,000 pieces per model. ABC 1:14 scale models are high quality plastic (or resin) kits. Miniland represents 1:18 scale plastic (or resin) kits. ABC trucks are beautifully rendered models mostly of vintage racing transporters in 1:43 scale. The primary ABC line represents some of the world's most unusual cars replicated in 1:43 scale, some available as kits as well as pre-assembled models. Autostile is a sub-grouping of ABC offerings. ABC & AMC is another sub-grouping of ABC offerings.

Carlo Brianza 1:14 Scale
1974 Ferrari 246 GTB Dino	$1,600
1974 Ferrari 246 GTS Dino	$1,600
Ferrari Dino 246 Coupe	$1,600
Ferrari Dino 246 Spider	$1,600
1960 Ferrari 250 SWB	$1,600
1961 Ferrari 250 GT SWB	$1,600
1962 Ferrari 250 GT SWB California Spyder	$1,600
1963 Ferrari 250 GTO Le Mans	$1,600
1965 Ferrari 250 LM Le Mans	$1,900
Ferrari 250 Le Mans	$1,600
Ferrari 250 Spider California	$1,600
1965 Ferrari 275 GTB Short Nose	$1,600
1967 Ferrari 275 GTB4	$1,600
1967 Ferrari 275 GTB4 Spyder N.A.R.T.	$1,600
Ferrari 275 GTS/4 Spider N.A.R.T.	$1,600
Ferrari 275 GTB/4 Coupe	$1,600
1984 Ferrari 288 GTO	$1,850
1967 Ferrari 330 P4 "Monza"	$1,650
1974 Ferrari 365 GTB4 Daytona	$1,600
1974 Ferrari 365 GTB4 Daytona Spyder	$1,600
1980 Ferrari 365 GT4 BB	$1,650

1984 Ferrari 512 BB $1,650
Ferrari 365 GTB/4 Daytona Spider .$1,600
Ferrari 365 GTB/4 Daytona Coupe...$1,600
1967 Ferrari P4 Monza Bandini-
    Amon $1,600

ABC 1:14 Scale by Carlo Brianza
1972–4 Alfa Romeo GTA Junior
    v.1 Ore Jarama...................$250–400
    v.2 Monza $250–400
    v.3 Paul Ricard $250–400
1992 Alfa Romeo 155 GTA
    v.1 C.I.V.T. $250–400
    v.2 Nannini.........................$250–400
1989 Lancia Delta 16V $250–400
1991 Lancia Delta Integrale 16V GR.A
    1000 Laghi $250–400
1964 Ferrari 250 GT Lusso Tour De
    France $250–400
1964 Ferrari 250 GT Lusso
    Stradale $250–400

ABC 1:24 Scale by Carlo Brianza
Ferrari 340 Mexico, kit or
    built..................................$250–400

ABC 1:43 Scale by Carlo Brianza
1928 Alfa Romeo 1500 Campari Mille
    Miglia Winner, #13C $240
1993 Alfa Romeo 155 V6 T.I.D.T.M.
    v.1 Nannini.........................$250–300
    v.2 Larini Campione D.T.M. ..$250–300
    v.3 Danner $250–300
    v.4 Francia Team Schubel $250–300
Alfa Romeo 155 GTA
    v.1 C.I.V.T. '92 Nannini $250–300
    v.2 C.I.V.T. '92 Larini $250–300
1930 Alfa Romeo 1750 Mille
    Miglia-Nuvolari/Guidotti, top down,
    #16 ....$240
1931 Alfa Romeo 1750
    Castagna $250–300
1931 Alfa Romeo 1750 GTC Coupe
    Royal Touring $250–300
1931 Alfa Romeo 6C 1750 G.S. "Flying
    Star" Touring $250–300
1931 Alfa Romeo 6C 1750 G.T.C
    "Flying Star" Touring $250–300
1932 Alfa Romeo 6C 1750 GTC Guida
    Interna Semirigida..............$250–300
1934 Alfa Romeo 6C 2300 Pescara
    24H $250–300
1934 Alfa Romeo 6C 2300 Touring
    "Soffio Di Satana" $250–300
1940 Alfa Romeo 6C 2500
    Farina $250–300
1940 Alfa Romeo 6C 2500
    Touring $250–300
1947 Alfa Romeo 6C 2500 Michelotti
    Nino Farina $250–300
1952 Alfa Romeo 6C 2500 Giardiniera
    Viotti "Woody Wagon" $250–300
Alfa Romeo G.P. Tipo 308
    v.1 Indianapolis 1940 ....$250–300
    v.2 Pintacuda 1º Assoluto Rio De Janeiro
    1938..................................$250–300

v.3 500 Miglia Di Indianapolis Louis
    Durant $250–300
Alfa Romeo G.P. Tipo 158A
    v.1 G.P Livorno 1938.........$250–300
    v.2 Villoresi.......................$250–300
1948 Ferrari 166 All Mille Miglia Winner,
    #12 ....$240
1949 Ferrari 166 Mille Miglia, red,
    #14 ....$240
1963 ATS 2500 GT1958 Ferrari 250 GT
    Liliama Di Rethy $250–300
Ferrari 212 Export Giardinetta
    Vignale $250–300
Ferrari 212 Inter Cabriolet
    "Abbott" $250–300
1952 Ferrari 250 Carrera Panameri-
    cana $250–300
1952 Ferrari 250 Le Mans........$250–300
1952 Ferrari 250 S Mille
    Miglia................................$250–300
1958 Ferrari 250 GT Liliama Di
    Rethy.................................$250–300
1953 Ferrari 342 America........$250–300
1954 Ferrari 375 Mille Miglia....$250–300
1959 Ferrari 400 S.A. $250–300
Ferrari 410 Ghia......................$250–300
1969 Ferrari 275P Berlinetta
    Michelotti $250–300
Ferrari Vignale Shooting Brake
    CH.N.7963 ....$250–300
1953 Fiat 8V $250–300
1953 Fiat 8V Le Mans Lurani-
    Mahe $250–300
Fiat 8V Zagato........................$250–300
1953 Fiat 8V Zagato Spider Mille
    Miglia................................$250–300
1953 Fiat 8V Zagato Spider Capelli-
    Veronelli $250–300
1954 Fiat 8V Stradale $250–300
1995 Fiat Barchetta
    v.1 Arancio (orange?) $250–300
    v.2 Gialla (?) $250–300
    v.3 Rossa (red?) $250–300
    v.4 Azzurra (blue?) $250–300
Lancia Aprilia Aerodinamica $250–300
1993 Lancia Delta Present-
    azione $250–300
1938 Lancia Astura Cabriolet Pinin
    farina................................$250–300
Maserati Grand Prix Transporter..........$900
Maserati Grand Prix Transporter with 3
    Maserati 250 F cars.................$1,650
1927 Om Superba-Minoja/Morandi, Mille
    Miglia Winner, red #15 ....$240
1954 Pontiac Chieftain Custom Catalina,
    tan, #22 ....$300
Scuderia Ferrari Transporter.................$900
Scuderia Ferrari Transporter with 3 Ferrari
    801 F1 cars..........................$1,650
1936 Scuderia Ferrari Classic Trans-
    porter $300
1971 Scuderia Ferrari Transporter O.M. 107
    Rolfo...................................$700

Scuderia Lancia Support Van Carrera
    Panamericana......................$650
1951 Team Alfa Romeo Transporter.....$300

ABC & AMC 1:43 Scale by Carlo Brianza
Ferrari 348 TS
    v.1 Massimo Presicci $250–300
    v.2 Ivan Benaduce $250–300
Ferrari 348 TB
    v.1 Merzario $250–300
    v.2 Paolo Rossi $250–300
    v.3 Gianluca Giraudi $250–300
    v.4 Benussiglio Mario $250–300

ABC Autostile 1:43 Scale by Carlo Brianza
1926 Alfa Romeo RLSS C.P
    Avus $250–300
1941 Alfa Romeo 16C Proto-
    type....................................$250–300
Alfa Romeo Disco Volante.........$250–300
1922 Alfa Romeo RLSS Stradale ..$250–300
Fiat 509 SM.............................$250–300
1935 Lancia Astura Stradale $250–300
1946 Lancia Astura G.P.
    Modena...............................$250–300

ABC Indy
Ferrari Indianapolis 1987, 1:43 .$75 – 125

ABC Ruby
Bugatti T59 Nuvolari 1934, 1:43.$75 – 125

ABC Trucks by Carlo Brianza
Alfa Romeo Transporto
    v.1 Auto G.P. Tripoli 1936...$250–400
    v.2 Coppa Vanderbilt Nuvolari
    1936 ....$250–400
Alfa Romeo, 500 Transporto Alfa Gran Prix
    1950–51 ....$250–400
Alfa Romeo 500 Cassonato
    1935 ....$250–400
Alfa Romeo Mille Cassonato $250–400
Autocarro Ceirano 47 CRA Scuderia Ferrari
    1929 ....$250–400
Camion Fiat 642 Scuderia Centro
    Sud $250–400
Camion Lancia Esatau P Scuderia Lancia
    1953 ....$250–400
Camion Thames Trader Scuderia
    Maranello $250–400
Fiat 642 NR2 Transporto
    v.1 Ferrari 1956 ....$250–400
    v.2 Maserati 1956 ....$250–400
Lancia Eptaiota Torpedoene 1930 Scuderia
    Ferrari $250–400
OM 71-107 "Rolfo" 1971 Transporto
    Ferrari $250–400

Miniland by Carlo Brianza
Ferrari 250 GT Lusso, 1:14 ...$1,200–1,400

Speed by Carlo Brianza
Alfa Romeo 166, 1:43.........$75–125
Fiat Fiorino 1996, 1:43..............$75–125

Abraham, L. D.
Vintage toy car enthusiast Staffan Kjellin of Sweden reports that L. D. Abraham models were made in London, England, in the late forties. The model Kjellin provided as an

example has a clockwork motor and was seen advertised in a January 1948 magazine.

Vauxhall 10 .... $25 – 40

A. C. Williams

It is historically interesting to note that the popularity of cast-iron toys declined around the same time that diecast toys, which offered lighter-weight more-detailed alternatives to the heavy iron models, established their initial dominance in the world toy market.

Adam Clark Williams purchased the J. W. Williams Company from his father in 1886, thus beginning of one of the more successful toy companies of the era. The Ravenna, Ohio, company specialized in cast-iron toys until 1938 when the company changed direction away from toys. Few A. C. Williams toys are marked, so most often the only clues to their heritage are turned steel hubs and starred axle peens. Most A. C. Williams toys were "so crude as to barely qualify as doorstops," according to Ken Hutchison and Greg Johnson in their book *The Golden Age of Automotive Toys 1925–1941*. But A. C. Williams did produce a few exceptional toys.

In fact, some are considered the best examples of cast-iron toys. A. C. Williams toys are steadily gaining in value, up to $1,100 for the rarest mint condition specimen, an 11¾ inch 1917 Touring Car with two passengers, and an average $400–600 for most other examples.

Chrysler Airflow, 4¾" $120–160
Chrysler Airflow, 6½" $500–600
Dodge Woody Pickup, 5" $150–175
Double Decker Fageol Bus, blue with gold trim,
7¾" $850–925
Fageol Bus, "Wisconsin Motor Bus Lines,"
7¾" $1250–1500
Ford, 1935, 4½" $350–450
Ford Model T Coupe, 6" .... $225 – 275
Ford Model T Express Truck, 7¼" $425–475
Ford Opera Coupe, 5" $275–350
Graham Sedan, 5" $110–130
Graham Coupe, 5" $110–130
Laundry Truck, 8" .... $750–$800
Lincoln Touring Car, 7" .... $350–$425
Lincoln Touring Car, 9¼" $900–1000
Lincoln Touring Coupe, 8¾" $1100–1300
Mack Gas Tanker, 3¾" $75–100
Mack Gas Tanker, 5⅛" $150–225
Mack Gas Tanker, 7¼" $250–325
Mack Stake Truck, 5⅛" $175–225
Mack Stake Truck, 7" $750–825
Mack Stake Truck, 8½" $375–425
Mack Stake Truck, 3½" $75–100
Mack Stake Truck, 4¼" $150–175
Packard 900 Light Eight Sedan, 1932,
7" $300–500
Packard 900 Light Eight Sedan, 1932,
8" $550–900

Packard 900 Light Eight Stake Truck, 1932,
8" $300–500
Packard Coupe, 4½" $125
Packard Roadster, 4½" $125
Packard Sedan, 4½" $125
Packard Stake Truck, 4½" $125
Plymouth Coupe, 1933, 5¼" $150
Plymouth Sedan, 5¼" $150
REO Sidemount Sedan, 5" $120
Rolls Royce, 3½" $75–90
Studebaker Coupe, two-tone, 4¼" $175–225
Studebaker Truck, 4½" $125

Academy Minicraft

The first I'd heard of this company was from a photo sent to me via e-mail of an unusual three-wheel 1935 Morgan Super Sports in 1:16 scale. Since then, I've found an assortment of these offered by Phoenix Model Company of Brooksville, Florida. According to a company representative, these are plastic models sold as kits. Minicraft models encompass the car and airplane assortment, while the Academy brand represents their military models.

Along with an assortment of vintage cars are also armored vehicles, steam locomotives, and airplanes.

11203 Triumph TR-3A, 1:24 .... $6–7
11204 1931 Ford Model A Pickup Truck,
1:16 .... $32–40
11206 1902 De Dion Bouton,
1:16 .... $8–10
11207 1919 Hispano Suiza Alfonso Roadster,
1:16 .... $16–20
11208 1933 Cadillac V-16 Town Car,
1:16 .... $24–30
11209 1961 Rolls Royce Silver Cloud,
1:24 .... $8–10
11210 Mako Shark Show Car,
1:20 .... $12–15
11211 1931 Ford Model A Sedan,
1:16 .... $20–25
11212 1935 Morgan Super-Sports Three-
Wheeler, 1:16 .... $16–20
11213 1948 MG TC Roadster $20–25
11214 1931 Ford Model A Delivery Van,
1:16 .... $20–25
11215 1907 Rolls Royce Touring Car,
1:16 .... $32–40
11216 1939 Jaguar SS-100,
1:16 .... $32–40
11217 1928 Lincoln Dietrich Convertible
Sedan $24–30
11218 1928 Mercedes-Benz SS,
1:16 .... $52–65
11219 1936 Mercedes-Benz 540K,
1:16 .... $52–65
11220 1955 Mercedes-Benz 300SL Gullwing,
1:16 .... $32–40
11221 1931 Ford Deluxe Roadster,
1:16 .... $24–30
11222 Bonneville A-V8, 1:16 .... $24–30

ACB (also see Le Phoenix)

23 Avenue Carnot
75017 Paris, France
phone: 00 33 1 56 68 99 75
fax: 00 33 1 56 68 99 76

ACB produces 1:10 scale resin models and kits, as well as 1:43 scale metal models and kits under Le Phoenix and Super Le Phoenix brands.

ACB 1:10 Scale Resin Models and Kits

ACBK001 Mercedes W 196 1954, kit.... $500
ACB002M Ferrari 250 TR 1957, limited serial
(20 units produced) De Conto, built .. $2,900

Accucast

Around the fifties or early sixties, a company called Accucast reproduced some early Tootsietoy models of the twenties, some from original dies, others from new dies. Thanks to Dave Weber of Warrington, Pennsylvania, for the information. The brand is occasionally confused with Authenticast.

Acme (also see Thomas Toys)

Acme Plastic Toys, Inc. manufactured Thomas Toys from 1945 to 1950 when Islin Thomas bought out Acme. After that, all the toys carried only the Thomas Toys trademark. Acme was based in New York City while Thomas Toys was located in Newark, New Jersey.

Aerocar PT 650, "Made in U.S.A. Plas-Tex,"
7½" $175–225
Airline Limousine, #29, 1947, 4½" $25–30
Airline Limousine, #138, "Thomas Toys Newark
N.J.," 4½" $25–30
Streamlined Convertible Coupe, #77,
4½" $15–20
Streamlined Sedan, #77, 4½" $15–20
Coupe and House Trailer, #30, 8¼" $20–25
Esso Gas Truck, #43 .... $40–60
Jeep with Hinged Windshield, #17, 4½" . $15–20
Limousine and Trailer, #55, 6¼" $30–35
Merry-Go-Round Truck, #74, 4¾" $25–30
Motorcycle with Rider, #72, 4" $50–60
Police - Fire Chief Radio Car, #67,
4½" $25–30
Service Motorcycle with Rider, #90, 4½" . $30–35
Texaco Gas Truck, #40, 4" $20–25

Action Performance

Action Performance Companies, Inc.
4707 E Baseline Rd.
Phoenix, AZ 85040
phone: 602-894-0100
fax: 602-894-6316
800-411-8404 Action Racing Collectibles
800-952-0708 Racing Collectibles Club of America
602-337-3700 Fan Fueler
602-337-3700 Action's Corporate Office
www.action-performance.com

Action Performance Companies Inc. markets and distributes products through a variety of channels, including the 100,000-member Action Racing Collectables Club of America (RCCA), trackside at racing events, mass retail department stores, and a nationwide wholesale network of approximately 5,000 specialty dealers and distributors.

Besides racing diecast models, Action also produces fulfillment products such as t-shirts, posters, and other racing-related promotional items through its group of companies and subsidiaries — Action Racing Collectables Club of America, Action Platinum Series Racing Collectables, Revell Collection, Fan Fueler, and Image Works.

In November 1997, the company announced that it had reached an agreement in principle to purchase the motorsports diecast collectibles business of Revell-Monogram Inc., a unit of Binney & Smith Inc. of Easton, Pennsylvania, for $15 million in cash, and also to form a broad-ranging and long-term strategic alliance with Revell-Monogram. The acquisition includes a ten-year licensing agreement that will provide Action with exclusive use of the trademarked brand names of Revell-Monogram's U.S. motorsports diecast product lines, Revell Racing and Revell Collection, and existing U.S. distribution channels.

Action will exclusively market and distribute Revell-Monogram's plastic model kits into its trackside distribution channel and assist Revell-Monogram in obtaining motorsports merchandise licenses with drivers and racing teams for plastic model products.

Revell-Monogram, the world leader in plastic model kits, was until recently a business unit of Binney & Smith, maker of Crayola and Liquitex brand products and a subsidiary of Hallmark Cards Inc. of Kansas City, Missouri. Revell-Monogram has since been purchased (in 2001) by Alpha International, producers of Gearbox Collectibles. Action Performance is the leader in the design, marketing, and distribution of licensed motorsports merchandise. Its products include a broad range of motorsports-related apparel, souvenirs, diecast car replica collectibles, and other memorabilia.

In August 1998, Action Performance also purchased a controlling percentage of Paul's Model Art. The purchase includes the acquisition of Minichamps, Danhausen, Lang, and other brands associated with Paul's Model Art. UT has since been purchased by Gateway Global, and the brand has been incorporated into their AUTOart and Gate assortments.

Action Racing Collectibles, 1:24 Scale

Larry Dixon/Miller/Black Splash $75
Larry Dixon/Miller/Silver Splash $75
Cory McClenathan/McDonalds Olympic .$55
Mike Dunn/Mopar.................................$55
Kenji Okszaki/Mooneyes.......................$55
John Force/Castrol................................$75

Action Racing Collectibles, Brickyard 400 Set, 1:64 Scale

Limited edition of 25,000, with collector cards, set includes: Dale Earnhardt #3, Jeff Gordon #24 ....$30

Action Products

Action Products International Inc. is based in Ocala, Florida. They are not connected with Action Performance or its affiliates, but produce essentially generic toys. The example found is a crude 3¼ inch space shuttle with pullback action. Value is not likely to rise on this novelty toy.

Space Shuttle $1

ADJ

ADJ is an obscure brand with just one known model, as listed in *Schroeder's Collectible Toys Antique to Modern*.

Citroën CX Fire Chief Station Wagon $30–35

Advanced Products Company

Cleveland, Ohio, is birthplace to Advanced Products Company, a farm toy producer that emerged after World War II. Best information places the demise of the company in the early sixties.

Cockshutt 30 Farm Tractor, 1946, 1:16..........................$200–250
  in original box $350–400
Cockshutt 40 Farm Tractor, circa late 1950s, 1:16, ...$350–500
  in original box $600–750
Ferguson TO-20 Farm Tractor, circa late 1940s, 1:12 ....$250–300
  in original box $400–450
New Holland Baler, circa late 1950s, 1:16..........................$350–400
New Holland Baler, circa late 1950s, 1:32..........................$275–325

Agat (also see Radon)

Agat is a brand of diecast models that has recently emerged from the reformation of the Radon company of Russia. Reportedly, Agat offers a series of GAZ replicas based on the noted Russian brand of cars and trucks.

AGM

AGM is a British firm that produced precision scale model kits made of white metal.

1948 DeSoto Taxi...............................$70
1948 DeSoto Sedan $70

Agritec (also see ROS)

According to Bill Molyneaux, diecast collector and dealer, Agritec of Spain is the producer of the ROS brand of construction and farm diecast models.

12 Fiat F2100/F130 Tractor, 1:25 ....$18
20 Fiat-Hitachi Excavator, 1:32, 12" $49
20 Fiat-Hitachi FH200 Backhoe, 1:32 ....$28
21 Fiat-Allis Wheel Loader, 1:32, 9" $39
21 Fiat-Allis FR130 Wheel Loader, 1:32 .....$28
22 Fiat-Allis Dozer, 1:32, 6" $39

22 Fiat-Allis FD14E Dozer, 1:32................$24
117 Ford New Holland Tractor, blue, 1:25.........................$30–40
202 Iseki 530 Tractor, 1:32...................$18
209 Fiat Hitachi 200.3 Excavator, orange, 1:32.........................$34–45
216 Fiat Allis FR 130.2 Wheel Loader, orange, 1:32.........................$34–45
223 Fiat Hitachi FD 175 Turbo Bulldozer, orange, 1:32.........................$34–45
259 Massey Ferguson 194F Tractor............$18
285 Pisten Bully Snow Plow, red, 1:32..$60–80
301 Fiat 80-90 Tractor, 1:32...................$18
384 Fiat Hitachi Bulldozer, Loader, and Excavator, yellow, 1:32.........................$85–110
391 Fiat Hitachi Bulldozer, Loader, and Excavator, orange, 1:32.........................$85–110
490 Merlo All-Terrain Forklift, green, 1:32.........................$50–60
503 Fiat Hitachi 200 Excavator, yellow, 1:32.........................$34–45
522 Fiat Allis FR 130 Wheel Loader, yellow, 1:32.........................$34–45
544 Fiat Allis FD 14E Bulldozer, yellow, 1:32.........................$34–45
568 Hyundai Robex 290 LC Excavator, yellow, 1:32.........................$34–45
575 Fiat Hitachi CX 500 Crane, orange, 1:32.........................$34–45
612 Fiat Hitachi Compactor Loader, orange, 1:32.........................$34–45
802 Olimpus Backhoe........................$28
10255 Lamborghini 1706 Tractor, 1:32....$18
10256 Hurlimann H-G170T Tractor, 1:25.........................$18
10257 Same Galaxy 170 Tractor, 1:25 ....$18
10258 Same Galaxy 170 Dual Rear Wheel Tractor, 1:25........................$18
10308 Fiat 180-90DT Turbo Tractor, 1:18.........................$28
10309 Carraro 7700 Reversible Tractor, 1:25.........................$18
30202 Iseki Farm Tractor, 1:32 ....$14
30302 Hesston 80-90 Tractor, 1:32 ......$14
30401 Massey Ferguson 1014 Tractor, 1:32.........................$14
30403 Massey Ferguson 3050/3090 Tractor, 1:32.........................$14
40505 Landini 783 Crawler, 1:32............$14
50302 Fiat-Laverda 3890 Combine, 1:43..$18
50303 Olimpus Turbo Combine, 1:43 ......$18
60114 Hesston 4700 Baler, 1:25............$14

Aguti-toys

Aguti-toys is known to have produced at least one diecast toy, a pirate copy of a Matchbox #33 Datsun 126X. By their own number, it would appear that there were at least eight other models in the series, but no record has been found so far.

#9 Datsun 126X....................................$1–2

AHC (also see Auto Pilen, Pilen)

Many AHC models are made from dies

obtained from the defunct Escuderia Pilen company of Spain, producers of 1:43 and 1:64 scale models known as Pilen or Auto Pilen. While based in the Netherlands, many of AHC's models are made in Spain and later China. AHC is also known as the manufacturer of Hess Oil collectibles. Models listed below are all 1:43 scale.

Ford Escort Van
   v.1 metallic medium blue $16
   v.2 red...$16
   v.3 silver..$16
   v.4 white..$16

Mercedes-Benz MB100 Van
   v.1 "Bundespost," orange and red $24
   v.2 "Telefonica," green, blue, and white ...$24

Nissan Maxima
   v.1 dark green $16
   v.2 dark maroon $16
   v.3 gold and silver $16
   v.4 white...$16

Nissan Micra
   v.1 black..$16
   v.2 deep red..$16
   v.3 graphite gray..................................$16
   v.4 green...$16
   v.5 light aqua blue................................$16
   v.6 metallic blue...................................$16
   v.7 red...$16
   v.8 silver..$16
   v.9 metallic light green, "Car of the Year 1993" on pewter plinth $40

Nissan Serena Space Cruiser
   v.1 blue $16
   v.2 metallic dark bronze $16
   v.3 graphite gray..................................$16
   v.4 red...$16

Opel Kadett
   v.1 "Rijkspolitie," white and orange $24
   v.2 Police, navy blue with strobe lights $16

Seat Ibiza 3-Door Hatchback
   v.1 metallic dark blue $16
   v.2 graphite gray..................................$16
   v.3 metallic green $16
   v.4 red...$16
   v.5 silver..$16
   v.6 white..$16

Seat Ibiza 4-Door Hatchback
   v.1 white..$16

Seat Toledo GT 4-Door
   v.1 red...$16

Suzuki Samurai
   v.1 blue and white................................$16
   v.2 cream and black.............................$16
   v.3 green and black..............................$16
   v.4 maroon and white...........................$16
   v.5 red and gray...................................$16
   v.6 silver and white...............................$16
   v.7 yellow and black $16

Toyota Celica 4x4 Twin Turbo
   v.1 cream...$16
   v.2 graphite gray..................................$16

Toyota MR2
   v.1 silver..$16

Vauxhall Astra Van
   v.1 blue $16
   v.2 dark brown on pewter plinth $32
   v.3 "Q8," blue......................................$16

Volvo 440
   v.1 black..$16
   v.2 chrome..$32
   v.3 dark maroon $16
   v.4 light blue $16
   v.5 silver..$16
   v.6 white..$16
   v.7 "Politie," orange stripes $24
   v.8 "Politie," orange and blue stripes $24

Volvo 460
   v.1 black..$16
   v.2 graphite gray..................................$16
   v.3 metallic light blue............................$16
   v.4 red...$16
   v.5 silver..$16
   v.6 white..$16
   v.7 "Taxi," black and yellow $16
   Volvo 480ES $32

Volvo 850
   v.1 dark blue $16
   v.2 dark green $16
   v.3 red...$16
   v.4 GLT "Polis," white and gray $16
   v.5 T5, dark graphite gray $16

Ahi

Ahi toys are 1:80 to 1:90 scale diecast toys produced in Japan in the late fifties and early sixties. The line offers an assortment of mostly American cars, but also includes some British and other European cars as well as 1:120 scale Dodge military trucks and some antique autos.

Alfa Romeo Giuletta Sprint, 1:90 ....$16
Austin A105, 1:90 ....$16
Austin-Healey, 1:90 ....$16
Buick, 1:90 ....$16
Cadillac, 1:90 ....$16
Chevrolet Impala, 1:90 ....$16
Chrysler, 1:90...$16
Citroën DS 19, 1:90 ....$16
Daimler, 1:90 ....$16
DeSoto Diplomat, 1:90 ....$16
Dodge, 1:90...$16
Ferrari 375 Coupe, 1:90 ....$24
Ferrari 500 Formula 2, 1:90 ....$24
Fiat 1800, 1:90 ....$16
Ford, 1:90..$16
Imperial, 1:90 ....$16
International Harvester, 1:90 ....$16
Jaguar Mk IX, 1:90 ....$16
Jaguar XK150 Roadster, 1:90 ....$16
Maserati Racer, 1:90...............................$16
Mercedes-Benz 220SE, 1:90 ....$16
Mercedes-Benz 300SL Roadster, 1:90 .....$16
Mercedes-Benz W 25 Racer, 1:90 ....$16
Mercedes-Benz W 196 Racer, 1:90 ....$16

Mercedes-Benz RW 196 Racer, 1:90.........$16
MG TF Roadster, 1:90 ....$16
MGA 1600, 1:90 ....$16
Midget Racer, 1:90 ....$16
Oldsmobile, 1:90 ....$16
Opel Kapitän, 1:90 ....$16
Plymouth, 1:90 ....$16
Pontiac, 1:90 ....$16
Porsche 356A, 1:90 ....$16
Rambler, 1:90 ....$16
Renault Floride, 1:90 ....$16
Rolls-Royce Silver Wraith, 1:90 ....$20
Simca Aronde P 60, 1:90 ....$16
Volkswagen 1200, 1:90 ....$20
Volvo Amazon 122 S, 1:90 ....$16
Volvo PV 544, 1:90 ....$16

Ahi Antique cars
1902 Ali Coold Frankline, 1:80............$12
1903 Cadillac, 1:80 ....$12
1903 Rambler, 1:80 ....$12
1904 Darracq, 1:80.............................$12
1904 Oldsmobile, 1:80 ....$12
1904 Oldsmobile Truck, 1:80 ....$12
1907 Vauxhall, 1:80 ....$12
1909 Stanley Steamer, 1:80 ....$12
1911 Buick, 1:80 ....$12
1914 Stutz Bearcat, 1:80 ....$12
1915 Ford Model T, 1:80 ....$12

Dodge Military Trucks
Ambulance, 1:120 ....$12
Barrel Truck, 1:120 ....$12
Cement Mixer, 1:120 ....$12
Covered Truck, 1:120 ....$12
Crane Truck, 1:120 ....$12
Lumber Truck, 1:120 ....$12
Missile Carrier, 1:120 ....$12
Radar Truck, 1:120 ....$12
Rocket Launcher, 1:120 ....$12
Searchlight Truck, 1:120 ....$12
Tank Carrier, 1:120 ....$12
Truck with Machine Gun, 1:120 ....$12

AHL (see American Highway Legends)

Albedo

Albedo-Forkel GmbH
Postfach 1155
D-91556 Heilsbronn, Germany
phone: +49 (0) 98 72/89 00
fax: +49 (0) 98 72/53 86

Collector Ron Gold sent me an Albedo catalog printed in German and featuring a beautiful assortment of 1:87 scale freight trucks. Previously unknown, Albedo models appear to be precision plastic replicas of contemporary semis with an emphasis on spectacular graphics. Values are listed in German Marks (DM), so conversion to US dollars is approximated.

Iveco "Jo Vonlanthen," catalog #220 012, DM49 ....$33 US
Iveco "Magneti Marelli," catalog #220 010, DM49 ....$33 US

Iveco Semi Freighter "For Motorsport 30 Years of Formula One Power," catalog #220 032, DM43.................................$24 US

MAN Freight Truck with Trailer "Löwenbräu," catalog #800 046, DM39.................$22 US

MAN Semi Freighter "Polizei Pferdetransporter," catalog #800 047, DM39 ....$22 US

Mercedes-Benz Actros Semi Freighter "Hansel & Gretel," catalog #600 001, DM69.$39 US

Mercedes-Benz Actros Semi Freighter "D & W," catalog #210 001, DM49 ....$28 US

Mercedes-Benz Actros Semi Freighter "Müller Drogerie," catalog #210 002, DM45 ....$25 US

Mercedes-Benz Freight Truck "ADAC Prüfdienst," catalog #200 377, DM25 ....$14 US

Mercedes-Benz SK Freight Truck with Trailer "Bitburger," catalog #200 376, DM43.................................$24 US

Mercedes-Benz SK Semi Freighter "Oro Di Parma," catalog #200 375, DM36 $20 US

Renault AE Benetton "Bitburger," catalog #220 001, DM79.................................$44 US

Renault AE Benetton "Drive," catalog #220 003, DM79 ....$44 US

Renault AE Equipment Transporter "elf F1," catalog #220 029, DM34 ....$19 US

Renault AE Equipment Transporter "Starbird Satellite Services," catalog #220 030, DM34 ....$19 US

Renault AE Freight Truck with Trailer "König-Pilsener," catalog #700 151, DM39.......$22 US

Renault AE Semi Freighter "elf F1," catalog #220 028, DM39.................................$22 US

Renault AE Semi Freighter "Lösche," catalog #700 150, DM43.......................$24 US

Renault AE Semi Freighter "Tishlen Deck Dich," catalog #600 005, DM69 ....$39 US

Renault AE Semi Freighter "Würth," catalog #700 152, DM36.......................$20 US

Renault AE SZ "F1 Equipment," catalog #220 006, DM59.................................$33 US

Renault Bus with Trailer "Williams Renault F1," catalog #220 027, DM43 ....$24 US

Renault Premium Semi Freighter "1 FC Kölsch," catalog #710 012, DM39 ....$22 US

Renault Premium Semi Freighter "Milka-Ostern 1998," catalog #710 016, DM49.$28 US

Renault Premium Semi Freighter "Prince De Bretagne," catalog #710 013, DM36 .$20 US

Renault Premium Semi Freighter "Rotkappchen," catalog #600 003, DM69 ....$39 US

Renault Premium Semi Freighter "Schneewittchen," catalog #600 006, DM69 ....$39 US

Renault Premium Semi Tank Container "P&O Tankmasters," catalog #710 014, DM36.................................$20 US

Scania Container Semi "Hyundai," catalog #111 126, DM36.................................$20 US

Scania Semi Freighter "Jordan," catalog #220 033, DM49 ....$28 US

Volvo FH Freight Truck with Trailer "Wernesgrüner Pils," catalog #320 029, DM45 .....$25 US

Volvo FH Semi Freighter "Frau Holle," catalog #600 002, DM69.........................$39 US

Volvo FH Semi Freighter "Frolic," catalog #320 033, DM39 ....$22 US

Volvo FH Semi Freighter "Milka-Ostern 1998," catalog #320 032, DM49 ....$28 US

Volvo FH Semi Freighter "Spedition Vendel," catalog #320 029, DM39 ....$22 US

Volvo FH Semi Freighter "Wernesgrüner Pils," catalog #320 028, DM43.................$24 US

Volvo XL Semi Freighter "750 Jahre Kölner Dom," catalog #600 007, DM43 ....$24 US

Volvo XL Semi Freighter "Aschenputtel," catalog #600 004, DM69.........................$39 US

Volvo XL Semi Freighter "Goodyear Racing," catalog #220 031, DM43.................$24 US

Volvo XL Semi Freighter "Interblumex," catalog #320 026, DM69.........................$39 US

Volvo XL Semi Freighter "Ouzo 12," catalog #320 027, DM43.........................$24 US

Volvo XL Semi Tractor "750 Jahre Kölner Dom," catalog #320 031, DM25 ....$14 US

Albedo German Democratic Republic (DDR) Banknote Edition

Volvo F12 Freight Truck "20 Mark," catalog #600 010, DM36 ....$20 US

Volvo F12 Freight Truck "50 Mark," catalog #600 011, DM36 ....$20 US

Volvo F12 Freight Truck "100 Mark," catalog #600 012, DM36 ....$20 US

Volvo F88 Freight Truck "5 Mark," catalog #600 008, DM36 ....$20 US

Volvo F89 Freight Truck "10 Mark," catalog 600 009, DM36 ....$20 US

Alezan

Alezan of France is another obscure brand of white metal models with just two known models.

Alfa Romeo Evoluzion, dark red $75–85
DeTomaso Pantera, white metal kit........$45–60

ALJ

ALJ models are 1:43 scale vehicles.

Late 1950s Ford 2-Door Convertible with top down, white/red $11

Delahaye 2-Door Roadster, metallic green...$11–14

Early 1950s Buick 2-Door Roadster, cream...$11

Late 1950s Ford 2-Door Convertible with top up, red and gray $11

Early 1950s Buick 2-Door Convertible with top up, pink $11

All-American

All-American of Los Angeles, California, is known to have produced just one model, in 1949.

All-American Hot-Rod, 9" long...................$400

All American Toy Company

Patrick Russell, president

540 Lancaster SE
Salem, OR 97301
503-399-8609 Mon–Fri 9–6 Pacific

Clay Steinke, founder of the All American Toy Company of Salem, Oregon, produced a total of 26,000 1:12 scale cast-metal toy trucks from its beginnings in 1948 to 1955. Its assortment of large scale toy trucks distinctive for their "air horn steering" includes the popular Timber Toter log truck, popular with children whose families worked in the Pacific Northwest logging industry. They originally sold for around $20, considered a high price for toys sold back in the 1950s. Today's values are in the hundreds, even thousands of dollars. Model numbers appeared on the box only, not on the model.

All American Originals

Play-Dozer, 9" long.............$1,000–1,500

Cattle Liner, 38" long, C-5....$1,500–2,000

Cargo Liner, 38" long, CL-8..$1,200–1,700

Dyna-Dump, 20" long, early sandcast cab, D-3 ....$800–1,500

Dyna-Dump, 20" long, diecast cab, D-3.................................$500–700

Hay-Grain-Feed-Seed with Trailer $1,000–1,500

Hay-Grain-Feed-Seed without Trailer $500–800

Heavy Hauler, 38" long, HH-9.$800–1,200

Midget Skagit Log Loader, 18" long, MS.................................$300–500

Play-Loader, 11" long, HD-6........$400–600

Scoop-A-Veyor, 16" long, S-1......$450–600

Timber Toter, 38" long, early sandcast cab, L-2.................................$800–1,000

Timber Toter, 38" long, diecast cab, L-2.................................$400–650

Timber Toter Jr. with Trailer, 20" long, LJ-4.................................$600–1,000

All American New Models

After a false restart in 1990, the All American Toy Company is back in business in its home town of Salem, Oregon, purchased lock, stock, and barrel in 1992 by Patrick Russell, with all the original tooling intact. The company is now reproducing some of those classic models. Here is a list of available new models and prices. As you will note, current second market values are already on the rise.

Founder's Edition Timber Toter, 1992 replica (original retail $595)........$900–1,000

"Rocky" Galion Dump Truck, 1995 Dyna-Dump replica, maroon cab, silver box (113 made) ($595 retail)....$700–1,000

"Rocky" Galion Dump Truck, 1995 Dyna-Dump replica, white cab, blue box (limited to 112) ($595 retail).......$700–900

The Heavy Hauler II, double axle "lowboy" trailer ($595 retail)...............$700–900

The Heavy Hauler II, triple axle "lowboy" trailer ($695 retail) $700–900

Motorcycle Hauler, only 100 made ($449 retail) $600–750

Custom Classic Motorcycle for Motorcycle Hauler...$60
1948 Indian Chief, maroon or yellow $60

Allied

Allied was based in Corona, New York, and made only plastic toys. Age and history is otherwise unknown.
Allied Furniture Moving Van with "Viso box" trailer, 10 pieces of furniture, #208, 5½"...$25–40
Auto Sales and Station with Five vehicles $125–150
Cement Mixer, #197, 4"....................$65–80
Delivery Service Truck $60–75
Dump Truck, #174, 5½".....................$60–75
Dump Truck, #191, 4½".....................$15–20
Emergency Truck, #129, 7".................$70–85
Stake Truck with eight farm animals and removable stakes, #193, 9½" $50–65
Station Wagon, 3½"...........................$10–15

All-Nu

A few lead alloy slush mold military vehicles were produced circa 1920–1940 by this obscure company. Models are marked "Made in USA." The brand also encompasses a few cardboard vehicles.
Field Kitchen, lead, 2½".....................$25–40
Searchlight, lead, 2¾".........................$25–40
Sound Detector, lead, 2¾"..................$25–40
Tank, lead, 3" $25–40

Alloy Forms, Inc.

Alloy Forms models are 1:87 scale kits intended for use with HO gauge train sets. Kits consist of unpainted white metal detail parts. Truck kits also include styrene, brass, and rubber parts.

Alloy Forms Automobiles

1953 Buick Skylark Convertible with Continental Package.................................$7
1949 Buick Roadmaster $7
1959 Cadillac Eldorado Convertible $7
1955 Cadillac Fleetwood $7
1950 Chevrolet 4-Door Fastback............$7
1953 Chevrolet Bel-Air.........................$7
1955 Chevrolet Bel-Air 2-Door $7
1957 Chevrolet Bel-Air Sport Coupe $8
1953 Chevrolet Corvette........................$7
1959 Chevrolet El Camino......................$7
1959 Chevrolet Impala Convertible $7
1955 Chevrolet Nomad Wagon $7
1949 DeSoto 4-Door $7
1949 Ford Club Coupe with Engine $8
1948 Ford Convertible............................$8
1956 Ford Thunderbird...........................$7
1949 Hudson 4-Door $7
1949 Mercury 2-Door.............................$7
1948 Studebaker Starline $7
Plymouth Coupe $8
Plymouth Coupe without Engine $8

Alloy Forms Trucks

Autocar Block Truck............................$20

1955 Chevrolet 2-Ton Stake Truck..........$10
Ford LTS Block Truck...........................$20
1951 Ford Panel Delivery Truck...............$8
1956 Ford Pickup $8
1956 Ford Pickup with Camper $10
1956 Ford Pickup with Rack..................$10
1954 Mack B-42 Flatbed Truck $18
Mack B-42 3-Axle Block Truck $20
Mack B-61 2-Axle Refrigerated Box Truck.$20
Mack BQ 3-Axle Box Truck...................$20
Mack BQ 3-Axle Stake Truck.................$18
Mack CJ COE 3-Axle Stake Truck $18

Alloy Forms Dump Trucks & Trailers
(Length indicated refers to the original length of the trailer on which the miniature replica is based.)

Autocar with 12' Dump Box $20
Autocar with 22' Dump Trailer $25
Autocar with Large Dumper $25
Autocar Special Dump Truck $35
Diamond REO with 7' Dump Bed $20
Diamond REO with 11' Dump Bed $20
Diamond REO with 22' Dump Trailer......$20
Ford LNT 2-Axle with 7' Dump Trailer......$20
Ford LNT 3-Axle with 7' Heil Dump Body..$20
Ford LNT 3-Axle with 30' 3-Axle Dump Trailer..$35
Ford LNT Coal/Gravel with Tandem Axle Dump Trailer $23
Ford LTS with 12' Heil Dump Bed $20
Ford LTS with Dump Body $23
Ford LTS with 22' Dump Trailer $25
GMC Astro with 22' Dump Trailer $25
Mack B-61 Dump Truck.......................$25
Mack B-61 2-Axle Dump Truck $20
Mack B-61 3-Axle Dump Truck $20
Mack B-71 with 30' 3-Axle Dump Trailer ..$35
Mack B-71 20' Coal/Gravel with Tandem Axle Dump Trailer $23
Mack Universal Chassis Dump Truck.......$20
22' 2-Axle Dump Trailer.......................$18
30' 3-Axle Dump Trailer.......................$25

Alloy Forms Semi-Tractor/Trailers
(Length indicated refers to the original length of the trailer on which the miniature replica is based.)

Autocar Chassis...................................$15
Autocar with Log Trailer $20
Autocar with 45' "Lowboy" Flatbed Trailer $30
Diamond REO BBC Refrigerated............$20
Diamond REO Delivery.........................$20
Diamond REO Universal Chassis............$15
Diamond REO with 40' Flatbed Trailer....$18
Ford LNT Cab with Universal Chassis $15
Ford LNT 2-Axle with Refrigerated Body ..$20
Ford LNT 3-Axle $18
Ford LTS with Universal Chassis $15
GMC Astro 2-Axle................................$15
GMC Astro 2-Axle with 40' "Lowboy" 16-Wheel Flatbed Trailer.......................$30
GMC Astro 3-Axle with Rectangular Gas Tanks $15

GMC Astro Short Cab 2-Axle................$15
GMC Astro Short Cab 3-Axle................$15
GMC Astro Short Cab with 16' body.....$20
GMC Astro Sleeper...............................$15
Mack B-61 Tank 2-Axle.......................$20
Mack B-61 Universal Chassis $15
Mack B-61 with 16' Body $20
Mack B-61 with Logging Trailer $30
Mack B-70 with Universal Chassis $15
Mack B-71 with Heavy Duty Flatbed Trailer $18
Mack CF/Pierce $30
Mack CF with Universal Chassis $20
Mack CF 4-Door $20
Mack DM-800 Offset Cab with Universal Chassis $15
30' Logging Trailer...............................$20
37' Depressed Center Flatbed Trailer......$20
45' 16-Wheel "Lowboy" Trailer............$20

Alloy Forms Emergency Equipment

Diamond REO Pierce Tanker $27
Ford LNT Fire Pumper...........................$27
Ford LS Fire Pumper.............................$27
Mack B-61 2-Axle Fire Pumper $30
Mack B-61 Fire Tanker $20
Mack B-61 Open Fire Truck..................$27
Mack CF NYC Fire Pumper $30
Pierce Ford LN Pumper $27
Pierce Ford LS Pumper $27

Alloy Forms Miscellaneous

1947 Clark Fork Lift $4

Alterscale

Alterscale Miniature Outboards
Karl E. Beisel
1965 Fountainbrook Ct.
Woodbridge, VA 22192
phone: 703-490-6649
e-mail: K2BEISEL@aol.com
website: www.alterscale.com

It seems there is (and apparently has been for over thirty years) a select group of collectors of scale model outboard boat motors. A book has been written about them, and there are just a few websites devoted to them. Two manufacturers come to light: K & O brand models apparently manufactured diecast and plastic boat motors from 1952 to 1962. Alterscale is the more recent brand to produce such models.

Alterscale now produces several precision scale models of Evinrude, Honda, and Johnson outboards.

You may consider purchasing *Toy Outboard Motors* by Jack Browning, $22.95, 150 pages of compiled articles with photos. Available only direct: Jack Browning; 214 16th Street; Roanoke, VA 24017; phone 540-982-1253. Comment: This is the only comprehensive work in existence on this subject. It covers principally the K&O motors (in detail) but touches on many other toy outboards. It includes a list of toy outboard collectors with names and addresses. Jack Browning is one of the world's premier collectors of toy outboards.

American Highway Legends (also see Hartoy)

Hartoy produces a series of 1:64 scale trucks of forties and fifties vintage called American Highway Legends that have become very popular with collectors. Models retail for $10 to $30 each, and sometimes bring higher prices at toy shows and from specialty dealers. The series has now been discontinued in lieu of Hartoy's introduction of a new series of commercial trucks called Precision Engineered Models (PEM). Hartoy is currently located in Lake Worth, Florida.

"Breyer's" Box Truck	$18
"Coca-Cola" Box Van	$18
"Coca-Cola" Mack City Delivery Truck	$18
"Coca-Cola" Mack Stake Truck	$18
"Coca-Cola" Ford Tractor Trailer	$18
"Evinrude" Box Truck	$18
"Ford Parts" Ford Tractor Trailer	$18
"Fram Filters" Mack Covered Truck	$18
"Kelly Springfield" GMC Box Truck	$18
"Mobil" GMC Tanker Truck	$18
"Pennzoil" Peterbilt Tanker Truck	$18
"Ray-O-Vac" Mack Stake Truck	$18
"Scott Paper" Mack Tandem Trailer	$18
"Shell Fuel Oil" Tractor Trailer	$18
"Timken" Mack Covered Stake Truck	$18
"Wrigley's" Mack Box Truck	$18

The Great American Brewery Collection from American Highway Legends

"Dixie Beer," Dixie Brewing Co. Peterbilt 260 Tandem Trailer Truck	$30
"Hamm's Beer," Pabst Brewing Co. Ford F-7 Freight Truck	$30
"Jax Beer," Jackson Brewing Co. (Pearl Brewing Co.) GMC T-70 Stake Truck	$12
"Olympia Beer," Olympia Brewing Co. (Pabst Brewing Co.) GMC T-70 Covered Truck	$12
"Pearl Lager Beer," Pearl Brewing Co. Ford F-5 Box Truck	$12
"Point Special Beer," Stevens Point Beverage Co. Ford F-5 Truck	$12

Other American Highway Legends, as extracted from www.hartoy.com, 01/10/99

AHL Straight Chassis

H04050 GMC T-70 Mr. Goodbar	$12 – 15
H05010 Ford F-5 Bitter-Sweet	$12–15
L01014 Mack BM Evinrude	$12–15
L02042 Mack CJ Royal Oak	$12–15

AHL 22' Bullnose T/T

H51100 Mack BM Hershey's	$15–18
H52100 Mack CJ Reese's	$15–18
L55103 Ford F-7 Maxwell House	$15–18
L55104 Ford F-7 Pennsylvania Railroad	$15–18

AHL 32' Van Trailer

L55403 Ford F-7 Eckerd Drug	$15–18
L57402 Ford C-Series Atlas Van Lines	$15–18

AHL 32' Tank Trailers

H55300 Hershey's Syrup Tank Trailer	$15–18

American National

American National started in Toledo, Ohio, around 1894 by brothers William, Walter, and Harry Diemer. Their products included many pedal cars and some spectacular pressed steel toys throughout the 1920s and 1930s. Values reflect the rarity of these incredibly realistic toys.

American Railway Express Truck, 27"	$1,750–2,500
Chemical Fire Truck, 28"	$4,000–4,500
Circus Truck, 27"	$1,500–2,000
Coal Truck	$3,500–4,000
Dump Truck, 28"	$1,500–2,000
Mack "Giant" Army Truck, 26½"	$1,500–2,000
Packard Convertible, red, 28"	$2,000–2,500
Packard Coupe, brown, 28"	$2,000–2,500
Richfield Gasoline Truck, 27"	$2,500–3,000

American Precision Models (APM)

P.O. Box 190
Buffalo, NY 14225 USA
fax: 716-634-7769
e-mail: info@modelbuses
website: www.modelbuses.com

American Precision Models (APM) is a leading manufacturer of Injection molded HO scale model buses based on American prototypes. Products are available as undecorated kits, painted and assembled, or custom decorated. APM also handles bus models by Herpa, Wiking, Praline, and Busch.

1951 Visicoach American Bus 1:87 Scale

v.1 blue	$16
v.2 green	$16
v.3 orange	$16
v.4 red	$16
AM001 Flexible Visicoach, unpainted kit (£11)	$17
AM002 Flexible Visicoach, five colors, built (£14)	$22
AM007 GM 4509 Old look coach, kit (£11)	$17
AM007 GM 4509 Old look coach, four colors, built (£14)	$22
SP-100 GM North Olmsted	$25–30
SP-101 GM Cleveland Transit	$25–30
SP-102 GM Toronto #1960	$25–30
SP-103 GM Toronto #1963	$25–30
SP-104 NJ Public Service #329	$25–30
SP-105 NJ Public Service #347	$25–30
39000-0 GM Transit, unassembled	$12 – 15
39000-1 GM Transit, blue	$16–20
39000-2 GM Transit, red	$16–20
39000-3 GM Transit, green	$16–20
39000-4 GM Transit, orange	$16–20
39000-99 GM Transit, decal	$3–4
39013-0 Flexible, unassembled	$10–12
39013-1 Flexible, blue	$15–18
39013-2 Flexible, red	$15–18
39013-3 Flexible, green	$15–18
39013-4 Flexible, orange	$15–18
39013-5 Flexible, maroon	$15–18

Ampersand

The release of a 1:43 scale model of Arie Luyendyk's 1990 Indy winning Lola T-90 punctuates the 1997 return of Ampersand resin cast kits. Previous issues of Indy racers were marketed a few years earlier. The Lola with Domino's Pizza livery is available in kit or factory-built form.

Lola T-90 Arie Luyendyk, Domino's Pizza, 1990 Indy 500 winner, kit	$40
built	$95

AMR – Century (also see Andre-Marie Ruf)

AMR models are hand-built white metal kits reportedly produced by Andre M. Ruff, a noted maker of hand-built models from France. The first AMR-produced replica was a Renault R8 Gordini.

Fiat Abarth 1300, limited edition, red	$375
Mercedes-Benz 500 SCL, off-white	$95
Morgan 2+2, white	$495
Renault Alpine, limited edition, red	$250
Renault R8 Gordini	$600

Century models are a less expensive assortment of models from AMR. A considerable assortment of these 1:43 scale Century white metal models are currently available.

3 1949 Volkswagen Split Window	$77
4 1986 Chevy Corvette Convertible, top down	$77
5 1986 Volvo 480 ES	$77
6 1966 Ford Mustang	$97
8 1987 Mercedes-Benz 300CE	$77–95
9 1950 Volkswagen Beetle Hebmueller Convertible	$77
10 1988 Porsche 911 Speedster	$97
12 1959 Volkswagen Karmann Ghia Coupe	$77
13 1959 Volkswagen Karmann Ghia Convertible	$77–97
14 1965 Lincoln Continental Convertible	$97
15 1951 Volkswagen Beetle Convertible	$77
16 1966 Ford Mustang Convertible	$77–97
18 1989 Porsche Carrera 4	$97
19 1989 Ferrari 348 GTB	$117
22 1989 Mazda MX5 Miata	$97
24 Volvo 480 Cabriolet	$97
30 1948 Lincoln Loewy	$97
135 Porsche Turbo Carrera, Martini / LeMans, silver, #22	$89
445 Porsche 917/920 #23 Pink Pig, pork cuts labeled in German	$89
901/902 1950 Volkswagen Beetle Hebmueller Convertible	$97

3004 1959 Volkswagen Karmann Ghia Coupe, chrome $117
3005 1959 Volkswagen Karmann Ghia Convertible, chrome $117
3010 1988 Porsche 911 Speedster Racer ..$97
3013 1948 Lincoln Mk 1 Loewy/Derham ..$117
3014 1949 Volkswagen Beetle 1200 Convertible $117
S3001 1950 Volkswagen Beetle Krankenwagen, white $97
S3002 1949 Volkswagen Beetle (only 250 made), chrome $97
S3003 1950 Volkswagen Beetle Hebmueller (only 250 made), chrome $97

AMT

AMT is best known for its plastic model kits. But for a short time around 1968, they produced an inexpensive series of diecast toys called "Pups," 1:64 scale boxed toy cars made in Hong Kong. No model list available.

Andre-Marie Ruf (Also see AMR)

Sarl ANDRE-MARIE RUF
B. P. 20 - Route de Violès
84850 - Camaret Sur Aygues
France
phone: 33 (0) 4 90 37 27 27
fax: 33 (0) 4 90 37 23 56

Besides models produced under the AMR brand, Andre-Marie Ruf produces 1:43 scale white metal model kits under his own signature brand.

AMR003A Ferrari 365 California 1966/67 avec roues "fil" (series limited to 250) $55
AMR025A Ferrari 250 LWB 'Interim' Le Mans 1959 #18, 20 ....$55
AMR025B Ferrari 250 LWB 'Interim' Tour de France 1959 #164 ....$55
AMR030K F 512S LM 1970 FILIPINETTI #14 & 15 ....$55
AMR030AK Ferrari 512S LM 1970 SEFAC #s 6, 7, 8 ....$55
AMR030BK Ferrari 512S LM 1970 NART #11 ....$55
AMR030CK Ferrari 512S LM 1970 SEFAC #5 ....$55
AMR030DK Ferrari 512S LM 1970 FRANCORCHAMPS #12 ....$55
AMR030EK Ferrari 512S LM 1970 NART #10 ....$55
AMR030FK Ferrari 512S LM 1970 FILIPINETTI #16 ....$55
AMR031AK Ferrari 250 GTO 1962 civile $55
AMR031BK Ferrari 250 GTO Tour de France 1964 #175 ....$55
AMR031CK Ferrari 250 GTO 1962 Targa Florio 1962 #86 ....$55
AMR031DK Ferrari 250 GTO 1962 rallye du Touquet 1965 ....$55
AMR031EK Ferrari 250 GTO 1962 Nürburgring 1965 ....$55

AMR031FK Ferrari 250 GTO 1962 Sebring 1963 ....$55
AMR031GK Ferrari 250 GTO 1962 Targa Florio 1964 #112 ....$55
AMR034K Ferrari Berlinetta Fantuzzi Targa 1965 ....$54
AMR035K Ferrari 250 GT 57 ch. 0677 1st TdF 57, 1st Reims 58 ....$54
AMR035AK Ferrari 250 GT 57 ch. 0607 TdF 57 ....$55
AMR036K Ferrari 512 S Spa 70 #20 ....$55
AMR037K Cadillac Cabriolet DeVille 1967 ....$70
AMR038K Ferrari Berlinetta Fantuzzi Spyder 1966 ....$54
AMR040AK Corvette C5R Le Mans 2000 ...$54
AMR041K Ferrari 290 Mille Miglia 1956 #548 - Eugenio Castellotti $55
AMR042K Ferrari Pininfarina 1980 ....$55

Anguplas Mini Cars

Made in Spain, Anguplas Mini Cars are small-scale plastic replicas of popular cars of the sixties. They were likely produced in the same era. Mostly produced in 1:86 scale, a few were made to 1:43 scale. They feature relatively accurate plastic bodies on a diecast chassis with separate plastic tires on metal hubs. Typical of plastic models, fatigue tends to deform the bodies of the vehicles over the years, making mint specimens rare. Original prices for models listed are in parentheses.

7 Ford Edsel Convertible, 1:86 ($.39) $10
38 VW Beetle, 1:86 ($.25) $10
47 1960 Studebaker Lark, 1:86 ($.29) $10
51 Mercedes-Benz Microbus, 1:86 ($.49) ..$10
56 Ford Falcon, 1:86 ($.29) $10
61 Jeep Wagon, 1:86 ($.39) $10
76 Jaguar Mark Nine, 1:86 ($.39) $10
83 Karmann Ghia, 1:86 ($.25) $10
86 Cadillac Fleetwood, 1:86 ($.49) $10
89 Ford Comet, 1:86 ($.39) $10
92 Studebaker Hawk, 1:86 ($.39) $10
99 Volvo Sport, 1:86 ($.29) $10

Anker

A few Anker 1:25 scale models from Germany are offered by Diecast Miniatures.

Alfa Romeo 1300 ....$18
Audi 100 ....$18
Barkas 153 Van $18
Jaguar XJS $18
Renault Rodeo Jeep $18

Anso (see Anson)

Anson

Ontrade Industrial Ltd.
702-5 New East Ocean Centre
9 Science Museum Road
T.S.T. East, Hong Kong, China
or

Anson Industries Ltd.
Unit 1308, Lippo Sun Plaza
28 Canton Rd., Tsim Sha Tsui,
Kowloon, Hong Kong
or
K H Simmonds
31 Priestgate
Peterborough PE1 1JP UK
or
Anson International Marketing Inc.
11181 Hidden Springs Ct.
Dubuque, IA 52003
phone: 319-582-1311
fax: 319-582-1807
toll-free: 877-239-7016
e-mail: usaanson@aol.com

According to Anson's own website at www.anson-scalemodel.com. Anson began their operations from Hong Kong in 1992. Because of the Anson logo with a displaced "N," some collectors have misread the name as "Anso." Ansons are larger scale limited edition diecast models made in China.

1:18 Scale Models

30301 Ferrari Dino 246 GT, red or yellow, 1:18 ....$25–40
30302 1969 Lamborghini Miura, available in several colors, 1:18 ....$25–40
30303 1992 Bugatti EB110, red, blue, or metallic silver, 1:18 ....$25–40
30305 1992 Porsche 911 Carrera 2 Targa, 1:18, white, red, purple, or green $25–40
30306 Porsche 911 Carrera 4 Cabriolet, roof raises and lowers, silver or red, 1:18 ....$25–40
30307 Saab 900 Turbo Cabriolet, red or dark gray, 1:18 ....$25–40
30308 Ferrari 328 GTS, Ferrari red or yellow, 1:18 ....$25–40
30309 1992 Porsche 911 Carrera 4 Cabriolet, 1:18, red, yellow, mint, silver, dark green, or black $25–40
30313 Porsche Carrera 4 Cabriolet with top down, 1:14 ....$95
30317 Lotus Caterham Super 7, metallic red or green, 1:18 ....$25–40
30318 Dodge Viper RT/10, yellow or black $25–40
30319 Dodge Ram 3500 Dually Pick Up $25–40
30320 Porsche 911 Twin Turbo, red or black, 1:18 ....$25–40
30321 Porsche 911 GT2 Street Version, yellow or silver, 1:18 ....$25–40
30322 Porsche 911 GT1 1996 Version, white with "Mobil" tempo accents, 1:18 ....$25–40
30323 Ferrari F550 Maranello, red or yellow, 1:18 ....$25–40
30325 Porsche 911 GT2 Stadler Motorsport, 1:18 ....$25–40

30326 Porsche 911 GT2 Rohr Motorsport, 1:18 ....$25–40

30327 Porsche 911 GT2 Team Taisan, 1:18 ....$25–40

30328 Mercedes-Benz E-Class Station Wagon, silver or dark blue, 1:18 ....$25–40

30329 Porsche 911 GT1 Street Version, silver or white, 1:18 ....$25–40

30330 Mercedes-Benz CLK, silver or quartz blue, 1:18 ....$25–40

30331 Plymouth Prowler, yellow with top up, 1:18 ....$25–40

30332 Porsche 911 GT2 Super Cup, 1:18 ....$25–40

30333 1997 Dodge "Copperhead" Concept Car, metallic orange, 1:18........$25–40

30334 1963 Ford Thunderbird Roadster, Rangoon red or silver mink, 1:18 ....$25–40

30335 1947 Cadillac Series 62 Convertible, ivory or black, 1:18 ....$25–40

30336 Ferrari 308 GTS, Ferrari red or yellow, 1:18 ....$25–40

30337 1998 Cadillac Seville, black or dark blue, 1:18 ....$25–40

30338 Mercedes-Benz CLK Cabriolet, silver or imperial red, 1:18 ....$25–40

30339 Porsche GTI 1997 Version, white with "Warsteiner" tempo print, 1:18 ....$25–40

30341 Renault Twingo, blue or dark green, 1:18 ....$25–40

30342 Renault Megane Cabriolet, red or yellow, 1:18 ....$25–40

30343 Mercedes-Benz CLK AMG, dark blue $25–40

30344 1963 Ford Thunderbird Hardtop, Rangoon red or silver mink, 1:18 ....$25–40

30345 1946 Cadillac Series 62 Hardtop, ivory or black, 1:18..............$25–40

30346 Renault Spider (Aeroscreen version) $25–40

30347 Renault Maxi Megane Rally "DIAC" France $25–40

30348 Renault Maxi Megane Rally "GB" UK $25–40

30349 Renault Maxi Megane Rally "Espagne" Spain $25–40

30350 Renault Spider (Street version) $25–40

30352 Renault Spider "Kicker" Racing $25–40

30353 Renault Spider "Cobra" Racing $25–40

30355 1973 Cadillac Eldorado Indy Pace Car $25–40

30357 1973 Cadillac Eldorado Hardtop, black $25–40

30360 Porsche 911 Turbo Polizei ...$25–40

30362 Mercedes-Benz E-Class Wagon Polizei $25–40

30363 Mercedes-Benz CLK Cabriolet, silver $25–40

30366 Plymouth Prowler Hot Rod "Flame" model $25–40

30367 Plymouth Prowler Hot Rod "Speed" model..............$25–40

30369 Mercedes-Benz CLK AMG Safety Car $25–40

30370 Mercedes-Benz E-Class Wagon Service Car $25–40

30371 1953 Cadillac Eldorado Convertible, white..............$25–40

30372 1953 Cadillac Eldorado Soft Top, red $25–40

30376 Renault Megane Coupe, yellow $25–40

30377 Renault Maxi Megane Rally Belgium..............$25–40

30379 Renault Maxi Megane Rally Italy $25–40

30381 Dodge Ram Dump Truck $25–40

30382 Dodge Ram Stake Truck $25–40

30383 1932 Cadillac V16 Sport Phaeton, black and silver or cream and burgundy $25–40

30384 1957 Studebaker Golden Hawk, metallic gold $25–40

30385 BMW X5 ....$25–40

30386 BMW 2002, red $25–40

30387 1973 Cadillac Eldorado Convertible, red or bronze..............$25–40

30388 Renault Spider (Aeroscreen version) $25–40

30389 1968 Mercedes-Benz 280SL Pagoda..............$25–40

30390 2000 Mercedes-Benz C-Class $25–40

30391 2000 GMC Sierra Pick Up.$25–40

30392 2002 Cadillac Escalade $25–40

30394 2000 Chevrolet Silverado Pick Up..............$25–40

Anson Motorcycles

80801 Ducati 916, red, 1:10 ....$25–40

80802 BMW K1200RS, yellow, 1:10 ....$25–40

Anson 1:43 Scale Models

80801 Ford F150 Lightning Pick Up..$8–12

80802 Ford F350 Supercab Pick Up.$8–12

80803 Lincoln Navigator $8–12

80804 Ford Expedition $8–12

80805 Ford Excursion......................$8–12

80806 2000 Chevrolet Silverado $8–12

80807 2000 GMC Sierra $8–12

80808 BMW X5..............................$8–12

80809 2002 Cadillac Escalade.......$8–12

Antex

Only a single model has so far been found to represent this brand.

Porsche 944, 1:43 ....$5

APM (see American Precision Models)

Aquli

Argentina is home to the Aquli brand, makers of Matchbox-like knockoffs, poorly cast but retaining some of the charm and accuracy of their legitimate counterparts.

Alfa Carabo..............$1

A.R.

A.R. is among the earliest of French manufacturers of miniature vehicles, dating back to the 1920s. A.R. produced toys in a variety of media, including tinplate, cast iron, lead, and zinc alloy. Its cars, mostly Peugeots, are valued at $100 and up. A series of Peugeot 301 trucks is listed as well, with models valued at $75 to $100 each.

Below is a sampling of models and values.

Bluebird Record Car, 5" $100

Peugeot Andreau Coupe $100

Peugeot Andreau Limousine $100

Peugeot 301 Mail Truck, 3⅜"..................$100

Renault Paris Bus, 3⅞".............................$100

Arbur

Among the many more prominent British toy companies was a comparatively obscure one known as Arbur Products. The products they manufactured in the late forties and early fifties were toys based on Dinky Toys and others.

Fire Truck, 1:50..............$50

MG Record Car, 1:43 ....$40

Scammell Tractor Trailer, 1:50 ....$35

Sunbeam Coupe, 1:43 ....$50

Tractor Trailer Flatbed Truck, 1:50 ....$35

Tractor Trailer Open Bed Truck, 1:50 ....$35

Tractor Trailer Van, 1:50.............................$35

Arcade

The most prominent name in cast-iron and zinc alloy toys, Arcade began in 1868 as the Novelty Iron Works in Freeport, Illinois. Arcade reached prominence in 1921 with the introduction of a series of Yellow Cab replicas. The company continued producing toys until the Second World War. Arcade's classic style and detailing creates a bridge between cast-iron toys of the day and diecast zinc alloy toys of the future. Here is just a sampling of the over 260 models offered.

A.C.F. Bus, 1927, 11½" $3,500

Ambulance, 1932, 7¾"..............$750

Car carrier with cars, 1931, 24½"........$2,000

Chevy Coupe $7,000

Double Decker Bus, 1929, 8½" $900

Double Decker Bus, Chicago Motor Coach, 1936, 8¼" $900

Greyhound Cruiser Coach Bus, 1941, 9⅛" $500

Greyhound Cruiser Coach Bus, 1937, 7¾" $400

Red Baby Truck, 1923, 10¾"..............$1,250

Yellow Cab, approx. 7½ to 8 inches, 1936 ....$8,500–10,000

Yellow Coach Double Decker Bus, 1925, 14" $4,000

Archer

The distinction of Archer plastic toys are their futuristic appearance. Inspired by the 1930s movie matinees of Flash Gordon and Buck Rogers, these streamlined toys were produced in both large and small versions. The Raymobile in particular is a sleek pickup truck with a deadly looking weapon perched in the back and an attendant on the tailgate.

Futuristic Auto Carrier with four 5" vehicles, #349, 14"...$175–225
Futuristic Convertible, 10" $75–90
Futuristic Convertible, 5" $30–35
Futuristic Coupe, 10" $75–90
Futuristic Coupe, 5" $30–35
Futuristic Gasoline Truck, 5" $50–65
Futuristic Pickup Truck, 10" $85–110
Futuristic Pickup Truck, 5" $30–35
Raymobile $60–75
Rocket, red, yellow and black, 13"....$125–150
Scopemobile..$60–75
Searchmobile $60–75

Argo

Argo is a brand of tin litho cars from the late forties and early fifties. While they are fairly simple toys with windows and doors printed on the metal exterior, each demonstrated a distinctive working feature such as wipers, ringing bells or, in the case of the taxi, a moving meter. All Argo cars are based on a single model with variations in colors, markings, and working features. They sold in 1955 for $2.98 each.

Ambulance, bell rings $15–20
Armored Car with cannon $15–20
Armored Car with machine gun $15–20
Chief Car, bell rings $15–20
Chief Car, fixed bell $15–20
Police Car, gun moves...........................$15–20
Sedan, windshield wipers work.............$15–20
Sedan, windows roll up and down........$15–20
Taxi with meter on roof..........................$15–20
Taxi with meter in windshield $15–20

Armour (also see Detail Cars, C.D.C.)

Armour models are mostly military vehicles made by C.D.C. S.r.l. (Detail Cars), Via F. Lippi No. 19, 20131 Milano, Italy.

CDC Armour Collection 1:72 Scale

3100 PZ KPFZ IV North Africa $29–32
3101 PZ KPFW IV Type F1 Tank.....$28–30
3102 PZ KPFZ IV G North Africa.....$29–32
3103 PZ KPFZ IV G Europe West ...$29–32
3104 PZ KPFZ IV G Europe West ...$29–32
3112 Hummer M 1025 European..$17–19
3114 Hummer M 998 European $17–19
3124 LAV 25 European 90MM Gun.$29–32
3130 Tank Sherman Europe West...$29–32
3131 Tank Sherman North Africa....$29–32
3132 Tank Sherman Europe West...$29–32
3133 Tank Sherman Europe West...$29–32
3135 Tank Sherman Pacific USMC .$29–32
3136 Tank Sherman Europe West FR.$29–32
3138 Tank Sherman Battle Dress $29–32
3143 Tank US 2.5T Cargo Truck Europe UK..$29–32
3144 US Army 2.5T Tanker Truck ...$25–27
3165 Tank Panther AUSF $29–32
3200 Flak PZ IV Wirbelwing $28–30
3210 Tank PZ KPFW IV Europe $29–32
3211 Tank PZ KPFW IV Europe $29–32
3212 Tank PZ KPFW IV Europe $29–32
3214 Tank PZ KPFW IV Europe $29–32

Arnold

Arnold toys are tin lithographed windup, friction, and battery-operated toys produced in Japan in the 1950s. Their military jeep with three figures seated inside is the most commonly seen model. The battery-operated jeep was connected by a cable to the remote control box. While the jeep is an attractive toy worth displaying, many collectors have cut the control cable to make the model more appealing. The unfortunate result is a drastic reduction in the value of the toy.

Fire Chief Car, friction with battery operated siren, 10" $300
Military Jeep, white with green stars, with remote control cable intact $500
    with cable cut off.............................$125
Military Jeep, green with white stars, with remote control cable intact $300
    with cable cut off...............................$75
Packard Convertible, 10" $175
Police Car, friction, 10" $500
Sparkling Fire Truck, U.S. Zone, windup, 4½" $500

Arnold, Bruce (see Bruce Arnold Models)

Arpra

Kits and ready-built models of plastic and metal are available under the Arpra brand of Brazil.

1 Mercedes-Benz 1513 Refrigerated Cargo Truck, 1:50 ....$20
2 Mercedes-Benz 1513 Refrigerator Van, blue/white $24
3 Mercedes-Benz 1513 Van, blue/white $24
4 Mercedes-Benz 608 ....$24
8 Scania LKS-141 Semi-Tractor with Tandem Axles, 1:50 ....$20
9 Scania LK-141 Semi-Cab, orange............$24
10 Scania LKS-141 Cab, orange $24
11 Scania LK-111 Semi-Cab, orange............$24
12 Scania T-112 Semi-Cab, orange $24
13 Scania R-142 Semi-Cab, orange $24
16 Trailer Refrigerator, white......................$24
19 Trailer Oil, white...................................$24
20 Trailer LP Gas, white............................$24
29 Dynapac CA25PD $24
30 Dynapac CA25D Roller, yellow............$24

37 Scania T112 Semi Gas Truck, orange....$45
39 Mercedes-Benz 1932 Semi-Cab, white ..$24
136 Scania T112 Semi-Cab, green............$24
302 Mercedes-Benz 0371 2-Axle Highway Bus, silver, orange, and red $75
304 Scania Fire Tanker $65
310 Scania L111 Semi Gas Truck, orange, 1:50 ....$65

ARS

ARS of Italy produces high quality 1:43 scale versions of Alfa Romeo automobiles.

101 Alfa Romeo Spider, top up, red, green, silver, yellow $24
103 Alfa Romeo 33 Boxer 16V, red, black..$24
104 Alfa Romeo 33 Sedan 1.5L 1E, dark green..$24
105 Alfa Romeo 33 Sedan Permanente, orange...$24

Art Model

Art Model miniatures are licensed 1:43 scale versions of various Ferrari models, manufactured in Pesaro, Italy. Art Model vehicles sell for $36 each.

Incidentally, "stradale" is Italian for street (as in Fiat Strada) as compared to "prova," which indicates a racing, proving grounds, or prototype version.

001 Ferrari 166 MM Coupe Prova, red......$36
002 Ferrari 166 MM Coupe Stradale, cream...$36
003 Ferrari 166 MM Coupe Stradale, black...$36
004 Ferrari 195 S Coupe Mille Miglia 1950, blue...$36
005 Ferrari 166 MM Spyder Prova, red......$36
006 Ferrari 166 MM Spyder Stradale, white..$36
007 Ferrari 166 MM Spyder Stradale, black...$36
008 Ferrari 166 MM Spyder Mille Miglia 1949, red...$36
009 Ferrari 195 S Coupe Le Mans 1950, blue...$36
010 Ferrari 166 MM Coupe Mille Miglia 1951, red...$36
011 Ferrari 166 MM Spyder Le Mans 1949, red...$36
012 Ferrari 166 MM Spyder 12 Ore di Parigi, yellow...$36
014 Ferrari 500 TRC 1956 Prova, red........$36
015 Ferrari 500 TRC Clienti, yellow............$36
016 Ferrari 166 MM Coupe Le Mans 1950, yellow...$36
017 Ferrari 166 MM Spyder Mille Miglia 1950, silver..$36
Ferrari 410 S 1955 ....$36
Ferrari 340 Mexico 1952 ....$36
Ferrari California 250 Spyder 1957, top up..$36

Asahi Model Pet

Asahi models are made in Japan. Asahi Toy Company first made tinplate toy cars in the late forties and early fifties. It wasn't until 1960 or so that the company produced diecast toys under the "Model Pet" brand. While production reportedly ended in the early seventies. The 1:43 scale Rolls Royce Camargue has been produced later, as recently as 1980 or so, and is the only recent offering known of the brand.

1 Toyota/Toyopet Crown Deluxe, 1:43 ....$125
1A Toyota Crown, gold plated, 1:43........$150
2 Toyota Masterline Station Wagon, 1:43.$125
2A Toyota Masterline Ambulance, white, 1:43 ....$225
3 Subaru 360, 1:40 ....$125
4 Toyota Land Cruiser, green, 1:43 ....$150
5 Datsun Bluebird, 1:42 ....$125
6 Prince Skyline Deluxe, 1:42 ....$125
7 Toyota Corona, 1:42 ....$100
8 Austin A50 Cambridge, 1:42 ....$150
9 Hillman Minx, 1:42 ....$150
10 Nissan Cedric, 1:42 ....$125
10A Nissan Cedric Taxi, 1:42 ....$150
11 Toyota Crown Station Wagon, 1:42 ...$100
12 Toyota Crown, 1:42 ....$125
12A Toyota Crown Police, 1:42 ....$175
13 Mazda R360 Coupe, 1:42 ....$125
14 Toyota Publica, 1:42 ....$100
15 Prince Skyline Sports Convertible, 1:42.$125
16 Prince Skyline Sports Coupe, 1:42........$125
17 Datsun Bluebird, 1:42 ....$100
18 Isuzu Bellett, 1:42 ....$125
19 Toyota Sports Coupe, 1:42 ....$100
20 Toyota Crown, 1:42 ....$100
20A Toyota Crown, gold plated, 1:42 .....$125
20B Toyota Crown Police, black and white, 1:42 ....$150
21 Toyota Masterline Station Wagon, 1:42 ....$100
21A Toyota Masterline Ambulance, white, 1:42 ....$150
22 Prince Gloria, 1:42 ....$100
22A Prince Gloria Taxi, 1:42 ....$150
23 Toyota Land Cruiser, green, 1:42 ....$150
24 Mitsubishi Colt 1000, 1:42 ....$75
25 Datsun Bluebird, 1:42 ....$75
26 Hino Contessa 1300, 1:42 ....$75
27 Toyota Corona, 1:42 ....$100
29 Hino Contessa 1300 Coupe, 1:42 ....$75
30 Mazda Familia, 1:42 ....$75
31 Toyota Sports 800, 1:42 ....$75
32 Nissan Silvia Coupe, 1:42 ....$75
33 Nissan Cedric, 1:42 ....$75
34 Honda S800 Roadster, 1:42 ....$100
35 Honda S800 Coupe, 1:42 ....$100
36 Toyota 2000GT Coupe, 1:42 ....$75
37 Honda N360, 1:40 ....$75
38 Toyota Crown Super, 1:42 ....$50
39 Toyota Crown Coupe, 1:42 ....$50
40 Mitsubishi Galant GTO, 1:42 ....$50
41 Toyota Crown Police, black and white, 1:42 ....$50
43 Honda RC162 Motorcycle, 1:35 ....$30
44 Suzuki 750GT Motorcycle, 1:35 ....$30

45 Nissan Skyline 2000GT Coupe, 1:35...$30
46 Yamaha 650XS Motorcycle, 1:35 ....$30
47 Datsun Sunny Coupe EX1400, 1:42......$50
48 Honda 750 Motorcycle, 1:35 ....$30
50 Honda 750 Police Motorcycle, 1:50 .....$30
51 Toyota Corona Mk. II 2000G SS, 1:42.$50
52 Datsun Bluebird UHT, 1:42 ....$50
54 Nissan Cedric 2600 GX, 1:42 ....$50
55 Toyota Crown Taxi, yellow, 1:42 ....$50
56 Toyota Crown Fire Car, red, 1:42 ....$50
57 Toyota Crown Ambulance, white, 1:42..$50
58 Mitsubishi Galant GTO Rally, 1:42 ......$50
59 Nissan Skyline 2000GT Rally, 1:42 ......$50
60 Yamaha Police Motorcycle with Sidecar, 1:35 ....$30
61 Yamaha Police Motorcycle, 1:35 ....$30
62 Yamaha Motorcycle with Sidecar, 1:35 .$30
101 Toyota Toyoace Truck, 1:48 ....$150
102 1963 Toyota Toyoace Covered Truck, 1:48 ....$150
103 Honda Motorcycle, 1:40 ....$75
Rolls Royce Camargue, yellow, orange, or gray, 1:42 ....$20

Ashton

Gerhard Klarwasser
Route 1 Scale Models
P O Box 1406
Attleboro Falls MA 02763-0406

Ashton Models of New England are finely detailed hand-built 1:43 scale fire fighting equipment. The most popular model is the Ahrens-Fox Fire Engine. Gerhard Klarwasser, previously the owner of Toys for Collectors, now produces these models and others under the auspices of Route 1 Scale Models.

Ashton Models Fire Trucks Scale 1:43

7020A 1951 Mack Pumper Type 95 "Chicago" $135
7022A Ahrens Fox Chemical Truck "Bristol" No. 3 (1927)............................$135
7025 FWD Model F50T Pumper "Cedarburg" (1951)............................$200
7027 Ahrens Fox Model J "Cincinnati" (1921)..$170
7027 Ahrens-Fox Piston Pumper "New Orleans" (1921) $109
7030 Mack Pumper "Centerport" L.I., NY (1953)..$170
7033 Ahrens Fox "Cincinnati" K.17 City Service Truck (1923) $195
7035 Ahrens-Fox Piston Pumper "Harrisburg" (1921)..............................$109
7038 Mack Pumper "Hanover" G.P.M. 750 (1952)..$95
7039 Ahrens Fox "Vandergrift" NS4 1000 G.P.M. Pumper (1925) $95
7040 Ahrens-Fox Aerial Ladder Truck "Clifton" $179
7044 Mack Type L "F.D.N.Y." Rescue Truck No. 1 (1948) $190
7046 Ahrens-Fox Ladder Truck "Nashua" (1923)..$189

7051 Ahrens Fox H.T. Pumper "F.D.N.Y. 264" (1938).............................$230
7052 Mack Fuel Tanker "F.D.N.Y." (1941)..$190
7053 Mack Pumper L Typ "Bridgeport PA" (1949)..$95
7057 Mack L Typ 95 Pumper "Chicago" (1954)..$95
7058 Mack Rescue Truck "Tuxedo Cheverly" (1952)..$190
7060 Ahrens-Fox Aerial Ladder Truck Buffalo N.Y. (1927)............................$260
7061 Mack with 1956 Rescue Body "Boston Engine No.11" (1947)..............$195
7062 Ahrens-Fox KS2 Pumper "Tokyo" (1924)..$195
7063 Ahrens-Fox PS2 "New South Wales Fire Brigade" Australia (1929).......$195
7066 GMC Pumper "Riegelsville, PA" (1961)..$195

Ashton "Gold Collection"

7031G Mack Tow Truck "Detroit" $175
7034G FWD Open Cab Truck "Cody" $175
7036G Ahrens-Fox Aerial Ladder Truck "Newark"....................................$229
7037G Mack Quad "Whitehall" $229
7041G Ahrens-Fox Pumper "Newark" $169
7042G Mack 95 1000 GAL. Pumper "Ellensburg" (1949)........................$280
7043G Mack LT 1000 GAL. Pumper "Glendale" CA (1954) $285
7045G Mack L Type Rescue Truck "Silver Springs" MD (1949)........................$285
7048G FWD High Pressure Foam Pumper "Chicago" (1949)........................$285
7049G Ahrens Fox HT Pumper "New Worlds Fair" (1938)........................$320
7050G Fire House display, 2 Fire Trucks + House (carton)............................$475
7055G Ahrens Fox Pawtucket (1938) No.1 ....$320
7056G Ahrens Fox Pawtucket (1938) No. 7 ....$340
7064G Mack with 1956 Rescue Body "Boston Engine No.14" (1947).....$320
7065G Mack with 1956 Rescue Body "Boston Engine No.45" (1947).....$320
7067G Mack (1947) $320

Auburn Rubber Company

Auburn, Indiana, was home to the Auburn Rubber Company, makers of some of the most popular toy cars of the '30s, '40s, and '50s. Auburn started in 1935 producing toy soldiers. The first rubber vehicle was produced in 1936 — a Cord sedan. Some ninety different rubber vehicles were produced in quantities numbering in the millions. By 1952, vinyl was substituted for rubber. The company continued producing such toys until 1969 when the Auburn went out of business. Below is a sampling of cars produced.

There were also trucks, military vehicles, and farm implements made.

Auburn Rubber Toys
1939 Buick Y Job Experimental Roadster, 9¾" $95
1948 Buick 2-Door fastback sedanette, 7¼" $95
1950 Cadillac 4-Door sedan, 7¼" $85
1936 Cord 4-Door sedan, 6" $150
1935 Ford 2-Door, 4" $60
1935 Ford Coupe, 4" $60
Futuristic Sedan with center tailfin, 5" $45
1946 Lincoln Convertible 2-Door, 4½" ...$45
1937 Oldsmobile 4-Door sedan, 4½" ...$60
1938 Oldsmobile 4-Door sedan, 5¾" ...$75
1940 Oldsmobile 4-Door sedan, open fenders, 6" $65
1940 Oldsmobile 4-Door sedan, fender skirts, 6" $55

Auburn Vinyl Toys
Airport Limousine, 7½" $25
Cadillac Convertible, 3½" $15
Cadillac Convertible, 5" $25
Ford Ranchero, 4¾" $25
Sedan, 4½" $45
Station Wagon, 4⅝" $25

Aurora Cigar Box
Aurora is best known for HO gauge slot cars. Their 1968 Cigar Box line of cars were so named for the clever box in which they were packaged. Each Cigar Box model featured a shiny-colored-chrome plastic body. A diecast metal chassis was held on with two screws so that it could be easily removed and replaced with slot car chassis and motor. The wheels were unimpressive, to say the least. But the cars themselves were fairly realistic for their original retail price, about 50–75 cents each. Popularity of these little cars has increased in just the last couple of years. Prices below represent new condition specimens in original box. Out of the box, models are worth about 60 percent of price listed.

AC Cobra, lavender $75
Buick Riviera...$35
Camaro $55
Chaparral, white, #6114 ....$35
Cheetah, yellow $55
Cobra GT $35
Corvette Stingray $60
Cougar, #6116 ....$50
Ferrari Berlinetta $35
Ferrari Dino, yellow, #6111 ....$35
Firebird..$55
Ford GT, metallic lavender/pink, #6105 .....$40
Ford J Car, yellow, #6104 ....$35
Ford XL-500
    v.1 white, #6107 ....$35
    v.2 red, #6207 ....$35
Jaguar XKE
Lola GT..$35
    Mako Shark, blue, #6103 ....$40
    Mangusta...$40

Mustang Convertible, purple $60
Mustang Hardtop $80
Porsche 904, red, #6112....................$35
Thunderbird, #6110
    v.1 yellow $55
    v.2 white $55
Volkswagen $75
Willy's Gasser, pink $75

Authenticast (see Comet)

AutoArt (also see Gateway Global)
AUTOart is a brand of precision scale diecast models from Gateway Global, the new parent company for UT, as well as new Gate and AUTOart brands. AUTOart models are available in 1:12, 1:18 and 1:43 scale.

1:12 AUTOart Signature
12001 1:12 Mercedes Benz CLK GTR FIA GT 1997 GT1 Champion B.SCHNEIDER / A.WURZ / K.LUDWIG #11 ....$50–70

1:12 AUTOart Motorcycle
12501 Vespa Scooter GS 150 ......$50–70

1:12 AUTOart Contemporary
79831 Snowmobile GT SE 2000, black $50–70
79832 Snowmobile GT SE 2001, blue $50–70
79811 Snowmobile MXZ 700 2001, yellow $50–70
79821 Snowmobile Mach Z 2001, black $50–70

1:18 AUTOart Movie

70020 Aston Martin DB5, silver, James Bond 007 Goldfinger.............................$55–70

70021 James Bond Aston Martin DB5 with weapons, silver $50–70
70060 For Your Eyes Only James Bond Lotus Esprit Turbo, metallic red $50–70
75300 The Spy Who Loved Me James Bond Lotus Esprit Type 79, white $50–70
75306 The Spy Who Loved Me James Bond Lotus Submarine.......................$50–70
73519 Jaguar XK-SS 1956 Steve McQueen version, green $50–70
70511 The World Is Not Enough James Bond BMW Z8 ....$50–70
80030 Porsche 917K Le Mans Steve McQueen version #20.............$50–70

1:18 AUTOart Millennium
71051 Chevrolet Corvette SS 1957, blue .$50–70
73541 Jaguar XJ 13, green $50–70
70501 BMW 2002 Turbo, white ...$50–70
74001 Jeep Grand Wagoneer 1989..$50–70
86496 Chaparral 2 "Sport Racer" 1965, #66 ....$50–70

1:18 AUTOart Contemporary
71061 Chevrolet Corvette Z06 2001, torch red $50–70
71062 Chevrolet Corvette Z06 2001, quick silver $50–70
71063 Chevrolet Corvette Z06 2001, millenium yellow $50–70
79731 VW New Beetle, reflex yellow..$50–70
79732 VW New Beetle, vapor blue ..$50–70
79711 VW New Beetle Dune, yellow..$50–70
79721 VW New Beetle RSI, silver ..$50–70
71521 Chrysler GT Cruiser, silver....$50–70
71522 Chrysler GT Cruiser, black...$50–70
71531 Chrysler Panel Cruiser, metallic blue.....................................$50–70
71532 Chrysler Panel Cruiser, metallic red.......................................$50–70

1:18 AUTOart Performance
70071 Lamborghini Diablo Coupe VT, titanium silver $50–70
70072 Lamborghini Diablo Coupe VT, metallic red $50–70
70081 Lamborghini Diablo SV, black...$50–70
70082 Lamborghini Diablo SV, metallic blue.....................................$50–70
70083 Lamborghini Diablo SV, yellow..$50–70
70091 Lamborghini Diablo Roadster, red $50–70
70092 Lamborghini Diablo Roadster, yellow $50–70
70093 Lamborghini Diablo Roadster, black $50–70
70041 Lexus GS 400, black, LH drive .$50–70
70042 Lexus GS 400, silver, LH drive ..$50–70
70045 Toyota V300 Aristo, silver, RH drive $50–70
70046 Toyota V300 Aristo, black, RH drive $50–70

71000 1959 Corvette Stingray Experimental Car, 1:18..............................$65–70

72710 Ford Mustang Super Stallion, blue $50–70
72831 Ford Forty Nine, black $50–70
72720 Saleen Mustang S351 Coupe, yellow $50–70
72721 Saleen Mustang S351 Coupe, white $50–70
72730 Saleen Mustang S351 Convertible, metallic red $50–70
72731 Saleen Mustang S351 Convertible, yellow $50–70
73201 Honda S 2000, yellow (LH driver) (European version)...................$50–70
73202 Honda S 2000, black (LH driver) (European version)...................$50–70

73203 Honda S 2000, white (LH driver) (European version)..................$50–70
73204 Honda S 2000, silver (LH driver) (European version)..................$50–70
73206 Honda S 2000, black (LH driver) (US version) $50–70
73207 Honda S 2000, white (LH driver) (US version) $50–70
73208 Honda S 2000, silver (LH driver) (US version) $50–70
73209 Honda S 2000, yellow (RH driver) (Japan version)..................$50–70
73210 Honda S 2000, black (RH driver) (Japan version)..................$50–70
73211 Honda S 2000, white (RH driver) (Japan version)..................$50–70
73212 Honda S 2000, silver (RH driver) (Japan version)..................$50–70
77151 Mitsubishi Lancer EVO VI, blue..................$50–70
77152 Mitsubishi Lancer EVO VI, white $50–70
77153 Mitsubishi Lancer EVO VI, silver..................$50–70
77156 Mitsubishi Lancer EVO VI "TOMMI MAKINEN" edition, red $50–70
77157 Mitsubishi Lancer EVO VI "TOMMI MAKINEN" edition, white........$50–70
77158 Mitsubishi Lancer EVO VI "TOMMI MAKINEN" edition, black $50–70
77301 Nissan Skyline R34 GTR 1999, blue..................$50–70
77302 Nissan Skyline R34 GTR 1999, titanium silver..................$50–70
77303 Nissan Skyline R34 GTR 1999, white $50–70
77304 Nissan Skyline R34 GTR 1999, midnight purple..................$50–70
78201 Panoz GTR-1 street car, ocean extreme $50–70
78202 Panoz GTR-1 street car, gold $50–70
78211 Panoz Roadster 1998, red..$50–70
78212 Panoz Roadster 1998, silver...$50–70
78213 Panoz Roadster 1998, yellow.$50–70
78601 Subaru Impreza 22B, metallic blue..$50–70
78611 Subaru Impreza WRX Type R, yellow.$50–70
78612 Subaru Impreza WRX Type R, blue ...$50–70
78621 Subaru Impreza WRX 4DRS, white...$50–70
78622 Subaru Impreza WRX 4DRS, blue...$50–70
71011 Callaway C12 1998, silver...$50–70
71012 Callaway C12 1998, red..$50–70
71013 Callaway C12 1998, yellow .$50–70
71014 Callaway C12 "MUKO" car, blue..................$50–70
70112 Mercedes Benz CL 600, black.$50–70
70113 Mercedes Benz CL 600, white.$50–70
70121 Mercedes Benz CL 500 "LORINSER VERINSER", silver..................$50–70
70125 Mercedes Benz CL 55 AMG "F1 limited edition," silver..................$50–70
78701 Lexus IS300 1999, yellow ..$50–70
78702 Lexus IS300 1999, blue $50–70
78703 Lexus IS300 1999, black ...$50–70

78707 Toyota RS200 Altezza 1999, yellow..................$50–70
78708 Toyota RS200 Altezza 1999, white $50–70
78709 Toyota RS200 Altezza 1999, silver..................$50–70
78711 Toyota MR2 Spyder 2000, red (LH drive)..................$50–70
78715 Toyota MR2 Spyder 2000, red (RH drive)..................$50–70
78712 Toyota MR2 Spyder 2000, silver (LH drive)..................$50–70
78716 Toyota MR2 Spyder 2000, silver (RH drive)..................$50–70
78713 Toyota MR2 Spyder 2000, yellow (LH drive)..................$50–70
78717 Toyota MR2 Spyder 2000, yellow (RH drive)..................$50–70
78721 Toyota Celica GTS 2000, silver (LH drive)..................$50–70
78722 Toyota Celica GTS 2000, red (LH drive)..................$50–70
78723 Toyota Celica GTS 2000, yellow (LH drive)..................$50–70
78726 Toyota Celica GTS 2000, silver (RH drive)..................$50–70
78727 Toyota Celica GTS 2000, red (RH drive)..................$50–70
78728 Toyota Celica GTS 2000, yellow (RH drive)..................$50–70
74821 BMW Mini Cooper, silver (with sunroof)..................$50–70
74822 BMW Mini Cooper, red (without sunroof)..................$50–70
74823 BMW Mini Cooper, racing green (without sunroof)..................$50–70
77811 Porsche 996 GT3, red $50–70
77812 Porsche 996 GT3, yellow ...$50–70
77821 Porsche 996 GT3R, white ...$50–70
77831 Porsche 996 Turbo, red $50–70
77832 Porsche 996 Turbo, silver $50–70
73432 Holden Commodore VT Coupe 2000, gold, w/certificate $50–70
74511 Lamborghini Murcielago, metallic yellow..................$50–70
74512 Lamborghini Murcielago, metallic orange..................$50–70
74513 Lamborghini Murcielago, metallic black $50–70

1:18 AUTOart Classics
70023 Aston Martin DB-5, green (LH drive)..................$50–70
70024 Aston Martin DB-5, green (RH drive)..................$50–70
70025 Aston Martin DB-5, metallic red (LH drive)..................$50–70
70026 Aston Martin DB-5, metallic red (RH drive)..................$50–70
70061 Lotus Esprit Turbo, black......$50–70
70062 Lotus Esprit Turbo, white......$50–70
70066 Essex Lotus Esprit Turbo, blue....$50–70
71000 Chevrolet Corvette Stingray 1959, silver $50–70

71001 Chevrolet Corvette Stingray 1959, red..................$50–70
71021 Chevrolet Corvette 1982 collector edition, silver..................$50–70
73500 Jaguar 120C (C-Type) 1951, green..................$50–70
73501 Jaguar 120C (C-Type) 1951, silver..................$50–70
73502 Jaguar 120C (C-Type) 1951, bronze..................$50–70
73510 Jaguar XK SS 1956, blue....$50–70
73511 Jaguar XK SS 1956, green..$50–70
73512 Jaguar XK SS 1956, cream.$50–70
73561 Jaguar D Type (short nose), green..................$50–70
75301 Lotus Esprit Type 79, yellow....$50–70
75302 Lotus Esprit Type 79, green ..$50–70

1:18 AUTOart Off Road
70010 Range Rover 4.6 HSE, metallic green (LH drive)..................$50–70
70011 Range Rover 4.6 HSE, metallic green (RH drive)..................$50–70
70012 Range Rover 4.6 HSE, metallic red (LH drive)..................$50–70
70013 Range Rover 4.6 HSE, metallic red (RH drive)..................$50–70
70014 Range Rover 4.6 HSE, silver (LH drive)..................$50–70
70015 Range Rover 4.6 HSE, silver (RH drive)..................$50–70
70016 Range Rover 4.6 HSE, metallic black (LH drive)..................$50–70
70017 Range Rover 4.6 HSE, metallic black (RH drive)..................$50–70
70031 Lexus RX 300, silver (LH drive) .$50–70
70032 Lexus RX 300, black (LH drive)..................$50–70
70035 Toyota Harrier, metallic red (RH drive)..................$50–70
70036 Toyota Harrier, bronze (RH drive)..................$50–70
72761 Lincoln Navigator, white......$50–70
72762 Lincoln Navigator, black......$50–70
72781 Ford Expedition Himalaya, white..................$50–70
74011 Jeep Grand Cherokee 1999, white..................$50–70
74012 Jeep Grand Cherokee 1999, black..................$50–70
74013 Jeep Grand Cherokee 1999, red..................$50–70
77101 Mitsubishi Pajero LWB 1998, metallic blue (RH drive)..................$50–70
77103 Mitsubishi Pajero LWB 1998, metallic blue (LH drive)..................$50–70
77102 Mitsubishi Pajero LWB 1998, metallic red (RH drive)..................$50–70
77104 Mitsubishi Pajero LWB 1998, metallic red (LH drive)..................$50–70
77105 Mitsubishi Pajero LWB 1998, white (RH drive)..................$50–70
77106 Mitsubishi Pajero LWB 1998, white (LH drive)..................$50–70

77121 Mitsubishi Pajero SWB 1998, silver $50–70
77122 Mitsubishi Pajero SWB 1998, black $50–70
77131 Mitsubishi Pajero EVO, black $50–70
77132 Mitsubishi Pajero EVO, red ..$50–70
77133 Mitsubishi Pajero EVO, white $50–70

1:18 AUTOart Police
72701 Ford Crown Victoria LAPD Police $50–70
72702 Ford Crown Victoria Des Plaines Police $50–70
72703 Ford Crown Victoria NYPD Police $50–70

1:18 AUTOart Racing
80031 Porsche 917K Daytona 24HR 1970 REDMAN / SIFFERT #1 ....$50–70
80032 Porsche 917K Le Mans 1970 Winner H.HERRMANN / R.ATTWOOD #23 ....$50–70
80033 Porsche 917K Daytona 24 Hr 1970 KINNUNEN / RODRIGUEZ #2.$50–70
80034 Porsche 917K Sebring Winner 1971 ELFORD & LARROUSSE #3 ....$50–70
80035 Porsche 917K KYAIAMI 1970 SIFFERT / AHRENS #2 ....$50–70
80036 Porsche 917K WATKINS GLEN LARROUSE / VAN LENNEP #35 ....$50–70
80010 Toyota racing truck '98 IVAN STEWART #11 ....$50–70
80011 Toyota racing truck '97 IVAN STEWART #1 ....$50–70
80020 Toyota Corolla WRC 1998 C.SAINZ / L.MOYA #5 (RALLY PORTUGAL) $50–70
80021 Toyota Corolla WRC 1998 F. LOIX / S.SMEETS #9 (RALLY PORTUGAL) $50–70
80022 Toyota Corolla WRC 1998 C.SAINZ / L.MOYA #5 (RALLY FINLAND) $50–70
80023 Toyota Corolla WRC 1998 D.AURIOL/D. GIRAUDET #6 (RALLY GREAT BRITAIN) $50–70
80024 Toyota Corolla WRC 1998 D.AURIOL / D.GIRAUDET #6 (RALLY AUSTRALIA) $50–70
80025 Toyota Corolla WRC 1998 D. AURIOL / D. GIRAUDET #9 (RALLY ESPANA) $50–70
80026 Toyota Corolla WRC 1998 C.SAINZ / L.MOYA #5 (RALLY ARGENTINA) $50–70
80027 Toyota Corolla WRC 1998 C.SAINZ / L.MOYA #5 (RALLY NEW ZEALAND) $50–70
80028 Toyota Corolla ASIA -PACIFIC RALLY CHAMPION 1998 Y.FUJIMOTO/SIRCOM #16 ....$50–70

89981 Toyota Corolla WRC 1999 D.AURIOL / D.GIRAUDET #4 (SAFARI RALLY KENYA) $50–70
89982 Toyota Corolla WRC 1999 C.SAINZ / L.MOYA #3 (SAFARI RALLY KENYA) $50–70
80081 Toyota Corolla WRC 2000 S.PREVOT / B.THIRY #18 (RALLY MONTE CARLO) $50–70
89986 Toyota TS020 LeMans 24TH 1999 M.BRUNDLE / E.COLLARD / V.SOSPIRI #1 ....$50–70
89987 Toyota TS020 LeMans 24TH 1999 T.BOUTSEN / R.KELLENERS / A.MCNISH #2 ....$50–70
89988 Toyota TS020 LeMans 24TH 1999 U.KATAYAMA / T.SUZUKI / K.TSUCHIYA #3 ....$50–70
89906 Chevrolet Corvette C5-R GT2 24 ROLEX HR AT DAYTONA R.FELLOWS /J.PAUL JR /C.KNEIFEL CAR #2 ....$50–70
89907 Chevrolet Corvette C5-R GT2 24 ROLEX HR AT DAYTONA S.SHARP /A.PILGRIM /J.HEINRICY #4 ...$50–70
80005 Chevrolet Corvette C5-R ALMS R FELLOWS /C KNEIFEL /J BELL #3 .$50–70
80006 Chevrolet Corvette C5-R ALMS A PILGRIM / K COLLINS / F FREON #4 ....$50–70
80007 Chevrolet Corvette C5-R ALMS 2000 TEXAS WINNER R.FELLOWS /C.KNEIFEL #3 ....$50–70
80106 Chevrolet Corvette C5-R GT2 CLASS 2001 ROLEX 24AT DAYTONA R.FELLOWS / C.KNEIFEL / J.O CONNELL / F.FREON #2 ....$50–70
80107 Chevrolet Corvette C5-R 2001 TEXAS 24AT WINNER LEMANS A.PILGRIM/K.COLLINS/F.FREON #64 ....$50–70
89721 Dodge Viper GTS-R 1997 SEBRING O.BERETTA / PH.GACHE #51 ....$50–70
89722 Dodge Viper GTS-R 1997 SEBRING T.ARCHER / J.BELL #52 ....$50–70
89723 Dodge Viper GTS-R 24HR AT DAYTONA 1997 SEBRING O.BERETTA / T.ARCHER / D.DUPUY #94 .....$50–70
89821 Dodge Viper GTS-R LE MANS 1998 1ST RUNNERS UP GT2 CLASS T.ARCHER / O.BERETTA / P.LAMY #51 ......$50–70
89822 Dodge Viper GTS-R LE MANS 1998 G.AYLES / J.HUGENHOLTZ / M.TURNER #56 ....$50–70
89823 Dodge Viper GTS-R LE MANS 1998 N.AMORIN / G.GOMES / M.MELLOBRYNER #55 ....$50–70
89824 Dodge Viper GTS-R LE MANS 1998 WINNER GT2 CLASS J.BELL / D.DONOHUE / L.DRUDI #53 .$50–70
89921 Dodge Viper GTS-R 1999 ZAKSPEED TEAM #53 ....$50–70

89922 Dodge Viper GTS-R PETITE LE MANS 1999 M.DUEZ / O.BERETTA / K.WENDLINGER #91 ....$50–70
80045 Dodge Viper GTS-R WINNER OF ROLEX 24 AT DAYTONA 2000 O.BERETTA / D.DUPUY / K.WENDLINGER #91 ....$50–70
80047 Chrysler Viper GTS-R WINNER OF LE MANS 2000 D.DUPUY / K.WENDLINGER / O.BERETTA #51 ....$50–70
89831 Mercedes Benz CLK GTR LE MANS 1998 D2 B.SCHNEIDER / K.LUDWIG / M.WEBBER #35 ....$50–70
89832 Mercedes Benz CLK GTR FIA GT 1998 "BYE BYE" K.LUDWIG / R.ZONTA #2 ....$50–70
89833 Mercedes Benz CLK GTR FIA GT 1998 CHAMPION K.LUDWIG / R.ZONTA #2 ....$50–70
89834 Mercedes Benz CLK GTR FIA GT 1998 ORIGINAL-TEILE BERND MAYLANDER / CHRISTOPHE BOUCHUT #11 .....$50–70
89835 Mercedes Benz CLK GTR FIA GT 1998 ORIGINAL-TEILE M.TIEMANN / J.M.GOUNON #12 ....$50–70
89851 Panoz Esperante GTR-1 LE MANS 1998 E.BERNARD / C.TINSEAU / J.O'CONNELL #44 ....$50–70
89852 Panoz Esperante GTR-1 LE MANS 1998 D.BRABHAM / A.WALLACE / J.DAVIES #45 ....$50–70
89853 Panoz Esperante GTR-1 FIA GT 1998 E.BERNARD / D.BRABHAM #3 ......$50–70
89854 Panoz Esperante GTR-1 FIA GT 1998 D.BRABHAM / A .WALLACE #4 ....$50–70
89910 Ford Focus WRC 1999 PRESENTATION CAR $50–70
89911 Ford Focus WRC 1999 C. MCRAE / N.GRIST #7 (RALLY MONTE CARLO) $50–70
89912 Ford Focus WRC Test Car ...$50–70
89913 Ford Focus WRC 1999 C MCRAE / N.GRIST #7 (RALLY PORTUGAL) $50–70
89914 Ford Focus WRC 1999 C.MCRAE / N.GRIST #7 (RALLY SAFARI KENYA WINNER) $50–70
80012 Ford Focus WRC 2000 C. MCRAE / N.GRIST #5 (RALLY MONTE CARLO) $50–70
80013 Ford Focus WRC 2000 C. SAINZ /L.MOYA #6 (RALLY MONTE CARLO) $50–70
80014 Ford Focus WRC 2000 C.MCRAE / N.GRIST #5 (WINNER OF RALLY CATALUNYA) $50–70
80111 Ford Focus WRC 2001 C. Sainz / L.Moya #3 (RALLY MONTE CARLO) $50–70
80112 Ford Focus "RS" WRC 2001, F.DELECOUR / D.GRATALOUP #17 (RALLY MONTE CARLO) $50–70

80016 Ford Mustang Cobra R 2000 (Proto-Type version)................$50–70
89941 Mitsubishi Lancer EVO VI WRC 1999 T.MAKINEN /R.MANNISENMAKI #1 (RALLY NEW ZEALAND) $50–70
89942 Mitsubishi Lancer EVO VI WRC 1999 S.HAYASHI / Y.KATAOKA #2 (WINNER OF RALLY CANBERRA)......$50–70
80041 Mitsubishi Lancer EVO VI WRC 2000 T.MAKINEN / R.MANNISENMAKI #1 (WINNER RALLY MONTE CARLO).$50–70
80141 Mitsubishi Lancer EVO VI WRC 2001 T.MAKINEN / R.MANNISEN-MAKI #7 (WINNER RALLY MONTE CARLO)...............$50–70
89992 Subaru Impreza WRC 1999 R. BURNS / R.REID #5 (RALLY MONTE CARLO)...............$50–70
89993 Subaru Impreza WRC 1999 R. BURNS / R.REID V-RALLY FRANCE #5 ....$50–70
89994 Subaru Impreza WRC '99 R.BURNS / R.REID #5 (RALLY MONTE CARLO/NIGHT RACE)............$50–70
80091 Subaru Impreza RALLY GERMAN 2000 TEAM A .KREMER / K.WICHA #4.................$50–70
80191 Subaru Impreza WRC 2001 R.BURNS/R.REID #5 (RALLY OF PORTUGAL)...............$50–70

1:43 AUTOart Street
55311 Lotus Esprit Type 79, yellow.$20–30
55312 Lotus Esprit Type 79, green ..$20–30
55313 Lotus Esprit Type 79, red $20–30
55301 Lotus Turbo Esprit, pearl white.$20–30
55302 Lotus Turbo Esprit, black.......$20–30
55303 Lotus Turbo Esprit, yellow $20–30
57151 Mitsubishi Lancer EVO 6, white $20–30
57152 Mitsubishi Lancer EVO 6, blue..................$20–30
57156 Mitsubishi Lancer EVO VI "TOMMI MAKINEN" edition street car, red .$20–30
58601 Subaru Impreza 22B, metallic blue...................$20–30
55401 Lotus Esprit V8 1996, red....$20–30
55402 Lotus Esprit V8 1996, black.$20–30
55403 Lotus Esprit V8 1996, yellow .$20–30
55404 Lotus Esprit V8 1996, racing green $20–30
51061 Chevrolet Corvette Mako Shark, dark blue...............$20–30
50201 Aston Martin DB7, silver $20–30
50202 Aston Martin DB7, red $20–30
50203 Aston Martin DB7, metallic blue..................$20–30
50204 Aston Martin DB7, metallic green .$20–30
53601 Jaguar XJR, black $20–30
53602 Jaguar XJR, white $20–30
53603 Jaguar XJR, silver $20–30
53571 Jaguar XJ8, blue $20–30
53572 Jaguar XJ8, red $20–30
53573 Jaguar XJ8, gold.................$20–30

53501 Jaguar C Type, green $20–30
53502 Jaguar C Type, silver............$20–30
53503 Jaguar C Type, bronze........$20–30
53551 Jaguar D-Type (long nose), racing green $20–30
53561 Jaguar D-Type (short nose), racing green $20–30
53631 Jaguar XK8 Coupe, blue $20–30
53632 Jaguar XK8 Coupe, red.......$20–30
53621 Jaguar XKR Coupe, green....$20–30
53622 Jaguar XKR Coupe, white $20–30
54511 Lamborghini Murcielago, metallic yellow...................$20–30
54512 Lamborghini Murcielago, metallic orange $20–30
54513 Lamborghini Murcielago, metallic black $20–30
53751 Jaguar XK SS 1956, blue....$20–30
53752 Jaguar XK SS 1956, green..$20–30
58611 Subaru Legacy B4 1999, gold $20–30
58612 Subaru Legacy B4 1999, white $20–30
58613 Subaru Legacy B4 1999, black $20–30
58621 Subaru Legacy GTB 1999, gold $20–30
58622 Subaru Legacy GTB 1999, white $20–30
58623 Subaru Legacy GTB 1999, silver $20–30
58641 Subaru Impreza WRX STI 2001, silver $20–30
54821 BMW Mini Cooper, silver...$20–30
54822 BMW Mini Cooper, red $20–30
54823 BMW Mini Cooper, racing green $20–30
54824 BMW Mini Cooper, blue....$20–30
54825 BMW Mini Cooper, black ..$20–30
54826 BMW Mini Cooper, yellow.$20–30
51001 Chevrolet Corvette Stingray 1959, silver $20–30
51002 Chevrolet Corvette Stingray 1959, red $20–30
57301 Nissan Skyline R34 GTR 1999, blue $20–30
57302 Nissan Skyline R34 GTR 1999, silver $20–30
57303 Nissan Skyline R34 GTR 1999, midnight purple..................$20–30
59731 VW Beetle (new version), bright blue $20–30
59732 VW Beetle (new version), green ..$20–30
59733 VW Beetle (new version), yellow..................$20–30
59734 VW Beetle (new version), red..$20–30
59711 VW New Beetle Dune, yellow.$20–30
59721 VW New Beetle RSI, silver ..$20–30
51511 Chrysler PT Cruiser 2001, red.$20–30
51531 Chrysler Panel Cruiser 2001, blue $20–30
51521 Chrysler GT Cruiser 2001, silver $20–30

51051 Chevrolet Corvette SS 1957, blue..................$20–30

1:43 AUTOart Off Road
54801 Range Rover 4.6 HSE, metallic green $20–30
54802 Range Rover 4.6 HSE, metallic red $20–30
54803 Range Rover 4.6 HSE, metallic silver $20–30
54804 Range Rover 4.6 HSE, metallic black $20–30
54901 Land Rover Discovery V8 1994, green $20–30
54902 Land Rover Discovery V8 1994, black $20–30
54903 Land Rover Discovery V8 1994, metallic blue $20–30
56101 Mercedes Benz G-Wagon SWB 80s–90s, blue $20–30
56102 Mercedes Benz G-Wagon SWB 80s–90s, purple / red $20–30
56103 Mercedes Benz G-Wagon SWB 80s–90s, black $20–30
56104 Mercedes Benz G-Wagon SWB 80s–90s, silver $20–30
56111 Mercedes Benz G-Wagon LWB 80s–90s, silver $20–30
56112 Mercedes Benz G-Wagon LWB 80s–90s, black $20–30
56113 Mercedes Benz G-Wagon LWB 80s–90s, metallic red $20–30
56114 Mercedes Benz G-Wagon LWB 80s–90s, metallic green $20–30
57101 Mitsubishi Pajero 1999 LWB, blue..................$20–30
57102 Mitsubishi Pajero 1999 LWB, red..................$20–30
57103 Mitsubishi Pajero 1999 LWB, white..................$20–30
57111 Mitsubishi Pajero 1999 SWB, black..................$20–30
57112 Mitsubishi Pajero 1999 SWB, purple..................$20–30
57113 Mitsubishi Pajero 1999 SWB, silver..................$20–30
57201 Mitsubishi Pajero EVO, white $20–30
57202 Mitsubishi Pajero EVO, black..................$20–30
57203 Mitsubishi Pajero EVO, red $20–30

11:43 AUTOart Racing
69851 Panoz Esperante GTR-1 FIA GT 1998 #3 ....$20–30
69852 Panoz Esperante GTR-1 FIA GT 1998 #4 ....$20–30
69981 Toyota Corolla WRC 1999 #4 ....$20–30
69982 Toyota Corolla WRC 1999 #3 ....$20–30
69941 Mitsubishi Lancer EVO 6 WRC 1999 #1 ....$20–30
69942 Mitsubishi Lancer EVO 6 WRC 1999 #2 ....$20–30

69991 Subaru Impreza WRC 1999 #5 ....$20–30
60091 Subaru Impreza WRC 2000 #4 ....$20–30
60191 Subaru Impreza WRC 2001 #5 ....$20–30
60031 Mercedes Benz CLK DTM 2000 #1 BERND SCHNEIDER $20–30
60032 Mercedes Benz CLK DTM 2000 #2 THOMAS JUGER $20–30
60033 Mercedes Benz CLK DTM 2000 #5 KLAUS LUDWIG $20–30
60034 Mercedes Benz CLK DTM 2000 #6 MARCEL FASSLER $20–30
60035 Mercedes Benz CLK DTM 2000 #14 PEDRO LAMY $20–30
60036 Mercedes Benz CLK DTM 2000 #15 DARREN TURNER $20–30
60037 Mercedes Benz CLK DTM 2000 #18 MARCEL TIEMANN $20–30
60038 Mercedes Benz CLK DTM 2000 #19 PETER DUMBRECK $20–30
60039 Mercedes Benz CLK DTM 2000 #24 PEDRO LAMY $20–30
60040 Mercedes Benz CLK DTM 2000 #42 DARREN TURNER $20–30
60131 Mercedes Benz CLK DTM 2001 #1 BERND SCHNEIDER $20–30
60132 Mercedes Benz CLK DTM 2001 #2 PETER DUMBRECK $20–30
60133 Mercedes Benz CLK DTM 2001 #5 UWE ALZEN $20–30
60134 Mercedes Benz CLK DTM 2001 #6 MARCEL FASSLER $20–30
60135 Mercedes Benz CLK DTM 2001 #9 BERND MAYLANDER $20–30
60136 Mercedes Benz CLK DTM 2001 #10 PATRICK HUISMAN $20–30
60137 Mercedes Benz CLK DTM 2001 #14 THOMAS JUGER $20–30
60138 Mercedes Benz CLK DTM 2001 #15 CHRISTIJAN ALBERS $20–30
60139 Mercedes Benz CLK DTM 2001 #24 DAVID SAELENS $20–30
60140 Mercedes Benz CLK DTM 2001 #42 DARRE TURNER $20–30
60111 Ford Focus WRC 2001 ......$20–30
60141 Mitsubishi Lancer EVO 6 WRC 2001 T.MAKINEN /R.MANNISENMAKI #7 (WINNER OF MONTE CARLO) .$20–30
66496 Chaparral 2 "Sport Racer" 1965 #66 ....$20–30

Auto Buff

This series of 1:43 scale vintage Ford models were hand built in California by Le Buff Stuff and produced in very small quantities. The series has long since been discontinued and models are now quite scarce. Auto Buff dies were sold to Oakland Models of Michigan in 1982.
Ford Model A Roadster, top down, blue/black ..$115
Ford Model A Convertible, top down, medium green $115

1930 Ford Model A Pickup $115
1930 Ford Model A Roadster $115
1940 Ford Pickup, red $115
1940 Ford Convertible, top down, brown .$115
1940 Ford Convertible, top up, maroon/tan $115
1948 Ford Coupe, black $115
1948 Ford Coupe, red $345
1948 Ford Coupe, maroon $115
1948 Ford Convertible, top up, black $115
1948 Ford Convertible, top down, dark green ...$115
1953 Ford Pickup, black $115
1953 Ford "Coke" Panel Van, red $345
1953 Ford Stake Truck, white/black $115

Autocraft (also see Hongwell)

Hongwell is a new discovery in the ever-expanding world of diecast and plastic toys. Their Autocraft Truck Monster series represents an assortment of trucks in approximately 1:34 scale, all conveniently measuring about 9 inches long. Only the cab is diecast; the rest is plastic. Features include opening compartments and other working parts. Detail is particularly nice for a toy priced around $14. All models are identified as Mercedes-Benz trucks by the prominent trademark three-pointed star on the grille.

Hongwell's Autocraft Road Monster series represents sets that include cars, 4x4s, trailers, and accessories.

Autocraft Road Monster Series

AC1101 Sedan and Travel Trailer $9
AC1102 Van and Racing Boat with Trailer $9
AC1103 SUV with Twin Engine Speedboat and Trailer $9
AC1104 SUV with Expedition Trailer and Kayaks $9
AC1105 SUV with 4 Wheel All Terrain Cycle and Trailer $9
AC1106 SUV with Animal Cage and Animal $9

Autocraft Truck Monster Series

AC2912, Fire Engine, red
  v.1 "Fire Dept. Fire and Rescue Service" $14
  v.2 "Feuerwehr" $14
AC2921, Cement Truck, yellow $14
AC2922, Dump Truck, silver cab, blue dumper $14
AC2931, Skip Truck, yellow with metallic gray skip container $14
AC2932, Garbage Truck, yellow $14
AC2941, Recycling Truck with bins and crane $14
AC2942, Super Transport Box Truck, blue $14
AC2951, Log Truck with crane and logs ..$14
AC2961, Auto Salvage Truck $14

Autohobby

Autohobby models are limited edition resin hand builts. Resin models are generally sold unfinished with rough, unfinished edges, for hobbyists

to finish, assemble, and customize to their liking.
610 1938 Citroën 11B Coca-Cola Van $58

Auto Pilen (also see Pilen)

Escuderia Pilen of Spain produces these toy cars under the brand names Pilen, Auto Pilen, and Escuderia Pilen. Dr. Craig S. Campbell, assistant professor of geography at Youngstown State University, reports that the predominant scale for these toys is 1:43. Many, but not all, of Pilen's superior line were recastings of French Dinkys, such as the Citroën DS Pallas and the Matra Simca Bagheera. After Pilen's demise in the eighties, some Pilen dies were used by AHC of the Netherlands. Pilens are comparable to Solido in detail, though their colors are brighter, comparable to SpectraFlame colors on the earliest Hot Wheels.

Auto Pilen 1:43 Scale

Adams Brothers Probe $65
Buggi Playero $45
Chevrolet Astro I $60
Chevrolet Corvette Stingray Split Window, 1967 ....$80
Citroën 2 CV $60
DeTomaso Mangusta $65
Ferrari 512 ....$50
Ferrari P5 ....$65
Ford Mark II $50
Ghibli Maserati $50
Javelin $80
Mercedes 250 Coupe $60
Mercedes Ambulance Sedan $60
Mercedes C-111 ....$50
Mercedes Taxi $50
Mini Cooper $50
Modulo Pininfarina $50
Monteverdi Hai 450 SS, yellow with black trunk and hood, #347 ....$50
Monza Spider $50
Oldsmobile Toronado Police $100
Oldsmobile Toronado $120
Porsche 917 ....$45
Porsche Carrera 6, shocking pink with clear windows, #303 ....$45
Renault R-12 S $45
Renault R-12 G. C. Trafico $45
Seat 124 Sport $50
Seat 127 ....$50
Seat 600 ....$50
Seat 850 Spyder $50
Stratos Bertone, #509 ....$45
Vauxhall SRV $50

Auto Pilen 1:64 Scale

Fiat 131 Wagon, 1:64 ....$12
Peugeot 504, 1:64 ....$12

Auto Replicas

Great Britain is where Auto Replicas are produced. The company, owned by foremost modelmaker Barry Lester, manufactures white metal kits.

1937 Packard Model 1507 Club Sedan $75

Autoreplica

Autoreplica is reportedly a brand of 1:43 scale diecast models made in Italy.

1	1934 ERA GP Racer "Romulus," light blue and yellow $59
4	1921 Bugatti Brescia Racer, #3, blue $59
8	1957 Porsche Speedster, unfinished metal, kit $59
16	1937 Packard 12 Roadster, top down, blue $59
24	1937 Packard Formal Sedan $59
24	1937 Packard Tourer/Town Car $59
28	1954 Sunbeam Alpine Roadster, top down $59
29	1932 Alfa 8C Roadster, top down, red..$59
33	1955 Chevrolet Bel Air Convertible, top down, sea green $39
38	1939 Morgan Plus 4 Tourer $59
42	1936-37 Tatra 77-77A, blue $59
44	1936 Morgan 2 Seater, green and black $59
101	1925 Austin Van, "Lucas," dark green..$59
Kit 1	1950 Fiat Panel Van $19
Kit 21	1925-26 Renault Record $19
	Amilcar Italiana $45

Aviva (also see Hasbro)

Hasbro has been a powerful force in the toy industry since the 1960s. Toys such as Mr. Machine, the see-through gear-driven walking, animated robot with a top hat, was possibly one of the best known toys of the period, at least if you watched Saturday morning cartoons. The most popular and sustaining line of toys for Hasbro has been G.I. Joe. They have since also purchased Kenner, the brand responsible for Fast 111s and Winners Circle diecast cars.

Collector Steve Reeson notes that one Aviva model he found, imprinted with "AVIVA - 1965 United Feature Syndicate Inc. Made in Japan" is approximately 1:64 scale, and looks very similar to a CAN-AM race car of that era.

"What is so interesting," says Reeson, "is that the wheels have a raised lip on the inside very similar to a certain Hot Wheels design. It also has a very springy suspension. Given that the car has 1965 on the bottom, could this design have influenced the design team at Mattel back then?" Good question.

Hasbro has continued through to the present, but it has been overshadowed by the giant called Mattel. In the late seventies and on, Hasbro has produced Aviva character toys usually sold at Hallmark shops. Predominantly models with Peanuts characters from the comic strip of the same name, Aviva at last word continues to market such items in diecast and plastic. Here is a brief sampling.

Aviva Hasbro Large Diecast

Snoopy drives a red hook and ladder fire truck, wearing a red helmet, Woodstock sits in the rear (Aviva #72039/1) .$8–12

Snoopy drives a yellow convertible with red and green accents, Woodstock sits on the back (Aviva #72039/2) $8–12

Snoopy as the Flying Ace pilots yellow biplane with red wings, "Snoopy," Woodstock's face is on the tail of the plane (Aviva #72039/3) $8–12

Lucy Van Pelt Jeep with opening hood, folding windshield $8–12

Charlie Brown driving a right-hand drive red and white #25 race car $8–12

Aviva/Hasbro Mini diecast

Snoopy wearing a black tuxedo and top hat, yellow Open Car (Aviva #72044-2) $6–8

Snoopy wearing a red hat drives a truck called "Cat Catcher" (Aviva #72044-5) $6–8

Snoopy as the flying ace drives a red racer (Aviva #72044-6) $6–8

Bandai

Bandai is best known for high quality, accurately scaled lithographed tin battery-operated models from Japan. Values are high for their tinplate models, but only a few diecast models are known to exist in this brand.

BMW 320i, No. 3, orange-red with cross and deer head in a circle, "Fagermeister" on roof and hood $8–12

Bandi

Another one of those obscure brands listed in *Schroeder's Collectible Toys Antique to Modern Price Guide*, possibly a misspelling of Bandii. Only one model is listed.

1962 Volkswagen Sedan #742 ....$195

Bandii

Although possibly related, Bandii is not the same Japanese company as Bandai, a brand famous for their tin friction and battery-operated toy cars and trucks of great detail and quality.

Bandii is a comparatively obscure company that did however produce an interesting assortment of diecast toys.

Hato Bus, blue/white, 4½" $16
Hino Gas Tanker "JAL," 1:87 scale $5
Lancia Stratos "Alitalia," 1:87 scale $5
Mazda RX7 252i, 1:64 scale $5
Mitsubishi Galant, 1:64 scale $5
Nissan "JAL" Vacuum Car, 1:87 scale $5
Nissan "KLM" Vacuum Car, 1:87 scale $5
Nissan "Nippon" Vacuum Car, 1:87 scale $5
Nissan Ambulance, 1:87 scale $5
Porsche 928, blue, 1:43 scale $16
Porsche 930, silver, 1:43 scale $16
Porsche 935, 1:64 scale $5

Tank Lorry "JAL," 1:87 scale $5
Tank Lorry "KLM," 1:87 scale $5
Tank Lorry "Nippon," 1:87 scale $5

Bang

When Box Model of Pesaro, Italy, reorganized in 1991, the result was several new companies, Art Model, Bang, and Best of Italy. All Bang models are manufactured to exacting 1:43 scale.

401	Ferrari 250 GTO Prova 1962–63, red	$40
402	Ferrari 250 GTO Le Mans 1962, white	$40
405	Ferrari 250 GT 1956–57 Prova, red	$40
406	Ferrari 250 GT 1956–57 Stradale, silver	$40
407	Ferrari 250 GTO 3 Ore di Pau, red	$40
409	Ferrari 250 GTO Tourist Trophy 1963, red	$40
410	Ford AC Cobra Spyder Stradale, red	$40
411	Ford AC Cobra Spyder Stradale, black	$40
412	Ford AC Cobra Spyder, with top up, turquoise, black/white	$35
414	Ford AC Cobra Sebring 1963	$40
415	Ferrari 250 GT, Mille Miglia 1957	$40
420	Ford AC Cobra Le Mans 1963	$40
421	Ford AC Cobra Laguna Seca, white	$40
422	Ford AC Cobra Spyder, Riverside 1962	$35
423	Ford AC Cobra, Targa Florio 1964, lavender	$35
424	Ferrari 250 Tour de France Prova, red	$35
425	Ferrari 250 Tour de France Stradale, silver	$40
426	Ferrari 250 Tour de France, Gran Prix de Paris 1960, red	$40
427	Ferrari 250 Tour de France 1959, white	$40
431	Ferrari 250 Tour de France 1958, gray	$40
432	Ferrari 250 GTO Sebring 1962, light blue	$40
433	Ferrari 250 GTO Laguna Seca 1963	$40
438	Ford AC Cobra 289 LeMans 1963, green	$35
441	Ferrari 250 Tour de France 1958, light blue	$40
444	Ferrari 250 GTO Spa 1965, yellow	$40
453	Ford GT40 LeMans 1966, white	$35
455	Ford GT40 Mallory Park 1968, red	$35
456	Ford GT40 Le Mans 1966, white	$40
458	Ferrari 250 GTO Tour de France 1964, gray	$40
464	Ferrari 250 GTO Le Mans 1962, red	$40
501	Ferrari 250 348TS, red	$24
501	Ferrari 250 348TS, white, "Cofradis"	$32
504	Ferrari 250SWB Coupe Tour De France 1961, blue	$40
1007	Ford GT40 LeMans 68 Race 1968, light blue	$35
1008	Ferrari 250SWB Coupe SportItalia #7, red	$35
1008	Ferrari 250 SWB, red	$40

1009 Ford GT40 Coupe SportItalia Limited, yellow.................................$40
1010 Ferrari 250GT Tour De France 1957, red..$39
1011 Mercedes-Benz 300SL Mille Miglia 1989, metallic red........................$40
1012 Ferrari 250 SWB Montlhery 1991, silver..$39
1013 Ferrari 250 GTO Thirty Years, chrome..$35
1014 Ferrari 250 Tour de France Mille Miglia 1958, red.................................$40
7071 Ford GT40 Stradale 1966, gold.......$35
7072 Ford GT40 LeMans 1968, "11" blue..$35
7073 Ford GT40 LeMans 1968, "10" blue..$35
7074 Ford GT40 LeMans 1969, "6" blue..$35
7075 Ferrari 250 GT SWB Prova 1961, red..$35
7076 Ferrari 250 GT SWB Stradale 1961, silver..$35
7077 Ferrari 250 GT SWB Stradale 1961, yellow..$35
7078 Ferrari 250 GT SWB Le Mans 1961, red..$35
7079 Ford Mk II Le Mans Stradale 1966, black..$35
7080 Ford Mk II Le Mans 1966, blue........$35
7081 Ford Mk II Le Mans 1966, black.......$35
7082 Ford Mk II Le Mans 1966, red.........$35
7083 Ferrari 250 GT SWB Le Mans 1961, blue...$26
7084 Ferrari 250 GT SWB Tour De France 1961, red................................$26
7085 Ferrari 250 GT SWB LeMans 1961, white..$35
7086 Ferrari 250 GT SWB LeMans 1961, silver..$26
7087 Mercedes-Benz 300 SL Gullwing 1954, cream.................................$35
7088 Mercedes-Benz 300 SL Gullwing 1954, red....................................$35
7089 Mercedes-Benz 300 SL Gullwing Coupe 1955, silver.........................$39
7090 Mercedes-Benz 300 SL Gullwing Coupe 1955, black.........................$39
7091 Ford Mk II Sebring 1966, metallic blue..$35
7092 Ford Mk II LeMans 1966, gold.........$35
7093 Ford Mk II LeMans 1966, yellow.......$35
7094 Ford Mk II Roadster Sebring 1966.....$35
7095 1962 Ferrari 250 GTO De Montlhery, red...$35
7096 1958 Ferrari 250 Tour De France 3 Ore di Pau 2D #59, blue.................$35
7097 Ferrari 330 P.4 Prova, red.............$40
7098 Ferrari 330 P.4 1967 24 Ore Le Mans, red..$40
7099 Mercedes-Benz 300SL Gullwing Mille Miglia 1989, "224", mint blue.........$35
7100 Mercedes-Benz 300 SL Gullwing Tour de France 1956, "81," red.............$40
7101 Mercedes-Benz 300 SL Gullwing Le Mans 1956, "7," silver...................$40
7102 Mercedes-Benz 300 SL Gullwing Tour de France 1956, "149," silver.........$40

8001 Ferrari 348ts Stradale TD 1991, red..$35
8002 Ferrari 348ts Stradale TD 1991, yellow..$39
8003 Ferrari 348ts Stradale TD 1991, black $35
8004 Ferrari 348tb Stradale, blue............$39
8005 Ferrari 348tb Stradale, red.............$39
8006 Ferrari 348tb Stradale, white...........$39
8007 1990 Ferrari 348tb Challenge #48, red..$35
8013 1993 Ferrari 456GT Prova, red........$44
9301 1993 Ferrari 348tb Challenge Cutrera #1, white.................................$39
9302 1993 Ferrari 348tb Challenge Giudici, white..$39
9303 1993 Ferrari 348tb Challenge Ragazzi #2, white.................................$39
9305 1993 Ferrari 348tb Challenge Rossi #5, yellow..$39
9306 1993 Ferrari 348tb Challenge Peitra #6, red..$39
9308 1993 Ferrari 348tb Challenge Benaduce #8, red..$39

BAM (see Boutique Auto Moto, Bruce Arnold Models)

Banner

Banner toys represent a wide assortment of vehicles, mostly trucks, produced in an amalgam of materials. Plastic and lithographed tin were often used in tandem to create these distinctive toys. The company's beginnings have been traced back to 1944 in the Bronx, New York. They later moved to Paterson, New Jersey, until going bankrupt in 1965. Stamped steel toys from Banner were produced from the cast-off waste product of the automotive and electronics industry.
Buick Sedan, 4½".................................$15
1948 Oldsmobile Station Wagon, plastic, 4"...$35
1950s Sedan, plastic, 4½".......................$15

Banthrico (also see National Products)

Banthrico Inc., "The Coin Bank People," started in Chicago, Illinois, in 1914. The main office moved to Golden Valley, Minnesota, by the 1980s. Whether or where Banthrico still produces models is unknown.

Models are generally antiqued brass-like 1:25 to 1:43 scale pot metal vehicles with a slot in the bottom for coins, often with printing on them for the various banks that gave them away to customers when they opened an account. Besides vehicles, Banthrico produced a huge variety of castings that included heads, buildings and monuments, animals, and other unusual items usually somehow associated with American history and heritage, such as Lindbergh's Spirit of St. Louis, cowboys, Indians, buildings, covered wagons, and more.

Older Banthrico castings were copper or bronze colored, usually with antique patina applied. Newer ones are brass in appearance, with the newest ones in pewter color.

Unlike the bank promos, the dealer promos originally produced by Banthrico under their National Products Division, were painted in the vehicle's authentic colors. The Nash in particular was a dealer promo model.

With the help of avid Banthrico collectors Bob and Robin La Rosa, Larry Stitt, and a book by Steve Butler on dealer promotional models, I am now able to offer this more extensive list with more current values.

Banthrico Car Banks, listed by make and year

1910 Baker Electric.......................$60–65
1928 Beer Truck..........................$50–65
1900 Buick Pillbox Coupe................$60–65
1908 Buick...............................$60–65
1924 Buick...............................$50–65
1953 Buick Special.......................$60–65
1954 Buick Skylark Convertible.........$60–65
1908 Cadillac............................$60–65
1930 Cadillac Convertible Roadster..$60–65
1954 Cadillac Sedan.....................$60–65
1915 Chevrolet...........................$60–65
1928 Chevrolet Pickup Truck...........$60–80
1951 Chevrolet...........................$50–65
1953 Chevrolet Corvette Coupe $50–60
1954 Chevrolet 4-Door Sedan........$60–65
1956 Chevrolet...........................$55–65
1957 Chevrolet Bel Air 2 door Convertible........................$90–100
1963 Chevrolet Corvette Coupe $60–65
1924 Chrysler............................$50–55
1946 Chrysler Town & Country.......$60–65
1926 Cord Phaeton......................$55–65
1936 Cord................................$60–70
1914 Dodge Touring Car...............$60–70
1930 Duesenberg........................$60–70
1902 Electric Car........................$60–65
Firetruck................................$50–60
1908 Ford, fixed wheels................$55–65
1912 Ford "T-Bucket"...................$50–60
1915 Ford Omnibus......................$55–75
1917 Ford Touring Car..................$50–60
1926 Ford Model "T" Sedan.........$60–65
1927 Ford Model "T" Sedan, fixed wheels..............................$75–85
1929 Ford Model "A"...................$60–65
1929 Ford Model "A" Convertible...$60–65
1934 Ford Coupe........................$60–65
1934 Ford Convertible..................$60–65
1934 Ford Panel Truck..................$55–65
1935 Ford English Taxi Cab......$140–160
1955 Ford Pickup Truck................$70–80
1955 Ford Thunderbird.................$70–80
1957 Ford Thunderbird.................$70–80
1965 Ford Mustang.....................$60–65
Horse Drawn Fire Pumper, no horse .$70–100
1955 Jaguar $50–75

1951 Kaiser $50–65
1930 La Salle Coupe $50–65
1908 Lincoln $60–75
1912 Lincoln Coach $60–65
1927 Lincoln Brougham $60–65
1941 Lincoln Continental $60–65
1969 Lincoln Continental $60–65
1906 Mack Truck $75–90
1954 Mercury 2-Door hardtop $60–65
1953 MG Convertible $55–60
1902 Nash Rambler $65–70
1949 Nash Airflyte $55–60
1906 Oldsmobile $60–65
1923 Oldsmobile $50–65
1953 Oldsmobile 88 ....$75–100
1954 Oldsmobile 88 ....$75–100
1956 Oldsmobile 98 Convertible ...$60–65
1937 Packard V-12 ....$50–60
1954 Packard 4-Door Sedan $60–65
1928 Pickup $50–65
1917 Pierce Arrow $50–65
1915 Police Wagon $50–65
1926 Pontiac $65–70
1964 Pontiac $50–65
1902 Rambler $60–70
1937 Rolls Royce $60–65
Stage Coach $55–70
1910 Stanley Steamer $75–80
1904 Studebaker $60–65
1957 Studebaker Golden Hawk $70–80
1919 U. S. Mail Truck, recalled by Postmaster General $250–275
1977 Volkswagen Beetle $70–75

Other Banthrico Products

Buildings, various historical structures.$95–125
Busts, various heads of historical figures $95–125
Cannon $75–90
Covered Wagon $90–100
Minute Man $65–80
Popcorn Cart $90–100
Robot $90–100
Spirit of St. Louis, Lindbergh's solo transatlantic airplane $90–125
Two-piece Train; engine and coal car $300–375

Banthrico Dealer Promos

1952 Buick Roadmaster 4-Door ..$250–300
1953 Buick Roadmaster 4-Door ..$250–300
1954 Buick Roadmaster 2-Door hardtop $350–400
    Reissue $100–125
1955 Buick Roadmaster 2-Door hardtop $375–425
1956 Buick Super 4-Door hardtop .$375–425
1952 Cadillac 62 4-Door $175–250
1954 Cadillac Fleetwood 4-Door .$250–325
    reissue $100–125
1955 Cadillac Biarritz 2-Door hardtop $300–350
    reissue $100–125
1956 Cadillac Biarritz 2-Door hardtop $275–350

1949 Chevrolet Fleetline 2-Door ..$325–375
1949 Chevrolet Fleetline 4-Door ..$325–375
1949 Chevrolet Styleline 2-Door ..$325–375
1949 Chevrolet Styleline 4-Door ..$325–375
1949 Chevrolet Styleline Coupe .$350–400
1950 Chevrolet Fleetline 2-Door ..$225–275
1950 Chevrolet Fleetline 4-Door ..$250–300
1950 Chevrolet Styleline 2-Door ..$225–275
1950 Chevrolet Styleline 2-Door hardtop $275–325
1950 Chevrolet Styleline 4 door ...$225–275
1950 Chevrolet Styleline Coupe .$275–325
1950 Chevrolet Styleline Convertible $225–275
1953 Chevrolet 210 4-Door $225–275
1954 Chevrolet Corvette Convertible, circa 1973 in red, white, or blue .$100–125
1954 Chevrolet 210 4-Door $225–275
1955 Chevrolet Bel Air 2-Door hardtop $200–250
    reissue $100–125
1950 Chrysler New Yorker 4-Door $250–300
1953 Chrysler New Yorker 2-Door hardtop $350–375
1954 Chrysler New Yorker 4-Door $400–450
1955 Chrysler New Yorker 4-Door.$325–375
    reissue $100–125
1955 Chrysler New Yorker 4-Door with dealer or color markings $400–450
1950 Dodge Coronet 4-Door $250–300
1951-52 Dodge Coronet 4-Door $250–300
1953 Dodge Coronet 4-Door $250–300
1954 Dodge Royal 4-Door $325–375
1950 Ford Custom 4-Door $175–225
1953 Ford Customline 4-Door $225–275
1953 Ford F-100 Pickup $300–350
    reissue $100–125
1955 Ford Fairlane 4-Door $250–300
    reissue $100–125
1956 Ford Customline 4-Door $250–300
1967 Jeep M-715 U. S. Army Stake Truck $150–175
1953 Kaiser Manhattan $400–450
1953 Lincoln Cosmopolitan 4-Door $400–450
1954 Lincoln Cosmopolitan 2-Door hardtop $250–300
    reissue $100–125
1951 Mercury 4-Door $275–325
1953 Mercury Monterey 4-Door .$400–450
1954 Mercury Monterey 2-Door hardtop $275–325
1955 Mercury Monterey 2-Door hardtop $375–425
1951–52 Nash Rambler 2-Door hardtop, single color $325–375
1951–52 Nash Rambler 2-Door hardtop, two-tone $350–400
1953–54 Nash Rambler 2-Door hardtop, single color $325–375

1953–54 Nash Rambler 2-Door hardtop, two-tone $350–400
1953 Oldsmobile 88 4-Door $375–425
1954 Oldsmobile 88 2-Door hardtop $250–300
    reissue $100–125
1955 Oldsmobile 98 2-Door hardtop $450–500
1953 Packard Clipper 4-Door $350–400
    reissue $100–125
1954 Packard Clipper 4-Door, single color $450–500
1954 Packard Clipper 4-Door, two-tone $475–525
1953 Plymouth Cranbrook 4-Door .$250–275
1955 Plymouth Belvedere 2-Door ..$325–375
1956 Plymouth Savoy 2-Door $300–350
1953 Pontiac Chieftain 2-Door hardtop $250–300
1955 Pontiac Starfire 2-Door hardtop $325–375
1953 Studebaker Commander 2-Door hardtop $375–425
1950 Willys 2-Door wagon $400–450

Bapro

As reported by collector Staffan Kjellin of Sweden, Bapro is a Swedish toy company that in the fifties produced a racing car (Mercedes circa thirties vintage) and a very futuristic "Mooncar."

Mercedes Racing Car $35–50
Mooncar $40–55

Barclay

From 1924 to 1971, Barclay produced a large assortment of toys from various headquarters in West Hoboken, Union City, and North Bergen, New Jersey, beginning with lead alloy models in the thirties and forties and later changing to zamac (zinc alloy). Most models are fairly common in appearance, but a few represent sleek, streamlined "futuristic" styling that reflects the Art Deco influence of the period. Below is just a sampling of models.

Anti-Aircraft Gun Truck, #198, 4" $35

Ambulance, #194, 3½" $40

Ambulance, #50, 5" $50
Armored Army Truck, #152, 2⅞" $25
Army Car with two soldiers lying down, gunner on right, driver on left $25
Army Car with two silver bullhorns, 2½" ..$40
Army Tractor (Minneapolis-Moline), 2¾" $25
Army Truck with Gun, #151, 2¾" $30
Army Truck with Anti-Aircraft Gun, #151, 2½" ..$25
Army Tank Truck, #197, 3⅛" $30

Auburn Speedster, #58 ....$30
Austin Coupe, 2" $30
Auto Transport Set, truck with small trailer, 4½"
   and 2 cars $60
Beer Truck, with barrels $50
Bluebird Racer $390
Buck Rogers Rocket Ship $900
Bus, Futuristic, 3" $25
Bus, "Coast to Coast," "Barclay Toy," two-piece,
   #405, 2⅞" $75
Cannon Car, battery powered light (1935), 3½" ..$200
Chrysler Airflow, 4" $85
Chrysler Imperial Coupe, #39 ....$25
Convertible with mother and five children,
   1920s–1930s $1,200
Cord Front Drive Coupe, #40, 3⅝" $35
Double Decker Bus, 4" $60
1937 Federal Truck $25
1940 Anti Aircraft $25
Mack Pick Up Truck, 3½" $25
"Milk & Cream" Truck, 3⅝", #377, white rubber
   tires $60
Milk Truck, 3⅝", #377, black rubber tires $40
Milk Truck shaped like a milk bottle, #567 .$250
"Parcel Delivery," #45, 3⅝" $100
Renault Tank, #47, 4" $35
Searchlight Truck, 4¹⁄₁₆" $150
Silver Arrow Race Car, 5½" $35
Station Wagon, 2-piece "Barclay Toy," #404,
   2¹⁵⁄₁₆" $60
Steam-Roller, 3¼," slush lead with tin roof $50
Streamline Car, #302, 3⅛" $35
Taxi, #318, 3¼" $20
Wrecker, two-piece diecast, #403, 2⅞" $70

Barlux

The Italian firm of Barlux started producing diecast toys around 1970 and continued until about 1983. Barlux toys failed to gain popularity due to their comparatively crude design. They weren't widely distributed, at least not outside of Italy, and are hard to find.

100 Fiat Wrecker, 1:24 ....$30
101 Fiat Ambulance, 1:24 ....$30
102 Fiat Carabinieri, 1:24 ....$30
705 Fiat 697 Fire Truck, 1:43 ....$16
739 Fiat 697 Flat Truck & Fork Lift, 1:43 ....$16
747 Fiat 697 Flat Truck & Trailer, 1:43 ....$16
762 Fiat 697 Dump Truck & Loader, 1:43 ..$16
73001 Matra MS-120, 1:66 ....$10
73002 Lotus-Ford 72, 1:66 ....$10
73003 BRM ,1:66 ....$10
73004 Tyrrell-Ford, 1:66 ....$10
73005 Ferrari B2, 1:66 ....$10
73006 March-Ford, 1:66 ....$10
73007 McLaren-Ford, 1:66 ....$10
73008 Brabham-Ford, 1:66 ....$10
73009 Surtees-Ford, 1:66 ....$10
73010 Lotus Turbine, 1:66 ....$10
73062 Land Rover and Caravan, 1:43 ......$16
73081 MTS-20 Shovel Loader, 1:43 ....$16
73082 MTS-10 Fork Lift, 1:43 ....$16
73083 MTS-30 Trencher, 1:43 ....$16

73084 MTS-20 Snowplow-Sander, 1:43....$16
73085 Garbage Truck, 1:43 ....$16
73086 Road Roller, 1:43 ....$16
73810 Public Works Vehicle with Snowplow,
   1:50 ....$16

Basteltip

Jeff Bray Jr.'s Diecast Miniatures of Amston, Massachusetts, listed one model from this otherwise unknown brand.

Raba Fire Crane, 24" $28

Bayshore Repli-Cars

According to information provided by collector Duane Kaufhold, Bayshore Repli-Cars are approximately 1:64 scale models that were made in Holland. He found two examples, a 1919 Ford Model T Crane Truck and a 1919 Ford Model T Pick-Up each in its own blisterpack, with most of 20 other vehicles listed on the back. Original price was 65 cents. Copyright date is 1967 by Bayshore Industries, Inc., New York, New York, a subsidiary of Miner Industries.

1 1919 "T" Ford Pickup..........................$5–10
2 Porsche $5–10
3 1919 "T" Ford Crane Truck.................$5–10
4 1919 "T" Ford Delivery Truck..............$5–10
5 1919 "T" Ford Two-Seater $5–10
6 1919 "T" Ford Sedan $5–10
7 BMW 2000 CS $5–10
8 Volkswagen 1600 TL $5–10
9 no model listed
10 Citroën ID 19 ....$5–10
11 Ford Taunus 17 M $5–10
12 no model listed
13 Jaguar E Type $5–10
14 Mercedes-Benz 230 SL $5–10
15 Opel Rekord 1900 ....$5–10
16 Mercedes-Benz 250 SE....................$5–10
17 Ferrari Formula 1 - 3L $5–10
18 Brabham Formula 1 - 3L $5–10
19 Cooper-Maserati Formula 1 - 3L.........$5–10
20 Lotus Formula 1 - 3L $5–10

BBR

EWA says it best in one of their recent catalogs: "BBR models are outstanding for their superb hand-built quality and detailing. The company was started just over ten years ago in a small town midway between Lake Como and Milan and not far from Monza, in the north of Italy. It quickly achieved world fame for its finely detailed 1:43 scale models with the super paint finish.

"The cars modeled, as befits an Italian company, are mostly race cars and mostly Ferraris, with some Alfa Romeos and Lancias. Other subjects have been covered too, including Porsche, McLaren, Benetton, Williams (and other F1 cars), and Nissan, plus some Lincolns as raced in the Carrera Pan Americana in the early '50s. Many of the cars modeled are also available as kits."

1938 Alfa Romeo 2900B 8C, maroon,
   "19" $194

1938 Alfa Romeo 2900B 8C, maroon,
   "8" $194
1939 Alfa Romeo 6c 2500 "Duxia" $159
1939 Alfa Romeo 2900 Berlinetta Touring
   Long $149
1949 Alfa Romeo 2500SS Villa d'Este
   Coupe $139
1949 Alfa Romeo Villa D'Este Coupe,
   silver $168
1950 Alfa Romeo 6C 2500 ....$159
1952 Alfa Romeo Villa D'Este, Convertible top
   down $154
1952 Alfa Romeo 2500SS Coupe Monte Carlo,
   burgundy $188
1956 Alfa Romeo 6C 2500 Street,
   maroon $184
1956 Alfa Romeo 6C 2500 MM Fangio,
   maroon, "730" $184
1993 Alfa Romeo 155 V6 DTM Nannini ..$229
1947 Ferrari 125S Street, red..................$178
1950 Ferrari 212 International Nurbr.-TD,
   blue $178
1951 Ferrari 212 Carrera Panamerican "No. 9
   Ascari" $154
1952 Ferrari 212 "Interpininfarina" $139
1952 Ferrari 212 International Pininfarina Bordeaux, black ....$154–$178
1951 Ferrari 212 Carrera Panamerican "No.
   3" $154
1954 Ferrari 250 Europa Street, red........$154
1954 Ferrari 250 Europa "Cabriolet Pininfarina" $149
1954 Ferrari 250 Europa NY Show,
   maroon/gray $194
1956 Ferrari 250 Europa "Boano" $159
1957 Ferrari 250GT PR Bernhard, black ...$184
1959 Ferrari 250 GTE $159
1959 Ferrari 250 "Enzo Ferrari" $159
1962 Ferrari 250 GTO $159
1965 Ferrari 275 GTB $169
1984 Ferrari 288 GTO $159
1984 Ferrari 288GTO 2-Door Coupe, red..$178
1982 Ferrari 308GTB Coupe, red $178
1982 Ferrari 308GTB Coupe, silver $178
1982 Ferrari 308GTB Coupe, blue $178
1982 Ferrari 308GTB Coupe, yellow $178
1965 Ferrari 330 GT 2+2, available in red,
   blue, metallic green, or dark gray $199
1967 Ferrari 330GTC Liliana Di R, blue....$178
1967 Ferrari 330 P4 LeMans #24 ....$198
1993 Ferrari 348 Cabriolet......................$159
1954 Ferrari 375 Am Vign- Turin, yellow...$184
1954 Ferrari 375 MM Pan Am Chinetti,
   red $129–144
1955 Ferrari 375 AM "Giovanni Agnelli"..$159
1955 Ferrari 375 Am Agnl-Torino, green...$178
1956 Ferrari 410SA di Parigi, beige $168
1985 Ferrari 412T 2+2, available in red, silver,
   blue, or metallic green.........................$199
1994 Ferrari 412 T1 Berger F1 Racer.......$219
1976 Ferrari 512BB Coupe, yellow $184
1997 Ferrari 550 Maranello, available in red or
   yellow $199

1991 Ferrari F40 Koenig Coupe, red $174
1991 Ferrari F40 Koenig Coupe, yellow ...$174
1996 Ferrari F50 Coupe, red $199
1996 Ferrari F50 Spyder, red $199
1987 Ferrari Testarossa "GioVanni Agnelli" Convertible, silver $138
1987 Ferrari Testarossa Straman Convertible, red $164
1988 Ferrari Testarossa "Koenig" $139
1953 Porsche 356A $188
1993 Porsche 911 Carrera $188

Bburago (also see Martoys)

Since Bburago (spelled with two Bs) entered the diecast miniature market as Martoys in 1974, their dominance on the US market has risen steadily. Producing precision scale models as well as toys, Bburago is one of the few diecast collectibles still manufactured in Europe instead of Asia — Milan, Italy, to be specific. The Bburago name was adapted in 1977.

Bburago models mostly replicate Italian sports cars such as Ferrari, Lamborghini, Alfa Romeo, and Bugatti. But also represented are Mercedes-Benz, Jaguar, Porsche, and even a couple of Dodge Vipers, with an ever-expanding assortment. Many models are available both as pre-assembled models and unassembled kits, as listed below.

In addition, one collector claims that Bburago made at least one 1:12 scale model, listed below.
1937 Jaguar SS100, 1:12 scale.

Bburago Series (model lists follow)
Super – 1:24 scale 0100 series models
VIP – 1:24 scale 0500 series models
Bijoux – 1:24 scale 1500 series models
Diamonds – 1:18 scale 3000 series models
DeLuxe – 1:18 scale 3500 series kits
Executive – 1:18 scale 3700 series kits
Pocket – 1:43 scale 4100 series models
Portachiavi – 1:87 scale 4500 series models
Kit Super – 1:24 scale 5100 series kits
Kit Bijoux – 1:24 scale 5500 series kits
Grand Prix – 1:24 scale 6100 series models
Kit Diamonds – 1:18 scale 7000 series kits

Bburago Super 1:24 Scale
0102 Porsche 911S, metallic blue or metallic silver $12–15
0104 Ferrari Testarossa $12–15
0105 Mercedes-Benz 190 E $12–15
0111 Mercedes-Benz 500 SEC $12–15
0112 Range Rover Safari $12–15
0115 Lancia Delta S4 ....$12–15
0116 Peugeot 205 Safari $12–15
0119 Alfa Romeo 75 Gr.A $12–15
0121 Porsche 959 ....$12–15
0125 Fiat Tipo $12–15
0129 Ferrari 348 TB Evoluzione $12–15
0130 Mercedes-Benz 300 SL........$12–15
0131 Peugeot 405 Raid $12–15
0133 Ferrari 512 BB $12–15
0137 Lamborghini Countach 5000 Quattrovalvole $12–15
0148 Ferrari 308 GTB $12–15

0163 Porsche 959 Turbo, metallic gray $12–15
0188 Alfa Romeo 75 Polizia $12–15
0189 Alfa Romeo 75 Carabinieri....$12–15
0190 Alfa Romeo 75 Guardia Di Finanza $12–15
0192 Ferrari GTO Rally $12–15
0194 Fiat Cinquecento $12–15
0198 Renegade Jeep CJ-7 ....$12–15
0199 Porsche 924 Turbo Gr.2 ....$12–15

Bburago VIP 1:24 Scale
0503 1936 Bugatti Atlantic............$12–15
0504 1984 Ferrari Testarossa $12–15
0506 1965 Ferrari 250 Le Mans $12–15
0510 1962 Ferrari 250 GTO $12–15
0511 1966 Ferrari 275 GTB 4 ....$12–15
0513 1965 Ford AC Cobra 427...$12–15
0522 1954 Mercedes-Benz 300 SL ..$12–15
0532 1987 Ferrari F40 ....$12–15
0535 1991 Bugatti EB 110 ....$12–15
0537 1988 Lamborghini Countach ..$12–15
0538 1932 Bugatti "Type 55" $12–15
0541 1990 Lamborghini Diablo $12–15
0542 1992 Ferrari F40 Evoluzione...$12–15
0563 1986 Porsche 959 Turbo $12–15
0572 1984 Ferrari GTO $12–15

Bburago Early 1500 Series
From 1974 to 1980, the 1500 series was represented by 1:43 scale Fiat 50 NC Trucks. These truck models were discontinued in favor of the newer Bijoux series.

1501 Covered Dump Truck $25
1502 Crane Truck............................$25
1503 Quarry Dump Truck $25
1504 Lumber Truck.........................$25
1505 Dump Truck...........................$25
1506 Cement Mixer.........................$25
1507 Lumber Truck.........................$25
1508 Tank Truck.............................$25
1509 Fire Ladder Truck $25
1510 Milk Tank Truck......................$25
1511 Fire Crane Truck.....................$25
1512 Flatbed with Boat $25

Bburago 1:14 Scale Formula One Models (issued from 1976 until 1981)
2101 1976 Ferrari 312T2 ....$50
2102 1976 Tyrell P34/2 ....$40
2103 1976 Brabham BT46.................$40
2105 1978 Lotus 79/JPS MK4 ....$40
2106 1981 Lotus Essex MK3 ....$40
2107 1979 Tyrell 009.......................$40
2108 1980 Ferrari 312T5 ....$50
2109 1980 Renault RE20...................$40

Bburago Bijoux 1:24 Scale
1501 1938 Citroën 15 CV TA.......$12–15
1502 1948 Jaguar XK 120 Roadster $12–15
1503 1936 Bugatti Atlantic............$12–15
1506 1966 Ferrari 250 LM "Monza" .$12–15
1507 1957 Ferrari Testa Rossa.......$12–15
1508 1948 Jaguar XK 120 Coupe ..$12–15
1509 1928 Mercedes-Benz SSK.....$12–15
1510 1962 Ferrari 250 GTO........$12–15

1511 1966 Ferrari 275 GTB 4......$12–15
1524 1957 Chevrolet Corvette $12–15
1532 1992 Ferrari 456 GT $12–15
1535 1991 Bugatti EB 110..........$12–15
1536 1992 Ferrari 456 GT $12–15
1539 1989 Ferrari 348 TB $12–15

Bburago Diamonds 1:18 Scale
3001 Rolls-Royce Camargue, 1:22 .$24–30
3002 1931 Mercedes-Benz SSKL Caracciola
    v.1 chrome $70–80
    v.2 other $24–30
3004 1984 Ferrari Testarossa $24–30
3005 1934 Bugatti "Type 59" $24–30
3006 1937 Jaguar SS 100 ....$24–30
3007 1957 Ferrari 250 Testa Rossa $24–30
3008 1932 Alfa Romeo 2300 Spider $24–30
3009 1928 Mercedes-Benz SSK $24–30
3010 1955 Lancia Aurelia B24 Spider $24–30
3011 1962 Ferrari 250 GTO........$24–30
3013 1954 Mercedes-Benz 300 SL $24–30
3014 1931 Alfa Romeo 8C 2300 Monza $24–30
3015 1954 Mercedes-Benz 300 SL.$24–30
3016 1961 Jaguar "E" Cabriolet $24–30
3018 1961 Jaguar "E" Coupe $24–30
3019 1984 Ferrari Testarossa $24–30
3020 1936 Mercedes-Benz 500 K Roadster $24–30
3021 1961 Porsche 356 B Coupe.$24–30
3022 1987 Ferrari F40 ....$24–30
3024 1957 Chevrolet Corvette $24–30
3025 1992 Dodge Viper RT/10....$24–30
3026 1961 Jaguar "E" Cabriolet $24–30
3027 1984 Ferrari GTO $24–30
3028 1990 Lamborghini Diablo $24–30
3029 1992 Ferrari 348 TB Evoluzione..........................$24–30
3031 1961 Porsche 356 B Cabriolet $24–30
3032 1987 Ferrari F40 ....$24–30
3034 1957 Chevrolet Corvette $24–30
3035 1991 Bugatti EB 110 ....$24–30
3036 1992 Ferrari 456 GT $24–30
3037 1988 Lamborghini Countach.$24–30
3038 1961 Jaguar "E" Coupe $24–30
3039 1989 Ferrari 348 TB $24–30
3041 1990 Lamborghini Diablo $24–30
3042 1992 Ferrari F40 Evoluzione .$24–30
3045 1991 Bugatti EB 110 ....$24–30
3047 1988 Lamborghini Countach.$24–30
3051 1961 Porsche 356 B Cabriolet $24–30
3055 1991 Bugatti EB 110 ....$24–30
3057 1986 Ferrari GTO Rally $24–30
3065 1992 Dodge Viper RT/10....$24–30

Bburago Deluxe 1:18 Scale Kits
3505 1934 Bugatti "Type 59" $24–30
3507 1957 Ferrari 250 Testa Rossa...................................$24–30

3509 1928 Mercedes-Benz SSK $24–30
3511 1962 Ferrari 250 GTO $24–30
3513 1954 Mercedes-Benz 300 SL.$24–30
3514 1931 Alfa Romeo 8C 2300 Monza $24–30
3516 1961 Jaguar "E" Cabriolet $24–30
3519 1984 Ferrari Testarossa $24–30
3520 1936 Mercedes-Benz 500K Roadster $24–30
3521 1961 Porsche 356 B Coupe .$24–30
3525 1992 Dodge Viper RT/10 ....$24–30
3527 1984 Ferrari GTO $24–30
3528 1990 Lamborghini Diablo $24–30
3529 1991 Ferrari 348 TB Evoluzione $24–30
3534 1957 Chevrolet Corvette $24–30

Bburago Executive 1:18 Scale Kits
3702 1931 Mercedes-Benz SSKL "Caracciola" $24–30
3718 1961 Jaguar "E" Coupe $24–30
3721 1961 Porsche 356 B Coupe.$24–30
3724 1957 Chevrolet Corvette $24–30
3725 1992 Dodge Viper RT/10 ...$24–30
3731 1961 Porsche 356 B Cabriolet.$24–30
3732 1987 Ferrari F40 ....$24–30
3735 1991 Bugatti EB 110 ....$24–30
3737 1988 Lamborghini Countach.$24–30
3739 1989 Ferrari 348 TB $24–30
3741 1990 Lamborghini Diablo $24–30
3746 1992 Ferrari 456 GT $24–30

Bburago 4000 Series 1:43 Scale Models issued in 1988
4001 Lancia Stratos $7–10
4002 Peugeot 205 ....$7–10
4003 Audi Quattro $7–10
4004 Ferrari 512 BB $7–10
4005 Fiat Panda $7–10
4006 Jeep Renegade $7–10
4007 BMW M1 ....$7–10
4008 Alfa Romeo 33 ....$7–10
4009 Saab 900 Turbo $7–10
4010 Ferrari 308 ....$7–10
4011 Range Rover $7–10
4012 Porsche 935 ....$7–10
4021 Lancia Stratos $7–10
4022 Peugeot 205 ....$7–10
4023 Audi Quattro $7–10
4024 Ferrari 512 BB $7–10
4025 Fiat Panda $7–10
4026 Jeep Renegade $7–10
4027 BMW M1 ....$7–10
4028 Alfa Romeo 33 ....$7–10
4029 Saab 900 Turbo $7–10
4030 Ferrari 308 ....$7–10
4031 Range Rover $7–10
4032 Porsche 935 ....$7–10

Bburago Pocket 1:43 Scale Models Box 4100 series, Blister 4800 series
4101 Saab 900 Turbo $7–10
4102 Mercedes-Benz 190 E $7–10
4103 Porsche 924 Turbo $7–10
4104 Ferrari Testarossa, red with white interior $7–10

4105 BMW M1 IMSA $7–10

4105 Dodge Viper RT/10, black with silver racing stripes $7–10

4106 Ferrari 512 BB Daytona $7–10
4107 Ferrari GTO Rally, red with Rally accents, white interior $7–10
4108 Lancia Stratos VSD $7–10
4108 Ferrari F40, red with silver gray interior $7–10
4109 Renault 9 ....$7–10
4109 Mercedes-Benz 300 SL Convertible, top down, metallic blue, cream interior $7–10
4110 Alfa Romeo Giulietta Alpilatte ...$7–10
4110 Porsche 928 Grand Am $7–10
4111 Porsche 924 Turbo Gr. 2 ....$7–10
4112 Renault R9 Rally $7–10
4112 Suzuki Vitara Raid $7–10
4113 Fiat Panda Rally $7–10
4114 Porsche 911 ....$7–10

4115 Dodge Viper GTS, metallic blue with white racing stripes $7–10

4115 Renault R5 Turbo $7–10
4116 Fiat Ritmo Totip $7–10
4116 Peugeot 205 Safari $7–10
4117 Ferrari 308 GTB $7–10
4118 Mazda RX7 ....$7–10
4119 Fiat Uno $7–10
4120 Fiat Uno Rally $7–10
4121 Fiat Regata $7–10
4122 Renegade Jeep $7–10
4123 Peugeot 205 Turbo 16 ....$7–10
4124 Alfa Romeo 33 Rally $7–10
4125 Peugeot 205 GTI $7–10
4125 Dodge Viper RT/10, red $7–10
4126 Porsche 959 Rally $7–10
4127 Lamborghini Countach 5000 ...$7–10
4128 Ferrari F40 ....$7–10
4129 Ferrari 348 TB Evoluzione, red with Rally decals, cream interior $7–10
4130 Renault Clio RT $7–10
4131 Land Rover 109 Aziza $7–10
4132 Jeep CJ5 Renegade $7–10
4133 Ferrari 512 BB $7–10
4134 Fiat Regata Rally $7–10
4134 Fiat Tipo Rally $7–10
4135 Lancia Delta S4 ....$7–10

4136 Ferrari 456 GT, red $7–10
4137 Lamborghini Countach 400S ...$7–10
4138 Fiat Cinquecento Rally $7–10
4139 Ferrari 348 TB, red with cream interior $7–10

4140 MCA Centenaire, metallic silver blue $7–10

4141 Lamborghini Diablo, yellow $7–10
4142 Porsche 935 Vaillant $7–10
4143 Ford Sierra Group A $7–10
4144 Fiat Punto $7–10
4146 Ferrari 456 GT, metallic dark blue with pale beige interior $7–10
4147 Porsche 911 Turbo $7–10
4148 Ferrari 308 GTB Rally, red "PIONEER" Rally accents, black interior, light gray steering wheel and Rally lights on nose $7–10
4149 Mercedes-Benz 190 E $7–10
4150 Peugeot 405 Raid $7–10
4151 Lamborghini Diablo, red with cream interior $7–10
4152 Chevrolet Corvette $7–10
4153 Porsche 911 Carrera Super Cup, yellow with Rally accents, light gray interior $7–10
4155 Citroën Xantia $7–10
4156 Range Rover T Castrol $7–10
4157 Ferrari Testarossa, yellow with cream interior $7–10
4158 BMW 535i, metallic dark champagne red with light gray interior $7–10
4159 Audi Quattro GT Sanyo $7–10
4160 Renault R5 Turbo Monte Carlo..$7–10
4160 Renault Clio 16V $7–10
4161 Porsche 959 ....$7–10
4164 Alfa Romeo Giulietta Group 2 ..$7–10
4165 Mercedes-Benz 450 SC Mampe $7–10
4165 Citroën Xantia $7–10
4165 Dodge Viper RT/10, yellow $7–10
4166 Lancia Stratos Pirelli $7–10
4167 BMW M3 GT Cup, green with "tic tac" Rally accents, gray interior.....$7–10
4168 Fiat Ritmo Abarth $7–10
4168 Ferrari F40 Evoluzione, red with Rally accents, silver gray interior $7–10
4169 BMW M1 ....$7–10
4170 Lancia Beta Martini $7–10
4170 MIG Georgia Centenaire $7–10
4171 Land Rover Raid $7–10
4172 Lancia Beta Alitalia $7–10
4174 Mazda RX7 Group 2 ....$7–10
4175 Ferrari GTO, yellow with cream interior $7–10

4176 Alfa Romeo Giulietta Polizia $7–10
4177 Alfa Romeo Giulietta Carabinieri ..$7–10
4178 BMW 535i.........................$7–10
4179 Fiat Tipo...........................$7–10
4180 Lancia Delta Rally $7–10
4181 Mercedes-Benz 300 SL...........$7–10
4183 Ford Sierra Group A Rally........$7–10
4184 Porsche 935 Momo $7–10
4185 Porsche 911 Carrera '93, red with
    light gray interior $7–10
4186 Alfa Romeo 33 Polizia $7–10
4187 Alfa Romeo 33 Carabinieri.....$7–10
4189 Ferrari 348tb $7–10
4190 Peugeot 405 Safari $7–10
4191 Porsche 928, red with light gray interi-
    or $7–10
4192 Chevrolet Corvette $7–10
4193 Alfa Romeo 33 ....$7–10
4193 Fiat Cinquecento $7–10
4194 Suzuki Vitara......................$7–10

Bburago Portachiavl 1:87 Scale
4513 Mercedes-Benz 300 SL.............$2–4
4519 Ferrari Testarossa $2–4
4532 Ferrari F40 ....$2–4
4563 Porsche 959 ....$2–4

Bburago Kit Super 1:24 Scale
5102 Kit Porsche 911 Armel $7–10
5105 Kit Mercedes-Benz 190 E $7–10
5106 Kit Peugeot 205 Turbo 16.......$7–10
5115 Kit Lancia Delta S4 ....$7–10
5119 Kit Alfa Romeo 75 ....$7–10
5121 Kit Porsche 959 Raid $7–10
5129 Kit Ferrari 348 TB Monteshell ...$7–10
5131 Kit Peugeot 405 Raid $7–10
5133 Kit Ferrari 512 BB Daytona......$7–10
5142 Kit Kremer Porsche 935 Turbo ..$7–10
5148 Kit Ferrari 308 GTB $7–10
5172 Kit Ferrari GTO Pioneer $7–10
5173 Kit BMW 635 CSi.................$7–10
5194 Kit Fiat Cinquecento Rally.........$7–10
5199 Kit Porsche 924 Turbo $7–10

Bburago Kit Bijoux 1:24 Scale
5501 Kit 1938 Citroën 15 CV TA $7–10
5502 Kit 1948 Jaguar XK 120
    Roadster $7–10
5504 Kit 1984 Ferrari Testarossa $7–10
5506 Kit 1966 Ferrari 250 LM
    Daytona............................$7–10
5507 Kit 1957 Ferrari Testa Rossa $7–10
5509 Kit 1954 Mercedes-Benz 300
    SL $7–10
5510 Kit 1962 Ferrari 250 GTO......$7–10
5513 Kit 1965 Ford AC Cobra 427 ..$7–10
5524 Kit 1957 Chevrolet Corvette $7–10
5532 Kit 1954 Mercedes-Benz 300
    SL $7–10
5537 Kit 1988 Lamborghini Countach..$7–10
5539 Kit 1989 Ferrari 348 TB $7–10
5540 Kit 1987 Ferrari F40.............$7–10

Bburago Grand Prix 1:24 Scale Formula One Racers
6101 Ferrari 64½, "27" $7–10
6102 Benetton Ford......................$7–10

6103 Grand Prix F.1 ....$7–10
6104 Race Champion $7–10
6108 Williams FW14.....................$7–10
6109 Burago Team $7–10
6110 Formula USA $7–10
6121 Formula 3000 ....$7–10
6122 Indy Team $7–10
6128 Ferrari 641/2, "28"..............$7–10

Bburago Kit Diamonds 1:18 Scale
7002 Kit 1931 Mercedes SSKL Mille
    Miglia $25–30
7005 Kit 1934 Bugatti "Type 59" Grand
    Prix $25–30
7006 Kit 1937 Jaguar SS 100 Targa Flo-
    rio...................................$25–30
7007 Kit 1957 Ferrari Testa Rossa Le
    Mans $25–30
7008 Kit 1932 Alfa Romeo 2300 Tour-
    ing..................................$25–30
7009 Kit 1928 Mercedes SSK Monte
    Carlo $25–30
7010 Kit 1955 Lancia Aurelia B24 Spi-
    der...................................$25–30
7011 Kit 1962 Ferrari 250 GTO Nurbur-
    gring................................$25–30
7013 Kit 1954 Mercedes-Benz 300
    SL $25–30
7014 Kit 1931 Alfa Romeo 8C G. P.
    Mon.................................$25–30
7016 Kit 1961 Jaguar "E" Cabriolet Tour de
    France...............................$25–30
7018 Kit 1961 Jaguar "E" Coupe ...$25–30
7019 Kit 1984 Ferrari Testarossa $25–30
7020 Kit 1936 Mercedes-Benz 500K Road-
    ster $25–30
7021 Kit 1961 Porsche 356 B
    Coupe...............................$25–30
7024 Kit 1957 Chevrolet Corvette ..$25–30
7025 Kit 1992 Dodge Viper RT/10.$25–30
7027 Kit 1984 Ferrari GTO...........$25–30
7032 Kit 1987 Ferrari F40 ....$25–30
7035 Kit 1991 Bugatti EB110 ....$25–30
7039 Kit 1989 Ferrari 348 TB $25–30
7041 Kit 1990 Lamborghini Diablo.$25–30

Bburago Disney Characters 1:18 Scale
For just one season at Disney World, two 1:18 scale character toy cars were offered for $20–25 each, as reported by collector Robert Birkenes of Tampa, Florida. Each was 10 inches long and now considered rare and very valuable.

#8005 Goofy ("Pippo" on package)...$75–90
#8006 Donald Duck ("Paperina" on pack-
    age) $75–90

Beaut
"It's A Beaut" is the company slogan for Beaut Manufacturing Company based in northern New Jersey. The company produced just a few simple models from 1946 until 1950. The cars were made of a single casting like Tootsietoys, with large tires. All models are based on a 1942 Chrysler Sedan.

Fire Chief Car.............................$20–30
Police Car.................................$20–30
Sedan $20–30
Taxi $20–30
Van $20–30

The Beckman Collection
Beckman Jr/Sr High School
1325 9th St. SE
Dyersville, IA 52040
phone: 319-875-7188.

Beckman Jr./Sr. High School took advantage of its location in Dyersville, Iowa, home of the world-renowned Ertl company, to offer an assortment of customized Ertl, Scale Models, and First Gear models for sale as a source of fundraising. As indicated in their ads, all proceeds from the sale of these items go to benefit the educational enrichment of Beckman students. If you have questions about any of the items listed below, or if you would like to order any of the items, call or write.

Tractor Trailors 1:64 Scale
Ertl International Harvester with "Chrysler" logos, per case (12) $192
    or ....$20 each
Ertl International Harvester COE with "Chrysler" logos, per case (12)......$192
    or ....$20 each
Ertl GMC with "GMC Motorsports" logos, per case (12) $192
    or ....$20 each
Spec Cast, "Goodyear," per case (12) ..$192
    or ....$20 each
Spec Cast, "Beckman Collection," per case (12)...............................$192
    or ....$20 each
Ertl, "Cadillac" logos, per case (12) $264
    or ....$27 each
Ertl, "Pontiac" logos, per case (12).......$264
    or ....$27 each

Other Toys Available
Ertl "Beckman 2nd Edition" 1913 Bank, 1:25, per case (12)...................$72
    or ....$8 each
Ertl "Beckman 3rd Edition" 1950 Bank, 1:25, per case (12).................$132
    or ....$15 each
Scale Models "Beckman 4th Edition" 1931 Bank, 1:25, per case (12)............$132
    or ....$15 each
Scale Models "Co-Op" Tanker Bank (Sampler), 1:25, per case (12)............$132
    or ....$15 each
Scale Models "Co-Op" Tanker Bank (Production), 1:25, per case (12)............$132
    or ....$16 each
Ertl "Mountain Dew" Delivery Truck, 1:64, per case (12)......................$180
    or ....$10 each
Ertl "Diet Pepsi" Delivery Truck, 1:64, per case (12) $180
    or ....$12 each

Ertl "7-Up" Beverage Delivery Truck, 1:64, per case (12)......................$228
or ....$20 each
First Gear "Dyersville" Grain Truck, 1:34, per case (12)......................$192
or ....$20 each
First Gear 1951 Ford Dry Goods Van, 1:34, per case (12)......................$192
or ....$22 each
Ertl International Harvester 90s School Bus Bank, 1:50, per case (12)...........$204
or ....$26 each
Ertl "University of Notre Dame" 1938 Panel Truck Bank, per case (12)...........$252
or ....$26 each
Ertl Premier Edition 1955 Ward LaFrance Firetruck Bank, "Dyersville, Iowa," per case (12) $242
or ....$26 each
Scale Models 1:16 Scale Tractor Series: John Deere A, Allis-Chalmers Series IV, D17 ....$37.50 (6 or more)

Belgium Trucks

Diecast Miniatures lists two versions of a Ford T-Bird under the Belgium Trucks brand. No other information is available as of this writing.
1960 Ford Thunderbird Convertible, green/yellow...........................$268
1960 Ford Thunderbird Convertible, pink/blue/black............................$268

Benbros

Benbros of Great Britain, originally known as Benson Brothers, was started by Nathan and Jack Benenson. The Benbros name was adopted in 1951. They produced diecast models around the same time as Lesney Products Co. introduced Matchbox toys and were similar in quality. A few models have even been confused with their Matchbox counterparts, especially the Coronation Coach. Some Benbros castings were reissues of Timpo toys produced from 1939 to 1952.

Several series evolved from the Benbros brand including the T.V. Series of 24 models introduced in 1954 with models packaged in little boxes resembling television sets of the period. By 1957, models were repackaged as Mighty Midgets, and the series continued through 1965. Qualitoys were larger scale items than other Benbros toys. Zebra Toys were introduced in the early sixties in order to offer models with more working features and more accurate castings for their size. In 1965, Benbros was taken over, and their toy line was discontinued.

Benbros numbered models

1 Horse Drawn Hay Cart $25
2 Horse Drawn Log Cart $25
3 Military Motorcycle and Sidecar, "AA" ..$30
4 Stage Coach with Four Horses $25
5 Horse Drawn Gypsy Caravan $15

6 Horse Drawn Milk Cart $25
7 Three-Wheeled Electric Milk Trolley $25
8 Foden Tractor and Log Trailer $25
9 Dennis Five Engine with Escape Ladder..$25
10 Crawler Bulldozer............................$15
11 Crawler Tractor with Hay Rake $15
12 Army Scout Car.............................$15
13 Austin Champ $15
14 Centurion Tank.............................$15
15 Vespa Scooter with Rider $25
16 Streamlined Express Locomotive (TV Series only) $25
16 Chevrolet Nomad Station Wagon (Mighty Midget only) $15
17 Crawler Tractor with Disc Harrow $15
18 Hudson Tourer $15
19 Crawler Tractor and Trailer $15
20 Foden 8-wheel Flat Lorry $15
21 Foden 8-wheel Open Truck $15
22 ERF Petrol Tanker $25
23 AEC Box Van $25
24 Field Gun $10
25 Spyker $10
26 1904 Vauxhall 5 HP $10
27 1906 Rolls-Royce $10
28 Foden 8-wheel Flatbed Truck with Chains $25
29 RAC Motorcycle and Sidecar...........$40
30 AEC Army Box Van $30
30 Bedford Army Box Van....................$25
31 AEC Lorry with Tilt..........................$15
31 Bedford Lorry with Tilt $25
32 AEC Compressor Lorry $15
32 Bedford Compressor Truck $25
33 AEC Crane Lorry $15
33 Bedford Crane Lorry $25
34 Land Rover, "AA" $25
35 Army Land Rover $25
36 Royal Mail Land Rover....................$25
37 Wolseley Six-Eighty Police Car $15
38 Daimler Ambulance $30
39 Bedford Milk Float $15
40 American Ford Convertible................$15
41 Army Hudson Tourer $25
42 Army Motorcycle and Sidecar...........$40
43 Bedford Articulated Box Van.............$25
44 Bedford Articulated Lowside Truck $25
45 Bedford Articulated Low Loader $25
46 Bedford Articulated Petrol Tanker.......$40
47 Bedford Articulated Crane Truck (number not confirmed) $15
48 Bedford Articulated Flatbed Truck with Chains $25
49 Karrier Bantam "Coca-Cola" Bottle Truck $55
50 RAC Land Rover (number not confirmed)......................................$40
220 AEC Flat Lorry with chains, "Sunderland," 5⅛"...............................$175
221 Articulated Low Loader, Timpo reissue, 6½".......................................$45
223 Land Rover, "Royal Mail E II R," red, 4⅜"..$175

224 Articulated Petrol Tanker, Timpo reissue...$55
225 AEC Dropside Lorry, "Sunderland," 5¼"...$150
226 Petrol Tanker, Timpo reissue, 4⅝"...$55
227 AEC Flat Lorry, Timpo reissue, "Sunderland," 5⅛"...............................$150
228 AEC Lorry with Tilt, 5¼"...............$150
310 Ruston-Bucyrus 10-RB Crane, 1½"..$125
311 Ruston-Bucyrus 10-RB Excavator, 1½"..$125

Benbros Army Vehicles

A101 Army Open Land Rover, 4⅜", and Field Gun, 4" $125
A102 Lorry with Anti-Aircraft Gun, 4⅝"..$45
A103 Lorry with Radar Scanner, 4⅝"....$45
A104 Lorry with Searchlight, 4⅝".........$45
A105 Armoured Car, 3¾", and Field Gun, 4"...$45
A106 Army AEC Lorry with Tilt, "Sunderland," 5¼"..................................$175
A107 Army Closed Land Rover, 4⅜"....$75

Benbros unnumbered models

AA Land Rover, "AA Road Service," same casting as #A107 and #223 ....$175
AA Motorcycle and Sidecar, 3¼"....$150
AEC Lorry with #310 Ruston-Bucyrus 10-RB Crane, "Sunderland" $175
AEC Lorry with #311 Ruston-Bucyrus 10-RB Excavator, "Sunderland" $175
Articulated Box Van, Timpo reissue, "Lyons Tea," 5¾"...........................$180
Caterpillar Bulldozer, 4⅝"..................$55
Caterpillar Excavator with driver, 5½".....$55
Caterpillar Tractor, 3⅞".....................$55
Coronation Coach with 8 horses, Souvenir of the Coronation of Queen Elizabeth II, 4½", 1953 ....$150
Covered Wagon with 4 bullocks, L. Brooks reissue, 7¼".............................$125
Covered Wagon with 4 horses, 7¼" ...$125
Daimler Ambulance, 1:43 ....$75
Dodge Army Radar Truck, 1:50 ....$85
Euclid Dump Truck, copy of Dinky #965, 5¾"...$85
Father Christmas Sleigh with 4 reindeer, 4"..$50
Ferguson Tractor with driver, 2⅞".........$50
Ferguson Tractor, 2⅞", and Log Trailer, 7"..$75
Ferguson Tractor with Cab and Shovel, 4"..$60
Ferguson Tractor 2⅞", with Roller Trailer, 4⅜"..$75
Ferguson Tractor 2⅞", with Harrow, 4⅜"..$75
Forward Control Box Van, Timpo reissue, "Pickfords Removals," 3⅞" $60
Horse Drawn Farm Cart with farmer, Timpo reissue..$85
Horse Drawn Log Wagon with log, 8¾"...$85

Horse Drawn Water Wagon, Timpo reissue $85
Muir Hill Dumper with driver, 4⅛" $80
RAC Motorcycle and Sidecar, 3¼" $150
Rickshaw with 2 passengers, pulled by Ostrich or Zulu, 6" $125
Roman Chariot with 2 horses and driver, 5¼" $125
Solo Motorcycle with Rider, 3¼" $55
State Landau with 4 horses, 2 separate footmen, 4" $50
Stephenson's Rocket Locomotive and Coal Tender, 4⅛" $55
Tanker, "Esso Motor Oil," 1:45 .... $75
Tanker, "Petrol Goes a Long Way," 1:45 .... $25

Zebra Toys by Benbros

Austin Mini Van, AA Patrol Service, #60 .... $250–325
Austin Mini Van, RAC $250–325
Bedford Cattle Transporter, #20, 3⅞" $85–100
Daimler Ambulance, #27 & #107, 4" $130–160
Field Gun, 4" $25–35
Foden Concrete Mixer, #16 & #100, 2¾" $85–100
Heinkel Bubble Car, #34 & #106, 3⅞" $130–160
Jaguar "E" Type, #10 & #103, 3½" $145–160
Lansing Bagnall Rapide 2000 Fork Lift Truck, 3½" $85–100
Routemaster Bus, "Fina Petrol," #30 & #104, 4⅜" $130–160
Scammell Scarab Articulated Van, "British Railways," #36 & #101, 4⅛" ... $160–200
Triumph Motorcycle Police Patrol, 3¼" $50–70
Triumph Motorcycle Rally, 3¼" $50–70
Triumph Motorcycle Army Dispatch, #3, 3¼" $50–70
Triumph Motorcycle Telegraph Boy, #4, 3¼" $50–70
Triumph Motorcycle and Sidecar, RAC, 3¼" $130–160
Triumph Motorcycle and Sidecar, AA, 3¼" $130–160

Best

There are actually four toy manufacturers named Best, all unrelated. One started in the 1930s in Kansas by John M. Best, Sr., another in just the past decade in Pesaro, Italy, by Marco Grassini. A third company called Best-Box is an obscure brand of miniature vehicles made in Holland. Their resemblance to Efsi toys of Holland may not be coincidental. A fourth company is based in Taiwan.

Best Toys of Kansas

It was in the midst of the hard economic times of the 1930s that John M. Best, Sr., start-ed Best Toy & Novelty Factory. His main business as a printer who worked with metal alloys lent itself to a sideline in lead alloy toys. The company started as a family hobby and continued until 1939 when Best was purchased by Ralstoy of Ralston, Kansas. In the meantime, Best maintained a close association with the Kansas Toy Company in John Best's home town of Clifton, Kansas, occasionally swapping dies.

Many early Best models are actually Ralstoy or Kansas Toy models. Unlike recent reproductions, Best originals are distinguished by white rubber wheels or embossing of the words "Made in USA." Several models used the metal wheels common to Kansas Toy originals, while others possessed wooden hubs with rubber tires. The familiar oversized white tires made of soft rubber eventually became a standard on Best models.

The original line of Best toys were an assortment of generic sedans, coupes, and racers typically 3½ to 4" long, along with an oil transport measuring 6¾".

Racer #76, 4¼" long $30
Racer #81, 4½" $30
Racer #85, record car with large square fin and driver, 4" $30
Sedan #86, 2-Door Fastback, slant grille with grid pattern, possibly a Lincoln, 4" $30
Sedan #87, possibly a Brewster $30
Sedan #90, 2-Door airflow, hood reaches front bumper with no grille, 3½" $30
Sedan #91, 2-Door airflow, high style vee grille, faired front fenders, possibly a Cadillac, 3½" $30
Coupe #92, chopped top, heart-shaped grille, possibly a Dodge, 3¾" $30
Coupe #93, streamlined with hood similar to #91, grid pattern grille, possibly a Cadillac, 3⅝" $30
Large Sedan Taxi #94, 2-Door airflow, similar to #90, 4½" $30
Sedan #95, 2-Door, similar to #94, with 3 headlamps, similar to a Chrysler-Briggs show car, 3½" $30
Sedan #95, same as #94 with "Police Dept." shield on doors, 3½" $30
Coupe #96, same as #93, 3⅝" $30
Large Bluebird Racer #97, record car with driver, large fin, 12 exhaust ports, 4½" $30
Coupe #98 .... $30
Coupe #99, similar to a Pontiac, 4" $30
Sedan #100 Pontiac, 4" $30
Oil Transport Cab Unit #101, sleeper cab, slanted grille, similar to an International, 3¼" .. $25
Oil Transport Trailer #102, streamlined "GASOLINE," attaches to #101 Cab Unit, 6¾" ... $30
Sedan, 2-Door airflow, similar to a DeSoto, 3⅞" $30

Best Model of Italy

Art Model / Bang / Best Model / Box Model
Via Toscana, 85
61100 Pesaro, Italy

New 1:43 scale precision models are currently being produced from Pesaro, Italy, by Marco Grassini under the Best brand name. They represent models of Porsches, Alfa Romeos, Jaguars, and Ferraris. While it would seem their product line is extensive, it is actually based on issuing many variations of just a few models.

An interesting observation is that Bang, Best Model, and Art Model replicas are all 1:43 scale, all three brands are based at Via Toscana, 85, 61100 Pesaro, Italy, and their catalogs are similar, as well as their models. Box Model seems to have a similar relationship.

Alfa Romeo TZ1 Clienti, red, #9059 .... $22
Alfa Romeo TZ1 Monza 1963, white, #9060 .... $22
Alfa Romeo TZ1 Targa Florio 1965, yellow, "60," #9061 .... $22
Alfa Romeo TZ1 Targa Florio 1965, red, "70," #9062 .... $22
Alfa Romeo TZ1 Targa Florio 1964, red, "58," #9067 .... $18
Alfa Romeo TZ1 Le Mans 1964, blue, "40," #9068 .... $18
Alfa Romeo TZ2 1965 .... $25
Ferrari P2 Prova, red, #9019 .... $25
Ferrari 250 GT Lusso 1964 .... $23
Ferrari 250 LM 1964 Prova, red, #9008 .... $25
Ferrari 250 LM Nurburgring 1964, red, #9009 .... $25
Ferrari 250 LM Le Mans 1965, yellow, #9010 .... $25
Ferrari 250 LM Le Mans 1965, red, #9025 .. $25
Ferrari 250 LM Le Mans Nurburgring 1965, green, "8," #9054 .... $25
Ferrari 250 LM Monza 1966, white, #9011 .... $25
Ferrari 250 LM Bridgehampton 1965, silver, #9017 .... $25
Ferrari 250 LM Kyalami 1966, yellow, #9018 .. $25
Ferrari 250 LM Tour de France 1969, red, #9023 .... $25
Ferrari 275 GTB/4 Stradale (Street) Hardtop, red, #9001 .... $25
Ferrari 275 GTB/4 Stradale Hardtop, yellow, #9002 .... $25
Ferrari 275 GTB/4 Convertible Spyder, top down, yellow, #9003R1 .... $25
Ferrari 275 GTB/4 Convertible Spyder, top down, red, #9003G2 .... $25
Ferrari 275 GTB/4 Convertible Spyder, top up, white, #9004 .... $25
Ferrari 275 GTB/4 Convertible Spyder, top down, black, #9005 .... $25
Ferrari 275 GTB/4 Rally Monte Carlo 1966, hardtop, yellow, #9006 .... $25
Ferrari 275 GTB/4 Targa Florio 1966, hardtop, red, #9007 .... $25
Ferrari 275 GTB/4 Tour de France 1969, silver, 9015 .... $25
Ferrari 275 GTB/4 Le Mans 1967, red, #9024 .... $25
Ferrari 290 MM Prova 1957, red, #9063 .. $22

Ferrari 290 MM Buenos Aires 1957, red, "10," #9064..$22
Ferrari 290 MM Mille Miglia 1956, red, "600," #9069..$25
Ferrari 290 MM Mille Miglia 1956, red, "548," #9070..$25
Ferrari 330 GTC 1966 ....$25
Ferrari 330 P2 Nurburgring 1965, red, #9020..$25
Ferrari 330 P2 Limited Edition, silver plated...$44
Ferrari 330 P2 Limited Edition, gold plated ...$44
Ferrari 365 P2 Le Mans 1965 "17," red, #9026..$25
Ferrari 365 P2 Le Mans 1965 "18," red, #9021..$25
Ferrari 750 Monza Prova, red, #9044 ......$25
Ferrari 750 Monza Daytona 1955, white, #9055..$25
Ferrari 750 Monza Carrera Panamericana 1954, black, "2," #9058 ....$25
Ferrari 750 Monza Goodwood 1955, red, #9045..$22
Ferrari 750 Monza Spa 1955, yellow, "34," #9046..$25
Ferrari 750 Monza Spa 1955, yellow, "33," #9049..$25
Ferrari 750 Monza Targa Florio 1955, red, #9047..$25
Ferrari 750 Monza Tourist Trophy 1955, red, #9048..$25
Ferrari 750 Monza MM #254 Alesi 1992..$28
Ferrari 750 Monza Limited Edition 1992, silver plated..$44
Ferrari 750 Monza Limited Edition 1992, gold plated..$44
Ferrari 860 Monza Prova, red, #9051 ......$24
Ferrari 860 Monza Sebring 1956, red, "17," #9052..$24
Ferrari 860 Monza Mille Miglia 1956, red, "556," #9053..$24
Ferrari 860 Monza MM "328" 1992 ......$28
Jaguar E Coupe Guida Sinistra, red, #9012R1..$25
Jaguar E Coupe Guida Sinistra, black, #9012N3..$25
Jaguar E Coupe Inglese Guida Destra, black, #9014V4..$25
Jaguar E Coupe Inglese Guida Destra, white, #9014B5..$25
Jaguar E Coupe Tourist Trophy 1962, blue, #9016..$25
Jaguar E Coupe Le Mans 1962, white, #9022..$25
Jaguar E Spyder, top down, black, red, or silver, #9027..$25
Jaguar E Spyder, top down, amaranth or green, #9028..$25
Jaguar E Spyder, top up, white with black top, #9029..$25
Jaguar E Spyder, hard top, red, #9030......$25
Jaguar E Spyder Tourist Trophy 1962, white, #9038..$25

Jaguar E Spyder Oulton Park 1961, blue, #9036..$25
Jaguar E Spyder Nurburgring 1963, silver, #9037..$25
Jaguar E Spyder Brands Hatch 1965, white, #9038..$25
Jaguar E Spyder 1961 ....$22
Jaguar E Spyder 1962 ....$22
Jaguar E Spyder 1963 ....$24
Jaguar E Spyder 1965 ....$24
Porsche 908/2 Prova, white, #9040 ....$25
Porsche 980/2 Brands Hatch 1969, "54," #9041..$25
Porsche 980/2 Brands Hatch 1969, "53," #9042..$25
Porsche 980/2 Brands Hatch 1969, "55," #9043..$25
Porsche 980/2 Watkins Glen 1972, yellow, #9065..$25
Porsche 980/2 Zeltweg 1970, white, #9066..$25
Porsche 908/3 Prova, red, #9033 ....$25
Porsche 908/3 Nurburgring 1970, white ...$25
Porsche 908/3 Targa Florio 1970, light blue, "40," #9034..$25
Porsche 908/3 Targa Florio 1970, light blue, "36," #9034..$25
Porsche 908/3 Targa Florio 1970, light blue, "12," #9039..$25
Porsche 908/3 1969 ....$24
Porsche 908/3 Targa Florio 1970, white with red, "20," #9050 ....$22

Best Model of Italy – Gold and Silver Series

1001 Ferrari 275 GTB/4 Coupe, silver..$60
1002 Ferrari 275 GTB/4 Spyder, silver..$60
1003 Ferrari 330 P2, silver $60
1004 Ferrari 750 Monza, silver............$60
2001 Ferrari 275 GTB/4 Coupe, gold.$75
2002 Ferrari 275 GTB/4 Spyder, gold.$75
2003 Ferrari 330 P2, gold $75
2004 Ferrari 750 Monza, gold............$75

Best-Box of Holland (also see Efsi)

Best-Box toys were made in Holland in the sixties. Even the crudest of these hard-to-find toys have features that make them distinctive. The Ford Model Ts are simple castings. But the plastic spoked wheels and black plastic tires add to their realism. The Porsche 911S features opening doors and represents a fairly accurate representative of the actual car after which the toy is styled. Later models were issued under the Efsi brand.

2 Porsche 911S, green $20
501 DAF 600 Saloon............................$25
502 DAF 1400 Refuse Truck $20
503 DAF 1400 Fire Engine $25
504 DAF Torpedo Dump Truck $25
505 DAF Torpedo Open Truck $20
506 DAF Torpedo Closed Truck $20

2501 Ford Model T Pickup......................$20
2502 Ford Model T Tanker......................$20
2502 Porsche 911S.............................$25
2503 1919 Ford Model T Breakdown Truck .$20
2504 1919 Ford Model T Delivery Van $20
2505 1919 Ford Model T Coupe $20
2506 1919 Ford Model T Sedan $20
2507 1919 Ford Model T Advertisement $20
2507 BMW 2000 CS $25
2508 Volkswagen 1600 TL......................$30
2509 Mercedes-Benz 220 SE Coupe........$20
2509 BRM Formula 1 ....$20
2510 Citroën ID19 Station Wagon $20
2511 Ford Taunus 17 M Super.................$20
2512 Opel Rekord $20
2512 Honda Formula 1 ....$20
2513 Jaguar E-Type Convertible $20
2514 Mercedes-Benz 230 SL Convertible ...$20
2515 Opel Rekord 1900.........................$20
2516 Mercedes-Benz 250 SE Coupe..........$20
2517 1966 Ferrari 312 Formula 1 ....$15
2518 Brabham Formula 1 ....$15
2519 Cooper-Maserati Formula 1 ....$15
2520 Lotus Formula 1 ....$15
2521 Citroën Dyane $20
2522 Ford Transit Van $20

Best Toy Co., Ltd.

No.9, Lane 410, Niu Pu Rd., Hsinchu, Taiwan, R.O.C.

Not much is known about this company. It is believed that it is not in any way connected with any of the other companies and does not produce any diecast toys.

Betal

Little is known of this brand other than the small amount of information provided by collector John Dean of Federal Heights, Colorado, who has had at least one example of a 1942 Packard Senior Series in his collection for some twenty years. Single cast with no base or interior, it is in a style reminiscent of Tootsietoys. Apparently, some Betal castings are reissues of Timpo Toys.

Austin 16 Saloon, brass wheel hubs, Timpo Toys reissue
v.1 no name on model, diecast body, no base, 3¾".............................$50–70
v.2 "A BETAL PRODUCT" under roof, diecast body, tin base, friction motor, 3¾" $50–70
v.3 "A BETAL PRODUCT" under roof, plastic body, tin base, friction motor, 3¾" $50–70
1942 Packard Senior Series................$12–18

Big River Models (also see Milestone Models)

Big River Models of Sydney, Australia, has just begun producing hand-built models of Australian prototypes. Working with Milestone Models, also of Sydney, Big River has released a

1937 Chevrolet Utility, featuring uniquely different styling than its U.S. counterpart. Streamlining is the difference. Holden originally produced this Australian Chevrolet just prior to the release of the first completely Australian-built FX. Retail is $180 Australian, or about $250 US.

1937 Chevrolet Ute . $180 Australian ($250 US)

Bijou (see Modelauto)

Bing

Tinplate toys were the staple for Bing Toy Works of Germany from the 1880s until 1932 when the company went into receivership. German toy manufacturer Karl Bub purchased the company soon afterwards. Bing toy cars are especially valued by collectors and hard to find.

Double Decker Bus, 10" $1,500–1,800
Ford Model T Coupe, clockwork motor, red with black and cream trim, circa 1924, 6½" $1,000–1,250
Ford Model T Doctor's Coupe, clockwork motor, black, 6½" $575–600
Ford Model T Roadster, clockwork motor, red with black and yellow trim, circa 1924, 6½" $1,000–1,250
Ford Model T Sedan, clockwork motor, blue with black and cream trim, circa 1924, 6½" $900–1,150
Ford Model T Touring Car, clockwork motor, circa 1924, 6½" $900–1,150
Limousine, maroon with yellow trim, clockwork motor, circa 1908, 14" $4,500–4,800
Limousine, blue and black, clockwork motor, circa 1915, 9½" $1,500–1,800
Yellow Taxi, clockwork motor, orange with black trim, circa 1924, 9" $2,100–2,250

Bison

Bison models are made in Germany.
Tatra Dump Truck, 1:43 .... $5

Bitsi-Toys (see Lehigh)

Blue Box

Writer/photographer Jeff Koch discovered an unusual Porsche Targa with retractable roof made by an obscure company known only as Blue Box. He paid less than a dollar for it in 1996. Since then, quality toy soldier sets have been found with this name on them.

Porsche Targa with retractable roof, 3" $1–2

Boley (also see High Speed, Smart Toys)

A seemingly new company, Boley of Los Angeles, California, is a marketing company for essentially generic toys, especially formula racers. Packaged as "Formular diecast," three sets of two cars each, upon removal from the package, reveal themselves as High Speed brand toys. Each body style of the six cars is different, not only in color, but in actual casting. two-car sets sell for $.99 each at popular retail chains. Other Boley toys have been found to be made by Sunnyside/Superior, High Speed, and Smart Toys.

Bonux (also see Cle)

Bonux is a brand of ready-made and kit models marketed by the Cle firm of France in the 1960s. Several models have been produced under this brand. While Cle primarily produced plastic models, their Bonux brand was devoted to diecast miniatures.

Fiat Torpedo 1901 .... $15
Ford 1903 .... $15
Isotta-Fraschini 1902 .... $6
Leyland Double Deck Bus 1920 .... $12
Packard 1912 Town Sedan $15
Peugeot 1898 Brougham $7
Peugeot 203 .... $12
Regal 1914 Sedan $15
Renault 1910 Truck $15
Road Roller $7
Rolls-Royce 1911 Silver Ghost Landau $15
Sizaire-Naudin 1906 Racing Car $15

Boss

Little is known of this company, but models are believed to be 1:43 scale white metal.

1970 AMC Javelin, gold $154
1970 Dodge Challenger TransAm HT, pink $134
1970 Dodge Challenger TransAm "Posey #77," green $134

Bossat Dermov

Just when I thought I'd seen the ultimate miniature cars in the name of Pocher 1:8 scale models (retail $499 and up), along comes Bossat Dermov! These French masterpieces are outrageously detailed and even more outrageously priced, as you will see from this list of 1:8 scale models listed in the January–March 1995 Exoto, Inc., quarterly publication called "Exoto Tifosi." Prices listed below are not typographical errors. They are actual prices for new unassembled models.

1929 Bentley "Le Mans" $19,900
Aston Martin DB4 Zagato $26,900
BMW 328 .... $19,900
Bugatti Type 13 Brescia $5,800
Bugatti Type 59/50B $16,400
Bugatti Type 55 .... $16,400
Bugatti Type 50 Coupe $19,900
Bugatti Atalante $26,900
Facel Vega III $26,900
Mercedes-Benz 540K $22,900
Ferrari 512M $22,900
Ferrari Daytona Group IV $26,900
1957 Ferrari 250 TR "Pontoon" $9,950

Bourbon

Two models of this obscure French toy manufacturer are known.

Peugeot D4A Van $25

Berliet Tanker Semi $30

Boutique Auto Moto (BAM)

Aaron Robinson reports that Boutique Auto Moto was a small shop in Paris, France, that at one time produced their own line of white metal models, most notably a line of IMSA Lolas and in particular a "Red Lobster" car from around 1981. Stephen Demosthenes provides a description of one model, a Porsche Carrera 3.0.

1 Porsche Carrera 3.0, orange, #5 Jagermeister, kit $75

Box Model (also see Art Model, Bang, Best)

Ferraris and Jaguars dominate the Box Model assortment, made in Italy, all 1:43 scale. Box Model precedes Best, Art Model, and Bang, brands that resulted from the reorganization of the company in 1991.

AC Cobra 289 Open, wire wheels, red, #8410 .... $20
AC Cobra 289 Open, alloy wheels, black, #8411 .... $20
Ferrari 250 GT, silver plated, #102 .... $28
Ferrari 250 GT, gold plated, #202 .... $38
Ferrari 250 GT Long, Mille Miglia, #8415 .. $22
1956 Ferrari 250 GT Prova Street, red, #8405 .... $22
1956 Ferrari 250 GT Prova, silver, #8406 .. $22
1957 Ferrari 250 GT Pau 3 Hours, red, #8407 .... $22
1958 Ferrari 250 GT Tour de France, silver, #8431 .... $22
1958 Ferrari 250 GT Tour de France Shell/Peron, #8441 .... $22
1959 Ferrari 250 GT Tour de France, white, #8427 .... $22
1960 Ferrari 250 GT Tour de France Street, blue, #8425 .... $8
1960 Ferrari 250 GT Tour de France, red, #8426 .... $8
Ferrari 250 GTO, gold plated, #201 .... $38
Ferrari 250 GTO, silver plated, #101 .... $28
1962 Ferrari 250 GTO Sebring, #8432 .... $22
1963 Ferrari 250 GTO Laguna Seca, #8433 .... $18
Ferrari 250 LM Street, red, #8434 .... $18
1966 Ferrari 275 GTB Spyder, top down, red, #8418R $18
1966 Ferrari 275 GTB Monte Carlo, #8429 .... $22
1966 Ferrari 275 GTB Spyder, top up, white, #8419 .... $22
1966 Ferrari 275 GTB Spyder, wire wheels, black, #8428 .... $18
1966 Ferrari 275 GTB4 Targa Florio, red, #8430 .... $22
1969 Ferrari 275 GTB4 Tour de France "142," silver, #8442 .... $22
1964 Ferrari 250 LM Nurburgring Rindt, red, #8435 .... $22

1965 Ferrari 250 LM LeMans Dumay, yellow, #8436 ....$22

1966 Ferrari 250 LM Monza, white with stripe, #8437 ....$22

1962 Ferrari GTO Coupe Street, red, #8401 ....$22

1962 Ferrari GTO Coupe LeMans '62, light green, #8402 ....$22

1963 Ferrari GTO Coupe TT '63, green, #8403 ....$22

1962 Ferrari GTO Targa Florio O/P, white/brown, #8408 ....$18

1963 Ferrari GTO Coupe TT '63, red, #8409 ....$22

1962 Jaguar E Coupe O/P, black, #8439N $22

1962 Jaguar E Coupe left hand drive, red, #8439R $22

1962 Jaguar E Coupe right hand drive, green/white, #8440 ....$22

1962 Jaguar E Coupe TT "14," blue, #8443 ....$22

BradsCars

Brighton, England, was home to Bradshaws Model Products, producer of a hard-to-find series of crude one-piece casted toy cars. Produced from around 1952 to 1954 to roughly 1:75 scale, or double O, they were priced higher than the better-made Matchbox toys of the same period, which was likely the reason for their quick demise.

Austin A30 (Austin A7 on base), black, red, or green $50

Morris 6, black, red, tan, blue, or light green $50

Riley 1.5, red, black, gray, or green $50

Brand S

Brand S models are relatively generic toys from Hong Kong.

2 Audi 100, white $5

3 Ford Sierra, yellow $5

9 Lancia Stratos, white $5

15 1911 Renault Truck, green $5

Bren L Toys

Vintage toy car enthusiast Staffan Kjellin of Sweden first reported on Bren L Toys in April 1999. Manufactured by W. H. Cornelius Ltd., Bren L Toys are hollow diecast cars with no interior or base.

Bentley Coupe? $25–40

Breslin

Breslin toys are lead alloy, mostly copies of Barclay and Manoil, manufactured in Toronto, Canada, and are distinguished from the originals by the words "Made in Canada" or "Canada" on them.

Brinks Armored Car, 9" $500

Brinks Truck Bank, aluminum, 8" $70

Motorized Machine Gunner $40

Tank $40

Truck with Cannon Wagon $40

Brianza (see A.B.C. Brianza)

Brimtoy Pocketoys

The pre-World War I English company of Wells-Brimtoy Distributors, Ltd., better known for tin and plastic toys, produced a series of diecast toys from the late forties to early fifties called Pocketoys. Some featured clockwork motors inside.

Bedford LWB Truck $50

Buick, blue, red, green, or cream $50

Sunbeam Talbot, cream, green, or blue $50

Vauxhall Coupe, blue, yellow, red, or green .$50

Vauxhall Saloon, red, or blue $50

Wolseley Sedan $50

Britains

William Britain introduced a line of hollow-cast toy soldiers in 1893. Britains Petite, Ltd. is still in business, still producing diecast soldiers, as well as a number of vehicles, mostly farm machinery and military vehicles. The company was purchased in 1998 by the Ertl Company of Dyersville, Iowa, itself now a division of Racing Champions as of April 15, 1999.

Armored Car #274 ....$75

Armored Car #1321 ....$400

Army Ambulance #1512, wounded man and stretcher, doors open, 6" $200

Army Lorry, caterpillar type, #1333 ....$250

Army Lorry, 4-wheel type, #1334 ....$200

Army Lorry with driver, #1335 ....$225

Army Staff Car with officer and driver, #1448 ....$350

   v.1 smooth white tires, black fenders $350

   v.2 white tires, khaki colored body and fenders $350

   v.3 rubber tires, 1948–1950 version, rectangular windshield $300

   v.4 lead tires, 1951–1957, gray colored $325

   v.5 black plastic tires, 1958–1959 ....$275

Army Tender, caterpillar type, covered, #1433 ....$175

Army Tender, 10-wheel covered, #1432 ....$175

Balloon Barrage Unit with lorry, winch and balloon, #1757 ....$1,500

BMW 600CC Motorcycle, black and chrome, #9694 ....$96

Bren Gun Carrier #876 ....$75

Corporation Motor Ambulance with driver, wounded patient and stretcher, #1514 ....$800

Covered Lorry with gun and drivers, #1462 ....$425

Dispatch Rider, #200 ....$40

Dispatch Rider, #1791 ....$175

Drag Racing Motorcycle with rider, blue $48

Greeves 250CC Scrambler Motorcycle, #9692 ....$64

Harley-Davidson, rider with guitar on back, #9689 ....$115

Heavy-Duty Lorry with driver, searchlight, battery and lamp, #1642 ....$700

Heavy-Duty Lorry, underslung, #1641 ....$500

Heavy-Duty Lorry, underslung with driver, #1643 ....$1,000

Howitzer 4.5", #1725 ....$30

Mobile Searchlight #1718 ....$60

Mobile Unit, 2-Pounder, #1717 ....$60

Motorcycle Machine Gun #199 ....$100

Police Car with two officers, #1413 ....$750

Range Rover Discovery, 1:32, 1996 ....$20

Regular Limber #1726 ....$25

Speed Record Car "The Bluebird," #1400 ....$350

Tank #1203 ....$200

British Motoring Classics

British Motoring Classics are 1:43 scale models. The Austin/Morris/Cooper legacy is similar to other car companies that manufacture several different brands of automobiles. British Motoring Classics presents high-quality replicas of Mini Coopers, Morris Minis, and Austin Minis with various liveries and colors. Models are currently offered at $88 each.

Brookfield Collectors Guild

16312 West Glendale Drive
New Berlin, Wisconsin 53151-9917

Brookfield Collectors Guild has been producing plastic scale promo models and diecast replicas since 1992. Most of their diecast models are coin banks, usually with a slot hidden in a trunk, under the chassis, or some other discreet location.

Meanwhile, back in 1980, even before Brookfield had a name, company president Kenneth Dahlke established a reputation for excellence when he produced lavish models of the 1908 Model T for the Henry Ford Museum in Dearborn, Michigan. Around the same time, his company released a replica of Louis Chevrolet's first car for the company that bears his name. These two early models were clad in silver plate and fitted with diamond headlights and ruby taillights, and manufactured in very limited edition.

Since then, an assortment of diecast banks have been produced. The first ones, Chevy Suburbans, had the coin slot in the top. Later versions put the slot on the bottom so as not to ruin the integrity of the model.

Presented here is a complete Brookfield product history, including production year, description, quantity produced (issue price), and current value. The reason some models list no price is that they were offered as incentive bonuses for dealers purchasing a certain quantity of the regular production models.

Brookfield Collectors Guild is now owned by Action Performance as of the summer of 1999.

Early Brookfield Models

1908 Model T Ford, issued in 1980, produced for the Henry Ford Museum (no pricing information available). Author's best guess $10,000–25,000

First Chevrolet, issued in 1980 as a commemorative for corporate executives of General Motors (no pricing information available). Author's best guess..........................$750–1,500

The Brookfield Collection

The April 1997 issue of *Brookfield Forecast*, published by Brookfield Collectors Guild, provides the most comprehensive list to date on Brookfield issues.

Dale Earnhardt/GM Goodwrench products are available through GM Goodwrench dealers first exclusively.

* These models are banks with a hidden coin slot in chassis.

** Only available to dealers when they purchase a case.

Brookfield Collectors Guild Chevrolet Suburbans*

N/A '92 Dale Earnhardt #3	$175
525 '93 Indy 500 Suburban Bank	$40
532 '93 Indy 500 Emergency Truck	$250
N/A '93 Jeff Gordon Rookie of the Year	$40
563 '94 Brickyard 400	$35
563A '94 Brickyard 400, white box, pre-production	$200
564 '94 Brickyard 400, yellow truck	$200
N/A '94 Chevrolet Racing Thunder	$45
572 '95 #3 Goodwrench, white truck	$400
N/A '95 John Force	$45
577 '95 Dale Earnhardt, 7 Time Champion	$75
577S '95 Dale Earnhardt, silver	$125
517 '95 Teal Chevrolet Suburban	$45
646 '95 Indy 500	$35
644 '95 Brickyard 400	$40

Brookfield Collectors Guild GMC Suburbans*

N/A '94 Don Prudhomme	$40
617 '95 #30 Pennzoil, M. Waltrip	$35
N/A '95 #30 Pennzoil Brickyard 400	$200
N/A '95 #30 Pennzoil, silver	$275
600 '95 #42 Mello Yello, Kyle Petty	$35
605 '95 #42 Mello Yellow, Thanks Fans	$35
602 '95 #42 Mello Yello, silver	$90
518 '95 Teal GMC Suburban	$45
643 '95 7&7 Split Petty/Earnhardt	$60
643R '95 7&7 Split, reverse colors	$80

Brookfield Collectors Guild GMC & Chevrolet*

633 '95 7&7 Twin Pack, Petty/Earnhardt	$75
656 '95 7&7 Twin Pack, reverse colors	$125

Brookfield Collectors Guild Chevrolet Dually* & Trailer (diecast crew cab truck/bank with opening rear trailer door)

528 '94 Dale Earnhardt Combination	$150

632 '94 Dale Earnhardt Combo, silver	$200
561 '94 Brickyard 400	$75
565 '94 Brickyard 400, yellow	$90
670 '95 Racing Thunder	$75
638 '95 Indy 500 Hauler	$65
N/A '95 Indy 500, silver special	$120

Brookfield Collectors Guild Chevrolet Dually*

636 '95 Brickyard 400 Pace Truck	$40

Brookfield Collectors Guild GMC Dually & Trailer (diecast crew cab truck/bank with opening rear trailer door)

599 '95 #42 Kyle Petty Mello Yello	$65
601 '95 #42 Kyle Petty, silver	$200
635 '95 7&7 Portrait: Earnhardt/Petty	$75
N/A '95 7&7 Portrait, reverse colors	$85
616 '95 #30 M. Waltrip Pennzoil	$60
618 '95 #30 M.Waltrip, silver	$175

Brookfield Collectors Guild Chrysler Diecast (opening hood, doors, trunk)

508 '93 Dodge Intrepid, Cherry	$55
506 '93 Chrysler Concorde, CharGold	$55
538 '94 Dodge Intrepid, Ram Blue	$45
537 '94 Chrysler Concorde, Green	$50
515 '94 Chrysler New Yorker, Black	$55
519 '94 Chrysler LHS, Char, Gold	$55
642 '95 Dodge Intrepid, Black	$50
649 '95 Chrysler Concorde, Red	$50
650 '95 Chrysler New Yorker, Wild Berry	$55
651 '95 Chrysler LHS, Spruce Pearl	$50
682 '96 Chrysler LHS, Dr. Gold	$50
680 '96 Chrysler Concorde, Spruce	$35
679 '96 Dodge Intrepid, Candy Apple Red	$50
642R '95 Dodge Intrepid, Rosewood	$75
649R '95 Chrysler Concorde, Rosewood	$75
650R '95 Chrysler New Yorker, Rosewood	$75
651R '95 Chrysler LHS, Rosewood	$75

Brookfield Collectors Guild Chrysler Diecast Banks

540 '93 Plymouth Minivan, gold wheels	$30
539B '93 Jeep Grand Cherokee, Black	$25
539R '94 Jeep Grand Cherokee, Red	$30
539W '94 Jeep Grand Cherokee, White	$30
539LD '94 Jeep Grand Cherokee, Orchid	$55
540 '94 Plymouth Minivan, silver wheels (4 mil.)	$30
540RE '95 Plymouth Minivan, red graphics	$55
539C '95 Jeep Grand Cherokee, Camp Jeep	$25
539G '95 Jeep Grand Cherokee, Orvis	$25

Brookfield Collectors Guild Plastic Promotional Models

558 '94 Brickyard 400 Monte Carlo, tan interior	$30

558A '94 Brickyard 400 Monte Carlo, black interior	$60
566 '94 Brickyard 400 Monte Carlo, T. George	$35
568 '94 Dodge Neon Sedan, Emerald Green	$20
544 '94 Plymouth Neon Sedan, Emerald Green	$20
542 '94 Dodge Neon Sedan, Nitro Green	$25
567 '94 Plymouth Neon Sedan, Nitro Green	$25
534 '94 Neon Sedan, White Racer	$20
545 '95 Neon Sedan, Special Black	$60
661B '95 Chevrolet Monte Carlo, Black	$25
661R '95 Chevrolet Monte Carlo, Red	$30
661S '95 Chevrolet Monte Carlo, Silver	$60
552 '95 Chrysler Cirrus, Med. Fern	$20
552R '95 Chrysler Cirrus, Rosewood	$60
551 '95 Dodge Stratus, Light Fern	$25
551R '95 Dodge Stratus, Rosewood	$150
694 '96 Plymouth Neon Coupe, White	$30
640 '96 Earnhardt Street Monte Carlo	$25

Brookfield Collectors Guild Special Racing Promotional Models (twin packs)

573 '95 Jeff Gordon Brickyard 400 Twin Pack: Monte Carlo Pace Car & Lumina Race Car	$60
662 '95 Earnhardt Racer & Custom Monte Carlo	$50
662S '95 Earnhardt Racer & Silver Monte Carlo	$90

Brookfield Collectors Guild Premiere Edition Models

726 Dodge Viper GTS Coupe, blue w/white stripe	$100
504 Dodge Viper RT/10 Convertible, Red	$100

Brookfield Collectors Guild Diecast Models 1:25 Scale

767R Chrysler Sebring Convertible, Red	$35
767N Chrysler Sebring Convertible, Green	$35
767G Chrysler Sebring Convertible, Gold	$35
758 Oldsmobile Bravada	$40
672W Chevrolet Express, White	$40
672B Chevrolet Express, Adriatic Blue	$40
717 Chevrolet Tahoe, Truck of the Year	$40
682 Chrysler LHS, DramaGold	$35
680 Chrysler Concorde, Spruce Blue	$35
679 Dodge Intrepid, Candy Apple Red	$35
672BF 1996 Brickyard 400 Chevy Express Van	$45

Brookfield Collectors Guild Plastic Promotional Models 1:25 Scale

743 Dodge Stratus, Candy Apple Red	$25
742 Chrysler Cirrus, Black	$25
736B Chevrolet Monte Carlo, Adriatic Blue	$25
736P Chevrolet Monte Carlo, Purple Pearl Metallic	$25

648T Oldsmobile Aurora, Dark Teal Metallic $30
648W Oldsmobile Aurora, White........$25
648C Oldsmobile Aurora, Champagne .$30
648R Oldsmobile Aurora, Garnet Red....$30
648S Oldsmobile Aurora, Silver Teal $60
648P Indy Racing League Aurora Pace Car....................................$30
718 Neon Celebrity Challenge Racer, Yellow.................................$30
696 Neon Celebrity Challenge Racer, Black....................................$25
678 Dodge Neon Coupe, Magenta $25
695 Dodge Neon Sedan, Light Iris........$25
693 Plymouth Neon Expresso Coupe, Lapis.....................................$25
669 Dodge Neon SCCA Club Racer, Black....................................$25

Brookfield Collectors Guild Winston Cup Racing Collectibles 1:25 Scale Diecast
575 Dale Earnhardt/Goodwrench Chevrolet. Tahoe..............................$45
579C Jeff Gordon/DuPont Crew Cab Truck (CCT)............................$75
580C Jeff Gordon/DuPont Chevrolet Suburban...............................$40
584C Bobby Labonte/Interstate Crew Cab (CCT).............................$70
585C Bobby Labonte/Interstate Chevy Suburban.............................$40
589C Terry Labonte/Kellogg's Crew Cab (CCT).............................$75
590C Terry Labonte/Kellogg's Chevrolet Suburban $40
594C Sterling Martin/Kodak Crew Cab CCT.................................$70
595C Sterling Marlin/Kodak Chevy Suburban.............................$40
600 Kyle Petty GMC Suburban.............$40
607C Ken Schrader/Budweiser Crew Cab (CCT).............................$75
607C Ken Schrader/Budweiser Chevrolet Suburban.............................$40
611C Darrell Waltrip/Parts America Crew Cab (CCT)...........................$70
612C Darrell Waltrip/Parts America Chevy Suburban.............................$40
636 Brickyard 400 Pace Truck $40
644 Brickyard 400 Chevy Suburban $40
646 Indy 500 Trackside Chevy Suburban $40
670 Earnhardt Chevrolet Racing Thunder (CCT).............................$75
700 Dale Earnhardt Victory Suburban $45
701 Dale Earnhardt Victory Crew Cab...$40
752 Ricky Craven/Budweiser Chevrolet Tahoe..............................$40
753 Terry Labonte/Kellogg's Chevrolet Tahoe..............................$40
754 Jeff Gordon/DuPont Chevrolet Tahoe..............................$40
764 Jeff Gordon/DuPont Trackside Crew Cab Truck, Trailer & Race Car........$75

765 Budweiser Trackside Crew Cab Truck, Trailer & Race Car $75
766 Terry Labonte Kellogg's Trackside Crew Cab Truck, Trailer & Race Car.........$75
708 Dale Earnhardt Show Car Trailer (CCT).................................$70
722 Dale Earnhardt Stars & Stripes, 3 car set......................................$135
723 Dale Earnhardt Olympic Trackside Tahoe.................................$45
724 Dale Earnhardt Olympic Combination Set...$85
744 Earnhardt AC Delco Replica (GM Dealer).....................................$55
755 Ken Schrader/Budweiser Chevy Express Van.....................................$40
756 Terry Labonte/Kellogg's Chevy Express Van.....................................$40
757 Jeff Gordon/DuPont Chevy Express Van.....................................$40

761 DaleEarnhardt/#3 Goodwrench Van $40

763 Dale Earnhardt Trackside Crew Cab Truck, Trailer & Race Car $75
776 Johnny Benson, Jr./Pennzoil GMC Suburban...............................$40
777 Johnny Benson, Jr./Pennzoil GMC Transporter..........................$70
784 Earnhardt AC Delco/Goodwrench Twinpack $95
785 Earnhardt AC Delco Trackside Combo. Set.....................................$100
788 Earnhardt AC Delco Replica (Distributor) $55
789 AC Delco Distribution Version.......$100
790 Earnhardt AC Delco Suburban $50

Brookfield Collectors Guild 1:32 Scale Corvette Series, 1992
1953 Corvette Convertible, white $35–50
1954 Corvette Convertible, black....$35–50
1955 Corvette Convertible, red.......$35–50
1956 Convertible, black and silver ..$35–50
1957 Corvette, green and beige.....$35–50
1958 Corvette, turquoise and white .$35–50
1959 Corvette, snowcrest white $35–50
1960 Corvette, Roman red and ermine $35–50
1961 Corvette, Fawn beige $35–50
1962 Corvette, Roman red $35–50
1963 Corvette, Daytona blue $35–50
1964 Corvette, Riverside red $35–50
1965 Corvette, Nassau blue $35–50

1966 Corvette, Rally red $35–50
1967 Corvette, G.W. green $35–50
1968 Corvette, Silverstone...........$35–50
1969 Corvette, Monza Red $35–50
1970 Corvette, Ontario orange $35–50
1971 Corvette, yellow $35–50
1972 Corvette, Elkhart green $35–50
1973 Corvette, medium blue $35–50
1974 Corvette, medium red $35–50
1975 Corvette, silver $35–50
1976 Corvette, classic white $35–50
1977 Corvette, black $35–50
1978 Corvette, silver on silver $35–50
1979 Corvette, light beige $35–50
1980 Corvette, dark brown $35–50
1981 Corvette, red $35–50
1982 Corvette, silver beige $35–50
1984 Corvette, bright red $35–50
1985 Corvette, gold metallic $35–50
1986 Corvette, yellow $35–50
1987 Corvette, medium blue metallic.$35–50
1988 Corvette, metallic dark red $35–50
1989 Corvette, metallic gray $35–50
1990 Corvette, metallic turquoise.....$35–50
1991 Corvette, metallic quasar blue ..$35–50
1992 Corvette, bright red $35–50

Brooklins

Brooklin Models Ltd.
Pinesway Industrial Estate
Ivo Peters Road
Bath, Avon
BA2 3QS England
e-mail: brooklin_models@talk21.com
website: www.brooklinmodels.co.uk

Brooklin, Lansdowne & Robeddie are all brands of Brooklin Models Limited of Brooklin, Ontario, Canada. Started in 1974 by John Hall in his basement, the company has since become the world's leading manufacturer of hand-built 1:43 scale collectible model automobiles. Brooklins are now manufactured in a 10,000 square foot factory in Bath, England.

While their replication of fifties and sixties vintage US cars makes them popular with collectors, Brooklins sometimes lack the fine detailing of comparable models, opting instead for heavy, solid construction and exacting scale. Some enthusiasts prefer to add chrome foil for finish trim, applying thin metallic film in a fashion similar to gold leaf. This preference leads back to the argument of the purist versus the hobbyist, as mentioned in the introduction to this book.

While Brooklins focus on American (US) cars, Lansdowne models are replicas of British cars. The series was introduced in 1993 to present a completely new line of models for collectors.

Robeddie models meanwhile concentrate on Swedish vehicles — Volvos mostly, with a 1969 Saab 99 thrown in for variety.

The Brooklin Collection — current regular issues $55 each; current special issues $75–115 each; obsolete issues $200–350 each. Richard O'Brien's book *Collecting Toy Cars & Trucks* presents a comprehensive listing of Brooklins, both the original Canadian issues and the newer British issues. Presented here is a survey of those issues. Since the book was published however, second market values have dropped considerably for Brooklins, probably due to increasing competition from other companies producing the same or similar models of equal or better quality for considerably less.

Listed immediately below is a list of color variations for the Brooklins #2 1948 Tucker (which, for some reason, Richard O'Brien's book lists as a 1949 Tucker for Canadian issues, 1948 Tucker for British issues). As with most things, Brooklins can be purchased for considerably less than the prices indicated below.

Brooklin 1948 Tucker Torpedo

v.1 medium blue with gray interior, Canadian issue #14......$150
v.2 dark blue with gray interior, Canadian issue #14......$150
v.3 very dark blue with gray interior, Canadian issue #14......$150
v.4 black with beige interior, Canadian issue #14......$150
v.5 black with light gray interior, Canadian issue #14......$150
v.6 maroon, Canadian issue #2..$200–225
v.7 metallic medium blue, Canadian issue #2......$150
v.8 metallic dark blue with gray interior, Canadian issue #2......$150
v.9 metallic light maroon, no gas cap, British issue #2......$95
v.10 metallic light maroon, with gas cap, British issue #2......$95
v.11 metallic maroon, British issue #2......$95
v.12 metallic dark maroon, with gas cap, British issue #2......$95
v.13 metallic gold with tan interior, British issue #2A......$45–65
v.14 metallic dark gold with tan interior, British issue #2A......$45–65
v.15 metallic maroon with tan interior, 500 m. Tucker Club, British issue #2A ...$150
v.16 metallic silver with tan interior, Harrah's, British issue #2A......$125
v.17 metallic light brown with gray interior, Harrah's, British issue #2A......$125
v.18 metallic gold with beige interior, Harrah's, British issue #2A......$125
v.19 metallic Lazer red, Paramount Pictures, British issue #2A......$100
v.20 metallic Stratus silver, Paramount Pictures, British issue #2A......$100
v.21 metallic turquoise, Paramount Pictures, British issue #2A......$100
v.22 green, prototype......$250–400
v.23 Sierra beige, prototype......$250–400
v.24 black, prototype......$250–400
v.25 Signa amber, prototype......$250–400
v.26 champagne, prototype......$250–400

v.27 zircon blue, prototype......$450–600
v.29 Jaguar coral, prototype......$250–400
v.30 white, prototype......$250–400
v.31 light blue, Tucker Club 2nd issue ..$100

Brooklin Canadian Issues

1 1933 Pierce Arrow Silver Arrow......$250–400
2 1948 Tucker Torpedo (see narrative)
3 1930 Ford Victoria 2-Door......$100–250
4 1937 Chevrolet Coupe......$125–275
5 1930 Ford Model A 2-Door Sedan, recalled due to "bad casting" (highly speculative)......$250
5 1930 Ford Model A 2-Door Coupe .$350
6 1932 Packard......$225
7 1934 Chrysler Airflow......$100
8 1940 Chrysler Newport 4-Door......$100
8A 1941 Chrysler Newport Pace Car .$275
9 1940 Ford Van......$300–450

Brooklin British Issues

1 1933 Pierce Arrow......$65–225
2 1948 Tucker Torpedo (see narrative)
3 1930 Ford Victoria 2-Door......$85–150
4 1937 Chevrolet Coupe......$100–250
5 1930 Ford Model A 2-Door Coupe......$80–200
6 1932 Packard Standard 8......$85–150
7 1934 Chrysler Airflow......$55–100
8 1940 Chrysler Newport......$85–100
8A 1941 Chrysler Newport Indy Pace Car......$50–200
9 1940 Ford Delivery......$65–350

10 1949 Buick Roadmaster Coupe ..$65–150

11 1956 Lincoln Continental Mark II......$65–150
12 1931 Hudson Greater 8 Boattail......$65–250
13 1957 Ford Thunderbird......$70–250
14 1940 Cadillac V16......$50–275
15 1950 Mercury Convertible......$55–150
16 1935 Dodge Van......$50–300
16 1935 Dodge Pickup......$65–250
17 1950 Studebaker Starlight......$50–100
18A 1941 Packard Super Clipper ..$65–300
19A 1955 Chrysler C300......$50–75
20 1953 Buick Skylark......$250
21 1963 Chevrolet Corvette......$55–300
22A 1958 Edsel Citation......$55–125
23 1956 Ford Fairlane Victoria......$55–90
23A 1956 Ford Mainline Police......$55–70
24 1968 Shelby Mustang......$150
24 1968 Ford Mustang......$150
25 1958 Pontiac Bonneville Convertible......$55–200
26 1955 Chevrolet Nomad......$55–225

27 1957 Cadillac Eldorado Brougham......$150
28 1957 Mercury Turnpike Cruiser..$55–200
29A 1953 Kaiser Manhattan......$55–225
30 1954 Dodge Royal 500 Convertible......$45–65
31 1953 Pontiac Van......$45–65
32A 1953 Studebaker Champion Starliner......$45–65
33 1938 Phantom Corsair......$45–65
34 1954 Nash Ambassador......$45–65
35A 1957 Ford Sunliner, top down..$45–65
36 1952 Hudson Hornet......$45–65
37 1960 Ford Sunliner......$45–65
38 1939 Graham "Sharknose"......$45–65
39 1953 Oldsmobile Fiesta......$45–65
40A 1948 Cadillac Series 62 Sedanet......$45–65
41A 1959 Chrysler 300E......$45–65
42 1952 Ford F1 Ambulance......$45–65
43A 1948 Packard Station Sedan...$45–65
44 1961 Chevrolet Impala......$45–65
45 1948 Buick Roadmaster......$45–65
46 1959 Chevrolet El Camino......$45–65
47 1965 Ford Thunderbird......$45–65
48 1958 Chevrolet Impala......$45–65
49 1954 Hudson Italia......$45–65
50 1948 Chevrolet Aero Sedan......$45–65
50A 1947 Chevrolet Aero Sedan Police......$55–70
51 1951 Ford Victoria......$45–65
52 1941 Hupmobile Skylark......$45–65
53 1955 Chevrolet Cameo Pick-Up Truck......$45–65
54 1953 Airstream Wanderer Travel Trailer......$45–65
55A 1951 Packard Mayfair......$45–65
56 no model assigned
57 1960 Lincoln Continental Convertible......$55–70
58 1963 Ford Falcon Sprint......$55–70
59 1957 Rambler Rebel......$55–70
60 no model assigned
61 1960 Chevrolet Impala Convertible.$55–70
62 no model assigned
63 1956 Plymouth Fury......$55–70
64 1959 Ford Thunderbird......$40–60
65 1947 Wesley Slumbercoach......$45–60
66 1956 Packard Patrician......$55–75
67 1961 Chrysler Imperial......$45–60
68 1954 Chevrolet Bel Air Sport Coupe......$55–70
69 1946 Mercury Sportsman Convertible Coupe......$55–70

1949 Dodge Wayfarer Coupe 55–70

71 1955 Classic American Speedboat and Trailer.................................$55–70
72 1958 Shasta Airflyte Travel Trailer..$55–70
73 1949 Oldsmobile 98 Coupe $55–70
74 1947 Cadillac Series 62 Convertible $55–70
75 1960 Edsel Ranger Convertible..$55–70
76 1948 Ford F-1 Pick Up $55–70
77 1959 Mercury Commuter Wagon ...$75
78 1936 Stout Scarab $75
79 1951 Chrysler Imperial Convertible $55–70
80 1937 Pierce Arrow Travel Trailer $55–70
81 1936 Pierce Arrow 1601 ....$55–70
82 1959 DeSoto Adventurer $55–70
83 1947 Ford V-8 Station Wagon .$55–70
84 1934 Lasalle Coupe...............$55–70
85 1941 Chrysler New Yorker Convertible $55–70

Lansdowne Models
1 1958 Austin-Healey Sprite Mk I....$45–65
2 1957 Vauxhall Cresta.................$45–65
3 1956 MG Magnette 2A.............$45–65
4 1962 Morris Mini Van Mk I.........$45–65
5 1957 Rover 90 P4 ....$45–65
6 1961 Wolseley 6-110 ....$45–65
7 1954 Ford Zephyr Zodiac...........$45–65
8 1954 Triumph Renown $45–65
9 1953 Austin Somerset.................$45–65
10 1956 Hillman Minx...................$45–65
11 1963 Sunbeam Alpine $45-65
12 1958 Austin A105 Westminster.......................$45–65
13 1963 Hillman Super Minx Convertible $45–65
14 1963 Singer Gazelle Series III ...$45–65
15 1965 Rover P5 Mk II $45–65
16 1961 Humber Super Snipe Series III................................$45–65
17 1956 Willerby Vogue Caravan .$45–65
18 1955 Austin A30 Countryman ...$45–65
19 1968 Triumph Vitess.................$45–65
20 1956 Ford Squire Estate...........$50–75
21 1950 Lea Francis Estate Car......$55–70

Rob Eddie Models
1 1969 Volvo P1800S, red $45–65
2 1973 Volvo 144GL, white $45–65
3 1969 Saab 99, red $45–65
4 1950 Volvo PV831 Disponent, blue.$45–65
5 1946-50 Volvo PV60, maroon.....$45–65
6 1964 Volvo PV544, yellow.........$45–65
7 1953 Volvo PV445 Duett Station Wagon, red and gray..........................$45–65
8 1953 Volvo PV445 Van, Scandinavian Airlines System, red and blue.........$45–65
9 1957 Volvo PV120 Amazon 4-Door, blue and gray two-tone...................$45–65
10 1969 Volvo PV 221 Amazon Station Wagon...............................$45–65
11 1972 Volvo 1800 ES $45–65
12 1935 Volvo PV 36 Carioca $45–65
13 1956 Volvo P1900 Sports $45–65

14 1937 Volvo TR 704 ....$45–65
15 1973 Volvo 145 Station Wagon.............................$45–65
15A 1973 Volvo 145 Express........$45–65

Bruce Arnold Models (BAM)
This collection is comprised of 1:43 scale white metal models. The newest offering (as of 01/2000) is a radically customized 1953 Eldorado dubbed "Aretha," the first in the new Celebrity Series (CS) from Bruce Arnold Models.
BAM2 1953 Cadillac 60 Special............$175
CS1 1953 Eldorado "Aretha" custom, pearlescent hot pink, 2000 ....$175

Brüder Spielwaren
Brüder Toys are high quality injected plastic toys with a lot of functioning parts for high play value. Founded in 1926, Brüder Toys is one of the largest family owned and operated manufacturers of high quality toys. Located in the small town of Burgfarnbach in southern Germany, the family business currently employs over 350 local townspeople and operates a factory with 368,000 square feet. In an extremely competitive marketplace, Brüder Toys refuses to use labor exploitation. Brüder has innovated top computer operated machinery and robots, making it possible to maintain all manufacturing and reliability tests in-house. Going into its ninth decade, Brüder Toys continues its commitment to remain one of the most reliable specialty toy manufacturers in Europe. The list below represents only a scant sampling of the hundreds of toys the company has produced over the years.
Porsche 911 Coupe, 1:25 ....$11

Land Rover Vacation Car, 1:32 ....$32

Volkswagen Golf, 1:43 ....$6
Brüder Mini 1:87 Scale Toys
An assortment of accurate toy cars was produced by Brüder about 10 years ago. They are single piece bodies with free-rolling wheels and no window glazing. Each was produced in a variety of colors. Here is a sampling.
Citroen CX Station Wagon......................$1–2
Porsche..$1–2
Volkswagen Transport Van.......................$1–2

Brumm
Brumm SNC
Mr. Rio Tattarletti
via Bizzarone 3
22070 Oltrona San Mamette
Como - Nord Italia
e-mail: brumm@brumm.it
website: www.brumm.it

Brumista was the name given towards the end of the nineteenth century to the hackney-coach drivers of Milan, those grandfathers of today's taxi drivers... and it is from this word, el Brumm, that the trademark BRUMM, miniature styling for collectors of models scale 1:43, was derived.

The Brumm Company of Oltrona S. Mamette (a small village near Como, Italy) was the creation of three friends who began production in 1972 of models of period horse-drawn carriages, with and without horses in the Brumm and Historical series.

Then in 1976, they expanded ranges to include steam-powered vehicles (Old Fire) and the first motor cars in the now famous Revival series, of which the three wheeler Morgan was the first.

Today the company manufactures some 250 different models, all faithfully reproduced in 1:43 scale. The car models produced by Brumm have been mainly dedicated to those of a more historical nature, the exception being one or two contemporary racing cars.

From 1986 onwards, the company has also produced a yearly series of limited edition models of 5,000 pieces each, all now eagerly sought after. Likewise, in 1987, production ceased on the first ten models in the Revival series which immediately became coveted collectors' items. Brumm will continue its policy of bringing to the collectors releases of interesting and well-made models, all of which may with pride be placed in any collection the world over.

Products List
BRUMM REVIVAL — classic cars
BRUMM LIMITED EDITION — limited edition cars
BRUMM BIS — Revival model variants
BRUMM — classic carriages
BRUMM HISTORICAL — classic carriages with horses
BRUMM OLD FIRE — steam powered fire engines

Brumm Revival
R001 Morgan sport (aperta) 1923 ....$24
R002 Morgan sport (chiusa) 1923 ....$24
R003 Darmont sport (aperta) 1929 ....$24
R004 Darmont sport (chiusa) 1929 ....$24
R005 Bedelia sport (aperta) 1913 ....$24
R006 Bedelia sport (chiusa) 1913 ....$24
R007 SanFord sport (aperta) 1922 ....$24
R008 SanFord sport (chiusa) 1922 ....$24
R009 Fiat 75 HP corsa 1904 ....$24
R010 Fiat 110 HP corsa 1905............$24
R011 Fiat S 74 Corsa 1911 ....$24
R012 Fiat 500 C 1949-55 (aperta) $24

Brumm

R013 Fiat 500 C 1949-55 (chiusa) $24
R014 Fiat Mefistofele 1923 ....$24
R015 Ford 999 1902 ....$24
R016 Fiat F2 1907 ....$24
R017 Fiat S 61 1903 ....$24
R018 Renault G.P. 3B 1906 ....$24
R019 Benz-Blitzen 1909 ....$24
R020 Locomobile 'Old 16' 1906 ....$24
R021 Fiat 500 I Serie 1936 (aperta) $24
R022 Fiat 500 I Serie 1936 (chiusa) $24
R023 Fiat 500 I Serie Metano $24
R024 Fiat 500 I Serie Vigili Del Fuoco $24
R025 Ford 999 Record 1905 ....$24
R026 Alfa Corsa 1911 ....$24
R027 Renault (Parigi-Madrid) 1903 ....$24
R028 Fiat 500 C Belvedere (aperta) $24
R029 Fiat 500 C Belvedere (chiusa) $24
R030 Fiat 1100 Monocolore 1937-39 ..$24
R031 Fiat 1100 Bicolore 1937-39 ......$24
R032 Fiat 1100 Metano $24
R033 Fiat 1100 (508C) Gasogeno
    1937-39 ....$24
R034 Fiat 1100 (508C) Forze Armate
    1937-39 ....$24
R035 Ferrari 500 F2 1952 ....$24
R036 Alfa Romeo 158 1950 ....$24
R037 Mercedes W154 1939 ....$24
R038 Auto Union 12 Cil. 1936 ....$24
R039 Bugatti "Brescia" (GB) 1921 ......$24
R040 Bugatti "Brescia" (F) 1921 ....$24
R041 Bugatti "Type 59" 1933 ....$24
R042 Bugatti "Type 59" Biposto 1933 ..$24
R043 Alfa Romeo 159 1952 ....$24
R044 Ferrari 500/F2 1952 ....$24
R045 Fiat 500B Furgoncino PT 1946-49..$24
R046 Fiat 500 B Furgoncino Stipel $24
R047 Fiat 500 A Mille Miglia 1937 .....$24
R048 Fiat 500 C Giardinetta (aperta) ...$24
R049 Fiat 500 C Giardinetta (chiusa) ...$24
R050 Fiat 500 A Furgoncino $24
R051 Fiat 500 C Furgoncino $24
R052 Fiat 500 A Ramazotti $24
R053 Fiat 500 C Ramazotti $24
R054 Fiat 500 A Campari $24
R055 Fiat 500 C Campari $24
R056 Fiat 500 A Isobella $24
R057 Fiat 500 C Isobella $24
R058 Lancia Aprilia 1936-48 ....$24
R059 Lancia Aprilia Metano 1939-48 ..$24
R060 Lancia Aprilia Gasogeno 1939-
    44 ....$24
R061 Lancia Aprilia Mille Miglia 1947 ..$24
R062 Fiat 1100 (508 C.) Taxi 1937-
    39 ....$24
R063 Fiat 1100 (508 C.) Vigili Del
    Fuoco $24
R064 Fiat 1100 B 1948-49 ....$24
R065 Fiat 1100 E 1949-53 ....$24
R066 Ferrari 815 Sport 1940 ....$24
R067 Ferrari 815 Mille Miglia 1940....$24
R068 Ferrari D 246 1958 ....$24
R069 Ferrari D 246 G.P. Italia 1958 ...$24
R070 Mercedes W 125 1937 ....$24

R071 Mercedes W 125 1938 ....$24
R072 Mercedes W 196 1954-60 ......$24
R073 Blitzen Benz 1911 ....$24
R074 Talbot Lago F1 1948 ....$24
R075 Maserati 8 Cil. 1939 ....$24
R076 Ferrari-Lancia D 50 1956 ....$24
R077 Alfa Romeo 2300 1931 ....$24
R078 Alfa Romeo 2300 Mille Miglia
    1932 ....$24
R079 Fiat 500 B Gilette $24
R080 Fiat 500 C Vigili Del Fuoco........$24
R081 Blitzen Benz Indy 1911 ....$24
R082 Bugatti "Brescia" 1921 ....$24
R083 Fiat 1100 (508C) Spider 1937-
    39 ....$24
R084 Fiat 1100 (508C) Chiuso
    1937-1939 ....$24
R085 Fiat 1100 (508C) Coloniale $24
R086 Fiat 1100 (508C) Corpo Diplomati-
    co $24
R087 Bugatti 57-S Blu $24
R088 Bugatti 57-S Nera $24
R089 Alfa Romeo 1900 ....$24
R090 Alfa Romeo 1900 Mille Miglia....$24
R091 Alfa Romeo 1900 Polizia $24
R092 Maserati 250 F 1957 ....$24
R093 Ferrari Testa Rossa Le Mans
    1957 ....$24
R094 Ferrari Testa Rossa $24
R095 Lancia Aurelia B20 1951 ....$24
R096 Lancia Aurelia B20 Mille Miglia ...$24
R097 Lancia Aurelia B20 Carrera
    Mexico $24
R098 Vanwall 1957 ....$24
R099 Bentley (aperta) 1930 ....$24
R100 Bentley (chiusa) 1930 ....$24
R101 Jaguar XK 120 Roadster (aperta)
    1948 ....$24
R102 Jaguar XK 120 Roadster (chiusa)
    1948 ....$24
R103 Jaguar XK 120 Roadster Mille
    Miglia $24
R104 Jaguar XK 120 Roadster Le
    Mans $24
R105 Jaguar XK 120 Coupe 1948 ......$24
R106 Jaguar XK 120 Linas-Montlhlery...$24
R107 Auto Union Rekordwagen 1935...$24
R108 Auto Union Rekordwagen Carenata
    1937 ....$24
R109 Auto Union Tipo D 1938............$24
R110 Auto Union 12 Cil. Ruote Gemellate
    1936 ....$24
R111 Maserati 8 Cil. Indianapolis 1940 ..$24
R112 Maserati 8 Cil. G.P. Tripoli 1938..$24
R113 Talbot LAGO F.1. Belgio 1951....$24
R114 Bentley Compressore 1932 ....$24
R115 Darracq V8 1905 ....$24
R116 Napier 6 1905 ....$24
R117 Porsche 356 Speedster 1952 ....$24
R117S Porsche 356 Speedster 1952 ....$24
R118 Porsche 356 Speedster (chiusa)
    1952 ....$24
R119 Porsche 356 Coupe 1952 ....$24

R120 Porsche 356 Coupe Mille Miglia
    1952 ....$24
R121 Porsche 356 Coupe' Tetto Aperto
    1952 ....$24
R122 Ferrari 801 1957 ....$24
R123 Ferrari 156 1961 ....$24
R124 Ferrari 156 G.P. Monza 1961 ....$24
R125 Ferrari 375 F1 1951 ....$24
R126 Ferrari 375 Indianapolis 1952 ...$24
R127 Lancia Ferrari D50 MONTECARLO
    1956 ....$24
R128 Lancia Ferrari D50 Belgio 1956...$24
R129 Jaguar D Type 1954 ....$24
R130 Jaguar D Type Le Mans Cunningham
    1954 ....$24
R131 Lancia B24 (aperta) 1955 ....$24
R132 Lancia B24 (chiusa) 1955 ....$24
R133 Lancia B24 America (aperta)
    1956 ....$24
R134 Lancia B24 America (chiusa)
    1956 ....$24
R135 Maserati 250F Muso Corto MONTE-
    CARLO 1957 ....$24
R136 Maserati 250F Muso Corto 1957.$24
R137 Maserati 250F Iniezione 1957 ....$24
R138 Alfa Romeo 2300 Bicolore 1931.$24
R139 Alfa Romeo 8C 2900 B 1938 ....$24
R140 Alfa Romeo 8C 2900 B 1938 ....$24
R141 Alfa Romeo 8C 2900 B Mille Miglia
    1938 ....$24
R142 Ferrari 126 C4 Alboreto Agosto
    1984 ....$24
R143 Ferrari 126 C4 Arnoux Gennaio
    1984 ....$24
R144 Porsche 356 Coupe Targa Florio
    1952 ....$24
R145 Alfa Romeo 1900 Carrera Mexico
    1954 ....$24
R146 Jaguar D Type Mille Miglia 1957.$24
R147 Jaguar D Type 1° Le Mans 1955 .$24
R148 Jaguar D Type Prototipo 1954......$24
R149 Jaguar D Type 1° Le Mans SC. Ecosse
    1956 ....$24
R150 Jaguar D Type Le Mans Biposto
    1956 ....$24
R151 Jaguar D Type SC. Belga 1956...$24
R152 Jaguar D Type Silverston SC. Ecosse
    1956 ....$24
R153 Jaguar D Type Le Mans Francia
    1957 ....$24
R154 Jaguar D Type Record 1960 ....$24
R155 Ferrari Testa Rossa Mexico $24
R156 Ferrari Testa Rossa P.Rodriguez ...$24
R157 Ferrari 330 P3 1° 1000km Spa
    1966 ....$24
R158 Ferrari 330 P3 Spider Le Mans
    1966 ....$24
R159 Ferrari 330 P4 1° 1000km Monza
    1967 ....$24
R160 Ferrari 330 P4 Spider Le Mans
    1967 ....$24
R161 Ferrari 330 P4 Le Mans Filipinetti
    1967 ....$24

R162 Lancia Aurelia B20 Le Mans 1951 ....$24
R163 Jaguar XK 120 Coupe Rally Alpi 1953 ....$24
R164 Jaguar XK 120 Roadster Rally Alpi 1953 ....$24
R165 Fiat 1400 B 1956–58 ....$24
R166 Fiat 1400 B Bicolore 1956–58 ...$24
R167 Ferrari 500 F.2 SC.EPADON 1953 ....$24
R168 Ferrari 375 Indianapolis 1952.....$24
R169 Bugatti 57S 8 Cil. 3900 C.C. 1936 ....$24
R170 Bugatti 57S (chiusa) 1936 ....$24
R171 Ferrari 312 F.1 Jacky Ickx 1968...$24
R172 Ferrari 312 F.1 Chris Amon 1968 .$24
R173 Bugatti Type 59 Ruote Gemellate 1933 ....$24
R174 Bugatti Type 59 1933 ....$24
R175 Mercedes W 154 Indianapolis 1947 ....$24
R176 Simca 5 1956 ....$24
R177 Fiat 1100 E Furgone 1947–48 ...$24
R178 Fiat 1100 E Furgone Vigili Fuoco 1947–48 ....$24
R179 Fiat 1100 E Furgone Croce Rossa 1947–48 ....$24
R180 Fiat 1100 E Furgone Croce Rossa Militare $24
R181 Fiat 1100 E Vigili Fuoco $24
R182 Ferrari 125 Mille Miglia 1947.....$24
R183 Ferrari 125 Circuito Di Pescara 1947 ....$24

R184 Bentley Speed Six "Barnato" 1928.$24

R185 Bentley Speed Six Bleu-Train Match 1928 ....$24
R186 Lancia B24 Mille Miglia 1955.....$24
R187 Mercedes 300 SLR Coupe 1955 ..$24
R188 Mercedes 300 SLR Le Mans 1955 .$24
R189 Mercedes 300 SLR Targa Florio 1955 ....$24
R190 Mercedes 300 SLR Mille Miglia 1955 ....$24
R191 Ferrari 375 G.P. Monza 1951....$24
R192 Ferrari 375 Thin Wall Special 1951 ....$24
R193 Porsche 550 Coupe Le Mans 1956 ....$24
R194 Porsche 550 Spider Le Mans 1955 ....$24
R195 Porsche 550 Spider Mille Miglia 1954 ....$24
R196 Ferrari Squalo 1953 ....$24

R197 Ferrari Squalo G.P. Italia 1953 ....$24
R198A Porsche 356 Polizia Tedesca 1952 ....$24
R198B Porsche 356 Polizia Olandese 1952 ....$24
R198C Porsche 356 Polizia Portoghese 1952 ....$24
R198D Porsche 356 Polizia Svizzera 1952 ....$24
R199 Vanwall F.1 G.P. Belgio 1957 ....$24
R200 Ferrari 512 S Daytona 1970.......$24
R201 Ferrari 512 S SC.Francorchamps 1970 ....$24
R202 Ferrari 512 S Spa 1970 ....$24
R203 Ferrari 512 S Buenos Aires 1970.$24
R204 Lancia D24 Ascari Mille Miglia 1954 ....$24
R205 Lancia D24 Fangio Carrera Mexico 1953 ....$24
R206 Porsche 356 Carrera Mexico 1952 ....$24
R207 Porsche 356 Spider Mille Miglia 1952 ....$24
R208 Porsche 356 Coupe Carrera 1952 ....$24
R209 Lancia D24 Taruffi Targa Florio 1954 ....$24
R210 Ferrari 512 BB LM Prototipo 1980 .$24
R211 Ferrari 512 BB LM Le Mans Sc. Rosso 1980 ....$24
R212 Ferrari 512 BB LM SC. Emka 1980 ....$24
R213 Ferrari 512 BB LM Le Mans Ch. Pozzi 1980 ....$24
R214 Ferrari 512 BB LM Le Mans 1980..$24
R215 Fiat 1100 E Taxi 1949–53 ....$24
R216 Fiat 1400 B Taxi 1956–58 ....$24
R217 Porsche 917 Prototipo 1970 ......$24
R218 Porsche 917 Le Mans Porsche-Salzburg $24
R219 Porsche 917 Monza Wyer/Gulf 1970 ....$24
R220 Porsche 917 Le Mans Martini Racing 1971 ....$24
R221 Porsche 917 Monza Wyer/Gulf 1971 ....$24
R222 Ferrari 156 Baghetti G.P. Francia 1961 ....$24
R223 Maserati 250/12 cil. Prova 1957 .$24
R224 Porsche 356 C Spyder 1963/65 .$24
R225 Porsche 356 C Spyder Chiusa 1963/65 ....$24
R226 Porsche 356 C Coupe 1963/65 .$24
R227 Ferrari 512 M Prototipo 1970 .....$24
R228 Ferrari 512 M 1000km Austria 1970 ....$24
R229 Ferrari 512 M Daytona 1971......$24
R230 Ferrari 512 M Le Mans 1971 ......$24
R231 Ferrari 512 M Watkins Glen 1971 ....$24
R232 Porsche 550 RS Stradale 1954....$24
R233 Porsche 550 RS Stradale Bicolore 1954 ....$24

R234 Porsche 550 RS America $24
R235 Porsche 550 RS Carresa Mexico 1953 ....$24
R236 Porsche 550 RS 1000km Nurburgring 1956 ....$24
R237 Alfa Romeo 33TT12 Prototipo 1974 ....$24
R238 Alfa Romeo 33TT12 1000Km Monza 1975 ....$24
R239 Alfa Romeo 33TT12 1000Km Monza 1975 ....$24
R240 Alfa Romeo 33TT12 1000Km Spa 1975 ....$24
R241 Alfa Romeo 33TT12 1000Km Spa 1975 ....$24
R242 Fiat 1100 E.I.A.R. 1948 ....$24
R243 Simca 5 Militare D-Day 1944 ......$24
R244 Simca 5 Furgoncino 1936 ....$24
R245 Fiat 1100 Furgone Campari 1952 ....$24
R246 Fiat 500B Furgone Vigili Del Fuoco 1946/49 ....$24
R247 Fiat 600 Hard Top 1955 ....$24
R248 Fiat 600 Soft Top Open 1955.....$24
R249 Fiat 600 Soft Top Closed 1955 ...$24
R250 Fiat 600 Multipla 1956 ....$24
R251 Fiat 600 Multipla 1956 Taxi de Milano $24
R252 Porsche 917K 1000 Km Monza (1971) Scuderia Martini Racing, Elford - Larrousse $24
R253 Porsche 917K 1000 Km Austria (1970) Scuderia Salzburg, Ahrens - Marko $24
R254 Porsche 917K Le Mans (1970) Scuderia Piper, Piper - Van Lennep $24
R255 Ferrari 312 F1 G.P. Italia (1967) Chris Amon $24
R256 Ferrari 312 F.1 G.P. Italia (1969) Pedro Rodriguez $24
R257 Ferrari 312 PB 1971 Prototype $24
R258 Ferrari 312 PB 1000 Km Buenos Aires (1971) Ignazio Giunti $24
R259 Ferrari 312 PB 1000 Km Monza (1971) Ickx - Regazzoni $24
R260 Ferrari 312 PB 6 Hours at Daytona (1972) Ickx - Andretti $24
R261 Ferrari 312 PB 1000 Km Monza (1972) Ickx - Andretti $24
R262 Simca Hult Le Mans (1938) Camerano - Loveau $24
R263 Porsche 550 RS Le Mans (1955) Olivier - Jeser $24
R264 Ferrari 125 Circuito di Parma (1947) Franco Cortese $24
R265 Fiat 600 Derivazione Abarth 750 1956 ....$24
R266 Fiat 500 C Furgoncino (MiniVan) Marmitte Abarth 1956 ....$24
R267 Ferrari 126 C2 Grand Prix San Marino (1982) Gilles Villaneuve $24
R268 Ferrari 126 C2 Grand Prix San Marino (1982) Didier Pironi $24

R269 Porsche 917K 6 Hours at Daytona (1970) Scuderia Wyer-Gulf, Siffert - Redman........................$24

R270 Porsche 917K Kyalami (1970) Scuderia Martini Racing, Siffert - Ahrens.....$24

R271 Porsche 917K 6 Hrs at Watkins Glen (1970) Scuderia Martini Racing, Larousse-Van Lennep............$24

R272 Ferrari 126 C2 Grand Prix Long Beach (1982) Gilles Villeneuve $24

R273 Ferrari 126 C2 Grand Prix Long Beach (1982) Didier Pironi $24

R274 Porsche 550 RS Carrera Mexico (1954) Salvador Lopez - Chavez.....$24

R275 Porsche 550 RS Carrera Mexico (1954) Fletcher Aviation, Pasadena CA, Hans Herrmann....................$24

R276 Porsche 550 RS Carrera Mexico (1954) Jaroslav Juan $24

R277 Porsche 550 RS Carrera Mexico (1954) Fernando Segura - Herbert Linge $24

R278 Cooper T51 Grand Prix Monaco (1959) Jack Brabham $24

R279 Cooper T51 Grand Prix Italia (1959) Stirling Moss $24

R280 Mercedes 196C Grand Prix Francia (1954) J. M. Fangio $24

R280b Mercedes 196C Grand Prix Francia (1954) Karl Kling $24

R280c Mercedes 196C Grand Prix Francia (1954) Hans Herrmann..................$24

R281 Mercedes 196C Monza (1955) Stirling Moss $24

R282 Alfa Romeo 33SC12 500 Km Monza (1977) Vittorio Branbilla $24

R283 Alfa Romeo 33SC12 Pergusa, Coppa Florio (1977) Arturo Merzario.........$24

R284 Fiat 1100E Furgone (Van) (1950) Rammazzotti............................$24

R285 Fiat 600 (1960) Ramazzotti.......$24

R286 Fiat 600 Multipla (1960) Ramazzotti........................$24

R287 Ferrari 126C2 Grand Prix Italia (1982) Patrick Tambay.......................$24

R288 Ferrari 126C2 Grand Prix Italia (1982) Mario Andretti.......................$24

R289 Ferrari 156 Grand Prix Austria (1964) Lorenzo Bandini $24

R290 Ferrari 158 Grand Prix Italia (1964) John Surtees $24

R291 Ferrari 158 Grand Prix Messico (1964) John Surtees $24

R291b Ferrari 158 Grand Prix Messico (1964) Lorenzo Bandini, Limited Edition 3,000 pieces $32

R292 Morgan MX-4 Super Sport Barrelback open (1935)......................$24

R293 Morgan MX-4 Super Sport Barrelback closed (1935).......................$24

LE-4 Morgan MX-4 Super Sport Barrelback (1935) 1980 USA Coast to Coast 7,500 pieces $28

R294 Ferrari 312 F1 Prova Modena (1969) with raised wings, Chris Amon $24

R295 Ferrari 312 F1 Prova Modena (1969) with small rear spoiler, Chris Amon...$24

R296 Ferrari 158 Grand Prix Italia (1965) Nino Vaccarella $24

R297 Ferrari 512 Grand Prix Italia (1965) Lorenzo Bandini......................$24

R298 Ferrari 512 Grand Prix Italia (1965) John Surtees $24

R299 Cooper T53 Grand Prix Gran Bretagna (1960) Bruce Mclaren..........$24

R300 Cooper T53 Grand Prix Gran Bretagna (1960) Jack Brabham $24

R301 Ferrari 312 F1 Grand Prix Spagna (1969) Chris Amon $24

R302 Ferrari 312 F1 Grand Prix Francia (1969) Chris Amon $24

R303 Ferrari 312 F1 Grand Prix Monte Carlo (1969) Chris Amon...............$24

R304 Fiat Abarth 750 Mille Miglia (1955) Domenico Ogna $24

R305 Fiat Abarth 750 500 Km Nurburgring (1962) $24

R306 Fiat Abarth 850 TC Pieve Santo Stefano (1962) Piero Falorni...............$24

R307 Fiat 1400 B Polizia Stradale (1956) $24

R308 Fiat 600 Polizia Stradale (1960) ..$24

R309 Fiat 600 Multipla Carabinieri (1956) $24

R310 Fiat 600 Multipla Enciclopedia Motta (1956) $24

R311 Fiat 1100E Furgone (Van) Olio Carli (1946) $24

Brumm Limited Edition

1986

S001 Porsche 365, Circuito Avus..........$35

S002 Fiat F1, Corsa $35

S003 Ferrari 815, Circuito Di Pescara ...$35

S004 Porsche 365, Rally Delle Alpi $35

1987

S005 Vanwall F1 '58.........................$35

S006 Mercedes W196 '54 ....$35

S007 Jaguar XK120 - '48.................$35

S008 Ferrari D246 - G.P. Belgio '48.....$35

1988

S009 Ferrari 156, G.P. Belgio '61 ....$35

S010 Alfa Romeo 2900, G.P. Bremgarten $35

S011 Benz Blitzen, Berlino-Avus '11 ....$35

S012 Bugatti 57-S, Tourist Trophy '35....$35

1989

S013 Ferrari 330, Piper-Atwood '66 ....$35

S014 Ferrari 330 P4 - NART '67 ....$35

S015 Ferrari 330 P4, Francorchamps '67 ....$35

S016 Ferrari 330 P4, Scud. Maranello ..$35

1990

S017 Porsche 356 Rally Delle Alpi '52 ....$35

S018 Porsche 356 Targa Florio '52 ......$35

S019 Porsche 356 Carrera Mexico '52 .$35

S020 Porsche 356 Rally Monte Carlo '52 ....$35

1992

S072/92 Ferrari 512 BB LM 1980, prodotta per il 20° anno di attività della ditta.................................$35

1993

Fangio World Champion F.1

S021 Alfa Romeo 159 (1951) $35

S022 Mercedes W196 (1954) $35

S023 Mercedes W196 (1955) $35

S024 Ferrari D50 (1956).............$35

S025 Maserati 250F '57.............$35

1994

Daytona 1967

S026 Ferrari 330 P4 Spider 1967 Daytona $35

S027 Ferrari 330 P4 Coupe 1967 Daytona $35

S028 Ferrari 330 P3 Coupe 1967 Daytona $35

Le Mans 1967

S029 Ferrari 330 P4 Coupe 1967 Le Mans $35

S030 Ferrari 330 P4 Coupe 1967 Le Mans $35

S031 Ferrari 330 P4 Coupe 1967 Le Mans $35

1995

79a Targa Florio

S032 Fiat 500C Copmmissari Di Gara 1954.............................$35

S033 Lancia D24 1954 ....$35

S034 Mercedes 300SLR 1955.......$35

S035 Ferrari TR59 1959.............$35

S036 Ferrari 330P3 1966.............$35

S037 Ferrari 330P4 1967 ....$35

Targa Florio 1995 5000 pieces Limited Edition

S032 Fiat 500C Belvedere, Commissari Di Gara, 38a Targa Florio 1954.............................$45

S033 Lancia D24, Commissari Di Gara, 38a Targa Florio 1954.................$45

S034 Mercedes 300SLR, 1° Piero Taruffi, 38a Targa Florio 1954.................$45

S035 Ferrari TR59, Behra-Brooks, 43a Targa Florio 1959.................$45

S036 Ferrari 330P3, Bandini-Vaccarella, 50a Targa Florio 1966.................$45

S037 Ferrari 330P4, Vaccarella-Scafiotti, 51a Targa Florio 1957.................$45

1998

S043 Ferrari 512M Le Mans 1971 N.A.R.T. Team.................................$45

S044 Ferrari 512M Le Mans 1971 Ecurie Francochamps.........................$45

S045 Ferrari 512M Le Mans 1971 Scuderia Filipinetti.............................$45

S046 Ferrari 512M Le Mans 1971 Escuderia Montjuich.............................$45

S047 Ferrari 512M Le Mans 1971 Gelo Racing Team........................$45

S048 Mercedes W196 Grand Prix Germania 1954 Juan Manuel Fangio $45
S049 Ferrari D50 Grand Prix Germania 1956 Juan Manuel Fangio $45
S050 Maserati 250F Grand Prix Argentina 1957 Juan Manuel Fangio $45
S051 Cooper T51 Grand Prix Gran Bretagna 1959 Jack Brabham $45
S052 Ferrari 512 Grand Prix Germania 1964 John Surtees......................$45

Brumm Champions, famous drivers ready to put behind the wheel of your favorite Brumm racecar

CH01 Gilles Villeneuve for Ferrari 126C2 1982 (R267/272)...................$10
CH02 Didier Pironi for Ferrari 126C2 1982 (R268/273).......................$10
CH03 Patrick Tambay for Ferrari 126C2 1982 (R287 ....$10
CH04 Mario Andretti for Ferrari 126C2 1982 (R288)..........................$10
CH05 Clay Regazzoni for Ferrari 312PB 1971 (R259/261)...................$10
CH06 Jacky Ickx for Ferrari 312PB 1971 (R259/261).........................$10
CH07 Mario Andretti for Ferrari 312PB 1972 (R260)..........................$10
CH08 Ignazio Giunti for Ferrari 312PB 1971 (R258).........................$10

Brumm Bis
1989 Out of Production
R22 bis Fiat 500A Stato Del Vaticano (1936)................................$50
R33 bis Fiat 1100 508c Versione Gasogeno (1937)..........................$50
R47 bis Fiat 500A Mille Miglia (1947)..$50
R67 bis Ferrari 815 Mille Miglia (1940)................................$50
R76 bis Ferrari D50 G.P. Italia - Monza (1956)................................$50
R77 bis Alfa Romeo 2300 Allestimento Speciale (1931)....................$50
R90 bis Alfa Romeo 1900 Mille Miglia (1954)................................$50
R120 bis Porsche 356 Mille Miglia (1952)................................$50
R145 bis Alfa Romeo 1900 Carrera Mexico (1954)................................$50

Brumm Bis 1992
R36 bis Alfa Romeo 159 Farina - G.P. Spagna (1951)......................$40
R37 bis Mercedes W154 S. Lang - G.P. Tripoli (193)........................$40
R58 bis Lancia Aprilia Prima Serie (1958)................................$40
R131 bis Lancia B24 Allestimento Speciale (1955)........................$40
R171 bis Ferrari 312/F.1 C.Amon-G.P. USA (1968)........................$40

Brumm Bis 1993
R13 bis Fiat 500C Mille Miglia (1937)..$40
R21 bis Fiat 500A Targa Florio (1948)................................$40

R117 bis Porsche 356 Speedster James Dean (1954)........................$40
R156 bis Ferrari Testa Rossa Governors Trophy Race (1960)....................$40
R183 bis Ferrari 125S Circuito Di Piacenza (1947)................................$40

Brumm Bis 1994
R101 bis Jaguar XK120 Stirling Moss Silverstone (1951)....................$40
R114 bis Bentley Speed Six Birkin-Chaasagne Le Mans (1930)...........$40
R162 bis Lancia Aurelia B20 Bonetto-Anselmi Le Mans (1952)...................$40
R173 bis Bugatti Type 59 G.P. Italia (1931) $40
R188 bis Mercedes 300SLR Levegh-Fich Le Mans (1955)......................$40

Brumm Classic Carriages
B01 Landaulet $65
B02 Landaulet (aperto) $65
B03 Coupe $65
B04 Coupe Dormeuse $65
B05 Landau $65
B06 Landau (aperto) $65
B07 Spyder $65
B08 Spyder (aperto) $65
B09 Phaeton $65
B11 Dog Cart $65
B12 Vis-A-Vis $65
B13 Vis-A-Vis (aperto) $65
B14 Milord $65
B15 Milord (aperto) $65
B16 Coupe A Huit Ressorts $65
B17 Mail-Coach $65
B18 Duc A Huit Ressorts $65
B19 "Brumm" De Milan $65
B20 Berlina Papale Da Viaggio.............$65
B21 Cab $65
B22 Dress Chariot $65
B23 "Post - Caise" $65
B24 Royal Mail-Coach.........................$65
B25 Tilbury $65
B26 Carrozza Napoleonica.................$65

Brumm Historical
H00 Cavallo Con Finimenti Ed Attacchi..$65
H01 Pariglia Eques. Con Finimenti Ed Attachi................................$65
H02 Doppia Pariglia Con Finimenti Ed Attachi................................$65
H03 "Brumm" De Milan Con Cavallo $65
H04 "Berlina Da Viaggio" Pio X $65
H05 "Duc A Huit Ressorts" of Napoleon III $65
H06 "Mail Coach" Vettura Da Posta Inglese $65
H07 "Cab" Dell'attrice Rejane...............$65
H08 "Coupe Dormeuse" of Paolina Bonaparte................................$65
H09 "Phaeton" of Emile Loubet $65
H10 "Vis-A-Vis Gran Gala" Nuziale.......$65
H11 "Dog Cart" of Guglielmo II of Germany................................$65
H12 "Botticella De Roma" $65

H13 "Dress Chariot" of Count of Caledonia $65
H14 "Milord" of Eugenia Montijo.........$65
H15 "Spyder" of Geroge Sand $65
H16 "Poste Chaise" Vettura Da Noleggio Inglese $65
H17 Landau Bavarese $65
H18 Royal Mail-Coach $65
H19 Tilbury $65
H20 Portantina Spagnolesca $65
H21 Carrozza Napoleonica Da Campo .$65

Brumm Old Fire steam powered vehicles
X01 Fardier Par "Cugnot" 1769...........$65
X02 Carro Di Newton 1680 ....$65
X03 Diligenza Di Gurney 1825 ....$65
X04 Carro Di Trevithick 1803 ....$65
X05 Carro Di Bordino 1854 ....$65
X06 Turbina Di Verbiest 1681 ....$65
X07 Vettura Di Pecquer 1828 ....$65
X08 Anfibio Di EVANS 1801 ....$65

Brumm 1996 Toy Fairs
S96/01 Fiat 600 1a serie (1955), Milan Toy Fair, qty. 1,000 pieces for the Italian market................................$75–90
S96/02 Fiat 600 1st serie (1955), Nuremberg Toy Fair, qty. 100 pieces numbered items $500–750

Brumm Limited Edition for Replicars, The Netherlands
S96/03 Ferrari 357 (1951), First Ferrari victory in F.1, Silverstone, 1951 with Gonzales, qty. 600 pieces $125
S96/04 Fiat 500A (1936), Roman Holiday, qty. 600 pieces $125

Brumm Limited Edition for Federico Motta Editore, Milan, Italy
S96/05 Fiat 600 Multipla (1956), Advertisment vehicol, qty. 1,000 pieces $75–90

Brumm Limited Edition for La Mini Miniera, Cuneo, Italy
S96/06 Ferrari 156 F1 G.P. Siracusa (1961), 1° classified Baghetti, qty. 1,000 pieces................................$75–90
S96/07 Fiat 500B Furgoncino, Expo Model Fossano 4-12/5/1996, qty. 1,000 pieces................................$75–90

Buby (also see Collector's Classics)

Reasonably priced but hard to find, Buby models were made in Argentina, and are nice models for the price. Many models are from old Solido dies, but some are original. Later models were issued as Collector's Classics to avoid a blatant connection with the Buby name when the company suffered through a few public relations issues. The last Collector's Classics models were produced in 1995.

Buby 1:64 Scale Models
10 Mercedes-Benz 1112 Dump Truck......$5
20 Fiat 1500 Rally $5
25 Fiat 128 Rally $5
27 Renault 12 Rally $5
1030 Maserati Indy.........................$5

1030 Peugeot 504 ....$5
1040 Mercedes-Benz 350SL..............$5
1041 Mercedes-Benz 350SL Rally..........$5
1050 Ford Mustang II $5
1051 Ford Mustang "Dukes of Hazzard"..$5
1052 Ford Mustang II Cobra.................$5
1060 Citroën 3CV $5
1070 Ford Sierra $5
1081 Chevrolet Nova $5
1090 Maserati Bora..........................$5
1091 Maserati Bora Rally...................$5
1120 Volkswagen Facel (Fox) $5
1140 Renault 12 ....$5
1141 Renault 12 Rally $5
1142 Renault 12 "Polizia" $5
1160 Renault 18 ....$5
1161 Renault 18 "Polizia" $5
1162 Renault 18 "Marlboro" $5
1170 Renault 12 Station Wagon $5
1171 Renault 12 Station Wagon
    "Rescue" $5
1180 1964 Opel Kapitän Ambulance $5
1190 Ford F100 Tow Truck $5
1212 VW Buggy...............................$5
1220 Ford Bronco $5
1221 Ford Bronco with roll bar $5
1224 Ford Bronco "NASA" $5
1227 Ford Bronco Wagon $5
1230 Ford Van "Marlboro" $5
1231 Ford Van "Coca Cola" $5
1233 Ford Van "John Player" $5
1234 Ford Van "Las Lenas" $5
1235 Ford Van "Peugeot" $5
1240 Renault Fuego $5
1241 Renault Fuego "Cazalis" $5
1250 Ford Sierra XR4 ....$5
1251 Ford Sierra XR4 "Bardahl"...........$5
1260 Renault Kombi $5
1261 Renault Kombi "Aerolineas"...........$5
1262 Renault Kombi Ambulance $5
1263 Renault Kombi School Bus $5
1264 Renault Kombi "World Tour" $5
1265 Renault Kombi "Lufthansa" $5
1270 Jeep CJ5 ....$5
2020 Chevrolet C60 "Esso" $5
2030 Chevrolet C60 Fire Pumper...........$5
2040 Chevrolet Semi Refrigerator $5
2050 Chevrolet Semi Cattle...................$5
2060 Fiat Cement Mixer $5
3010 Ford Van 4x4 "Thunder" $5
3020 Ford Van 4x4 "Cracker"...............$5
3030 Jeep CJ5 4x4 "Mad Mex"............$5
3040 Jeep CJ5 4x4 "Vagabond" $5
3050 Ford Bronco 4x4 "Old Iron"..........$5
3060 Ford Bronco 4x4 "Outlaw" $5

Buby 1:43 Scale Models
1000 Buick Century Ambulance, white ..$100
1000A Buick Century Army Ambulance,
    green...................................$100
1001 Buick Century Station Wagon, blue
    and white..............................$100
1002 Ford Fairlane 500, blue and
    white $100

1002A Ford Fairlane 500 Rally, red....$100
1003 Ford Fairlane 500 Policia, blue and
    white $100
1004 Ford F100 Pickup, red $60
1004A Army Pickup, green $60
1004B Covered Pickup, blue and black, or
    green and black.........................$60
1023 Ika Torino Rally.........................$45
1033 1968 Chevrolet Nova Rally $45
1036 Fiat 128 ....$18
1037 Fiat 128 Rally...........................$18
1046 1967 Chevrolet Camaro $45
1047 1967 Chevrolet Camaro Rally $45

Buccaneer

Until collector Steve Mason provided photos of a toy 1937 Packard with the brand name "Buccaneer" stamped into the base, I had never heard of Buccaneer brand. Latest information indicates that Buccaneer is actually a mid- to late-seventies pirate of early Tootsie-toys and Dinky Toys, hence the name Buccaneer (another name for pirate). What distinguishes Buccaneer from the original is the weight. Buccaneer models are white metal and are therefore considerably heavier than their zinc alloy counterparts.

According to Martin Van de Logt of the Netherlands, Buccaneer models started out as "easy" white metal kits costing around £5 (about $8 US) and that they were never meant to fool collectors.

Armstrong Siddeley Typhoon, #28 ....$20–25
1934 Armstrong Siddeley 30HP, #15 ..$20–25
1938 Bedford Van "Use Kodak
    Film," #40 ....$20–25
1934 Bentley 3.5 l Coupe, #14 ....$20–25
1938 Bedford Van "Wakefield's Castrol Motor
    Oil" $20–25
1937 Bentley, #8.............................$20–25
1937 Buick Limousine, #23 ....$20–25
1934 Caravan, #31 ....$20–25
1934 Chrysler Airflow, #2...................$20–25
1937 Chrysler Royal Limousine, #20.....$20–25
1939 Chrysler $20–25
1934 Daimler Limousine, #7...............$20–25
Graham Saloon, #17 ....$20–25
1935 Ford Van "Bisto," #37 ....$20–25
1935 Ford Van "Dunlop Tyres," #38 ....$20–25
1935 Ford Van "Hovis for Tea," #36....$20–25
1935 Ford Van "Virol for your Child,"
    #39 ....$20–25
1939 Frazer Nash, #26 ....$20–25
1933 Humber Vogue Saloon, #11.......$20–25
Jaguar SS 1, #16............................$20–25
1939 Jaguar SS100, #27 ....$20–25
1935 La Salle Sedan, #9...................$20–25
1937 Lincoln Zephyr Coupe, #5 ....$20–25
MG EX 135 Record Car, #25 ....$20–25
1953 MG TF, #3 ....$20–25
1934 Morris Van "Carter Patterson,"
    #33 ....$20–25
1934 Morris Van "Crawford's Biscuits,"
    #35 ....$20–25

1934 Morris Van "Meccano Engineering,"
    #32 ....$20–25
1934 Morris Van "PickFords," #34 ......$20–25
1937 Oldsmobile Super Six, #22 ....$20–25
1937 Packard Super 8 Limousine, #21 .$20–25
1934 Rolls Royce Phantom Coupe, #4..$20–25
Rolls Royce Phantom Town Sedan,
    #10.......................................$20–25
1938 Rolls Royce Thunderbolt Record
    Car $20–25
1934 Rover 14HP Streamline Saloon,
    #12.......................................$20–25
1933 Salmson 4-Seater, #18 ....$20–25
1937 Salmson, #2...........................$20–25
1937 Studebaker State Commander,
    #19.......................................$20–25
1935 Vauxhall Limousine, #6.............$20–25

Budgie (also see Morestone)

Like Corgi, Dinky, Impy, and other diecast toys of the fifties and sixties, Budgies are a product of Great Britain. While Corgi is named after the Welsh Corgi, a popular dog in Wales, Budgie is named after a budgerigar (parakeet), another popular pet for many Brits as well as bird lovers around the world.

Budgie was originally owned by Morris and Stone (Morestone), who introduced the first castings as Esso promotional models before changing their name to Budgie The brand was later purchased by Guitermans.

Budgie toys were popular in England and the US in the sixties, but were eclipsed by Corgi, Dinky, and especially Matchbox, eventually going out of business.

Latest news indicates dies and castings have been purchased by a new company in England called Autocraft that is reproducing Budgie models in small quantities.

Twin Pack with Standard London Taxi, black, and
    London Bus, red $45–60
Crane Truck, red with blue crane, 4"..........$20
1 1960 Volkswagen Pickup "Coca-Cola,"
    1:43 ....$115
5 Police Car, 1:64 ....$25–30
8 Volkswagen 1200 Saloon, 1:64......$25–30
12 1960 Volkswagen Micro Van, 4" $25
18 Dump Truck, 1:64 ....$20
30 Rover Squad Car...........................$12
57 "REA Express" Parcel Delivery Van $30–40
102 Rolls-Royce Silver Cloud $30–40
224 Railway Engine $25–30
236 Routemaster Double Decker Bus, 4" ..$25–30

Bugattiana (see Modelauto)

Burago (see Bburago with two B's)

Busch/Praliné

Busch/Praliné models are precisely exact 1:87 scale plastic models made in Germany. The brand is now owned by Sieper Werke

GmbH, manufacturer of Siku toys. Of particular note is article 3452, a 1954 Cadillac Ambulance, exquisitely detailed and neatly packaged in a clear plastic display box. Walthers HO catalog devotes seven pages of their catalog to this brand.

#3452 1954 Cadillac Ambulance, cream with chrome plastic trim, 1:87 ....$8–10

Bush

Bush was a producer of diecast promotional models during the fifties. Not much is known by this author, but collectors of dealer promos will no doubt have more information.

Cam-Cast

Cam-Cast produced just a few toy trucks from Edgerton, Ohio, in the fifties. They appear to be one fairly thick, crude lump of metal with details painted on or applied with decals. They carry a high value for such simple toys, mostly due to rarity.

Van, "Western Auto" $40–75
Van, "North American Van Lines" $40–75
Van, "Pillsbury's Best" $40–75
Van, "Evan Motor Freight" $40–75
Oil Tanker, "Gulf" $40–75
Oil Tanker, "Marathon Oil" $40–75
Oil Tanker, "Sunoco" $40–75

Carette, Georges

Georges Carette was born in France, but went to Nuremburg, Germany, in 1886 to start manufacturing toys, particularly tinplate clockwork vehicles. The company remained in business until 1917. Carette fled back to France at the beginning of World War I, and his company was taken over by Karl Bub.

Landaulet Limousine $6,000
Limousine with clockwork motor, 16" $5,000
Limousine with opening doors and roof rack, 12¼" $4,000
Limousine with chauffeur, 12½" $3,000
Limousine with driver, high headlamps and luggage rack, 15" $6,000
Limousine with driver and passenger, clockwork motor, 12½" $5,000
Open car with clockwork motor, tinplate driver, forward and reverse gears, 6½".......$2,000
Open car with driver, 9" $1,500
Open Phaeton with driver, 12" $5,500
Open Tourer 4-Seater with bisque driver and passenger, wind-up, 12½" $17,500
Phaeton 4-Seater with driver and passenger, 9" $3,500

Carlo Brianza (see A.B.C. Brianza)

Carmania

Currently available is an assortment of Carmania models of France in 1:64 scale for $5 each, and one 1:43 scale model for $15.

Carmania 1:64 Scale

10 1976 Chevrolet Camaro Z28, pink....$5
11 1981 Chevrolet Camaro, yellow........$5
12 Chevrolet Corvette Convertible, silver...$5
13 Chevrolet Corvette Coupe, maroon $5
14 1974 Ferrari 308 Coupe, blue..........$5
15 1974 Ferrari 308 Coupe, maroon $5
16 1974 Ferrari 308 Roadster, red $5
17 Ferrari 365 GT, yellow or pink $5
18 Ferrari Testarossa, red......................$5
19 1989 Ford Thunderbird Rally, orange..$5
21 Ford F250 4WD Pickup, white $5
22 Honda CRX Coupe, red $5
23 Lamborghini Countach, blue..............$5
26 Mercedes 307 Van, yellow/white......$5
27 Morgan Plus 4 Roadster, green..........$5
28 Nissan Mid 4 Coupe, black $5
32 1969 Pontiac GTO Hardtop $5
33 1981 Pontiac Firebird Convertible $5
34 1976 Pontiac Firebird T-Top..............$5
36 Porsche 928, blue $5
37 Porsche 928, "Pennzoil" $5
39 Suzuki Samurai $5
40 Toyota Extended Cab Pickup $5
42 1920 Vauxhall $5
43 1980 Camaro Z28, purple...............$5
44 Volkswagen Beetle Baja Bug, yellow...$5

Carmania 1:43 Scale

100 Schnauzer Team P7 "Esso," white...$15

Carousel 1

Mason Distributing Company
2203 Patterson Ave.
Roanoke, VA 24016
toll-free: 800-777-3977

The first I'd heard of this brand was in August 1999 when I received e-mails from two different people asking about them. Vintage Indy cars are the focus of this new brand of highly detailed precision 1:18 scale models.

#3 Rodger Ward, white and red $100–110
#6 Bob Swelkert, pale pink and white.$100–110
#98 Parnelli Jones, white and blue $100–110

Castle Art (also see Gaiety)

Collector Paul Starck wrote via e-mail of a brand called "Castle Art." He indicates that they are diecast cars also known as "Gaiety" toys made in Birmingham, West Midlands, England, in the fifties. "I have two racers from them," writes Starck. "One is a silver Morgan (three wheeled wind-up) and could have been a promo for the Morgan Car Company. The other seems to be cast iron." This is all that's known about this brand.

C. A. W. Novelty Company

C.A.W. Novelty Company was started in 1925 in Kansas by Charles A. Wood. His fine examples of "slushmold" (lead alloy) toys were not fully appreciated by collectors until as late as 1990 when one collector named Chic Gast described a group of unidentified toys as "orphans." The toys were also marketed by the name of Mid-West Metal Novelty Manufacturing Company in 1929.

World War II brought lead casting to a halt in 1940 and C.A.W. went with it. The last employee of the company, Rod Hemphill, and newfound partner Howard Clevenger purchased the company assets and started C&H Manufacturing Company.

C.A.W. toys originally sold for 10 cents to a dollar.

Air Drive Coach, #25, 3⅞" $30–40
DeSoto Sedan, #32, 3⅞" $30–40
Dump Truck, 3⅛" $30–40
Fuel Tanker, 3¾" $30–40
Marvel Racer, #31, 3⅜" $30–40
New Design Racer, #38, 3⅜" $30–40
Overland Bus, 3¾" $30–40
Sport Roadster, 3½" $30–40
Streamline Coupe, #30, 3" $30–40
Tank Truck, 3³⁄₁₆" $30–40
Transparent Windshield Racer, #39, 3" .$30–40
Wonder Special, #33, 3⅜" $30–40

C.B.Car

From Milan, Italy, Esci produces a series of 1:24 scale cars called Real Cars under the C.B.Car brand.

#105 Porsche 959, opening doors and engine compartment, wheels steer $16

C.B.G. Mignot (see Mignot, C.B.G.)

CCC

Collector Bill Cross reports that these are resin models, hand made in France. The range now includes "unusual" European cars like Ford Vedettes, Peugeot 203, and the tiny Rovin Microcar.

1936 Ford Roadster..............................$125
1955 Ford Crown Victoria.....................$125
Ford Vedette.......................................$130
Delahaye Fire T-140 ....$135
Peugeot 203......................................$130
Rovin Microcar $130

C.D.

One of the most obscure French toy companies, C.D. produced a small assortment of cast toy vehicles in the 1920s.

Bugatti Sports Car $100
Chenard & Walker Ambulance..............$100
Chenard & Walker Limousine $100
Chenard & Walker "Ricard" Van $100
Chenard & Walker Wrecker, 3⅜"..........$100
Delage Limousine $100
Delahaye Ambulance $100
Delahaye Fire Truck $100
Delahaye Limousine $100
Delahaye Torpedo $100
Delahaye Van $100
Ford Model T $100
Hotchkiss Limousine $100
Latil Farm Truck $100

Latil Van, 3¾" $100
MG Record Car $100
Panhard Tractor $100
Peugeot Sans Soupape.......................$100
Renault 40CV Berline $100
Renault 40CV Coupe $100
Renault 40CV Limousine $100
Renault 40CV Torpedo $100
Renault 40CV Ambulance $100
Renault 40CV Truck $100
Renault Vivaquatre Coupe $100
Rosengart Super Traction Fastback............$100
Rosengart Super Traction Roadster $100

CDC (see Detail Cars)

Century (see AMR)

Chad Valley

Chad Valley, as the name implies, is a brand of scale model cars made by a British firm based in South Africa beginning in the late forties. Some models were especially made for the Rootes Group as promotionals at dealerships. Diecasting continued until 1956.

220 Rolls-Royce Razor Edge Saloon, 1:43.$165
221 Rolls-Royce Razor Edge Traffic Control, 1:43 ....$165
222 Rolls-Royce Razor Edge Police Car, 1:43 ....$165
223 Record Car, 1:43 ....$175
224 Double Decker Bus, 1:76 ....$250
225 Commer open Truck $150
226 Commer Flat Truck $150
227 Commer Timber Wagon $150
228 Commer Cable Layer.....................$165
229 Commer Breakdown Truck...............$165
230 Commer Milk Truck with eight milk cans $175
231 Commer Fire Engine $175
232 Commer Tower Repair Wagon $150
233 Commer Milk Tanker......................$175
234 Commer Petrol Tanker....................$150
235 Tractor, 1:43 ....$150
236 Hillman Minx, 1:43.......................$140
237 Humber Super Snipe, 1:43 ....$125
238 Sunbeam-Talbot, 1:43...................$150
239 Dust Cart $150
240 Commer Avenger Coach, 1:76 ....$200
241 Karrier Public Health Vehicle..............$150
242 Commer Truck...............................$175
243 Bulldozer $150
244 Farm Trailer..................................$40
245 Manure Spreader $75
247 Stacutrac $175
500 Guy Van, "Chad Valley" $225
500 Guy Van, "Guy Motors" $225
503 Fordson Tractor, 1:43 ....$175
504 Guy Ice Cream Truck, 1:43 ....$250
507 Humber Hawk, 1:43......................$200
509 Hay Rake $60
550 Saloon, 1:70................................$35

551 Single Decker Coach, 1:70.............$35
552 Van, 1:70....................................$35
553 Post Office Van $35
554 Ambulance $35

Champion

Champion is a brand of 1:66 scale models reportedly made in France in the 1970s. Their 1:43 scale models were marketed as Super Champions.

Champion 1:66 Scale

Porsche 917 Monza, gulf blue, Car #7 Rodriguez & Oliver, 1:66 ....$10
Porsche 917 Nurburgring, yellow, Car #3 Atwood & Muller, 1:66..................$10
Porsche 917 Spa, white, martini, Car #22 Van Lennep & Mario, 1:66............$10
Porsche 917 Le Mans, red, Car #23 Larrousse & Kaunsen, 1:66.................$10

Super Champion 1:43 Scale

Porsche 917 #19, 1:43 ....$25–40
Lola T70 Mk. 3B, 1:43..................$25–40

Champion Hardware Company

In business from 1883 to 1954, the Champion Hardware Company of Geneva, Ohio, produced toys during the years of 1930 to 1936 while under the operation of C. I. Chamberlin. Among those toys was an assortment of cast-iron toy cars and trucks.

Airflow, 4¾" $800
Coupe, based on a Plymouth, with opening rumble seat, 7½" $800
Coupe, based on a Reo, 7½" $1,000
Delivery Truck, #536, 8" long...................$800
Gas and Motor Oil Truck, 8" $750
Mack Dump Truck, 7" $350
Mack Express Truck, 7½" $250
Mack Stake Truck, 4½" $200
Mack Stake Truck, 7½" $750
Mack Wrecker, 9" $800
Panel Delivery Truck, 7¾" $2000
Race Car with driver and passenger, 5½" ..$400
Race Car with removable driver, 6" $400
Race Car, 9" $325
Sedan, 5¼" $225
Wrecker, 4" $225
Wrecker, 7½" $500
Wrecker, 8¼" $2,000
Wrecker, 9" $500

Champ of the Road (also see Universal)

This obscure brand represents the American marketing division of Universal toys of Hong Kong.

Charbens

Leslie and John Barker of Guelph, Ontario, Canada, report that Charbens were made in England probably in the fifties and early sixties. The accuracy of scale is average, quality of casting is good. Some cars are cast in two

pieces. While casting detail is low, fenders are attached separately. Detailing was likely by hand. Wheels are painted on outside only. Lights and grill, if present, are painted.

Charbens Old Crock Series

OC1 1894 Darracq Genevieve, red, orange, or blue $20
OC2 1904 Spyker, yellow & black.......$20
OC3 1914 "Old Bill" Double Decker Bus
v.1 cast in two halves.....................$20
v.2 single cast..............................$30
OC4 1907 Ford Model T, blue $20
OC5 1907 Vauxhall, green $20
OC6 1906 De Dion Bouton.................$20
OC7 1898 Panhard, blue, light green & silver, or brown & silver $20
OC8 1906 Rolls-Royce Silver Ghost, silver...$20
OC9 1903 Standard 6 HP...................$15
OC10 1902 Wolseley, turquoise $20
OC11 1908 Packard Runabout, light green $20
OC12 1905 Packard Runabout............$20
OC13 1900 Straker Steam Lorry $20
OC14 Stephenson's Rocket Locomotive ..$20
OC15 Rocket Tender..........................$20
OC16 1909 Albion Pickup...................$20
OC17 1912 Rover Roadster $20
OC18 1911 Mercedes-Benz $20
M19 Bedford Horse Transport.............$25
OC20 1910 Lanchester $20
OC21 1922 Morris Cowley Roadster ...$20
OC22 1900 Daimler...........................$20
OC23 1904 Autocar............................$20
OC24 1870 Grenville Steam Carriage .$20
OC25 1905 Napier Record Car..........$20
OC26 Fire Engine...............................$25
OC27 Articulated Breakdown Truck......$20
OC28 1913 Mercer Runabout $20
M30 Mobile Searchlight $20
M31 Mobile Twin Bofor Gun $20
M32 Mobile Radar $20
M33 Mobile Field Gun $20
M34 Mobile Rocket Gun $20
M35 Armored Car $20

Other Charbens

6 Farm Tractor $65
8 Tipping Truck $50
9 Motor Coach $75
10 Royal Mail Van $65
11 Ambulance $65
12 Van, "Carter Paterson" $60
13 Police Van $65
14 Post Office Van $65
15 Dennis Fire Engine $75
17 Tractor and Three Trailers.................$75
18 Tractor and Grass Cutter.................$75
19 Tractor and Harvester.....................$75
20 Mobile Crane $45
21 Muir Hill Dumper $50
26 Armored Car $50
28 Steam Roller.................................$45
31 Cable Truck..................................$65

32 Alfa Romeo Racing Car	$100
33 Cooper-Bristol Racing Car	$100
34 Ferrari Racing Car	$100
36 Horse Transport Box	$75
37 Rocket Gun on Truck and Trailer	$70
Javelin Saloon	$100
Morris Fire Engine	$75
Morris Station Wagon	$75
Morris Van, "Esso"	$65
Pedestrian Electric Vehicle, "Dairy Milk"	$100
Pedestrian Electric Vehicle, "Hovis"	$100
Scammell GWR Mechanical Horse	$65
Tanker	$65
Van	$50

Charmerz (also see Playart)

According to Dave Weber of Warrington, Pennsylvania, Playart at one time produced a series of models called Charmerz for New York distributor Charles Merzbach. As it turns out, they were repackaged Playart models. Charles Merzbach also served as one of the first US distributors for Majorettes.

Chein

In 1903, Julius Chein founded the New Jersey company which produced lithographed wind-up metal toys. The company continued producing toys until 1979. The company remains in business today in Burlington, New Jersey.

Airflow with garage, wind-up	$625
Greyhound Bus, wind-up, 9"	$425
Greyhound Bus, push toy, 9"	$325
Limousine, wind-up, 7"	$575
Peanuts Bus, "HAPPINESS IS AN ANNUAL OUTING," lithograph illustrated with Snoopy driving, Peanuts comic strip characters as passengers	$250
Roadster, 8½"	$650
Six Window Sedan, 8½"	$700
Taxi, wind-up, 7"	$450
Touring Car, 7"	$500
Woodie Sedan, 5¼"	$100
Woodie Station Wagon	$200

Cherryca Phenix (also see Taiseiya, Micro Pet)

Taiseiya of Japan originally marketed these exceptional 1:43 scale diecast models, some with battery-operated lights, under the Micropet brand in the early sixties. Taiseiya was later purchased by Yonezawa, known for Diapet diecast models.

1 Hino Contessa	$250
2 Nissan Cedric Station Wagon	$250
3 Mercedes-Benz 300 SL Roadster	$275
4 Datsun	$100
5 Chevrolet Impala	$275
6 Buick Electra	$275
7 Ford Falcon	$275
8 Volkswagen 1200	$275
9 Volkswagen Karmann Ghia Roadster	$325

10 Dodge Polara	$235
11 Mercedes-Benz 300 SL Hardtop	$275
12 Datsun 1200 Station Wagon	$250
13 Datsun 1200 Pickup	$250
14 Isuzu Bellel 2000 De Luxe	$275
15 Ford Thunderbird	$275
16 Datsun Fairlady Roadster	$275
17 Lincoln Continental	$300
18 Mercedes-Bent 220 SE	$275
19 Citroën DS 19 Convertible	$325
20 Cadillac 62 Special	$300
21 Chevrolet	$125
22 Datsun Bluebird	$425
23 Jaguar Type E Roadster	$250
24 Prince Gloria	$250
25 Nissan Cedric	$250
26 Toyota/Toyopet Crown	$250
27 Toyota/Toyopet Crown Station Wagon	$250
28 Toyota/Toyopet Corona	$250
29 Mercedes-Benz 300 SL Roadster	$275
30 Isuzu Bellett	$250
31 Prince Skyline 1500	$250
32 Datsun Bluebird	$225
33 Mitsubishi Colt 1000	$225
34 Hino Contessa	$225
35 Nissan Cedric Taxi	$275
36 Toyota/Toyopet Crown Police Car	$275
37 Toyota/Toyopet Crown Taxi	$275
38 Honda S 600 Roadster	$225
39 Prince Sprint Coupe	$225
40 Toyota/Toyopet Corona Coupe	$225
41 Daihatsu Berlina/Compagno	$200
42 Mitsubishi Debonair	$200
43 Nissan Cedric Police Car	$250
44 Mazda Luce	$225
45 Mitsubishi Colt 1000 Rally	$250
46 Datsun Bluebird Rally	$250
47 Nissan Prince Skyline Rally	$250
48 Prince Gloria Rally	$250
50 Isuzu Bellet GT	$250
001 Fordson Major Tractor and Trailer	$225
OT1 1892 Peugeot	$75
OT2 1896 Peugeot	$75
OT3 1898 Peugeot Victoria	$75
OT4 1899 Peugeot Victoria	$75
OT5 1901 Decauville Vis-a-Vis	$75
OT6 1901 Delahaye Vis-a-Vis	$75
FL-1 Buick Electra	$275
FL-2 Ford Falcon	$275

Chico (see Tekno)

Chrono

Chrono - A Model Collection Co. Ltd.
Room 3105, Diamond Square
Shun Tak Centre
168-200 Connaught Road
Central Hong Kong, China
fax: +852-2785-3901

The specialty for this obscure Hong Kong-based company, just now gaining more prominence, is 1:18 scale diecast models.

791001 Aston Martin DB5, green, 1998	$25–35
791002 Aston Martin DB5, dark red, 1998	$25–35
791003 Aston Martin DB5, light blue metallic, 1998	$25–35
791020 1998 Lotus Elise Spider, yellow, offen, 1998	$25–35
791021 1998 Lotus Elise Spider, blue, offen, 1998	$25–35
791022 1998 Lotus Elise Spider, black, offen, 1998	$25–35
791030 1998 Lotus Elise Hardtop, red, 1998	$25–35
791031 1998 Lotus Elise Hardtop, green, 1998	$25–35
791032 1998 Lotus Elise Hardtop, silver, 1998	$25–35
791040 1969 Triumph Spitfire MK IV Cabrio, white, 1998	$25–35
791041 1969 Triumph Spitfire MK IV Cabrio, green, 1998	$25–35
791042 1969 Triumph Spitfire MK IV Cabrio, black, 1998	$25–35
791050 1969 Triumph Spitfire MK IV Hardtop, red, 1998	$25–35
791051 1969 Triumph Spitfire MK IV Hardtop, blue, 1998	$25–35
791052 1969 Triumph Spitfire MK IV Hardtop, yellow, 1998	$25–35
791060 1953 Porsche 550 RS, silver, 1998	$25–35
791061 1953 Porsche 550 RS, blue, 1998	$25–35
791062 1953 Porsche 550 RS, red, 1998	$25–35
791070 1953 Porsche 550 RS, silver, Nr. 40, 1998	$25–35
791080 Aston Martin DB5, silver, James Bond, 1998	$25–35
791080 1953 Porsche 550 RS, silver, James Dean, 1998	$25–35
791090 1968 Fiat 24 Spider, red, offen, 1998	$25–35
791091 1968 Fiat 24 Spider, yellow, offen, 1998	$25–35
791092 1968 Fiat 24 Spider, black, offen, 1998	$25–35
791100 1968 Fiat 24 Spider, white, Hardtop, Abarth, 1998	$25–35
791101 1968 Fiat 24 Spider, red, Hardtop, Abarth, 1998	$25–35
791110 1968 Fiat 24 Spider, metallic blue, Pininfarina, 1998	$25–35
791111 1968 Fiat 24 Spider, metallic green, Pininfarina, 1998	$25–35
Nissan Primera STW-CUP, Asch, 1998	$25–35
Nissan Primera STW-CUP, Massen, 1998	$25–35
Opel Vectra STW-CUP, Alzen, 1998	$25–35
Opel Vectra STW-CUP, Thiim, 1998	$25–35

Ciba

The only models issued by Ciba appear to be 1:43 scale Mercedes-Benz cars.

Mercedes-Benz 300E, blue, green, red, or yellow..$11

Cigar Box (see Aurora)

C.I.J.

Compagnie Industrielle du Jouet, better known as C.I.J. of France, first produced 1:43 scale models in 1933 out of plaster and flour. Other materials used in producing models included tinplate, lead cast and, from 1938 to 1964, diecast. The firm of J.R.D. was purchased in 1963, and a few C.I.J. models were reissued unchanged as J.R.D. models and vice versa. Here is an assortment of known models. Introduction year and current value follows the description.

Berliet GLR 19 Tank Truck, #3/23, 1959 ...$75
Berliet GLR 19 "Shell" Tanker, #3/24, 1959 ....$75
Berliet Semi-Trailer Truck, #3/77, 1965 ....$110
Berliet Weitz Mobile Crane, #3/84, 1964–65..$90
Caravan Trailer, #3/27, 1959 ....$55
Cattle Trailer, #3/28, 1962....................$55
Chrysler Windsor Sedan, #3/15, 1956...$140
Citroën AMI 6, #3/6, 1964,....................$55
Citroën ID19 Ambulance, #3/41, 1964 ....$85
Citroën ID19 Estate Car, #3/4, 1958–59..$85
Citroën 11CV, #3/11, 1964–65 (reissued as J.R.D. #112)......................................$55
Citroën 1200KG Van, #3/89, 1965 ....$90
Citroën 1200KG Police Van, #3/89, 1964–65..$90
Citroën 2CV Mail Van, #3/76, 1965.........$80
Crane Truck, #3/81, 1956 ....$90
De Rovin Open Two-Seater, #3/1, 1954 ...$85
Facel Vega Facellia, #3/3, 1958–60........$90
Fire Engine, #3/30, 1959......................$110
Mercedes-Benz 220 Sedan, #3/12, 1959 ..$55
Panhard "BP" Tank Truck, #3/20, 1951 .....$60
Panhard Dyna 130, #3/47, 1950...........$70
Panhard Dyna 54, #3/54, 1955.............$70
Panhard Dyna Junior, #3/5, 1954 ....$85
Peugeot 403 Break, #3/46, 1955...........$60
Peugeot 403 Ambulance, #3/46, 1962 ....$75
Peugeot 403 Police Car, #3/46, 1960 .....$55
Peugeot 404 Sedan, #3/13, 1965 (reissued as J.R.D. #151)....................................$55
Plymouth Belvedere Sedan, #3/16, 1957 ..$140
Renault 1000KG Van, #3/60, 1955.........$55
Renault 1000KG Astra Van, #3/60, 1957.$90
Renault 1000KG Boucherie Van, #3/60, 1960 ....$90
Renault 1000KG Mail Van, #3/60, 1957..$90
Renault 1000KG Belgian Mail Van, #3/60, 1957 ....$125
Renault 1000KG "Shell" Van, #3/60, 1956 ....$90
Renault 1000KG Van and Trailer, #3/60, 1957 ....$115
Renault 1000KG Ambulance, #3/61, 1955 ....$110

Renault 1000KG Army Ambulance, #3/61, 1959 ....$110
Renault 1000KG Bus, #3/62, 1955 ....$90
Renault 1000KG Police Van, #3/63, 1955 ....$80
Renault 2.5 Ton Bottle Truck, #3/94, 1963 ..$95
Renault 2.5 Ton Fire Engine, #3/95, 1963 ....$120
Renault 2.5 Ton Gun Truck, #3/99, 1964 ....$100
Renault 2.5 Ton Radar Truck, #3/98, 1964 ....$100
Renault 300KG Van, #3/67, 1957..........$55
Renault 300KG Mail Van, #3/68, 1957 ...$70
Renault 4CV, #3/48, 1950.....................$70
Renault 4CV Police Car, #3/49, 1950.....$70
Renault 7-Ton Covered Truck, #3/25, 1953 ....$40
Renault Alpine Coupe, #3/50, 1958–59...$55
Renault Atomic Pile Transporter, #3/75, 1957 ....$180
Renault Bus, #3/40, 1954 ....$80
Renault Colorale Ambulance, #3/55, 1956..$80
Renault Colorale, #3/44, 1953...............$55
Renault Covered Trailer, #3/26, 1953.......$40
Renault Domane Break, #3/53, 1958......$60
Renault Domane Ambulance, #3/53, 1960..$75
Renault Dauphine, #3/56, 1956 ....$60
Renault Dauphine Taxi, #3/56, 1958 ....$60
Renault Dauphine Police, #3/57, 1958.....$60
Renault Dauphinoise Break, #3/66, 1956–57 ....$55
Renault Dauphinoise Police Car, #3/69, 1955 ....$80
Renault Dump Truck, #3/80, 1955 ....$80
Renault E-30 Farm Tractor, #3/33, 1959..$110
Renault E-30 Tractor and Trailer, #3/34, 1959 ....$165
Renault Estafette Bus, #3/92, 1961...........$70
Renault Estafette Van, #3/90, 1963.........$75
Renault Estafette Police Bus, #3/93, 1962 ..$75
Renault Estafette Police Van, #3/91, 1963..$75
Renault Etoile Filante Record Car, #3/2, 1957 .$90
Renault Excavator, #3/88, 1964–65 ....$75
Renault Floride, #3/58, 1960 ....$55
Renault Fregate, #3/51, 1951 ....$60
Renault Fregate Grand Pavois, #3/52, 1958 ....$60
Renault Police Pickup and Trailer, #3/65, 1962 ....$100
Renault Prairie, #3/42, 1953...................$55
Renault Prairie Taxi, #3/45, 1955 ....$55
Renault Savane, #3/43, 1953.................$55
Renault Searchlight Truck and Trailer, #3/96, 1963 ....$100
Renault Semi-Trailer Truck, #3/70, 1955.....$80
Renault Semi-Trailer Tank Truck, #3/72, 1958 ....$100
Renault Semi-Trailer Log Truck, #3/73, 1956 ....$80
Renault "Shell" Tank Truck, #3/21, 1952....$60
Renault Tractor and Sling Cart Trailer, #3/39, 1959..$160

Renault Tractor and Trailer, #3/38, 1959 .$160
Renault Wrecker, #3/83, 1964 ....$90
Sailboat on Trailer, #3/76, 1964............$55
Saviem Bottle Truck, #3/79, 1965 ....$100
Saviem Missile Launcher, #3/97, 1964 ...$100
Seed Trailer, #3/32, 1959......................$55
Shovel Truck, #3/82, 1958 ....$90
Simca 1000 Coupe Bertone, #3/9, 1964.$55
Simca 1000 Sedan, #3/7, 1962–63.......$55
Simca 1000 Police Car, #3/8, 1963.......$55
Sling Cart Trailer, #3/36, 1959...............$60
Sugar Beet Trailer, #3/31, 1959.............$60
Tipping Farm Trailer, #3/37, 1959...........$60
Unic Cab and Trailer with railroad car, #3/78 ....$140
Volkswagen, #3/10, 1954 ....$65
Water Tank Trailer, #3/35, 1959 ....$55

Circle N Toys

Similar in appearance to Tootsietoys, Circle N Toys is a previously unknown company until collector Jarek Skonieczny discovered a toy jeep with the name and logo on the underside in September 1999. More research is needed.
Jeep, 3" $2-6

City (see Vitesse)

CKO

The trademark logo on the bottom of CKO models is all that identifies these models. The C forms an arc around the K with the O to the right. Models are made in Germany and are quite rare for their vintage, having been produced sometime between the mid-sixties and mid-seventies. As it turns out, these are all tinplate models.
Ferrari Formula 1, red $125
Mercedes-Benz SL 350, metallic light blue, #440 ....$125
Mercedes-Benz Taxi, cream $125
Porsche 911, #432, metallic gold tinplate, 1:40 ....$125
Volkswagen Pickup, blue........................$145
Volkswagen Beetle, #425, yellow............$45

Classic Construction Models
6590 SW Fallbrook Place
Beaverton, OR 97008
phone: 503-626-6395
fax: 503-646-1996
website: www.teleport.com/~ccmodels

Brass construction comprises these impressive precision scale construction vehicles from Classic Construction Models made in Beaverton, Oregon. The series represents models issued in limited edition of 1,000 each.

Classic Construction Models 1:87 Scale
    Caterpillar 325 L.........................$30–40
    Caterpillar D8R............................$30–40
Classic Construction Models 1:48 Scale
    American Hoist & Derrick Model 518 Self-

Slewing Steam Derrick $595
Dresser TD-40B Crawler Tractor with Cargo
Winch or 3 Shank Ripper $140
Link Belt HC-268 Truck Crane $1,195

Classic Construction Models 1:48 Scale Excavator Attachments
Esco Rock Breaker $30
Hendrix Compaction Wheel $30
Kent Vibrating Plate Compactor $30

Classic Construction Models Classic Collectibles
1911 Marmon Wasp, detailed pressed steel replica of the first car to win the Indianapolis 500 ....$496

Classic Construction Models Country Classics
#1 1929 Kenworth Lumber Truck Bank...$40
#2 1929 Kenworth Log Truck Bank $40

Classic Metal Works
6465 Monroe Street
Suite 204
Sylvania, OH 43560-1302
phone: 419-885-1448
fax: 419-882-1253
website: www.classicmetalworks.com

Incorporated in 1997, Classic Metal Works, Inc. are distinguished by their quality and detail. According to the monthly trade magazine *The Toy Book* (December 1998, page 10), Classic Metal Works models are hand-assembled vehicles with more than 50 parts, including spark plug wiring, a separate engine, opening doors and hood, steerable wheel, packaged in full-color corrugate window packages. Each vehicle comes with its own collectors' stackable display case. Prices listed are suggested retail.

Classic Metal Works Blueprint Series 1:24 Scale limited edition of 15,000 numbered pieces
10101 1970 Chevelle SS454, introduced in 1998 ....$30
10102 1967 Corvette L-71 Roadster, introduced in 1998 ....$30
10103 1949 Mercury Deluxe Coupe, introduced in 1998 ....$30
10104 1971 Plymouth 426 Hemi 'Cuda, introduced in 1998 ....$30

Classic Metal Works Police Interceptor Series 1 1:24 Scale 1999 Ford Crown Victorias, limited edition of 25,000 numbered pieces
State Pursuit Cars
20101 California Highway Patrol, introduced in 1999 ....$34
20102 Ohio Highway Patrol, introduced in 1999 ....$34
20103 Illinois State Police, introduced in 1999 ....$34
20104 Wisconsin State Police, introduced in 2000 ....$34
20105 New York State Police, introduced in 2000 ....$34

20107 Texas Highway Patrol, introduced in 2000 ....$34
20108 Michigan State Police, introduced in 2000 ....$34
20109 Florida Highway Patrol, introduced in 2000 ....$34

Municipal Pursuit Cars
25101 New York City Patrol, introduced in 2000 ....$34
25102 Chicago City Patrol, introduced in 2000 ....$34
25103 Denver Patrol, introduced in 2000 ....$34
25104 Dallas City Police, introduced in 2000 ....$34
25105 Cleveland City Police, introduced in 2000 ....$34
25106 Los Angeles Police, introduced in 2000 ....$34

Other Classic Metal Works 1:24 Scale 1999 Ford Crown Victoria models
50101 New York City Taxicab, introduced in 2000 ....$34

Classic Metal Works Mini Metals — precision 1:87 scale models with diecast body and chassis, real rubber tires, opening hoods, detailed engines, and factory official paint colors, introduced in 2000

30101 1953 Ford Victoria Convertible $8

30102 1948 Ford Convertible $8

1952 Ford Crown Victoria, 1:87 ....$8

1953 White 3000 Fuel Tanker, 1:87 ....$8

30103 1961 Chevrolet Impala $8
30104 1950 Ford Pickup...................$8
30105 1941 Plymouth Coupe $8
30106 1955 Chevrolet Bel Air...........$8
30107 1948 Ford Woody...................$8
30108 1970 Chevrolet Chevelle...........$8

Classy Chassies (see MegaMovers)

Clau-Mar
One of the many obscure brands currently available is a series of 1:43 scale Clau-Mar models from Argentina, all variations of a particular bus with various liveries.
Camello 3-Deck Bus
v.1 silver, "Chevalier" $15
v.2 white, "El Condor" $15
v.3 white, Expreso Rojas" $15
v.4 white, "Expreso Singer"..................$15
v.5 silver, "International"......................$15
v.6 white, "La Estrella" $15
v.7 white, "Rio Del Plata".....................$15
v.8 white, "Siera Cordoba" $15

Cle (also see Bonux)
Clement Gaget founded the Cle firm of France, manufacturer of plastic toy vintage cars since 1958. The company also produced a series of diecast models under the Bonux brand. For a listing of models and values, see the Bonux section of this book.

Clover (also see New Clover)
Clover models are manufactured in Korea, China, and other Asian manufacturing centers.
Bobcat X225 Skid Loader, 1:25 ....$35
Bobcat 743B Skid Loader, 1:19 ....$25
Bobcat 753 Skid Loader, 1:50 ....$10
Bobcat 753 Skid Loader, 1:25 ....$25
Bobcat 7753 Skid Loader, 1:25 ....$25
1959–1962 Melroe (Bobcat) M-200 Loader, 1:25 (replica of 1st machine built by Melroe Company)...............................$18
Semi Flatbed with three Bobcat 753 Skid Loaders, 1:50 ....$55
Kiamaster Ambulance, 1:43.....................$18
Kiamaster Kombi, 1:43 ....$18
Pontiac Firebird Coupe, 1:59 ....$5

CMA (also see Creative Masters)
CMA is reputed to make a number of top-quality 1:24 scale diecast. They are more expensive than the Mints — Franklin and Danbury — in the $600 to $2,000 range. Marshall Buck is the reported owner of the company. Attention to exact detail is apparently what sets CMA models apart from the rest. No listing available as of this writing, but EWA lists "CMA" as an abbreviation for "Creative Masters."

CMC
CMC of Germany is one of the more recent arrivals on the diecast scale model

scene. Their precision scale models are offered by just a few dealers. The price is already rising on these exceptionally fine models.

Exoticar and Toys for Collectors both offer a 1:24 scale model of The Black Prince. Created and built from a 1930 Mercedes SSK chassis as a one-of-a-kind sports car by Count Trossi, The Black Prince survived sixty years and many different owners. Now owned by Ralph Lauren, it won the Concours d'Elegance at Pebble Beach.

The 1:24 scale model offers amazing detail that includes a beautiful black lacquer finish, photo etched metal wire wheels, brakes, grille and exhaust, hand-painted engine detail with exposed metal exhaust headers, complete with leather bonnet strap and photo etched metal buckle. The interior is leather and fully carpeted with accurately detailed gauges and steering wheel, and an opening trunk with spare tire.

In addition, TfC offers another 1:24 scale CMC model of a 1936 Mercedes-Benz 500 K Spezialroadster of which only 25 of the real car were ever made. Only five of the original cars remain, but the miniature model is just as beautiful. Hand assembled from over 200 parts, it has exquisite engine and chassis detail and real leather seats. The red body is offset with 30 chrome moldings and chrome wire wheels with whitewall tires.

Besides the remarkable models so far mentioned, CMC also provides an assortment of 1:43 scale Jie Fang trucks for the Chinese market and highly detailed 1:12 scale BMW motorcycle models with real leather seats.

Below is a list of models so far offered by CMC.

Benz Patent Motorwagen 1886, 1:10 scale...................................$175–225
Mercedes-Benz 500 K Spezialroadster in red or blue, 1:24 scale......................$145–160
Mercedes-Benz 540 K Cabriolet B 1936, in red and black or blue and silver, 1:24 scale.......................................$145–160
Mercedes SSK Trossi "Schwarzer Prinz" (Black Prince), 1:24 scale.................$135–150
Mercedes W 196 Silberpfeil (Monoposto) 1954, 1:18 scale...................$150 – 175
Porsche 550 Spyder 1954–55, 1:24 scale...$135–150

CMC 1:43 Scale Jie Fang Trucks, hand built in China for Germany

Jie Fang fire tanker, red with "Beijing" on tank, £40...$62 US)
Jie Fang tanker truck, blue with white tank, £40...................................($62 US)
Jie Fang high lift truck, yellow, £40..($62 US)
Jie Fang military missile launcher truck, green, £40...................................($62 US)
Jie Fang military troop carrier truck, green, £40...................................($62 US)
Jie Fang Open Cargo truck, blue-gray £40...................................($62 US)

CMC 1:24 Scale Models

Mercedes-Benz 450SL, red.................$130
Mercedes-Benz 450SL, silver $130
Mercedes-Benz 300SL-S.....................$130
CMC 1:12 scale BMW R 1100 RS Motorcycle
v.1 silver.................................$50–75
v.2 green $50–75
v.3 white................................$50–75
v.4 red..................................$50–75

Code 3 Collectibles
6115 Variel Avenue
Woodland Hills, CA 91367-3727
phone: 818-598-2298
website: www.code3.net

One of the newest emerging diecast model companies is Code 3 Collectibles of Woodland Hills, California. The first model to appear on the market, in the summer of 1997, was a 1:64 scale Seagrave fire engine. It is beautifully packaged in an elegant clear display package and sold for around $20. Code 3 Collectibles is the diecast division of the same company that makes Funrise electronic toy cars and trucks.

Code 3 Seagrave Fire Engines, 1:64, 1997
v.1 City of Los Angeles, April 1997, 25,000 issued, sold out......................$25–30
v.2 Houston Fire Department, July 1997, 25,000 issued, sold out $25–30
v.3 Philadelphia Fire Department, September 1997, 25,000 issued, sold out.$25–30
v.4 Fire Department of New York, November 1997, 25,000 issued, sold out.$25–30
v.5 Honolulu Fire Department, November 1997, 15,000 issued $25–30
v.6 Louisville Fire Department, November 1997, 15,000 issued $25–30
v.7 Denver Fire Department, February 1998 ....$20
Code 3 GMC Suburbans, 1:64, 1998
v.1 Boston, January 1998 ....$20
v.2 New York, March 1998 ....$20
v.3 Los Angeles, May 1998 ....$20
v.4 Baltimore EMS, June 1998.............$20
Code 3 Saulsbury Heavy Rescue Trucks, 1:64, 1998
v.1 New York.................................$20
Code 3 Seagrave Tractor Drawn Aerial, 1:64, 1998
v.1 Washington D.C., January 1998.....$35
v.2 Honolulu, April 1998 ....$35
v.3 Baltimore, June 1998 ....$35
Code 3 Ford Crown Victoria Police, 1:24, 1998
v.1 California Highway Patrol, February 1998 ....$25
v.2 Georgia State Patrol, February 1998..$25
v.3 Florida, February 1998 ....$25
v.4 Massachusetts, April 1998.............$25
v.5 Nevada, April 1998.....................$25
v.6 Buffalo, NY, April 1998 ....$25
v.7 New York State Police, June 1998 ...$25

Cofalu

In the sixties, Cofalu of France produced an assortment of Tour De France models both in diecast metal and plastic in various scales ranging from 1:32 to 1:40.

Cofradis

Two Cofradis models are currently known. They are listed as 1:43 scale models. Most Cofradis issues are modified Solido models.
100 Shelter Euro Missile $24
117 Mack "Danone" Van.........................$24

Collector Case

Most unpainted models such as Collector Case resemble pewter, but are likely made of cast aluminum or the more common "zamak," the zinc alloy common to diecast models. If these didn't cost so much, I would think the intent would be for the collector to paint them. But I would be very hesitant to alter a model that costs $60 to $80. Unless expertly done, it would likely render the model worthless. Diehard hobbyists, however, would likely consider it a challenge to do a good job of customizing.

Collector Case models are available in unpainted base metal, except where noted.

Collector Case 1:43 Scale
602 1963 Chevrolet Corvette Coupe....$65
604 1974 Chevrolet Corvette Convertible, top down $65
606 1974 Chevrolet Corvette T-Top $55
607 1936 Ford Phaeton 4-Door, top up, black & tan...................................$47
608 1936 Ford Convertible 4-Door, top down $47
609 Shelby Cobra 427.......................$60
612 1937 Mercedes-Benz 540 K $47
614 1948 Ford Convertible 2-Door, top down $65
615 1936 Ford Roadster $65
616 1956 Ford Thunderbird Coupe......$47
617 1966 Ford Mustang GT Coupe.......$60
618 1948 MG TC................................$55
619 1986 Chevrolet Corvette Coupe....$47
620 1986 Chevrolet Corvette, top down $47
621 1953 Austin Healy 3000 RDS, top down $65
622 Porsche 928...............................$47
624 1932 Ford Coupe $47
625 1936 Auburn Speedster...............$47
628 1956 Ford Thunderbird Convertible, top down..$60
629 1933 Duesenberg SJ...................$47
631 1961 Chevrolet Stingray Racer......$65
633 1957 Porsche 356 Speedster, top down..$60
701 1956 Chevrolet Corvette, red........$47

Collector Case 1:72 Scale Airplanes
901 F4U-1 Corsair.............................$65
902 P-51 Mustang.............................$65

903 F4F Wildcat.................$65
904 P-40 Warhawk..............$65
905 Douglas DC-3...............$65
907 F-15 "Desert Storm"........$65

Collector Case 1:76 Scale

A series of Chevrolet Corvette coupes and convertibles from 1963 to 1982 are currently offered for $18 each, with the exception of a 1964 Corvette on a pewter-like base for $30.

Collector's Classics (also see Buby)

These fabulous 1:43 scale models of American cars from the forties, fifties, and sixties were made up until 1995 in Argentina by Buby. They are later issues of Buby models renamed to avoid a blatant connection with the Buby name amidst some public relations problems. The last Collector's Classics models were produced in 1995.

1955 Chevrolet Bel Air hard top.............$55
1955 Chevrolet Bel Air Convertible, top down.................$55
1969 Chevrolet Camaro RS Convertible, top down.................$55
1956 De Soto Adventurer, white & gold......$55
1956 De Soto Adventurer, black & gold......$55
1956 De Soto Fireflite hard top................$55
1956 De Soto Fireflite Convertible, top up....$55
1956 De Soto Fireflite Convertible, top down.................$55
1956 De Soto Indy Pace Car...................$55
1953 Ford Sunliner Convertible, top up.......$55
1953 Ford Sunliner hard top...................$55
1953 Ford Sunliner Convertible, top down...$55
1953 Ford Indy Pace Car, limited.............$55
1946 Lincoln Continental Convertible, top up.................$55
1946 Lincoln Continental Convertible, top down.................$55
1946 Lincoln Continental Indy Pace Car......$55

1954 Mercury Monterey, top up.............$55

1954 Mercury Sun Valley Coupe $55
1956 Packard Caribbean Convertible, top up.................$55
1956 Packard Caribbean hard top............$55
1956 Packard Caribbean Convertible, top down.................$55
1964 Studebaker Avanti Sports Coupe, #21 ....$55

Collectors Mint

These are pewter models in 1:43 scale made by Richardi Auto Models of New Jersey.

Collectoy

Collectoy of Japan produces diecast toys, some with friction drive, in a wide range of styles. Inaccuracy of scale is mostly due to oversized wheels on some of the models. As with many Japanese brands, Collectoy was discovered by Bob Speerbrecher in a Japanese language book on diecast cars issued in 1998. Included in the assortment are several vintage American and European cars. At least one friction toy, circa 1958 Ford Station Wagon, has mention of Line Mar Toys on the box. Vintage of cars would indicate the toys to be produced in the sixties, but may be much newer.

DeSoto.................................$20–35
Mercedes 300SL Convertible $20–35
Mercedes 300SL Gullwing $20–35
Triumph TR-3.......................$20–35
Porsche 356......................$20–35
Jaguar XK-150..................$20–35
Ford Edsel.....................$20–35

Comet - Authenticast

Comet - Authenticast (not to be confused with Accucast or Comet Miniatures) started in Queens, New York, as "Comet Metal Products" by the Slonim family around 1940. Starting with toy soldiers, Comet switched to producing 1:108 scale identification models of military vehicles for the government on the verge of World War II. They continued selling them as toys after the war until the early 1960s.

Reissues have recently been produced by Quality Castings of Alexandria, Virginia, using the original molds. Original models are currently valued at $25–50. Reissues are worth around $10–20.

5008 Daimler Armored Car, original.....$25–50
  reissue $10–20

Comet - Authenticast WWII Japanese Vehicles

5051 Amphibian Tankette, original..$25–50
  Quality reissue.........................$10–20
5052 Tankette, original...................$25–50
  Quality reissue.........................$10–20
5053 Medium Tank, original..........$25–50
  Quality reissue.........................$10–20
5054 Medium Tank, original..........$25–50
  Quality reissue.........................$10–20
5055 Tankette, original...................$25–50
  Quality reissue.........................$10–20
5056 Light Tank, original................$25–50
  Quality reissue.........................$10–20
5057 Heavy Medium Tank, original.$25–50
  Quality reissue.........................$10–20

Comet - Authenticast WWII German Vehicles

5100 PzKw III, original $25–50
  Quality reissue.........................$10–20
5101 PzKw I, original....................$25–50
  Quality reissue.........................$10–20
5102 Panzerjager, original............$25–50
  Quality reissue.........................$10–20

5103 PzKw IV G, original $25–50
  Quality reissue.....................$10–20
5104 PzKw IV F, original...............$25–50
  Quality reissue.....................$10–20
5105 PzKw II, original...................$24
  Quality reissue.....................$10–20
5106 PzKw III, original $25–50
  Quality reissue.....................$10–20
5107 Tiger, original.......................$25–50
  Quality reissue.....................$10–20
5108 8-Wheeled Armored Car, original $25–50
  Quality reissue.....................$10–20
5109 Pz35T, original.....................$25–50
  Quality reissue.....................$10–20
5110 Panther, original..................$25–50
  Quality reissue.....................$10–20
5111 Sturmgeschutz, original........$25–50
  Quality reissue.....................$10–20
5112 Half-track, original...............$25–50
  Quality reissue.....................$10–20

Comet - Authenticast US ID Models

5150 75mm Gun on Half Track, original $25–50
  Quality reissue.....................$10–20
5151 Heavy Tank M6, original $25–50
  Quality reissue.....................$10–20
5152 Sherman Tank, original.........$25
  Quality reissue.....................$10–20
5153 Greyhound Armored Car, original $25–50
  Quality reissue.....................$10–20
5154 Half-track, original...............$25–50
  Quality reissue.....................$10–20
5155 Hellcat, original...................$25–50
  Quality reissue.....................$10–20
5156 Priest, original.....................$25–50
  Quality reissue.....................$10–20
5156 General Pershing Tank, original .$25–50
  Quality reissue.....................$10–20
5157 General Scott, original $25–50
  Quality reissue.....................$10–20
5158 General Stuart, original $25–50
  Quality reissue.....................$10–20
5159 Wolverine, original...............$25–50
  Quality reissue.....................$10–20
5160 Jeep, original......................$25–50
  Quality reissue.....................$10–20
5161 Weasel, original..................$25–50
  Quality reissue.....................$10–20
5162 Scout Car, original..............$25–50
  Quality reissue.....................$10–20
5163 Quack, original...................$25–50
  Quality reissue.....................$10–20
5164 King Kong, original..............$25–50
  Quality reissue.....................$10–20
5166 General Chaffee Tank, original $25–50
  Quality reissue.....................$10–20
5167 Slugger II Tank, original........$25–50
  Quality reissue.....................$10–20
5168 Slugger Tank, original..........$25–50
  Quality reissue.....................$10–20

5169 76mm Sherman Tank, original $25
   Quality reissue...................$10–20
5170 Airborne Tank, original.........$25–50
   Quality reissue...................$10–20
5171 Staghound Armored Car,
   original $25–50
   Quality reissue...................$10–20
5172 Twin 50 Armored Car,
   original $25–50
   Quality reissue...................$10–20
5173 DUKW, original...................$25–50
   Quality reissue...................$10–20
5174 M32 Tank Recovery, original.$25–50
   Quality reissue...................$10–20
5175 LVTAA Amphibian Tank,
   original $25–50
   Quality reissue...................$10–20
5176 LVT Amphibian, original........$25–50
   Quality reissue...................$10–20
5177 Utility Tank, original $25–50
   Quality reissue...................$10–20
5178 Medium Tank, original...........$25–50
   Quality reissue...................$10–20
5179 General Patton, original.........$25–50
   Quality reissue...................$10–20
5180 Walker Bulldog, original $25–50
   Quality reissue...................$10–20
5181 6 x 6 Truck, original $25–50
   Quality reissue...................$10–20
5182 Command Car, original $25–50
   Quality reissue...................$10–20
5183 Troop Carrier, original $25–50
   Quality reissue...................$10–20
5184 Trailer, original....................$25–50
   Quality reissue...................$10–20
5185 Weapons carrier, original $25–50
   Quality reissue...................$10–20
5186 M67 Tank, original...............$25–50
   Quality reissue...................$10–20
5187 M48 Tank, original $25–50
   Quality reissue...................$10–20
5188 M103 Heavy Tank, original ..$25–50
   Quality reissue...................$10–20
5189 Atomic Cannon, original $25–50
   Quality reissue...................$10–20
5190 T98 S.P. 105mm Gun, original.$25–50
   Quality reissue...................$10–20
5191 S.P. 155mm Howitzer, original.$25–50
   Quality reissue...................$10–20
5192 M3 Medium Tank, original $25–50
   Quality reissue...................$10–20
5193 Hawk Missile Transporter, Launcher,
   Mobile Radar & crew, original ..$25–50
   Quality reissue...................$10–20
5194 Honest John Launcher and crew,
   original $25–50
   Quality reissue...................$10–20
5195 Nike-Ajax Launcher and crew,
   original $25–50
   Quality reissue...................$10–20
5196 M42 duster Twin 40mm AA,
   original $25–50
   Quality reissue...................$10–20

5197 Ontos S.P. Rocket Launcher,
   original $25–50
   Quality reissue...................$10–20

Comet - Authenticast WWII Russian Vehicles

5200 KV-1 Heavy Tank, original $25–50
   Quality reissue...................$10–20
5201 KV-2 Heavy Tank, original $25–50
   Quality reissue...................$10–20
5202 Josef Stalin Tank, original $25–50
   Quality reissue...................$10–20
5203 T34 Medium Tank, original ...$25–50
   Quality reissue...................$10–20
5204 T70 Light Tank, original $25-50, Quality reissue $10–20
5205 ST2 Armored carrier, original .$25–50
   Quality reissue...................$10–20
5206 T34/85 Medium Tank, original.$25–50
   Quality reissue...................$10–20
5207 Josef Stalin III Tank, original $25–50
   Quality reissue...................$10–20

Quality Castings New Issues of German Vehicles

4017 Wespe $10–20
4018 7.5 PAK $10–20
4023 Opel Blitz.........................$10–20
4026 88 Flak on or off bogie wheels..$10–20
4027 2 cm FLAF on or off trailer $10–20
4031 3.7 PAK...........................$10–20
4035 7.5 INF Gun $10–20
4036 Kubelwagen......................$10–20
4037 BMW Cycle.......................$10–20
4041 Pz38t..............................$10–20
4042 Wirblewing FLAK $10–20
4044 Hetzer $10–20
4045 Marder III $10–20
4046 250/I Half-track $10–20
4049 Hummell $10–20
4051 5 cm PAK $10–20
4052 222 Armored Car.................$10–20
4054 Brumbar $10–20
4055 234/I Armored Car $10–20
4058 Tiger II with Porsche Turret $10–20
4061 7/2 Half-track with 3.7 FLAK.$10–20
4062 2 cm Quad FLAF and trailer...$10–20
4063 3.7 FLAK on trailer................$10–20
4064 88 PAK $10–20
4065 105 Howitzer......................$10–20
4066 Ferdinand..........................$10–20
4067 Elefant $10–20
4068 250/7 Mortar Half-track.......$10–20

Comet Miniatures (also see Simba)

Comet Miniatures is an English company that has reportedly produced a pair of replicas, under the Mini Metal brand, of the Seaview and Flying Sub from the popular seventies TV series *Voyage to the Bottom of the Sea*. The models, according to R. C. Johnston of White Rock, British Columbia, were produced in 1988. The Mini Metalls brand is also used by Simba, a company

that offers 1998 Volkswagen New Beetle models in various colors and styles, as reported by collector Tjeng-Bo Lie of Plano, Texas. (See Simba.)
Voyage to the Bottom of the Sea Seaview Submarine, MM-07, 1988.................$20–35
Voyage to the Bottom of the Sea Flying Sub, MM-03, 1988 ....$20–35

Con-Cor

Con-Cor vehicles are 1:87 scale pre-painted plastic models that feature full-color lettering on sides and ends. All vehicles are pre-assembled. Included in the series are semis with trailers, separate semi trailers, rail containers, cars, and buses, all designed for use with HO gauge railroad layouts.

Con-Cor Semi with Trailer

Atchison, Topeka & Santa Fe Freight Truck $8
Brillion Freight Truck....................$8
Chiquita Freight Truck..................$9
Evergreen Freight Truck................$8
Hi-Way Dispatch Freight Truck.................$8
Mayflower Moving Van.................$12
Miller Truck Log Truck..................$8
Pacific Fruit Express $8
Palumbo Open Back Truck............$8
Pepsi Freight Truck.......................$8
Registered Texas Longhorns $8
Riteway Double Freighter $11
Rollins Freight Truck.....................$8
Safety Kleen Tanker.....................$10
Texaco Tanker............................$10
Texas Oil Tanker..........................$8
Transcon Double Freight Truck..............$11
Union Tanker................................$8
US Mail Freight Truck $9

Con-Cor "America 500 Years" Semi with Trailer, Special Edition

Columbus....................................$17
Monuments.................................$17
New York Skyline.........................$17
Space...$17
US Capital...................................$17
Wild West...................................$17

Con-Cor Bluebird School Buses

Camp Woebegon $11
County #4..................................$11
Good Shepherd $11
Helping Hand Temporary Labor...........$11
Maintenance-of-Way.....................$11
Unified School Dist. #2....................$11
US Army $11
Washington HS $11

Con-Cor Autos and Others

'57 Chevy...................................$8
'69 Mustang................................$8
Ferrari Testarossa $8
Fire Chief 4x4 ....$3.50
Ford Mustang.............................$8
Lamborghini...............................$8
Mercedes-Benz 300E $3

Conquest

Conquest models are exquisite 1:43 scale cars hand built in England.

1 1954 Oldsmobile Starfire 98 Convertible, top down, two-tone.................................$189
1a 1954 Oldsmobile Starfire 98 Convertible, top down, one-tone.........................$169
2 1960 Chevrolet Impala Convertible, top down...$189
2a 1960 Chevrolet Impala Convertible, top up...$189
3 1955 Buick Super hard top, three-tone ...$210
4 1963 Ford Galaxie 500 XL Convertible, top down...$189
4a 1963 Ford Galaxie 500 XL hard top, limited...$210
5 1954 Oldsmobile 98 Holiday hard top .$198
6 1957 Imperial Crown Southhampton 4-Door hard top...$198
7 1957 Buick Roadmaster 75 Riviera 4-Door hard top...$198
8 1954 Pontiac Star Chief Convertible, top down...$198
9 1963 Ford Country Squire station wagon...$198
10 1950 Lincoln Cosmopolitan 4-Door Sedan...$198
11 1955 Buick Super Convertible, top down...$198
11a 1955 Buick Super Convertible, top up...$198
11D 1955 Buick Super Convertible, top down, continental kit.................................$279
12 1960 Cadillac Fleetwood Sixty Special 4-Door hard top......................................$198
13 1956 Plymouth Savoy 4-Door Sedan ...$179
14 1948 Pontiac Torpedo Eight Deluxe Convertible, top down................................$189
14a 1948 Pontiac Torpedo Eight Deluxe Convertible, top up.................................$189
15 1956 Buick Special Convertible, top down...$198
16 1957 Ford Thunderbird hard top.........$189
17 1954 Pontiac Star Chief Custom Catalina hard top...$189
18 1958 Cadillac Fleetwood.....................$235
19 1955 Oldsmobile 98 Holiday 4-Door hard top...$235
20 1960 Plymouth Fury.............................$210
30 1947 Cadillac Fleetwood 75.............$275
32 1962 Cadillac Series 62 Convertible, heather and maize.............................$270

Conrad (also see Gescha)

Conrad of Germany is a brand name applied in the seventies to a line of heavy equipment models originally introduced under the Gescha brand in the 1960s. Conrad models are currently available. Gescha models meanwhile are no longer made, rare, and highly valued.

1000 Mercedes-Benz 230 C-280 CE, 1:35 ....$18
1001 Mercedes-Benz 200-280 T Wagon, 1:35 ....$18
1002 Mercedes-Benz 280-450 Sedan, 1:35 ....$18
1010 Volkswagen Passat GLS, 1:43 ....$18
1011 Volkswagen Passat Variant, 1:43 .....$18
1012 Audi 80 Coupe, 1:43 ....$9
1013 Volkswagen Scirocco GLI, 1:43 ....$60
1014 Volkswagen Polo C, 1:43 ....$9
1015 Volkswagen Santana GL, 1:43 ....$18
1016 Volkswagen Kombi, 1:43...............$24
1017 Volkswagen Kombi with Glass Rack, 1:43 ....$24
1018 1917 Graf & Stift Fire Truck, 1:43.....$60
1018 OAF Fire Truck, 1:43.....................$52
1019 American LaFrance Fire Truck, 1:43 ...$60
1020 Audi Quattro Coupe, 1:43 ....$18
1021 Volkswagen Polo Coupe, 1:43 ....$18
1022 Audi 100, 1:43.................................$9
1023 American LaFrance Fire Truck, 1:43 ...$78
1024 American LaFrance Fire Truck, 1:43 ...$94
1025 1910 Dennis Fire Truck, 1:43...........$52
1026 1928 Volvo Flat Truck, 1:43.............$60
1027 1921 MAN Old Timer Fire Engine, 1:43 ....$55
1028 1947 Volvo LV153 Stake Truck, 1:43 .$46
1029 1949 Volvo LV293 C2LF Stake Truck, 1:43 ....$49
1030 1928 Volvo Old Timer Fire Engine, 1:43 ....$49
1031 1902 White Old Timer Pie Wagon, 1:43 ....$32
1032 MAN KVB "Messer Griesheim" Gas Van, 1:50 ....$35
1033 1958 Magirus Stetter Old Timer Concrete Mixer, 1:43 ....$54
1034 1955 Mercedes-Benz Racing Transporter, 1:43 ....$45
1035 1920 MAN Gas Tanker "Messer Griesham," 1:43 ....$44
1035 Mercedes-Benz Liquid Truck, 1:43 .....$38
1036 1950 Magirus Low Side Dump Truck, 1:43 ....$42
1037 Volvo Titan L395 Flatbed Truck, 1:43.$48
1076 Mercedes-Benz 280-450, 1:35........$18
1282 Case 580D Construction King Loader/Backhoe, 1:35, Silver Anniversary 1957–1982...............................$90-120
1501 Mercedes-Benz 230 C-280 CE $18
1502 Mercedes-Benz 200-280 T Wagon, 1:35 ....$18
1503 Mercedes-Benz 200 TD-300 TD Wagon, 1:35 ....$34
1504 Mercedes-Benz 300CE Coupe, 1:35 .$34
1601 Mercedes-Benz 230 C-300 CE, 1:35 ....$18
1602 Mercedes-Benz 207 D Bus, 1:50......$18
1603 Mercedes-Benz 207 D Van, 1:50.....$18
1604 Mercedes-Benz Van, 1:50 ....$18
1605 Mercedes-Benz 100/130/150 Bus, 1:50 ....$60
1606 Mercedes-Benz 170 Van, 1:50 ....$34
1607 Mercedes-Benz 206 Van, 1:50 ....$34

1608 Mercedes Van Type 208, 1:50........$34
1620 Mercedes-Benz 507D Van, 1:43......$18
2000 Condecta Mobile Crane, 1:87.........$85
2010 Peiner Tower Crane, 1:87................$85
2011 Potain Truck Crane, 1:87 ....$79–88
2012 Zeppelin ZBK 100 Truck Crane, 1:87...$79–88
2013 BPR Cadillon GT2210 Truck Crane, 1:87...$79–88
2014 Potain GMR Crane, 1:50...........$79–88
2020 Liebherr HC120 Tower Crane, 1:87...$69–78
2021 Liebherr 21K Tower Crane, 1:50...$75
2022 Liebherr 112 HC-K Tower Crane, 1:87...$104
2023 Liebherr 28K Mobile Tower Crane, 1:50...$87–94
2030 MAN-Wolff Tower Crane, 1:87........$85
2040 Putzmeister Cement Pump, 1:50......$100
2070 Krupp 80T Crane Truck, 1:50..........$85
2071 P & H T-1300 Crane Truck, 1:50......$85
2072 Liebherr Crane Truck, 1:50.............$85
2073 Clark 720 Crane Truck, 1:50............$85
2074 Gottwald Hydraulic Crane, 1:50......$85
2075 P & H Omega Crane, 1:50...............$85
2076 Liebherr LTM 1030 Crane, 1:50.......$85
2077 Krupp 250 GMT Crane, 1:50...........$85
2078 Wirth Rotary Drill Truck, 1:50..........$95
2079 Liebherr LT 1060 Crane, 1:50..........$95
2080 Krupp 70 GMT Crane, 1:50..............$95
2081 Demag AC435 Superlift Crane, 1:50...$109–118
2082 Liebherr 1160 Truck Crane $109
2083 Liebherr LTM1025 Truck Crane, 1:50...$69–78
2084 Faun Mobile Crane, 1:50...........$89–98
2085 Liebherr 1090 Crane, 1:50......$99–108
2086 Demag AC155 Truck Crane, 1:50...$79-88
2110 Peiner Container Lift, 1:87 ....$75
2410 Terex 72/71 Wheel Loader, 1:43 ...$85
2411 Terex TS-14B Scraper, 1:43 ....$85
2420 Dresser Wheel Loader, 1:50...........$65
2421 Furukawa 345 Wheel Loader, 1:50...$64
2422 O&K L55 Wheel Loader, 1:50...$58–65
2425 Hanomag 70E Wheel Loader, 1:50 .$60
2426 Case 621 Wheel Loader with attachments, 1:35.................................$60
2427 Hanomag 15F Wheel Loader, 1:50...$38–42
2428 Hanomag CL310 Compactor/ Bucket...$65–70
2430 GHH LF12 Wheel Loader, 1:50......$65
2501 Tamrock Tunnel Drill....................$50
2502 Grove AMZ66 Manlift, 1:50......$35–64
2701 Voest-Alpine Road Roller, 1:35......$60
2702 Losenhausen Vibromax Roller, 1:35...$60
2703 Case Vibromax 1102 Roller, 1:35....$58
2704 Case Vibromax 854K Roller, 1:35...$45–58
2705 Case W102 Roller......................$32
2710 Bomag BW213D Roller, 1:50 ....$48

2711 Bomag BW120 AD-2 Roller, 1:50.................................$34–55
2721 Dresser 830E 200 Ton Dumper, 1:50...........................$109–118
2722 Dresser 210M 55 Ton Mining Dump Truck, 1:50.....................$69–78
2741 Caterpillar PS500 Compactor..........$49
2762 Terex Articulated Dump Truck............$52
2771 O&K RH120C Shovel, 1:50..........$124
2772 Demag H135S Hydraulic Shovel, 1:50..................................$108
2801 Liebherr 731 Dozer-Ripper, 1:50.......$55
2802 Liebherr Track Loader, 1:50..............$60
2803 Liebherr 722 Dozer, 1:50..............$54
2804 Liebherr RL422 Pipe Layer, 1:50.......$58
2810 Sennebogen Mobile Crane, 1:50.....$60
2812 Sennebogen Backhoe, 1:50.............$60
2814 Sennebogen 526 Excavator, 1:50.....$60
2815 Zeppelin ZR28 ABI Pile Driver Excavator, 1:50..................................$79–88
2817 Sennebogen Backhoe with Blade......$60
2817 Zeppelin ZM15 Wheel Excavator, 1:50..................................$42–54
2817 Hanomag Wheel Loader, 1:50.....$42
2818 Furukawa W625E Wheel Backhoe, 1:50......................................$54
2818 Dresser Wheel Excavator, 1:50.......$36
2819 Furukawa 625E Track Backhoe, 1:50.$54
2819 Dresser Track Excavator, 1:50..........$40
2821 Liebherr 921 Excavator, 1:50..........$60
2822 Liebherr 912 Excavator, 1:50..........$60
2823 Liebherr 991 Backhoe, 1:50..........$60
2824 Liebherr 991 Excavator, 1:50..........$60
2825 Liebherr 922 Hydraulic Excavator, 1:50..$65
2826 Liebherr 952 Excavator, 1:50..........$60
2827 Liebherr 984 Shovel, 1:50...............$88
2828 Liebherr 984 Backhoe, 1:50.............$88
2829 Liebherr R912 Track Hoe, 1:50........$58
2830 Liebherr A912 Lit. Wheel Clam, 1:50..$64
2831 Liebherr HS881 Hydraulic Cable Excavator, 1:50...............................$109
2831 Liebherr HS882 Track Lat Crane, 1:50....................................$118
2832 Liebherr A932 Scrap Grapple Excavator, 1:50..$65
2833 Liebherr A310 Wheel Backhoe, 1:50.$58
2834 Liebherr 954 Backhoe, 1:50............$65
2835 Liebherr 932 Track Scrap Hand, 1:50..$65
2840 Caterpillar 950 Loader, 1:25.........$90
2841 Caterpillar 950 Loader-Ripper, 1:50..$65
2842 Fuchs Excavator with Magnet Lift, 1:50..$64
2850 Caterpillar D10 Dozer-Ripper, 1:50...$65
2851 Caterpillar D6H Bulldozer, 1:50.......$65
2852 Caterpillar D11N Dozer-Ripper, 1:50..$65
2853 Hanomag Dozer, 1:50.....................$42
2854 Caterpillar D11 Dozer, 1:50............$99
2862 Caterpillar D400 Dump Truck, 1:50..$62
2873 1931 Caterpillar 60 Diesel, limited numbered edition, 1:25.....................$75
2882 Liebherr L522 Wheel Loader, 1:50...$44

2883 Liebherr L507 Wheel Loader, 1:50...$40
2886 Caterpillar 936 Wheel Loader, 1:50.$42
2887 Liebherr 531 Wheel Loader, 1:50....$64
2889 Caterpillar CS653 Roller, 1:50.........$44
2892 Case-Poclain 1088 Maxi Backhoe, 1:50..$48
2893 Case-Poclain 81P Excavator, 1:50....$52
2894 Case 2188 Track Excavator, 1:50....$54
2901 Atlas Wheel Backhoe with Blade, 1:50..$60
2902 Atlas 1704 Track Excavator, 1:50....$60
2903 Atlas 1704 Track Backhoe, 1:50....$48
2904 Atlas 1304 Wheel Excavator/Clam, 1:50..$54
2910 Fiat-Allis Dozer-Ripper, 1:50...........$65
2920 Scheid PV 60 Roller, 1:50...............$75
2931 Case 580 D Tractor Loader, 1:35.$70–85
2932 Case 580 G Tractor Loader, 1:35....$80
2933 Case 580 E Tractor Loader, 1:35....$80
2934 Case 580 Super K with serial number, gold, 1:35............................$88
2935 Case 580 K Tractor Loader, 1:50.....$65
2936 Case 590X Tractor Backhoe Load, 1:35..$78
2951 Massey Ferguson 50B Loader, 1:35..$75
2952 Massey Ferguson 50D Loader, 1:35.$75
2954 Massey Ferguson 60HX Loader/Backhoe, 1:35..$92
2960 Case Drott 50 Track Backhoe, 1:35..$75
2961 Case Drott 980B Track Backhoe, 1:35..$75
2962 Case 1280 Track Excavator, 1:35....$75
2963 Case DH4B Trencher, 1:32.............$75
2964 Case 1085B Wheel Backhoe, 1:35.$65
2965 Case 125B Track Backhoe, 1:35.....$65
2966 Case 760 Trencher, 1:35.................$65
2970 Clark H500 Forklift, 1:25...............$45
2971 Clark ECA Forklift, 1:25.................$45
2972 Clark Forklift, 1:25........................$29
2980 Caterpillar Forklift, 1:25................$35
2981 Linde R14 Forklift, 1:25.................$64
2982 Linde R16 Forklift, 1:25.................$54
2983 Fenwick T20 Forklift, 1:25.............$32
2983 Linde Lift Truck, 1:25....................$25
2984 Jungheinrich ECE Forklift, 1:25..........$34
2985 Linde E25 Forklift, 1:25.................$58
2990 Yale Forklift, 1:25.........................$65
2991 Kalmar LMV 22 Forklift, 1:50.........$65
2992 Yale Forklift, 1:25.........................$65
2993 Case 586E Forklift, 1:35................$65
2994 Jungheinrich Forklift, 1:25...............$64
2995 Jungheinrich Forklift, 1:25...............$64
2996 Lansing Forklift, 1:25.....................$42
2997 Jungheinrich EJC 12.5 Forklift, 1:25..$48
2998 Yale Forklift, 1:25.....................$42–58
2999 Kalmar Forklift 40' Container, 1:50....$88
3009 Mercedes-Benz Titan Truck Tractor, 1:50..$90
3010 Mercedes-Benz Low Loader Semi, 1:50..$90
3011 Mercedes-Benz Truck & Trailer "BayWa," 1:50..$90
3012 Mercedes-Benz Truck & Trailer, 1:50 .$90

3013 Mercedes-Benz Truck & Trailer "Spedition Lueg," 1:50..............................$90
3014 Mercedes-Benz Spitzer Silo Semi, 1:50..$90
3015 Mercedes Semi Bulker L Hoist, 1:50 ..$84
3016 Mercedes-Benz Truck & Trailer "Mobelspedition" or "Pfenning" logo, 1:50.....$90
3019 Mercedes-Benz Gas Cylinder Semi "Air Products," 1:50..........................$90
3020 Mercedes-Benz Container Semi, 1:50..$90
3021 Mercedes-Benz Pipe Carrier, 1:50....$90
3022 Mercedes-Benz Tanker Semi, 1:50....$90
3023 Mercedes-Benz Gas Tanker Semi "L'Air Liquide" or Fedgas"......................$90
3024 Mercedes-Benz Gas Cylinder Semi "Messer Griesheim," 1:50....................$90
3025 Mercedes-Benz Low Loader Semi, 1:50..$90
3026 Mercedes-Meiller Dump Truck, 1:50..$90
3027 Mercedes-Benz Semi Tanker "Linde," 1:50..$78
3029 Mercedes-Benz Semi Trailer Truck, 1:50..$90
3030 Mercedes-Benz Open Semi, 1:50.....$90
3030 Mercedes-Benz Covered Semi, 1:50.$90
3031 Mercedes-Benz Covered Truck & Trailer, 1:50..$90
3032 Mercedes-Benz Covered Truck, 1:50.$90
3033 Mercedes-Kuka Garbage Truck, 1:50$90
3034 Mercedes-Hegla Glass Truck, 1:50 ..$90
3037 MAN Small Truck, 1:43..................$18
3038 Mercedes-Benz Refrigerator Truck, 1:50..$90
3039 Mercedes-Haller Garbage Truck, 1:50..$90
3040 Mercedes-Benz Dump Truck, 1:50.....$90
3041 Mercedes-Leach Garbage Truck, 1:50..$90
3042 Mercedes-Schorling Sweeper, 1:50..$90
3043 Mercedes-Benz 1300 Tractor, 1:50..$60
3044 Mercedes-Benz Cement Mixer, 1:50.$90
3045 Mercedes-Benz Cement Mixer, 1:50.$90
3046 Mercedes-Benz Open Semi, 1:50.....$90
3047 Schorling Street Sweeper, 1:50........$90
3048 Mercedes-Benz Container Truck, 1:50..$90
3049 Mercedes-Faun Garbage Truck, 1:50.$90
3050 Mercedes-Liebherr Cement Mixer, 1:50..$90
3052 Mercedes-Benz Putzmeister Mixer/Pumper, 1:50..$94
3053 Mercedes-Benz Tank Truck, 1:50......$90
3054 Mercedes-Benz Single Car Transporter, 1:50..$90
3060 Mercedes-Benz Semi Suction Unit, 1:50..$94
3064 Mercedes-Benz Mixer "Blank Betonova," 1:50..$72
3066 Mercedes-Benz Suction Vehicle Vacuum TA, 1:50....................................$64
3069 Mercedes-Benz Schorling P17 Snow Sweeper, 1:50..........................$98

3079 Mercedes-Benz Faun Drain Cleaner Vacuum, 1:50 .... $68
3085 Ericsson Radar, 1:50 .... $39
3086 Mercedes-Benz Putzmeister 52/5 5-Axle Concrete Pump, 1:50 .... $94
3088 Liebherr LTF1030 Crane, 1:50 .... $94
3093 Mercedes-Benz Schwing 32XL Pump, 1:50 .... $84
3095 Putzmeister 3-Axle Concrete Pump, 1:50 .... $78
3245 Magirus Liebherr Mixer, 1:50 .... $46
3264 Iveco Stetter 4-Axle Mixer, 1:50 .... $78
3274 Iveco 4-Axle Dump, 1:50 .... $68
3274 Magirus 4-Axle Dump, 1:50 .... $39
3330 Bedford Semi Flatbed, 1:50 .... $72
3464 Steyer/Stetter 4-Axle Mixer, 1:50 ..... $72
3519 Freightliner with "Air Products" Trailer, 1:50 .... $59
3520 Freightliner T/T Container, 1:50 .... $92
3523 Mercedes-Benz "Messer Griesheim" Bulk Gas Semi, 1:50 .... $78
3640 Mack Dump Truck, 1:50 .... $65
3641 Mack Refuse Truck, 1:50 .... $55
3669 Mack Airport Plow and Sweeper, 1:50 .... $109
3744 Volvo NL12 Concrete Mixer, 1:50 ... $78
3755 Volvo NL12 Atlas Gondola Truck, 1:50 .... $72
3775 Volvo NL12 Conventional Dump Truck, 1:50 .... $72
3776 Volvo Low Sideboard Truck, 1:50 ..... $49
3777 Volvo NL10 Water Truck, 1:50 .... $72
3812 Freightliner Conventional "Talbert," 1:50 .... $78
3819 Freightliner Conventional "Air Products," 1:50 .... $92
3820 Freightliner Truck with Box Trailer, 1:50 .. $59
3826 Freightliner Conventional Dump Trailer, 1:50 .... $65
3912 Volvo Semi With Talbert Lowboy, 1:50 .... $78
3928 Volvo NL12 Semi with Refrigerator Trailer, 1:50 .... $92
4111 MAN Schmitz Heavy Haulage Trailer, 1:50 .... $94
4127 MAN Semi Linde TVTS30 Tanker, 1:50 .... $72
4150 MAN Semi Concrete Mix Stetter, 1:50 .... $72
4165 MAN 4-Axle Mixer "Liebherr," 1:50 .. $64
4166 MAN Haller Suction Truck, 1:50 .... $78
4167 MAN 4-Axle Roll-Off, 1:50 .... $58
4178 Huffermeister Roll-Off, 1:50 .... $75
4179 MAN Drain Cleaner, 1:50 .... $55
4196 Mercedes-Benz Silo Transporter, 1:50 .... $72
4199 MAN Atlas 130.1 Crane Truck, 1:50 .... $64
4220 Iveco Transporter, 1:50 .... $39
4236 Iveco Euro Cargo Truck, 1:50 .... $48
4298 Iveco Eurotech Truck, 1:50 .... $58
4315 Volvo F12 Semi Bulk Carrier, 1:50 .... $69–92

4317 Volvo F16 Logging Truck/Trailer, 1:50 .... $69–94
4327 Volvo Double Trailer truck, 1:50 .... $55
4372 Volvo Euro Trotter, 1:50 .... $59
4392 Volvo F12 Air Crash Tender, 1:50 .... $78
4564 Volvo FL10 3X Concrete Mixer, 1:50. $64
4589 Volvo FL6 Container Tailgate Lift, 1:50 .... $65
4594 Volvo Schwing KVM52 Concrete Pump, 1:50 .... $118
4608 Volvo FH12 with Refrigerator Trailer, 1:50 .... $88
4609 Volvo FH16 with 4-Axle Trailer, 1:50. $94
4840 Iveco Euro Trekker Dump Truck, 1:50. $44
4961 Iveco Eurostar with Tank Trailer, 1:50. $72
4898 Iveco Euro Truck, 1:50 .... $45
5016 Mercedes Farm Tractor, 1:43 .... $25
5017 Mercedes-Benz 800 Tractor, 1:43 ... $18
5018 Steyer Farm Tractor, 1:43 .... $25
5066 Elgin Pelican Street Sweeper, 1:50 ... $68
5068 Multicar Utility, 1:50 .... $42
5201 Kassbohrer Pisten Bully Snow, 1:43 . $92
5401 Case 1845C Uniloader, 1:50 .... $42
5402 Putzmeister Worm Pump, 1:50 .... $35
5403 Rosenbauer Fox Fire Pump, 1:50 ..... $38
5404 Mercedes-Benz Messer Griesheim Acetylene Cutte, 1:50 .... $98
5405 Putzmeister Concrete Mixer Trailer, 1:35 .... $54
5406 Demag SC40DS-2 Compressor, 1:24 .... $42
5421 Mercedes-Benz Highway Bus, 1:50 .. $55
5422 Mercedes-Benz Articulated Bus, 1:50. $98
5423 MAN Luxury Coach Bus, 1:50 .... $78
5505 E-1 Hush 95' Ladder Fire Truck, 1:50. $84
5506 E-1 Hush 80' Ladder Fire Truck, 1:50. $84
5507 E-1 Titan III, 1:50 .... $75
5510 E-1 Hush Pumper Fire Truck, 1:50 ... $84
5512 Falcon Fire Truck, 1:50 .... $75
6036 MAN Type L2000 Truck, 1:50 .... $44
6107 MAN F2000 Semi Container Truck, 1:50 .... $84
6165 MAN F2000 Liebherr 904 Mixer, 1:50 .... $62
9996 Liebherr Boom Extensions, 1:50 ...... $14
9997 Lattice Tower Extensions for 2011 Potain Tower Crane, 1:87 .... $14
9998 Lattice Tower Extensions for 2012 Zeppelin ZBK100 Tower Crane, 19:50 1:87 .... $14
9999 Lattice Tower Extensions for 2013 BPR Cadillon GT2210 Tower Crane, 1:87 .. $14

COPy Cars

Jeff Mantyak reports that COPy Cars are similar to Road Champs police cars (likely customized off Road Champs chassis), but are produced by a Canadian model company. The models are Chevrolet Caprices representing an assortment of Canadian police vehicles, with opening doors and trunks, and pullback action. Order from Coppers Collectibles, 2514-23 Avenue South, Lethbridge, Alberta T1K 1K9

Canada, phone: 403-329-8378, fax: 403-329-4055, email: coppers@telusplanet.net
Ontario Provincial Police $15–20
Peel Regional Police $15–20

Cor-Cor

It was 1925 when Louis A. Corcoran started Cor-Cor, later changing the name to Corcoran Metal Products after a plant fire and a move to a new location. The company continued until 1941 when Corcoran retired for health reasons.
Chrysler Airflow $1,250
DeSoto Airflow $1,250
Graham Paige Sedan, electric, 20" $1,600

Corgi (also see Original Omnibus Co., Oriental Omnibus Co., Race Image, Husky, Detail Cars)

The Corgi legacy is a rich one, beginning in 1934 with parent company Mettoy of Swansea, South Wales. In 1956 Mettoy merged with Playcraft Ltd. to form Mettoy Playcraft Ltd. In 1993, Mattel bought the Corgi brand and attempted for a short time to maintain the tradition of producing Corgi quality collectible toys. Shortly afterward, employees of the British manufacturing center reportedly bought back the Corgi Collectibles line. Corgi has since been purchased (as of July 1999) by Zindart, an American-owned company based in Hong Kong. Visit Corgi's new Corgi Shop website at www.corgi-shop.co.uk.

Several books have been written about Corgis, and the multitude of models produced certainly could fill a book or more. So instead we present a survey of the models produced over the years, along with current collector values.

Popular Corgi models such as the Beatles' Yellow Submarine are now being reproduced to give new collectors a second chance at getting the good ones at a reasonable price.

A Survey of Corgi Models Through the Years

Aston Martin DB4, #309, 1962–1965 .... $50–65

Aston Martin DB5 (see James Bond)

The Avengers Gift Set #40, 1966–1969 ....$250–300
Includes John Steed & Emma Peal figures, #318 Emma's Lotus Elan, #9001 John Steed's Bentley

The Avengers 1927 Bentley with John Steed figure, #9001, 1964–1969 ......$125–150

The Avengers 1927 Bentley with John Steed figure, 1998 reissue $40

Batmobile, #267, 1966 ....$450–500

Batboat, #107, 1967 ....$350–375

Batmobile and Batboat, Gift Set #3, 1967–1981 ....$850–900

The Beatles Yellow Submarine, #803, 1969–1970 ....$600–750

The Beatles Yellow Submarine, 1997 reissue $55–70

Cadillac Superior Ambulance, #437, 1962–1968 ....$65–80

Chevrolet Astro 1 Experimental Car, #347 ....$45–60

Chevrolet Camaro SS 350, #338, 1968–1970 ....$80–100

Chipperfield's Circus Karrier Booking Office Truck, #426, 1962–1964...$125–150

Chipperfield's Circus Chevrolet Booking Office Truck, #426, 1978–1981 ....$45–60

Chipperfield's Circus Cage Wagon, #1123, 1961–1968 ....$75–90

Chipperfield's Circus Crane Truck, #1121, 1960–1968 ....$90–110

Chipperfield's Circus Crane Truck, #1144, 1969–1972 ....$100–125

Chipperfield's Circus Giraffe Truck, #503, 1964–1971 ....$90–110

Chipperfield's Circus Horse Van, #1130, 1962–1972 ....$100–125

Chipperfield's Circus Land Rover and Elephant Cage, Gift Set #19, 1962–1969 ....$125–150

Chipperfield's Circus Parade Vehicle, #487, 1969–1979 ....$75–90

Chipperfield's Circus Performing Poodles Truck and Ring, #487, 1967–1979 ....$75–90

Chipperfield's Circus Transporter, #1139, 1968–1972 ....$100–125

Chitty Chitty Bang Bang Car, #266, 1968–1972 ....$450–600

Chitty Chitty Bang Bang Car, 1992 reissue $175–225

Citroën Ski Team Car with skier, #475, 1964–1967 ....$45–60

Ecurie Ecosse Racing Transporter, #1126, 1961–1965 ....$90–120

Ford Holmes Wrecker, #1142, 1967–1974 ....$100–125

Ford Express Semi-Trailer Truck, #1137, 1965–1970 ....$80–110

1957 Ford Thunderbird, #810, 1983 ....$50–65

Garbage Truck, #1116, 1979......$30–40

Green Hornet's Black Beauty, #268, 1967–1972...$425–450

Heinkel $30–40

Jaguar XJ12C, #286, 1974–1979 .$25–40

Jaguar XJS Motul, #318, 1983 ....$20–30

James Bond Aston Martin DB5, 1st issue #261 metallic gold, 1965–1968 ....$125–175

James Bond Aston Martin DB5, 2nd issue #270 metallic silver with red tire rippers, 1968 ....$90–120

James Bond Aston Martin DB5, 3rd issue #271 metallic silver with Whizzwheels, 1978 ....$45–65

James Bond Aston Martin DB5, 4th issue with spoked wheels, 1997 reissue..........$40

James Bond Citroën 2CV, #272, 1981–1982 ....$50–65

James Bond Citroën 2CV, 1997 reissue .$40

James Bond Lotus Esprit, #269, 1977 ....$60–75

James Bond Lotus Esprit, 1997 reissue $40

James Bond Moon Buggy, 1972 ....$600

James Bond Moon Buggy, 1997 reissue $40

James Bond Toyota 2000 GT, 1967...$625

James Bond Toyota 2000 GT, 1997 reissue $40

Lincoln Continental Stretch Limousine with lighted TV in back seat, #262, 1967–1969 ....$100–125

Man from U.N.C.L.E. Blue Oldsmobile, #497, 1966.........................$450

Mazda B1600 Pickup, #493, 1975–1978 ....$25–40

1956 Mercedes-Benz 300S, Convertible Top Down, #806, 1983 ....$35–50

1956 Mercedes-Benz 300S Convertible Top Up, #805, 1983 ....$35–50

MGB GT, #327, 1967–1968......$60–75

MGC GT, #345, 1969.............$60–75

The Monkees Monkeemobile, #277, 1968 ....$525

The Muppets Kermit's Car, #2030...$30–45

The Muppets Fozzie Bear's Truck, #2031 ....$30–45

The Muppets Miss Piggy's Sports Car, #2032 ....$30–45

The Muppets Animal's Percussionmobile, #2033 ....$30–45

NSU Sport-Prinz, 1:43........................$60–75

Plymouth Sports Suburban Station Wagon, #219, 1959–1963 ....$100–125

Plymouth Sports Suburban Station Wagon, #445, 1963–1965............$75–90

Plymouth Sports Suburban Station Wagon Mail Car, #443, 1963–1966.$65–80

Popeye's Paddle Wagon, #802, 1969 ....$650

Rolls-Royce Corniche, #279, 1979 .$30–40

The Saint's Volvo P1800, #258, 1965 ....$225–275

Studebaker Golden Hawk, #211, 1958–1965 ....$65–80

Tour de France Citroën, #510, 1970–1972 ....$65–80

Volkswagen Fire Van $20–30

Tour de France Commer TV Camera Van, #479, 1967–1972 ....$60–75
Tour de France Renault, Gift Set #13 includes bicyclist and car with movie camera, 1968–1972 ....$65–80

Corgi Truckers

In the early eighties, Corgi issued a series of 1:64 scale contemporary trucks marketed as Corgi Truckers that have since been incorporated into Mattel's Corgi Auto-City line. New models as of 1997 are called Hot Wheels Haulers.

"Unsung Heroes" Utility Truck, 1:43 $20–30

Ford "Pepsi" Cargo Truck $5–6
Ford "Kraft Dairylea Cheese Spread" Cargo Truck $5–6
Ford Dump Truck $5–6
Ford "Duckham's" Tanker $5–6
Kenworth "7UP" $5–6
M.A.N. "Raleigh" Truck $5–6
M.A.N. Dump Truck $5–6
M.A.N. "BP" Tanker $5–6

Corgi Greyhound Buses

Greyhound's "Dog and Target" design was first used to demonstrate solidarity with Great Britain during the attack on London by the Germans in 1939. Below are listed several variations of one bus style. All of these models were currently available as of this writing.

Greyhound Coach
v.1 "Philadelphia" $35
v.2 "New York Central RR" $30
v.3 "Pennsylvania RR" $30
v.4 "Trailways," teardrop design $30
v.5 "Trailways," pinstripe design $30
v.6 "Champlain," with billboard $30
v.7 "Los Angeles" $35
v.8 "New York" Public Service Coach $35
v.9 "WACS" $30

v.10 "WAVES" $30
v.11 New York/Albany/Montreal Coach with billboard $30

Corgi Mack Fire Trucks

Mack Pumper, "Chicago," 1994 ....$25
Mack "B" Pumper," Paxtonia," 1995 .....$35

Corgi Race Image Collectibles

According to Corgi's website, "The Corgi brand has been the hallmark of high-quality diecast models for over 40 years and, as a result, has worldwide following for both old and new production. All products are designed in Britain to the highest standards and traditions which guarantee the authenticity of every model.

"Corgi now brings this considerable experience to the US racing collectibles market and offers the following features on exciting models at an affordable price:

"Super detailed 1:64 scale semi's, strictly limited editions, numbered certificates of authenticity, chromed stack and wheels, diecast cabs, chrome mirrors, soft tires, twin wheels, Ford Aeromax and Kenworth T800 cabs." The Race Image brand is now associated with Lucky Plan. Corgi Race Image models are now out of production.

Corgi Race Image Transporter & Car 1:64 Scale
The Family Channel Racing Team $15–20
Kellogg's Corn Flakes Racing $15–20
Kodak Racing $15–20
La Victoria/Winnebago with rail dragster $20–25
Maxwell House/Bobby Labonte ...$15–20
Mopar Xpress/Tommy Johnson Jr. Top Fuel with rail dragster $20–25
Quaker State/Brett Bodine $15–20
Slick 50/Ricky Smith $15–20
Slick 50/Western Auto.............$15–20
Slick 50/Winston Drag Racing.....$15–20
Syntec with rail dragster $20–25
Texaco Havoline/Davey Allison ...$15–20
Valvoline/Mark Martin $15–20
Winn Dixie Racing $15–20
La Victoria/Mike Dunn..............$40
Pennzoil /Eddie Hill $40
Castrol Syntec/Pat Austin $40
Valvoline/Joe Amato $40
Western Auto/Al Hofmann $40
Mooneyes/Kenji Okszaki $40
Kendall/Chuck Etchells $40
Corgi Race Image Cars only 1:64 Scale
John Force, 2 Car Set.................$45
Don Prudhomme / Skoal Bandit $45
NHRA 40th U.S. Nationals Drags ...$45

Corgi Rockets

#906 Jensen Interceptor, 1:64 ....$15-18

Husky Models

Corgi produced a series of small, inexpensive models in the sixties called Husky, later changed to Corgi Jrs. Here are just a few examples of Husky models. Typically,

current values are around $15 to $20 each, with a few notable exceptions as listed below.

Batmobile, Husky Extra, 1966............$350
Bedford TK 7-Ton Skip Truck, #27 (model courtesy of Brad Intermill, Eugene, Oregon) $25
Chitty Chitty Bang Bang, 1967 ....$400
James Bond Silver Aston Martin, 1966 ....$400
Jeep, #5, with #19 Boat and Trailer......$30
Man from U.N.C.L.E., 1966 ....$375
Monkeemobile, 1967 ....$400

Corgi Jrs.

Corgi Jrs., successors to the Husky line, are still being produced today. Current models are available for about $2 to $4 each. Here is a sampling of current and past models. While the prices on a few models may seem extremely high, they are nevertheless what at least one dealer is asking for these apparently hard-to-find items. When Mattel purchased Corgi, Corgi Jrs. became Corgi Auto-City models.

Hertz Bus..$5

Jaguar Racer..$3

"Pointers" Van $10

Batmobile, 1967 ....$325
Batboat, 1967 ....$325
BMW $3
BP Van $3
Buick Regal Police $3

Chitty Chitty Bang Bang, 1968 ....$275
Corvette $3
Garbage Truck $3
Helicopter..$3
Ironside Police Van, 1970 ....$325
James Bond Silver Aston Martin, 1966 .$400
Mercedes-Benz Ambulance $3
Mercedes Convertible $3
Mercedes Taxi $3
Military Jeep..$3
Monkeemobile, 1968 ....$275
Popeye's Paddle Wagon, 1971 ....$275
Porsche Targa $3
Shell Tanker $3
Stagecoach $12
Stern Wheeler $12

T-Bird...$5

Team Racing Van $3
Tipping Lorry $3

Corgi Classics, 1:43 scale

Bentley $20–30

Jaguar $25–30

Mercedes-Benz, blue $25–30

Mercedes-Benz, red $25–30
Rolls-Royce Corniche $30–35
T-Bird $25–30
Triumph TR-3 ....$20–25

Kiko Toys from Corgi
Kiko is the Mexican division of Corgi Jrs. Here is a small sampling of models from this series.

Austin Metro, #55, white $4–5
Caravan, #61, red $4–5
Caravan Fire, #806, red $4–5
Caravan Police, #821 ....$4–5
Chevy Van "Monica" $4–5
Renault 4 Van, #M5, red $4–5
Rover 3500 Fire Chief, #805 ....$4–5
Scania Van "Cascao" $4–5
Simca 1308, #M9 ....$4–5
Volkswagen Golf, #51, red $4–5
Volkswagen Golf Fire Chief, #809, red .$4–5
Volkswagen Van "Correios," #M6 ....$4–5

Corgi 1:18 Scale
95102 1996 MGF Convertible, green, introduced in 1996 ....$39

Courtland
"Prepared" cardboard was the material used for the first toys produced by Walter Rudolph Reach in 1943. The density of the material was nearly that of wood, and a lot cheaper. The success of those toys prompted Reach to start the Courtland Manufacturing Company the next year. The first Courtland brand toy was a wooden truck tractor and trailer. It wasn't long before wood was rejected in favor of inexpensive tin, thanks to Reach's connection with the Campbell's Soup Company and "rejected" tin from their canning operations.

Courtland prospered by obtaining huge orders from Sears, Roebuck and Company, along with big orders from several other companies in 1946.

The company suffered after Reach started producing toys with a mechanical motor that included a lifetime guarantee. That in itself wasn't the downfall. It was the counterfeit copies that showed up on the market with the Courtland name on them, most with inferior motors, that created a problem. Reach couldn't back out of his lifetime guarantee, and ended up replacing motors on toys his company didn't even produce.

Even so, Reach tried in 1953 to resurrect the company after moving to Philadelphia, hence the Courtland Toy Company was born. He attempted to capitalize on the popularity of Courtland toys by remanufacturing several of the original toys and a few new ones. It was plastic that did him in this time as tin toys were being phased out of the market in favor of the new, versatile material which Reach didn't have the capital to invest in retooling for plastic injection molding equipment. So it was in the same year, 1953, that the manufacture of Courtland toys ceased.

Checker Cab, green and yellow, 7¼" $300
Fire Chief Car, red and white, 7¼" $125
Space Rocket Patrol Car, 7¼" $250
State Police Car, mechanical with siren, 7¼" $250
Woody Sedan, 7¼" $125

Cougar (see Solido)

CPM
This series of vehicles, presumably made in England, comprised of 1:43 scale models.
Austin-Healey 100-6 Roadster.....................$39
1939 Buick 4-Door Sedan $39
Daimler SP250 Roadster $39
Guy "Eveready" Van $125
Jensen 541 Coupe $39
Morris 1000 4-Door Sedan, gray $39
Morris 1000 Convertible, white $39
1939 Studebaker Commander 2-Door Sedan, navy blue $39
Sunbeam Alpine Roadster, red/white/green .$39
Sunbeam Tiger Roadster $39
Triumph Spitfire Roadster, red $39

Craftoys
Omaha, Nebraska, was the home of Craftoys, an assortment of slush mold (lead alloy) toys similar to the early Best, Ralstoy, and Kansas Toy models. A short-lived company, it lasted just a few years before World War II set in and the lead was needed for the war.
Cement Mixer, #78, 3¾" $16
Fire Truck, #101, 4½" $30
Fordson Tractor, #17, 2½" $16
Freight Train, #3600, 16½", includes:
 Locomotive 0-6-4 "KT&N RR," 4½" $12
 Railroad cars, 3¼" ....$12 each
 Caboose, 2¾" $12
Miller FWD Indy Racer, #81, 4½" $20
Oil Truck, #104, 3¾" $30
Racer, #100, 4¼" $30
Speed Car, #103, 4¼" $30
Station Wagon, #105, 3¾" $30
Streamlined 2-Door Sedan, #92, 4" $30
Tanker, #102, 6¾" $30

Cragstan (Also see Gamda Koor, Sabra)
Cragstan is best known for battery operated robots, of which Mr. Atomic is most highly valued. In the late sixties to early seventies, Cragstan dabbled in diecast and produced some noteworthy 1:43 scale models under the Detroit Seniors brand.

Around the rest of the world, these models were sold as Gamda Koor or Sabra models, but in the US, they were sold under the Cragstan "Detroit Seniors" brand.

Dr. Craig S. Campbell, professor in the Department of Geography at Youngstown State University, collects diecast toys and finds that it relates well to his field of teaching. He reports that his Cragstan "Detroit Senior" is a 1:43 scale 1966 Chevrolet Impala Sedan police car with an opening trunk. "It is just a tad lighter in shade than a Navy blue, with a chrome plastic base," he reports. "The kicker is that it was made in Israel. On both sides are red shields with blue stars within the shields. I don't know if all

Cragstans were made in Israel, but this one was and I believe that they may have been made under contract by the Israeli diecast company Gamda Koor-Sabra, whose name I've seen in several places. The model has good detail and proportion and looks like an old Corgi or Dinky. Perhaps it is a casting borrowed from another diecast company. Does anyone know of a 1966 Chevy Impala Sedan that was made by Dinky or Solido or some other company?" Further research may reveal the facts.

1966 Buick Riviera
    v.1 various colors, #8108 .... $30–45
    v.2 Israeli Presidential Car, #8108/1 .$35–50
Cadillac De Ville Convertible, #8123 ....$35–50
Cadillac Eldorado
    v.1 various colors, #8110 .... $35–50
    v.2 Israeli Presidential Car, #8110/1 .$35–50
    v.3 Sheriff's Car, dark blue, #8110/2 .$35–50
Chevrolet Camaro SS, various colors, #8120 .... $35–50
1966 Chevrolet Chevelle Station Wagon
    v.1 various colors, #8100 .... $35–50
    v.2 Police, #8100/1 .... $35–50
    v.3 United Nations, #8100/2 ....$35–50
    v.4 Israeli Military, #8100/3 .... $35–50
    v.5 Israeli Post Service, #8100/4 ...$35–50
    v.6 Sabra Diving Club, #8100/5 ...$35–50
    v.7 Ambulance, white with red cross, #8101 .... $35–50
    v.8 Ambulance Israeli Magen David, cream with star, Hebrew text, #8101/1.$35–50
    v.9 Ambulance Israeli Military Ambulance, beige with white label, #8101/2 .... $35–50
    v.10 Fire Chief, red "Fire Chief," #8102 .... $35–50
    v.11 Israeli Fire Service, #8102/1 ..$35–50
1967 Chevrolet Corvair Monza Coupe, #8113 .... $30–45
1968 Chevrolet Corvette Stingray
    v.1 various colors, #8105 .... $30–45
    v.2 stock car, #8105/1 .... $35–50
1966 Chevrolet Impala
    v.1 various colors, #8103 .... $30–45
    v.2 Fire Chief, red, #8103/1 .... $30–45
    v.3 Israeli Police, blue, #8103/2 ....$30–45
    v.4 Police, dark blue, #8115 .... $35–50
    v.5 Israeli Police, red, #8115/1 ..... $35–50
    v.6 Taxi, yellow, #8116 .... $35–50
    v.7 Israeli Taxi, #8116/1 .... $35–50
Chevrolet Pickup
    v.1 various colors, #8122 .... $35–50
    v.2 Israeli Police, #8122/1 .... $35–50
    v.3 Israeli Military, #8122/2 .... $35–50
    v.4 Coastguard with boat, #8122/3 .... $35–50
    v.5 Wrecker, Israeli Police Breakdown truck, #8122/4 .... $35–50
    v.6 Wrecker, Breakdown Truck, #8122/5 .... $35–50
    v.7 Wrecker, Israeli Military Breakdown Truck, #8122/6 .... $35–50

Chrysler Imperial Convertible, various colors, #8111 .... $35–50
1966 Dodge Charger
    v.1 various colors, #8112 .... $35–50
    v.2 United Nations, white, #8112/1 .$35–50
    v.3 Flower Power, #8112/2 .... $35–50
    v.4 Israeli Police, #8112/3 .... $35–50
Ford GT, #8104 .... $35–50
Ford Mustang
    v.1 various colors, #8106 .... $35–50
    v.2 psychedelic colors, #8106/1 ...$35–50
Ford Thunderbird
    v.1 various colors, #8118 .... $35–50
Ford Torino, various colors, #8121 ....$35–50
Oldsmobile Toronado
    v.1 various colors, #8109 .... $35–50
    v.2 Israeli Police, red, #8109/1 ..... $35–50
1965 Plymouth Barracuda
    v.1 various colors, #8114 .... $30–45
    v.2 Israeli Military, white, #8114/1 .$35–50
Pontiac Firebird, various colors, #8119 ..$35–50
1967 Pontiac GTO
    v.1 various colors, #8107 .... $30–45
    v.2 Israeli Tourist Bureau, cream with red label, Hebrew text, #8107/1 ..$35–50
Volkswagen Beetle
    v.1 various colors, #8117 .... $35–50
    v.2 Hippie, with Flower Power decoration, #8117/1 .... $35–50
    v.3 Polizei, green and gray, #8117/2 .... $35–50
    v.4 Deutsches Bundes Post, yellow, #8117/3 .... $35–50
    v.5 PTT (Swiss), yellow, #8117/4 ...$35–50
    v.6 Airport "Follow Me," #8117/5 .$35–50

Creative Master (also see Creative Masters)

Creative Master International, Inc.
Guangdong Province
People's Republic of China
CEO: Carl Ka Wing Tong (as of 10/21/98)

    You won't see this brand on anything the company makes. They contract their work to other companies whose name goes on the model.

    Creative Master International, Inc., founded in 1986 by Carl Tong and Leo Kwok, is a Hong Kong-based company with manufacturing facilities in Guangdong Province of the People's Republic of China, according to a 1998 company prospectus. Creative Master manufactures premium collectible car replicas in the $20–22 price range sold by such companies as Danbury Mint, Hallmark, Mattel, and Action Performance.

    The company was recently awarded the prestigious Hong Kong Productivity Council Industry Award in the Productivity Category.

Creative Masters (also see Creative Master)

    In December 1995, Revell, now a subsidiary of Action Performance, introduced a

1:20 scale "Creative Masters" diecast replica of the original 1989 Dodge Viper R/T 10 Roadster. Revell is so serious about faithfully reproducing this model in miniature that a miniature price sheet is included on the model on the windshield. The connection between Revell and Creative Master is somewhat complex, but in a nutshell, Revell obtained permission to use the name (with the "s" added to make the name plural) for US marketing of their products. It wasn't long before the two companies had a "falling out," the result of which is still unclear.
Shelby Cobra, red, 1:20 .... $125–150
1989 Dodge Viper R/T 10 Roadster, 1:20 .... $175–190
Shelby Mustang GT350, "incorrect" black engine, #8820 .... $200–250
Shelby Mustang GT350, "correct" blue engine, #8820 .... $175–190

Crescent Toys (also see D.C.M.T.)

    The Crescent Toy Company was born in a 30 square foot backyard workshop in London, England, in 1922. Through the twenties and thirties, Henry Eagles and Arthur Schneider manufactured lead alloy toy soldiers, cowboys, kitchen sets, and other items.

    After World War II, Crescent resumed making their toys, adding "DCMT" into the casting, evidence of their marketing of toys from the firm of Diecasting Machine Tools Ltd.

    The DCMT mark was removed from models made in 1948 and later. DCMT meanwhile went on to make Lone Star models. Crescent continued making toys until 1981.
155 Artillery Gun $32
223 forties Race Car $48
235 Cannon, operable $75
422 forties Nash Roadster $45
423 forties Petrol Tanker $25
424 forties Flat Truck $25
425 forties LaSalle Sedan $40
650 Military Set, includes two 696 British Tanks, 698 Scout Car, 699 Russian Tank $225
695 Howitzer, unpainted, with spring and plunger $15
696 British Tank $50
698 Scout Car $40
800 forties Jaguar $40
804 forties Jaguar Police Car $36
1221 forties Fire Engine with Extending Ladder $64
1268 Mobile Space Rocket $120
1269 Mobile Crane $68
1272 Scammell Scarab Articulated Truck...$116
1274 Scammell Scarab and Low Loader Trailer $116
1276 Scammell Scarab and Oil Tanker, Shell or Esso $150
1284 Mercedes-Benz W196 Racing Car .$100
1285 B.R.M. Mk II Racing Car $100
1286 Ferrari 625 Racing Car $100

1287 Connaught A Series Racing Car $100
1288 Cooper Bristol Racing Car $100
1289 Gordini 2.5 Litre Racing Car $100
1290 Maserati 25OF Racing Car $100
1291 Aston Martin DB3S Racing Car $80
1292 Jaguar D-Type Racing Car $85
1293 Vanwall Racing Car.....................$150
1350 seventies Container Truck..........$32
1351 seventies Petrol Tanker................$32
1352 seventies Girder Truck.................$32
1353 seventies Platform Truck...............$32
1360 seventies Cement Mixer................$16
1361 seventies Covered Truck...............$10
1362 seventies Tipper Truck..................$16
1363 seventies Recovery Vehicle...........$16
1364 seventies Super Karner.................$10
1813 Horse Drawn Timber Wagon.........$136
1814 PloughTrailer $24
1815 Hayloader $20
1816 Roller Harrow..............................$16
1817 Timber Trailer..............................$16
1818 Tipping Farm Wagon $16
1819 Large Farm Wagon $36
1822 Bulldozer.....................................$30
2700 Western Stage Coach $110
2705 Scammell Scarab Set $350
6300 Set 1, includes 1284 through 1289.........................$600
6300 Set 2, includes 1285 through 1290.........................$600

Cristian

The Cristian brand represents inexpensive 1:43 scale models made in Argentina.
Renault Dauphine $4
Ifa Torino Coupe $4
1960 Mercedes 220 ....$4
Fiat 1500 Ramco Coupe $4
1960 Fiat Car Transporter.................$4
DAF Car Transporter $4

Crossway Models

Crossway Models
2 Salem St.
Gosberton, Spalding, Lincs
PE11 4NQ England
phone/fax: 011-44-1775-841-171

Every Crossway Model is hand finished and exquisitely detailed. Meanwhile, Jemini models, a white metal model car manufacturer in England, at one time produced some unusual British car models. Now Jemini has merged with Crossway Models of England. Issues are limited from 10 to 500 of each model.

Crossways CK Series
CK 01 Austin/Morris 11/1300 ....(£60 UK) $90 US

Crossways CM Series
CM 01 Rover 75 Saloon
v.1 black..................(£64 UK) $96 US
v.2 Connaught green. (£60 UK) $90 US
v.3 ivory..................(£60 UK) $90 US

Crossways CMM Series, 25 produced of each model
CMM 1 Austin A70 Saloon, black ....(£60 UK) $90 US
CMM 2 Austin 1100 MK2, flame red ....(£60 UK) $90 US
CMM 3 MG TD, red with wire wheels ....(£60 UK) $90 US

Crossways CP Series
CP 10 Sunbeam Rapier, velvet/sage green ....(£60 UK) $90 US

Crossways JMR Series, 500 of each model in each color, except JMR 002 of which 150 are to be issued
JMR 002 Wolseley Six, black .... (£64 UK) $96 US
JMR 003 Wolseley 1300 MK2, teal, harvest gold, green mallard, or black tulip ....(£60 UK) $90 US
JMR 006 Austin 1300 GT, flame red ....(£60 UK) $90 US
JMR 007 MG 1300 GT MK2, Bermuda blue or snowberry white ....(£60 UK) $90 US

Crossways JSE Series
JSE 002 Standard Vanguard Estate, black, 50 issued .... (£66 UK) $100 US
JSE 002 Standard Vanguard Van, black, 100 issued .... (£60 UK) $90 US
JSE 003 Morris 100 Traveler, green and red, 100 issued .... (£60 UK) $90 US
JSE 004 Sunbeam Tiger, open, white (Metropolitan Police) .... (£60 UK) $90 US
JSE 004 Sunbeam Tiger, closed, white (Metropolitan Police)......... (£60 UK) $90 US
JSE 007 MGB, black....... (£60 UK) $90 US
JSE 008 Austin A70, black .(£60 UK) $90 US
JSE 009 Austin 1100 MK3, Bermuda blue and white (Metropolitan Police)...................(£60 UK) $90 US

Other Crossway Models
Triumph Dolomite Sprint, carmine, pageant blue or vermilion, limited edition of 600..........................(£70 UK) $90 US
Riley RMA Saloon, black or dark red, limited edition of 600 ....(£70 UK) $90 US

Crown Premiums

3310 East Woodview Avenue
Oak Creek, WI 53154
website: crownpremiums.com
e-mail: brenda@crownpremiums.com

Crown Premiums entered the diecast bank replica industry in 1981 designing promotional items for Harley-Davidson, Snap-On Tools, Lennox, CITGO, Conoco, Tropicana, and other notable companies. In 1996, Crown Premiums introduced the first pedal car bank replica. Each issue is limited to 5,000 units. For more information, contact Brian O'Hara at 941-495-6964 or Mark Hoeger at 319-875-2694. Below is a sampling of models.

1:6 Scale Pedal Car Bank Replica Banks
1941 Garton Fire Engine $120–130
1948 BMC CT Convertible $120–130
1947 BMC Racer $120–130
1948 BMC Stake Truck $120–130
1947 BMC Car Racer $120–130

1:12 Scale diecast Petite Metal Car Banks
1941 Garton Fire Engine $60–70
1948 BMC CT Convertible $60–70
1947 BMC Racer $60–70
1948 BMC Stake Truck $60–70
1947 BMC Car Racer $60–70

C-Scale

C-Scale represents 1:43 scale white metal kits made in Great Britain.

Cursor

Although the Cursor line consists mainly of plastic models, these models from Germany are practically indistinguishable from diecast models in their precision, scale, and appearance. Newer Cursor models are diecast as well.

Cursor models represent a variety of German and other European cars and trucks, including the first Daimler and Benz cars produced in 1886. Cursor models are available from Diecast Miniatures, Toys for Collectors (TfC), and other fine scale model dealers.

VW Bus, light gray, 1:43 ....$120
1 1886 Benz First Three-Wheel Car, 1:43..................................$15
2 1896 Daimler Fire, red, 1:43 ....$18
3 1897 Daimler Taxi, blue, 1:43 ....$18
8 1911 Benz Blitzen Racer, silver, 1:43 ......$18
14 1904 Bussing Bus, 1:35 ....$18
100 Mercedes-Benz Unimog, 1:50 ....$18
189 Graft & Stift Kaiser Wagon, 1:40.......$49
266 Matador Van Pickup, blue $70
280 Iveco Dump Truck, 1:50................$25
311 Panther 6x6 Fire Truck.................$120
312 Panther 8x8 Fire Truck................$129
484 Holder Farm Tractor, 1:35 ....$25
569 Hanomag Wheel Loader...............$30
677 Fendt LS Farm Tractor, green, 1:43 .....$18
678 Fendt LB Farm Tractor, green, 1:43 .....$18
780 Magirus Oil Truck.......................$20
880 Holder Culitrac Farm Tractor, 1:35 ......$25
982 Double Decker Bus, 1:35 ....$39
982T 1903 MAN Truck......................$39
986 Kaessborer Setra S8 Bus, 1:60 ....$49
1084 Mercedes-Benz 300E $19
1182 Mercedes-Benz 190E, 1:35 ....$19
1300 Mercedes-Benz L408D, silver, 1:43...$18
2911 Mercedes-Benz 500 with closed sunroof, 1:43....................................$27
2912 Mercedes-Benz 500 with open sunroof, 1:43....................................$27
12932 MAN Truck, 1:35, new model for 1995 ....$27
12935 MAN Wood Transporter, 1:35, new model for 1995 ....$27

Custom Miniatures

One limited edition model is available from this brand, of which only 500 were made.

1957 Chevrolet Bel Air 2-Door Hardtop, 5-spoke mag wheels, maroon, white, silver, 1:43 ....$119

Dale Model Company

According to collector Jarek Skonieczny, Frank Dale originally worked for H. L. Framberg, manufacturer of cast metal World War II identification models used by the military to assist in recognizing military vehicles from a distance. Frank Dale left the Chicago-based company to form his own firm called Dale Model Company and continue producing military toys. More information is needed on both the Dale Model Company and H. L. Framberg. Original ID models were sold without a package. Later souvenir models were sold in boxes, most notably from F.A.O. Schwarz.

Dale Military Identification Models

Jeep MB.................................$70
Stuart M5 Tank....................$40–50
T-17 Armored Car $40–50
1/2 Track............................$40–50
Duck Amphibious.................$40–50
M715 Jeep, 1960s...............$40–50

Dale Jr./Dale Sr. Models (also see Revell)

In January 1999, Bryan Roy Hawthorne, bryanroy@mail.utexas.edu, listed the following Dale Jr. items, plus a few Sr. items, for sale on rec.toys.cars newsgroup. These are apparently completely unrelated to Dale Model Company however, likely referring instead to race car driver Dale Earnhardt.

Mr. Hawthorne wrote that these are "rare, hard-to-find 1997 Revell Collection Wrangler cars, which come in an acrylic case with a certificate of proof out of 5,004 produced. These were the first Dale Jr. cars besides his RCCA Mom n Pop's cars in 1994."

Dale Jr. Sets

1:43 scale 1997 Wrangler Revell Collection...$50
1:24 scale 1997 Wrangler Revell Collection...$200
1:18 scale 1997 Warngler Revell Collection...$175

Dale Sr. Models

ARC/RCCA
  1:64 1994 HO Lumina $20
ARC
  1:24 1996 Olympic Goodwrench Box.......................................$70
  1:24 1997 GW Plus $45
  1:24 1997 GW Plus black window bank..$50
  1:64 1997 GW Plus $10
  1:64 1997 AC Delco Japan...........$10
  1:24 1998 GW Plus.....................$45
  1:64 1998 GW Plus.....................$10

Dalia (also see Tekno, Solido)

Dalia of Spain was begun in the 1920s. By World War II, Dalia had produced a number of diecast toys. By the late 1950s, Dalia produced a series of 1:38 scale Vespa and Lambretta scooters. Around the same time, the company became the licensed distributor for Solido in Spain. About a decade later, Dalia established a working relationship with Tekno of Denmark to produce a group of 1:43 scale models made in Spain. While the original box says "Dalia-Tekno," the models only say Tekno on the base.

1 Vespa Scooter, green $75
2 Lambretta A Scooter, blue and orange $75
3 Lambretta B Scooter, gray and pink $75
4 Lambretta Motor Tricycle, beige and green .$75
5 Vespa Scooter with Sidecar, light blue $75
6 Lambretta A Scooter with Sidecar, silver $75
7 Lambretta B Scooter with Sidecar, orange and black..$75
8 Lambretta Motor Tricycle "Butano," orange $75
9 Vespa Scooter Red Cross, white and gray $75
10 Vespa Scooter with Sidecar Red Cross, white and gray..................................$75
11 Lambretta A Scooter, orange and black ..$75
12 Lambretta A Scooter with Sidecar, orange and black...$75
13 Lambretta Motor Tricycle with Buckets, orange and beige $75
14 Lambretta Motor Tricycle with Drums, orange and beige $75
15 Lambretta Motor Tricycle Milk Delivery, white and beige $75
16 Lambretta Motor Tricycle Wine Delivery, light blue and beige $75
17 Lambretta Motor Tricycle Water Delivery, silver and beige...............................$75
18 Vespa S Scooter, white and green $75
19 Vespa S Scooter with Sidecar, green and yellow $75
20 Lambretta A Army Scooter, olive............$75
21 Lambretta A Army Scooter with Sidecar, olive $75
22 Vespa S Army Scooter, olive $75
23 Vespa S Army Scooter with Sidecar, olive $75
24 Vespa Scooter "Policia," black...............$75
25 Vespa Scooter "Policia" with sidecar, black $75
26 Go-kart, red and blue $90
27 Lambretta Army Motor Tricycle, olive.......$75
28 Vespa Scooter "Telegrafos," beige $75
29 Vespa Scooter with Sidecar, "Telegrafos," beige $75
30 Lambretta Motor Tricycle with Cases, white and beige $75
31 Vespa Scooter, "Iberia," silver $75
32 Vespa Scooter with Sidecar, "Iberia," silver $75
33 Lambretta Motor Tricycle "Coca-Cola," white and orange $75

34 Vespa Scooter Rally, blue.....................$75
35 Vespa Scooter with Sidecar, Rally, blue...$75
36 Lambretta Motor Tricycle, Red Cross, gray and white...$75
37 Lambretta A Scooter, "Coca-Cola," white and orange $75
38 Lambretta A Scooter with Sidecar, "Coca-Cola," white and orange $75
39 Vespa Scooter, "Mop," yellow and beige $75
40 Vespa Scooter with Sidecar "Mop," yellow and beige $75
41 Lambretta Scooter, "Butano," orange $75
42 Lambretta Scooter with Sidecar, "Butano," orange $75

Dalia 1:66 Scale Cars

501 Porsche Carrera 6 ....$40
502 Ford GT Le Mans $40
503 Chaparral 2F $40
504 Seat 850 Coupe $40
505 De Tomaso Mangusta $40
506 Renault Alpine $40

Dalia-Solido Models

1 Jaguar D Le Mans, red, green, or blue .$100
2 Maserati 250F, red, yellow, or green .$100
3 Vanwall Racing Car, light blue, or green $100
4 Ferrari Testa Rossa, red, white, cream $150
5 Porsche 550/1500 RS (red, and black, yellow and black, or silver and green...$125
6 Cooper 1500 F.Z, tan, white and blue, or yellow and white $100
7 Porsche F.2, silver and red, yellow and black, or orange and silver $125
8 Seat 1400-C, black and green, black and silver, red, or green and yellow $150
9 Renault Floride Convertible, copper, red, or blue $100
10 Mercedes-Benz 190SL Roadster, copper, silver, or white.................................$100
11 Lotus F.1, yellow or black $75
12 Lancia Flaminia Coupe Pinin Farina, red, silver, blue, or green.....................$100
13 Fiat Abarth Record, orange, red, or white $100
14 Seat 1400-C Taxi, Barcelona, black, and yellow $150
15 Seat 1400-C Taxi, Madrid, black, and red $150
16 Alfa Romeo Giulietta Roadster, red, orange, light blue, or green............$75
17 Ferrari 250 GT 2+2, red, green, or yellow $125
18 Aston Martin DB4, blue, yellow, red, silver, copper...$100
19 Citroën Ami 6, white and green or white and blue $100
20 Ferrari 156 F.1, light blue or red $100
21 Fiat Abarth 1000, orange, silver, or tan $100
22 Mercedes-Benz 220 SE Coupe v.1 "Autopistas," orange $150

v.2 "Falck," white $150
v.3 "Policia," black $150
v.4 "PTT," white $150
v.5 blue or red $100
v.6 Red Cross, white $150
23 Alfa Romeo 2600 Coupe Bertone, cream, dark red, blue, green, or silver.................$100
24 Seat1400-C "Policia," black $150
25 Panhard DB Le Mans, blue, silver, or white $75
26-1 Aston Martin DB 5 Vantage, white, cream, blue, green, or copper .$100
26-2 Aston Martin DB 5 Vantage, "The Saint," white $175
27 Seat 1400-C, "Iberia," silver $150
28 NSU Prinz, red, blue, green, or orange and black.................$75
29 Porsche GT Le Mans, green, blue, silver $125
30 Fiat 2300 S Ghia Convertible
    v.1 "Autopistas," orange $150
    v.2 green, red, blue, or white $100
31 Ford Thunderbird, red, blue, tan, metallic green.................$100
32 Ferrari 2.5 L, red $100
33 Seat 1500
    v.1 "Policia," black $150
    v.2 Taxi Barcelona, black and yellow $150
    v.3 Taxi Madrid, black and red $150
    v.4 white, green, or metallic blue.................$125
34 Harvey Indianapolis, dark green or yellow $75
35 Simca Oceare Convertible, green or metallic blue $100
36-1 Maserati 3.5 L Mistral
    v.1 copper, beige, yellow, or metallic blue $100
    v.2 "NASA," orange.................$150
37 Ford Mustang, red, white, metallic light blue $100
38 B.R.M. F.1, yellow or metallic green .$75
39 Alpine F.3, dark green ....$ 75
40 Lola Climax V8 F.1, tan and red.......$70
41 Porsche Carrera 6, yellow and red ...$75
42 Ford GT 40 Le Mans, yellow and blue.................$70
43 Ferrari 330 P3, light blue.................$100
44 Alfa Romeo Giulia TZ, blue or orange $90
45 Oldsmobile Toronado, orange or green $65
46 Panhard 24 BT
    v.1 "Urgencias," white.................$125
    v.2 silver.................$60
47 Chaparral Z D, red.................$50
48 BMW 2000 CS, white $65
49 Simca 1100, yellow.................$75
50 De Tomaso Mangusta, tan.................$60
51 Chaparral 2F, blue and red, blue and black, or white and red $60

52 Citroën Ami 6 S.W.
    v.1 "Butano," orange $150
    v.2 "Falck," white $150
    v.3 Ambulance, white $150
    v.4 blue, green.................$75
54 Opel GT 1900, metallic blue, metallic green.................$75
55 Ford Thunderbird Taxi, black and yellow $125
56 Ford Thunderbird, "Policia," black ...$150
57 Ford Mustang Rally, red.................$75
58 Ford Mustang "Policia," black $125
59 Ford Mustang Taxi Barcelona, black and yellow.................$125
60 Ford Mustang Taxi Madrid, black and red $125
61 Oldsmobile Toronado Rally, orange $75
62 Simca 1100 Red Cross, white $150
63 Simca 1100 Taxi, black and yellow $125
64 Alfa Romeo 2600 Coupe "Iberia" silver $120
65 Alfa Romeo Carabo Bertone, orange $75
66 Alpine Renault, yellow $75
67 Maserati 3.5 L Mistral Rally, yellow and black $75
68 Lola T70 MK 3B, red.................$50
69 Mclaren M8 B Can Am, orange $65
70 Matra 650, blue.................$65
71 Porsche 914/6, yellow.................$60
72 Ferrari 365 GTB4, red.................$75
73 Buggy Bertone, metallic green $50

Dalia-Tekno
415 Ford Taunus Van
    v.1 "Autopistas," orange $250
    v.2 "Butano".................$250
    v.3 "Iberia," black.................$250
    v.4 "Mop Projectos," yellow and tan $250
    v.5 "Policia," black $250
    v.6 "Tekno".................$250
    v.7 "Telegrafos".................$250
    v.8 Ambulance, white $250
829 Lincoln Continental.................$65
832 M.G. 1100 ....$50
833 Ford Mustang Hardtop.................$50
834 Ford Mustang Convertible.................$50
914 Ford D 800 Truck.................$50
915 Ford D 800 Stake Truck $50
928 Mercedes-Benz 230SL Hardtop $50
929 Mercedes-Benz 230SL Roadster $50
930 Monza GT Coupe.................$50
931 Monza GT Roadster $50
933 Oldsmobile Toronado $50

Danbury Mint
47 Richards Avenue
Norwalk, CT 06857

Danbury Mint was established in 1969 as a producer of fine precision scale automobiles. With a focus on accuracy, it remains a produc-

er of some of the best miniature automotive replicas ever produced.
    Aston Martin DB7, James Bond.....$140–150

1920s Borden's Milk Truck, white with black trim, 1:24 ....$140–145

1930s Borden's Milk Truck, white with black trim, 1:24.................$140–145
1955 Borden's Delivery Truck, white with yellow top, 1:24.................$140–145
1969 Brawner-Hawk Mario Andretti Indy Car, 1:18.................$260–$275
1938 Budweiser Delivery Truck, 1:24.................$155–160
1955 Budweiser Delivery Truck, 1:24.................$155–160
1953 Buick Skylark Convertible, blue with blue-gray interior, 1:24.................$115–120
1953 Buick Skylark Convertible, burgundy, 1:24.................$115–120
1932 Cadillac V-16 Sport Phaeton, green, 1:24.................$115–120
1953 Cadillac Eldorado Convertible, pearl white with red interior, white hardtop, 1:16.................$200–210
1959 Cadillac Series 62 Convertible, red with red interior, 1:24.................$115–120
1932 Cadillac V-16 Sport Phaeton, green with beige interior, 1:24.................$115–120
1920s Campbell's Soup Delivery Truck, red, 1:24.................$125–130
1931 Campbell's Soup Delivery Truck, red, 1:24.................$125–130
1940s Campbell's Soup Delivery Truck, red, 1:24.................$125–130
1950s Campbell's Soup Delivery Truck, red, 1:24.................$125–130
1931 Chevrolet Roadster Pickup, turquoise blue with black bed, 1:24.................$115–120
1941 Chevrolet Pickup, blue with black fenders, 1:24.................$115–120
1941 Chevrolet Special DeLuxe, beige, Convertible top down, 1:24.................$115–120
1953 Chevrolet 3100 Pickup, green, 1:24.................$115–120
1953 Chevrolet Wrecker, red, 1:24.................$140–145
1955 Chevrolet Bel Air, burnt orange and white, 1:24.................$115–120
1955 Chevrolet Bel Air, red and white, 1:18.................$200–210
1955 Chevrolet Nomad, blue and white, 1:24.................$115–120

1955 Chevrolet Nomad, turquoise with white roof, 1:24 ....$115–120
1955 Chevrolet Nomad Street Machine, red, 1:24 ....$115–120
1957 Chevrolet Bel Air Convertible, teal blue, 1:24 ....$115–120
1957 Chevrolet Cameo Carrier Pickup, red with white bed, 1:24 ....$115–120
1957 Chevrolet Bel Air Convertible, blue with light and dark blue interior, 1:24 ....$115–120
1958 Chevrolet Apache Pickup, bright blue, 1:24 ....$115–120
1958 Chevrolet Impala Convertible, turquoise with blue interior, 1:24 ....$115–120
1962 Chevrolet Corvette Convertible, red, 1:24 ....$115–120
1966 Chevrolet C-10 Pickup, dark blue with white roof, 1:24 ....$120–125
1968 Chevrolet Chevelle SS-396, red, 1:24 ....$115–120
1968 Chevrolet El Camino SS-396, black $120–130
1969 Chevrolet SS/RS Camaro Convertible, blue with white interior, 1:24 ......$115–120
1969 Chevrolet SS/RS Camaro Convertible, white with orange stripes, 1:24 ....$115–120
1972 Chevrolet Cheyenne, red and white, 1:24 ....$125–130
1942 Chrysler Town & Country Station Wagon, black and wood, 1:24 ....$115–120
1948 Chrysler Town & Country Convertible, maroon and wood with maroon interior, 1:24 ....$115–120
1957 Chrysler 300C, cream, 1998, 1:24 ....$115–120
1927 Coca-Cola Delivery Truck, yellow and black, 1:24, 1995 ....$150–160
1928 Coca-Cola Delivery Truck, yellow and black, 1:24 ....$150–160
1931 Coca-Cola Delivery Truck, yellow and black, 1:24 ....$150–160
1938 Coca-Cola Delivery Truck, red, 1:24 ....$150–160
1929 Cord L-29 Special Coupe, turquoise blue with tan top, 1:18 ....$200–210
1950 Divco Borden's Milk Truck, white, yellow, gray with red trim $140–145
1929 Dodge Pickup, black with yellow stripe, 1:24 ....$115–120
1957 Dodge Sweptside, red and white two-tone, 1:24 ....$115–120
1935 Duesenberg SSJ Speedster, gray-red with beige interior, 1:24 ....$115–120
1958 Edsel Bermuda Station Wagon (see Ford Edsel)
1958 Ferrari 250 Testa Rossa, red with red interior, 1:24 ....$115–120
1920s Ford Model T Paddy Wagon, black, 1:24 ....$115–120
1925 Ford Model T Coupe, black, 1:24 ....$115–120

1925 Ford Model T Pickup, black with wood bed, 1:24 ....$115–120
1927 Ford Coca-Cola Delivery Truck, yellow and black, 1:24 ....$130–140
1931 Ford Borden's Delivery Truck, red.$135–145
1931 Ford Campbell's Soup Delivery Truck, red $125–135
1931 Ford Model A Deluxe Roadster, black-brown, 1:24 ....$115–120
1931 Ford Model A Deluxe Roadster, light brown, 1:24 ....$115–120
1931 Ford U.S. Mail Truck, dark green $130–140
1936 Ford Deluxe Cabriolet, dark blue, 1:24 ....$115–120
1938 Ford Pickup, dark blue, 1:24 ..$115–120
1940 Ford Deluxe Coupe, red with beige interior, 1:24 ....$115–120
1940 Ford Hot Rod, black with yellow flames, 1:24 ....$115–120
1942 Ford Pickup, dark green, 1:24 ..$115–120
1952 Ford F-1 Pickup, dark green, 1:24 ....$115–120
1955 Ford Fairlane Crown Victoria, two-tone cream and black, 1:24 ....$115–120
1956 Ford F-100 Pickup, red, 1:24 .$115–120
1956 Ford Sunliner Convertible, two-tone red and white, 1:24 ....$115–120
1956 Ford Thunderbird, red with red and white interior, 1:24 ....$115–120
1956 Ford Thunderbird, white, 1:24 .$115–120
1958 Ford Edsel Bermuda Station Wagon, orange and off-white with wood paneling, 1:24 ....$115–120
1962 Ford Thunderbird Sports Roadster, cream with red interior, 1:24 ....$115–120
1966 Ford Mustang Convertible, cream, blue-cream, 1:24 ....$115–120
1966 Ford Mustang Hardtop, maroon with black roof, 1:24 ....$115–120
1938 GMC Car Carrier, dark blue, 1:24 ....$145–150
1938 GMC Coca-Cola Delivery Truck, red $130–140
1953 Good Humor Truck, white, 1:24 ....$135–140
1940s Heinz Delivery Truck, white with red fenders, 1:24 ....$125–130
1934 Hispano Suiza J-12, blue, 1:24 ..$115–120
1938 Indian Four Motorcycle, 1:10 .$125–130
1948 Indian Chief, 1:10 ....$125–130
1949 Jaguar XK120, sand with red interior, 1:24 ....$115–120
1949 Jaguar XK120, metallic silver with red interior, 1:24 ....$115–120
1926 Mack AC Rotary Pumper Fire Engine, 1992, 1:32 ....$180–190
1931 Mercedes-Benz SSKL, white with black interior, 1:24 ....$115–120
1949 Mercury Club Coupe, black with beige interior, 1:24 ....$115–120
1949 Mercury Fire Chief's Car, red, 1:24 ....$115–120

1949 Mercury Police Cruiser, black with white doors, 1:24 ....$115–120
1950 Mercury Custom, plum/magenta, 1:24 ....$115–120
1920s Morton's Salt Delivery Truck, 1:24 ....$125–130
1930s Morton's Salt Delivery Truck, 1:24 ....$125–130
1940s Morton's Salt Delivery Truck, 1:24 ....$125–130
1950s Morton's Salt Delivery Truck, 1:24 ....$125–130
1955 Oldsmobile Super 88, red and white two-tone, 1:24 ....$115–120
1934 Packard V12 LeBaron Speedster, red and black, 1:24 ....$115–120
1933 Pierce Silver Arrow, silver, 1:24 ....$115–120
Plymouth Prowler, purple, top up, 1:24 ....$115–120
1965 Pontiac GTO, lavender, 1:24.$115–120
1969 Pontiac GTO "The Judge," Carousel red, 1:24 ....$115–120
1938 Rolls Royce Phantom III, maroon and black, 1:24 ....$115–120
1937 Studebaker Pickup, red, 1:24.$115–120
1957 Studebaker Golden Hawk, gold, 1:24 ....$100–110
1927 Stutz Black Hawk Speedster, black, 1:24 ....$115–120
1927 Stutz Black Hawk, Custom Series, black and red, 1:24 ....$115–120
1956 Texaco Pickup Truck, red, 1:24 .$130–135
1925 U.S. Mail Truck, 1:24 ....$135–140
1931 U.S. Mail Truck, 1:24 ....$135–140
1935 U.S. Mail Truck, 1:24 ....$135–140

Danbury Mint Pewter Models
1936 Alvis Speed 25 ....$80–110
1935 Auburn 851 Speedster $80–110
1953 Austin-Healey 100 ....$80–110
1927 Bugatti Royale $80–110
1913 Cadillac Roadster $80–110
1937 Cord 812 ....$80–110
1938 Delahaye $80–110
1934 Duesenberg SJ $80–110
1926 Fiat $80–110
1909 Ford Model T $80–110
1912 Hispano Suiza $80–110
1926 Isotta Fraschini $80–110
1906 Itala Targa Florio $80–110
1936 Jaguar SS/100 ....$80–110
1941 Lincoln Continental $80–110
1939 Mercedes-Benz 540K $80–110
1948 MG-TC $80–110
1912 Packard $80–110
1905 Rolls Royce 10 HP $80–110
1907 Rolls Royce Silver Ghost $80–110
1909 Rolls Royce Silver Ghost $80–110
1911 Rolls Royce Silver Ghost 40/50 HP Limousine $80–110
1913 Rolls Royce Alpine Eagle $80–110
1923 Rolls Royce Springfield Silver Ghost $80–110

1936 Rolls Royce Park Ward........$80–110
1939 Rolls Royce Silver Wraith $80–110
1954 Rolls Royce Silver Dawn III ...$80–110
1968 Rolls Royce Phantom VI........$80–110
1912 Simplex $80–110
1909 Stanley Steamer $80–110
1914 Stutz Bearcat $80–110
1907 Thomas Flyer $80–110
1924 Vauxhall............................$80–110
1934 Viosin 17CV.......................$80–110

Danhausen (also see Max Models and Paul's Model Art)

Danhausen Modelcar
Postfach 485
5100 Aachen, Germany

Danhausen models and kits come from Aachen, Germany, near the border of Belgium and the Netherlands. Besides the proprietary Danhausen line, Danhausen also offered models from Pocher, ABC Brianza, and some Russian-made diecast. Like many current models produced in Europe, obtaining them in the U.S. is nearly impossible.

1931 Mercedes SSK L, 1:43 kit.................$17
Ferrari BB Spyder, red, 1:43 ....$65
Porsche 917/930, Sunoco, unfinished white metal, 1:43 kit....................................$17

Dapper (also see Bandai)

Dapper is a division of Bandai of Japan. One diecast model, produced in the 1980s, is known from this brand.

203 Hato Bus, 4½", 1980........................$20

Darda

Dardas of Germany are mostly plastic-body toy cars with a distinction. Pullback action and the wildest track this side of Hot Wheels helps Dardas fly around loops and curves at a scale speed of 500–600 scale miles per hour! A huge assortment of Darda models are available, along with a large assortment of track sets.

Corvette..$7
Porsche $7
Sonic Shifter $8
State Police Car $7
Stop N Go Camaro $7
Stop N Go Mercedes Police Car $7
Stop N Go Nissan 300 ZX...........................$7
Stop N Go BMW 850i $7
Turbo Racer $7
Ultra Porsche Boxter $8
Ultra Speed Camaro Z-28 ....$8
Ultra Speed Corvette $8
Ultra Speed Lamborghini Diablo...................$8
Ultra Speed Mercedes SLK $8
Ultra Speed Mustang..................................$8
Ultra Speed Panther....................................$8
Ultra Speed Stop N Go Jaguar $8
Ultra Speed Stop N Go Porsche $8
Volkswagen Beetle $7
Yellow Canon Ultra Speed Formula 1........$8

David Deanstyne

This American brand is known for one hollow-cast metal bus.

GM 3702 Coach, Adirondack Transit Lines, 8½"...$200

Day, John (see John Day Models)

Days Gone (see Lledo)

D.C.M.T. (also see Crescent, Impy, Lincoln, Lone Star, River, and Roadmaster)

Diecasting Machine Tools Ltd. of Great Britain started producing toys as a sideline in the 1940s in North London in order to demonstrate the potential of their equipment. While most of their toys were produced under the Crescent brand, a few were simply marked "D.C.M.T." Some had friction motors in them.

The Crescent Toy Company originated from England in 1922. Through the twenties and thirties, Henry Eagles and Arthur Schneider manufactured lead alloy toy soldiers, cowboys, kitchen sets, and other items.

After World War II, Crescent resumed making their toys, adding "DCMT" into the casting, evidence of their marketing of toys from the firm of Diecasting Machine Tools Ltd. Crescent became the marketing firm for these models as well as their own Crescent brand.

One brand of which there is some dispute is a series of toys issued under the River brand. Neither the model or the box had any mention of Lone Star, Crescent, or D.C.M.T., and the castings were inferior to the other lines produced, which led to metal fatigue with which D.C.M.T. models were not so plagued. Regardless of such controversy of whether D.C.M.T. produced them or not, the author lists them below.

The D.C.M.T. mark was removed from models made in 1948 and later. D.C.M.T. meanwhile went on to make Lone Star models. Crescent continued making toys until 1981. Here are a few models made under the D.C.M.T. mark, followed by the River series. Lincoln Industries of Auckland, New Zealand, reportedly produced remakes from old D.C.M.T. tooling.

D.C.M.T. Models

Low Loader Tractor Trailer...............$45–60
Military Truck...............................$45–60
Tanker Truck................................$45–60
Timber Truck with real "log" $60–75

River Models

Austin A40 Somerset......................$60–75
Buick Roadmaster $75–90
Daimler Conquest $60–75
Ford Prefect.................................$60–75
Standard Vanguard Saloon.............$60–75
Standard Vanguard Station Wagon $60–75

DDR

As it turns out, DDR toys are wooden toys made in East Germany (DDR = Deutsche Demokratische Republik) prior to reunification. The toys are similar to Brio but with more accuracy, according to collector Brian Willoughby.

1950 Deutz Dump Truck............................$5
1950 Deutz Fire Ladder.............................$5
1950 Deutz Lumber Truck..........................$5
1950 Deutz-Fahr Farm Tractor $5
1980 Zetor Tractor $5
1985 IFA Semi Fish Van.............................$5
1985 IFA Van "Fernverkehr" $3
Deutz Fire Trailer $5

Deanstyne, David (see David Deanstyne)

Dehanes

Dehanes brand models are 1:55 scale models, mostly of freight trucks, with a few exceptions.

001 1939 Dodge Airflow.....................$155
101 Mack B "Heinz 57" $69
103 White 3000 "Threemor" $69
103 White 3000 "Mason Dixon" $69
104 Ford C600 "Johnny Walker" $69
105 Ford C600 "UPS" $69
106 Mack COE "Johnny Walker" $69
205 Mack B80 Dump Truck $69
801 Mack L Oil Truck "Hooker"................$69
914 1955 Mack H63T "Hennis" $145
915 International Conventional "PIE" $145
916 White 3000 Semi "Mason Dixon" $135
956 Mack "Coca Cola" Van $69
957 Mack Semi "Navajo" $115
SPC 1946 Chevrolet "Western Pacific" $155
WISE 1955 White Semi "Wise" $115

Deles

Discovered in a drug store recently is an assortment of inexpensive toy cars in roughly 1:43 scale with the name Deles on the bottom and made in China. A couple of late model Mercedes-Benz Coupes, a Porsche 356 Convertible, and a few other models sell for $1.25 each. Typically models have very lightweight bodies, plastic chassis, and rubber tires on crude wheel hubs.

The Porsche 356 Convertible is arguably the most charming and attractive of the bunch.

Mercedes-Benz Coupe $1–2
Porsche 356, pale blue...........................$1–2

Del Prado

The Edizioni del Prado Car Collection offers seventy 1:43 scale diecast model cars made in China for Del Prado of Italy. Each model includes a history of the car represented. Several appear to be copies of models from Jouef of France, Vitesse of Portugal, and The Dinky Collection from Matchbox. Here is a partial list in alphabetical order.

Alfa Romeo 156......................................$30
1976 Alpine A110, French blue $30
Aston Martin DB5, metallic gray................$30
Audi A4..$30
1970 BMC Mini Cooper, red with a white
    roof..$30
BMW 507, cream...................................$30
BMW 850i...$30
Bugatti T41 Royale..................................$30
Cadillac Eldorado...................................$30
Cadillac Seville, gold with tan roof $30
1964 Citroen DS19, black with white roof...$30
1963 Corvette Stingray, metallic light blue ...$30
Dodge Viper $30
Facel Vega HK 500..................................$30
Ferrari 512 Testarossa $30
1965 Fiat 500F, light blue.........................$30
1967 Ford Mustang Fastback, red (Dinky-Match-
    box copy)...$30
Hispano Suiza H6B $30
Honda Civic $30
1961 Jaguar E Type Spider, British racing
    green..$30
Jaguar XJ220...$30
Jeep Grand Cherokee, dark green $30
1966 Lamborghini Miura, yellow................$30
Lancia Delta Integrale $30
Maserati Bora $30
Mercedes 300SL Gullwing, metallic gray.....$30
Mercury Coupe $30
MGB $30
Morgan Plus 4 ....$30
Oldsmobile Toronado..............................$30
Opel Calibra $30
1989 Porsche 911 Carrera Cabriolet,
    black..$30
Rolls-Royce Silver Cloud $30
Saab 900S $30
Toyota Celica GT4 ....$30
Triumph TR3 ....$30
Vauxhall Viva $30
Volkswagen 1303, white (Jouef copy).........$30

Dent Hardware Company

Since 1895, Dent Hardware Company operated out of Fullerton, Pennsylvania. Dent toys are historically significant for their contribution to the toy market of the early twentieth century. Their first cast-iron vehicles emerged in 1898. In the 1920s, Dent attempted to market aluminum toys, but they failed to catch buyers' attention and were quickly phased out. Even though the company survived until 1973, toy production ceased during the Great Depression of the 1930s. Very few, if any, of Dent's toys were marked. Experts recognize them because of extensive experience in buying, selling, and trading. Richard O'Brien's book *Collecting Toy Cars and Trucks* provides a list of known Dent models. If identifiable as Dent cast-iron models, values start at $110 and go up to $10,000 for the rarest models.

Mack American Oil Co. Tanker, 10½"...$1,600
Mack American Oil Co. Tanker, 15"......$2,700
Bus, 6¼"..$750
Coast to Coast Bus, 7½"..........................$250
Coast to Coast Bus, 15"........................$1,500
Coupe, 5"...$250
Mack Junior Supply Company, New York -
    Philadelphia, 16" $10,000
Public Service Bus, 13½" $4,500

Deoma Micromodels (or Micro-toys) of Italy

A series of military models were sold under the Deoma Micromodels name during the late 1950s and early 1960s. Some models are crude copies of Dinky models of that era.

1 T-34 Tank, 2½"..............................$20–30
2 Daimler Armored Car, 1⅝" $20–30
3 Austin 1-Ton Open Truck, 1¾" $20–30
4 Bedford Open Truck, 2¼" $20–30
5 Bedford Covered Truck, 2¼" $20–30
6 Austin 1-Ton Covered Truck, 1¾"........$20–30
7 General Patton Tank, 2⅝" $20–30
8 Combat Car, 2" $20–30
9 Jeep, 1⅝" $20–30
10 High Speed Tractor, 2¼" $20–30
11 Three-Axle Open Truck, 2⅜"............$20–30
12 Three-Axle Civilian Truck, 2⅜"..........$20–30
14 Tank Transporter, 2¾"....................$20–30
15 Three-Axle Covered Truck, 2⅜" $20–30
16 "Long Tom" 155mm Cannon, 3¾"...$20–30
23 Austin 1-Ton Covered Truck, 1¾" $20–30

Design Studio (see Motor City USA)

Desormeaux

Two 1:43 scale lead alloy vehicles are known to have been produced by Desormeaux of France. Description, production year, and value are indicated below.

1923 Citroën 5CV, 1957 ....$125
1910 Le Zebre, 1958 ....$125

Detail Cars — CDC (Corgi Detail Cars, also see Armour)

Collector Bill Cross reports that these are mass produced in China, often looking as if they come from the same source as Minichamps. They are marketed by CDC in Italy and by Corgi in Great Britain. Armour is a division of CDC that produces military models.

As of January 1997, the US distributor for CDC is Dual Connection, P O Box 569, Gibsonia, PA 15044. Phone 412-381-1143 or 800-351-1141. Fax 412-381-1006.

110 1990 Lamborghini Diablo, yellow $27
111 1994 Lamborghini Diablo S, red........$27
112 1992 Lamborghini Diablo Roadster, yel-
    low..$27
113 1990 Lamborghini Diablo Roadster,
    blue...$27

114 1993 Lamborghini Diablo Coupe,
    black..$27
131 1992 Jaguar XJS Convertible, top down,
    blue...$27
132 1992 Jaguar XJS Convertible, top up, sil-
    ver..$27
133 1992 Jaguar XJS Coupe, red $27
140 1993 Ferrari 512 TR Coupe, red $27
142 1993 Ferrari 512 TR, top down,
    yellow...$27
144 1993 Ferrari 512 TR, top up, yellow ...$27
150 1987 Ferrari F-40, red $27
151 1987 Ferrari F-40 LeMans, red $27
153 1991 Ferrari F-40, Italian Racing Club,
    red..$27
154 1993 Ferrari F-40 Monte Shell, multi-
    color..$27
155 1994 Ferrari F-40 Totip, multicolor......$27
160 1991 Nissan 300ZX Coupe, black.....$27
161 1991 Nissan 300ZX Convertible, red...$27
162 1991 Nissan 300 ZX Soft Top, blue ...$27
163 1991 Nissan 300 ZX Convertible, red ..$27
164 1991 Nissan 300ZX Coupe, silver $27
165 1991 Nissan 300 ZX Monza, multi-
    color..$27
170 1993 Jaguar XJ220 Coupe, silver $27
171 1993 Jaguar XJ220 Coupe, green $27
172 1993 Jaguar XJ220 GT LeMans $27
174 1993 Jaguar XJ220 GT Martini $27
190 1993 Ferrari 456GT, metallic blue $27
191 1993 Ferrari 456GT, metallic red $27
193 1993 Ferrari 456GT, red.................$27
200 1958 Alfa Romeo Giulietta Spyder, red..$27
201 1958 Alfa Romeo Giulietta Spyder,
    white..$27
202 1958 Alfa Romeo Giulietta Spyder,
    blue...$27
203 1958 Alfa Romeo Giulietta Spyder Hard-
    top, red...$27
204 1958 Alfa Romeo Giulietta Spyder Hard-
    top, white...$27
205 1958 Alfa Romeo Giulietta Spyder Soft
    Top, gray...$27
206 1958 Alfa Romeo Giulietta Monoposto
    Mille Miglia, red $27
210 1993 Chevrolet Corvette ZR1 Coupe,
    white..$27
211 1993 Chevrolet Corvette ZR1 Convertible,
    top down, red $27
212 1993 Chevrolet Corvette ZR1 Convertible,
    top up, yellow...................................$27
213 1993 Chevrolet Corvette ZR1, metallic
    blue...$27
214 1993 Chevrolet Corvette ZR1 Convertible,
    top down, green $27
215 1993 Chevrolet Corvette ZR1 Coupe 40th
    Anniversary, red $27
220 1959 Porsche 356A Coupe, red $27
221 1959 Porsche 356A Coupe, silver $27
222 1959 Porsche 356A Convertible, top up,
    red..$27
223 1959 Porsche 356A Convertible, top
    down, silver......................................$27

224 1959 Porsche 356A Convertible, top up, blue.............$27
225 1959 Porsche 356A Convertible, top down, metallic yellow.............$27
226 1959 Porsche 356A Coupe Mille Miglia, silver.............$27
227 1959 Porsche 356A Coupe Carrera Panamerica #200, white.............$27
228 1959 Porsche 356A Coupe Carrera Panamerica #153, silver.............$27
229 1959 Porsche 356A Convertible, silver.$27
230 1994 Mercedes-Benz 320 SL Convertible, metallic silver.............$27
231 1994 Mercedes-Benz 320 SL Convertible, red.............$27
233 1994 Mercedes-Benz 320 SL Coupe, metallic blue.............$27
234 1994 Mercedes-Benz 320 SL Coupe, blue.............$27
235 1994 Mercedes-Benz 320 SL Coupe, gray.............$27
240 1952 BMW 502 Coupe, black.............$27
241 1952 BMW 502 Coupe, red.............$27
242 1952 BMW 502 Convertible, top down, blue.............$27
243 1952 BMW 502 Convertible, top up, silver.............$27
244 1952 BMW 502 Convertible, top down, red.............$27
245 1952 BMW 502 Coupe, two-tone gray.............$27
246 1952 BMW 502 Convertible, cream..$27
250 1959 BMW 503 Coupe, red.............$27
251 1959 BMW 503 Coupe, silver.............$27
252 1959 BMW 503 Coupe, black.............$27
253 1959 BMW 503 Convertible, red......$27

260 1994 Volkswagen Concept 1, yellow $27

261 1994 Volkswagen Concept 1, red......$27
262 1994 Volkswagen Concept 1, green...$27
263 1994 Volkswagen Concept 1 Convertible, yellow.............$27
264 1994 Volkswagen Concept 1 Convertible, red.............$27
265 1994 Volkswagen Concept 1 Convertible, green.............$27
266 1994 Volkswagen Concept 1 Convertible, silver.............$27
270 Volkswagen Golf, red.............$27
271 Volkswagen Golf, silver.............$27
272 Volkswagen Golf, white.............$27
273 Volkswagen Golf Cabriolet, red.............$27
274 Volkswagen Golf Cabriolet, silver.......$27
275 Volkswagen Golf Cabriolet, yellow.....$27

277 Volkswagen Golf Silverstone, multi-color.............$27
280 1994 Ford Mustang GT, red.............$27
281 1994 Ford Mustang GT Coupe, yellow.............$27
282 1994 Ford Mustang GT, blue.............$27
285 1994 Ford Mustang GT Convertible, bright blue.............$27
287 1994 Ford Mustang Indy Pace Car, red.............$27
290 1994 Ferrari F355 Berlinetta Coupe, red.............$27
291 1994 Ferrari F355 Berlinetta Coupe, yellow.............$27
292 1994 Ferrari F355 Berlinetta Coupe, blue.............$27
293 1994 Ferrari F355 Berlinetta Spyder, red.............$27
294 1994 Ferrari F355 Berlinetta Convertible, yellow.............$27
295 1994 Ferrari F355 Berlinetta Convertible, blue.............$27
296 1994 Ferrari F355 Berlinetta TS, top up, gray.............$27
305 1973 Ford Capri 2600 GT, metallic red with black roof.............$27
311 1964 Fiat 600 D, white.............$27

DG

DG stands for Dave Gilbert, the producer of white metal hand builts and kits from Great Britain. Two series, one regular and one Dinky style, were produced, although numbers may be intermingled. DG was started in 1973. The DG Dinky series represents models Dinky could have made in the thirties and forties but didn't. Thanks to Harv and Kay Goranson for updates and information.

Collector and dealer Noel Glucksman adds that "DG Models continue to this day by Dave Gilbert under his company name of AUTOCRAFT - Hand Made White Metal Models - 101 Enville Road, Kinver, West Midlands, England. Phone/Fax 011-44-1384-873-239 (from USA).

"He has been making an exquisite line of motorcycles with hand-painted riders for about three years or so," adds Glucksman. "A firm in the USA that sells them is MOTO Mini, McKinney, Texas."

2 1944 Dodge 4x4 Army Ambulance........$35
3 1934 Morris "Chivers"............$35
4 1930 Bentley Speed 6 ....$35
5 1936 Cord $35
1938 MG Tickford (kit)............$50
MG Y Saloon (kit) $50
1921 Murphy Duesenberg (kit) $50

DG Productions
760 Florida Central Parkway
Suite 212
Longwood, FL 32750
customer service: 407-331-1195

DG Productions is a Florida-based manufacturer of a high-quality plastic 1997 GM Topkick model coin banks with working lights and extensive details. D.G. Productions has plans on a series of these trucks. Some have shortened wheel bases, some with different markings, etc., according to wiseg@msdlouky.org in May 1998.
Schwan's Ice Cream and Fine Foods Delivery Truck, production limit 5,000 ....$50–65

Diamond
Russell Alameda provides the following information on this otherwise unknown brand.
1964 Shelby Cobra 427 SC, white, 1:18, limited edition of 2,100 ....$75

Diapet (also see Yonezawa)
Diapet is a popular Japanese brand of quality diecast vehicles produced by Yonezawa Toys.
Acura NSX, 1:40 ....$20
Airport Bus, B32 ....$20
Bus, 3-Axle Double-Decker, 4½", 11 ....$30
Bus "Hishi Nippon," 231 ....$20
Cordia XG1600 Turbo, G13 ....$20
Corvette, G76 ....$75
Datsun 280Z, G3, G116 ....$20
Datsun 280Z Police, P53 ....$20
Datsun F2 Coupe, G15 ....$20
Datsun Leopard 4-Door Sedan, G2 ....$20
Datsun Mail Van, 271 ....$20
Datsun Silvia 200SX, G39/G125 ....$20
Datsun Tow Truck, 272 ....$20
1930 Duesenberg, G124, 1:27 ....$34
DP2 Backhoe, K23 ....$20
DP2 Backhoe/Loader, K24 ....$20
Fuso Bus, B36 ....$20
Fuso Truck Crane, K30 ....$20
Hato Bus, B40 ....$24
Hato Double Decker Bus, B47, 1:75 ....$24
Honda Acura NSX, SV26, 1:40 ....$25–32
Honda Beat, SV33, 1:35 ....$19
Honda Prelude, SV34, 1:40 ....$21
Honda Prelude 2.0 SI, G55, 1:40 ....$20
Ihi 1600 Clamshell Bucket Crane, K21, 1:40 ....$34
Ihi IS-110 Power Shovel, K3, 1:50 ....$20
Ihi IS-110 Clamshell (Bucket), K5, 1:50 ....$22
Ihi IS-110 Track Backhoe, K4, 1:50 ....$22
Ihi IS-220 Track Backhoe, K17, 1:40.............$34
Infiniti Q45, SV18, 1:40 ....$24–34
Isuzu "Shell," 107 ....$20
Isuzu Shovel, K53 ....$20
Isuzu Mixer, 109 ....$20
Isuzu Semi TV, B47 ....$20
Jr. Highway Bus, B5, 1:60 ....$24
Kawasaki 88 ZII Wheel Loader, K31, 1:28.$28
Komatsu D20QF Track Loader, K31, 1:28 ..$22
Kubota Tractor, 1:23 ....$20
Lexus Coupe, SV22 ....$30
Lincoln Continental Mk IV, 01427 ....$30

Mack Car carrier, T54, 1:40 ....$37
Mazda Cosmo 2-Door Hardtop, 1:40 ....$20
Mazda Miata MX 5, SV14, 1:40 ....$21
Mazda RX7, SV35, 1:40 ....$24
Mazda RX7 Police, P57 ....$20
Mercedes-Benz 230S 4-Door Sedan, 167 ...$25
Mercedes-Benz 560SEL, G8, 1:40 ....$24
Mini Cooper 1000, SV3 ....$24
Mitsubishi Crawler Crane, K39, 1:60 ....$22
Mitsubishi GTO, SV27, 1:40 ....$21
Mitsubishi MS280 Track Backhoe, K42, 1:60 ....$22
Mitsubishi School Bus, B35 ....$20
Mitsubishi Starion 2000 GSR Coupe, silver, G17 ....$38
Neoplan Skyliner Bus, B41, 1:60 ....$28
Nissan Ambulance, P13, 1:35 ....$22
Nissan Cedric Ambulance, 283 ....$20
Nissan Cedric Police, P64 ....$20
Nissan Cedric Taxi, P65 ....$20
Nissan Cedric Ultima Station Taxi, P29 ....$35
Nissan Cherry Camper, T8 ....$20
Nissan Kombi "1008," T4 ....$20
Nissan Kombi Police, P3 ....$20
Nissan Fairlady 300 ZX, red, SV15 ....$27
Nissan Infiniti, SV18, 1:40 ....$25
Nissan Prairie, G22 ....$20
Nissan S&B 30 Mini Backhoe, K16, 1:26 ..$32
Nissan Safari, T1 ....$20
Nissan Silvia Coupe, G37 ....$20
Nissan Skyline Police Car, P43, 1:30 ....$20
Nissan Taxi, P16/P65, 1:40 ....$20
1980 Pontiac Firebird, G67 ....$20
Porsche 911S, red with black interior, 248, 1:40 ....$20
Porsche Turbo, metallic brown/silver, blue windows, black interior, G-47, 1:40 ....$20
Porsche 911S, metallic gold, #0158, 1:43 .$20
Rolls-Royce Silver Shadow, G71, 1:40 ....$25
Sakai Roller, K8 ....$20
Sakai TS150 Tire Roller, K12, 1:40 ....$22
School Bus, B4 ....$20
Seibu Tour Bus, B1, 1:75 ....$20
Sightseeing Bus, B39 ....$20
Subaru Leon 2-Door Hardtop, G128 ......$20
Subaru Mail Van, 462 ....$20
Sumitomo-FMC LS3400 Track H, K37, 1:42 ....$34

Sunny Coupe 1200 GL, #212....................$24

Suzuki Fronte Police, 296 ....$20
Toyota 2000GT, 162 ....$20
Toyota Carib (Tercel) 4x4 Wagon, G23 .....$20
Toyota Carib (Tercel) Radio Car, P5 ....$20

Toyota Celica 2800 GT/G5 ....$20
Toyota Corolla 1500SR 3-Door Sedan, G21 ....$20
Toyota Corolla Levin Coupe, G29 ....$20
Toyota Crown Police, 613/P62 ....$20
Toyota Crown Taxi, P63 ....$20
Toyota Fire Chief's Car, P17, 1:40 ....$22
Toyota Hiace Ambulance, P43/P55, 1:36 ....$12–20
Toyota Hiace Camper, T6 ....$20
Toyota Jobsun 7 Skid Loader, K11, 1:22 ....$24
Toyota Landcruiser FJ-60, T-100, 1:30 ......$30
Toyota Landcruiser Army, T2, 1:30 ......$20
Toyota Lexus SC, SV22, 1:40 ....$25
Toyota Mini School Bus, B37 ....$20
Toyota Pickup 4x4, T3 ....$20
Toyota Police Van, P42 ....$20
Toyota Previa Van, T-70, 1:40 ....$25
Toyota Soarer (Lexus) Coupe, G1/G27 .....$20
Toyota Supra 3.0GT Turbo, G50, 1:40 .....$20
Volkswagen 1300 Beetle, 165 ....$20
Volkswagen 1600TL, 157 ....$20
Yamaha Snowmobile, 287 ....$20

Dicascale

Dicascale of Japan is known to have produced a number of diecast cars.
212 Nippon Kotsu Coach, 1:100 ....$10

Dimension 4 (also see Specialty Diecast, Lucky Plan, Speedway Collection, Mark One, Hot Pursuit)

c/o Specialty Diecast Company
370 Miller Road
Medford, NJ
phone: 800-432-1933

First discovered in January 1998, the Speedway Collection is a series of 1:43 scale diecast NASCAR models manufactured by Lucky Plan Industries, produced by Specialty Diecast Company, distributed by Dimension 4 of Bell California and packaged in a clear plastic display box with the name "Mark One Collectibles" on top. Confused? I am. It would appear to be a marketing collaboration to offer yet another line of racing collectibles to an apparently starved market. In fact, there appears to be a glut of new diecast racing collectibles flooding the market in recent months, from Kenner's Winner's Circle collection to numerous Racing Champions' permutations and Mattel's Hot Wheels Pro Racing series, not to mention Racing Collectibles Club of America, Action Racing, and others.

The distinction, if indeed there is any, is that the Speedway Collection is the first high-quality low-priced series offered in mass-market retail stores such as Wal-Mart. Models sell for about $5 each. Listed below is just one of those models. Most recent models from Lucky Plan are being sold under the Race Image brand, which also happens to be a brand produced by Corgi.

Dimension 4 purchased Hot Pursuit Collectibles in 1997 shortly after Hot Pursuit was started. Latest information indicates that Dimension 4 is now out of business as of December 13, 1999.
97018 Pontiac Grand Prix, Bobby Labonte #18 "Interstate Batteries" $5

Dimestore Dreams

Binary Arts Corporation
1321 Cameron Street
Alexandria, VA 22314
phone: 703-549-4999
fax: 703-549-6210

Reproductions are common in the toy industry, but in 2000, Binary Arts Corporation started capitalizing on it in a big way. The result is Dimestore Dreams, reproductions of plastic toys originally made in the 1940s by Pyro Plastics, Thomas Toys, and Precision Plastics.
Ambulance, #20000, Precision Plastics reproduction $6–7

Convertible with Speedboat and Trailer, #20200, Precision Plastics reproduction $8–10

Motorcycle with Driver and Sidecar, #20310, Thomas Toys reproduction $6–7

Police Car, #20030, Thomas Toys reproduction $6–7

Spaceship X-100, #20400, Pyro Plastics reproduction $6–7
Station Wagon, #20060, Thomas Toys reproduction $6–7

Dinkum

It was previously assumed that Dinkum toys of Australia were given their name to capitalize on the similar-sounding Dinky brand name of England. But as collector Bill Cross reports,

Dinkum is Australian vernacular which, roughly translated, means "good," or "true," as in "fair dinkum, mate!"

Ford Falcon GT, red & black	$95
1969 Ford Mustang Boss, red, 1:43	$68
1985 Holden Commodore, white, 1:43	$35
Holden FJ Panel Van, dark blue	$85

Dinky

Excellent collector reference books have already been written on these great little gems from Great Britain, as indicated in this book's bibliography section. So, instead of trying to duplicate those works, this book will present a short history and highlight only a few of the numerous models produced.

Dinky Toys started out in 1933 as Modelled Miniatures, produced and marketed under the Frank Hornby name, the original manufacturer. Hornby also produced electric trains, and the first models produced were intended as accessories to these train sets.

Simultaneously in Liverpool, England, and Bobigny, France, the British and French Dinky Toys were put into production in 1934. French-made Dinky Toys, particularly the post-war models, are more highly valued in the U.S., and perhaps Europe, because the French models focused on American cars of the era, and serve as accurate models of the era.

The advent of Hot Wheels by Mattel in 1968 posed a major threat to companies such as Dinky Toys, contributing to the close of the French facility in 1972, although Pilen of Spain continued to produce some French Dinky models later in the seventies, while Solido of France attempted a similar feat in 1981.

The British firm, meanwhile, attempted to stay in business by farming out production of some models to Polistil of Italy and to Universal of Hong Kong. Universal eventually purchased the rights, and incorporated the brand into the Matchbox line, which Universal had purchased in 1982.

Several other firms staked a claim on the Dinky brand from time to time, including Tri-Ang of England in 1963, Mercury of Italy, Mercury Industries based in the US and Canada, Gibbs of Ohio, Best Box/Efsi of the Netherlands, and most notably Meccano of England.

The Dinky brand vanished with the purchase of Matchbox in 1992 by Tyco. All that is now left of Dinky models are their frequent appearance as Matchbox Collectibles out of Beaverton, Oregon, a division of Tyco that markets models through mail-order advertising in such publications as *Parade*, and in specialty magazines such as *Collecting Toys*, *Diecast Digest*, and others.

For a more complete detail of the complete line, Dr. Edward Force's book on *Dinky Toys* is available in bookstores or by special order.

The Dinky Collection from Matchbox is featured in *Matchbox Toys 1947 to 1996* by Dana Johnson from Collector Books ($18.95 retail), as well as in the third book in a four-volume set on Matchbox toys, *Universal's Matchbox Toys*, by Charles Mack.

Modelled Miniatures — The First Dinky Toys, 1933

Sports Roadster	$350
Sports Coupe	$250
Motor Truck	$175
Delivery Van	$300
Farm Tractor	$200

A Survey of Dinky Toys Through the Years

Austin A105, 1958	$20
Berliet Dump Truck, 1961	$125
Bristol Canadian Pacific Airline, 1959	$95
Brockway Pontoon Bridgelayer Truck, #884, 1961–1970	$1250
Buick Riviera, 1965–1967	$90–120
Buick Roadmaster, 1954	$225–240
Cadillac Superior Ambulance, 1974	$75–90
Corvair Monza, 1965	$90–110
Ford GT, 1966	$50–65
Hudson Hornet, 1958	$150–175
Jaguar XK120, 1954	$125
Johnson Street Sweeper, 1977	$45
Lady Penelope's Fab 1 Limousine (from *Thunderbirds* TV Series), #100, 1966–1976	$125–150
Maserati 2000, 1958	$90
Meccano Delivery Van, 1934	$250
Mercury Seaplane, 1939	$100
Oldsmobile 88, 1965	$90
Packard Super 8, 1939	$250
Plymouth Belvedere, 1957	$150
Pontiac Police Car, 1971	$75
Rambler Classic, #006, 1965–1967	$90
Rambler Cross Country, 1961	$95
Riley Saloon, 1947	$85
Rolls-Royce Silver Wraith, 1959	$90
Rover 3500 Police, 1979	$50

Speed of the Wind, 1936 ....$125

Star Trek Klingon Battle Cruiser, large, #357, 1980	$550
Star Trek Klingon Battle Cruiser, small, 804, 1980	$100–125
Star Trek U.S.S. Enterprise, large, #358, 1976–1980	$600–700
Star Trek U.S.S. Enterprise, small, #803, 1980	$100–125

Studebaker Commander, 1949	$425–450
Studebaker Golden Hawk, 1958	$150–175
Talbot Lago, 1953	$75–90
Viceroy 37 Bus, 1972	$25–40

Mini-Dinky

10 Ford Corsair	$25
11 Jaguar E-Type	$25
12 Corvette Stingray	$35
13 Ferrari 250 LM	$25
14 Chevrolet II	$25
15 Rolls Royce Silver Shadow	$25
16 Ford Mustang	$25
17 Aston Martin DB 6	$25
18 Mercedes 230 SL	$25
19 MGB Sports Car	$25
20 Cadillac	$25
21 Fiat 2300 Station Wagon	$25
22 Oldsmobile Toronado	$35
23 Rover 2000	$25
24 Ferrari Superfast	$25
25 Ford Zephyr 6	$25
26 Mercedes 250SE	$25
27 Buick Riviera	$25
28 Ferrari F1 Racing Car	$25
29 Ford GT	$25
30 Volvo 1800S	$25
31 Volkswagen 1600 TL	$25
32 Vauxhall Cresta	$25
33 Jaguar Mark 10	$25
94 International Bulldozer	$25
95 International Skid Shovel	$25
96 Payloader Shovel	$25
97 Euclid R40	$25
98 Michigan Scraper Earth Mover	$25
99 Caterpillar Grader	$25

DMP Studios

DMP is a Canadian company that specializes in custom hand-built or "studio" models and factory-approved conversions of Brooklins. DMP models are distributed in the US by Brasilia Press, P O Box 2023, Elkhart, IN 46515.

1961 Chevrolet Impala Convertible (converted Brooklin Impala Sports Coupe), Honduras maroon..................$125

Doepke

At the end of World War II, The Charles Wm. Doepke Mfg. Co., Inc. of Rossmoyne, Ohio, began manufacturing large, durable toys called Doepke (pronounced DEP-key) "Model Toys." Production continued until 1959. The full story of Doepke Model Toys can be found in Richard O'Brien's book *Collecting Toy Cars and Trucks* from Krause Publishing, and in Don & Barb DeSalle's book *The DeSalle Collection of Smith-Miller & Doepke Toys*. Doepke toys are sturdy large scale cast-metal and pressed steel toys with heavy rubber tires.

#2000 Wooldridge Heavy Duty Earth Hauler, 25" long..................$275
#2001 Barber-Greene High Capacity Bucket Loader, 13" high..................$350

#2002 Jaeger Concrete Mixer, 15" long...$350

#2006 Adams Diesel Road Grader, 26" long......................................$200

#2007 Unit Mobile Crane, 11½"............$250

#2008 American LaFrance Aerial Ladder Truck......................................$475

#2009 Euclid Earth Hauler Truck, 27" long......................................$325

#2010 American LaFrance Pumper Fire Truck, 18" long........................$350

#2011 Heiliner Earth Scraper, 29" long $300

#2012 Caterpillar D6 Tractor and Bulldozer, 15" long...................................$500

#2013 Barber-Greene Mobile High-Capacity Bucket Loader, 22" long....................$450

#2014 American LaFrance Aerial Ladder Fire Truck, 23" long.......................$500

#2015 Clark Airport Tractor and Baggage Trailers......................................$450

#2017 MG, 1954, 15" long.........$500–700

#2018 Jaguar, 1955............$700–900

#2023 Searchlight Truck, 1955...........$1,200

Doorkey

Doorkey models are mostly 1:43 scale diecast made in various worldwide factories for the Holland-based company. Note that besides being marketed under the Doorkey brand, they are also produced for AHC.

Doorkey Models Made in China

DO150 Toyota Celica, 1:43..(£13) $21 US

DO151 Toyota Landcruiser, 1:43 ....(£13) $21 US

DO152 Toyota MR-2, 1:43 ...(£13) $21 US

DO153 Toyota Supra, 1:43...(£13) $21 US

DO154 BMW 2000 Saloon, 1:43 ....(£13) $21 US

DO155 BMW 507 sports, 1:43.......................£(13) $21 US

DO401 1994 BMW 325i, 1:43...................(£5) $8 US

DO402 1994 Mercedes 500SEL, 1:43...................(£5) $8 US

DO403 1994 Lexus SC 400, 1:43.......................(£5) $8 US

Doorkey Models Made in Spain

DO101T Mercedes 100 Van plain colors, 1:50 ....(£15) $24 US

DO101T Mercedes 100 Van Spanish Telephones, 1:50 ....(£15) $24 US

DO101C Mercedes 100 Van Spanish Post, 1:50 ....(£15) $24 US

DO104 Suzuki Samurai 4 x 4 ..(£15) $24 US

DO106 Opel Kadett Combo Van lhd ....(£15) $24 US

DO108Q Vauxhall Astramax Van Q8 Lubricants......................(£19) $30 US

DO108Q Vauxhall Astramax Van rhd ....(£15) $24 US

DO110 Ford Escort Van 1993 various colors ....£(15) $24 US

DO114 Nissan Maxima with spoiler ....(£15) $24 US

DO115 Nissan Maxima....(£15) $24 US

DO116 Nissan Serena people carrier......................(£15) $24 US

DO117 Nissan Micra 3-Door RHD or LHD ....(£15) $24 US

DO118 Nissan Micra 5-Door RHD or LHD ....(£15) $24 US

DO125 SEAT Ibiza Hatchback ....(£15) $24 US

DO126 SEAT Toledo various colors ....(£15) $24 US

DO130 Volvo 440 GL 1994 restyle ....(£15) $24 US

DO131 Volvo 440 Turbo 1994 restyle ....(£15) $24 US

DO133 Volvo 480 Turbo 1994 restyle ....(£15) $24 US

DO135 Volvo 850 GLT (10 colors) ....(£15) $24 US

DO136 Volvo 850 Estate Car 1996......................$27 US

DO139 Volvo 850 T-5 (10 colors) stock ....(£15) $24 US

DO1xx Volvo 460 Saloon 1996 .....$27 US

Doorkey Made for AHC of Spain, 1:43, made in Spain, refinished in Holland

D130DP Volvo 440 Politie, Dutch police ....£29 ($45 US)

D135SP Volvo 850 GLT Polis, Swedish police..............£24 ($38 US)

D135D Volvo 850 GLT Douane (Customs)....................£24 ($38 US)

D135DP Volvo 850 GLT Politie, Dutch police................£24 ($38 US)

D200SM Volvo B10M bus Maastricht (300 made)..£39 ($61 US)

D200LP DAF MB230 bus Lila Pause (300 made) ....£39 ($61 US)

D200DP DAF-den Oudsten bus Politie (300 made) ....£39 ($61 US)

Dragon Wings

Dragon Models
B1-10/F., 603-609 Castle Peak Rd.
Kong Nam Industrial Building
Tsuen Wan, N. T., Hong Kong
phone: (852) 2493-0215
fax: (852) 2411-0587
e-mail: info@dragon-models.com
website: www.dragon-models.com

Dragon Wings are 1:400 scale precision diecast airliner miniatures of exceptional quality from Dragon Models of Hong Kong.

Druge Brothers

Druge Brothers Manufacturing Company of Oakland, California, produced a couple of scale model lumber yard "straddle buggies" designed for hauling lumber. The company produced just a few models around 1948, original price $9.75. Models appear to be in 1:50 scale.

Cari-Car Lumber Carrier, yellow $175–200

Hyster Lumber carrier, yellow $200–225

Dugu

One of the premier miniature model companies of Italy was known as Dugu, a company that produced some beautiful models in 1:43 to 1:50 scale. The company started in 1963 by marketing Miniautotoys and Museo models. They represented real cars from the Automotive Museum of Torino, Italy.

Miniautotoys are high-quality 1:43 scale models similar to Rio, while Museo models are 1:50 scale simplified, less expensive models. A third series called Sispla was also produced in 1974.

Dugu Miniautotoys 1:43 Scale

1 1911 Fiat 4 Closed Tourer, 1962......$50

2 1925 Lancia Lambda Sedan, 1962...$50

3 1911 Fiat 4 Open Tourer, 1963 ....$50

4 1907 Fiat Grand Prix, 1964 ....$55

5 1925 Lancia Lambda Torpedo, 1964..$50

6 1907 Itala Palombella, 1966...........$50

7 1912 Itala 25/35HP Closed Tourer, 1965.......................$50

8 Itala 25/35HP Open Tourer, 1965 ...$50

9 1896 Bernardi 3.5HP, top up, 1967.$50

10 1896 Bernardi 3.5HP, top down, 1966.......................$50

11 1899 Fiat 3.5HP, top down, 1966 .$45

12 1899 Fiat 3.5HP, top up, 1966......$45

13 1967 Duesenberg SJ Town Car, 1967.......................$140

14 1925 Fiat 509 2-Door Sedan, 1967.......................$50

15 1925 Fiat 509 Open Tourer, 1967.$50

16 1909 Itala 35/45HP Limousine, 1968.......................$50

17 1934 Fiat Balilla Coppa D'Oro, 1968.......................$55

18 1936 Cord Phaeton, top up, 1968.......................$180

19 1931 Duesenberg SJ, 1968 ....$135

20 1936 Cord Phaeton, top down, 1968.......................$180

21 1934 Rolls-Royce Silver Ghost, top up, 1969.......................$120

22 1934 Rolls-Royce Silver Ghost, top down, 1969.......................$120

23 Fiat-Eldridge Grand Prix, 1975........$80

24 1911 Fiat S-76 Record Car, 1971 ..$80

Dugu Museo 1:50 Scale

M1 1893 Benz Victoria, 1964 ....$40

M2 1894 Peugeot Vis-a-Vis, 1964........$40

M3 1899 Benz Estate Car, 1964.........$40

M4 1902 Darracq Tourer, 1964.........$40

M5 1903 De Dion-Bouton Populaire, 1964.......................$40

M6 1908 Legnano 6/8HP Spider, top up, 1965.......................$40

M7 1908 Legnano 6/8HP Spider, top down, 1965.......................$60

M8 1936 Fiat 500A Coupe, 1966......$60

M9 1908 Brixia Zust Phaeton, 1967....$40

M10 1948 Cisitalia 202 Coupe, 1968 .$55
M11 1914 Lancia Theta, 1968 ....$40
M12 1923 Ansaldo 4C Open Tourer, 1970 ....$40
M13 1936 Fiat 500A Convertible Coupe, 1969 ....$60
M14 1923 Fiat 519S Tourer, 1971 .....$40

Dugu Sispla, 1:43 Scale, 1974
1 Same Centauro Farm Tractor...........$260
2 Fiat 56 550HP Farm Tractor $260
3 Fiat 697N Dump Truck $90
4a Fiat 90NC Dump Truck $90
4b OM Dump Truck $90
5 Fiat Tank Truck $90

Duravit
Duravit models are made in Argentina. Not much else is known as of this writing.
Mercedes Semi Oil Truck, 23" $18

Durham Classics
A small assortment of Durham Classics of Canada are currently available. These American classic cars are exquisitely represented in 1:43 scale. These are some of the best detailed and most accurate 1:43 scale models on the market.
1F 1934 Chrysler Airflow Two-Door 30th Anniversary $119
1G 1934 Chrysler Airflow "California Highway Patrol" $119
2 1953 Ford Pick-Up, blue $99
2H 1953 Ford Pick-Up, red with "Wurlitzer" juke box $119
3S 1939 Ford Panel Delivery "Sacramento Bee" $119
4 1938 Lincoln Zephyr Coupe, black....$95–99
5 1941 Chevrolet Coupe, blue $95–99
5D 1941 Chevrolet "Michigan State Police" .$99
5E 1941 Chevrolet Coupe "Idaho State Police" $99
6A 1953 Ford Telephone Repair Truck "General" $109
7 1954 Ford Panel Wagon "Canadian Colonial Airways" $99
7A 1954 Ford Panel Wagon "Prairie Airways" $99
9 1938 Lincoln Zephyr Convertible, top down $95–99
9D 1938 Lincoln Zephyr Convertible, top up $95
10A 1941 Chevrolet Convertible, top down ..$99
12 1941 Chevrolet Panel Delivery Van...$99
12B 1941 Chevrolet Panel Delivery Van "Labatts" $99
13A 1939 Ford Panel Delivery "The Sacramento Bee" $99
14A 1951 Ford Monarch 2-Door Coupe $99
15A 1941 Ford Coupe $99
17 1941 Chevrolet Suburban "Niagara Tours" $109

Dust & Glory (see Great American Dreamcars)

Duvi
Albert Sattler of Melbourne, Australia, wrote by e-mail, "I have recently acquired an exquisite 1:43 scale Renault Dauphine from DUVI. I can only tell you what's on the box: 'Vente Interdite Aux Moins De 14 ANS.' Does that help at all?" Unfortunately it doesn't since it appears to be French for "Not intended for children under 14 years." Mr. Sattler didn't mention what price he paid, so an educated guess is all I can provide.
Renault Dauphine, 1:43......................$40–50

Dux
An otherwise unknown company, Dux of Germany at one time produced a large-scale diecast Studebaker model and a Mercedes W196 Gullwing.
Studebaker..............................$25–60
Mercedes-Benz W196 Gullwing $25–60

Dyna-Mo
Dyna-Model Products Co.
93 South Street
Oyster Bay
Long Island, NY
Dyna-Mo brand 1:87 scale models are manufactured on Long Island, New York, specifically for use with HO gauge railroad layouts. They feature cast-metal bodies with separate tires and wheels. (Some assembly required.) Models are available pre-painted or unpainted.
Airport Platform Tractor & Two Baggage Wagons, painted $8
unpainted $6
1908 Buick, painted $7
unpainted $4
Caterpillar Bulldozer, painted...........$10
unpainted $6
Caterpillar Crawler, painted $8
unpainted $5
Coal Conveyor, painted $7
unpainted $4
1947 Ford Pickup Truck, painted $7
unpainted $4
Fork Lift (2-pack), painted...........$10
unpainted $6
1911 Maxwell, painted $7
unpainted $4
1916 Packard Twin Six, painted........$7
unpainted $4
1909 Stanley Steamer, painted $7
unpainted $4
1914 Stutz Bearcat, painted $7
unpainted $4

Dyna-Model Products Company (see Dyna-Mo)

Dynamic
A recent find revealed a toy car in a blisterpack labeled Dynamic. The package's resemblance to a Majorette blisterpack was obviously more than coincidental. It is an obvious attempt to copy Majorette's packaging and capitalize on Majorette's popularity.

Eagle Collectibles (formerly Eagle's Race)
Eagle's Race is from Universal Hobbies of Hong Kong introduced in 1998. The company has since changed the name to Eagle Collectibles.

Eagle's Race/Eagle Collectibles 1:18 Scale
3019 Ford GT 40 #2, black, 1ST 24H Le Mans 1966 ....$20
3039 Ford GT 40 #1, blue, 2ND 24H Le Mans 1966 ....$20
3040 Ford GT 40 #5, gold, 3RD 24H Le Mans 1966 ....$20
3101 1965 Ford Mustang GT 350 Shelby, white & dark blue $20
3154 1965 Ford Mustang GT 350 Hertz, white & gold $20
3159 1965 Ford Mustang Fastback, red with blue stripes $21
3801 1940 Ford Deluxe Coupe, black $22
3802 1940 Ford Deluxe Coupe, red $22
3804 1940 Ford Deluxe Hot Rod, red with yellow flames $22
3805 1940 Ford Deluxe Hot Rod, blue with pink flames $22
3806 1940 Ford Deluxe Hot Rod, black with yellow flames $22
3807 1940 Ford Deluxe Hot Rod, yellow with red flames $22
3808 1940 Ford Deluxe Coupe, white $22

Eagle's Race 1:43 Scale
1005 1:43 Mustang Mach III, red...........................$18–20
1006 1:43 Triumph TR3A Convertible, Limited Edition, red $18–20
1007 1:43 Triumph TR3A Convertible, Limited Edition, bright green $18–20
1008 1:43 Triumph TR3A Hardtop, Limited Edition, black $18–20
1009 1:43 Triumph TR3A Hardtop, Limited Edition, silver $18–20
1018 1:43 1973 Porsche 911 2.4L, green $18–20
1019 1:43 1973 Porsche 911 2.4L, red $18–20
1020 1:43 MGB Mk II Convertible, Limited Edition, light blue $18–20
1021 1:43 MGB Mk II Convertible, Limited Edition, bright green $18–20
1024 1:43 VW Beetle Convertible, red $18–20
1025 1:43 VW Beetle Convertible, black $18–20
1027 1:43 VW Beetle Soft Top, light blue $18–20
1041 1:43 Porsche 911S #15 Monte Carlo $18–20
1044 1:43 Porsche 911S #80 Le Mans...............................$18–20

1049 1:43 Mustang Mach III, black...$18–20

1050 1:43 Mustang Mach III, yellow...............................$18–20

1059 1:43 MGB Mk II Soft Top, orange...............................$18–20

1060 1:43 MGB Mk II Convertible, Limited Edition, light blue.............$18–20

1062 1:43 MGB Mk II Soft Top, yellow...............................$18–20

1063 1:43 MGB Mk II Police, black...............................$18–20

1064 1:43 MGB Mk II Police, white...............................$18–20

1065 1:43 MGB Mk II, black/silver, Limited Edition...............................$20–22

1066 1:43 MGB Mk II, bronze/gold, Limited Edition...............................$20–22

1070 1:43 MGF 1.8L Convertible, red...............................$18–20

1071 1:43 MGF 1.8L Convertible, bright green...............................$18–20

1072 1:43 MGF 1.8L Convertible, purple...............................$18–20

1073 1:43 MGF 1.8L Convertible, orange...............................$18–20

1074 1:43 MGF 1.8L Soft Top, light gray...............................$18–20

1075 1:43 MGF 1.8L Soft Top, blue...............................$18–20

1076 1:43 MGF 1.8L Soft Top, burgundy...............................$18–20

1081 1:43 Triumph TR3A #25 Le Mans...............................$18–20

1082 1:43 Triumph TR3A #26 Le Mans...............................$18–20

1083 1:43 Triumph TR3 Convertible, light yellow...............................$18–20

1084 1:43 Triumph TR3 Convertible, light blue...............................$18–20

1085 1:43 Triumph TR3 Tour De Corse...............................$18–20

1086 1:43 Triumph TR2 Convertible, pearl white...............................$18–20

1087 1:43 Triumph TR2 Convertible, black...............................$18–20

1088 1:43 Triumph TR2 #28 Le Mans...............................$18–20

1089 1:43 Triumph TR3A #27 Le Mans...............................$18–20

1090 1:43 Porsche Carrera, white/blue...............................$18–20

1092 1:43 MGB #47 Marathon 1966...............................$18–20

1093 1:43 Triumph TR3 Hardtop, beige...............................$18–20

1094 1:43 Porsche Carrera, blue/black...............................$18–20

1095 1:43 Triumph TR3 Soft Top, green...............................$18–20

1096 1:43 1973 Porsche 911 2.4L, yellow...............................$18–20

1097 1:43 Triumph TR3A Rochester NY Fire...............................$18–20

1098 1:43 Triumph TR2 #29 Le Mans...............................$18–20

1099 1:43 Triumph TR2 #68 Le Mans...............................$18–20

1101 1:43 VW Beetle, yellow/black, Limited Edition...............................$20–22

1103 1:43 VW Beetle "JEANS," yellow...............................$18–20

1104 1:43 VW Beetle "CITY," red, Limited Edition...............................$20–22

1105 1:43 VW Beetle "BIG," green, Limited Edition...............................$20–22

1106 1:43 VW Beetle "JEANS," yellow, Limited Edition...............................$20–22

1107 1:43 VW Beetle Soft Top, gold...............................$18–20

1108 1:43 VW Beetle "POLIZEI"....$18–20

1109 1:43 VW Beetle "FIRE BRIGADE"...............................$18–20

1110 1:43 VW Beetle "ROAD PATROL"...............................$18–20

1111 1:43 VW Beetle, orange......$18–20

1112 1:43 VW Beetle, apple green...............................$18–20

1114 1:43 VW Beetle Soft Top, silver...............................$18–20

1115 1:43 VW Beetle Convertible, light yellow...............................$18–20

1120 1:43 Ford GT40 #98 Daytona 1966...............................$18–20

1124 1:43 VW Beetle "FLOWER POWER"...............................$18–20

1125 1:43 VW Beetle "FLOWER POWER"...............................$18–20

1128 1:43 Triumph TR3A Hardtop, blue/white...............................$18–20

1130 1:43 Porsche 911 2.4L, silver.$18–20

1131 1:43 Porsche Carrera "GALLIA"...............................$18–20

1132 1:43 Porsche Carrera RSR #66...............................$18–20

1133 1:43 Porsche Carrera RSR #69...............................$18–20

1134 1:43 Porsche Carrera RSR #65...............................$18–20

1135 1:43 Porsche Carrera RSR #53...............................$18–20

1136 1:43 Porsche Carrera RSR #14...............................$18–20

1137 1:43 PORSCHE Carrera RSR, tart...............................$18–20

1138 1:43 Ford GT40 #22 Sebring 1969...............................$18–20

1139 1:43 Ford GT40 Mk II #57 Le Mans...............................$18–20

1140 1:43 MGB #202 Targa Florio 1968...............................$18–20

1150 1:43 MGB GT East Sussex Police...............................$18–20

1151 1:43 MGB GT, red............$18–20

1152 1:43 MGB GT, purple $18–20

1153 1:43 MGB GT, white $18–20

1154 1:43 MGB GT, Limited Edition.$20–22

1155 1:43 MGB GT "JUBILEE," Limited Edition...............................$20–22

1201 1:43 1932 Ford Roadster, yellow...............................$18–20

1202 1:43 1932 Ford Roadster, black...............................$18–20

1203 1:43 1932 Ford Roadster, light blue...............................$18–20

1204 1:43 1932 Ford Roadster, red/yellow...............................$18–20

1205 1:43 1932 Ford Roadster, white/purple...............................$18–20

1206 1:43 1932 Ford Roadster, black/yellow...............................$18–20

1207 1:43 1932 Ford Coupe, purple/pink...............................$18–20

1208 1:43 1932 Ford Coupe "SHARK"...............................$18–20

1209 1:43 1932 Ford Coupe, black/blue...............................$18–20

1210 1:43 1932 Ford Coupe, red..$18–20

1211 1:43 1932 Ford Coupe, blue/red...............................$18–20

1212 1:43 1932 Ford Coupe "EAT MY DUST"...............................$18–20

1401 1:43 Dodge Charger Daytona #71...............................$18–20

1402 1:43 Dodge Charger Daytona Chrysler Race...............................$18–20

1403 1:43 Dodge Charger Daytona #22...............................$18–20

1404 1:43 Dodge Charger Daytona #99...............................$18–20

1405 1:43 Dodge Charger Daytona #6...............................$18–20

1406 1:43 Dodge Charger Daytona Start, red...............................$18–20

1407 1:43 Dodge Charger Daytona Start, dark blue...............................$18–20

1408 1:43 Dodge Charger Daytona Start, white...............................$18–20

1409 1:43 Dodge Charger Daytona Start, blue...............................$18–20

1410 1:43 Dodge Charger Daytona Start, black...............................$18–20

1501 1:43 Land Rover Freelander, open, black...............................$18–20

1502 1:43 Land Rover Freelander, open, red...............................$18–20

1503 1:43 Land Rover Freelander, open, silver...............................$18–20

1504 1:43 Land Rover Freelander, closed, light green...............................$18–20

1505 1:43 Land Rover Freelander, closed, light purple...............................$18–20

1506 1:43 Land Rover Freelander, closed, light gold...............................$18–20

1550 1:43 1949 Mercury Coupe, black...............................$18–20

1551 1:43 1949 Mercury Coupe, red...............................$18–20

1552 1:43 1949 Mercury Police, black/white...............................$18–20

1553 1:43 1949 Mercury Fire Chief, red $18–20

1554 1:43 1949 Mercury Custom, purple/yellow $18–20

1555 1:43 1949 Mercury Custom, silver/green $18–20

1556 1:43 1949 Mercury Custom, black/yellow $18–20

1557 1:43 1949 Mercury Custom, red/yellow $18–20

1601 1:43 Porsche 1973 AFRICA SAFARI, Limited Edition $25–27

1602 1:43 Porsche 1974 AFRICA SAFARI, Limited Edition $25–27

1603 1:43 Porsche 1971 AFRICA SAFARI, Limited Edition $25–27

1701 1:43 Renault 5 Turbo, red $18–20

1702 1:43 Renault 5 Turbo, blue....$18–20

1703 1:43 Renault Turbo #9 Monte Carlo $18–20

1704 1:43 Renault #7 Tour De Corse $18–20

1705 1:43 Renault Tour De France $18–20

1706 1:43 Renault #598 Tour Italy $18–20

1707 1:43 Renault Corte Ingles ...$18–20

1801 1:43 Renault Corte Ingles ...$18–20

1802 1:43 Renault Sport Trophy ..$18–20

1803 1:43 1999 Renault Sport Trophy $18–20

1804 1:43 1999 Renault Sport Trophy $18–20

1805 1:43 1999 Renault Sport Trophy $18–20

2001 1:43 Grand Sport #2 Sebring $18–20

2002 1:43 Grand Sport #3 Sebring $18–20

2003 1:43 Grand Sport #80 Nassau $18–20

2004 1:43 Grand Sport Roadster #12 ....$18–20

2005 1:43 Grand Sport Roadster #10 ....$18–20

2006 1:43 Grand Sport #67 Road America $18–20

2007 1:43 Grand Sport Roadster #7 ....$18–20

3008 1:18 Ford GT40 #6 Le Mans 1969 ....$30–32

3019 1:18 Ford GT40 #2 Le Mans 1966 ....$30–32

3039 1:18 Ford GT40 #1 Le Mans 1966 ....$30–32

3040 1:18 Ford GT40 #5 Le Mans 1966 ....$30–32

3101 1:18 1965 Ford Mustang GT350, white/blue $30–32

3116 1:18 1965 Ford Mustang GT350, red/white $30–32

3118 1:18 1966 Ford Mustang HERTZ, black/gold $30–32

3124 1:18 1966 Ford Mustang HERTZ, red/gold $30–32

3128 1:18 1965 Ford Mustang GT350, blue/white $30–32

3130 1:18 Shinoda Boss Mustang Coupe, yellow, Limited Edition $35–37

3131 1:18 1994 Ford Mustang Convertible, black $30–32

3135 1:18 1994 Ford Mustang Coupe, black/gold $30–32

3138 1:18 1994 Ford Mustang Convertible, orange/black $30–32

3143 1:18 Shinoda Boss Mustang Coupe, black, Limited Edition $35–37

3144 1:18 Shinoda Boss Mustang Convertible, blue, Limited Edition.........$35–37

3145 1:18 Shinoda Boss Mustang Coupe, orange, Limited Edition $35–37

3146 1:18 Shinoda Boss Mustang Convertible, red, Limited Edition $35–37

3147 1:18 Shinoda Boss Mustang Convertible, black, Limited Edition $35–37

3152 1:18 1966 Ford Mustang GT350, blue/dark blue $30–32

3153 1:18 1966 Ford Mustang GT350, green/yellow $30–32

3154 1:18 1966 Ford Mustang HERTZ, white/gold $30–32

3155 1:18 Ford Mustang Coupe, blue/white $30–32

3156 1:18 Ford Mustang Coupe, white/blue $30–32

3157 1:18 Ford Mustang Coupe, red/gold $30–32

3158 1:18 Ford Mustang Coupe, blue $30–32

3159 1:18 1966 Ford Mustang GT350, red/blue $30–32

3164 1:18 Ford GT40 Mk II #8 Le Mans $30–32

3166 1:18 1966 Ford Mustang GT350, pink/white...........................$30–32

3167 1:18 1966 Ford Mustang GT350, black/red $30–32

3168 1:18 Ford GT40 Mk II #3 Le Mans $30–32

3169 1:18 1965 Mustang Fastback, dark green $30–32

3170 1:18 1965 Mustang Fastback, light blue $30–32

3171 1:18 Ford GT40 Mk II #6 Le Mans $30–32

3172 1:18 Ford GT40 Mk II #68 Le Mans $30–32

3173 1:18 Ford GT40 Street, silver ..$30–32

3174 1:18 Ford GT40 Street, green/black $30–32

3175 1:18 1966 Ford Mustang HERTZ, green/gold $30–32

3176 1:18 1994 Ford Mustang Convertible, metallic blue....................$30–32

3177 1:18 1994 Ford Mustang Coupe, silver $30–32

3178 1:18 1965 Ford Mustang Fastback, yellow $30–32

3201 1:18 1973 Porsche Carrera, white/red $30–32

3203 1:18 1973 Porsche Carrera, yellow/green $30–32

3204 1:18 1973 Porsche Carrera, black/red $30–32

3205 1:18 1973 Porsche Carrera, red $30–32

3206 1:18 1973 Porsche Carrera, green/black $30–32

3207 1:18 1973 Porsche Carrera, blue $30–32

3208 1:18 Porsche 911 #80 Le Mans $30–32

3209 1:18 Porsche 911 #48 Le Mans $30–32

3210 1:18 1973 Porsche Carrera, silver $30–32

3211 1:18 1973 Porsche Carrera, light blue $30–32

3212 1:18 Porsche 911 Tour De France $30–32

3214 1:18 1973 Porsche Carrera, orange $30–32

3215 1:18 1973 Porsche Carrera, orange/black $30–32

3301 1:18 Alfa Romeo Spyder, red $30–32

3302 1:18 Alfa Romeo Spyder Hardtop, red $30–32

3304 1:18 Alfa Romeo Spyder, black $30–32

3305 1:18 Alfa Romeo Spyder, yellow $30–32

3306 1:18 Alfa Romeo Spyder Hardtop, silver $30–32

3307 1:18 Alfa Romeo Spyder, white, Limited Edition $35–37

3308 1:18 Alfa Romeo Spyder, metallic green $30–32

3601 1:43 Dodge Viper GTS 1996, blue/white $18–20

3603 1:43 Dodge Viper GTSR #5, white/blue $18–20

3604 1:43 Dodge Viper GTSR #49 Le Mans $18–20

3605 1:43 Dodge Viper GTSR #51 Le Mans $18–20

3606 1:43 Dodge Viper GTSR #98 Daytona $18–20

3607 1:43 Dodge Viper GTSR #48 Le Mans $18–20

3608 1:43 Dodge Viper GTSR #50 Le Mans $18–20

3609 1:43 Dodge Viper RT/10 #40 Le Mans $18–20

3610 1:43 Dodge Viper RT/10 #41 Le Mans $18–20

3611 1:43 Dodge Viper GTSR, black.$18–20

3612 1:43 Dodge Viper GTSR #64 Le Mans $18–20

3614 1:43 Dodge Viper GTSR #62 Le Mans $18–20

3615 1:43 Dodge Viper GTSR #63 Le Mans $18–20

3616 1:43 Dodge Viper GTSR #52 GT2 Champion $18–20

3617 1:43 Dodge Viper GTSR #61 Le Mans $18–20

3618 1:43 Dodge Viper GTSR Taisan 1997 ....$18–20

3620 1:43 Dodge Viper RT/10 1996, white/blue $18–20

3621 1:43 Dodge Viper RT/10 Soft Top, black $18–20

3624 1:43 Dodge Viper RT/10 1996, blue/white $18–20

3627 1:43 Dodge Viper RT/10 1996, silver/blue $18–20

3628 1:43 Dodge Viper GTS 1998, red/white $18–20

3630 1:43 Dodge Viper GTS 1998, silver/blue $18–20

3631 1:43 Dodge Viper GTS 1999, black/silver $18–20

3640 1:43 Dodge Prowler Convertible 1999, purple $18–20

3641 1:43 Dodge Prowler Soft Top 1999, purple $18–20

3642 1:43 Dodge Prowler Convertible 1999, yellow $18–20

3643 1:43 Dodge Prowler Soft Top 1999, yellow $18–20

3644 1:43 Dodge Prowler Convertible 1999, black $18–20

3645 1:43 Dodge Prowler Soft Top 1999, black $18–20

3646 1:43 Dodge Prowler Convertible 1999, red $18–20

3647 1:43 Dodge Prowler Soft Top 1999, red $18–20

3648 1:43 Dodge Prowler Convertible PPG $18–20

3651 1:43 Dodge Ram 2500 V10, black $18–20

3652 1:43 Dodge Ram 2500 V10, gray/silver $18–20

3653 1:43 Dodge Ram 2500 V10, green/silver $18–20

3654 1:43 Dodge Ram 2500 V10, red/silver $18–20

3655 1:43 Dodge Ram 2500 V10, amethyst $18–20

3656 1:43 Dodge Ram 2500 V10, chestnut $18–20

3660 1:43 Dodge Viper GTS4 #53 Le Mans $18–20

3661 1:43 Dodge Viper GTSR #51 Le Mans $18–20

3662 1:43 Dodge Viper GTSR #51 GT2 Champion $18–20

3663 1:43 Dodge Viper GTSR #53 GT2 2nd $18–20

3664 1:43 Dodge Viper GTSR TAISAN 1998 ....$18–20

3665 1:43 Dodge Viper GT2 Champion, Limited Edition $20–22

3666 1:43 Dodge Viper GTS PPG Pace Car $18–20

3667 1:43 Dodge Viper ACR Record $18–20

3801 1:18 1940 Ford Coupe, black $30–32

3802 1:18 1940 Ford Coupe, red .$30–32

3803 1:18 1940 Ford Coupe, dark metallic blue $30–32

3804 1:18 1940 Ford Hot Rod, red/yellow $30–32

3805 1:18 1940 Ford Hot Rod, blue/pink $30–32

3806 1:18 1940 Ford Hot Rod, black/yellow $30–32

3807 1:18 1940 Ford Hot Rod, yellow/red $30–32

3808 1:18 1940 Ford Coupe, cream $30–32

3810 1:18 1940 Ford Coupe, burgundy $30–32

3811 1:18 1940 Ford Coupe, gray $30–32

3812 1:18 1940 Ford Hot Rod, purple/red $30–32

3814 1:18 1940 Ford Hot Rod, green/yellow $30–32

3901 1:18 Porsche 917K #22 Le Mans 1971 ....$30–32

3902 1:18 Porsche 917L #23 Le Mans 1970 ....$30–32

3903 1:18 Porsche 917K #2 Monza 1971 ....$30–32

3904 1:18 Porsche 917K #2 Daytona 1970 ....$30–32

3905 1:18 Porsche 917K #3 Sebring 1971 ....$30–32

3906 1:18 Porsche 917K #57 Le Mans 1971 ....$30–32

3907 1:18 Porsche 917K #3 Daytona 1970 ....$30–32

3908 1:18 Porsche 917K #2 Kyalami $30–32

4301 1:18 Ford Model T Touring, black $30–32

4302 1:18 Ford Model T Touring, red $30–32

4303 1:18 Ford Model T Touring, dark blue $30–32

4304 1:18 Ford Model T Police $30–32

4305 1:18 Ford Model T DREYERS.$30–32

4306 1:18 Ford Model T Ford Service $30–32

4351 1:18 1941 Chevrolet Convertible, red $30–32

4352 1:18 1941 Chevrolet Convertible, black $30–32

4353 1:18 1941 Chevrolet Deluxe Soft Top $30–32

4350 1:18 1941 Chevrolet Convertible, beige $30–32

4354 1:18 1941 Chevrolet Deluxe Soft Top $30–32

4355 1:18 1941 Chevrolet Convertible Hot Rod $30–32

4401 1:18 Land Rover Hardtop AA Rescue $30–32

4402 1:18 Land Rover Hardtop, beige/brown $30–32

4403 1:18 Land Rover Soft Top, bright green $30–32

4404 1:18 Land Rover Soft Top Medic $30–32

4405 1:18 Land Rover Pickup, red/white $30–32

4406 1:18 Land Rover Pickup, black .$30–32

4701 1:18 Porsche 956L #1 ROTHMANS $30–32

4702 1:18 Porsche 956L #2 ROTHMANS $30–32

4703 1:18 Porsche 956L #21 KREMER $30–32

4704 1:18 Porsche 956L #7 NEWMAN 1984 ....$30–32

4705 1:18 Porsche 956L #7 NEWMAN 1985 ....$30–32

4706 1:18 Porsche 956L #8 Sport America $30–32

4707 1:18 Porsche 956 #19 IMOLA 1984 ....$30–32

Eagle's Race (see Eagle Collectibles)

Ebbro

c/o Great Eagle Trading Co.
Unit 5, 5/F, Favor Industrial Centre,
2-6 Kin Hong St.,
Kwai Chung, N.T.,
Hong Kong
Danny Ngan, sales manager
website: www.ebbro.com.hk

First seen in *Model Auto Review* (June 1999), Ebbro is a brand of 1:43 scale diecast models made in Japan and exported exclusively by Great Eagle Trading Company of Hong Kong.

Datsun Fairlady SRL311, 1967, 1:43

   v.1 red with black interior and soft top, white hard top, #430116 ....$32

   v.2 white with red interior, black soft top and hard top, #430123 ....$32

   v.3 silver with black interior, soft top and hard top, #430130 ....$32

Datsun Fairlady Z, 1:43.............................$32
Datsun Fairlady 2000, 1:43......................$32
Nissan Fairlady Z 432, yellow with black spoked rims, #31, 1:43.................................$32
Nissan Fairlady Z 2000Z-L, white with black steel rims, #32, 1:43.................................$32
Nissan Fairlady Z 240Z, dark green with stock hubcaps, #33, 1:43............................$32
Nissan Fairlady Z 240Z-G, maroon with stock hubcaps, #55, 1:43............................$32
Honda N360, 1:43....................................$32

Edil

Edil Toys of Italy are detailed 1:43 scale models produced from 1965 to 1970. Models reproduced afterwards in Turkey by Meboto still hold the Edil brand name but are comparably inferior castings with crude finishes that give them away as later models. Below is a list of original models.

1 Alfa Romeo Giulia GT, 1965...........$45–75
2 Fiat 850, 1966..............................$45–75
3 Lancia Flavia Coupe, 1966..............$45–75
4 Alfa Romeo Giulia TI, 1966..............$45–75
5 Alfa Romeo Giulia Police Car, 1966..............................$45–75
6 Fiat 1500 Sedan, 1966.................$45–75
7 Fiat 124 Sedan, 1967...................$45–75
8 Fiat 850 Coupe, 1967...................$45–75
9 Ferrari 275 GTB, 1967..................$45–75
10 Lamborghini Miura, 1968...............$45–75
11 Mercedes-Benz 250SE..................$45–75
12 Iso Grifo, 1968...........................$45–75
13 Lamborghini Bertone Marzal, 1968 .$45–75

Edocar (also see Zee Toys / Zylmex)

Edocar is a trademark of the Netherlands-based company of Fred Beheer BV, or Edor BV. Edor is evidently a reseller of various brands within the "Benelux," the tax union of Belgium, Netherlands, and Luxembourg, later known as the Common Market.

A set of Coca-Cola race cars from Edocar were determined to be castings from Action/Racing Collectibles, according to David Weber of Warrington, Pennsylvania. He indicates that these were unauthorized alterations of the latter suspected to be illegally obtained from the Action/Racing Collectibles factory in China.

A 1988 Edocar catalog provided by collector Werner LeGrand of Brecht, Belgium, features models issued in the US as M C Toys Mini Racers (later reissued as Maisto Turbo Treads), Yat Mings currently offered as Ja-Ru Real Wheels. Also included in the catalog are models that are recognizable as Lledo models of England.

Price is in US dollars for models in original Edocar packages, otherwise models are worth $1 each. Brand name in parentheses indicates manufacturer.

EM-1 Audi Quattro (M C Toys)....................$3
EM-2 Citroën 2CV (M C Toys).....................$3
EM-3 Corvette (Yat Ming).........................$4
EM-4 Ford Escort (M C Toys)......................$3
EM-5 Rolls Royce (M C Toys).....................$4
EM-6 VW Golf GTi (M C Toys)....................$3
EM-7 Lancia Rally (M C Toys)....................$4
EM-8 Ford Granada (M C Toys)..................$3
EM-9 Ford Lorry (Yat Ming).......................$4
EM-10 Lorry Trailer (Yat Ming)...................$6
EM-11 1986 Corvette Convertible (M C Toys) $3
EM-12 4 x 4 Jeep Hardtop (Yat Ming)...........$4
EM-13 Mercedes 500 SLC (M C Toys)...........$3
EM-14 Buick Le Sabre (M C Toys)................$3
EM-15 Nissan 300 ZX (M C Toys)................$3
EM-16 Chevy Blazer (Yat Ming)..................$3
EM-17 1957 Corvette (Yat Ming).................$5
EM-18 Volvo 760 GLE (M C Toys)................$3
EM-19 Renault 25 Turbo (M C Toys).............$3
EM-20 Datsun (Yat Ming)..........................$3
EM-21 Mercedes 560 (M C Toys).................$3
EM-22 Mobile Crane (Yat Ming)..................$5
EM-23 4 x 4 Open Military Jeep (Yat Ming) ...$3
EM-24 Extending Ladder Fire Engine (Yat Ming)..$4
EM-25 Mercedes Van (M C Toys).................$3
EM-26 Porsche 928 (M C Toys)...................$3
EM-27 Peugeot 309 (M C Toys)..................$3
EM-28 Jaguar XJ6 (M C Toys)....................$3
EM-29 Ford Station Wagon (Yat Ming)..........$6
EM-30 Tipper Truck (Yat Ming)....................$3
EM-31 Ferrari Testarossa (M C Toys).............$3
EM-32 Mazda RX-7 (Yat Ming)...................$4
EM-33 Tow Truck (Yat Ming)......................$5
EM-34 Cadillac Seville (Yat Ming)................$3
EM-35 Toyota MR-2 (M C Toys)..................$3
EM-36 Mercedes 500 SEC (M C Toys).........$3
EM-37 Porsche 959 (M C Toys)...................$3
EM-38 Ford Mustange (Yat Ming)................$3
EM-39 Ambulance (Yat Ming).....................$3
EM-40 Porshce Turbo (M C Toys)................$3
EM-41 Dodge Sheriff (Yat Ming)..................$5
EM-42 Suzuki SJ413QJX Sidekick (M C Toys) .$3
EM-43 Military Lorry (M C Toys)...................$4
EM-44 Porsche 956 (M C Toys)...................$3
EM-45 4x4 Open Jeep (Yat Ming)................$3
EM-46 BMW M1 (M C Toys).......................$3
EM-47 Peugeot 205 GTI (M C Toys).............$3
EM-48 Ferrari 308 GTB (M C Toys)..............$3
EM-49 Ford Sierra XR4i (M C Toys)..............$3
EM-50 VW Scirocco (Yat Ming)...................$4
EM-51 Formula 1, white with red accents, "Valvo-line" (M C Toys) $3
EM-52 Formula 1, black with white, blue, and red accents (M C Toys) $3

Edocar Coca-Cola Licenses

CC-1 Porsche...$6
CC-2 Chevrolet Van (Yat Ming)..................$4
CC-3 Chevy Blazer (M C Toys)...................$4
CC-4 Delivery Truck (Yat Ming)..................$4
CC-5 4x4 Pickup (M C Toys)......................$4
CC-6 Bedford Van (Yat Ming).....................$4

CC-7 Corvette...$6
CC-8 1986 Firebird $6

Edocar Oldtimer Series (Lledo)

EA-1 Ford Model T Petrol Tanker.............$10
EA-2 Dennis Fire Engine.........................$10
EA-3 Ford Taxi.....................................$10
EA-4 Dennis Van..................................$10
EA-5 AEC Autobus................................$10
EA-6 Packard Ambulance........................$10
EA-7 Rolls Royce Phantom II...................$10
EA-8 Chevrolet Van...............................$10

Edocar Zee Toys

Mercedes-Benz 500 SL, #13, marked as a Zee Toy on the base, package marked with Edocar brand $2

EFE (see Exclusive First Editions)

Efsi / Holland-Oto (also see Best-Box)

Efsi toys are well made but crude toys from Holland. They are durable, authentic replicas representing mostly European vehicles that sell for about $4 each. Each of the dozen or so Efsi models manufactured is available in many different variations and liveries. What they lack in accuracy they make up for in charm. Older models were produced under the Best-Box brand. In April 2000, collector Jan Scholten reported that Efsi now goes by the name of Holland-Oto, although the Efsi brand continues in Germany.

1010 1919 Ford Model T Truck $10
1020 1919 Ford Model T Tanker..............$10
1030 1919 Ford Model T Crane Truck.......$10
1040 1919 Ford Model T Van..................$10
1050 1919 Ford Model T Two Seater........$10
1060 1919 Ford Model T Sedan...............$10
1070 1919 Ford Model T Ambulance........$10
1100 1919 Ford Model T Fire Van............$10
2010 B.R.M. Formula I...........................$10
2020 Honda Formula I...........................$10
2030 Ferrari Formula I...........................$15
2040 Brabham Formula 1.......................$10
2050 Mclaren Formula I..........................$10
2060 Lotus 49 C Formula I......................$10
3020 Commer Van................................$15
3021 Commer Ambulance.......................$15
3022 Commer ServiceVan.......................$15
3023 Commer Fire Van...........................$15
3024 Commer Army Ambulance...............$15
3021 Commer U.S.A. Army Van...............$15
3030 Mercedes-Benz Open Truck.............$10
3040 Mercedes-Benz Covered Truck.........$10
3041 Mercedes-Benz Red CrossTruck.......$10
3042 Mercedes-Benz Army Truck.............$10
3050 Mercedes-Benz Dump Truck............$10
3051 Mercedes-Benz Army Dump Truck......$10
3060 Trailer...$10
3061 Red Cross Trailer $10
3062 Army Trailer $10
3080 Mercedes-Benz Fire Engine.............$10

3090 Mercedes-Benz Tanker "SHELL" $15
3091 Mercedes-Benz Tanker "ELF" $15
3092 Mercedes-Benz Tanker "ARAL" $15
3093 Mercedes-Benz Army Tanker $15
4010 Ford Taunus 17 M $15
4011 Ford Taunus Stock Car $15
4020 Porsche 911 S $15
4021 Porsche 911 S Dutch Police Car $15
4022 Porsche 911 S Rally $15
4030 Jaguar E Type $15
4040 Mercedes-Benz 280SL $15
4050 Opel Rekord 1900 ....$15
4060 Mercedes-Benz 250 SE Coupe $15
4061 Mercedes-Benz 250 SE Coupe Rally .$15
4070 BMW 2000 CS $15
4071 BMW 2000 CS Rally $15
4080 Volkswagen 1600 TL $20
4090 Citroën ID 19 ....$15
4091 Citroën ID 19 Ambulance $15
4100 Citroën Dyane 6 ....$15
4110 Ford Transit Van $15
4111 Ford Transit Ambulance $15
4112 Ford Transit Police Van $15

E.G.M.

E.G.M. toys were manufactured in Italy in 1959.
Alfa Romeo Giulietta Spyder (if ever actually pro-
duced)...............................$175–250
Dean Van Lines Special $125
Tarf Speed Record Car............................$125

EiDAI (also see Grip Zechin)

EiDAI Corporation
2.8.7. Higashiogu, Arakawaku
Tokyo, Japan

Made in Japan, EiDAI scale models are
occasionally sold under the Model Power
brand. Many EiDAI models replicate those sold
under the Grip Zechin, Madmax, and World
Zechin brands, all produced by EiDAI.
Airport Bus, 1:100.......................$14–17
Boom Truck, 1:87.......................$12–15
DeTomaso Pantera GT-35, 1:28 (Technica
series).............................$25–30
Ladder Truck, 1:87......................$12–15
March 761B "Rothmans" #10 Ian,
1:43................................$18–24

E J Enterprises

15736 E. Valley Blvd.
City of Industry, CA 91744

Recently discovered are these larger scale
pull-back action diecast toys in a black box
with colorful graphics and the name E J Enterprises. The models looked familiar, so I
removed them from the box and looked at the
base. They're made by Sunnyside of Hong
Kong.

Eko

Eko Diecast

Two diecast models are known to have
been produced by Eko of Spain.

6005 Hispano Suiza Alphonso XIII Convertible, red & cream $15
6010 1911 Daimler Convertible, silver ..$10

Eko HO Gauge Plastic Models

Eko 1:87 scale models are appropriately
colored molded plastic, imported from Spain,
with painted details, available from Walthers.
They serve as exquisite additions to any HO
gauge collection or train layout.

Eko cars

Alfa Romeo Giulietta Sprint......................$3
BMW 501 ....$3
BMW Coupe $3
Borgward Isabella $3
Chevrolet El Camino $3
Citroën 2CV $3
Citroën AMI $3
Citroën Break $3
Citroën DS 19 ....$3
Commer Beer Barrel $3
Commer Dump Truck $3
Commer Soda Truck $3
DAF Coupe $3
DAF Daffodil $3
DeSoto Diplomat $3
Dodge Dart $3
Fiat 124 ....$3
Fiat 1500 ....$3
Fiat 1800 Station Wagon $3
Fiat 600 Multipla $3
Fiat 850 ....$3
Fiat Seat 124 ....$3
Ford Anglia $3
Ford Comet $3
Ford Consul $3
Ford Falcon $3
Ford FK Kombi Ambulance......................$3
Ford Thunderbird $3
Ford Zephyr $3
Jaguar D...$3
Jaguar E Coupe $3
Jaguar Mark Nine $3
Jaguar Racer $3
Jeep $3
Karrier Garbage Truck $3
Karrier Gass Bottle $3
Land Rover (Open Top) $3
Leyland Double Decker Bus $3
Mercedes-Benz 190SL Convertible...........$3
Mercedes-Benz 190SL Coupe.................$3
Mercedes-Benz 220 ....$3
Mercedes-Benz 300 ....$3
Mercedes-Benz Racer $3
MG 1600 ....$3
Morris Mini $3
Opel Rekord $3
Pegaso "CAMPSA" Oil Truck $3
Renault 4-L $3
Renault 4/4 ....$3
Renault Dauphine.................................$3
Renault R-8 ....$3
Rover 3/L $3
Saab 96 ....$3

Seat 1400 Panel Truck..........................$3
Seat Coupe 600 ....$3
Seat Sedan 1400 ....$3
Seat Sedan 1400C $3
Skoda Coupe $3
Studebaker Avanti................................$3
Studebaker Hawk.................................$3
T245 Army Tanker/Dozer $3
Volkswagen Beetle $3
Volkswagen Beetle Convertible $3
Volkswagen Karmann Ghia $3
Volvo Sport $3

Eko 2-Axle Trucks

"Eko Cola" Truck $3
Ford Flat Bed $2
Ford Flat Bed with Canvas Top $2
Ford Thames Flat Bed Truck $2
Gas Oil Tank Truck Ford $2
Magirus Flat Bed $2
Magirus Flat Bed with Canvas Top $2
Magirus Tank Truck $2
Panel Truck Fourgon $2
Pegaso Cement Delivery Truck $2
Pegaso Delivery Truck $2
Pegaso Tank $2
"Piper Cola" Truck $2
Sava Butano Delivery Truck $2
Sava Garbage Truck..............................$2
Thames Beer Delivery Truck $2
Thames Flatbed Truck $2
Thames Soda Delivery Truck $2

Eko Semi Trucks

Pegaso Semi Tank Truck $4
Titan Semi Lo-Boy with Cargo Tank...........$5
Pegaso Auto Transport with 5 autos $8

Eko Buses

Pegaso Motor Bus $3
Alco Double Decker Bus $3
Chausson Motor Bus $3

Elegance

Fabulous 1:43 scale model Cadillacs are
offered under the Elegance brand. The 1951
Cadillac Pullman in particular (Elegance #117)
was produced in 1986 and modeled after the
car owned by King Ibn Saud of Saudi Arabia.
Coachwork on the original car was done by
Hess and Eisenhardt.
1951 Cadillac Pullman 6-Door Limousine, midnight blue, mirrored passenger windows,
#117................................$450–500
1975 Cadillac 86 El Clasico..........$475–500
1976 Cadillac Fleetwood $400–425
1976 Cadillac Silverhawk 6-Door
Limousine...........................$525–550

Eligor

Eligor France
Paul and Anne-Marie Vullierme, owners
605n Zi La Plaine
01580 Izernore
France
phone: 4-74-76-56-56

Eligor

e-mail: eligor@wanadoo.fr
Eligor USA
Airport Office Center
1540 Airport Road - Suite 207
Charlottesville, VA 22911
phone: 804-973-7638
website: www.eligor.com

Eligor represents a series of popular vintage 1:43 and a few 1:25 scale models, mostly diecast but a few resin models as well, originally manufactured by Jacques Greilsamer in Martignat, France, starting in 1976. Eligor models are available from finer hobby shops and mail order houses. The company used many of Norev's original tooling. In 1986, Greilsamer sold the brand to Louis Surber, who had been producing Eligor models for Greilsamer. In 1996, Eligor was acquired by Paul and Anne-Marie Vullierme. In 1998, Eligor relocated to a newly designed facility in Izernore, France. Eligor currently offers over 300 models and variations of vintage and modern cars selling for around $25 each, and nearly 300 modern and vintage semi-tractor trailers and commercial trucks for $89 suggested retail price.

Eligor 1:43 Scale Vintage Cars

1965 Austin Mini 850, green with black roof, #1110 ....$25
1965 Austin Mini Parisienne, black with rattan doors, #1113 ....$25
1965 Austin Mini Police, white, #1112 ....$25
1967 Bentley T Berline, #1048 ....$25
1975 Bentley Berline, metallic brown, #100092 ....$25
1967 BMW 2000 Berline, gray, #100505 ....$25
1967 BMW 2000 Fire Chief, red, #1118 ....$25
1967 BMW 2000 Fire Chief, red, #100408 ....$25
1967 BMW 2000 Polizei RFA, green and white, #1116 ....$25
1967 BMW 2000 Polizei RFA, green and white, #100406 ....$25
1967 BMW 2000 Rallye, white, #1117 ....$25
1967 BMW 2000 Rallye, white, #100407 ....$25
1967 BMW 2000 Taxi, black, #1115 ....$25
1967 BMW 2000 Taxi, black, #100405 ....$25
1967 BMW 2000 Tilux Berline, blue, #1114 ....$25
1927 Bugatti 35 B Course, #1025 ......$25
1928 Bugatti 35 B Course, blue, #100044 ....$25
1928 Bugatti 35 B Sport, #1045 ....$25
1928 Bugatti 35 B Sport, red, #100089 ....$25
1962 Chevrolet Corvair Monza, green, #1136 ....$30

1962 Chevrolet Corvair Monza, beige, #100510 ....$23
1962 Chevrolet Corvair Monza, red, #100512 ....$23
1962 Chevrolet Corvair Monza Police USA, black and white, #100274 ....$25
1962 Chevrolet Corvair Monza Fire Dept. Los Angeles, red and white, #100275 ....$25
1958 Chrysler New Yorker Convertible, top down, baby blue, #1100 ....$25
1958 Chrysler New Yorker Convertible, top down, pink, #100509 ....$23
Citroën 3 CV Fire Dept. Paris, #100394 ....$25
Citroën 3 CV Michelin, #100396 ....$25
Citroën 3 CV Camionette, gray, #100518 ....$23
1925 Citroën 5 CV Torpedo, top down, #1017 ....$25
1925 Citroën 5 CV Torpedo, top down, #100032 ....$25
1925 Citroën 5 CV Torpedo, top up, #1037 ....$25
1926 Citroën 5 CV Camionette, "Bally," #1057 ....$25
1926 Citroën 5 CV Camionette, "Michelin," #1054 ....$25
1926 Citroën 5 CV Pompiers (Fire Van), #1056 ....$25
1926 Citroën 5 CV Pompiers (Fire Van), #100117 ....$25
1925 Citroën 5 HP Covered, yellow with black trim, #100073 ....$25
1925 Citroën 5 HP Camionette, "Michelin," #100113 ....$25
1925 Citroën 5 HP Camionette, Postes, #100090 ....$25
1925 Citroën 5 HP Fire Department, #100115 ....$25
1934 Citroën 500 KG, yellow, #100014 ....$25
1934 Citroën 500 KG, "Caran D'Ache," #1015 ....$25
1934 Citroën 500 KG, "Lion Noir," #1026 ....$25
1934 Citroën 500 KG, "Phillips," #100097 ....$25
1934 Citroën 500 KG, "PTT," #100005 ....$25
1934 Citroën 500 KG Ambulance, #1021 ....$25
1934 Citroën 500 KG Ambulance, #100040 ....$25
1934 Citroën 500 KG Juragruyere, #100012 ....$25
1934 Citroën 500 KG Nicolas, #100022 ....$25
1934 Citroën 500 KG Postes, green, #100004 ....$25
1934 Citroën 500 KG Service Des Sapeurs Pompiers (Fire Pumper) with ladder and hoses, #100039 ....$25

1934 Citroën 500 KG Saint Raphael, #100038 ....$25
1934 Citroën 500 KG Start Pilote, red, #100016 ....$25
Citroën AMI 6 Fire Department #100450 ....$23
Citroën AMI 6 Berline, blue, #100521 ..$23
Citroën AMI 6 Berline, two-tone green, #100525 ....$25
Citroën AMI 6 Break, brown, #100526 ..$25
Citroën Berlingo, green, #100646 ....$25
Citroën Berlingo Fire Department, #100658 ....$25
Citroën Berlingo Reseau Citroën, #100659 ....$25
Citroën Berlingo Poste, #100677 ....$25
Citroën Berlingo Multispace, blue, #100704 ....$25
Citroën C 15 Fire Department, #100379 ....$25
Citroën C 15 Poste, yellow, #100381 ..$25
Citroën C 15, white, #100542 ....$25
1967 Citroën DS 21, black, #100531 ....$23
1967 Citroën DS 21 Administration, #100227 ....$25
1967 Citroën DS 21 Berline, bronze, #1119 ....$25
1967 Citroën DS 21 Etat-Major Des Pompiers, black, #1126 ....$25
1967 Citroën DS 21 Fire Department Lyon, #100231 ....$25
1967 Citroën DS 21 Fire Chief, red, #1122 ....$25
1967 Citroën DS 21 Gendarmerie, blue, #1123 ....$25
1967 Citroën DS 21 Gendarmerie, #100232 ....$25
1967 Citroën DS 21 Ministerielle, #1120 ....$25
1967 Citroën DS 21 Police Parisienne, black and white, #1121 ....$25
1967 Citroën DS 21 Police of Paris, #100228 ....$25
1967 Citroën DS 21, "Rallye Du Maroc," #100700 ....$25
1967 Citroën DS 21 "Rallye Monte Carlo," light blue, #1124 ....$25
1967 Citroën DS 21 Taxi Parisienne, #1125 ....$25
Citroën H Van, gray, #100338 ....$25
Citroën H Van Fire Dept. PTT "Bureau Mobile," #100363 ....$25
Citroën H Van Fire Dept. Lyon with ladder, #100355 ....$25
Citroën H Van Gendarmerie, #100352 ....$25
Citroën H Van "Kodak," #100435 ....$25
1933 Citroën Rosalie Berline, #1005 ....$25
1933 Citroën Rosalie Berline, yellow with black fenders, #100513 ....$23
1933 Citroën Rosalie Fire Dept., #100009 ....$25

1934 Citroën Rosalie Taxi, #1035 ....$25

1934 Citroën Rosalie 60th Anniversary, black, #100007 ....$25

1933 Citroën Rosalie Taxi, red and black, #100069 ....$25

1934 Citroën Secours Pompiers (Fire Truck), #1020 ....$25

Citroën SM Gendarmerie, #100444.....$25

1938 Citroën T.A.V. Berline 11 BL, #1031A.................................$25

1947 Citroën T.A.V. Berline 11 BL, #1031B.................................$25

1948 Citroën T.A.V. Berline Pompiers (Fire Chief), #1033 ....$25

1938 Citroën T.A.V. Cabriolet, top down, #1001 ....$25

1938 Citroën T.A.V. Cabriolet, top up, #1002 ....$25

1939 Citroën T.A.V. Taxi, #1053.........$25

1938 Citroën Traction 11 BL Covered Cab, #100002 ....$23

1934 Delage D8 Cabriolet, top down, #1038 ....$25

1934 Delage D8 Cabriolet, top up, #1039 ....$25

1934 Delage D8 Cabriolet, #100074 .$25

1962 Ferrari GTO $25

1965 Ford Cortina Berline, red, #1102.$25

1965 Ford Cortina Police, blue, #1104.$25

1965 Ford Cortina Police Autoroute G.B., #1105 ....$25

1965 Ford Cortina Rallye, white, #1103 ....$25

1932 Ford Roadster Fire Chief $25

1932 Ford Roadster, baby blue $25

1932 Ford Roadster Police $25

1932 Ford Sedan, green $25

1932 Ford Sedan Police $25

1932 Ford V-8 Berline "Tudor," maroon, #1205 ....$30–35

1932 Ford V-8 Limousine "Fordor," green, #1204 ....$30–35

1932 Ford V-8 Roadster, top up, yellow, #1201 ....$30–35

1932 Ford V-8 Roadster, top down, maroon, #1200 ....$30–35

1932 Ford Van Police.........................$25

1933 Ford V-8 Covered Pickup, "Boots The Chemist Express Delivery," #1068..$25

1933 Ford V-8 Covered Pickup, "Guinness," #1066 ....$25

1933 Ford V-8 Covered Pickup, "Texaco Motor Oil," #1069 ....$25

1933 Ford V-8 Pickup, "Texaco" $35

1933 Ford V-8 Pickup, "Goodrich" $25

1933 Ford V-8 Pickup, black, #1080....$25

1933 Ford V-8 Pickup, green with wooden cargo box, #1059......................$30

1934 Ford V-8 Ambulance, #1081 .....$25

1934 Ford V-8 Fire Truck, "Trenton," #1082....................................$25

1934 Ford V-8 Fire Truck, "Washington," #1084....................................$25

1934 Ford V-8 Panel Van, "Ford Service," #1070....................................$25

1934 Ford V-8 Panel Van, "Air Show" ...$25

1934 Ford V-8 Panel Van, "Castrol," #1072....................................$25

1934 Ford V-8 Panel Van, "Cobham's," #1079....................................$25

1934 Ford V-8 Panel Van, "Crosse & Blackwell," #1073 ....$25

1934 Ford V-8 Panel Van, "Firestone" $25

1934 Ford V-8 Panel Van, "Guinness," #1076....................................$25

1934 Ford V-8 Panel Van, "Lindt," #1071....................................$25

1934 Ford V-8 Panel Van, "Longines," #1075....................................$25

1934 Ford V-8 Panel Van, "Lyons Tea," #1074....................................$25

1934 Ford V-8 Panel Van, yellow "Mobiloil," #1077....................................$25

1934 Ford V-8 Panel Van, "RCA His Master's Voice," #1092 ....$25

1934 Ford V-8 Panel Van, "Stephens," #1078....................................$25

1934 Ford V-8 Pickup, covered, green and white, "Carlsberg Beer," #1085 .....$25

1934 Ford V-8 Pickup, open, green and white, "Carlsberg Beer," #1086 .....$25

1934 Ford V-8 Tanker, blue and white, "Milkmaid," #1088 ....$25

1934 Ford V-8 Tanker, yellow, "Mobiloil," #1090....................................$25

1934 Ford V-8 Tanker, red, "Trenton No. 8 Fire Dept.," #1091 ....$25

1934 Ford V-8 Wrecker, yellow and green, #1087....................................$25

1934 Ford V-8 Wrecker, red, "Fire Dept.," #1087P...................................$25

1934 Ford Sedan, green $25

1960 Jaguar 3.4 L Berline, red, #1127.$25

1960 Jaguar 3.4 L "Tour De France," #1128....................................$25

1960 Jaguar 3.4 L Police Autoroute G.B., white, #1129 ....$25

1960 Jaguar 3.4 L Police G.B., dark blue, #1130....................................$25

1960 Jaguar Mk 1 ....$25

1960 Jaguar E-Type $25

1964 Jaguar E-Type Roadster, top down, red, #1152 ....$25–30

1958 Lancia Aurelia B 20 Coupe, gray bronze, #1143 ....$25

1958 Lancia Aurelia B 20 Coupe "Mille Miglia," black, #1144 ....$25

1963 Lancia Flaminia Berline, blue, #1132....................................$25

1959 Lotus Elite $25

1929 Mercedes-Benz Nurburg Limousine, #1043....................................$25

1931 Mercedes-Benz Taxi D'Hotel "Kaiserhof," #1044................................$30

1965 Mini Cooper "Rally Monte Carlo," #1111 ....$25

1965 Mini Cooper "Rally Monte Carlo," #100215................................$25

Mini 850 Parisienne, #100218.....$25

1925 Opel Laubfrosch Camionette, "Kaffee Hag," #1060 ....$25

1925 Opel Laubfrosch Camionette, "Ovomaltine," #1064 ....$25

1925 Opel Laubfrosch Fire Truck #1095 ....$25

1925 Opel Laubfrosch Torpedo, top down, #1093 ....$25

1925 Opel Laubfrosch Torpedo, top up, #1094 ....$25

1937 Panhard Dynamic Berline, #1006..$35

1937 Panhard Dynamic Berline, gray and black, #100010 ....$25

1937 Panhard Dynamic Taxi, #1006T..$35

1963 Panhard PL 17 Break, Poste, yellow, #100220................................$25

1963 Panhard PL 17 Break, green, #100580................................$23

1931 Peugeot 201 Berline, #1016 ......$25

1931 Peugeot 201, gray, #100582....$23

1931 Peugeot 201 Fire Department, #100030................................$25

1954 Peugeot 203 Berline, blue, #100587................................$23

1954 Peugeot 203 Fire Dept. Loiret, #100309................................$25

1954 Peugeot 203 Taxi G7, red and black, #100397................................$25

Peugeot 204 Break, green, #100597...$23

Peugeot 204 Break Fire Dept., #100438................................$25

Peugeot 204 Break Gendarmerie, #100439................................$25

1965 Peugeot 403 Berline, blue, #1145....................................$25

1965 Peugeot 403 Berline, beige, #100591.................................$23

1964 Peugeot 403 Break Fire Dept. Lyon, #100430................................$25

1965 Peugeot 403 Taxi G7, black with red roof, #1146 ....$25

1965 Peugeot 403 Taxi G7, black with red roof, #100428 ....$25

1954 Peugeot 404 Coupe, red, #1101....................................$25

1954 Peugeot 404 Coupe, white, #100595................................$25

1964 Peugeot 404 Break, beige, #1137.$25

1964 Peugeot 404 Break, black, #100601................................$23

1964 Peugeot 404 Break Ambulance, white, #1141 ....$25

1964 Peugeot 404 Break Fire Dept. Soultz, #100261................................$25

1964 Peugeot 404 Break Gendarmerie, blue, #1139 ....$25

1964 Peugeot 404 Break Gendarmerie, #100259................................$25

1964 Peugeot 404 Break Police, black, #1138....................................$25

1964 Peugeot 404 Break Police Municipale, #100258 ....$25
1964 Peugeot 404 Break Poste, yellow, #100256 ....$25
1964 Peugeot 404 Break Secours Pompiers, red, #1140 ....$25
1964 Peugeot 404 Break Taxi, black, #1142 ....$25
1964 Peugeot 404 Pickup Fire Dept. Lyon, #100286 ....$25
Peugeot Partner, blue, #100667 ....$25
Peugeot Partner Fire Dept., #100699 ....$25
1968 Porsche 911 Targa, metallic blue, #1147 ....$25
1968 Porsche 911 Targa Rallye, white with rally markings, #1148 ....$25
Porsche 917 24 Hrs. Du Mans, No. 12, #100312 ....$25
Renault 1000 KG Camionette, #100486 ....$32
Renault 1000 KG Fire Dept. 4x4, #100632 ....$35
1954 Renault 4 CV, green, #100610 ..$23
1954 Renault 4 CV Berline, tan, #1106 .$25
1954 Renault 4 CV Fire Chief, red, #1109 ....$25
1954 Renault 4 CV Police, black, #1108 ....$25
1954 Renault 4 CV "Renault Service," #100421 ....$25
1954 Renault 4 CV "Tour De France," #1107 ....$25
Renault 5, green, #100616 ....$23
Renault 5 Fire Department Marseille, #100462 ....$25
1938 Renault Juvaquatre Berline, #1014 .$30
1938 Renault Juvaquatre Berline, yellow, #100608 ....$25
1938 Renault Juvaquatre Camionette Tolee, blue, #100643 ....$23
1938 Renault Juvaquatre Fire Dept. with boat and trailer, #100703 ....$25
1938 Renault Juvaquatre Pompiers (Fire Chief), #1014P $25
1928 Renault KZ Coupe Chauffeur, #1041 ....$25
1928 Renault KZ Pompiers (Fire Truck), #1048 ....$25
1928 Renault KZ Fire Department with ladder, #100702 ....$25
1928 Renault KZ Taxi, #1042 ....$25
1927 Renault NN Torpedo, covered, blue and black, #100076 ....$23
1928 Rolls Royce Limousine 20/25, #1030 ....$30
1930 Rolls Royce Limousine DeVille, #1055 ....$30
1975 Rolls Royce Silver Shadow, #100091 ....$25
1976 Rolls Royce Silver Shadow Berline, #1047 ....$30
1929 Rolls Royce Taxi D'Hotel "Carlton," #1051 ....$30

Simca Break 1500, burgundy, #100620 ....$23
Simca Break Marly, yellow, #100617 ...$25
Simca Break Marly Ambulance Fire Dept., #100412 ....$25
1930 Talbot Pacific Limousine, #1036 ..$25
1930 Talbot Pacific Limousine, #100070 ....$25
1930 Talbot Pacific Hotel Taxi, "Hotel De France," #1052 ....$25
1930 Talbot Pacific Hotel Taxi, brown and red, #100109 ....$25
1968 Triumph TR5 Cabriolet, top down, dark green, #1133 ....$25
1968 Triumph TR5 Cabriolet, top up, red, #1134 ....$25
1968 Triumph TR6 "Coupe Des Alpes, blue, #1135 ....$25

Eligor 1:25 Scale
Citroën Fire $55

Eligor 1:43 Scale Truck Collection
DAF XF 95 Super Space "gefco," #111416 ....$89
DAF XF 95 DHOLLANDIA, #111424....$89
Dekra Euro Truck, #110981 ....$119
Iveco Eurotech MP 2x4 "Ferrari 1995," #110948 ....$89
Iveco Eurotech "Martini Racing," #110970 ....$89
Iveco Eurostar, "Iveco," 111267 ....$89
Kenworth W 900 "DHL," 110936........$89
Kenworth W 900 Timber Truck, 111559 ....$79
Man 19.422 "Total," 110953 ....$89
Man F 2000 King of the Mountain, #111221 ....$89
1948 Mercedes, "Berlin 2000," #110932 ....$89
Mercedes Actros Mory N.L., #111100 .$89
Mercedes Actros Deflecteur Ferlay, #111384 ....$89
Renault B 120 Fire Dept., #110028 ......$29
Renault B 120 Reanimation, #110045 ..$29
Renault B 120 Fire Dept. Izernore, #110439 ....$29
Renault R 350 "Auto Ecole Alain," #110063 ....$89
Renault G 340 TI Citerne Dentressangle N.L., #111049 ....$89
Renault Premium Norbert Directionel, #110569 ....$89
Renault Premium Norbert Auto-Porte, #110570 ....$89
Renault Premium Lamberet, #110749 ....$89
Renault Premium Distribution Poste, #111246 ....$65
Renault Premium Porteur Danzas, #111412 ....$65
Renault AE 500 "A.F.T. - I.F.T.I.M.," #110766 ....$89
Renault AE 430 Restyle Bils Deroo, #111372 ....$89
Renault Car Iliade Bus, #130042 ....$89

Renault R 312 Bus, "S.T.V.U.," #130046 ....$89
Scania Series 3 TRPS Jarlaud, #110997 .$89
Scania Series 4 Peugeot Sport F1 97, #111125 ....$89
Scania Series 4 Toit Bas Pivoin, #111237 ....$89
Scania Topline Boreal Services, #111395 ....$89
Volvo FH "KLM Cargo," #111003 ....$89
Volvo FH Peugeot Sport 1998, #111371 ....$89

Elysee
Likely made in France, more information is needed on this brand, although one model is known.
1940 Dodge Coupe, 1:43 ....$55

Emek
EMEK-MUOVI OY
Kapulametsäntie 9
09430 Saukkola, Finland
phone: + 358-(0)19-371 500
fax: + 358-(0)19-371 502
e-mail: emek@pp.kolumbus.fi
Emek represents plastic collectible quality 1:25 scale models made in Saukkola, Finland. Below is just a short sampling.
1014 Scania T-Cabin dumper $15–20
1018 Volvo FL10 dumper $15–20
2045 Scania T-Cabin tipper with tipper trailer $15–20
6070 Lännen excavator $15–20
2095 Volvo FL 10 tipper $15–20

Empire (see Zaugg)

Enchanted (see Enchantment Land Coach Builders)

Enchantment Land Coach Builders
Specializing in 1:43 Scale limousines and hearses, these custom hand-built cars are created both on and off major model manufacturers' chassies. The home base for the company is believed to be in New Mexico (Land of Enchantment). The fact that Enchanted and Enchantment Land Coach Builders list the same Packard models indicates the two companies are one.
B5 1947 Buick Flexible Landau Hearse, black $139
B6 1947 Buick Flexible Limousine Hearse, black $139
B7 1947 Buick Flexible Limousine Ambulance, white $139
C1 1947 Chrysler Durham Continental Hardtop $109
C2 1947 Chrysler Town & Country Coupe ..$99
C3 1947 Chrysler Windsor Convertible $99
C4 1978 Cadillac Seville $99

C6 1947 Chrysler Stretch Limousine, maroon $119
C7 1947 Chrysler Hearse, maroon $119
C8 1947 Chrysler Flower Car, maroon.....$119
C10 1931 Cadillac Indy 500 Pace Car, white $139
C11 1957 Chevrolet Nomad Wagon $109
C12 1947 Cadillac Meteor Hearse Limousine, black $139
C13 1947 Cadillac Series 75 Ambulance, white $139
C14 1947 Cadillac Series 75 Limousine, black $139
C16 1966 Cadillac Superior Hearse, black..$139
D1 1947 DeSoto Convertible $99
D2 1940 Dodge Station Wagon, tan.......$119
F2 1951 Ford Victoria Hardtop $99
F3 1935 Ford Siebert Hearse Limousine, gray $129
F4 1935 Ford Siebert Ambulance, white ...$139
G1 1940 Graham Hollywood Sedan, maroon $139
K1 1954 Kaiser Darrin Roadster, top down, yellow $119
K2 1951 Kaiser Henry J Sedan $99
K3 1953 Kaiser Manhattan $89
K5 1953 Kaiser Manhattan $89
L1 1941 Lincoln Mark 1 Two-Door Hardtop ..$119
L4 1938 LaSalle Carved Panel Hearse, black $149
L5 1938 LaSalle Limousine Hearse, black ..$149
L6 1938 LaSalle Limousine Ambulance, white $149
M2 1988 Ford Mustang GT Convertible $99
M4 1986 Mustang Convertible, top down ..$99
M5 1982 Ford Mustang Notchback Coupe .$99
P1 1937 Packard Dual Cowl Phaeton.........$89
P1 1968 Pontiac Convertible $99
P2 1937 Packard Town Car........................$99
P3 1937 Packard Station Wagon, beige $99
P4 1937 Packard Continental Sedan $79
P5 1937 Packard Landaulet $89
P6 1937 Packard Club Coupe $89
P7 1937 Packard Pickup $89
P8 1937 Packard Stretch Limousine, black .$119
P9 1937 Packard Panel Delivery $89
P10 1937 Packard Victoria $79
P11 1937 Packard Hollywood Darrin Convertible $99
P13 1937 Packard Victoria, top down $89
P14 1937 Packard 4-Door Taxi $109
P15 1937 Packard 12-Passenger Coach bus........................$119
P16 1937 Packard Club Sedan $99
P17 1937 Packard Coupe Fire Service $129
P18 1937 Packard Pickup Fire Service......$129
P19 1937 Packard Coupe Police Service $99
P20 1937 Packard Art-Carved Hearse, black $119
P21 1937 Packard Art-Carved Flower Car, black $119
P22 1937 Packard Van Police Service......$129
P23 1937 Packard Van Fire Service $129

P24 1937 Packard Van Funeral Service, black $119
T1 1960 Ford Thunderbird 2-Door Hardtop..$99
T2 1965 Ford Thunderbird Convertible, top down $99
W1 1937 Willys Coupe $99
W21 1950 Meteor Convertible................$99
W22 1948 Ford Convertible....................$79
W23 1957 Chevrolet Nomad $109
Z10 1949 Buick Riviera $139
Z11 1956 Lincoln Mark 2 Convertible $139
Z19 1955 Chrysler Convertible................$119
Z20 1953 Buick, top down....................$119
Z22 1958 Ford Edsel Convertible $119
Z23 1956 Ford Convertible $139

Enco

In late March 1999, collector Peter Max Polshek inquired about the Enco Model Company of England, of which I had not previously known. He reports of one model, a Jensen Interceptor FF in 1:43 scale. EWA's Internet search engine (http://ewa1.com/models.html) has no models listed, but does include Enco in their abbreviation chart http://www.ewacars.com/tx/wabbrev as "ENC." More information is needed.
Jensen Interceptor FF, 1:43 ....$40–55

Enstone Emergency Models

British hand-built white metal models and kits in 1:48 scale are produced under the Enstone brand.
Daimler DC27 Ambulance...................$75–90

EPI Sports Collectibles

EPI Group Limited
250 Pequot Ave.
Southport, CT 06490
phone: 203-255-1112
Chris Reynolds is president of EPI Group. The EPI Sports Collectibles division is known to have produced at least one very accurate Shell oil tanker in approximately 1:43 scale. As with most diecast models in recent years, EPI models are manufactured in China.
1995 Shell Oil Company's Diecast Collectible Tanker Truck, short tanker truck with tandem tanker, yellow and chrome, 1:43, 10,000 produced..................................$25–30

Epoch (also see MTech)

MTech models are produced by Epoch, Ltd., of Japan. More information can be found under the section on MTech.

Equipe Gallois

Although Bryan Garfield-Jones of Great Britain produced a number of white metal kits under the Equipe Gallois brand, no list of models is available.
6 1949 Buick Roadmaster $60–90

Eria

Eria of France produced ten 1:46 scale models between 1957 and 1961.

31 Peugeot 403, 1957 ....$25
32 Renault Dauphine, 1958 ....$25
33 Simca P60 Aronde, 1959 ....$25
34 Panhard PL17, 1960 ....$25
35 Renault Estafette Van, 1960 ....$30
36 Jaguar D Type, 1960..........................$25
37 Peugeot 404, 1961............................$25
38 Citroën ID19 Ambulance, 1961..........$25
39 Citroën ID19 Break, 1961 ....$25

Erie

Parker White Metal Company of Erie, Pennsylvania, was the source for Erie toys manufactured prior to World War II. The founder was F. W. Ziesenheim in 1935. Most Erie models are unpainted shiny aluminum alloy with wooden wheels.
Cabover Truck, 1937, 3¼".................$35–45
Champion Coal Truck, 1935, 5"........$85–100
Ford Ice Truck, 1935, 5"...................$75–90
Ford Pickup Truck, 1935, 5"..............$65–75
Ford Tow Truck, 5" $75–90
Futuristic Sedan, 1939, 4¼"..............$65–75
Lincoln Zephyr Sedan, 1936, 5½".......$90–125
Lincoln Zephyr Sedan, 1936, 3½"........$65–75
Packard Roadster, 1936, 6"...............$90–125
Packard Roadster, 1936, 3½"............$65–75
Tow Truck, 1939, 4¼".......................$65–75

Ertl

Fred J. Ertl Sr. started The Ertl Company in 1945 from his Dubuque, Iowa, home. He applied the diecasting techniques he had learned in his homeland of Germany to manufacture licensed farm toys from John Deere and International Harvester's original blueprints. Soon after, he moved operations to Dyersville, Iowa, where the company remains today. From diecast farm toys, Ertl has expanded to the manufacture of pressed steel and diecast toy trucks, diecast scale model cars, and an assortment of other toys. Their large assortment of diecast vehicle banks has been extremely popular for decades.

On February 1, 1999, Racing Champions announced it would purchase the Ertl Company. The arrangement was completed by April 15, 1999.

Ertl's immense product line represents thousands of models, all designed after real vehicles. As you might guess, an entire book is needed to present the broad range of models produced. Ertl collectors are an elite group, many of whom only collect special issue limited edition models. Others specialize in just Ertl tractors or Ertl banks.

Several collectors' clubs exist for Ertl models. While the official Ertl Collectors Club no longer exists, Ertl still published *The Replica* newsletter. *The Replica* is a full-color publication featuring product previews from the farm toy and collectibles lines. It is a bi-monthly magazine that also includes subscriber exclusives, feature articles related to the industry, as well as a classified ad/show listing section. Circulation is around 30,000 worldwide and current subscription rates are U.S. $12 for 1 year (6 issues); outside the U.S. $16 for 1 year (6 issues). The address for subscriptions is Ertl A/R Replica Subscriptions, P.O. Box 500, Dyersville, IA 52040.

Ertl previously was a subsidiary of Kidde, Inc., makers of fire extinguishers, smoke detectors, and a broad range of other products. Other brands such as Spec-Cast, Liberty Classics, First Gear, and a few others have sprung up in Iowa, inspired by Ertl's success. Spec-Cast, in fact, is a direct offspring of the Ertl Company.

While Ertls were originally made in Iowa, most are now manufactured in China, Korea, or other Asian manufacturing centers. A confusing numbering system on the package is rarely reflected on the model, so an alphabetical listing is therefore presented by description, followed by model number, scale, introduction year, where made, and current value. Many models are reissued year after year, so information is often incomplete. Here is just a sampling.

Ertl 1:18 Scale American Muscle Collection
1935 Auburn 851 Boattail Speedster
   v.1 red....................................$35–40
   v.2 black................................$35–40
   v.3 cream..............................$45–55
1970 Buick GSX, yellow/red/black.....$30
1971 Buick GSX, black/gold..............$30

1957 Chevrolet Bel Air $30

1969 Chevrolet Camaro SS 396, orange/white $30
1969 Chevrolet Camaro Z-28, red/white $30
1996 Chevrolet Camaro Z28 Convertible, green or red..........................$25
1970 Chevrolet Chevelle SS 454 LS6
   v.1 metallic blue with white accents.$30
   v.2 yellow with black accents.........$30
1967 Chevrolet Corvette L-71 Roadster, Sunfire yellow..................................$40
1963 Chevrolet Corvette Stingray, dark blue...$30
1964 Chevrolet Impala SS, black.........$25
1994 Chevrolet Lumina, Western Auto, D. Waltrip.....................................$30
1994 Chevrolet Lumina, Goodwrench, Earnhardt.....................................$30
1994 Chevrolet Lumina, Interstate, Jarrett $30

1994 Chevrolet Lumina, #24 Dupont, Jeff Gordon....................................$75
1995 Chevrolet Monte Carlo, Goodwrench #3, Dale Earnhardt........................$75

1970 Dodge Challenger, T/A....................$30

1970 Dodge Challenger, R/T....................$30

1978 Dodge Li'l Red Truck $30
1995 Dodge Ram Truck, red or black....$25
1978 Dodge Warlock pickup truck $30
Ferrari 275 GTB4, red $30
1940 Ford Deluxe Coupe, maroon........$25
1996 Ford F-150 Pickup, red or green...$25

1970 Ford Mustang Boss 302, yellow with black accents $30

1970 Ford Mustang Boss 429, Grabber green $40
1995 Ford Smokin' Joes #23, Jimmy Spencer $75
1992 Ford Thunderbird, #1 Baby Ruth, Jeff Gordon...................................$75
1992 Ford Thunderbird, Budweiser, Elliott $30
1992 Ford Thunderbird, Valvoline, Martin $30
1970 Plymouth AAR 'Cuda, lime green $30

1969 Plymouth GTX $30

1969 Plymouth Hemi Roadrunner, yellow.$30

1969 Plymouth Hemi Roadrunner, limited edition Scorch red $30
1990 Pontiac Grand Prix, STP, R. Petty...$30
1990 Pontiac Grand Prix, Miller Genuine Draft #27, Rusty Wallace $75
1993 Pontiac Grand Prix, Pennzoil, M. Waltrip $30
1993 Pontiac Grand Prix, Miller Genuine Draft #2, Rusty Wallace $75
1993 Pontiac Grand Prix, Mello Yello, K. Petty $30
1969 Pontiac GTO "The Judge"
   v.1 metallic light blue $30
   v.2 green/yellow/white.............$30
1996 Pontiac TransAm Coupe, metallic red or burgundy $25
Shelby Cobra 427 S/C, red/white $30

Ertl 1:43 Scale Amerian Muscle
Class of 1967 - Set $30
1967 Camaro SS396, metallic teal blue.$10
1967 Pontiac Firebird, black............$10
1967 Ford Mustang Shelby GT350, red.$10
Class of 1970 - Set $30
1970 Olds 442, metallic gold.............$10
1970 Chevrolet Nova SS396, deep green $10
1970 Ford Torino Cobra, bright orange-red $10

Other 1:43 Scale American Muscle
1957 Chevrolet BelAir $10
1957 Chrysler 300C $10
1957 Mercury Turnpike Cruiser.............$10
1964 Chevrolet Impala SS $10
1969 Plymouth Barracuda......................$10

Ertl 1:64 Scale Amerian Muscle
1957 Chrysler 300C, black or metallic green..................................$8

1959 Ford Starliner, blue $30

1960 Ford Starliner, silver.....................$8

Ertl Air & Space
Army Helicopter...................................$3
Coast Guard Helicopter, #1509, AIR & SPACE series $3
Space Shuttle with Booster Rockets & Launch Pad, #1515, 1:500, Hong Kong $5

Ertl Farm Machines 1:64 Scale
Allis-Chalmers 8070 Tractor, #1703-1819, China $6
Case 2594 Tractor, #1704, 1986, Korea $6
Ford TW-20 Tractor with Cab, #1703-1621, China $6
Ford TW-35 Tractor with Cab, #1703-832, Korea $6
International Harvester 5088 Tractor with Cab, #1703-1797, Korea.............$6

John Deere Tractor with Cab, #1703-1619, Hong Kong......................................$6
Massey-Ferguson 2775 Tractor, #1703-1622, China....................................$6
Anhydrous Ammonia Tank, #1589-1550, Hong Kong....................................$3
International Harvester Farm Wagon, #1589-1755, Korea.............................$3
International Harvester Mixer Mill, #1589-1551, Korea................................$3
International Harvester Round Baler, #1589-1758, Korea............................$3
New Holland Forage Wagon, #1589AO, 1986, Korea.................................$3
John Deere Forage Wagon....................$3
International COE Grain Hauler, #1518-1238, China...................................$8

Ertl John Deere Tractor Collection
1892 Froelich.............................$6–8
1914 Waterloo Boy.....................$6–8
1923 John Deere Model D..............$6–8
1939 John Deere Model A Row Crop..$6–8
1952 John Deere Model 60.............$6–8
1958 John Deere 730 Row Crop......$6–8
1960 John Deere 4010 Row Crop....$6–8

Ertl Mighty Movers 1:64 Scale
Case 1845C Uni-Loader......................$8
Caterpillar Road Grader, #1848, China ..$8
International Excavator 640, #1854.......$8
International Hauler 350 Dump Truck, #1852, China...............................$8
International Scraper 412B, #1855 Earth Mover, China...........................$8
International TD20 Series E Crawler, #1851, China..............................$8
International Wheel Loader 560, #1850, China..............................$8

Ertl Vintage Vehicles 1:43 Scale
#1 1932 Ford Roadster, #2501, China..$15

#2 Ta-Pat-Co Brand, 1:43.................$15

#3 1930 Chevrolet Stake Truck, #2503, China.................................$15

#5 1912 Buick, #2516, 1985, 1:43.............$15

#4 1932 Ford Panel Truck "Perfection Stoves," #2504......................$15
#6 1940 Ford Woody Station Wagon, #2517, China......................$15
#7 1930 Chevrolet ½-Ton Delivery Truck, #2518..............................$15

#8 Ford Fordor, 1:43.....................$45

#10 1930 Packard Boat Tail Speedster, #2542..............................$15
#12 1952 Cadillac Coupe DeVille Model 62 4-Door, #2541, China............$15
#14 1960 Corvette, #2588.............$15
#16 1959 Checker Cab, #2587........$15
#17 1957 Ford Thunderbird, #2802....$15
F-2 1936 Massey-Harris Challenger, #2511..............................$15
F-4 International Harvester Farmall 300, #2513..............................$15

Ertl Batman, The Movie Collectibles
Batmobile, 1:64.............................$5
Batmobile, 1:43............................$15
Joker Van, 1:43............................$12

Ertl Batman, The Animated Series Collectibles, 1:64 Scale
Batmobile...................................$6
Bruce Wayne's Car........................$6
Police Helicopter..........................$6

Ertl Dick Tracy Movie Replicas 1989, 1:64 Scale
Dick Tracy's 1936 Ford Fordor Police Car, #2676..............................$8
Itchy and Flattop's 1939 Chevrolet, 1990, #2677..............................$8
Tess's 1937 Plymouth, 1990, #2678......$8
Dick Tracy's 1936 Ford, #2679.............$8

Ertl Dukes of Hazzard TV Series Replicas 1:64 Scale
Dukes' Dixie Challenger....................$15
Cooder's Pickup Truck.....................$10
Hazzard County Sheriff's Car..............$10
Boss Hogg's Cadillac.....................$10

Ertl The Cannonball Run Movie Replicas 1:64 Scale
Ferrari Dino 246 GT.......................$8

Ertl Made in America Series
Corvette, Made in USA.....................$1
Charger, Made in USA......................$1
Fiero, Made in USA........................$1
Firebird, Made in USA.....................$1

Other Ertl Models
1951 Chevrolet, 1:64......................$6
Chevy Stepside Pickup "Bell System," 1:64..............................$15

Britains Land Rover Discovery, 1:18..$25–30

British Taxi, 1:43.....................$10–12

1950 Chevrolet 3100 Pickup, 1:24 scale.............................$15–20

#11 1955 Chevrolet Bel Air 2-Door Hardtop, #2540, China, 1:24....................$15

1931 Hawkeye Flatbed, "True Value," 1:43 scale.............................$15–20

1931 Hawkeye Truck, Fred Meyer, 1:43..............................$10–12
Horse-Drawn Van "Telephones 5¢ Per Day" and "New Nickel Service"........$60–75
Land Rover, 1:64.........................$3
Lamb Chops Train, 1994..................$5
Mack 1926 Bull Dog "Let Your Fingers Do The Walking" Yellow Pages delivery truck..............................$60–75

Pontiac GTO, 1:43 ....$8

Ertl NASA Commemoratives
"Columbia" Command Module-Apollo
11 ....$10–12
"Friendship 7" Mercury Capsule $10–12
Lunar Rover-Apollo 15 ....$10–12
"Eagle" Lunar Module-Apollo 11 ......$10–12

Esci (see C.B.Car)

Esdo
Dominique Esparcieux is the founder of Esdo of France which offers a series of 1:43 scale models. One representative model is known.
Oldsmobile Omega Sedan, gold...............$65

Eska
What little is known about this brand is that Eska Company Inc. was based in Dubuque, Iowa, and produced at least one diecast promotional bank, a 1961–1971 International Scout Metro Mite Convertible. The brand is also associated with Tru-Scale toys from Carter Machine Company, later sold to Ertl.
1961–1971 International Scout Metro Mite, top
down $100–150

Espewe
Espewe of Germany makes these models of various scales, some or all are plastic.
1911 Horch 4-Door Car, 1:43 ....$18
1913 Audi Convertible, top down, 1:43.....$18
Ifa Truck, 1:120 ....$5
Stake Truck with load, blue plastic, 1:87 ....$5

Estetyka
Estetyka is a manufacturer from Poland that produces an assortment of 1:43 scale models of mostly Italian vehicles.
1 1926 Bugatti 35 Roadster $8
2 1926 Isotta Fraschini $8
4 1904 Wanderer Roadster $8
5 Ferrari P4...$11
6 Ferrari Dino $11
7 Fiat 126 2-Door Sedan $8
8 Polonez 4-Door Sedan $8
9 Ursus C385 Tractor..............................$18

Evrat 87 - LP Creations
Evrat 87
Yves Evrat
Apis Technology
10 Avenue du Quebec
BP 537 Courtaboeuf
Cedex 91946 France
phone: 011-33-169-86-12-09
fax: 011-33-169-29-03-18
Evrat 87 has recently appeared as a producer of 1:43 scale racing models. Whether made of white metal or resin is yet unknown. Gerfaut Carbone is said to be the producer. Evrat 87 is one of the many French companies

associated with the model auto artisans union known as MAFMA.
Maclaren Mercedes MP4/13, 1st Australian
Grand Prix 1998 ....$80–100

Excel (also see Goodee)
1950 Jeep CJ2, 5" $20

Excite (also see Magic)
Excite / Magic
1270 Champion Circle
Carrollton, TX 75006
Excite offers an assortment of 1:32 scale stretch limos with an uncanny resemblance to Majorette 3045-series limousines. The copy is so blatant that the box even indicates the same number 3045 on the back. While the Excite models are the same length as the Majorettes, about 9 inches long, they are wider than the Majorettes, giving them more accurate proportions.

Upon removal from the package however, the base of the Excite model bears the unmistakable "Flying S" logo that identifies it as a Superior model from Sunnyside. So it appears that Excite simply repackages Superiors with their own name on the box. Similarly, E.J. Enterprises also has repackaged Superior models as their own.

Another diecast toy assortment that goes by the Magic brand curiously bears the same address on the back of their package as Excite models. Closer inspection, particularly of the Chevy Caprice fire department command car, reveals them to be Welly toys. Apparently this practice of repackaging and re-branding diecast toys is not as uncommon as we might think.

Exclusive First Editions (EFE)
Bill Cross reports that Exclusive First Editions are 1:76 scale diecast models, in tune with the scale of British "00" gauge model trains. They now produce a very extensive range of vintage and modern British buses and trucks. The brand was started in 1989 in Milton Keyes, England. Models are produced in Asia.

Exclusive First Edition Automobiles
401 Triumph Roadster $10–12
403 Triumph Roadster $10–12
501 MGB.......................................$10–12
503 MGB.......................................$10–12
601 Triumph Vitesse.......................$10–12
603 Triumph Vitesse $10–12
701 Austin-Healey Sprite $10–12
703 Austin-Healey Sprite $10–12

Exclusive First Edition Commercial Service Vehicles
10101 AEC RT London Transport Bus "Duracell" $12–15
10102 AEC RT Greenline Bus
"Buxted" ....$12 – 15
10103 AEC RT London Country Bus "Birds Eye" $12–15

10104 AEC RT London Transport Bus
"Schweppes" $12–15
10107 AEC RT London Transport Bus
"Dulux" $12–15
10109 AEC RT London Transport Bus "Bird's Custard" $12–15
10111 AEC RT London Transport Bus "Barclays".................................$12–15
10112 AEC RT London Transport Bus "Vernons"..................................$12–15
10113 AEC RT Dundee Bus
"Courier".................................$12–15
10114 AEC RT Bradford Bus..........$12–15
10201 AEC RT Open Top Bus "Beachy Head" $12–15
10202 AEC RT Open Top Bus "Colemans" $12–15
10203 AEC RT Open Top Bus "Coronation" $12–15
10204 AEC RT Open Top Bus "Typhoo Tea" $12–15
10301 AEC Mammoth Major 6 Wheel Dropside "Fenland" $12–15
10302 AEC Mammoth Major 6 Wheel Dropside "Cyril Ridgeon & Son".$12–15
10303 AEC Mammoth Major 6 Wheel Dropside "J. D. Lown".............$12–15
10401 AEC Mammoth Major 8 Wheel Flatbed "Bath & Portland".........$12–15
10402 AEC Mammoth Major 8 Wheel Flatbed "London Brick".............$12–15
10501 AEC Mammoth Major Box Van "London Carriers".....................$12–15
10502 AEC Mammoth Major Box Van "Startrite"...................................$12–15
10503 AEC Mammoth Major Box Van "BRS".....................................$12–15
10504 AEC Mammoth Major Box Van "PEK".....................................$12–15
10505 AEC Mammoth Major Box Van "Oxydol".................................$12–15
10601 AEC Mammoth Major 8 Wheel Tanker "Century Oils" $12–15
10602 AEC Mammoth Major 8 Wheel Tanker "J. & H. Bunn" $12–15
10604 AEC Mammoth Major 8 Wheel Tanker "Mobilgas" $12–15
10605 AEC Mammoth Major 8 Wheel Tanker "Regent" $12–15
10701 AEC Mammoth Major 6 Wheel Flatbed "Furlong Bros." $12–15
10702 AEC Mammoth Major 6 Wheel Flatbed "Blue Circle".............$1215
10703 AEC Mammoth Major 6 Wheel Flatbed "Wimpey" $12–15
10703R AEC Mammoth Major 6 Wheel Flatbed "Wimpey" $12–15
10801 AEC Mammoth Major 8 Wheel Dropside "British Steel" $12–15
10802 AEC Mammoth Major 8 Wheel Dropside "Whitbread".............$12–15
10803 AEC Mammoth Major 8 Wheel Dropside "Marley" $12–15

10804 AEC Mammoth Major 8 Wheel Dropside "Macready's" $12–15

10901 AEC Mammoth Major 6 Wheel Tanker "Haygates" $12–15

10902 AEC Mammoth Major 6 Wheel Tanker "Lord Rayleighs Farms" $12–15

10903 AEC Mammoth Major 6 Wheel Tanker "LPG Transport" $12–15

10908 AEC Mammoth Major 6 Wheel Tanker "Welch's" $12–15

11001 AEC Mammoth Major Box Van "Croft" $12–15

11002 AEC Mammoth Major Box Van "Pickfords" $12–15

11005 AEC Mammoth Major Box Van "Lacons" $12–15

11106 AEC Mammoth Major Box Van "Rose's" $12–15

11104 RTL Double Decker Bus "Lockey's" $12–15

11105 RTL Double Decker Bus "Brylcreem" $12–15

11901 Harrington Cavalier Coach $12–15

11903 Harrington Cavalier Coach "Grey Green" $12–15

12001 AEC Mammoth Major 8 Wheel Tipper "Wimpey" $12–15

12002 AEC Mammoth Major 8 Wheel Tipper "Tarmac" $12–15

12101 Harrington Cavalier Coach .$12–15

12102 Harrington Cavalier Coach "East Yorkshire" $12–15

12103 Harrington Cavalier Coach "Hebble" $12–15

12201 Harrington Grenadier Coach $12–15

12202 Harrington Grenadier Coach "Premier Travel" $12–15

12301 Harrington Grenadier Coach $12–15

12302 Harrington Grenadier Coach "Grey Cars" $12–15

12501 Atkinson 6 Wheel Box Van "Wells" $12–15

12601 Atkinson 6 Wheel Dropside "McNicholas" $12–15

12701 Atkinson 8 Wheel Tanker "Charringtons" $12–15

12801 Atkinson 8 Wheel Flatbed "McPhees" $12–15

12901 Atkinson 8 Wheel Box Van "Fyffes" $12–15

13001 Atkinson Car Transporter......$12–15

13002 Atkinson Car Transporter "Swift's" $12–15

13303 Atkinson Car Transporter "Midlands" $12–15

13301 Atkinson 8 Wheel Tipper "St. Albans" $12–15

13402 Leeds Horsefield Tramcar "CWS/Tizer" $12–15

13403 Leeds Horsefield Tramcar "Jacob's" $12–15

15623 AEC Routemaster London Transport $12–15

16312DL Bristol LS Wilts & Dorset ...$12–15

18501 Bristol VR Open Top Southern National $12–15

19901 Tate & Lyle 3-Piece Gift Set ..$12–15

19902 Rank Hovis 3-Piece Gift Set..$12–15

19904 Taylor Woodrow Gift Set $12–15

19003 RTL 3-Piece Gift Set $12–15

19006 Fisherman's Friend 3-Piece Gift Set $12–15

19808 Daimler CVG6 West Bromwich $12–15

24310 B.E.T. Halifax $12–15

24702 Manchester MCW Atlantean Devon General $12–15

99903 Deluxe Road Transport Set ...$12–15

Exem (also see Progetto K)

This unusual brand from Portugal offers an assortment of 1:43 scale Austin-Healey Sprites in diecast resin.

#7004 Austin-Healey "Bugeye" Sprite, 1:43, red, open top $30

#7005 Austin-Healey "Bugeye" Sprite, 1:43, British racing green, open top $30

#7006 Austin-Healey "Bugeye" Sprite, 1:43, black, top up $30

Exemplers

No information is available except for a single model produced under this brand name.

DeTomaso Pantera, silver, 1:45 ....$15–20

Exoto

Exoto Inc. offers a broad assortment of precision scale models in their Exoto Tifosi catalog. Exoto Models represent highly detailed precision models, mostly in 1:18 scale, mostly of race cars.

For 1998, Exoto expands their offerings with a new series called ThunderTrac, a line of 1:18 scale models showcased by variations of the popular AM General High Mobility Multipurpose Wheeled Vehicle, abbreviated HMMWV and better known as the Humvee or Hummer.

Cobra Daytona Coupe

v.1 1964 Gurney/Bondurant LeMans Class Winner #5, Viking blue $130

v.2 1965 Sutcliffe and Harper #59, red $130

1963 Corvette Grand Sport

v.1 metallic blue $110

Grand Prix Tyrell 003

v.1 1971 Jackie Stewart #2 ....$110

v.2 Francois Cevert #9 ....$110

1967 Lotus Ford 49

v.1 J. Clark #5 ....$110

Lotus Ford 49B

v.1 1968 G. Hill #9 ....$130

v.2 1968 G. Hill #10 ....$130

v.3 1968 M. Andretti #12 ....$130

v.4 1968 Siffert #22 ....$130

Exoto ThunderTrac Series

Humvee Civilian Soft Top, 1:18 ....$80

Humvee Military Command Car, 1:18...$80

Humvee Desert Storm, 1:18 ....$80

Humvee Civilian Wagon, 1:18 ....$80

F & F

Starting in 1954 and continuing until 1967, Fiedler and Fiedler of Dayton, Ohio, produced inexpensive cereal premiums for Post cereals under the auspices of F & F Mold and Die Works. The three inch long cars are one piece plastic with no interior, base, or window glazing. A preponderance of Fords is evident in the assortment.

1950 Ford 4-Door Sedan $40

1951 Ford 4-Door Sedan $40

1954 Ford Crestline Hardtop $25

1954 Ford Crestline Sunliner $25

1954 Ford Customline Ranchwagon $25

1954 Ford Customline 2-Door Sedan $25

1955 Ford Country Sedan Station Wagon ..$25

1955 Ford Customline 2-Door Sedan $25

1955 Ford Fairlane Crown Victoria $25

1955 Ford Thunderbird Convertible $25

1957 Ford Ambulance $25

1957 Ford Convertible $25

1957 Ford Fire Chief $25

1957 Ford 4-Door Hardtop Sedan $25

1957 Ford Highway Patrol $25

1959 Ford Thunderbird Convertible $25

1961 Ford Thunderbird Convertible $25

1961 Ford Thunderbird Hardtop $25

1961 Ford Thunderbird Single Seat Roadster ..$25

1966 Ford Mustang Convertible $25

1966 Ford Mustang Fastback $25

1966 Ford Mustang Hardtop $25

1967 Mercury Cougar Hardtop $25

1969 Mercury Cougar Hardtop $25

1969 Mercury Cyclone Fastback $25

1969 Mercury 2-Door Hardtop $25

1969 Mercury 4-Door Sedan $25

1954 Mercury Monterey Convertible $25

1954 Mercury Monterey 4-Door Sedan $25

1954 Mercury Monterey 2-Door Sedan $25

1954 Mercury XM-800 Show Car $25

1960 Plymouth Convertible $25

1960 Plymouth Hardtop Coupe $25

1960 Plymouth Station Wagon $25

Faie

It is unknown who is the US distributor for Faie models of Hong Kong. It is common for such "generic" models to be widely sold in drugstores and supermarkets, among other places. You'll likely notice that once removed from the package, these models have no identifying marks. The maximum value these toys will likely reach is about a buck, owing mostly to being cheaply made, having no discernable markings, and being mass produced in quantities nearing a million of each. Note the misspelling of McLaren on the package back ("Mc Larem"). Such mistakes indicate they were produced and marketed for the English-speaking market by non-English-speaking manufacturers, a common trait of cheaply made Asian knock-offs, whether of diecast toys or other products.

Ferrari 412 M	$1
Fox Bat FW 1	$1
Heskith B 52	$1
Lotus TPS76, yellow with Goodyear #9	$1
McLaren M32, red with Dunlop/Goodyear F1 #2	$1
Porsche Audi	$1
Porsche Turbo 936	$1
Simca Matra 670	$1
Tiager Jawg 18, orange with Agip/Lucas #4	$1

Fairfield Mint

1004 Hope Street
Box 4185
Stamford CT, 06907-0185
or
20 Academy Street
Norwalk, CT 06852-7100
phone: 203-854-9109

Fairfield Mint of Norwalk, Connecticut, entered the diecast model market around 1995. The company has contracted with several companies to produce models for them, including Solido, Redbox, Yat Ming, Ertl, Motor City Classics, and others. The difference is in color variations supposedly issued exclusively under the Fairfield Mint brand name.

The first in the series of 1:12 scale models is a white '58 Chevy Corvette produced for Fairfield by Solido of France, now a division of Majorette. It sells for $94, according to the December 1995 Diecast Car Collectors Club newsletter.

Other models include a 1959 Chevy Impala Convertible in 1:18 scale and a 1955 Ford Fairlane Crown Victoria in 1:18 scale, both produced for Fairfield by Yat Ming. Variations of these models are also packaged as Road Legends. They sell for $20–35 each.

Also available is a 1953 Chevrolet Pickup in 1:18 scale that appears to be one produced by Mira of Spain.

1958 Chevrolet Corvette, 1:12, white with silver side scoops	$50–94
1959 Chevrolet Impala Convertible, 1:12, top down, metallic cornflower blue with white interior	$25–40
1955 Ford Crown Victoria, 1:12, bright pink and white	$25–40
1953 Chevrolet Pickup, 1:12, red	$30–45

Faller

Among a large number of plastic models, Faller of Germany has produced several beautifully rendered 1:18 scale diecast Mercedes-Benz models.

4310 Mercedes-Benz 220 SE cabriolet, top down, white	$39
4311 Mercedes-Benz 220 SE cabriolet, top down, burgundy	$39
4312 Mercedes-Benz 220 SE cabriolet, top up, limited edition	$42
4315 Mercedes-Benz 220 SE Coupe, blue or white	$39
4321 Mercedes-Benz 220 S, 1956, black or gray	$39
4322 Mercedes-Benz 220 S Taxi	$42
4325 Mercedes-Benz 220 S, two-tone, open sun roof	$39
4326 Mercedes-Benz 220 S, two-tone, closed roof	$39

Faller offers smaller diecast vehicles as well. Here is a small sampling.

Citroen DS-21	$15–20
Porsche 904 GT	$15–20
Volkswagen Polizei	$15–20

Other Faller models are motorized plastic vehicles designed to travel on special roadways as part of an HO gauge railroad layout.

Faracars

Faracars is a brand of 1:43 scale diecast race cars made in France for a Chicago company. They produced only one car, a Parnelli Jones Indy 500 STP Turbine car similar to a Hot Wheels Shelby Turbine. Nicely detailed, it was one of two models planned. The second car, reportedly a Novi Special, was planned but something went wrong and it never happened. Thanks to Greg Ford for the information.

Indy 500 STP Turbine Car, 1:43	$20–25

Fastwheel (see Yat Ming)

Feeling43

Feeling43 is one of the brands that belong to the French model manufacturers union MAFMA. Feeling43 offers 1:43 scale "super kits" and built models. No model list is currently known.

Feil

Richard Feil of Rhode Island, a German-American goldsmith, produced 1:43 scale mostly pewter replicas in the 1970s and early 1980s. He has long since returned to Europe.

1934 Auto Union Racer, 1:43	$45
1938 BMW 328, 1:43	$45
Cugnot 3-wheel, 1:43	$60
Horse-Drawn Fire Wagon, 1:43	$45
Steam Roller, 1:43	$45

Fidart

Any clue to the background of this brand would be greatly appreciated.

1 Volkswagen Dune Buggy, 1:64	$3
2 Lola GT Coupe, 1:64	$3
3 Super Turbo, 1:64	$3

Fimcar

Fimcar models are from Australia. Only a few other notable brands hail from there, Fun Ho!, Top Gear Trax, Micro Models, and probably one or two others. Where Fimcar fits into the picture, I don't know. But based on the $35 price tag, they must be fairly nice representations of the real thing.

1948 Holden Pickup, light blue, 1:43	$35
1953 Holden Pickup, 1:43	$35

Fine Art Models

Post Office Box 225
Birmingham, Michigan 48012
phone: 248-288-5155
fax: 248-288-4412
e-mail: info@fineartmodels.com

No one tells the story of Fine Art Models better than Gary Kohs, president, as extracted from their website at www.fineartmodels.com.

"Fine Art Models produces museum-quality limited-edition scale models that many feel are the finest available in the world today. These are the products of a small Royal Oak, Michigan, company formed in 1990 with the singular goal of being the best in the world at what we do. Our focus is producing the finest models available at a price that represents a value and providing customer service without equal. We have no dealers, only one price, and our models can be found in museums and private collections around the world.

"We focus on transportation models including trains, planes, ships, and automobiles. Our models are not limited to American subjects, as Fine Art Models has a presence in the European market with specific models. In as many situations as possible, we personally deliver our models. The scale of our models corresponds to accepted museum standards and, in every case, it is a scale that allows us to replicate the subject without compromise to detail.

"Our models contain no plastic and, in most cases, are made of brass, nickel silver, or stainless steel. The wood on the models is real wood, and the glass in the windows is real scale glass. You will never find a compromise in the design or construction of our models.

"Our ship models have no equal. Period! We feel we have elevated the art of ship model building in many ways, including high-definition resin hulls that reproduce every detail of a real hull, laser-cut and etched wood decks with every detail of a real wood deck and photo-etched brass superstructures that provide every detail of the real ship's superstructure. To understand the level of this detail, you only have to look at our ship models including USS Arizona, USS Missouri, Bismarck, Edmund Fitzgerald, PT Boat, and many more. And now we have introduced the first model ever of RMS Titanic built in cooperation with the original builders of Titanic, Harland & Wolff. This has already been called the model of the century.

"Our train models are 1:32 scale "Gauge 1" — the original gauge for all trains going back to the late 1800s. We have produced several train models that have sold out and continue to appreciate in value in the secondary market. Our present locomotive, the New York Central J-3a Hudson, is considered the finest train model ever produced, with our patented sound system replicating every sound of the original locomotive. Models on the drawing board include the Union Pacific Big Boy, Pennsylvania 11 Decapod, Pennsylvania B6sb Switcher, Norfolk & Western Class A, and the German Bay S3/6. The sign of a great model is that one's eye is not drawn to any one feature on the model while viewing it, yet one can study the model for hours and continually find something new. This describes our models in every respect.

"Our automobile models are built around the Bugatti marque. Rather than try to be everything to everyone, we chose what we consider to be the finest automobile ever built from all points of view. We will make our name in automobile models by building Bugatti. Our Bugatti models are 1:8 scale and are made entirely of hand-fabricated brass — there is no plastic anywhere. The bodies are formed over wooden bucks as were the real Bugattis seventy years ago. We don't feel there are finer automobile models anywhere at any price.

"Having risen to the top in these respective areas, we focused on airplanes, perhaps the greatest challenge of all. These are all-metal airplanes with working control surfaces, operating controls and virtually every detail found on the real airplane whether one can see it or not. Our 1:15 scale FG-1D Corsair may be the most difficult airplane model of all, and we chose it to be our first for this reason. It is all-metal with fabric-covered outer wings, wood ailerons, fabric-covered tail surfaces, folding wings with working controls, and every other detail found in the original airplane. Following the Corsair, we will do the P-51D Mustang, P-38 Lightning, Spitfire Mark I, and many more.

"As a company, we will never become larger than we are today and we will never increase the size of our limited editions regardless of demand. With few exceptions, that maximum number is 139 pieces, the edition size of our very first model.

"Fine Art Models has a 100-plus-page catalog detailing the more than one hundred different model editions we have built over these years, and we publish a quarterly newsletter that keeps everyone informed of our new releases — we invite you to contact us for additional information. One of our many customers best described our models as truly fine art that

has a tendency to elevate everything around them. Please give us a call any time."

Fine Art Models 1:8 Scale Automobiles

1904 Mercedes Simplex, white with red or black interior, 1994, 50 built, sold out $16,500
1913 Mercer J Raceabout, yellow or blue, 1994, 25 built, sold out.........$16,500
1909–1921 Bugatti Type 13 Brescia, black or red, 1996, 14 built, sold out .$8,500
1924–1926 Bugatti Type 35A, 1999, 50 built $8,500
1924–1925 Bugatti Type 35B, 1999, 50 built $8,500
1926 Bugatti Type 37, 1999, 50 built.......................................$8,500
1927–1931 Bugatti Type 37A, 1999, 50 built.......................................$8,500
1927–30 Bugatti Type 43, 1999, 50 built.......................................$9,500
1931–32 Bugatti Type 50/59, 1999, 50 built...........................$10,000
1931–34 Bugatti Type 51, 1999, 50 built.......................................$9,000
1931–35 Bugatti Type 55, 1999, quantity and price not provided
1938 Bugatti Type 57C, 1998, 50 built.................................$16,000

Fine Model

Collector Robert Speerbrecher (see Silver Pet) reports that these models are likely 1:43 scale and represent mid-sixties to early seventies Japanese cars. Four models are shown in a Japanese language book. They appear to be a Datsun 240Z, Datsun 240Z Police, and two versions of an unidentified two-door sedan.

A phone number, 03 (3806) 1219, is shown in the book as a contact for the company, and values are shown as 9000 Japanese yen each, which converts to around $65–66 US.
Datsun 240Z $66
Datsun 240Z Police $66
Two-Door Japanese Sedan (two color variations)................................$66 each

Finoko

Russia, 644083, Omsk, Glinki street, 4 - 41
contact: Fisyn Alexsander Olegovich

Finoko buses are made-to-order 1:43 scale models produced by Finoko workshop, Omsk, Russia. Material is tin-lead castings, with windows of "organic glass" inside, and bottom equipment is available. Quality is good, quantity is limited, prices are moderate, according to Andrey U. Pogorely, e-mail: pogorely@infopro.spb.su, website: http://nt.isc.nw.ru/finoko/.

First Choice

Since about 1987, First Choice has produced plastic toys with electronic lights and

sounds. In 1997, the Canadian company produced their first diecast vehicle, a Seagrave Fire Pumper in two current Windsor, Ontario, liveries. A limited production of 1,000 of the first color and 2,500 of the second will assure a high resale value for collectors and dealers.

First Gear

First Gear models are 1:34 scale trucks made of heavy diecast metal that are often customized to the buyers requirements. Various clubs and companies contract First Gear to produce a limited edition model or series of models that feature their company logo or advertising (known as livery). Just a few base models are used, but the variations are numerous.

First Gear Toy Collector Club of America 1994 Remington Arms Company Commemorative Series

1st in the Series: "Mallard" #10-1082 '52 GMC................................$45
2nd in the Series: "Dove" #10-1098 '51 Ford................................$45
3rd in the Series: "Pheasant" #10-1139 '51 Ford................................$45
4th in the Series: "Quail" #10-1094 '51 Ford $45
5th in the Series: "Goose" #10-1134 '52 GMC................................$45
6th in the Series: "Turkey" #10-1133 '51 Ford $45

Other First Gear Models

1949 Chevrolet variations:
    "Genuine Chevrolet" $30
    "Mercy Hospital" Ambulance $30
    "Pepsi Big Shot" $40
    "Rock Solid Chevrolet"....................$30
1951 Ford variations:
    "GlasUrit Autolack System" Box Van .$45
    "1995 Hershey" Stake Bed $45
    "Auto Value" Box Van $60

"Barq's Root Beer" $40

    "Navajo" Box Van........................$35
    "Red Star" Box Van $50

"Royal Crown Cola" Beverage Truck $40

1952 GMC variations:
    "Burlington" Box Van $35

"Carstar" Wrecker $40
Chicago Fire Wrecker $100
"Falstaff Beer" $40
"FDNY Oxygen" Stake Bed...........$40
"Harley Custom Chrome" $50
"McLean Trucking" $100
Montgomery County Wrecker.........$45
"Morton Salt" Stake Bed $35
"O'Doul's Oasis Beer" $35
Philadelphia Rescue........................$50
"Railway Express" Stake Truck.........$40
"Stroh's Beer" $40

U. S. Mail Stake Truck $40

"Whitney Volunteer" Tanker $40
1953 Ford C600 variations:
  "Roadway" Box Van $35
1957 International Harvester variations:
  "AAA of Sacramento" Wrecker........$45
  "Atlas Van Lines" $70
  Boston Engine #54 Fire Truck $70
  "Campbell Soup" Box Van $40
  "Dart Towing of the Bronx" $40
  "Esso" Tanker $35
  "FDNY Garage" Tow Truck $45
  "Gulf Oil Refinery" Fire Truck $40
  "Gulf Oil" Wrecker $50
  "Hershey Chocolate" Van $55
  "Mobil Oil Refinery" Fire Truck.........$45
  "Paul Arpin" Double Freighter Moving
    Van.......................................$50
  Philadelphia Tow Truck $60
  "Shell" Aviation Tanker $35
  "SOCAL" Tanker...........................$45
  "Tow Times" Wrecker $60
  US Army Wrecker $45
  "Von Der Ahe" Double Freighter Moving
    Van.......................................$50
  Zephyr Lubes" Box Van $30
1960 Mack variations:
  "Adley Express" $90
  "Campbell Soup" $70
  "Columbian" Moving Van $80
  "Eagle Snacks" $55
  "Eastern Express" $55
  "Great Northern" $90
  "Hershey Anniversary" $65
  "Humble Oil" $90
  "Mack Trucks" $140
  "New York Central" $55
  "Pepsi Cola" $90
  "Red Star" $130
  "Smith & Wesson" $90
  "St. Johnsbury" $60
1:54 Scale Series, 1997

Freightliner FLD 120 conventional tractor
  with 48-foot trailer $65–80
International 4900 series trucks ..$65–80
Refrigerated Box Truck $65–80
Fuel Tanker..............................$65–80
Stake Truck..............................$65–80

Fisher-Price

Most of what Fisher-Price has produced is preschool toys, and along with so many other companies, they've also marketed diecast-and-plastic diecast toys. Fisher-Price is now a brand owned by Mattel, along with Tyco, Matchbox, and others, as well as their own original Hot Wheels. Below is a list of the Sesame Street toys produced under the Fisher-Price brand.

Previously, Hasbro had the license to produce Sesame Street preschool toys. For 1998, Mattel has issued twelve diecast-and-plastic models under the Tyco Preschool / Matchbox brand. Models are made in China, distributed by Mattel Australia Pty., Ltd., and sold (in the US) in sets of three for $5.99 or individually for $1.97 each. The 1999 models are packaged under the Fisher-Price brand, but on the base is printed either "Matchbox" or "Tyco."

Baby Bear's Buggy, lime green with orange roll bar and base, blue wheels $2–3
Bert's Tow Truck, lime green with blue boom, orange base, yellow wheels................$2–3
Big Bird's Buggy, lime green with blue roll bar, orange base, yellow wheels................$2–3
Big Bird's Fire Engine, red and white with yellow wheels $2–3
Big Bird's Mail Truck, red cab, white container, blue base and wheels $2–3
Cookie Monster's Airplane, white with yellow trim and propeller, red base, blue wheels....$2–3
Cookie Monster's School Bus, yellow with blue base, red wheels $2–3
Elmo's Cement Mixer, blue and red with yellow base, silver barrel, red wheels $2–3
Elmo's Dump Truck $2–3
Elmo's Locomotive, blue with red smokestack and wheels, yellow trim $2–3
Elmo's Taxi, yellow with red base, blue wheels..$2–3
Ernie's Cement Mixer, yellow with red barrel and wheels $2–3
Ernie's Dump Truck $2–3
Ernie's Police Car $2–3
Fozzie Bear's Dump Truck, blue with red dumper, yellow base, red wheels $2–3
Fozzie Bear's Police Car, white with black doors, orange base, blue wheels..................$2–3
Grover's Helicopter, red and yellow with blue skids, silver propeller and tailfin $2–3
Oscar the Grouch's Garbage Truck, silver with orange container, yellow base, lime green wheels $2–3
Telly's Front Loader, yellow with lime green scoop and wheels.....................................$2–3

Zoe's Convertible, red with yellow base, blue wheels $2–3

Fletcher, Barnhardt & White
327-B W. Tremont
Charlotte, NC 28203

Fletcher, Barnhardt & White is not so much a brand as an advertising and marketing firm. The offerings listed below are collectible premiums sold only at Shell gas stations. Thanks to collector Dave Lehrer for the information.

Reports Mr. Lehrer, "I also discovered a generic Porsche 959 Shell Promo made in China, similar in quality and construction to Summer models. It even sports wheels similar to some I have seen on Summer models. However, inside the baggie was a card that said that defective merchandise could be exchanged by writing FBW, 327-B W. Tremont, Charlotte, NC 28203."

Lehrer continues, "A quick web search turned up a listing for this company in North Carolina, although not at the address above. It is listed as an advertising/specialties firm. I would be interested in hearing anything regarding the source of these models and if there are any more to be had."

Chevrolet Monte Carlo Stock Car, #18 Dale Jarrett, Interstate Batteries, approx. 1:43, black painted metal chassis $8–10
Ford Mustang Stock Car #3 Tommy Archer, Shellzone, approx. 1:43, black plastic chassis $8–10
Honda Indy Car, #10 Motorola, approx. 1:50, black painted metal chassis..............$8–10
Honda Indy Car, #4 Rahal-Hogan Racing, approx. 1:50, black painted metal chassis $8–10
Porsche 959 ....$8–10

Fly

The name is all that's known about the Fly brand.

Forma

An assortment of 1:43 scale models were marketed by this Italian firm under the Forma name which became Yaxon of Italy after 1977.

300 Fiat 130 Semi-Trailer Truck $30
301 Fiat 170 Overhead Service Truck $30
302 Fiat 170 Garbage Truck....................$30
303 Fiat 170 Lumber Semi-Trailer Truck $30
304 Fiat 170 Open Semi-Trailer Truck $30
305 Fiat 170 Covered Semi-Trailer Truck $30
306 Fiat 170 Container Semi-Trailer Truck ...$30
311 Mercedes-Benz 2232 Truck and Trailer .$30
317 Mercedes-Benz 2232 Container Truck .$30
355 Fiat 780 Farm Tractor......................$30
356 Fiat 880 Farm Tractor......................$30
370 Two-Wheel Open Farm Trailer $30
371 Manure Spreader $30
372 Tank Trailer $30

381 Four-Wheel Open Farm Trailer.............$30
382 Hay Loader Trailer $30
385 Same 130 Farm Tractor $30
386 Lamborghini Farm Tractor $30

43rd Avenue / Gems 'N' Cobwebs

Sinclair's Auto Miniatures is one of the few sources for this eclectic British brand of hand-built white metal replicas of US cars. In addition, 43rd Avenue's assortment of English replicas called Gems & Cobwebs features a 1997 release of a 1938 prototype Jaguar SS-100 Coupe in 1:43 scale which was showcased in an article in the February 1997 issue of *Mobilia* magazine. The fact that this model even exists celebrates the rarity of the real car which was never put into production.

43rd Avenue

1959 Cadillac Flattop 4-Door Sedan, 1:43 ....$100
1968 Ford Torino 2-Door Convertible, 1:43 ....$100
1951 Studebaker Business Coupe 2-Door, 1:43 ....$100
1951 Studebaker Coupe 2-Door, 1:43 ....$100

43rd Avenue Gems 'n' Cobwebs

Alvis TF21, open $95
Alvis TF21, Saloon $95
Austin A60 Pickup $95
Austin A60 Van $95
Ford Zephyr Convertible $95
Humber Super Snipe $95
Jaguar 420 G $95
Jaguar Mk II $95
Jaguar Mk IX $95
Jaguar Mk IX Hearse $95
Jaguar MX $95
Jaguar S Type Saloon $95
Jaguar S Type Police $95
1938 Jaguar SS-100 Prototype Coupe .$110
Jaguar V12 E Type Hardtop....................$95
Jaguar V12 E Type Convertible................$95
Jaguar XJ6 ....$95
1994 Jaguar XJR $95
Jaguar XK150S Coupe $95
Jaguar XK150S Roadster $95
Riley Pathfinder Saloon $95
Riley Pathfinder Police $95

Fournier Enterprises

1884 Thunderbird St.
Troy MI 48084
phone: 800-501-3722
fax: 810-362-2866

Fournier produces hand-built 1:8 scale models of Kurtis Indy Roadsters. These all-metal models represent momentous times in Indianapolis history and feature hand-fabricated aluminum bodies, leather seats, and treaded rubber tires. Models measure approximately 21 inches long and are limited editions of 500 each.

Trio Brass Special, Johnnie Parsons ....NPA

Fuel Injection Special, Bill Vukovich ....NPA

Framberg, H. L. (also see Dale Model Company)

H. L. Framberg manufactured World War II identification models for use during the war in identifying military vehicles from a distance. More research is needed on this Chicago-based company. After W.W.II, Frank Dale left the firm to form his own Dale Model Company and continue making cast-metal military toys based on those made by H. L. Framberg. Nothing more is known about either company except that values on H. L. Framberg models are reportedly around $100 each. The Dale counterparts are valued around $70 each.

France Jouets

Marseilles, France, was the home of France Jouets, founded in 1959. When production was discontinued in 1969, the dies were sold to Safir, also of France. Just six basic chassis provided the basis for a variety of models.

France Jouets 100 Series — Berliet GAK Trucks

101 Tank Truck, 1962 ....$75
102 Lumber Truck, 1962 ....$75
103 Covered Truck, 1962 ....$75
104 Dump Truck, 1962 ....$75
105 Grocery Truck, 1962 ....$75
106 Street Sweeper, 1962 ....$75
107 Cement Mixer, 1962 ....$75
108 Crane Truck, 1964 ....$75
109 Garbage Truck, 1964 ....$75
110 Overhead Service truck, 1964.......$75
111 Farm Truck, 1964 ....$75
112 Pipe Truck, 1964 ....$75
113 Glass Truck, 1964 ....$75
114 Crane Truck, 1964 ....$75
115 Tow Truck, 1964/65....................$75
116 Bucket Truck, 1965 ....$75

France Jouets 200 Series — Pacific Heavy Truck

201 Crane Truck, 1967 ....$125
202 Pipe Carrier Truck, 1959 ....$125
203 Rocket Launcher Truck, 1959......$125
204 Transformer Carrier, 1965..........$125
205 Cement Truck, 1966 ....$125
206 Atomic Cannon Truck, 1966/67.$125
207 Atomic Cannon, not mounted on a truck, 1967 ....$125
208 Atomic Cannon Truck, 1967 ....$125

France Jouets 300 Series — GMC Truck

301 Ambulance Truck, 1959 ....$75
302 Covered Truck, 1961 ....$75
303 Anti-Aircraft Gun Truck, 1959........$75
304 Lance-Rocket Truck, 1959.............$75
305 Rocket Carrier Truck, 1965...........$75
306 Dump Truck with Shovel, 1961 ......$75
Crane Truck, 1961............................$75
Dump Truck, 1961 ....$75
Dump Truck and Trailer, 1961 ....$75

Fire Truck, 1961 ....$75
Lumber Truck, 1959..........................$75
Quarry Dump Truck, 1961 ....$75
Radar Truck, 1959...........................$75
Road Repair Truck, 1961.....................$75
Searchlight Truck, 1959.....................$75
Sweet Sweeper, 1961 ....$75
Tank Truck, 1961 ....$75
Troop Carrier, 1959.........................$75

France Jouets 400 Series — Dodge Truck

401 Open Army Truck, 1960...............$75
402 Army Troop Carrier, 1964 ....$75
403 Covered Army Truck, 1960...........$75
404 Anti-Aircraft Truck, 1960............$75
405 Radar Truck, 1960......................$75
406 Searchlight Truck, 1960...............$75
407 Fire Truck, 1966 ....$75
408 Lance-Rocket Truck, 1966...........$75
409 Ambulance Truck, 1966 ....$75

France Jouets 500/600 Series — Jeep

501 Open Army Jeep, 1961 ....$65
502 Covered Army Jeep, 1964...........$65
503 Army Jeep with Anti-Aircraft Guns, 1961 ....$65
504 Army Jeep with Lance-Rockets, 1961 ....$65
505 Army Radar Jeep, 1961 ....$65
506 Army Jeep with Searchlight, 1961 ....$65
507 Fire Jeep, 1961 ....$65
508 Police Jeep, 1965 ....$65
601 Jeep and Anti-Tank Gun, 1961 ......$65
602 Jeep and Generator Trailer, 1961 ..$65
603 Jeep and Open Trailer, 1961 ....$65
605 Anti-Tank Gun without Jeep, 1961 ..$65
Anti-Aircraft Gun Trailer, 1960............$65
Lance-Rocket Trailer, 1960.................$65
Radar Trailer, 1960.........................$65
Searchlight Trailer, 1960...................$65

France Jouets 700 Series — Berliet Stradair Truck

701 Dump Truck, 1967 ....$75
702 Grocery Truck, 1967 ....$75
703 Tow Truck, 1967 ....$75
704 Glass Truck, 1967 ....$75
706 Street Sweeper, 1967 ....$75
707 Garbage Truck, 1967 ....$75
708 Coca-Cola Truck, 1967..............$75

Franklin Mint

Ruth Gessner
Franklin Mint Precision Models
Mail Drop 185
Franklin Center, PA 19091

Between Danbury Mint and Franklin Mint, some of the most popular and collectible precision models have been produced. Jay Olins, editor of Precision Diecast Car Collectors Club newsletter, is perhaps the most avid collector of both. Every three months, he publishes a complete up-to-date list of models produced by each company. Collectors are very critical of authenticity and detail, so they often write to the manufacturer and to Mr. Olins regarding any discrepancies discovered. Olins apparently has the inside track with both companies, and he relays all such comments to the manufacturer.

Below are listed Franklin Mint models currently available as of March 10, 1995, except where noted by italics. Because of their lack of availability and resulting rarity, some models may be considerably more valuable than indicated herein. Prices listed indicate approximate retail value.

1:6 Scale
1957 Corvette 283HP Engine $125–140

1:8 Scale
1886 Benz Patent Motorwagen ..$125–140

1:10 Scale
1942 Indian 442 Motorcycle $120–140
1957 Harley-Davidson XL Sportster Motorcycle $120–140
1985 Harley-Davidson Heritage Softail Classic Motorcycle $120–140

Franklin Mint 1:16 Scale
1931 Bugatti Royale Coupe De Ville $115–135
1930 Ford Model A $115–135
1913 Ford Model T $115–135
1905 Rolls Royce 10HP $115–135
1911 Stanley Steamer 62 Runabout $115–135

Franklin Mint 1:24 Scale
1938 Alvis Speedster 4.3 Litre, green-silver/beige $85–125
1935 Auburn 851 Speedster, white/red $85–125
1949 Buick Skylark Convertible, pale yellow/red $85–125
1949 Buick Riviera, light blue-gray/gray $85–125
1936 Bugatti Atalante Type 57 SC, red-black/beige $85–125
1930 Bugatti Royale Coupe Napoleon 2, black-blue $85–125
1953 Cadillac Eldorado, white/red $85–125
1959 Cadillac Eldorado Biarritz, light blue/white $85–125
1957 Cadillac Eldorado Brougham, black-stainless/blue-white $85–125
1910 Cadillac Thirty Roadster, black/beige $85–125
1932 Cadillac V-16, blue 2-tone, canvas top/brown $85–125
1955 Chevrolet Bel Air Hardtop, red-white/red-white $85–125
1955 Chevrolet Bel Air Hardtop, blue-white/blue-white $85–125
1955 Chevrolet Bel Air Convertible, gypsy red-white/red-white $85–125
1955 Chevrolet Bel Air Fire Chief #12, red/red & white $85–125
1955 Chevrolet Bel Air Police Chief #67, black & white $85–125
1956 Chevrolet Bel Air Convertible, green-white/green-white $85–125

1957 Chevrolet Bel Air Hot Rod, black-flames/black $85–125
1957 Chevrolet Bel Air Hardtop, red-white/red $85–125
1957 Chevrolet Bel Air Convertible, black/red-silver, issued March 1995 ....$85–125
1957 Chevrolet Bel Air Convertible, red/red-silver $85–125
1953 Chevrolet Corvette, cream/red $85–125
1955 Chevrolet Corvette, metallic blue/beige $85–125
1956 Chevrolet Corvette, turquoise-white/white $85–125
1957 Chevrolet Corvette, red/white $85–125
1957 Chevrolet Corvette Fuel Injected, black-silver/red $85–125
1959 Chevrolet Corvette, red/red, issued March 1995 ....$85–125
1963 Chevrolet Corvette Sting Ray, black-blue/black $85–125
1967 Chevrolet Corvette Sting Ray, black-blue/black $85–125
1967 Chevrolet Corvette L-88 Sting Ray, blue/blue $85–125
1978 Chevrolet Corvette Silver Anniversary Edition, silver/silver $85–125
1986 Chevrolet Corvette, yellow/black $85–125
1986 Chevrolet Corvette, white/white-black $85–125
1960 Chevrolet Impala, white/white $85–125
1960 Chevrolet Impala, red $85–125
1912 Christie Front Drive Steamer Fire Engine $85–125
1948 Chrysler Town & Country Convertible, dark green-wood/red-beige $85–125
1937 Cord 812 Phaeton Coupe, light yellow/black $85–125
1933 Duesenberg Twenty Grand SJ, silver-beige/green $85–125
1930 Duesenberg J Derham Tourist, maroon-beige/gray $85–125
1930 Duesenberg J Derham Tourist (Gary Cooper), silver-black / black $85–125
1933 Duesenberg J Victoria (Greta Garbo), blue-black/blue $85–125
1935 Duesenberg Model J550 Convertible, maroon/white $85–125
1958 Edsel Citation (see Ford Edsel)
1989 Ferrari F40, red/red $85–125
1958 Ford Edsel Citation, pink/pink $85–125
1913 Ford Model T, black $85–125
1932 Ford Deuce Coupe, black with beige interior $95–105
1955 Ford Fairlane Crown Victoria, pink-white/pink-white $85–125

1957 Ford Fairlane 500 Skyliner, white-red/white/red $85–125
1956 Ford Thunderbird, turquoise/turquoise $85–125
1949 Ford "Woody" Wagon, maroon/beige $85–125
1924 Hispano Suiza Tulipwood Speedster, wood/copper $85–125
1925 Hispano Suiza Kellner H6B, maroon/white $85–125
1938 Jaguar SS-100, cream/brown ..$85–125
1961 Jaguar XKE, gray/beige $85–125
1985 Lamborghini Countach 5000S, red/beige $85–125
1985 Lamborghini Fraternal Order of Police, black-white $85–125
1941 Lincoln Continental Mark I, maroon/red $85–125
1939 Maybach Zeppelin, black/gray $85–125
1904 Mercedes Simplex, white/brown $85–125
1935 Mercedes-Benz 500K Roadster, red-beige/red-black $85–125
1935 Mercedes-Benz 770K Pullman Limousine, red-black $85–125
1954 Mercedes-Benz Gullwing 300SL, silver/plaid $85–125
1954 Mercedes-Benz Gullwing 300SL, red/plaid $85–125
1926 Mercedes-Benz Model K, midnight blue/burgundy and paisley $85–125
1954 Mercedes-Benz W196 Racer, silver/red $85–125
1957 Mercedes-Benz 300 SC Roadster, burgundy/tan & black $85–125
1948 MG TC Roadster, red/beige $85–125
1956 Nash Metropolitan, aqua-white/aqua/white $85–125
1977 Oldsmobile Petty NASCAR, blue-red "43" $85–125
1912 Packard 1-48 Victoria, white with black top $85–125
1970 Plymouth Superbird Petty NASCAR, blue "43" $85–125
1988 Porsche 911 Carrera targa, red/black $85–125
1988 Porsche 911 Carrera targa, black $85–125
1907 Rolls Royce Silver Ghost, silver with green seats $85–125
1911 Rolls Royce Tourer, white with tan top $85–125
1925 Rolls Royce Silver Ghost Tourer, silver-black/black $85–125
1929 Rolls Royce Phantom I Cabriolet De Ville, black-blue/black $85–125
1992 Rolls Royce Corniche IV, white/beige $85–125
1992 Rolls Royce Corniche IV, blue/tan $85–125

1911 Stanley Steamer 62 Runabout, red with black top.............................$85–125
1915 Stutz Bearcat, yellow.........$85–125
1928 Stutz Black Hawk, red/black.......................$85–125
1948 Tucker, light blue/gray.......$85–125
1962 Volkswagen Microbus, salmon & cream/cream.....................$85–125
1967 Volkswagen Cabriolet, red/black..$85–125
1967 Volkswagen Beetle, yellow/white.............................$85–125
1967 Volkswagen Beetle, white....$95–105

Franklin Mint 1:32 Scale
1922 Ahrens Fox R-K-4 Pumper Fire Engine..............................$65–75
1954 American LaFrance Fire Engine.$65–75
1988 Peterbilt Truck Model 739 - Cab & Trailer............................$65–75

Franklin Mint 1:43 Scale Classic Cars of the 50s
1953 Buick Skylark.....................$45–60
1959 Cadillac Eldorado...............$45–60
1955 Chevrolet Bel Air................$45–60
1957 Chevrolet Bel Air Convertible..$45–60
1953 Chevrolet Corvette..............$45–60
1957 Chevrolet Corvette..............$45–60
1956 Chevrolet Nomad................$45–60
1958 Chevrolet Corvette..............$30–40
1950 Chrysler Town & Country......$45–60
1952 DeSoto.............................$45–60
1958 Edsel Citation....................$45–60
1955 Ford Crown Victoria............$45–60
1959 Ford Skyliner....................$45–60
1950 Ford Station Wagon............$45–60
1956 Ford Thunderbird................$45–60
1958 Ford Thunderbird................$45–60
1951 Hudson Hornet..................$45–60
1956 Lincoln Continental Mark II....$45–60
1951 Mercury Monterey...............$45–60
1950 Nash...............................$45–60
1956 Oldsmobile Starfire.............$45–60
1955 Packard...........................$45–60
1953 Packard Caribbean.............$45–60
1957 Plymouth Fury...................$45–60
1953 Studebaker Starliner............$45–60

Franklin Mint 1:43 Scale Classic Cars of the 60s
1963 Buick Riviera.....................$45–60
1963 Cadillac Eldorado...............$45–60
1967 Chevrolet Camaro...............$45–60
1960 Chevrolet Corvair...............$45–60
1963 Corvette Sting Ray..............$45–60
1968 Dodge Charger..................$45–60
1964 Ford Mustang....................$45–60
1962 Ford Thunderbird................$45–60
1961 Lincoln Continental.............$45–60
1964 Pontiac LeMans GTO...........$45–60
1963 Rambler Classic 660...........$45–60
1963 Studebaker Avanti..............$45–60

Franklin Mint 1:43 Scale Luxury Car Series
1931 Bugatti Royale Berline De-Voyage..............................$45–60

1930 Cadillac V-16.....................$45–60
1931 Cord L-29.........................$45–60
1929 Duesenberg J....................$45–60
1928 Hispano Suiza H6B.............$45–60
1928 Isotta Fraschini..................$45–60
1946 Jaguar Mark IV...................$45–60
1927 Lincoln Sport Touring...........$45–60
1939 Mercedes-Benz 770K Grosser Cabriolet.............................$45–60
1934 Packard...........................$45–60
1933 Pierce Silver Arrow.............$45–60
1922 Rolls Royce Silver Ghost........$45–60

Freeway Flyers (see Playart)

Freewheels
Details regarding this brand are nearly nonexistent. Only one model is known.
Mercedes 190E, silver.............$10

Frobly
According to collector Bill Cross, "Frobly models are hand-built resin/white metal models made in France. The proprietor has recently discontinued the range — he is associated with a French collector's model shop, the name of which escapes me at present. The first model in the Frobly range was an incredibly ugly Packard Hawk."
Citroën DS19 4-Door Sedan.......$65
Citroën DS19 Convertible............$65
Citroën ID19 4-Door Sedan.........$65
1961 Ford Econoline Van............$79
1961 Ford Econoline Pickup........$79
1951 Mercury Convertible..........$89
Packard Hawk.......................$100

Fun Ho! (also see Streamlux)
Fun Ho! Museum
PO Box 14, Inglewood
Taranaki, New Zealand
contact Barry Young
e-mail: fun.ho!toys@xtra.co.nz
In a recent book by Ellis David Daw of Australia entitled *Fun Ho! Miniature Vehicles, A Collector's Guide*, the author reports that Fun Ho! castings were first produced in 1939 by H. J. Underwood of Underwood Engineering Company of New Zealand. The first ten Fun Ho! models (always with an exclamation point) consisted of lead hollow-cast vehicles hand-poured into molds and sold in association with lead soldiers, farm and other animals, trees, fences, and similar items. The fact that they were hand poured resulted in inconsistencies in thickness of the castings.
Ian Cousins of New Zealand reports that the models are not called Fun Ho! because they approximate HO scale but because the manufacturer wanted a name that conjured up the concept of toys that were a lot of fun... the name therefore arose in a similar way to the wagoner's or military call "forward ho!"

The original series of Fun Ho! midgets were produced starting in 1940 using the Streamlux dies from Australia — many of these early Fun Ho! models still have the Streamlux markings on the base plate making it sometimes difficult to establish whether the model was made in New Zealand or Australia. From 1952 on, plastic wheels replaced the crude rubber ones.
After 1945, health regulations fairly well ended the use of lead in the alloys, but production of the large aluminum cast toys continued into the 1970s. Accuracy varied from one model to the next.
A zinc alloy diecast range of toys was introduced in 1962 in a promotional arrangement with Mobil oil and marketed as Fun Ho! Mobil Midgets. This new range featured chromed and coppered finishes in the beginning, but later gave way to more conventional paint finishes. Production of the original line ended in 1982. For a short time afterwards, Asian imported toys, including Zee toys, were marketed as "Distributed by Fun Ho!" but lacked the distinctiveness of the originals.
In 1964, Underwood Engineering acquired the dies from the Streamlux range of Australian toys and applied the Fun Ho! Midgets brand name to them along with some upgrades to the castings.
At one time, Fun Ho! models were being reproduced through the Fun Ho! Museum, PO Box 14, Inglewood, Taranaki, New Zealand, by Barry Young.
Ian Cousins adds, "I have no information on the items produced by Message Models, but it was my understanding that, for the last few years, Barry Young of Inglewood had been producing replacement parts and replicas of the original models from the original dies through his Fun Ho! Museum. I understand that this museum has now been sold to the local tourism board but that Barry is available to talk to groups of visitors by prior arrangement."

Fun Ho! Original Castings
#1 Massey-Ferguson 35 Tractor, copper finish, chromed wheels, towbar, 1⅝", 1964–1970.........................$55–60
#2 Holden FE (EK) Special Sedan, marked as EK but is actually an FE, 2⅛", 1964–1972.........................$55–60
#3 Austin Open Back Truck, 2", 1964–1972.........................$55–60
#4 Austin Petrol Tanker, 2", 1964–1972.........................$55–60
#5 Volkswagen Combi Bus, 2⅛", 1964–1982.........................$55–60
#6 Mercedes-Benz W196 Racer, 2", 1964–1972.........................$55–60
#7 Commer Coach, 2⅛", 1964–1972
v.1 British Overseas Airways Corporation (BOAC) Bus.............$55–60

v.2 Australian National Airways (ANA) Coach $55–60

#8 Austin Tip Truck, 2", 1964–1972 ....$70–75

#9 Volkswagen Sedan, 1⅝", 1964–1972 ....$55–60

#10 Ford Falcon Sedan, 2⅛", 1965–1972 ....$50–55

#11 Morris 850 Mini-Minor, 1⅜", 1965–1972 ....$50–55

#12 Vauxhall Velox, 2⅛", 1965–1972 ....$50–55

#13 Morris 1100, 1¾", 1965–1972 ....$50–55

#14 Ford Cortina Estate Car, 1⅞", 1966–1972 ....$50–55

#15 Hillman Imp, 1½", 1966–1972 ....$50–55

#16 Fordson Super Major Tractor, 1¾", 1965–1982 ....$50–55

#17 Austin-Mini, 1⅜", 1965–1972 ..$50–55

#18 Austin Articulated Truck, 3" with trailer, 1966–1972 ....$75–80

#19 Land Rover, 1¹³⁄₁₆", 1966–1978 ....$40–45

#20 Ford Thames Freight Van, 2", 1966–1979 ....$40–45

#21 Fire Engine, 2⅜", 1966–1982 ....$40–45

#22 Bedford Articulated Truck, 3⁹⁄₁₆", 1966–1982 ....$60–70

#23 Jaguar Mk X (Mark 10), 2½", 1966–1982 ....$40–45

#24 Chevrolet Bel Air, 2¹¹⁄₁₆", 1966–1982 ....$45–45

#25 MGB Sports Car, 1⅞", 1966–1970 ....$40–45

#26 Ford Thames Freighter Pickup (Ute), 2", 1966–1982 ....$40–45

#27 Bedford Articulated Tanker, 3⅝", 1966–1982 ....$40–45

#28 Morris J2 Pickup, 2⅛", 1966–1971 ....$40–45

#29 Bedford Truck, 2⅜", 1966–1982 ....$40–45

#30 Car Trailer, 1½", 1966–1982 ....$40–45

#31 White Heavy Duty Tip Truck, 2¼" $40–45

#32 Austin 1100, 1¾", 1966–1972 ....$40–45

#33 Rolls Royce Phantom V, 1⅝", 1967–1982 ....$40–45

#34 Holden HR Sedan, 2⅜", 1967–1982 ....$40–45

#35 Holden HR Ambulance Panel Van, 2¼", 1967–1982 ....$40–45

#36 Holden HR Police Panel Van, 2¼", 1967–1982 ....$40–45

#37 Aveling Road Roller, 2¾", 1967–1982 ....$40-45

#38 Car Trailer, 1⅝", 1967–1978 .$20–25

#39 Farm Trailer, 2⅛", 1967–

1982 ....$20–25

#40 Bedford Articulated Milk Tanker, 3⅝", 1967–1982 ....$40-45

#41 Ford Zephyr Mk 4, 2½", 1969–1977 ....$30–35

#42 Caterpillar D8 Tractor, 2", 1969–1982 ....$30–35

#43 Jaguar E-Type, 2⅛", 1969–1982 ....$30–35

#44 Caterpillar Front End Loader, 2¹⁵⁄₁₆", 1969–1982 ....$30–35

#45 Mercedes-Benz 230, 2½", 1969–1982 ....$30–35

#46 Caterpillar Bulldozer, 2¹¹⁄₁₆", 1969–1982 ....$30–35

#47 Forklift Truck, 2⅜", 1970–1982 ....$30–35

#48 Ford D 6-Wheel Truck, 3½", 1970–1982 ....$30–35

#49 Ford D Sand Dumper, 3¾", 1970–1982 ....$30–35

#50 Ford D Dump Truck, 2¾", 1970–1982 ....$30–35

#51 Ford D Low Loader, 3½", 1970–1982 ....$30–35

#52 Sand Dump Trailer, 3¼", 1970–1982 ....$30–35

#53 Breakdown Truck, 2⅜", 1971–1982 ....$30–35

#54 Front End Loader, 2¹³⁄₁₆", 1972–1982 ....$30–35

#55 Tractor Scraper, 3⅝", 1971–1982 ....$30–35

#56 Landliner Bus, 3⅝", 1971–1982 ....$30–35

#57 Holden HR Ute, 2⅝", 1971–1982 ....$30–35

#58 Jeep, 2⅜", 1976–1982 ....$30–35

#59 Armored Jeep, 2⅜", 1977–1982 ....$30–35

#60 Road Grader, 4", 1978–1982 .$45–50

#61 Holden HR Panel Van, 2¼", 1978–1982 ....$30–35

#62 Army Ambulance, 2¼", 1977–1982 ....$30–35

#63 Army Jeep, 2⅜", 1977–1982 .$30–35

#64 Army Bulldozer, 2⅜", 1977–1982 ....$30–35

#65 Army Road Roller, 2¾", 1977–1982 ....$30–35

#66 Army Grader, 4⅛", 1978–1982 .$40–45

#67 Army Transporter, 3½", 1977–1982 ....$30–35

#68 Army Dump Truck, 2⅞", 1977–1982 ....$30–35

#69 Army Each Scraper, 3⅝", 1977–1982 ....$30–35

#70 Army Tractor Shovel, 2⅞", 1977–1982 ....$30–35

#71 Army Tanker, 3¾", 1977–1982 ....$30–35

#72 Army Front End Loader, 2¹⁵⁄₁₆", 1977–1982 ....$30–35

#76 Racing Car, 1941 ....$75–80

#81 Oliver Tractor, 1941 ....$75–80

Fun Ho! King Size

K-1 International Articulated Truck, 5½", 1973–1982 ....$50–55

K-2 International Dump Truck, 1976–1982 ....$50–55

K-3 International Army Supply Truck, 1978–1982 ....$50–55

K-4 International Army Dump Truck, 1978–1982 ....$50–55

Fun Ho! Recasts from Message Models

#5 VW Combi Bus, approximately 1,000 produced, 1996–present $15–20

#16 Fordson Tractor, approximately 400 produced, 1996–present $18–24

#19 Land Rover, approximately 600 produced, 1996–present $15–20

#21 Fire Engine, approximately 1,200 produced, 1996–present $15–20

#23 Jaguar Mk X (Mark 10) Saloon, approximately 400 produced, 1991–present..$15–20

#24 Chevrolet Bel Air, approximately 500 produced, 1996–present $15–20

#26 Ford Thames Ute, approximately 2,500 produced, 1991–present $15–20

#33 Rolls Royce Phantom V, approximately 4,500 produced, 1996–present $15–20

#34 Holden HR Sedan, approximately 2,500 produced, 1996–present $15–20

#35 Holden HR Ambulance Panel Van, approximately 1,000 produced, 1996–present $15–20

#36 Holden HR Police Panel Van, approximately 1,000 produced, 1996–present $15–20

#38 Car Trailer, approximately 1,500 produced, 1996–present $12–15

#39 Farm Trailer, approximately 5,000 produced, 1996–present $10–12

#43 Jaguar E-Type, approximately 1,400 produced, 1996–present $15–20

#45 Mercedes-Benz 230, approximately 700 produced, 1996–present ..$18–24

#47 Fork Lift, approximately 3,000 produced, 1996–present $15–20

#57 Holden HR Ute, approximately 1,500 produced, 1996–present $15–20

#61 Holden Panel Van, approximately 300 produced, 1996–present $25–28

Funmate

Funmate toys were packaged in laundry detergent in the seventies, according to collector John Dean. One model is of a Volkswagen Beetle in shiny metallic copper-tinted chrome. Value is likely to remain low on these fairly generic and unremarkable toys.

Funrise (also see Code 3 Collectibles)

While Funrise is mostly known for plastic toys with electronic sirens, sound effects, and lights, the company has apparently produced a few diecast toys as well, according to Loraine Price whose son has a collection of them. Here are some models she has listed.

Airport Fire Truck $8
Ford Ranger Police Truck $8
Rescue Helicopter................................$8
Ambulance $8
Metro Tow Truck $8
Fire Engine...$8
Chevrolet Police Car............................$8
Fire Rescue Truck $8
Ford Explorer $8
Van Ambulance $8
Chevrolet Tahoe $8

FYP

Harvey Goranson reports that Yves Pebernet produced this range of resin models from 1986 until 1995.

Rolls Royce Phantom V Landaulet, white & black $450
Rolls Royce Silver Wraith "Gulbenkian," dark green $385

Gabriel

A lesser-known toy company of the sixties and early seventies, Gabriel apparently produced a few diecast model kits similar to Hubley. I find it surprising that I can find no information on this company in any other reference book.

1929 Ford Model A Station Wagon, unassembled in sealed box........................$45–60
assembled or partly assembled with original box $25–30

Gad (see Great American Dreamcars)

Gaffe

Gaffe belongs to the French model Artisans union known as MAFMA. Resin kits of 1:43 scale Paris-Dakar rally vehicles comprise the series. No model list is known.

Gaia

Model Power, Inc., has repackaged Gaia brand American LaFrance fire trucks as models for 1:87 (HO scale) railroad sets. Other models from Model Power are made by Playart, another manufacturer famous for repackaging their models under a different brand.

American LaFrance Fire Pumper, 1:87 ....$13
American LaFrance Ladder Truck, 1:87........$15
American LaFrance Snorkel Truck, 1:87 ......$15

Gaiety (also see Castle Art)

Collector Paul Starck wrote via e-mail of a brand called Castle Art. He indicates that they are diecast cars also known as Gaiety toys, made in Birmingham, West Midlands, England, in the fifties. "I have two racers from them," writes Starck. "One is a silver Morgan (three wheeled wind-up) and could have been a promo for the Morgan Car Company. The other seems to be cast iron." This is all that's known about this brand.

Galgo

An interesting assortment of these inexpensive models manufactured in Argentina are available in 1:43 and 1:64 scale.

Galgo 1:64 Scale

Dodge Challenger "A-Team," white & red .$3
Fiat Dump Truck $3
Fiat Snorkel Fire Truck $3
Fiat Semi "BJ Bear" $3
Lancia Stratos $3
Scania Oil Tanker "Aeronafta" $3
Scania Oil Tanker "Agip" $3
Scania Oil Tanker "Esso" $3
Scania Oil Tanker "Shell" $3
Scania Semi "Camel Cigarettes" $3
Scania Semi "Cazalis" $3
Scania Semi "Coca Cola" $5
Scania Semi "Fargo" $3
Scania Semi "Frigor" $3
Scania Semi "Lee" $3

Galgo 1:43 Scale

1 BMW 3.5 "1st National" $14
2 Cametal Luxury Bus $14
26 Mercedes School Bus $14
27 Peugeot 505 4-Door Sedan.............$14
29 Porsche 935 "Canon" $14
30 Porsche 935 "Rothmans" $14
31 Porsche 935 "Jagermist" $14
32 Renault Alpine "Elf" $14
33 Renault 18 4-Door Sedan $14
34 Renault 18 Fire Chief $14

35 Scania Semi "Adidas" $8
36 Scania Semi Van..............................$8
37 Scania Semi "Cheese" $8
38 Scania Semi "A-Team" $8
39 Scania Semi "Coca Cola" $8
40 Scania Semi "Paint" $8
42 Scania Semi "Wine" $8
43 Scania Semi "VW Parts" $8
44 Ford Falcon 4-Door Sedan Rally........$8
45 Dodge Dart 2-Door Hardtop Rally, orange..$8
46 Volkswagen Van "Bagley" $8

Galoob (see Micro Machines)

Gama

Gama models were manufactured in Furth, Bavaria, by the Georg Adam Mangold company. Begun in 1882, Gama only started producing diecast models in 1959. Gama models have been issued under the Schuco brand starting in 1994. Gama models remain some of the more distinctive models of our time.

1 Porsche Carrera Six, 1:63, 1968...........$24
5 NSU Ro-80, 1:63, 1968.....................$24
13 Volkswagen 1302, 1:63, 1969..........$24
31 Henschel Wrecker, 1969...................$24
890 Opel Kadett, 1:43, 1979 ....$30
892 Porsche 924, silver with black interior, 1:43..$25
893 Opel Rekord, 1:43, 1978 ....$30
901 Ford Taunus 17M, 1959 ....$48
907 BMW 600, 1959............................$48
919 Faun Cement Truck, 1962 ....$54
925.1 Demag Excavator, 1969 ....$54
960.1 Porsche Carrera 6, bronze, #2, 1:39...$25
960.5 Porsche 917, blue, #5, 1:42 ....$30
973 Porsche 911, metallic green with tan interior, license # FU-GA555, 1:42 ....$30
973 Porsche 911, green with black hood, 1:42 ....$30
973 Porsche 911R, metallic dark green with tan interior, checker stripe, #10, 1:42.........$30
973.4 Porsche 911 Police, white with black hood, 1:43...................................$30
973.5 Porsche 911 Rallye, green with black hood, black and white check stripe, #2, 1:43 ....$30
973.6 Porsche 911 Police, white and green with blue light on roof, 1:43 ....$30
982.0 Porsche 914, silver, 1:43...............$30
982.1 Porsche 914 Police, white with green hood and top, 1:43 ....$30
1003 Opel Frontera, 1:43 ....$15
1005 Opel Corsa, 1:43 ....$15
1007 Messerschmitt Tiger, red, closed, 1:43 ....$21
1008 Messerschmitt Tiger, yellow, open, 1:43 ....$21
1009 Messerschmitt Tiger, silver, closed, 1:43 ....$24
1010 Messerschmitt Tiger, black, open, 1:43 ....$24

1011 BMW 525i Touring Wagon, 1:43 ...$15
1013 Opel Astra GSi, 1:43 ....$30
1020 Ford Mondeo, 1:43 ....$15
1021 BMW 325i Coupe, 1:43 ....$15
1026 Opel Astra Cabriolet, 1:43 ....$15
1133 Opel Senator, 1:43 ....$15

1168 Mercedes-Benz 300CE, Limousinse, 1:43 ....$15

1173 Audi 80, 1:43 ....$15
1150 BMW Isetta, 1:43 ....$35
2103 BMW 325i, 1:24 ....$42
2105 BMW M3, 1:24 ....$42

Gama for AHC

1:43 diecast in Germany, refinished in Holland.

GA001R Opel Kadett, boot, Rijkspolitie (Dutch police) ....(£18) $28 US
GA001R Opel Kadett hatch, Marechausee (Dutch customs police).......(£18) $28 US

Gamda Koor (also see Crescent, D.C.M.T., Impy, Lone Star, Sabra, Cragstan)

An Internet bulletin board posting on America OnLine was from a collector seeking Gamda diecast cars and trucks made in Israel in the early to mid 1960s, alternately known as Gamda Sabra, Gamda Koor, and a small line of US cars produced under the Cragstan Detroit Seniors brand.

Collector Bill Cross reports, "There was an article in a recent issue of *Model Collector* on this range. If memory serves, the range had its beginnings in the Lone Star products of the D.C.M.T. company in Great Britain. There were few models in the range and were, I think, mostly post-WW2 British vehicles." If my latest research is any indication, it seems a lot of brands originated from D.C.M.T., including Crescent and Lone Star. Some Gamda models are in fact enhanced versions of D.C.M.T. models, with windows added and better paint jobs applied. Reissues of Dinky toys also made it into the Gamda line-up. In addition, the brand name Gamda-Sabra can be found on the bases of several models. Cragstan is yet another associated brand.

25-Pounder Gun, tan $30
Armored Car, tan $50
Articulated Flat Truck, blue and red $75
Articulated Tanker, "DELEK" $100
Articulated Tanker, "PAZ" $100
Articulated Tanker, "SONOL" $100
Articulated Tanker, "TNUVA" $100
Articulated Tanker, UN, white $100
Articulated Timber Truck, blue and red $75
Bedford "Driving School" Truck.................$90

Centurion Tank, 1:45, tan $60
Centurion Tank, 1:90, tan $45
Centurion Tank, 1:120, tan $30
Covered Dairy Truck, "TNUVA," blue and cream $75
Covered Mail Truck...............................$75
Covered Truck, "AMCOR" $60
Daimler Conquest Saloon, gray $100
Dump Truck...$50
Ford Prefect, cream or green.....................$65
Leyland "Egged" Bus, blue and gray..........$150
Massey Ferguson Tractor, red $60
Military Covered Truck, tan.....................$75
Military Truck, tan.................................$50
Mobile Canteen Truck $75
Roadmaster Coupe, white and red $80
Tank Transporter, tan $85
Tipping Truck.......................................$65
Truck...$65
Truck with Gas Cylinders........................$75
Quicklime Spreader $30
Vanguard Ambulance, white $90
Vanguard Military Ambulance, tan $75
Willys Jeep, white or red.........................$45
Willys Jeep, UN, white $55
Willys Military Ambulance, tan $60
Willys Military Jeep, tan $45
Willys Military Police Jeep, green $45
Willys Station Wagon Ambulance, white ...$100
Willys Station Wagon Army Van, tan $100
Willys Station Wagon Police Van, green....$100
Willys Station Wagon Van, orange...........$100

Gasqui (or Gasquy)

Belgium is the source for these quality toys, first produced around 1947. The company only lasted a few years before going out of business in the early fifties.

Army Bus, green $150
Buick Coupe, green, blue or red $125
Buick Coupe with clockwork motor, red $175
Bus, red, yellow, green, or gray................$150
Chevrolet Sedan, red, blue, or gray..........$325
FN Breakdown Truck, gray or green..........$100
FN Covered Military Truck, green $100
FN Military Breakdown Truck, green..........$100
FN Open Truck, green, red, or gray..........$100
FN Stake Truck, red or green $100
FN Tanker, green, red, gray and green, gray and red, gray and yellow...................$100
Ford Tudor, blue, gray, red, or green.........$325
Maserati Race Car, green, red, or cream $75
Mercury Ambulance, white, cream, and red .$150
Mercury Army Ambulance, green $125
Mercury Mail Van, yellow $225
Mercury Van, red.................................$150
Mercury Van with clockwork motor, red......$150
Plymouth Sedan, red, brown, green, gray, or chrome-plated $125
Plymouth Staff Car, green $200
Studebaker Champion, blue, brown, gray, or green $450
Tatra, blue, red, brown, green, or gray $450

Willys Army Jeep, green $75
Willys Jeep, red...................................$100
Willys Jeep Station Wagon, red and yellow $325
Willys Red Cross Jeep, white $75

Gate (also see Gateway Global)

It was around May 1999 that Gateway Global, a new company, introduced their Gate line of low-end 1:18 scale diecast models, starting with several color variations each of the Mazda Miata and Volkswagen New Beetle.

01011 Mazda MX-5 Miata, red...............$20
01013 Mazda MX-5 Miata, blue $20
01015 Mazda MX-5 Miata, silver.............$20
01017 Mazda MX-5 Miata, emerald green ..$20
01021 Peugeot 406 Coupe, red $20
01022 Peugeot 406 Coupe, yellow...........$20
01023 Peugeot 406 Coupe, metallic blue ..$20
01024 Peugeot 406 Coupe, silver.............$20
01041 Porsche 996 Coupe, red $20
01042 Porsche 996 Coupe, silver $20
01043 Porsche 996 Coupe, black.............$20
01044 Porsche 996 Coupe, yellow............$20
01051 Porsche 996 Convertible, red $20
01052 Porsche 996 Convertible, silver $20
01053 Porsche 996 Convertible, black $20
01054 Porsche 996 Convertible, yellow $20
01031 1998 Volkswagen New Beetle Coupe, light blue $20
01032 1998 Volkswagen New Beetle Coupe, green $20
01033 1998 Volkswagen New Beetle Coupe, black..$20
01034 1998 Volkswagen New Beetle Coupe, dark blue $20
01035 1998 Volkswagen New Beetle Coupe, white..$20
01036 1998 Volkswagen New Beetle Coupe, yellow $20
01037 1998 Volkswagen New Beetle Coupe, red..$20
01038 1998 Volkswagen New Beetle Coupe, silver..$20

Gateway Global, Inc.

(Includes AutoArt, Gate and UT models)
Gateway Global of Europe GmbH
Postfach 485
D-52005
Aachen, Germany
• Gateway Global Limited
  3/F, 8 Yip Cheong Street
  On Lok Tsuen, Fanling
  New Territories, Hong Kong
• Gateway Autoart Canada
  9620 Ignace Local L
  Brossard, Quebec
  J4Y 2R4 Canada

Gateway Global is the new (1999) parent company to UT models, and the new Auto Art and Gate brands. See their listings under their separate brand name headings.

Gaz (see Volga)

Gearbox
4515 20th Avenue SW
Cedar Rapids, IA 52404
phone: 319-390-1405
fax: 319-390-1413

Gearbox is a recent entry into the diecast market that an eclectic assortment of diecast models, as the product list below illustrates.

Gearbox 12" 1920s Wayne Gas Pump Mechanical Coin Banks
- v.1 Amoco Regular.......................$40–50
- v.2 Amoco Silver..........................$40–50
- v.3 Amoco Ultimate.....................$40–50
- v.4 British Petroleum....................$40–50
- v.5 Ford Benzol...........................$40–50
- v.6 Gulf.....................................$40–50
- v.7 International Harvester.............$40–50
- v.8 John Deere............................$40–50
- v.9 John Deere, 24 karat gold plated.............................$120–150
- v.10 Mobilgas............................$40–50
- v.11 Pennzoil.............................$40–50
- v.12 Phillips 66..........................$40–50
- v.13 Shell..................................$40–50
- v.14 Skelly................................$40–50
- v.15 Skelly Aromax......................$40–50
- v.16 Texaco Fire Chief.................$40–50
- v.17 Texaco Fire Chief, 24 karat gold plated............................$120–150
- v.18 Texaco Sky Chief, red...........$40–50
- v.19 Texaco Sky Chief, yellow........$40–50
- v.20 Union 76............................$40–50

Gearbox 1950s Tokheim Gas Pump Coin Banks
- v.1 John Deere, available from John Deere dealers only.........................$35–45
- v.2 Mobil Regular........................$30–40
- v.3 Mobil Special........................$30–40
- v.4 Phillips 66............................$30–40
- v.5 Phillips 66 Flite Fuel...............$30–40
- v.6 Shell...................................$30–40
- v.7 Skelly Powermax....................$30–40
- v.8 Skelly Premium......................$30–40
- v.9 Super Shell...........................$30–40
- v.10 Texaco Fire Chief, red...........$30–40
- v.11 Texaco Fire Chief, red and white................................$30–40
- v.12 Texaco Sky Chief, red with Texaco Star globe.........................$30–40
- v.13 Texaco Sky Chief, red with Sky Chief Wing globe.......................$30–40
- v.14 Texaco Sky Chief, silver with Sky Chief Wing globe....................$30–40

Gearbox 8" 1920s Wayne Gas Pumps
- v.1 Amoco Regular......................$15–20
- v.2 Amoco Silver.........................$15–20
- v.3 Amoco Ultimate.....................$15–20
- v.4 British Petroleum....................$15–20
- v.5 Ford Benzol..........................$15–20
- v.6 Gilmore...............................$15–20
- v.7 Gulf....................................$15–20
- v.8 John Deere...........................$15–20
- v.9 Magnolia.............................$15–20
- v.10 Mobil Regular......................$15–20
- v.11 Mobil Special......................$15–20
- v.12 Pennzoil............................$15–20
- v.13 Phillips 66..........................$15–20
- v.14 Shell.................................$15–20
- v.15 Skelly...............................$15–20
- v.16 Skelly Aromax.....................$15–20
- v.17 Socony.............................$18–24
- v.18 Texaco Fire Chief.................$15–20
- v.19 Texaco Sky Chief, red...........$15–20
- v.20 Texaco Sky Chief, silver.........$15–20
- v.21 Wadhams..........................$18–24
- v.21 White Eagle........................$18–24
- v.22 White Star..........................$18–24

Gearbox Diecast Vehicle Coin Banks
1912 Ford Delivery Car
- v.1 Campbell's..........................$20–25
- v.2 Hershey.............................$20–25
- v.3 Pepsi-Cola..........................$20–25
- v.4 Pepsi-Cola Keystone Cops...$20–25
- v.5 Red Crown.........................$20–25
- v.6 Shell.................................$20–25

1912 Ford Oil Tanker
- v.1 Ford Benzol........................$25–30
- v.2 Red Crown.........................$25–30
- v.3 Skelly...............................$25–30

Gearbox Diecast Aircraft Coin Banks
1932 Stearman Biplane
- v.1 Pepsi-Cola Keystone Cops...$40–50
- v.2 Pepsi-Cola Sterling Silver..$125–150
- v.3 RCA Victor.........................$40–50

1938 Grumman Goose
- v.1 Campbell's Soup.................$45–55
- v.2 Gearbox............................$45–55
- v.3 Gulf.................................$45–55
- v.4 Shell................................$45–55
- v.5 U. S. Coast Guard...............$45–55
- v.6 U. S. Navy.........................$45–55

Stinson Detroiter
- v.1 Shell................................$45–55
- v.2 Gulf.................................$45–55
- v.3 Mobilgas..........................$45–55
- v.4 Pennzoil...........................$45–55
- v.5 Lone Star..........................$45–55

Stinson Reliant
- v.1 Royal Navy........................$45–55
- v.2 Gulf.................................$45–55
- v.3 U. S. Army Air Corps..........$45–55
- v.4 U. S. Army Air Force...........$45–55
- v.5 U. S. Coast Guard..............$45–55

Waco Biplane
- v.1 Amoco Regular...................$45–55
- v.2 Amoco Silver......................$45–55
- v.3 Amoco Ultimate..................$45–55

Gearbox Precision Vehicles
1912 Ford Model T Delivery Van
- v.1 Campbell's Soup...........$150–175
1913 Ford Model T Delivery Van
- v.1 brown, Texaco..............$150–175
- v.2 black, Texaco...............$150–175

1953 Ford F-100 Pick-Up, Texaco Fire Chief..............................$150–175
1953 Ford F-100 Delivery Van, Texaco Fire Chief........................$175–200
1965 Mustang Hardtop, 1:18...$150–175
1965 Mustang Convertible, 1:18..$150–175
1940 Ford Coupe Hardtop, 1:18..$150–175
1940 Ford Coupe Convertible, 1:18............................$150–175
1958 Chevrolet Bel Air Hardtop, 1:18............................$150–175
1958 Chevrolet Bel Air Convertible, 1:18............................$150–175
1963 Chevrolet Impala SS Hardtop, 1:18............................$150–175
1963 Chevrolet Impala SS Convertible, 1:18............................$150–175
1950 Buick Roadmaster Hardtop, 1:18............................$150–175
1950 Buick Roadmaster Convertible, 1:18............................$150–175

Gearbox Precision Aircraft
1917 Sopwith Pup Biplane
- v.1 British Military.....................$75–90
- v.2 German Military...................$75–90
- v.3 Military, blue......................$75–90
- v.4 U. S. Army.........................$75–90
- v.5 U. S. Military......................$75–90
1918 AIRCO DH4 Biplane
- v.1 British Military.....................$75–90
- v.2 U. S. Air Mail......................$75–90
- v.3 U. S. Navy.........................$75–90
Grumman Wildcat F4F-3.............$75–90
Grumman Tigercat F7F-3.............$75–90
Vought Corsair XF4U..................$75–90

Gearbox Mailbox Banks
- v.1 Express Mail, white...............$25–30
- v.2 Priority Mail, red...................$25–30
- v.3 U. S. Mail, dull green.............$25–30
- v.4 Zippy Zip Code, blue.............$25–30

Gearbox Texaco 4" Pedal Cars
Four different models comprise this assortment, each in three different liveries and three different colors, packed sixteen red versions, sixteen black, and four green to each carton, making the green ones the least plentiful and therefore the most highly valued on the collector market.

1940 Ford Coupe
- v.1 Texaco Fire Chief, red.........$12–16
- v.2 Texaco Fire Chief, black......$12–16
- v.3 Texaco Fire Chief, green.....$16–20
- v.4 Texaco Sky Chief, red.........$12–16
- v.5 Texaco Sky Chief, black......$12–16
- v.6 Texaco Sky Chief, green.....$16–20
- v.7 Texaco Star, red................$12–16
- v.8 Texaco Star, black.............$12–16
- v.9 Texaco Star, green............$16–20
1955 Chevy Bel Air
- v.1 Texaco Fire Chief, red.........$12–16
- v.2 Texaco Fire Chief, black......$12–16
- v.3 Texaco Fire Chief, green.....$16–20
- v.4 Texaco Sky Chief, red.........$12–16

v.5 Texaco Sky Chief, black......$12–16
v.6 Texaco Sky Chief, green $16–20
v.7 Texaco Star, red...............$12–16
v.8 Texaco Star, black.............$12–16
v.9 Texaco Star, green $16–20

1956 Ford T-Bird
v.1 Texaco Fire Chief, red $12–16
v.2 Texaco Fire Chief, black......$12–16
v.3 Texaco Fire Chief, green $16–20
v.4 Texaco Sky Chief, red $12–16
v.5 Texaco Sky Chief, black.......$12–16
v.6 Texaco Sky Chief, green $16–20
v.7 Texaco Star, red...............$12–16
v.8 Texaco Star, black.............$12–16
v.9 Texaco Star, green $16–20

1957 Chevy Bel Air
v.1 Texaco Fire Chief, red $12–16
v.2 Texaco Fire Chief, black.....$12–16
v.3 Texaco Fire Chief, green $12–16
v.4 Texaco Sky Chief, red $12–16
v.5 Texaco Sky Chief, black.......$12–16
v.6 Texaco Sky Chief, green $16–20
v.7 Texaco Star, red $12–16
v.8 Texaco Star, black $12–16
v.9 Texaco Star, green $16–20

Gearbox Texaco 9" Pedal Car Coin Banks

Sold in 12 packs of 11 black and 1 green versions.

1940 Ford Coupe
v.1 Texaco Fire Chief, black......$40–50
v.2 Texaco Fire Chief, green $65–80
v.3 Texaco Sky Chief, black.......$40–50
v.4 Texaco Sky Chief, green $65–80
v.5 Texaco Star, black $40–50
v.6 Texaco Star, green $65–80

1955 Chevy Bel Air
v.1 Texaco Fire Chief, green $65–80
v.2 Texaco Fire Chief, black.....$40–50
v.3 Texaco Sky Chief, green $65–80
v.4 Texaco Sky Chief, black.....$40–50
v.5 Texaco Star, green $65–80
v.6 Texaco Star, black $40–50

1956 Ford T-Bird
v.1 Texaco Fire Chief, black......$40–50
v.2 Texaco Fire Chief, green $65–80
v.3 Texaco Sky Chief, black.......$40–50
v.4 Texaco Sky Chief, green $65–80
v.5 Texaco Star, black $40–50
v.6 Texaco Star, green $65–80

1957 Chevy Bel Air
v.1 Texaco Fire Chief, black......$40–50
v.2 Texaco Fire Chief, green $65–80
v.3 Texaco Sky Chief, black.......$40–50
v.4 Texaco Sky Chief, green $65–80
v.5 Texaco Star, black $40–50
v.6 Texaco Star, green $65–80

Gearbox 4" Factory Color Pedal Cars

1955 Chevy Bel Air two-tone
v.1 blue and black................$15–20
v.2 green and beige $15–20
v.3 green and black $15–20
v.4 plum and beige...............$15–20

v.5 red and white $15–20
v.6 turquoise and white............$15–20

1957 Chevy Bel Air
v.1 black $15–20
v.2 blue.........................$15–20
v.3 green $15–20
v.4 red $15–20
v.5 turquoise $15–20

1956 Ford T-Bird
v.1 black $15–20
v.2 blue.........................$15–20
v.3 coral $15–20
v.4 red $15–20
v.5 tan $15–20
v.6 white $15–20
v.7 yellow.......................$15–20

Gearbox 9" Factory Color Pedal Car Coin Banks

1940 Ford Coupe
v.1 plum $40–50
v.2 gray $40–50
v.3 black $40–50
v.4 dune beige $40–50
v.5 white $40–50
v.6 red $40–50

1955 Chevy Bel Air two-tone
v.1 black and blue................$40–50
v.2 black and green $40–50
v.3 green and beige $40–50
v.4 plum and beige...............$40–50
v.5 red and white $40–50
v.6 turquoise and white...........$40–50

1956 Ford T-Bird
v.1 black $40–50
v.2 blue.........................$40–50
v.3 coral $40–50
v.4 red $40–50
v.5 tan $40–50
v.6 white $40–50
v.7 yellow.......................$40–50

1957 Chevy Bel Air
v.1 black $40–50
v.2 blue.........................$40–50
v.3 green $40–50
v.4 red $40–50
v.5 turquoise $40–50

Other Gearbox products

Gearbox 5" Wayne Gas Pump $15
Gearbox 4" Stearman Bi-Plane $15
1:48 Scale 1912 Tanker $25
1:48 Scale 1912 Delivery Truck.................$25

Gege

Plastic bodies and diecast chassis typify these 1:20 and 1:43 scale Gege toys from France. Just a few 1:43 scale models exist, all produced in 1956.
Citroën DS19.........................$72
Ford Vendome.........................$72
Ford Vedette.........................$72
Peugeot 203.........................$72
Peugeot 403.........................$72
Renault Fregate Amiral $72
Simca Aronde $72

Simca Versailles.....................$72

Gemini Jets

GeminiJets Incorporated/Airliners Distributing Inc.
6414 Windy Street
Las Vegas, Nevada 89119
phone: 702-614-0900
fax: 702-914-8036
e-mail: feedback@geminijets.com
website: www.geminijets.com

Precision diecast commercial jet models are produced under the Gemini Jets brand of Las Vegas, Nevada.

Gems 'N' Cobwebs (see 43rd Avenue)

Generic

So-called "generic" diecast toys are those that, while the package in which they were originally sold may be marked with one brand or another, the model itself is basically unmarked, other than "made in Hong Kong" or "made in China." A few, such as Zee Toys and M C Toys, may have just a logo and perhaps a model number on the base. Often, these generic models are unlicensed copies, or "knockoffs," of established brands such as Matchbox or Tomica, matching size and sometimes even markings.

Brands such as Imperial Diecast, Rhino, Superior Racers, Sunshine (usually designated only with an "SS" number), and MegaMovers are only identified by the package they come in. Once removed from the package, they become unbranded generic toys, some nicely produced, others made cheaply.

Listed below and pictured is a sampling of generic models with no markings to indicate brand or manufacturer. Because it is difficult to determine brand or manufacturer, their value is not due to rise, but some are especially good copies of name brand models.

Ambulance, based on Mercedes 280G, pullback action 1:43 ....$4
Bulldozer, 1:64.....................$0.75
Cadillac Stretch Limousine (identical to Majorette 300 Series models except for raised plastic chassis to accomodate pullback mechanism)................$2
Crane, 1:100, made in China $1
Double Decker Buses, pull-back action...........$2
Esso Tanker, made in Hong Kong $0.75
Mini Cooper Rally, made in China, pull-back action $1
Mini Loader, 1:64, made in China $0.75
1988 Mitsubishi Eclipse GS, made in Taiwan, 1:16 (promotional model)..............$25–40

Gescha (also see Conrad)

Since 1923, Gescha has manufactured a variety of toys, but they didn't start producing diecast models until the 1960s. In the seventies, the line of Gescha diecast toys was renamed Conrad, while the Gescha name continued with its mechanical tinplate and other toys.

Because the Gescha name is not included on diecast models produced after 1977, it becomes easier to recognize these earlier models, now considered quite valuable.

Fiat-Allis 41-B Dozer $100–125

Caterpillar 769B Quarry Truck...........$75-90

Gingell

Gingell Diecasting Manufacturing Ltd. produces a line of inexpensive generic diecast toys manufactured in China and packaged in 25-car sets for $5. As with typical budget toys, they are cheaply produced, lack much detail, and are lightweight metal with plain plastic chassis. Value of these will not likely rise, and identification of individual models is difficult or impossible, which also detracts from any future collector value. Gingell toys are best considered as a novelty rather than a serious addition to a collection.

Giodi (also Techno Giodi)

Giodi is a relatively obscure Italian manufacturer of mostly Fiat models. Below is a list of models and current values. The company produced models until 1993 when they went bankrupt.

1 Ferrari Daytona Coupe, black, 1:18 ....$30
1 Ferrari Daytona Coupe, yellow, 1:18 ....$30
3 Ferrari Daytona Spyder, red, 1:18 ....$30
73030 Fiat "Jumbo" Farm Tractor, yellow/black, 1:28 ....$17
73035 Fiat Turbo DT 180-90 Farm Tractor, brown/white/black, 1:28 ....$17
73038 Fiat Farm Tractor/Loader, 1:28 ....$17
73039 Fiat Farm Tractor/Backhoe, 1:28 ....$17
73051 Fiat Jeep "Grand Canyon," blue/white, 1:25 ....$15
73053 Fiat Jeep "Algiers-Cape Town," orange/white, 1:25 ....$15
73056 Fiat Jeep "Police," blue/white, 1:25 .$17
73062 Fiat Jeep/Camper "Expedition," orange/white, 1:25 ....$17
73064 Fiat Jeep "Safari," tan, brown, camouflage, 1:25 ....$17
73070 Fiat Snorkel Fire Engine, 1:35 ....$22

73073 Fiat Flatbed Truck with Load, orange/black/silver, 1:35 ....$17
73074 Fiat Flatbed with Trailer & 2 Loads, orange/black/silver, 1:35 ....$22
73076 Fiat Dump Truck with Tractor, yellow/black/red, 1:35 ....$17
73077 Kenworth Conventional Semi-Cab & Load, 1:35 ....$15
73082 Fiat MTS-10 Forklift with Pallet, yellow/silver/orange, 1:43 ....$17
73084 Fiat 4WD Tractor with Snowplow, orange, 1:43 ....$17
73085 Fiat MTS-40 Road Roller, orange/black, 1:43 ....$17
73091 Fiat Jeep "SOS" Road Service Tow, orange/yellow, 1:25 ....$17
73092 Fiat Jeep "Ambulance," white, 1:25 .$17
73093 Fiat Jeep/Camper "Grand Canyon," blue/white, 1:25 ....$17
73104 Kenworth Semi Milk Truck, orange/blue/gray, 1:35 ....$22
73106 Kenworth Cement Truck, orange, 1:35 ....$17
73107 Kenworth Flatbed Semi with F. Dump, red/black/yellow, 1:35 ....$17
73109 Fiat Crane Truck, 1:35 ....$17
74002 Ferrari Daytona Spyder, black, 1:18.$30
74003 Ferrari Daytona Spyder, yellow, black top, 1:18 ....$30
74011 Ferrari Daytona Coupe, red, 1:18 ...$30
99999 1968 Mercedes 280SL, silver cabriolet, 1:18 ....$30

Gloor

The improbable and otherwise unknown Gloor brand is represented by one model.
1960 Chevrolet Stepvan "UPS," 1:43 ....$35

Golden Classics (see Golden Wheel)

Golden Wheel (U.S.A.) Inc.

200 Fifth Avenue, Suite 618
New York, NY 10010
website: www.goldenwheeldiecast.com

Golden Wheel toys represent inexpensive miniature replica cars and trucks made by Golden Wheel Die Casting of China.

Golden Classics Ford Model T gift banks from the same company are so similar to Ertl banks that they can be easily mistaken for them at first glance. Closer inspection shows a few differences, most notably a plastic roof secured to the windshield by a crudely melted post, and the distinctive phrase "Coins Bank" in script on each model. These models are such a blatant attempt to capitalize on the popularity of Pepsi-Cola collectibles and coin banks that they even say gift bank on the box, and the tanker even declares "Collectable Models" right on the tank.

Still, considering the $12 price tag, they are comparably nice models to the more

expensive $20–35 Ertl versions, and they do make attractive, affordable gifts.

Other models in the ever-expanding Golden Wheels catalog represent a diversity of diecast toys and replicas, many of them promotional models intended to advertise various products. Their website illustrates a huge catalog of models. Here is a small sampling.

Ford Model T Delivery Van, white with blue roof and fenders "Drink Pepsi-Cola" $12–15
Ford Model T Tanker, white with red roof and fenders, "Pepsi-Cola" $12–15
Ford Model T Tanker, "Mountain Dew" ..$12–15
Tractor Trailer, 1:87, "Pepsi" $4–5
Tractor Trailer, 1:87, "Mountain Dew" $4–5
Tractor Trailer, 1:64, "Pepsi" $9–12
Tractor Trailer, 1:64, "Mountain Dew" $9–12

Golden Wheel 3" Models

Mercedes-Benz, in various colors, 3"...$2–4

Mercedes-Benz, in various colors, 3"...$2–4

Ferrari, in various colors, 3"...................$2–4

Ferrari, in various colors, 3".....................$2–4

Goldvarg

Sergio & Mariana Goldvarg
The Goldvarg Collection
Mendoza 1059 1º "A" CP: 1428
Capital Federal
Republica Argentina
phone: 54-11-4749-6551
fax: 54-11-4749-6601
e-mail: goldvarg@sminter.com.ar
website: www.thegoldvargcollection.com

The Goldvarg Collection is a series of 1:43 scale American cars of the forties, fifties, and sixties. The white metal assortment was first produced by Mariana and Sergio Goldvarg of Buenos Aires, Argentina, in 1989. As of January 1, 2000, after being out of production for nearly three years, The Goldvarg Collection models are again being produced in cooperation with SMTS (Scale Model Technical Services) of England.

GC1 1957 Oldsmobile Starfire 98 hardtop, blue.....................$89
GC1-F 1957 Oldsmobile Starfire 98 Fire Chief $89
GC2 1946 Chevrolet Stylemaster 4-Door $89

GC3 1951 Chrysler Crown Imperial Limousine LWB, blue.....................$62–89

GC4 1956 Lincoln Premiere Hardtop Coupe $89
GC5 1955 Pontiac Star Chief Convertible, red $89
GC6 1950 Packard Woody Station Wagon, green $89
GC7 1956 Mercury Montclair Coupe $89
GC8 1954 Chevrolet Bel Air 4-Door Sedan.....................$89
GC9 1952 Nash Golden Airflyte Ambassador Sedan Pininfarina $89

GC10 1959 Pontiac Bonneville 2-Door Hardtop $89
GC11 1959 Mercury Park Lane 2-Door Hardtop $89
GC12 1951 Henry J Kaiser 2-Door Sedan, dark gray $89
GC12-B 1951 Henry J Standard $89
GC13 1949 Plymouth Commercial Utility Station Wagon $89
GC14 1958 Oldsmobile Sedan $89
GC15 1949 Cadillac Series 62 4-Door Sedan.....................$89
GC16 1946 Ford Deluxe Sedan $89
GC17 1960 Plymouth Fury.....................$89
GC18 1952 Nash Golden Airflyte.............$89

Gonio

These 1:24 scale tin-plate military models from Czechoslovakia are made to the highest degree of authenticity. Though they do not exactly fit the definition of "diecast," they represent an important contribution to the area of highly collectible authentic scale models. Examples below are provided by Toys for Collectors and Diecast Miniatures. Features include steerable wheels and other working parts.

Dodge WC-51 with foldable side guards, #1007.....................$100
Dodge WC-51 Powerwagon Weapons Carrier, #08657, USA, olive drab $88
Dodge WC52A, Arctic white $150
Dodge WC52A, olive drab.....................$130
Jeep Kommando with trailer and supplies, #1010 .... (sold out) $125
M3A1 Halftrack Armored Personnel Carrier, #1011 ....$190
M3 Halftrack, olive drab.....................$160
M3T Tunis Halftrack $180
VW T-82 Porsche Ambulance Kubelwagen East, #1002, top down $59
VW T-82 Porsche Kubelwagen, #086XX, sand $82
VW T-82 Porsche Kubelwagen, #1001, top down, Africa Corps, sand $54
VW T-82 Porsche Kubelwagen, #1001L, top up, camouflage, limited edition $69
VW T-82 Porsche Kubelwagen East, #1004, top down $54
VW 166 Porsche Schwimmwagen (Amphibious Vehicle),# 08655, olive drab.............$100
VW 166 Porsche Schwimmwagen West (Amphibious Vehicle), #1006 ....$100
White 160AX Powered M-3 Halftrack, #08661, USA, olive drab $128
Willys Jeep, foldable windshield, #1008, opening hood.....................$79

Goodee

Goodee toys are very similar to Tootsietoys in that they generally are single-cast bodies with no chassis or windows. Goodee diecast vehicles were manufactured by Excel Products Company of New Jersey in the 1950s. Six-

inch and three-inch models were produced, some of the larger models with windup motors.

6" Models

1953 GMC Pickup Truck.....................$25
1953 Ford Police Cruiser $25
1954 DeSoto Station Wagon.............$25
1955 Ford Fuel Truck.....................$25
American LaFrance Fire Pumper $25

Box Truck $20

Military Jeep.....................$25

3" Models

1953 Ford Police, 2-Door Sedan...........$28
1953 GMC Pickup Truck $15
1953 Studebaker Coupe $20
1953 Lincoln Capri Hardtop.............$15
1953 Cadillac Convertible $15
1954 DeSoto Station Wagon.............$15
1954 Ford C600 Oil Truck $28
1955 Ford Fuel Truck.....................$15
American LaFrance Fire Pumper $15
Military Jeep.....................$15
Moving Van.....................$15
Step Van $15
Land Speed Racer $15

Govroski (also see Russian models)

Quality diecast toys from Russia, Govroski is represented in *Schroeder's Collectible Toys* by just one model.
Volga Sedan, metallic blue.....................$35

Gran Toros (also see Hot Wheels, Mebetoys, Johnny Lightning)

When Mattel purchased Mebetoys of Italy around 1970, they applied the Hot Wheels name to several 1:43 scale models and dubbed them Gran Toros. The Gran Toros name was later acquired by Playing Mantis who currently issues their own small line of 1:43 scale diecast cars dubbed Gran Toros by Johnny Lightning.

Grand Prix

Grand Prix models are from Great Britain and produced by Brian Harvey, available in 1:43 scale white metal kits.

Austin Seven Twin Cam (kit) $18
Ford Escort "Castrol" (kit) $18
Lotus Elan Roadster (built) $45
1983 Ferrari "Martini" (kit) $18

Great American Dreamcar / Dust & Glory / Quarter Mile

Great American Dreamcars, occasionally also known as Great American Dream Machines or simply "Gad," are 1:43 scale white metal models marketed by Phil Alderman's Autofare of New Jersey. He also offers Dust & Glory, a line of vintage American racers, and quarter mile dragster replicas. Original models are casts of SMTS, MCM, and possibly a few others.

1903 Packard Gray Wolf $200
1M Don Garlits Swamp Rat 1 Dragster......$179
2 1954 Chevrolet Corvette Nomad, blue ..$179
3 1939 Buick Y Job Show Car, black $179
3MC 1939 Buick Y Job - Exc 4 Minicar, gray $179
4 1955 Lincoln Futura Show Car, green $179
5 1954 Cadillac La Espada Show Car, yellow $179
6 1965 Chevrolet Corvette Mako Shark II, dark blue $179
7 1954 Cadillac El Camino 2-Door Coupe, silver $179
8 1951 Chrysler K-310 Show Car, 2-tone blue $179
9 1956 Packard Predictor Show Car, pearl white $179
12 1956 Buick Centurion 2-Door Show Car, red/white/clear $179
14 1952 Chrysler C-200 Convertible Show Car, black/green $179

Grip Zechin (also see Eidai)

EiDAI Corporation
2.8.7. Higashiogu, Arakawaku
Tokyo, Japan

Grip Zechin is a hard-to-find brand of unusual toys made in Japan by Eidai. Recently, Jeff Kopis of Clallam Bay, Washington, reports a few models found in 1977 in a Seattle, Washington, Bon Marche department store, where he recalls that the store had a complete line of Grip Zechin models. Unfortunately, he only purchased three at the time, all Caterpillar models. Nevertheless, his additional information is invaluable.

Most Grip Zechin models were also sold under the Madmax Grip and World Zechin brands, according to Roy Ferguson of Manchester, Iowa. He reports that the models were available in all three names but some were only available in one name. The models were available in the early seventies, and from price stickers on the box, Ferguson concludes that they may have been a little pricey for the time, and that this may have led to their demise. Some of the dies were reused by Tomica, and a larger model, a four-axle crane in 1:75 scale, showed up in the Diapet line.

Grip Zechin

DeTomaso Pantera GT-35, Eidai/Grip Technica series, 1:28 ....$45–60
1 Caterpillar 769 B Dump Truck, 1:98 ....$30–40
2 Sakai Vibration Roller SV-100, 1:60 ....$35–45
3 Nakamichi Truck Backhoe, 1:62 ..$30–40
4 Caterpillar D5 Snowplow Bulldozer, 1:56 ....$25–30
5 Caterpillar D5 Bulldozer, 1:56 .....$25–30
6 Prinoth Snow Groomer with Snowmobile, 1:70 ....$35–45
7 Caterpillar 920 Wheel Loader, 1:76 ....$30–35
8 Caterpillar D5 Rakedozer, 1:56 ...$25–30
9 Aichi Crane Auger E-600, 1:62 ...$30–35
10 Hovercraft MV PP-5, 1:210 ....$40–45
11 Caterpillar 920 Snowplow Wheel Loader, 1:76 ....$30–35
12 Hino Fire Engine, 1:100 ....$30–35
13 Fuso Mixer Car, 1:70 ....$25–30
14 Kato Oil Pressure Crane, 1:140 .$40–50
15 Fuso Sewage Truck, 1:70 ....$25–30
16 Hino TC30 Snorkel Fire Engine, 1:100 ....$25–30
17 Isuzu Racing Carrier with Racing Car, 1:100 ....$35–40
18 Hino Snorkel Car, 1:100 ....$30–40
19 Caterpillar Motor Grader, 1:96 .$25–35
20 Isuzu Lift Truck, 1:62 ....$25–30
21 Hitachi UH 03 D Shovel, 1:70 ..$30–35
22 Carferry Sunflower, 1:1600 ......$50–65
23 Caterpillar 14E Snowplow Motor Grader.............................$30–35
24 P & H Machinery Crane, 1:100 ..$35–40
25 Hitachi UH 03 D Crumshell, 1:70 ....$30–35
26 Hitachi Wheel Crumshell, 1:70..$30–35
27 Fuso Vacuum Car, 1:70............$25–30
28 Hitachi Earth Auger, 1:70 ....$35–40
29 Hitachi Wheel Shovel, 1:70 ......$35–40
30 unknown
31 Jeep J 52, 1:42 ....$25–35
32 unknown
33 Jeep J 52 Army with gun, 1:42 ..$30–35
34 Isuzu Bulldozer Carrier, 1:100 ...$35–45
35 Bullet Train $30–40
36 Caterpillar 621 Motorscraper, 1:111 ....$30–40
37 Road Sweeper, 1:85.................$30–40
38 Hino Shell Semi Tanker.............$30–40
39 Isuzu Bulk Powder Transport, 1:100 ....$25–30
40 Aichi Skymaster AS-C2, 1:62 ....$30–40
41 unknown

42 Police Accident Investigation Truck .$30–40
43 Ambulance $30–40
44 Isuzu Cargo Trailer, 1:100 ....$35–45
45 Semi with Container "Japan National Rail"...............................$30–40
46 unknown
47 Yamaha Policeman Side Car, 1:43 ..$45

World Zechin

2 Sakai Vibration Roller SV-100, 1:60, red $35–45
4 Hino 3 Axle Ladder Truck, red $30–40
16 Hino Tractor with Trailer.............$30–40
20 Caterpillar 620 Wheel Loader, blue...............................$30–40
21 "Hino Suction Truck...................$30–40
24 Caterpillar D5 Rotary Rake, red ..$30–40
25 Aichi Basket Truck $30–40
26 Jeep with Roll Bar, red $30–40
28 Airport Bus $30–40

Madmax Grip

1 Caterpillar 769 Quarry Truck $30–40
2 Caterpillar D5 Dozer $30–40
8 Scissor Lift Airport Truck $30–40
12 Hino Semi Tanker "Shell" $30–40
20 Hino Suction Truck $30–40
26 School Bus, yellow $30–40

GTS (See Le Mans Miniatures)

Guiloy

Guiloy is a brand of models made in Spain. They are best known for their great miniature renditions of motorcycles. But they also produced a truck series called Mini Camiones and an assortment of car models.

Guiloy Mini Camiones, circa 1970s

Guiloy Mini Camiones are a series of trucks in 1:66 scale, all based on the same truck tractor with various backs or trailers attached to create a variety of models. Based on photocopied catalogs from Dr. Craig Campbell, assistant professor of geography at Youngstown State University, I was able to translate the Spanish descriptions of most models by the pictures. Some however remain a mystery, such as #50 "Bomber." The 50-66 series represents the same truck with different backs. The 1000 series represents the same truck with various trailers attached.

Guiloy 1:66 Scale Trucks

50 Bomber - Ladder Fire Truck (?).....$10–15
51 Gria - Crane Truck $10–15
52 Gasolina - Texaco Tanker $10–15
53 Misil - Missile Launcher $10–15
54 Ametralladora - Military Anti-Aircraft Gun Truck $10–15
55 Cateon - Military Cannon Truck ..$10–15
56 Dumper $10–15
57 Toldo - Covered Lorry $10–15
58 Toldo Militar - Military Covered Lorry $10–15

59 Contenedor Mudanzas - Container Truck......$10–15
60 Contenedor Frigorifico - Refrigerator Truck......$10–15
61 Contenedor Militar - Military Container Truck......$10–15
62 Cajón Militar - Military Open Lorry......$10–15
63 Cajón Normal - Open Lorry......$10–15
64 Vigas - Flatbed Truck with I-Beams.$10–15
65 Tubos - Pipe Truck......$10–15
66 Troncos - Log Truck......$10–15

Guiloy 1:66 Scale Tractor/Trailers
1000 Campsa Gasoline Tanker......$15–20
1001 Toldo - Covered Lorry......$15–20
1004 Cajón - Open Lorry......$15–20
1005 Tubos - Pipe Truck......$15–20
1008 Tanques Militar - Military Tank Transporter with two armored tanks....$25–30
1009 Planeador Militar - Military Glider Transporter with glider......$15–20
1013 Cemento - Pressurized Tanker .$15–20
1014 Amoniaco - Pressurized Tanker......$15–20
101? Esso Gasoline Tanker......$15–20
1018 Elf Gasoline Tanker......$15–20
10?? Crane Truck......$15–20

Guiloy Motorcycles
G15 1948 Indian Motorcycle Anniversary Edition, burgundy or yellow......$50
GY17227 1948 Indian Chief, 1:10 scale......$30
GY2802 Honda "Repsol," 1:18......$16
GY2803 Honda "Campsa," 1:18......$16
GY2804 Kawasaki "Metzeler," 1:18....$16
GY2807 Suzuki "Pepsi" racer, 1:18......$16
GY2815 Harley Davidson Custom Classic, 1:18......$18
GY2872 Harley Davidson Custom Sport, 1:18......$18
GY2896 BMW R1000RS street bike, 1:18......$16
GY3106 Honda racing motorcycle, 1:10......$45
GY3147 BMW R 100RT street bike, 1:10......$45
GY3163 BMC Ecureuil motocross bike, 1:10......$45
GY3166 Honda "Castrol," 1:10......$45
GY3187 Suzuki "Pepsi," 1:10......$45
GY3118 BMW R-80 motocross bike, 1:10......$45
GY3146 Yamaha "Garriga" racer, 1:10......$45
GY3801 Harley Davidson Custom Classic, 1:10......$50
GY6244 Yamaha, 1:6......$100
GY6247 Yamaha, 1:6......$100

Guiloy 1:18 Scale Models
G1 1995 Aston Martin DB-7, wine, green, black, or blue......$35–40
G2 1993 McLaren F-1, red, blue, silver, or metallic burgundy......$35–40

G16 1969 Mercedes C111, metallic orange or silver......$35–40

Guiloy 1:25 Scale Models
50 Mercedes-Benz 350SL Coupe......$24
51 Porsche 911 Coupe......$24
524 Porsche 911 Rally, "Rothmans," white, blue, red, green......$24
525 Porsche 911 Rally, Martini," yellow ..$24

Guiloy 1:64 Scale Models
1 Land Rover Range Rover Wagon......$3
2 Fiat Ritmo 4-Door Sedan......$3
3 Talbot 150 4-Door Sedan......$3
4 Renault 4 Van......$3
5 Ford Fiesta 2-Door Sedan......$3
6 Peugeot 504 4-Door Sedan......$3
7 Fiat (Seat) 131 Wagon......$3
8 1976 Ford Torino......$3

Guiloy Gold Series Scale 1:18
67501 Mercedes C-111, gold color......$30
67502 Ferrari GTO -64, red metallic......$30
67520 Mercedes C-111, green......$30
67521 Mercedes C-111 aluminum color......$30
67007 Aston Martin DB7, black......$30
67510 Prototype LM, orange......$30
67511 Ferrari Mythos, red......$30
67512 Ferrari Mythos, blue......$30
67517 Aston Martin DB7, black......$30
67524 Ferrari Mythos, yellow......$30
67526 Ferrari 250 GTO -64, yellow $30
67525 Ferrari 250 GTO -64, red......$30
67530 Prototype LM, red......$30
67537 Aston Martin DB7, dark green ...$30
67538 Ferrari Mythos, aluminum color...$30
67539 Prototype LM, yellow......$30
67540 Ferrari 250 GTO -64, green......$30
67550 Aston Martin DB7, violet......$30
67558 Prototype LM, aluminum color.....$30

Guiloy Premier Series Scale 1:24
64516 Lamborghini Countach 5000, red......$11
64544 Aston Martin DB7 Coupe......$11
64501 Mercedes 500 SL Coupe......$11
64515 Ferarri Testarossa, red......$11
64517 Ferrari Testarossa, yellow......$11
64518 Mercedes 500 SL, Cab, violet...$11
64531 MB 500 SL, Coupe, red metallic......$11
64532 Ferrari Testarossa, aluminum color......$11
64535 Mercedes 500 SEC, blue......$11
64540 Mercedes 500 SL, Cab, green..$11
64549 Mercedes C-111, -69, gold color......$11
64505 Porche 911 Carrera 4 Targa, red......$11
64508 Ferrari F-40, aluminum color......$11
64514 Ferrari F-40, light blue......$11
64519 Ferrari F-40, red......$11
64521 Ferrari F-40, yellow......$11
64527 Porche 959 Turbo, blue......$11
64542 Porche 911 Targa, white......$11
64569 Porche 959, red......$11

Guiloy Top Line Series 1:18 Scale
68560 1937 BMW 327 Coupe......$70
68565 1937 BMW 327 Cabriolet......$70
68570 Chrysler Atlantic......$70

Guiloy Superbike 1:6 Scale
Classic American Iron......$50
Blue American Custom......$50
Custom Cherokee......$50
Custom Angel......$50
Yamaha Custom New York......$50

Guisval

Guisval of Spain offers an assortment of vehicles in an unusual variety of scales that include 1:30, 1:37, 1:43, 1:66, and 1:80. Some are said to be direct knockoffs of Matchbox Models of Yesteryear, such as the Mercedes 540K. Guisval started in 1967 and survives to this day.

Ferrari Testarossa, 1:30......$24
Porsche 959, 1:30......$24
1 Goofy Train, 1:43......$15
1 Chaparral, 1:66......$15
2 Daffy Duck Plane, 1:43......$15
5 Ford Lotus 40, 1:66......$15
8 Ferrari 330 P2, 1:66......$15
13 Morris Mini with skis, 1:66......$15
14 Land Rover with missile, 1:66......$15
15 Hot Rod, 1:66......$15
16 Mini Cooper, 1:66......$15
17 Refuse Truck, 1:80......$15
18 Ferrari P4, 1:66......$15
19 Land Rover Circus, 1:66......$15
20 Horse Box, 1:80......$15
21 Dune Buggy, 1:66......$15
23 Go Bug, 1:66......$15
24 Go Bug Fire, 1:66......$15
25 Chevrolet Corvair Monza, 1:66......$15
26 MG 1100, 1:66......$15
27 Seat 124, 1:66......$15
28 Morris 1100, 1:66......$15
29 Seat 124 Policia, 1:66......$15
30 Seat 850 Coupe, 1:66......$15
31 Renault 16, 1:66......$15
32 Seat 850 Coupe Rally, 1:66......$15
33 Ford Lotus STP, 1:66......$15
34 Lotus 63/2, 1:66......$15
35 1971 Ford Mustang, 1:66......$15
36 Ford Lotus V8 Racer, 1:66......$15
37 1971 Ford Mustang Circus, 1:66 ...$15
38 Lotus 49B Racer, 1:66......$15
39 Ferrari Dino Pininfarina, 1:66......$15
40 Porsche 917, 1:66......$15
41 Lamborghini Marzal, 1:66......$15
42 Hatra Shovel, 1:80......$15
43 Chevrolet Corvair Monza, chrome plated, 1:66......$15
44 Alfa Romeo Osi Scarabeo, 1:66......$15
45 Panther Bertone, 1:66......$15
46 Ford 4000 Tractor, 1:66......$15
47 Case Bulldozer, 1:80......$15
48 Taylor Crane, 1:80......$15
49 Hatra Dumper, 1:80......$15
50 Hatra Cement Truck, 1:80......$15

72 Kenworth Fire Ladder, 1:64.............$3–5
95 1926 Hispano Suiza Convertible, top down, 1:64.............$3–5
96 1926 Hispano Suiza Convertible, top up, 1:64.............$3–5
97 1931 Cadillac Roadster, 1:64.............$3–5
98 Caravan Ambulance, 1:64.............$3–5
99 Audi Quattro Ambulance, 1:64.............$3–5
101 Chevrolet Astro, 1:37.............$15
101 Renault 12 TS Familian, 1:37.............$15
102 Ferrari Can-Am, 1:37.............$15
102 Citroën 2 CV Berline, 1:37.............$15
103 Ford Capri, 1:37.............$15
104 Citroën SM Ambulance, white, 1:37 ...$20
105 Ford Capri Ski Club, 1:37.............$15
105 Citroën 2 CV Sahara Travesta, 1:37 ...$15
106 Citroën SM Tour De France, 1:37.............$15
107 Ford Capri Rally, 1:37.............$15
107 Porsche Carrera, 1:37.............$15
108 1979 Chevrolet Camaro, 1:37.............$15
109 Ford Capri Policia, 1:37.............$15
109 Renault R12 TS Policia, 1:37.............$15
110 Fiat 130 Coupe, 1:37.............$15
111 Volvo Wrecker, 1:37.............$15
112 Renault 17 Safari Rally, 1:37.............$15
113 Mercedes Club Regatta, 1:37.............$15
114 Volvo Ladder Truck, 1:37.............$15
115 Renault 17 Coupe, 1:37.............$15
115 Mercedes 350 SL Rally, 1:37.............$15
116 Chevrolet Camaro Rally Safari, 1:37 ...$15
117 Mercedes 406 Van, 1:37.............$15
117 Mercedes Radio Van, 1:37.............$15
118 Volvo Military Rescue Truck, 1:37.............$15
119 Volvo Military Gun Truck, 1:37.............$15
119 Fiat 100 Policia, 1:37.............$15
120 Jeep Policia, 1:37.............$15
122 Porsche with Skis, 1:37.............$15
123 Volvo Street Maintenance Truck with signs, 1:37.............$15
124 Jeep with Ladder, 1:37.............$15
125 Fiat 100 Taxi, 1:37.............$15
126 Military Jeep with gun, 1:37.............$15
127 Jeep Renegade, 1:37.............$15
128 Chevrolet Van "Moto Club," 1:37.............$15
129 BMW Deportivo, 1:37.............$15
130 Volvo Elevator Truck, 1:37.............$15
131 Magirus Cement Truck, 1:37.............$15
132 Mercedes Policia Van, 1:37.............$15
134 Mercedes Ambulance Van, 1:37.............$15
135 Rescue Helicopter, 1:37.............$15
136 Magirus Covered Transporter, 1:37.....$15
137 Red Cross Helicopter.............$15
138 Mercedes Red Cross Van, 1:37.............$15
139 Magirus Troop Carrier.............$15
139 Chevrolet Van "Paris Dakar", 1:37.............$15
140 Military Helicopter, 1:37.............$15
144 Renault 17 Coupe, 1:37.............$15
151 Scammell Articulated Truck with 2 tractors, 1:50.............$15
152 Scammell Articulated Truck with 2 cars, 1:50.............$15
153 Scammell Articulated Truck with 2 trucks, 1:50.............$15

156 Scammell Articulated Truck with 2 racers, 1:50.............$15
157 Scammell Articulated Truck with 2 trucks, 1:50.............$15
171 Scammell Breakdown Truck, 1:50 ....$20
172 Scammell Fire Engine, 1:50.............$20
173 Scammell Stake Truck, 1:50.............$20
174 Scammell Dump Truck, 1:50.............$20
175 Scammell Cement Truck, 1:50.............$20
331 Lancia 037 "Marlboro".............$15
332 Lancia 037 "Mobil".............$15
333 Lancia 037 "Bridgestone".............$15
337 Toyota Celica "Esso".............$15
338 Toyota Celica "Avis".............$15
339 Toyota Celica "Avis".............$15
402 Ford Sierra 4-Door Sedan.............$15
403 Citroën BX 4-Door Sedan.............$15
404 Peugeot 505 4-Door Sedan.............$15
406 Ford Sierra "Esso".............$15
441 Citroën BX "Autoveri".............$15
442 Ford Sierra "Esso".............$15
444 Citroën BX "Shell".............$15
446 Ford Escort "Goodyear".............$15
447 Audi Quattro Coupe.............$15
449 Ford Sierra "Gitnes".............$15
450 Mercedes Covered Truck.............$40
451 Mercedes Crane Truck.............$40
452 Mercedes Bottle Truck.............$40
453 Mercedes Log Carrier.............$40
453 Peugeot 505 "Esso".............$40
454 Mercedes Animal Transporter.............$40
457 Ford Sierra Police.............$25
461 Renault 9 "Road Services".............$25
462 Ford Sierra "NASA".............$25
463 Peugeot 505 Ambulance.............$25
467 Ford Escort Ski.............$25
501 1907 Adler.............$25
502 Fiat Zero Roadster, top up.............$25
503 1924 Isotta Fraschini 8A Town Car.............$25
504 1924 Isotta Fraschini 8A Convertible ...$25
505 1907 Adler Tow Car.............$25
506 Fiat Zero Roadster, top down.............$25
516 Chevrolet Fire Van.............$15
523 Caravan Ski.............$15
529 Chevrolet Van "Polar".............$15
665 Peterbilt Semi Cow Transporter.............$3–5
707 Datsun Pickup with Cage, 1:64.........$3–5
752 Bugatti T50 Coupe, 1:64.............$15
754 Mercedes 540K.............$15
755 1928 Lincoln 4-Door Sedan.............$15
802 Renault 5 2-Door Sedan, 1:64.............$3–5
803 Fiat Ritmo/Strada 4-Door Sedan, 1:64.............$3–5
805 Plymouth Horizon 4-Door Sedan, 1:64.............$3–5
901 Nissan Jeep Tow Truck.............$15
903 Nissan Jeep with Plow.............$15
904 Renault Espace School Bus.............$15
905 Nissan Fire Jeep.............$15
906 Renault Espace Police.............$15
917 Porsche 959.............$15
918 Ferrari Testarossa.............$15

922 Mercedes Unimog Fire.............$15
923 Mercedes Unimog Safari.............$15

Gulliver

Four models were produced by Gulliver of France, three in the late 1930s, one in 1950.
Berliet Bus, 6".............$130
Berliet Covered Truck, 5¼".............$90
Renault Celtaquatre, 4".............$130
Renault 4CV, 1950.............$145

H. L. Framberg (see Framberg, H. L.)

Hallmark (also see Kiddie Car Collectibles)

Hallmark has produced numerous promotional and novelty items for their stationery stores. Among the offerings are a few whimsical diecast toys called Road Rovers, not much more than a heavy lump of zamak, in simplified shapes for toddlers or as novelties. On the other hand, their recent offerings of miniature pedal cars are just short of spectacular. See a list of them under the Kiddie Car Collectibles heading. Value is based on a March 1999 eBay auction of #2 Banana Bus in mint condition with original box that sold for $15. Note that the assortment is labeled Series I. What Series II is and if it was ever issued is not known.

Hallmark Series I Road Rovers — Diecast Metal, Hand Painted

1 Chocolate Mouse.............$5–8
   in original box.............$15
2 Banana Bus.............$5–8
   in original box.............$15
3 Fuzz Mobile.............$5–8
   in original box.............$15
4 Blue Blob.............$5–8
   in original box.............$15
5 Little Dumpy.............$5–8
   in original box.............$15
6 Red Rover.............$5–8
   in original box.............$15
7 Merry Mover.............$5–8
   in original box.............$15
8 Purple Squash.............$5–8
   in original box.............$15
9 Scuttle Bug.............$5–8
   in original box.............$15
10 Firey Fred.............$5–8
   in original box.............$15
11 Fudge Drudge.............$5–8
   in original box.............$15
12 Flash, The Garbage Eater.............$5–8
   in original box.............$15

Hartoy (also see American Highway Legends, Precision Engineered Models)

1967 10th Avenue North
Lake Worth, Florida 33461
phone: 561-586-5556
fax: 561-586-5558
toll free: 800-245-1264

e-mail: hartoyinc@aol.com
website: www.hartoy.com

Hartoy is an American promotional company that, besides producing its own American Highway Legends series of 1:64 scale trucks in various liveries, takes basic models from Lledo and others and, through a licensing agreement with numerous companies, customizes them with advertising and logos. A series of Coca-Cola vehicles and Chevron gas station promotionals are some of the better-known models from Hartoy.

American Highway Legends is the most prominent series from Hartoy, and is dealt with in its own section. (See American Highway Legends.)

Precision Engineered Models (PEM) is the next generation of promotional trucks. (See Precision Engineered Models.)

Lledo and Days Gone models marketed by Hartoy are likewise listed with the rest of the Lledo models. (See Lledo.)

Hasbro (also see Aviva, Kenner, Playskool, Winner's Circle)

Hasbro has been a powerful force in the toy industry since the 1960s. Toys such as Mr. Machine, the see-through gear-driven walking, animated robot with a top hat, was possibly one of the best known toys of the period, at least if you watched Saturday morning cartoons. But Hasbro's solid claim to fame is G. I. Joe action figures and accessories, a perennial favorite for some thirty years.

Hasbro has continued through to the present, but it has been overshadowed by the giant called Mattel. In fact, Mattel failed in an attempt to purchase Hasbro in 1995.

G. I. Joe aside, Hasbro's product line at one time included a line of Aviva character toys usually sold at Hallmark shops. Predominantly Peanuts characters from the comic strip of the same name, Aviva at last word continues to market such items in diecast and plastic. See Aviva for a sampling of a few of the diecast items issued.

Most recently, Hasbro has issued Kenner Winner's Circle NASCAR models and Playskool diecast vehicles featuring Barney the Purple Dinosaur and friends. Go to the respective brands for a product listing.

Hasegawa

If not for the fact that they are exquisite for 1:24 scale plastic model kits, Hasegawa would receive no mention at all in this book on toy cars. Their new VW Samba 23-Window Minibus is the kicker and one worth having, even in a diecast collection.

Herpa

Herpa Miniaturmodelle GmbH

LeonrodstraBe 46/47
D-90599
Dietenhofen, Germany
website: www.herpa.de

Among the wide assortment of models available under the Herpa brand name is a series of 1:87 scale cars and trucks with plastic bodies. The accuracy and detail of these diminutive vehicles is remarkable, and are listed in this book because of their value as scale model miniatures. In the larger 1:43 scale, Herpa produces an assortment of diecast models that are especially nice, although they feature no working parts such as opening doors, hood, or trunk.

Herpa 1:43 Scale Diecast Models

BMW 740i, arctic white	$18
BMW 740i, bright red	$18
BMW 740i, metallic blue	$18
BMW 740i, Oxford green	$18
Ferrari 288 GTO, red	$18
Ferrari 288 GTO, yellow	$18
Mercedes-Benz E320 Sedan, metallic blue	$18
Mercedes-Benz E320 Sedan, metallic gray	$18
Mercedes-Benz E320 Sedan, red	$18
Mercedes-Benz E320T, black	$18
Mercedes-Benz E320T, blue	$18
Mercedes-Benz E320T Convertible, blue	$18
Mercedes-Benz E320T Convertible, white	$18
Mercedes-Benz 320 Convertible	$20
Mercedes-Benz 320 Coupe	$20
Mercedes-Benz 320 Sedan	$20

Mercedes-Benz 600 SEL, green.............$18

Mercedes-Benz 320 wagon	$20
Mercedes-Benz 600 SEL, gray	$18
Mercedes-Benz 600 SEL, purple	$18
Mercedes-Benz 600 SEL, red	$18
Volkswagen Polo 4-Door	$20
Volkswagen Polo 2-Door	$20

Herpa Hitech 1:43 Scale Diecast Models

Ferrari F40, black	$45
Ferrari F40, red	$45
Ferrari F40, yellow	$45
Ferrari Testarossa, red	$45
Ferrari Testarossa Convertible, red	$45
Ferrari Testarossa Coupe, yellow	$45
Ferrari Testarossa Spyder, yellow	$45
Ferrari Testarossa Spyder, silver	$45
Ferrari 348tb, black	$45
Ferrari 348tb, metallic blue	$45
Ferrari 348tb, red	$45

Ferrari 348tb, red	$45
Ferrari 348tb, yellow	$45
Ferrari 348ts, metallic green	$45
Mercedes-Benz 600AMG	$40
Mercedes-Benz 600SEL	$40

Herpa Jr. 1:66 Scale Models

BMW 528 Fire Chief Car (plastic), red	$5
BMW 325i, blue	$5
BMW 325i, green	$5
BMW 325i, red	$5
BMW 325i, yellow	$5

Hess

While Hess trucks are plastic, they represent a large portion of the scale model truck collector market, and are mentioned here due to their popularity. Hess trucks are issued by the Hess Oil Company.

Information provided below is from the *1996 Hess Price Guide* by Thomas G. Nefos, publisher & editor of *The National Toy Connection*, reprinted by permission.

Hess Promotional Toys [Original Selling Prices in brackets]

1964 - B-Model Mack Tanker Truck, made in Hong Kong (Same tanker was used by Service, Wilco, Gant, Billups, Etna & Travelers) [$1.39] $1,900

1965 - same as 1964

1966 - "Hess Voyager" Tanker Ship, made in the U.S.A. by Marx Toys [$1.89] $2,300

1967 - Split Window Tanker Truck with "Red Velvet" base on box, no rivets on battery switch, made in the U.S.A. [$2.89] $2,400

1968 - same as 1967 except no velvet box was used, no rivets on battery switch, made in Hong Kong [$1.49].......$675

1969 - same as 1968

1969 - Split Window Tanker "Amerada Hess" - Made in Hong Kong, rare, not sold to public $2,500

1970 - Red Pumper Fire Truck, made in Hong Kong by Marx Toys [$1.69] $695

1971 - same as 1970 except box was labeled "Season's Greetings" [$1.69] $3,000

1972 - Split Window Tanker Truck - same as 1968 except has "rivets" on battery switch [$1.79] $375

1973 - no promotion offered

1974 - same as 1972 [$1.89] $375

1975 - Semi Box Truck, 3 oil drums, no Hess labels on drums, 1pc. cab on tractor, made in both U.S.A. & Hong Kong [$1.99] $395

1976 - same as 1975 except oil drums have Hess labels & tractor cab is made in 2 pieces [$2.29] $395

1977 - Semi Tanker Truck, large rear label 1.5" x 1", made in Hong Kong

[$2.39]....................................$175

1978 - same as 1977 except small rear label 1" x ⅞" [$2.49]................$185

1979 - no promotion offered

1980 - GMC Training Van - dated 1978 sold but sold in 1980 - Made in Hong Kong [$3.29]........................$395

1981 - no promotion offered

1982 - '33 Chevy "Home Delivery" Tanker Truck, box marked "First Hess Truck," not a bank, made in Hong Kong [$4.69]...........................$95

1983 - same as 1982 (reissued), not a bank, made in Hong Kong [$5.29]..........$95

1984 - similiar to 1977-78 Semi Tanker Truck except made into a bank, made in Hong Kong [$4.99]....................$95

1985 - '33 Chevy "Home Delivery" Tanker bank, distributed in the North........$125

1985 - reissued 1984 Tanker, distributed in the South.............................$95

1986 - White Semi Box Truck with 3 Hess labeled oil drums, made in both Hong Kong & China [$5.49]..............$100

1987 - same as 1986 [$5.99]...........$75

1988 - White "Toy Truck & Racer," made in both Hong Kong & China [$6].......$70

1989 - White Aerial Ladder Fire Truck with dual siren sounds, made in China [$8.99]..................................$65

1990 - White Semi Tanker Truck, back up and air horn sounds, made in China [$9.99]..................................$45

1991 - same as 1988 except different style race car, larger truck cab, made in China [$10.99].........................$35

1992 - White "18 Wheeler" Box Truck with racer, made in China [$11.99]......$40

1993 - Hess Patrol Car, white and green, sirens & lights, larger scale toy [$11.99]..............................$28

1993 - Hess Premium Diesel Tanker given as a gift to Hess bulk diesel dealers, reissue of the 1990 semi tanker with new graphics, special box wrapped in green paper, and special gift card from the Hess company, not sold to public...........$1,000

1994 - same as 1993, not sold to public......................................$1,000

1994 - Hess Rescue Truck, white and green with red ladder, larger scale toy [$14.99]..............................$25

1995 - Hess Toy Truck & Helicopter, white, green, flatbed semi with detachable helicopter [$15.99]...................$20

National Toy Connection offers a full-color photo album of all of the above described toys and their boxes. This album can be updated each year with the purchase of only 1 photo... it's never out of date! To get yours send $26 + $3 shipping and handling U.S.A. (foreign orders please send International Postal Money Order in U.S. $34) to:

National Toy Connection
Suite 2346
779 E. Merritt Island Causeway
Merritt Island, FL 32952
800-704-1232 Nationwide Toll Free Order Line
(Sorry, phone number only available in the U.S.A.)

High Speed

Whether High Speed brand toys can be considered diecast is debatable. These inexpensive generic toys are mostly plastic. On the samples found, only the truck cab and upper chassis are diecast. Nevertheless, they possess the charm of a well-designed toy, while lacking the identity of a scale model.

While suggested retail of $2.49 seems high to me, the $.99 paid at Toy Liquidators makes them reasonably priced. Values will not likely rise on such toys in the near future, let's say the next twenty years, but they are "cute" additions to a well-rounded diecast toy collection.

Box Truck....................................$1–2
Cement Truck...............................$1–2
Dump Truck.................................$1–2
Utility Truck.................................$1–2
F1 Racer.....................................$1–2

Highway Travelers

P O Box 187
Oakdale, NY 11769-0187

Highway Travelers are white-metal models whose "finish, craftsmanship, and attention to detail are as good as you'll find," according to Toys for Collectors of Attleboro Falls, Massachusetts, the only known source for these models.

102P 1962 Studebaker Lark Convertible Indianapolis 500 Pace Car.....................$170

102S 1962 Studebaker Lark Daytona with sunroof..$160

103C 1951 Frazier Manhattan Convertible.....................................$220

103S 1951 Frazier Manhattan Softtop......$220

104C 1961 Plymouth Fury Convertible.....$190

104H 1961 Plymouth Fury Hardtop..........$220

104S 1961 Plymouth Fury Softtop...........$190

105C 1987-93 Cadillac Allante Convertible.....................................$155

105H 1987–93 Cadillac Allante Hardtop $155

105P 1992 Cadillac Allante Indianapolis 500 Pace Car..$170

Holland-Oto (see Efsi)

Hongwell (also see Autocraft)

Hongwell is a new discovery in the ever-expanding world of diecast-and-plastic toys. Their Autocraft Truck Monster series represents an assortment of trucks in approximately 1:34 scale, all conveniently measuring about 9 inches long. Only the cab is diecast; the rest is plastic. Features include opening compartments and other working parts. Detail is partic-

ularly nice for a toy priced around $14. All models are identified as Mercedes-Benz trucks by the prominent trademark three-pointed star on the grille.

Since its introduction, Hongwell has deferred most of its assortment to the Autocraft brand. For a model list, go to the Autocraft section in this book.

Horsman

Fiero fanatic Ray Paulk first contacted me in March 1999 regarding this brand. "Horsman King of the Road World Class Series" is the complete name on the box of these approx. 1:32 scale models. On the end of the box is printed
(c) 1988 Horsman
Division of Gata Box Ltd.
New York NY 10010
Made in Macao

As for the spelling of Macau, Paulk notes, "I typed exactly what was on the box." Paul adds, "This particular box shows "NO. 07900." The sample model is a rather heavy diecast metal white 1988 Corvette with opening doors and hood. The interior is all black plastic but nicely detailed and under the hood is a chrome engine insert. The back of the box pictures the Corvette in red along with a silver BMW and a black Pontiac Fiero notchback."

The original price sticker still remains on the box. This model was originally sold at Farm + Fleet for $4.49. Paulk recently won it in an eBay auction for a winning bid of $10.51. As an avid collector of Fiero toys and memorabilia, Paulk wants to find the Fiero model pictured on the back.

BMW..$5–10
Fiero...$5–10
Corvette......................................$5–10

Hot Wheels

The author of this book purposely makes no attempt to present the full Hot Wheels line in this book. To do justice to the entire line of toys, it would take an entire book, of which there are several. For more information on these and other books on diecast toys, send 2 first class stamps to Dana Johnson, P O Box 1824, Bend OR 97709-1824.

It is an interesting comparison to note that collectors in Europe have little interest in Hot Wheels, finding them crude, unrealistic, and unappealing. Martin Van de Logt of the Netherlands says this book devotes way too much on Hot Wheels, Majorette, and, for that matter, Hot Pursuit models. "Why list so many?" is his query. Indeed, it is difficult to explain the fanaticism for these trendy toys.

Nevertheless, since 1968, Mattel's Hot Wheels line has maintained a solid lock on the diecast toy car market, at least in the US. While many other toy manufacturers, even Matchbox, suffered the humiliation of lost market share, near

103

bankruptcy and repeated buyout, Hot Wheels toys have remained market-stable. Prototypes and production models alike from Hot Wheels' first few years are commanding high prices, as are new special issues and even some regular issues. Much speculation — and some would say overspeculation — and debate ensues over the value of new regular production issues.

One such prototype is a 1969 issue #6274 Beach Bomb, a Volkswagen Van with two surfboards projecting out the back window. While the production model with side panels added to the cast to hold the surfboards is fairly common and priced at $40 to $80, only some 14–20 specimens of the prototype are believed to exist. The latest edition of *Tomart's Price Guide to Hot Wheels* (Second Edition, 1997) lists the value of this rarest Hot Wheels model at $3,500, but one such specimen sold at Christy's auction house in February 1995 for $4,025.

In late 1996, Mattel made the announcement that the company was working on purchasing Tyco Toys, the current owner of Matchbox, Dinky, and several other toy brands. By mid-1997, the sale was complete.

A few years earlier, Mattel purchased the Corgi brand and incorporated many of the Corgi Jrs. into the Hot Wheels line. Eventually, though, the original employees of Corgi in Swansea, South Wales, bought back the larger scale Corgi Collectibles series from Mattel. Will the same thing happen to Matchbox? Will some Hot Wheels take on the look of Matchbox models? Or will the Matchbox series be kept distinct from the Hot Wheels offerings?

As of 1998, Matchbox toys reportedly had already been seen in Hot Wheels five-packs, and retail advertising had Matchbox five-packs shown with the Hot Wheels logo on them.

Hot Wheels Alphabetical Listing, 1968 through 1972 — The First Five Years

Models listed below represent the first five years, from 1968 through 1972. Values are for mint specimens not in original blister pack. Values are usually considerably higher for packaged models. Due to space restrictions, the entire Hot Wheels product line cannot be represented here.

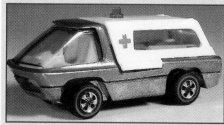

Ambulance #6451, 1970-1972............$35–40
except white enamel.....................$110

Alive '55 Chevy Nomad #6968, plain enamel colors, 1973 ....$80–90

Alive '55 #9210, flame accents, 1973 ....$10–95
AMX/2 #6460, 1971.................$35–45
except metallic pink........................$65

Beatnik Bandit #6217, 1968–1971.....$10–25

Boss Hoss #6407, metallic colors, 1971 ....$50–75
Brabham Repco F1 Racer #6264, 1969–1971 ....$10–15
Bugeye #5178, 1971–1972 ....$35–40
except metallic pink........................$90
Buzz Off #6976, plain colors, 1973 ....$90–100
Buzz Off #6976, pinstripes, 1973.....$40
Buzz Off #6976, gold chrome, 1973 ....$20
Bye-Focal #6187, 1971–1972 .....$65–80
Carabo #6420, 1970–1971........$25–30
except metallic pink........................$70
Cement Mixer #6452, 1970–1972 .$25–35
except white enamel $95
Chaparral 2G #6256, 1969–1971.$15–25
except metallic pink........................$80
Classic Cord #6472, 1971–1972 ....$100–140
except metallic pink......................$190

Classic '31 Ford Woody #6251, 1969–1971 ....$15–25

Classic '32 Ford Vicky #6250, 1969–1971 ....$25–35

Classic '36 Ford Coupe #6253, 1969–1971 ....$10–20
except metallic light blue.......................$50
& metallic pink..................................$90

Classic '57 T-Bird #6252, 1969–1971 ....$20–30
except metallic pink....................$90

Classic Nomad #6404, 1970–1971..$40–50
except metallic pink $70

Cockney Cab #6466, 1971–1972 ....$35–50
Custom AMX #6267, 1969–1971 $35–60
Custom Barracuda #6211, 1968–1969 ....$45–65
Custom Camaro #6208, 1968–1969 ....$40–60
except white enamel version.........$400
Custom Charger #6268, 1969–1971 ....$50–80
except metallic pink......................$75

Custom Continental Mark III #6266, 1969–1971..................................$20–35

Custom Corvette #6215, 1968–1971 ....$50–75

Custom Cougar #6205, 1968–1969 ....$50–70
Custom Eldorado #6218, 1968–1971 ....$35–45
except metallic pink.................$75
Custom Firebird #6212, 1968–1969 ....$40–55
Custom Fleetside #6213, 1968–1969 ....$40–65
Custom Mustang #6206, 1968–1969 ....$60–200
Custom Police Cruiser #6269, 1969–1972 ....$60
Custom T-Bird #6207, 1968–1969 .$45–60
except metallic pink......................$90
The Demon, #6401, 1970–1971 ..$15–20
Deora #6210, 1968–1969 ....$40–60
Double Header #5880, 1973 ....$70–80
Double Vision #6975, 1973 ....$70–90
Dump Truck #6453, 1970–1972 ......$20

Custom Volkswagen #6220, 1968–1971 ....$10–25
except metallic pink & enamel colors....$70

Dune Daddy #6967, 1973 ....$25–65
except orange...........................$120
or Wisconsin Toy Co. $3
Evil Weevil #6471, 1971–1972 ...$35–40
Ferrari 312P #6417, metallic colors,
1970–1971 ....$10–35
except met. red w/white interior $175
Ferrari 312P #6973, enamel colors,
1973 ....$120

Ferrari 512S #6021, 1972.................$80–100

Fire Chief Cruiser #6469, 1970–
1971 ....$10–15
Fire Engine #6454, 1970–1972.$35–55
Ford J-Car #6214, 1968–1971 ....$10–15
Ford Mark IV #6257, 1969–1971.$10–15
Fuel Tanker #6018, 1971 ....$65
Funny Money #6005, 1972 ....$50

Grass Hopper #6461, 1971.................$30–45
except metallic pink...........................$65

Hot Heap #6219, 1968–1971 ....$10–20
except metallic pink $80

Hairy Hauler #6458, 1971 ....$30–40
except metallic pink.....................$60
Heavy Chevy #6408, metallic colors,
1970–1971 ....$35–45
Heavy Chevy #6189, chrome,
1970–1971 ....$45
Hiway Robber #6979, 1973................$65
The Hood #6175, 1971–1972.....$25–45
except metallic pink.....................$75

**Ice "T" #6184, metallic colors, 1971–
1972** **$45**

Ice "T" #6980, enamel colors with no
accents, 1973 ....$100
Ice "T" #6980, enamel colors with accents,
1973 ....$20–40
except yellow w/orange & olive ...$145
Indy Eagle #6263, 1969–1971 ....$10–25
except gold chrome $50

**Jack "Rabbit" Special #6421, 1970–
1971** **$15**
**except "Jack in the Box,"
unopened** **$150–180**

Jet Threat #6179, 1971–1972 ......$45–75
King 'Kuda #6411, metallic colors,
1970–1971 ....$35–45
King 'Kuda #6190, chrome, 1970–1971 .$45

Light My Firebird #6412, 1970–1971 .$15–25

Lola GT70 #6254, 1969–1971....$10–15
Lotus Turbine #6262, 1969–1971 .$10–15
Mantis #6423, 1970–1971 ....$15–35
Maserati Mistral #6277, 1969–
1971 ....$45–55
McLaren M6A #6255, 1969–
1971 ....$10–25
Mercedes-Benz 280SL #6275, metallic col-
ors, 1969–1971 ....$20–30
Mercedes-Benz 280SL #6962, enamel col-
ors, 1973 ....$95–110

Mercedes-Benz C-111 #6169, metallic colors, 1972 ....$80–100
Mercedes-Benz C-111 #6978, enamel colors with no accents, 1973 ...$175–200
Mercedes-Benz C-111 #6978, enamel col-
ors with accents, 1973 ....$15–40
Mighty Maverick #6417, 1970–
1971 ....$35–45
Mod Quad #6456, 1970–1971 ..$15–30
except metallic pink.....................$75
Mongoose #6410, 1970..................$55
except with no plastic windows &
#6969 on roof underside............$550
Mongoose 2 #5954, 1971–1972 .....$90
Mongoose Rail Dragster #5952, 1971–
1972 ....$70
Moving Van #6455, 1970–1972.$40–45
Mutt Mobile #6185, 1971–1972..$45–75
except metallic pink.....................$110

Nitty Gritty Kitty #6405, 1970–1971 ....$35–45

Noodle Head #6000, 1971–1972.$50–85
Odd Job #6981, 1973..............$85–100
Olds 442 #6467, 1971.........$150–195
Open Fire #5881, 1972..............$85–95
Paddy Wagon #6402, 1970–1979....$15
Paddy Wagon #6966, 1973........$10–30
Peepin' Bomb #6419, 1970–1971.$10–15
except metallic pink.....................$25
Pit Crew Car #6183, 1971–1972.......$70

**Police Cruiser Olds 442 #6963,
1973** **$40–75**

**Porsche 917 #6416, metallic colors,
1970–1971** **$15–25**
except metallic pink...........................$50

Porsche 917 #6972, enamel colors,
1973 (depending on variation).$25–200
Power Pad #6459, 1970–1971....$35–45
Prowler #6965, 1973 (depending on variation) $25–190
Python #6216, 1968–1971.........$12–20
except metallic pink.....................$70

Racing Rig #6194, 1971 ....$75–85
Rear Engine Mongoose #5699, 1972.$160
Rear Engine Snake #5856, 1972.......$160
Red Baron #6400, red with black interior, 1970-1979 ....$15–20
Red Baron #6400, red with white interior, 1970-1979 ....$135
Road King Truck #7615, yellow, 1974 (model courtesy of Jo R. Fujise) $600
Rocket-Bye-Baby #6186, 1971–1972 ....$50–70
Rolls-Royce Silver Shadow #6276, 1969–1971 ....$30–55
    except metallic pink.............$100
Sand Crab #6403, 1970–1971 ...$10–25
    except metallic pink.............$35)
Sand Witch #6974, 1973 (depending on variaton).............$35–100
S'Cool Bus #6468, 1971 ....$100
Scooper #6193, 1971 ....$75–80
Seasider #6413, 1970–1971 ....$50–70
Shelby Turbine #6265, 1969–1971..$10–25
Short Order #6176, 1971–1972 ..$40–45
    except metallic purple.............$60
Show-Off #6982, 1973.............$90–120
Side Kick #6022, 1972 ....$75–85
    except metallic pink.............$100
Silhouette #6209, 1968–1971 ......$10–20
    except metallic pink.............$75
Six Shooter #6003, 1971–1972 ...$50–60
    except metallic magenta $85
Sky Show Deora #6436, 1970 ......$1,000
Sky Show Fleetside #6436, 1970–1971 ....$400
Snake #6409, 1970 ....$75
Snake #6969, #6969 under roof, only 30 known to exist, 1973.............$550
Snake 2 #5953, 1971–1972.............$50
Snake Rail Dragster #5951, 1971–1972.............$70
Snorkel #6020, metallic colors, 1971 ....$60–70
Snorkel #6020, enamel, 1971.............$85
Special Delivery #6006, 1971–1972 ..$50
Splittin' Image #6261, 1969–1971 .$10–15
    except metallic pink.............$80
Street Snorter Maverick #6971, 1973 ....$90–100
Strip Teaser #6188, 1971–1972...$50–80

**Sugar Caddy #6418, 1971 ....$35–50
except metallic pink.............$95**

Superfine Turbine #6004, 1973.$190–225
Sweet 16 #6007, 1973.............$85–100
Swingin'Wing #6422, 1970–1971 $20–30
    except metallic pink.............$55
T-4-2 #6177, 1971–1972.............$40–60

Team Trailer #6019, 1971 ....$70
TNT-Bird #6407, 1970–1971 ....$25–40
Torero #6260, 1969–1971 ....$10–20
    except metallic pink.............$50
Tow Truck #6450, 1970–1972.....$25–30
    except metallic pink.............$65
Tri Baby #6424, 1970–1971 ....$15–25
    except metallic pink.............$35
Turbofire #6259, 1969–1971 ....$10–20
    except metallic pink.............$70
Twin Mill #6258, 1969–1971 ......$10–25
    except metallic pink.............$70
Volkswagen Beach Bomb #6274, hybrid prototype with surfboards out back window, wide chassis intended to be used with side slot production version, 1969–1971 ....$50,000

Volkswagen Beach Bomb #6274, surfboards in side slots, 1969–1971 ....$40–50

Volkswagen Beach Bomb #6274, prototype with surfboards out back window, 1969–1971 ....$4,000
Waste Wagon #6192, 1971 ....$75–90
What-4 #6192, 1971–1972.......$60–85
Whip Creamer #6457, 1970–1971 .$20–30
    except metallic pink.............$40

Hot Pursuit

There seems to be no shortage of new diecast companies. Hot Pursuit Collectibles is one of those. Based in Cherry Hill, New Jersey, Hot Pursuit Collectibles offers these 1:24 scale coin banks through various specialty outlets, particularly Budget-Minders, Specialty Diecast Company, and Joel's Toys. The models, introduced in 1997, are similar to the 1:43 scale Chevrolet Caprice police cars first introduced by Road Champs a few years ago, except that opening the trunk reveals a hidden coin slot. Why a bank? It immediately appeals to more collectors — those that collect diecast models and those that collect diecast banks, as well as those that collect model police cruisers.

Latest information (December 14, 1999) indicates that Hot Pursuit went out of business in 1997, the same year they started, and that existing inventory was purchased by Dimension 4, now also rumored to be out of business.

New York Police Department.............$25
California Highway Patrol.............$25
Michigan State Police.............$25
Oklahoma Highway Patrol.............$25

Ohio State Highway Patrol.............$25
Arkansas State Trooper.............$25
New York City Taxi.............$25
New Jersey.............$25
Virginia.............$25
Florida.............$25
Alabama.............$25
Georgia.............$25
New York.............$25
Maryland Police (2 car set).............$40–45
Chicago Fire Department.............$25
New York Fire Department.............$25
San Francisco Fire Department.............$25
Philadelphia Fire Department.............$25

HP Toys

The fact that HP Toys were made in Denmark sometime in the mid-1980s is all the author so far knows about this brand. More information would be greatly appreciated.
1984 Leyland Farm Tractor, 1:25.............$22

Hubley

Hubleys were made in Lancaster, Pennsylvania, and remain some of the most popular and collectible toys on the collector market. The first Hubley toys were cast iron. The company that made them has been traced back to 1892. By 1940, lighter diecast zinc alloy replaced heavy cast iron, thus cutting the cost of worldwide shipping. Plastic toys make up a significant portion of the Hubley line. Richard O'Brien's book *Collecting Toy Cars and Trucks* provides a detailed history of Hubley toys.

Besides the assembled toys, Hubley also produced diecast model kits in the sixties. These kits, unassembled and still in the original box, are gaining renewed popularity with collectors.

In the mid-1980s, Hubley was purchased by Ertl, and a few Hubley toys and kits have been reissued by them.

A good example is the classic Hubley school bus. The original Hubley version featured clear plastic labels and no windows. The earlier Ertl version is windowless while a later issued by Ertl has dark tinted plastic windows. The Hubley version is priced around $45–55. The two Ertl versions were recently available for around $12–17.

A Survey of Hubley Toys

Airflow Car, 5¼".............$85
Bell Telephone Truck with telephone pole trailer, 24".............$185
Jaguar, 7½".............$190
Motorcycle Delivery Van with Driver, "Say It With Flowers" (extremely rare).............$42,000
Packard Sedan, 1939–1940, 5½".......$75
Packard Dietrich, 1:22.............$75
Panama Digger, 3½".............$600
Panama Digger, 9½".............$1650

Mighty Metal Airport Set..$45–60

Hubley Kiddietoys

A popular series of Hubley toys were marketed as Kiddietoys. Here is a sampling.

Dump Truck, #476 ....$140
Dump Truck, #510 ....$250
MG Sport Car, 9" $190
Racer, #457, 6½" $55
Sedan, #452, 7" $29
Taxi, #5 ....$25
Tractor..$40–55
1946 Ford Stake Truck, #461 ....$170

Hubley Model Kits

1932 Chevrolet Roadster, #4862-400 ....$75–90
Duesenberg SJ, #4864 ....$60–75
Duesenberg Model SJ Town Car, #4868-70001930................................$80–110
1930 Packard Roadster, #4860-500 ....$75–90

Hubley Real Toys (U.S.A.)/Real Types (Canada), 1:60 scale

A few toys representing U.S. cars were issued around 1958 to 1960 in 1:60 scale. They were marketed in the U.S. as Real Toys, and in Canada as Real Types, a series of cars of approximately 3"–3½" long.

Ford Country Squire, #RT250, two-tone cream and brown $55–70
Chevrolet Corvair, #RT340, turquoise .$55–70
Buick, #RT 90, light blue $55–70
Studebaker Hawk, #RT 50, red $65–80
GMC Firebird III, #RT 350, red $60–75
Ford Fairlane, #RT 20, mint green $55–70
RT 80 Chevrolet Corvette, red $45–70

Husky (also see Corgi)

Husky toys were the first series of smaller toys produced by Corgi. Later the line would be renamed Corgi Juniors. Husky toys were lightweight and inexpensive, but highly accurate renderings of common European vehicles of the mid-sixties, considering their original price of 39 to 49 cents each. For a sample list-ing of Husky models, go to the Corgi section of this book.

Icibi

Icibi is a brand of 1:25 scale models of undetermined quality made in Greece.
270 Deutz Fire Ladder Truck, 1:25 ....$7
900 McLaren CanAm, 1:25....................$7
1431 Porsche 911 Police, 1:25 ....$7
5020 Deutz Fire Engine, 1:25 ....$7

Igra

Igra models are quality 1:38, 1:43, and 1:87 scale plastic models from the former Czech Republic (Czechoslovakia). These rare models are offered by Modelauto and others.
1 1924 Tatra Sedan....................$15
2 1924 Tatra Phaeton.................$15
6 1906 Laurin/Klement.............$15
7 1907 Praga Charon.................$15
9 1906 Velox Car......................$15
12 Zetor Crystal Tractor $15
13 Zetor Tractor/Loader $15
14 Zetor Manure Spreader $15
IG463 Skoda 120 LS Saloon Car ....(£4) $6 US
IG464 Tatra T613 Saloon Car........(£4) $6 US
IG465 Bugatti T35 (Yesteryear copy).(£4) $6 US
IG999 Selection pack of veteran and vintage cars:
Laurin & Klement, Tatra, Praga etc, different from above listed items, approx 1:43 scale ....(£3) ea $5 US
Or pack of 10 different assorted.(£20) $31 US

IHC (see International Hobby Corp.)

Ilario

Ilario of France produces 1:43 scale Ferrari resin kits and built models. No model list is known.

Imperial Diecast

Imperial Toy Corporation has its US headquarters in Los Angeles, California. Other international headquarters include Imperial Toy Canada Ltd, in Mississauga, Ontario, and its Great Britain distributor Titan Toys International Ltd. The distinction of these models may lie mostly in their colorful packages and regal logo. The actual models are made better than most generics, and sell for comparably more. Featured are pull-back action motorcycles with tiny "training wheels" to propel them, nicely made commercial jets, a series of helicopters that are also equipped with pull-back action, and various other somewhat attractive toys. While these models possess more charm than most generic toys, as with most generic diecast toys, value will likely remain at retail price of $1 to $2 each, partly due to the fact that the name is only on the package but not on the toy.

An exception to the generic offerings from Imperial are the distinctive models issued under the Imperial Toys Freeway Flyers brand. The bases are the dead giveaway that these were produced by Playart. What distinguishes them as Imperial Toys is the package. Out of the package, they are unidentifiable as anything but Playarts. They are more valuable as Playarts in Imperial packaging than they are as Imperial toys.

Imperial Toys — Freeway Flyers (Playart models with chrome hubcaps) Values are for new models in original package.

706-00 Batmobile $15–20
706-01 Plymouth Barracuda $10–12
706-02 Porsche Carrera 910 ....$10–12
706-03 Thunderbird $10–12
706-04 Opel GT $10–12
706-05 Mangusta 5000 Ghia $10–12
706-06 Mako Shark $10–12
706-07 Javelin SST $10–12
706-08 Lamborghini Miura $10–12
706-09 Chevrolet Camaro SS $10–12
706-10 AMX "390" $10–12
706-11 Jensen FF $10–12
706-12 Alfa Romeo P33 ....$10–12
706-13 Carabo Bertone $10–12
706-14 Mercedes-Benz C111 ......$10–12
706-15 Cadillac Eldorado $10–12
706-16 Mustang Hardtop $10–12
706-17 Toyota 2000 GT Convertible $10–12
706-18 Fire Chief $10–12
706-19 Man From U.N.C.L.E. Car..$15–20
706-20 Mustang $10–12
706-21 Chevrolet Astro-1 ....$10–12
706-22 Toyota 2000 GT...............$10–12
706-23 Jaguar 'E' Type 2+2 ....$10–12
706-24 Volkswagen Beetle...........$10–12
706-25 Maserati Marzal $10–12
706-26 Cement Mixer $10–12
706-27 Pickup Truck $10–12
706-28 Dump Truck $10–12
706-29 Wrecker Truck $10–12
706-30 Fire Truck $10–12
706-31 Gasoline Truck $10–12
706-32 Police Car $10–12
706-33 Rolls Royce $10–12

706-34 Fiat Dino $10–12
706-35 BMW 2002 ....$10–12
706-36 Corvette Stingray $10–12
706-37 Datsun 240Z $10–12
706-38 VW Porsche 914 ....$10–12
706-39 Honda N360.....................$10–12
706-40 Honda S800.......................$10–12
706-41 Corona Mark II 1900 Hardtop
    SL $10–12
706-42 Celica 1600 GT.................$10–12
706-43 Toyota Crown Hardtop SL ..$10–12
706-44 Porsche Targa 911S $10–12
706-45 Isuzu 117 Coupe $10–12
706-46 Corolla Sprinter SL $10–12
706-47 Nissan Sunny 1200 Coupe
    GX $10–12
706-48 Yamaha Super Discmatic Rotary
    Coupe $10–12
706-50 Ford Capri 1600 GT........$10–12
706-51 Rover 2000 TC.................$10–12
706-52 Honda 2 GS (Honda Civic).$10–12
706-54 Mercedes-Benz 350 SL......$10–12
706-55 Ford Cortina GXL..............$10–12
706-56 Hipup Coupe Galant GTO
    MR..$10–12
706-57 Austin Mini Cooper S MK II.$10–12
706-58 Fiat 124 Sport $10–12

Mighty Machines Ford Hot Rod Hauler Set, 2000 ....$5–8

Mighty Machines Ford Street Rod from Ford Hot Rod Haulers Set......................$2–3

Impy (also see Crescent, D.C.M.T. and Lone Star)

A British company called Lone Star produced a series of toys known as Impy toys. But the actual name on the base is "Lone Star Road-Master Impy Super Cars." No wonder everyone called them Impy. For more on Impy models, see Lone Star.

Imra (or IMRA)

Likely originating in southern California, these white metal models are likely prepainted kits, according to Harvey Goranson. As

nearly as Goranson can recall, several Imra molds may have ended up as Precision miniatures kits.

1975 Indy 500 Winner Jorgenson #48, 1:40 ....$275
Eagle Dan Gurney/Bobby Unser, 2-tone blue, 1:40..$275

Integral

Integral is a brand of 1:43 and 1:24 scale resin "superkits" and built models. Integral is part of the MAFMA consortium of France. No model list is known.

InterCar (see Auto Pilen)

International Hobby Corp. (IHC)

IHC, otherwise known as International Hobby Corp., caters to the HO gauge hobby market in providing various plastic model vehicles, buildings and accessories in 1:87 scale. Quality varies from model to model but is generally good considering the very reasonable price. Below is a sampling of vehicles offered.

Cement Mixer, #916 ....$3
Harvester, #903 ....$3
Livestock Transporter, #918 ....$3
School Bus, 1940s Style, 911 ....$3

Intex (see Zee Toys)

Irwin

Beginning with celluloid baby rattles and pinwheels, Irwin Cohn started the Irwin company in 1922. Toy cars and trucks produced by Irwin were made of an assortment of materials. In 1973, Irwin was purchased by Miner Industries. Recent models have been sold under the Joal brand by Irwin and listed separately in this book under Joal heading as well as below.

Army Bus, plastic.....................................$45
Barney Rubble Car, plastic, circa mid-sixties..$30
Buick Convertible, plastic, 1948, 5"...........$15
Chevrolet Panel Delivery, plastic, 6"...........$15
Chevrolet Pickup Truck, plastic, 1952, 5¼" ..$15
Dream Car Convertible, metal, 16" $350
Ford Sunliner, plastic friction, 9"..................$75
Ice Cream Truck, plastic $80
Ives Horseless Carriage Runabout, plastic, 6½" $4000
Ives Steamer, cast iron, 19½" $800
Jaguar Roadster, plastic, 6".......................$55
Packard Sedan, plastic friction, 1952, 9".....$30
Pontiac Hardtop Coupe, plastic friction, 1952, 6"..$20
"Skipper" Convertible, plastic, 1962 ....$250
Steeraway Wonder Car, plastic $160

Joal Classics Collection by Irwin (See illustrations under Joal listing.)

50100 Jaguar E Cabriolet, British racing green with beige interior $6

50107 Mercedes-Benz 300SL Cabriolet, black with red interior $6
50109 Mercedes-Benz 230SL, white with black roof, red interior $6
50111 Porsche Carrera 6 Deslizante, white with blue doors and hood $6
50114 Ferrari 250 LeMans, red $6
50125 Lamborghini Miura 6 P-400 Deslizante, yellow............................$6

Ites

Ites is an obscure brand from Czechoslovakia of which more information would be greatly appreciated.

Mirage Racer, 1:32...............................$18

J43 Kawabatakikaku (see Kawabatakikaku)

Jaco

Listed below is a small assortment of these 1:43 scale models of construction equipment of which little else is known.

531 Shovel...$11
532 Compactor.......................................$11
534 Bulldozer...$11
535 Loader...$11
544 Road Roller $11
733 Dozer/Ripper $11
933 Compactor/Loader...........................$11

Jane Francis Toys

Jane Francis started making toys in 1942, during World War II. Her first toys were stuffed handmade gingham dogs, calico cats, and Jumbo the Elephant toys for a Pittsburgh hospital gift shop. When Gimbel's department store requested 12 dozen stuffed toys, Jane Francis Toys was begun.

Her husband joined the operation towards the end of the war to introduce a line of crude diecast cars and trucks, among other items. In 1945, the first models reached the market. By 1949, the last diecast toys were produced, but the Francis' daughter Jane Francis Vanyo continued her father's business, the A. W. Francis Company, in producing diecast lawn and garden accessories. As of 1993, the company was still in operation from its headquarters in Somerset, Pennsylvania.

This author found one Jane Francis toy buried in some backyard with only a vestige of its original beige paint left on it but with no rust or corrosion, and with axles and wheels missing. It has since been repainted in red. On the underside of this single-cast toy is clearly marked "Jane Francis." Value in this condition is only a $1 to $4 at best, but in near mint original condition, wheels, axles, and paint intact, it would be worth around $20. Below is a list of the models produced from 1945 to 1949, with length and associated current collector values.

Gulf Box Truck with tin Cargo cover, 5"........$45

Pickup Truck, 5"	$25
Pickup Truck, 5"	$25
Pickup Truck, 6½"	$45
Sedan, futuristic, 6½"	$35
Sedan, futuristic with wind-up motor	$45
Tow Truck, 5"	$35

Ja-Ru (also see Golden Wheels)

Ja-Ru, Inc.
4030 Phillips Hwy.
Jacksonville, FL 32207
phone: 904-733-9311
toll-free: 800-231-3469
contact: Dennis Wit

Jacksonville, Florida, is home base for Ja-Ru toys made in China. Several lines of toys appear to exist under the Ja-Ru brand. Golden Wheels are inexpensive toy cars and trucks made by Golden Wheel diecasting of China for Ja-Ru. Golden Classics Ford Model T gift banks are so similar to Ertl banks that they can be easily mistaken for them at first glance. But closer inspection shows a few qualitative differences, most notably a plastic roof secured to the windshield by a crudely melted post, and the distinctive phrase "Coins Bank" in script on each model. These models are such a blatant attempt to capitalize on the popularity of Pepsi-Cola collectibles and Ertl coin banks that they even say gift bank on the box. The Model T tanker truck even declares "Collectable Models" right on the tank. Talk about obvious!

Still, considering the $12 price tag, they are comparably nice models to the more expensive $20–35 Ertl versions, and they do make attractive, affordable gifts.

Ja-Ru has also recently produced some fairly attractive "Matchbox" size models called Real Wheels. Among the assortment are some fairly nice models of military vehicles labeled "Fighting Army" and some notable toy cars sold under the "Collectors" moniker. Removed from the brightly colored package, the models are rendered generic, with no markings on them to distinguish them from other such generic toys, except for some models which feature a number on the base and the words "Made In China."

Lately, many Ja-Ru Real Wheels have turned out to be repackaged Yat Ming and Zylmex models.

Ja-Ru Golden Wheels

Ford Model T Delivery Van, white with blue roof and fenders, "Drink Pepsi-Cola" $12–15
Ford Model T Tanker, white with red roof and fenders, "Pepsi-Cola" $12–15
Ford Model T Tanker, "Mountain Dew" $12–15
Tractor Trailer, 1:87, "Pepsi" $4–5
Tractor Trailer, 1:87, "Mountain Dew" ..$4–5
Tractor Trailer, 1:64, "Pepsi" $9–12
Tractor Trailer, 1:64, "Mountain Dew" .$9–12

Diet Pepsi Tanker, white with red and blue accents, opaque silver-gray windows and base, 2½" $1–2
Pepsi Nissan Pathfinder, white with red and blue accents, opaque silver-gray windows, rally lights and base, 2¼" $1–2

Ja-Ru Real Wheels

Army Jeep, No. 1608, army green with tan and dark green camouflage markings, 2¾" $1–2

Military Covered Truck, #1362, army green with tan and dark green camouflage.....$1–2

Military Helicopter, army green with tan and dark green camouflage.................$1–2

Military Tank, #1102, army green with tan and dark green camouflage....................$1–2

Cadillac Seville, metallic blue with gold, silver and black stripe accents on sides.$1–2

Toyota Supra, white with red accents, "36," "yatming no.1036" on base $1–2
Audi Quattro, white with two-tone blue accents, "35" $1–2

BMW, metallic gray to magenta with rally markings, #1029..........................$1–2

F1 Racer, green, #1312 ....$1–2
F1 Racer, white, #1308......................$1–2
F1 Racer, pale orange, #1311 ....$1–2

Je Toys

Like so many inexpensive toys, Je Toys is a manufacturer of an assortment of generic toys that includes cars, motorcycles, airplanes, racers, etcetera. Quality and scale are not issues with these miniatures. They are strictly low-budget toys built for play and throw away. As collectibles, they are an oddity. In terms of collector value, they are worthless. Once removed from the vaguely identifiable packaging, they are rendered anonymous.

Regardless of that fact, Je Toys have produced a "cute" set of miniature antique vehicles in roughly 1:43 scale called Classic Cars that sell for about $2 a piece.

Jemini

Jemini models are white models made in England. Most recently, Jemini merged with Crossways Models of England. See Crossways for a list of current and recent models.

JEP (see Jouets de Paris)

Jet/Jet Wheels

Best information indicates that "Jet" and "Jet Wheels" toys are produced by Jet Mechanics of Argentina.

Buick Riviera....................................$12–15
Camaro, metallic blue-green, 1:64..........$8–10
Dodge Charger $8–10
1976 Ford Taunus, 1:64......................$8–10
Lamborghini Countach, red $12–15
Mercury Cougar $10–12

JNG

From an otherwise unknown brand comes a replica DeTomaso Pantera in 1:45 scale.

DeTomaso Pantera, lime green, 1:45 ....$18–30

Joal

Joal Juguetes y Herrajes
JOAL, S.A.
Avda. de la industria, 12 Apdo.
47 03440 IBI (Alicante) SPAIN
phone: (96) 555 08 01 or 555 08 02
fax: (96) 555 07 65
website: www.joal.es

Since 1949, Juguetes Joal S.A., primarily manufacturers of 1:50 and 1:32 scale diecast construction models, has been based in Spain. Recently, Irwin Toy Limited of Toronto, Canada, established a short-lived marketing agreement whereupon they issued a set of six vintage sports cars dubbed the Joal Classics Collection. The models are detailed, accurate, and realistic, with opening doors, hoods, and trunks. Models possess an ephemeral charm that is not often reproduced these days. Gaps in numbering indicates there may be other models from which these six were selected.

Joal models are currently manufactured in Macau and marketed in the U.S. by Intermarket-Carmania
Skylake Industrial Park
19591 NE 10th Ave., Bay E
North Miami Beach, FL 33179
phone: 305-651-8887
fax: 305-651-7131
contact Gus Moris

Joal Classics Collection by Irwin

50100 Jaguar E Cabriolet, British racing green with beige interior $8–10

50107 Mercedes-Benz 300SL Cabriolet, black with red interior..........................$8–10

50109 Mercedes-Benz 230SL, white with black roof, red interior............................$8–10

50111 Porsche Carrera 6 Deslizante, white with blue doors and hood....................$8–10

50125 Lamborghini Miura 6 P-400 Deslizante, yellow.....................................$8–10

50114 Ferrari 250 LeMans, red $8–10

Joal Heavy Equipment and Other Models

100 Jaguar E Type Roadster, 1:43 ....$30
101 Simca 1000 ....$25
102 Renault R 8 ....$25

103 Seat 850 Coupe $25
104 Renault R 10 ....$25
105 Alfa Romeo Giulia TZ1 Canguro $25
106 Seat 124 ....$25
107 Mercedes-Benz 300SL..............$25
108 Chevrolet Monza $25
109 Mercedes-Benz 230SL Hardtop $25
110 Mercedes-Benz 230SL Roadster $25
111 Porsche Carrera 6 ....$25
112 Alfa Romeo Giulia 55 ....$25
113 Chaparral 2F............................$25
114 Ferrari 250 Le Mans $25
115 Iso Rivolta Coupe, 1:43 ....$25
116 Ferrari 612 Can-Am $25
117 Mercedes-Benz C-III $25
118 Adams Probe 16 ....$25
119 Ferrari 512S, 1:43 ....$35
120 Twin Mill $25
121 Porsche 917K............................$25
122 McLaren M80 ....$25
123 Fiat (Seat) 132 4-Door Sedan, 1:43 ....$16
124 Mercedes 350SL Coupe, 1:43 .....$16
125 Lamborghini Miura Coupe, 1:43 ...$16 (see 50125 above)
126 Citroën SM $25
127 Citroën CX Pallas $25
128 Chrysler 150 ....$25
129 Ford Fiesta $25
149 Volvo Coach, 240mm, 1:50........$18
151 Mercedes-Benz 230SL and Trailer ..$25
152 Citroën CX Pallas and Trailer..........$25
153 Citroën SM, Ford Fiesta and Trailer .$25
154 Wrecker and Ford Fiesta $25
155 Chrysler 150, Ferrari Formula I and Trailer $25
160 Akerman H-7C Digger, 160mm, 1:50 ....$16
161 JCB-930 Tough Terrain Forklift, 146mm, 1:35 ....$16
162 JCB-801 Mini Backhoe Excavator, 146mm, 1:35 ....$16
163 Volvo L-70 with Pallet Fork, 170mm, 1:50 ....$16
164 Volvo-70 with Snow Blade, 173mm, 1:50 ....$16
165 Volvo-70 with Handing Arm, 215mm, 1:50 ....$16
166 JCB 525-58 with Pallet Fork, 210mm, 1:35 ....$16
167 Volvo A-35 Cement Mixer, 245mm, 1:50 ....$19
168 PPM 530 ATT Crane, 1:50..........$40
169 PPM Superstacker, 1:50 ....$34
170 Volvo A-35 Grapple Stacker, 260mm, 1:50 ....$22
171 Carmix Mixer, 161mm, 1:50........$16
172 Akerman H-25D Excavator, 210mm, 1:50 ....$22
173 Fire Engine, 215mm, 1:50............$24
174 CAT D5C Tractor, 79mm, 1:50 ....$14
175 JCB 4CX Sitemaster Backhoe Loader, 345mm, 1:35 ....$28

176 International Transport, 350mm, 1:50..$16
177 CAT 918F Wheel Loader, 265mm, 1:25..$30
178 Valmet 4-Wheel Tractor, 140mm, 1:35..$14
179 Valmet 8-Wheel Tractor, 140mm, 1:35..$16
180 Akerman EC620ME Digger, 250mm, 1:50..$24
181 Volvo L70C Wheel Loader, 1:50....$16
182 Agusta Helicopter, 220mm $14
183 Komatsu PC400 LC Excavator, 425mm, 1:32..................................$48
184 CAT IT18F Loader, 280mm, 1:25 .$32
185 JCB 4CX Centermount Backhoe Loader, 345mm, 1:35..................................$30
186 Komatsu PC400 EX, 1:32............$58
187 BT Forklifts and Pallet Lift, 1:25 ....$24
188 BT RT1350SE Forklift $16
189 Caterpillar 375 Excavator, 1:50....$24
191 Valmet Pulling Tractor, 1:35 ....$16
192 Massey Ferguson Skat 516 Load, 1:32..$16
200 Aveling Dump Truck, 1:43............$14
200 Leyland Dumper $25
200 Leyland Dumper "Construccion" $25
201 Taylor Crane Truck $25
201 Taylor Crane Truck "Autopistas"......$25
202 Albion Cement Mixer, 1:43 ....$14
203 Massey Ferguson Tractor $25
204 Farm Trailer $12
205 Farm Pulverisator..........................$12
206 Massey Ferguson Tractor with Mechanical Shovel $25
207 Pegaso Truck with Boat Motor $25
208 Pegaso Tanker, "BUTANO"..........$25
209 Pegaso Tanker, "CAMPSA"..........$25
210 Bulldozer $25
211 Pegaso Multibucket......................$25
212 Pegaso Articulated Truck..............$25
213 Caterpillar 935 Traxcavator..........$25
213 CAT-955/L Track-Type Loader, 100mm, 1:50..................................$18
214 CAT-920 Wheel Loader, 123mm, 1:50..$16
215 CAT-V80F Lift Truck, 113mm, 1:25 ..$16
216 CAT-225 Hydraulic Excavator, 216mm, 1:43..$18
217 CAT-12-G Leveller/Road Grader, 168, 1:50..$18
218 Cat 825-B Compactor, 147mm, 1:43..$16
219 CAT 631-D Wheel Tractor Scraper, 204mm, 1:70..................................$18
220 CAT D-10 Chain Tractor, 150mm, 1:70..$18
221 Steam Roller, 114mm, 1:50..........$12
222 CAT-631 Tilt Tractor, 173mm, 1:70 .$16
223 CAT-773 Truck, 133mm, 1:70......$14
224 CAT-591 Pipelayer, 105mm, 1:50.$22
225 CAT Digging Crane, 260mm, 1:43..$20

226 CAT-518 Grapple Skidder, 193mm, 1:43 ....$16

227 Volvo BM L-160 Wheel Loader, 160mm, 1:50 ....$16

228 Euclid R-32 Dump Truck, 160mm, 1:50 ....$16

229 CAT "V" Snow Plough with Spreader, 175mm, 1:43 ....$16

230 Volvo BM 6300 Excavator Loader, 210mm, 1:50 ....$22

231 Volvo BM A-25 Articulated Dump Truck, 195mm, 1:50 ....$16

232 Akerman EW200 Wheel Backloader/Excavator, 1:50 ....$16

233 CAT Challenger 65 Tractor, 122mm, 1:50 ....$16

234 Volvo L-70 Wheel Loader, 148mm, 1:50 ....$16

235 Volvo L-70 Skidder, 160mm, 1:50.$16

236 Akerman Telescopic Crane, 205mm, 1:50 ....$18

237 Volvo BM L-160 High Lift, 212mm, 1:50 ....$19

238 Volvo BM A-35 Articulated Dumper, 216mm, 1:50 ....$18

239 Michigan L-320 Wheel Loader, 217, 1:50 ....$19

240 New Holland TX-34 Combine Harvester, 227mm, 1:42 ....$22

241 Volvo L-160 Compactor, 160mm, 1:50 ....$16

242 Euclid R-858 Dump Truck, 205mm, 1:50 ....$24

243 JCB 435 Track-Type Loader, 211mm, 1:35 ....$19

244 CAT CB-534 Compactor with Cab, 99mm, 1:50 ....$14

245 JCB 525-58 Telescopic Loader, 210mm, 1:35 ....$16

246 JCB 712 Dump Truck, 72mm, 1:35 ....$16

247 New Holland TX-34 Combine Harvester with Maice (Corn) Head, 254mm, 1:42 ....$22

248 CAT CB-534 Compactor, 99mm, 1:50 ....$14

249 Akerman H7C with Hydraulic Hammer, 160mm, 1:50 ....$16

250 Ebro 6100 Tractor, 117mm, 1:38.$16

251 Ebro 6100 Tractor and Trailer with Hay Bails, 255mm, 1:38 ....$24

252 Ebro 6100 Tractor with Sprayer, 260mm, 1:50 ....$14

253 CAT Challenger 65 with Disc Harrow, 230mm, 1:50 ....$22

254 Valmet Tractor with Grapple Skidder Trailer, 363mm, 1:35 ....$29

320 Heavy Duty Transporter with #216, 363mm $29

321 Heavy Duty Transporter with #220, 363mm $29

322 Heavy Duty Transporter with #229, 363mm $29

323 Heavy Duty Transporter with #225, 363mm $29

324 Heavy Duty Transporter with #227, 363mm $29

325 Heavy Duty Transporter with #237, 363mm $29

326 Heavy Duty Transporter with #182, 363mm $24

387 CAT IT18F Tool Carrier, 1:25........$39

John Day Models (also see Precision Autos)

When it comes to precision handmade models, John Day's name seems to keep cropping up. The latest is a miniature Shelby Cobra allegedly from John Day Models. As reported by its owner Bob Shapton, it has no markings and is very heavy for its size. Evaluation is difficult, so the value below is an educated guess.

Shelby Cobra, 1:43 scale, blue $250–500

John Smith (see Smith Family Toys)

Johnny Lightnings (also see Topper Toys)

Johnny Lightnings were originally produced by Topper Toys, owned by Henry Orenstein, from 1969 to 1971. But charges of business fraud forced Orenstein out of business.

Twenty-three years later, Thomas E. Lowe, a businessman who remembers as a kid the toy cars that beat Hot Wheels on their own track, purchased the Johnny Lightnings license to reproduce several of the original designs in a commemorative series under the new company name of Playing Mantis. The series has proven itself so popular with collectors that ten color variations, limited to 10,000 each, have been issued during 1994, and indicated as series A through J.

In 1995, Playing Mantis made a major departure from its original direction by creating all-new models called Muscle Machines, relying on the popularity of the brand name and the passion for American muscle cars. Each model/color variation is produced in limited quantities of 20,000 or less.

Johnny Lightnings really took off in 1996, with many new issues. Dragsters USA feature popular funny cars from the seventies, eighties, and nineties. Indy Race Cars and Pace Cars consist of a two-pack of one Indy winning race car and the corresponding pace car for that year. Wacky Winners are the brainchild of Tom Daniel, noted automotive designer with a flair for the bizarre.

Aside from all the regular production models, several promotional models were issued as well. By special order, private individuals, groups, and dealers had various models reproduced with special markings to designate them as promotionals for their business or organiza-tion. All are listed below following a chronology of the original Topper line.

Johnny Lightnings by Topper, 1969 to 1971

1969 (Prices listed first are for mint condition out of package, then for models in original blister pack.)

Leapin Limo $35–40; $75

Custom GTO $125–150; $250
Custom El Camino.....$125–150; $250
Custom T-Bird.............$80–100; $150
Custom Toronado........$80–100; $175
Custom Eldorado...........$60–80; $125
Custom Mako Shark, doors open $75–100; $125
Custom Mako Shark, doors don't open $25–30; $50
Custom XKE, doors open .$75–100; $125
Custom XKE, doors don't open $25–30; $50
Custom Ferrari, doors open $90–110; $135
Custom Ferrari, doors don't open $25–30; $50
Custom Turbine, painted interior $75–100; $125
Custom Turbine, unpainted interior $15–20; $30
Custom Dragster $15–25; $35
Custom '32 Ford $25–30; $40

1970
Nucleon $30–40; $60
Vicious Vette..................$30–35; $45
Frantic Ferrari $15–20; $30
Jumpin Jag $20–25; $35
Sand Stormer $15–20; $30
Vulture $40–50; $70
Sling Shot $25–30; $45
Flame Out $35–40; $55
TNT...............................$25–30; $40
Al Unser Indy Special $30–35; $65
A.J.Foyt Indy Special $30–35; $65
Parnelli Jones Indy Special .$30–35; $65
Double Trouble...............$35–40; $75
Triple Threat $20–30; $40
Bug Bomb $25–35; $45
Condor $70–85; $120
Movin Van.....................$15–25; $35
Mad Maverick $20–30; $45
Wasp $35–45; $65
Baja $35–45; $70
Whistler $45–55; $100
Custom Spoiler...............$15–25; $35
Smuggler.......................$20–30; $40
Stiletto $10–20; $35

1970 Jet Powered Cars
Flying Needle $20–30; $40
Wedge $20–30; $40
Screamer $20–25; $35
Glasser $25–35; $45
Monster $15–20; $30
Bubble $20–25; $35
1971 Custom Cars
Wild Winner $40–50; $90
Pipe Dream $40–50; $90
Big Rig $40–50; $90
Twin Blaster $40–50; $90
Prototypes (cars planned but never put into production)
Custom Mustang $2,000–3,000
Custom Camaro $2,000–3,000
Custom Charger $2,000–3,000
Custom Continental $2,000–3,000

Johnny Lightning Commemoratives by Playing Mantis, 1994

Each model has been produced in ten different color variations and designated Series A through J. Polished metalflake colors include cherry red, emerald green, slate blue, light purple, and chocolate, while high-gloss enamel colors are black, yellow, turquoise, and hot pink. Aside from the regular issues listed below, exclusive sets were issued by FAO Schwarz in red, gold, silver, or blue chrome colors.

101 Custom El Camino, 1994 .... $4–6
for FAO Schwarz version $12–15
102 Custom GTO, 1994 .... $4–6
for FAO Schwarz version $12–15

103 Custom XKE, 1994 .... $4–6
for FAO Schwarz version $12–15

104 '32 Roadster, 1994 .... $4–6
for FAO Schwarz version $12–15
105 Bug Bomb, 1994 .... $4–6
for FAO Schwarz version $12–15
106 Movin' Van, 1994 .... $4–6
for FAO Schwarz version $12–15
107 Vicious Vette, 1994 .... $4–6
for FAO Schwarz version $12–15
108 The Wasp, 1994 .... $4–6
for FAO Schwarz version $12–15

Johnny Lightning Commemoratives Round 2 by Playing Mantis, 1995

111 Custom T-Bird, 1995 .... $5–8
113 Custom Spoiler, 1995 .... $4–6
114 Custom Mako Shark, 1995 .... $4–6
115 Custom Turbine, 1995 .... $4–6
116 Triple Threat, 1995 .... $4–6
117 Nucleon, 1995 .... $4–6

118 T.N.T., 1995 .... $4–6

109 Custom Continental, 1995 .... $4–6

110 Custom Toronado, 1995 .... $4–6

112 Custom Mustang, 1995 .... $4–6

Johnny Lightning Cartoon Network by Playing Mantis, 1998

Speed Buggy $5
Fred Flintstone's Sports Car $5
Penelope Pitstop's Compact Pussycat $5
Dick Dastardly's Mean Machine $5

Johnny Lightning Classic Customs Corvettes by Playing Mantis, 1997

This series documents some of the classic prototypes devised by Chevrolet Corvette designers.

Sting Ray III $6–8
Corvette Indy $6–8
Aerovette $6–8
1954 Nomad $6–8
1965 Mako Shark $6–8
1967 Coupe 427 .... $6–8
1962 Roadster $6–8
1957 Roadster $6–8
1995 ZR-1 .... $6–8
1982 T-Top $6–8

Johnny Lightning Classic Gold by Playing Mantis, 1998–1999

'70 Cougar XR-7
Release 1 - red $4–5
Release 2 - grabber green $4–5
Release 3 - orange $4–5
'63 Impala
Release 1 - red $4–5
Release 2 - black $4–5
Release 3 - white $4–5
'69 SC/Rambler
Release 1 - snow white $4–5
Release 2 - white $4–5
Release 3 - white $4–5
'56 Chevy
Release 1 - copper $4–5
Release 2 - blue bottom $4–5

Release 3 - white (top) /coral (bottom) . $4–5
33 Willys Gasser
Release 1 - pale orange $4–5
Release 2 - red $4–5
Release 3 - blue $4–5
T-Type/Grand National
Release 1 - silver $4–5
Release 2 - black $4–5
Release 3 - black/silver $4–5
'65/66 Shelby Mustang $4–5
Release 1 - dark green $4–5
Release 2 - white $4–5
Release 3 - red $4–5
'69 Camaro
Release 1 - orange-red $4–5
Release 2 - red $4–5
Release 3 - blue $4–5
'70 Olds 442/Cutlass
Release 1 - blue $4–5
Release 2 - red $4–5
Release 3 - black $4–5
'74 Olds Cutlass
Release 1 - light blue $4–5
Release 2 - gold $4–5
Release 3 - almond beige $4–5

Johnny Lightning Dragsters U.S.A. by Playing Mantis, 1996

Commemorating the wildest funny cars on the dragstrip are these 1:64 scale replicas. Each one is issued in its original color plus several other color combinations.

Shirley Shahan's '69 Drag-On Lady $3–4
Roland Leong's '71 Hawaiian $3–4
Raymond Beadle's '71 Blue Max $3–4
Roger Lindamood's '72 Color Me Gone . $3–4
Al Bergler's '71 Motown Shaker $3–4
Pat Minick's '72 Chi-Town Hustler $3–4
Ed McCulloch's '71 Revellution $3–4
Richard Earle's '58 Christine $3–4
Tony Foti's '92 LAPD $3–4
Norm Wizner's '55 Jukebox $3–4
Ronnie Sox's '71 Sox & Martin $3–4

Johnny Lightning Dragsters U.S.A. Round 2 by Playing Mantis, 1997

Why I've never seen or heard of these models until August 1997 is beyond me. They are modern funny cars offered through Full Grid Racing & Diecast, and possibly nowhere else. Only 20,000 of each model and color variation are produced.

Pioneer $5
Rug Doctor $5
Otter Pops $5
Sentry Gauges $5
Kendall $5
Burnouts $5
Mooneyes $5
Western Auto $5
Fast Orange $5

Johnny Lightning Dragsters U.S.A. Round 3 by Playing Mantis, 1997

More models commemorating the wildest funny cars on the dragstrip are these 1:64

scale replicas. Each one is issued in its original color plus several other color combinations.

Jungle Jim Liberman	$3–4
Texas Gene Snow's Snowman	$3–4
Wild Willy Borsch's Wildman	$3–4
Big Daddy Don Garlits	$3–4
Ramchargers	$3–4
Barry Setzer	$3–4
Don Schumacher's Wonder Wagon	$3–4
Mr. Norm's Super Charger	$3–4
Bob Banning Dodge	$3–4
Trojan Horse	$3–4
White Lightning Funny Car	$8–12

Johnny Lightning Dragsters USA Summerfest by Playing Mantis, 1997

Special "stars & stripes" decorative accents set these models apart from the usual "Dragsters" line-up. Two models issued in two color versions comprise this four-car set for around $25. Only 15,000 sets produced.

Johnny Lightning Dragsters USA Platinum Issue by Playing Mantis, 1997

Not available at any mass-market stores, these dragsters consist of all diecast bodies, Cragar rims, Goodyear rubber tires, and more. Only 10,000 produced.

Pabst Blue Ribbon	$12–15
Pure Hell	$12–15

Johnny Lightning Funny Car Legends by Playing Mantis, 1998–1999

Jungle Jim, Jim Liberman	$4–5
USA-1, Bruce Larson	$4–5
Flying Dutchman, Al Vander Woude	$4–5

Johnny Lightning Frightning Lightning by Playing Mantis, 1996

Scarier and scarier is Johnny Lightning's Frightning Lightning series featuring some bizarre inventions from some of this planet's most innovative custom car designers. Tom Daniel's influence is seen in this series that includes the famous car from *Ghostbusters* fame and the possessed homicidal Plymouth named Christine from the horror thriller *The Car.*

Haulin Hearse	$4–6
Elvira Macabre Mobile	$4–6
Boothill Express	$4–6
Vampire Van	$4–6
The Mysterion	$4–6
Christine	$4–6

Johnny Lightning Holiday Dragsters by Playing Mantis, 1996

Series A:
Nitro Santa, red	$10–15
Roarin' Rudolph, silver	$10–15

Series B:
Nitro Santa, gold	$10–15
Roarin' Rudolph, green	$10–15

Johnny Lightning Hollywood on Wheels by Playing Mantis, 1998 – 2000+

Back to the Future Delorean	$5–6
Blues Brothers Bluesmobile	$5–6

Austin Powers Shaguar $3

Lost in Space Chariot $5

Lost in Space Jupiter 2 ....$5

Lost in Space Robot $5

Nash Bridges $5

Blues Brothers 2000 Bluesmobile	$5–6
Dragnet Detective's Car	$5–6
The Monkee's Monkeemobile	$8–10
Partridge Family Bus	$5–6

Sheriff Taylor's Squad Car from the Andy Griffith Show	$5–6
Starsky and Hutch's Torino	$7–8

Johnny Lightning Hot Rods by Playing Mantis, 1997

These are 1:64 scale diecast replicas of

Walker, Texas Ranger $5

real street rods. Production of 15,000 or less is guaranteed for each model.

'29 Crew Cab	$4–5
Rumblur	$4–5
Bumongous	$4–5
Frankenstude	$4–5
Tom Hammond's '69 Pro Street Chevelle	$4–5
Mike Lloyd's '72 Goin' Goat GTO	$4–5
Pro Street Camaro	$4–5
'62 Bad Bird T-Bird	$4–5
Beastmobile	$4–5
Flathead Flyer	$4–5

Johnny Lightning Hummer Series, 1999

Civilian Wagon	$4–5
Off Road Racer	$4–5
Military Humvee	$4–5
Rescue Vehicle	$4–5

Johnny Lightning Indy 500 Champions and Pace Cars by Playing Mantis, 1996

Two-packs include the winning Indianapolis 500 racer for the selected year, along with the pace car for that race.

1969 Mario Andretti and 1969 Chevy Camaro	$5–6
1970 Al Unser and 1970 Olds 442	$5–6
1974 Johnny Rutherford and 1974 Hurst Olds	$5–6
1975 Bobby Unser and 1975 Buick Century	$5–6
1977 A. J. Foyt and 1977 Olds Delta 88	$5–6
1978 Al Unser and 1978 Chevy Corvette	$5–6
1979 Rick Mears and 1979 Ford Mustang	$5–6
1992 Al Unser Jr. and 1992 Cadillac Allante	$5–6

Johnny Lightning James Bond 007 by Playing Mantis, 1998

"Dr. No" Sunbeam Convertible, Atlantic blue	$5–6
"Thunderball" 1964 Aston Martin, platinum pearl	$5–6
"Goldeneye" 1964 Aston Martin, platinum pearl	$5–6
"Goldfinger" Mustang Convertible, white	$5–6

"You Only Live Twice" Toyota 2000GT Convertible, white $5–6

"On Her Majesty's Secret Service" Cougar Convertible, red $5–6

"Diamonds are Forever" Mustang Mach 1, red $5–6

"The Spy Who Loved Me" Lotus Espirit, white...$5–6

"For Your Eyes Only" Lotus Espirit, apricot .$5–6

"The Living Daylights" 1987 Aston Martin, black...$5–6

Johnny Lightning MAGMAs, 1:43 Scale by Playing Mantis

1968 Chevy Camaro $8
1970 Dodge Challenger T/A...............$8
1971 Ford Mustang Boss 351 ....$8
1971 Ford Mustang Mach 1 ....$8
1971 Plymouth Roadrunner..................$8
The Munsters Drag-U-La......................$8
Al Unser Johnny Lightning Special $8
T'rantula $8

Johnny Lightning Muscle Cars by Playing Mantis, 1995

According to the package, "each car is painted in several of these 16 famous Musclepaint™ colors mixed from GM, Ford & Chrysler's original paint formulas!" ...Grabber Blue, Plum Crazy, Daytona Yellow, Sublime, Gold Rush, Vitamin-C Orange, Blue Fire, Starlight Black, Moulin Rouge, Glacier Blue, Rallye Green, Tor-Red, Quicksilver, Aspen Green, Cameo White, Champagne.

'70 Superbird..................................$4–5
'71 Hemi 'Cuda $4–5
'70 Boss 302 ....$4–5
'70 Super Bee $4–5
'69 GTO "The Judge" $4–5
'70 Chevelle SS $4–5
'69 Cougar Eliminator $4–5
'69 Olds 442 ....$4–5
'65 GTO Ragtop $4–5
'72 Nova SS $4–5

Johnny Lightning Muscle Cars Round 2 by Playing Mantis, 1996-97

So popular was this series that Tom Lowe decided to continue it with all new castings and a larger number of colors.

'66 Chevrolet Malibu $3–4
'68 Ford Shelby GT-500 Mustang $3–4
'68 Dodge Charger $3–4
'69 Pontiac Firebird...........................$3–4
'69 Plymouth Roadrunner $3–4
'70 Dodge Challenger $3–4
'70 Buick GSX $3–4
'72 AMC Javelin AMX $3–4

Johnny Lightning Muscle Cars USA by Playing Mantis, 1998–99

'67 Pontiac GTO...............................$4
'68 Chevy Chevelle $4
'70 Plymouth AAR 'Cuda $4
'71 Pontiac GTO "The Judge" $4
'70 AMC Rebel Machine $4
'65 Chevy II Nova $4

'70 Dodge Challenger T/A $4

Johnny Lightning Mustang Classics by Playing Mantis, 1998

1963 Mustang II Concept $4–5
1967 Mustang Shelby GT $4–5
1968 Mustang GT $4–5
1969 Mustang Mach $4–5
1973 Mustang Mach I $4–5
1975 Mustang Cobra II Racer $4–5
1977 Mustang Cobra II $4–5
1988 Mustang GT $4–5
1994 Mustang Boss $4–5
1998 Mustang Saleen Racer $4–5

Johnny Lightning Official Pace Cars by Playing Mantis, 1999

1968 Ford Torino $3–4
1969 Camaro $3–4
1970 Oldsmobile 442 ....$3–4
1971 Dodge Challenger $3–4
1972 Hurst Oldsmobile $3–4
1973 Cadillac Eldorado $3–4
1974 Hurst Oldsmobile $3–4
1977 Oldsmobile Delta 88 ....$3–4
1978 Chevrolet Corvette $3–4
1979 Ford Mustang $3–4
1992 Cadillac Allante........................$3–4
1998 Chevrolet Corvette Convertible ...$3–4

Johnny Lightning Racing Dreams by Playing Mantis, 1998

Playing Mantis produced a series for their Johnny Lightning line called "Racing Dreams," race cars with imaginative markings of your favorite cereal, candy, movie, or TV show. One of the cars commemorates the James Bond movie *Goldfinger*. Release A offers a series of funny cars, Release B is an assortment of stock cars.

Release A

Nintendo Star Fox 64 ....$5–7
Pepsi $5–7
DQ Dilly Bar $5–7
Army $5–7
Trix $5–7
James Bond Goldfinger $5–7
Jurassic Park The Ride $5–7
Popsicle $5–7
Mooneyes...................................$5–7
Hershey's $5–7

Release B

Super Mario 64 ....$5–7
Lucky Charms $5–7
T.G.i. Fridays..............................$5–7
U.S. Coast Guard $5–7
Planters $5–7
Pez $5–7

Johnny Lightning Showstoppers Series 1 by Playing Mantis, 1998

Chuck Poole's Chuck Wagon..............$5–6
Bill "Maverick" Golden's L'il Red Wagon .$5–6
Bob Riggle' Hemi Express $5–6
Dodge Rebellion $5–6

Johnny Lightning Showstoppers Series 2 by Playing Mantis, 1998

Bob Riggle's Hemi Under Glass $5–6

Joe Schubeck's Hairy Olds $5–6
Arnie Beswick's Tameless Tiger $5–6
Bill Shrewsberry's L.A. Dart $5–6

Johnny Lightning "Speed Racer" Series by Playing Mantis, 1997

Commemorating the cult classic cartoon, Playing Mantis has issued several models from the Japanese animated TV series introduced to America in 1967. Four 1:64 scale models have been produced in the original colors as sets for $16 or in single packs with various colors for $4 each. Sets include:

1. The Mach 5 (Speed Racer's car)......$5–6
2. Racer X's (Speed's long-lost brother, Rex Racer) $5–6
3. The "Fastest Car" (the GR-X) $5–6
4. The "Assassin Car".........................$5–6

Johnny Lightning Speed Rebels by Playing Mantis, 1997

"10 great cars in a brand new scale" is how Fred Blood of Full Grid describes these models of classic custom American cars, although just what scale that is he doesn't say.

Vicious Villain $2–3
Street Freak $2–3
Speed King.....................................$2–3
Dominator.......................................$2–3
Rat Attack $2–3
Wing Thing $2–3
Big Boss $2–3
Goat Buster $2–3
Alley Cat $2–3
Spoiler $2–3

Johnny Lightning Stock Car Legends, 1998
Johnny Lightning Top Fuel Legends, 1999
Johnny Lightning Truckin' America, 1998

Classic Pickup Trucks in 1:64 scale.

1929 Ford Model A $4–5
1940 Ford $4–5
1950 Ford F-1 ....$4–5
1955 Chevrolet Cameo $4–5
1958 Chevrolet El Camino $4–5
60s Studebaker Champ $4–5
1971 Chevrolet El Camino $4–5
1978 L'il Red Express $4–5
1991 GMC Syclone $4–5
1998 Dodge Ram $4–5

Johnny Lightning United States Postal Service American Truck & Samp Collection, 1999

These are promoted as authentic replicas of America's most famous truck and U. S. postage stamps.

Space Fantasy................................$4–5
Dramatic Dinosaurs $4–5
Riverboats......................................$4–5
Endangered Species $4–5
Prehistoric Animals...........................$4–5
Space Discovery $4–5

Johnny Lightning Wacky Winners by Playing Mantis, 1996

Tom Daniel has designed some crazy cars for Monogram Model Company, but this is his first venture into diecast miniatures. Some of his wackiest creations are captured in these Johnny Lightning replicas from Playing Mantis.

Root Beer Wagon.............................$3–4
Badman $3–4

Bad Medicine.................................$3–4

Bad News $3–4

Cherry Bomb.................................$3–4

Draggin' Wagon.............................$3–4

Garbage Truck..............................$3–4

Tijuana Taxi.................................$3–4

T'rantula.....................................$3–4

Trouble Maker..............................$3–4

Johnny Lightning Exclusive Sets by Playing Mantis, 1996

Dragsters USA at Service Merchandise and Hills, Limited Edition of 4,800 each packaged in display box ....$15–20 each
VW VANS at Venture, 4,800 each, two-tone black and red, or two-tone sky blue and antique white ....$20–25 each
'56 Chevys at Ames, 4,800 each, 2-tone Nassau Blue & Harbour Blue, or 2-tone India Ivory & Matador Red .$20–25 each

Johnny Lightning "Members Only" Cars by Playing Mantis

Subscribres to the NewsFlash newsletter have an opportunity to purchase exclusive variations of Johnny Lightning models not offered anywhere else. Many are already sold out and only available from second market dealers. Values are rising steadily on these very limited edition models.

1956 Chevrolet BelAir (sold out) $25–30
1965 Dodge A-100 Pickup (sold out) .$25–30
1960s Volkswagen Van (sold out)....$25–30
1996 White Lightnings (set of 10, sold out)....................................$40–50
1996 Toy Fair Car, "Ride the Storm" (only 800 made, sold out)..............$75–100
Plymouth Prowler............................$10–12
1965 Dodge A-100 Little Red Wagon..............................$15–20

1998 Volkswagen Concept One $10–12
Volkswagen "Thing" Kubelwagen.....$10–12
1933 Hot Rod Willy's...................$10–12

Johnny Lightning Promotional Models by Playing Mantis

Several businesses and dealers have contracted with Playing Mantis to issue special promotional models especially made for them. Below are listed the models with color variation, production quantity, markings, who the promoter is, and their phone number to reach them.

1956 Chevy BelAir
v.1 Hot Pink, 5000 made, "Sweet Little Rock n Roller," $25–40
Mike Stead, 1-818-558-8099
v.2 Seafoam, 5000 made, car hop picture $25–40
Mike Stead, 1-818-558-8099
v.3 Cherry Red, 5000 made, "Steadly Quickwheels," $25–40
Mike Stead, 1-818-558-8099

Dodge A-100 Pickup
v.1 Pearl White, 5000 made, blue flames with "Pyromaniac," ...$25–40
Bob Goforth, 1-510-889-6676
v.2 Purple, 5000 made, "Purple Hazed Express," $25–40
Mike Stead, 1-818-558-8099
v.3 Black, 5000 made, "Bad to the Bone,"..............................$25–40
Mike Stead, 1-818-558-8099
v.4 Red with Astroblades wheels, 10,000 made, Little Red Wagon.......$20–30
Bill "Maverick" Golden
v.5 Red with Cragar SS wheels, 10,000 made, Little Red Wagon, Playing Mantis..............................$20–30

1954 Sedan Delivery
v.1 Cherry Red, 5000 made, Lane Automotive Logo $25–40
Lane Automotive, 1-800-772-2682
v.2 *Gold Rush and Purple, 2,500 made, "Johnny Lightning" ....$
Eastwood Company, 1-800-343-9353
v.3 *Quick Silver and Purple, 2,500 made, "Johnny Lightning" .$90–120
Eastwood Company, 1-800-343-9353
*both packaged with Lionel train
v.4 Cherry Red, 5000 made, "Steadly's Toy Fair '96,"...................$40–50
Steadly Quickwheels, 1-818-558-8099

1987 Buick Grand National
v.1 Black with Astroblades wheels, 5,000 made, no markings..$40–50
Toy Time, 1-508-827-5261
v.2 Black with Cragar SS wheels, 5,000 made, no markings............$40–50
Toy Time, 1-508-827-5261

Custom XKE
v.1 Cherry red, 3500 made $40–50
Steadly Quickwheels, 1-818-558-8099

Johnny Lightning Miscellaneous Models

1970 Ford Torino Cobra, 1:64 ....$7–9

American Chrome 1958 Chevrolet Impala..$5–7

American Chrome 1955 Ford Crown Victoria $5–7

American Chrome 1957 Lincoln Premiere $5–7

America's Finest – Michigan State Police GMC Suburban $5–7

Shelby AC Cobra.............................$4–6

Show Rods Barris Kopper Kart $7–10

Johnny Lightning Sizzlers by Playing Mantis, 1996–97

The original Sizzlers by Mattel represented the first commercial application of Nickel Cadmium (NiCad) rechargeable batteries. Now, since Mattel has abandoned the Sizzlers name, it was then purchased by the Centuri/Estes model rocket company. Playing Mantis has since negotiated a licensing contract with Centuri/Estes for the exclusive right to market toy cars using the trademark. The first of the new Sizzlers from Playing Mantis showed up in WalMart on December 1, 1996. As with most Johnny Lightnings, each Sizzlers model is issued in at least eight color variations.

'68 Racing Camaro $8–10
Trans Am Firebird.............................$8–10
'71 Hemi 'Cuda $8–10
Camaro Highway Patrol $8–10
Viper GTS.......................................$8–10
Sting Ray III $8–10
Whistler Mustang..............................$8–10
Rain-X Camaro $8–10

For more information on Johnny Lightnings and how to receive the quarterly NewsFlash newsletter, contact:

Playing Mantis
P O Box 3688
3600 McGill Street, Suite 300
South Bend, IN 46619-3688
phone: 800-MANTIS-8

Jolly Roger

Jolly Roger diecast toys are made in England. The line includes a few Gasquy-Septoy reissues.

Jouef

Until its bankruptcy in 1996, the head office for Jouef was in Champagnole, France, with US distribution based in Mequon, Wisconsin.

Plastic models were once the predominant Jouef product, but recently the company has produced an exceptional assortment of diecast models in 1:18, 1:24, and 1:43 scale. Dubbed Jouef Evolution, named after their flagship model Ferrari GTO Evoluzione, the models represented are high-quality replicas for a reasonable price.

Jouef 1:18 Scale
3002 Ferrari 250 GTO 64 ....$40
3005 Ferrari 330 P4 Spyder $40
3008 Ford GT 40, #6 Le Mans Winner 1969 ....$40

3001 Ferrari GTO Evoluzione $40

3012 Ferrari 250 GT SWB, Le Mans 1961 ....$40
3016 Ferrari 250 GTO, #27 Le Mans 1964 ....$40
3017 Ferrari 330 P4 Coupe B, #21 Le Mans 1967 ....$40
3018 Ferrari 412 P, #23 Le Mans 1967 (Limited Edition).........................$55
3019 Ford GT 40 Mk II, #21 Le Mans Winner 1966 ....$40
3021 Ford Mk II Street Version $40
3022 Ferrari 250 GT SWB, 1961, red.$40
3023 Ferrari 250 GT SWB, 1961, yellow $40
3024 Ferrari 412 P, #25 "N.A.R.T." Le Mans 1967 ....$40
3029 Ferrari 330 P4 Coupe $40
3030 Ferrari 330 P4 Coupe, #24 Le Mans 1967 ....$40
3031 Ferrari 330 P4 Spyder, Targa Florio 1976 ....$40
3101 Ford Mustang 350 GT, 1965 .....$40
3108 Ford Mustang Cobra Convertible 1994 Indy Pace Car, red $45
3110 Ford Mustang GT Convertible, 1994, red, teal, or yellow....................$40
3111 Ford Mustang GT Coupe, 1994, red, teal, or yellow $40
3119 Ford Mustang Cobra Coupe, 1994, Rio red, white, or black $40
3201 Porsche 911 RS 2.7 L, 1973, white/red $40
3203 Porsche 911 RS 2.7 L, 1973, yellow/black $40
3204 Porsche 911 RS 2.7 L, 1973, black/red $40
3205 Porsche 911 S 2.4, 1973, red ...$40
3301 Alfa Romeo Spyder $40
3302 Alfa Romeo Spyder with hard top .$40
3303 Alfa Romeo Spyder with soft top ...$40
3304 Alfa Romeo Spyder, open top $40
3501 Nissan 300 ZX, red $40
3502 Honda NS-X, gray $40
3503 Nissan 300 SX, gray.................$40
3504 Nissan 300 SX, yellow............$40

Jouef 1:24 Scale
3003 Ferrari 250 GTO 64 ....$25
3007 Ford GT 40.............................$25
3027 Ferrari 330 P 4 Spyder $30
3028 Ferrari 250 GTO, #25 Le Mans 1964 ....$35

Jouef 1:43 Scale
3000 Ferrari GTO Evoluzione..............$15
3004 Ferrari 250 GTO 64 ....$15
3006 Ford GT 40.............................$15

3009 Ferrari 330 P4.............................$15
3011 Ferrari 250 GT SWB, 1961 ....$15
3025 Ferrari 330 P 4, #2 Le Mans Winner
1966 ....$15
3026 Ford GT 40 Mk II, #2 Le Mans Winner 1966 ....$15
3202 Porsche 911 RS 2.7 L 73 ....$15

MGB MK 11 ....$15

Triumph, TR3.................................$15

Jouets de Paris (JEP)

The Societe Industrielle de Ferblanterie was founded in 1899. In 1928, the name Jouets de Paris was adopted, then later changed to Jouets en Paris (abbreviated J.E.P.), until 1965 when the company went out of business. A variety of models and materials make up this eclectic collection of toys from France, with a predominance of tinplate models. *The Golden Age of Automotive Toys 1925–1941* by Ken Hutchison and Greg Johnson showcases an exquisite assortment of rare tinplate JEPs in 1:11 and 1:16 scale valued at $1,500–10,000.

Delage Limousine, 13½", circa 1929.....$2,000
"Madeline-Bastille" Autobus, 10¼", circa
1928..................................$2,000
Peugeot, 1:43, 1958, plastic body, diecast
chassis.................................$150–200
Citroën DS19, 1:43, 1958, plastic body,
diecast chassis $150–200
Simca Versailles, 1:43. 1958, plastic body,
diecast chassis $150–200
Panhard Dyna, 1:43, 1958, plastic body,
diecast chassis $150–200
Renault Dauphine, 1:43, 1958, plastic body,
diecast chassis $150–200
Renault Town Car 40HP President of the Republic,
tinplate, 1:11 scale, 17".....$6,000–10,000

Joustra

The resemblance of Joustra diecast models of France to early Gama trucks indicates that Joustra may have manufactured these models under license from Gama, since most Joustra toys are tin windups.
Meiller Excavator Truck, 6¼".....................$40
Meiller Dump Truck, 4⅜".............................$40

JPS

BP 25
58130 - Guerigny
France
phone: 33 (0) 3 86 37 36 74
fax: 33 (0) 3 86 37 00
JPS008 JULES 6 roues Paris Dakar 1984......$40
JPS011 ALPINE A110 Ronde CÈvenome
1975 ....$40
JPS012 ALPINE GTA Production 1986 ....$40
JPS017 PEUGEOT DANGEL Paris Dakar
1986 ....$40
JPS018 2CV Proto $40
JPS020 MOTOR HOME RENAULT F1 ......$110
JPS021 RENAULT ESPACE "RENAULT F1," trans-
port motors $45
JPS022 RENAULT ESPACE phase 2, 4
colors $40
JPS023 SPICE C2 Le Mans 1990 #102 .....$40
JPS024 SPICE C2 Le Mans 1990 #116 .....$40
JPS025 ALPINE A110 Championnat Course de
Cûte 1977 ....$40
JPS027 MATRA 530 LX, 4 colors..............$40
JPS034 RENAULT 5 Turbo, 4 colors.........$40
JPS035 4CV Proto $40
JPS036 MATRA 530 "SONIA DELAUNAY" $40
JPS037 AUSTIN HEALEY "FROGEYES".......$40
JPS041 ALPINE A110 Rallye du Maroc
1974 ....$40
JPS042 HOTCHKISS 686GS Coach 1939, 3
colors $40
JPS045 N. S. U. Silhouette GR5 ....$40
JPS046 RENAULT ESPACE "Magy cours"....$40
JPS047 SALMSON 2300S CHARBONNEAUX .$40
JPS048 ALPINE A 610 ....$40
JPS049 ALPINE A 610 "Magy cours" $40
JPS050 BUGATTI 332 GP de Tours 1923...$40
JPS051 RENAULT ESPACE "Pompiers du Loir et
Cher" $45
JPS054 A. L. D. C289 Le Mans 1990 ....$40
JPS055 SPICE Le Mans 1993 #24 ....$40
JPS056 MATRA 530 SX $40
JPS057 HOTCHKISS 686GS Coupe 1939, 3
colors $40
JPS059 JEEP CHEROKEE "CHIEF" 2 portes, 2
colors $40
JPS061 JEEP CHEROKEE "LIMITED" Pompiers
Meurthe et Moselle $45
JPS062 RENAULT ESPACE Ambulance Pompiers
Meurthe et Moselle $45
JPS065 A. C. R. Le Mans 1980 ....$40
JPS071 ALPINE A 610 Le Mans 1994 ....$40
JPS073 Berlinette ECHAPPEMENT, 2 colors .$40
JPS074 VESPA 400, 3 colors....................$35
JPS075 CITROEN U55 "Chamboursy," camion
au 1/43 ....$75

JPS076 DEBORA Le Mans 1994................$40
JPS078 NISSAN TERRANO 2 Chassis court.$40
JPS079 PANHARD RIFFARD Le Mans 1953 #50
or 61 ....$40
JPS080 BUGATTI 251, version A, B, C $40
JPS081 Coffret BUGATTI 251, 3 versions + per-
sonnage $105
JPS082 CHEVRON B16 Le Mans 1970, version
A, B, C..............................$40
JPS083 Coffret CHEVRON B16 Le Mans 1970,
3 versions $100
JPS084 BUGATTI 32 "Juneck" avec person-
nage..............................$40
JPS086 ALPINE A 110 Rallye du Bandama
Pescarolo $40
JPS088 RENAULT 5 Turbo Rallye de Lorraine Didi-
er AURIOL $40
JPS089 RENAULT 5 Alpine Turbo Groupe 2 Didi-
er AURIOL $40
JPS090 Coffret RENAULT 5 Didier AURIOL, 2 kits
+ personnage $70
JPS091 RENAULT 5 Turbo 1, 2colors $40
JPS094 PEUGEOT 201C, a: coupe - b : décou-
vrable $40
JPS095 A. L. D. Le Mans 1994 ....$45
JPS096 ALPA Le Mans 1994 ....$40
JPS097 MAZDA KUDZU Le Mans 1995 .....$40
JPS103 WM P78 Le Mans 1978 ....$40
JPS105 DEBORA Le Mans 1995 ....$45
JPS107 TALBOT coupe 2,5l 1955 ....$45
JPS108 ALPINE A 310 Le Mans 1978 ....$45
JPS111 ALPINE A 610 1993, dernière version .$45
JPS100 N. S. U 1300 Groupe 2 J-P
SCHWARTZ $40
JPS112 RENAULT CLIO 16S GR N Tour de
Corse 1995 Mc OUDRY $45
JPS116 Barquette HOMMEL, 2 colors $45
JPS117 SPIDER RENAULT LEGEAY SPORT Essais
Le Mans 1996 #31 red $45
JPS118 SPIDER RENAULT LEGEAY SPORT Essais
Le Mans 1996 #32 blue $45
JPS121 CITROEN ZX KITCAR Rallycross 1996
Caty Caly $40
JPS122 ALPINE A110 Rallye des 1000 pistes
1976 Andruet $40
JPS124 RENAULT 5 Alpine GR 2 Monte Carlo
1978 #12 or 19.......................$40
JPS126 SPIDER RENAULT RJ RACING Warm Up
Le Mans 1996 ....$45
JPS127 DEBORA Le Mans 1996 or 4h du Mans
1996 ....$45
JPS128 PANHARD RIFFARD Le Mans 1954 #58
ou 59 ....$45
JPS129 SPIDER RJ RACING 4 Heures du Mans
1996 ....$45
JPS130 RENAULT PRIMAQUATRE "SAPRAR"
1939 Roadster $45
JPS131 RENAULT PRIMAQUATRE "SAPRAR"
1939 Cabriolet $45
JPS132 ALPINE A 110 Rallycross 1977 Bruno
Saby $45
JPS134 CITROEN ZX KITCAR Championnat d'Es-
pagne 1997 ....$40

JPS135 PANHARD RIFFARD Le Mans 1954 #60, coupe $40
JPS136 SPICE Le Mans 1991 #45 "Finantial Times" $45
JPS137 ALPINE A 310 V6 1st Var 1976.....$40
JPS138 JOEST 1st Le Mans 1997 ....$45
JPS140 A. L. D. C289 Le Mans 1989 ....$45
JPS141 PORSCHE 934 Le Mans 1978 #68 "Jagermeister" $45
JPS142 Barquette HOMMEL record du monde 100 000 km $45
JPS143 SPICE Le Mans 1991 #39 ....$45
JPS144 HELEM V6 RJ RACING Essais Le Mans 1997 #36 ....$45
JPS145 HELEM V6 RJ RACING Essais Le Mans 1997 #37 ....$45
JPS147 RENAULT 5 Turbo GR B Monte Carlo 1983 Ragnotti.....................................$45
JPS148 RENAULT 5 Turbo GR B Monte Carlo 1983 Ragnotti.....................................$45
JPS149 NISSAN MICRA 3 portes "Lagoon ou Cypia" $40
JPS150 PORSCHE 934 kit non peint pour décalcs BAM, SOLIDO etc. $35
JPS152 DAEWOO PROMETECH ANDROS #12 ....$45
JPS155 PORSCHE 934 Le Mans 1978 "URCUN" $45
JPS154 RENAULT DAUPHINE QUERON Cévennes 1971 ....$45
JPS156 RENAULT 5 Turbo GR B Tour de Corse 1986 Manzagol $45
JPS157 NISSAN MICRA ANDROS 1998 or 24 H de Chamonix $45
JPS158 NSU SPIDER Wankel.................$45
JPS159 PORSCHE 934 Le Mans 1976 #57 "Gelo" $45
JPS160 RENAULT TWINGO V6 ANDROS 1998 ....$45
JPS161 PEUGEOT 306 16S 24H de Spa "Laffite - Witmeur".................................$45
JPS162 PEUGEOT 306 16S, 2 colors $40
JPS163 PEUGEOT 306 16S "Magny-cours" ...$40
JPS164 PEUGEOT 306 16S "Gendarmerie" ..$40
JPS165 ALPINE A 310 V6 GR5 "Carlberson" ..$45
JPS166 RENAULT 5 Alpine GR2 Monte Carlo 1980 Saby....................................$40
JPS167 CHEVROLET STYLELINE 1952, berline $40
JPS168 NSU PICK-UP $40
JPS169 MERCEDES SLK "Carlsson" 1998 ...$45
JPS170 ALPINE A 310 V6 GR5 Tour de France 1976 ....$40
JPS171 DEBORA LMP296 Le Mans 1998...$45
JPS172 MATRA 630 Le Mans 1968, Pescarolo - Servoz-Gavin......................................$45
JPS174 NSU 1000 C..............................$40
JPS177 RENAULT Megane Andros 1999, Ragnotti..$45
JPS178 RENAULT Twingo V6 ANDROS 1999, phase 2 ....$45
JPS179 CHEVROLET Styleline 1952, cabriolet...$40

JPS180 MATRA 630 Le Mans 1967 #29/30...$45
JPS181 DAEWOO Prometech Andros 1999 #19 / 45 ....$45
JPS182 DAEWOO Prometech Andros 1999 #11 ....$45
JPS184 BMW 2002 Le Mans 1975 ....$45
JPS185 PORSCHE 908/03 Le Mans 1976 "EGON EVERTZ" $45
JPS186 NISSAN Micra Andros phase 2, 3 portes $45
JPS187 MERCEDES SLK "Carlsson" Presentation.......................................$45
JPS188 SIMCA 1100 Breack 5 portes $40
JPS189 SIMCA 1000 Beack 5 portes "Gendarmerie" $45
JPS190 NISSAN Micra phase 2, 3 portes ...$40
JPS191 FACEL VEGA Excellence................$45
JPS192 CHEVRON B8 LM 1969 ....$45
JPS193 LEYLAND MATRA camion utilisé par l'Équipe MATRA SPORTS $110
JPS195 WM P176 Le Mans $45
JPS196 CHEVROLET Styleline 1952, coupe fastback $40
JPS197 PEUGEOT 306 GR. N Tour de Corse 1999 ....$45
JPS198 LOLA T298 Le Mans 1980 #27, 1981 #31-33 ....$45
JPS199 LOLA T298 Le Mans 1981 #31 .....$45
JPS200 PANHARD DB "Le Mans" Cabriolet...$45
JPS201 PEUGEOT104 ZS Gr.2 Tour de Corse 1977 ....$45
JPS202 PORSCHE 924 Le Mans 1980 #2-3-4 ....$45
JPS203 JIDE 1600 RENAULT Cévennes 1971 ....$45
JPS205 PEUGEOT 406 Coupe 100 000 kms $45
JPS206 NISSAN Micra Andros 2000 #4 Collard Malcher......................................$45
JPS207 RENAULT Mégane Andros 2000 #33 Pierrot Gourmant $45
JPS208 RENAULT Mégane Andros 2000 #12 Fina $45
JPS209 NISSAN Micra Andros 2000 #7 Richelmi Balas $45
JPS210 RENAULT Clio Trophy Andros 2000 L. Fouquet...$45
JPS211 MARCH 75S LM 75 ....$45
JPS212 LOLA T298 LM 79 #20.................$45
JPS214 LEYLAND Transporteur Ligier Gitanes...$110
JPS215 PEUGEOT J7 Matra, camion atelier .$65
JPS216 CHEVRON B12 REPCO Le Mans 1968 ....$45
JPS217 TOJ SC206 BMW Le Mans 1979..$45
JPS218 MERCEDES SLK "Carlsson" 24 H Nurburgring 2000 ....$45
JPS219 COURAGE C52 "Pescarolo Sports" Le Mans 2000...$45
JPS220 PORSCHE 934 Le Mans 1980 #80 ....$45

JPS221 CHEVROLET STYLELINE coupe BEL AIR $40
JPS223 OPEL Astra "Silhouette" Champ. 2000 ....$45
JPS224 DEBORA Le Mans 2000............$45
JPS225 MOYNET SIMCA XS Le Mans 1969 ....$45
JPS226 BERLIET Stradair Transporteur Matra Gitanes...$70
JPS227 LEYLAND Transporteur Matra Gitanes...$110
JPS228 LOLA T292 1er Gr6 Le Mans 1976..$45
JPS229 MATRA 660 Le Mans 1971 ....$45
JPS230 PORSCHE 934 Le Mans 1976 #54 "Meznaries" $45
JPS231 LOLA T212 Le Mans 1971#50 "Camel - Philips" $45
JPS232 PEUGEOT 607 HDI Raid endurance 500 000 Km $45
JPS233 INALTERA Le Mans 1976 #1 or 2...$45
JPS234 RONDEAU M482 Le Mans 1983 "Concessionnaires Ford"...............................$45
JPS235 PEUGEOT 205 GTI Gr.N Var 1987, Delecour...$45
JPS236 TRIUMPH 1800 Roadster 1949, maquette C.P.C. $45

JRD

From 1935 to 1962, J. R. D. produced toys from Montreuil, France. Beginning in 1958, J.R.D. started marketing diecast models. Prior to that time, they were made of plaster and flour. When J.R.D. failed in 1962, C.I.J., also of France, purchased the dies and packaging, and marketed them as their own, sometimes by placing a simple label over the previous brand name on the package.

106 Citroën 1200 KG Police Van, 1:45, 1962 ....$80
107 Citroën 1200 KG Red Cross Van, 1:45, 1958 ....$90
108 Citroën 2CV EDF Van, 1:45, 1958 ....$80
109 Citroën 2CV Fire Van, 1:45, 1958 ....$90
110 Citroën 2CV Sedan, 1:45, 1958 ....$80
111 Citroën 2CV Van, 1:45, 1958 ....$75
112 Citroën 11CV Sedan, 1:45, 1958 ....$90
113 Citroën 1200 KG Van "Esso," 1:45, 1958 ....$100
114 Citroën P55 Covered Truck, 1:45, 1958 ....$75
115 Citroën P55 Army Truck & Trailer, 1:45, 1958 ....$90
116 Citroën DS19 Sedan, 1:45, 1958......$80
117 Citroën 2CV Road Service Van, 1:45, 1958 ....$90
118 Citroën 2CV "Air France" Van, 1:45, 1958 ....$90
120 Berliet Semi-Trailer "Kronenbourg," 1:45, 1958 ....$175
121 Berliet Semi-Trailer Tanker "Total," 1:45, 1958 ....$160
122 Unic Tank Truck "Antar," 1:45, 1958 .$145
123 Unic Cab, Trailer & Railroad Car, 1:45, 1958 ....$200

124 Unic Izoard Circus Train, 1:45, 1958 .$200
125 Berliet Weitz Crane Truck, 1:45, 1959 ....$145
126 Unic Van "Hafa," 1:45, 1959.........$175
127 Unic Van "Transports Internationaux," 1:45, 1959 ....$175
128 Unic Milk Tank Truck, 1:45, 1959 ....$165
129 Fruehauf Truck Trailer, 1:45, 1959 ....$120
130 Unic Liquid Transporter, 1:45, 1960..$145
131 Berliet Garbage Truck, 1:45, 1960 ..$145
132 Berliet Semi-Trailer "Antargaz," 1:45, 1961 ....$165
133 Berliet Fire Truck, 1:45, 1961 ....$175
134 Berliet Bottle Truck, 1:45, 1962 ....$165
151 Peugeot 404 Sedan, 1:45, 1962......$75
152 Citroën DS19 Cabriolet, 1:45, 1962..$75
153 Mercedes-Benz 220S Sedan, 1:45, 1962..$75
154 Citroën Ami 6, 1:45, 1962............$75
155 Simca 1000 Sedan, 1:45, 1962......$75

J.R.D. 1980s Reissues from C.I.J.

111 Citroën DS19, previously 116 ....$25
112 Citroën DS19 Convertible, previously 152 ....$25
211 Citroën 2CV Sedan, previously 110 ..$25
221 Citroën 2CV Fire Van, previously 109 .$25
223 Citroën 2CV Van, previously 111...$25
301 Citroën HY Van, previously 113.....$25
401 Citroën 11CV Sedan, previously 112.$25

JRI (see Road Champs)

JRL Collectibles

JRL Toys
23158 Bernhardt St
Hayward, CA 94545

JRL has offered just a few precision detailed diecast models. The specimen I acquired as an example is a 1:18 scale Dodge Ram 3500 "Dually" pick up that has opening doors, hood, and tailgate, functional steering, fully detailed engine, drive train, and exhaust system, and Goodyear Wrangler AT blackwall tires. The model is copyright dated 1995; the box is copyrighted 1997. The price marked from a local collectibles dealer was $40, but I purchased it for 25 percent off during an after-Christmas sale. EWA listed the same model in black and red, and a 1:12 scale Viper in red or black. At last check, JRL was out of business.

1995 Dodge Ram 3500 "Dually" Pickup, black and red, 1:18, #01 ....$45

1995 Dodge Ram 3500 "Dually" Pickup, white, 1:18, #01 ....$45

Dodge Viper RT/10, black, 1:12, #7120B $150
Dodge Viper RT/10, red, 1:12, #7120R..$150

JTE

A single model has been identified from JTE. Harvey Goranson reports that John Day produced an Inaltera, among hundreds of other early crude white metal kits. There may be a connection.
1978 Inaltera Team, blue, 1:43 ....$25–50

Juguinsa

Juguinsa models are made in Venezuela.
Monteverdi Coupe, 1:43 ....$18
Fiat 124 Coupe, 1:43 ....$18
AMC Javelin 343 Coupe, 1:43 ....$18

Jupiter

Jupiter is a brand of 1:43 scale white metal models from Belgium. When the brand was introduced and whether they are still in business is not known. What is known is that they produced a 1960 Plymouth Valiant and a T-Bird in the early 1990s. Dick Brown, who reported these models via e-mail (DICKATL@aol.com) in March 2000, says they are an offshoot of a firm called Gaston that makes truck models. They are quite expensive even by 1:43 scale white metal standards.

1960 Plymouth Valiant, c. 1993 ......$200–250
1960 Ford Thunderbird, c. 1993
   v.1 convertible, top up $200–250
   v.2 convertible, top down $200–250
   v.3 hardtop with sunroof............$200–250
   v.4 2-seat roadster $200–250

Jurgens

Jurgens models are hand-built 1:43 scale models.
1937 Packard Wagon $65
1940 Dodge Wagon $65
1948 Chrysler Town & Country Convertible .$65
1950 Buick Wagon $65

K&M

K&M Planning Co., Ltd., of Japan is known to have issued just one model, a 1979 Dome-O RL LeMans entry, according to Harvey Goranson, who attended LeMans in 1981 and witnessed a single such car sponsored by Amada. ("The team had cool samurai shirts!")
1979 Hayashi Dome-O Exotic Car, white with orange and black stickers, sponsored by Roland, 1:43 ....$38

K&O

From 1952 to 1962, K & O was the premiere manufacturer of toy boat motors in both metal and plastic. A list of models produced is on Alterscale's website at www.alterscale.com/kolist.html and in a book entitled *Toy Out-*

board Motors by Jack Browning $22.95, 150 pages of complied articles (by Jack Browning) with photos. Available only direct: Jack Browning, 214 16th Street, Roanoke, VA 24017 (phone: 540-982-1253). Comment: This is the only comprehensive work in existence on this subject. It covers principally the K&O motors (in detail) but touches on many other toy outboards. It includes a list of toy outboard collectors with names and addresses. Jack Browning is one of the world's premier collectors of toy outboards. Values are otherwise unknown.

K&R

K&R represents 1:43 scale white metal kits and hand-built models, mostly of British sports cars. Harvey Goranson reports that they have been around since the late seventies to early eighties, and may have been at one time connected with Abington Classics. No representative models are known.

K-Line

Primarily known for their electric trains, K-Line also produces a series of HO gauge (1:87 scale) semi tractor/trailers in various liveries, intended as accessories for HO gauge train sets. Here is an assortment of models offered by K-Line Electric Trains, Inc., Chapel Hill, North Carolina.

K-665603TT Ringling Bros. and Barnum & Bailey Circus Tractor Trailer $30
K-666703TT Diet Coke Tractor Trailer with railroad flat car..$30
K-811201TT Hershey's "Take a Bite"..........$30
K-811202TT Hershey's "The Great American Chocolate Bar" $30
K-811203TT Hershey's "Life is Sweet!" $30
K-811204TT Hershey's "First Love" $30
K-813301TT Ferrara Nougat Candy Tractor Trailer..$30
K-8201 K-Line Electric Trains Vintage Delivery Truck Bank $30
K-820202 Special Addition Vintage Truck Bank (Boy)..$30
K-820301 Father's Day Bank $30
K-820302 Valentine's Gift Bank $30
K-820801 Special Addition Vintage Truck Bank (Girl)...$30
K-82601 K-Line Oil Company Vintage Tanker...$30
K-826101 Happy Birthday Gift Bank $30

Kaden

Kaden Ltd. models are 1:43 scale replicas of Skoda Octavia sedans and station wagons in various rally and commercial liveries. Price and materials used are unknown. Information was extracted from a review of the 1999 Nuremburg Toy Show in the May 1999 issue of *Diecast Collector* magazine, published in Great Britain.

Kado

Kado represents 1:43 scale models from Japan (not to be confused with Kato, also of Japan).

F-1 Racer	$40
Hayashi Dome-O Exotic Car	$40
Porsche 930 Coupe	$40
Porsche 356 Speedster, silver with brown seats, chrome bumper	$40
Porsche 356 Speedster, blue with brown seats, chrome bumper	$40
Porsche 356 Speedster, red, with brown seats, chrome bumper	$40
Porsche 930 Turbo, metallic green with black interior, wipers, mirror	$40
Porsche 930 Turbo, metallic gold with black interior, wipers, mirror	$40
1957 Opel Rekord (tin)	$40

Kansas Toy & Novelty Company

Kansas Toy & Novelty Company started in 1923 when Arthur Haynes, an auto mechanic, began making toys out of his Clifton, Kansas, shed. Kansas Toy, Ralstoy, and others based in the Midwest in the thirties and forties swapped dies with each other to establish a partnership. This makes discerning one brand from another very difficult since models were usually not marked.

Army Tank #74, 2¼"	$50
Austin Bantam Sedanette #58, 2¼"	$35
Bearcat Racer #26, 4"	$75
Bearcat Racer #33, 3"	$50
Buick Roadster with rumble seat #54, 2⅜"	$20
Buick Roadster with no trunk #54, 2¼"	$35
Case Steam Tractor #25, 3"	$70
Chevrolet Sedan, 2⅞"	$30
Chevrolet Sedan, 2¼"	$40
Chrysler Convertible Coupe #8, rear mount spare, 3⅛"	$40
Chrysler Convertible Coupe #8, no rear mount spare, 3⅛"	$60
Chrysler Convertible Coupe, 5"	$75
Chrysler Roadster #14, 3⅛"	$35
Chrysler Roadster, no number, 3⅛"	$50
Convertible Coupe, 2⅞"	$60
Convertible Coupe #35, 2¼"	$50
Coupe, 3⅛"	$60
Dump Truck #42, 3½"	$70
Fageol Overland Bus #9, 3½"	$75
Fageol Overland bus, no number, 3½"	$60
Farm Dirt Scraper #65, 3⅝"	$50
Farm Dirt Tumble #64, 4"	$40
Farm Disc Harrow #62, 4"	$70
Farm Planter #61, 4"	$70
Farm Plough #63, 4"	$60
Farm Tractor #17, 2⅞"	$50
Farm Tractor, no number, 2⅝"	$60
Fire Engine #70, 2¼"	$75
Ford Pickup Truck #51, 2¾"	$50
Ford Stake Truck Semi & Trailer #55, 4"	$65

Fordson Farm Tractor #57, 1¾"	$25
Golden Arrow Record Car Racer #46, 2⅞"	$25
Indy Racer #10, 3⅛"	$50
John Deere Model D Large Farm Tractor, no number, 4⅞"	$75
Large Lady Racer with driver, 6"	$60
Midget Racer with no driver, 3"	$40
Midget Racer with driver, 3"	$80
Midget Racer #31, 2⅛"	$20
Midget Racer #67, 1½"	$90
Pickwick 1928 COE Nite Coach Tour Bus #49, 2⅜"	$60
Pickwick COE Tour Bus #59, 3⅜"	$50
Racer, 1"	$35
Railroad Box Car #38, 3¼"	$40
Railroad Caboose #40, "KT&N RR," 2¾"	$60
Railroad Livestock Car #41, "KT&N RR"	$60
Railroad Locomotive Tender #36, 4⅜"	$15
Railroad Pullman Car #37, 3½"	$40
Railroad Tank Car #39, "KT&N RR," 3⅛"	$60
Sedan Limousine, 3⅜"	$60
Sedan #60, 3½"	$45
Separator-Thresher #27, 3"	$70
Separator-Thresher #72, 2"	$50
Steam Road Roller #43, 3¼"	$20
Steam Tractor #71, 2½"	$20
Three-Wheel Coupe #66, 3½"	$60
Truck #20, 3⅛"	$30
Warehouse Tractor #48, 3"	$35

Kawabatakikaku (or J43 Kawabatakikaku)

As reported by Robert Speerbrecher (see Silver Pet), this Japanese brand is represented by mid-sixties Japanese sports cars in 1:43 scale. Such a brand name as this begs more research.

Datsun Fairlady 200P	$58–60
Honda S600	$58–60

Kawada

Kawada is one of those brands mentioned by collector Henry McFarland inquiring via e-mail in February 1997. This is the first I've heard of this brand from Japan. No model list is known.

Kazan

Only since the fall of the Iron Curtain have we in the USA discovered such a goldmine of diecast toys from the former Soviet Union. Kazan models are named after the town in which they were produced. Started in 1979, Kazan's main focus was on the many variations of the Kamaz truck introduced in 1978. The following list offers the various versions of this workhorse truck.

43105 Military Truck 6x6	$24
5320 Dropside Truck	$24
5320 Dropside Truck "1945–1985"	$24
5320 Dropside Truck "1917–1987"	$24
5320 Dropside Truck with Tilt	$24
5320 Dropside Truck with Tilt "Lada Spares"	$24
53212 Long Wheelbase Truck	$24
53212 Long Wheelbase Truck with Tilt	$24
53212 Long Wheelbase Truck with Tilt "Sovtransavto"	$24
53212 Tanker "Moloko"	$24
5325 4x2 Dropside Truck	$24
5325 4x2 Dropside Truck with Tilt "Sovtransavto"	$24
5410 Tractor Unit	$12
5410 Tractor Unit and Trailer	$24
5410 Tractor Unit, Trailer and Tilt	$32
55105 Dump Truck	$24
5511 Dump Truck	$24
5511 Dump Truck "Mocctpon"	$24
5511 Dump Truck "Moscow 1980"	$24

Kemlows

Kemlows Diecasting Products Ltd. was one London, England, toy manufacturer that remains relatively unknown. The box is typical of fifties diecast from Great Britain. The distinction is that it is marked "A Wardie Product," likely indicating its distributor B. J. Ward Ltd. Master Model and Wee World Series are other monikers applied to the model's box.

Recognizing such models out of their respective boxes is a bit more difficult. Here is a list of known models.

Armored Car, 1:60	$50
Articulated Lumber Truck, 1:50	$50
Caravan, 1:43	$50
Field Gun, 1:60	$25
Flat Truck, 1:50	$50
Ford Zephyr Mark I, 1:43	$100
Removal Van "PickFord's," 1:60	$100
Thornycroft Mighty Antar, 1:43	$75
Thornycroft Mighty Antar, 1:60	$50
Tractor and Farm Cart	$50

Kenna

Pete Kenna makes these beautiful 1:43 scale hand-built models in the United Kingdom.

MG TD, top up, side curtains	price unavailable
Austin A40 Van	$110
Austin Devon Estate	$120
Austin Devon Saloon	$120
Austin Devon Van	$120
Austin Dorset	$120
Austin Estate	$120
Austin HereFord Saloon	$120
Austin HereFord Convertible	$120
Austin "Woody"	$120
Standard Vanguard Ph 1/2 Ambulance	$100
Standard Vanguard Ph 1/2 Estate	$100
Standard Vanguard Ph 1/2 Pickup	$100
Standard Vanguard Ph 1/2 Saloon	$100
Standard Vanguard Ph 1/2 Van	$100
Triumph Herald 12/50	$120
Triumph Herald 13/60	$120
Triumph Vitesse	$120

Kenner

Kenner, now owned by Hasbro (who also now owns Tonka and several other venerable toy brands), is well known for its huge assortment of toys. It's Girder & Panel and Bridge & Turnpike construction sets were extremely popular in the sixties and seventies. Hasbro in turn is sustained by the popularity of its G. I. Joe action figures.

Most familiar of the Kenner diecast line is Kenner Fast 111's, produced around 1980 and styled after the wildest Hot Wheels and Johnny Lightnings. But their popularity (and speed) could never compete much with either of them. Still, Kenner Fast 111's are slowly and steadily gaining popularity as a collectible and can still be purchased very cheaply, around $2 a piece or less.

Kenner has recently produced a five-car set of 1:64 scale vehicles based on the movie *Batman Forever* which is slowly rising in value. The set is currently worth about $8–10.

Currently, the Kenner brand mostly encompasses Star Wars figures and playsets. In March of 1996, Mattel failed in an attempt to buy out Hasbro, securing the integrity of the Kenner brand as well.

The most recent offering (1997) from Kenner is a line called Winner's Circle. The 1997 Stock Car Series Winner's Circle cars are 1:64 scale with a trading card depicting the driver. Also produced are a couple of rail dragsters and funny cars.

Kenner Fast 111's
1980 Firebird	$4–6
Trans Am	$4–6
1980 Mustang Cobra	$4–6
1980 Corvette Stingray	$4–6
NA 217	$4–6
Chevy Monza "Fun 'E'" Car	$4–6
Shark Car with fins	$4–6
Gravel Grinder Jeep, white with yellow stars, blue stripes	$4–6
Pipe Dreamer, red with blue and black stripes	$4–6
T R Terrific, blue with yellow and green stripes, yellow "8" on hood	$4–6
Rallye Champ, white with red, blue, purple flames, "Rallye" on spoiler	$4–6
Sporty Shifter, orange with blue, white, black race tampos	$4–6
Street Boss, black with rebel flag	$4–6
Master Blaster	
v.1 red with white, black, yellow tampo, yellow "2" on hood	$4–6
v.2 white with blue, black, red tampo, red "2" on hood	$4–6

Kenner Winner's Circle — 1:64 Scale Stock Assortment
Ward Burton	$3–4
Ward Burton (paint special)	$3–4
Dale Earnhardt	$3–4
Dale Earnhardt (Wheaties)	$3–4
Dale Earnhardt (Japan)	$3–4
Dale Earnhardt '78	$3–4
Dale Earnhardt '80 (Olds 442)	$3–4
Dale Earnhardt '81	$3–4
Dale Earnhardt '82	$3–4
Dale Earnhardt '83	$3–4
Dale Earnhardt '84	$3–4
Dale Earnhardt '86	$3–4
Dale Earnhardt '88	$3–4
Dale Earnhardt '88 Camaro	$3–4
Dale Earnhardt '89 Pontiac	$3–4
Dale Earnhardt '95	$3–4
Jeff Gordon	$3–4
Jeff Gordon (Career Series 1)	$3–4
Jeff Gordon (Career Series 2)	$3–4
Jeff Gordon (Career Series 3)	$3–4
Jeff Gordon (Career Series 4)	$3–4
Jeff Gordon (Career Series 5)	$3–4
Jeff Gordon (Career Series 6)	$3–4
Jeff Gordon (Jurassic Park)	$3–4
Jeff Gordon (Prem Chroma)	$3–4
Dale Jarrett	$3–4
Dale Jarrett (paint special)	$3–4
Robert Presley (Scooby Doo)	$3–4
Robert Presley (Yogi Bear)	$3–4
Mike Skinner	$3–4
Mike Skinner (paint special)	$3–4
Mike Bliss (truck)	$3–4
Brett Bodine	$3–4
Ron Hornaday	$3–4
Bobby Labonte	$3–4
Jeremy Marfield	$3–4
Sterling Marlin	$3–4
Ricky Rudd	$3–4
Jay Suter	$3–4
Kenny Wallace	$3–4

Kenner Winner's Circle — 1:64 Scale Drag Racing Assortment
Joe Amato	$4–5
Shelly Anderson	$4–5
Pat Austin	$4–5
Kenny Bernstein	$4–5
Larry Dixon	$4–5
Mike Dunn	$4–5
Tom McEwen	$4–5
Al Hofman	$4–5
Tom Hoover	$4–5
Scott Kalitta	$4–5
Shirley Muldowney	$4–5
Mark Oswald	$4–5
John Force	$4–5
John Force (paint special 1)	$4–5
John Force (paint special 2)	$4–5
John Force (paint special 3)	$4–5
John Force (Life Series 1)	$4–5
John Force (Life Series 2)	$4–5
John Force (Life Series 3)	$4–5
John Force (Life Series 4)	$4–5
John Force (Life Series 5)	$4–5
John Force (Life Series 6)	$4–5
John Force (Pomona)	$4–5

Kenner Winner's Circle — 1:24 Scale Circle Top Assortment
Joe Amato	$14–16
Shelly Anderson	$14–16
Pat Austin	$14–16
Kenny Bernstein	$14–16
Larry Dixon	$14–16
Mike Dunn	$14–16
Scott Kalitta	$14–16
Shirley Muldowney	$14–16

Kenton
Kenton Hardware Company produced cast-iron toys from 1890 to 1952. Sales sagged by 1931, so a partnership was formed between Kenton and Kingsbury. See Kingsbury.

Kibri
Walthers devotes several pages to their extensive assortment of 1:87 scale plastic Kibri models, worth mentioning for their detail and accuracy. Kibri of Germany at one time produced at least one diecast model as listed below.
Auto-Union Streamlined Racing Car, 4⅛"	$50

Log Truck, 1:87 precolored plastic kit..$10

Kidco
When Kidco of Illinois started is unknown. But somewhere around 1985, Kidco was purchased by Universal while Universal still owned the Matchbox brand. The Burnin' Key Cars and Lock-Ups assortments were originally a Kidco product that was incorporated into the Matchbox line-up for a short time in the eighties. Burnin' Key Cars are now owned by Maisto.
Firebird Trans Am V8, 1981, Hong Kong	$1
'57 Corvette, white with red stripes, hood opens, 1977	$1

Kiddie Car Classics
Hallmark offers these exquisite miniature replicas of vintage pedal toys made of heavy diecast metal and great paint jobs. They are working models with pedals that turn the wheels and functional steering. Values indicated are Hallmark retail prices.
1935 American Airflow Coaster, Limited Edition of 29,500 made, 5" long	$45
1964½ Ford Mustang, 7" long	$55
1940 Garton Aero Flite Wagon, Limited Edition of 24,500 made, 7" long	$48
1959 Garton Deluxe Kidillac, issued 3/95, retired 1/97, 7½" long	$55
1961 Garton Casey Jones Locomotive, issued 3/95, retired 1/97, 6½" long	$55
1950 Garton Delivery Cycle, 6¾" long	$38
1956 Garton Dragnet Police Car, Limited Edition of 24,500 made, 6¼" long	$50

1956 Garton Hot Rod Racer, 5½" long $55
1956 Garton Kidillac, issued 7/94, retired 12/94, 7⅜" long................................$50
1956 Garton Mark V, Limited Edition of 24,500 made, 6¼" long................................$45
1963 Garton Speedster, 5" long $38
1966 Garton Super-Honda, 6¼" long $45
1964 Garton Tin Lizzie, 5¾" long $50
1941 Keystone Locomotive, 5" long $45
1939 Mobo Horse, 3⅞" long $45
Late 1940s Mobo Sulky, Limited Edition of 29,500 made, 7" long....................$48
1941 Murrary Airplane, Limited Edition of 14,500, issued 10/92, retired 10/93, 7¼" long....................................$50
1958 Murray Atomic Missile, Limited Edition of 24,500 made, 7¾" long.............$55
1968 Murray Boat Jolly Roger, Limited Edition of 19,500 made, issued 3/93, retired 2/96, 6⅛" long....................$50
1955 Murray Champion, Limited Edtion of 14,500, issued 10/92, retired 10/93, 6⅛" long....................................$45
1961 Murray Circus Car, Limited Edition of 24,500 made, 7" long....................$48
1953 Murray Dump Truck, yellow, Limited Edition of 14,500, issued 10/92, retired 10/93, 7½" long....................$48
1955 Murray Dump Truck, orange/black, Limited Edition of 19,500, issued 3/94, retired 3/96, 7½"..................$48
1955 Murray Fire Chief, Limited Edition, issued 9/93, retired 1/96, 6⅛" long............$45
1955 Murray Fire Truck, red, Limited Edition of 14,500 made, issued 10/24, retired 10/93, 7" long....................$50
1955 Murray Fire Truck, red/white, Limited Edition of 19,500 made, issued 3/94, retired 1/96, 7" long....................$50
1958 Murray Police Cycle, Limited Edition of 29,500 made, 5½" long....................$55
1948 Murray Pontiac, 5⅞" long $50
1955 Murray Ranch Wagon, Limited Edition of 19,500, issued 1/94, retired 2/96, 6⅛" long....................$48
1955 Murray Red Champion, Limited Edition of 19,500, issued 3/94, retired 3/96, 6⅛" long....................$45
1955 Murray Royal Deluxe, Limited Edition of 29,500 made, 6¼" long....................$55
1961 Murray Speedway Pac Car, Limited Edition of 24,500 made, 6⅛" long.............$45
1962 Murray Super Deluxe Fire Truck, 7½" long....................................$55
1961 Murray Super Deluxe Tractor with Trailer, 7¼" long tractor, 4¼" long trailer $55
1950 Murray Torpedo, issued 3/95, retired 1/96, 6¼" long....................$50
1955 Murray Tractor and Trailer, Limited Edition of 14,500, issued 10/92, retired 12/93, 11⅛" long $55
1935 Sky King Velocipede, 5" long.........$45

1937 Steelcraft Airflow by Murray, Luxury Edition, 24,500 made, 6⅞" long $55
1935 Steelcraft Airplane by Murray, Limited Edition of 29,500 made, 7¾" long.........$50
1937 Steelcraft Auburn, Luxury Edition, 24,500 made, issued 7/95, retired 4/96, 8½" long................................$65
1935 Steelcraft by Murray, Luxury Edition, 24,500 made, 7¼" long....................$65
1939 Steelcraft Lincoln Zephyr by Murray, Limited Edition of 24,500, 6¾" long.........$50
1941 Steelcraft Spitfire Airplane by Murray, Limited Edition, 19,500, issued 3/94, retired 1/96, 7¼"................................$50
1937 Steelcraft Streamline Scooter by Murray, 6¼" long................................$35
1935 Steelcraft Streamline Velocipede by Murrary, 4½" long $45

Kiddietoy (see Hubley)

Kiko (see Corgi)

Kilgore

Westerville, Ohio, was home to Kilgore, a company that produced some of the most elegant toys of the 1930s. These cast iron cars were accurate representations of vehicles of the period, comparable to the best diecast of any era. Graham models were the specialty for these high quality miniature marvels.

Ken Hutchison and Greg Johnson have written a delightful book entitled *The Golden Age of Automotive Toys 1925–1941* in which they showcase these and other rare and beautiful toy cars and trucks in spectacular photos, with entertaining and informative text. The hardbound edition from Collector Books is a prize to cherish at just $24.95 suggested retail price.

1932 Graham Blue Streak Coupe, 6½"................................$2,200–2,500

1932 Graham Blue Streak Roadster, 6½"................................$2,200–2,500

1932 Graham Blue Streak Sedan, 6½"................................$2,200–2,500
1932 Graham Blue Streak Coupe, 4".$175-350
1932 Graham Blue Streak Roadster, 4"................................$175–350
1932 Graham Blue Streak Sedan, 4". $175–350
Graham Stake Truck, 4"..................$100–150
Graham Wrecker, 4"..................$100–150
Graham Dump Truck, 4"..................$100–150
Pierce Arrow-styled Coupe, 4" $100–150

Pierce Arrow-styled Roadster, 4" $100–150
Pierce Arrow-styled Sedan, 4"........$100–150
Pierce Arrow-styled Coupe, 5"........$125–175
Pierce Arrow-styled Roadster, 5"........$125–175

Kim Classics

From England come these new 1:43 scale white metal models.
2 Cadillac Limousine "Maloney" $198
3Z GMC Sierra Police Suburban $149
6 1992 Jaguar XJ6 Sedan $115
7 1960 Chrysler Saratoga $129
1972 Buick Electra 225 Sedan.............$229

King K (also see Xonex)

c/o Ken Kovach
8300 W. Sauk Trail
Frankfort, IL 60423
phone: 815-469-5937

Since 1987, King K has been the business of Ed and Ken Kovach from Frankfort, Illinois, producing some of the most exquisite miniature cars, buses, and flivvers ever made. So when Ken Kovach made his first resin-cast miniature pedal car in 1990, a 1955 Champion, he started the newest trend in collectible toys. His replicas average about 12 inches long (1:3 scale), bigger than average for such models. (Compare to Kiddie Car Classics at approximately 6 inches.) Limited production runs of 10, 50, or 100 make these rare and highly collectible.

Newer models are also produced in a much smaller 1:18 scale. Xonex has since reproduced King K's models in diecast, and in larger production runs of 10,000 for around $60–80 each.
1955 Champion, 1:3 scale, 1990, original price................................$165
current value..........................$250–400
1940 Silver Pursuit Plane, 1991, original price................................$300
current value..........................$250–450

King of the Road (see Horsman)

Kingsbury

The Kingsbury company dates back to 1886 in Keene, New Hampshire. Around 1910, Harry Kingsbury purchased the Wilkins Toys Company. After World War I, he changed the Wilkins brand name to Kingsbury to produce toys usually made of pressed steel with windup motors. While the firm remains in business, toy production apparently ceased after 1942. Values range from $400 to $2,500. In 1931, Kenton formed a partnership with Kingsbury to bolster sagging sales of its cast iron toys and products. See Kenton.

King Star

King Star toys of Korea, while lightweight and low priced, are relatively accurate scale models. Here is a sampling of models produced.
Mercedes-Benz 450 SLC 5.0, 1:50 ....$5
Mercedes-Benz 450 SLC Police Car.........$5

Pontiac Firebird	$5
Fuso Van	$5
Fuso Cement Truck	$5

Kinsmart (see Kintoy)

Kintoy

Kintoy Die-Casting Manufactory Ltd. of China is known to produce several color variations of a 1:43 scale BMW Isetta with pull-back action for around $6 each. Other models include several color variations of a new VW Beetle, 5 inches long with pull-back action, recently found for just $2 each. Identification of these models requires referencing the package, as most Kintoy and Kinsmart toys have no identifying marks other than "Made In China" on the base, rendering them generic. Both Kintoy and Kinsmart toys are sold in bulk display packs and have no individual packaging.

Kintoys

BMW Isetta, 1:43	$4–6
Humvee Power Climber, 2¾", pullback action	
v.1 blue	$2–4
v.2 metallic red	$2–4
v.3 black	$2–4
v.4 yellow	$2–4
v.5 red	$2–4
v.6 white	$2–4
v.7 metallic green	$2–4
New VW Beetle, 5"	$2–4

Kinsmart

1950 Chevrolet Corvette, 1:64.....................$3

Toyota RAV4, 1:32...$6

Ford Thunderbirds with pullback action motors, 1:64.......................................$3 each

---

1955 Chevrolet Stepside, 1:64 with pullback action	
v.1 red	$2
v.2 metallic red	$2
v.3 yellow	$2
v.4 cream	$2
v.5 black	$2
v.6 metallic blue	$2
v.7 metallic green	$2
1950 Chevrolet Suburban, 1:36 with pull-back action	$2–4

Kirby

An Atlas Backhoe is the only known model by Kirby.

Atlas 2004LC Track Backhoe, 1:87............$26

Kirk

The Kirk brand of Denmark is hard to find, since most of the models they marketed were first produced by other companies. The connection is somewhat confusing, but Tekno and H. Lange are two Danish companies whose products ended up in the Kirk product line. Even though Kirk produced models since 1960, it wasn't until 1969 that the company actually put the Kirk name on the base. Here is a list of models issued under the Kirk brand.

Chevrolet Monza GT	$60
Chevrolet Monza Spyder	$45
Ford D 800 Tipper Truck	$45
Ford D 800 Covered Truck	$45
Ford D 800 Lumber Truck	$45
Ford D 800 Brewery Truck	$65
Jaguar E Type	$65
Mercedes-Benz 0302 Bus	$60
Mercedes-Benz 0302 Bus, "PTT"	$75
Mercedes-Benz 280 SL	$65
Mercedes-Benz 280 SL Police	$45
Oldsmobile Toronado	$65
Porsche 911 S	$45
Saab 99	$65
Toyota 2000 GT	$60

Kookaburra

Kookaburra is the name brand of 1:43 scale white metal models from Melbourne, Australia, as recently reported by Australian collector Gary Hallett.

001 Holden EK Taxi, RSL Cabs, Sydney, 100 made	Price unavailable
005 1962 Holden EK Station Sedan	Price unavailable

Kyosho

Kyosho Corporation
Atsugi Operation Center
153 Funako, Atsugi
Kanagawa 243-0034, Japan

These fine quality diecast precision scale models from Japan are part of a line of toys that include radio-controlled cars, boats, and planes, and detailed plastic model kits.

Kyosho 1:18 Scale Models

0300 Austin Countryman, blue	$50–60
0201 Ferrari 512 BB, yellow, limited edition	$100
0202 Ferrari 512 BB, black, limited edition	$100
0203 Ferrari 512 BB, silver limited edition	$100
08171R Ferrari 512 BB, red	$50–60
08171Y Ferrari 512 BB, yellow	$50–60
7001 1991 Honda Acura NSX, red or silver with black roof	$90–100

7001R 1991 Honda Acura NSXR, white...$50–60

0171 Lancia Stratos, Rally	$50–60
08132A Lancia Stratos HF Rally "Alitalia"	$50–60
08131R Lancia Stratos HF Rally, red	$50–60
08131Y Lancia Stratos HF Rally, yellow	$50–60
7015 Lotus Caterham Super 7, British racing green, red, blue, or yellow	$50–60
0190 Lotus Europa Special, white	$50–60
0191 Lotus Europa Special, black	$50–60
0192 Lotus Europa Special, green	$50–60
08151K Lotus Europa Special, black	$50–60
08151G Lotus Europa Special, green	$50–60
08151W Lotus Europa Special, white	$50–60
0400 Mazda Miata MX, 5 LHD, yellow	$50–60
0401 Mazda Miata MX, 5 LHD, light blue	$50–60
7009 Mazda RX7, red or silver	$90–100
7010 Mazda RX7, black or yellow	$90–100
7011 Mazda Miata MX5, top down, Superman blue	$40–50
7005 Mercedes-Benz 300 SL Gullwing, silver	$90–100
7017 1966 MGB Mk-1, green, red, or white	$50–60
7008 Mini Cooper 1275S, green, red, white, or British flag	$80–90
08111G Morgan 4/4 Series-II, green	$50–60

08111W Morgan 4/4 Series-II, white $50–60
08111B Morgan 4/4 Series-II, blue..$50–60
08111R Morgan 4/4 Series-II, red .$50–60
0301 Morris Traveler, green $50–60
0500 Nissan 300ZX, yellow $50–60
7002 1992 Nissan 300ZX Twin Turbo, red or metallic blue $50–60
7002J 1993 Nissan Skyline GTR, Unisea or Multicolor $50–60
7003 Nissan 300ZX T-Top, red....$90–100
7007 Porsche 356A/1600, red or silver $80–90
08041S Shelby Cobra 427S/C Racing, silver $50–60
0600 Shelby Cobra 427 S/C, red.$50–60
7006RW Shelby Cobra 427S/C, red with white stripe $50–60
7006G Shelby Cobra 427S/C, green..$50–60
7006Z Shelby Cobra 427S/C, blue.$50–60
7013 Toyota Supra with wing, red.$90–100
7014 Toyota Supra with wing, red, black, or silver $90–100

Kyosho Museum Collection

In addition, Kyosho has recently added 1:43 scale models to their offerings, dubbed the Museum Collection. Models offered include those mentioned below:

03011R Shelby AC Cobra 427 S/C, red $25–30
03011S Shelby AC Cobra 427 S/C, silver $25–30
03021S Nissan Skyline 2000 GTR, silver $25–30
03021W Nissan Skyline 2000 GTR, white $25–30
03022B Nissan Skyline 2000 GTR Racing, white with blue and red accents.$25–30
03031R Toyota 2000 GT Hardtop, red.$25–30
03032Y Toyota 2000 GT Hardtop Trial Car, yellow..$25–30
03033W Toyota 2000 GT Convertible, white..$25–30
03151G Caterham Super Seven, green.$25–30
1601 Jaguar E-Type Roadster, green $30

Lacquer & Leather (or Lack & Ledder)

This German brand reportedly offers an unauthorized custom version of Maisto's Mercedes-Benz Concept Car in 1:18 scale.

Lada

Lada, also known as Vaz is a brand of diecast models from Russia. Quality is exceptional for the price, and models are 1:43 scale except where noted.

1116 AWA scale 1:66 ....$5
2101 Saloon standard $8
2101 Saloon traffic police $8
2101 Saloon Rally Car $8
2101 Saloon standard + luggage rack $8

2101 Saloon training car $8
2102 estate standard............................$8
2102 estate Rally support car $8
2102 estate standard + luggage rack $8
2102 fire chief $8
2102 estate with symbols $8
2105 Saloon standard $9
2105 std. + lugg. rack $9
2105 traffic police $12
2107 Saloon standard $9
2107 Saloon std.+ lugg.rack $12
2109 5 door traffic police with beacon $12
2121 NIVA standard $12

Lansdowne (see Brooklin)

Lansing Slik-Toys

Lansing, Iowa, was the home of Lansing Slik-Toys, mostly one-piece cast aluminum toys, with a few plastic models. The company is no longer in business.

Bulldozer $130
Combine $300
Fastback Sedan, #9600, 7" $40
Fastback Sedan Taxi, #9600, 7" $40
Firetruck, #9606, 6" $35
Firetruck, #9700, 3½" $35
Grader, 9½" $100
Metro Van, #9618, 5" $40
Oliver 77 Tractor, 7¾" $400
Open Stake Truck, #9602, 7" $40
Pickup Truck, #9601, 7" $40
Pickup Truck, #9605, 6" $35
Pickup Truck, #9703, 4" $35
Roadster, #9701, 3½" $35
Sedan 4-Door, #9604, 6" $35
Semi Tractor Trailer Flatbed Truck, #9613, 8"..$40
Semi Tractor Trailer Grain Truck, #9611, 8".$40
Semi Tractor Trailer Log Truck, 8" $40
Semi Tractor Trailer Milk Truck, #9610, 8" .$45
Stake Truck, #9500, 11" $60
Station Wagon, #9704, 4" $30
Tank Truck, #9603, 7" $35
Tank Truck, #9705, 4" $30
Wrecker, #9617, 5" $30

L. D. Abraham (see Abraham, L. D.)

L'Eau Rouge

Considering the great number of 1:43 scale models and kits available, especially in Europe, it is natural to expect that someone would produce dioramas and figures to complement the models. L'Eau Rouge of France, one of the brands comprising MAFMA, nicely fills that niche. No model list is available.

Lee Toys

A recent offer on the Internet revealed a set of diecast farm toys by a company called Lee Toys. The set includes a tractor and five other farm implements vacuum sealed in an attractive display box. The set sold on eBay Internet auction site for $20.

Le Jouet Mecanique

Dating from around 1955, just one reference to Le Jouet Mecanique has been found, a diecast model with clockwork motor.
Panhard Dyna, 1:45 ....$60

Legends of Racing

While not diecast, Legends of Racing resin models deserve mention, according to Russell Alameda of San Jose, California. These 1:43 scale models are made in China for the Huntersville, North Carolina, company. Each car is packaged in a clear display box with card that provides a few paragraphs of details on the model inside.

1974 Chevrolet Malibu, "Buddy Baker".$10–20
1955 Chrysler 300 ....$10–20
1969 Dodge Daytona, "Jim Vandiver"...$10–20
1965 Ford Galaxie 500, "#41," "Curtis Turner," "Harvest Ford," white and red, 1:43, issued 1992 ....$10–20
1965 Ford Galaxie 500, "Ned Jarrett" $10–20
1965 Ford Galaxie 500, "Fred Lorenzen".$10–20
1952 Hudson Hornet, "Flock" $10–20
1969 Mercury Cyclone (independent driver)...$10–20
1969 Mercury Cyclone, "Woods Brothers" $10–20
1960 Pontiac Bonneville $10–20
1962 Pontiac Bonneville, "Fireball Roberts" $10–20

Lehigh Bitsi-Toys

Around the year 1950, a company called Lehigh produced a small assortment of heavy diecast toys known as Bitsi-Toys. Here are the only two known models.

1949 Chevrolet Coupe, 2½" $20
1948 Reo Tractor/Trailer, 5½" $30

Leksakshust

Greyhound Bus, 1:43 ....$24

Le Mans Miniatures

Mike Burt of Ridgefield, Washington, relayed this information to me from the manufacturer of Le Mans Miniatures of Foulletourte, France. Figurines and dioramas are the main offerings from Le Mans Miniatures. An assortment of 1:43 scale models from their GTS Collection is also available.

Le Mans Miniatures — 1:87, 1:43, 1:24 Scale Resin

Driver running at start of Le Mans, 1:24, FLM124001 ....$10–15
French Fireman of the 80s and 90s, 1:24, FLM124005 ....$10–15
1994 Dauer Porsche Le Mans Winner diorama $50–65
1996 Joest Porsche WSC Le Mans diorama, 12 figurines, race car and accessories $45–60

1968 Ford GT 40 Le Mans, 1:24, 124019..............$35–50

Le Mans Miniatures GTS Collection — 1:43 Scale Resin

Peugeot 206 WRC, "Présentation," Réf: GS508.R..............$30–45

Peugeot 406 Coupe, metallic gray, GTS, #02.0 ....$25–30
Peugeot 406 Coupe, metallic blue, GTS, #02.1 ....$25–30
Peugeot 406 Coupe, yellow, GTS, #02.2 ....$25–30
Peugeot 406 Coupe, metallic green, GTS, #02.3 ....$25–30
Peugeot 406 Coupe, metallic red, GTS, #02.4 ....$25–30
Peugeot 406 Coupe, Cosmos gray, GTS, #02.5 ....$25–30
Peugeot 406 Coupe, Riviera blue, GTS, #02.6 ....$25–30
Peugeot 406 Coupe, metallic green, GTS, #02.7 ....$25–30
Peugeot 406 Coupe, metallic red, GTS, #02.8 ....$25–30
1985 Renault R8 GT Turbo, pearly white, GTS, #01.0 ....$25–30
1985 Renault R5 GT Turbo, red, GTS, #01.1 ....$25–30
1985 Renault R5 GT Turbo, white, GTS, #01.2 ....$25–30
1985 Renault R5 GT Turbo, black, GTS, #01.3 ....$25–30
1985 Renault R5 GT Turbo, blue, GTS, #01.4 ....$25–30
1985 Renault R5 GT Turbo, silver, GTS, #01.5 ....$25–30
Renault 12, Gordini blue, GTS, #04.0 ....$25–30
Renault 12, Gordini orange, GTS, #04.1 ....$25–30
Renault 12, Gordini yellow, GTS, #04.2 ....$25–30
Renault Alpine A 310 Pack GT, marine blue, GTS, #05.0 ....$25–30
Renault Alpine A 310 Pack GT, white, GTS, #05.1 ....$25–30
Renault Alpine A 310 Pack GT, red, GTS, #05.2 ....$25–30
1973 Simca 1000 Rallye 2, green, GTS, #03.0 ....$25–30
1973 Simca 1000 Rallye 2, Tacoma white, GTS, #03.1 ....$25–30
1973 Simca 1000 Rallye 2, red, GTS, #03.2 ....$25–30

Lemeco

Based in Sweden, Lemeco produced a series of diecast models based on Dinky Toys, according to collector Staffan Kjellin of Sweden. Other toys produced by the company include a board game called Bonanza, plastic toy jigsaw and other plastic toys.

Ford Sedan $40–65
Austin Devon $40–65

Le Phoenix

Exoticar lists these as the finest quality 1:43 scale hand-built models from France that feature leather interior, full photo-etched metal and trim, detailed cockpit, limited between 100 and 200 piece production run of only 10 units per item are available.

1966 Ferrari Dino 206 Le Mans 2-car set in elegant presentation case with metal Dino emblem, limited to 120 pieces..............$1,295
1964 Ferrari 250 GTO Le Mans #26 ....$595
1959/1960 Ferrari 250 TR Le Mans #11..............$595
Ferrari 275 NART Spyder, available in red, yellow, or metallic gray..............$595
1972 Ferrari 365 GTB/4 Daytona Le Mans #39..............$595
1966 Ferrari 500SF, metallic blue or maroon..............$595

Lesney (see Matchbox)

Les Rouliers

The obscure French toy company Les Rouliers is known to produce only one model.
Renault Etoile Filante, 1:43, 1961..............$50

Les Routiers

A diminutive series of 1:90 scale diecast vehicles were produced in 1959 under the French firm name Les Routiers.

1 Panhard Tank Truck $50
2 Unic Semi Trailer..............$50
3 Berliet Dump Truck $50
4 Citroën Wrecker..............$50
5 Citroën Dump Truck $50
6 Caterpillar Dumping Tractor $50
7 Richier Road Rollre $50
8 Caterpillar Road Grader $50
9 Caterpillar Quarry Bucket $50
10 Tractomotive Excavator $50
11 Renault Byrrh Tank Truck..............$50
12 Renault Etoile Filante $50
13 Bus $50
14 Mobile Crane $50

Liberty Classics (also see Spec-Cast)

428 6th Avenue NW
P O Box 368
Dyersville, IA 52040-0368
questions e-mail to: es@libertyclassics.com
dealers e-mail to :jm@libertyclassics.com
website: www.libertyclassics.com

The Liberty Classics website tells the story the best: "Liberty Classics was formed in 1991 by industry veteran Jack Stoneman and his son Eric. Jack's resume includes twenty years with the Ertl Co., from where he moved up to become president of Revell-Monogram.

"Eric started in the toy business after graduating from college and spent several years 'in the trenches' of the diecast business before partnering with his father to start Liberty. Two years after they started the company, they were joined by Paul, son and brother, who left a retail service company he had started after leaving college.

"The original mission of the company was to produce diecast for the ad specialty and premium markets, a business that had been dominated by the Ertl Co. for years. One of the goals from the beginning was to produce the highest quality diecast available. Jack and Eric called upon an old friend and business relationship in Hong Kong that had been established almost thirty years earlier. In partnership with their good friend, they established a state-of-the-art factory to produce diecast. Collectively the Liberty team has more than one hundred years of experience and has been producing diecast for thirty years.

"The Liberty team has developed and introduced over 85 unique items, most of which had never been tooled in scale diecast before and all of which were distributed by SpecCast. There have been airplanes, tractor-trailers, vintage pickup trucks and vehicles, engines, motorcycles, log splitters, tractors, pedal cars, industrial machines, and even a newspaper vending machine. In 1998, Liberty Classics dedicated themselves, their experience, and their resources to develop a line for retail...a line specifically for the diecast collector.

"The same experience, processes, and attention to detail have been brought to bear in developing our retail line. Our first introduction was our line of vintage police vehicles. Monty McCord, the well known police historian, collaborated with us to help insure that our police vehicles were the most authentic available. Our second introduction was our line of hot rods. These weren't just new paint schemes on old tools. Our hot rods were researched and then tooled from scratch. Our most recent introduction, the Power Plant Series of engines, aptly demonstrates our commitment to scale, authenticity, and innovation.

"We will carry on our tradition and serve the needs of collectors with a high quality, affordable, and unique line of diecast. As long as we're in business we will work to set standards in our industry."

326 Travel REA "Goodyear Racing #1"	$24
1026 White New Idea Crate Pickup	$18
1547 1932 Ford Model A Roadster "Fina"	$16
1553 1932 Ford Model A Roadster "A&W"	$27
2004 1929 Ford Tanker "Fina Petroleum"	$15
2005 1929 Ford Tanker "Amalie Motor Oil"	$26
12516 1937 Chevrolet Pickup, red	$20
35018 Lockheed VGA Airplane "Signal"	$31
35021 Lockheed VGA Airplane "Magnolia"	$31
35040 Lockheed VGA Airplane "Mountain Dew"	$16

Lincoln (see Lincoln Industries, Lincoln International, Lincoln Toys, Lincoln White Metal)

Lincoln Industries

During the 1950s, Lincoln Industries of Auckland, New Zealand, produced a line of models thought to be made from D.C.M.T. castings.

Austin A Somerset, 1:43	$50
Buick Roadmaster, 1:43	$75
Bus, 1:87	$20
Dumper, 1:87	$20
Fire Engine, 1:87	$25
Ford Prefect, 1:43	$75
Jaguar XK120, 1:87	$25
Land Rover, 1:87	$40
Massey Ferguson Tractor	$20
Pickup Truck, 1:87	$25
Racing Car, 1:87	$20
Tanker, 1:87	$25
Van, 1:87	$20
Wrecker, 1:87	$20

Lincoln International

This Hong Kong-based company produced some stylish trucks and tractors of late fifties to early sixties vintage. Their Major series offers durable and attractive diecast toys measuring around 8 inches long. Lincoln International also produced some fairly plain tinplate toys.

Dump Truck, red cab, silver painted grille, black chassis, yellow dumper	$60–75
Front End Loader Tractor, red with yellow loader and wheel hubs, black engine with silver accents	$60–75
Timber Truck, red cab, silver painted grille, yellow bed, black chassis, scored wooden block simulates load of lumber	$60–75

Lincoln Toys

Lincoln Toys of Windsor, Ontario, Canada, produced several pressed steel toys, valued by collectors from $100 to $600.

Lincoln White Metal Works

Lincoln White Metal Works of Lincoln, Nebraska, has produced models that more appropriately fit the definition of "diecast." From 1931 to 1940, Lincoln White Metal Works sold toys to Woolworth, Kress, Kresge, and Schwartz Paper Co., and many other markets. Identifying these models becomes difficult since not all of them are specifically marked.

Bluebird Record Car with V-8 engine, 6"	$150–175
Bluebird Record Car with V-8 engine, 4"	$100–125
Bluebird Record Car with V-12 engine, 4⅜"	$125–150
Chrysler or DeSoto Airflow Sedan, 3¾"	$75–100
Fire Engine, Graham-like grille, "Made in USA," 3½"	$75–100
Miller FWD Special Indy Racer, 5⅛"	$125–150
Pierce-Arrow Silver Arrow Sedan, 3½"	$75–100
Wrecker Car, Graham-like grille, "Made in USA," 3½"	$75–100
Tanker Truck, COE, "Made in USA," 3¾"	$75–100
Streamlined Railcar, 4½"	$100–125

Lindberg

Lindberg is best known for plastic kits of airplanes. In the mid sixties to early seventies, they produced a small assortment of fairly realistic 1:64 scale plastic kits with diecast chassis called Mini-Lindy. Thanks to Steve Mellon for the complete list. Values are for unassembled kits in their original packaging.

No. 1 Porsche Carrera, white with blue stripes, red interior and chrome engine	$12–15
No. 2 Ford Pick-Up, 30's vintage, green with black bed interior and brown chassis	$12–15
No. 3 Corvette Stingray, yellow with black stripes	$12–15
No. 4 Jaguar XK-E, red with twin white racing stripes and brown interior	$12–15
No. 5 '67 Mustang Fastback with black interior	$12–15
No. 6 Jeepster	$12–15
No. 7 Volkswagen Camper Van	$12–15
No. 8 Chevy Van	$12–15
No. 9 Camaro SS	$12–15
No. 10 Fire Engine	$12–15
No. 11 Dump Truck	$12–15
No. 12 Highway Bus, "Greyhound"	$12–15
No. 13 Mail Truck	$12–15
No. 14 Cement Mixer	$12–15
No. 15 MG TD Sports Car, blue with brown top	$12–15
No. 16 Tow Truck	$12–15
No. 17 1968 Corvette	$12–15
No. 18 Austin-Healey 3000	$12–15
No. 19 Volkswagen	$12–15
No. 20 Mercedes SSK	$12–15
No. 21 1930 Packard	$12–15
No. 22 Ford Camper	$12–15
No. 23 School Bus	$12–15
No. 24 Tractor Trailer	$12–15
No. 25 Pontiac Firebird	$12–15
No. 26 Porsche Targa	$12–15
No. 27 Dune Buggy	$12–15
No. 28 Jaguar D Type	$12–15
No. 29 Bobtail "T"	$12–15
No. 30 Ford GT	$12–15
No. 31 Oldsmobile Vista-Cruiser	$12–15
No. 32 Stake Truck	$12–15
Buick Riviera	$12–15

Line Mar

Line Mar (also spelled "Linemar") of Japan produced the Collectoy series of diecast friction toys representing American cars and trucks. Linemar has had a close affiliation with Marx, which is hinted at in the name.

Lintoy

Until I received in the mail a diecast "1:64" scale Mercedes-Benz C-111 made by Lintoy, I had forgotten ever having heard of them before. Model measures 3" and is metallic red with flat black painted metal base, black plastic interior, made in Hong Kong, and the rear engine compartment opens. As it turns out, Lintoys are made by Bachmann, the German model maker and producer of electric trains and sets, in the early to mid-seventies. The toy cars resemble a Playart, Tomica, or Matchbox of that period. Excellent detail and fair wheels punctuate this little model. Several others were listed with the letter of inquiry included with the model. Thanks to Helen Shaffer for the information and the model.

BMW Turbo, orange	$8–12
Mercedes-Benz C-111, metallic red	$8–12
Ford Mk IV, white	$8–12
Fiat Abarth, avocado	$8–12
Porsche 911, yellow	$8–12
Mercedes-Benz 350SL	$8–12

Lintoy Super Metal Mini-Planes

Besides cars, Bachmann also produced eight diecast airplanes dubbed "Bachmann / Lintoy Super Metal Mini-Planes."

Douglas A20 Boston / Havoc	$20–25
Grumman F-11A Tiger, #11	$25–35
Messerschmitt ME262	$25–35
Messerschmitt ME410	$25–35
Mig-21, #08	$30–40
NA-P-51D	$30–35
Saab 35X Draken, #07	$25–35
Sepecat Jaguar, #10	$25–35

Lion Car (see Lion Toys)

Lion Toys

Lion Toys of Holland were originally sold as Lion Car, a brand of simple diecast models from the Netherlands. While the company was founded in the mid-1940s, production of diecast toys started in 1956. Some models are refinished in the UK. Since 1995, the brand has been ressurected under new management, the new name and a new approach to scale and accuracy. Current models are detailed accurate replicas of European freighter semi-trucks in 1:50 scale. Thanks to Jan Scholten for the updates.

Currently Available Lion Toys

LN001 DAF 2300 Articulated Van Placketts, 1:50 ....(£18) $28 US
  DAF 2800 Dump Truck, 1:43........$24 US
LN002 Commer Walkthru Rutland Fire Brigade, 1:43 ....(£15) $24 US
LN003 Commer Walkthru Amusements: Fairground, 1:43.................(£25) $38 US
LN004 Commer Walkthru Marples Construction (1:43).....................(£25) $38 US
LN005 Commer Walkthru BRS Parcels (1:43)..........................(£25) $38 US

Obsolete Lion Cars

10 Volkswagen 1200 ....$125
11 Renault 4 CV $125
12 Opel Rekord............................$100
13 D.K.W. 316...............................$100
14 Renault Dauphine $75
20 DAF 1300 Chassis and Cabin $100
21 DAF 1300 Flat Truck....................$75
22 DAF 1300 Truck $100
22 DAF 1400 Truck $50
23 DAF 1400 Truck with tilt $75
23 DAF 1400 Army Truck with tilt.........$50
24 Trailer $15
25 Trailer with tilt $20
26 DAF 1300 Breakdown Lorry $100
26 DAF 1400 Breakdown Lorry $65
27 Renault Goelette Van $125
28 Commer Van $75
29 DAF 600 ....$100
30 DAF Daffodil $125
30 DAF Daffodil, gold-plated $300
31 DAF 750 Pickup $75
31 DAF 750 Pickup with tilt $75
32 DAF Torpedo Truck $75
33 DAF 33 ....$125
33/34 DAF Torpedo Semi-Trailer $75
33/35 DAF 1400 Semi-Trailer $25
33/35 DAF 1400 Semi-Trailer Army, olive $25
36 DAF 2600 Eurotrailer.....................$50
37 DAF 2600 Tank Trailer $50
38 DAF SE 200 Bus $50
39 DAF 33 Van $50
39 DAF 33 Van "REMIA" or "GROENPOL"......................$125
40 DAF 55 Coupe...........................$75
40 DAF 55 Coupe "CAMEL DAF RACING TEAM"............................$150

40 DAF 55 Coupe "LYONS INTERNATIONAL"..............................$150
40 DAF 66 SL Coupe $50
41 DAF 44 Station Wagon $50
42 DAF Pony Semi Trailer $65
42 DAF 55 Coupe with DAF emblem $75
43 DAF 20001Z200 Covered Truck......$50
43 DAF 2000/2200 Military Covered Truck, olive $50
44 DAF 44 ....$75
44 DAF 44 "GVB AMSTERDAM" or "MARATHON" $175
45 DAF Pony Truck $65
46 DAF 750 Pickup with hood.............$65
46 DAF 46 ....$65
47 DAF 2000/2200 Bulk Carrier $50
48 DAF 2000/2200 Truck & Trailer $50
49 Commer Van "TECHNISCHE UNIE".$75
50 DAF 2600 Car Carrier $75
54 Commer Van "Van GEND & LOOS".$40
55 Commer Van "POSTERIJEN" $40
55 Commer Van 3 ....$25
56 DAF 2000/2200 Tipping Truck $45
57 DAF 2600 Container Trailer $50
58 DAF 2800 Covered Truck $45
59 DAF 2800 Eurotrailer.....................$45
60 DAF 2800 Car Transporter $45
61 DAF 2800 Container Trailer $40
62 DAF 2800 Tank Trailer $25
63 DAF 2800 Truck and Trailer $25
64 DAF 2800 6-W.Truckand Trailer $25
66 DAF 2800 6-W. Covered Truck.......$25
67 DAF 2800 6-W. Tanker...................$25
68 DAF 2300 Covered Truck $25
68 DAF 2300 Military Covered Truck, olive $25

Lion Models

Lion Models are 1:87 scale diecast kits from Germany, according to Werner Legrand of Belgium. He comments that, to the best of his knowledge, Gunther Frieherr (Baron) von Dobeneck founded the company that is reportedly still in business.

3 Fiat 500 A Topolino 1936–48 ...$12–15
4 Fiat 500 Luxus 1961 ....$12–15
7 Glas Goggomobil Coupe 1964–69 ....$12–15
8 Glas Goggomobil S35 Coupe Prototype 1959 ....$12–15
10 NSU Fiat 500 Weinsberg Coupe 1960–63 ....$12–15
11 Fiat 500 Giardiniera Familiare 1961 ....$12–15
12 Lloyd LP 300 1950–51 ....$12–15
13 VW Porsche 914 1969–74......$12–15
14 Lloyd LC 300 Coupe 1952.......$12–15
15 Glas Goggomobil Cabrio Prototype..............................$12–15
17 NSU Fiat 500 C 1952–55.......$12–15
18 NSU Fiat 500 Spyder-Sport Weinsberg 1939 ....$12–15
19 Peugeot 205 1983–present $12–15

20 Ford Taurus Special G-73 A 1950–51 ....$12–15
21 Veritas Saturn Coupe 1950.......$12–15
22 Veritas Comet Roadster 1950 ...$12–15
25 Austin-Healey Sprite 1958–61 ...$12–15
26 Lloyd LS 300 Kombi 1952........$12–15
27 Peugeot 205 Turbo 16 1985....$12–15
28 Isdera Imperator 108 i 1984–91.$12–15
29 Isdera Spyder 033 i 1982–present.$12–15
30 Bugatti Type 55 Coupe 1932–35 .$12–15
32 Lotus Super Seven 1961–66......$12–15
33 Bugatti T 41 Royale Cabriolet 1931.$12–15
34 Jaguar XK 150 Roadster 1957–60 ....$12–15
35 AC Cobra Shelby 427 1965–present......................................$12–15
36 Stutz Royale 1979–88..............$12–15
37 Studebaker President Speedster 1955 ....$12–15
38 Jaguar XK 150 Roadster 1957–60 ....$12–15
39 Rometsch Beeskow Cabrio 1951–54 ....$12–15
40 Mini 1000 Mk III $12–15
41 Ford Fiesta 1989–96 ....$12–15
42 Marcos Mantula 3500 V8 1985–93 ....$12–15
43 Fiat Panda 1000 CL 1986–present.$12–15
44 VW Polo 1981–90.................$12–15
45 Mazda MX-5 Miata 1989–present.$12–15
46 Riley Elf Mk III 1966–69 ....$12–15
47 Ferrari 250 GT Spyder 1961–63 ....$12–15
48 Bugatti T-41 Royale Fiacre Coupe 1928 ....$12–15
49 Tucker Torpedo 1948 ....$12–15
50 Jaguar MK-2 1959–67 ....$12–15
51 Mini Pick-Up 1961 ....$12–15
52 MG Midget Mk III 1966–69.....$12–15
53 Ford Taurus Cabriolet 1951.......$12–15
54 Ferrari 365 GTS-4 Daytona Spyder 1969–73 ....$12–15
55 Mini Cabrio 1990 ....$12–15
56 Mini Clubman Saloon 1969–80 .$12–15
57 Mazda 121 1990–96 ....$12–15
58 Mini Morris Minivan 1960 ....$12–15
59 Mini Clubman Estate 1969–80..$12–15
60 Mini Morris Traveler 1960–69...$12–15
61 Mini Broadspeed GT Coupe 1966–68 ....$12–15
62 Honda Beat 1991–95 ....$12–15
63 Triumph TR 3 1955–57 ....$12–15
64 Ferrari 365 GTB-4 Daytona Coupe 1969–73 ....$12–15
65 Bugatti T 55 Roadster 1932–35 ..$12–15
66 Ferrari 250 GT Berlinetta SWB 1959–62 ....$12–15
67 Nissan Figaro 1991 ....$12–15
68 Ghia Fiat 500 Jolly $12–15
69 Borgward Isabella Coupe 1957–61 ....$12–15
70 Autobianchi Bianchina Trasformabile 1957–62 ....$12–15

Lionel

Lionel has set the standard for electric toy trains for most of this century. Now they produce a number of vehicles for use with train sets, specifically HO gauge semi trucks and trailers with various liveries. These are recently introduced models that are still available from hobby shops and specialty dealers for $65 to $80 each.

In addition, an assortment of Lionel plastic 1955 Ford Custom 2-door sedans is also offered in blue, red, white, or yellow for $15 each.

Lionel is also the producer of "Revolvers," reversible cars that convert from one car to another when flipped over. A growing interest in these unusual toys has sparked several Hong Kong-based companies to produce knockoff versions, including Ja-Ru Real Wheels and Imperial Diecast.

Lit'l Toy (Mercury Industries U.S.A.)

In March 1999, collector Bruce Mibeck of Illinois reported of an unusual toy among his collection of Matchbox, Budgie, Husky, Lone Star, Penny, and other toys. It has the designation "Lit'l Toy by Mercury Inds. U.S.A." on the base. This is the first and only reference to this brand I've seen so far. Value is highly speculative since I've never seen the particular model and have found no other reference to the brand.

No. 101 International Dozer $15–40

Litan

Litan is one of the emerging model manufactures to originate from Russia. Their line of models includes Samara and Lada vehicles and Belarus tractors.

Lixin

Lixin models are made in China, and little else is known about them. Any details are appreciated.

1932 Dong Feng 4-Door Sedan (tin), 1:25 ..$20	
1950 Army Jeep CJ2, 1:32 ....$20	
1950 Buick Super Convertible, top down (tin), 1:25 ....$20	
1950 Buick Super Coupe (tin), 1:25 ....$20	
1950 Cadillac 2-Door Hardtop, 1:25 ....$20	
1950 Cadillac Convertible, top down, 1:25 .$20	
1950 Harley Davidson with Sidecar, 1:25 ..$20	
1955 Chevrolet Corvette Convertible, top up (tin), 1:25 ....$20	
1955 Chevrolet Corvette Convertible, top down (tin), 1:25 ....$20	
1957 Chevrolet Corvette Convertible, top down, 1:25 ....$20	
1957 Chevrolet Corvette Convertible, top up, 1:25 ....$20	
1960 Toyota Crown Ambulance (tin), 1:25 ..$20	
1961 Ford Thunderbird 2-Door Hardtop, 1:25 ....$20	
1970 Volkswagen Bus, 1:43 ....$20	
Beijing Fire Ladder Truck (tin), 9" $20	
Beijing Double Decker Bus (tin), 9" $20	

BMW 507 Convertible, top down, 1:25 ....$20
BMW 507 Convertible, top up, 1:25 ....$20
Douglas DC3 Overseas Airplane, 9" $20
Jaguar E-Type 2+2 Coupe, 1:25 ....$20
Jaguar E-Type Convertible, top down, 1:25 ..$20
Mercedes-Benz 300SL Gullwing Coupe, 1:25 ....$20
Mercedes-Benz 450 4-Door Sedan, 1:25 ...$20
Volkswagen Karmann Ghia Coupe, 1:25 ....$20

LJN (also see Hallmark)

LJN has produced a number of inexpensive diecast toys that are essentially generic in form and markings and of generally low quality. A few such toys were made for Hallmark in the seventies, sometimes marked as Road Rovers. See Hallmark for list and values.

At least one vehicle has been found with the LJN mark on its base, as reported via e-mail by Larry Johnston.

Police S.W.A.T. Van, blue, 3", "Spelling Goldberg Prod. LJN Toys Hong Kong" on base $1-2

Lledo

When Lesney sold the Matchbox line of diecast toys to Universal Holding Company of Hong Kong in 1982, John W. "Jack" Odell left the firm, of which he was a partner for many years, to form Lledo (Odell spelled backwards). Lledo models are also known as Days Gone and designated as DG.

Every one of the hundreds of Lledo models produced for the first six years are variations of approximately 30 base models. Color and markings are what differentiate each model. Here is a list of the basic models, from which the numerous variations have arisen through the years. The value of each model depends on the number of each variation produced from year to year.

Most regular production models sell for $7 to $10 each. Limited edition models vary considerably, depending on availability and quantity produced. Dr. Force's book Lledo toys serves as an excellent source for variations and values.

The latest addition to the Lledo product line is the Vanguard series. These fifties and sixties British vehicles are strongly reminiscent of the kinds of toys issued by Corgi and Dinky some thirty years ago.

In 1999, Lledo filed for bankruptcy and went into receivership. By November 1999, Lledo was purchased by the same newly-formed Zindart of Hong Kong, the same company that only a month earlier had purchased the Corgi brand.

Schwan's Truck $10–12

UPS Truck..............................$15–18

Lledo Models Introduced in 1983
DG1 Horse Drawn Tram...................$9–12
DG2 Horse Drawn Milk Float...........$9–12
DG3 Delivery Van $9–12
DG4 Omnibus $9–12
DG5 Fire Engine...............................$9–12
DG6 Ford Model T $9–12

Lledo Models Introduced in 1984
DG7 Ford Woody Wagon $9–12
DG8 Ford Model T Tanker..............$9–12
DG9 Ford Model A Touring Car with top down $9–12
DG10 Albion Single Decker Coach ...$9–12
DG11 Large Horse Drawn Van $9–12
DG12 Fire Engine $9–12
DG13 1934 Ford Model A Van $9–12

Lledo Models Introduced in 1985
DG14 Ford Model A Touring Car, top up $9–12
DG15 AEC Double Deck Bus..........$9–12
DG16 Heavy Goods Van $9–12
DG17 Long Distance Coach $9–12
DG18 Packard Van $9–12
DG19 Rolls Royce Phantom II $9–12

Lledo Models Introduced in 1986
DG20 1930 Ford Model A Stake Truck...................................$9–12
DG21 Chevrolet Van $9–12
DG22 Packard Town Van $9–12

Lledo Models Introduced in 1987
DG23 Scenicruiser Bus..................$18–20
DG24 Rolls Royce Playboy Convertible Coupe $9–12
DG25 Rolls Royce Silver Ghost Tourer $9–12
DG26 1934 Chevrolet Bottle Truck....$9–12
DG27 Mack Breakdown Truck..........$9–12
DG28 1934 Mack Canvas Back Truck...................................$9–12

Lledo Models Introduced in 1988 and later
DG29 1942 Dodge Truck...............$9–12
DG30 1939 Chevrolet Pickup Truck ..$9–12
DG31 Brewer's Dray $9–12
DG33 1920 Model T Ford Car $9–12
DG36 1938 Chevrolet Pickup $9–12
DG41 1928 Karrier E6 Trolley Bus $9–12
DG42 1934 Mack Tanker Truck $9–12
DG43 1931 Morris Van $9–12
DG44 1937 Scammell 6-Wheeler $9–12
DG46 1930 Bentley 4.5 Litre $9–12
DG47 1933 Austin Taxi.................$9–12
DG48 1939 Chevrolet $9–12

DG49 1931 AEC Renown Double Deck Bus $9–12
DG50 1926 Bullnose Morris Van $9–12
DG52 1935 Morris Truck $9–12
DG57 1939 Ford Tanker $9–12
DG58 1950 Morris Van $9–12
DG59 1950 Bedford 30cwt Truck $9–12
DG60 1955 Dennis F8 Fire Engine ...$9–12
DG61 1953 Pontiac Van $9–12
DG62 1935 Ford Tanker $9–12
DG63 1950 Bedford 30cwt Delivery Van $9–12
DG65 1960 Morris Traveller $9–12
DG66 1926 Dennis Delivery Van $9–12
DG67 1935 Ford 3 Ton Articulated Truck...$9–12
DG68 1932 AEC Regent Open Top Bus $9–12
DG71 1959 Morris LD 150 Van $9–12

DG73 1955 VW Transporter Van $9–12

DG75 1957 Bristol LD6G Lodekka Bus $9–12
DG77 1937 Scammell Tanker $9–12
DG78 1939 Dodge Airflow $9–12
DG79 1939 Ford Fire Engine $9–12
DG80 1937 Scammell Tanker $9–12
DG82 1930 Ford Model A Coupe ...$9–12
DG85 1912 Renault Van $9–12
DG86 1955 VW Camper $9–12
DG87 1951 M.A.N. Van $9–12
DG88 1931 Sentinel DG4 Steam Wagon.........................$9–12
DG90 1966 GMC Tanker................$9–12
DG91 1930 Foden Steam Wagon ...$9–12
DG92 Bentley 'S' Series $9–12

Lledo Rolls-Royce Collection

SL32 1907 Rolls-Royce 40/50 hp Ghost
v.1 SL32000 silver $9–12

v.2 SL32002 red with silver cowl...$9–12
SL53 1926 Rolls-Royce 20 hp Landaulet
v.1 SL53000 mushroom and maroon..........................$9–12
v.2 SL53002 cream and brown ..$9–12
SL54 1929 Rolls-Royce Phantom II 'D' Back
v.1 SL54000 white and brown....$9–12

v.2 SL54001 yellow and black ...$9–12
v.3 SL54005 two-tone green.......$9–12
SL89 1959 Rolls-Royce Silver Cloud
v.1 SL89000 metallic gray and silver $9–12
v.2 SL89001 black $9–12

Lledo Bentley Collection

SL46 1930 Bentley 4½ Litre 'Blower'
v.1 SL46000 dark green.........................$9–12

SL46 1930 Bentley 4½ Litre 'Blower'
v.2 SL46001 blue $9–12
v.3 SL46002 red $9–12
v.4 SL46004 gray.....................$9–12
SL92 Bentley 'S' Series
v.1 SL92000 maroon and silver...$9–12

Lledo Vanguard Models
VA1002 Ford Anglia, white and maroon $22
VA2000 Volkswagen Cabriolet, red $22
VA2001 Volkswagen Cabriolet, light blue...............................$22
VA3000 Austin A40 Van, dark green, Ransome's Lawnmowers $22

Gold Jaguar E-Type $20–25

VA4002 Ford Anglia Van, pale blue, Hotpoint $22
VA5000 Triumph Herald, red $22
VA5002 Triumph Herald, yellow $22
VA6000 Ford Thames Trader Van, Martini..............................$27
VA7000 Bedford "S" Type Tanker, Regent $27
VA7001 Bedford "S" Type Tanker, Shell-BP $27
VA8000 Bedford "S" Type Van, Heinz 57 Varieties $27
VA9000 Ford Thames Trader Tanker, North Eastern Gas $27
VA12000 Volkswagen Beetle, beige $22

Lledo Vanguard 1:43 Scale Car Range

Gold Lotus Europa $9–12

Gold Shelby Cobra $9–12

Ford Classic 109E............................$9–12

VA22 Regal Reliant............................$30
VA23 Austin A35 ....$30
VA24 Karrier Boxback $30
VA25 Mini Cooper $30
VA26 Hillman Imp $30
VA28 Commer Boxback $30

Lledo Land Speed Legends
LP4903 Thrust SSC............................$40

LP5267 Bluebird $20

LP5268 Thrust 2 ....$20

LP5269 Railton Mobil Special $20

LP5270 Sonic 1 ....$20

Lledo Chevron Promotional Models
1990:
1934 Mack Tanker, Red Crown Gasoline $18–24
1928 Chevrolet Van, Zerolene Motor Oil............................$18–24

1930 Ford Model A Stake Truck, Atlas Tire Truck $18–24

1991:
1920 Ford Model T, Red Crown ...$15–20
1934 Dennis Fire Engine, Refinery Fire Dept. $15–20
1938 Chevrolet Pickup, Standard Oil $15–20

1992:
1936 Packard Van Broadcast Car, Standard Oil Announcer $12–15
Horse Drawn Tanker, Polarine $12–15
1930 Ford Model A (High Roof), Atlas Tires $12–15

1993:
1927 Gasoline Truck, Red Crown (Standard Oil) $15–20
Chain Drive Tank Truck, Zerolene ... $15–20
1936 Ford Model A Van, Atlas Tires $15–20

1994:

1935 Ford Articulated Semi Truck and Trailer, Chevron $12–15

Streamlined Tank Truck, Standard $12–15

Horse Drawn Tank Wagon, Standard Oil $12–15

1995:

1939 Ford Flatbed Truck and Barrels, Standard Oil Roof Paint $10–12

1937 Scammell Six-Wheel Refined Oil Truck, Supreme Chevron Gasoline $10–12

1920 Ford Model T Van, Red Crown $10–12

1996:
1942 Dodge 4 x 4 Chevron Exploration Van $9–10
1939 Ford Fire Engine, Richmond Refinery $9–10
Ford Atlas Tire Service Vehicle $9–10

1997:

1963 GMC Fuel Delivery Truck, Chevron $8–9

1934 Mack Crane Truck, Standard Oil Well Repair $8–9

REO Lubricant Delivery Truck, Standard Lubricants $8–9

1950 Bedford 30CWT, Standard Oil $8–9

1998:
1935 Ford Articulated Tanker, Crown Gasoline $8–9

Other Lledo Promotionals

1926 Dennis Delivery Van, Campbell's Condensed Soups $10–12

1955 Volkswagen Kombi Van, Pepsi-Cola $10–12

1955 Volkswagen Kombi Van, 7-Up ... $10–12

Loden Aquli

Three Loden Aquli 1:64 scale models from Argentina are known and listed below.
Dodge Charger Show Car $5
Renault 12 Sedan $5
Renault 12 Taxi $5

Lomo

ZIS and GAZ models dominate the product line of this Russian manufacturer of 1:43 diecast models.

Londontoy

From 1945 to 1950, Londontoy diecast toys were produced in London, Ontario, and in the US by the Leslie Henry Company. The difference can be found in the absence or presence of the words "Made In Canada." Tires are usually white rubber or wood. Bodies are similar to Tootsietoys, with no chassis or base and no interior. Thanks go to Paul Voorhis for providing additional details, including model numbers and correct length.

Mr. Voorhis writes, "All the 6" Chevrolets that I have seen have a wind-up motor geared to the front axle. All were painted white with 'POLICE' decals on doors and trunk. Does M stand for motorized or mechanical as in early Corgi toys? Was there a version of this without the motor, a plain #54? There are also black rubber wheels, and on the 6" Chevrolets they appear with large, shiny axle ends to simulate hubcaps. Some Londontoys have white wheels made of what appears to be thick cardboard."
Beverage Truck, #15, 1941 GMC Cabover, 4" $25
Beverage Truck, #41, 5", marked "ARMY SERVICE TRUCK" underneath, 1941 GMC Cabover, 5" $30

Canadian Greyhound Bus, #33, 5" $40
1941 Chevrolet Master Deluxe Coupe, #14, 4" $25
1941 Chevrolet Master Deluxe Coupe, #54M, 6" $30
City Bus, 4" $30
City Bus, 6" $30
1941 Ford Fire Truck, 6" $30
1941 Ford Open Cab Firetruck, #16, 4" $25
1941 Ford Pickup Truck, #12, 4" $25
1941 Ford Pickup Truck, 6" $30
Hawker Hurricane Airplane, #11, 4" $40
Large Car Transporter $100
Large Dump Truck $100
Large Lumber Truck $100
Large Moving Van with tin body $100
Large Stake Truck $100
Large Tractor and Van Trailer $100
Oil Tanker, 1941 GMC Cabover, #13, 4"
    v.1 plain $30
    v.2 Imperial Esso $30
Oil Tanker, 6" $30
Panel Delivery, #32, 1941 Ford, 5" $40
Six-Window Sedan, #31, 1939 Ford Deluxe or 1940 Ford Standard, 5" $40
Steam Switch Locomotive, possibly #1, 3"....$50
Thunderbolt Racer, 6" $40

Lone Star (also see Crescent, D.C.M.T., Impy, Roadmaster)

While Lone Star of Great Britain has produced many toys, perhaps the most popular models were those better known as Impy toys. The complete name for one series of toys is "Lone Star Road-Master Impy Super Cars," so it is no wonder that they are better known as Impy toys. "Roadmaster" was spelled with a hyphen in 1956 (Road-Master), and later without the hyphen beginning in 1962.

The Lone Star brand was originated in 1951 by Diecasting Machine Tools Ltd., otherwise known as D.C.M.T. Besides toy cars, Lone Star specialized in cap pistols and cowboy outfits, hence the reference. The Road-Master line of toy cars debuted in 1956. A second offering, combining the hyphenated words into "Roadmaster," was released in 1962.

Flyers

In response to the introduction of Hot Wheels in 1968, Lone Star issued newer models dubbed Road-Master "Flyers" Super Cars. They lacked the rhinestone headlights and the "Impy" name of the earlier models. This models issued in 1956 had no number designation, while those issued in 1962 were given numbers in the 1400 range. Later Impy Roadmaster models were given just a two-digit designation.

Tuf-Tots

The Lone Star Tuf-Tots series, 1:118 scale trucks and 1:86 scale cars of comparatively crude castings, were introduced in 1969. Around the same time as Tuf-Tots (1969),

Lone Star also introduced Roadmaster Majors, 1:43 scale trucks of simple castings.

D.C.M.T.

D.C.M.T. was founded in 1940 by engineers Sidney Ambridge and Aubrey Mills. Besides producing products under the Lone Star brand, D.C.M.T. also manufactured diecasting machinery for Lesney (the original company that produced Matchbox toys) and Kemlows. The first toys manufactured by D.C.M.T. were marketed by Crescent of England. D.C.M.T. and Lone Star went out of business in 1983.

Lone Star Chronology

1940 – D.C.M.T. manufacturing firm founded
1951 – Lone Star brand introduced
1956 – Road-Master series begun
1960 – D.C.M.T. strikes a deal with Tootsietoys to produce Classic Series of 1:50 scale American cars
1962 – Roadmaster name adopted, new models added to the line
1966 – Impy Roadmaster name adopted, more new models offered
1968 – Flyers introduced with new wheels and axles to compete with Hot Wheels, Impy trucks renamed Lone Star Commercials
1969 – Tuf-Tots, Roadmaster Majors introduced
1976 – Flyers, Commercials discontinued, cheaper series of new Impy toys introduced
1983 – Lone Star and parent company D.C.M.T. go out of business

Lone Star Model Listing A to Z, including Road-Master, Roadmaster, Flyers, and Commercials

Alfa Romeo Giulia Spyder, Roadmaster #23 ....$30–40
Alfa Romeo Giulia Spyder, Flyers #23 ....$15–25
Austin Western Mobile Crane, #33 .$25–35
Builder's Supply Truck, Commercials #41 ....$15–25
Cadillac 62 Sedan, #1472, 1962 ....$65–80
Cadillac Coupe de Ville, white & blue $95–120
Cadillac Eldorado, Flyers #40 ....$25–30
Case International Harvester 946 Farm Tractor $18–25
Chevrolet Corvair, #1470, 1962, coral $65–80
Chevrolet Corvair, #1470, 1962, white $90–110
Chevrolet Corvair Fire Car, #1479, 1962 ....$45–60
Chevrolet Corvair Feuerwehr, #1479, 1962 ....$55–70
Chevrolet Corvair Staff Car, #1480, 1962 ....$45–60
Chevrolet Corvette, 1964, teal $25–30
Chevrolet Corvette, Flyers #38 ....$20–30
Chevrolet Corvette Gran Turismo Coupe, Roadmaster #11 ....$30–45

Chevrolet Corvette Gran Turismo Coupe, Flyers #11 ....$20–35
Chevrolet El Camino, #1474, 1962.$60–75
Chrysler Imperial, Roadmaster #12, metallic blue $60–75
Chrysler Imperial, Flyers #12 ....$25–40
Citroën DS 19, #1482, 1962 ....$55–70
Daimler (1904), 1956 ....$35–50
Daimler Conquest Roadster, 1956, 1:40 ....$65–80
Darracq Genevieve (1904), 1956 ..$35–50
Dodge Dart Phoenix, #1475, 1962, metallic blue $95–120
Dodge Dart Phoenix Police, #1477, 1962 ....$45–60
Dodge Dart Phoenix Polizei, #1477, 1962 ....$60–75
Euclid 82-80 Crawler Tractor, #34 ..$20–35
Fiat 2300 S Coupe, Roadmaster #21 ....$25–35
Fiat 2300 S Coupe, Flyers #21 ......$15–25
Foden COE Tilt Cab 8-Wheel Dump Truck, Roadmaster #24, 1962 ....$20–35
Foden Half-Cab High-Side Lorry, Commercials #47 ....$20–30
Foden Half-Cab Hopper Lorry, Commercials #48 ....$20–30
Foden Half-Cab Tipper, Commercials #49 ....$20–30
Foden Half-Cab Tipper, Commercials #42 ....$15–25
Foden Tipper, Commercials #24, 1968 ....$18–25
Foden Fuel Tanker, "Mobil," Roadmaster #26, 1962 ....$25–40
Foden Fuel Tanker, "Mobil," Commercials #26, 1968 ....$20–30
Foden Truck, "Express Freight" or "Lucas Batteries," Roadmaster #29 ....$25–35
Foden Truck, "Express Freight" or "Lucas Batteries," Commercials #29 ....$15–25
Ford 7610 Farm Tractor $18–25
Ford Corsair, Roadmaster #18 ....$25–35
Ford Corsair, Flyers #18 ....$20–30
Ford Corsair Fire Chief Car, #32 .....$25–35
Ford Zodiac Estate Car, Roadmaster #14 ....$30–45
Ford Zodiac Estate Car, Flyers #14 ..$20–35
Ford Zodiac Estate Police Car, Roadmaster #16 ....$30–45
Ford Zodiac Estate Police Car, Flyers #16 ....$20–35
Ford Model T (1912), 1956 ....$45–60
Ford Mustang Fastback, Flyers #39 ....$25–30
Ford Sunliner Convertible, #1473, 1962, pale blue $115–140
Ford Taunus 12M, Roadmaster #27 ....$25–40
Ford Taunus 12M, Flyers #27 ....$20–30
Ford Thunderbird, 1:40 ....$65–80
Ford Transit Breakdown Truck, Roadmaster #31, 1962 ....$25–35

Ford Transit Breakdown Truck, Commercials #31, 1968 ....$15–25
Ford Zodiak Estate $35–40
Garage Ramp, #401 ....$30–45
Garage, lock-up, #402 ....$20–35
International Harvester 946 Farm Tractor with shovel, #25 ....$20–30
Jaguar Mk. 10, Roadmaster #10 .....$35–40
Jaguar Mk. 10, Flyers #10 ....$25–30
Leyland Drop-Side Lorry, Commercials #46 ....$20–30
Leyland High-Side Lorry, Commercials #47 ....$20–30
Leyland Hopper Lorry, Commercials #48 ....$20–30
Locomotive $25–30
London Taxi, 1:50 ....$25–30
Lotus Europa, Flyers #36 ....$20–30
Marine Transport Truck with plastic boat, Commercials #44 ....$20–30
Maserati Mistral, Flyers #9 ....$20–30
Massey Ferguson 3070 Tractor $18–25
Mercedes-Benz 220SE, #17 ....$25–35
Mercedes-Benz 220SE Police Car, Roadmaster #16M $25–35
Mercedes-Benz 220SE Police Car, Flyers #16M $20–30
Merryweather Turntable Fire Engine, Commercials #30 ....$30–40
MG TF, 1:35, 1956 ....$65–80
Military Jeep, olive drab $65–75
Morris Bullnose (1912), 1956 ....$35–50
Peugeot 404, Roadmasters #28 ......$20–30
Peugeot 404, Flyers #28 ....$15–25
Pumps and Sign, "Mobil," #404 .....$20–35
Rambler Ambulance, #1478, 1962 .$45–60
Rambler Army Ambulance, #1481, 1962 ....$45–60
Rambler Army Station Wagon, #1471, 1962 ....$50–65
Rambler Station Wagon, #1471, 1962 ....$45–60
Rolls-Royce Silver Cloud, #1476, 1962 ....$55–70
Rolls-Royce Silver Cloud Convertible, Roadmaster #22 ....$25–35
Rolls-Royce Silver Cloud Convertible, Flyers #22 ....$15–25
Routemaster Double Decker Bus $18–25
Toyota 2000 GT, Flyers #13 ....$20–30
Vauxhall Firenza Coupe, Flyers #7 ...$25–30
Volkswagen Microbus, Roadmaster #15 ....$40–55
Volkswagen Microbus, Flyers #15 ...$25–35
Volkswagen Microbus Ambulance, Roadmaster #20 ....$25–40
Volkswagen Microbus Ambulance, Flyers #20 ....$25–40
Volvo P1800S, Roadmaster #19 .....$25–35
Volvo P1800S, Flyers #19 ....$20–30

Tuf-Tots Series, 1969
Big L Dump Truck, #607 ....$7–9
Caravan, #625 ....$15–18

Cement Mixer Truck, #615 ....$7–10
Circus Cage Truck, #626 ....$7–10
Citroën Coupe, #619 ....$12–15
Citroën DS Sports, #602 ....$12–15
City Refuse Truck, #614 ....$7–10
Dodge Dart Coupe, #621 ....$12–15
Dodge Dart Sport, #604 ....$12–15
Earth Mover, #627 ....$7–10
Esso Tanker, #601 ....$15–20
Express Freight Truck, #611 ....$7–10
Fire Engine, #624 ....$7–10
Herts Farms Jeep and Trailer, #608 ..$12–15
Horse Box, #617 ....$12–15
L.S. Construction Tipper Truck, #610 ..$7–10
London Bus, #623 ....$12–15
Low Loader, #612 ....$12–15
M Autos Truck with Petrol Pumps, #609 ....$12–15
Mercedes Coupe, #622 ....$15–18
Mercedes Sport, #605 ....$12–15
Milk Delivery Truck, #616 ....$12–15
Speedboat and Trailer, #613 ....$12–15
Stingray Coupe, #620 ....$15–18
Stingray Sports, #603 ....$12–15
Tow Truck, #606 ....$12–15
Waste Disposal Truck, #618 ....$7–10

New Impy Series, 1976
Articulated Transporter with pipes and water tank, #184 ....$12–15
Boat Transporter, #188 ....$15–18
Breakdown Truck with Lotus Europa, #186 ....$15–18
Bulk Carrier and Trailer, #191 ....$12–15
Cadillac, #72 ....$12–15
Cadillac with speedboat on trailer, #185 ....$15–18
Cement Mixer and Trailer, #192 .....$12–15
Corvette GT Rally, #76 ....$12–15
Corvette Stingray Fastback, #74 ......$12–15
Crane Truck, #181 ....$10–12
Esso Fuel Tanker, #182 ....$10–12
Ford Mustang, #79 ....$15–18
Jaguar, #77 ....$15–18
Jaguar with cabin cruiser on trailer, #185 ....$15–18
Lotus Europa, #80 ....$12–15
Low Loader with Tuf-Tots Car, #183 .$15–18
Maserati Mistral, #78 ....$15–18
Mercedes-Benz, #82 ....$10–12
Petrol Tanker and Trailer, #190 ....$15–18
Range Rover, #71 ....$12–15
Range Rover Police Car, #75 ....$10–12
Range Rover with speedboat on trailer, #185 ....$15–18
Six-Wheel Bulk Carrier, #51 ....$10–12
Six-Wheel Cement Mixer, #54 ....$10–12
Six-Wheel Crane Truck, #52 ....$10–12
Six-Wheel Express Freight Truck, #55 .$10–12
Six-Wheel Low Sided Truck, #56 .....$10–12
Six-Wheel Marine Transporter, #53 .$10–12
Six-Wheel Petrol Tanker, #61 ....$10–12
Six-Wheel Sand Truck, #58 ....$10–12
Six-Wheel Timber Truck, #60 ....$10–12

Six-Wheel Tipper, #50 ....$10–12
Six-Wheel Water Pipe Truck, #59 ...$10–12
Six-Wheel Water Tank Truck, #57 ...$10–12
Timber Truck, #189 ....$10–12
Toyota Coupe, #73 ....$12–15
Volvo 264 Coupe, #81 ....$10–15

LP Creation (also see Evrat 87)
LP Creation is one of many brands associated with MAFMA, the French model auto artisans union. The brand encompasses high quality Formula One replicas. See more details at Evrat 87.

Lucky Plan Industries, Ltd. (see Specialty Diecast)

Luso
These are diecast and plastic models made in Portugal in the early to mid-eighties. Harvey Goranson reports that they made a nice racing version of the BMW 320 in Liechtenstein livery as raced at LeMans.
BMW 320 ....$35
Citroën GS Pallas "Michelin," yellow $35
Porsche 935, Martini racing, Car #4, blue 7, red stripes, #M8, 1:43 ....$35

M C Toys (see Maisto)

The Ma Collection
A brochure from Sinclair's Mini-Auto (see resource directory in back of this book) describes the 1:43 scale 1946 "Rita Hayworth" Delahaye 135M as "the sensuously-bodied convertible that Prince Ali Khan gave to Hollywood star Rita Hayworth. Custom coachwork by Figoni Falaschi, this fabulous 1:43 scale miniature is by the famous Ma Collection of Switzerland." Only 150 copies of this model have been made promising high resale value. Other 1:43 scale Ma models are made in France.

Also produced for the Ma Collection were some resin hand-built models back in the mid-seventies.
1953 Bugatti 101 Antem, red and black $350–395
1937 Bugatti 57 Milord, yellow and black $350–395
1939 Bugatti 57, available in yellow and black or green and black $350–395
1946 Delahaye 135M "Rita Hayworth" $350–395
1949 Delahaye 135M Guillore, blue .$350–395
1938 Delahaye V12 Roadster, red ...$350–395
1945 Hispano Suiza K6 ....$350–395
1948 Talbot Lago T26 GS, blue, white, or black $350–395

Madison
How I missed this brand up until now is a mystery. White metal 1:43 scale models are what comprise this quality assortment. More

information forthcoming soon.

1952 Buick Super 2-Door Hardtop ...$100–150
1952 Buick Super Convertible.........$100–150

Madmax (see Grip Zechin)

MAFMA

Les Meilleurs Artisans Français du Modélisme Automobile
(French Model Automobile Artisans)
website: www.mafma.com

MAFMA is a French consortium for manufacturers of resin and metal kits and built models by ACB, Le Phoenix, Andre-Marie Ruf, Piranha Models, Plan 43X, L'Eau Rouge, Evrat87, LP Creation, Feeling43, Gaffe, JPS, Tenariv, Renaissance, Integral, Provence Moulage, Profil 24, Le Mans Miniatures, GTS, and Ilario. For French model car artisans, MAFMA represents strength through unity.

Magic (also see Excite)

Magic / Excite
1270 Champion Circle
Carrollton, TX 75006

A diecast toy assortment that goes by the Magic brand curiously bears the same address on the back of their package as Excite models. Closer inspection, particularly of the Chevy Caprice fire department command car, reveals it to be made by Welly. Apparently this practice of repackaging and re-branding diecast toys is not as uncommon as we might think.

Magnuson Models

Although not diecast, Magnuson models, manufactured by Wm. K. Walthers, Inc., are such superb miniatures that they deserve mention. These HO scale (1:87) model kits are intended for use with HO train sets. As stated in the Walthers HO catalog, "Whether parked at the curb or on the roll, these detailed autos bring HO scale streets to life! These American classics make the perfect super-detail for steam or diesel era scenes, and help set the time and place of your entire layout. Each model is a one-piece resin casting with all details molded in place. Cast-metal wheels are included, and some models feature separate metal bumpers. Just assemble and paint, and these easy-to-build kits are ready for the road."

439-910 '48 Coupe, pkg. of 2 ....$7.98
439-911 '39 Sedan Delivery, pkg. of 2...$7.98
439-912 '53 Hardtop, pkg. of 2.........$7.98
439-913 '41 Convertible with top up, pkg. of 2 ....$7.98
439-914 '59 Checker Marathon Taxi, pkg. of 2 ....$7.98
439-917 Divco Milk Truck, pkg. of 2 ......$7.98
439-919 '41 Pickup Truck, pkg. of 2 ......$7.98
439-920 '40 Traveler 4-Door Sedan, pkg. of 2 ....$7.98
439-921 '53 Tank Truck, each $7.98
439-922 '54 Panel Truck, pkg. of 2 ......$7.98

439-923 Railway Express Agency Delivery Truck, each $7.98
439-924 '56 Semi Tractor, pkg. of 2.......$7.98
439-926 '56 Delivery Truck, pkg. of 2.....$7.98
439-928 '40 Panel Truck, pkg. of 2 ....$7.98
439-929 Model "R" Semi Tractor, pkg. of 2 ....$7.98
439-930 Oil Truck, each $7.98
439-931 1964 Step Van, pkg. of 2........$7.98
439-932 '48 Diamond T Coal Truck, each..$7.98
439-933 Crew Cab Pickup Truck, each ...$7.98
439-934 '57 LP Gas Delivery Truck, each .$7.98
439-935 '53 Flatbed Truck, each...........$7.98
439-936 Heavy Duty Coal Truck, each....$7.98
439-946 '56 Hardtop, pkg. of 2............$7-98

Maisto

Maisto International, Inc., based in Fontana, California, is the US division of Master Toy Co. Ltd. of Thailand, with May Cheong Toy Products Factory Ltd. of Kowloon as the Hong Kong subsidiary. The company also encompasses May Tat, the budget toy division. Previously marketed in the US under the brand name of M C Toys, Maisto has become a dominant force in the precision scale model market as well as the diecast toy industry. Previously, their smallest toys, comparable to Matchbox toys and Hot Wheels in size and price, were called M C Toys Mini Racers. Since unifying the product line to the Maisto brand in 1994, these approximately 1:64 scale toys have been renamed Maisto Turbo Treads, and have been produced with new color variations and packaging.

Meanwhile, Maisto has made a huge impact in the larger scale model industry, starting with their Trophy series models of approximately 1:43 scale that sell for $4 or less, and crowning the product line with 1:12 scale diecast masterpieces that retail for over $100 each. Every Maisto model shows exquisite attention to detail that establishes the company as a strong competitor to the big name brands. In fact, Maisto has become one of the big name brands.

As is the case with many brands, M C Toys, Intex Recreation, and Zee Toys were all related in one way or another. The intermixing of models and castings blurred the lines that demarcated one company's product from the others'. Maisto's willingness to market their wares under retailer's proprietary brands is a major factor in their success. K-Mart sells them as MegaMovers. Wal-Mart offers them as Road & Track models, commemorating the fiftieth anniversary of the magazine of the same name.

In 1998, to commemorate Tonka's fiftieth anniversary, Maisto has begun a series of 3¼ inch long miniature versions of classic Tonka vehicles that sell for $1.99 each. Models are listed at the end of this section. Larger renditions in diecast are also available for around $5 each.

Also in 1998, Maisto introduced a series of farm implements in approximately 1:64 scale dubbed Countryside Farm & Field. These are an obvious attempt to capitalize on the popularity of Ertl's similar 1:64 scale offerings and cut into their market with similar models and sets competitively priced.

Maisto 1:10 Scale Motorcycles, suggested retail price $19.99

31601 1995 BMW R1100R, red or blue.....................................$30–35
31602 1995 Honda Shadow VT1100C2, turquoise or red $30–35
31603 1995 Moto Guzzi California 1100, yellow or red.........................$30–35
31604 Indian Chief Roadmaster, red & white, yellow or light blue $30–35

Maisto 1:18 Scale Motorcycles, suggested retail price $3.99

BMW R1100R $5–6
BMW R1100RS $5–6
Honda NR $5–6
Honda Valkyrie $5–6
Honda VT1100C2 ....$5–6
Indian Chief $5–6
Indian Four $5–6
Kawasaki KLX250SR $5–6
Kawasaki Ninja ZX-9R $5–6
Malaguti Phantom F-12 ....$5–6
Moto Guzzi V10 Centauro $5–6
Yamaha FZ600R $5–6
Yamaha TT250R $5–6
Yamaha V-Max $5–6
Yamaha XV1000 Virago $5–6

Maisto Scale 1:12, suggested retail price $119.99

33201 1992 Jaguar XJ220, metallic dark blue, silver, turquoise, green, red, yellow, or white $125
33202 1959 Cadillac Eldorado Biarritz Convertible, red, pink, or white......$125
33203 1992 Jaguar XJ220, yellow with XJ220 graphics on sides...............$125

Maisto Scale 1:18, suggested retail price $14.99–19.99

1965 Pontiac GTO Hurst Edition............$20

1971 Chevrolet Chevelle SS454 ....$20

30806 1955 Mercedes 300S Convertible, custom airbrushed \$25–30

30811 1966 Mercedes-Benz 280SE Convertible, custom airbrushed \$25–30

30817 1955 BMW 502 Convertible, custom airbrushed \$25–30

31801 1989/1990 Mercedes-Benz 500 SL, aqua, lilac, silver, cranberry, black, or white \$15–20

31802 1989 Porsche 911 Speedster, red, yellow, or white.....................\$15–20

31803 1990 Lamborghini Diablo, red, or yellow.............................\$15–20

31804 1990 Ferrari 348ts, red or yellow.............................\$15–20

31805 1990 BMW 850i, metallic red, teal, blue, or black.......................\$15–20

31806 1955 Mercedes-Benz 300S, burgundy, metallic green, black, or white \$15–20

31807 1992 Jaguar XJ220, metallic dark blue or silver....................\$15–20

31808 1992 Bugatti EB110, red or blue.............................\$15–20

31809 1992 Corvette ZR-1, burgundy, red, or white.............................\$15–20

31810 1992 McLaren F1, gray, metallic gold, or silver \$15–20

31811 1966 Mercedes-Benz 280SE, burgundy or white \$15–20

31812 1993 BMW 325i Convertible, black, silver, or red \$15–20

31813 1959 Cadillac Eldorado Biarritz, pink, red, or white....................\$15–20

31814 Porsche Boxster, black or silver..\$15–20

31815 1994 Mustang Mach III, red or dark blue \$15–20

31816 1993 BMW 325i, red, white, blue, or black.............................\$15–20

31817 1955 BMW 502, dark blue or cream \$15–20

31818 1994 Porsche 911 Carrera, red, blue, or yellow \$15–20

31819 Lamborghini Diablo SE, metallic purple or green.........................\$15–20

31820 1951 Volkswagen Export Sedan (Beetle), gray, black, or green....\$15–20

31821 1952 Citroën CV15, black, gray, black, or burgundy..................\$15–20

31822F 1995 Ferrari F50 Coupe, yellow, silver, or red \$15–20

31823 1995 Ferrari F50 Barchetta, yellow or red.............................\$15–20

31824 1955 Mercedes-Benz 190SL Convertible, red or white.................\$15–20

31826 1951 Volkswagen Cabriolet, baby blue or pink..........................\$15–20

31827 1995 Corvette Indy Pace Car, burgundy and white \$15–20

31827/9 1994 Ford GT-90 Concept Car, white or black \$15–20

31828 1996 Dodge Viper GTS Coupe Indy Pace Car, blue with white stripes ..\$15–20

31829L 1996 Lamborghini Jota, metallic purple or blue \$20–25

31830 1996 Corvette LT-4 Convertible, magenta, blue and silver...........\$15–20

31831 Alfa Romeo Spider, red or black \$15–20

31832 1996 Dodge Viper GTS Coupe, blue with white stripes..............\$15–20

31833 1959 Jaguar Mark II, green or cream \$15–20

31834 1952 Citroën 2CV, closed top, gray or cream \$15–20

31835 1952 Citroën 2CV, Open top, gray or cream \$15–20

31836 Jaguar XK 8, green or blue ..\$15–20

31837 1952 Citroën 15CV 6 Cyl, black or gray \$15–20

31838 Mercedes-Benz SLK, silver or yellow.............................\$30–40

31839 Ferrari F550 Maranello, red or yellow.............................\$15–20

31840 1996 Corvette Coupe, red or green.............................\$15–20

31841 Mercedes-Benz A140, red or black \$15–20

31842 Mercedes-Benz SLK 230 Cabriolet, red or white \$15–20

31843 Porsche 550A Spyder, silver ..\$15–20

31844 Lamborghini Diablo SV, white.\$15–20

31845 Dodge Viper GTS-R, white with blue stripes \$15–20

31846 1998 Corvette Convertible, red or white \$15–20

31850 1971 Alpine Renault 1600S, metallic blue \$15–20

31851 Dodge Concept Vehicle (Copperhead)....................................\$15–20

31852 "smart," red, yellow, white, or black (1998)...................................\$18–24

31853 1948 Porsche No. 1 Type 356 Roadster (1998).....................\$18–24

31854 1948 Chevrolet Fleetmaster "Woody," brown, burgundy, or gray (1998)....................................\$30

31913 1996 Dodge Caravan, burgundy or green....................................\$15–20

31921 Ford F-150 Pickup, burgundy, silver, or blue \$15–20

35817 1955 BMW 502 Convertible, two-tone blue and white \$15–20

35820 1951 Volkswagen Beetle Coupe, two-tone light blue and white, or pink with flowers \$15–20

35821 1952 Citroën 15CV, two-tone burgundy and black, or yellow with Rally markings................\$15–20

35821T 1952 Citroën 15CV Taxi, red and black \$18–24

35826 1951 Volkswagen Beetle Convertible, two-tone dark green and yellow................\$15–20

35841 Mercedes-Benz A Class Formula 1, metallic silver with red and black accent trim \$18–24

35850 1971 Alpine Renault 1600S, blue with Rally markings................\$18–24

Snowmobile with pullback action \$4

Mercedes A Class \$15

Maisto 1:24 Scale (except where noted)

31901 Mercedes-Benz 500SL, burgundy, light blue, or metallic dark gray \$10–12

31902 Porsche 911 Speedster, red, blue, or white \$10–12

31903 Lamborghini Diablo, red or yellow................\$10–12

31904 Ferrari 348ts, red or yellow .\$10–12

31905 '94 Mustang GT, red, green, dark blue, or goldenrod.................\$10–12

31906 1992 Ford Explorer, burgundy, dark blue, green, white, or metallic teal, with or without "Eddie Bauer" on doors \$10–12

31907 Jaguar XJ220, metallic dark blue or silver \$10–12

31908 Bugatti EB110, blue or red ..\$10–12

31909 1995 Ford Explorer, black or green................\$10–12

31910 McLaren F1, red or silver.....\$10–12

31911 1993 Ford F-150, red, black, or metallic teal, with or without ATV in back & driver, 1:25................\$10–12

31912 1995 Dodge Ram Pickup, red or black, 1:26................\$10–12

31912I 1995 Dodge Ram Pickup Indy Pace Truck, blue with white stripes, 1:26................\$15–18

31913 1996 Dodge Caravan/Chrysler Voyager, maroon or green, 1:26.....\$10–12

31914 1996 Dodge Viper RT/10, white with blue stripes.......................\$10–12

31915 1995 Dodge Viper RT/10, yellow or green \$10–12

31915I 1995 Dodge Viper RT/10 Pace Car, red \$15–18

31916 1996 Ford F150 Indy Pace Truck, red $15–18

31917 1994 Ford Mustang Pace Car, red $15–18

31919 1994/1995 Lamborghini Diablo SE, metallic magenta or metallic green $10–12

31921 1997 Ford F150 Flareside, silver or dark blue, 1:26 ....$10–12

31922 Ferrari F50 Convertible, red or silver $10–12

31923 Ferrari F50 hard top, yellow or red $10–12

31924 1996 Camaro Z28, white or teal, 1:25 ....$10–12

31925 1996 Ferrari F355 Coupe, red or yellow $10–12

31927 Ferrari F355 Cabriolet, white or black $10–12

31928 Chrysler Plymouth Voyager, white or blue, 1:26 ....$10–12

31929 Lamborghini Jota, purple or blue $10–12

31930 Dodge Ram Supersport SS/T, black with white stripes, 1:26 ....$10–12

31931 Plymouth Prowler, purple $10–12

31932 1997 Dodge Viper RT/10, blue $10–12

31933 Porsche Boxster, red or silver .$10–12

31936 Jaguar XK8 ....$10–12

31937 1999 Ford F-350 Super Duty Pickup, silver with flatbed, 1:27 ....$10–12

31937 1999 Ford F-350 Super Duty Pickup, red with stake bed, 1:27 ....$10–12

31939 Ferrari 550 Maranello, red or silver $10–12

31940 1997 Corvette, red or white $10–12

31942 Mercedes-Benz SLK 230 Cabriolet, red or yellow $10–12

31947 Mercedes-Benz ML-320, silver or black $10–12

31951 1995 Ferrari F50 Coupe, red or yellow $10–12

B0600 1995 Dodge Viper GTS Coupe, blue with white stripes $10–12

1998 Mercedes-Benz S 500, 1:26 ......$10

Maisto Trophy/Special Edition, suggested retail price $1.99

Aston Martin DB7, 1:40, metallic purple .$3–4

Aston Martin Virage, metallic green ...$3–4

BMW Z1 Cabriolet, metallic silver $3–4

BMW 325i Cabriolet, 1:37, white......$3–4

BMW 850i, metallic red $3–4

Audi TT Roadster, 1:36 ....$4

Bugatti EB110, blue $3–4

1957 Chevrolet Corvette, 1:39, black with white trim $3–4

[Image of 1957 Chevrolet Corvette]

1957 Chevrolet Corvette, 1:39, silver with red trim $3–4

1963 Chevrolet Corvette Stingray, 1:38, metallic silver $3–4

Chevrolet Corvette ZR-1, 1:38, white or yellow $3–4

Dodge Viper RT/10, 1:39, red $3–4

Ferrari 288 GTO, 1:36, red $3–4

Ferrari 348ts, 1:38, yellow $3–4

Ferrari 456GT, 1:39, red $3–4

Ferrari F40, 1:39, red $3–4

Ferrari F50, 1:39, red $3–4

Ferrari Testarossa, 1:39, red $3–4

Jaguar E Cabriolet, British racing green .$3–4

Jaguar XJ220, 1:40, metallic dark blue $3–4

Jaguar XJS V12 Cabriolet, 1:40, red $3–4

Jaguar XJS V12 Cabriolet, 1:40, metallic silver/blue w/ blue interior $3–4

Lamborghini Diablo, 1:40, yellow........$3–4

Lotus Elan, 1:36 scale, metallic blue $3–4

Lotus Esprit, 1:38, metallic silver $3–4

Mercedes-Benz 500SL, black $3–4

Mercedes-Benz 500SL, metallic blue $3–4

Mercedes-Benz 500SL, metallic teal $3–4

MG RV8, 1:37, metallic green $3–4

Porsche 911 Carrera, 1:38, yellow $3–4

Porsche 911 Speedster Cabriolet, 1:38, red $3–4

Porsche 911 Speedster Cabriolet, 1:38, silver $3–4

Porsche 911 Turbo Flat Nose Cabriolet, white $3–4

Porsche 959, 1:36, silver $3–4

Maisto Motorized Models, suggested retail $2.99

Pullback action makes these models different from their Trophy counterparts. Many Trophy models are duplicated in this series. Here is just a sampling.

Aston Martin DB7, purple $3–4

Jaguar XJ220, silver...................$3–4

Lotus Esprit Turbo, silver $3–4

Maisto Mini Transporters, 1:87 Scale Semi Tractor-Trailers, suggested retail price $2.99

M57 Semi Rescue Helicopter Transporter.$3–4

M58 Semi Racing Boat Transporter $3–4

M59 Fire Engine Semi...................$3–4

M60 Tanker Semi "Shell" $3–4

M61 Freighter Semi "Trans America Express"...................$3-4

M61 Freighter Semi "North American"..$3-4

M62 Semi Police Helicopter Transporter.$3–4

M63 Semi Car Transporter...................$3–4

M64 Semi Boat Transporter...................$3–4

Maisto Turbo Treads / M C Toys Mini Racers, $0.50 to $1 each

These toys match Matchbox regular series models in size and accuracy of scale. In fact, before they were Maistos, collectors quipped that "M C" stood for "Matchbox Copy." While most models have no moving parts, such as opening doors, their quality is remarkable for their usual price of $1 each or less.

While most models are currently available, their quality and rising popularity should make them more valuable as collectible toys over the years. The fact that the value has already risen from $1 to $2 for these models attest to their popularity and quality, although the value will likely not soon rise above that figure. In addition, they can often still be purchased for 75 cents each or less.

Ambulance Truck $1–2

Audi Quattro, #8447...................$1–2

BMW M1, #8448 ....$1–2

BMW 750il, #8742 ....$1–2

BMW 850i, #9005...................$1–2

Buick LeSabre Stock Car, #8618........$1–2

Caterpillar Quarry Dump Truck...........$1–2

Chevrolet Corvette, #8617...................$1–2

Chevrolet Corvette ZR-1 ....$1–2

Chevrolet Corvette, 1997 ....$1–2

Chrysler Concept Vehicle (Dodge "Copperhead"), 1998 ....$2–3

[Image of Citroën 2CV]

Citroën 2CV, #8732 ....$1–2

Commando Hum-V, yellow $1–2

Dodge Concept Vehicle...................$1–2

Dodge Viper GTS...................$1–2

Dodge Viper RT/10 ....$1–2

Ferrari F40, #9001 ....$1–2

Ferrari Testarossa, #9010...................$1–2

Ferrari 250 GTO, #8736 ....$1–2

Ferrari 308 GTB, #8445 ....$1–2

Ferrari 348ts, #9101 ....$1–2

Ferrari 365 GTB, #9004 ....$1–2
Fire Ladder Truck.............................$1–2
Ford Econovan, #9008.....................$1–2
Ford Escort 1.6i, #8449 ....$1–2
Ford Explorer.................................$1–2
Ford Granada 2.8 GL, #8451 ....$1–2
Ford Pick-Up, #8739 ....$1–2
Ford Sierra XR4Ti, #8441 ....$1–2
Formula 1 Racer, #8733 ....$1–2
Formula 1 Racer, #8734 ....$1–2
Garbage Truck................................$1–2
Jaguar XJ-S V-12, #8613 ....$1–2
Jaguar XJ220 ....$1–2
Lamborghini Countach, #8735 ....$1–2
Lamborghini Diablo, #9006 ....$1–2
Lincoln Continental Mark VII $1–2
Mazda RX-7, #8738 ....$1–2
Mercedes-Benz 260 SEL, #8615 ....$1–2
Mercedes-Benz 500 SL, #9011 ....$1–2
Mercedes-Benz 500 SL, #8452 ....$1–2
Mercedes-Benz ML-320 ....$1–2
Mercedes-Benz CLK-GTR....................$1–2
Motorcycle....................................$1–2
Mustang Mach III............................$1–2
Nissan MID-4, #8737 ....$1–2
Nissan 4x4 Dirt Truck $1–2
Nissan 300ZX, #8620 ....$1–2
Peugeot 205 GTI, #8611 ....$1–2
Peugeot 309, #8614 ....$1–2
Peugeot 405 Turbo 16, #8741 ....$1–2
Pontiac Firebird, #8443 ....$1–2
Porsche Turbo, #8444 ....$1–2
Porsche 356A, #9003 ....$1–2
Porsche 911 Speedster, #9012 ....$1–2
Porsche 956, #8442.........................$1–2
Porsche 959, #9009 ....$1–2
Renault 25V6 Turbo, #8612 ....$1–2
Suzuki SJ413Q Samurai, #8622.........$1–2
Toyota MR-2, #8619 ....$1–2
Toyota SR5, #8621 ....$1–2

Trabant, #9002 ....$1–2

Volkswagen Dune Racer, #8740.........$1–2
Volkswagen Eurovan $1–2
Volkswagen Golf GTi, #8446.............$1–2
Volkswagen NR-1060, #9007 ....$1–2
Volkswagen 1300 Beetle, #8731 ....$1–2
Volvo 760 GLE, #8616 ....$1–2

Maisto Dirt Mover Sets
224200 Set 1, includes wheel loader with
    excavator, crane with ripper, and wheel
    loader with pile driver....................$29
224300 Set 2, includes snow plow with rip-
    per, wheel loader with ripper, and fork lift
    with log loader..............................$29

Maisto Airline Series — Commercial Airliners, 4"–5" long, in attractive window box
Swissair $4
British Airways $4
Japan Air Lines $4
Lufthansa $4
Alitalia...$4
Air France $4
United $4
Cathay Pacific $4

Maisto 2-Wheelers — 1:18 Scale Motorcycles, highly detailed, working suspension.
Honda NR, red, silver, and black.............$3
Kawasaki KLX250SR Dirt Bike, lime green with
    bright yellow, pink & purple accents......$3
Kawasaki Ninja ZX-9R, red and silver.......$3
Suzuki GSX750 Police Motorcycle, white and
    chrome..$3
Yamaha XV1000 Virago Chopper, metallic
    red and chrome..............................$3

Maisto Tonka Series

This series of diecast and plastic models started out in 1998 with four 3¼" miniatures of classic Tonka vehicles. In 1999, the series was expanded to fifty models, most of which are reissues of Maisto models in new color schemes. A #51 is also mentioned on the back of the package as "Collectors Search - Big Mike." An educated guess is that this emulates the Hot Wheels Treasure Hunt models, Racing Champions Chase Cars, Matchbox Challenge Cars, and Johnny Lightning White Lightnings in that the particular model in question is hard-to-find and highly collectible.

Other Maisto issues include 4½" versions of assorted Tonka toys.
#1 Mighty Tonka Quarry Truck, yellow
    dumper with black cab, grill and chassis
    v.1 unnumbered blisterpack, 1998.$4–5
    v.2 numbered blisterpack, 1999 ....$2–3
#2 Mighty Tonka Road Grader, yellow with
    black and white accents
    v.1 unnumbered blisterpack, 1998.$4–5
    v.2 numbered blisterpack, 1999 ....$2–3
#3 Tonka Classic 1956 Pickup Truck, dark
    blue
    v.1 unnumbered blisterpack, 1998.$4–5
    v.2 numbered blisterpack, 1999 ....$2–3
#4 Tonka Classic 1949 Dump Truck, red
    with green dumper
    v.1 unnumbered blisterpack, 1998.$4–5
    v.2 numbered blisterpack, 1999 ....$2–3
#5 Front End Shovel $2–3
#6 LAX Crash Tender Command Truck..$2–3
#7 Rescue 4 Ambulance, red, "Emergency
    Response Vehicle" $2–3
#8 M-923 A1 Big Foot Storm Truck, "El Nino
    Storm Relief" $2–3
#9 Cement Mixer $2–3
#10 Coast Guard Helicopter, MH-60K
    Night Hawk, red $2–3
#11 Chevy Silverado, black.................$2–3
#12 Dog Recovery Van, silver $2–3
#13 Mercedes-Benz ML 320 SUV $2–3

#14 Front End Loader.......................$2–3
#15 Baja Bug..................................$2–3
#16 Mighty Tonka Crane $2–3
#17 MT Towing, purple with black ramp,
    gray plastic side trim.....................$2–3
#18 Camp Tonkawa Bus, khaki $2–3
#19 Prerunner Toyota SR5 4x4 Pick Up, yellow
    with black, white and silver accents...$2–3
#20 Chevy Caprice Sheriff $2–3
#21 Mighty Tonka Backhoe.................$2–3
#22 Party Supply Truck, white with red interi-
    or, "Party Supplies 555-PRTY" $2–3
#23 Bulldozer, green with silver-gray
    plow...$2–3
#24 Ocean Gear Ford Econovan, green with
    wave graphics, "Ocean Gear".......$2–3
#25 Ford GP Trailblazer......................$2–3
#26 Hummer Commando Hum-V $2–3
#27 Rumblin' Dump, metallic burgundy
    with gray dumper, "Rumblin' Dump
    Co." $2–3
#28 Police Ranger............................$2–3
#29 Sportsman Camper......................$2–3
#30 Auto Club Tow $2–3
#31 Tractor.....................................$2–3
#32 Cable Vision Bucket.....................$2–3
#33 Dodge Dakota $2–3
#34 Police Launch $2–3

Jumbo Crane, 2001 copy of toy from the 1960s $2–3

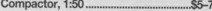

Compactor, 1:50 ....$5–7

Power Shovel, 1:50..............................$5–7

Road Roller, 1:50 ....$5–7

#35 Fire Engine $2–3
#36 Locksmith Van.........................$2–3
#37 Fertilizer Van $2–3
#38 City Recycler $2–3
#39 Tonka Tanker $2–3
#40 Quarry Dump $2–3
#41 Ford Pickup $2–3
#42 Pipe Truck $2–3
#43 Traffic Equipment Truck $2–3
#44 News Copter $2–3
#45 Super Duty..............................$2–3
#46 Fire Support $2–3
#47 Ford Explorer $2–3
#48 Mountain Dew Delivery $2–3
#49 Forest Ranger $2–3
#50 Daimler Tour Bus......................$2–3
#51 Big Mike $12–16
Maisto Tonka "Big 10" Pack, contains 10
   Maisto Tonka toys for $7.99 (Target):
   v.1 contains:
      Cement Truck, yellow with silver gray
         drum and black frame, "Tonka
         Cement Mix 2000" on drum .$1
      MH-60K Night Hawk Helicopter,
         blue with white trim, "Atlantic
         Coast Air Reconnaissance" $1
      Dump Truck, silver with yellow
         dumper, "Rumblin' Sons Gener-
         al Contractors" $1
      Commando Hum-V, silver with black
         trim, "Cincinnati" $1
      Bulldozer, silver with black plow, "Rum-
         blin' Sons General Contractors"..$1
      Chevrolet Caprice Police Car, black,
         "Force Rhode Island" $1
      Quarry Truck, white with yellow
         dumper, black trim................$1
      Search Truck, white with black and
         gold trim, "LA Surveillance Los
         Angeles Task Force".............$1
      Front End Loader Tractor, silver lower,
         black upper, "Rumblin' Sons
         General Contractors" $1
      Crash Tender, dark gray with blue ram,
         "Fontana Swat Dept. Ram Unit"..$1
   v.2 contains:
      Beverage Truck, red with white back,
         "Tonka Dairy – Got Milk?" $1
      Dodge Dakota, red $1
      School Bus, yellow with white roof,
         "TUSD Tonka Unified School
         District"................................$1

Mercedes-Benz ML-320, black with
   metallic silver-gray interior.......$1
Garbage Truck, red cab, black con-
   tainer $1
Chevy Silverado, metallic blue......$1
Fire Ladder Truck, metallic blue with sil-
   ver trim, metallic gray ladder....$1
Ford Explorer, silver....................$1
Ambulance, white with red windows,
   lime green trim, "Paramedic
   Emergency Vehicle" $1
Ford F350 Super Duty Pick Up, yel-
   low with black and silver trim..$1

Maisto Countryside Farm & Field
Trucks and Trailers (Assortment
   #15091) retail, $4.79
   Ford F350 Super Duty Cattle Carrier...$5
   Ford F350 Super Duty Horse Transport .$5
   Ford F350 Super Duty Tractor Trailer...$5
Implements (Assortment #15093) retail, $2.39
   Bale Throw Wagon $3
   Ford Tractor (Harvester) $3
   Ford Tractor with Front End Loader (Mulcher).$3
   Hay Rake.......................................$3
   Hydra-Push Spreader $3
   Mower Conditioner $3
   Mulch Tiller....................................$3
   Rectangular Baler $3
   Rotary Cutter...................................$3
   Round Baler....................................$3
   Row Crop Planter $3
   Sprayer $3
   Wing Disc $3
Workin' Trucks (Assortment #15094)
   retail, $4.79
   AG Service Sprayer Truck...................$5
   Dairy Transport Truck $5
   Delivery Truck with Tractor $5
   Dealership Implement Truck................$5
   Farm Feed Delivery Truck...................$5
Tractors (Assortment #15095) retail, $3.99
   Ford Tractor, blue $4
   Ford Tractor, blue with cab $4
   Ford Tractor, blue with front end loader .$4
   Ford Tractor, green...........................$4
   Ford Tractor, green with cab $4
   Ford Tractor, green with front end loader..$4
   Ford Tractor, red $4
   Ford Tractor, red with cab $4
   Ford Tractor, red with front end loader.$4
   Ford Tractor, yellow $4
   Ford Tractor, yellow with cab.............$4
   Ford Tractor, yellow with front end loader.$4

Majorette
History and Heritage
   Some of the world's most popular, or at
least most proliferous, diecast toy cars and
trucks come from the French company known
simply as Majorette F, founded by Emile Veron,
one-time candidate for Premier of France and
brother of M. Veron, founder of Norev ("Veron"
spelled backwards).

The company started producing diecast toy
cars and trucks in 1961. During the early
years, availability of Majorettes was very limited. Models often showed up as promotional
models for various retailers. In 1982,
Majorettes became more readily available in
the US with the establishment of Majorette
USA, with headquarters in Miami, Florida.

It was not the best of times for introducing a
new diecast toy line in the US, as the 1980s
saw the downfall, merger, or sellout of many
popular toy companies such as Matchbox,
Corgi, Dinky, and Solido. Nevertheless,
Majorette created a niche in the US market that
remains today perhaps as strong as ever,
despite bankruptcy, receivership, and eventual
sale of the company.

Solido of France, meanwhile, was almost
one of the casualties of the era. This venerable
brand of toys had existed independently since
1930. But as with other toy companies, Solido
suffered financially, eventually being purchased
by Majorette in 1980. Fortunately the Solido
line survives, as does Majorette.

In 1990, bankrupt Majorette was purchased by Ideal Loisirs (pronounced ee-dee-ALL
LEE-zhurs), a French toy conglomerate. In turn,
Playmates toy company of Hong Kong purchased a 37.5 percent interest in Ideal Loisirs
in mid-1992.

Playmates made its mark in the toy industry
with its popular licensed line of Teenage Mutant
Ninja Turtles action figures. Since then, the company has been held together by the powerful
force and extraordinary popularity of its Star
Trek, Next Generation, and Deep Space Nine
action figures, models, and play sets.

About the same time, a Portuguese brand
of small, accurately scaled, mostly plastic toy
vehicles called Novacars was assimilated into
the Majorette line, becoming the new
Majorette Novacars 100 Series. A listing of
these models can be found separately under
the Novacar listing.

The latest change in the business occurred
when TA Triumph-Adler of Nuremberg, Germany, took a controlling share in the Ideal
Loisirs Group. Triumph-Adler Toy Division is
known for the Zapf brand of dolls, Tronico
radio-controlled cars, Cartronic car racing
tracks, Europlay summer toys, and Kidtech children's computers.

The result of this merger/buyout is that
Majorette now belongs to one of the largest toy
conglomerates in Europe, and one of the leading toy manufacturers in the world.

The Majorette Line-Up
The backbone of the Majorette line of toys
is the 200 Series, models approximately 3
inches long mimicking the Matchbox 1-75
series. In many ways, as you will see,
Majorette has taken a marketing approach
very similar to Matchbox.

Like Matchbox's Two-Packs, Majorette's 300 Series offers vehicle and trailer in a single package, occasionally throwing in a second trailer and calling it a "bonus pack."

And like Matchbox's Convoy/Super Rigs series, Majorette's 600 Series replicates semi tractors and trailers in 1:87 scale.

Many sub-series, such as Road Eaters, Smelly Speeders, and Sonic Flashers are created from regular series models.

Other Majorette series feature models on a larger scale that offer a wide assortment of vehicles and sets. All of these models are covered in depth in the information that follows.

While Solido is now a subsidiary of Majorette, they remain distinctive in their own right, and are detailed in the section of this book devoted to Solido toys.

The Origin of the Majorette 200 Series

Originally, the 200 Series of 1:55 to 1:100 scale models started out in 1962 as Rail-Route brand models, bearing numbers between 1 and 15. The following year offered the same models in different colors and markings, or with trailers attached, in a 100 Series. By 1965, a third number designation was added to create the 200 Series. By 1966, the Rail-Route name was dropped entirely and the Majorette 200 Series was born. Later, several of these older models have been reintroduced into the 200 Series as new models.

A second 100 Series dubbed "Globe Toys" was introduced for the German market consisting of previously released toys with the model number and Majorette name obscured from the base.

The newest 100 Series designation was applied to Novacars, an assortment of accurate model cars and trucks acquired by Majorette from a company based in Portugal. Cars feature plastic bodies and metal chassis, except for the F1 Racers, which have metal bodies and plastic chassis. A list of Novacars can be found under its own heading below.

101-A BRM Formula 1 Racer
   v.1 unchromed $15
   v.2 chromed $15
102-A Porsche Formula 1 Racer
   v.1 unchromed.............................$15
   v.2 chromed................................$15
107-A Hotchkiss Jeep with Cable Carrier..$12
109-A Ferrari LeMans
   v.1 unchromed $15
   v.2 chromed $15
110-A Ferrari Formula 1 Racer
   v.1 unchromed $15
   v.2 chromed $15
113-A Citroën DS 21 ....$20
114-A Magirus Multi Benne Skip Truck
   1:100 (later reissued as 222-A)
   v.1 orange with red skip $16
116-A Peugeot 404 Saloon..................$20
Unnumbered Peugeot 404 Station Wagon
   v.1 metallic slate blue $25–30

The New Majorette 100 Series Novacars

Novacar models, previously from Minia Porto Jogos E Brinquedos Lda. of Paredes, Portugal, were originally packaged in either a display blister card or a hook blisterpack. The list below combines the original models along with new Majorette variations. Currently, models are marketed in a four-car blisterpack set. Many of these models have been incorporated into the 200-Series for 1997.

101 Ferrari 308
   v.1 light yellow with red interior $2
   v.2 darker yellow with red interior.......$2
   v.3 red tan interior (1996)................$2
102 Nissan 300 ZX
   v.1 light blue with red interior, black and gold accents $2
   v.2 darker blue with red interior, black and gold accents $2
   v.3 clear with silver flecks, blue-gray and yellow interior $2
   v.4 clear with silver flecks, purple and white interior..........................$2
   v.5 bright green with yellow and black racing accents (1996) $2
103 Chevrolet Corvette
   v.1 white with black "23," green and red accents $2
   v.2 white with red "23," green and red accents $2
   v.3 black with white accents.............$2
   v.4 black with silver "Corvette" and Chevrolet logo $2
   v.5 clear with red flecks, dark red and white interior $2
   v.6 clear with silver flecks, purple and pink interior $2
   v.7 yellow with red and black "Grand Prix" accents $2
104 Ferrari Testarossa
   v.1 red with "Ferrari" and logo on hood...............................$2
   v.2 red with "S RACING" on hood.....$2
   v.3 yellow with "S RACING" on hood (1996) $2
105 Mercedes-Benz 500SL
   v.1 silver with red interior, "500SL" on doors $2
   v.2 silver with red interior, no markings .$2
   v.3 black with gray interior, no markings (1996) $2
106 Peugeot 605
   v.1 white with black interior $2
   v.2 white with red interior $2
   v.3 blue with red and white "Rallye 5" accents (1996)........................$2
107 Nissan Pathfinder/Terrano
   v.1 red with black and white rally markings...................................$2
   v.2 green with black and white rally markings...................................$2
   v.3 white with black and gold "SHERIFF" markings $2

   v.4 red with "FIRE DEPT." markings $2
108 Kenworth Semi Tractor
   v.1 blue with red and white stars and stripes..................................$2
   v.2 red (1996) $2
109 Chevrolet Impala Police Car
   v.1 white with blue and gold markings.$2
   v.2 black with white and gold markings..$2
110 Renault Espace Van
   v.1 red with "Espace" on sides in script lettering................................$2
   v.2 white with blue "Ambulance" markings, orange accents $2
   v.3 yellow with blue and red rally accents $2
111 Porsche LeMans GT Racer/Sport proto
   v.1 black with white accents, "TOP DRIVERS" on nose, silver-gray windows...................................$2
   v.2 clear with yellow flecks, lime green interior $2
   v.3 clear with silver flecks, blue-gray interior $2
   v.4 turquoise with white and coral racing accents, coral windows (1996) ...$2
112 F1 Racer
   v.1 yellow with red and black accents, red plastic base $2
   v.2 black with gold and red accents, white plastic base $2
113 Volkswagen Caravelle Van
   v.1 red with black and gold accents ...$2
   v.2 red with "Surf" accents................$2
114 Ford Escort GT yellow with red and black rally accents $2
116 Chevrolet Extended Cab Pickup
   v.1 black with white accents.............$2
   v.2 clear with red flecks, dark red and white interior..........................$2
   v.3 clear with yellow flecks, lime green and pink interior $2
   v.4 white with blue "POLICE" accents (1996) $2
   v.5 black with tan mudsplash accents (1996) $2
117 Honda Acura NSX
   v.1 red with black interior $2
   v.2 red with white interior $2
119 Jeep
   v.1 blue with black top, yellow accents (1995) $2
120 Ferrari F40
   v.1 red $2
121 Ford Van
   v.1 purple with flame accents............$2

Majorette 200 Series

Like Matchbox, Majorette replaces various models every year, resulting in new models with the same model number as old ones. So a letter code has been assigned to each model number to designate each successive model change.

Several sub-series have been marketed, which are included in the variations below. One of those is Kool Kromes, models in various colors of chrome. Another is Road Eaters, models with advertising for food and candy on them. A third sub-series is Smelly Speeders ("Not Stinky — Just For Kids"), each with distinctive scents and appropriate trademark names. These models are repeated in their own section for easier cross-reference.

In 1995, another sub-series was introduced called Supers, models that steer. Since they have been assigned new numbers that don't coincide with the regular 200 series, they have been listed following the 200 Series.

Majorette 200 Series Wheel Variations

Twenty-one distinctive wheel types have been documented so far on Majorette 200-Series models. Below is a key to the abbreviations used to identify them. Unless otherwise noted, spokes, circles and rings are raised chrome portions of a wheel.

3kk – inner and outer rings with three inner "knobs" or "bumps" alternating with three outer "knobs" or "bumps"

3spb – three broad spokes that taper from center to outside, enclosed by a ring

3spn – three slightly narrower spokes that taper from center to outside, enclosed by a ring

4c – "four leaf clover" in contoured circle

5d – five dashes (arcs) between an inner and outer circle

5pw – five-pointed pinwheel

5sp – five broad spokes that widen from center to outer ring

6sp – six spokes in a circle

6spk – six spokes in a circle with "knobs" or "bumps" on inside of circle between each spoke

8h – eight holes within a broad chrome circle .$

8hr – variation of 8h in red chrome, other colors also produced

8sp – eight spokes in a circle, or four pairs of V-pattern spokes

atv – solid rubber tire used on six-wheel all-terrain vehicle

bw1 – single piece black plastic wheel used on many Majorettes from the 1960s

bw2 – single piece black wheel with separate black hubcap, usually a front wheel on a Bernard truck

bw3 – one-piece black wheel, usually a rear wheel assembly on a Bernard truck; hub extends out further than the side of the tire and has eight lug nuts molded in; the axle is visible in the center of the wheel

bw4 – dual wheels, but together as one piece; axle doesn't show, so the outside wheel is attached to the inside wheel after the inside wheel is attached to the axle; hub has eight lug nuts, and a molded cap over the axle

ct* – construction tire, typically found on construction vehicles and equipment, several types found

ct3c – "three leaf clover" in a circle

ct4sp – four spokes in a circle

ctb – single piece black construction wheel with four unchromed spokes

ctsc – construction tire with square inside of a circle, commonly used as front wheels on current farm tractor models

ft1 – farm tire, from rear axle of farm tractor, single piece plastic wheel

ft2 – farm tire, from rear axle of farm tractor, tire separate from colored plastic wheel hub

rt – racing tire with separate hub used on 1960s Majorette F1 racers

rw – wide racing wheel with chrome circle, usually projects out well beyond wheel well

spiral – chrome spiral wheel

thc – single piece tire with chrome hubcap

Majorette 200 Series

201-A St. Tropez Travel Trailer, 1:68
    v.1 yellow with blue decals $5
    v.2 white with water and beach tampos $4

201-B Citroën GS
    v.1 red with white interior, thc $6

201-C Citroën Visa Chrono, rear hatch opens 1:52
    v.1 white with red and blue accents, light blue interior, blue windshield, "CHRONO," 6sp $2
    v.2 white, "4 ROUES MOTRICES" $2
    v.3 yellow, "4 ROUES MOTRICES" $2

201-D Ford Model A Van, 1:60
    v.1 metallic red, 5d, gold trim, cream canopy, "TEA SHOP" $4
    v.2 blue with gold trim, cream canopy, "TEA SHOP" $4

v.3 orange, "Willy Wonka Runts," Road Eaters $3

    v.4 red, "Campbell's Teddy Bears," Road Eaters $3
    v.5 blue, "Cadbury Dairy Milk" $6
    v.6 blue, "Cadbury Buttons" $6
    v.7 blue, "Orange Company" $3
    v.8 blue-green with black fenders and running board, "Toys Shop," white canopy, 5d, 1999 ....$3

201-E Fiat Coupe
    v.1 yellow with tan interior $4
    v.2 silver with red interior, black and blue tampos $4

202-A Volkswagen 113 ....$8
202-B Volkswagen 1302 Beetle / Coccinelle, trunk opens, 1:60 (compare to 202-E, 203-D)

v.1 red with yellow lightning bolt on trunk.$6

    v.2 red with yellow flower on trunk......$9
202-C Triumph TR7
    v.1 red with blue and white "TR7" and "35" markings, butterscotch interior, rw $2
    v.2 red, no markings, rw $2
    v.3 orange "TR7 and "35" markings, rw $2

202-D Peugeot 405 T16
    v.1 orange with white interior, charcoal gray bumpers, Kool Kromes $3
    v.2 blue, Kool Kromes $3
    v.3 yellow with rally graphics, red interior, yellow bumpers, 6sp $2
    v.4 red with no graphics, red interior, yellow bumpers, 6sp $2

202-E Volkswagen 1302 Beetle / Coccinelle, trunk doesn't open, 1:60
    v.1 silver, "CIBIE" stickers, blue windows, number 202 on base, 3kk $3
    v.2 blue, 3sp, part of 311 set...........$3

203-A Etalmobile Warehouse Vehicle 1:50 ....$15
203-B Fiat 127, doors open, dog on back seat looking out left rear window 1:55

v.1 hot pink $8

    v.2 blue...$6
    v.3 metallic blue................................$6
    v.4 red with white interior, 3sp..........$8
    v.5 red with white interior, thc $8
    v.6 lime green with white interior, thc ..$8
    v.7 metallic yellow-green $6
    v.8 yellow with white interior, thc........$9
    v.9 orange with white interior, 5sp $8

203-C Police Motorcycle
    v.1 bright blue with dark blue rider, white saddle bags, chrome engine & exhaust pipes $20

203-D Volkswagen 1302 Beetle/Coccinelle, trunk doesn't open (compare to 202-B)
    v.2 blue, 3kk...................................$3

v.1 lime green, 3kk **$3**

v.3 light blue, 3kk $4
v.4 orange with blue and white accents, 3kk, blue tires $5
v.5 purple, 3kk, 'Cadbury Dairy Milk Buttons' on doors..........................$6
v.6 yellow, 3kk..................................$4
v.7 light blue with random design, 3kk, 1999...$3

203-E, 1996 Ford Mustang GT Coupe
v.1 yellow with red interior, black bumpers $2
v.2 black with red interior, "17" $2

204-A Bernard Fire Engine Ladder Truck, 3 axles
v.1 red, "Grand Echelle" on ladder base, "Ville de MEGEVE" cast on doors, red base under cab, bw3 and bw4 ....$10–12

204-B Fire Rescue, red 4 headlights, 1:80
v.1 3kk, no tampos $6
v.2 3kk, "fire brigade" tampo with coat of arms on doors......................$6

204-C Bank Security Armored Truck with rear door that slides up to open, 1:57 (reissued as 231-C, 1999)
v.1 yellow with green "Bank Security" label $3
v.2 yellow with red, white, and blue "Bank Security" tampos $3
v.3 white, 5d, red and blue accents, black rear door $2
v.4 silver..$5
v.5 yellow with white and blue decals.$3
v.6 yellow with white and blue "POST" stickers..................................$5
v.7 blue, "BANK SECURITY," red circle with dollar sign, black rear door, 5d, 1999 (231-C) $2

204-D Ferrari 456 GT, 1994
v.1 red $2

204-E Ferrari F50 Coupe, 1997
v.1 red with black interior $2

205-A Bernard Dump Truck
v.1 blue, silver dump, 3 axles, bw1, gray base extends over rear axles $8

205-B Saab Scania Dump Truck
v.1 yellow with red dumper $6
v.2 silver with red dumper $6
v.3 orange, 3kk, "58" sticker on hood, orange dumper.........................$6

205-C Renault Super Cinq GT Turbo 1:51
v.1 black with red and yellow graphics, light gray interior and trim (1988 version)...$2

v.2 blue, 6sp, pink interior and bumpers (1989 version)...........................$2
v.3 red, 6sp, white interior and bumpers, "Racing Team" on hood, white "VH" accents, "45" $2
v.4 metallic blue, 6sp, gray interior and bumpers, red and yellow "NRJ" accent $2
v.5 metallic silver, 6sp, gray interior and bumpers, black,yellow and white rally accents, "19," "MONTE CARLO" $2

205-D Jaguar XJ6 Police, 1994
v.1 white, 4c, red and yellow side stripe, "Police" on hood and trunk $3
v.2 white, 8h, red and yellow side stripe, "Police" on hood and trunk $3

205-E, 1996 Ford Mustang GT Convertible
v.1 red with black interior, "Special Pace Car" $2
v.2 black with tan interior $2

205-F Peugeot 206, 1999
v.1 yellow $2

206-A Bernard Flat Truck with Racks 1:100 ....$12

206-B Bernard Flat Truck with Scraper 1:100 ....$12

206-C Bernard Cattle Carrier Stake Truck, compare to 219-A, 1:100

v.1 blue with brown cargo sides..............**$12**

206-D Peugeot 404 Ambulance............$12

206-E Citroën Ambulance with flags on front fenders
v.1 white, 3kk, red cross sticker on hood, blue flags $8
v.2 white, 5sp, "Ambulance" sticker and red cross behind side doors $8
v.3 white, 3kk, "Ambulance" sticker and red cross behind side doors $8

206-F Pontiac Fiero
v.1 white, rw, blue bottom, red interior, black "3" and "FIERO" on hood, black "turbo" on roof, red accents $3
v.2 orange, rw, black bottom, white interior, yellow windshield, "42," white and black accents $3
v.3 yellow, rw, red interior................$3
v.4 yellow, rw, blue bottom, red interior, yellow windshield, "#3 Turbo" $3
v.5 red, rw, black bottom, white interior, white side stripe, "#42," yellow windshield $3

v.6 red, rw, black bottom, red interior, red side stripe, "#42," yellow windshield $3

206-G Renault Twingo Minivan, 1995

v.1 blue..**$4**

v.2 baby blue.....................................$3
v.3 light green $3
v.4 yellow...$3

206-H Peugeot 206, 1999
v.1 metallic silver-gray.......................$2

207-A Jaguar XKE 2+2 Coupe.............$10

207-C Jaguar Type E V12, engine can be same color as body of the car, unpainted metal, or painted silver; all have decal of a jaguar on hood, hood opens, 1:60
v.1 dark metallic blue, 3sp $8
v.2 light metallic blue, 3sp $8
v.3 bright red, 3sp $8
v.4 dark metallic red, 3sp $8
v.5 dark metallic red, thc..................$8

207-C Rock Motorcycle $15

207-D Extending Ladder Fire Truck (Pompier), 1:100, 1986
v.1 red with no lettering, white ladder .$4
v.2 red with gold lettering, 4c, "F.D.S.F.," wheat laurel insignia, white ladder $2
v.3 red with gold lettering, 4c, "F.D.N.Y.," four petal insignia, medium gray ladder $2
v.4 same as v.3, dark gray ladder, slightly darker shade of red than v.2 ....$2

207-E Renault Clio 1:53
v.1 metal flake blue with white interior and bumpers, "5" $2
v.2 metal flake teal with gray interior, white "Clio" script on sides, Supers steerable................................$2

208-A Bernard Snow Plow, 1:50.........$12

208-B Chrysler 180, 4-Door, front doors open, 1:60

v.1 bright green, thc, white interior, blue windshield **$10**

v.2 metallic red, 3kk, white interior, yellow windshield ....$10 v.3 orange, 3sp, white interior, clear windshield $10

208-C Farm Tractor 1:65
  v.1 light blue with black engine and fenders, cultivator, ft1 yellow rear hubs, 1999 ....$3
  v.2 blue with yellow engine and fenders, no cultivator, ft2 ....$2
  v.3 green with black fenders, cultivator, ft2 ....$2
  v.4 green with yellow fenders, no cultivator, ft2 ....$2
  v.5 green with green fenders, no cultivator, ft2 ....$2
  v.6 green with black engine and fenders, yellow rear hubs, no cultivator, ft2 .$2
  v.7 green with black engine and fenders, chrome hubs, no cultivator, ft2 ......$2
  v.8 red with black fenders, cultivator, ft2, black wheels $2
  v.9 yellow with green fenders, no cultivator, ft2 ....$2

209-A Camper
  v.1 orange pickup truck with white camper shell $12

209-B Porsche 911 Turbo, doors open, 1:57
  v.1 black with red and white "911" accents, white interior, rw $3
  v.2 bright blue with white interior, bright blue rw, Kool Kromes $2
  v.3 bronze with white interior, bronze rw, Kool Kromes $2
  v.4 copper with white interior, copper rw, Kool Kromes $3
  v.5 fluorescent orange with white interior, white accents, "SWANSON KIDS FUN FEAST," Road Eaters, rw $3
  v.6 red with Porsche logo on hood, white interior, rw...............................$2
  v.7 red with black and silver accents, "16," "Porsche," "turbo," rw $3
  v.8 red with "CAMPBELL'S DINOSAUR VEGETABLE SOUP," Road Eaters, chrome rw $3
  v.9 white with "22" on doors and hood, orange and black rally accents, chrome rw, 1999 ....$2
  v.10 yellow with orange and blue accents, 6sp $6
  v.11 yellow, red base, blue interior, light brown tires, chrome rw, "CHOCOLATE WAVE," Smelly Speeders $3
  v.12 pink, white interior, "HIT PARADE," blue and silver accents, red base, chrome rw $2

209-C Ferrari 456 GT
  v.1 black with tan interior, "33," red and white tampos $2

209-D Porsche 996, doors open, 1999
  v.1 yellow with red interior, black plastic base, 5pw $2

210-A Volkswagen K70, doors open, 1:60
  v.1 yellow...............................$8

v.2 red $8
v.3 bright red-orange $8
v.4 blue...............................$8

v.5 metallic blue $8

v.6 metallic red, 3spb, white interior ...$8
210-B Volkswagen Golf, rear hatch opens, 1:60
  v.1 red with yellow "GOLF" on sides ..$4
  v.2 red with silver "GOLF" on sides.....$4

v.3 metallic lime green, no graphics $5

v.4 blue, 3sp...............................$3
210-C Peugeot 205 CTI/GTI Cabriolet (also 281-B, compare to 210-D, 281-A), 1:53
  v.1 blue with white interior and midline, red and white accents.................$2
  v.2 white with red interior and midline, black CTI and accent stripe on sides $2
  v.3 white with red interior and midline, no markings...............................$2
  v.4 silver with pink interior and midline, blue, orange, and yellow splatter accents...............................$2
210-D Peugeot 205 GTI/CTI Hardtop (see 281-A, compare to 210-C, 281-B), 1:53
211-A Hotchkiss Jeep with Cattle Trailer...............................$16
211-B Tracto-Pelle Wheel Loader, with cast or separate plastic steering wheel, canopy
  v.1 orange with unpainted silver bucket, cast steering wheel, silver plastic base and engine...............................$8

v.2 orange-yellow, painted silver bucket, plastic steering wheel, silver plastic base and engine $8

v.3 pale yellow, yellow bucket, gray plastic base and engine, plastic steering wheel...............................$8
211-C Tracto-Pelle Wheel Loader, steering wheel cast into interior, cast cab (compare to 263-A)
  v.1 orange with gray plastic interior and stack, chrome wheel hubs $6
  v.2 orange with chrome plastic interior and stack, black wheel hubs, #263 .....$6
211-D Tractor with Plow (var. of 211-B, 263-A Tractor Shovel)
  v.1 red with silver metal snow plow, metallic gray interior, ct4s with black rims...............................$10
211-E Road Grader Shovel....................$4
211-F Ferrari GTO, 1:56
  v.1 red with Ferrari logo on hood, rw..$2
  v.2 red with white lower body, gold "23" on doors, rw $2
  v.3 red with gold "23" on doors, rw...$2
211-G Ferrari Testarossa, 1997
  v.1 red...............................$2
  v.2 yellow, 8h, black interior $2
211-H Ford Mondeo
  v.1 silver, 8h, tan interior $2
  v.2 blue, 8h, white tampos "15"........$2
  v.3 silver, 8h, light brown interior, Supers steerable...............................$3
212-A Bernard Circus Truck $16
212-B Wrecker/Service Truck, produced with dual or single headlights, same casting as 204-B
  v.1 white with blue roof light $6
  v.2 red, 3kk, unpainted metal boom, yellow roof light $6
  v.3 orange, 3kk, "Service" stickers on doors, unpainted metal boom, dual headlights $10
  v.4 orange, 3kk, "Service" stickers on doors, yellow boom $10
212-C Ford Escort XR3, rear hatch opens, 1:52
  v.1 black with red and white accents, wide tires $2
  v.2 yellow with red and black accents ..$2
  v.3 red with black, yellow and orange accents, narrow tires $2
  v.4 black with gold accents $2
212-D Pontiac Firebird, hood opens, 1995
  v.1 yellow, 8h, red interior $2
  v.2 blue, 4c, racing tampos, bright pink interior, 1999...............................$2
  v.3 blue, 8h, red interior, red and white rally accents, "3"........................$2
213-A Citroën DS19
  v.1 blue with red interior $12
213-B Citroën DS21 ....$10
213-C Mercedes-Benz 350SL Convertible, trunk opens, 1:60
  v.1 silver with red-orange accents, light green interior $4
  v.2 yellow, 3sp, black interior, yellow windshield $6

v.3 silver, 3kk, yellow interior, yellow windshield, yellow accents, "Team 8" on hood $6

v.4 white, 5sp, yellow windshield, no accents $6

213-D Mercedes-Benz 450 SL $4

213-E Mercedes-Benz Stake Truck with hay bales, 1:100 (compare to 254-B)

v.1 red, 3sp, brown stake bed, yellow bales $6

v.2 red, 3kk, brown stake bed, yellow bales $6

213-G F1 Racer, 1995

v.1 yellow, rw $2

v.2 purple, rw $2

v.3 orange, rw $2

v.4 red, rw $2

v.5 blue, rw, yellow and red accents, white wing and interior, red base and front wing, no markings $2

v.6 blue, rw, yellow and red accents, white wing and interior, red base and front wing, "19," "FAT," "Performance" $2

v.7 blue, rw, gold and red accents, white wing and interior, red base and front wing, "19," "FAT," "Performance" ..$2

213-F Chevrolet Impala Taxi (also 219-A, compare to 240-B), 1:69

v.1 yellow, 8h, "444-4444," "Yellow Cab" .$3

v.2 black and yellow, 8h, "444-4444," "Yellow Cab" $3

213-H Roadster (designed after a Dodge Viper)

v.1 metal flake blue with black interior, white and black stripes...............$2

v.2 red with black interior, silver wheels $2

214-A Citroën DS21 with Boat $16

214-B Saviem Modular Site Office Truck

v.1 yellow with brown office module $8–10

v.2 metallic blue with cream office module $8–10

214-C Saviem Container Truck

v.1 white with "PEPSI" logo, 3kk........$6

v.2 white and blue with "ADIDAS" logo, 3kk $5

v.3 white cab, 3kk, white container, blue and green accents, "chambourcy," "YOGHOURTS" $8

214-D 20 Panel Truck $6

214-E Nissan 300ZX Turbo T-Roof, doors open, headlights raise and retract, 1:62

v.1 white with black, red and blue "MOBIL 1" accents $3

v.2 white with red interior, red "300ZX" accents...........................$3

v.3 yellow with red interior, blue and white accents $3

v.4 yellow, 8h, red and black accents, "17" on hood........................$3

v.5 yellow, 8h, red interior $3

v.6 red, 8h, white interior, "7 Racing Team" on white panel on hood....$3

v.7 red with bright green interior, black and white accents, "17 Racing Team" $3

v.8 red with bright green interior, yellow and white accents $3

v.9 orange with red interior, no accents, 8h $3

214-F 6x6 Pumper, 1999

v.1 red, "Sapeurs Pompiers," gray rotating nozzles on roof...................$3

215-A Citroën DS21 with Caravan........$16

215-B Unimog with Fork Lift, 1:82

v.1 white, 8sp, blue canopy, "AIR FRANCE" label, yellow forks, blue windshield $6

v.2 red, 8sp, green canopy, yellow forklift.....................(eBay auction) $28

v.3 orange, 5d, blue windshield and light, yellow forks (1999) Construction Set $3

215-C Chevrolet Grand Prix Corvette, doors open (also 268-B), 1:57

v.1 black with gold and black accents .$2

v.2 black with gold and white accents .$2

v.3 black with silver and gold accents .$4

v.4 black upper, white lower body, rw, yellow windshield, red interior, red and white accents, red "3" on roof and hood $3

v.5 black with red and white accents, "43, tsp, GOODYEAR" $3

v.6 black, rw, "ZR1" on doors, yellow interior, "Corvette" on hood $3

v.7 black, rw, yellow windshield, silver and gold accents, "61 Turbo" on roof and hood $3

v.8 blue with red and white accents, "43, tsp, GOODYEAR" $3

v.9 blue with gold and black accents..$4

v.10 cream with red and black accents, "500 Miles" on hood, yellow windshield (Color Pack)...................$3

v.11 orange, "15," blue and white accents, rw $2

v.12 orange, "15," blue and white accents, orange rw $3

v.13 red with black and gold accents, "500 MILES" $2

v.14 red with black and gold accents, "ZR1" $3

v.15 red with white and blue rally accents, green interior, "4" on hood..................................$3

v.16 red with white, blue and yellow racing tampos, "4" on doors and roof $2

v.17 red with silver and gold accents..$3

v.18 red with pink and gold accents, "500 MILES" $2

v.19 red with "ZR1" on doors, "CORVETTE" and logo on hood, black interior..............................$2

v.20 red, rw, yellow interior, rally markings, yellow/white/blue doors and roof, "4 Roadlifter Speed" on hood $3

v.21 red, rw, silver accents, "19 Turbo" on hood $3

v.22 pearl with red and black accents, "500 MILES, 6" $3

v.23 white with "2000" on hood, "18" $4

v.24 yellow with red and black accents, "500 MILES, 6" $3

216-A Peugeot 404 Police $10

216-B 1970 Plymouth Fury Police

v.1 black, 3spb, star and "2" on hood, emblem on sides, clear windows $10–15

v.2 metallic dark blue, 3spb, star and "2" on hood, emblem on sides, clear windows...............................$10–15

v.3 metallic blue, 3spb, star and "9" on hood, emblem on sides, clear windows...............................$10–15

v.4 metallic blue, 3spb, emblem on hood, white "POLICE" side tampos, blue windows...................$10–15

v.5 metallic blue, 3kk, white interior, star and "6" on hood $30

v.6 yellow, 3kk, police markings $20

216-C Toyota Lite Ace Van Wagon, 1:52

v.1 black with gold accents $3

v.2 blue with no markings $3

v.3 metallic teal blue with yellow and orange accents $3

v.4 silver with red accents, 6sp, "Eagle," yellow windshield......................$3

v.5 metallic blue with silver and orange accents $3

v.6 mustard yellow with bluebird accent on sides $3

v.7 white with red accents $3

v.8 white with red, blue, and yellow accents $3

v.9 blue with "First Sport Turbo" accents $3

216-D Mercedes A Class, 1999

v.1 red...$3

217-A Peugeot 404 Saloon with Alpine .$16
217-B BMW Turbo, gullwing plastic doors open
  v.1 silver, 3sp, black doors, yellow interior, "LIEGE SOFIA LIEGE" $8
  v.2 blue, 3sp, black doors and white "BMW" tampos......................$8
  v.3 white, 3sp, blue doors, blue interior, dark and light blue accents, "BMW Turbo" on hood $8
  v.4 red, 3sp, black doors, white interior .$8
217-C Ford Thunderbird Turbo, hood opens, 1:67, 1986
  v.1 red with black trim and interior......$2
  v.2 metallic red with black trim and interior $2
  v.3 blue with yellow accents $2
  v.4 blue, 8h, red interior, gold and red "THUNDERBIRD" on sides, "3" on hood and roof $2
  v.5 blue, 8h, black trim and interior $2
  v.6 yellow, 8h, black interior, "GAMBLER," red, blue, and black accents, "4" $2
  v.7 black with hot pink trim and interior, gold "GAMBLER" graphics $2
  v.8 white with white tires, brown trim and interior, "COOL COCONUT," Smelly Speeders $3
217-D Chevrolet Extended Cab Pickup, 1997
  v.1 black with no markings................$2
  v.2 black with "Sheriff," "911" markings in white, shield on hood, amber windshield, 8h.......................$2
  v.3 white with "RACING CHAMPION" livery, yellow "90" outlined in blue, 1999....................................$2
217-E Stock Car
  v.1 white with yellow interior, red and black tampos, "71" $2
  v.2 blue with black interior, red and white tampos, "28" $2
  v.3 black, 6sp, yellow interior, white roll cage $2
217-F Chevrolet Pick Up 1:76
  v.1 black with red interior, amber windows...................................$2
218-A Bernard Sanitation Truck (compare to 218-B, 247-C)
  v.1 metallic green cab, metallic gray plastic container, bw1 ....$12

  v.2 yellow cab, metallic gray plastic container, bw1 ....$12
  v.3 blue cab, metallic gray plastic container, bw1 ....$12
  v.4 red cab, metallic gray plastic container, bw1 ....$12
  v.5 green cab, metallic gray plastic container, bw1 ....$12
218-B Mercedes-Benz Sanitation Truck, 1:100 (compare to 218-A, 247-C)
  v.1 green with metallic gray container, "VILLE DE PARIS," 3kk $4
  v.2 orange cab, metallic gray container, "VILLE DE PARIS," 3kk $4
  v.3 orange cab, gray container, "VILLE DE PARIS," 3kk $6
  v.4 orange cab, gray container, no sticker, no raised area for sticker, 3kk..$3
  v.5 green cab, gray container, hippo on sticker, 3kk $2
218-C Peugeot 405 Mi 16, 1:62
  v.1 red, 8h, black plastic trim and interior $2
  v.2 blue, 8h, white plastic trim and interior $2
  v.3 white, 8h, red plastic trim and interior, "Peugeot" on sides $2
  v.4 white, 8h, pink plastic trim and interior, multicolored "Mi 16" on doors and hood $2
218-D Peugeot 406, 1997
  v.1 metallic blue..............................$2
  v.2 white, 8h, blue and red accents, "POLICE," black base and bumpers, gray interior................................$2
219-A Bernard Stake Truck, removable stake (compare to 206-C)
  v.1 blue with light brown stake $8
219-B Matra Simca Bagheera, 1:55
  v.1 blue with white interior, "62" on roof, "RALLYE" on doors, 3spb.............$5
  v.2 blue with "K Way Groupe Sportif" on hood in black and dark blue, 3spb......................................$5
  v.3 blue with "Bagheera" on doors, 3spb......................................$5
  v.4 white with black and red decals, 3spb......................................$5
  v.5 yellow, yellow windshield, 5sp.....$5
  v.6 yellow, yellow windshield, 3spb ...$5
  v.7 orange, 3spb............................$5
219-C Honda Accord, doors open, 1:59
  v.1 metallic mint green with white accents, red interior $3
  v.2 metallic green with white accents, red interior $3
  v.3 yellow with blue accents, 6sp, red interior $3
  v.4 Kool Kromes metallic yellow $3
219-D Chevrolet Impala Taxi (see 213-F, compare to 240-B)
219-E Lamborghini Diablo, 1:58
  v.1 yellow, Kool Kromes $3

  v.2 red, Kool Kromes......................$3
  v.3 black "CRY BABY" candy logo, Road Eaters $3
  v.4 white "PEPSI" logo, Road Eaters....$4
  v.5 yellow "Willy Wonka Everlasting Gobstopper," Road Eaters...........$4
  v.6 yellow with no markings $2
  v.7 yellow with logo on hood $2
  v.8 red with logo on hood.................$2
219-F Porsche Boxster
  v.1 metal flake teal with red interior, clear headlights, Porsche shield on hood $3
  v.2 yellow, rw, white interior, blue accents, red "8" $3
220-A Volvo 245 DL Station Wagon, 1:60
  v.1 red, 3sp, white interior, trailer hitch $6
  v.2 green with black dashboard and grille, white interior $6
  v.3 brown with yellow "Touring Club de France" tampos.........................$6
  v.4 white $6
  v.5 gold/brown, 3sp, white interior, no trailer hitch $6
  v.6 white, 3sp, yellow and black "Tour De France" accents, "OFFICIALS" on sides, trailer hitch..................$6
220-B Mustang SVO, 1:59, 1986
  v.1 metallic periwinkle blue with no markings, narrow tires......................$4
  v.2 metallic periwinkle blue with no markings, oversized tires................$4
  v.3 metallic periwinkle blue with red and white accents, oversized tires $2
  v.4 metallic turquoise, oversized tires...$2
  v.5 white with red accents, oversized tires $2
  v.6 white with black and red "Mustang 1" accents, narrow tires $3
  v.7 white with bright blue front half, red diagonal stripes on sides, oversized tires $3
  v.8 white with blue front half, red diagonal stripes on sides, oversized tires $3
  v.9 white with metallic blue front half, red diagonal stripes on sides, oversized tires $3
  v.10 red with horse and "MUSTANG" on sides, narrow tires $2
  v.11 red with horse and "MUSTANG" on sides, oversized tires.............$2
  v.12 Oregon State Police cruiser, one-of-a-kind customized by Richard Burns...................................$25
220-C Honda Acura NSX, 1997
  v.1 plastic body, red, 8h...................$4
  v.2 metal body, red, 8h....................$3
  v.3 metal body, yellow with racing graphics, checkered flag, "2," "BandL," 8h $3
  v.4 metal body, yellow, red interior, "2," rally tampos, 8h.......................$3

221-A Renault R16 ....$10
221-B Citroën GS Bertone Camargue
  v.1 metallic maroon with yellow base ...$6
  v.2 metallic blue, unpainted base, Union Jack on hood, "Jack MacKeen," light blue interior $6

v.3 metallic blue, unpainted base, Union Jack on hood, "Jack MacKeen," light green interior......................$6

  v.4 metallic blue with no markings $6
  v.5 white, 3sp, "Holiday Inn" $6
221-C Audi Quattro, 1:58
  v.1 white with multicolor "MONTE CARLO" Rally markings $3
  v.2 blue with black and gold accents..$3
  v.3 white with no markings $3
  v.4 white "AUDI SPORT" $3
  v.5 white with yellow, black, gray, and red accents, "IN:NY 35 MICHELIN," wide tires $3
221-D Renault X54 ....$3
221-E Renault Safrane, 1:63
  v.1 v.1 blue, 6sp, black interior $2
  v.2 white, 8h, red interior, red rally markings, "8 RALLYE" $2
222-A Fiat Skip Truck Multi Benne (reissue of 114-A), 1:100
  v.1 red with yellow skip, "SERVICE" sticker, black base $6
  v.2 orange with blue skip, "SERVICE" sticker, "8" on hood in yellow circle, black base, 3kk $8
  v.3 orange with blue skip, "SERVICE" sticker, no sticker on hood, black base, 3kk $8
  v.4 orange with green skip, gray base, 3kk $8
222-B Renault 25 V6, front doors open, 1:63
  v.1 metallic burgundy $2
  v.2 metallic pale green $2
  v.3 metallic blue, 6sp, orange and yellow flames $2
  v.4 metallic dark gray $2
  v.5 metallic deep blue $2
  v.6 metallic silver, 8h, gray interior and bumpers $2
223-A Mobile Office $8
223-B Crazy Car 4x4
  v.1 lime green $6
  v.2 gray blue, ct4sp, orange interior ...$4
223-C Desert Raider 4x4
  v.1 black with red and gold accents $3

223-D '57 Chevy Hot Rod
  v.1 Road Eaters, white with "CHEE-TOS CHESTER CHEETAH" logo..........$3
  v.2 Road Eaters white with "PETER PAN CREAMY" logo.........................$3
  v.3 Kool Kromes, copper $3
  v.4 red with orange flame accents......$2
  v.5 baby blue with magenta and white accents "FIFTIES" $2
  v.6 metallic teal blue with flames $2
  v.7 pale yellow, 6sp, mauve and white accents..................................$3
  v.8 pink, 6sp, blue and white accents, "FIFTIES" $3
  v.9 red, 8sp, "Fire Service," red canopy, "T3" on blue sunroof, blue windshield $6
224-C Fourgon Ice Cream Truck (Glacier) (see 259-D)
224-A Unimog Snow Plow, 1:82 (also 259)

v.1 green, 8sp, orange canopy, yellow windshield, unpainted metal plow $6

  v.2 orange with orange canopy, three white trees on sides, unpainted metal plow $6
224-B Fourgon Motor Home, 1:67

v.1 white $8

  v.2 beige...$8
224-D Jeep Cherokee Limited with surfboards on roof (compare to 285-B), 1:60
  v.1 black with gold accents, orange surfboards, charcoal interior $2
  v.2 black with gold accents, hot pink surfboards, charcoal interior $2
  v.3 black with gold accents, 5s, "Limited" on doors, red surfboards $2
  v.4 black with blue and white waves, orange surfboards, translucent pink interior $2
  v.5 dark blue with yellow fenders, orange surfboards, 5d black tires $2

  v.6 dark blue with yellow fenders, 5d dark blue tires, red surfboards, "Surf" on sides (5-pack)......................$2
  v.7 metallic green with tan lower body, 1998................................$2
  v.8 metallic blue with yellow fenders, "Surf," fish graphics, 1999 ....$2
224-E Jeep Cherokee Sheriff (see 285-B)
225-A Safari Truck, 1:80, brush bar on front, same casting as 242-A
  v.1 yellow, 3kk, brown plastic canvas, paint streaks off hood, black brush bar $10
  v.2 orange, 3kk, brown plastic canvas, paint streaks off hood, black brush bar $10
225-B BX4TC
  v.1 white with red and blue accents, "TOTAL 15" $5
225-C Renault 19 Convertible
  v.1 metallic silver............................$3
  v.2 white, 6sp, "RENAULT" on door, red interior $3
  v.3 metallic blue, 6sp, red interior.......$3
226-A Repco F1 Racer with driver, 1:55

v.1 metallic green with white tampo, "5" on nose $10

  v.2 metallic red with "8" decal........$10
226-B Volkswagen Panel Van (Fourgon VW Tole), rear tailgate opens, 1:66
  v.1 red, 5sp, "Café Hag," white accents, white interior............................$10
  v.2 pink, 3sp, white interior............$10
226-C Road Roller
  v.1 light yellow $2
  v.2 darker yellow with black roller and interior $2
227-A Lotus F1 Racer with driver
  v.1 metallic orange-copper with black accents, "2" $10
227-B Magirus Beton Cement Mixer, 1:100
  v.1 red cab, orange body, blue and yellow mixer $8
  v.2 red cab, orange body, yellow and pale orange mixer......................$8
  v.3 red cab, orange body, blue mixer with yellow and black stripe around mixer $6
227-C Ford Mustang GT Convertible, hood opens, 1:59
  v.1 yellow "OFFICIAL PACE CAR" $2
  v.2 lime green "OFFICIAL PACE CAR" .$2

v.3 yellow, 6sp, "MUSTANG GT," black interior $2
v.4 bright blue $2
v.5 metallic purple, 6sp, orange interior, white and orange accents, "TURBO" on hood $2
v.6 metallic blue, 6sp, orange interior, black, red, and white accents $2
v.7 metallic blue, orange rw, orange interior, black, red, and white accents $3
227-D Ford Ka, 1998
v.1 metallic purple $3

v.2 metallic silver **$3**

v.3 metallic teal $3
228-A BRM F1 Racer $10
228-B Chevy Blazer Wrecker, ct4s (Depanneuse) (compare to 228-D, 291-A), 1:62
v.1 silver with yellow, red, and black accents, "auto assistance" on hood $2
v.2 silver with no markings $4
v.3 blue with silver sticker on hood "Express 24/24" $2
v.4 red with blue, white, and black accents "auto assistance" on hood $2
v.5 blue with yellow, red, and white accents "Express 24/24" on hood $2
v.6 fluorescent orange with blue, white, and black accents "Express 24/24" on hood $2
v.7 fluorescent orange with black and white "24 HR SERVICE" on hood and doors $2
v.8 fluorescent orange with black and white checkerboard pattern on sides "SERVICE" $2
v.9 red with black and white accents "EMERGENCY ROAD SERVICE" ..$2
v.10 red, no markings (blue "24/24 quick TOWING" stickers are from MajoKit set) $3
v.11 white with blue lettering, red accents, "EMERGENCY ROAD SERVICE" $2
v.12 red ct4sp, "24 HR SERVICE" on hood and doors, black and white accents, yellow windows $3
228-C Chevy Blazer Pickup 4x4 (see 291-A)
228-D Chevy Blazer Pepsi Truck, Sonic Flashers (compare to 228-C)
v.1 red with opaque white windows and cargo, makes "breaking glass" sound when bumped $5

228-E Saviem Grue, with extending crane (Crane Truck)
v.1 orange with green and black crane, yellow hook, 3sp, 3 axles, black plastic base $8
229-A Ferrari F1 Racer
v.1 metallic purple with checkered stripe $10
229-B Datsun 260Z, 1:60
v.1 black, 3sp, white interior, no accents $3
v.2 metallic light green $5
v.3 metallic turquoise $5
v.4 red, 3sp $4
v.5 white with green and red "SOS" decals on doors $4
v.6 yellow with red accents $3
v.7 yellow with red, black, and yellow accents $3
229-C BMW 325i, front doors open, 1:56
v.1 white with red and blue accents, black interior $3
v.2 white with red, blue, and black accents $3
v.3 silver with red and black accents, black interior $3
229-D Aston Martin DB7, doors open, 1994
v.1 metallic blue, 6sp, no markings, black interior $3
v.2 metallic blue, 6sp, rally graphics, 1999 ....$2
230-A Peugeot 204C Roadster, doors open

v.1 metallic bright blue with cream interior **$10**

230-B Renault 4L Delivery Van, 1:55
v.1 red, 3sp, yellow coat of arms on hood $4
v.2 yellow $4
v.3 blue with white telephone dial logo $4
230-C Volvo 760 GLE, 1:61
v.1 silver, 3kk, red and black accents, without markings $3
v.2 silver, 3spb, red and black accents, without markings $3
v.3 silver, 8h, red and black accents, diagonal markings across doors ...$3
v.4 metallic periwinkle blue, 3spb, red and black accents, no diagonal markings, white interior $3
v.5 metallic dark green, no markings...$3
v.6 metallic green, no markings..........$3
v.7 metallic teal blue, 8h, no markings, black interior $3
v.8 metallic teal blue, 8h, no markings, white interior $3

230-D Ford Transit Custom Tow Truck
v.1 white, 6sp, "TOTAL" logo, amber windshield $2
v.2 red with "Jack's 24 HR. Service" ...$2
230-E Toyota RAV4, 1999
v.1 metallic green with silver lower body, cream interior $3
231-A Citroën Dyane Raid
v.1 white with red unchromed 3spb wheels, red interior and brush bar, "3" on sides $8
v.2 metallic brown with black 3spb wheels, interior and brush bar $8
v.3 light green, red 3spb, black brush bar, cream sunroof $3
231-B Mercedes-Benz 190E 2.3-16, 1:59, 1986
v.1 metallic green with red interior $3
v.2 metallic green with yellow interior..$3
v.3 metallic pewter gray with red interior $3
v.4 metallic bronze-gray with yellow interior $3
v.5 metallic silver, 8h, red interior $3
v.6 white, 8h, black interior, blue and orange rally accents, "13"..........$2
v.7 white with blue and burnt orange rally accents, red interior $2
231-C Bank Security, 1999 (see 204-C)
232-A Porsche LeMans Racer, 1:65

v.1 metallic red..............................**$9**

v.2 yellow......................................$9
v.3 red, 3kk, "3" on front, "elf" on back fender $9
232-B Formula 1 Brabham, 1:53, 1986
v.1 blue and white, "parmalat" $2
v.2 black and light gray, "parmalat" ...$2
232-C Dune Buggy, rw, compare to 248-A
v.1 hot pink with white roof "FUN BUGGY," chrome engine and headlights $4
v.2 hot pink with white roof, "ICE CREAM," chrome engine and headlights $3
v.3 pink with white roof, "Buggy," "3" on roof, chrome engine and headlights $4
v.4 red with white roof, rally tampos on roof, chrome engine and headlights $4
v.5 red with yellow roof, blue engine and headlights, 1999 ....$4

v.6 red, white roof, "Buggy," "3" on roof, chrome engine and headlights $4

v.7 red, white roof, "ICE CREAM" on roof, chrome engine and headlights $4

v.8 blue, white roof, "ICE CREAM" on roof, chrome engine and headlights $4

232-D Mercedes CLK+ GTR, 1999
v.1 silver, "M2" $3

233-A Panther Bertone Course Racer, 1:65
v.1 lime green with yellow base, gray spoiler $10
v.2 orange with yellow base, gray spoiler $10
v.3 metallic blue with yellow base $10
v.4 red with light blue base $10

233-B Mercedes Public Works Truck (Trax Publics), 1:70
v.1 orange with cream tow bar, blue canopy, amber windows $5
v.2 orange with white tow bar, blue canopy, light blue windows.........$5
v.3 orange, 3kk, amber windshield, white canopy with "works" stickers, blue "1" on roof......................$5
v.4 metallic light blue with white canopy.....................$4

233-C Renault Express Van, 1:53
v.1 orange, 6sp, "europcar rentacar," black rear doors.........................$5
v.2 white, 6sp, "europcar rentacar" $5
v.3 red, 6sp, "AVIS," white rear doors ..$4
v.4 red, 6sp, "AVIS," red rear doors ...$4
v.5 red, 6sp, "AVIS," yellow rear doors $8
v.6 blue, 6sp, "SATELLITE SERVICE," yellow rear doors $3

234-A Locomotive $15

234-B Simca 1100 T1, rear hatch opens, 1:60
v.1 dark blue, white "Police" tampos...$4
v.2 black, white "Police" tampos, unpainted metal trailer, white police boat (from 300-Series)......................$4
v.3 blue, 3sp, white interior, yellow windshield, red and yellow flame accents .$4

234-C Ford Fourgon Van, no side windows, 6sp, 1:53 (compare to 234-D, 234-E, 250-B, 279-A)
v.1 white with "Fruits" label, red rear doors $2
v.2 white with "Fruits" tampo, white rear doors $2
v.3 white with "Hawaiian Surfer" label, red rear doors $3
v.4 yellow with "racing team" label, red rear doors $2
v.5 yellow with red trim, "ELEPHANT RESERVE" (part of 344 Elephant Cage Transporter) $2

v.6 yellow with red trim, "MAGIC CIRCUS" sticker $3
v.7 white with "RACING TEAM" markings......................$2
v.8 white with blue fenders, "BASEBALL" $2
v.9 white with blue fenders, "SKATE BOARD" $2
v.10 red "Coca-Cola," sun, 1995 .....$4
v.11 blue "Cadbury Dairy Milk Buttons" $6
v.12 red, "Avis," no side doors or window, 1998 ....$2
v.13 blue, "Cadbury's Dairy Milk," blue rear doors $5
v.14 yellow, "Cadbury's Mini Eggs," purple accents $5
v.15 yellow, "Magic Circus," red rear doors, yellow windshield $2
v.16 red, red tires, "Surf" graphics and scene same as 248 VW, 1999 ....$2

234-D Ford Fourgon Van, porthole side windows (compare to 234-C and E, 250-B, 279-A)
v.1 red, "Avis," side doors, 1998 ......$2
v.2 yellow with red flames, blue running boards, 6sp wheels.....................$3

234-E Ford Fourgon Van, rectangular side windows (compare to 234-C and D, 250-B, 279-A)
v.1 white with red base, red "Canon" tampos $4

234-F Ford Fourgon Police Van (see-279-A)

235-A BMW 2800CS Coupe $7

235-B Motorboat and Trailer.................$15

235-C BMW 3.0 CSI, 1:60
v.1 yellow.......................$4
v.2 metallic bluish green.....................$4
v.3 metallic yellowish green $4
v.4 metallic red.......................$4
v.5 orange, 5sp, white interior, yellow windshield $4

235-D Citroën Acadiane Service Van, 1:53
v.1 yellow, 3kk, white rear doors, white envelope insignia on sides...........$4
v.2 blue.......................$4

235-E Volkswagen Golf GTI 16S, 1:56
v.1 yellow, 6sp, dark blue and white accents $2
v.2 yellow, 8h, light blue and white accents $2
v.3 lime green, 6sp, blue and white accents $2
v.4 lime green, 6sp $2
v.5 lime green, 8h $2
v.6 green, 8h $2
v.7 green, 6sp, "4," "Champions," "Racing" tampos, copper and white accents $2
v.8 red, 6sp $2

235-F Sport Proto Racer, 1997
v.1 white with yellow and black accents $2

236-A Sterckeman Lovely 400 Travel Trailer, 1:65
v.1 gold and white two-tone, yellow windows, bw1 ....$12

236-B Bernard Truck with Chalet $12

236-C Peugeot 604 (also 238-A)............$4

236-D Jeep Cherokee 4x4, tailgate opens, 1:64. Early versions featured a dog in the back, double side window trim, and ribbed roof. Later versions eliminated the dog. Most recent versions feature simplified side window casting and no roof ribs.
v.1 black with "CHEE-TOS CHESTER CHEETAH," no dog, plain roof, ct4s, Road Eaters................................$3
v.2 blue with "Franco American SpaghettiOs/TeddyOs," Road Eaters.......$3
v.3 fluorescent green with red and white flames, no dog, plain roof $2
v.4 fluorescent orange with blue and white flame accents, ribbed roof................................$2
v.5 fluorescent orange, "Big Chief," red and black accents, ribbed roof, black tailgate, ct4sp..........................$2
v.6 green with ribbed roof, white interior, 5d................................$2
v.7 light brown, "BIG CHIEF," dog in back, ribbed roof $3
v.8 metallic brown with "BIG CHIEF," dog in back, ribbed roof.............$5
v.9 red with black "MAD BULL" accents, ribbed roof, ct4s $4
v.10 red with gold and black "MAD BULL" accents, ribbed roof, ct4s ...$4
v.11 red with white and black, orange and blue rally accents, dog in back $3
v.12 red with white and black, orange and blue rally accents, no dog in back $2
v.13 white with "Coca-Cola" polar bear, ct4sp................................$10
v.14 white, ct4sp, black irregular shaped spots all over $2
v.15 yellow with red and black accents, Indian on hood, dog in back, ribbed roof................................$3
v.16 yellow "ROCKIN' BANANA," plain roof, yellow tires, Smelly Speeders $3
v.17 yellow with western motif, "INDIAN" on roof $2
v.18 yellow with "Safari" on sides and hood, animal tracks, ct4sp $2
v.19 yellow, ct4sp, black irregular shaped spots all over $2
v.20 yellow, ct4sp $2

237-A Mercedes-Benz 280SE $10

237-B Maharajah, modified Citroën Dyane with rotating umbrella and elevated chair with steps, 5sp wheels on back axle drive cogs that turn umbrella as car rolls across a hard surface v.1 yellow, 3sp front, 5sp rear, white interior, white umbrella with orange and yellow accents $8

v.2 green, 3kk front, 5sp rear, white interior, white umbrella with red and green accents $8

237-C Lamborghini Countach, 1:56

v.1 red with black spoiler, black and yellow accents, white interior, rw $2

v.2 red with red spoiler, no markings, white interior.................................$2

v.3 red with red spoiler, white "COUNTACH" accents, white interior $2

v.4 red with yellow spoiler, black and white checkered accents, "78" on sides $2

v.5 red with "Lamborghini" on yellow spoiler, black and white checkered accents, "78" on sides $3

v.6 red with plain yellow spoiler, gold and white accents, bull logo $3

237-D Audi TT, 1999

v.1 metallic gold $2

238-A Peugeot 604, hood opens (also 236-C)

v.1 black, 3kk, white interior $5

v.2 black, 3sp, white interior $5

v.3 metallic blue, no markings...........$5

v.4 metallic blue, white stripes along sides $5

v.5 metallic brown $5

v.6 metallic red, 3sp, white interior $5

v.7 gold, 3kk, yellow interior, yellow windshield $5

v.8 gold, 3sp, yellow interior, yellow windshield $5

238-B Formula 1 Racer, rw, 1:55, 1986

v.1 green with red base, red and white accents, "Benetton," black wing, "8".$6

v.2 green with black base, red spoiler and interior, "HOT WINNER" $4

v.3 green, red and white accents, "62," red wing $2

v.4 light blue with red base, black "Ral"lye" on yellow accents, blue "41" on red accent............................$2

v.5 silver, red base, red, blue, and green accents, "RACING,""2," black wing $2

v.6 yellow with red base, red and blue accents, "2," "RACING".............$2

v.7 yellow, red base, red and black accents, "WARNING" (Portugal)............................$4

v.8 yellow with blue accents, "Shell" logo on back, "Tictel,""12," black wing $2

238-C Dodge Concept Car ("Copperhead"), 1999

v.1 metallic gold $2

239-A Peugeot 504 with opening doors, hood and trunk

v.1 metallic blue $12

239-B Matra Simca 670

---

v.1 metallic blue, "10, Goodyear, Shell" $5

239-C Fiat Ritmo / Strada

v.1 yellow with black accents, "ABARTH 2000" $4

v.2 red with black accents, "ABARTH 2000" $4

v.3 red with no markings $5

239-D Audi 90, doors open, 1:60 (also 259-E)

v.1 black with white and yellow tampos, white interior, pale blue windows.....................................$2

v.2 yellow with "AUDI 90" and logo on sides, black interior, 8h $2

239-E Chevrolet Blazer 4x4, 1995 (also 249-D GMC Jimmy)

v.1 red with "Racing Team 3"............$2

v.2 red with no markings...................$2

v.3 orange with blue and white rally graphics, "ROCO," "10," 1999 .$2

v.4 yellow "Pinder Circus" $5

v.5 metallic blue, ct4sp, gray lower body $2

v.6 orange, ct4sp, blue lower body....$2

240-A Simca 1308, 1:60, rear hatch opens

v.1 metallic dark silver.......................$6

v.2 metallic bright blue, gray interior, 3spb.......................................$6

v.3 metallic bright blue, gray interior, 3kk $6

v.4 metallic light silver with "Chrysler Simca" and Chrysler logo on sides, 3spb ...$8

v.5 burnt orange with "Chrysler Simca" and Chrysler logo on sides, 3spb .$8

v.6 burnt orange with "Chrysler Simca" and Chrysler logo on sides, 3kk ...$8

v.7 orange with black "Europe 1" on sides, "E 1 Europe 1" on hood, 3spb.......$8

240-B Chevrolet Impala Police Car, 1:69 (compare to 213-F, 219-A), 1986

v.1 white with black accents, "POLICE N 31" $3

v.2 black and white with gold accents, "HIGHWAY PATROL N 31"..........................$3

---

v.3 black with white doors, "POLICE N31".......................................$2

v.4 bright blue with white roof, 1999 .$2

v.5 black, "Police" shields, wide gold stripes from front to back over car...$4

241-A DAF 2600 Canvas Top Truck, 1:100

v.1 green with silver platform sides and orange canopy, "Services Rapide Lempereur and Cuparc" $7

v.2 green with gray platform sides and orange canopy, "Services Rapide Lempereur and Cuparc" $7

241-B Saviem Canvas Top Truck, 3kk

v.1 orange with red canopy, "JOE CIRCUS" $4

v.2 blue with white canopy, "SERNAM" $3

v.3 blue, 3kk, yellow canopy, "SAVIEM SERVICE" $5

v.4 red with cream canopy, "Majorette Metal" $4

v.5 green with cream canopy, "Majorette Metal" $4

v.6 blue, 3kk, yellow canopy, "MICHELIN" $5

241-C Ford Covered Truck, long narrow side windows on cab, 1:100

v.1 green body, yellow canopy, "super cargo" label $2

v.2 white body, metallic gray canopy, "majorette" tampo $2

v.3 white body, white canopy, "majorette" tampo $2

v.4 red body, 3spb, yellow canopy, "super cargo" label $2

241-D Ford Covered Truck, no narrow side windows on cab, 1:100

v.1 white body blue canopy, "MOVING STUDIO" tampo.........................$2

v.2 white body, "ELF Competition" $2

v.3 red with white cargo cover, "Coca-Cola" $4
v.4 blue "Cadbury Roses Chocolates".$6
241-E Ford Tanker (see 245-C, 245-D)
242-A Snow Top Truck, with or without plow
v.1 orange with plow, orange canopy, "SERVICE" stickers on doors, blue sticker on hood, single headlights .$6

v.2 orange, no plow, 3sp, orange canopy, "SERVICE" stickers on doors, blue sticker on hood, single headlights.....................$5

v.3 orange with plow, no door label $6

242-B Power Shovel (Pelle Mechanique, Pelleteuse), 1:100
v.1 red body, yellow base, yellow shovel......................................$3
v.2 yellow body, black base and shovel..$2
243-A DAF Covered Trailer $12
243-B Shadow DN5 F1 Racer, 1:50
v.1 black with white base..................$4
v.2 dark blue.....................................$4
243-C Ford Transit Van, right side door slides open, 1:60 (compare to 295-A)
v.1 blue with silver and gold accents, blue interior and bumpers, "CITY BUS"...$4
v.2 metallic pale green with blue interior and bumpers $3

v.3 metallic pale green with hot pink interior and bumpers.........................$3
v.4 metallic pale green with red interior and bumpers $4
v.5 pearl white with hot pink interior and bumpers, tropical accents $3
v.6 red with blue and white accents, white interior and bumpers...........$3
v.7 red with blue and white accents, red interior and bumpers $3
v.8 red with yellow interior and bumpers, "City Bus" in script, "210291" on sides $2
v.9 red with blue and white accents, yellow interior and bumpers $2
v.10 white, 6sp, blue and red accents, blue interior and bumpers, "CITY BUS," yellow windshield $4
v.11 white with black interior and bumpers, "CITY BUS" $3
v.12 white with red and blue diagonal stripes..................................$3
v.13 white with red, metallic blue and green accents, pink interior and bumpers $2
v.14 white with red interior and bumpers, "LE MANS SPORT SERVICE Assistance" $2
v.15 white with pink interior and bumpers, "Splish Splash" accents .$2
v.16 white ambulance with orange stripes, red lights on top, door doesn't open, Sonic Flashers....................$5
v.17 yellow "School Bus" with red interior and bumpers $3
v.18 yellow, 6sp, "BCR," blue and red accents, black bed, yellow interior, white bumpers, in Construction Set with yellow #323 trailer.................................$4
244-A Volkswagen Ambulance
v.1 metallic blue with white interior, "POLICE" $8
v.2 orange with white interior, "SERVICE AUTOROUTE," 3spb...................$6
v.3 white with red cross, "AMBULANCE" tampo, thc $6
v.4 white with red cross, "AMBULANCE" tampo, 3sp $6
244-B Jeep 4x4, modified (raised) chassis, plastic roof (compare to 268-A, 290-A), 1:54
v.1 black, ct4sp, yellow roof, eagle logo on hood $3
v.2 black, ct4sp, white roof, rally markings..$3
v.3 hot pink, ct4sp, black roof, yellow interior, black and white graphics on hood $2
v.4 metallic light green, ct4sp, black roof, red interior, black/green/light blue accents, "RENEGADE" $2
v.5 red, ct4sp, white roof, rally markings, black interior.............................$3

v.6 red, ct4sp, black roof and interior, black/red/blue/light blue accents, "RENEGADE"............................$3
v.7 red, ct4sp, black roof and interior, black and white graphics on hood $3
v.8 metallic copper, ct4sp, white roof and interior, yellow "golden eagle" decal on hood.........................$3
244-C BMW Z3 Coupe, 1999

v.1 metallic blue $4

245-A DAF 2600 Tanker, 1:100
v.1 "SHELL" $6
245-B Saviem Tanker, 1:100
v.1 orange and red..........................$8
v.2 red, 3kk, yellow tank, "Shell"........$8
v.3 red, 3kk, white tank, "Shell" $6
v.4 red, 3kk, white tank, "ESSO" $6
v.5 red, 3sp, white tank, "ESSO" $6
v.6 red, 3kk front wheels, 3sp back wheels, white tank, "ESSO".........$6
v.7 blue, 3kk, white tank, "GULF".......$6
v.8 red-orange, 3kk, white tank, "EWING OIL CO." $20
v.9 "TEXACO" $24
245-C Ford Tanker (Citerne), long narrow side windows on cab, 1:100
v.1 blue with white tank, "Milky the good milk"...$3
v.2 white with white tank, "Shell" $4
v.3 pale blue with white tank, cartoon cow and grass picture $2
245-D Ford Tanker (Citerne), no narrow side windows on cab, 1:100
v.1 Cadbury Caramel $4
v.2 Cadbury Creme Eggs $4
v.3 white with cow, milk can, and grass $2
v.4 Petrol Company $2
v.5 yellow with white tank, "Shell" $5
v.6 light blue with white tank, 4c, cow and grass $2
v.7 orange, 4c, gray tank, "GT Gas Tanker," Construction Set.............$2
245-E Ford Transit Wrecker
v.1 yellow with red interior, "BCR Enterprises" in red $2
v.2 red with white interior, "24," "Emergency Road Service" $3
246-A DAF 2600 Bucket Truck, 1:100
v.1 red, bw1, yellow bucket and crane base, red arm on crane $15
246-B Range Rover Rescue Unit with open rear section, 1:60

v.1 red, white interior and ladder, blue windshield, blue riders in back (part of 376-A)..............$4

246-C Range Rover Rescue Unit with closed rear section, 1:60
v.1 red, black interior, silver ladder, gold "DISTRICT 3 FIRE DEPT.," 5d $2
v.2 red, black interior, white ladder, gold "RESCUE UNIT," 8sp $2
v.3 red, white interior, white ladder, blue shield, 5d $2
v.4 red, black interior, white ladder, gold "DISTRICT 3 FIRE DEPT.," 5d $2
v.5 red, black interior, dark gray ladder, gold "DISTRICT 3 FIRE DEPT.," 5d $2

247-A DAF 2600 Crane Truck, 1:100
v.1 yellow with black crane, gray plastic base $12
v.2 metallic light green with black crane, gray plastic base $12

247-B Porsche 924, 1:60
v.1 green with white "Porsche" accents, amber windows..................$6
v.2 red, 3sp, silver "Porsche" accents, amber windows, red interior $6
v.3 metallic blue, 3kk, orange "Porsche" accents, clear windows, red interior...................$4
v.4 silver, 3kk, black "Porsche" accents, amber windshield.....................$5

247-C Refuse Truck (Benne Ordures), 1:100 (compare to 218-A, 218-B)
v.1 green body, gray container, no markings..................................$5
v.2 green body, orange container, no markings..................................$4
v.3 lime green body, orange container, hippo on sides..........................$3
v.4 lime green body, tan container with 3 hippos on sides....................$2
v.5 red body, yellow container, "CITY of NEW YORK"......................$2
v.6 white body, orange container with 3 hippos on sides....................$2
v.7 red body, fluorescent yellow container, 3 hippos on sides................$2
v.8 yellow body, green container, "Clean World" logo in black, 1998 ....$2
v.9 green body, yellow container, cartoon singing trash cans on sides ...$2
v.10 green body, gray container, single hippo on sides, yellow windshield, 3kk..................................$2

248-A Dune Buggy, random flower and lightning decals on roof, Jaguar on nose, 1:55 (compare to 232-C)
v.1 red with black roof, spiral $8
v.2 lime green with white roof, spiral...$8
v.3 lime green with black roof, spiral...$8
v.4 metallic blue with white roof, 8sp ..$6

248-B Pontiac Firebird Trans Am, hood opens (compare to 258-C, also 293-A), 1:62

v.1 black with brown and gold firebird insignia on hood, amber windows, red interior $2
v.2 metallic blue with brown and gold insignia on hood $2
v.3 metallic blue with black and gold insignia on hood $2
v.4 pink $2
v.5 red with black and white racing accents, "8, TURBO RACING"....$2
v.6 red with gold firebird insignia on hood $2
v.7 red with silver and black firebird insignia on hood $2
v.8 green, rw, silver accents, "19" on hood, yellow windshield and interior $2
v.9 red, small rw, no tampos, yellow windshield $2
v.10 red, small rw, yellow windshield, "Pringles"....................................$2

248-C Volkswagen Combi/Van
v.1 red plastic body, "Surf" graphics...$2

249-A Moto-Neige / Ski-Doo Nordic Snowmobile, with tread (compare to 259-G, 284-B, also see 352-A)
v.1 red with silver skis and handlebars...............................$16
v.2 yellow with silver skis and handlebars...............................$16
v.3 orange with orange skis, silver handlebars...............................$16

249-B Mercedes-Benz 450 SE, front doors open, 1:60
v.1 metallic gold with red interior $3
v.2 metallic lime green with red interior.$3
v.3 metallic silver.............................$2

249-C Toyota Celica 2.0 GT, doors open, 1:58
v.1 red with white "CELICA" accent on sides, yellow interior, headlights open and retract $3
v.2 white with red and green rally accents, headlights cast closed.....$2

249-D GMC Jimmy, 1995 (see 239-E Chevrolet Blazer)

250-A Citroën Maserati SM
v.1 blue, 3sp, white interior $10

250-B Ford US Van, with large rectangular window and two smaller ones on left side, circular window on right side, exhaust pipe on left side (compare to 234-C, 234-D, 234-E, 279-A), 1:65
v.1 black $5
v.2 yellow with white bordered red flames, blue fenders....................$5

250-C Mercedes-Benz 300TE Station Wagon, hatch opens, 1:63
v.1 blue with charcoal gray interior and bumpers, no markings.................$3
v.2 white with charcoal gray interior and bumpers, blue and white "Mercedes-Benz SERVICE"..........................$3

v.3 blue with white interior and bumpers, white accents, "ASSISTANCE"......$3
v.4 blue, 6sp, white interior and bumpers, no tampos..................$3
v.5 blue, 6sp, black interior and bumpers, Mercedes tampo on hood $3
v.6 light gray/blue, 6sp, no tampos ...$3
v.7 blue, 6sp, light blue interior and bumpers, white accents, "Assistance", "Mercedes" logo on hood $3
v.8 pale green, charcoal interior, blue accents, "Sport Assistance," bicycle tampo on hood, 6sp $3

251-A Ford Capri
v.1 light blue with white roof, dark blue, light blue and white hood stripes, 3spb...$6
v.2 red, white roof, 3spb $6
v.3 orange with black roof, 3spb $6

251-B Ford Bronco 4x4, 1:56
v.1 black with silver accent and gold stars on sides, no sunroof $2
v.2 black with silver and gold accents, no sunroof $2
v.3 black with silver and gold accents, with sunroof $2
v.4 mustard yellow, no markings $4

251-C Service Boom Truck/Utility Truck, 1998 (compare to 283-A, also 283-B)
v.1 blue, 4c, white crane and boom, white "PHONE" on doors $2
v.2 yellow, 4c, black boom and base..$2

252-A Dune Buggy Surfer JP4 with surfboard, 1:47
v.1 blue with pink plastic trim, yellow roll cage, 3spb $4
v.2 blue with pink plastic trim, yellow roll cage, 6sp $4
v.3 red with white plastic trim, black roll cage, blue surfboard, 3spb $4

252-B Honda Prelude 4WD, doors open, 1:58
v.1 red with black and silver accents, black interior, silver Honda logo on hood $3

252-C Morgan convertible, top off, 1999 (compare to 261-A)
v.1 cherry red, 5d, white interior, blue windshield $2
v.2 metallic teal, rw, white interior, blue windshield $2
v.3 metallic blue, rw, white interior, blue windshield $2
v.4 metallic red, rw, white interior, blue windshield $2

253-A Ford 5000 Farm Tractor, 1:55
v.1 blue with white fenders and wheel hubs...$8
v.2 red with white fenders, black wheels...$6

253-B Oldsmobile Omega, 1:75
v.1 metallic blue, 3spb, white interior..$6
v.2 white with black and red accents,

"Firestone 23 SEIKO" $6
v.3 silver, 3spb, red interior, black and red "ZZ" stripes on sides.............$6

253-C Cadillac Allante
v.1 Kool Kromes, yellow with black interior $2
v.2 Kool Kromes, light green with black interior $2
v.3 Kool Kromes, light blue $2
v.4 hot pink with white interior, no markings, 8h $2
v.5 silver with red roof.....................$5
v.6 hot pink with white interior, blue/orange/green/yellow accents $2
v.7 Road Eaters fluorescent lime green with white interior, "Franco American SpaghettiOs" $3
v.8 green, 8h, red/white/blue/pink accents, white interior, "FUN" on trunk $2
v.9 red with white interior, no markings, 8h $3

254-A Mercedes-Benz Stake Truck with Hay Load, 1:100
v.1 red and brown, 3kk.............$6

254-B Mercedes Cattle truck, 1:100 (compare to 213-E)
v.1 yellow with light brown box, gray door, 1 black, 1 cream steer, 254/213 on base, 3kk $6
v.2 light yellow with dark brown box and gray door, 1 black, 1 white steer, 254 on base.....................$4

254-C Citroën XM, hood opens, 1:61
v.1 metal flake silver, 4c, black interior ..$3
v.2 metal flake silver, 8h, black interior ..$3
v.3 white, 4c $2
v.4 metallic light green, 4c, green interior, 8h $3

255-A Hanomag Bulldozer, 1:70
v.1 red, silver blade and base, green plastic cab $6
v.2 red, silver blade with red and white sticker, silver base, green plastic cab....................$6
v.3 red, yellow blade and base, yellow plastic cab, gray interior.............$6
v.4 yellow, silver blade and base $6
v.5 yellow, yellow blade and base.....$6

255-B Renault R5 Turbo, 1:53
v.1 red with yellow interior and lower body, "TURBO," 6spk $4

255-C Renault Maxi 5 Turbo, 1985, 1:53
v.1 blue with red interior and lower body, red and white rally accents, "PHILLIPS, elf, 3," thc.............$3

255-D Ambulance Truck, 1:60
v.1 white, 4c, orange accents, blue "NYC EMS AMBULANCE," "222" on doors $2
v.2 white, 8h, orange accents, blue "NYC EMS AMBULANCE," "222" on doors $2

256-A Amphibie ATF/ATV All Terrain Vehicle, six-wheel amphibious one-man all-terrain vehicle, 1:35
v.1 green with white interior and base, black plastic gear, decal of eyes on front $12
v.2 orange-red with yellow interior and base, decal of eyes on front $12

256-B BMW 733, with or without sunroof outline on roof, front doors open, 1:60
v.1 burgundy, 3kk, cream interior, yellow "FEDERATION EQUESTRE FRANCAISE" on hood, sunroof $5
v.2 metallic light green, 3kk, no markings, sunroof, white interior, green tinted windows....................$5
v.3 silver, no markings $5
v.4 white with green/orange/yellow horse and horseshoe label on hood, no sunroof....................$5

256-C Mack Tow Truck (also 297-B, compare to 297-A), 1:100
v.1 red with gray plastic deck and base, black boom, silver metal hook, 1996 ....$2

257-A Renault 5 LeCar with antenna and rear view mirrors, 1:55 (compare to 280-A)
v.1 metallic silver with chrome mirrors $8
v.2 pale yellow with chrome mirrors....$8
v.3 red with white "RTL" on blue and yellow accents, black mirrors, "RTL" on sides only $8
v.4 red with white "RTL" on blue and yellow accents, chrome mirrors, "RTL" on hood and sides....................$8
v.5 metallic red, 3kk, white interior, no tampos $8

257-B Mazda RX7 Daytona, doors open, 1:56
v.1 blue with silver "21," black "MAZDA," red interior, wide tires .$2
v.2 orange with blue accents, blue interior, wide tires $3
v.3 orange with blue accents, blue interior, narrow tires $4
v.4 orange with black and silver "21 MAZDA" $3
v.5 orange with black and silver "RX7," blue interior, rw $4
v.5 white with black and red accents, "23" $2
v.6 white with "Mobil 1" accents $2
v.7 black with silver and gold "21 MAZDA" $2

257-C BMW 325i, doors open 1995, 1:56
v.1 metallic dark olive green with dark gray interior and bumpers.............$2
v.2 burgundy....................$2
v.3 white, 8h, red interior and bumpers, "Star 3" racing markings $2
v.4 metal flake teal with blue interior....$2
v.5 metallic blue, 8h, gray interior $2

v.6 white, 8h, blue and red rally accents, "3," "STAR," "Bolids" $2
v.7 white, 8h, green doors with "Polizei," dark gray interior (1999) Rescue Force 3 pack) $2

257-D BMW 325 Polizei, 1999
v.1 white with green doors and hood, pale blue windows and roof light .$2

258-A Dune Buggy with awning and amber windshield, chrome spiral wheel design
v.1 yellow with white awning, yellow flower design on roof with red outline, green leaf, white interior $10
v.2 yellow with white awning, dark blue pansy design on roof, white interior $10
v.3 red with white awning, red and yellow flower design on roof, white interior....................$10

v.4 red with white awning, dark blue pansy design on roof, white interior $10

v.5 red with white awning, rt wheels, black interior $15

258-B Mercedes-Benz Fire Engine (Pompier Aeroport), 1:70
v.1 red and white, 3sp, "No. 4 Fire and Rescue" on yellow/orange sticker, blue windshield, gray water cannon $6
v.2 red and white, 3kk, no sticker, blue windshield, black water cannon ...$6

258-C Pro Stocker Firebird with Oversized Engine (compare to 248-B, 293-A), 1:62
v.1 white with red and blue stars and stripes....................$2
v.2 yellow with black and red accents ..$2

259-A Unimog Snow Plow, 1:82 (see 224-A)
259-B Camping Trailer....................$6
259-C Fourgon Ice Cream Van (Glacier) (compare to 224-C)
v.1 green with yellow awning and interior $5
v.2 metallic red with pale blue windows, yellow awning and interior $5
v.3 pale green with yellow star graphics, yellow awning, 1999 ....$2
v.4 pink with pale blue windows, yellow awning and interior $5
v.5 red with clear windows, yellow awning and interior $5

v.6 red with pale blue windows, yellow awning and interior $5

v.7 yellow with pink windows, white awning with blue graphics, cream interior $6

v.8 yellow with blue windows, white awning with no graphics, cream interior $6

v.9 white with red awning $4

v.10 white, 4c, yellow interior, orange awning, pictures of cones on roof (1998) $2

v.11 pale green, 4c, yellow interior, red awning, yellow stars and "Ice Cream" on roof (1999) $2

259-D Fourgon Motor Home (see 224-C)

259-E Audi 90 (see 239-D), 1:60

259-F British Bus (also 286-A), 1:125

v.1 red, 3kk, amber windows, white interior, "British Airways" labels $6

v.2 red, 3kk, clear windows, white interior, dark blue, red and white stickers, white "Visit London" on blue part of labels $6

v.3 red, 3kk, amber windows, white interior, light blue, red and white stickers, large black "Visit London" across entire label $6

259-G Moto-Neige / Snowmobile, same casting as 249-A but without tread (also 284-B)

v.1 white with amber windshield, silver skis and handlebars, red and blue accents, "92" $6

v.2 white with amber windshield, red skis and handlebars, "Olympic Racing" $6

v.3 white with amber windshield, dark brown-gray skis and handlebars, "Olympic Racing" $6

v.4 white, Olympic symbols, "6" on front, amber windshield, red skis $4

v.5 red, yellow windshield, blue and white accents, "92," black plastic base $5

v.6 red, amber windshield, white snowflakes, white handlebars and skis, black seat (1999) $3

260-A Renault 17

v.1 orange, 3kk, white interior, yellow windshield, gas tampos (Esso, Mobil, BP, etc.) $9

v.2 orange, 3kk, white interior, yellow windshield, no tampos $6

260-B Explorateur 4x4, 1:59 based on a Volvo P2304, this all-terrain, four-wheel drive vehicle was used by the Swedish Armed Forces and the United Nations in the 1970s

v.1 gold with cream canopy with green design, brown interior $5

v.2 metallic blue with white canopy and interior, "TUNIS 483 DAKAR" $5

v.3 metallic blue, ct4sp, white canopy and interior, "PARIS DAKAR," "340," "RB" $5

v.4 metallic blue, ct3c, white canopy and interior, "PARIS DAKAR," "340," "RB" $5

260-C Mercedes-Benz 500SL Roadster 1:58

v.1 deep red with maroon interior $3

v.2 Kool Kromes, light green-blue with metallic gray interior and bumpers $2

v.3 Kool Kromes, red $2

v.4 Kool Kromes, teal blue $2

v.5 metallic light gold with beige interior and bumpers $2

v.6 Road Eaters, bright red, "Willy Wonka NERDS" $3

v.7 Smelly Speeders, hot pink with white interior, red tires, "STRAWBERRY SPEEDSTER" $2

v.8 metallic silver with maroon interior and bumpers $2

v.9 black, 6sp, dark gray interior $2

v.10 metallic silver, 6sp, gray interior and bumpers $2

261-A Morgan convertible, top on, 1:50 (compare to 252-C)

v.1 blue chrome, white interior, clear windshield, 5d blue hubs, Kool Kromes / Top Chromes $3

v.2 metallic blue, 5d, white roof and interior, amber windshield $2

v.3 green chrome, 5d green hubs, white interior, clear windshield, Kool Kromes $3

v.4 dark green, 8sp, cream roof and interior, amber windshield $3

v.5 dark green, 8sp, white roof and interior, amber windshield $3

v.6 dark green, 8sp, white roof and interior, clear windshield $3

v.7 dark green, 8sp, brown roof and interior, clear windshield $3

v.8 pale green, 5sp, white interior and roof (Color Pack) $3

v.9 metallic green, 5d, cream roof and interior, amber windshield $2

v.10 metallic mint green, 5d, white roof and interior, light blue windshield $2

v.11 dark red, 8sp, cream roof and interior, yellow windshield $3

v.12 dark red, 8sp, cream roof and interior, amber windshield $3

v.13 red with white interior, cream top .$2

v.14 cherry red, 8sp, black top, gray interior, clear windshield $3

v.15 lavender, 5sp, white interior and roof, blue windshield (Color Pack) $3

261-B Explorer, 1995 (see 260-B)

262-A Airport Minibus, 1:87

v.1 white with blue and red "AIR FRANCE" tampos $6

v.2 white with red "TWA" tampos $6

v.3 white with "AIRPORT" tampos $2

v.4 red lower body, yellow upper body .$3

v.5 red "Coca-Cola" sun $5

v.6 white with red and black abstract pattern on sides, pale blue windows .$2

v.7 white upper, green lower, soccer graphics $2

v.8 white upper and lower, "JAPAN AIR LINES" tampos $4

v.9 white lower, red upper, "JAPAN AIR LINES" tampos $4

v.10 white upper and lower, red and black abstract design on sides $2

v.11 white lower, red upper, "AIRPORT" tampos $2

v.12 orange lower, white upper, "AIRPORT" tampos $2

263-A Front End Loader (also see 211 Plow), 1:87

v.1 orange, ct3c $3

v.2 yellow, ct4sp, light gray engine and stack $2

v.3 orange, ct3cb, black hubs $3

v.4 yellow, ct3c, dark gray engine and stack $2

v.5 yellow, ct4sp, dark gray engine and stack $2

v.6 light blue, ct3c, dark gray engine and stack $2

264-A Alpine A310 Special Team Unit

v.1 dark blue, 3sp, blue windows, white interior, red/white/blue "POLICE" markings $8

v.2 white, 3sp, blue windshield, blue interior, "SOS" on sides $8

v.3 white, 3sp, blue windows, red/white/blue "POLICE" markings $8

264-B Custom Ford Transit Van Pickup

v.1 red with white bumper and interior, "RACING SERVICE" $4

264-C Volkswagen Golf, 1:56

v.1 red, 8h $2

v.2 silver, 4c $2

v.3 teal, 8h $2

v.4 silver, 8h $2

v.5 blue, 8h, yellow interior, green bumpers $2

v.6 blue, 8h, black interior $2

v.7 blue, 8h, black interior, "12," rally tampos $2

264-D Volkswagen Golf IV, 1999

v.1 metallic light green $2

265-A Citroën CX, 1:60

v.1 burgundy, 3sp, cream interior $6

v.2 metallic light gold-brown, 3sp, white interior $6

v.3 silver $6

265-B Container Truck with air deflector on cab roof, 3 axles, 1:100

v.1 lime green body, white container, 4c, "Yoplait" $3

v.2 red body, 4c, white container, "WEST LINES" ....$3 v.3 red body, 4c, white container, "RESTAURANT PIZZA DEL ARTE" ..$3

v.4 white, 4c, "DIET PEPSI," Road Eaters $4

v.5 white cab, 4c, white container, "PETER PAN," Road Eaters $3

v.6 red cab, 4c, white container, "PETER PAN," Road Eaters................$3

v.7 fluorescent orange, 4c, "Swanson Kids Growlin' Grilled Cheese Fun Feast Barnie Bear," Road Eaters ...$3

v.8 white, 4c, "ROQUEFORT SOCI-ETE" $3

v.9 white, 4c, "TOTAL" $4

v.10 red, 4c, "Coca-Cola" $6

v.11 blue, 4c, "Cadbury Roses Choco-lates" $6

v.12 blue, 4c, "Cadbury Dairy Milk" ..$6

v.13 blue with white container, 4c, clown print on sides $2

v.14 white, 4c, gold "FUTURA MOTORS PTY. LTD." (Australian promotional issue) $15–20

v.15 blue with white container, dancing clowns graphics, 4c, 1998........$2

v.16 lime green cab and chassis, white unmarked container, 4c $4

v.17 white with blue "Clairgel," white "Notre qualite, C'est la qualite" on blue background, 4c $8

v.18 yellow "Leon's" Canada's Only Furniture Superstores," premium, no package, 4c $16

v.19 white, 4c, white container, no markings (1999)........................$2

266-A Renault 18, 1:60

v.1 dark yellow with "TAXI" sign on roof, "radio taxi" $4

v.2 light yellow with "TAXI" sign on roof, "radio taxi" $4

v.3 metallic blue with yellow spoiler on roof (part of 368-A) $4

v.4 metallic silver.......................$6

v.5 yellow with passenger, no markings..............................$6

v.6 light metallic blue with white spoiler on roof $6

266-B Land Rover 4x4, opening plastic rear door, 1:60

v.1 cream with black roof rack and interior..$3

v.2 red with black roof rack and interior..$3

v.3 tan with "4x4 SAFARI" graphics on hood, black roof rack and rear door...................................$2

v.4 tan with black zebra stripes $2

v.5 white with black and white zebra stripes, black roof rack $3

v.6 white body with "4x4 Safari" tampo on hood, black roof rack and rear door .$3

v.7 white with red light bar on roof, "NASA" $2

v.8 white, 5d, black roof rack, red "Safari" on yellow background on hood, gray and brown splash marks on body $2

v.9 yellow with "SAFARI" graphics on sides and hood, black roof rack and rear door $2

v.10 black, 5d, "4 Rallye Oil" on hood, brown roof rack, in set 328........$3

v.11 white, 5d, no roof rack, red light rack, "Police"......................$3

267-A Excalibur, 1:56

v.1 metallic light blue, 8sp, white interior, black roof $5

v.2 metallic brown, 8sp $4

v.3 yellow with passenger, 8sp $6

v.4 silver, 8sp, black roof $4

v.5 red, 8sp, black roof $6

v.6 red, 8sp, light gray roof, white interior, yellow windshield.................$5

v.7 red, 8sp, light gray roof, dark gray interior $5

v.8 white, 8sp, black top $5

267-B Crazy Car, 1:55 (1995 reissue of 223-B)

v.1 black with white interior, red steering wheel and exhaust pipes, "FUNNY" on roof, "CRAZY CAR" on hood .$3

268-A Jeep CJ with conventional (low) chassis, open, with roll bar (compare to 244-B, 290-A), 1:54

v.1 black with red interior, black roll bar, gold accents, red 4x4 on hood $3

v.2 metallic light brown $4

v.3 yellow with bright green interior and roll bar, abstract green and black accents on hood $3

268-B Chevrolet Corvette Turbo Racer (see 215-C), 1:57

268-C Pontiac Trans Sport SE, 1:55

v.1 red, 6sp, gray lower body, white interior..$2

v.2 red, 8h gray lower body, white interior..$2

v.3 blue, 8h, gray lower body, white interior..$2

269-A Jeep Cherokee Ambulance, rear doors open, 1:64

v.1 white with blue accents, blue six-armed cross on hood, bright blue interior, 5d $3

v.2 white with no markings on sides, red cross on hood, 5d.....................$4

v.3 white with red accents, red cross on hood, bright blue interior, 5d $3

269-B Ford Mondeo, 1994 ....$2

269-C Porsche Boxster, 1998

v.1 yellow with blue accents, red "8" ..$2

v.2 pale gray with cream interior, no graphics, 1999 ....$2

v.3 metallic silver, 6sp, red interior, 1999 ....$2

270-A Autobianchi A112, rear hatch opens, 1:53

v.1 metallic gold with black interior, black and red accents.........................$6

v.2 red, 3spb, black interior, white and green "A112," yellow windshield.$6

270-B Renault Clio, rear hatch opens, 1:53

v.1 red, 8h, black interior, black stripe on side with white "Clio".................$3

270-C Ford Econoline Ambulance, 1998

v.1 white with brown and gold trim $3

271-A Alfa 75

v.1 red with black accents, black interior, no trim on grille.....................$6

v.2 red with black accents, black interior, silver trim on grille.....................$4

v.3 red with tan interior $3

v.4 red, 8h, "FORZA ITALIA," green and white accents, white interior.........$3

271-B Alfa Romeo Giulietta, 1:55

v.1 blue "POLIZIA" with white base and interior $4

v.2 red, 3sp, black and silver accents, black interior $3

271-C Ford Econoline Van/Saloon Car, 1998

v.1 metallic teal blue with hot pink interior $2

271-D Alfa Romeo Polizia, 1999 ....$2

272-A Ford Tempo/Sierra, 1:58

v.1 metallic blue, 8h, yellow windshield, silver accents, "Sierra".................$2

v.2 silver, 3sp, yellow windshield, red accents.............................$2

v.3 white with blue accents.................$2

v.4 light yellow with red accents.........$2

v.5 yellow with red accents $2

272-B Renault Espace, 1997

v.1 white plastic body with orange trim, blue "AMBULANCE" and logo $2

273-A Toyota Tercel 4WD, 1:55

v.1 blue with black interior, silver accents.............................$4

v.2 metallic sea green with black accents.............................$4

v.3 metallic periwinkle blue with black accents.............................$4

v.4 red with black accents and interior ..$4

v.5 bright orange, no markings $4

v.6 metallic gold with black "4WD" ...$4

273-B Roadster, 1994, based on a Dodge Viper, 1:58

v.1 red with black interior $2

273-C Forklift, 1999

v.1 yellow with steel gray cage and lift $2

274-A Super Dump Truck (Benne Carriere), 1:100

v.1 yellow, ct3c chrome hubs, silver dumper.............................$2

v.2 yellow, ct3c black hubs, silver dumper.............................$2

275-A Renault 11 Encore, sliding sunroof, 1:54
  v.1 dark maroon with yellow interior, yellow "11" and stripe..................$4
  v.2 red with yellow interior and accents, black lower body......................$3
  v.3 white, 8h, black plastic lower body, red interior, yellow windshield, black/yellow/red/light blue rally accents, "25"...........................$3
  v.4 metallic green with black/orange/silver rally accents.........................$5
275-B Ford Escort GT, doors open, 1:55
  v.1 yellow with green interior, red and black rally tampos, "5," 4c.........$2
276-A Toyota 4x4 Runner (4Runner), conventional (low) chassis, 1994
  v.1 red with black interior, black stripe, silver "4X4 Runner" on sides, 5d.....$2
  v.2 metallic maroon, 5d....................$2
  v.3 yellow with racing and checkerboard graphics, 5d, 1998...................$2
276-B Toyota 4x4 Runner (4Runner), modified (raised) chassis
  v.1 red with rally tampos, ct4sp.........$2
277-A Toyota Landcruiser, conventional (low) chassis, back window opens, 1:53
  v.1 beige with green accents "RAID 86" and map of Africa on roof, "African safari, Kenya"...........................$4
  v.2 red with yellow interior and accents, black lower body......................$3
  v.3 white with black zebra stripes, black interior....................................$4
  v.4 metallic green with black/orange/silver "Rallye" accents....................$5
  v.5 white with "Jungle King" on roof, red interior...................................$4
277-B Toyota Landcruiser 4x4, modified (raised) chassis, back window opens, 1:53
  v.1 beige, ct4sp, red interior, "AFRICAN SAFARI"....................................$3
  v.2 black, ct4sp, gold accents, "RAID 86" and map of Africa on roof, "African safari, Kenya"................$4
  v.3 bright green, ct4sp, yellow interior, "AFRICAN SAFARI"....................$3
  v.4 red, ct4sp, black and gold accents, "Rally 43," yellow interior............$3
  v.5 white, ct4sp, red and gold "Rallye" accents, green and black "STAR 80"..$2
  v.6 red, ct4sp, black zebra stripes, black interior.................................$4
  v.7 white, ct4sp, black zebra stripes, black interior.............................$4
  v.8 metallic brown, ct4sp, red, yellow and orange decals....................$4
  v.9 white, ct4sp, red interior, green accents, "RAID 86" and map of Africa on roof, "KENYA" and "african safari" on sides..............$3
277-C Harvester, 1999
  v.1 light green $2

278-A Western Locomotive, 1:87
  v.1 metallic blue with red cowcatcher.$10
  v.2 metallic green with red cowcatcher.$10
  v.3 black with red cowcatcher, Sonic Flashers $12
278-B Mobile Home Camping Car, pickup truck camper (compare to 313-B)
  v.1 hot pink with beige camper..........$4
  v.2 lime green, 8h, white camper.......$4
  v.3 blue, 4c, white camper $4
  v.4 blue, 8h, white camper $4
  v.5 red, 8h, white camper, blue and white mountain scene $3
  v.6 hot pink, 6sp blue tires, beige camper..$4
  v.7 hot pink, 8h, white camper $2
  v.8 red, 8h, "Coca Cola," no camper on back, black air deflector on roof, part of set with 5th wheel trailer (see 313-B)
279-A Fourgon Police Van, windows all around, 1:65 (compare to 234-C, 234-D, 234-E, 250-B)
  v.1 blue, 6sp, white interior/grille/fenders, label on sides has red outer stripes, wide white stripe in the middle with blue "POLICE," clear light and windshield $3
  v.2 blue, 6sp, white interior/grille/fenders, two blue and one thin red stripe on top of wide white stripe, blue "POLICE," clear light and windshield.....................................$3
  v.3 blue, 6spk, white interior/grille/fenders, blue "POLICE" on white rectangle on sides of van, blue light and windshield $3
  v.4 white with blue and red "POLICE" accents, blue interior/grille/fenders $3
  v.5 white, 6sp, "Canon," red interior/grille/fenders/rear doors .$3
279-B Stock Car, 1:60
  v.1 metallic blue with red and white accents, pink interior, yellow roll cage...$2
  v.2 metallic blue with red and white accents, yellow interior, pink roll cage...$2
  v.3 green with orange and white accents, yellow interior, pink roll cage...$2
  v.4 green with orange and white accents, pink interior, yellow roll cage...$2
  v.5 bright blue with red and white racing accents, yellow interior, hot pink roll cage...$2
279-C '56 Corvette, 1999
  v.1 bright blue with white accents.......$4
280-A Renault 5 LeCar, no rear view mirrors or antenna, front doors open, 1:51 (compare to 257-A)

  v.1 metallic light olive green with yellow interior, black/orange/yellow accents..$6
  v.2 white, 4c, yellow windshield and interior, black/orange/yellow stripes on sides...$6
  v.3 white, 4c, yellow windshield and interior, yellow accents + tennis racquet, "Tennis" $6
280-B Ferrari F40, 1:58
  v.1 red with no plastic rear window....$2
  v.2 red with plastic rear window $2
  v.3 Kool Kromes, red.........................$3
  v.4 Kool Kromes, yellow $3
281-A Peugeot 205 GTI/CTI Hardtop Sedan (also 210-D, compare to 210-C, 281-B), 1:53
  v.1 black with red plastic trim and interior, gold insignia on hood................$2
  v.2 red with black plastic trim and interior, black insignia on hood $2
  v.3 white with black plastic trim and interior, black and red accents...........$2
  v.4 yellow, 6sp, black plastic trim and interior, red/black/blue accents, "205" on roof $2
  v.5 yellow, 6sp, red accents, "FLASH TEAM, saphi ligner," "17".........$2
  v.6 white, 6sp, red and blue accents, "POLICE" $3
  v.7 white with red and black graphics, black interior.............................$2
281-B Peugeot 205 GTI/CTI Cabriolet, 1:53 (see 210-C, compare to 210-D, 281-A)
281-C Mack Cement Truck, 1998
  v.1 yellow cab, 6sp, red with blue barrel..$2
  v.2 yellow cab, 6sp, red with orange barrel (1999) $2
282-A F1 Ferrari, 1986
  v.1 red with yellow and black accents, "Agip 27"...............................$2
  v.2 green and red with "Benetton 23".$4
  v.3 green and red with "Benetton 8"...$4
  v.4 red, white and black with "TAG 1".$2
  v.5 blue and white with "Parmalat 2"..$2
  v.6 red, rw, "FIAT," "Agip" $2
  v.7 red, rw, "FIAT," "1," Shell logo, "Agip 27"...............................$2
283-A Crane Truck, 1:100 (compare to 251-C)
  v.1 red, 4c, blue crane, black boom, black hook $2
  v.2 yellow, 4c, yellow crane, black boom, red hook..........................$2
  v.3 yellow, 4c, yellow crane, black boom, silver hook.....................$2
283-B Utility Truck, 1:100, 1998 (see 251-B)
284-A Saab 900 Turbo, front doors open, 1:62
  v.1 black with red interior, amber windows, silver "TURBO" on sides.....$3
  v.2 metallic blue, 4c, cream interior, pale yellow windows, white "TURBO" on sides $3

v.3 metallic green with cream interior, pale yellow windows, white "TURBO" on sides $3

v.4 metallic green, 4c, cream interior, pale yellow windows, silver "TURBO" on sides $3

284-B Snowmobile (Moto-Neige) identified as #284 only on package (see 249-A, 259-C)

285-A Lancia Monte Carlo, 1:50

v.1 mustard yellow, 6sp, black interior, amber windows, black "MONTE CARLO" $4

v.2 white, 6sp, red accent, amber windows, black "68" on doors and hood $3

v.3 white, 6sp, "Tour de Course," "Guillaume," blue and red accents $4

285-B Jeep Cherokee Sheriff (compare to 224-C)

v.1 white with blue accents, red roof light..$2

v.2 white with blue accents, orange roof light..$2

v.3 white and blue with red roof light ..$2

286-A British Bus (also 259-E), 1:125

v.1 red with amber windows, white interior, "British AIRWAYS" label $6

v.2 red with amber windows, yellow interior, "VISIT LONDON" $6

286-B Fiat Tipo, 1:54

v.1 metallic blue, 8h, white accents and interior, "TIPO" on sides $3

v.2 red, 8h, white interior, white accents..$3

v.3 yellow, 8h, red interior, racing accents, "1" $3

287-A Toyota Hi-Lux Pickup, conventional chassis (compare to 292-A), 1:56

v.1 orange, ct4sp, silver, black and yellow accents, "4 x 4" $6

v.2 orange, ct4sp, black interior, dark green, yellow and dark orange accents, "Toyota 4x4" $6

287-B Toyota Hi-Lux Pickup 4x4, modified 4x4 chassis (see 292-A)

287-C Bulldozer

v.1 yellow with black plastic cab, light gray plastic plow $3

v.2 yellow with black plastic cab, dark gray plastic plow $2

288-A Renault Kangoo Van/Saloon Car, windows on sides, 1998

v.1 yellow with graphics, bright blue interior..$4

289-A F1 MacLaren, 1986

v.1 white, rw, red and black accents ..$3

v.2 orange, rw, red and black accents, "HONDA," black wing (COLOR PACK) $3

289-B Renault Kangoo Panel Van, no windows on sides behind door, 1998

v.1 red with bright blue interior $4

290-A Jeep 4x4 Rallye CJ, modified (raised) chassis, open, with roll bar (compare to 244-B, 268-A)

v.1 black with red interior and roll bar, gold accents and red "4x4" on hood $2

v.2 black with red interior, black roll bar, gold accents and red "4x4" on hood $2

v.3 black with red interior, black roll bar, red/orange/yellow accents $2

v.4 yellow with black and green abstract design on hood, green interior, black roll bar $2

v.5 fluorescent lime green with black and green abstract design, bright green interior and roll bar $2

290-B '57 T-Bird, 1999

v.1 red with white flames on hood and front fenders, white roof $3

291-A Chevy Blazer Pickup 4x4 (also 228-D, compare to 228-C, 228-E), 1:62

v.1 blue with yellow interior, black and gold accents $3

v.2 red, ct4sp, black and white horses on sides, "WILD MUSTANG" on hood, yellow windshield, black light bar .$2

v.3 yellow with red interior, red and black accents, black rally lights behind cab $3

v.4 black, ct4sp, multicolor "INTERNATIONAL FOUNDATION" on hood, yellow windshield and interior $2

v.5 red ct4sp, "Coca-Cola," yellow interior, black light bar, sun accent $3

v.6 black, ct4sp yellow wheels, multicolor "INTERNATIONAL FOUNDATION" on hood, yellow windshield and interior..$2

v.7 red, ct4sp, "4WD" on doors and hooh, yellow windshield..............$2

v.8 yellow, ct4sp, black and red accents, "4WD" on hood and doors, yellow windshield, black light bar...........$2

v.9 yellow, ct4sp black hubs, black and red accents, "4WD" on hood and doors, yellow windshield, black light bar $2

v.10 black, ct4sp, bovine skull on hood, red, white and yellow accents, "TEXAS" on doors, red lamps, no ridges on roof............................$2

292-A Toyota Hi-Lux Pickup with modified (raised) 4x4 chassis (compare to 287-A)

v.1 fluorescent green, ct4sp, red and black "WESTERN RODEO" $2

v.2 metallic gold, ct4sp, silver, black and red "4X4 Toyota" $3

v.3 metallic blue, ct4sp, red and yellow accents "NIGHT HAWK" $3

v.4 red, ct4sp, black interior, yellow, black and silver accents $3

v.5 yellow, ct4sp, black interior, rally accents.................................$4

v.6 black and red, ct4sp, red interior and wheels, "APPLE JAZZ," Smelly Speeders $3

v.7 metallic pink, ct4sp, blue, black and silver accents, "Toyota 4x4" white interior $3

v.8 hot pink, ct4sp, yellow flames, "GLADIATOR" $2

v.9 metallic blue, ct4sp, black interior..$2

v.10 white, ct4sp, orange, black and red accents............................$2

293-A Pontiac Firebird Turbo (see 248-B, compare to 258-C)

293-B Jaguar XJ6, front doors open, 1:65

v.1 black, 8h, red interior..................$2

v.2 silver with red interior.................$2

v.3 metallic green, 4c, red interior $2

v.4 metallic green, 8h, red interior $2

293-C Jaguar Police, 1999

v.1 white with red and blue accents....$2

294 Not issued

295-A Ford Transit TUG Custom Tow Truck (compare to 243-C)

v.1 red, white interior and bumpers, "JACK'S TOWING 24 HR SERVICE," amber windows..............$2

v.2 fluorescent orange with "RACING SERVICE" $3

296-A Chevrolet El Camino SS Pickup, 1:59

v.1 red chrome with pink flames, white interior, Kool Kromes..................$3

v.2 red with white interior, white "EL CAMINO SS" on sides $2

v.3 blue, 8h, white interior, "EL CAMINO" $2

v.4 metallic blue with white interior, white "EL CAMINO SS" on sides $2

v.5 dark blue, 8h, "Willy Wonka DWEEBS" candy, Road Eaters.....$3

v.6 fluorescent lime green, 8h, "CRY BABY" candy, Road Eaters $3

v.7 white with red interior, red and blue accents, "AMERICAN THUNDER" $2

v.8 white with red interior, orange and green paint splash accents, "INDY CRASH" $2

v.9 white, 8hbl, red and blue accents, "American Off Road" (blue wheels) from Glider set........................$2

v.10 hot pink with white interior, white and blue paint splash accents, "INDY CRASH" $2

v.11 bright green with white interior, "EL CAMINO" $2

297-A Mack Dump Truck, 1:100 (compare to 256-C)

v.1 metallic blue, 6sp, metallic silver dumper.................................$2

v.2 yellow, 6sp, metallic silver dumper ..$2

297-B Mack Wreck Truck, 1:100 (see 256-C)

297-C Ford Skip Truck, 1998

v.1 blue with green skip $2

v.2 blue with orange skip $2

298-A Ford Recycling Lorry, 1998
  v.1 green with red and blue recycling
      containers $2
  v.2 green with yellow and blue recycling
      containers $2

Majorette Supers

These are selected 200 Series models, with newly assigned model numbers followed by an "S," that are steerable.

201.S Fiat Coupe, yellow $3
202.S Fiat Coupe Racing, silver $3
203.S Mustang Convertible, black...........$3
204.S Mustang Convertible, red $3
205.S Mustang Hardtop, yellow $3
206.S Mustang Hardtop Sport, black.......$3
207.S Renault Clio, turquoise $3
208.S Renault Clio Rallye, blue $3
209.S Ferrari 456 GT, red $3
210.S Ferrari 456 GT Racing, black........$3
211.S Ford Mondeo, silver......................$3
212.S Ford Mondeo Rallye, blue $3
213.S Roadster, red $3
214.S Roadster Sport, metallic teal...........$3
215.S Ferrari GTO, yellow $3
216.S Ferrari GTO Racing, red $3
217.S Stock Car
  v.1 white $3
  v.2 red $3
218.S Stock Car
  v.1 light blue $3
  v.2 black $3
219.S Porsche Boxster
  v.1 silver, 1996..............................$3
  v.2 metallic blue, 1998 ....$3
220.S Porsche Boxster Sport
  v.1 metallic teal, 1996 ....$3
  v.2 metallic silver with red accents $3
221.S Mondeo Police, 1998
  v.1 black with white trim, bumpers......$3
222.S Peugeot 406
  v.1 red, 1997.................................$3
223.S Peugeot 406, 1998
  v.1 orange with racing accents $3
224.S Volkswagen Golf IV, 1999..........$2
225.S Dodge Concept Car ("Copperhead"),
      1999 ....$2
226.S BMW Z3 Coupe, 1999.............$2

Majorette Special Forces Series 220 — military versions of 200-series models

220.1 4x4 Chevy Pickup
  v.1 dark green, CT4sp, white star on
      hood, black gun, blue windows ...$2
  v.2 dark green, CT4sp, tan camouflage,
      black gun, blue windows $2
  v.3 tan, CT4sp, dark green camouflage,
      black gun, blue windows $2
220.2 Missile Launcher
  v.1 dark green, 4c, dark gray missiles,
      black missile base, dark gray roof
      unit, white star on doors $2
  v.2 tan, 4c, dark green camouflage,
      black missiles, dark gray missile
      base, tan roof unit $2

220.3 Tank with Cannon
  v.1 dark green..................................$2
  v.2 dark green, tan camouflage $2
  v.3 tan, dark green camouflage $2
220.4 Military Ambulance
  v.1 dark green, 4c, 'AMBULANCE' on
      hood, dark green cross on white
      background..................................$2
  v.2 dark green, 8h, 'AMBULANCE' on
      hood, dark green cross on white
      background..................................$2
  v.3 dark green, 8h, tan camouflage,
      'AMBULANCE' on hood, dark green
      cross on white background; the tan
      camouflage can be either light or
      dark $2
  v.4 tan, 8h, dark green camouflage,
      'AMBULANCE' on hood, tan cross
      on white background..................$2
220.5 Impala Military Police
  v.1 dark green, 4c, 'Military Police' on
      doors and hood, blue windshield
      and emergency light...................$2
  v.2 dark green, 8h, 'Military Police' on
      doors and hood, blue windshield
      and emergency light...................$2
  v.3 dark green, 8h, tan camouflage, 'Mil-
      itary Police' on doors and hood, blue
      windshield and emergency light ...$2
  v.4 tan, 8h, dark green camouflage, 'Mil-
      itary Police' on doors and hood, blue
      windshield and emergency light ...$2
220.6 Tank Rocket Launcher
  v.1 dark green..................................$2
  v.2 tan, dark green camouflage, black
      missile launcher...........................$2
  v.3 dark green, tan camouflage, black
      missile launcher...........................$2
220.7 Military Jeep
  v.1 dark green, CT4s, black roof, white
      star on hood $2
  v.2 dark green, 5d, tan camouflage,
      black interior and roll bar, no roof.$2
  v.3 tan, 5d, dark green camouflage,
      black interior and roll bar, no roof.$2
220.8 Anti-Aircraft
  v.1 dark green, 4c, tan camouflage,
      black cannon, white star on door .$2
  v.2 dark green, 4c, tan camouflage,
      black cannon, light gray roof unit..$2
  v.3 dark green, 4c, tan camouflage,
      black cannon, dark gray roof unit .$2
  v.4 tan, 4c, dark green camouflage,
      black cannon $2
220.9 6x6 with Cannon
  v.1 dark green, 4sc, green cannon, white
      star on front $2
  v.2 dark green, 4cs, green cannon, tan
      camouflage.................................$2
220.10 6x6 Missile Launcher
  v.1 dark green, 4sc, black missile launch-
      er $2
  v.2 tan, 4sc, black missile launcher.....$2

  v.3 tan, 4sc, dark green camoflage,
      black missile launcher $2
220.11 Unimog
  v.1 dark green, 5d, tan camouflage, blue
      windshield and roof lights............$2
220.12 Unimog
  v.1 tan, 5d, dark green camouflage, blue
      windshield and roof lights...........$5
220.13 4x4 Command Car Jeep, 1998
  v.1 khaki $2
220.14 Military Police Van, 1999 ....$2
  v.1 tan, 6sp, dark green camouflage,
      "MILITARY POLICE," black interior,
      star on door $3
  v.2 dark green, 6sp, tan camouflage,
      "MILITARY POLICE," black interior,
      star on door $3
900.5 50-piece Special Forces set, 1999 .$50

Majorette 300 Series

While the 300 Series consists mostly of 200 Series vehicles with trailers, it also features buses, stretch limos and semi-tractor/trailers. Many early sets were called Super Tandems. Since it is possible to mix and match some vehicles and trailers, the values indicated represent models sealed in their original package. Many of the trailers are only available in 300 Series sets and are indicated as such by an asterisk (*). Many models were issued in various color combinations and with different markings.

310-A Autobus Saviem Paris Bus, open deck
      on the back, 1:87
  v.1 green lower, white upper, amber win-
      dows, 3spb $8
310-B Scraper Earth Mover, 1993
  v.1 yellow...$5
311-A BMW 733 (256-B) and Horse
      Trailer*
  v.1 white car, white trailer with khaki trail-
      er cover $7
  v.2 burgundy car and trailer with khaki
      trailer cover $7
311-B Volvo 760 GLE (230-B) and Horse
      Trailer*
  v.1 metallic dark green car, metallic dark
      green trailer with white trailer cover,
      1988 ....$5
311-C Chevy Blazer 4x4 Pickup and Horse
      Trailer*
  v.1 metallic blue...............................$4
311-D Peugeot 205 GTI Hardtop (281-A)
      and Horse Trailer*
  v.1 red with black trim and interior, black
      insignia on hood, red horse trailer
      with white canopy......................$2
312-A Magirus Fighter Plane Transporter,
      1:100, 1989
  v.1 blue tractor, silver trailer, blue/white
      airplane with red wings.............$4
  v.2 dark green cab, silver trailer, white
      over black jet, from Special Forces 3-
      pack $4
313-A Wrecker and Sedan $14

313-B Camping Car Pickup Truck with Fifth Wheel Trailer (pickup is a variation of 278-B), 1992
- v.1 hot pink pickup with "4x4 Country" on hood, mountain print on sides, cream trailer $5
- v.2 red, 8h, "Coca Cola," black air deflector on roof, part of Coca-Cola set..................$8
- v.3 hot pink pickup with no markings, cream trailer $5
- v.4 red pickup with "4x4 Country" on hood, mountain print on sides, white trailer $5
- v.5 lime green pickup with mountain print on sides, white trailer $5

314-A Volkswagen 1302 (#202-B) and Boat Trailer
- v.1 red with lightning bolt on trunk with orange and white boat on blue trailer..................$16
- v.2 red with lightning bolt on trunk with orange and white boat on red trailer $16

314-B Citroën DS21 (213-A) and Boat Trailer* $16

314-C Peugeot 204C (230-A) and Boat Trailer*
- v.1 metallic light blue car, red hull, white upper on boat $12

314-D Saab 900 Turbo Sedan (284-A) and Boat Trailer*
- v.1 metallic blue car, boat has blue hull and white deck..................$8
- v.2 black car, boat has white hull and red deck $8

314-E Honda Accord with Boat and Trailer
- v.1 metallic mint green with red interior, boat has red hull, white deck, silver trailer..................$6

314-F Magirus Dump Truck, 1993 ....$3
- v.1 dark green cab, 4c, metallic silver dump, from Special Forces 3-pack .$4

315-A Citroën DS21 (213-A) and Sterckeman Lovely 400 Travel Trailer (236-A)..................$20

315-B Volkswagen K70 (210-A) and Sterckeman Lovely 400 Travel Trailer (236-A)
- v.1 with pink car..................$20
- v.2 with blue car..................$20
- v.3 with yellow car..................$20
- v.4 with red car..................$20

315-C Volkswagen Golf (210-B) with Sterckeman Lovely 400 Travel Trailer..................$20

315-D Mercedes 280SE (237-A) and House Trailer (236-A)..................$12

315-E Western Train (278-A) and Passenger Coach*
- v.1 green with red cowcatcher, red passenger coach with white roof $20
- v.2 metallic blue with red cowcatcher, red passenger coach with white roof..................$20
- v.3 black with red cowcatcher, black and red passenger coach with white roof, Sonic Flashers..................$24

315-F Tow Truck with Construction Trailer, 1997
- v.1 yellow..................$4

316-A Farm Tractor (208-C) and Dump Trailer*
- v.1 dark green tractor with yellow fenders, yellow trailer with green tailgate..................$6
- v.2 dark green tractor with black fenders, yellow trailer with green tailgate ...$6
- v.3 red tractor with black fenders, red trailer with black tailgate..................$5
- v.4 light green tractor with black fenders, green trailer with black tailgate $4
- v.5 light yellow tractor with bright green fenders, yellow trailer with unpainted frame, green tailgate $4

317-A Renault R17 TS (260-A) with Lotus F1 (227-A) and Trailer* $12

317-B Fiat 127 (203-A) with Alpine F3 Racer* and Trailer*
- v.1 hot pink with aqua racer, "5" on nose, and metallic yellow-green trailer ..$12
- v.2 hot pink with aqua racer, "3" on nose, and red trailer $12
- v.3 blue with aqua racer, "3" on nose, and red trailer..................$12
- v.4 metallic blue with aqua racer, "3" on nose, and yellow trailer $12
- v.5 lime green with aqua racer, "4" on nose, and yellow trailer..................$12

317-C Fiat Ritmo / Strada (239-C) and Kayak Trailer* $6

317-D Ford Thunderbird (217-A) and Kayak Trailer*, 1986
- v.1 metallic red car $5

317-E Renault Super Cinq GT Turbo (205-C) and Kayak Trailer* $3

317-F Ford Econoline Van with Covered Trailer, 1999 ....$4

318-A Jeep 4x4 (290-A) and F1 Racer (238-B), 1986
- v.1 green jeep with yellow roof, white racer $6
- v.2 black jeep with no roof, green racer $3
- v.3 black jeep with no roof, yellow racer, 1989 ....$3
- v.4 yellow jeep with no roof, green racer, 1993 ....$3
- v.5 black jeep with beige roof, yellow racer, 1995..................$3

319-A Mercedes Car Transporterm, 1:100
- v.1 red cab and lower trailer, yellow upper trailer..................$8
- v.2 yellow cab and upper trailer, red lower trailer, two silver plastic cars .$8

319-B Extending Ladder Fire Engine, 1:86..$4

320-A Bernard Semi Log Trailer with 3 textured dowel "logs," 1:100
- v.1 light green with blue log trailer $16
- v.2 light green with red log trailer $16
- v.3 red with blue log trailer..................$16

320-B Alfa Romeo (271-A) and Glider Trailer*, 1986
- v.1 red car with silver accents, black trim, 3spb..................$4

320-C Volkswagen Rabbit 210-B) and Glider Trailer*
- v.1 silver with black "GOLF" accents, 3spb..................$4

320-D Toyota Tercel (273-A) and Glider Trailer*
- v.1 metallic blue car..................$6
- v.2 red car..................$6

320-E El Camino and Glider Trailer*, 1993
- v.1 hot pink pickup..................$3
- v.2 bright green pickup..................$3
- v.3 white, 8hb, red and blue accents, "AMERICAN OFFROAD," red interior..................$3

320-F GMC Jimmy and Glider Trailer*, 1995 ....$4

321-A Mercedes Covered Utility Truck and Utility Trailer, 1:100 ....$4

321-B Magirus Power Boat Transporter (Bateau), 1:100
- v.1 yellow tractor, boat has red hull, white deck..................$4
- v.2 red tractor, boat has red hull, white deck..................$4
- v.3 dark green cab, 4c, yellow over black boat, silver trailer, from Special Forces 3-pack..................$4

322-A Bernard Semi Low Loader Trailer, 1:100
- v.1 yellow..................$18
- v.2 red..................$18
- v.3 pale blue..................$18

322-B Bernard Semi Low Loader Trailer with Crane, 1:100, variations include wide single wheels or narrower dual wheels on trailer, and with or without rear loading ramp
- v.1 orange with red flatbed trailer, black crane..................$16
- v.2 yellow with yellow flatbed trailer, black crane..................$16
- v.3 yellow with red flatbed trailer, black crane..................$16
- v.4 blue with blue flatbed trailer, black crane, dual wheels..................$16

322-C Dauphin 2SA365 Helicopter, 1:87, 1988
- v.1 Coast Guard $6
- v.2 Police..................$4

323-A Renault and Glider Trailer* $12

323-B Fiat (#203) and Glider Trailer with orange and white "Wasmer 26 Squale" glider
- v.1 metallic yellow-green with orange trailer..................$12
- v.2 metallic yellow-green with yellow trailer..................$12
- v.3 red with orange trailer..................$12
- v.4 lime green with metallic yellow-green trailer..................$12

v.5 blue with metallic yellow-green trailer $12

323-C Tractor (208-A) and Livestock Trailer*
  v.1 red tractor with black fenders, light gray seat and steering wheel, red trailer with black bull $6

323-D Toyota Pickup (287-A) and Livestock Trailer*, 1986
  v.1 orange truck, orange trailer $6
  v.2 blue truck with red/yellow "Night Hawk" accents, blue trailer with white bull $6
  v.3 yellow truck with "Western" accents, red trailer $3
  v.4 pink truck with "Gladiator" accents, yellow trailer.................................$3
  v.5 red truck with "Gladiator" accents, yellow trailer.................................$3
  v.6 blue truck with yellow trailer $3

324-A Bernard Semi Open Trailer, 1:100
  v.1 red with blue and red open trailer, red trailer base, bw1 ....$12
  v.2 red with red open trailer, red trailer base $12
  v.3 yellow with red open trailer, orange trailer base $12
  v.4 pale blue with red and gray open trailer.................................$12
  v.5 metallic blue with red open trailer..$12

324-B Magirus Semi Open Trailer, roof light cast into cab roof, 1:100
  v.1 blue cab, 3kk, white upper tank body, blue tank cover, "L'AIR LIQUIDE," 4c wheels on trailer $6

324-C Magirus Pressurized Tanker (Citerne), 1:100
  v.1 blue cab, white upper tank body, blue tank cover, "L'AIR LIQUIDE" ...$6

324-D Volvo Pressurized Tanker (Citerne), 1:100
  v.1 yellow cab, white upper tank body, yellow lower tank body, "SHELL" label on tank $4
  v.2 yellow cab, 4c, white upper tank body, yellow lower tank body, "TOTAL" label on tank.................$4
  v.3 white cab, white upper tank body, yellow lower tank body, "SHELL" label on tank $4
  v.4 white cab, white upper and lower tank body, "elf" label on tank.......$3

324-E Renault Kangoo with Boat and Trailer, 1999 ....$4

325-A Peugeot 404 (206-A) and Horse Trailer* $12

325-B Mercedes-Benz 450SE (249-A) and Travel Trailer* $6

325-C Ford Sierra (272-A) and Travel Trailer*, 1986
  v.1 yellow car with red accents, red lower trailer body, white upper.....$4

325-D Volkswagen Golf and Travel Trailer*
  v.1 blue Golf, 4c, with matching blue and white trailer $4

325-E Ford Mustang GT Convertible (227-C) and Travel Trailer*
  v.1 yellow lower, white upper on trailer, yellow Mustang $4
  v.2 red lower, white upper on trailer, metallic blue Mustang $4

325-F Chevrolet El Camino Pickup (296-A) and Travel Trailer*
  v.1 red lower, white upper on trailer, red pickup with white interior $4

326-A Western Stagecoach drawn by three horses
  v.1 metallic gold-brown with cream plastic top and harness, brown plastic horses $16
  v.2 metallic green with red plastic top and harness, brown horses.................$16

326-B Mercedes-Benz Stretch Limo, 1:58
  v.1 metallic teal with amber windows, black base $3
  v.2 metallic teal with amber windows, gray base $3
  v.3 metallic silver with amber windows.$3
  v.4 white with amber windows $3

327-A Ford Double Tanker (245-C with Tanker Trailer*)
  v.1 blue cab, white tanks, "Milky, the good milk" $4
  v.2 yellow cab, white tanks, "Shell" $3
  v.3 yellow with whit tanks, "Petrol Company," 1998 ....$3

327-B Ford Tanker (245-D with Tanker Trailer)
  v.1 Esso.................$4
  v.2 Petrol Company $4
  v.3 Shell $4

328-A Chrysler 180 (208-A) and Sailboat Trailer* $12

328-B Safari Toyota Landcruiser (277-A) and Lion Cage Trailer* $4

328-C Land Rover with Lion Cage Trailer*
  v.1 white with black and white zebra stripes, white trailer with black cage, brown lion $6

329-A Bernard Semi-Log Trailer, 1:100
  v.1 realistic logs held by metal chains, dual tires on trailer $8
  v.2 textured dowel logs held by plastic bands, dual tires on trailer $8

329-B Scania Semi-Log Trailer, 1:100
  v.1 textured dowel logs held by plastic bands, single tires on trailer..........$8

329-C Spacecraft Shuttle Transporter, 1:100 ....$4

330 not issued

331-A Peugeot 204 (230-A) and Kayak Trailer* $12

331-B Volkswagen 1302 (202-B) and Kayak Trailer*
  v.1 red with lighting bolt on trunk, orange and white kayaks on metallic yellow-green trailer.................$16
  v.2 red with flower on trunk, orange and white kayaks on red trailer.........$16

v.3 metallic blue, orange and white kayaks on unpainted metal trailer $16

331-C Road Grader Leveling Scraper
  v.1 yellow.................$8

332 not issued

333-A Ford Transit TUG (295-A) and Motorcycle Trailer* $4

333-B GMC Jimmy (249-D) and Motorcycle Trailer* $4

334-A Ford 5000 Farm Tractor (253-A) and Log Trailer, 1970s
  v.1 red trailer.................$16
  v.2 blue trailer $16

334-B Tractor and Log Trailer, 1994
  v.1 green tractor with black and yellow trailer.................$8

335-A Toyota 4-Runner and Moto Trailer with motorcycle, 1995.................$8

336-A El Camino and Bicycle Trailer with two bicycles, 1995.................$8

336-B Mercedes 300 TE and Bicycle Trailer with two bicycles, 1997.................$6

337 not issued

338-A DAF 2600 Crane Truck with Sloop Trailer
  v.1 yellow truck $18
  v.2 metallic light green truck.................$18

338-B Mercedes and Sloop Trailer* $12

338-C Chrysler 180 (#208-B) and Sloop Trailer*
  v.1 metallic green car with blue and white boat $16

338-D Honda Accord (219-B) and Sloop Trailer*
  v.1 yellow with blue accents, red interior, boat has yellow hull, light blue deck, silver trailer $4

338-E Volkswagen Golf GTI (235-E) and Sloop Trailer*
  v.1 green with blue and white graphics, VW logo, boat has orange hull, white deck, silver trailer $4
  v.2 green with orange and white rally graphics, boat has orange hull, white deck, silver trailer.................$4

338-F Blazer and Sloop Trailer* $4

338-G Volkswagen Golf GTI (264-C) and Sloop Trailer*
  v.1 metalflake blue, 8h $4

339-A Cadillac Stretch Limo, 1:58
  v.1 black $3
  v.2 white $3
  v.3 metallic gray $3
  v.4 metallic blue.................$3
  v.5 purple $4
  v.6 two-tone white/steel blue.................$4

340-A BMW 3.0 CSI and Digue Baronette GT Travel Trailer
  v.1 yellow car, white trailer with light blue windows $16

340-B Peugeot 504 (239-A) and House Trailer (236-A) $12

340-C Chrysler 180 (208-A) and House Trailer (236-A).................$16

340-D Volvo Semi-Container Truck
- v.1 red with red trailer, red/white/black "CHALLENGE COMPANY" label.$3
- v.2 red with yellow trailer, "HOLLY-WOOD" $3
- v.3 "Coca-Cola" polar bear scene $8
- v.4 blue "Cadbury Dairy Milk Buttons" .$8
- v.5 yellow cab, red trailer, "Cadbury Creme Eggs" $8
- v.6 red with red trailer, "Majorette" "metal" $5
- v.7 red "Majorette Mini Transport" $5

341 not issued

342-A DAF 2600 Covered Truck (241-A) and Covered Trailer (243-A) $24

343-A Safari Truck (225-A) with Dinghy and Raft Trailer*
- v.1 red with paint streaks, gray inflatable raft on orange trailer $16
- v.2 orange with paint streaks, gray inflatable raft on orange trailer $16
- v.3 yellow with paint streaks, gray inflatable raft on orange trailer $16
- v.4 yellow with paint streaks, gray inflatable raft on metallic yellow-green trailer $16
- v.5 yellow with paint streaks, gray inflatable raft on yellow trailer $16

343-B Dune Buggy JP4 (252-A) with Dinghy and Raft Trailer*
- v.1 red with white fenders and interior, red and white raft on silver trailer ..$6

343-C Renault 25 (222-A) with Dinghy and Raft Trailer* $4

343-D El Camino (296-A) with Dinghy and Raft Trailer* $4

343-E Peugeot 205 (281-A) with Dinghy and Raft Trailer*
- v.1 white with red and black graphics, red and white raft on silver metal trailer $4

344-A DAF 2600 Tanker (245-A) and Tanker Trailer* $12

344-B Circus Caravan Fourgon (234-A) and Animal Trailer* $4

345-A Ford Skip Truck and Trailer, 1998
- v.1 blue with green and yellow skips ..$4
- v.2 blue with orange and red skips.....$4

346-A Recycling Lorry and Trailer, 1998
- v.1 green with yellow, white, blue, and red recycling containers..............$4

347 thru 349 not issued

350-A Power Boat Transporter, 1:100, 1988 ....$4

351-A Dodge Tow Truck with Traffic Signs, 1:80
- v.1 orange with yellow boom, red and white striped "Service" sticker on sides $16

351-B Citroën SM (250-A) with Traffic Signs $16

351-C Volkswagen Van (244-A) with Trailer and Traffic Signs $20

352-A Ski-Doo Snowmobile (249-A) and Sled*
- v.1 yellow with light green sled, clear windshield $25
- v.2 yellow with light green sled, amber windshield $25
- v.3 yellow with red sled, amber windshield $25
- v.4 red with red sled, clear windshield, "Shell" decal on right side, tiger's head on left side $25

352-B Farm Tractor (#253) with Log Trailer $20

353 not issued

354-A Ford 5000 Tractor (253-A) and Log Trailer
- v.1 blue tractor with white fenders, red trailer $16
- v.2 blue tractor with white fenders, blue trailer $16

355-A Volvo Semi Oil Tanker, 1:100 ....$4
- v.1 white cab, 4c, white upper tank body, yellow lower tank body, "TOTAL" label on tank.................$4
- v.2 white cab, white upper tank body, yellow lower tank body, "SHELL" label on tank $4
- v.3 white cab, white upper and lower tank body, "elf" label on tank.......$3
- v.4 yellow cab, white upper tank body, yellow lower tank body, "SHELL" label on tank $4

356 through 360 not issued

361-A Bernard Semi with Container Trailer
- v.1 blue with white trailer, "MAJORETTE CONTAINER" $16
- v.2 "TWO GUYS STORES" $16
- v.3 "Chambourcy - Youghourt - Desserts - Frommage Frais".....................$16
- v.4 blue, "MAJORETTE CONTAINER," dual wheels.....................$16

361-B Magirus Freight Truck, 1:100
- v.1 red cab, white container $6
- v.2 blue cab, white container "Express LINES".......................$4
- v.3 blue cab, white container "Alloin Transports" $5

362-A Fire Rescue (204-A) with Barge and Trailer*
- v.1 red, 3spb..............................$16

362-B Land Rover 4x4 (266-B) with NASA Radar Trailer*
- v.1 white with blue accents, red light bar, circle-dash-circle wheels, white trailer with black radar.......................$12
- v.2 white with blue accents, red light bar, 8-spoked wheels, white trailer with black radar $12

363-A BMW 2800 CS Coupe (235-A) with Racer and Trailer* $12

364-A Bernard Tanker, 1:100
- v.1 "Esso," red cab with white tank trailer $12
- v.2 "Shell," red cab, 5sp on cab and trailer $12

364-B Magirus Tanker, 1:100
- v.1 "Shell"...............................$4
- v.2 "Texaco" $16
- v.3 "Agip" $6
- v.4 white cab, white tank, "Petro Canada" $6

365-A Bernard Sloop Hauler, 1:100
- v.1 lime green cab, red trailer, boat has yellow hull, white deck..............$8

365-B Magirus Sloop Hauler, 1:100
- v.1 red cab, yellow trailer, boat has white hull, red deck $5
- v.2 red cab, silver trailer, boat has red hull, white deck $5
- v.3 red cab, silver trailer, boat has white hull, yellow deck $6
- v.4 pink cab, silver trailer, boat has lime hull, pink deck $5
- v.5 red cab, silver trailer, boat has blue hull, white deck $4
- v.6 red cab, silver trailer, boat has yellow hull, white deck.................$4

365-C Magirus Fighter Plane Transporter (see 312-A)

366-A Saviem Canvas Back Truck (241-B) and Trailer*
- v.1 "Majorette Metal" $8
- v.2 "Sernam".............................$6

366-B Ford Covered Truck (241-C) and Trailer*
- v.1 green with yellow cargo covers, "majorette" $4
- v.2 green with yellow cargo covers, "super cargo" $4
- v.3 white with blue cargo covers, "majorette" $4
- v.4 white with white cargo covers, "majorette" $4
- v.5 white with white cargo covers, "elf" $4
- v.6 red with white cargo covers, "Coca-Cola" ice cubes, 1995 ....$6
- v.7 blue, "Cadbury Roses Chocolates" ..$8

366-C Ford Covered Truck (241-D) and Trailer*
- v.1 "elf competition" $4
- v.2 "Moving Studio" $4

367-A Mercedes Tractor with Covered Trailer, 1:100
- v.1 red with white container "Renault" .$4

367-B Covered Truck, 1999 ....$4

368-A Renault 18i (266-A) and Trailer (201-A)
- v.1 blue car with yellow trailer............$6

369-A Farm Tractor (208-A) and Hay Trailer* $6

370-A Caravane Residentielle (House Trailer), 1:100
- v.1 dark cream with amber and clear windows, yellow floor, red interior....$16

370-B Deep Sea Explorer Transporter, 1:100
- v.1 blue with yellow submarine $4
- v.2 purple with yellow submarine $5

371-A Gazelle Rescue Helicopter, 1:70
  v.1 red base, white upper, "RESCUE" .$6
  v.2 red base and upper, "RESCUE" $6
  v.3 red base and upper, "TURBO" $4
372-A Renault (275-A) and Kayak Camper Trailer* $4
372-B Peugeot Cabrio (210-C) and Kayak Camper Trailer*
  v.1 silver with pink interior and midline, blue, orange, and yellow splatter accents, black and white trailer with red hull and white upper on kayak $4
  v.2 blue, white trim and interior, red and white graphics, white and light blue trailer, white and red kayak $4
372-C Peugeot Hardtop (281-A) and Kayak Camper Trailer*
  v.1 black, red plastic trim and interior, gold insignia on hood, red and black trailer, yellow and kayak $4
373-A Neoplan Autocar Airport Bus, 1:87
  v.1 green lower, white upper body, "FRANKFURT BERN ROMA" in red $6
  v.2 white with pale amber windows, "IBERIA" label $6
  v.3 white lower, red upper body, amber windows, "croisiere" label $4
  v.4 red lower, white upper body, pale blue windows, "croisiere" label $4
  v.5 yellow lower, white upper body, pale blue windows, "croisiere" label $4
  v.6 yellow lower, white upper body, amber windows, "Happy Holidays" label $6
  v.7 blue lower, white upper body, pale blue windows, cream interior, "MIAMI BEACH" label $4
  v.8 blue lower, white upper, pale blue windows, hot pink interior, "MIAMI BEACH" $4
  v.9 blue lower, yellow upper body, "TRAVEL" $4
  v.10 red "Coca-Cola" ice cubes, 1995 ....$6
  v.11 white lower, red upper, "Happy Holidays" label $4
  v.12 blue lower, white upper, blue planets, red stars, red interior $4
  v.13 black lower, white upper, red/yellow/blue abstract accents, 1993 ....$4
  v.14 blue lower, yellow upper, "TRAVEL" sunset horizon logo, 1995 ....$4
  v.15 yellow "School Bus," 4c, 1996 ..$4
  v.16 beige "Air France," 3sp $6
374-A Toyota Landcruiser (277-A) and Covered Trailer* $4
375-A Ford Transit (295-A) and F1 Racer $4
376-A Range Rover Rescue Team (246-B) and Tank Trailer* $6

377-A Semi-Sand Truck (Semi-Senne Carriere), 1:100 ....$5
378-A Racing Team Van (234-A) and Motorcycle Trailer*
  v.1 yellow van with red interior, red and black "racing team" stickers $4
378-B Ford US Van (250-B) and Motorcycle Trailer*
  v.1 black van with red/orange/yellow flame stickers, black trailer with green and yellow motorcycles $6
379-A Hopper Tank Truck, 1:100 ....$6
379-B Magirus Powder Transporter, 1997 .$4
  v.1 dark green cab, 4c, red tank with gray tank base, from Special Forces 2-pack $4
380 and 381 not issued
382-A Mercedes Utility Truck with Compressor
  v.1 yellow $15
382-B Toyota Pickup (292-A) with Compressor
  v.1 orange $10
  v.2 white $12
382-C Land Rover with Compressor
  v.1 yellow $4

Majorette 600-Series 1:87 Scale (HO Gauge) Semi-Tractor/Trailers

601-A Helicopter Transporter with 371-A Gazelle Rescue Helicopter
  v.1 blue cab, orange and yellow graphics, yellow airfoil, gray trailer, red and white helicopter $7
  v.2 red cab, "Engine #45 District 2 Fire Dept.," no airfoil, gray trailer, red helicopter $4
602-A Payloader Transporter with 263-A Front End Loader
  v.1 metallic blue cab, orange and yellow graphics, white foil, gray trailer with 211-B Wheel Loader $7
603 not issued
604-A Kenworth Semi Freight Truck
  v.1 "BORG WARNER" $8
  v.2 "NIGHT HAWK" $8
  v.3 western sunset scene on trailer $4
604-B Kenworth Sleeper Cab Semi Freight Truck
  v.1 blue tractor with red trailer, red/white/blue "EAGLE TRUCK" stars and stripes, 1995 ....$4
  v.2 white tractor with blue trailer, "Shark Monster" $4
605-A Double Tanker
  v.1 "Shell" $6
605-B Mercedes Double Tanker, 1995
  v.1 "Shell" yellow tractor, black visor and grille, white tanks with black base .$6
606-A Kenworth Semi Tanker, metallic silver cab, hood opens, realistic red wheel hubs
  v.1 metallic silver "TEXACO" tank with black ends, Texaco 'Star T' logo upright $4
  v.2 metallic silver "TEXACO" tank with black ends, Texaco 'Star T' logo upside down $25

606-B Kenworth Sleeper Cab Tanker, metallic silver cab, hood doesn't open, six-spoke wheel hubs
  v.1 gray "TEXACO" tank with gray ends..$4
607-A Double Freighter
  v.1 "ROAD DRAGON" $8
607-B 2-Container Transporter, 1999 ......$4
609-A Kenworth Auto Transporter
  v.1 light yellow cab, green and black accents, black trailer, yellow upper deck, "auto line" stickers..............$8
610-A Kenworth Rocket Transporter
  v.1 NASA $4
611-A Semi Circus Trailer with two cages, plastic animals inside
  v.1 red cab, yellow, black and gold "Magic Circus" graphics, red and yellow cages, black base..........$10
  v.2 red cab, red, white, and blue "CIRCUS" graphics, red and white cages, blue base $4
  v.3 yellow cab, yellow cages, "MAGIC CIRCUS" graphics, blue trailer base $4
  v.4 white cab, white cages $4
  v.5 red cab, yellow, black, and gold "Magic Circus" graphics on cab, none on yellow and red cages.....$4
  v.6 yellow cab, yellow and red cages, blue trailer base, green and gradient red "Magic Circus" graphics $4
612-A Hook and Ladder Fire Engine, 1986 ....$6
613-A Power Boat Hauler.......................$4
614-A Kenworth Cattle Transporter
  v.1 yellow trailer, metallic green cab...$6
  v.2 light brown trailer, lime green cab, "KANSAS" $4
614-B Kenworth Sleeper Cab Cattle Transporter
  v.1 green cab, light brown trailer........$4
  v.2 bright green cab, tan trailer $4
615-A Pro Stock Firebird Transporter.........$4
616-A Bulldozer Transporter
  v.1 green cab with "BLUE'S TRUCKING CO." on doors $4
616-B Bulldozer Transporter (new cab), 1995 ....$4
617-A Crane Truck
  v.1 yellow with black accents, black boom $4
618-A Seaplane Transporter
  v.1 fluorescent green cab, red graphics, black trailer, red seaplane, fluorescent green wings and nose..........$4
619-A Car Carrier $4

Majorette 800 Series — Airport, New for 1995

801-A Boeing 747/400
  v.1 Cathay Pacific............................$4
  v.2 Air France..................................$4
  v.3 Thai Airways...............................$4

802-A Airbus
v.1 Singapore Airlines $4
v.2 Air France.............................$4
v.3 Alitalia $4
v.4 Swissair $4
803-A Boeing 767
v.1 KLM $4
v.2 Delta Airlines $4
v.3 Air Canada $4
v.4 Japan Air Lines (JAL) $4
v.5 SAS $4
804-A Douglas MD 80
v.1 Alitalia $4
v.2 Iberia $4
v.3 SAS $4
805-A Douglas DC 10
v.1 Iberia $4
v.2 Japan Air Lines (JAL) $4

Majorette 1000 Series — Deluxe Collection, approximately 1:60 scale
1001 Jaguar XJ-SC
v.1 blue.................................$8–10
v.2 green................................$8–10
1002 Ferrari F40
v.1 red..................................$8–10
v.2 yellow...............................$8–10
1003 Porsche 911
v.1 white................................$8–10
v.2 silver................................$8–10
1004 Lamborghini Countach
v.1 black................................$8–10
v.2 red..................................$8–10
1005 Ferrari Testarossa
v.1 white................................$8–10
v.2 red..................................$8–10
1006 Rolls Royce Corniche II
v.1 metallic red.........................$8–10
v.2 metallic bronze......................$8–10
1007 Mercedes 500 SL
v.1 metallic silver......................$8–10
v.2 metallic bronze.....................$8–10

Majorette 2400 Series — Legends, approximately 1:38 scale
2401 1957 Chevy Bel Air $5
2402 1956 T-Bird
v.1 red, red roof, white interior...........$5
v.2 yellow, yellow roof $5
2403 1963 Corvette Stingray Split Window
v.1 yellow................................$5
v.2 red $5
2404 1965 Mustang
v.1 red, red roof $5
v.2 blue, white roof.....................$5
v.3 GT 350, white, blue stripes, black interior $6
2405 Mercedes 300SL Gullwing............$5

Majorette 2500 Series — Grand Sport, approximately 1:38 scale
2501 Porsche 959............................$5
2502 Ferrari 328 GTB $5
2503 Pontiac Trans Am.......................$5
2504 Lamborghini Countach $5

Majorette Hot Rods
2601 '32 Ford Coupe with removable engine cowl
v.1 orange, blue, black, and white accents....................................$4
v.2 red $4
v.3 green, black, yellow, and white accents....................................$4
2602 '41 Willys Coupe with removable engine cowl
v.1 yellow, red flames on side $4
v.2 yellow, black and white checkered flag on side...............................$4
2603 '34 Ford Sedan with removable engine cowl
v.1 black, red, and yellow flames.......$4
v.2 black, white, red, and gold stripe accents....................................$4
v.3 blue, light blue flames on side.......$4
2604 '57 Chevy with 2 interchangeable turbo engines
v.1 red $4
v.2 white, flames on side, black interior..$4
2605 Pickup Hot Rod with removable engine cowl
v.1 orange, black fenders, "HOT ROD" on doors $4
v.2 blue, blue fenders, white accents, "HOT TRUCK" on doors..............$4
v.3 black, red, and yellow accents $4

Majorette 3000 Series
Recent information from collector Ron Gold indicates a Texaco tanker was produced in the 3000 series, but he is unable to identify which one. Several model numbers have been applied to what has only been described as a generic tanker in researched text, including #s 3040, 3041, and 3044. The speculative value below reflects the collectability and undocumented rarity of this model.
30xx Scania Super 140 Texaco Tanker.................................$30–35
3006-A Kenworth Semi Tractor, 1995 .....$6
3007-A Dune Buggy, 1986 ....$6
3008-A Impala Police, 1986
v.1 white with black doors.................$6
v.2 light blue, "Police NYPD" $6
3009-A Impala Taxi, 1986
v.1 yellow with black fender panels & hood $6
3010-A Magirus Dump Truck
v.1 blue cab, gray dumper................$6
v.2 yellow cab, gray dumper.............$6
3011-A Crane Truck $6
3011-B 4x4 Chevrolet Blazer Hawaii, 1999
v.1 blue with yellow trim and topper ...$6
3012-A Farm Tractor with side mower
v.1 red with white cab, black roof $6
3012-B Farm Tractor
v.1 lime green $6
3013-A Safari Land Rover......................$6
3013-B Toyota Raid, 1986

v.1 cream, green roof, black roof & roof rack, black luggage, "Trans Africa," 1986................................$10
3014-A Mercedes E 280 Wagon, 1997..$6
3015-A Blazer Pickup
v.1 teal with white topper.................$8
v.2 green with white topper..............$8
v.3 teal with black topper, "Fruit of the Loom," "T-Shirts," 1986 ....$8
3015-B Mercedes M-Class, 1999
v.1 light maroon $6
3015.1-A Mercedes M Class Fire Van, 1999
v.1 red with white bumpers and trim ...$6
3016-A CJ7 Jeep
v.1 blue with shark graphics, white roof, red seats................................$6
v.2 white with black roof, red interior, "kleber racing cross," "elf," 1986.$8
3017-A Mercedes 230GE 4x4 Police, 1:53 ....$6
3018-A Range Rover
v.1 bright blue with fluorescent splash graphics $6
v.2 blue with rally graphics...............$6

v.3 blue with no graphic $6
3019-A Renault Master T35 Road Repair Truck, 1:45 ....$6
3020-A Excalibur

v.1 blue..$6

v.2 gold......................................$6

3021-A Ambulance
v.1 white with black roof, amber windows, orange & blue accents $6
3022 not issued

3023-A Armored Security Truck, coin slot in roof, doors open
    v.1 red with white roof $6
3023-B Mercedes E280 Van, 1997 ....$6
3023.1-A Mercedes E280 Bicycle Racing Team Assistance with 2 bicycles on back, 1999 ....$6
3024-A TV Service Van
    v.1 yellow with green & red accents, red roof, silver ladder on roof, 1986 ....$6
3025-A Renault Master T35 Breakdown Truck 1:45, 1986 ....$6
3026-A Crane Truck $6
3026-B Ford Mustang, 1995 ....$4
3027 Camaro, 1995 ....$4
3028 Racing Semi-Tractor, 1:60 ....$6
3029 Ford Model A Van $6
3030 Front End Loader $10
3030.1-A Winnebago Minnie Winnie Camping Car, 1994 ....$10
3030.2-A Holiday Van, 1995 ....$7
3030.3-A Ambulance Van, 1995 ....$7
3030.4-A Fire Truck, 1995 ....$7
3031-A Cement Truck $10
3031-B Peugeot 806 Van, 1997 ....$6
3031.1-A Peugeot 806 Taxi Van, 1999 ..$6
3031.2-A Peugeot 806 Police Van, 1999 ....$6
3032-A Heavy Duty Transporter (with 226-A Road Roller and 263-A Front End Loader) $12
3032.1-A Ford F350 Wrecker, 1999
    v.1 red, "Rainbow Heavy Duty Towing" $6
3032.2-A Ford F350 Pickup, 1999
    v.1 metallic blue $6
3033-A Fire Engine $10
3034-A Power Shovel $10
3034-B Renault Premium Container Truck
    v.1 red cab, "Majorette" logo on white container with red roof $6
3035-A Kenworth Wrecker $10
3036-A Kenworth Dump Truck, 1986 ....$10
3037 Toyota Garbage Truck $10
3037.1 Scania Garbage Truck, 1999 ..$10
3038-A Road Roller $10
3038-B Bank Security, 1999 ....$10
3039-A Bulldozer $10
3040-A White Scania Tanker, 1986
    v.1 cream cab, white tank, silver-gray chassis, "elf" "antar" $10
    v.2 white cab, tank has SHELL logo and name $15
    v.3 white cab, white tank, Petro-Canada $15
    v.4 yellow cab, white tank, "Shell" ...$15
3041-A Scania Super 140 Tanker Truck
    v.1 "Ewing Oil Co. Dallas" (based on the "Dallas" TV show)...............$30–45
    v.2 Green cab, tank has BP logo and red stripe $20–25
3041-B Jeep 4x4 with Bass Boat

    v.1 red with yellow roof, boat has blue hull, white deck $10
3042-A Covered Freighter $14
3042-B Mercedes 4x4 and Racing Boat Trailer
    v.1 blue with white roof, red boat.....$12
3042-C Jeep 4x4 and Racing Boat Trailer $12
3043-A Helicopter..............................$8
3044-A Scania Super 140 Tanker Truck
    v.1 yellow cab, white tank with yellow chassis, "Shell" $12
    v.2 grayish brown cab and tank with silver-gray chassis, "Mobil" $12
    v.3 red cab and tank with silver-gray chassis, "Texaco" $12
    v.4 blue cab, tank has FINA name with red and blue stripes $18
    v.5 light tan cab and tank with silver-gray chassis, "Petro-Canada" $12
3044-B Renault Premium Covered Trailer Semi, 1999
    v.1 "Michelin," blue and yellow $10
3045-A Lincoln Super Stretch Limo
    v.1 white with white landau roof $15
    v.2 silver with black landau roof $12
    v.3 black with black landau roof $15
    v.4 metallic blue with blue landau roof .$12
3046-A Neoplan Metro Bus
    v.1 black with abstract graphics $8
    v.2 blue with abstract graphics...........$8
    v.3 white, "PARIS" with Paris landmarks depicted $8
3047 and 3048 not issued
3049-A Toyota Truck and Trailer...........$10
3049-B Tractor and Tank Trailer $10
3050-A Mercedes 4x4 and Racing Boat .$10
3050-B Unimog and Trailer, 1999 ....$10
3051-A Tractor and Hay Trailer.............$12
3052-A Toyota Landcruiser and Horse Trailer
    v.1 olive green, yellow roof with no luggage rack, large 4c wheels, olive green and yellow horse trailer $16
    v.2 bright blue, black roof with luggage rack, brown luggage, tires on plastic chrome rims, black and cream trailer, light brown horse, chrome contour rims ..$12
3052-B Jeep and Horse Trailer $12
3052-C Mercedes M Class and Horse Trailer, 1999
    v.1 metallic dark green $12
3053-A Blazer 4x4 and Camping Trailer .$12
3053-B Range Rover and Camping Trailer
    v.1 metallic red, trailer has metallic red lower, white upper $12
3054-A Tractor and Dumping Trailer, 1999
    v.1 lime green $10
3055-A Volvo Semi Container..............$12
3056 not issued
3057-A Camaro and Racing Boat.........$10
3058 and 3059 not issued
3060-A Sailboat Transporter, 1986.......$16
3061-A Renault Car Carrier without cars (compare to 3092) $16

3062-A GM Double Container Trailer Semi
    v.1 red cab with yellow plastic trim, yellow containers with red roof, "Fast Trucking" $16
3062-B Double Container Trailer Semi, new "Euro" style cab
    v.1 pale blue cab, "Trans World" $10
3063-A Semi Dump Truck, 1986 ....$16
3064-A Travel Bus
    v.1 white upper, blue lower, yellow, orange, and red stripe down side $12
    v.2 white upper, red lower, yellow, red and blue stripe down side $12
3065-A Racing Car Transporter, 1986 ..$12
3066-A Van and Motorcycle Trailer $16
3067-A GM Semi Horse Trailer $16
3068-A Pepsi Freighter......................$16
3069-A Dune Buggy Set $16
3070-A Jeep and Dune Buggy Trailer, 1986 ....$16
3070-B Renault Premium Semi with Covered Trailer
    v.1 blue with yellow cover, Michelin ...$8
3071-A Volvo Car Carrier without cars...$13
3071-B Car Carrier without cars
    v.1 blue cab $12
    v.2 yellow cab $12
    v.3 red cab...............................$12
3072-A Mercedes 230GE and Porsche 959 Trailer $16
3073-A Volvo Racing Boat Transporter
    v.1 bright blue cab, boat has yellow hull, blue deck $16
3074-A Jet Plane Transporter $16
3075-A Dragster Transporter $7
3076-A Oil Tanker Truck
    v.1 orange cab, light gray tank with red top, "GT" $7
3077-A Jeep 4x4 with Motorcycle Trailer
    v.1 white with red roof, rally graphics .$12
3078 through 3089 not issued
3090.1-A Kenworth Log Transporter and Land Rover (266-B) $12
3090.2-A Boat Transporter
    v.1 Coast Guard, red, white, and blue $12
    v.2 Beach Patrol, red, yellow, and blue $12
3091-A Snorkel Fire Engine $12
3091-B Fiat Monospace with Motorcycle and Sea-Doo Trailer, 1997............$12
3092-A Renault Car Transporter with five cars (compare to 3061) $20
3092-B Van with Hot Rod and Trailer.....$12
3093-A Building Transporter, carries Majokit house to assemble $24
3093-B Racing Truck Transporter $12
3094-A Super Helicopter Transporter and Land Rover.....................$24
3094-B Kenworth Helicopter Transporter and Land Rover
    v.1 black and white, Police $16

3095-A Magirus Car Carrier with five cars......................................$20

3095-B Kenworth Car Carrier with four cars......................................$16

3096-A Fire Engine with extension ladder......................................$24

3096-B Snorkel Fire Engine, 1997.......$12

3097-A Semi Bulldozer Transporter........$16

3098-A Racing Car Transporter with 4 F1 Racers......................................$16

3099-A Chevrolet Custom Pickup with Beach Buggy and Trailer......................$12

Majorette 4x4 Super Movers, 1986

4x4 vehicles with oversized tires and modified raised chassis

3101 Jeep Night Hawk

v.1 black with red roof, "night hawk" accents......................................$8

3102 Blazer Sheriff

v.1 blue with white topper, "N845 Sheriff"......................................$8

3103 Blazer Demon Killer

v.1 red with silver roll bar, white "Demon Killer" accents, "12"......................$8

3104 Toyota Desert Fox

v.1 white with black roof, orange & black "Desert Fox" accents..................$8

Majorette All-American Road Kings, 1:32 Scale Models, new for 1995

3201 '95 Mustang GT, yellow...............$4

3202 '95 Camaro Convertible, bright blue......................................$4

3203 Chevy Sportside Extended Cab, white with black lower body......................$4

3204 Chevy Sportside and Camper Top, red with black lower body and camper top......................................$4

3205 Chevy Dooley Custom Pickup.........$4

3206 Chevy Dooley Custom Pickup with Camper Top......................$4

3231 Mustang and Motorcycle Trailer.....$8

3232 Camaro and Sea-Doo Trailer.........$8

3233 Chevy Pickup and Motorcycle Trailer......................................$8

3234 Chevy Dooley Custom Pickup and Sea-Doo Trailer......................$6

Majorette Ultra Custom, 1:32 Scale custom vehicles, introduced in 1995

3221 '95 Mustang.............................$4

3222 '95 Camaro..............................$4

3223 Custom Chevy Dually....................$4

3224 Custom Chevy Dually and Camper Top......................................$4

Majorette Club / Super Club 1:24

With the purchase of Solido in 1993, Majorette gained access to the superb large-scale models to incorporate at will into the Majorette collectibles assortment. Some Club 1:24 and Club 1:18 models are representatives of this merger.

4101 Bugatti 55 de la Chapelle, red....$12

4102 Jaguar E Type............................$10

4103 Ferrari 365 GT Daytona.............$10

4104 AC Cobra 427, top down (compare to 4212)

v.1 dark blue.................................$10

v.2 white......................................$10

4105 Bugatti 55 de la Chapelle, green.$12

4106 Mustang Hardtop, 1995..............$8

4107 Chevrolet Silverado Pickup, 1995..$8

4108 Jeep Grand Cherokee Limited, 1995.$8

4109 Jeep Grand Cherokee Laredo, 1995.$8

4110 Jeep Grand Cherokee Sheriff, 1996..$8

4111 Chevrolet Silverado Rescue, 1996..$8

4112 Chevrolet Silverado Rallye, 1996...$8

4113 Jeep Grand Cherokee Rallye, 1997.$8

4114 Jeep Grand Cherokee Fire Chief, 1997......................................$8

4151 Ferrari Daytona, red, 1997...........$8

4152 Ferrari Daytona, yellow, 1997.......$8

4153 Porsche 944 Coupe, yellow, 1997.$8

4154 Porsche 944 Coupe, red, 1997....$8

4155 Ford GT 40, white, 1997.............$8

4156 Ford GT 40, light blue, 1997........$8

4157 Formula 1, red, 1997.................$8

4158 Formula 1, white, 1997..............$8

4159 Formula Indy, black, 1997...........$8

4160 Bugatti Roadster, red, 1997.........$8

4161 Lamborghini Countach, orange, 1997......................................$8

4162 Proto "Baja," white, 1997.............$8

4201 Porsche 944 Turbo.....................$8

4202 Chevrolet Corvette Coupe.............$8

4203 Lamborghini Countach 5000 Quattrovalvole

v.1 red......................................$8

v.2 white......................................$8

4204 Chevrolet Corvette Roadster.............$8

4205 Porsche 944 Turbo Coupe.............$8

4208 Porsche 944 S2 Cabriolet.............$8

4209 Peugeot 405 Turbo 16.................$8

4210 Mercedes-Benz 500 SL Roadster....$8

4211 Lamborghini Diablo

v.1 red......................................$8

v.2 yellow......................................$8

4212 AC Cobra 427, top up (compare to 4104)

v.1 metallic red................................$8

v.2 metallic teal.................................$8

4213 Mercedes 500 SL Coupe.............$8

4214 Ford GT 40

v.1 light blue LeMans........................$8

v.2 red......................................$8

4215 1993 Porsche 911, 1995.............$8

4217 Ford Mustang Convertible, 1995...$8

4218 Ferrari 550 Maranello, red, 1997...$10

4219 Ferrari 550 Maranello, yellow, 1997......................................$10

Majorette Club 1:24 Metal Kit Easy-to-assemble metal kits

4301 Porsche 944 Turbo......................$8

4302 Jaguar Type E..........................$8

4303 Ferrari 365 GT Daytona.............$8

4304 AC Cobra 427..........................$8

4305 Chevrolet Corvette Coupe.............$8

4306 1993 Porsche 911, 1995.............$8

4311 Lamborghini Diablo.....................$8

4312 Ferrari 365 GTB Daytona, 1997......................................$8

4313 Porsche 944 Coupe, 1997.........$8

4314 Ford GT 40, 1997.....................$8

4315 Formula 1, 1997.......................$8

4316 Bugatti Roadster, 1997..............$8

4317 Lamborghini Countach, 1997.......$8

4318 Proto "Baja," 1997.....................$8

Majorette Club 1/18 Majorette/Solido Models - 1994

4401 Peugeot 605, 1994.................$24

4402 1964 Mini Cooper, 1994.........$24

4403 Ferrari 365 GTS Convertible, 1994......................................$24

4404 1936 Ford Pickup Truck, 1994......................................$24

4405 1955 Cadillac Eldorado, 1994......................................$24

4406 1958 Volkswagen Beetle, 1994......................................$24

4407 Citroën ZX Rallye Raid, 1994......$24

4408 BMW 850i, 1994.....................$24

4409 Lexus LS 400, 1994.................$24

4410 Mercedes 500 SL Convertible, 1994......................................$24

4411 AC Cobra 427 Convertible, 1994......................................$24

4412 1958 Chevrolet Corvette Convertible, 1994......................................$24

4413 Ford Thunderbird, 1995.............$24

4414 Jeep Grand Cherokee Laredo, 1995......................................$24

4415 Jeep Grand Cherokee Limited, 1995......................................$24

4416 1957 Chevrolet Nomad, 1995......................................$24

4417 Toyota Land Cruiser, 1995.........$24

4418 Mercedes 600 S Coupe, 1995......................................$24

4421 Jeep Wrangler Californian with surfboard, 1997......................$24

4422 Jeep Wrangler, 1997..............$24

4423 Jeep Wrangler Rallye, 1997.......$24

4424 Jeep Grand Cherokee Rallye, 1997......................................$24

4451 Lotus / Caterham Super Seven......................................$24

4452 Ferrari Dino 246 GT..................$24

Majorette Platinum 1:18

4453 Lamborghini Miura, 1997..........$24

4454 Bugatti EB 110, 1997..............$24

4455 Porsche 911 Carrera 4 Cabriolet, 1997......................................$24

4456 Ferrari 328 GTS, 1997............$24

4457 Porsche 911 Turbo, 1997.........$24

Majorette Construction / Super Construction

4501 Front End Loader......................$10

4502 Cement Mixer..........................$10

4503 Heavy Duty Transporter with Wheel Loader......................................$10

4504 Roller......................................$10

4505 Bulldozer with Payloader and Rear Drag Claw $10
4506 Wheeled Excavator....................$10
4507 Dump Truck, 1997.....................$10
4508 Truck with Crane, 1997............$10
4509 Unimog Road Maintenance Sand Truck, 1999 ....$10
4511 Telescoping Mobile Crane $14
4512 Road Grader Leveling Scraper $14
4513 Crawler Shovel $14
4514 Dump Truck and Land Rover........$14
4515 Caterpillar Tracked Crane $14
4517 Earth Mover Scraper...................$14
4518 Maxi Dump Truck, 1997 ....$14
4519 Excavator Loader Tractor, 1999...$14

Majorette Collector Cruisers, reissues of 1:43 scale Solido castings, 1999

1957 Cadillac Eldorado Convertible, red with white interior..............................$6
1961 Ford Thunderbird Convertible, powder blue with white interior.......................$6
1964 Ford Mustang Convertible, red with black interior $6
1984 Chevrolet Corvette Convertible Coupe, black with red interior $6
1965 Ford Mustang GT Hardtop, black with white roof $6
1969 Chevrolet Corvette Hardtop Coupe, yellow...$6

Majorette 6000 Series "MOTOS," motorcycle models, new for 1999

6015 Kawasaki 1500 Classic Cruiser, 1999 ....$10–12
6016 MV Agusta, 1999 ....$10–12
6017 Kawasaki VN1500, 1999...$10–12
6018 Voxan Roadster, 1999 ....$10–12
6019 Voxan Cafe' Racer, 1999.....$10–12

Majorette Road Eaters

Variations of 200 and 600 series models with candy, soft drink and prepared food advertising
201 Ford Model A Delivery Van
  v.1 Campbell's Soup Teddy Bear.......$2
209 Porsche 911
  v.1 Campbell's Soup Dinosaur Vegetable.................................$2
  v.2 Swanson Kids Fun Feast Larry Lion.$2
219 Lamborghini Diablo
  v.1 Cry Baby candy.........................$2
  v.2 Willy Wonka Gobstopper candy .$2
223 '57 Chevy Hot Rod
  v.1 Peter Pan Creamy Peanut Butter $2
  v.2 Frito-Lay Chee-Tos Chester Cheetah $2
236 Jeep Cherokee
  v.1 Spaghetti Os Teddy Os...............$2
  v.2 Frito-Lay Chee-Tos Chester Cheetah $2
253 Cadillac Allante
  v.1 Spaghetti Os $2
  v.2 Willy Wonka Nerds candy $2
260 Mercedes-Benz 500 SL Roadster
  v.1 Willy Wonka Nerds candy $6
265 Volvo Container Truck

  v.1 Peter Pan Extra Crunchy Peanut Butter...$2
  v.2 Swanson Kids Growlin' Grilled Cheese Fun Feast Barnie Bear......$2
  v.3 Diet Pepsi Uh Huh.......................$3
296 Chevrolet El Camino
  v.1 Cry Baby candy.........................$2
  v.2 Willy Wonka Dweebs candy.......$2
604 Freight Truck (Kenworth Conventional or Kenworth C.O.E. tractor)
  v.1 Cry Baby candy.........................$3
  v.2 Peter Pan Extra Crunchy Peanut Butter $3
  v.3 Frito-Lay Chee-Tos Chester Cheetah $3
  v.4 Campbell's Soup Dinosaur Vegetable $3

Majorette Magic Cars, Series 290 vehicles with Magic Motion decorations

Many of the new 100 Series Novacar models have been adapted for this 1995 series with clear roofs for displaying Magic Motion images underneath.
  Corvette Big Mouth Bruno $4
  Corvette Swamp Thing $4
  Ford Escort Monster Maniac......................$4
  Honda Acura NSX Bird Barian $4
  Honda Acura NSX Future Freak $4
  Nissan 300ZX Skull Pirate.......................$4
  Nissan 300ZX Turkey Tom $4
  Volkswagen Eurovan Melting Mel $4

Majorette Super Rockers, Series 2010 Monster Trucks

2011 Toyota Hilux "American Monster Truck"
  v.1 white with blue stars, red stripes $4
2012 Blazer "Crazy Monster"
  v.1 red with flame accents.................$4
2013 Cherokee "Mad Bull"
  v.1 yellow.....................................$4
2014 Toyota Hilux
  v.1 orange with black/red/gold accents...................................$6
  v.2 red with black/red/gold accents..$4
2015 Blazer "4WD"
  v.1 green.....................................$4
  v.2 bright blue $4
2016 Cherokee "Big Chief"
  v.1 blue.......................................$4
  v.2 green.....................................$4
Blazer American Monster
  v.1 silver with red stripes, blue field of stars $4
Blazer Gator Baiter
  v.1 metallic yellow $4
Blazer Heavy Metal
  v.1 metallic red..............................$4
Jeep Cherokee Big Mudder
  v.1 metallic green $4
Jeep Cherokee Cheyenne
  v.1 metallic green $4
Jeep Cherokee Roarin' Monster
  v.1 metallic red..............................$4

Jeep Cherokee Monster Crasher
  v.1 metallic blue..............................$4
Jeep Cherokee Snake
  v.1 metallic purple...........................$4

Majorette Super Crystal, Series 280

Assorted 100-Series Novacar plastic models and plastic versions of 200-Series models with translucent metal flake bodies comprise this sparkling collection.
  Chevrolet Caprice Police, yellow with pink interior or blue with yellow interior $0.75
  Chevrolet Corvette ZR1, pink with white interior or yellow with pink interior........$0.75
  Chevrolet Extended Cab Pickup Truck, blue with red interior or yellow with white interior...$0.75
  Ferrari Testarossa, red with white interior or purple with white interior $0.75
  Honda Acura NSX, red with yellow interior or purple with pink interior...............$0.75
  Kenworth Truck, blue or yellow $0.75
  Mercedes 500SL Convertible, red with yellow interior or light blue with khaki interior..$0.75
  Nissan 300ZX, red with yellow interior or yellow with red interior $0.75
  Nissan Pathfinder, blue with red interior or purple with white interior $0.75
  Renault Espace, yellow with pink interior or pink with white interior.................$0.75
  Sport Prototype Racer, pink or blue $0.75
  Volkswagen Eurovan, blue with pink interior or clear with red interior.....................$1

Majorette Crazy Roadsters, Series 450 Character models intended for French market

451 Tom Dog....................................$4–5
452 Croco Bill..................................$4–5
453 Teddy Bear $4–5
454 Bip the Turtle $4–5
455 Big Bebert $4–5
456 Elliot the Cat $4–5
457 Noddy in his Car $4–5
458 Big Ears in his plane...................$4–5

Majorette Smelly Speeders/Tutti Frutti Series 460

Scented, colored tires distinguish these models from their 200 Series counterparts. The US version is called "Smelly Speeders — Not Stinky, Just For Kids." The French version is packaged as "Tutti Frutti."
  Porsche 911 Chocolate Wave (see 209-B) ...$2–3
  Ford Thunderbird Cool Coconut (see 217-C) ..$2–3
  Ford Mustang Dunkin' Orange (see 227-C)....$2–3
  Jeep Cherokee Rockin' Banana (see 236-D) ...$2–3
  Mercedes-Benz 500SL Roadster Strawberry Speedster (see 260-C) $2–3
  Toyota Hilux 4x4 Apple Jazz (see 292-A).......$2–3

Majorette Kool Kromes/Top Chromes, 250 Series

Various transparent colors applied to a base chrome finish on assorted 200-Series models make up this striking sub-series of models. Values are listed within the 200-series section.

163

Peugeot 405 T16 (see 202-D)
  v.1 orange
  v.2 dark blue
Porsche 911 Turbo (see 209-B)
  v.1 light brown
  v.2 bright blue
'57 Chevy Hot Rod (see 223-D)
  v.1 orange
  v.2 bright blue
Mercedes-Benz 500SL Convertible Roadster (see 260-C)
  v.1 turquoise
  v.2 red
Cadillac Allante Convertible (see 253-C)
  v.1 light green
  v.2 yellow
Morgan (see 252-C)
  v.1 dark blue
  v.2 bright blue
Ferrari F40 (see 280-B)
  v.1 red
  v.2 yellow
El Camino (see 296-A)
  v.1 blue
  v.2 red

Majorette Sonic Flashers

An assortment of Majorette vehicles have been altered to accommodate an electronic device that emits a siren or other appropriate sound, accompanied by flashing lights. Besides the altered regular series vehicles, Majorette also presents a series of preschool toys called Baby Sonics, each made in primary colors with a smiling driver wearing the appropriate hat of his trade, and a series of tiny toys less than one inch long called Micro Sonic Flashers.

Majorette Sonic Flashers, "The Original"
2302 Ford Bronco II Sheriff 4x4, white with siren and lights $4
2303 Ford Transit Van Ambulance, white with alert siren and roof lights $4
2304 Porsche 928 Japan Police, white with pictograms on sides, siren and lights $4
2306 Ford Bronco II
  v.1 Fire 4x4, red with siren and roof lights.................................$5
  v.2 Police 4x4, red with machine gun and gun flash $4
2308 Porsche 928 Mafia Escape Car, dark metallic gray, cannon sound and gun flash $4
2309 Chevrolet Caprice Police Car, white with siren and roof lights $4
2310 Fire Engine, red with siren and roof lights $4
2312 Ambulance, white with siren and roof lights $4
2313 BMW 535i, red with rally accents, car horn and headlights ..$4
2314 Corvette Coupe, screeching brakes, brake lights $4

2315 Chevrolet 4x4 Tow Truck, orange with truck horn and roof lights.......$4
2316 Sebring Team, gear shifting engine sound, back lights $4
2317 Corvette ZR1, black, gear shifting engine sound, back lights............$4
2318 Daytona Team, screeching brakes, brake lights...............................$4
2319 Semi Tractor, truck horn and headlights $4
2320 Ferrari Testarossa Super GT, turn signal, headlights and rear lights...$8
2322 Chevrolet 4x4 Beverage Truck, breaking glass sound
  v.1 yellow with black load...........$6
  v.2 red with white load, "Pepsi" logo $4
2323 Ford Bronco 4x4 Crash Car, breaking glass sound $6
2324 Fire Rescue, bright red with siren and roof lights.............................$4
2325 6x6 S.W.A.T. Vehicle, missile launcher, roof lights $6
2326 Rocket Launcher, missile launcher, roof lights $6
2327 Corvette, screeching brakes and back lights................................$4
2328 Porsche, "Texas Ranger" with screeching brakes and back lights .$4
2331 Chevrolet Blazer 4x4 with Machine Gun, olive drab, machine gun sound $5
2332 Missile Launcher, olive drab camouflage, missile launcher $4
2333 Tank with Cannon, cannon sound $4
2334 Military Ambulance, fire siren, roof lights $4
2335 Chevrolet Impala Military Police, olive drab, siren, roof lights $4
2336 Anti-Aircraft, olive drab camouflage, anti-aircraft gun sound $4
2337 Tank Rocket Launcher, olive drab camouflage, missile launcher $4
2338 Ford Van Commando Truck, olive drab, siren, roof lights $4
2339 6x6 All Terrain with Cannon, olive drab camouflage, cannon sound..$4
2341 Western Train, steam whistle, engine sound, ringing bell, clickety-clack sound
  v.1 red and black......................$8
  v.2 yellow and black $8
2342 Space Craft Transporter, intergalactic search sound, siren, probe light, roof lights $8
2343 Cadillac Mafia Stretch Limo, car horn, machine gun sound, headlights, gun flash (variation of #339)
  v.1 black with red and white "Jazz in the Night" accents..............$12
  v.2 red with black and gold "Story" accents $12

  v.3 turquoise with white "scratch" markings $12
  v.4 black with white "scratch" markings $12
2351 Coast Guard Boat, siren, roof light $12
2352 Fire Boat, fire siren, roof light ..$12
2353 Security Boat, siren, roof light..$12
2360 Turbo Flash Copter $12
2362 Turbo Flash Copter $12
2363 Turbo Copter $12
2364 Turbo Snake Copter............$12
2381 Police Helicopter $12
2383 Coast Guard Helicopter $12
2386 Black Eagle Jet $12
2387 Air Patrol Jet $12

Majorette Super Sonic Flashers
3301 Chevrolet Impala Police.........$12
3302 Ford Van Ambulance $12
3303 Chevrolet Impala Fire Chief....$12
3304 Range Rover Alarm Car.........$12
3305.1 Ferrari F40, red...............$10
3305.2 Lamborghini Countach, yellow $10
3305.3 Honda Acura NSX, blue $10
3306 Mercedes 4x4 + Warning ...$12
3307 Police Van $12
3309 Fire Van $12
3311 Ambulance...........................$12
3312 Fire Truck.............................$12

Majorette Traffic Jammers – #3351 through 3354 are designated as Traffic Jammers and play "music."
3351 '57 Chevy.........................$8
3352 Corvette Stingray $8
3353 Chevy Sportside Pickup $8
3354 Chevy Pickup Custom...........$8
3391 Transporter with Sonic Helicopter..................................$15
3392 Transporter with Sonic Boat ..$15
3393 Transporter with Sonic Airplane..................................$15
3401 Range Rover $10
3402 Range Rover Rally $10
3403 4x4 Roarin' Monster $10
3404 Bank Security $10

Majorette 3600 Sonic Flashers – The system for numbering these is not clear but are listed as such in the 1997 catalog.
3600 Fire Truck............................$10
3600 4x4 Police $10
3600 Cement Mixer $10
3600 Ambulance...........................$10
3600 Farm Tractor $10
3600 Dump Truck..........................$10
3651 Farm Tractor with front end bucket loader and accessories $12
3652 Dump Truck with figure and accessories $12
3653 Cement Mixer with figure and accessories $12
3654 4x4 Police with figure and accessories $12

3655 Helicopter with figure and accessories $12

3656 Humvee Armored Truck with figure and accessories................$12

3657 Tank with figure and accessories $12

3661 Fire Truck with figure and accessories $12

Majorette Turbo Sonic – Turn car on, press on body of car, engine roars. Release car, it accelerates away with gear change sounds and flashing headlights. When car hits something, you hear smashing glass sound and engine switches off. Requires 4 type LR6 1.5 volt batteries not included.

3451 Ferrari F40, red..............$14

3452 Ferrari F40, black...........$14

3453 Ferrari F40, yellow $14

Majorette Micro Sonic Flashers 1300 Series

1301 Police Car $3

1302 Ambulance Van $3

1303 Wrecker..........................$3

1304 Sheriff 4x4......................$3

1305 Fire Chief Car $3

1306 S.W.A.T. Van $3

1307 Fire Engine......................$3

1308 Military Police 4x4 ....$3

1309 Lamborghini Countach Sports Car.$3

1310 Ferrari F40 Sports Car $3

1311 Porsche 959....................$3

1312 Mercedes-Benz 600 SL $3

1313 Corvette ZR1 ....$3

1314 Ferrari Testarossa Sports Car $3

1315 Missile Launcher $3

1316 Tank with Cannon $3

1317 Anti-Aircraft $3

1318 Tank Rocket Launcher $3

1319 Military Car $3

1320 Military Tow Truck...........$3

1321 Military Van $3

Majorette Baby Sonics/MajoBaby 1400 Series

1401 Police Car, white with police siren and roof light $6–8

1402 Fire Chief Car, red with fire siren and roof light $6–8

1403 Ambulance, white with siren and roof light $6–8

1404 Police, red with police siren and roof light $6–8

1405 Fire Car, yellow with fire siren and roof light $6–8

1406 Emergency, pink with siren and roof light $6–8

1407 Red and Yellow Train, roof light, engine sound, ringing bell, clickety-clack sound, steam whistle $6–8

1408 Blue, Yellow and Pink Train, roof light, engine sound, ringing bell, clickety-clack sound, whistle $6–8

Majorette Majo Baby 1500 Series

1501 Police Van, siren and roof light ..$7–9

1502 Fire Truck, siren and roof light....$7–9

Majorette Licenses

Coca-Cola is one of the major brands that have licensed Majorette to produce models with the Coca-Cola marque. The assortment is comprised of models from various Majorette series.

234 Ford Van, red, Coca-Cola Sun $4

236 Jeep Cherokee 4x4, white, Coca-Cola Polar Bear......................$4

262 Minibus, red, Coca-Cola Sun...........$4

265 Volvo Container Truck, red, Coca-Cola Ice Cubes....................$4

265.10 Volvo Container Truck, white, Coca-Cola Ice Cubes.....................$4

291 Blazer 4x4, red, Coca-Cola Sun $4

313 Deluxe Fifth Wheel Camping Car, red pickup with white trailer, Coca-Cola Sun $6

321 Magirus Semi-Boat Trailer, Coca-Cola Sun $6

326 Mercedes Stretch Limousine, red, Coca-Cola Sun $6

340 Volvo Semi-Container, red with white trailer, Coca-Cola Polar Bear.............$6

355 Volvo Semi-Tanker, white, Coca-Cola Ice Cubes.......................$6

604 Kenworth Container Truck, white with red container, Coca-Cola Sun $8

606 Kenworth Tanker, red with white tank, Coca-Cola Polar Bears.....................$8

613 Semi Speed Boat Transporter, Coca-Cola Sun $8

3042 Jeep 4x4 with Racing Boat and Trailer, Coca-Cola $15

3055 Volvo Semi Container Truck, Always Coca-Cola $15

3073 Volvo Semi Offshore Racing Boat Transporter, Coca-Cola $15

3076 Semi Tanker, Coca-Cola $15

Majorette Majo-Kits

Besides the wide variety of diecast models produced over the years, Majorette has also produced high-quality durable plastic modular playsets designed to be used with most Majorette toys. Curbs, sidewalks, park benches, buildings, people, signs, and more are included.

701 Postal Drop, 44 pieces..................$15

702 City Park, 57 pieces $15

703 Parking Lot, 52 pieces $15

704 Intersection, 50 pieces $15

705 Shell Gas Station, 56 pieces..........$15

706 Border Crossing, 46 pieces $15

707 Bus Stop, 47 pieces $15

708 Esso Gas Station, 51 pieces..........$15

709 Intersection, 60 pieces $15

710 Fire Brigade, 60 pieces $15

711 Self-Serve Gas Station and Car Wash, 58 pieces..............................$15

712 City Park, 60 pieces $15

715 Border Crossing $20

716 Shell Gas Station..........................$20

717 City Park $20

718 City Parking..................................$20

731 City Streets, 158 pieces $25

732 City Streets, 151 pieces $25

733 City Streets, 157 pieces $25

734 City Streets, 160 pieces $25

748 Restaurant and Bus Stop $45

749 Majorette Garage $45

761 City Streets, 309 pieces $40

762 City Streets, 317 pieces $45

779 Fire Station $50

7403 Bank, over 100 pieces including Armored Car, 1986 ....$25

7404 Farm, over 100 pieces including live-stock wagon, 1986....................$25

7416 Gas Station, over 100 pieces including wrecker.........................$25

7417 Park, over 100 pieces including Jeep and Dump Trailer......................$25

7601 Fire Station, over 150 pieces including 2 vehicles, 1986 ....$40

7648 Fast Food Restaurant, over 150 pieces..$40

7649 Super Garage, over 150 pieces ..$40

7701 Giant Farm, over 200 pieces, 1986 ....$50

7702 Jumbo Construction Site, over 200 pieces, 1986 ....$50

7801 Triple Decker Garage, over 245 pieces, 1986 ....$60

Majorette Action Figure Sets

Four figures, a vehicle and various accessories complement Majo-Kits.

781 Firemen $10

782 Policemen $10

783 Auto Mechanics $10

784 Farmers $10

785 Construction Workers....................$10

786 Paramedics..................................$10

Majorette Motors

These cars are slightly larger than the 200 series cars, with push down/pull back motorized action. They are made in France. The chassis is screwed onto the body, and the motor is visible through the windows. All have a variety of six spoke wheel that is different from that of the 200 series. The spokes are wider at the hub than at the rim. The rear tires are grooved to accept a black rubber band used for traction.

Porsche 911

   v.1 orange, "24" $4

   v.2 black $4

Rover Truck

   v.1 red, "Fire Service," blue windows ..$4

BMW M1

   v.1 light blue, "18" $4

   v.2 white, "6"................................$4

Renault Alpine

   v.1 green, "12" $4

   v.2 blue, "15" $4

Renault 5 Turbo

   v.1 yellow, "20" $4

   v.2 red, "10" $4

Majorette Turboom

These cars are slightly larger than the 200 series cars, with push down/pull back motorized action. They are made in France. All have a variety of six spoke wheel that is different from that of the 200 series. The spokes are wider at the hub than at the rim. The rear tires are grooved to accept a black rubber band used for traction. The car is made to compress when hit on the front, such that the hood and doors open. The car can then be pulled back into shape to "fix" the damage.

    Peugeot 205
        v.1 white, "Shell," "MICHELIN".........$6

Majorette Wild Wheels, 1988

A storyline goes along with these wacky 4x4 modified fantasy vehicles with adjustable axles and oversized balloon tires. Here is the unlikely story as told in a 1988 Majorette catalog: "At the beginning of the 23rd century appeared strange vehicles. Half vehicle, half wild animal, there were called Wild Wheels. No one knew where they cam from but everyone feared them. Ferocious, powerful and fast over any and all obstacles. The Wild Wheels kept their animal instinct and the power of the vehicles in which they took form. Nothing can resist these fearsome mutants, made invincible by their incredible mutation. The Wild Wheels fight for their survival on the destroyed world turned jungle where they rule." Yeah, sure.

  2101 Mustang, modified Ferrari 308 GTS with chrome horse's head mounted to hood, yellow.................$5
  2102 Panther, modified Excalibur with chrome panther's head mounted to hood, black.................$5
  2103 Bull, modified Lamborghini Countach with chrome bull's head mounted to hood, red.................$5
  2104 Rhino, modified Jeep Cherokee with chrome rhinoceros' head mounted to hood, blue.................$5
  2105 Elephant, modified semi-tractor with chrome elephant's head mounted to hood, red with black cargo container on back that opens to form ramps for other vehicles in series.................$8

Majorette Gift Sets, 1986

Such gift sets have likely been offered prior to 1986, but the earliest documentation of such sets by the author is from a 1986 catalog, the earliest dealer catalog in his possession. Value indicated is for complete boxed set.

  Emergency Center Set, over 35 pieces, includes 5 emergency vehicles, 1 Majikit building to assemble.................$15
  Super Builders Set, over 60 pieces, includes 3 heavy duty construction vehicles, 4 action figures with accessories, 1 Majokit building to assemble.................$25

Mandarin

This series made in Singapore represents 1:64 scale models, except for two character models. Some are Playart reissues.

Disney Uncle Scrooge, 7".................$14
Hanna Barbera Yogi Bear, 4".................$14
101 1967 Chevrolet Camaro Coupe.........$5
103 Datsun Skyline.................$5
104 Datsun 280Z.................$5
107 Honda 9 Coupe.................$5
108 Leyland Double Decker Bus, green.........$5
109 Leyland Double Decker Bus, "London Express".................$5
110 Leyland Double Decker Bus, "Singapore Air".................$5
111 Leyland Double Decker Bus, "World Travels".................$5
112 Mitsubishi Colt.................$5
113 Mercedes-Benz 230SL Coupe.................$5
114 Toyota Celica Mk 1.................$5
115 Toyota Celica Mk2.................$5
116 Toyota 2000GT.................$5

117 Volkswagen Van Ambulance $5

119 Volkswagen Van "Mandarin Toy".........$5
120 Volkswagen Van "Police.................$5

Mangalick

Mangalick models are offered as cast-iron toys of unknown vintage and heritage, but are apparently newer models based on prices and description.

1900 "Coca-Cola" Truck, 12".................$29
1930 Allis Tractor, 8".................$19
1930 Ford Farm Tractor, 5".................$19
1930 Ford Model A "Coke," 5".................$19
1930 Ford Model AA "Coke," 9".................$19
1930 John Deere Tractor, 12".................$19
1930 John Deere Tractor, 8".................$19
1930 Mack Dump Truck, 8".................$19
8-Horse Beer Wagon, 24".................$29
Horse Drawn Fire Wagon, 7".................$19
Horse Drawn Wagon, "Coke," 7".............$19
Horse Drawn Wagon, "US Mail," 7".........$19
Horse Drawn Van, "Bond Tea," 12".........$19

Manoil

Jack and Maurice Manoil started the Manoil legacy from Manhattan, New York, in 1934. Sculptor Walter Baetz is the source of the wonderful classic streamlined Art Deco styling of these attractive models. The company later moved to Brooklyn, then Waverly, New York, where it continued until 1955.

Now, authentic reproductions of these classics are being manufactured from the original molds by Pride Lines of Lindenhurst, New York.

Below is a listing of the original models and current values.

Maniol Pre-War Models, 1935–1941
    700 Sedan.................$90
    701 Sedan.................$90
    702 Coupe.................$90
    703 Wrecker.................$90
    704 Roadster.................$90
    705 Sedan.................$90
    706 Rocket Bus.................$120

Manoil Military Vehicles, 1941–1945
    70 Soup Kitchen.................$18–19
    71 Shell Carrier with Soldier on Shell Box.................$20–22
    72 Water Wagon.................$18–20
    73 Tractor.................$22
    74 Armored Car with Anti-Aircraft Gun...$55
    75 Armored Car with Siren.................$50–65
    95 Tank.................$17
    96 Large Shell on Truck.................$18
    97 Pontoon on Wheels.................$36
    98 Torpedo on Wheels.................$20
    103 Gasoline Truck.................$20
    104 Chemical truck.................$24
    105 Five Barrel Gun on Wheels.................$22

Manoil Post-War Models, 1945–1955
    707 Sedan.................$50
    708 Roadster.................$35–50
    709 Fire Engine.................$30
    710 Oil Tanker.................$25
    711 Aerial Ladder.................$400
    712 Pumper.................$400
    713 Bus.................$24
    714 Towing Truck.................$20
    715 Commercial Truck.................$20
    716 Sedan.................$20
    717 Hard Top Convertible.................$24
    718 Convertible.................$20
    719 Sport Car.................$20
    720 Ranch Wagon.................$20

Märklin

Märklin has long been one of the most prominent German toy makers of the twentieth century. While better known for toy trains, in the 1930s Märklin produced a beautiful assortment of construction kits that, when assembled, resulted in a stylish period vehicle. Chassis, body, electric light set, and motor were each sold separately.

New Märklin commemorative models, pre-assembled, are being offered for hundreds of dollars. The original Märklin construction kit models are currently worth $200 to $900.

99R Driver (composition).................$75
1101C Basic Chassis.................$50
1103St Streamlined Coupe Body.................$250
1104 Pullman Limousine Body.................$250
1105L Lorry Body.................$250
1106T Tanker Body.................$400
1107R Racing Body.................$200

1108G Armored Car Body $250
1109M Clockwork Motor $80
1110B Electric Lighting Set $40
1133R Mercedes Racing Car, complete with chassis and motor $200
1133AL Mercedes Racing Car, aluminum, complete with chassis and motor $200
Mercedes Racing Car, 12" windup $250
Road Working Machine, 3⅝" $200
Kubelwagen, diecast, 3½" $650
Troop Carrier, 6-Wheel diecast, 4½" $650
Troop Carrier, 10-Wheel diecast, 5" $900
L1500 1936 Mercedes Truck, new model, 1994 ....$450

Märklin 1:43 Scale

Beginning in the 1950s, Märklin produced an assortment of excellent 1:43 scale diecast, a few of which are listed below.

Mercedes-Benz 350 SL $80–95
Porsche 356, red, no interior $80–95
Porsche 356, cream, no interior $80–95
Porsche 911T Targa, #1800, gold $80–95
Porsche 911T Targa, #1800, red $80–95
Porsche 910, #1810, red, Car #16 ....$80–95
Porsche 910, #1810, white, Car #17 ....$80–95
Porsche 910, #1810, brown and mustard, Car #19 ....$80–95
Porsche 907, #1815, orange, Car #19 ....$80-95
Porsche 907, #1815, yellow, Car #19 ....$80-95
Porsche 914, #1826, silver $80–95
Porsche 914, #1826, orange $80–95

Marque

Stephen Demosthenes reports of this brand of 1:43 white metal models and kits.
#1 Porsche 1948 Prototype 1, white metal kit $70
#2 Porsche 1949 Gmund Coupe, Le Mans 1951, white metal kit $70
Porsche 917/30, red, yellow w/ black stripes, Car #6, "Cam 2" decals $70

Mars, Inc.

A few promotional race car toys have been made for Mars, Inc., the candy company. Models were made in China by an unnamed manufacturer, and were distributed by KMS, 1445 N. Rock Rd., Wichita, KS 67206.
Buick Regal Stock Car Racer, 1:48, white with brown and red accents, "SNICKERS" number 8 ....$2–4
Ford Thunderbird Stock Car Racer, 1:48, white with red accents, "BABY RUTH" number 1 ....$2–4

Marsh

Marsh models are 1:43 scale replicas from England that feature full photo-etched metal cockpits, dashboards, engines, and wheels.
1962 Cobra 260, Billy Krause #98 ....$199

1963 Cobra 289 Sebring, Gurney #15 ....$199
1964 Cobra 289 Road America, Miles/Bucknum/Johnson $199
1964 Cobra 289 Sebring, Gurney #11 ...$199
1964 Cobra "Flip Top," Miles Nassau $199
1964 Corvette GS Sebring $199
1963 Corvette GS Sportster $199
1966 Corvette GS Roadster $199
1966 Ford Mk II LeMans $199
1967 McLaren $199
1970 McLaren $199
1971 McLaren $199
1968 McLeagle $199

Martino Models

Marty Martino has made some resin hand-built models in the USA.
1954 Buick Skylark Convertible, 1:43 ....$65
1986 Chevrolet Corvette Indy, silver-gray, 1:25 ....$65
1957 Oldsmobile $50

Martoys (also see Bburago)

Martoys of Spain began in 1974, later becoming Bburago of Italy in 1977.
Alpine Renault, 1:24 ....$35
Alpine Renault Rally, 1:24 ....$35
Audi 80 GT, 1:24 ....$35
BMW 3.0 CS, 1:24 ....$35
Fiat 127, 1:24 ....$35
Fiat 127 Vigili Urbani, 1:24 ....$35
Lancia Beta, 1:24 ....$35
Lancia Stratos, 1:24 ....$35
Porsche 911S, #0102, 1:24, red with black interior $45
Porsche 911 Police, #0111, white with green hood, Police decals $45
Porsche Carrera RS, #0114, yellow with Martini decals, Car #8 ....$45
Porsche Carrera RS, #0114, silver with Martini decals, Car #8 ....$45
Range Rover, 1:24 ....$45
Renault 5 Le Car, 1:24 ....$40

Marusan

Marusan Shoten Ltd. of Japan, better known for superb tin toys in the 1950s which are now highly valued, produced a few diecast toys in 1960 and 1961. Models are identified by the name "San" on the base. Their resemblance to Dinky toys may not be a coincidence. The Avenue Bus and Morris J Van appeared the year after the Dinky versions went out of production.
8501 Panhard Semi Truck $75–125
8502 Morris J Mail Van $75–125
8503 Daimler Ambulance $75–125
8504 Ford Milk Truck $7–125
8505 Avenue Bus $7–125
8506 Euclid Dump Truck $75–125
8507 Austin Van $75–125
Toyota Truck $75–125

Marushin

Marushin models are made in Japan. The only automotive models currently known to have been produced by Marushin are a 1:43 scale Lancia Stratos and a 1:8 scale Porsche engine kit. In addition, several Japanese fighter planes were at one time also produced in diecast.
Lancia Stratos, white/red/green, 1:43 ....$15

Marx

Marx has made a lot of toys in its long life, but it was only in the mid- to late sixties that the company produced a small line of diecast toys. They are crude and heavy with very little detail, but they are rare. Here are a few.
1967 Mercury Cougar $15–20
1967 Cadillac Eldorado $15–20
1969 Chevrolet Camaro $15–20
1967 Mustang Convertible $15–20
Volkswagen Beetle $15–20

Mascot

1950 Chrysler Town & Country, 1:43 ....$85

Master Models

1960 Autocar Rolloff Flatbed, 1:43 ....$135
1960 Chevrolet Ambulance, 1:43 ....$85
1960 Chevrolet C80 Fire Ambulance, 1:43 ..$85

Masterpieces in Miniature

Masterpieces in Miniature are HO gauge (1:87 scale) diecast models made in England.
American Motors Jeep Gladiator Pickup Truck, yellow $10

Master Toy Company (see Maisto)

Masudaya

What else this Japanese company makes aside from one distinctive miniature of Robby The Robot from the classic movie *The Forbidden Planet* is a mystery. But this massive little replica weighs in at well over a pound, pretty heavy for its size - just 5½ inches tall. This hard-to-find diecast collectible may still be available from just a few sources for $30 retail. Value below reflects second-market value.
Robby The Robot, 5½" $40–45

Matchbox

Since 1947, Lesney and Matchbox toys have been the most universally popular diecast toys since Tootsietoys. Only Hot Wheels has overshadowed Matchbox in worldwide brand name recognition. The complete story of Matchbox toys can be found in Dana Johnson's book *Matchbox Toys 1947 to 1996* from Collector Books ($18.95 retail). Presented below is a brief survey of Matchbox toys over the years. Broad ranges in values indicate that there are several variations of which some are more valuable than others. Further research is recommended.

Early Lesney Toys

Lesney Products Company started manufacturing toys in 1948, a year after the company was begun. As industrial orders declined, Leslie and Rodney, with the help of their friend Jack Odell, started experimenting with the manufacture of diecast toys. Many of the early models created were later reproduced in smaller versions as the first of the Matchbox series. Here is a chronology of those early models.

1948

Aveling Barford Diesel Road Roller, 4⅜", 1948 .... $300–700

Caterpillar Bulldozer with blade, 4½", 1948 .... $250–700

Caterpillar Tractor, no blade, 3⅛", 1948 .... $225–650

Cement Mixer, 3⁹⁄₁₆", 1948 ... $300–375

1949

Horse Drawn Milk Float, 5⅜", 1949 .... $750–1,200

Rag and Bone Cart, 5¼", 1949 .... $1,000–1,750

Ruston Bucyrus 10RB Power Shovel Excavator 4", 1949 .... $400–500

Soap Box Racer, gold painted, 3⅛", 1949 .... $2,000–2,500

1950

Jumbo the Elephant, lithographed tin windup with key, 4" 1950 .... $500–600

Prime Mover with Trailer & Bulldozer, 18" 1950 .... $400–700

1951

Muffin the Mule, cast metal marionette, 5½" $200–250

1952

Large Coronation Coach, 15¾", 1952 .... $450–1250

1953

Small Coronation Coach, 4½", 1953 .... $100–200

1954

Massey Harris Tractor, red with beige wheels, black rubber tires, 7¹³⁄₁₆" $600–700

Bread Bait Press, 2", 1954 .... $60–80

1955

Conestoga Wagon, 4⅞", 1955 .... $100–120

Matchbox Miniatures 1-75 Series

From 1953 to the present, the mainstay of the Matchbox toys has been the 1-75 series, or regular series, also referred to as Matchbox Miniatures. Below is a numerical list of Matchbox Miniatures with current value (mint in original container). Length of each model is provided as an aid to identification.

Major model changes are designated by letters, indicating successive models (A=1st, B=2nd, C=3rd, etc.). For instance, 31-A, represents the first model issued as model number 31, in this case a Ford Customline Station Wagon

introduced in 1957. In comparison, 31-G, represents the seventh model issued as model number 31, a Mazda RX-7 introduced in 1979.

1-A Diesel Road Roller, 1⅞", 1953 (compare to 1-B 1955, 1-C ,1958)

v.1 dark green $40–55

v.2 light green $80–100

1-B Road Roller, 2¼", 1955

v.1 green with either dark tan or light tan driver $60–80

1-C Road Roller, 2⅜", 1958 (compare to 1-A 1953, 1-B 1955)

v.1 green with red metal wheels. $50–65

1-D Aveling BARFORD Road Roller, 2⅝", 1962

v.1 green with red plastic rollers . $15–20

1-E Mercedes-Benz Lorry, black plastic wheels, 3", 1968

v.1 mint green with orange canopy. $5–10

v.2 mint green with yellow canopy $10–15

1-F Mercedes-Benz Lorry, Superfast wheels, 3", 1969

v.1 metallic gold with orange canopy $15–20

v.2 metallic gold with yellow canopy $15–20

v.3 red with yellow canopy, "Transcontinental Haulage" $3–6

v.4 olive with tan canopy, "USA48350" $10–12

v.5 olive drab with tan canopy, "USA48350" $40–50

v.6 olive with tan canopy, "4TS 702K" $5–8

v.7 blue with orange yellow canopy, "IMS" $15–20

1-G Mod Rod, 2⅞", 1971

v.1 red wheels, "WILDCAT" label $20–25

v.2 black wheels, "WILDCAT" label............................. $12–15

v.3 black wheels, flower label.... $15–18

v.4 black wheels, spotted cat label............................. $9–12

v.5 black wheels, scorpion label .. $20–25

v.6 black wheels, chrome body, stripes $20–25

1-H Dodge Challenger with hood grilles, no scoop, 2¹⁵⁄₁₆", 1976 (compare to 1-I, 1982, 1-J, 1983 & 34-H, 1983)

v.1 red with silver interior $5–8

v.2 red with white interior $5–7

v.3 red with red interior $8–12

v.4 blue with red interior................ $5–7

1-I Revin' Rebel Dodge Challenger, cast hood scoop, 2⅞", 1982

v.1 orange with blue roof, "REVIN' REBEL" tampos $5–7

v.2 orange with blue roof, no markings $9–12

v.3 orange with white roof, "REVIN' REBEL" tampos $8–10

1-J Dodge Challenger Hot Rod, separate hood scoop, 2⅞", 1983, (compare to 1-H, 1976, 1-I, 1982)

v.1 yellow with black roof, "TOYMAN," England cast...................... $3–5

v.2 yellow with black roof, "TOYMAN," Macau cast..................... $2–4

v.3 yellow with black roof, "TOYMAN," China cast..................... $2–4

v.4 yellow with black roof, no markings, China cast..................... $3–5

v.5 white with white roof, no markings, Graffic Traffic..................... $5–7

v.6 light blue with black roof, "CHALLENGER," Action Pack with accessories.............................. $4–6

v.7 white with black roof, "TOYMAN," China cast $4–6

v.8 metallic blue with white roof, "HEMI," "CHALLENGER" (1993)......... $2–4

v.9 fluorescent yellow with black spatter accents, black roof, hot pink interior (1994) $1–2

v.10 white with purple spatter accents, black roof, fuscia interior (1996).. $1–2

1-K Jaguar XJ6, 3", 1987 (see 41-I, 1987)

1-L Diesel Road Roller, commemorative replica of 1-A, made in China, 1⅞", 1988

v.1 green (1988) from 40th Anniversary Gift Set...................... $8–12

v.2 dark blue (1991) Matchbox Originals...................................... $4–5

1-M Jaguar XJ6 Police, 3", 1991

v.1 white with "POLICE" tampos, blue and yellow stripes.................. $4–6

v.2 white with "POLICE" tampos, checkerboard pattern and stripes........ $4–6

1-N Dodge Viper GTS Coupe, 1997

v.1 metallic blue with white stripes (1997).......................... $2–3

v.2 white with blue stripes (1998)... $1–2

2-A Dumper, 1⅝", 1953

v.1 green metal wheels........ $120–150

v.2 unpainted metal wheels $45–60

2-B Dumper, 1⅞", 1957

v.1 with driver $45–60

2-C Muir Hill Dumper, red with green dumper, black plastic wheels, 2³⁄₁₆", 1961

v.1 "Laing" decals.................... $20–25

v.2 "Muir Hill" decals $65–80

2-D Mercedes Trailer, black plastic wheels (goes with 1-E), 3½", 1968

v.1 mint green with orange canopy. $7–10

v.2 mint green with yellow canopy. $10–12

2-E Mercedes Trailer, Superfast wheels (goes with 1-F), 3½", 1969

v.1 metallic gold with orange canopy $15–20

v.2 metallic gold with yellow canopy $15–20

v.3 red with yellow canopy, "Transcontinental Haulage"................... $4–6

v.4 olive with tan canopy, "USA48350" $10–12
v.5 olive drab with tan canopy, "USA48350" $40–50
v.6 olive with tan canopy, "4TS 702K" $4–6
v.7 blue with orange yellow canopy, "IMS" $15–20
2-F Jeep Hot Rod, 2⁵⁄₁₆", 1971
v.1 pink $12–18
v.2 red $12–18
v.3 olive $7–10
v.4 olive drab $35–45
2-G Hovercraft, 3⅛", 1976 .... $5–10
2-H S-2 Jet, 2⅞", 1981
v.1 black with yellow base and wings $5–7
v.2 light blue with white base and wings $4–6
v.3 light blue with white base, gray wings $4–6
v.4 dark blue with white base and wings, Macau cast $12–15
v.5 dark blue with white base and wings, China cast $3–5
v.6 army green, black base, army green wings $4–6
2-I Pontiac Fiero, 2¹³⁄₁₆", 1985
v.1 white upper, blue lower, "GOODYEAR," silver wheels ... $2–4
v.2 white upper, blue lower, "GOODYEAR," gold wheels . $4–6
v.3 white upper, red lower, "GT FIERO" $2–4
v.4 yellow upper, orange lower, "PROTECH," New Superfast wheels $3–5
v.5 yellow upper, orange lower, "PRO-TECH," silver wheels $20–25
v.6 yellow upper, gold lower, "PRO-TECH," Laser wheels $3–5
v.7 black upper, red lower, "2 DOG RACING TEAM" $10–12
2-J Rover Sterling, 2¹⁵⁄₁₆", 1988 (see 31-J 1988)
2-K Corvette Grand Sport, 3", 1990 (also 15-K, 1990, 3-I, 1998)
v.1 metallic blue, "15" on doors $3–5
v.2 metallic blue, "Corvette" on doors $3–5
v.3 metallic blue, "HEINZ 57" ... $20–25
v.4 metallic blue, "2" on doors, from 40th Anniversary Corvette Collection (1993) $5–7
v.5 metallic red, chrome windows, black base, World Class $12–16
v.6 metallic red, chrome windows, chrome base, World Class $4–6
v.7 white and blue, "9" and red stripes, Goodyear tires $6–8
v.8 white with red accent stripe, "Corvette" (1993) $2–4
v.9 orange with black tire tread pattern (1994) $1–2
v.10 white with black widow tampo (1995) $1–2
v.11 black with black widow tampo (1996) $1–2
2-L Mazda Savanna RX7, "Made in Japan" cast 1981
v.1 green with stripe and "RX7" tampo $12–15
v.2 yellow with strip and "RX7" tampo $12–15
2-M Corvette Stingray III, 1998 (see 38-K 1994)
3-A Cement Mixer, 1⅝", 1953
v.1 blue with orange metal wheels $30–40
v.2 blue with gray plastic wheels .. $40–50
3-B Bedford Ton Tipper, gray cab, 2½", 1961
v.1 maroon dumper, gray wheels . $90–100
v.2 red dumper, gray wheels $30–40
v.3 maroon dumper, black wheels . $15–20
v.4 red dumper, black wheels $15–20
3-C Mercedes-Benz "Binz" Ambulance, 2⅞", 1968 .... $6–9
3-D Mercedes-Benz "Binz" Ambulance with SF wheels, 2⅞", 1970
v.1 off-white or cream, rear hatch opens $12–15
v.2 off-white, rear hatch doesn't open $6–9
v.3 olive, rear hatch doesn't open ... $6–9
3-E Monteverdi Hai, 2⅞", 1973
v.1 orange with unpainted base, ivory interior $5–10
v.2 orange with silver-gray base, ivory interior $9–12
v.3 orange with unpainted base, yellow interior $5–10
v.4 orange with black base, "3" labels $5–10
v.5 orange with black base, "6" labels $12–18
3-F Porsche 911 Turbo, 3", 1978
v.1 metallic brown with unpainted base $12–18
v.2 metallic brown with black base . $6–8
v.3 metallic silver $5–9
v.4 gray with red interior $6–8
v.5 metallic green $4–9
v.6 red with clear windows $3–6
v.7 red with opaque windows $8–10
v.8 black $2–4
v.9 white $8–10
v.10 metallic dark blue, "Wrangler 47" $7–9
v.11 metallic dark blue, "Porsche" .. $2–4
v.12 light blue $3–5
v.13 yellow $2–4
v.14 light yellow $2–4
3-G Hummer (HMMWV), 1994
v.1 tan camouflage with bright orange cross on rear hatch (1994) $2–4
v.2 tan camouflage with bright orange vertical bar on rear hatch (1995) $1–2
v.3 army green with white star on doors and hood (1996) $1–2
v.4 army green with brown and black camouflage (1996, 5-pack) $2–4
3-H Alfa Romeo 155, 1997 (also 62-N 1998) $1–2
3-I Corvette Grand Sport, 1998 (see 2-K 1990) $4–5
4-A Massey Harris Tractor, with fenders, 1⅝", 1954 .... $60–75
4-B Massey Harris Tractor, no fenders, 1⅝", 1957 .... $50–70
4-C Triumph Motorcycle and Sidecar, 2⅛", 1960
v.1 silver with black plastic tires .. $45–50
4-D Dodge Stake Truck with regular wheels, 2⅞", 1967
v.1 blue-green stakes $60–75
v.2 green stakes $6–9
4-E Dodge Stake Truck with SF wheels, 2¾", 1970 .... $15–20
4-F Gruesome Twosome, 2⅞", 1971
v.1 gold with amber windows ... $60–80
v.2 gold with purple windows $12–18
v.3 red with purple windows $9–12
4-G Pontiac Firebird, 2⅞", 1975
v.1 metallic blue with dual chrome hood scoops $5–8
4-H '57 Chevy Bel Air, 2¹⁵⁄₁₆", 1979 (reissued as 43-G, 1990, compare to 31-N, 1998)
v.1 metallic magenta $6–8
v.2 red with "CHERRY BOMB" tampos $4–6
v.3 black with red hood, flame tampos $2–3
v.4 pink with red hood, flame tampos $6–8
v.5 pale green with red hood, flame tampos $5–8
v.6 peach with red hood, flame tampos $5–8
v.7 metallic rose red with red hood, flame tampos $3–5
v.8 metallic purple with red hood, flame tampos $4–7
v.9 red with red hood, "HEINZ 57 CHEVY" tampos $15–20
v.10 metallic purple with "MILKY WAY" tampos $15–20
v.11 black with dark red hood, flame tampos $2–4
v.12 metallic red with red hood, chrome windows, silver stripe tampos (World Class) $4–6
v.13 red with yellow flame outlines, silver trim, chrome interior $2–4
v.14 white with pink and blue accents, chrome interior and grille $1–2
4-I Austin FX4R London Taxi (European model), 2⅝", 1987
v.1 black with no markings $4–6
v.2 black with "GREAT TAXI RIDE LONDON TO SIDNEY" $6–8

v.3 yellow with "ABC TAXI," Preschool series $5–7
v.4 black, "LONDON TAXI" and British flag on left side only................$3–5

4-J Massey Harris Tractor, commemorative replica of 4-A, made in China, 1⅝", 1988
v.1 red (1988), from 40th Anniversary Gift Set $8–10
v.2 green (1991), Matchbox Originals $2–4

4-K '97 Corvette, 1997 (also 58-J, 1998)
v.1 metallic blue.........................$1–2

4-L Mustang Mach III, 1998 (see 15-N, 1994)

5-A London Bus, red, 2", 1954 (compare to 5-B, 1957, 5-C, 1961, 5-D, 1965)
v.1 "BUY MATCHBOX SERIES," metal wheels.................................$60–70

5-B London Bus, 2¼", 1957 (compare to 5-A, 1954, 5-C, 1961, 5-D, 1965)
v.1 metal wheels, "BUY MATCHBOX SERIES" $45–60
v.2 gray plastic wheels, "BUY MATCH-BOX SERIES" $65–80

5-C London Bus, red body, plastic wheels, 2⁹⁄₁₆", 1961 (compare to 5-A, 1954, 5-B, 1957, 5-D, 1965)
v.1 "Player's Please," gray wheels.................................$100–125
v.2 "Visco Static," gray wheels...$35–45
v.3 "Drink Peardrax," gray wheels.................................$150–175
v.4 "Drink Peardrax," black wheels.................................$150–175
v.5 "Baron of Beef," gray wheels.................................$175–200
v.6 "Baron of Beef," black wheels.................................$175–200
v.7 "Visco Static," black wheels .$30–40

5-D London Bus, 2¾", 1965 (compare to 5-A, 1954, 5-B, 1957, 5-C, 1961)
v.1 "Longlife" decals...................$9–12
v.2 "Visco Static" decals or stickers...............................$9–12
v.3 "Baron of Beef" $180–200

5-E Lotus Europa with SF wheels, 2⅞", 1969
v.1 metallic blue, does not say "Superfast" on base.....................$60–75
v.2 metallic blue, says "Superfast" on base...............................$9–12
v.3 metallic lavender....................$9–12
v.4 black $12–16

5-F Seafire Boat, 2¹⁵⁄₁₆", 1975
v.1 white deck, blue hull................$5–8
v.2 red deck, white hull................$5–8
v.3 red deck, blue hull $15–20
v.4 white deck, brown hull with trailer.............................$65–80
v.5 red deck, yellow hull with trailer.............................$20–25
v.6 black deck, yellow hull with trailer.............................$12–18

5-G U.S. Mail Jeep (Sleet 'N' Snow), 2⅜", 1978
v.1 "U. S. MAIL" tampo $4–6
v.2 "GLIDING CLUB" labels $9–12
v.3 army green $12–18

5-H Jeep Eagle/4x4 Golden Eagle Off-Road Jeep/Jeep Wrangler, 2⁷⁄₁₆", 1982 (reissued as 56-K, 1990, compare to 20-F, 1982)
v.1 metallic tan with "GOLDEN EAGLE" tampo..............................$3–5
v.2 red with "GOLDEN EAGLE" tampo, metal base..........................$2–4
v.3 red with "GOLDEN EAGLE" tampo, plastic base..........................$1–3
v.4 army green with plastic gun, no roll bar...............................$6–8
v.5 yellow "50th Anniversary Jeep" tampo $14–17
v.6 fluorescent pink with white interior, Dream Machines (1993).........$3–5
v.7 metallic blue with pink and yellow accents (1993) $2–4
v.8 metallic purple with "BAD TO THE BONE" on hood, teal blue interior (1995) $1–2
v.9 metallic gray with "BAD TO THE BONE" on hood, black interior (1996) $1–2

5-I Peterbilt Petrol Tanker, 3", 1985 (see 56-G, 1982)

5-J London Bus, commemorative replica of 5-A, made in China, 2", 1988
v.1 "BUY MATCHBOX SERIES" (1988), from 40th Anniversary Gift Set .$8–10
v.2 "MATCHBOX ORIGINALS" (1991), Matchbox Originals................$2–4

5-K Nissan Fairlady Z ("Made in Japan" cast), 1981
v.1 red $12–15
v.2 pearly silver $12–15

5-L BMW Z3, 1998 (see 25-M, 1997)

6-A 6-Wheel Quarry Truck, 2⅛", 1955
v.1 metal wheels.....................$40–55
v.2 gray plastic wheels $150–200

6-B Euclid Quarry Truck, 2½", 1957
v.1 yellow with gray plastic wheels.....................$175–225
v.2 yellow with black plastic wheels.....................$25–50

6-C Euclid Quarry Truck, 2⅝", 1964
v.1 yellow...........................$10–15

6-D Ford Pickup, 2¾", 1968
v.1 white grille $9–12

v.2 silver grille.........................**$12–15**

6-E Ford Pickup with SF wheels, 2¾", 1970 ....$15–20

6-F Mercedes-Benz 350SL Convertible, 3", 1973
v.1 orange with black roof $6–10
v.2 yellow with black roof............$5–8
v.3 silver-gray with black roof.....$20–25
v.4 metallic orange with black roof .$5–10
v.5 metallic orange with white roof .$5–10
v.6 maroon with white roof $5–8
v.7 red with white roof $5–8
v.8 blue with no roof $5–10
v.9 plum with no roof $5–10
v.10 white with no roof, translucent red interior $5–8
v.11 pale gray with no roof, translucent white interior $35–50
v.12 beige with no roof, translucent white interior $35–50
v.13 red with no roof, translucent white interior $35–50

6-G IMSA Mazda, 3", 1983
v.1 dark blue with white and orange tampos, Macau cast....................$2–4

6-H F1 Racing Car, 2⅞", 1985 (Europe; see 16-H, 1984 & 65-G, 1984 U.S.)

6-I Ford Supervan II, 2¹⁵⁄₁₆", 1985 (rest of world; 72-K, 1987 US)
v.1 white with "Ford Supervan" tampos...........................$3–5
v.2 white with "STARFIRE" tampos...$4–6
v.3 white with "FUJI RACING TEAM" tampos $4–6
v.4 white with roof lights, "AMBULANCE," Siren Force $12–16
v.5 white with roof lights, "AMBULANCE/RESCUE 911" $12–16
v.6 white with no markings, Graffic Traffic $4–6
v.7 red with roof lights, "FIRE OBSERVER," Siren Force $12–16
v.8 red with roof lights, "FIRE OBSERVER/RESCUE 911" $12–16
v.9 red with "TIZER FLAVOURED SOFT DRINK" tampos $4–6
v.10 dark blue with "DUCKHAM'S QXR ENGINE OILS" tampos $4–6
v.11 dark blue with lights, "POLICE CONTROL UNIT," Siren Force.............................$12–16
v.12 dark blue with lights, "POLICE CONTROL UNIT/RESCUE 911" $12–16
v.13 dark gray, "DANGER HIGH EXPLOSIVE/HEAVY LOAD," weapons, Roadblasters....................$3–5
v.14 light gray, "DANGER HIGH EXPLOSIVE/HEAVY LOAD," weapons....................$15–20
v.15 yellow with "SERVICE CAR BP OIL" tampos $12–15
v.16 yellow with "GOODYEAR PIT STOP" tampos $4–6

6-J Alfa Romeo, 2⅞", 1991 (rest of world; see 15-M U.S., 1991)

6-K Quarry Truck (replica of 6-A), Matchbox Originals, 2⅛", 1993 ....$4–6

6-L Excavator, Atlas, 3", 1992 (see 32-G, 1981)

7-A Horse Drawn Milk Cart, 2¼", 1955
   v.1 orange with silver bottles, metal wheels $100–125
   v.2 orange with white bottles, metal wheels $125–150
   v.3 orange with orange bottles, metal wheels $50–75
   v.4 orange with gray plastic wheels $75–100

7-B Ford Anglia, light blue, 2⅝", 1961
   v.1 gray plastic wheels $20–25
   v.2 silver plastic wheels $20–25
   v.3 black plastic wheels $15–20

7-C Ford Refuse Truck, 3", 1966
   v.1 black plastic wheels $8–10

7-D Ford Refuse Truck with SF wheels, 3", 1970 ....$15–20

7-E Hairy Hustler, 2⅞", 1971
   v.1 metallic orange-red with purple windows, "5" labels $65–80
   v.2 metallic orange-red with amber windows, "5" labels $12–18
   v.3 metallic orange-red with amber windows, scorpion label $20–25
   v.4 white with amber windows, no labels $35–50
   v.5 white with amber windows, checkers and stripes tampo...............$12–18
   v.6 yellow with amber windows, flames tampo $30–50

7-F Volkswagen Rabbit with rack and surfboards, 2⅞", 1976
   v.1 metallic green with yellow interior $5–8
   v.2 yellow with "ADAC" labels, roof light and antenna, no rack $30–35
   v.3 metallic green with red interior ..$9–12
   v.4 yellow with red interior $4–6
   v.5 red with yellow interior.............$3–5
   v.6 metallic silver with red interior....$4–6
   v.7 metallic silver with tan interior..$20–25
   v.8 metallic silver with blue interior $85–100
   v.9 black with red stripe tampo, no rack...............................$3–5
   v.10 black with red and orange stripe, "9" tampo, no rack $9–12

7-G Volkswagen Rompin' Rabbit, 4 x 4, 2⅞", 1982
   v.1 white with "ROMPIN' RABBIT" tampos $4–6
   v.2 yellow with "RUFF RABBIT" tampos..............................$3–5

7-H Volkswagen Ruff Rabbit 4 x 4, 2⅞", 1983.......................................$3–5

7-I IMSA Mazda (Europe; 6 - G, U.S.), 3", 1983 (see 6-G, 1983)

7-J Porsche 959, 2⅞", 1987 (reintroduced as 51-L, 1994)

   v.1 metallic pearl gray with "Porsche" tampos on doors $2–4
   v.2 white with "Porsche" tampos on doors, white wheels...............$4–6
   v.3 white with "Porsche" tampos on doors, silver wheels $2–4
   v.4 gray with "Porsche 959" tampos..................................$2–4
   v.5 white with "Porsche 959," red, yellow, and black stripes $8–10
   v.6 pink with Porsche 959 tampos ..$3–5
   v.7 purple with "Porsche 959" tampos $3–5
   v.8 white with "REDOXON" tampos $18–22
   v.9 white with "PACE CAR/SHELL" tampos $3–5
   v.10 white with "PIRELLI GRIPPING STUFF 313" tampos $4–6
   v.11 black with "Porsche" logo $2–4
   v.12 chrome with no markings...$15–18
   v.13 white with "LLOYDS" tampos $10–12
   v.14 magenta with "RAGE" tampo, black and yellow accents.................$1–2

7-K Horse Drawn Milk Float, commemorative replica of 7-A, made in China, 2¼", 1988
   v.1 orange (1988), from 40th Anniversary Gift Set $8–10
   v.2 light blue (1991), Matchbox Originals $3–5

7-L T-Bird Stock Car, 3", 1993 (also 64-I, 1998)
   v.1 white with "MAUI 17" tampos (1993) $1–3
   v.2 blue with "RACETECH" tampos (1994) $1–3
   v.3 bright pink, "10" and checkered flag tampos $1–3
   v.4 blue with "Kyle Wieder 11" racing accents $1–3
   v.5 black with "Evan Carr" racing accents $1–3

7-M Refuse Truck, 1998 (see 36-G, 1980)

8-A Caterpillar Tractor, no blade, 1½", 1955 (compare to 8-B, 1959)
   v.1 orange with orange driver .$80–100
   v.2 light yellow with red driver .$80–100
   v.3 dark yellow with dark yellow driver.............................$30–40

8-B Caterpillar Tractor, 1⅝", 1959 (compare to 8-A, 1955)
   v.1 yellow with metal rollers.......$50–60

8-C Caterpillar Tractor, 1⅞", 1961
   v.1 metal rollers $45–60
   v.2 silver plastic rollers..............$65–80
   v.3 black plastic rollers...............$40–60

8-D Caterpillar Tractor, 2", 1964
   v.1 yellow with black plastic rollers $15–20

8-E Ford Mustang Fastback, 2⅞", 1966
   v.1 white $12–15
   v.2 orange.........................$100–125

8-F Ford Mustang Fastback with SF wheels, 2⅞", 1970
   v.1 white, red interior...............$30–35
   v.2 red, red interior $40–45
   v.3 red, ivory interior...............$30–35

8-G Ford Mustang Wildcat Dragster, 2⅞", 1970
   v.1 "Wildcat" labels $12–15
   v.2 "Rat Rod" labels $20–25
   v.3 no labels $12–15

8-G Ford Mustang Wildcat Dragster, 2⅞", 1970
   v.1 "Wildcat" labels $12–15
   v.2 "Rat Rod" labels $20–25
   v.3 no labels $12–15

8-H DeTomaso Pantera, 3", 1975
   v.1 white with blue base, "8" label on hood $4–6
   v.2 white with unpainted base, "8" label on hood $4–6
   v.3 white with blue base, "9" label on hood $8–12
   v.4 white with blue base, sunburst label on hood $8–12
   v.5 white with lavender base, "8" label on hood $30–45
   v.6 blue with black base $4–6

8-I Rover 3500 Police (European model), 3", 1982
   v.1 metallic red $5–7
   v.2 white with "POLICE" tampo, roof lights, England cast $4–6
   v.3 white with "POLICE" tampo, roof lights, China cast $4–6
   v.4 white with "POLICE" tampo, roof lights, Manaus cast $25–30
   v.5 white with no markings, roof lights, England cast (Graffic traffic) $4–6

8-J Greased Lightning DeTomaso Pantera, 3", 1983
   v.1 red with black interior $4–6

8-K Scania T142, 3", 1986 (also 71-H, 72-J, other variations exist in Convoy series)
   v.1 white with red, orange, and yellow stripes $3–5
   v.2 blue with red, orange, and yellow stripes $3–5

8-L Vauxhall Astra/Opel Kadett Police (European model), 2⅞", 1987 ....$4–6

8-M Mack CH600, 3", 1990 (also 39-I, 1990, other variations in Convoy and White Rose series)
   v.1 white with black and red stripes $2–4

8-N Airport Fire Tender, 3", 1992 (also 24-L, 1992)
   v.1 fluorescent orange-red with blue and white checkerboard pattern......$2–4

8-O Mazda RX-7, 1994 (also 67-J, 1998)
   v.1 yellow with black and red accents (1994) $1–2
   v.2 red with yellow accents (1996).$1–2
   v.3 gradient metallic gold front to metallic red back (1996) $1–2

8-P Peterbilt Cement Truck, 1998 (see 19-H, 1982)

9-A Dennis Fire Escape, 1955
  v.1 no front bumper, no number cast, 2¼".................$45–60

9-B Dennis Fire Escape, with front bumper, number 9 cast, 2⅜", 1957
  v.1 metal wheels.................$50–60
  v.2 gray plastic wheels........$125–150

9-C Merryweather Marquis Fire Engine, red, 2¼", 1959
  v.1 tan ladder, gray plastic wheels.................$30–40
  v.2 gold ladder, gray plastic wheels.................$30–40
  v.3 gold ladder, black plastic wheels.................$10–12
  v.4 silver ladder, black plastic wheels.................$20–25
  v.5 tan ladder, black plastic wheels.................$20–25

9-D Boat and Trailer, 3¼", 1966
  v.1 dull blue deck.................$12–15
  v.2 bright blue deck.................$5–8

9-E AMX Javelin, 3", 1971
  v.1 lime with silver hood scoop, doors open.................$9–12
  v.2 lime with black hood scoop, doors open.................$4–6
  v.3 metallic blue, black hood scoop, doors open.................$4–6
  v.4 metallic blue black hood scoop, doors don't open.................$4–6
  v.5 metallic green, black hood scoop, doors open.................$4–6
  v.6 metallic blue, black hood scoop, doors don't open.................$4–6
  v.7 red with black hood scoop, doors don't open.................$20–25

9-F Ford Escort RX2000, 3", 1978
  v.1 white with tan interior, "DUNLOP" labels.................$3–5
  v.2 white with red interior, "DUNLOP" labels.................$80–90
  v.3 white with tan interior, "PHANTOM" labels.................$4–6
  v.4 blue with tan interior, "PHANTOM" labels.................$4–6
  v.5 green with tan interior, "DUNLOP" labels.................$3–5
  v.6 green with tan interior, seagull labels.................$3–5
  v.7 green with white interior, seagull labels.................$3–5
  v.8 green with red interior, seagull labels.................$80–90

9-G Fiat Abarth, 2¹⁵⁄₁₆", 1982 (also 74-G 1984)
  v.1 white with red interior, "MATCHBOX" tampo.................$3–5
  v.2 white with black interior, "MATCHBOX" tampo.................$100–120
  v.3 white with "ALITALIA" tampo.....$2–4

  v.4 white with red, orange, and yellow stripe tampo, Macau cast......$9–12
  v.5 white with "MATCHBOX 11" tampo, Manaus cast.................$30–40

9-H Caterpillar Bulldozer, 2⅝", 1983 (see 64-F, 1979)

9-I Toyota MR2, 2⅞", 1987 (also 74-H, 1987)
  v.1 white with "MR2 PACE CAR" tampos.................$2–4
  v.2 blue with "MR2" tampos and pink stripes, New Superfast wheels..$3–5
  v.3 metallic blue with "MR2" tampos and pink stripes, Laser Wheels.......$5–7
  v.4 green with "7 SNAKE RACING TEAM" tampos.................$10–12

9-J Dennis Fire Escape, commemorative replica of 9-A, made in China, 2¼", 1988
  v.1 red reels (1988), from 40th Anniversary Gift Set.................$8–10
  v.2 yellow reels (1991), Matchbox Originals.................$2–4

9-K Faun Earth Mover Dump Truck, 2¾", 1989 (see 58-F 1976, also 53-H, 1989)

9-L Utility Truck, 1998 (see 74-I, 1987, also 33-J, 1989)

10-A Mechanical Horse and Trailer 1955
  v.1 red cab, gray trailer, metal wheels, 2⅜".................$60–75

10-B Mechanical Horse and Trailer, red cab, tan trailer, 2¹⁵⁄₁₆", 1958 (compare to 10-A, 1955)
  v.1 metal wheels.................$45–60
  v.2 gray plastic wheels.................$50–60

10-C Sugar Container Truck "TATE & LYLE," 2⅝", 1961
  v.1 crown decal on back, gray wheels.................$65–80
  v.2 no crown decal, gray wheels.$30–40
  v.3 silver wheels.................$65–80
  v.4 black wheels.................$30–40

10-D Leyland Pipe Truck with six pipes, black plastic wheels, 2⅞", 1966
  v.1 silver grille.................$8–10
  v.2 white grille.................$12–15

10-E Leyland Pipe Truck with six pipes, SF wheels, 2⅞", 1970.................$15–20

10-F Mustang Piston Popper (Rolamatic), 2¹³⁄₁₆", 1973 (reissued as 60-E, 1982)
  v.1 metallic blue, "SUPERFAST" cast on base.................$55–80
  v.2 metallic blue, "ROLAMATIC" cast on base.................$4–6
  v.3 white.................$200–250
  v.4 yellow, "HOT POPPER".................$5–8

10-G Plymouth Gran Fury Police, 3", 1979
  v.1 white with "POLICE" tampos with shield.................$2–4
  v.2 white with "METRO" tampos.....$3–5
  v.3 white with blue "POLICE" tampos...$2–4
  v.4 white with "POLICE SFPD" tampos, dark blue windows.................$2–4
  v.5 white with "POLICE SFPD" tampos, green windows.................$60–70

10-H Buick LeSabre Stock Car, 3", 1987
  v.1 black with white base, "4" and "355 CID" tampos.................$2–4
  v.2 purple and white, "KEN WELLS/ QUICKSILVER," Laser wheels....$6–8
  v.3 light green with white base, "4" and "355 CID" tampos.................$3–5
  v.4 light brown with white base, "4" and "355 CID" tampos.................$3–5
  v.5 orange with white base, "4" and "355 CID" tampos.................$6–8
  v.6 red with white base, "4" and "355 CID" tampos.................$6–8
  v.7 yellow with red base, "10/ SHELL/MARSHALL" tampos.....$2–4
  v.8 white with red base, "10/ SHELL/MARSHALL" tampos.....$2–4
  v.9 red with white base, "07"/TOTAL RACING" tampos.................$2–4

10-I Dodge Viper RT/10, 1994 (also 56-K, 1998)
  v.1 red, gold wheels.................$2–4
  v.2 red, silver wheels.................$1–2

10-J Peterbilt Quarry Truck, 1998 (see 30-H, also 23-H, 1982)

11-A Road Tanker, 1¾", 1955 (compare to 11-B, 1958)
  v.1 green with metal wheels..$400–500
  v.2 dark yellow with metal wheels.................$75–100
  v.3 yellow with metal wheels.....$50–60
  v.4 red with metal wheels, "ESSO" decal on rear.................$50–60
  v.5 red with metal wheels, "ESSO" decal on sides.................$125–150

11-B Road Tanker "ESSO," red, 2½", 1958 (compare to 11-A, 1955)
  v.1 gold trim, metal wheels.................$40–50
  v.2 silver trim, metal wheels.....$30–40
  v.3 gray plastic wheels.................$30–40
  v.4 silver plastic wheels.................$150–175
  v.5 black plastic wheels.................$80–100

11-C Taylor Jumbo Crane, 3", 1965
  v.1 yellow weight box.................$15–20
  v.2 red weight box.................$12–15

11-D Mercedes-Benz Scaffold Truck with black plastic wheels, 2½", 1969 .$9–12

11-E Mercedes-Benz Scaffold Truck with SF wheels, 2½", 1969.................$15–20

11-F Flying Bug, 2⅞", 1972.................$15–20

11-G Bedford Car Transporter, 3", 1976 $4–8

11-H Mustang Cobra, 2⅞", 1982.................$5–8

11-I IMSA Mustang, 3", 1983 (also 67-G, 1983)
  v.1 black with red and white stripes, "Ford MUSTANG" tampo.................$2–4
  v.2 black with yellow and green flames.................$2–4
  v.3 black with yellow and green stripes.................$2–4
  v.4 yellow with black and red strips, "47" tampos.................$3–5
  v.5 red with no markings.................$10–12

v.6 light orange with yellow flames (1993) $2–4

v.7 bright red with spatter accents (1994)...............................$1–2

11-J Lamborghini Countach LP500S, 3", 1985 (see 67-H, 1985)

11-K Chrysler Atlantic, 1997 (also 19-J, 1998)...............................$2–4

11-L Maintenance Truck, 1998 (see 45-G, 1990, also 69-I, 1990)

12-A Land Rover with driver, 1¾", 1955 (compare to 12-B, 1959)

v.1 olive green, metal wheels $40–50

12-B Land Rover without driver, no roof, olive green, 2¼", 1959 (compare to 12-A, 1955)

v.1 gray plastic wheels $85–100

v.2 black plastic wheels $25–30

12-C Safari Land Rover, 2⅜", 1965

v.1 green with brown luggage on roof $9–12

v.2 blue with brown luggage on roof $9–12

v.3 blue with tan luggage............$9–12

v.4 gold with tan luggage.......$80–100

12-D Safari Land Rover, with luggage on roof, SF wheels, 2⅜", 1970

v.1 bright blue with Superfast wheels.....................$600–700

v.2 metallic gold with Superfast wheels.....................$20–25

12-E Setra Coach, 3", 1970

v.1 metallic gold with tan roof....$15–20

v.2 metallic gold with white roof...$9–12

v.3 yellow with white roof..........$8–10

v.4 burgundy with white roof $8–10

12-F Big Bull Bulldozer, 2⅜", 1975

v.1 orange rollers $4–7

v.2 yellow rollers $4–7

v.3 black rollers...........................$6–9

12-G Citroën CX Station Wagon, 3", 1979

v.1 metallic blue with blue windows $10–12

v.2 metallic blue with clear windows $4–6

v.3 metallic dark blue with red interior, clear windows..............$120–140

v.4 yellow $5–7

12-H Citroën CX Ambulance (European model), 3", 1980

v.1 white with "AMBULANCE" tampos..............................$4–6

v.2 white with "MARINE DIVISION POLICE" tampos.....................$5–8

12-I Pontiac Firebird S/E, 3", 1982 (also 51-I, 1984)

v.1 red with no markings $3–5

v.2 black with firebird tampo..........$3–5

v.3 black with "HALLEY'S COMET" tampo.................................$6–8

v.4 blue with stripes $4–6

v.5 red with "MAACO" labels $6–8

v.6 metallic blue with stripes, Laser Wheels.................................$3–5

v.7 powder blue with white stripes $9–12

v.8 purple with firebird tampo $3–5

12-J Firebird Racer Halley's Comet Commemorative Car, 3", 1986 (see 60-G, 1984, also 51-I, 1984).................$6–8

12-K Modified Racer, 2¹⁵⁄₁₆", 1989 (also 32-H, 1990)

v.1 orange with chrome exhaust pipes $2–3

v.2 orange with black exhaust pipes .$2–3

v.3 purple, Action Pack, with accessories $4–6

v.4 white with no markings, Graffic Traffic $6–8

v.5 chrome $16–20

v.6 orange to red, Super Color Changers...............................$3–5

v.7 red with "MIKE 15" tampos......$5–7

v.8 red with "36" $5–7

v.9 red with "12" and stripes $5–7

v.10 dark blue with "12" $5–7

(Note: All variations listed below were produced for Nutmeg Collectibles under license from Matchbox.)

v.11 yellow, "REGGIE 44/MAGNUM OILS".............................$5–8

v.12 white, "U2 JAMIE" $5–8

v.13 white, "TONY 1/UNIVERSAL JOINT SALES" $5–8

v.14 white and blue, "ADAP 15" ...$5–8

v.15 white, "41".........................$5–8

v.16 red, "JERRY COOK" $5–8

v.17 white, "MAYNARD TROYER" .$5–8

v.18 dark blue, "RON BOUCHARD" .$5–8

v.19 orange-yellow, "4 BUGS" $5–8

v.20 red, "JAMIE TOMAINO" $5–8

v.21 orange-yellow, "SATCH WIRLEY".$5–8

v.22 dark blue, "DOUG HEVERON" ..$5–8

v.23 black, "GEORGE KENT" $5–8

v.24 blue, "MIKE McLAUGHLIN" ...$5–8

12-L Mercedes-Benz 500SL Convertible, 3", 1990

v.1 metallic gray $2–3

v.2 black with chrome windows, World Class...................................$4–6

v.3 white with gray accents $2–4

12-M Dodge Cattle Truck, 3", 1992 (reissue of 4-E Dodge Stake Truck, 1970)

v.1 green with yellow stake, two black steers $4–6

12-N Audi Avus, 1995

v.1 silver chrome $2–3

v.2 red chrome $1–2

12-O School Bus, 1998 (see 47-H, 1985)

13-A Bedford Wreck Truck, 2", 1955 (compare to 13-B, 1958)

v.1 tan $45–60

13-B Bedford Wreck Truck, tan, 2⅛", 1958 (compare to 13-A, 1955)

v.1 metal wheels....................$40–50

v.2 gray plastic wheels $50–60

13-C Ford Thames Trader Wreck Truck, 2½", 1961

v.1 gray wheels.....................$40–50

v.2 black wheels....................$30–40

13-D Dodge Wreck Truck, "BP," with black plastic wheels, 3", 1965

v.1 green cab, yellow body, prototype $900–1,000

v.2 yellow cab, green body $10–15

13-E Dodge Wreck Truck, "BP," with SF wheels, 3", 1970 ....$20–25

13-F Baja Dune Buggy, 2⅝", 1971

v.1 metallic light green with flower label...............................$9–12

v.2 metallic light green with police shield label $20–25

v.3 metallic green with flower label.$9–12

v.4 metallic green with sunburst label..............................$12–18

v.5 bright green with flower label..............................$175–200

13-G Snorkel Fire Engine with closed cab, 3", 1977 ....$5–10

13-H 4x4 Mini-Pickup, Dunes Racer, with roll bar and Rally lights, 2¾", 1982

v.1 orange $3–5

v.2 yellow $3–5

v.3 white with "BOB JANE T-MART" tampo..............................$12–16

v.4 white with "63" tampo $2–4

13-I 4x4 Mini-Pickup with roof foil, 2¾", 1983 ....$2–4

13-J Bedford Wreck Truck (replica of 13-A) Matchbox Originals, 2", 1993......$4–5

13-K The Buster, stylized pickup truck, 1996 (also 20-K, 1998)

v.1 metallic blue upper, bright yellow lower, hot pink accents...........$1–2

13-L Shovel Nose Tractor, 1998 (see 29-F, 1976)

14-A Daimler Ambulance, 1⅞", 1956 (compare to 14-B, 1958) $50–65

14-B Daimler Ambulance, 2⅛", 1958 (compare to 14-A, 1956)

v.1 metal wheels....................$35–45

v.2 gray plastic wheels $30–40

v.3 silver plastic wheels.........$100–125

14-C Bedford Lomas Ambulance, 2⅝", 1962

v.1 gray plastic wheels $100–125

v.2 silver plastic wheels $50–60

v.3 black plastic wheels $15–20

14-D Iso Grifo sportscar with chrome hubs, 3", 1968 (compare to 14-E, 1969)......$6–9

14-E Iso Grifo sportscar with Superfast wheels, 3", 1969 (compare to 14-D, 1968)
- v.1 dark blue $15–20
- v.2 metallic dark blue $15–20
- v.3 light blue $9–12
- v.4 powder blue $12–15

14-F Rallye Royale, 2⅞", 1973 ....$5–10

14-G Mini Ha Ha Mini Cooper, 2⅜", 1975 ....$12–18

14-H Leyland Tanker (European model), 3⅛", 1982
- v.1 red cab with "ELF" and red stripe tampo...................................$4–6
- v.2 yellow cab with "SHELL," white tank with yellow base $6–8
- v.3 red cab with "SHELL," white tank with red base $40–50
- v.4 black cab tank, "GAS" tampo ..$4–6

14-I 1983 Corvette Convertible, 3", 1983
- v.1 metallic silver with red interior....$3–5
- v.2 red upper, light gray lower $2–4
- v.3 red upper and lower, "350 CID" tampo...$2–4
- v.4 red and white upper, red lower, "CHEF BOYARDEE" $10–12
- v.5 red and white upper, red lower, "350 CID" tampos $3–5
- v.6 gray upper, lavender lower, interior replaced by gold chrome armament, Roadblasters........................$6–8
- v.7 maroon with yellow and pink graphics, yellow interior $1–2

14-J 1984 Corvette Convertible, 3", 1984 (compare to 14-I, 1983)..............$3–5

14-K Jeep Eagle/Laredo, 2⅝", 1987 (see 20-F, 1982)

14-L 1987 Corvette Convertible, 3", 1987 (reissued as 28-L, 1990)
- v.1 yellow with "Corvette" and logos $2–4
- v.2 white and red with "350 CID," Laser wheels....................................$3–5
- v.3 white and red with "350 CID," New Superfast wheels $3–5
- v.4 red with "Corvette" and logo $2–4
- v.5 orange with "Corvette" and logo..$3–5
- v.6 metallic blue with chrome windshield, World Class....................$4–6
- v.7 red with flame tampos $6–8
- v.8 white with stripes and zigzag tampos $2–4
- v.9 lime green with rubber tires, "Rally OFFICIAL" $7–9
- v.10 burgundy with silver "Corvette," side vents and logo, 40th Anniversary Corvette Collector Set (1993) ..$4–6
- v.11 burgundy with yellow and magenta scribble design, yellow interior (1994) $2–4
- v.12 white with blue and orange scribble design, blue interior (1996) $1–2

14-M 1988 Corvette Convertible, 3", 1988 (see 14-L, 1987)

14-N Grand Prix Racer, 3", 1989 (see 74-J, 1988)

14-O Bulldozer, 1998 (see 64-F, 1979)

15-A Prime Mover Truck Tractor, 2⅛", 1956 (goes with 16-A or 16-B, compare to 15-B, 1959)
- v.1 yellow with metal wheels..$500–700
- v.2 orange with metal wheels $25–50
- v.3 orange with plastic wheels .$175–200

15-B Atlantic Super Prime Mover Truck Tractor, orange, 2⅝", 1959 (goes with 16-A or 16-B, compare to 15-A, 1956)
- v.1 gray plastic wheels $350–425
- v.2 black plastic wheels $30–45

15-C Dennis Refuse Truck, dark blue with gray container, 2½", 1963
- v.1 no porthole in rear hatch......$45–50
- v.2 porthole in rear hatch $15–20

15-D Volkswagen 1500 Saloon, off-white with "137" on doors, 2⅞", 1968 $9–12

15-E Volkswagen 1500 Saloon with SF wheels, 2⅞", 1970
- v.1 cream $15–20
- v.2 metallic red $20–25

15-F Hi Ho Silver! Volkswagen, 2½", 1971 (1981 variation of 31-E Volksdragon 1971)...................................$9–12

15-G Fork Lift Truck, 2½", 1972
- v.1 steering wheel, "Lansing Bagnall" labels, gray forks $9–12
- v.2 steering wheel, "T6AD" labels, gray forks.............................$100–125
- v.3 no steering wheel, "Lansing Bagnall" labels, gray forks $8–10
- v.4 no steering wheel, "Lansing Bagnall" labels, long red forks $15–20
- v.5 no steering wheel, "Lansing Bagnall" labels, black forks $9–12
- v.6 no steering wheel, "Lansing Bagnall" labels, yellow forks $9–12
- v.6 cast steering wheel, "HI LIFT" labels, with roof, black forks.............$9–12
- v.7 cast steering wheel, "HI LIFT" labels, no roof, black forks...............12–18

15-H Ford Sierra XR4Ti, 3", 1983 (also 40-G, 1990, see 55-J, 1983)

15-I Peugeot 205 Turbo 16 (European model, reissued as 25-M, 1991), 2¹¹⁄₁₆", 1985
- v.1 white with "205" and stripes, Macau cast $3–5
- v.2 white with "205" and stripes, China cast $3–5
- v.3 white with "205" tampos, Manaus cast $25–30
- v.4 orange-red with "MICHELIN/BILSTEIN/48" tampos $2–4
- v.5 green with no markings $10–12
- v.6 yellow with "Peugeot 205/BILSTEIN/48" tampos $2–4

15-J Saab 9000, 2¹⁵⁄₁₆", 1988 (also 22-J, 1989)
- v.1 metallic red $3–5

v.2 metallic blue, Laser wheels $8–10
- v.3 white $4–6
- v.4 metallic gray $10–12

15-K Corvette Grand Sport, 3", 1990 (see 2-K 1990)

15-L Alfa Romeo, 2⅞", 1991 (US; 6-J rest of the world 1991)
- v.1 red with black roof, no markings, China cast $2–4
- v.2 red with red roof, no markings, China cast..................................$10–12
- v.3 red with black roof, "ALFA ROMEO," China cast $2–4
- v.4 red with red roof, "ALFA ROMEO," China cast $2–4
- v.5 lime with lime roof, "ALFA ROMEO," China cast $4–6

15-M Sunburner (loosely based on Dodge Viper), 3", 1992 (also 41-K, 1992)
- v.1 fluorescent yellow with sun and flames tampo on hood $2–4
- v.2 white with sun and flames tampo on hood..$4–6
- v.3 metallic blue with white racing stripes (1993) $2–4
- v.4 fluorescent yellow....................$4–6

15-N Mustang Mach III Convertible, 1994 (also 4-L, 1998)
- v.1 red with stars and stripes pattern..$1–2
- v.2 black with stars and stripes pattern (1996) $1–2
- v.3 white with red and white stars & stripes pattern (1997).............$1–2

15-O Faun Mobile Crane, 1998 (see 42-H, 1985)

16-A Atlantic Trailer, 3⅛", 1956 (goes with 15-A Prime Mover, compare to 16-B, 1957)
- v.1 tan with metal wheels......$175–200

16-B Atlantic Trailer, 3¼", 1957 (goes with 15-A or 15-B Prime Mover, compare to 16-A, 1956)
- v.1 tan with tan towbar, gray plastic wheels...................................$35–45
- v.2 orange with black towbar, gray plastic wheels $100–125
- v.3 orange with black towbar, black plastic wheels......................$30–40
- v.4 orange with unpainted towbar, black plastic wheels $30–40
- v.5 orange with orange towbar, black plastic wheels $40–50

16-C Scammell Mountaineer Snowplow, 3", 1964
- v.1 gray plastic wheels $80–90
- v.2 black plastic wheels $15–20

16-D Case Bulldozer, 2½", 1969
- v.1 green treads.......................$9–12
- v.2 black treads $12–15

16-E Badger Exploration Truck with Rolamatic radar, 2⅞", 1974
- v.1 metallic orange-red..................$4–6
- v.2 army green $4–6

v.3 olive drab.................$35–45

16-F Pontiac Firebird Trans Am, 3", 1979 $5–7

16-G Pontiac Trans Am, 3", 1982
  v.1 metallic tan $4–6
  v.2 metallic gold $3–5
  v.3 white $3–5

16-H Formula Racer, 3," 1984
  v.1 red with black "PIRELLI" on airfoil, "Fiat 3" tampo $2–4
  v.2 white, orange, green, yellow "WATSON'S" on foil, "MR. JUICY/SUNKIST" tampo $20–25
  v.3 yellow with dark red "GOODYEAR" on foil, "MATCHBOX RACING TEAM" $2–4
  v.4 white with blue "SHELL" on foil, "MATCHBOX/GOODYEAR" tampo................................$3–5

16-I Pontiac Trans Am T-Roof, 3", 1985 (see 35-F, 1982)

16-J Ford LTD Police, 3", 1990 (see 51-K, 1988)

16-K Land Rover Ninety, 2½", 1990 (rest of world; see 35-H, 1990, U.S.)

16-L Street Streak concept car, 1998 (see 62-M, 1996)

17-A Bedford "MATCHBOX REMOVAL" Van, 2⅛", 1956
  v.1 maroon or blue body $150–180
  v.2 green.............................$30–50
  v.3 light green $60–75

17-B Austin London Taxi, maroon, 2¼", 1960
  v.1 gray plastic wheels $40–50
  v.2 silver plastic wheels $65–75

17-C Hoveringham Tipper, 2⅞", 1963
  v.1 red cab, orange tipper $15–20

17-D AEC Ergomatic Horse Box with black plastic wheels, 2¾", 1969............$6–9

17-E AEC Ergomatic Horse Box with SF wheels, 2¾", 1970 ....$16–24

17-F The Londoner London Bus with solid door in left side center, 3", 1972 (compare to 17-G ,1982, with double doors on left side)
  v.1 red, "SWINGING LONDON" labels, black or gray base $7–12
  v.2 red, "SWINGING LONDON" labels, unpainted base........$15–20
  v.3 gold chrome, "SWINGING LONDON" labels..................$275–350
  v.4 silver chrome, "SWINGING LONDON" labels..................$275–350
  v.5 red, "PRESTON GUILD MERCHANT 1972" $100–125
  v.6 red, "LONDON KENSINGTON HILTON" $100–125
  v.7 red, "TYPHOO TEA".......$100–125
  v.8 red, "IMPEL 73" $100–125
  v.9 red, "BERGER PAINTS" $5–12
  v.10 red, "ICP INTERCHEMICALS & PLASTICS" $200–250
  v.11 red, "BORREGARD PAPER" $200–250

v.12 red, "SELLOTAPE SELBSTKLEBEBANDER" $200–250
v.13 red, "SELLOTAPE PACKAGING SYSTEMS" $100–125
v.14 red, "SELLOTAPES ELECTRICAL TAPE" $200–250
v.15 red, "SELLOTAPE INTERNATIONAL OPERATIONS" $200–250
v.16 red, "CHAMBOURCY YOGURT" $80–100
v.17 red, "ESSO EXTRA PETROL"...$25–40
v.18 butterscotch and cream, "BERGER PAINTS" $100–125
v.19 butterscotch and cream, "IMPEL 76" $65–75
v.20 red, "SELFRIDGES" $65–75
v.21 red, "AVIEMORE CENTRE/SANTA CLAUS LAND"...................$65–75
v.22 red, "AMCEL" $100–125
v.23 red, 'BARON OF BEEF' .$100–125
v.24 yellow and red, "SWINGING LONDON"....................$150–175
v.25 red, "AIM BUILDING FUND 1976" $35–55
v.26 red with no labels $5–10
v.27 white and red, "BERGER PAINTS" $150–175
v.28 white and blue, "BERGER PAINTS" $200–250
v.29 yellow and blue, "BERGER PAINTS" $200–250
v.30 metallic red, "LUFTHANSA".$200–250
v.31 red, "ARMY & NAVY" $50–65
v.32 red, "EDUSCHO KAFFEE".$200–250
v.33 orange, "JACOB'S BISCUIT MAKERS" $35–50
v.34 red, "JACOB'S BISCUIT MAKERS" $45–60
v.35 red, "Ilford Hp5 FILM"...$150–175
v.36 red, "MUSEUM OF LONDON" $150–175
v.37 red, "SILVER JUBILEE" $45–60
v.38 metallic gray, "SILVER JUBILEE" $12–15
v.39 metallic gray, "BERGER PAINTS" $50–75
v.40 blue, "DEUTSCHLANDS AUTO-PARTNER"..........................$35–50
v.41 blue, "MATCHBOX 1953–1978" $35–50
v.42 orange, "MATCHBOX 1953–1978" $55–80
v.43 red, "MATCHBOX 1953–1978" $7–10
v.44 red, "BUSCH GARDENS" .$35–50
v.45 red, "THE BISTO BUS" $8–15

17-G London Bus with large windows, 3", 1982 (reissued as 51-H, 1984, 28-K, 1990)
  v.1 Red, "BERGER PAINTS" labels .$9–12
  v.2 red, "LAKER SKYTRAIN" labels .$8–10
  v.3 white upper, light blue lower, "MATCHBOX No. 1/Montepna" $25–30

v.4 red, "MATCHBOX No. 1/Montepna," England cast...............$80–90
v.5 dark green, "CHESTERFIELD CENTENARY" labels $10–15
v.6 red, "MATCHBOX LONDON BUS," England cast.....................$5–8
v.7 red, "MATCHBOX LONDON BUS," Macau cast.....................$2–4
v.8 red, "NICE TO MEET YOU! JAPAN 1984," England cast...............$10
v.9 red, Japanese writing on labels, England cast.........................$10–12
v.10 red, "YORK FESTIVAL & MYSTERY PLAYS," England cast............$8–10
v.11 dark blue, "NESTLE MILKYBAR," England cast.....................$6–8
v.12 red, "NESTLE MILKYBAR," Macau cast.........................$8–10
v.13 dark green, "ROWNTREE FRUIT GUMS," Macau cast $8–10
v.14 red, "ROWNTREE FRUIT GUMS," England cast.....................$8–10
v.15 dark blue, "KEDDIES No. 1 IN ESSEX," England cast $40–50
v.16 maroon, "RAPPORT," England cast $9–12
v.17 white upper, black lower, "TORVALE FISHER ENGINEERING CO.," Macau labels...................$8–10
v.18 white upper, orange lower, "W H SMITH TRAVEL," Macau cast.$9–12
v.19 red, "YOU'LL ♥ NEW YORK"...................$2–4
v.20 "SPACE FOR YOUTH 1985/STAFFORDSHIRE POLICE," Macau cast...................$9–12
v.21 blue, "CITYRAMA," Macau cast $8–10
v.22 red, no labels, England cast...$4–6
v.23 red, no labels, China cast......$6–8
v.24 red, "NUREMBERG 1986," Macau cast.........................$70–80
v.25 red, "FIRST M.I.C.A. CONVENTION," Macau cast $180–200
v.26 red, "FIRST M.I.C.A. CONVENTION," England cast......$180–200
v.27 red, "FIRST M.I.C.A. CONVENTION," England cast......$180–200
v.28 "M.I.C.A. MATCHBOX INTL COLLECTORS ASSOCIATION" .$10–12
v.29 red, "AROUND LONDON TOUR BUS," China cast $2–4
v.30 blue, NATIONAL TRAMWAY MUSEUM," China cast.........$8–10
v.31 white upper, red lower, "MIDLAND BUS TRANSPORT MUSEUM," China cast................................$8–10
v.32 red, "BAND-AID PLASTERS PLAY-BUS," China cast $8–10
v.33 blue, "NATIONAL GIROBANK," China cast $8–10
v.34 red, "MATCHBOX-NIAGARA FALLS," China cast...............$6–8

v.35 red, "FERIA DEL JUGUETE VALENCIA," "12 FEBRERO 1987" $140–160

v.36 beige upper, blue lower, "WEST MIDLANDS TRAVEL," China cast $8–10

v.37 white, "DENNEY-HAPPY 1000TH BIRTHDAY, DUBLIN" $8–10

v.38 red, "123abc," "MY FIRST MATCHBOX-NUREMBERG 1990" $9–12

v.39 red, "123abc," Matchbox Preschool $6–8

v.40 yellow, "IT'S THE REAL THING-COKE," China cast $8–10

v.41 maroon, "CORNING GLASS CENTER," China cast $2–4

v.42 chrome, "CELEBRATING A DECADE OF MATCHBOX CONVENTIONS" $25–30

v.43 red, "MARKFIELD PROJECT SUPPORT APPEAL 92," China cast $8–10

v.44 red, "LONDON WIDE TOUR BUS," China cast $2–4

v.45 white, no labels, China cast, Graffic Traffic $4–6

17-H AMX Pro Stocker, 2⅝", 1983
v.1 metallic silver with red and black stripes, "AMX" tampo $2–4
v.2 maroon with "Dr. Pepper" tampo .$4–6

17-I Ford Escort XR3 Cabriolet, 2¾", 1985 (also 37-K)
v.1 white with "XR3i" tampos, silver wheels, Macau cast $2–4
v.2 white with "XR3i" tampos, gold wheels, Macau cast $4–6
v.3 white with "XR3i" tampos, Thailand cast $2–4
v.4 white with "3" and stripes, New Superfast wheels $4–6
v.5 red with "XR3i" and "Ford" tampos $8–10
v.6 metallic blue with "3" and stripes, Laser wheels $4–6
v.7 metallic blue with white and orange spatter tampos $2–4
v.8 dark blue with "XR3i" tampos, Macau cast...................$2–4
v.9 dark blue with "XR3i" tampos, Thailand cast $2–4

17-J Dodge Dakota Pickup, 3", 1990 (see 50-I, 1989)

17-K Ferrari 456 GT, 1994
v.1 metallic blue, "456 GT" in yellow on sides (1994)...................$3–5
v.2 metallic purple with white tampo on sides, roof and hood (1995) $1–2
v.3 metallic purple with white tampo on sides, no markings on hood or roof (1996) $1–2
v.4 metallic red with no markings (1996) $1–2

17-L VW Concept 1, 1998 (see 49-K, 1996)

18-A Caterpillar D8 Bulldozer with blade, 1⅞", 1956 (compare to 18-B 1958, 18-C, 1961)
v.1 yellow with red blade..........$40–60

18-B Caterpillar Dozer, yellow, no blade braces, 2", 1958 (compare to 18-A, 1956, 18-C, 1961)
v.1 yellow with yellow blade $55–70

18-C Caterpillar Bulldozer, yellow with blade braces, 2¼", 1961 (compare to 18-A, 1956, 18-B, 1958)
v.1 metal rollers $30–40
v.2 silver plastic rollers...............$85–95
v.3 black plastic rollers.............$20–30

18-D Caterpillar Crawler Bulldozer, 2⅜", 1964
v.1 silver plastic rollers $90–100
v.2 black plastic rollers.............$15–20

18-E Field Car with tires on plastic hubs, 2⅝", 1969
v.1 green wheel hubs...........$250–300
v.2 red wheel hubs, unpainted base .$6–9
v.3 red wheel hubs, black painted base $9–12

18-F Field Car with SF wheels, 2⅝", 1970
v.1 yellow...........................$12–15
v.2 olive $4–6
v.3 olive drab.......................$40–50
v.4 white $300–400
v.5 orange $3–5
v.6 metallic red $3–5

18-G Hondarora Motorcycle, 2⅜", 1975
v.1 red with silver handlebars and seat...................$8–12
v.2 red with black handlebars and seat...................$4–6
v.3 red with black handlebars and white seat...................$75–90
v.4 orange with black handlebars and seat...................$8–12
v.5 olive drab with black handlebars and seat...................$40–50
v.6 army green with black handlebars and seat $4–6
v.7 metallic red with black handlebars and seat $40–50
v.8 metallic green with black handlebars and seat $4–6
v.9 yellow with no driver $3–5
v.10 yellow with tan driver $3–5
v.11 yellow with brown driver........$3–5
v.12 yellow with green driver.....$40–50

18-H Extending Ladder Fire Engine, 3", 1984 (also 23-J, 1998)
v.1 red with white ladder, no markings $1–2
v.2 red with white ladder, "FIRE DEPT," "7," shield tampos...................$1–2
v.3 red with white ladder, Japanese lettering.......................$8–10
v.4 red with white ladder, "3" and crest tampo...................$3–5
v.5 red with white ladder, "FIRE DEPT," no origin cast.....................$8–10

v.6 red with yellow ladder, Live 'N' Learn/Preschool $6–8
v.7 yellow with white ladder, no markings...................$3–5
v.8 fluorescent orange with "4" and checkered bar accents (1994)...................$1–2
v.9 fluorescent orange with "5" and INTERCOM CITY" tampo......$8–10
v.10 fluorescent orange with white accents $1–2
v.11 red with white upper, gold and black accents, "FD No.1" on shield (1996 5-Pack) $2–4
v.12 red with white "12TH," gold "RESCUE SQUAD," gold trim (1995)...................$1–2
v.13 red with white "12TH RESCUE SQUAD," white trim (1996).....$1–2
v.14 white with orange ladder (1996)...................$1–2

18-I Plymouth Prowler, 1998 (see 34-L, 1995)

19-A MG Midget Sports Car with driver, 2", 1956 ....$50–75

19-B MGA Sports Car, white, 2¼", 1958
v.1 metal wheels, gold grille....$80–100
v.2 metal wheels, silver grille......$60–80
v.3 gray plastic wheels $80–100
v.4 silver plastic wheels........$125–150

19-C Aston Martin Racing Car, metallic green, 2½", 1961
v.1 gray driver, "52" decal $40–50
v.2 gray driver, "41" decal $40–50
v.3 gray driver, "5" decal $40–50
v.4 gray driver, "19" decal $25–35
v.5 white driver, "19" decal $25–35
v.6 white driver, "3" decal $40–50
v.7 white driver, "53" decal $40–50

19-D Lotus Racing Car, 2¾", 1966
v.1 orange.........................$25–30
v.2 green.........................$15–20

19-E Lotus Racing Car with SF wheels, 2¾", 1970 ....$30–35

19-F Road Dragster, 2⅞", 1970
v.1 red $10–15
v.2 purple.........................$15–20
v.3 metallic red.........................$15–20

19-G Badger Cement Truck, Rolamatic, 3", 1976.........................$3–5

19-H Peterbilt Cement Truck, 3", 1982 (reissued as 8-P, 1998)
v.1 metallic green with orange barrel, "BIG PETE" tampos $3–5
v.2 blue with yellow barrel, "KWIK SET CEMENT" tampos..................$2–4
v.3 yellow with orange barrel, "DIRTY DUMPER" tampos $45–60
v.4 yellow with gray barrel, "PACE CONSTRUCTION" tampos.........................$2–4
v.5 red with lime green barrel $5–7
v.6 pink with white barrel, "READYMIX" tampo $8–10

v.7 red with orange barrel, Manaus cast $35–40

v.8 yellow with red barrel, "PACE CONSTRUCTION" tampos $2–4

v.9 orange with black barrel $1–3

v.10 red with black barrel, white barrel base (1996)......................$1–2

19-I MG Midget Sports Car (commemorative replica of 19-A) Matchbox Originals, 2", 1993..$3–5

19-J Chrysler Atlantic, 1998 (see 11-K, 1997)

20-A Stake Truck, maroon, 2⅜", 1956

v.1 gold grille and fuel tanks, metal wheels..............................$80–100

v.2 silver grille and fuel tanks, metal wheels..............................$30–50

v.3 maroon grille and fuel tanks, metal wheels..............................$30–50

v.4 silver grille and fuel tanks, gray plastic wheels $100–125

v.5 dark red grille and fuel tanks, gray plastic wheels..................$90–120

20-B ERF 686 Truck "EVEREADY FOR LIFE," blue, 2⅝", 1959

v.1 gray plastic wheels $40–50

v.2 silver plastic wheels............$85–95

v.3 black plastic wheels............$45–55

20-C Chevrolet Impala Taxi Cab, 3", 1965

v.1 orange with gray wheels, ivory interior $250–350

v.2 orange with black wheels, ivory or red interior....................$20–25

v.3 yellow with black wheels, ivory or red interior....................$10–15

20-D Lamborghini Marzal with SF wheels, 2¾", 1969

v.1 metallic red $12–15

v.2 salmon $12–15

v.3 yellow..............................$30–40

v.4 pink $12–15

20-E Range Rover Police Patrol (Rolamatic), 2⅞", 1975

v.1 white with "POLICE" labels, frosted windows $5–12

v.2 olive drab, "AMBULANCE" .$40–50

v.3 olive drab, "POLICE" $40–50

v.4 light olive, "AMBULANCE" $4–7

v.5 light olive, "POLICE" $4–7

v.6 orange, "SITE ENGINEER" ..$15–18

v.7 orange, "POLICE" $9–12

v.8 white, "COUNTY SHERIFF" ...$8–12

v.9 blue, "PARIS DAKAR 81" $30–45

v.10 metallic tan, "PARIS DAKAR 83" $5–8

v.11 beige, PARIS DAKAR 83" $5–8

20-F 4x4 Jeep, Desert Dawg, 2⅝", 1982 (reissued as 14-K, 1987)

v.1 white with red roof, "DESERT DAWG" tampo, England cast .$2–4

v.2 metallic copper with red roof, England cast..............................$3–5

v.3 black with white roof, "LAREDO" tampo, Macau cast $2–4

v.4 black with white roof, "LAREDO" tampo, Hong Kong cast......$15–20

v.5 black with white roof, "LAREDO" tampo, Thailand cast $2–4

v.6 dark tan with red roof, "GOLDEN EAGLE," England $15–20

v.7 red with white roof, "GOLDEN EAGLE," Macau cast $7–10

v.8 army green with tan roof, camouflage tampo, Macau cast $4–6

v.9 yellow with lime green roof, Macau cast......................................$7–10

v.10 black with red roof, "LAREDO" tampo, Macau cast............$10–12

v.11 tan with tan roof, brown camouflage $1–3

v.12 yellow with black roof, pink and blue accents $2–4

v.13 army green with army green canopy, white star, "V-9872-3" (1996) $1–2

20-G Jeep Laredo/Eagle/Wrangler 4x4, 2⅝", 1983 ....$2–4

20-H Volvo Container Truck, 3", 1985 (see 23-I, 1985, also 62-J, 1990)

20-I Volkswagen Transporter/Ambulance Vanagon, 2⅞", 1986 (not issued in US)

v.1 white with ambulance markings and roof lights $3–5

v.2 black with green markings, Commando series $4–6

v.3 white with no markings, Graffic Traffic series $4–6

20-J '97 Firebird Formula, 1997 ....$1–2

20-K The Buster stylized pickup, 1998 (see 13-K, 1996)

21-A Bedford Duplé Long Distance Coach, 2¼", 1956 (compare to 21-B, 1958)..............................$45–55

21-B Bedford Duplé Long Distance Coach, 2⅝", 1958 (compare to 21-A, 1956)

v.1 light green $45–60

v.2 dark green $80–100

21-C Commer Milk Delivery Truck, 2¼", 1961

v.1 silver wheels $25–35

v.2 gray wheels.......................$65–75

v.3 black wheels $15–25

21-D Foden Concrete Truck, 3", 1968 .$6–9

21-E Foden Concrete Truck with SF wheels, 2⅞", 1970..............................$20–25

21-F Rod Roller, 2⅝", 1973

v.1 yellow with metallic red rear wheels $15–20

v.2 yellow with red rear wheels..$12–18

v.3 yellow with black rear wheels $8–12

v.4 orange-yellow $8–12

21-G Renault 5TL, 2¹¹⁄₁₆", 1978

v.1 yellow with tan interior, "LeCar" tampos $4–6

v.2 yellow with red interior, "LeCar" tampos $8–10

v.3 blue with no markings............$6–10

v.4 metallic gray with tan interior, no markings $8–10

v.5 metallic gray with red interior, "A5" tampos $15–18

v.6 metallic gray with red interior, no markings $4–6

v.7 metallic gray with red interior, "LeCar" tampos $6–8

v.8 white with "Renault" tampos ...$7–10

v.9 white with "Roloil" tampos, black base......................................$4–6

v.10 white with "Roloil" tampos, red base....................................$12–15

v.11 red with "Turbo" tampos $12–18

21-H Corvette Pace Car, 3", 1983

v.1 metallic gray with blue accents, "PACE CAR" on sides $4–6

v.2 white with red accent and "Corvette" tampos, Thailand $3–5

21-I Breakdown Van, 3", 1986

v.1 red with white boom, "24 HOUR SERVICE" $2–4

v.2 yellow with black boom, "AUTO RELAY 24 HR. TOW"............$2–4

v.3 black with gray boom, yellow stripes, Commando series $4–7

v.4 red with green boom, blue wheels, Preschool series $6–8

v.5 orange with orange boom, "AUTO RELAY 24 HR. TOW"............$3–5

v.6 orange with black boom, "AUTO RELAY 24 HR. TOW"............$2–4

v.7 white with no markings, Graffic Traffic $4–6

v.8 fluorescent orange, "INTERCOM CITY AUTO SERVICES"........$8–10

21-J GMC Wrecker, 2⅞", 1987 (also 71-J, 1989, 72-M, 1989, 63-J, 1998)

v.1 white with "FRANK'S GETTY," Macau, Thailand or China cast............$2–4

v.2 white with "FRANK'S GETTY," no origin cast..............................$4–6

v.3 white with "ACCESSORY WHOLESALERS INC." $16–20

v.4 black with "INDY 500" $8–10

v.5 metallic purple with yellow accents, "PARKHILL TOWING" (1995)..................................$1–2

21-K Nissan Prairie, 2⅞", 1991 (rest of world, see 31-L, U.S., 1991)

J-21-L Toyota Celica XX, "Made in Japan" and "J-21" cast on base, 1979

v.1 cream $12–15

v.2 red $12–15

21-M Mack Heavy Rescue Auxiliary Power Truck, 3", 1998 (see 57-K, 1991, also 50-J, 1991)

22-A Vauxhall Cresta Sedan, 2½", 1956 (compare to 22-B, 1958)

v.1 red with white or cream roof, no windows..............................$30–50

22-B Vauxhall Cresta Sedan, 2⅝", 1958 (compare to 22-A, 1956) v.1 cream, no windows, metal wheels $40–50

v.2 cream, no windows, gray plastic wheels........................$40–50

v.3 cream, green windows, gray plastic wheels $45–55

v.4 cream and turquoise, green windows, gray plastic wheels $350–400

v.5 gray and turquoise, green windows, gray plastic wheels.............$65–75

v.6 bronze and turquoise, green windows, gray plastic wheels ...$65–75

v.7 gray and pink, green windows, gray plastic wheels $50–60

v.8 gray and pink, green windows, silver plastic wheels $50–60

v.9 gold, green windows, gray plastic wheels...........................$50–60

v.10 gold, green windows, silver plastic wheels...........................$50–60

v.11 copper, green windows, gray plastic wheels...........................$50–60

v.12 copper, green windows, silver plastic wheels..........................$50–60

v.13 copper, green windows, black plastic wheels.........................$35–45

22-C Pontiac Grand Prix, 3", 1964

v.1 red with black plastic wheels .$15-18

22-D Pontiac Grand Prix with SF wheels, 3", 1970

v.1 red with Superfast wheels................$1,600–2,000

v.2 purple with Superfast wheels ..$30–40

22-E Freeman Inter-City Commuter Coach, 3", 1970

v.1 metallic purple....................$12–16

v.2 metallic gold $12–16

v.3 metallic magenta $12–16

22-F Blaze Buster Fire Engine, 3", 1975

v.1 red with white ladder, silver interior $175–200

v.2 red with black ladder, silver interior $15–20

v.3 red with yellow ladder, silver interior...........................$5–12

v.4 red with yellow ladder, white interior...........................$3–5

v.5 red with orange-yellow ladder, "FIRE" labels $3–5

v.6 red with orange-yellow ladder, "No. 32" labels.........................$8–12

22-G Toyota Mini Pickup Camper, 2¾", 1982

v.1 silver with white stepped roof, "BIG FOOT" tampos $4–6

v.2 silver with white flat roof, "BIG FOOT" tampos $3–5

v.3 silver with black roll bar, "BIG FOOT" tampos.........................$30–40

v.4 red with white flat roof, "ASPEN SKI HOLIDAYS," metal base.........$3–5

v.5 red with white flat roof, "ASPEN SKI HOLIDAYS," plastic base $2–4

v.6 white with white flat roof, "SLD PUMP SERVICE" tampo $10–12

22-H Toyota Mini Pickup Camper, Bigfoot 4x4, 2¾", 1983 ....$2–4

22-I Jaguar XK120, 3", 1984

v.1 dark green with red interior, no markings......................................$4–6

v.2 cream with red interior, "414" tampo $2–4

v.3 white with maroon interior, chrome windshield, World Class $4–6

v.4 white with blue and fluorescent orange flames, Dream Machines......$2–4

22-K Opel Vectra/Chevrolet Cavalier GS, 3", 1990 (also 41-J, 1991)

v.1 metallic red $3–5

v.2 green..................................$10–12

22-L Lamborghini Diablo, 3", 1992 (also 49-I, 1992)

v.1 yellow $2–3

v.2 red with chrome windows, rubber tires, World Class....................$3–5

v.3 metallic blue with pink and white accents (1994) $1–2

v.4 bright yellow with black spots, bright pink interior (1995)................$1–2

v.5 red with black spots, fluorescent yellow interior (1996) $1–2

J-22-M Mitsubishi Galant Eterna ("Made in Japan" and J-22 cast on base), 1979

v.1 red $12–15

v.2 yellow.................................$12–15

22-N 4X4 Chevy Blazer Police, 1998 (see 50-H, 1985)

23-A Berkeley Cavalier Travel Trailer, 2½", 1956

v.1 pale blue..........................$30–40

v.2 lime green $40–60

v.3 metallic green $275–325

23-B Bluebird Dauphine Travel Trailer, 2½", 1960

v.1 metallic green with gray plastic wheels $300–350

v.2 metallic tan with gray plastic wheels $50–60

v.3 metallic tan with silver wheels .$50–60

v.4 metallic tan with black plastic wheels $80–100

23-C Trailer Caravan, 2⅞", 1965

v.1 yellow...............................$12–16

v.2 pink $12–16

23-D Volkswagen Camper with opening roof, 2⅛", 1970

v.1 blue with orange interior and roof $12–15

v.2 orange with orange interior and roof............................$100–125

v.3 orange with white interior, orange roof $12–16

v.4 olive with no interior $6–10

v.5 white with no interior, "PIZZA Van"...............................$12–15

23-E Atlas Dump Truck, 3", 1975

v.1 blue with orange dumper.......$6–10

v.2 red with metallic silver dumper $6–10

v.3 blue with yellow dumper $8–12

23-F Mustang GT350, 2⅞", 1979 ..$10–12

23-G Audi Quattro, 3", 1982 (also 25-J, 1982)

v.1 white with "AUDI 20" tampo, England cast $2–4

v.2 white with "AUDI 20" tampo, Macau cast $2–4

v.3 white with "AUDI 20" tampo, Manaus cast.............................$25–30

v.4 white with DUCKHAM'S/PIRELLI tampo..................................$3–5

v.5 purple with "QUATTRO 0000" tampo..................................$4–6

v.6 blue with "QUATTRO 0000" tampo..................................$8–10

v.7 metallic dark gray with pictogram and "AUDI 2584584" $20–25

23-H Honda ATC, 1985

v.1 red $9–12

v.2 fluorescent green.....................$5–8

23-I Peterbilt Quarry Truck, 3", 1982 (rest of world, see 30-H US, 1982)

23-J Volvo Container Truck, 3", 1985 (also 20-H, 1985, 62-J, 1990, 44, 1998)

v.1 blue with white container, "COLDFRESH" labels $3–5

v.2 white with white container, "SCOTCH CORNER" labels .$8–10

v.3 gray with gray container, "SUPER-SAVER DRUGSTORES" $8–10

v.4 blue with white container, "MB1-75 #1 IN VOLUME SALES" $35–40

v.5 white with white container, "FEDERAL Express".......................$2–4

v.6 white with white container, "UNIC" $8–10

v.7 blue with white container, I "UNIC" $8–10

v.8 blue with blue container, "CROOKE'S HEALTHCARE".............$6–8

v.9 white with white container, "KELLOGG'S/MILCH-LAIT-LATTE".$35–40

v.10 blue with white container, "KELLOGG'S/MILCH-LAIT-LATTE".$35–40

v.11 white with white container, "TNT IPEC"...............................$3–5

v.12 green with gray container, "HIKKOSHI SEMMON CENTER" $10–12

v.13 blue with blue container, "ALLDERS" $6–8

v.14 white with white container, "XP PARCELS" $6–8

v.15 blue with blue container, "COMMA PERFORMANCE MOTOR OILS".................$8–10

v.16 red with brown container, "MERKUR KAFFEE" labels $10–12

v.17 green with white container, "M" and green stripes ....$10–12 v.18 red with white container, "DEN-NER" $10–12

v.19 white with white container, "FAMILY TRUST" $8–10

v.20 blue with red container, "CHRIS-TIANSEN" $8–10

v.21 white with white container, "KIT KAT" $30–35

v.22 white with white container, "YORKIE" $30–35

v.23 red with white container, "BIG TOP CIRCUS" $2–4

v.24 blue with white container, "BIG TOP CIRCUS" $4–6

v.25 white with light blue container, "CO-OP PEOPLE WHO CARE" $7–9

v.26 white with light blue container, "99 TEA" $6–8

v.27 black with black container, "COOL PAINT CO." (1993) $2–4

v.28 bright orange with "MATCHBOX" logo on doors, "GET IN THE FAST LANE" $1–2

v.29 bright orange without logo on doors, "GET IN THE FAST LANE" $1–2

v.30 bright orange with yellow container, "NORTH AMERICAN DIECAST TOY COLLECTORS ASSOCIATION 2ND ANNIVERSARY NOVEMBER 1995" (unlicensed commemorative)...$8–10

23-K Extending Ladder Fire Truck, 1998 (see 18-H, 1984)

24-A Weatherhill Hydraulic Excavator, yellow, 2⅜", 1956
v.1 orange with metal wheels $60–80
v.2 yellow with metal wheels ...$80–100

24-B Weatherhill Hydraulic Excavator, 2⅝", 1959
v.1 yellow with gray plastic wheels $30–40
v.2 yellow with black plastic wheels $20–30

24-C Rolls Royce Silver Shadow, 3", 1967
v.1 metallic red with chrome hubs $6–9

24-D Rolls Royce Silver Shadow with SF wheels, 3", 1970
v.1 metallic red $9–12
v.2 metallic gold $12–15

24-E Team Matchbox Formula 1 Racer, 2⅞", 1973
v.1 yellow with white driver, "8" label................................$225–275
v.2 yellow with white driver, "4" label $225–275
v.3 metallic blue with white driver, "1" label $275–325
v.4 metallic blue with white driver, "5" label $35–50
v.5 metallic green with white driver, "5" label $35–50
v.6 red with white driver, "8" label .$4–8
v.7 red with white driver, "44" label .$4–8

v.8 red with yellow driver, "44" label..............................$12–18
v.9 orange with tan driver, "44" label, with trailer $35–50
v.10 orange with yellow driver, "44" label $35–50

24-F Diesel Shunter Locomotive, 3", 1978
v.1 dark green............................$7–9
v.2 yellow with red undercarriage...$4–6
v.3 yellow with metallic red undercarriage $25–35

24-G Datsun 280ZX, 3", 1982 (hood doesn't open, compare to 24-H, 1983)
v.1 black with white interior $2–4
v.2 black with red interior $3–5

24-H Datsun 280ZX 2+2, 3", 1983 (compare to 24-I, 1987)
v.1 black with gold pin stripes $2–4
v.2 black with "TURBO ZX" tampos, silver wheels $2–4
v.3 black with "TURBO ZX" tampos, gold wheels $6–12
v.4 white with red and blue "TURBO 33" tampo $8–10
v.5 black with orange, yellow and white "TURBO" tampo $3–5
v.6 gray with orange, yellow and white accents, Laser Wheels $6–8
v.7 red with black and orange tampos with armaments, Roadblasters ..$5–7

24-I Nissan 300ZX Turbo, hood opens, 2⅞", 1987
v.1 pearl gray with gold stripes and "TURBO" tampos $2–4
v.2 white with "FUJICOLOR" tampos..............................$2–4
v.3 red with red and orange stripes.$3–5
v.4 metallic red with red and orange stripes $3–5
v.5 white with "96/BP RACING TEAM"..............................$10–12
v.6 yellow with "4 MONKEY RACING TEAM" $10–12

24-J Ferrari F40, 3", 1989 (also 70-H, 1989)
v.1 red with clear windows, black interior $2–4
v.2 red with chrome windows, World Class $3–5
v.3 chrome with clear windows..$15–20
v.4 red with chrome and black windows, Lightning series $3–5
v.5 yellow with blue chrome and black windows, Lightning series $3–4
v.6 white with blue chrome and black windows, Lightning series $4–6
v.7 black with black and chrome windows, Lightning series $4–6
v.8 red with black windows, Triple Heat series $4–6
v.9 yellow white chrome windows, World Class........................$3–5
v.10 red with black spots, opaque yellow windows (1994) $2–4

v.11 gradient metallic purple to metallic pink (1996).........................$1–2

24-K Lincoln Town Car, 3", 1990 (see 43-F, 1989)

24-L Airport Fire Tender, 3", 1992 (see 8-N, 1992)

24-M LTD Police Car, 1998 (see 51-K, 1988, also 16-J, 1990)

25-A Bedford "DUNLOP" 12CWT Van, 2⅛", 1956 ....$40–55

25-B Volkswagen 1200 Sedan, metallic light blue, 2½", 1960
v.1 gray plastic wheels, clear windows..............................$40–50
v.2 gray plastic wheels, green windows..............................$40–50
v.3 silver plastic wheels, green windows..............................$50–60
v.4 black plastic wheels, green windows..............................$100–120

25-C Bedford Petrol Tanker with tilt cab, 3", 1964
v.1 yellow cab, "BP," gray plastic wheels..............................$140–160
v.2 yellow cab, "BP," black plastic wheels..............................$15–20
v.3 dark blue cab, "ARAL," black plastic wheels $80–100

25-D Ford Cortina GT with regular wheels, 2⅞", 1968
v.1 metallic light brown, no roof rack..................................$6–9
v.2 metallic light brown with roof rack..................................$9–12

25-E Ford Cortina GT with SF wheels, 2⅝", 1970
v.1 metallic light brown $30–40
v.2 metallic blue $15–20

25-F Mod Tractor, 2⅛", 1972 ....$6–12

25-G Flat Car with container, 3", 1978
v.1 tan container, "NYK" labels......$5–7
v.2 tan container, "UNITED STATES LINES" labels....................$10–12
v.3 tan container, "SEA/LAND" labels $5–7
v.4 tan container, "OCL" labels....$8–10
v.5 light brown container, "NYK" labels $12–15
v.6 beige container, "SEA/LAND".$8–12
v.7 blue container, "UNITED STATES LINES" labels....................$20–25
v.8 blue container, "SEA/LAND" labels $20–25
v.9 orange container "OCL" labels.$30–35
v.10 red container, "NYK" labels...$20–25
v.11 white container, no labels (labels included with playset).............$6–9
v.12 yellow container, no labels (labels included with playset).............$6–8

25-H Toyota Celica GT, small rear wheels, 2¹⁵⁄₁₆" 1978
v.1 blue with "78" tampos.............$4–6
v.2 yellow with "YELLOW FEVER" tampos $30–40

25-I Toyota Celica GT with oversized rear wheels, 2¹⁵⁄₁₆", 1982 (compare to 25-H, 1978)
  v.1 yellow with "YELLOW FEVER" tampo $4–6

25-J Audi Quattro, 3", 1982 (see 23-G 1982)

25-K Ambulance, Chevrolet, 2¹⁵⁄₁₆", 1983 (also 41-F)
  v.1 white with "PACIFIC AMBU-LANCE" $3–5
  v.2 white with orange accents, "PARA-MEDICS E11" $2–4
  v.3 white with "EMT AMBULANCE". $3–5
  v.4 white with no markings, Graffic Traffic $6–8
  v.5 yellow with "PARAMEDICS E11" $4–6
  v.6 fluorescent orange with "AMBULANCE 7/INTERCOM CITY" $8–10
  v.7 red with white, gold and black accents, blue windows (1996 5-Pack) $2–4
  v.8 white with blue and orange accents, "AMBULANCE/DIAL 911" (1996) $1–2

25-L Peugeot Quasar, 2¾", 1985 (also 49-H, 1987)
  v.1 white with "QUASAR" tampos.... $2–4
  v.2 dark blue with New Superfast wheels, "9" and pink stripes $4–6
  v.3 metallic blue with Laser wheels, "9" and pink stripes $4–6
  v.4 black with bright green and orange stripes, Roadblasters $3–5
  v.5 purple with "QUASAR" tampos ... $2–4
  v.6 yellow with "3" tampos, stripes and flames, Preschool $6–8
  v.7 maroon with yellow accents $1–2

25-M BMW Z-3, 1997 (also 5-L, 1998)
  v.1 blue with white accents bordered in red $1–2

25-N Ford Ambulance, 1998 (see 51-M, 1997)

26-A Foden "READY-MIX" Concrete Truck, 1¾", 1956
  v.1 metal wheels, gold grille $65–85

v.2 metal wheels, silver grille $35–50

  v.3 silver plastic wheels $135–160

26-B Foden "READY MIX" Concrete Truck, orange, 2½", 1961
  v.1 gray mixer, gray wheels .. $400–450
  v.2 orange mixer, gray wheels ... $35–45

  v.3 orange mixer, silver wheels . $130–150
  v.4 orange mixer, black wheels ... $15–20

26-C GMC Tipper Truck with regular wheels, 2⅝", 1968 .... $6–9

26-D GMC Tipper Truck with SF wheels, 2⅝", 1970 .... $15–20

26-E Big Banger, 3", 1972 (compare to 26-G Cosmic Blues, 1980, and 48-E Pi-Eyed Piper, 1972)
  v.1 red with unpainted base, blue windows $12–18
  v.2 red with unpainted base, amber windows $12–18

26-F Site Dumper, 2⅝", 1976
  v.1 yellow with yellow dumper, black interior $3–5
  v.2 yellow with red dumper, black interior $4–7
  v.3 orange-red with orange-red dumper, white interior $30–40
  v.4 orange-red with with metallic gray dumper, white interior $4–8

26-G Cosmic Blues, 3", 1980 (reissued as 41-H, 1993)
  v.1 white with blue accents, England cast $9–12
  v.2 white with blue accents, Macau cast $3–5
  v.3 white with blue accents, China cast $3–5
  v.4 blue with white accents, China cast $2–4
  v.5 bright orange-yellow with magenta and black accents (1993) $1–2
  v.6 black with fluorescent orange and white flames (1996) $3–5

26-H Volvo Covered Tilt Truck, 3", 1984 (reissued as 49-K, 1990)
  v.1 metallic blue with yellow canopy, no markings, England cast $20–30
  v.2 metallic blue with yellow canopy, "FRESH FRUIT CO.," Macau cast $2–4
  v.3 yellow with yellow canopy, "FERRY-MASTERS" $2–4
  v.4 white with white canopy, "FEDERAL Express" $2–4
  v.5 dark blue with yellow canopy, "MICHELIN" $2–4
  v.6 army green with tan canopy, "LS2020" $16–20
  v.7 black with dark gray canopy, "LS1506" $16–20
  v.8 blue with blue canopy, "HENNEIZ" $10–12
  v.9 red with green canopy, yellow wheels, Live 'N' Learn/Preschool $6–8
  v.10 red with no canopy, "123" tampo on doors, Live 'N' Learn/Preschool $6–8
  v.11 white with white canopy, "PIRELLI GRIPPING STUFF" $2–4

26-I Volvo Cable Truck (rare variation of 23-I, 1985), 3", 1984
  v.1 yellow with two metallic gray cable spools on back $15–20

26-J BMW 5-Series 535i, 3", 1989 (also 31-K ,1990)
  v.1 metallic dark gray $2–4
  v.2 white with "FINA 31/BMW TEAM" $3–5

26-K "READY MIX" Concrete Truck (replica of 26-A) Matchbox Originals, 2½", 1993 .... $3–5

26-L Chevy Van, 3", 1993 (reissue of 68-E, 1979)

26-M Snorkel Fire Engine with open cab, 1998 (see 63-H, 1982)

27-A Bedford Low Loader, 1⅜", 1956
  v.1 light blue cab, dark blue trailer $625–800
  v.2 dark green cab, tan trailer $35–60

27-B Bedford Low Loader, 3¾", 1959
  v.1 light green cab with metal wheels $40–50
  v.2 light green cab with gray plastic wheels $65–75
  v.3 dark green cab with gray plastic wheels $75–95

27-C Cadillac Sixty Special, 2¾", 1960
  v.1 metallic light green with white roof $275-325
  v.2 metallic gray with white roof. $35–45
  v.3 lavender with pink roof $40–50

27-D Mercedes-Benz 230SL Convertible with regular wheels, 3", 1966
  v.1 cream $6–8
  v.2 white $8–10

27-E Mercedes-Benz 230SL Convertible with SF wheels, 2⅞", 1970
  v.1 cream or off-white with red interior $15–20
  v.2 yellow with red interior $15–20
  v.3 yellow with black interior $12–15

27-F Lamborghini Countach with opening rear cowl, 2⅞", 1973
  v.1 yellow with chrome interior $6–9
  v.2 red with silver interior $6–9
  v.3 red with gray interior, black base $7–11
  v.4 red with gray interior, unpainted base $6–9
  v.5 red with yellow interior $6–9
  v.6 red with white interior $6–9
  v.7 red with tan interior $6–9
  v.8 yellow with light gray interior .. $45–65
  v.9 dark green $275–325

27-G Swing Wing Jet, 3", 1981
  v.1 red with white base and wings $2–4
  v.2 red with white base, gray wings. $4–6
  v.3 black with gray base and wings. $4–6

27-H Jeep Cherokee, 2⅞", 1987 (reintroduced as 73-K 1994)
  v.1 white, "QUADTRAK" $2–4

v.2 beige, "HOLIDAY CLUB" $2–4

v.3 yellow, "FOREST RANGER COUNTY PARK" $5–7

v.4 yellow, "BP CHIEF," green and red stripes $10–12

v.5 yellow, "MR. FIXER" $2–4

v.6 light green, "MR. FIXER" $3–5

v.7 brown, "MR. FIXER" $3–5

v.8 white, "NATIONAL SKI PATROL" .$3–5

v.9 metallic silver, "SPORT," "JEEP" $2–4

v.10 purple with orange and cream flames (1994) $1–2

v.11 red with black lower body, gold trim and shield (5-Pack) $2–4

27-I Mercedes-Benz 1600 Turbo Farm Tractor, 2¾", 1991 (see 73-I, 1990)

27-J Tailgator 1994

v.1 green (1994) $1–2

v.2 dark green (1996) $1–2

v.3 purple (1997) $1–2

27-K Camaro Police 1998 (see 59-K, 1995)

28-A Bedford Compressor Truck, 2¼", 1956 ....$35–55

28-B Thames Trader Compressor Truck, yellow, 2¾", 1959

v.1 gray plastic wheels $160–180

v.2 black plastic wheels $30–40

28-C Mark 10 Jaguar, 2¾", 1964

v.1 gray plastic wheels $140–160

v.2 black plastic wheels $15–20

28-D Mack Dump Truck with regular wheels, 2⅝", 1968 ....$9–12

28-E Mack Dump Truck with SF wheels, 2⅝", 1970

v.1 metallic dull gold $20–25

v.2 olive drab $30–40

v.3 olive $6–12

28-F Stoat Armored Truck, 2⅝", 1974

v.1 metallic gold $8–12

v.2 army green with black hubs $4–7

v.3 olive drab, chrome hubs $45–50

28-G Lincoln Continental Mark V, 3", 1979

v.1 red with white roof $4–7

28-H Formula Racing Car, 3⅛", 1982

v.1 metallic tan, England cast $3–5

v.2 metallic tan, Macau cast $3–5

v.3 metallic tan, Manaus cast $25–30

v.4 metallic red, Manaus cast $35–40

28-I 1984 Dodge Daytona Turbo Z, 2⅞", 1984

v.1 metallic burgundy with metallic gray lower body, England cast $4–6

v.2 metallic burgundy with metallic gray lower body, Macau cast $30–35

v.3 metallic silver with black lower body, red and black stripes $4–6

v.4 white with blue lower body, red and blue stripes $3–5

v.5 metallic burgundy with gold lower body, plastic armament, Roadblasters $6–8

v.6 dark blue with black lower body, "5 GOAT RACING TEAM" $10–12

v.7 red with yellow and blue "TURBO Z" tampos, silver wheels $2–4

v.8 red with yellow blue "TURBO Z" tampos, New Superfast wheels $4–6

28-J T-Bird Turbo Coupe, 3", 1988 (see 59-H, 1988, also 61-F, 1988)

28-K Leyland Titan London Bus, 3", 1990 (see 17-F, 1982, reissued as 51-H, 1984)

28-L Corvette Convertible, 3", 1990 (see 14-I, 1983)

28-M Fork Lift Truck, 3", 1991 (also 61-H, reissue of 48-F Sambron Jack Lift 1977, see 48-F, 1977)

28-N Mitsubishi Spyder, 1995 (also 69-J, 1998)

v.1 metallic blue with pale green interior, light green accents on sides and hood $1–2

v.2 metallic blue with pale green interior, no markings $1–2

v.3 metallic blue with white interior, no markings $1–2

28-O Ford Crown Victoria Police Car, 1998 (see 54-K, 1997)

29-A Bedford Milk Delivery Van, 2¼", 1956 ....$45–60

29-B Austin A55 Cambridge, two-tone green, 2¾", 1961

v.1 gray wheels $35–45

v.2 silver wheels $20–30

v.3 black wheels $20–30

29-C Fire Pumper with regular wheels, 3", 1966

v.1 "Denver" decals $9–12

v.2 shield labels $9–12

v.3 no labels $8–10

29-D Fire Pumper with SF wheels, 3", 1970

v.1 no water gun cast $20–25

v.2 water gun cast $9–12

29-E Racing Mini, 2¼", 1970

v.1 metallic orange $12–15

v.2 orange $9–12

29-F Shovel Nose Tractor/Tractor Shovel, 2⅞", 1976 (reissued as 13-L, 1998)

v.1 light yellow with red shovel, chrome hubs $9–12

v.2 yellow with red shovel, black hubs $12–18

v.3 lime green with yellow shovel .$150–175

v.4 dark yellow with red shovel $4–8

v.5 dark yellow with maroon shovel ..$3–5

v.6 dark yellow with black shovel ...$4–6

v.7 dark orange with red shovel .$35–45

v.8 dark orange with black shovel ..$8–12

v.9 light orange with black shovel .$8–12

v.10 purple with black shovel, Macau cast $6–8

v.11 dark yellow with red shovel, Macau cast $3–5

v.12 yellow with black shovel, "THOMAE MUCOSOLVAN," Macau $18–24

v.13 light orange with black shovel, "THOMAE MUCOSOLVAN," Macau $25–30

v.14 blue with red shovel, Macau cast .$6–8

v.15 yellow with black shovel, "THOMAE MUCOSOLVAN," Thailand $30–40

v.16 blue with black shovel, "SPASMO MUCOSOLVAN" $10–15

29-G Helicopter, 1998 (see 75-F 1982)

30-A Ford Prefect Sedan, 2¼", 1956

v.1 light blue $100–125

v.2 gray-brown or olive brown ...$35–50

30-B Magirus Deutz 6-Wheel Crane Truck, 2⅝", 1961

v.1 tan with gray plastic wheels .$800–850

v.2 silver with silver plastic wheels $40–50

v.3 silver with gray plastic wheels $40–50

v.4 silver with black plastic wheels ..$30–40

30-C 8-Wheel Crane Truck with regular wheels, 3", 1965

v.1 mint green $900–1,000

v.2 dark green $5–10

30-D 8-Wheel Crane Truck with SF wheels, 3", 1970

v.1 red with orange boom $175–200

v.2 red with gold boom $20–25

30-E Beach Buggy, 2⅝", 1971

v.1 pink with white interior $20–25

v.2 pink with yellow interior $12–15

v.3 lavender with yellow interior .$12–18

30-F Swamp Rat airboat, 3", 1976

v.1 army green with tan hull, "SWAMP RAT" labels $4–6

v.2 army green with tan hull, camouflage, tan driver $4–6

v.3 army green with tan hull, camouflage, black driver $10–15

30-G Leyland Articulated Truck, 3", 1981

v.1 blue cab, metallic gray trailer, no markings $3–5

v.2 blue cab, metallic gray trailer, "INTERNATIONAL" tampos $5–7

v.3 red cab, metallic gray trailer ...$7–10

v.4 blue cab, yellow trailer, "INTERNATIONAL," England cast $7–10

v.5 blue cab, yellow trailer, "INTERNATIONAL," Macau cast $3–5

v.6 blue cab, blue trailer, "PAUL'S" tampos $30–40

30-H Peterbilt Quarry Truck, 3", 1982 (US, also 23-H rest of world 1982) v.1 yellow with gray dumper, "DIRTY DUMPER," England cast.........$4–6

v.2 yellow with gray dumper, "DIRTY DUMPER," Macau cast...........$2–4

v.3 yellow with gray dumper, "PACE," Macau cast.....................$2–4

v.4 yellow with gray dumper, "PACE," Thailand cast...................$2–4

v.5 orange with gray dumper, "LOSINGER," Macau cast ..$10–12

v.6 white with gray dumper, "CEMENT COMPANY," Manaus $30–40

v.7 yellow with red dumper, "PACE," INTERCOM CITY," China cast.$8–10

v.8 yellow with red dumper, "PACE CONSTRUCTION"...............$2–4

30-I Mercedes-Benz 280GE G-Wagon, 3", 1984

v.1 red with white roof, "RESCUE UNIT" and checkerboard pattern.......$3–5

v.2 orange with white roof, "LUFTHANSA" tampo............$3–5

v.3 white with white roof, "POLIZEI" and checkerboard pattern.............$4–6

v.4 army green with tan roof, "LS 2014" tampo, Commando................$4–6

v.5 white with orange roof, "AMBU-LANCE" and checkerboard pattern $3–5

v.6 white with white roof, "AUTO RES-CUE 24 HR. TOWING" $2–4

v.7 red with red roof, "FIRE METRO AIR-PORT" $8–10

v.8 dark blue with dark blue roof, "SWAT UNIT TEAM SUPPORT".......$8–10

v.9 white with green roof and doors, "POLIZEI" $4–7

v.10 white with white roof, "LUFTHANSA" tampo............$4–6

v.11 fluorescent orange with white roof, "AUTO RESCUE 24 HR. TOW-ING" $2–4

30-J Toyota Supra, 1995

v.1 white with red and yellow flames on sides and hood.....................$1–2

v.2 white with red and yellow flames on sides, not on hood.................$1–2

v.3 red with white and orange flames on sides, not on hood.................$1–2

30-K Chevy Tahoe Police, 1998, new

v.1 white with blue accents, Police mark-ings.....................$1–2

31-A Ford Customline Station Wagon, 2¾", 1957 (compare to 31-B, 1960)

v.1 yellow with metal wheels $35–45

v.2 yellow with gray plastic wheels.....................$40–50

31-B Ford Fairlane Station Wagon, 2¾", 1960 (compare to 31-A, 1957)

v.1 yellow, silver plastic wheels.....................$100–120

v.2 green with pink roof, silver plastic wheels.....................$40–50

v.3 green with pink roof, gray plastic wheels.....................$40–50

v.4 green with pink roof, black plastic wheels $100–120

31-C Lincoln Continental, black plastic wheels, 2¾", 1964

v.1 metallic blue.....................$8–12

v.2 mint green $6–10

v.3 metallic lime green.........$500–600

31-D Lincoln Continental with SF wheels, 2¾", 1969

v.1 mint green with Superfast wheels.................$1,700–2,000

v.2 green-gold $20–25

31-E Volks Dragon, 2½", 1971 (compare to 15-F Hi Ho Silver!, 1971).........$12–15

31-F Caravan Travel Trailer, 2¹¹⁄₁₆", 1977 ....$3–6

31-G Mazda Savannah RX-7 without spoiler, 3", 1979 (compare to 31-H, 1982)

v.1 white $3–6

v.2 black with gold stripes on sides..$4–6

v.3 black with gold striped hood and roof $3–5

v.4 black with "RX7" and "MAZDA" tampos, Manaus cast $20–30

v.5 blue, England cast $12–15

31-H Mazda Savannah RX-7 with spoiler, 3", 1982 (compare to 31-G, 1979)

v.1 black with gold stripe accents, Macau cast.....................$4–6

v.2 white with "7" and stripe accents, Macau cast.....................$3–5

v.3 black with "RX7" and "MAZDA" tampos, Manaus cast $25–30

31-I Rolls Royce Silver Cloud, 3", 1987 (rest of world; see 62-I, 1985 US)

31-J Rover Sterling, 2¹⁵⁄₁₆", 1988 (also 2-J, 1988)

v.1 metallic red with no markings....$3–5

v.2 metallic pearl gray with red, white, and blue stripes, Laser wheels ..$4–6

v.3 blue with yellow base, blue wheels, ho hood, Preschool.................$4–6

v.4 yellow with no markings $10–12

v.5 metallic gray with "ROVER STER-LING" tampos.....................$2–4

v.6 white with no markings, Graffic Traffic $6–8

31-K BMW 5-Series 535i, 3", 1990 (see 26-J, 1989)

31-L Nissan Prairie, 2⅞", 1991 (also 21-K, 1991)

v.1 metallic blue, silver side tampos.$3–5

v.2 metallic silver, "NISSAN" tampos.....................$3–5

v.3 white, no markings, Graffic Traffic $6–8

v.4 red, "NISSAN" tampos $4–6

31-M Jaguar XJ220, 3⅛", 1993

v.1 metallic silver (1993).............$3–5

v.2 metallic blue (1993)................$2–4

v.3 fluorescent yellow and orange with bright blue accents (1994).......$1–2

v.4 metallic purple with chrome windows, Goodyear tires, World Class ...$3–5

v.5 fluorescent orange with black accents (1996).....................$1–2

31-N '57 Chevy Bel Air Hardtop, new cast-ing, 1998 ....$2

32-A Jaguar XK140 Coupe, 2⅜", 1957

v.1 cream $40–50

v.2 red.....................$75–100

32-B Jaguar XKE, 2⅝", 1962

v.1 metallic red, clear windows, gray plastic wheels.....................$40–50

v.2 metallic red, green windows, gray plastic wheels.....................$30–40

v.3 metallic red, clear windows, black plastic wheels.....................$25–35

v.4 metallic bronze, clear windows, black wheels.....................$40–50

32-C Leyland Petrol Tanker with regular wheels, 3", 1968

v.1 green with "BP" labels, silver grille.....................$6–9

v.2 green with "BP" labels, white grille.....................$9–12

v.3 dark blue with "Aral" labels, silver grille.....................$40–50

32-D Leyland Petrol Tanker with SF wheels, 3", 1970

v.1 blue cab, white tank, "ARAL".....................$45–60

v.2 green cab, white tank, "BP" ...$12–15

v.3 red cab, white tank, "National Association of Matchbox Collec-tors".....................$250–300

v.4 purple cab, metallic gray tank, "National Association of Matchbox Collectors".....................$200–225

32-E Maserati Bora, 3", 1972

v.1 burgundy.....................$8–15

v.2 gold $12–18

32-F Field Gun, 3", 1978

v.1 dark green.....................$4–12

v.2 green.....................$30–35

32-G Atlas Excavator, 3", 1981 (reissued as 6-L, 1990)

v.1 orange with black deck, boom and scoop, England cast.............$7–10

v.2 orange with gray deck, boom and scoop, England cast.............$7–10

v.3 yellow with black deck, boom and scoop, England cast.............$2–4

v.4 yellow with black deck, boom and scoop, Macau cast.................$1–3

v.5 yellow with yellow deck, black boom and scoop, Macau cast........$8–10

v.6 yellow with black deck and boom, red scoop $1–3

v.7 red with white trim.................$1–3

v.8 bright green with black deck and boom, bright green scoop (1998).....................$1–2

32-H Modified Racer, 2¹⁵⁄₁₆", 1990 (see 12-K, 1989)

32-I Jaguar XK140 Coupe (replica of 32-A) Matchbox Originals, 2⅜", 1993 ...$3–5

32-J '62 Corvette, 2¹⁵⁄₁₆", 1994 (reissue of 71-G, 1982)
- v.1 blue with white and magenta accents on sides and hood (1994) $1–2
- v.2 blue with white and magenta accents on sides, not on hood (1996) ..$1–2

32-K '70 El Camino, 1998, new
- v.1 metallic gold with black accent stripes on hood.............................$1–2

33-A Ford Zodiac Mk II Sedan, 2⅝", 1957
- v.1 light blue or light blue-green, no windows, metal wheels...........$30–40
- v.2 dark green, no windows, metal wheels.................................$30–40
- v.3 dark green, no windows, gray plastic wheels.................................$40–50
- v.4 silver-gray and orange, no windows, gray plastic wheels.............$40–50
- v.5 tan and orange to light orange, no windows, gray plastic wheels......$40–50
- v.6 tan and orange with green windows, gray plastic wheels.............$40–50
- v.7 tan and orange with green windows, silver plastic wheels $40–50

33-B Ford Zephyr 6 Mk III Sedan, 2⅝", 1963
- v.1 gray plastic wheels $30–35
- v.2 silver plastic wheels $35–40
- v.3 black plastic wheels $60–70

33-C Lamborghini Miura with chrome or spoked hubs, 2¾", 1969
- v.1 yellow with ivory interior.......$60–75
- v.2 yellow with red interior............$6–9
- v.3 metallic gold with ivory interior $60–75

33-D Lamborghini Miura with SF wheels, 2¾", 1970
- v.1 yellow..............................$45–60
- v.2 metallic orange $15–20
- v.3 metallic gold $12–15

33-E Datsun 126X, 3", 1973
- v.1 yellow with orange base, no tampo.............................$8–12
- v.2 yellow with unpainted base, no tampo.............................$12–18
- v.3 yellow with orange base, orange and red flame tampo...........$12–18
- v.4 yellow with orange base, black and red flame tampo $12–18

33-F Police Motorcyclist, Honda CB750 with rider, 2½", 1977
- v.1 cream with "POLIZEI" label, wire wheels.............................$30–40
- v.2 white with "POLIZEI" label, wire wheels.............................$12–16
- v.3 white with "POLIZEI" label, mag wheels.............................$12–15
- v.4 white with "POLICE" label, wire wheels.............................$3–5
- v.5 white with "POLICE" label, mag wheels, white seat.................$3–5
- v.6 white with "POLICE" label, mag wheels, green seat $12–15
- v.7 white with "POLICE" label, mag wheels, black seat...............$8–10
- v.8 black with "L.A.P.D." label $8–10
- v.9 white with "4" label, mag wheels, red seat, no rider $12–15
- v.10 white with Japanese lettering tampo $8–10

33-G Volkswagen Golf GTi, 2⅞", 1986 (also 56-H, reissued as 63-J 1991)
- v.1 red $3–5
- v.2 white, "FEDERAL Express" $3–5
- v.3 white, "Quantum" $6–8
- v.4 dark gray $2–4
- v.5 yellow, "PTT" $9–12
- v.6 white, "ABSTRACT" and graphics..........................$3–5
- v.7 white, "LIPPISCHE LANDES-ZEITUNG" $15–20

33-H Renault 11 Alliance, 2¹⁵⁄₁₆", 1987 (see 43-J, 1987)

33-I Mercury Sable Wagon, 3", 1988 (see 55-L ,1988)

33-J Ford Utility Truck, 3", 1989 (see 74-I, 1987, also 9-L, 1998)

33-K '69 Camaro SS 396, 1998 (see 40-K, 1997)..........................$3

34-A Volkswagen Van, blue "MATCHBOX Express," 2¼", 1957
- v.1 metal wheels......................$45–55
- v.2 gray plastic wheels $55–65
- v.3 silver plastic wheels...........$80–100
- v.4 black plastic wheels........$125–150

34-B Volkswagen Caravette Camper, light green, 2¾", 1962
- v.1 gray plastic wheels $40–50
- v.2 black plastic wheels $40–50

34-C Volkswagen Camper, silver with raised 6-windowed roof, 2⅝", 1967.....$9–12

34-D Volkswagen Camper, silver with low windowless roof, 2⅝", 1968 ......$7–10

34-E Formula One Racing Car, 2⅞", 1971
- v.1 metallic pink with "16" label only.............................$12–18
- v.2 metallic pink with "16" and WYNN'S labels...............$35–45
- v.3 metallic blue with "15" label ...$12–15
- v.4 blue $12–15
- v.5 orange $9–12
- v.6 yellow..............................$9–12

34-F Vantastic, 2⅞", 1975
- v.1 orange with exposed engine, unpainted base.............................$8–12
- v.2 orange with exposed engine, white base....................................$4–6
- v.3 orange, no exposed engine, white base, "34" on hood $4–6
- v.4 orange, no exposed engine, white base, sunburst label...........$20–25
- v.5 orange, no exposed engine, white base, "JAFFAMOBILE" label $225–275
- v.6 orange, no exposed engine, white tab base, "34" label $18–24
- v.7 orange, no exposed engine, white tab base, "3" label............$65–80

34-G Chevy Pro Stocker, 3", 1981
- v.1 white with no markings........$12–16
- v.2 white with "34" tampo, metallic gray base................................$5–8
- v.3 white with "34" tampo, red base................................$12–16
- v.4 white with "34" tampo, unpainted base................................$5–8
- v.5 light orange with "4" and strip tampos.............................$2–4
- v.6 white with "PEPSI 14" tampo, red interior $3–5
- v.7 white with "PEPSI 14" tampo, black interior $60–70
- v.8 white "SUPERSTAR 217" tampos .$4–6
- v.9 black with "HALLEY'S COMET" tampos $6–8
- v.10 white and orange with "21," "355 CID" tampo.....................$4–6
- v.11 white with "7-Up" tampo, red interior $5–7
- v.12 white with "7-Up" tampo, black interior $60–70
- v.13 blue and white with "70 Bailey Excavating" tampo $4–6

34-H Toyman Dodge Challenger, 3", 1983 (see 1-J, 1983)

34-I Chevy Pro Stocker Halley's Comet Commemorative Car (variation of 34-G), 3", 1986 ....$6

34-J Ford RS200, 2⅞", 1987
- v.1 white with "7" tampos $1–3
- v.2 blue with "2" tampos...........$1–3
- v.3 white with no markings, Graffic Traffic series $6–8
- v.4 dark blue with no markings ..$10–12

34-K Sprint Racer, 2¹⁵⁄₁₆", 1990
- v.1 red, "ROLLIN THUNDER 2"......$2–4
- v.2 metallic blue, "ROLLIN THUNDER 2" $4–6
- v.3 metallic blue, "LUCKY 7," Action Pack $3–5
- v.4 red, "LUCKY 7" $2–4

(Note: All variations listed below were produced for Nutmeg Collectibles under license from Matchbox.)
- v.5 red, "WILLIAMS 5M" in blue letters..$5–7
- v.6 red, "WILLIAMS 5M" in white letters................................$5–7
- v.7 black, "TMC 1" $5–7
- v.8 white, "Maxim 11" $5–7
- v.9 white, "SCHNEE 8D" $5–7
- v.10 yellow, "BEN COOK & SONS 33X" $5–7
- v.11 blue, "BEN ALLEN 1A".........$5–7
- v.12 red, "JOE GAERTE 7" $5–7
- v.13 red, "GAMBLER 4" $5–7
- v.14 yellow, "F&G CLASSICS EAST 17" $5–7

v.15 yellow, "D. BLANEY/VIVARIN 7C" $5–7

v.16 light blue, "SCHNEE-D. KRIETZ 69" $5–7

v.17 black, "DOUG WOLFGANG 49" $5–7

34-L Plymouth Prowler, 1995 (also 18-I 1998)

v.1 purple with gray interior $2–5

34-M '33 Ford Street, Rod, 1998, new

v.1 metallic hot pink with accents....$1–2

35-A Marshall Horse Box Truck, red cab, brown horse box, 2", 1957

v.1 metal wheels....................$35–45

v.2 gray plastic wheels $40–50

v.3 silver plastic wheels..........$80–100

v.4 black plastic wheels.......$215–150

35-B Snow Trac Tractor, 2⅜", 1964

v.1 white treads, "Snow Trac" decals $20–25

v.2 white treads, plain sides $20–25

v.3 white treads, "Snow Trac" cast into sides $20–25

v.4 gray treads, "Snow Trac" cast into sides $30–40

35-C Merryweather Fire Engine (SF only), 3", 1969

v.1 metallic red....................$10–12

v.2 bright red $10–15

35-D Fandango, 3", 1975

v.1 white with "6" label $12–15

v.2 white with "35" label $8–12

v.3 red with "35" label (except with black base, blue fan)............$8–12

v.4 red with sunburst label $8–12

v.5 purple with "35" label.....$275–325

v.6 red with "35 label, black base, blue fan......................$30–45

35-E Volvo Zoo Truck (rare variation of 23-I), 3", 1981

v.1 red with blue cage................$6–8

v.2 red with gray cage, tan or brown lions $6–8

v.3 red with gray cage, white lions $12–16

v.4 orange with gray cage........$14–18

35-F Trans Am T-Roof, Pontiac, 3", 1982 (also 16-I, 1985)

v.1 black with firebird design on hood, "Turbo" tampos, England cast ...$4–6

v.2 black with firebird design on hood, "TRANS AM" tampos, Macau cast $2–4

v.3 black with tiger stripes, Macau cast $12–16

v.4 metallic silver with firebird design on hood, Macau cast.................$2–4

v.5 red with "3 ROOSTER RACING TEAM" tampo, Macau cast ...$9–12

35-G 4x4 Pickup Camper, 3", 1986 (see 57-H, 1982)

35-H Ford Bronco II, 3", 1989 (also 39-H, 1990, 51-N, 1998)

v.1 white with "BRONCO" and stripes .$2–4

v.2 white with "COAST GUARD BEACH PATROL" $2–4

v.3 metallic blue with white splash, orange "BRONCO 4X4" $2–4

v.4 dark brown with "BRONCO" and stripes $3–5

v.5 orange with "BRONCO" and stripes $3–5

v.6 yellow with red flames and "4X4" .$6–8

v.7 red with yellow tires, Preschool series $6–8

v.8 white with "POLICE PD-22," from 1995 5-Pack...................$2–4

v.9 black with orange piranha design, orange interior, orange "Piranha" on hood $2–3

v.10 silver with orange piranha design, blue interior $1–2

35-I Land Rover Ninety, 2½", 1990 (U.S.; 16-K rest of world 1990)

v.1 blue with white roof, yellow and orange stripes $2–4

v.2 yellow with white roof, "PARK RANGER" $2–4

v.3 green with white roof, yellow and orange stripes $2–4

v.4 red with white roof, blue and gray stripes, "COUNTRY" $2–4

v.5 white with white roof, black and red stripes, "COUNTRY" $2–4

v.6 white with white roof, no markings, Graffic Traffic....................$6–8

v.7 dark blue with white roof, "ROYAL NAVY" $3–5

v.8 black with gray roof, gray and yellow camouflage, Commando series $4–6

v.9 light gray and navy blue with light gray roof, red stripes $3–5

v.10 white with blue roof, "KLM" $4–6

v.11 white with blue roof, "SAS" $4–6

v.12 white with blue roof, "ALITALIA"..$4–6

v.13 whit with white roof, "BACARDI RUM" $12–15

v.14 red with white roof, "RED ARROWS/ROYAL AIR FORCE"..$3–5

v.15 white with white roof, "RESCUE POLICE," checkerboard pattern ...$2–4

v.16 white with white roof, "CIRCUS CIRCUS" $4–6

v.17 white with green roof, "GARDEN FESTIVAL WALES" $6–8

35-J Pontiac Stock Car, 3", 1993

v.1 yellow, "SEASIDE 15" (1993).....$2–4

v.2 yellow, "PRO AUTO 10" (1994)........................$2–4

v.3 black upper, blue lower, light blue interior, "7 OUTLAW" $1–2

35-K Mercedes GTC stock car, 1996

v.1 metallic cornflower blue with white and coral pink Rally accents.....$1–2

35-L '56 Ford Pick-Up, 1998, new

v.1 orange with chrome trim $1–2

36-A Austin A50 Sedan, blue-green, 2⅝", 1957

v.1 metal wheels....................$35–45

v.2 gray plastic wheels $35–45

36-B Lambretta TV175 Scooter & Sidecar, 2", 1961

v.1 metallic green, black wheels ..$60–75

36-C Opel Diplomat with regular wheels, 2⅞", 1966

v.1 metallic gold with gray motor..$8–10

v.2 metallic gold with chrome motor..$6–9

v.3 sea green with gray motor.$700–800

36-D Opel Diplomat with SF wheels, 2⅞", 1970 ....$15–20

36-E Hot Rod Draguar, 2¹³⁄₁₆", 1970 ....$15–20

36-F Formula 5000, 3", 1975

v.1 red with "5000" labels..........$7–10

v.2 orange with "5000" labels $7–10

v.3 red with "TEXACO" on hood..$8–12

v.4 white with "TEXACO" on hood........................$250–300

36-G Refuse Truck, 3", 1980 (also 7-M 1998)

v.1 red with yellow container, no "Colectomatic" on container.........$16–20

v.2 red with yellow container, "Colectomatic" on container $3–5

v.3 magenta with yellow container .$2–4

v.4 blue with orange container, "METRO" labels $3–5

v.5 white with blue container, "METRO" labels $2–4

v.6 white with blue container, Chinese lettering............................$10–12

v.7 white with blue container, no labels $2–4

v.8 green with yellow container, "STATE CITY" tampos $1–3

v.9 orange with gray container, "REFUSE DISPOSAL" tampos $1–3

v.10 green with yellow container, "REFUSE DISPOSAL" tampos....$1–3

v.11 red with yellow container, "REFUSE DISPOSAL" tampos.............$4–6

v.12 yellow with white container, "DISPOSAL UNIT" tampos $1–3

v.13 fluorescent pale orange with white container, no markings...........$1–2

v.14 orange-red with light gray container, black recycle logos (1996)......$1–2

v.15 orange with "Metro" on doors, recycle symbol on container (1998).$1-2

36-H '57 Chevy Bel Air Convertible, 1998, new

v.1 baby blue with pink and white accents $1–2

37-A Coca-Cola Lorry, 2¼", 1957 (compare to 37-B, 1957, 37-C, 1960)

v.1 no base, uneven cases......$75–100

37-B Coca-Cola Lorry, 2¼", 1957 (compare to 37-A, 1957, 37-C, 1960)

v.1 no base, even cases $60–75

37-C Coca-Cola Lorry, black base, even load, 2¼", 1960 (compare to 37-A, & 37-B, 1957)

v.1 gray plastic wheels $50–60
v.2 silver plastic wheels........$125–150
v.3 black plastic wheels $50–60

37-D Dodge Cattle Truck with regular wheels, 2½", 1966
v.1 metal base............................$6–9
v.2 plastic base $9–12

37-E Dodge Cattle Truck with SF wheels, 2½", 1970
v.1 gray box $12–15
v.2 silver-gray box....................$20–25

37-F Soopa Coopa, 2⅞", 1972
v.1 blue $12–15
v.2 pink with unpainted base, flower label $15–18
v.3 pink with red base, flower label............................$25–30
v.4 orange with "JAFFA MOBILE" label............................$90-100

37-G Atlas Skip Truck, 2¹¹⁄₁₆", 1976
v.1 red with yellow skip................$4–7
v.2 red with blue skip...............$75–100
v.3 orange with red skip $75–100
v.4 orange with yellow skip.......$75–90
v.5 blue with yellow skip............$4–6
v.6 dark blue with yellow skip .$175–200

37-H Sunburner Maserati Bora, 3", 1982
v.1 black with yellow and red flame tampos, England cast.................$4–6
v.2 black with yellow and red flame tampos, Macau cast....................$2–4
v.3 black with yellow and red flame tampos, Hong Kong cast.............$2–4

37-I Matra Rancho (European model), 2⅞", 1982
v.1 light blue $5–7
v.2 yellow $4–6
v.3 dark blue with "SURF RESCUE" tampos $5–7
v.4 dark blue with no markings $7–10
v.5 black with "SURF RESCUE" tampos $4–6
v.6 orange with "SURF 2" tampos ..$3–5
v.7 fluorescent yellow with "MARINE RESCUE" tampos.......................$2–4
v.8 white with no markings, Graffic Traffic (stickers included with set) $6–8

37-J Jeep 4x4 with roll cage and winch, 2⅞", 1984 (compare to 20-G, 1982)...$1–2

37-K Ford Escort XR3i Cabriolet, 2⅞", 1986 (see 17-I, 1985)

37-L Nissan 300ZX, 3", 1991 (see 61-G, 1990)

37-M Mercedes-Benz 600SL, 3", 1992 (see 38-J, 1992)

37-N '70 Boss Mustang, 1998, new
v.1 metallic purple with accents $1–2

38-A Karrier Refuse Truck, 2⅜", 1957
v.1 grayish brown with metal wheels........................$100–125
v.2 dark gray with metal wheels..$30–40
v.3 dark gray with gray plastic wheels..............................$30–40

v.4 silver with gray plastic wheels .$40–50

38-B Vauxhall Victor Estate Car, yellow, 2⅝", 1963
v.1 green interior, gray plastic wheels............................$30–35
v.2 green interior, silver plastic wheels............................$35–40
v.3 green interior, black plastic wheels............................$25–30
v.4 red interior, silver plastic wheels.$25–30
v.5 red interior, black plastic wheels............................$25–30

38-C Honda Motorcycle and Trailer with regular wheels, 2⅞", 1967
v.1 orange with no decals.........$20–25
v.2 orange with "Honda" decals .$30–35
v.3 yellow with "Honda" decals...$9–12

38-D Honda Motorcycle and Trailer with SF wheels, 2⅞", 1970
v.1 yellow trailer with blue motorcycle $12–15
v.2 yellow with purple motorcycle $15–20
v.3 yellow trailer with pink motorcycle $15–20
v.4 orange trailer with blue-green motorcycle $6–9
v.5 yellow trailer with blue-green motorcycle $6–9

38-E Stingeroo Cycle (3-wheel motorcycle), 3", 1973
v.1 purple with chrome handlebars $300–350
v.2 purple with purple handlebars $12–18
v.3 purple with blue-gray handlebars $15–20

38-F Jeep (with or without top), 2⅜", 1976
v.1 army green with star label, no gun or roof cast $12–18
v.2 olive drab with "21★11" label, no gun or roof cast $45–60
v.3 army green with "21★11" label, no gun or roof cast....................$8–12
v.4 army green with 21★11 label, gun cast $5–8
v.5 green.................................$120-140
v.6 yellow.................................$6–9
v.7 blue with white roof, "U.S. MAIL" tampo...................................$5–8
v.8 light blue with white roof, "U.S. MAIL" tampo $8–10

38-G Ford Camper Pickup Truck, 3", 1980
v.1 amber windows on camper, "35" on base $40–50
v.2 no windows on camper...........$4–6

38-H Ford Model A Truck, 3", 1982 (over 280 variations known, a representative sampling is listed below)
v.1 blue, "CHAMPION" $3–5
v.2 blue, "KELLOGGS" labels $8–10
v.3 blue, "MATCHBOX ON THE MOVE IN '84" $75–125

v.4 white, "PEPSI"........................$4–8
v.5 white, "MATCHBOX USA" ..$25–30
v.6 white, "BEN FRANKLIN" .$450–600
v.7 blue, "MATCHBOX SPEEDSHOP," nonchrome-lettered wheels $2–4
v.8 blue, "MATCHBOX SPEEDSHOP," chrome-lettered wheels $60–75
v.9 black, "2nd M.I.C.A. CONVENTION"...................$200–250
v.10 blue, "KELLOGGS RICE KRISPIES" $9–12
v.11 yellow, "MATCHBOX SERIES MODEL A Ford Van" $2–4
v.12 blue, "MATCHBOX 40TH ANNIVERSARY 1990" $8–10

38-I Ford Courier Delivery Van, 3", 1992 (European model)
v.1 light purple, "MILKA" tampos, side cast windows......................$2–4
v.2 white with "COURIER" tampos, side cast windows $12–15
v.3 dark blue, "MATCHBOX-THE IDEAL PREMIUM," side cast windows.............................$20–25
v.4 red, no markings, no side cast windows.............................$12–15

38-J Mercedes-Benz 600SL, 3", 1992 (also 37-M 1992)
v.1 metallic silver.......................$2–4

38-K Corvette Stingray III Convertible, 1994
v.1 metallic purple with white and magenta accents (1994) $1–2
v.2 white with red and yellow accents (1996) $1–2
v.3 red with white and blue accents (1997) $1–2

38-L Pontiac GTO "The Judge," 1998 (see 70-J 1996)

39-A Ford Zodiac Convertible, pink, 2⅝", 1957
v.1 tan interior and base, metal wheels..........................$100–125
v.2 turquoise interior and base, metal wheels............................$30–50
v.3 turquoise interior and base, gray plastic wheels...................$45–60
v.4 turquoise interior and base, silver plastic wheels...................$60–80

39-B Pontiac Convertible, 2¾", 1962
v.1 metallic lavender $80–100
v.2 yellow $30–40

39-C Ford Tractor, 2⅛", 1967 ....$9–12

39-D Clipper, concept car with opening cockpit, 3", 1973
v.1 metallic magenta $9–12
v.2 hot pink $50–75

39-E Rolls Royce Silver Shadow II, 3¹⁄₁₆", 1979
v.1 metallic silver-gray $4–6
v.2 metallic red $4–6
v.3 metallic tan $4–6

39-F Toyota Celica Supra, 3", 1982 (also 60-H)
v.1 white $2–4
v.2 red with "TWIN CAM 24" tampos $8–10

v.3 white with "SUPRA" tampos......$2–4
v.4 white with red, blue, and yellow tampos $9–12

39-G BMW 323i Cabriolet, 2¾", 1985
v.1 metallic silver blue with "323i" tampos $2–4
v.2 red with "323i" tampos $2–4
v.3 white with "BMW/323i" tampos $10–12
v.4 red with "GLIDING CLUB" tampos $3–5
v.5 white with "ALPINA" tampos ..$4–6
v.6 dark blue with "323i/BP" tampos $10–12
v.7 white with purple, orange, and blue tampos $2–4

39-H Ford Bronco II 4x4, 3", 1990 (see 35-H, 1989)

39-I Mack CH600, 3", 1990 (see 8-M, 1990)

39-J Mercedes-Benz 600SEL, 3", 1991
v.1 metallic silver $2–4

39-K '71 Camaro, 1998, new
v.1 metallic green with white stripes ..$1–2

40-A Bedford Tipper Truck, red with tan dumper, 2⅛", 1957
v.1 metal wheels.....................$30–45
v.2 gray plastic wheels $30–45
v.3 black plastic wheels $25–30

40-B Leyland Royal Tiger Coach, metallic blue, 3", 1961
v.1 gray wheels $35–45
v.2 silver wheels $25–35
v.3 black wheels $20–30

40-C Hay Trailer, 3¼", 1967 ....$6–9

40-D Vauxhall Guildsman, with SF wheels only, 3", 1971
v.1 pink $12–18
v.2 red $9–12

40-E Bedford Horse Box with two horses, 2¹³⁄₁₆", 1977
v.1 red with beige box, green windows..........................$16–20
v.2 red with light brown box, green windows..........................$8–12
v.3 orange with green windows.....$4–6
v.4 orange with clear windows ...$8–10
v.5 orange with purple windows ...$5–8
v.6 metallic green......................$5–8
v.7 yellow with light brown box......$6–8
v.8 dark orange with beige box.....$6–8
v.9 dark orange with light brown box $4–6
v.10 blue with yellow box, lime wheels with red hubs $6–9
v.11 blue with yellow box, lime wheels with blue hubs $16–20
v.12 red with dark tan box, "Manaus" cast on base $25–30
v.13 white with white box, "CIRCUS CIRCUS" tampo..................$5–7

40-F Corvette T-Roof, 3¹⁄₁₆", 1982 (also 62-G, 1982, reissued as 58-I, 1992, 74-L, 1998)

v.1 white with stripes, England cast.$3–5
v.2 white with stripes, Macau cast ..$2–4
v.3 blue with flame tampos, without "New Superfast" rear wheels ...$3–5
v.4 blue with flame tampos, with "New Superfast" rear wheels $30–40
v.5 yellow with "Corvette" tampo....$2–4
v.6 blue with stripes, Manaus cast .$30–40
v.7 orange with chrome windshield, World Class....................$4–6
v.8 red with "VETTE" and "CHEVY" logo, China cast $2–4
v.9 metallic blue with chrome windshield, World Class....................$4–6
v.10 black with chrome windshield, World Class....................$6–8
v.11 red with white strip, yellow "VETTE" (58-I, 1993)....................$2–4
v.12 metallic blue with white and red accents (58-I, 1994)..............$2–4
v.13 metallic dark gray, from 40th Anniversary set $2–4

40-G Ford Sierra XR4Ti, 3", 1983 (also 15-H, 1983, see 55-J 1983)

40-H NASA Rocket Transporter, 3", 1985 (also 60-J, 1990, variation of 65-H, 1986, 72-I, 1985)
v.1 white with "NASA" logo, U.S. flag $1–2
v.2 white with "NASA" logo and checkerboard tampos $1–2
v.3 black with gray camouflage, Commando $30–35
v.4 army green camouflage with army green missile (1996 5-Pack).....$2–4
v.5 army green with army green missile..........................$1–2

40-I Road Roller, 3", 1991 (reissue of 72-F Bomag Road Roller, 1979, see 72-F, 1979)

40-K '69 Camaro SS 396, 1997 (also 33-K, 1998)....................$1–2

40-L '68 Mustang Cobra Jet, 1998 (see 69-J, 1997)

41-A D-Type Jaguar, green, "41" decal, 2³⁄₁₆", 1957 (compare to 41-B, 1960)
v.1 metal wheels.....................$30–40
v.2 gray plastic wheels $40–50

41-B D-Type Jaguar, green, 2⁷⁄₁₆", 1960
v.1 gray plastic wheels, "41" decal....................$40–50
v.2 silver plastic wheels, "19" decal....................$125–150
v.3 black plastic tires on spoked hubs $40–50
v.4 black plastic tires on red hubs $175–200

41-C Ford GT (tires will separate from hubs), 2⅝", 1965
v.1 white with red wheels, "6" decal $100–120
v.2 white with yellow wheels, "6" decal..........................$8–12

v.3 white with yellow wheels, "9" decals $12–16
v.4 yellow with yellow wheels, "6" decals $60–80
v.5 white with yellow wheels, "6" label..........................$7–12
v.6 white with yellow wheels, "9" label..........................$7–12

41-D Ford GT with SF wheels, 2⅝", 1970
v.1 white $12–15
v.2 metallic orange $12–15
v.3 yellow $550–650

41-E Siva Spider, 3", 1972
v.1 red with silver trim $15–20
v.2 red with black trim $12–18
v.3 dark blue with black trim $15–20
v.4 light blue with black trim $15–20

41-F Chevrolet Ambulance, 2¹⁵⁄₁₆", 1978 (reissued as 25-J, 1983)
v.1 white, various markings, no tab on base.........................$4–6
v.2 white, "AMBULANCE" and cross labels, tab on base $25–30
v.3 metallic gray with "PARIS DAKAR 81" labels $20–25
v.4 red, "NOTARZT" tampos $6–8
v.5 white, "PACIFIC AMBULANCE" tampo..........................$6–8
v.6 red with gold and white trim, "FIRE RESCUE," from 1996 5-Pack...$2–3

41-G Kenworth Conventional Aerodyne, 2¾", 1982 (other variations exist as part of Convoy and White Rose Race Transporter series)
v.1 red with stripes, England cast....$2–4
v.2 black with stripes, England cast $3–5
v.3 metallic gray with red and blue stripes, Macau cast...............$2–4
v.4 blue, Macau cast..................$4–6

41-H Porsche 935, Racing Porsche, Super Porsche, 3", 1983 (see 55-I)

41-I Jaguar XJ6, 3", 1987 (also 1-K, 1987)
v.1 metallic red......................$2–4
v.2 black with "W&M" and crest tampos $30–35
v.3 green with "REDOXON/Jaguar" tampos $16–20
v.4 white with no markings, Graffic Traffic $6–8

41-J Opel Vectra/Chevrolet Cavalier, 3", 1991 (see 22-K, 1990)

41-K Sunburner, 3", 1992 (see 15-M, 1992)

41-L Cosmic Blues, 3", 1993 (reissue of 26-G, see 26-G, 1980)

41-M Stinger, 1998 (see 68-J, 1995)

42-A Bedford "EVENING NEWS" Van, yellow-orange, 2¼", 1957
v.1 metal wheels.....................$40–50
v.2 gray plastic wheels $40–50
v.3 black plastic wheels $40–50

42-B Studebaker Lark Wagonaire with hunter and 1 or 2 dogs, 3", 1965..........$12–16

42-C Iron Fairy Crane with regular wheels, 3",
1969 (compare to 42-D, 1970) $6–9
42-D Iron Fairy Crane with SF wheels, 3", 1970
   v.1 red with yellow boom $60–75
   v.2 red with lime green boom ..$90–100
   v.3 orange-red with yellow or lime green
     boom $30–45
42-E Tyre Fryer, 3", 1972
   v.1 blue..............................$12–18
   v.2 orange "JAFFA MOBILE" $80–100
42-F Mercedes-Benz Container Truck, 3",
1977
   v.1 red with beige container,
     "SEA/LAND" labels $5–7
   v.2 red with beige container, "N.Y.K."
     labels $5–7
   v.3 red with beige container, "O.C.L."
     labels $8–10
   v.4 yellow with yellow container,
     "DEUTSCHE BUNDESPOST" .$25–30
   v.5 red with beige container, "CON-
     FERN" labels $30–40
   v.6 red with white container, "MATCH-
     BOX" labels $8–10
   v.7 red with white container,
     "MAYFLOWER" labels $6–8
   v.8 red with white container, "CONFERN"
     over "MAYFLOWER" $16–20
   v.9 green with green container, "CON-
     FERN" over "MAYFLOWER" .$80–90
42-G 1957 T-Bird, 3", 1982
   v.1 red $4–6
   v.2 cream and red two-tone $3–5
   v.3 black $2–4
42-H Faun Mobile Crane, 3", 1985 (also
15-O, 1998)
   v.1 yellow with "REYNOLDS CRANE
     HIRE," England cast $2–4
   v.2 yellow with "REYNOLDS CRANE
     HIRE," Macau cast $2–4
   v.3 yellow with "REYNOLDS CRANE
     HIRE," China cast $2–4
   v.4 yellow with no markings, yellow plas-
     tic crane cab $2–4
   v.5 yellow, road and bridge design, red
     plastic crane cab....................$2–4
   v.6 yellow with fluorescent orange
     crane cab, "IC" and checkerboard
     pattern $8–10
   v.7 orange with black crane, light gray
     boom (1996) $1–2
42-I Rotwheeler, 1998 (see 73-L, 1995)
43-A Hillman Minx Sedan, 2⅝", 1958
   v.1 green with metal wheels ..$200–225
   v.2 blue-gray with gray roof, metal
     wheels $40–50
   v.3 blue-gray with gray roof, gray plastic
     wheels $40–50
   v.4 turquoise with cream roof, gray plas-
     tic wheels............................$30–40
43-B Aveling Barford Tractor Shovel, 2⅝", 1962
   v.1 yellow with yellow shovel, base and
     driver................................$40–50

   v.2 yellow with yellow shovel, red base
     and driver $25–35
   v.3 yellow with red shovel, yellow base
     and driver $25–35
   v.4 yellow with red shovel, base and dri-
     ver $40–50
43-C Pony Trailer with two horses and regular
wheels, 2⅝", 1968 ....$6–9
43-D Pony Trailer with two horses and SF
wheels, 2⅝", 1970
   v.1 yellow..............................$15–20
   v.2 orange..............................$6–9
   v.3 beige..............................$6–10
   v.4 white with blue-gray tailgate,
     "POLIZEI" $3–6
   v.5 white with lime green tailgate ...$2–4
   v.6 green with white roof, "POLIZEI" .$3–5
   v.7 white with red roof $3–5
43-E Dragon Wheels, 2¹³⁄₁₆", 1972 .$15–20
43-F 0-4-0 Steam Locomotive, England cast unless
noted, 3", 1978 (reissued as 63-J, 1992)
   v.1 red with "4345" labels............$3–5
   v.2 red with "NP" labels............$8–10
   v.3 metallic red with "4345"
     labels $125–140
   v.4 green with "4345" labels $8–10
   v.5 green with "NP" labels $6–8
   v.6 green with "British RAILWAYS"
     tampo, Macau cast $8–10
   v.7 red with "4345" labels Macau
     cast $3–5
   v.8 green with "4345" labels, Macau
     cast $3–5
   v.9 green with "WEST SOMERSET RAIL-
     WAY" tampo $6–8
   v.10 red with white "NORTH YORK-
     SHIRE MOORS RAILWAY,"
     Macau $6–8
   v.11 red with white and black
     "NORTH YORKSHIRE MOORS
     RAILWAY" $21–16
   v.12 yellow with "123/efg" tampo,
     China cast $5–7
   v.13 blue with "HUTCHINSON" tampo,
     Macau cast $6–8
   v.14 green with white emblem tampo,
     Macau cast....................$16–420
   v.15 dark green with "GWR" tampo,
     Macau cast $6–8
   v.16 black with "British RAILWAYS"
     tampo $9–12
   v.17 blue with red accents, Macau
     cast $5–7
   v.18 yellow with 123/456" tampo,
     China cast $2–4
   v.19 green with "British RAILWAYS,"
     China cast $2–4
   v.20 red with "4345" tampo, China
     cast $2–4
   v.21 green with Kellogg's rooster head
     tampo, China cast $40–50
   v.22 white with no markings, China cast
     (Graffic Traffic version)..........$7–10

43-G '57 Chevy Bel Air, 2¹⁵⁄₁₆", 1990
(reissue of 4-H, 1979, compare to 31-
N, 1998)
43-H Peterbilt Conventional, 2¾", 1982
(other variations exist as part of Convoy
and White Rose Race Transporter series)
   v.1 black ....$.2–4
   v.2 white with "NASA" tampos $2–4
43-I AMG Mercedes-Benz 500SEC, 2⅞",
1984
   v.1 black with "500SEC" tampos ...$2–4
   v.2 black with "REDEXON/500SEC"
     tampos $15–20
   v.3 black with "PACE CAR HEUER"
     tampo, "RESCUE 911," Siren
     Force $8–10
   v.4 black with "PACE CAR HEUER"
     tampo, Siren Force $6–8
   v.5 cream with "EMERGENCY DOC-
     TOR," "RESCUE 911," Siren
     Force $8–10
   v.6 cream with "EMERGENCY DOC-
     TOR," Siren Force $6–8
   v.7 red with "AMG" tampo, Macau
     cast $2–5
   v.8 red with green and yellow
     stripes $10–12
   v.9 metallic red with "AMG" tampos and
     stripes $3–5
   v.10 white with "AMG" tampo, blue inte-
     rior $2–4
   v.11 white with "AMG" tampo, black
     interior $6–8
   v.12 white with red and blue "7" tampos,
     without New Superfast wheels .$2–4
   v.13 white with red and blue "7" tampos,
     with New Superfast wheels .$35–45
   v.14 white with "1 PIG RACING
     TEAM"............................$10–12
   v.15 white with chrome windows, World
     Class $4–6
   v.16 white with red and blue stripes,
     "POLICE," RESCUE 911" tampos,
     Siren Force $8–10
   v.17 white with red and blue stripes,
     "POLICE," Siren Force............$6–8
43-J Renault 11 Turbo Alliance, 2¹⁵⁄₁₆", 1987
(also 33-H)
   v.1 black $2–4
43-K Lincoln Town Car, 3", 1989 (also 24-K,
1990)
   v.1 white with metal base............$2–4
   v.2 white with plastic base............$2–4
   v.3 black with chrome windows, white-
     wall tires, World Class $3–5
   v.4 metallic silver with pink and yellow
     accents, Dream Machines series...$2–4
   v.5 yellow with blue wheels, Preschool
     series $10–12
43-L Camaro Z-28, 1994
   v.1 black with white, magenta, and
     cyan stripes on sides and hood
     (1994)..............................$1–2

v.2 black with white, magenta, and cyan stripes on sides, not on hood (1995) $1–2

v.3 metallic gray with white, magenta, and cyan stripes on sides, not on hood (1996) $1–2

44-M Rhino Rod, 1998 (see 53-J, 1994)

44-A Rolls Royce Silver Cloud, metallic blue, 2⅝", 1958

v.1 metal wheels.....................$30–40

v.2 gray plastic wheels $40–50

v.3 silver plastic wheels............$40–50

44-B Rolls Royce Phantom V, 2⅞", 1964

v.1 metallic tan, gray plastic wheels $80–100

v.2 metallic tan, black plastic wheels $15–20

v.3 metallic gray, black plastic wheels $30–40

44-C GMC Refrigerator Truck with regular wheels, 3", 1967 ....$6–9

44-D GMC Refrigerator Truck with SF wheels, 3", 1970

v.1 red with turquoise container..$30–40

v.2 yellow with red container...$$20–25

v.3 yellow with turquoise container, black axle covers $1,750–2,000

44-E Boss Mustang, 2⅞", 1972

v.1 yellow..........................$5–8

v.2 dark green......................$7–10

44-F Railway Passenger Coach, England cast unless noted, 3¹⁄₁₆", 1978

v.1 red with "431 432" labels $3–6

v.2 red with "NYK" labels $75–80

v.3 red with "GWR" labels..........$8–10

v.4 red with "5810-6102" labels.$9–12

v.5 green with "431 432" labels.$8–10

v.6 green with "5810-6102" labels.$6–9

v.7 red with "431 432" tampos, Macau cast.................................$2–4

v.8 red with "431 432" tampo, China cast.................................$2–4

v.9 lime green yellow and red, China cast.................................$7–10

v.10 green with "British RAILWAYS" tampo, China cast.................$2–4

v.11 red with "Kellogg's" label, "431 432" tampo, China $15–18

v.12 white, China cast (Graffic Traffic) $7–10

44-G 4x4 Chevy Van, 2⅞", 1982 (reissue of 68-E, 1979, also reissued as 26-L, 1993)

v.1 metallic light green with "RIDIN' HIGH" tampos.................$3–5

v.2 metallic dark green, black horse-shoes, white "4x4" on hood $3–5

v.3 metallic dark green, white horse-shoes, black "4x4" on hood ..$8–10

v.4 metallic emerald green, black horse-shoes, white "4x4" on hood..$12–16

v.5 white with "MATCHBOX RACING" tampos $2–3

v.6 white with "TOKYO GIANTS" tampos $10–12

v.7 white with "CASTROL RACING TEAM" tampos $8–10

v.8 white with "MATCHBOX MOTOR-SPORTS" tampos (26-K, 1993) ..$2–4

v.9 white with no markings, Graffic Traffic (stickers included with set) $6–8

v.10 fluorescent yellow with red and blue graphics (26-K, 1993)............$2–3

v.11 black with pink and light green graphics $2–4

44-H Citroën 15CV (European model), 3", 1983

v.1 black with chrome base..........$2–4

v.2 black with gray base..............$4–6

44-I Skoda 130LR Rally (European model), 2⅞", 1988

v.1 white, "SKODA 44" $2–4

44-J 1921 Ford Model T Van, 2⅞", 1990

v.1 yellow with red roof, blue base, "BIRD'S CUSTARD POW-DER".................................$2–4

v.2 light blue with black roof, dark blue base, "GOODYEAR TIRE & RUBBER CO".................................$2–4

v.3 red with black hood and roof, "ROYAL MAIL GR" $8–10

v.4 cream, dark blue roof and base, "3RD MICA NA CONVENTION 1990" $8–10

v.5 cream with dark blue roof and base, "5TH MICA CONVENTION 1990" $8–10

v.6 black, "MICA NA CONVENTION/DETROIT MOTOR CITY" $10–12

v.7 white, light blue roof and base, "MICA 7/I COULD HAVE DANCED ALL NIGHT" $12–15

v.8 cream, dark blue roof, "GREETINGS FROM PHILADELPHIA 1992/MICA NA"................................$12–15

v.9 white, light blue roof and base, "PARA 90" $8–10

v.10 white, light blue roof, "CHESTER DOLL HOSPITAL/WORLD'S LARGEST MATCHBOX DISPLAY"..........$8–10

v.11 dark green with black roof, dark gray base, "SWARFEGA" ...$30–40

v.12 black, "MARS"................$10–12

v.13 red with red roof, black base, "MARS" $10–12

v.14 cream with red roof, green base, "PG TIPS".........................$18–21

v.15 white with red roof, dark blue base, "LLOYDS" $10–12

v.16 black, "WILLIAMS LUSTY" $6–8

44-K Ford Probe GT, 1994

v.1 metallic red with orange and yellow side accents (1994) $1–2

v.2 black with blue and pink accents (1995) $2–3

v.3 purple with green and white accents (1996) $1–2

44-L Volvo Container Truck, 1998 (see 23-I, 1985, also 20-H, 1985, 62-J, 1990)

45-A Vauxhall Victor Sedan, 2⅜", 1958

v.1 red with no windows, metal wheels..................$900–1,000

v.2 yellow with no windows, metal wheels............................$30–40

v.3 yellow with no windows, gray plastic wheels............................$30–40

v.4 yellow with green windows, gray plastic wheels $30–40

v.5 yellow with clear windows, gray plastic wheels $30–40

v.6 yellow with green windows, silver plastic wheels $40–50

v.7 yellow with green windows, black plastic wheels $20–30

45-B Ford Corsair with boat and rack on roof, 2⅝", 1965

v.1 gray wheels.....................$30–40

v.2 black wheels....................$12–16

45-C Ford Group 6 with SF wheels only, 3", 1970

v.1 dark green $90–100

v.2 metallic green $12–15

v.3 purple $9–12

45-D BMW 3.0 CSL, 2⅞", 1976

v.1 orange..............................$6–8

v.2 white with amber dome light, "POLIZEI" label $30–40

v.3 white with blue dome light, "POLIZEI" label $30–40

v.4 white with green tampo $60–70

v.5 white with "BMW" and "Manhalter" label..........................$40v50

v.6 red with "BMW" label $55–65

45-E Kenworth COE Aerodyne, 2¾", 1982 (other variations exist as part of Convoy series)

v.1 white with brown and blue stripes, England cast....................$3–5

v.2 white with brown and blue stripes, Macau cast.....................$2–4

v.3 metallic silver with purple and orange tampos $2–4

v.4 white with "CHEF BOYARDEE" labels $30–40

v.5 red with yellow, orange, and white stripes $2–4

45-F Ford Cargo Skip Truck, 2¹³⁄₁₆", 1988 (see 70-G, 1988)

45-G Chevrolet Highway Maintenance Truck, 3", 1990 (also 69-I, 1990)

v.1 yellow, yellow dumper & plow, "INTERNATIONAL AIRPORT AUTHORITY 45".................$2–4

v.2 yellow, red dumper and plow, "INTERNATIONAL AIRPORT AUTHORITY 45".................$2–4

v.3 red, gray dumper and plow, "ASPEN SNOW REMOVAL".............$2–4

v.4 dark orange, red dump & plow, "INTERNATIONAL AIRPORT AUTHORITY 45".................$2–4

v.5 white, blue dumper and plow, red "HIGHWAY DEPT." tampos (1995)..............................$1–2
45-H Tailgator, 1998 (see 27-J, 1994)
46-A Morris Minor 1000, 2", 1958
v.1 light tan with metal wheels.$700–900
v.2 dark green with metal wheels..........................$50–60
v.3 dark green with gray plastic wheels..........................$60–80
v.4 dark blue with gray plastic wheels........................$80–100
46-B Pickford Removal Van, plastic wheels, 2⅝", 1960
v.1 dark blue, "Pickford's Removers & Storers," gray wheels..........$60–75
v.2 dark blue, "Pickford's Removers & Storers," silver wheels $100–120
v.3 green, "Pickford's Removers & Storers," gray wheels..............$40–50
v.4 green, "Pickford's Removers & Storers," silver wheels..............$75–90
v.5 green, "Pickford's Removers & Storers," black wheels.............$20–25
v.6 tan, "Beales Bealson," sunburst, black wheels $300–325
46-C Mercedes-Benz 300SE with regular wheels, 2⅞", 1968
v.1 green.................................$9–12
v.2 metallic blue........................$7–10
46-D Mercedes-Benz 300SE with SF wheels, 2⅞", 1970
v.1 metallic blue $60–75
v.2 metallic orange $20–25
v.3 metallic gold $9–12
v.4 olive with "STAFF" labels....$80–100
v.5 metallic silver-gray..............$20–25
46-E Stretcha Fetcha, Ambulance, 2¾", 1972
v.1 white $12–18
v.2 red, "UNFALL RETTUNG" label.............................$35–50
v.3 bright green, "VIPER Van".....$12–18
46-F Ford Tractor, 2³⁄₁₆", 1978
v.1 blue $2–5
v.2 green $4–6
v.3 dark blue..........................$40–50
v.4 yellow $2–4
46-G Hot Chocolate Volkswagen Beetle, 2¹³⁄₁₆", 1982
v.1 black with metallic brown sides.$4–6
v.2 metallic blue..........................$3–5
46-H Big Blue Volkswagen Beetle, 2¹³⁄₁₆", 1983.......................................$3–5
46-I Mission Chopper with retractable tail, 3", 1985 (see 57-I, 1985, also 49-L, 1998)
v.1 dark blue with metallic gray base and skids, orange tampos.............$1–3
v.2 dark blue with metallic gray base and skids, bullseye tampos............$1–3
v.3 red with white base and skids, "SHERIFF/AIR 1" tampos.........$1–3
v.4 army green with tan base and skids, Skybusters SB-12-C 1992 ....$1–3
v.5 army green with black base and skids, "AC15," Commando.....$4–6
v.6 black with gray base and skids, "AC99" Commando $4–6
v.7 red with white base and skids, "REBELS/RESCUE/AIR 1" $2–4
v.8 white with blue base and skids, "POLICE" and crest................$1–3
v.9 green with white base and skids, "POLIZEI" tampos $2–4
v.10 black with white base and skids, "POLICE" tampos $2–4
v.11 tan with brown camouflage (1993)..............................$1–3
v.12 green with brown and black camouflage (1996 5-Pack) $2–4
v.13 army green, "AT-7521" (1996)..............................$1–2
46-J Mercedes Sauber Group C Racer, 3", 1985 (also 66-H, 1985)
v.1 red with black airfoil, "BASF CASSETTES" tampo $4–6
v.2 white with black airfoil, "JR. COLLECTORS CLUB" $8–10
v.3 white with black airfoil, "CASTROL SAUBER 61" $2–4
v.4 yellow with blue airfoil, orange and blue accents $3–5
v.5 black with black airfoil, "CARGANTUA"................................$8–10
v.6 pale red with armaments, no airfoil, Roadblasters.........................$3–5
v.7 white and orange with orange airfoil, "BISOTHERM/BAUSTEIN"..$10–12
v.8 red with red foil, "ROYAL MAIL SWIFTAIR" $5–7
v.9 pale blue with black foil, "GRAND PRIX 46" $4–6
v.10 white with black airfoil, "GRAND PRIX 46" $2–4
v.11 chrome with black airfoil, no markings................................$15–20
v.12 fluorescent pink and blue with blue airfoil, Lightning......................$4–6
v.13 fluorescent orange and yellow with fluorescent yellow airfoil, Lightning $4–6
v.14 blue and fluorescent pink with blue foil, Lightning $4–6
v.15 "MATCHBOX USA 11TH ANNUAL CONVENTION & TOY SHOW 1992" $12–15
46-K '97 Chevy Tahoe, 1998, new
v.1 metallic red with white accents..$1–2
47-A Trojan 1-Ton "BROOKE BOND TEA" Van, red, 2¼", 1958
v.1 metal wheels.....................$30–40
v.2 gray plastic wheels $40–50
47-B Commer Ice Cream Canteen, 2⁷⁄₁₆", 1963
v.1 blue with gray plastic wheels.......................$150–175
v.2 blue with black plastic wheels..$30–35
v.3 metallic blue with black plastic wheels......................$100–120
v.4 cream with square roof decal, striped side decals, black wheels....$60–70
v.5 cream with oval roof decal, plain side decals, black plastic wheels.$40–50
47-C DAF Tipper Container Truck with regular wheels, 3", 1968
v.1 blue with yellow container, gray container cover $25–30
v.2 silver with yellow container, gray container cover $6–9
47-D DAF Tipper Container Truck with SF wheels, 3", 1970...................$20–25
47-E Beach Hopper (Rolamatic), 2⅝", 1974 ....$12–18
47-F Pannier Tank Locomotive, 3", 1979 .$4–6
47-G Jaguar SS100, 3", 1982
v.1 red with partially painted hood, England cast.............................$7–9
v.2 red with red hood, England cast.$3–5
v.3 red with red hood, Macau cast.................................$2–4
v.4 blue, Macau cast....................$3–5
v.5 blue with gray hood $2–4
v.6 dark green, Thailand cast.......$9–11
47-H School Bus, 3", 1985 (also 12-O, 1998)
v.1 yellow, "SCHOOL DISTRICT 2" .$1–2
v.2 army green, "GOVT PROPERTY".........................$10–12
v.3 yellow, "SCHOOL DISTRICT 2," "CHEF BOYARDEE" $8–10
v.4 orange-yellow, "1+2=3/abc," Preschool $6–8
v.5 orange-yellow, "ST. PAUL PUBLIC SCHOOLS" $55–60
v.6 blue, "POLICE 88".................$3–5
v.7 blue, "HOFSTRA UNIVERSITY".$10–12
v.8 yellow, "HARVEY WORLD TRAVEL" $6–8
v.9 orange, "SCHOOL DISTRICT 2"..$4–6
v.10 white and dark blue, "PENN STATE/THE LOOP"...............$6–8
v.11 bright pink, 1994 Collectors Choice from White Rose Collectibles..............................$5–7
47-I M2 Bradley Tank, 1998, new
v.1 khaki with black star on front and sides $1–2
48-A Meteor Sports Boat and Trailer, tan deck, blue hull, 2⅜", 1958 (compare to 48-B, 1961)
v.1 metal wheels.....................$40–50
v.2 gray plastic wheels $60–80
v.3 silver plastic wheels...........$80–100
48-B Sports Boat & Trailer with outboard motor, 2⅝", 1961
v.1 gray wheels.......................$60–75
v.2 black wheels......................$30–40
48-C Dodge Dump Truck with regular wheels, 3", 1966 ....$6–9
48-D Dodge Dump Truck with SF wheels, 3", 1970

v.1 blue cab, yellow dumper.....$15–20

v.2 metallic blue cab, yellow dumper.....................$15–20

48-E Pi-Eyed Piper, 2⅞", 1972 (compare to 26-E Big Banger, 1972, and 26-G, Cosmic Blues, 1980)

v.1 blue.........................$12–18

v.2 red, "BIG BANGER" decals, blue windows.....................$80–100

48-F Sambron Jack Lift, 3¹⁄₁₆", 1977 (reissued as Fork Lift Truck 28-M, 1991, 61-H, 1992)

v.1 yellow, no tampo.................$4–7

v.2 yellow, "SAMBRON" tampo .$175–200

v.3 lime green with red and white stripes (1991).....................$2–4

v.4 white with red stripes (1993).....................$3–5

v.5 bright green with red and white stripes (1994).....................$2–4

v.6 orange-yellow with red stripes (1994).....................$3–5

48-G Red Rider (variation of 48-E Pi-Eyed Piper, 1972), 2⅞", 1982

v.1 red, England cast..................$4–6

v.2 red, Hong Kong cast.............$4–6

v.3 red, Macau cast...................$2–4

v.4 red, China cast $2–4

48-H Mercedes-Benz Unimog with snow-plow, 3", 1984

v.1 yellow with "RESCUE" tampo ...$3–5

v.2 red with "UR83" tampo $3–5

v.3 white with red and blue tampos, plastic armament, Roadblasters $4–6

v.4 white with "C&S" tampos........$3–5

48-I Vauxhall Astra GTE (European model), 2¾", 1987

v.1 red with "GTE" and stripes $2–4

v.2 white with "AC DELCO 48," silver wheels.....................$2–4

v.3 white with "AC DELCO 48," white wheels.....................$3–5

v.4 white with "STP/SPHERE DRAKE" tampos.....................$2–4

v.5 yellow with "MOBILE PHONE/TELE-COM" tampos $3–5

v.6 yellow with no markings $10–12

v.7 black with "BP 52," "7," yellow stripe.....................$10–12

48-J Pontiac Firebird Racer S/E, 3", 1993 (also 12-I, 1982, 12-J, 1986, 51-I, 1984, 60-G, 1984)

v.1 black with hot pink and bright blue accents.....................$2–4

v.2 hot pink with fluorescent yellow accents on sides and hood (1994).....................$1–2

v.3 hot pink with fluorescent yellow accents on sides, not on hood (1996) $1–2

48-K '56 Ford Pickup, 1997.............$1–2

48-L Hummer, 1998 (see 3-G, 1994)

49-A M3 Army Halftrack Personnel Carrier, 2½", 1958

v.1 metal front wheels and rollers..$40–50

v.2 gray plastic front wheels, metal rollers $45–60

v.3 gray plastic front wheels and rollers $90–100

v.4 gray plastic front wheels, silver plastic rollers $70–80

v.5 black plastic front wheels and rollers $30–40

49-B Mercedes-Benz Unimog with regular wheels, 2½", 1967

v.1 tan with turquoise chassis $9–12

v.2 blue with red chassis $7–10

49-C Mercedes-Benz Unimog with SF wheels, 2½", 1970

v.1 blue.........................$15–20

v.2 metallic light blue $15–20

v.3 olive with star label $60–75

v.4 olive with "A" label $7–10

49-D Chop Suey Motorcycle, 2¾", 1973

v.1 magenta with silver handle-bars $275–325

v.2 magenta with orange handle-bars $15–20

v.3 magenta with red handle-bars $12–15

v.4 magenta with black handle-bars $15–20

v.5 magenta with dark red handle-bars $12–18

49-E Crane Truck, 2¹⁵⁄₁₆", 1976

v.1 yellow..............................$5–10

v.2 red $65–75

49-F Sand Digger Volkswagen Beetle, 2¹³⁄₁₆", 1983

v.1 metallic green, "SAND DIGGER" $3–5

v.2 red, "DUNE MAN" $4–6

49-G Dune Man Volkswagen Beetle, 2¹³⁄₁₆", 1984.....................$4–6

49-H Peugeot Quasar, 2¾", 1987 (rest of world, see 25-L, 1987 US)

49-I Lamborghini Diablo, 3", 1992 (see 22-L, 1992)

49-J BMW 850i, 3", 1993

v.1 metallic silver $2–4

v.2 white, no markings $3–5

v.3 maroon with pink and yellow streak tampos (1994) $1–2

v.4 silver with chrome windows, World Class.....................$3–5

v.5 red with "RIPPER" on sides, skull and crossbones on hood (1995) $1–2

v.6 red with "RIPPER" on sides, no markings on hood (1996) $1–2

49-K VW Concept 1, 1996 (also 17-L, 1998)

v.1 red with black roof $3–4

v.2 green with black roof.............$2–3

49-L Mission Chopper, 1998 (see 46-I, also 57-I, 1985)

50-A Commer Pickup, 2½", 1958

v.1 dark tan with metal wheels ...$40–50

v.2 light tan with metal wheels ...$40–50

v.3 light tan with gray plastic wheels.....................$40–50

v.4 dark tan with gray plastic wheels.....................$40–50

v.5 dark tan with silver plastic wheels.....................$80–100

v.6 red & white with silver plastic wheels.....................$275–300

v.7 red & gray with silver plastic wheels.....................$80–100

v.8 red & gray with gray plastic wheels.....................$60–80

v.9 red & gray with black plastic wheels.....................$60–80

50-B John Deere Tractor, 2⅛", 1964

v.1 gray plastic tires.................$25–30

v.2 black plastic tires $20–25

50-C Ford Kennel Truck with four dogs and regular wheels, 2¾", 1969 ....$6–9

50-D Ford Kennel Truck with four dogs and SF wheels, 2¾", 1970 ....$15–20

50-E Articulated Truck with removable trailer, 3¹⁄₁₆", 1973

v.1 orange-yellow cab and trailer, light blue trailer $4–6

v.2 yellow cab, light blue trailer, yellow trailer base $4–6

v.3 yellow cab, dark blue trailer, yellow trailer base with tow hook $80–100

v.4 red cab, blue trailer, blue trailer base.....................$25–40

v.5 red cab, silver-gray trailer, red trailer base $9–12

50-F Articulated Trailer, 3", 1980 (goes with 50-E Articulated Truck)

v.1 blue container, yellow trailer base (from Two Pack) $4–6

v.2 metallic gray container, red trailer base (from Two Pack).............$7–9

50-G Harley Davidson Motorcycle, 2¹¹⁄₁₆", 1980.....................$4–6

50-H Chevy Blazer 4x4 Police, 3", 1985 (also 22-N, 1998)

v.1 white with "SHERIFF 7" tampos, Macau cast $2–4

v.2 white with "SHERIFF 7" tampos, Thailand cast $2–4

v.3 white with "SHERIFF 7" tampos, Manaus cast $50–60

v.4 purple with orange, red and black tampos, Roadblasters.............$4–6

v.5 blue with black and white accents, orange "50" on roof, blue windows $1–2

v.6 blue with black and white accents, orange "50" on roof, red windows $1–2

50-I Dodge Dakota Pickup, 3", 1989 (also 17-J, 1990)

v.1 bright red with black and white stripes ....$2–4 v.2 bright red with "DAKOTA ST," black and white stripes $2–4

v.3 dark red with "DAKOTA ST," black and white stripes $2–4

v.4 metallic green with "MB CONSTRUCTION," Action Pack $4–6

v.5 white with no markings, Graffic Traffic $6–8

v.6 blue with "DAKOTA ST" and stripes $4–6

v.7 fluorescent orange, "FIRE CHIEF 1/INTERCOM CITY" $8–10

50-J Mack Floodlight Heavy Rescue Auxiliary Power Truck, 3", 1991 (see 57-K, 1991, also 21-M, 1998)

50-K '97 Ford F-150, 1998, new (compare to 65-J, 1995)

v.1 red $1–2

51-A Albion Chieftain Flatbed Transporter, "PORTLAND CEMENT," 2½", 1958

v.1 metal wheels $30–40

v.2 gray plastic wheels $30–40

v.3 silver plastic wheels $60–80

v.4 black plastic wheels $80–100

51-B John Deere Trailer with three barrels, 2⅝", 1964

v.1 gray plastic tires $25–30

v.2 black plastic tires $20–25

51-C AEC Ergomatic 8-Wheel Tipper with regular wheels, 3", 1969

v.1 white grille, "Douglas" $20–25

v.2 silver grille, "Douglas" $12–15

v.3 silver grille, "Pointer" $9–12

51-D AEC Ergomatic 8-Wheel Tipper with SF wheels, 3", 1970 .... $15–20

51-E Citroën SM, 3", 1972

v.1 metallic orange with orange interior $20–25

v.2 metallic orange with cream interior $8–12

v.3 metallic orange with yellow interior $8–12

v.4 metallic orange with tan interior $8–12

v.5 metallic blue, no markings $15–20

v.6 metallic blue, "8" tampo $8–15

v.7 metallic blue with roof rack $35–50

51-F Combine Harvester, 2¾", 1978

v.1 red $5–7

v.2 dark green $275–325

v.3 yellow $4–7

v.4 lime green and blue $7–10

51-G Midnight Magic (variation of 53-E Tanzara), 3", 1982

v.1 black with silver sides, England cast $3–5

v.2 black with silver sides, Macau cast $2–4

v.3 black with silver sides, Hong Kong cast $2–4

51-H Leyland Titan London Bus, 3", 1984 (see 17-G, 1982, reissued as 28-K, 1990)

51-I Pontiac Firebird S/E, 3", 1984 (also 12-I, 1982, 48-J, 1993, see 60-G, 1984)

51-J Camaro IROC Z, 3", 1985 (also 68-G, 1987)

v.1 green with "IROC Z" $6–8

v.2 blue with "IROC Z" on sides only $3–5

v.3 blue with "IROC Z" on sides and hood $3–5

v.4 red with "CARTER/GOODYEAR" . $4–6

v.5 metallic red with "CARTER/ GOODYEAR" $4–6

v.6 yellow with "IROC Z" $2–4

v.7 metallic orange with "CARTER/GOODYEAR" $4–6

v.8 green with "BP STUNT TEAM" and stripes $10–12

v.9 black with "Z28," red accents .. $2–4

v.10 black with "Z28," orange accents $2–4

51-K Ford LTD Police, 3", 1988 (also 16-J, 1990)

v.1 white with black accents, "POLICE PD-21" $1–2

v.2 white with blue accents, "POLICE PD-21" $1–2

v.3 purple, "POLICE PD-21" $3–5

v.4 red, "POLICE PD-21" $3–5

v.5 red, "FIRE DEPT/FIRE CHIEF" $2–4

v.6 white, "policeman caricature, Matchbox Preschool $6–8

v.7 white with no markings, Graffic Traffic $4–6

v.8 dark blue, "POLICE R-25" $3–5

v.9 white, "POLICE PD-21," "INTERCOM CITY" $8–10

v.10 bright blue with yellow accent stripe on sides, "STATE POLICE" (1996) $1–2

v.11 metallic blue with yellow accent stripe on sides, "STATE POLICE" (1996) $1–2

51-L Porsche 959, 2⅞", 1994 (reissue of 7-J 1987)

v.1 hot pink with "RAGE" on doors, accent on hood and roof $1–2

51-M Ford Ambulance, 1997 (also 25-N, 1998) $1–2

51-N Ford Bronco II, 1998 (see 35-H 1989, also 39-H, 1990)

52-A Maserati 4CL T/1948 Racer, 2½", 1958

v.1 red with black plastic wheels . $50–70

v.2 red with black plastic tires on spoked wheels $100–125

v.3 yellow with black tires on spoked wheels $60–80

52-B BRM Racing Car with black tires on plastic hubs, 2⅝", 1965

v.1 blue with "5" decal or label ... $8–12

v.2 blue with "3" decal $40–50

v.3 red with "5 decal or label $20–25

52-C Dodge Charger Mk III concept car (SF only), 2⅞", 1970

v.1 metallic magenta with metallic green base $7–10

v.2 metallic red with metallic green base $7–10

v.3 metallic light green with red base, "CASTROL" label $300–350

v.4 metallic light green with red base, no label $12–15

52-D Police Launch Boat, 3", 1976

v.1 white deck, blue hull with no tab, light blue figures $5–7

v.2 white deck, blue hull with tab, light blue figures $30–40

v.3 white deck, red hull, orange-yellow figures $7–9

v.4 white deck, red hull, light blue figures $12–15

v.5 black deck, dark gray hull and figures $5–7

v.6 white deck, blue hull, red figures . $6–8

v.7 white deck and hull, white figures $6–8

52-E BMW M1 with opening hood, 3", 1981

v.1 metallic gray with "52" tampo, clear windows $4–6

v.2 metallic gray with "52" tampo, smoke windows $4–6

v.3 metallic gray with "52" tampo, amber windows $9–12

v.4 metallic gray with "52" tampo, green windows $70–80

52-F BMW M1, hood doesn't open, 3", 1982 (compare to 52-E, 1981)

v.1 white with "BMW M1" $2–4

v.2 black with "Pirelli 59" $3–5

v.3 yellow with "11" and stripes $2–4

v.4 red with "1" and stripes $2–4

v.5 dark yellow with chrome windows, World Class $4–6

v.6 chrome plated $12–18

52-G Isuzu Amigo, 2⅞", 1991

v.1 metallic blue, "ISUZU AMIGO" tampos $4–6

v.2 light yellow, pink stripes and patterns $3–5

v.3 red, "AMIGO," silver and orange stripes $3–5

52-H Escort Cosworth, 1994

v.1 white with Rally accents, "Mobil 1" $1–2

52-I Jeep 4X4, 1998 (see 20-F, 1982, also 14-K, 1987)

53-A Aston Martin DB2 Saloon, 2¹⁵⁄₁₆", 1958

v.1 metallic light green with metal wheels $35–45

v.2 metallic light green with gray plastic wheels $30–40

v.3 metallic red with gray plastic wheels $130–150

v.4 metallic red with black plastic wheels $80–100

53-B Mercedes-Benz 220 SE, 2¾", 1963
  v.1 maroon with gray plastic wheels $25–30
  v.2 red with gray plastic wheels .$25–30
  v.3 maroon with silver plastic wheels $30–35
  v.4 maroon with black plastic wheels $25–30
  v.5 red with black plastic wheels $100–120
53-C Ford Zodiac Mk IV Sedan with regular wheels, 2¾", 1968

v.1 metallic silver blue.............................$6–9

  v.2 light metallic green..........$500–600
53-D Ford Zodiac Mk IV Sedan with SF wheels, 2¾", 1970
  v.1 metallic light blue............$300–350
  v.2 metallic green $20–25
  v.3 lime green $20–25
53-E Tanzara, 3", 1972
  v.1 orange with chrome interior..$12–15
  v.2 white with chrome interior $15–20
  v.3 white with red interior $20–25
53-F Jeep CJ6, 2¹⁵⁄₁₆", 1977 ....$3–7
53-G Flareside Pickup, 2⅞", 1982 (also 55-O, 1998)
  v.1 metallic blue with "326 BAJA BOUNCER" tampo $4–6
  v.2 orange with "326 BAJA BOUNCER" tampo.....................$2–4
  v.3 yellow with white interior, 8-spoke wheels $100–120
  v.4 yellow with black interior, 8-spoke wheels $35–40
  v.5 yellow with black interior, racing slicks $2–4
  v.6 khaki green with purple and blue design, racing slicks...............$5–7
  v.7 white with "DEB" tampo, racing slicks $30–35
  v.8 red with "326 BAJA BOUNCER" tampo, 8-spoke wheels $25–30
  v.9 lime green $6–8
  v.10 red with "BILL ELLIOTT 11" tampo, racing slicks.....................$6–8
  v.11 red with yellow flames, racing slicks (1994) $2–4
  v.12 red with yellow and orange flames on hood..........................$2–4
  v.13 fluorescent orange with black front end $2–4
53-H Faun Dump Truck, 2¾", 1989 (also 9-K, 1989, reissue of 58-F, 1976, see 58-F, 1976 for variations)

53-I Ford LTD Taxi, 3", 1992 (also 56-I, 1992)
  v.1 yellow with "RADIO XYZ CAB" and checkerboard pattern $3–5
53-J Rhino Rod, 1994 (also 43-M, 1998)
  v.1 gray....................................$1–2
  v.2 white $1–2
  v.3 black $1–2
53-K Ford F-150 4X4 1998 (see 65-J, 1995)
54-A Army Saracen Personnel Carrier, 2¼", 1958

v.1 black plastic wheels $20–35

54-B Cadillac S&S Ambulance, with regular wheels, 2⅝", 1965 ....$8–12
54-C Cadillac S&S Ambulance, with SF wheels, 2⅞", 1970 ....$20–25
54-D Ford Capri, 3", 1971 ....$9–15
54-E Personnel Carrier, 3", 1976........$5–8
54-F Motor Home, 3¼", 1980 (compare to 54-G, 1982, 54-H, 1985)
  v.1 beige...............................$4–7
54-G NASA Tracking Vehicle (variation of 54-F, 1980), 3¼", 1982
  v.1 white $3–5
54-H Airport Foam Pumper (variation of 54-F, 1980), 3¼", 1985
  v.1 red with white roof, "FOAM UNIT" and checkerboard..............$10–12
  v.2 yellow with "FOAM UNIT/METRO AIRPORT" $2–4
  v.3 red with "FOAM UNIT/METRO AIRPORT" $2–4
54-I Chevrolet Lumina Stock Car, 3", 1990 (Days of Thunder, White Rose Collectibles, and Hot Stocks comprise the majority of variations of this model, as indicated below.)
Days of Thunder variations:
  v.1 dark blue, "MATCHBOX MOTORSPORTS 35"........$2–4
  v.2 fluorescent green, "MATCHBOX MOTORSPORTS 35".......$2–4
  v.3 white with no markings, Graffic Traffic $6–8
  v.4 pink and white, "SUPERFLO 46," Macau cast $6–8
  v.5 pink and white, "SUPERFLO 46," China cast.......................$3–5
  v.6 green and lime, "CITY Chevrolet 46," Macau cast..............$6–8
  v.7 green and lime, "CITY Chevrolet 46," China cast $3–5
  v.8 bright orange and blue, "HARDEES 18," Macau cast $6–8
  v.9 bright orange and blue, "HARDEES 18," China cast $3–5

  v.10 black, "EXXON 51," with signature, Macau cast...........$6–8
  v.11 black, "EXXON 51," with signature, China cast $3–5
  v.12 black, "EXXON 51," without signature, Macau cast...$30–35
  v.13 black, "MELLO YELLO 51," Macau cast $6–8
  v.14 black, "MELLO YELLO 51," China cast.....................$3–5
White Rose Collectibles variations:
  v.15 black, "GOODWRENCH 3/GM," no trunk tampo, no "WESTERN STEER" $12–15
  v.16 black, "GOODWRENCH 3/GM," trunk tampo, no "WESTERN STEER" $8–10
  v.17 black, "GOODWRENCH 3/GM,"trunk tampo, "WESTERN STEER," Goodyear slicks $5–7
  v.18 black, "GOODWRENCH 3/GM," trunk tampo, "WESTERN STEER," rubber tires.$45–60
  v.19 orange-yellow, "KODAK FILM 4 RACING," rubber tires.......$5–7
  v.20 orange-yellow, "KODAK FILM 4 RACING," Goodyear slicks.$4–6
  v.21 yellow, "MAC TOOL DISTRIBUTORS 10" $16–20
  v.22 yellow, "MAC TOOLS 10".$8–10
  v.23 fluorescent orange and white, "PUROLATOR 10" $4–6
  v.24 black, "3/GM PARTS," rubber tires $45–60
  v.25 white and green, "HENDRICKS 25," rubber tires $6–8
  v.26 white and orange, "FERREE Chevrolet 49" $4–6
  v.27 dark purple and white, "WHITE ROSE COLLECTIBLES 29/MATCHBOX"...........$4–6
  v.28 dark purple and white, "PHIL PARSONS RACING 29/MATCHBOX" $20–25
  v.29 maroon, "PENNROSE 44/FIRECRACKER SAUSAGE/BIG MAMA" $6–8
  v.30 lime and black, "INTERSTATE BATTERIES 18" $4–6
  v.31 metallic blue and white, "RAYBESTOS 12" without "TIC TAC" $80–100
  v.32 metallic blue and white, "RAYBESTOS 12," "TIC TAC" $4–6
  v.33 black, "STANLEY TOOLS 92" $4–6
  v.34 maroon, "SLIM JIM 44"....$4–6
  v.35 lemon and white, "TEXAS PETE/LOZITO'S 87"........$4–6
Hot Stocks variations:
  v.36 red and yellow, "MATCHBOX RACING 7" $3–5

v.37 white and metallic blue, "MATCHBOX RACING 1".$3–5
v.38 white, "TEAM GOODYEAR 11"...............................$3–5
v.39 orange, "TEAM GOODYEAR 22"...............................$3–5
v.40 black, "CHAMPION 4"...$3–5
Lightning variations:
v.41 white and fluorescent yellow.$8–10
v.42 white and black...........$8–10
v.43 yellow and orange..........$3–5
v.44 green and white $3–5
Other variations:
v.45 white, "PG TAGS," England mail-away offer $80–90
v.46 chrome plated, no markings, Code 2 model.............$15–20
54-J Abrams M1 Tank, 1995
v.1 tan camouflage (1995) $1–2
v.2 army green (1996).................$1–2
v.3 army green with brown and black camouflage (from 5-pack 1996)..............................$2–4
54-K Ford Crown Victoria Police Car, 1997 (also 28-O, 1998).......................$1–2
54-L Chevy K-1500 4X4, 1998 (see 72-N, 1996)
55-A DUKW Army Amphibian, 2¾", 1958
v.1 metal wheels......................$30–45
v.2 gray plastic wheels $30–45
v.3 black plastic wheels...........$30–45
55-B Ford Fairlane Police Car, 2⅝", 1963
v.1 dark blue with black plastic wheels.......................$180–200
v.2 light blue with gray plastic wheels........................$80–100
v.3 light blue with silver plastic wheels........................$80–100
v.4 light blue with black plastic wheels..........................$30–35
55-C Ford Galaxie Police Car, 2⅞", 1966
v.1 blue dome light.................$50–60
v.2 red dome light...................$16–20
55-D Mercury Parklane Police Car with regular wheels, 3", 1968
v.1 red dome light...................$50–60
v.2 blue dome light $7–10
55-E Mercury Parklane Police Car with SF wheels, 3", 1970...................$10–15
55-F Mercury Commuter Police Station Wagon, 3", 1971
v.1 red roof light......................$12–18
v.2 amber roof light.................$45–60
55-G Hellraiser, 3", 1975.............$10–15
55-H Ford Cortina 1600 GL, 3$\frac{1}{16}$", 1979
v.1 metallic green, doors open.......$4–6
v.2 metallic red, doors open $5–7
v.3 metallic tan, doors open...........$5–7
v.4 metallic red, doors cast shut, opaque white windows $12–16
v.5 metallic gold $20–25
v.6 metallic peach...................$15–20
v.7 metallic orange $15–20
v.8 red with white & orange flame tampos $90–120
55-I Porsche 935, Racing Porsche, Super Porsche, 3", 1983 (also 41-H)
v.1 light blue with "ELF 71 SACHS" tampo, silver wheels $2–4
v.2 light blue with "ELF 71 SACHS" tampo, gold wheels............$35–40
v.3 white with "CADBURY BUTTONS" tampo $8–10
v.4 red with "AUTOTECH 35" tampo................................$3–5
v.5 metallic red with "AUTOTECH 35" tampo..................................$3–5
v.6 white with "Porsche 10" tampo, gold wheels.................................$3–5
v.7 white with "Porsche 10" tampo, silver wheels.................................$2–4
v.8 black with "11 OX RACING TEAM" tampo $10–12
v.9 red with "41 Porsche" tampo.$10–12
v.10 red with "Porsche" logo $2–4
v.11 light yellow with chrome windows, World Class.........................$4–6
v.12 pearly cream with chrome windows, World Class $3–5
v.13 white with fluorescent orange accents, blue "935" tampo, chrome and black windows $3–5
v.14 black with chrome and black windows...................................$3–5
v.15 yellow with "Porsche 10" tampo.$2–4
v.16 light blue with "FAR Porsche 71 SACHS," Manaus cast $25–30
55-J Ford Sierra XR4i, 3", 1983 (also 15-H, 1983, reissued as 40-I, 1990)
v.1 white with white interior $80–100
v.2 white with red interior $2–4
v.3 metallic gray with dark gray lower body....................................$2–4
v.4 black with dark gray lower body, white and green stripes $3–5
v.5 yellow with black lower body, black roof tampo $2–4
v.6 yellow with dark gray lower body, gray roof tampo................$25–30
v.7 cream with dark gray lower body .$7–9
v.8 metallic green upper, dark gray lower $3–5
v.9 dark blue with black lower body, "DUCKHAM'S RACE TEAM"...$4–6
v.10 white with red lower body, "VIRGIN ATLANTIC" $4–6
v.11 black with "TEXACO," "PIRELLI" tampos $2–4
v.12 red with "TIZER THE APPETIZER" tampo....................................$4–6
v.13 red, "FIRE DEPT," Lasertronics .$8–10
v.14 yellow-orange, "AIRPORT SECURITY," red roof lights, Lasertronics $16–20
v.15 yellow-orange, "AIRPORT SECURITY," green roof lights, Lasertronics $8–10
v.16 white, "SHERIFF," Lasertronics.$8–10
v.17 red upper, yellow lower, blue roof tampo $12–16
v.18 white upper, black lower, "GEMINI/N COOPER/1"...............$2–4
55-K Mercury Parklane Halley's Comet Commemorative Car, 3", 1986 ....$6
55-L Mercury Sable Wagon, 3", 1988 (also 33-I 1988)
v.1 white with gray base..............$2–4

55-M Rolls Royce Silver Spirit, 3", 1990 (see 66-I, 1988)..$2–4

55-N Ford Model A Hot Rod, 3", 1993 (reissue of 73-H, see 73-H, 1980)
55-O Flareside Pickup, 2⅞", 1994 (see of 53-G, 1982)
56-A London Trolley Bus, red, 2⅝", 1958
v.1 black rods, metal wheels .$180–200
v.2 red rods, metal wheels $35–45
v.3 red rods, gray plastic wheels..........................$25–40
56-B Fiat 1500 with luggage on roof, 2½", 1965
v.1 turquoise.............................$8–12
v.2 red $80–90
56-C BMC 1800 Pininfarina (SF only), 2¾", 1970 ....$15–20
56-D High-Tailer Team Matchbox Racer, 3", 1974 ....$6–10
56-E Mercedes-Benz 450SEL, 3", 1979 (compare to 56-F, 1980)
v.1 metallic blue with tan interior.....$3–5
v.2 metallic blue with red interior.....$5–7
56-F Mercedes-Benz 450SEL Taxi/Polizei, 3", 1980 (compare to 56-E 1979)
v.1 beige with cream "Taxi" sign on roof $3–5
v.2 white with blue roof light..........$4–7
v.3 white and green with "POLIZEI" tampo, blue roof light..............$5–8
v.4 white and green with roof light, no markings $4–6
56-G Peterbilt Tanker, 3", 1982 (also 5-I)
v.1 blue with white tank, "MILK" tampos $4–6
v.2 blue with white tank, no markings $4-6
v.3 red with chrome tank, "GETTY" tampos $2–4
v.4 red with chrome tank, "AMOCO" on tank, "GETTY" on door.$40–50
v.5 white with gray tank, "SHELL" tampos $2–4
v.6 white with gray tank, "AMPOL" tampos $8–10

v.7 white with chrome tank, "SHELL" tampos $2–4

v.8 white with chrome tank, "SHELL" with "IC" on doors $8–10

v.9 white with yellow tank, "SUPERGAS" tampos $16–20

v.10 white with white tank, "AMOCO" tampos $4–6

v.11 white with white tank, chrome pipes, no markings $35–40

v.12 white with white tank, gray pipes, Graffic Traffic $6–8

v.13 black with black tank, "AMOCO" tampos $5–7

v.14 black with black tank, INDY RACING FUEL" $12–15

v.15 black with black tank, "MATCHBOX," "GETTY," Manaus cast $35–40

v.16 black with white tank, "AMOCO" tampos $60–70

v.17 black with yellow tank, "SUPERGAS" tampos $3–5

v.18 black with chrome tank, "SUPERGAS" tampos $60–70

v.19 army green, "GAS" tampos....$4–6

v.20 lime green with red tank, Thailand cast $6–8

56-H Volkswagen Golf GTi, 2⅞", 1986 (see 33-G)

56-I Ford LTD Taxi, 3", 1992 (see 53-I, 1992)

56-J Isuzu Rodeo, 1995

v.1 black with bright pink mud splash pattern on sides and hood $1–2

v.2 white with bright pink mud splash pattern on sides $1–2

56-K Dodge Viper RT/10, 1998 (see 10-I, 1994)

57-A Wolseley 1500 Sedan, 2⅛", 1958

v.1 pale yellow-green with gold grille $60–80

v.2 pale yellow-green with silver grille $40–50

v.3 pale green with silver grille...$40–50

v.4 pale gray with silver grille $110–120

57-B Chevrolet Impala, metallic blue with light blue roof, 2¾", 1961

v.1 gray plastic wheels $30–40

v.2 silver plastic wheels $30–40

v.3 black plastic wheels $30–40

57-C Land Rover Fire Truck with regular wheels, 2⅞", 1966

v.1 gray plastic wheels $180–200

v.2 black plastic wheels $9–12

57-D Land Rover Fire Truck with SF wheels, 2⅞", 1970..........................$25–40

57-E Eccles Caravan Travel Trailer, 3", 1970 ....$6–10

57-F Wildlife Truck (Rolamatic) with lion under transparent canopy, 2¾", 1973

v.1 yellow with amber canopy $4–6

v.2 yellow with blue canopy $4–6

v.3 yellow with clear canopy $4–6

v.4 yellow with smoke canopy $4–6

v.5 white with blue canopy............$4–6

v.6 white with clear canopy..........$4–6

v.7 white with smoke canopy.........$4–6

57-G Carmichael Commando (European model), 3", 1982

v.1 white with "POLICE RESCUE" tampos $7–9

v.2 red with "FIRE" tampos.............$6–8

57-H 4x4 Mini Pickup, Mountain Man, 2¾", 1982..........................$2–4

57-I Mission Chopper with retractable tail, 3", 1985 (also 46-I, 1985, 49-L, 1998)

v.1 dark blue with metallic gray base and skids, orange tampos $1–3

v.2 dark blue with metallic gray base and skids, bullseye tampos $1–3

v.3 red with white base and skids, "SHERIFF/AIR 1" tampos.........$1–3

v.4 army green with tan base and skids, Skybusters SB-12-C 1992 ....$1–3

v.5 army green with black base and skids, "AC15," Commando.....$4–6

v.6 black with gray base and skids, "AC99" Commando $4–6

v.7 red with white base and skids, "REBELS/RESCUE/AIR 1" $2–4

v.8 white with blue base and skids, "POLICE" and crest.................$1–3

v.9 green with white base and skids, "POLIZEI" tampos $2–4

v.10 black with white base and skids, "POLICE" tampos $2–4

v.11 tan with brown camouflage (1993)..............................$1–3

v.12 green with brown and black camouflage (1996 5-Pack) $2–4

v.13 army green, "AT-7521" (1996)..............................$1–2

57-J New Ford Transit Van, 3", 1990 (see 60-I, 1987)

57-K Mack Heavy Rescue Auxiliary Power Truck, 3", 1991 (also 50-J, 1991, 21-M, 1998)

v.1 yellow $2–4

v.2 fluorescent orange, "FIRE RESCUE UNIT 2" $1–2

v.3 white with no markings, Graffic Traffic $6–8

v.4 fluorescent red, "FIRE RESCUE UNIT 2" $4–6

v.5 red with white and gold accents (1996 5-pack) $2–4

57-L Ferrari F40, 1998 (see 24-J, 1989, also 70-H, 1989)

58-A BEA Coach, 2½", 1958

v.1 "British European Airways" decals, gray plastic wheels..............$30–40

v.2 "BEA" decals, gray plastic wheels $40–50

v.3 "BEA" decals, silver plastic wheels $80–100

v.4 "BEA" decals, black plastic wheels $80–100

58-B Drott Excavator, 2⅝", 1962

v.1 red with silver motor and base, metal rollers $25–35

v.2 red with silver motor and base, silver rollers $80–100

v.3 red with silver motor & base, black rollers $25–35

v.4 orange with silver motor and base, black rollers $35–45

v.5 orange with orange motor and base, black rollers $35–45

58-C DAF Girder Truck with regular wheels, 2⅝", 1968 ....$6–9

58-D DAF Girder Truck with SF wheels, 2⅝", 1970..........................$20–25

58-E Woosh-N-Push, 2⅞", 1972.....$12–18

58-F Faun Earth Mover Dump Truck, 2¾", 1976 (reissued as 9-K, 1989, 53-H, 1989)

v.1 orange-yellow, orange-yellow dumper, no markings, England cast $3–5

v.2 yellow, yellow dumper, no markings, England cast..........................$3–5

v.3 yellow, yellow dumper, "CAT" tampos, England cast.................$5–7

v.4 yellow, metallic silver dumper, orange stripes, Macau cast.................$1–2

v.5 yellow, metallic silver dumper, orange stripes, China cast..................$1–2

v.6 blue, yellow dump, orange stripes and tools tampo, China cast....$3–5

v.7 orange-yellow, orange-yellow dumper, orange stripes, China cast $2–4

v.8 orange-yellow, red dumper, no markings, China cast $1–2

v.9 bright orange, bright orange dumper $1–2

v.10 bright orange, black dumper (1996) $1–2

58-G Corvette T-Top 3¹⁄₁₆", 1982 (see 40-F, 1982, also 74-L, 1998)

58-H Ruff Trek Holden Pickup, with tires in back, 2⅞", 1983 (compare to 60-E, 1977)

v.1 metallic tan with "RUFF TREK" tampo..............................$2–4

v.2 white with "RUFF TREK" tampo..$2–4

v.3 white with "217" tampo $3–5

v.4 white with black interior, "BRUT/FABERGE" tampo $3–5

v.5 white with red interior, "BRUT/FABERGE" tampo ...$40–50

v.6 dark blue with "STP/GOODYEAR" tampo..............................$40–50

v.7 white with "7-UP" tampo $4–6

v.8 brown with red, yellow and blue tampos, Roadblasters.................$6–8

v.9 white with flame tampos $8–10

v.10 yellow with "MATCHBOX RESCUE TEAM SUPPORT" tampo $3–5

58-I Mercedes-Benz 300E, 3", 1987

v.1 metallic light blue $2–4

v.2 white with green stripe, "POLIZEI 5075"...$5–7

58-J '97 Corvette, 1998 (see 4-K, 1997)

59-A Ford Thames "Singer" Van, 2⅛", 1958
- v.1 light green with gray plastic wheels...........................$30–40
- v.2 light green with silver plastic wheels.....................$$80–100
- v.3 dark green with gray plastic wheels........................$100–120
- v.4 dark green with silver plastic wheels........................$110–135

59-B Ford Fairlane Fire Chief Car, 2⅞", 1963
- v.1 red with gray plastic wheels.$80–100
- v.2 red with silver plastic wheels.$125–150
- v.3 red with black plastic wheels..$20–25

59-C Ford Galaxie Fire Chief Car with regular wheels, 2⅞", 1966...........$15–20

59-D Ford Galaxie Fire Chief Car with SF wheels, 2⅞", 1970.................$20–25

59-E Mercury Parklane Fire Chief, 3", 1971
- v.1 red with clear windows, with driver & passenger............................$8–12
- v.2 red with clear windows, no driver & passenger............................$8–12
- v.3 white with purple windows, "POLICE" labels..............................$35–45
- v.4 white with blue windows, "LOS ANGELES POLICE" tampo.......$5–8
- v.5 white with clear windows, "LOS ANGELES POLICE" tampo.......$5–8
- v.6 white with clear windows, "POLICE" tampo.........................$5–8
- v.7 white with blue windows, "METRO POLICE" tampo...................$8–12
- v.8 white with blue windows, "LOS ANGELES POLICE" on hood, "METRO POLICE" on sides..$15–20
- v.9 red with purple windows.....$30–40
- v.10 white with gray base, bar lights, "STATE POLICE"....................$3–5
- v.11 white with black base, bar lights, "STATE POLICE".................$9–12
- v.12 black Halley's Comet commemorative car (1986)....................$7–10
- v.13 metallic blue, bar lights, yellow/blue/red tampo..........$4–7

59-F Planet Scout, 2¾", 1971
- v.1 metallic green upper, lime lower, amber windows.................$12–15
- v.2 metallic green upper, apple green lower, amber windows.......$12–15
- v.3 red upper, beige lower, amber windows..........................$12–15
- v.4 avocado upper, black lower, amber windows..........................$20–25
- v.5 avocado upper, black lower, purple windows..........................$20–25
- v.6 metallic blue upper, black lower, purple windows $40–50

59-G Porsche 928, 3", 1980
- v.1 metallic tan $5–7
- v.2 metallic blue.........................$4–6

v.3 black with brown interior, "Porsche" and stripe tampos.................$8–10
v.4 black with red interior, "Porsche" and strip tampos $4–6

59-H T-Bird Turbo Coupe, 3", 1988 (also 28-J, 1988, 61-F, 1988)
- v.1 purple, "TURBO Coupe" $3–5
- v.2 metallic gold, "MOTORCRAFT," Laser wheels.............................$3–5
- v.3 light green, "TURBO Coupe" $3–5
- v.4 brown, "TURBO Coupe"...........$3–5
- v.5 pink, "TURBO Coupe".............$3–5
- v.6 red $2–4
- v.7 metallic gray, red interior, chrome windows, World Class $4–6
- v.8 metallic gray, black interior, chrome windows, World Class.....$60–$65
- v.9 metallic blue with purple and pink stripes............................$2–4

59-I Porsche 944, 3", 1991 (see 71-I, 1988)

59-J Aston Martin DB-7, 1994
- v.1 metallic green, "DB-7" on sides...$2–4
- v.2 metallic green, no markings........$2–4

59-K Camaro Police Pursuit, 1995 (also 27-K, 1998)
- v.1 black with white accents $3–5

59-L Ferrari F50, 1998 (see 75-H, 1996)

60-A Morris J2 "BUILDERS SUPPLY" Pickup, light blue, 2¼", 1958
- v.1 rear window, gray plastic wheels, red & black decals $30–40
- v.2 rear window, silver plastic wheels, red & black decals $40–50
- v.3 rear window, gray plastic wheels, red & white decals $30–40
- v.4 rear window, silver plastic wheels, red & white decals $40–50
- v.5 rear window, black plastic wheels, red & white decals $30–40
- v.6 no rear window, black plastic wheels, red & white decals $30–40

60-B Leyland Site Office Truck with regular wheels, 2½", 1966 ....$15–20

60-C Leyland Site Office Truck with SF wheels, 2½", 1970 ....$25–30

60-D Lotus Super Seven, 3", 1971
- v.1 orange.............................$15–20
- v.2 yellow.............................$20–25

60-E Holden Pickup, 2⅞", 1977
- v.1 maroon with yellow motorcycles, "500" labels $12–15
- v.2 red with yellow motorcycles, "500 labels $6–8
- v.3 red with yellow motorcycles, star label...............................$15–20
- v.4 red with olive motorcycles, sunburst label $9–12
- v.5 cream with "SUPERBIKE" label ..$6–8
- v.6 white with "SUPERBIKE" label ...$9–12
- v.7 cream with "Honda" label ...$12–15
- v.8 metallic blue with "Paris Dakar" labels $30–35

60-F Mustang Piston Popper (Rolamatic), 2¹³⁄₁₆", 1982 (also 10-F)
- v.1 yellow with red interior, no markings.................................$8–10
- v.2 yellow with red interior, "60" tampo.................................$5–7
- v.3 yellow with white interior, "60" tampo.................................$10–12
- v.4 orange with "SUNKIST" tampo .$3–5

60-G Pontiac Firebird S/E, 3", 1984 (also 12-J, 1986, 48-J, 1993, 51-I, 1984)
- v.1 yellow, "SON OF A GUN 55" .$4–6
- v.2 yellow, "PIRELLI 56" $4–6
- v.3 yellow, "10," red and white tampos, plastic base.....................$16–20
- v.4 light blue, "10," blue and yellow tampos, metal base $3–5
- v.5 light blue, "10," blue and yellow tampos, plastic base.............$8–10
- v.6 metallic blue, "10," blue and yellow tampos, metal base, Laser Wheels.............................$8–10
- v.7 metallic blue, "10," blue and yellow tampos, metal base, Laser Wheels.............................$8–10
- v.8 white, "FAST EDDIES 15," metal base..................................$2–3
- v.9 white, "FAST EDDIES 15," plastic base..................................$4–6
- v.10 white, "6 HORSE RACING TEAM"...............................$10–12
- v.11 dark brown, "FAST EDDIES 15"..................................$8–10
- v.12 pale green, "FAST EDDIES 15"..................................$8–10

60-H Toyota Celica Supra, 3", 1984 (see 39-F, 1982)

60-I New Ford Transit, 2⅞", 1987 (also 57-G , 1990, left hand drive unless noted)
- v.1 red, "MOTORSPORT" $2–4
- v.2 red, right hand drive, no markings $40–45
- v.3 red, left hand drive, no markings ...$2–4
- v.4 red, "AUSTRALIA POST" $6–8
- v.5 red, right hand drive, "ROYAL MAIL" $6–8
- v.6 red, right hand drive, "AUSTRALIA POST - WE DELIVER" $6–8
- v.7 red, "BUICK" $10–12
- v.8 white, "FEDERAL Express" $2–4
- v.9 white, right hand drive, "ORMOND ST. APPEAL" $6–8
- v.10 white, "WELLA" $6–8
- v.11 white, "AUSTRALIA TELECOM"..$6–8
- v.12 white, "XP Express PARCELS" ..$4–6
- v.13 white, right hand drive, "FEDERAL Express" $4–6
- v.14 white, "PETER COX PRESERVATION" $8–10
- v.15 white, "KIOSK" $10–12
- v.16 white, left or right hand drive, "KELLOGGS" $70–80
- v.17 white, "DCS" $80–90

v.18 white, no markings, Graffic Traffic $6–8

v.19 white, "SUPERTOYS" $20–25

v.20 white, "McKESSON" $70–80

v.21 white, "GARDEN FESTIVAL WALES" $7–9

v.22 white with red cross and stripes.$3–5

v.23 white, "UNICHEM" $8–10

v.24 white, right hand drive, "JCB JOB SITE" $6–8

v.25 white, right hand drive, XP Express PARCELS" $6–8

v.26 white, "WIGWAM" $8–10

v.27 lime green with no markings..$14–18

v.28 orange, "OVALMALTINE" ..$10–12

v.29 silver and gray, "ISOTAR/PER-FORM/POWERPLAY" $9–12

v.30 yellow, "British TELECOM" $3–5

v.31 yellow, "RYDER" $2–4

v.32 yellow, "CADBURY FLAKES" ..$2–4

v.33 metallic green, "TARONGA ZOOMOBILE" $6–8

60-J NASA Rocket Transporter, 3", 1990 (see 40-H, 1985, var. of 65-H, 72-I Airplane Transporter 1985)

60-K Lamborghini Countach LP500S, 1998 (see 67-H, 1985, also 11-J, 1985)

61-A Ferret Scout Car, 2¼", 1959

v.1 olive green with black plastic wheels $15–25

61-B Alvis Stalwart "BP EXPLORATION," 2⅝", 1966

v.1 yellow wheels $30–40

v.2 green wheels $9–12

61-C Blue Shark, 3", 1971

v.1 "86" label $12–18

v.2 "69" label $12–18

v.3 "scorpion label $20–25

61-D Ford Wreck Truck, 3", 1978

v.1 red with amber windows $4–7

v.2 red with blue windows $8–10

v.3 yellow $4–7

v.4 white $275–300

v.5 orange-red $125–150

61-E Peterbilt Wreck Truck, 3", 1982

v.1 blue with black booms, no markings, amber windows..............$80–100

v.2 orange with black booms, "EDDIE'S WRECKER" tampo $4–6

v.3 orange with dark green booms, black stripes $7–9

v.4 white with black booms, Macau cast $2–4

v.5 white with black booms, Manaus cast $25–30

v.6 white with blue booms, "9" tampo .$2–4

v.7 white with blue booms, "911" tampo $2–4

v.8 white with orange booms, "SFPD" tampo $2–4

v.9 army green with black booms....$3–5

v.10 red with black booms, "POLICE" tampo, Manaus cast..........$30–40

61-F T-Bird Turbo Coupe, 3", 1988 (also 28-J, 1988, see 59-H, 1988)

61-G Nissan 300ZX, no opening parts, 3", 1990 (also 37-L, 1991)

v.1 yellow, "300ZX" on doors $1–2

v.2 yellow, "NADTCA 1ST ANNIVER-SARY NOVEMBER 1994" ..$12–15

v.3 metallic teal blue with yellow accents, hot pink interior (1994) $2–4

v.4 metallic blue with silver/black riveted-steel-plate design on hood, pink interi-or (1995).............................$1–2

v.5 black with orange-red and white graf-fiti design, orange-red interior ...$1–2

61-H Fork Lift Truck, 3⅛", 1992 (also 28-M, 1991, reissue of 48-F Sambron Jack Lift, see 48-F, 1977)

61-I Formula Racer, 1998 (see 74-K, 1996)

62-A General Service Lorry, 2⅝", 1959

v.1 olive green with black plastic wheels $40–50

62-B TV Service Van with ladder, antenna, and three TV sets, 2½", 1963

v.1 gray plastic wheels, "RENTASET" decals $125–150

v.2 gray plastic wheels, "RADIO RENTALS" decals...........$180–200

v.3 black plastic wheels, "RENTASET" decals $30–35

v.4 black plastic wheels, "RADIO RENTALS" decals $40–50

62-C Mercury Cougar with chrome hubs and doors that open, 3", 1968

v.1 pale yellow $750–800

v.2 metallic pale green.................$6–9

62-D Mercury Cougar with SF wheels and doors that open, 3", 1970........$12–15

62-E Mercury Cougar Rat Rod, doors don't open, 3", 1970

v.1 "Rat Rod $12–15

v.2 "Wildcat" $20–25

62-F Renault 17TL, 3", 1974

v.1 "9" label on hood...................$5–8

v.2 "6" label on hood...................$5–8

v.3 "FIRE" label on hood $12–15

62-G Corvette T-Roof, 3⅟₁₆", 1980 (also 40-F, 58-I)

v.1 red with white accents, no "Corvette" cast on front or rear $35–45

v.2 red with white accents, "Corvette" cast on front and rear $4–6

v.3 black with clear windows, green and orange stripes $3–5

v.4 black with opaque windows, green and orange stripes.................$8–10

v.5 black with clear windows, yellow and orange stripes...................$2–4

v.6 black with gray interior, "THE FORCE" tampo $2–4

v.7 black with red interior, "THE FORCE" tampo, Manaus cast..........$20–30

v.8 green with "BRUT/FABERGE" tam-pos $8–10

v.9 metallic red with "TURBO VETTE" tam-pos, Laser Wheels................$8–10

v.10 black with "TURBO VETTE" tam-pos $4–6

v.11 various baseball team logos (29 variations)..........................$4–6

62-H Corvette Hardtop, 3⅟₁₆" ,1983....$4–6

62-I Rolls Royce Silver Cloud, 3", 1985 (US; 31-I, 1987 rest of world)

v.1 metallic silver-gray $6–8

v.2 cream $2–4

v.3 metallic gold, chrome windows, World Class...........................$4–6

62-J Volvo Container Truck, 3⅟₁₆", 1985 (see 23-I, 1985, also 20-H, 1986, 44-L, 1998)

62-K Volvo 760 (European model), 3", 1987

v.1 metallic pearl gray $3–5

v.2 metallic dark gray $3–5

v.3 purple $3–5

v.4 white, Graffic Traffic...............$6–8

v.5 burgundy $8–10

62-L Oldsmobile Aerotech, 3", 1989 (also 64-H)

v.1 metallic silver $3–5

v.2 fluorescent orange $2–4

v.3 metallic purple and white $1–2

62-M Street Streak concept car, 1996 (also 16-L, 1998)

v.1 metallic purple upper, white lower..$1–2

v.2 bright orange upper, black lower...$1–2

62-N Alfa Romeo 155, 1998 (see 3-H, 1997)

63-A Ford 3-Ton 4x4 Army Ambulance, 2½", 1959

v.1 olive green with black plastic wheels $40–50

63-B Airport Foamite Crash Tender, 2¼", 1964

v.1 silver nozzle $5–10

v.2 gold nozzle $20–25

63-C Dodge Crane Truck with regular wheels, 2¾", 1968

v.1 red hook.............................$6–9

v.2 yellow hook........................$8–12

63-D Dodge Crane Truck with SF wheels, 2¾", 1970.............................$20–25

63-E Freeway Gas Tanker, 3", 1973 (goes with 63-F, 1978)

v.1 "Burmah" $5–8

v.2 "Chevron" $5–8

v.3 "Shell" $5–8

v.4 "Exxon" yellow and white $5–8

v.5 "Exxon" red and white........$50–65

v.6 "BP" yellow....................$30–45

v.7 "BP" white and yellow $5–8

63-F Freeway Gas Tanker Trailer, 3", 1978 (goes with 63-E, 1973)

v.1 "CASTROL" label...............$60–80

v.2 "BURMAH" label $5–8

v.3 "OCTANE" label.................$7–10

v.4 French flag label................$60–75

v.5 Canadian flag label $80–100

v.6 "ARAL" label $20–25

v.7 "CHEVRON" label $6–8
v.8 "SHELL" label $6–8
v.9 "EXXON" label, white cab $7–10
v.10 "EXXON" label, red cab ...$45–55
v.11 "BP" label, yellow base $30–40
v.12 "BP" label, black base, green trailer base $8–10

63-G Dodge Challenger / Mitsubishi Galant Eterna, 2⅞", 1980 ....$10–12

63-H Snorkel Fire Engine with open cab, 2¹³⁄₁₆", 1982
v.1 red, "LOS ANGELES" tampos, England cast $6–8
v.2 red, "METRO FIRE" tampos, Macau cast $2–4
v.3 red, "METRO FIRE" tampos, China cast $2–4
v.4 red, "FIRE DEPT" and shield tampos, China cast $2–4
v.5 red, Japanese lettering, China cast $10–12
v.6 fluorescent lime yellow, "FIRE DEPT" and shield, China cast $4–6
v.7 fluorescent orange, "RESCUE UNIT FIRE 1" and checked bars, China cast $1–3
v.8 fluorescent orange, "RESCUE UNIT FIRE 1" and "IC" logo $8–10
v.9 red, "RESCUE UNIT FIRE 1" and checked bars, China cast $4–6
v.10 white, no markings, Graffic Traffic (stickers included in set) $6–8
v.11 red, "12th RESCUE SQUAD," gold trim (1995) $1–2
v.12 red lower, white upper, gold and black trim (1996 5-Pack) $2–3

63-I Dunes Racer 4x4 Pickup, 3", 1984 ....$4–6

63-J GMC Wrecker, 1998 (see 21-J, 1987, also 71-J, 1987, 72-M, 1989)

64-A Scammell Breakdown Truck, olive green, black plastic wheels, 2½", 1959

v.1 green metal hook $30–40

v.2 silver metal hook $30–40
v.3 gray plastic hook $25–35

64-B MG 1100 with driver and dog, regular wheels, 2⅝", 1966 ....$9–12

64-C MG 1100 with driver and dog, SF wheels, 2⅝", 1970
v.1 green with Superfast wheels.$125–175
v.2 blue with Superfast wheels ...$20–25

64-D Slingshot Dragster, 3", 1971
v.1 pink $12–18

v.2 orange $100–125
v.3 metallic blue $12–18

64-E Fire Chief Car (resembles a Ford Torino), 3", 1976 ....$10–12

64-F Caterpillar Bulldozer with plastic roof, 2⅝", 1979
v.1 yellow with yellow blade, tan canopy $4–6
v.2 yellow with yellow blade, black canopy, England cast $4–6
v.3 yellow with yellow blade, black canopy, Macau cast $1–2
v.4 yellow with yellow blade, black canopy, Thailand cast $1–3
v.5 yellow with black blade, black canopy $8–10
v.6 yellow with black blade, tan canopy $8–10
v.7 yellow with no blade, black canopy $12–16
v.8 red with yellow blade, blue canopy $7–10
v.9 orange with orange blade, black canopy, "LOSINGER" $9–12
v.10 red with lime green blade, blue canopy $7–10
v.11 yellow with yellow blade, red canopy $1–3

64-G Dodge Caravan, 2⅞", 1985 (see 68-F, 1984)

64-H Oldsmobile Aerotech, 3", 1990 (see 62-L, 1989)

64-I T-Bird Stock Car, 1998 (see 7-L, 1993)

65-A 3.4 Litre Jaguar, gray plastic wheels, 2½", 1959
v.1 metallic blue $30–40
v.2 blue $30–40

65-B Jaguar 3.8 Litre Saloon, 2⅝", 1962
v.1 red with gray wheels $25–35
v.2 red with silver wheels $35–45
v.3 metallic red with silver wheels .$35–45
v.4 red with black wheels $20–30

65-C Claas Combine Harvester (regular wheels only), 3", 1967 ....$6–9

65-D Saab Sonnet, 2¾", 1973
v.1 blue $9–12
v.2 white $200–250

65-E Airport Coach, 3", 1977
v.1 metallic blue, "AMERICAN AIRLINES," no tab on base $4–6
v.2 metallic blue, "AMERICAN AIRLINES," tab on base $20–25
v.3 metallic blue, "British AIRWAYS," no tab on base $4–6
v.4 metallic blue, "British AIRWAYS," tab on base $20–25
v.5 metallic blue, "LUFTHANSA," no tab on base $4–6
v.6 metallic blue, "LUFTHANSA," tab on base $20–25
v.7 red, "QANTAS" $9–12
v.8 red, "TWA," England cast on base $8–10

v.9 red, "TWA," Manaus cast on base $25–30
v.10 orange, "SCHULBUS" $30–40
v.11 metallic blue, "British" $8–10
v.12 white, "ALITALIA," England cast on base $8–10
v.13 white, "ALITALIA," Macau cast on base $4–6
v.14 white, "LUFTHANSA" $25–30
v.15 orange, "LUFTHANSA" $4–6
v.16 orange, "PAN AM" $4–6
v.17 white, "STORK SB" $8–10
v.18 red, "VIRGIN ATLANTIC" $5–7
v.19 metallic blue, "AUSTRALIAN" ..$8–10
v.20 metallic blue, "GIROBANK" .$8–10
v.21 white with blue roof, "KLM" $5–7
v.22 white with green roof, "ALITALIA" $5–7

65-F Tyrone Malone Bandag Bandit, 3", 1982
v.1 black, England cast $3–5
v.2 black, Macau cast $2–4
v.3 black, China cast $4–6

65-G Indy Racer, 3", 1984
v.1 blue with red "GOODYEAR" airfoil, "STP BOSCH 20" tampos $4–6
v.2 yellow with red "GOODYEAR" airfoil, "MATCHBOX RACING TEAM" .$2–4
v.3 pink with red "GOODYEAR" airfoil, "MATCHBOX RACING TEAM" .$3–5
v.4 light green with red "GOODYEAR" airfoil, "MATCHBOX RACING TEAM" $3–5
v.5 light peach with red "GOODYEAR" airfoil, "MATCHBOX RACING TEAM" $3–5
v.6 red with red "GOODYEAR" airfoil, "MATCHBOX RACING TEAM" .$3–5
v.7 orange with red "GOODYEAR" airfoil, "MATCHBOX RACING TEAM" $3–5
v.8 white with red airfoil, blue wheels, "123456," Matchbox Preschool $6–8
v.9 white, hot pink and blue with pink "RAIN-X" airfoil, "AMWAY/SPEEDWAY 22" $3–5
v.10 blue and white with blue "VALVOLINE" airfoil, "VALVOLINE 5" ...$3–5
v.11 orange-yellow and blue with yellow "KRACO" airfoil, "KRACO/OTTER POPS 18" $3–5
v.12 lemon yellow and black with lemon yellow "GOODYEAR" airfoil, "INDY 11" $3–5
v.13 black with black "HAVOLINE" airfoil, "HAVOLINE 86" $3–5
v.14 chrome with red "GOODYEAR" airfoil $16–20
v.15 blue and white, blue "MITRE 10" airfoil, "MITRE 10/LARKHAM/TAUBMANS 3" $6–8
v.16 white with fuchsia "HYFLO EXHAUSTS" airfoil, "HYFLOW EXHAUSTS 5" ..$2–4

65-H Plane Transporter "RESCUE," 3",
1986 (variation of NASA Rocket
Transporter, see 72-I, 1985)
65-I Cadillac Allante, 3", 1988 (also 72-L,
1988)
v.1 metallic silver $2–4
v.2 black with red and silver stripes, Laser
wheels.................................$3–5
v.3 pink with gray interior, "CADILLAC"
tampos $1–2
v.4 pink with white interior, bright green
and blue accents...................$1–2
v.5 white with red interior, rubber
tires $100–120
v.6 metallic gray, chrome windshield,
World Class........................$3–5
65-J Ford F-150 4x4 Pickup, 1995
v.1 red with white accents on sides
(1995) $2–4
v.2 metallic blue with silver accents on
sides (1996)......................$2–3
65-K Opel Calibra DTM, 1998 (see 66-J,
1997)
66-A Citroën DS19, yellow, 2½", 1959
v.1 gray plastic wheels $50–60
v.2 silver plastic wheels........$120–130
66-B Harley Davidson Motorcycle and Sidecar, 2⅝", 1962
v.1 metallic bronze with black
tires $85–95
66-C Greyhound Bus with regular wheels, 3",
1967
v.1 clear windows $60–75
v.2 amber windows $7–10
66-D Greyhound Bus with SF wheels, 3",
1970 ....$15–20
66-E Mazda RX-500, 3", 1971
v.1 orange with amber windows .$45–60

v.2 orange with purple windows.........$5–10

v.3 red with purple windows $12–15
v.4 red with amber windows $5–10
v.5 green with amber windows....$9–12
66-F Ford Transit, 2¾", 1977
v.1 orange, no tab on base..........$5–8
v.2 orange, tab on base $30–40
66-G Tyrone Malone Super Boss, 3", 1982
v.1 white with green windows, England
cast $2–4
v.2 white with red windows, England
cast $8–10
v.3 white, Macau cast $2–4
v.4 white, China cast..................$3–5
v.5 tan, gray armament replaces spoiler,
Macau cast..........................$6–8
66-H Mercedes Sauber Group C Racer, 3",
1985 (see 46-J, 1985)

66-I Rolls Royce Silver Spirit, 3", 1988 (also
55-M, 1990)
v.1 metallic red $2–4
v.2 metallic tan $4–6
v.3 metallic green-gold.................$5–7
66-J Opel Calibra, 1997 (also 65-K,
1998).......................................$1–2
66-K '97 MGF, 1998, new
v.1 lime green $1–2
67-A Saladin Armoured Car, 2½", 1959

**v.1 olive green with black plastic
wheels $30–40**

67-B Volkswagen 1600TL with chrome hubs,
2¾", 1967
v.1 red with no roof rack $6–9
v.2 red with maroon roof rack....$12–15
v.3 metallic purple, no roof rack.$100–110
67-C Volkswagen 1600TL with SF wheels,
2¾", 1970
v.1 red $30–40
v.2 metallic purple...................$15–20
v.3 pink...................................$12–15
67-D Hot Rocker Mercury Capri, 3",
1973 ....$9–12
67-E Datsun 260Z 2+2, 3", 1978
v.1 metallic burgundy, doors open..$3–5
v.2 metallic purple, doors open $8–12
v.3 metallic magenta, doors open ..$6–9
v.4 metallic blue, doors open $6–9
v.5 metallic gray, doors open $2–4
v.6 black, doors cast shut $2–4
v.7 metallic gray, doors cast shut, England cast................................$5–8
v.8 metallic gray, doors cast shut, China
cast.....................................$70–85
67-F Flame Out (variation of 48-E, 1972, 48-
G, 1982), 3", 1983
v.1 white with red and orange flame tampos $4–6
67-G IMSA Mustang, 3", 1983 (see 11-I)
67-H Lamborghini Countach LP500S, 3",
1985 (also 11-J, 1985)
v.1 red with Lamborghini logo on hood,
silver wheels $2–4
v.2 red with Lamborghini logo on hood,
gold wheels $10–12
v.3 black with "5" and stripes, silver
wheels $2–4
v.4 black with "5" and stripes, gold
wheels $4–6
v.5 white with "LP500S" and stripes,
New Superfast wheels $3–5
v.6 pearl silver, Laser wheels $4–6

v.7 red with green "15" and "BP" tampos $10–12
v.8 yellow with "10 TIGER RACING
TEAM" tampos $10–12
v.9 yellow with "LAMBORGHINI" and
"COUNTACH" tampos $2–4
v.10 yellow with "LP500S", chrome windows, World Class $4–6
v.11 black with "LP500" and stripes,
New Superfast wheels $12–16
v.12 chrome with no markings...$16–20
v.13 red with "COUNTACH," chrome
windows, World Class $4–6
v.14 white with no markings, Graffic Traffic $6–8
v.15 pearl cream with "COUNTACH"
and logo...............................$4–6
v.16 bright yellow and metallic blue with
pink interior (1994)...............$1–2
v.17 metal flake red with white "lamborghini" and bull logo on sides
(1996) $2–4
67-I Icarus Bus (European model), 3", 1987
v.1 white with orange roof, "VOY-
AGER".................................$4–6
v.2 white with red roof,
"GIBRALTAR" $6–8
v.3 white with green roof, "CITY LINE
TOURIST" $3–5
v.4 white with green roof, pictograms,
"2384584" $20–25
v.5 white with white roof, "CANARY
ISLAND" $8–10
v.6 white with white roof,
"ESPAÑA" $2–4
v.7 white and orange with white roof,
"AIRPORT LIMOUSINE" $10–12
v.8 white with no markings, Graffic Traffic $10–12
v.9 cream with cream roof,
"IKARUS" $3–5
v.10 beige with brown roof,
"MARTI" $10–12
67-J Mazda RX-7, 1998 (see 8-O, 1994)
68-A Austin Mk 2 Radio Truck, 2⅜", 1959

**v.1 olive green with black plastic
wheels $40–50**

68-B Mercedes-Benz Coach, 2⅞", 1965
v.1 turquoise $60–80
v.2 orange.................................$8–12
68-C Porsche 910 (SF wheels only), 2⅞", 1970
v.1 metallic red $12–15

v.2 white $20–25

68-D Cosmobile, 2⅞", 1975
- v.1 metallic blue upper, yellow lower, amber windows $12–18
- v.2 metallic red upper, beige lower, amber windows $15–20
- v.3 metallic avocado upper, black lower, purple windows $20–25
- v.4 metallic avocado upper, black lower, amber windows $25–30

68-E Chevy Van, 2¹⁵⁄₁₆", 1979 (reissued as 44-G, 1982 and 26-L, 1991)
- v.1 orange with clear windows, blue and red stripes $25–35
- v.2 orange with blue windows, blue and red stripes $3–6
- v.3 orange with blue windows, blue and white stripes.........$4–7
- v.4 orange with blue windows, red and black stripes $4–7
- v.5 orange with orange windows, red and black stripes $3–6
- v.6 orange with red windows, red and black stripes $3–6
- v.7 orange with green windows, red and black stripes $7–10
- v.8 dark orange with blue windows, red and black stripes $12–16
- v.9 orange with blue windows, red and black stripes $7–10
- v.10 orange with blue windows, "MATCHBOX COLLECTORS CLUB" $25–30
- v.11 white with blue windows, "USA 1" tampos $8–10
- v.12 white with blue windows, "ADIDAS" tampo $30–35
- v.13 green with blue windows, "CHEVY," yellow stripes $9–12
- v.14 green with blue windows, "CHEVY," brown stripes $9–12
- v.15 metallic gray with blue windows, "VANPIRE" tampos $3–5
- v.16 yellow with "MATCHBOX COLLECTING" tampos..............$16–20
- v.17 yellow with "PEPSI CHALLENGE" tampos $5–7
- v.18 white and maroon with "Dr. Pepper" tampos $8–10
- v.19 yellow with "STP SON OF A GUN" tampos $50–60
- v.20 black with "GOODWRENCH RACING TEAM PIT CREW" tampo .$5–7
- v.21 orange-yellow with 'KODAK FILM 4 RACING" tampos $6–8
- v.22 white with "25" and green accent tampo................................$4–6
- v.23 "GOODRICH 5 TIME NATIONAL CHAMPION DALE EARNHARDT" $5–7
- v.24 yellow with "PENNZOIL 30" tampo................................$6–8
- v.25 blue and fluorescent orange with "43 STP OIL TREATMENT" $5–7

- v.26 black with "PONTIAC EXCITEMENT 2" tampos $4–6
- v.27 black and green with "MELLO YELLO 42" tampos $5–7
- v.28 fluorescent orange and white with "PUROLATOR 10" tampos.......$5–7
- v.29 white with purple and lime green graphics (1996).....................$1–2

68-F Dodge Caravan, 2⅞", 1984 (also 64-G, 1985)
- v.1 burgundy with black stripes, England cast....................$16–20
- v.2 silver with black stripes, England cast $6–8
- v.3 black with no stripes, England cast .$4–6
- v.4 black with silver stripes, England cast $3–5
- v.5 black with silver stripes, Macau cast $2–4
- v.6 black with silver and gold stripes, China cast $2–4
- v.7 black with silver and gold stripes, Manaus cast $25–430
- v.8 white with "PAN AM," Macau cast $4–6
- v.9 white with "Caravan" and stripes, Macau cast $2–4
- v.10 white with "FLY VIRGIN ATLANTIC," Macau cast $3–5
- v.11 black with silver stripes, "ADIDAS" on hood, England cast.........................$175–200
- v.12 black with green and yellow stripes, Macau cast......................$10–12
- v.13 white with "NASA SHUTTLE PERSONNEL," Macau cast $3–5
- v.14 gray and blue with "British AIRWAYS," Thailand cast $3–5
- v.15 red with "RED ARROWS/ ROYAL AIR FORCE," Thailand cast $3–5

68-G Camaro IROC Z, 3", 1987 (see 51-J, 1985)

68-H TV News Truck, 3", 1989 (also 73-J)
- v.1 dark blue with metallic gray roof, "75 NEWS/MBTV MOBILE ONE".................................$2–4
- v.2 white with white roof, no markings, Graffic Traffic series $6–8
- v.3 white with dark blue roof, "SKY SATELLITE TELEVISION" $2–4
- v.4 blue and white with gray roof, "ROCK TV" $2–4

68-I Road Roller, 3", 1992 (reissue of 72-F Bomag Road Roller, see 72-F, 1979)

68-J Stinger, 1995 (also 41-M, 1998)
- v.1 yellow and black helicopter-style fantasy vehicle...........................$1–2

68-K Porsche 911, GT1, 1998 new
- v.1 white $1–2

69-A Commer 30 CWT "NESTLE'S" Van, gray plastic wheels, 2⅜", 1959

- v.1 maroon $30–40
- v.2 dark red $30–40
- v.3 red $60–70

69-B Hatra Tractor Shovel, 3", 1965
- v.1 orange with orange wheels, gray tires $20–30
- v.2 orange with orange wheels, black tires $12–16
- v.3 orange with red wheels, black tires $12–16
- v.4 orange with yellow wheels, black tires $12–16
- v.5 yellow with red wheels, black tires $12–16
- v.6 yellow with yellow wheels, black tires $10–15

69-C Rolls Royce Silver Shadow Convertible Coupe (SF wheels only), 3", 1969
- v.1 metallic blue $15–20
- v.2 metallic gold $15–20
- v.3 metallic lime-gold $15–20

69-D Turbo Fury, 3", 1973
- v.1 "69" label $12–18
- v.2 "86" label $12–18

69-E Armored Truck, 2¹³⁄₁₆", 1978
- v.1 red, "WELLS FARGO," clear windows....................$25–35
- v.2 red, "WELLS FARGO," blue windows....................$4–7
- v.3 green, "DRESDNER BANK" .$35–45
- v.4 dark army green, "DRESDNER BANK".............................$55–65

69-F 1933 Willys Street Rod, 2¹⁵⁄₁₆", 1982
- v.1 white with flame tampos, "313" on roof $3–5
- v.2 blue with flame tampos, "313" on roof, Hong Kong cast $2–4
- v.3 blue with flame tampos, "313" on roof, Macau cast...................$2–4
- v.4 black with flame tampos, "313" on roof, China cast $6–8
- v.5 pearly white with blue, pink and yellow tampos (1993) $2–3

69-G 1983 Corvette, 3", 1983 (see 14-I, 1983)

69-H Volvo 480ES (European model), 2⅞", 1989
- v.1 metallic pearl gray with green stripes, Laser wheels $4–6
- v.2 white, Macau cast $2–4
- v.3 white, China cast $5–7

69-I Chevrolet Highway Maintenance Truck, 3¹⁄₁₆", 1990 (see 45-G, 1990, also 11-L, 1998)

69-J '68 Mustang Cobra Jet, 1997 ......$1–2

69-K Mitsubishi Spyder, 1998 (see 28-N, 1995)

70-A Ford Thames Estate Car, yellow & turquoise, 2⅛", 1959
- v.1 no windows, gray plastic wheels $30–40
- v.2 clear windows, gray plastic wheels $30–40

v.3 green windows, gray plastic wheels $30–40

v.4 clear windows, silver plastic wheels $30–40

v.5 green windows, silver plastic wheels $30–40

v.6 green windows, black plastic wheels $25–35

70-B Atkinson Grit Spreader with regular wheels, 2⅝", 1966 ....$6–12

70-C Ford Atkinson Grit Spreader with SF wheels, 2⅝", 1970 ....$20–25

70-D Dodge Dragster, 3", 1971

v.1 pink with snake label $15–20

v.2 pink with "RAT ROD" label...$20–25

v.3 pink with "WILDCAT" label ..$20–25

v.4 pink with star flame label $50–75

v.5 pink with "CASTROL" label...$375–425

70-E Self-Propelled Gun, Rolamatic, 2⅝", 1976...............................$5–8

70-F Ferrari 308 GTB, 2¹⁵⁄₁₆", 1981 (versions 1 through 5, England cast)

v.1 red body and base, clear windows, no markings...........................$3–5

v.2 orange-red body and base, clear windows, no markings $3–5

v.3 orange-red body and base, clear windows, "FERRARI" logo $3–5

v.4 orange-red body and base, amber windows, "FERRARI" logo $4–6

v.5 orange-red with metallic gray base, clear windows, "FERRARI" logo $10–12

(versions 6 through 15, Macau cast unless noted)

v.6 orange-red with metallic gray base, clear windows, "FERRARI" $2–4

v.7 red with blue base, "PIONEER" tampos $2–4

v.8 yellow with red base, "FERRARI 308 GTB" tampos $3–5

v.9 orange with blue base, "RAT RACING TEAM" tampos...........$10–12

v.10 red body and base, "DATA EAST/SECRET SERVICE" tampos $60–70

v.11 red body and base, chrome windows, World Class $3–5

v.12 red body and base, "FERRARI" logo on hood......................$2–4

v.13 red body and base, "FERRARI" logo, Thailand cast $2–4

v.14 white body and base, green windows, Graffic Traffic $6–8

v.15 yellow with geometric design, Dream Machine (1993).........$2–4

70-G Ford Skip Truck, 2¹³⁄₁₆", 1988 (also 45-F, 1988)

v.1 yellow with gray metal skip $2–4

v.2 blue with red metal skip, Preschool series $6–8

v.3 yellow with gray plastic skip $2–4

v.4 yellow with red plastic skip $2–4

70-H Ferrari F40, 3", 1989 (see 24-J, 1989)

70-I Military Tank, 2⅞", 1993 (reissue of 73-F, Weasel 1974)

v.1 tan (khaki) camouflage.............$1–2

v.2 army green (olive) (1996) $1–2

70-J Pontiac GTO "The Judge," 1996 (also 38-L, 1998)

v.1 orange $2–3

70-K '97 Mercedes E Class, 1998, new

v.1 metallic charcoal gray $1–2

71-A Austin 200-Gallon Water Truck, 2⅜", 1959

v.1 olive green with black plastic wheels...............................$30–40

71-B Jeep Gladiator Pickup Truck, 2⅝", 1964

v.1 green interior $40–50

v.2 white interior $20–25

71-C Ford Heavy Wreck Truck, "ESSO," with regular wheels, 3", 1968

v.1 amber windows $60–75

v.2 green windows $6–9

71-D Ford Heavy Wreck Truck, "ESSO," with SF wheels, 3", 1970

v.1 red cab, white body, "ESSO" .$20–25

v.2 olive green $12–15

v.3 blue.............................$100–120

71-E Jumbo Jet Motorcycle, 2¾", 1973 ....$15–20

71-F Dodge Cattle Truck with cattle, 3", 1976 (reissue of 4-E, 1970; reissued as 12-M, 1992).............................$4–9

71-G 1962 Corvette, 2¹⁵⁄₁₆", 1982 (reintroduced as 32-J, 1993)

v.1 blue with white accents............$4–6

v.2 white with white base, red accents, blue interior $8–10

v.3 white whit white base, red accents, silver interior......................$3–5

v.4 white with blue base, red accents, silver interior $8–10

v.5 white with white base, red flames, Macau cast $2–4

v.6 white with white base, orange flames, Macau cast $2–4

v.7 white with white base, red flames, Hong Kong cast....................$2–4

v.8 bright blue with "FIRESTONE" tampo, Macau cast.......................$8–10

v.9 orange with "11" and white stripe tampo, Macau cast $3–5

v.10 red with "454 RAT" tampo, Macau cast.................................$2–4

v.11 metallic orange, "11" and white stripes, Laser Wheels $3–5

v.12 metallic green, "11" and white stripes, Laser Wheels $3–5

v.13 red, "HEINZ 57" tampo, Macau cast.................................$20–25

v.14 turquoise with white roof, chrome windows, World Class $4–6

v.15 white with white base, no markings, Graffic Traffic........................$6–8

v.16 metallic orange with black roof, "4" tampo..................................$4–6

v.17 metallic blue with magenta and white accents, chrome interior (1994)................................$1–2

71-H Scania T142, 3", 1986 (see 8-K, 1986, also 72-J, 1986)

71-I Porsche 944 Racer, 3", 1988, also 59-I, 1991)

v.1 red with "944 Turbo" on sides..$2–4

v.2 black with "944 Turbo" on sides, chrome windows, World Class .$3–5

v.3 red with "944 Turbo" and "CREDIT CHARGE" tampos.............$8–10

v.4 white with "DUCKHAM'S" tampos $16–20

v.5 metallic green......................$2–4

71-J GMC Wrecker, 2⅞", 1989 (see 21-J, 1987, also 72-M, 1989)

71-K Mustang Cobra, 1995 (also 73-M, 1998)

v.1 metallic red with black hood accents, cobra logo on hood (1995) $1–2

v.2 black with gray hood accents, cobra logo on hood (1996) $1–2

71-L '97 Jaguar XK-8, 1998, new

v.1 metallic blue with accents.........$1–2

72-A Fordson Power Major Farm Tractor, blue, 2", 1959

v.1 gray front wheels, gray rear tires on orange wheels..................$40–50

v.2 black front wheels, black rear tires on orange wheels.................$35–45

v.3 gray front & rear tires on orange wheels.............................$40–50

v.4 gray front & rear tires on yellow wheels.............................$90–100

v.5 black front & rear tires on yellow wheels.............................$90–100

v.6 black front & rear tires on orange wheels.............................$40–50

72-B Standard Jeep CJ5 with plastic wheel hubs, 2⅜", 1966 ....$6–9

72-C Standard Jeep CJ5 with SF wheels, 2⅜", 1970.........................$15–20

72-D Hovercraft SRN6, 3", 1972.......$4–6

72-E Maxi Taxi Mercury Capri, 3", 1973 ....$8–12

72-F Bomag Road Roller, 2¹⁵⁄₁₆", 1979 (reissued as 40-I, 1991, 68-I, 1992)

v.1 yellow with red interior, England cast $4–6

v.2 orange with blue stripes (1991)...$2–4

v.3 yellow with red stripes, bridge and road tampos (1992)..............$2–4

72-G Dodge Delivery Truck (European model), 2¾", 1982

v.1 red with white container, "PEPSI" labels $4–6

v.2 red with white container, "SMITH'S" labels $5–7

v.3 red with white container, KELLOGG'S" labels...................$3–5 v.4 white with white container, "STREET'S ICE CREAM" tampos $6–8

v.5 red with white container, "KELLOGG'S/MILCH-LAITE-LATTE" .$30–40

v.6 white with white container, "JETS-PRESS ROAD Express" $6–8

v.7 green with white container, "MINTIES" tampos $6–8

v.8 orange yellow with yellow container, "RISI" tampos.................... $20–25

v.9 blue with blue container, "MITRE 10" tampos............................ $6–8

v.10 red with red container, "NESTLES CHOKITO" tampos $6–8

v.11 red with red container, "KIT KAT" tampos $8–10

v.12 blue with blue container, "YORKIE" $8–10

v.13 white with white container, "PIRELLI GRIPPING STUFF" $3–5

v.14 red with white container, "MATCHBOX USA SHERATON INN 1989" $15–18

v.15 white with white container, "XPRESS PARCELS SYSTEMS" $4–6

v.16 dark green with orange container, "C PLUS ORANGE" $10–12

v.17 light gray and dark blue, "British AIRWAYS CARGO" $4–6

v.18 white with white container, "WIGWAM" $8–10

v.19 red with white container, "BIG TOP CIRCUS" $2–4

72-H Sand Racer, 2¹¹⁄₁₆", 1984
v.1 white with "GOODYEAR/UNION 211" tampo, Macau cast.................... $16–20

72-I Plane Transporter "RESCUE" (also 65-H 1986, variation of NASA Rocket Transporter), 3", 1985
v.1 yellow with "RESCUE" and checkerboard pattern........................ $6–8
v.2 army green with black and tan camouflage, Commando $45–50

72-J Scania T142, 3", 1986 (see 8-K, 1986, also 71-H, 1986)

72-K Ford Supervan II, 2¹⁵⁄₁₆", 1987 (US; see 6-I, 1985 rest of world)

72-L Cadillac Allante, 3", 1988 (see 65-I, 1988)

72-M GMC Wrecker, 2⅞", 1989 (see 21-J, 1987, also 71-J, 1989)

72-N Chevrolet K-1500 Pick-Up, 1996
v.1 black with yellow and pink accents $1–2

72-O '97 Firebird Ram Air, 1998, new
v.1 black.................... $1–2

73-A RAF 10-Ton Pressure Refueling Tanker, 2⅝", 1959
v.1 blue-gray with gray plastic wheels.................. $5–10

73-B Ferrari F1 Racing Car, red, 2⅝", 1962
v.1 white driver...................... $20–30

v.2 gray driver......................... $20–30

73-C Mercury Commuter Station Wagon with chrome hubs, 3⅛", 1968....... $6–9

73-D Mercury Commuter Station Wagon with SF wheels, 3", 1970
v.1 metallic lime green $10–15
v.2 red $15–20

73-E Mercury Commuter Station Wagon with raised roof, 3", 1972
v.1 metallic lime green $12–18
v.2 red $15–20

73-F Weasel Armored Vehicle, 2⅞", 1974
v.1 metallic green...................... $4–7
v.2 olive drab......................... $45–50
v.3 army green $5–8
v.4 metallic light green $5–8

73-G Ford Model A, spare tire cast, 2¹³⁄₁₆", 1979 (compare to 73-H, 1980, reissued as 55-O, 1991)
v.1 cream with dark green fenders .$8–10

73-H Ford Model A with no spare tire cast into fender, 2¹³⁄₁₆", 1980
v.1 cream with dark green fenders, green windows............................ $4–6
v.2 metallic light green with dark green fenders, green windows $4–6
v.3 metallic light green with dark green fenders, no windows $4–6
v.4 beige with brown fenders, amber windows............................... $3–5
v.5 beige with brown fenders, clear windows............................... $3–5
v.6 red with black fenders, clear windows............................... $3–5
v.7 black with black fenders, flame tampos $2–4
v.8 purple with yellow fenders, flame tampos $3–5
v.9 yellow with red fenders, "PAVA" tampo $10–12
v.10 red with dark green fenders.... $16–20
v.11 orange-yellow with white fenders, "GT" and yellowjacket tampos.. $7–10
v.12 light blue $8–12

73-I Mercedes-Benz 1600 Turbo Farm Tractor, 2¾", 1990 (also 27-I, 1991)
v.1 light green, no markings, green interior.................................. $2–4
v.2 light green, no markings, light yellow interior $2–4
v.3 light green, "MB Trac" tampos.. $2–4

73-J TV News Truck, 3", 1990 (see 68-H, 1989)

73-K Jeep Cherokee, 2⅞", 1994 (reissue of 27-H, see 27-H, 1987)

73-L Rotwheeler, big dog face, lower jaw moves when rolled, fantasy vehicle, 1995 (also 42-I, 1998)
v.1 brown $1–2
v.2 red $1–2
v.3 black $1–2

73-M Mustang Cobra, 1998 (see 71-K, 1995)

74-A Mobile Canteen Refreshment Bar, 2⅝", 1959
v.1 white with blue base & interior, gray wheels $300–350
v.2 pink with light blue base & interior, gray wheels $400–500
v.3 coral cream with blue base & interior, gray wheels $300–350
v.4 cream with blue base & interior, gray wheels $300–350
v.5 silver with gray wheels......... $30–40
v.6 silver with silver plastic wheels $30–40
v.7 silver with black plastic wheels $30–40

74-B Daimler London Bus with regular wheels, "ESSO EXTRA PETROL," 3", 1966
v.1 cream $12–15
v.2 green.................................. $9–12
v.3 red..................................... $7–10

74-C Daimler London Bus with SF wheels, 3", 1970
v.1 green, "ESSO EXTRA PETROL" $1,600–2,000
v.2 red, "ESSO EXTRA PETROL"... $12–15
v.3 red, "BARON OF BEEF" .$100–125
v.4 red, "INN ON THE PARK"......................... $100–125
v.5 red, "THE MINIATURE VEHICLE/N.A.M.C." $100–125

74-D Toe Joe Wreck Truck, 2¾", 1972
v.1 metallic lime green with green booms, red hooks $4–6
v.2 metallic lime green with green booms, black hooks $15–20
v.3 metallic lime green with white booms, black hooks................. $65–80
v.4 yellow with green booms, black hooks $15–20
v.5 yellow with red booms, black hooks $3–5
v.6 yellow-orange with red booms, black hooks $3–5
v.7 yellow-orange with "HITCHHIKER" label $100–120
v.8 red with green booms, black hooks $100–120
v.9 red with red booms, black hooks $100–120
v.10 red with red boom, red hooks $100–120

74-E Mercury Cougar Villager Station Wagon, 3", 1978
v.1 metallic green......................... $3–6
v.2 metallic blue......................... $5–8
v.3 army green.................... $275–325

74-F Orange Peel Dodge Charger, 3", 1981 .... $4–6

74-G Fiat Abarth, 2¹⁵⁄₁₆", 1984 (see 9-G, 1982)

74-H Toyota MR2, 2⅞", 1987 (see 9-I, 1987)

74-I Ford Utility Truck, 3", 1987 (rest of world, also 33-J, 1989 US) v.1 gray with orange front end, "ENERGY INC" $2–4

v.2 red with "53," yellow wheels, Preschool $6–8

v.3 yellow with red front end, "ENERGY INC," Action Pack.................$3–5

v.4 yellow with "TELEPHONE CO" $1–3

v.5 beige with bright green base and boom, green "TREE CARE" and tree tampos (1995) $1–2

v.6 metallic green with metallic gray base, white "TREE CARE" and tree tampos (1996) $1–2

74-J Williams Honda F1 Grand Prix Racer, 3", 1988 (also 14-N, 1989)

v.1 white and light blue, "GOODYEASR/SHELL/15"....$3–5

v.2 red, "Fiat/27," metal base $2–4

v.3 red, "Fiat/27," plastic base ...$8–10

v.4 red, "SCOTCH, TARGET"........$3–5

v.5 yellow, "PENNZOIL/2" $3–5

v.6 yellow, "PENNZOIL/4" $3–5

v.7 dark orange and white, "INDY/4" ...$3–5

v.8 chrome with no markings $16–20

v.9 blue, "PANASONIC/7" $3–5

v.10 white and blue, "INDY/76" ..$3–5

v.11 white and black, "HAVOLINE/Kmart/6" $3–5

v.12 orange, lavender and white, "INDY" $4–6

v.13 white and pink with blue spots, "7" (1994) $1–3

74-K Formula Racer, 1996 (also 61-I, 1998)

v.1 white with red spoiler, "MB RACING 1" $1–2

74-L Corvette T-Top, 1998 (see 40-F, 1982, also 58-G, 1982)

75-A Ford Thunderbird, cream & pink, 2⅝", 1960

v.1 gray plastic wheels $50–60

v.2 silver plastic wheels $50–60

v.3 black plastic wheels $80–100

75-B Ferrari Berlinetta with spoked or chrome wheel hubs, 3", 1965

v.1 metallic light blue, spoked wheels $60–80

v.2 metallic green, spoked wheels..............................$12–15

v.3 metallic green with chrome hubs $9–12

v.4 red with chrome hubs........$500–600

75-C Ferrari Berlinetta with SF wheels, 3", 1970

v.1 metallic green $60–80

v.2 red $20–25

75-D Alfa Carabo, 3", 1971

v.1 metallic pink with no tampo..$12–18

v.2 pink with no tampo.................$20–25

v.3 pink with tampo.................$15–20

v.4 red with tampo.................$8–12

75-E Seasprite Helicopter with small windows, 2¾", 1977

v.1 white $3–5

v.2 dark cream....................$275–325

v.3 dark green $275–325

75-F Helicopter with pilot and large windows, 3", 1982

v.1 white with orange base, "MBTV NEWS" $2–4

v.2 white with black base, "MBTV NEWS" $4–6

v.3 white with black base, "POLICE 36" $3–5

v.4 white with black base, "RESCUE" $2–4

v.5 white with black base, Japanese lettering............................$10–12

v.6 white with red base, "FIRE DEPT" $2–4

v.7 white with red base, "NASA" ...$2–4

v.8 white with red base, "VIRGIN ATLANTIC" $3–5

v.9 white with yellow base, "JCB" ...$4–6

v.10 white with yellow base, "FIRE DEPT" $2–4

v.11 white with orange base, "RESCUE" $2–4

v.12 black with black base, "AIR CAB" $2–4

v.13 red with white base, "RED REBELS" $2–4

v.14 red with white base, "FIRE DEPT" $2–4

v.15 metallic gray with orange base, "600" tampo $2–4

75-G Ferrari Testarossa, 3", 1987

v.1 red with "FERRARI" logos..........$2–4

v.2 black with silver accents, New Superfast wheels $3–5

v.3 metallic pearl gray, gold accents, Laser wheels $3–5

v.4 yellow with red, blue, and yellow accents, Roadblasters..............$3–5

v.5 yellow, "9 RABBIT RACING TEAM"..............................$10–12

v.6 metallic red with silver accents, Laser wheels $3–5

v.7 white with no markings, Graffic Traffic $6–8

v.8 red with chrome windows, World Class $3–5

v.9 white with chrome windows, World Class $3–5

v.10 fluorescent yellow with black accent stripes, hot pink flames $1–2

75-H Ferrari F50, 1996 (also 59-L, 1998)

v.1 red $1–2

75-I Ferrari F50 Coupe, 1997 ....$1–2

75-J '94 Camaro Z-28, 1998, new

v.1 purple with accents $1–2

76-A Mazda SAVANNAH RX7, 1981

v.1 light green, no markings.........$4–6

v.2 blue, no markings $4–6

v.3 blue with black stripe, "RX7" tampo........................$12–15

v.4 blue with red and white stripes $5–8

76-B Dunes Racer, 1996 (accidental reissue of 13-H, 1982), if in original package $2–3

77-A Toyota Celica XX, 1981

v.1 red, no markings.................$4–6

v.2 red with "SUNBURNER" tampo..............................$5–8

77-B Weasel Tank, 1996 (accidental reissue of 73-F, 1974), if in original package $2–3

78-A Nissan Fairlady Z, 1981

v.1 black, no markings.................$4–6

v.2 black with "Z" tampo..............$5–8

v.3 pearly white, no markings $12–15

78-B Ferrari Testarossa, 3", 1996 (accidental reissue of 75-G, 1987), if in original package $2–3

79-A Mitsubishi Galant Eterna, 1981

v.1 light green, no markings.........$4–6

v.2 dark green, no markings $4–6

v.3 light green with cream and red "HOT POINTS" tampo....................$5–8

v.4 light green with white and red "HOT POINTS" tampo....................$5–8

Mark One Collectibles (see Speedway Collection)

Mattel (see Hot Wheels)

Max Models (see Paul's Model Art)

Maxwell Mini Auto Toys (Matchbox of India)

Maxwell Mini Auto Toys of Calcutta, India, was a subsidiary of Matchbox of London, England, in the 1970s. Notably odd wheels and somewhat boxy shapes typify these toys intended for the local market in India. Several models are recognizable as Matchbox castings, although comparatively more crude.

501 Military Tank $10–12

502 Road Roller $10–12

503 Greyhound Luxury Coach $10–12

504 Formula One Racing Car..............$10–12

505 Lincoln Continental $10–12

506 MG 1100 (marketed as Mercedes 1100)...............................$10–12

507 Fiat 1100 Premier President 4-Door Sedan $10–12

508 Jeep with exposed engine $10–12

509 Vauxhall Guildsman $12–15

510 Ambassador Mark II 4-Door Sedan $10–12

511 Racing Mini $10–12

512 Volvo P 1800 ....$10–12

513 Lincoln Police Car, red.................$10–12

514 Lincoln Fire Chief $10–12

515 Lincoln Ambulance Car, yellow....$10–12

516 Hovercraft SRN6 ....$10–12

517 Double Decker Bus......................$10–12
518 Jeep with bonnet.......................$10–12
519 Jeep Ambulance.........................$10–12
520 Ambassador Mark II Fire Service $10–12
521 Ambassador Mark II State Patrol $10–12
522 Ambassador Mark II Yellow Cab Taxi...................$10–12
523 Fiat 1100 Premier President Taxi $10–12
524 Tata Mini Bus............................$10–12
525 Freeman Intercity Commuter Coach ..$10–12
526 Tata Van..................................$10–12
527 Tata School Bus.........................$10–12
528 Setra Coach..............................$10–12
529 Aircraft Carrier..........................$12–15
530 Tata Indian Airlines Passenger Coach...................$10–12
531 Jeep Fire Service with ladder $10–12
532 Tata B.O.A.C. Passenger Coach...$10–12
533 Tata Ambulance Bus...................$10–12
534 Pipe Carrier..............................$10–12
535 Freight Carrier...........................$10–12
536 Tata Circus Van.........................$10–12
537 Tata "Cold Spot Cola" Truck.........$10–12
538 Tata Brake Van Service Tow Truck...................$10–12
539 Boeing Passenger Jet Lufthansa.......$10–12
540 Tata Fruit Carrier Stake Truck $10–12
541 MIG Jet...................................$10–12
542 Mirage Jet...............................$10–12
543 Boeing Passenger Jet B.O.A.C....$10–12
543 Mini Jeep.................................$5–7
544 Honda Motorcycle......................$10–12
545 Boeing Passenger Jet "BOAC"......$12–15
546 Boeing Passenger Jet "Swissair" $12–15
547 Tata "Coca-Cola" Truck...............$12–15
548 Animal Carrier..........................$15–18
549 Ford Tractor.............................$12–15
550 Jeep CJ3................................$10–12
551 Jeep Ambulance.........................$10–12
552 Racing Car..............................$5–7
553 Volkswagen Beetle......................$5–7
554 Jeep Carrier.............................$5–7
555 Two Seater Coupe......................$5–7
557 Boeing Passenger Jet Air-India........$12–15
558 1959 Chevrolet Impala..............$12–15
559 1959 Chevrolet Impala Highway Patrol, black and white...................$12–15
560 1959 Chevrolet Impala Fire Chief, red and white...................$12–15
561 1959 Chevrolet Impala Police, red and white...................$12–15
562 1959 Chevrolet Impala Taxi, yellow and black...................$12–15
563 Tata Petrol Tanker "HP Oil"...........$15–18
564 Tata Petrol Tanker "IBP Oil"...........$15–18
565 Tata Petrol Tanker "Indian Oil" $20–25
566 Tata Petrol Tanker "Esso"..............$20–25
567 Tata Petrol Tanker "Caltex"............$20–25
568 Tata Petrol Tanker "Burmah - Shell" ..$10–12
569 Ford 3600 Tractor.....................$15–18
570 H.M.T. Zetor Tractor...................$15–18
571 Jeep Armoured Car.....................$10–12
572 Escort 335 Tractor.....................$15–18

573 Douglas Skyhawk Navy Jet $10–12
574 1934 Riley MPH Vintage Car $10–12
575 Tata Dump Truck........................$10–12
576 Helicopter...............................$10–12
577 Tata "Campa Cola".....................$10–12
578 Tata "Thums Up Cola"..................$10–12
579 Hindusthan Mini Tractor................$12–15
580 Rescue Helicopter......................$10–12
581 Small Petrol Tanker "HP"..............$10–12
582 Small Petrol Tanker "IBP".............$10–12
583 Small Petrol Tanker "Indian Oil".....$10–12
584 Small Petrol Tanker "Esso"............$10–12
585 Small Petrol Tanker "Caltex"..........$10–12
586 Small Petrol Tanker "Burmah - Shell" ..$10–12
587 Field Gun and plastic base...........$10–12
588 Field Gun................................$10–12
589 007 James Bond Lotus Esprit.........$12–15
590 Ford Mustang with opening doors...................$12–15
591 Tata Medium Petrol Tanker "HP" $20–25
592 Tata Medium Petrol Tanker "IBP" $20–25
593 Tata Medium Petrol Tanker "Indian Oil"...................$20–25
594 Tata Medium Petrol Tanker "Esso" ..$20–25
595 Tata Medium Petrol Tanker "Caltex"...................$20–25
596 Tata Medium Petrol Tanker "Burmah - Shell"...................$20–25
597 Tata Medium Petrol Tanker "Bharat Petroleum"...................$20–25
598 Tata Medium Petrol Tanker "Assam Oil"...................$20–25
599 Eicher Tractor...........................$15–18
601 Swaraj Tractor..........................$15–18
602 World War I Bi-Plane...................$15–18
603 Tata Big Petrol Tanker "Bharat Petroleum"...................$20–25
604 Tata Big Petrol Tanker "Assam Oil"...................$20–25
605 Big Jeep Highway Patrol..............$12–15
606 Big Jeep Fire Ladder Truck...........$12–15
607 Big Jeep Police.........................$12–15
608 Big Jeep Armoured Car $12–15
610 Jeep FC150 Pickup....................$10–12

May Cheong (see Maisto)

May Tat (also see Maisto)

May Tat is the bottom-of-the-line budget division of Maisto, producing unidentifiable unmarked toys in the so-called 1:60 scale. Since they bear no markings except on the package, they are considered generic, and are therefore valueless to the collector for anything other than a curiosity.

One example of May Tat toys is a series called Fun Wheels, six vehicles sold in a twelve-car display box — no individual packages. The models are barely recognizable due to drastically shortened bodies and exaggerated styling. Typical is the pull-back-action featured on these toys, available for $1 or less each.

McGregor (also see Politoys, Polistil)

McGregor is the Mexican subsidiary of Politoys, later known as Polistil, of Italy. Here is just a small sampling of models produced. Models are distinguished by the McGregor name on the base, the unusual 1:45 scale in which they are produced, and the words "Hecho en Mexico."

200 BRM F1, purple, 1:41 ....$11
201 De Sanctio F3, green, 1:41...............$11
203 Honda F1, brown & white, 1:41........$11
1919 Fiat 501 S. Sport, green with black fenders and black top...................$15–20
1929 Fiat 525 S. Reale, silver with black fenders and black top...................$15–20
Isotta Fraschini, kind of a dark mustard yellow, black top...................$15–20
Berliet, light yellow with black roof.........$15–20
Lancia Landa, yellow with black fenders and black top...................$15–20
1911 Fiat, sky blue with black fenders and black top, nice car...................$15–20
Bentley, British green with black fenders and black top...................$15–20
Fiat Balilla, black with off-white fenders ...$15–20
1899 Fiat, dark blue with red top, white interior...................$15–20
1902 Isotta Fraschini, dark blue with off-white fenders, white interior.....................$15–20
Itala Palombella, cream-colored body, black roof, yellow fenders...................$15–20

Mebetoys (also see Hot Wheels Gran Toros)

Now a subsidiary of Mattel, Mebetoys of Italy was originally an independent toy manufacturer based in Italy. It arrived on the scene in 1966. Mebetoys was purchased by Mattel around 1970 and have been referred to as "overgrown Hot Wheels."

Models continued to be produced under the Mebetoys brand name even as recently as 1985.

The 6600 series in particular echoes a number of Hot Wheels trademark names, although their resemblance to their namesake is minimal. Nevertheless, they bore the Hot Wheels name on the base and were produced between 1970 and 1972. The series was dubbed Gran Toros, a name now owned by Playing Mantis and issued under the Johnny Lightning brand.

A-1 Fiat 850, 1:42, 1966 ....$30
A-2 Fiat 1500, 1:42, 1966 ....$30
A-3 Alfa Romeo Giulia TI, 1:42, 1966.......$30
A-4 Alfa Romeo 2600, 1:43, 1966..........$30
A-5 Autobianchi Primula, 1:43, 1966........$30
A-6 Lancia Flavia, 1:43, 1966 ....$30
A-7 Alfa Romeo Giulia TI Carabinieri, 1:42, 1966...................$30
A-8 Alfa Romeo Giulia TI Policia, 1:42, 1966...................$30

A-9 Fiat 1100R, 1:43, 1967 ....$30
A-10 Maserati Mistral, 1:43, 1967 ....$40
A-11 Lancia Fulvia Coupe, 1:43, 1967 ......$30
A-12 Porsche 912, 1:43, 1967 ....$40
A-13 Opel Kadett Fastback, 1:43, 1967 ....$30
A-14 Ferrari Berlinetta Le Mans (not issued)
A-15 Fiat 1500 Policia, 1:42, 1967 ....$30
A-16 Fiat 124, 1:43, 1967 ....$30
A-17 BMW 2000CS, 1:43, 1967 ....$30
A-18 Alfa Romeo Duetto Spyder, 1:43, 1967 .....$30
A-19 Mercedes-Benz 250SE, 1:43, 1967 .....$30
A-20 Lamborghini Miura P400, 1:43, 1967 .....$30
A-21 Fiat 1500 Fire Chief, 1:42, 1967 ......$30
A-22 Corvette Rondine, 1:43, 1967 ....$40
A-23 Chapparal 2F, 1:43, 1968 ....$40
A-24 Ford GT Mark II, 1:43, 1968 ....$40
A-25 Porsche Carrera 10, 1:43, 1968 ......$40
A-26 Rolls-Royce Silver Shadow, 1:43, 1968 .....$50
A-27 Ferrari P4, 1:43, 1968 ....$40
A-28 Innocenti Mini-Minor, 1:43, 1968 .....$30
A-29 Toyota 2000GT, 1:43, 1968 ....$30
A-30 Iso Rivolta S4, 1:43, 1968 ....$30
A-31 Innocenti Mini-Minor Rally, 1:43, 1969 .....$30
A-32 Lancia Fulvia Rally, 1:43, 1969 ....$30
A-33 Porsche 912 Rally, 1:43, 1969 ....$40
A-34 Opel Kadett Rally, 1:43, 1969 ....$30
A-35 Yogi Bear & Boo Boo Character Car, 1969 .....$60
A-36 Fiat Nuova 500, 1:43, 1969 ....$30
A-37 NSU Ro 80 Wankel, 1:43, 1969 ....$30
A-38 Matra 530 Vignale, 1:43, 1969 ...$30
A-39 Lotus Europa, 1:43, 1969 ....$40
A-40 Land Rover Trans American, 1:43, 1969 .....$30
A-41 Fiat 124 Safari, 1:43, 1970 ....$30
A-42 Land Rover Ambulance, 1:43, 1970...$40
A-43 Fiat 124/128 Taxi, 1:43, 1970 ....$30
A-44 Bertone Runabout, 1:43, 1970 ....$30
A-45 Alfa Romeo Iguana, 1:43, 1970 .....$30
A-46 Alfa Romeo Junior Zagato, 1:43, 1971 .....$30
A-47 Lamborghini Urraco, 1:43, 1971 .....$30
A-48 Autobianchi A112, 1:43, 1971 .....$30
A-49 Stratos HF Bertone, 1:43, 1971 .....$30
A-50 Ferrari 365GTC-4, 1:43, 1972 ......$40
A-51 Porsche London-Sydney Rally, 1:43, 1972 .....$40
A-52 Fiat Dino with Boat, 1:43, 1972 ...$30
A-53 Ford Escort, 1:43, 1972 ....$30
A-54 Fiat 127, 1:43, 1972 ....$30
A-55 Ford Escort Mexico, 1:43, 1972 .....$30
A-56 Ferrari 312BB, 1:43, 1972 ....$40
A-57 Alfasud, 1:43, 1972 ....$30
A-58 Autobianchi Abarth A112, 1:43, 1972 .....$30
A-59 Fiat 128, 1:43, 1972 ....$30
A-60 Fiat 128 Rally, 1:43, 1972 ....$30
A-61 Morris Mini-Minor, 1:43, 1973.........$30

A-62 Fiat 126, 1:43, 1972 ....$30
A-63 BMW 2800 CS Alpina, 1:43, 1972.$30
A-64 Porsche 912 with Skis, 1:43, 1973....$40
A-65 Alfa Romeo Duetto with Bicycles, 1:43, 1972 .....$30
A-66 Autobianchi Primula with Oil Drums, 1:43, 1972 .....$30
A-67 U. S. Army Land Rover, 1:43, 1972 ...$30
A-68 Fiat 127 Rally, 1:43, 1972 ....$30
A-69 Renault 5TL, 1:43, 1974 ....$30
A-70 Volkswagen 1303, 1:43, 1974 .....$30
A-71 Innocenti Mini-Minor Hippy, 1:43, 1974 .....$40
A-72 Maserati Bora, 1:43, 1973 ....$40
A-73 Lancia Fulvia Marlboro, 1:43, 1974...$30
A-74 Land Rover Fire Truck, 1:43, 1974 ...$45
A-75 Fiat 124 Raid, 1:43, 1974 ....$30
A-76 Alfa Romeo Alfetta, 1:43, 1974 .....$30
A-77 Fiat 128 Coupe, 1:43, 1974...........$30
A-78 Porsche 912 Rally, 1:43, 1974 .....$40
A-79 Willys Military Jeep, 1:43, 1974 .....$30
A-80 Willys Baja Jeep, 1:43, 1974 ....$30
A-81 Willys Fire Jeep, 1:43, 1974 ....$40
A-82 Alfetta Carabinieri, 1:43, 1974 ....$30
A-83 Alfetta Polizia, 1:43, 1974 ....$30
A-84 Citroën Dyane, 1:43, 1974 ....$30
A-85 Fiat 131, 1:43, 1975 ....$30
A-86 BMC Mini 90, 1:43, 1976 ....$30
A-87 Volkswagen Golf, 1:43, 1976 ....$30
A-88 Volkswagen 1303 Jeans, 1:43, 1975..$30
A-89 Willys Police Jeep, 1:43, 1975 ....$30
A-90 Alfasud TI Rally, 1:43, 1975 ....$30
A-91 Lancia Fulvia Alitalia, 1:43, 1975 .$30
A-92 Alfetta Fire Chief, 1:43, 1975 ....$40
A-93 Porsche 924, 1:43, 1976 ....$40
A-94 Renault 5TL Rally, 1:43, 1975 ....$30
A-95 Willys Carabinieri Jeep, 1:43, 1976 ..$30
A-96 Willy United Nations Jeep, 1:43, 1976 .....$30
A-97 Alfasud Trofeo, 21:43, 1976 ....$30
A-98 Fiat 131 Rally, 1:43, 1976 ....$30
A-98 Porsche 924, 1:43, orange with brown interior $40
A-99 Citroën Dyane Vacation Car, 1:43, 1976 .....$30
A-100 Ferrari 512S Pininfarina, 1:43, 1976 .....$40
A-101 Porsche 917 Gulf, 1:43, 1976 ......$40
A-102 DeTomaso Ford Pantera, 1:43 ......$30
A-103 BMW 320, 1:43 ....$30
A-105 Alfasud Sprint, 1:43....................$30
A-106 Ford Fiesta, 1:43 ....$30
A-107 Simca 1308, 1:43.....................$30
A-108 Innocenti Mini DeTomaso, 1:43 .....$30
A-109 Citroën Dyane Rally, 1:43 ....$30
A-110 Fiat Abarth 131, 1:43 ....$30
A-111 Alfa Romeo Giulietta, 1:43 ....$30
A-112 Autobianchi A112 Abarth, 1:43 ......$30
A-112 Fiat 126, 1:43 (not known to exist)
A-113 BMW 320 Rally, 1:43 ....$30
A-114 Volkswagen Golf ADAC, 1:43.........$30
A-115 Volkswagen Golf Polizei, 1:43 ....$30
A-117 Alfasud Vacation Car, 1:43, 1980 ..$30

A-118 Audi 100 GLS, 1:43, 1980............$30
A-119 Fiat Ritmo 65, 1:43, 1980............$30
A-120 BMW 730, 1:43, 1980.................$30
A-121 Ford Granada, 1:43 ....$30
A-122 Desert Jeep, 1:43, 1980..............$30
A-123 Matra Rancho, 1:43, 1980 ....$30
A-124 Opel Monza Coupe, 1:43, 1980 ...$30
A-125 Fiat Panda 30, 1:43, 1980 ....$30
A-126 Volkswagen Golf Rally, 1:43, 1980.$30
A-127 Ford Fiesta Special, 1:43, 1980......$30
A-128 Simca 1308 GT, 1:43, 1980..........$30
A-129 Talbot Simca Horizon, 1:43, 1981 ..$30
A-130 Volvo 343, 1:43, 1981 ....$30
A-131 Fiat Abarth 131 Rally, 1:43, 1981...$30
A-133 Peugeot 305, 1:43, 1981 ....$30
A-134 Citroën Visa, 1:43, 1981 ....$30
A-135 Alfa Romeo Giulietta Carabinieri, 1:43, 1981 .....$30
A-136 Alfa Romeo Giulietta Polizia, 1:43, 1981 .....$30
A-138 Alfa Romeo Giulietta Special, 1:43, 1981 .....$30
A-139 Fiat Ritmo Special, 1:43, 1981 ......$30
A-140 Audi 100 Polizei, 1:43, 1984 ....$30
A-141 Audi 100 ADAC, 1:43, 1984 ....$30
A-142 Talbot Horizon Special, 1:43, 1981 $30
A-143 Opel Monza Special, 1:43, 1981...$30
A-145 Ford Granada Special, 1:43, 1981.$30
A-149 Jeep Rally Service Car, 1:43, 1981..$30
A-152 Fiat 131 Rally, 1:43, 1981 ....$30
1 Alfa Romeo 158-159 Grand Prix, 1:24, 1977 .....$30
2 Alfa Romeo P2 Grand Prix, 1:24, 1977...$30
2501 Fiat Farm Tractor, 1:43 ....$12
2510 Fiat 170 Garbage Truck, 1:43 ....$12
2512 Fiat 170 Container Truck, 1:43 ....$12
2514 Fiat 170 Semi-Trailer Truck, 1:43.......$12
2517 Fiat 170 Lumber Semi, 1:43 ....$12
2519 Fiat 170 Container Semi, 1:43 ....$12
6050 Fiat Uno "Wrangler Jeans," 1:43, 1985 .....$30
6051 Maserati Biturbo Racing, 1:43, 1985..$30
6065 Porsche 911 Turbo "Coca-Cola," 1:43, 1985 .....$30
6067 Porsche 911 Turbo "Gitanes," 1:43, 1985 .....$30
6069 Matra Murena Rally, 1:43, 1985 .....$30
6071 Matra Murena Rally, 1:43, 1985 .....$30
6073 Chevrolet Corvette 1984, 1:43, 1985 .....$30
6082 Volkswagen Golf Cabriolet Rally, 1:43, 1985 .....$30
6091 Audi Quattro Rally, 1:43, 1985 .....$30
6097 Jeep CJ7 Renegade, 1:43, 1985 .....$30
6099 Ford Sierra XR4, 1:43, 1985 ....$30
6103 Alfa Romeo 33 Turbo, 1:43, 1985...$30
6116 Audi Quattro Rally, 1:25, 1984 ....$30
6117 Opel Kadett Rally, 1:25, 1984 ....$30
6119 Porsche 956 Canon, 1:25, 1984 ....$30
6121 Ferrari PB, 1:43, 1984 ....$30
6186 Kenworth Tanker Semi, 1:43, 1985..$30
6188 Kenworth Container Semi, 1:43, 1985 .....$30

6191 Kenworth Dumper Semi, 1:43, 1985 ..$30
6192 Volvo Container Semi, 1:43, 1985 ...$30
6194 Volvo Livestock Semi, 1:43, 1985 .....$30
6196 Volvo Auto Transporter Semi, 1:43, 1985 ....$30
6420 Fiat Uno, 1:43, 1985 ....$30
6423 Mercedes-Benz 500 SEC Rally, 1:43, 1985 ....$30
6425 Alfa Romeo 33 Rally "Agip," 1:43, 1985 ....$30
6427 Pontiac Firebird, 1:43, 1985 ....$30
6430 Ford Sierra XR4 Rally, 1:43, 1985 ....$30

Hot Wheels Gran Toros by Mebetoys (6600 Series)

6601 Ferrari Can-Am, 1:43, 1970 .$80–90
6602 Chevrolet Astro II, 1:43, 1970 ..$65–75
6603 T'rantula Dragster, 1:43, 1971 .$65–75
6604 Torpedo Dragster, 1:43, 1971 .$65–75
6605 Lamborghini Miura, 1:43, 1971 ....$65–75
6606 Chaparral 2F, 1:43, 1971 ...$80–90
6607 Ford GT Mark II, 1:43, 1971 .$80–90
6608 Abarth 695 SS, 1:43, 1971 ..$65–75
6611 Ford Boss Mustang 302, 1:43, 1971 ....$100–120
6612 Alfa Romeo 33/3, 1:43, 1971 ....$65–75
6613 Porsche Carrera 10, 1:43, 1971 ....$80–90
6614 Ferrari P4, 1:43, 1971 ....$65–75
6615 Twin Mill, 1:43, 1971 ....$65–75
6616 Silhouette, 1:43, 1971 ....$65–75
6617 Toyota 2000GT, 1:43, 1971 .$65–75
6618 Lotus Europa, 1:43, 1971 ....$80–90
6621 Ferrari 512S Pininfarina, 1:43, 1971 ....$80–90
6622 Mercedes-Benz C-111, 1:43, 1971 ....$65–75
6623 Porsche 917, 1:43, 1971 ....$80–90
6624 Abarth 3000 SP, 1:43, 1971 ..$80–90
6625 Mantis, 1:43, 1971 ....$65–75
6626 McLaren Can-Am, 1:43, 1972 .$65–75
6627 DeTomaso Ford Pantera, 1:43, 1972 ....$65–75
6628 Chapparal 2J, 1:43, 1972 ...$80–90
6629 Lola T-212 Can-Am, 1:43, 1972 ....$65–75
6670 Matra MS 120, 1:28, 1972 .$65–75
6671 Ferrari 312 B2, 1:28, 1972 .$65–75
6672 BRM P160, 1:28, 1972 ......$65–75
6673 Lotus-Ford 72, 1:28, 1972 .$65–75
6674 Tyrrell-Ford, 1:28, 1972 ....$65–75
6675 Brabham BT 34, 1:28, 1973 .$65–75
6676 March-Ford, 1:28, 1973 .....$65–75
6677 Lotus JPS, 1:28, 1973 ....$65–75

Mebetoys 6700 Series and Higher

6700 Mercedes-Benz 280 SE, 1:28, 1981 ....$30
6702 Land Rover, 1:25, 1980 ....$30
6708 Mercedes-Benz 280 SE, 1:28, 1982 ....$30
6709 Volkswagen Golf 4-Door, 1:24, 1981 ....$30

6711 Citroën Dyane, 1:25, 1981 ....$30
6713 Porsche 924, 1:25, 1981 ....$30
6715 Lancia Beta Giro D'Italia, 1:25, 1981 ....$30
6719 BMW 320, 1:25, 1981 ....$30
6722 Alfa Romeo Giulietta, 1:25, 1981 ..$30
6726 Fiat 242 Safari, 1:25, 1980 ......$30
6728 Fiat 131 Abarth, 1:25, 1981 .....$30
6731 BMW 320 Rally, 1:25, 1980 ....$30
6732 Porsche 924 Rally, 1:25, 1980 ..$30
6733 Ford Granada 1978, 1:25, 1980 .$30
6734 Opel Monza, 1:25, 1981 ....$30
6737 Porsche 928 Rally, 1:25, 1980 ..$30
6739 BMW 730 Sedan, 1:25, 1980 .$30
6740 Audi 100 GLS, 1:25, 1980 ....$30
6741 Volkswagen Golf Rally, 1:25, 1980 .$30
6742 Ford Fiesta Rally, 1:25, 1980 .....$30
6743 Fiat 131 Abarth Parmalat, 1:25, 1981 ....$30
6745 Mercedes-Benz 280 SE Rally, 1:28, 1981 ....$30
6747 Talbot Matra Rancho, 1:25, 1980 ..$30
6748 Fiat Ritmo, 1:25, 1981 ....$30
6755 Volvo 343, 1:25, 1981 ....$30
6756 Volvo 343, 1:25, 1981 ....$30
6757 Fiat Ritmo Special, 1:25, 1981 ...$30
6758 Alfa Romeo Giulietta Special, 1:25, 1981 ....$30
6761 Alfa Romeo Giulietta Carabinieri, 1:25, 1981 ....$30
6762 Alfa Romeo Giulietta Polizia, 1:25, 1981 ....$30
6764 Porsche 924 Turbo, 1:25, 1980 .$30
6765 BMW 320 Alpina, 1:25, 1980 .$30
6766 Peugeot 305, 1:25, 1981 ....$30
6767 Citroën Visa, 1:25, 1981 ....$30
6784 Fiat Ritmo Alitalia, 1:25, 1981 ....$30
6785 Fiat Panda, 1:25, 1981 ....$30
6787 Opel Monza Special, 1:25, 1981 .$30
6788 Talbot Horizon Special, 1:25, 1981 ....$30
6792 Citroën Dyane Special, 1:25, 1981 ....$30
6797 Willys Jeep, 1:25, 1981 ....$30
6800 Fiat-Abarth Ritmo Rally, 1:25, 1981 .$30
6802 Fiat 240 Flat Truck with Kart, 1:25 .$30
6803 Volkswagen Golf Cabriolet, 1:25 ..$30
6804 BMW 320 Wind Surfer, 1:25, 1981 ....$30
6805 Lancia Beta Fire Squad, 1:25, 1981 ....$30
6807 Lancia Squadra SK, 1:24, 1981 .$30
6808 Porsche 911 Targa, 1:25, 1981 .$30
6810 Matra Rancho Rally, 1:25 ....$30
6823 Porsche 928 Rally, 1:25, 1983 ..$30
6830 Audi 100 NASA, 1:25, 1983 ....$30
6844 Maserati Biturbo, 1:25, 1983 ....$30
6845 Lancia 037 Turbo, 1:25, 1983 ...$30
6846 Ferrari 250 GT, 1:25, 1983 ......$30
6849 Fiat Uno, 1:43, 1983 ....$30
6850 Fiat Uno, 1:25, 1985 ....$30
6858 Ferrari Formula 1, 1:25, 1983 ....$30
6860 Ligier Formula 1, 1:25, 1983 ......$30

6861 Brabham Formula 1, 1:25, 1983 ..$30
6862 Arrows MP4 Formula 1, 1:25, 1983 ....$30
6863 Williams Formula 1, 1:25, 1983 ..$30
6864 Lotus Formula 1, 1:25, 1983 .....$30
6866 Renault Formula 1, 1:25, 1983 ...$30
6867 Audi Quattro Rally, 1:25, 1983 ..$30
6868 Opel Kadett Rally, 1:25, 1983 ...$30
6869 Fiat Panda Rally, 1:25, 1983 .....$30
6870 Alfa Romeo Giulietta Rally, 1:25, 1983 ....$30
6871 Fiat Ritmo Rally, 1:25, 1983 .....$30
6872 Citroën Visa Rally, 1:25, 1983 ...$30
6873 Talbot Horizon Rally, 1:25, 1983 ..$30
6874 BMW 735 Rally, 1:25, 1983 ....$30
6875 Porsche 928 Pirelli, 1:25, 1983 ..$30
6876 Volvo 343, 1:25, 1983 ....$30
6877 Lancia Delta, 1:25, 1983 ....$30
6878 Citroën Dyane, 1:25, 1983 ....$30
6879 Porsche 911 Targa, 1:25, 1983 .$30
6880 Peugeot 305, 1:25, 1983 ....$30
6881 Fiat 242 Pickup with Kart, 1:25, 1983 ....$30
6882 Audi 100 with Rubber Boat, 1:25, 1983 ....$30
6883 Ford Fiesta with Skiers, 1:25, 1983 ....$30
6884 Opel Monza with Surfboard, 1:25, 1983 ....$30
6885 Ford Granada Giro D'Italia, 1:25, 1983 ....$30
6886 Jeep Renegade with Motocross Cycle, 1:25, 1983 ....$30
6899 Talbot Matra Mureno Rally, 1:43, 1983 ....$30
6900 Mercedes-Benz 500 SEC Rally, 1:43, 1983 ....$30
6901 Maserati Biturbo Rally, 1:43, 1983 ..$30
6903 Pontiac Firebird, 1:43, 1983 .....$30
6904 BMW 635 Rally, 1:43, 1983 ....$30
6905 Lancia 037 Turbo Martini, 1:43, 1983 ....$30
6906 Audi Quattro Rally, 1:43, 1983 ..$30
6907 Porsche 911 Turbo Rally, 1:43, 1983 ....$30
6908 Chevrolet Corvette 1983, 1:43, 1983 ....$30
6909 Volkswagen Golf Cabriolet, 1:43, 1983 ....$30
6910 Ferrari PB Prototype, 1:43, 1983 .$30
6911 Jeep Laredo, 1:43, 1983 ....$30
8551 Ford Escort, 1:43, 1973 ....$30
8552 Ford Escort Mexico, 1:43, 1973 .$30
8553 Ferrari PB Prototype, 1:43, 1973 .$40
8554 Maserati Bora, 1:43, 1973 ....$40
8555 Alfa Romeo Alfasud, 1:43, 1973 ..$30
8556 Fiat 126, 1:43, 1973 ....$30
8558 Ferrari 312 BB, 1:32 ....$30
8563 Ford Mirage, 1:28, 1973 ....$30
8564 Fiat 126, 1:28 ....$30
8565 Ferrari Boxer, 1:43, 1973 ....$30
8567 Alfa Romeo Alfetta Carabinieri, 1:25 ....$30

8568 Ferrari 312 PB, 1:25..................$30
8573 Porsche 911 Targa, 1:25...........$30
8574 Volkswagen 1302, 1:25............$30
8582 Lancia Beta Coupe, 1:25..........$30
8595 Mercedes-Benz 280 SE, 1:28.....$30
8596 Volkswagen Golf 4-Door, 1:25....$30
8599 Citroën Dyane 6, 1:25.............$30
8612 Porsche 924, 1:25..................$30
8616 Alfa Romeo Alfasud Sprint, 1:25 ..$30
8618 Simca 1307, 1:25..................$30
8619 BMW 316, 1:25.....................$30
8620 Ford Fiesta, 1:25..................$30
8623 Alfa Romeo Giulietta, 1:25.........$30
8637 Volkswagen Golf Polizei, 1:25 ....$30
8638 BMW 320 Alpina, 1:25.............$30
8640 Porsche 924 Martini, 1:25, 1979 ..$30
9553 Peterbilt Tanker Semi "BP," 1:43,
    1985..................................$30
9554 Peterbilt Box Semi "Goodyear," 1:43,
    1985..................................$30
9557 Peterbilt Livestock Semi, 1:43,
    1985..................................$30
9558 Peterbilt Dumper Semi, 1:43,
    1985..................................$30
9560 Volvo Box Semi "Martini," 1:43,
    1985..................................$30
9561 Volvo Container Semi "Sea-Land,"
    1:43, 1985...........................$30
9562 Volvo Auto Transporter Semi, 1:43,
    1985..................................$30
9564 Volvo Dumper Semi, 1:43, 1985 ..$30
9606 Mercedes Livestock Semi, 1:43,
    1985..................................$30
9607 Mercedes Container Semi "Hapag-
    Lloyd," 1:43, 1985...................$30
9609 Mercedes Tanker Semi "Shell," 1:43,
    1985..................................$30
9610 Mercedes Auto Carrier Semi, 1:43,
    1985..................................$30

Mebetoys Jolly Series
Lotus-Climax Formula 1, 1:66...............$12

Meboto (see Moboto)

Meccano (see Dinky)

MegaMovers
MegaMovers, distributed by Megatoys of Los Angeles, California, produce a great assortment of five 1:55 scale pickup trucks and six 1:24 scale models called Luxury Classics. Evidence of the care put into producing these larger toys is seen in remnants of car wax found on one model purchased, the BMW 850i from the Luxury Classics series. The latest MegaMovers are repackaged Maistos.

They also produce a series of smaller models that are basically scrap metal and plastic, lacking detail and accuracy but low priced.

3½" Trucks approximately 1:55 Scale
1955 Chevy Stepside, yellow.................$1
Chevy S-10, bright pink.......................$1
1953 Ford Pickup Street Machine, red.....$1
Chevy C-150 Sportside, metallic silver......$1
Chevrolet C-1500 454SS, metallic charcoal
    gray..................................$1

Luxury Classics approximately 1:24 Scale
Porsche 959, black.........................$6
Lamborghini Diablo, yellow.................$6
BMW 850i, metallic red.....................$6
Ferrari F40, red...........................$6
Mercedes-Benz 500SL, metallic gray........$6
Mercedes-Benz 500SL Convertible, white .$6

Two- and Three-Piece Vehicle Sets
Cheaply-made models that are essentially worthless generic models.

ACTION TEAM includes car with boat and
    trailer, van, and horse trailer $1
ARMY SET includes van, tank, utility vehicle,
    and pickup truck.......................$1
POLICE SET includes police car, police van,
    and police helicopter....................$1
CONSTRUCTION SET includes car, fork lift,
    cement truck, and signs..................$1
CONSTRUCTION SET includes car, fork lift,
    soft drink truck, and signs $1
EMERGENCY SET includes utility vehicle,
    pickup, and ladder truck $1
MOTORCYCLE SET includes silver motorcy-
    cle, yellow motorcycle, and two signs .$1
MOTORCYCLE SET includes green Army
    motorcycle, blue motorcycle, and two
    signs..................................$1

Classy Chassies
A series of 12 pull-back action 1:38 scale cars called Classy Chassies have been especially manufactured in China for Kmart by a company called Road Runners. These toys are relatively accurate renderings of actual cars, considering they sell for around $3. The 1995 versions of these cars have been repackaged as MegaMovers 4¾" cars.

Camaro, white.............................$3
'57 Chevy, red $3
'56 Corvette, red.........................$3
Corvette Sting Ray, silver.................$3
Ferrari F-40, black.......................$3
Ferrari Testarossa, metallic blue $3
Ferrari 250GTO, red.......................$3
Ferrari 318S, metallic gold................$3
Ford Mustang, metallic green...............$3
Ford Thunderbird Convertible, white $3
Ford Thunderbird Hardtop, black $3
Lamborghini Diablo, yellow.................$3

Megatoys (see MegaMovers)

Mego
Best known for its Star Wars merchandise, Mego at one time produced 1:64 scale diecast cars made in Hong Kong. They have been variously marketed as A.M.T. Pups, Tuffy, and Jet Wheels.

Mercury
Torino, Italy, has been the home of Mercury since 1932. Once the premier manufacturer of diecast miniature vehicles, Mercury suffered in the face of increasing competition from Politoys, Mebetoys, and others. By 1980, the last Mercury models were made and the company folded.

1 Aero, 1:40, 1945 ....$100
1 Fiat Nuova 500, 1:48, 1958 ....$30
1 Fiat 131 Mirafiori, 1:43, 1974 ....$25
2 Farina, 1:40, 1946 ....$100
2 Fiat 1800, 1:48, 1959 ....$35
2 Fiat 131 Rally, 1:43, 1974 ....$25
3 Lancia Aprilia, 1:40, 1946 ....$35
3 Alfa Romeo Giulietta Sprint, 1:48, 1956 ..$45
3 Fiat 131 Polizia, 1:43, 1975 ....$25
4 Americana, 1:40, 1946 ....$100
4 Lincoln Continental Mark II, 1:48, 1957.$175
4 Alfa Romeo Giulia Ti, 1:43, 1966 ....$30
4 Fiat 131 Fire Chief, 1:43, 1971 ....$25
5 Lincoln Continental, 1:40, 1947 ....$175
5 Lancia Appia 3, 1:48, 1959 ....$35
5 Fiat 131 Carabinieri, 1:43, 1975 ....$35
6 Studebaker Commander, 1:40, 1947 ...$225
6 Autobianchi Bianchina, 1:48, 1958 ....$25
6 BMW 320, 1:43, 1976.................$25
7 Caravan Trailer, 1:40, 1946 ....$50
7 Fiat 1500 Spider, 1:48, 1960 ....$40
7 Fiat 131 Ambulance, 1:43, 1976 ....$25
8 Willys Jeep, 1948.....................$150
8 Lancia Flaminia, 1:48, 1957 ....$45
8 Fiat 128 Polizia, 1:43, 1974 ....$25
9 Cadillac 62 Sedan, 1:40, 1949 ....$150
9 Fiat 1300, 1:48, 1961 ....$35
9 Fiat 128 Fire Chief, 1:43, 1974 ....$25
10 Fiat 500C, 1:40, 1950 ....$50
10 Innocenti 950, 1:48, 1961 ....$25
10 Fiat 128 Carabinieri, 1:48, 1974 ......$25
11 Fiat 1400, 1950 ....$90
11 Bianchina Panoramica, 1:48, 1962 ....$25
11 Fiat 131 Taxi, 1:43, 1975 ....$25
12 Lancia Aurelia, 1950.................$60
12 Fiat 850 Bertone, 1:43, 1965 ....$30
12 Fiat 131 with Skis, 1:43, 1976 ....$25
13 Fiat Nuova 1100, 1:48, 1954 ....$50
14 Lancia Appia I, 1:48, 1955 ....$50
14 Fiat Abarth SS595, 1:43, 1970 ....$30
15 Volkswagen, 1:48, 1955 ....$90
15 Volkswagen Swiss Mail Car, 1:48, 1956.$125
16 Alfa Romeo 1900, 1:48, 1955 ....$55
17 Alfa Romeo Giulietta, 1:48, 1956........$50
17 Fiat 500L, 1:43, 1967 ....$30
18 Fiat 600, 1:48, 1955 ....$40
19 Fiat 600 Multipla, 1:48, 1957 ....$40
20 Limousine, 1:40, 1947 ....$120
20 Alfa Romeo Giulietta Ti, 1:43, 1975 ....$40
21 Spider, 1:40, 1947 ....$125
21 Ferrari 750, 1:50, 1960 ....$60
21 Ranger Ferves, 1:43, 1969 ....$25
22 Dump Truck, 1:40, 1947 ....$100
22 Mercedes-Benz Formula 1, 1:50, 1960.$60
22 Fiat 128, 1:43, 1969 ....$30
23 Crane Truck, 1:40, 1947 ....$90
23 Fiat 2300 S, 1:43, 1962 ....$40
23 Innocenti 90-120 Rally, 1:43, 1975 ....$40

24 Tank Truck, 1:40, 1947......................$90
24 Maserati 3500 GT, 1:43, 1964..........$45
24 Innocenti 90-120 with Skis, 1:43, 1976..$25
25 Saurer Bus, 1951..............................$90
25 Saurer Swiss Mail Bus, 1957..............$120
25 Fiat 125, 1:43, 1969.........................$30
25 Fiat 125 Rally, 1:43, 1957..................$25
26 Lancia D-24, 1:48, 1957....................$90
26 Fiat 130, 1:43, 1971.........................$25
27 Studebaker Golden Hawk, 1:48, 1957..$200
27 Lancia Fulvia Coupe, 1:43, 1965.........$35
28 Cadillac Eldorado, 1:48, 1956..........$150
28 Ferrari 330 P2, 1:43, 1967................$35
28 Fiat Campagnola ACI Service Car, 1:43, 1975..........................$25
29 Rolls-Royce Silver Cloud, 1:48, 1957....$90
29 Alfa Romeo Giulia Canguro, 1:43, 1965..$40
29 Fiat Campagnola Polizia, 1:43, 1975...$25
30 Bentley S Series, 1:48, 1957..............$90
30 Chapparal 2F, 1:43, 1968..................$60
30 Fiat Campagnola Fire Car, 1:43, 1975..$25
31 Maserati Grand Prix, 1:40, 1947.........$90
31 Lancia Flavia, 1:43, 1964..................$40
31 Fiat Campagnola Carabinieri, 1:43, 1975..........................$25
32 Auto-Union Grand Prix, 1:40, 1947....$100
32 Lancia Flavia Coupe, 1:43, 1964.........$35
32 Fiat Campagnola Ambulance, 1:43, 1975..........................$25
33 Mercedes Grand Prix, 1:40, 1947.......$95
33 Lancia Fulvia, 1:43, 1964..................$40
33 Fiat Campagnola Safari, 1:43, 1975....$25
34 Maserati Grand Prix, 1:40, 1951.........$95
34 Maserati 3500GT, 1:43, 1964..........$40
34 Fiat Campagnola with Snowplow, 1:43, 1975..........................$25
35 Alfa Romeo Grand Prix, 1:40, 1951.....$90
35 Fiat 1300 Polizia, 1:43, 1964.............$30
36 Ferrari Grand Prix, 1:40, 1951.........$125
36 Mercedes-Benz 230 SL, 1:43, 1965....$35
37 Cisitalia 1100, 1:40, 1951.................$90
37 Mercedes-Benz 230 SL Coupe, 1:43, 1965..........................$35
38 Cisitalia Grand Prix, 1:40, 1951.........$90
38 Fiat 850, 1:43, 1965.........................$25
39 SVA Racer, 1:40, 1951......................$90
39 Ferrari 250LM, 1:43, 1964................$40
40 Mercedes-Benz Racer, 1:40, 1951.....$100
40 Alfa Romeo Giulia GT, 1:43, 1965......$35
41 Fiat Abarth 1000 Bialbero, 1:43, 1966..$35
41 Aero, 1:80, 1950.............................$25
41A Farina, 1:80, 1950..........................$25
41B Lancia Aprilia, 1:80, 1950................$25
41C Americana, 1:80, 1950....................$25
41D Studebaker, 1:80, 1950..................$25
42 Fiat Abarth 1000, 1:43, 1965............$35
42A Maserati, 1:80, 1950.......................$25
42B Auto-Union, 1:80, 1950...................$25
42C Mercedes-Benz, 1:80, 1950.............$25
43A Open Truck, 1:80, 1950...................$25
43B Tank Truck, 1:80, 1950
   v.1 "Esso".......................................$25
   v.2 "Agip".......................................$25

   v.3 "Petrolea"..................................$25
   v.4 "Aquila"....................................$25
   v.5 "Galbani"..................................$25
   v.6 "Shell".......................................$25
   v.7 Standard".................................$25
   v.8 "Petrocaltex".............................$25
44A Maserati, 1:80, 1951.......................$25
44B Alfa Romeo, 1:80, 1951...................$25
44C Ferrari, 1:80, 1951.........................$25
44D Cisitalia 1100, 1:80, 1951...............$25
44E Cisitalia Grand Prix, 1:80, 1951........$25
44F SVA Formula 3, 1:80, 1951...............$25
44G Mercedes-Benz, 1:80, 1951.............$25
44 Fiat 850 Coupe, 1:43, 1967..............$35
45 Ferrari Dino Sport, 1:43, 1966............$35
46 Fiat 124, 1:43, 1976.........................$35
47A Covered Truck, 1:80, 1951...............$25
47B Crane Truck, 1:80, 1951..................$25
47C Saurer Bus, 1:80, 1951...................$25
48A Cadillac, 1:80, 1950........................$25
48B Fiat 500C, 1:80, 1950.....................$25
48C Fiat 1400, 1:80, 1950.....................$25
48D Lancia Aurelia, 1:80, 1950...............$25
48 Fiat Dino Pininfarina, 1:43, 1967.........$35
49A Ercole Semi-Trailer Truck, 1:80, 1951..$25
49B Ercole Semi-Trailer Tanker, 1:80, 1951..$25
49C Ercole Flatbed Semi-Trailer Truck, 1:80, 1951..........................$25
50 Mercedes-Benz 230SL Safari, 1:43, 1967..........................$35
50 Fiat Ritmo, 1:43, 1978......................$25
51 Lancia Fulvia Coupe, 1:43, 1966.........$35
51 Lancia Fulvia Rally, 1:43, 1973............$25
52 Maserati, 1:43, 1956........................$75
52 Lancia Beta Coupe Rally, 1:43, 1974...$30
53 Ferrari Supersqualo, 1:43, 1956..........$85
53 Alfa Romeo 33, 1:43, 1970................$35
53 Alfa Romeo Alfetta GT Rally, 1:43, 1976..........................$25
54 Lancia D-50, 1:43, 1956....................$85
54 Lancia Beta with Skis, 1:43, 1976........$25
55 Mercedes-Benz, 1:43, 1956...............$25
55 Alfa Romeo Alfetta with Roof Rack, 1:43, 1976..........................$25
56 Mercedes-Benz Formula 1, 1:43, 1956.$85
56 BMW 320 Monte Carlo Rally, 1:43, 1966..........................$25
57 Ferrari 330P Sebring, 1:43, 1966........$75
58 Alfa Romeo Alfetta Carabinieri, 1:43, 1966..........................$25
59 Ferrari 330P Sebring, 1:43, 1966........$75
59 BMW 320 Police Car, 1:43, 1976.....$25
60 Lancia Aprilia, 1:25, 1946.................$75
60 Ferrari 330P Nurburgring, 1:43, 1966..$50
61 Lancia Aurelia, 1:25, 1950.................$75
61 Porsche Carrera 6, 1:43, 1967............$40
63 Fiat Dino Bertone, 1:43, 1967............$40
63 Fiat 131 Familiare Carabinieri, 1:43, 1976..........................$25
64 Heavy Tractor, 1952.........................$75
64 Alfa Romeo 33, 1:43, 1968................$35
65 Ferrari 330 P4, 1:43, 1969................$35
66 M24 Tank, 1954..............................$35

66 Ferrari 512S Pininfarina, 1:43, 1971...$35
67 Alfa Romeo Montreal Bertone, 1:43, 1969..........................$30
68 Bertone Panther, 1:43, 1969..............$30
69 Jack's Demon Dragster, 1:43, 1969......$25
70 Fiat Balilla, 1:43, 1967......................$35
80 Fiat Campagnola, 1:35, 1977.............$25
81 Fiat Campagnola Mexico, 1:35, 1977..$25
82 Fiat Campagnola Ambulance, 1:35, 1977..........................$25
83 Fiat Campagnola Police Car, 1:35, 1977..$25
84 Fiat Campagnola Fire Truck, 1:35, 1977..$25
88 Saurer Moving Van, 1:65, 1957..........$75
89 Saurer Dump Truck, 1:65, 1957..........$75
89 Saurer Flatbed Truck, 1:65, 1957........$75
90 Americana with Steering, 1:40, 1950..$85
90 Fiat 238 Truck, 1:43 1970.................$75
91 Fiat 238 Truck, 1:43, 1970................$75
91 Pluto Dump Truck, 1948....................$75
91 Pluto Cattle Truck, 1948...................$75
92 Golia-Ercole Open Truck, 1948.........$120
92 Golia-Ercole Cattle Truck, 1948.......$120
92 Fiat 238 Truck, 1:43, 1970................$75
93 Golia-Ercole Open Truck, 1948.........$120
93 Golia-Ercole Cattle Truck, 1948.......$120
93 Fiat 238 Truck, 1:43, 1970................$75
94 Ciclope Flat Truck, 1:40, 1948.........$100
94 Ciclope Dump Truck, 1:40, 1948......$100
94 Ciclope Ladder Truck, 1:40, 1948......$100
94 Ciclope Crane Truck, 1:40, 1948......$100
95 Vulcano Truck Trailer, 1:40, 1948........$60
96 Viberti Tank Truck, 1:48, 1953...........$60
97 Fiat 682N Dump Truck, 1:50, 1956.....$75
97 Fiat 682N Covered Truck, 1:50, 1956.$75
98 Fiat 682N Bus, 1958.........................$75
99 Fiat 682N Car Transporter, 1:50, 1957..$75
100 Car Transporter Trailer, 1:50, 1957....$45
100 Fiat 697 Tank Truck, 1:50, 1977........$45
101 Fiat 697 Cement Truck, 1:50, 1977....$45
102 Fiat 697 Dump Truck, 1:50, 1977......$45
103 Fiat 697 Dump Truck, 1:50, 1977......$45
104 OM 90P Open Truck, 1:50, 1977.......$45
105 OM 90P Bucket Truck, 1:50, 1977.....$45
106 OM 90P Dump Truck, 1:50, 1977.......$45
107 OM 90P Dump Truck with Digger, 1:50, 1977..........................$45
121 Bisonte Crane Truck, 1945...............$85
124 Titano Crane, 1945.........................$85
130 Ursus Crane, 1947..........................$85
132 Fiorenti Power Shovel, 1:20, 1957.....$85
134 Fiat 682N Truck with Controls, 1:50, 1957..........................$85
135 Cable Conveyor..............................$85
201 Fiat Campagnola Wrecker, 1:43, 1976..........................$25
202 Fiat Campagnola Safari, 1:43, 1976...$25
203 Lancia Beta Rally, 1:43, 1976............$25
204 Fiat 131 Wagon with Skis, 1:43, 1976..........................$25
205 Fiat 131 Wagon with Luggage Rack, 1:43, 1976..........................$25
206 Fiat Campagnola African Tour Car, 1:43, 1976..........................$25

207 Rembrandt Caravan, 1:43, 1976.......$25
208 Fiat 131 with Boat, 1:43, 1976........$25
209 Fiat 131 with Roof Rack, 1:43, 1976..$25
210 Fiat 131 Polizia, 1:43, 1976...........$25
211 Alfetta Kenya Safari Car, 1:43, 1976 .$35
212 Vespa 125 Motorbike, 1952 ....$35
212 Fiat 131 Wagon with Boat, 1:43, 1976 ....$35
213 Lambretta 125C Moped, 1952.........$35
213 Fiat Campagnola with A-Gun, 1:43, 1977 ....$45
214 Ariete Field Gun, 1951 ....$25
214 Lambretta 125 LC Moped, 1952.......$35
214 Fiat Campagnola with Lance-Rockets, 1:43, 1977 ....$35
215 Ape Triporteur, 1952 ....$35
215 Fiat Campagnola with Radio, 1:43, 1977 ....$35
216 Lambretta Triporteur, 1952 ....$35
216 Fiat Campagnola with Searchlight, 1:43, 1977 ....$35
217 Lambretta 125 LC, 1952 ....$35
217 BMW 320 Rally, 1:43, 1977 ....$35
218 BMW 320 with Luggage Rack, 1:43, 1976 ....$35
219 BMW 320 with Boat, 1:43, 1976.....$35
221 Fiorentini Excavator, 1955 ....$35
231 Army Tank, 1952 ....$35
232 Cannon, 1952 ....$35
300 Fiat 124 Coupe, 1:43, 1969 ....$35
301 Horse Drawn Flat Wagon, 1950 ....$75
301 Sigma Gran Prix, 1:43, 1969 ....$35
302 Horse Drawn Covered Wagon, 1950.$75
302 Fiat 214 Sport Coupe, 1:43, 1969 ....$35
303 Carabo Bertone, 1:43, 1969..........$35
303 Lancia Beta Coupe, 1:43, 1974 ....$35
304 Alfa Romeo Montreal, 1:43, 1970.....$35
304 Fiat 131 Familiare, 1:43, 1976........$35
305 Ital Design Manta, 1:43, 1970 ....$35
305 Fiat Campagnola, 1:43, 1975 ....$35
306 Horse Drawn Log Cart, 1950 ....$75
306 Ferrari 312P, 1:43, 1970 ....$35
306 Alfa Romeo Alfetta GT, 1:43, 1975 ....$35
307 Stake Trailer, 1950 ....$35
307 Mercedes-Benz C-111, 1:43, 1969 ...$35
308 Porsche 917, 1:43, 1970 ....$35
309 Porsche 908/03, 1:43, 1970..........$35
310 Chapparal 2J, 1:43, 1971 ....$35
311 Fiat 127 Rally, 1:43, 1971 ....$35
312 Horse Drawn Open Cart, 1950..........$75
312 Fiat 214 Rally, 1:43, 1972 ....$35
313 Horse Drawn Tank Cart, 1950 ....$35
313 Fiat 132 GLS, 1:43, 1973 ....$35
314 Fiat 128 SL, 1:43, 1972 ....$35
315 Fiat 128 SL, 1:43, 1972 ....$35
316 Fiat 128 SL Rally, 1:43, 1973 ....$35
317 Fiat 132 Rally, 1:43, 1973 ....$35
318 Fiat 127 Rally, 1:43, 1972 ....$35
320 Fiat 132 Police Car, 1:43, 1975 ....$35
401 Fiat 131 & Caravan, 1:43, 1977 ......$35
402 Fiat 131 & Caravan, 1:43, 1977 ......$35
403 Fiat Campagnola African Tour & Caravan, 1:43, 1977................................$35

404 Alfa Romeo Alfetta GT & Caravan, 1977 ....$35
405 Fiat 131 Wagon with Skis & Caravan, 1:43, 1977..............................$35
406 Fiat 131 Wagon & Caravan, 1:43, 1977 ....$35
408 Fiat 131 with Skis & Caravan, 1:43, 1977 ....$35
409 Lancia Beta with Skis & Caravan, 1:43, 1977.................................$35
413 Fiat Campagnola Army Ambulance & Trailer, 1:43, 1977...........................$35
414 Fiat Campagnola Fire & Trailer, 1:43, 1977 ....$35
415 Alfa Romeo Alfetta GT & Trailer, 1:43, 1977 ....$35
416 BMW 320 & Trailer, 1:43, 1977 ......$35
418 Fiat 131 Wagon & Trailer, 1:43, 1977 ....$35
419 Alfa Romeo Alfetta GT & Trailer, 1:43, 1977 ....$35
420 BMW 320 & Caravan, 1:43, 1977 ..$35
423 Fiat Campagnola & Boat Trailer, 1:43, 1977 ....$35
431 Fiat 131 Wagon & Trailer, 1:43, 1977 ....$35
501 Michigan 375 Tractor Shovel, 1958 ...$55
501 Fiat 697 Dump Truck, 1:43, 1977......$55
502 Michigan 380 Tractor Plow, 1958......$55
502 Fiat 607 Container Truck, 1:43, 1977 ..$55
503 Michigan 310 Road Scraper, 1958....$55
503 Fiat 242 Camper, 1:43, 1977 ....$55
504 Caterpillar 12 Road Grader, 1958 .....$55
505 Euclid Twin Axle Dump Truck, 1959 ....$55
506 Caterpillar Giant Road Grader, 1959..$55
506 Fiat 242 Crane Truck, 1:43, 1977 .....$55
507 Lima Power Shovel, 1959 ....$55
507 Fiat 242 Fire Truck, 1:43, 1977 ....$55
508 Autocar Twin Axle Dump Truck, 1959..$55
508 Autocar Single Axle Dump Truck, 1959..$55
508 Fiat 242 Camper with Luggage Rack,1:43, 1977 ....$55
509 Lorain Crane Truck, 1959 ....$55
509 Fiat 697 Cement Mixer, 1:43, 1977 ..$55
510 Massey-Ferguson Farm Set, 1960........$55
510 Fiat 607 Tank Truck, 1:43, 1977 ....$55
511 Massey-Ferguson Farm Wagon, 1960.$55
512 Massey-Ferguson Hay Baler, 1960......$55
513 Euclid TS-24 Road Scraper, 1960.......$55
514 Drott Tractor Shovel, 1960.................$55
514 International Bulldozer, 1960 ....$55
515 Blaw-Knox Cement Mixer, 1960 ....$55
517 Allis-Chalmers Bulldozer, 1961...........$55
518 Austin-Western Road Roller, 1961 ......$55
519 Euclid C-6 Bulldozer, 1961 ....$55
520 Euclid L-30 Tractor Shovel, 1961 ....$55
521 Warner & Swasey Gradall, 1961.......$55
522 Austin-Western Road Grader, 1961.....$55
523 Landini Farm Tractor, 1961.................$55
531 Fiat 692 Container Semi, 1:43, 1977 ..$55
532 Fiat 692 Tanker Semi, 1:43, 1977 .....$55
534 Fiat 692 Car Transporter Semi, 1:43, 1977 ....$55

651 Ferrari Modulo Pininfarina, 1:32, 1971 ..$35
652 Lancia Fulvia Stratos Bertone, 1:32, 1972 ....$35
653 Alfa Romeo Alfasud 1200, 1:32, 1972 ....$35
751 Fred Flintstone's Car, 1971...............$150
801 Porsche Carrera 6, 1:66, 1969.........$55
801 Fiat Campagnola, 1:66 ....$35
802 Chapparal 2F, 1:66, 1969 ....$35
802 Fiat Tank Truck, 1:66 ....$35
803 Ferrari 330 P4, 1:66, 1969 ....$35
803 Fiat Open Truck, 1:66 ....$35
804 Ford GT 40, 1:66, 1969 ....$55
804 Caravan Trailer, 1:66 ....$55
805 Lamborghini Marzal, 1:66, 1969 ......$55
806 Ferrari 250 Le Mans, 1:66, 1969 ....$55
806 Fiat 217, 1:66 ....$55
807 Osi Silver Fox, 1:66, 1969 ....$55
807 Fiat 131 Rally, 1:66 ....$55
808 Alfa Romeo 33, 1:66, 1969 ....$55
809 Alfa Romeo Montreal, 1:66, 1969.....$55
809 Fiat Cement Truck, 1:66 ....$55
810 Dino Pininfarina, 1:66, 1969 ....$55
810 Fiat Farm Tractor, 1:66 ....$55
811 Lamborghini, 1:66, 1969 ....$55
811 Lancia Stratos Rally, 1:66 ....$55
812 Matra Djet, 1:66, 1969 ....$55
812 Porsche 935 Turbo, 1:66 ....$55
813 Ford Mustang, 1:66, 1969 ....$55
814 Lola T-70 GT, 1:66, 1969 ....$55
815 Ferrari P5, 1:66, 1969 ....$55
816 Sigma Grand Prix, 1:66, 1969 ....$55
817 Lotus Europa, 1:66, 1969 ....$55
818 Mercedes-Benz C-111, 1:66, 1969 ..$55
850 Covered Wagon, 1:66, 1969 ....$75
851 Stagecoach, 1:66, 1969 ....$75
870 Fiat 238 Van, 1:66, 1969 ....$55
872 Fiat 238 School Bus, 1:66, 1969......$55
873 Fiat 238 High-Roof Van, 1:66, 1969..$55
1201 Grand Prix Car: Jarama, 1:66 ....$55
1202 Grand Prix Car: Monte Carlo, 1:66 ..$55
1203 Grand Prix Car: Zeltweg, 1:66 ....$55
1204 Grand Prix Car: Hockenheim, 1:66...$55
1205 Grand Prix Car: Zandvoort, 1:66 ......$55

Mercury Aircraft

401 Fiat G-59 ....$40
402 Fiat G-212 ....$40
403 Fiat G-80 ....$40
404 Vampire..................................$40
405 Lockheed F-90 ....$40
406 Avro 707A $40
407 DH 106 Comet $40
408 Mystere $40
409 Missile $40
410 North American Sabre F86 ....$40
411 Piaggio P-148 ....$40
412 MIG-15 ....$40
413 Convair XF-92A Jet $40
414 Piaggio P136 ....$40
415 Boeing B-50 Superfortress.............$40
416 Convair XF-92A Six-Pusher Propeller Plane $40
417 Sikorsky Helicopter $40

418 Boeing B-47 Stratojet	$40
419 Douglas D559-2 Skyrocket	$40
420 MIG-19	$40
421 Convair XFY-1	$40
422 F7U-3 Cutlass	$40
423 F4U-5N Corsair	$40
424 F94-C Starfire	$40
425 P-38 Lightning	$40

Mercury Ships

451 Australia	$40
452 Cristoforo Colombo	$40
453 Federico C	$40
454 Venezuela	$40
455 Leonardo Da Vinci	$40
456 Victoria	$40
457 Bianca C	$40
458 Franca C	$40
459 Andrea	$40
460 Anna C	$40

Mercury Motorcycles

601 Bultaco Mark 4, 1971	$40
602 MV 350CC, 1971	$40
603 Guzzi V7, 1971	$40
604 Chopper Wildcat, 1971	$40
605 Laverda 750 SF, 1972	$40
606 Yamaha Scrambler, 1972	$40
607 BMW R75 750cc, 1972	$40
608 Honda CB750, 1972	$40
609 Honda US90 Army 3-Wheeler, 1972	$40
610 Kawasaki 750cc Mach IV H2, 1972	$40
611 Guzzi V7 Army Motorcycle	$40
612 Guzzi V7 Police Motorcycle	$40
613 Ducati Scrambler 250cc	$40
614 Harley-Davidson Electra	$40
615 Honda 750 Police Motorcycle	$40
616 Harley-Davidson Police Motorcycle	$40
1010 Benelli 750 Cycle & Sidecar, 1:18	$40

Mercury Industries USA (see Lit'l Toy)

Message Models (also see Fun Ho!)

Message Books and Models (also known as Message Models and Books) is reportedly the new owner of old Fun Ho! castings and tooling. Contact:

John Robinson
The Trans-Sport Shop
Message Models and Books
P O Box 239 Northbridge
New South Wales, 2063
Australia

Metalcar

Metalcar (or Metal Car) is a brand of models from Hungary.

Metal Car 1:64 Scale

1 Datsun 126X	$4
3 Futura Container Dump Truck	$4
4 Futura Tow Truck	$4

5 Honda 750 Motorcycle	$4
6 Mercedes-Benz 406 Police	$4
7 Mercedes-Benz 406 Bank Police	$4
8 Mercedes-Benz 406 Service	$4
9 Porsche 928 Coupe	$4
10 Volkswagen Dune Duggy	$4
11 Helicopter, USA	$5
12 Opel Senator 4-Door Sedan	$5
13 Mercury 406 Police	$5
14 Mercury 406 Ambulance	$5
15 Audi 2000 4-Door Sedan	$5
16 Steam Train Engine	$5
17 Lamborghini Espada Coupe	$5
18 Futura Oil Truck "SHELL"	$5
19 Futura Oil Truck "MOBIL"	$5
20 Futura Garbage Truck	$5
21 Futura Dump Truck	$5
22 Futura Tow Truck	$5
23 Jeep CJ5 Hardtop	$5
24 Jeep CJ5 Open	$5
25 Jeep CJ5 4x4	$5
26 Citroën SM Coupe	$5
27 Mercedes-Benz 190 4-Door Sedan	$5
28 Batmobile	$25
29 Porsche 928 Police	$5
30 Motorboat	$5
31 Alpine A310 Police	$5
32 Ferrari 275 Coupe	$5
33 Hanomag Truck	$5
34 Metchy F1 Racer	$5
35 Cessna Plane Police	$5
36 Cessna Plane Military	$5
37 Unimog 406 Truck	$5
38 Scania Bus	$5

Metalcar 1:43 Scale

1 BMW 3.0 Turbo	$20
2 Mercedes-Benz SeaLand Truck	$20
3 Mercedes-Benz Truck	$20
4 Mercedes-Benz Garbage Truck	$20
5 Mercedes-Benz Fire Ladder Truck	$20
6 Mercedes-Benz Tow Truck	$20
7 Surtees F1 FIRESTONE	$20
8 Volkswagen Golf JPS	$20
9 Volkswagen Golf Police	$20
10 BMW 525 Ambulance	$19
11 BMW 525 Polizei	$19
12 Dodge Van Police	$19
13 Audi Quattro Coupe	$19
14 Opel Kadett Police	$19

Metalcar 1:25 Scale

15 Mustang Police	$25

Metal Cast Products Company

From 1929 to 1940, Metal Cast Products Company produced slush-mold toy vehicles as an outgrowth of the S. Sachs company, producer of toy soldiers.

Manufacture of these models were franchised to various other smaller firms, while Metal Cast handled the marketing and distribution. Models are well made and nicely painted. Values are currently low for their vintage, but could rise somewhat as more collectors become

aware of them. The problem sometimes is in identifying models, since franchisers didn't always put a manufacturer name on the models. Fred Green Toys is one of the franchisers whose name is most often found on the base.

Cadillac 2-Door Sedan, #40, 5¼"	$45
Convertible Coupe, #63	$15
Dump Truck, #42, 5¼"	$15
Fire Engine Ladder Truck, #61, 4½"	$20
Fire Engine Steam Pumper with water cannon, #65, 4"	$20
Fire Engine Steam Pumper with no water cannon, no number, 3⅞"	$20
Packard 2-Door Convertible, top down, #41, 5¼"	$30
Racer, #62, Bluebird-style Record Car, 4½"	$30
Streamline Airflow-style Sedan, #60, 4"	$25
Stake Truck, #64, 4¼"	$20
Truck and Moving Van Trailer, #01-02, 6"	$15
Truck and Tank Trailer, #01-03, 6"	$15
Truck and Open Rack Stake Trailer, #01-04, 6"	$15
War Tank, #08, 4"	$65

Metal Masters

It is curious that more information is not written about Metal Masters. They seem to have been prolific toys during the 1940s and 1950s, at least in the eastern United States, originating from Pottstown, Pennsylvania. Identifying them is easy since every model is imprinted on the underside with "Metal Masters Co." and "Made In U.S.A." Although cast from a single mold similar to Tootsietoys and Midgetoys, Metal Masters differentiate themselves by their sleek, angular contours and classic lines.

Metal Masters are prototypical toys, which means that, while hinting at real cars from the 1930s, the toys make no attempt to replicate a particular vehicle. They instead reflect the styling of such great marques as Bugatti, Packard, Stutz, LaSalle, Duesenberg, Cord, and Auburn, combining elements from each to create a unique look all their own.

Like many toys made in the first half of the twentieth century, distribution of Metal Masters was limited to the general region from which the toys are produced. While they are apparently still easy to find in some parts of the eastern U.S., you'll rarely find them anywhere in the West, particularly in the Pacific Northwest. While visiting my family in Michigan and Wisconsin, I went to an antique shop where I was able to find Metal Masters toys by the dozen, although I couldn't afford to buy any at $35-60 a pop. Back here in Oregon, I've never seen a single one.

Since Metal Masters are stylized and represent no particular automobile, it is impossible to list them by make and model. So they are listed below by vehicle type, however nondescript. Identification is made simpler by the fact that there were only six basic castings, with some of them modified to create different models. The station wagon was produced without and without a wind-up motor, and was also adapted into an ambulance by applying a different paint scheme. The pick-up truck was also modified to serve as a tow truck and a fire truck.

Values below represent models in new condition with little or no visible wear.

Bus, 7¼", circa 1938	$45
Fire Truck, 10 inches long, circa 1940	
v.1 with removable ladders	$75
v.2 with wind-up motor and ladders	$120
Jeep, 5½", circa 1947	$50
Roadster, 7", circa 1938	$45
Station Wagon, 8½", circa 1940	
v.1 without wind-up motor	$60
v.2 with wind-up motor	$65
v.3 Ambulance	$65
Pickup Truck, 7", circa 1938	
v.1 Pickup Truck	$45
v.2 Tow Truck	$45
v.3 Fire Truck	$65
Tow Truck	
v.1 "ABC Towing Service," 10", circa 1940	$95
v.2 with wind-up motor, 10", circa 1940	$105
Tractor with driver, 5", vintage not reported	$105

Metal Miniatures

These are unpainted one-piece highly detailed cast-metal vehicles in 1:87 scale (HO gauge), of which one is listed as available from Walthers.

Caterpillar Tractor, 340-44	$2

Metosul

Metosul is a Portuguese brand of toys resembling Corgi and Dinky Toys, possibly from some older castings purchased from another producer, according to Dr. Craig S. Campbell, an avid collector of less common diecast cars. Metosul cars are typically 1:43-1:45 scale, while their trucks are 1:50 and buses 1:72.

Peter Foss adds that the Osul company of Portugal produced plastic toy cars starting in 1932. In 1964, they started a line of diecast metal Osul toys and dubbed them "Metosul." The company continued producing Metosul cars until around 1980. Foss says that Metosul castings are of lesser quality than Dinky or Corgi, and that there aren't many unique models offered in the assortment.

The reason for the variance in quality is due to several models that are recastings of old Matchbox Models of Yesteryear dies, and at least one former CIJ casting, a Notin Rulote Camping Caravan.

Metosul 1:43 Scale

Alfa Romeo Giulietta Roadster, #3, 1:43	$32
Alfa Romeo Giulietta Roadster Policia, #3, 1:43	$32
Alfa Romeo Giulietta Roadster GNR, #3, 1:43	$32
Alfa Romeo Giulietta Roadster GNR BT, #3, 1:43	$32
Citroën DS19, #2, 1:43	$40
Citroën DS19 Aluguer, #22, 1:43	$32
Citroën DS19 Bombieros, #48, 1:43	$32
Citroën DS19 Feuerwehr, #82, 1:43	$32
Citroën DS19 GNR, #61, 1:43	$32
Citroën DS19 Policia, #22, 1:43	$32
Citroën DS19 Taxi Lisbon, turquoise & black, #20, 1:43	$35
Citroën DS19 Taxi Portugal, #120, 1:43	$32
Citroën DS19 and Caravan, #43, 1:43	$64
Mercedes-Benz 190D, #9, 1:43	$48
Mercedes-Benz 190D Policia, #9, 1:43	$48
Mercedes-Benz 190D Taxi, #9, 1:43	$48
Mercedes-Benz 200, #10, 1:45	$27
Mercedes-Benz 200 Aluguer, #16, 1:45	$27
Mercedes-Benz 200 Army, #27, 1:45	$32
Mercedes-Benz 200 Bombieros, #52, 1:45	$27
Mercedes-Benz 200 Emergencia, #51, 1:45	$27
Mercedes-Benz 200 Policia, #25, 1:45	$24
Mercedes-Benz 200 Polizie, #30, 1:45	$24
Mercedes-Benz 200 Taxi, #10, 1:45	$27
Mercedes-Benz 200 Taxi Amsterdam, #110, 1:45	$27
Mini Cooper, #108, 1:43	$32
Morris Mini Minor, #7, 1:43	$32
Notin Rulote Camping Caravan, #19, 1:43 (former CIJ casting)	$27
Peugeot 204 4-Door Sedan, #24, 1:43	$24
Peugeot 204 Aluguer, #32, 1:43	$27
Peugeot 204 Taxi, #31, 1:43	$27
Peugeot 304 Estate Wagon, #49, 1:43	$27
Peugeot 304 Estate Wagon Bombieros, #60, 1:43	$27
Peugeot 304 Estate Wagon JAE Municipal, #58, 1:43	$27
Peugeot 304 Estate Wagon Policia, #55, 1:43	$27
Peugeot 304 Estate Wagon Police, #59, 1:43	$27
Renault Floride, #1, 1:43	$24
Renault R16, #14, 1:43	$24
Renault R16 GNR, #14, 1:43	$24
Renault R16 Taxi, #15, 1:43	$24
Renault R16 Aluguer, #16, 1:43	$24
Rolls-Royce Silver Ghost, #12, 1:43	$18
Volkswagen 1200, #4, 1:43	$32–64
Volkswagen 1200 Army, #4, 1:43	$64
Volkswagen 1200 Bombeiros, #57, 1:43	$32
Volkswagen 1200 GNR, #8, 1:43	$30–60
Volkswagen 1200 GNR BT, #6, 1:43	$32–64
Volkswagen 1200 Policia, #5, 1:43	$32–64
Volkswagen 1200 Polis, #56, 1:43	$32
Volkswagen Transporter, #42, 1:43	$20
Volvo P1800 Coupe, #11, 1:43	$27
Volvo P1800 Coupe GNR BT, #18, 1:43	$24
Volvo P1800 Coupe Policia, #17, 1:43	$24
Volvo P1800 Coupe Polis, #117, 1:43	$27

Metosul 1:50 Scale

Mercedes-Benz 1113 Army Cargo Transport Truck, light green & olive, #38, 1:50	$35
Mercedes-Benz 1113 Bombeiros, #53, 1:50	$27
Mercedes-Benz 1113 Correios, #50, 1:50	$32
Mercedes-Benz 1113 Dump Truck, #26, 1:50	$32
Mercedes-Benz 1113 EGT Truck, #37, 1:50	$32
Mercedes-Benz 1113 GNR Truck, #39, 1:50	$32
Mercedes-Benz 1113 JAE Truck, #41, 1:50	$32
Mercedes-Benz 1113 Policia Truck, #40, 1:50	$32
Mercedes-Benz 1113 Tanker, "GALP," #46, 1:50	$24
Mercedes-Benz 1113 Tanker, "SACOR," #28, 1:50	$36
Mercedes-Benz 1113 Tanker, "SONAP," #29, 1:50	$36
Mercedes-Benz 1113 Tanker Bombeiros, #54, 1:50	$36

Metosul 1:72 Scale

Leyland Atlantean Double Decker Bus, "Carris," #23, 1:72	$32
Leyland Atlantean Double Decker Bus, "Carris," #45, 1:72	$24
Leyland Atlantean Double Decker Bus, "Gazcidla," #36, 1:72	$32
Leyland Atlantean Double Decker Bus, maroon & gray, 1:72	$32
Leyland Atlantean Double Decker Bus, "SMC," #34, 1:72	$32
Leyland Atlantean Double Decker Bus, "STCP," #33, 1:72	$32
Leyland Atlantean Double Decker Bus, "STCP," #44, 1:72	$24
Leyland Atlantean Double Decker Bus, "Transul," #35, 1:72	$32

Mettoy (also see Corgi)

Richard O'Brien lists just a few of these early Mettoy models in his book. The connection between Mettoy and Corgi is explored more thoroughly in Dr. Edward Force's book on Corgi toys.

Motorcycle, circa 1940	$800
Racer, 7"	$2,000
Rolls Royce, 14"	$1,200
Sedan, 14", circa 1930	$600
Steam Roller, clockwork	$200

Miber

Miber models are plastic 1:87 scale models, often plain with stickers included for detailing, reportedly made in Nuremberg, Germany. According to Pantera model collector Markus R. Karalash, this company has produced HO scale (1:87) DeTomaso Panteras along with some other models. In addition, Mazda model collector Werner Legrand of Brecht, Belgium, offered this additional information: "Miber definitely had produced more than only the Pantera.

"I have a few (of course) Mazda models in my small collection, but I also know somebody with some Miber Toyotas. The finishing of those items is very poor in comparison to some other 1:87 scale manufacturers as Herpa, Wiking, etc.

"The interesting part is that they produced models that no others did, and the price wasn't bad either. They even promised (in 1992) a model of the NSX, too.

"I also found an extract of a Dutch article, dated 1985, on Miber models made by LH Industries. Briefly, it says that Miber often has announced items but, unfortunately, didn't always keep their promises."

1152 DeTomaso Pantera, 1:87	$4–8
2152 DeTomaso Pantera, 1:87	$4–8
9152 DeTomaso Pantera, 1:87	$4–8
1271 Mazda 323, white, 1:87	$4–8
1271 Mazda 323, cream, 1:87	$4–8
2042 Toyota Celica 2000 GTR, white, "Monte Carlo '89" stickers	$4–8
2043 Toyota Celica 2000 GTR, teal, "BP," "Leyton House Formula One Racing Team" tampos	$4–8
Toyota Celica 2000 GTR, red	$4–8

Micro Machines

Lewis Galoob Toys, Inc.
South San Francisco CA 94080
website: www.galoob.com

Galoob is the toy company best known for producing the world's smallest series of toy vehicles, numbering in the thousands of models. Up until the imminent re-release of the Star Wars motion picture in 1997, Micro Machines had produced only vinyl and plastic models in very small scale. As the enhanced version returned to theaters with new scenes added and an audio upgrade to THX Dolby surround sound, Galoob introduced its first series of diminutive diecast models to commemorate the event, as listed below. Models are made in China. Galoob is now a division of Hasbro. Later, with the release of Star Wars Episode 1, The Phantom Menace, Micro Machines offered another series of quality diecast models along with their vinyl and plastic assortment.

While rarely involving any diecast components, Galoob's Micro Machines are nevertheless an intriguing assortment of tiny plastic toys. For 1999, Micro Machines offered a new Collector Edition series of very accurate scale models in approximately 1:87 scale. The first to show up in stores was the Corvette Series 1, an exceptional assortment of high-quality replicas with opening hoods or removable roofs.

Galoob continued reissuing existing models and producing new ones, mixing and matching them in 3-, 4- and 5-piece theme sets retailing for $5 each. Forty different sets were issued each year especially from 1996 through 1998.

Galoob Micro Machines Collector Edition Corvette Series 1, 1:87 Scale, plastic

Manta Ray Experimental with opening hood, blue with silver accents	$2
1963 Grand Sport Racer with opening hood, white and blue with red accents	$2
1968 Convertible with removable top, white	$2
1968 Convertible with removable top, red	$2
1978 T-Top Coupe with removable T-Top, black with silver and red accents	$2
1996 Grand Sport with removable top, royal blue with white racing stripe	$2
1997 Coupe with opening hood, red	$2

Galoob Micro Machines Star Wars, diecast metal

Millenium Falcon	$8
Imperial Star Destroyer	$8
Imperial Tie Fighter	$8
Jawa Sandcrawler	$8
X-wing Starfighter	$8
Y-wing Starfighter	$8
Royal Starship of the Naboo Princess	$8
Trade Federation Battleship	$8
Trade Federation Droid Starfighter	$8
Gian Landspeeder	$8

Micro Models

Micro Models — six attempts in 42 years

The First Range — The first successful producer of quality diecast toy cars in Australia was Micro Models, a company whose success was and still is strongly connected with the success of the Holden automobile. From 1952 to 1960, Micro Models produced beautifully rendered toys in roughly 1:43 scale, with trucks produced in approximately 1:72 scale. Current collector value places these early models right around the $100–200 range.

But they weren't all Holdens. In fact the first toy produced by Micro Models was a Vauxhall Velox, a British car, designated GB-1. It was followed by a Holden Utility, more popularly known as a Ute, the Australian version of a pick-up truck — and designated GB-2. This was followed by yet another British replica, a Jaguar XK-120, marked GB-3. Two British Bedford trucks followed, both using the same chassis. GB-4 was a flatbed, or tray, truck, and GB-5 was a dump truck. GB-6, a four-wheel trailer, rounded out the first offering from Micro Models.

Many popular models followed, until 1958 when import barriers to Australia were lifted, and toys from around the world began seeping into the previously isolated continent. Because of increasing competition from foreign producers, Micro Models ceased operation in Australia in 1958.

The Second Range — Meanwhile in 1956, a second range of Micro Models had begun in New Zealand by Lincoln Industries, originally under an arrangement with the Australian company. The New Zealand series continued through 1960 and is strongly connected with the current series of Micro Models reissues from New Zealand. Lincoln Industries is believed to have had a connection with the British firm of D.C.M.T. (Diecasting Machine Tools Ltd.).

The Third Range — Kevin F. Meates of New Zealand purchased the brand in 1962 but didn't resume producing models until 1970. The Micro Models brand was finally resurrected in 1970 by the Meates family of New Zealand under the company names of Matai and Torro, and celebrated limited success in the manufacturing and marketing of new models through 1976.

The Fourth Range — In 1982, a company based in Western Australia obtained the rights to use the Micro Models brand to launch a series of plastic versions of the Holden FJ Panel Van in five different colors. The series was met with only meager interest and the company ceased production shortly afterward. Plastic renditions produced during this time are now worth around $40–70.

The Fifth Range — Weico Models Australia took the first stab at reproducing early Micro Models in white metal, in both kit and built form. On their bases were marked the words "Micro Reproductions." When properly assembled and painted, they were indistinguishable from the originals until inspected more closely. Their weight and inscription then became the obvious give-away of a reproduction. Their limited production capacity meant few were made, and current collector values of $100–200 reflect their rarity.

The Sixth (and present) Range — In 1994, after two years of preparation, Micro Models Ltd of Christchurch, New Zealand, unveiled authentic replicas of the original series offered between 1952 and 1958. The reason they could so faithfully reproduce the originals is that the company retained much of the original component dies and tooling, most in good condition, from the first company. Today's Micro Models commemorate those first quality offerings from the Australian manufacturer with new castings from original molds. Current prices place them around $30–35 Australian, quite a bit more in the States. When you can find them, they will likely cost you $65–95 US each.

For more information, write to Micro Models, Ltd., P O Box 815, Christchurch, New Zealand, or call 64-3-365-5016 (fax 64-3-366-6292). Values, in brackets [ ] represent wholesale prices in Australian dollars, while remaining price indicates retail value in U.S. funds.

The First Range, Australia 1952–1961

GB-1 Vauxhall Velox Sedan $175–200
GB-2 Holden FX Utility (Pickup) with tow hook $125–150
GB-3 Jaguar Sports XK120 ....$120–135
GB-4 Bedford Tray (Flatbed) Truck.$140–160
GB-5 Bedford Tipper Truck..........$140–160
GB-6 Small Trailer.........................$80–95
GB-7 Ford Zephyr Sedan $105–120
GB-8 International Delivery Van, Micro Models..................$145–160
GB-8 International Delivery Van, Peters Ice Cream $145–160
GB-9 Holden FX Sedan.............$145–160
GB-9 Holden FX Taxi $145–160
GB-9 Holden FX Police............$145–160
GB-10 Humber Super Snipe $130–145
GB-11 Commer 7-Ton Dump Truck..$145–160
GB-12 Talbot-Lago Racing Car....$145–160
GB-13 Morris Fire Engine $120–135
GB-14 Repair Hoist.......................$65–80
GB-15 Vanguard Estate Car $120–145
GB-16 International Drink Truck....$140–150
GB-17 Holden FJ Sedan.............$120–145
GB-17 Holden FJ Police.............$120–145
GB-17 Holden FJ Taxi...............$120–145
GB-18 Semi-Trailer $120–145
GB-19 Large Trailer $120–145
GB-20 International Ambulance ...$120–145
GB-21 Holden FJ Panel Van, Taxi Trucks $120–145
GB-21 Holden FJ Panel Van, Royal Mail $120–145
GB-21 Holden FJ Panel Van, PMG (Post Master General) $120–145
GB-22 Commer Tanker................$120–145
GB-23 International Tow Truck.....$120–145
GB-24 Vickers Viscount 700 Passenger Airliner, Trans-Australia Airlines $160–175
GB-25 Volkswagen Sedan $120–145
G-26 Ferguson Tractor $120–145
G-27 Commer Articulated Tanker, Shell $160–175
G-27 Commer Articulated Tanker, Mobilgas $160–175
G-27 Commer Articulated Tanker, Peters Ice Cream $160–175
G-28 Ferguson Tractor Front End Loader $120–140
G-29 Ford O.H.V.-V-8 Truck.......$125–140
G-30 Mobilgas Petrol Pump $60–80
G-31 Bedford SB Suburban Bus $90–110
G-32 MGA Sports Car $140–160
G-33 Holden FE Sedan.............$125–140
G-34 Ford Customline Sedan 1956.$125–140
G-35 Ford Mainline Utility..........$125–140
G-36 Volkswagen Bus $125–140
G-37 Ford O.H.V.-V-8 Dump Truck.$125–140
G-38 Holden FE Coupe Utility with tow hook..................$125–140
G-39 Ford O.H.V.-V-8 Tray (Flatbed) Truck............................$125–140
G-40 Chrysler Royal Sedan $160–175

G-41 Vauxhall Cresta Sedan 1958 .$125–140
G-42 Holden FC Station Wagon $125–140

The Second Range, New Zealand 1956–1960

4301 Vauxhall Velox Sedan $125–140
4302 Holden FX Coupe (Utility)...$125–140
4303 Jaguar XK-120.................$125–140
4304 Bedford S Tray Truck........$125–140
4305 Ford Zephyr Six Sedan $125–140
4306 Humber Super Snipe Sedan .$125–140
4307 Bedford S Tip Truck $125–140
4308 Small Trailer $125–140
4309 Holden FX Sedan Police....$125–140
4310 Talbot-Lago Racing Car.....$125–140
4311 Holden FX Sedan.............$125–140
4312 Holden FX Sedan Taxi $125–140
4313 Garage Repair Hoist............$45–60
4314 Commer 7 Ton Dump Truck..................$125–140
4315 Commer Tanker, Shell.......$125–140
4316 Commer Articulated Semi-Trailer $125–140
4317 Commer Articulated Tanker, Shell $125–140
4318 Morris Fire Engine $125–140
4319 Standard Vanguard Estate Car $125–140
4320 Holden FJ Panel Van $125–140
4321 Large Trailer $125–140
4322 Massey Harris Tractor $125–140
4323 Ford Zephyr Zodiak Sedan .$125–140
4327 International Ambulance $125–140
4328 International Tow Truck......$125–140
4329 Vicker Viscount Passenger Aircraft, TAA.........................$125–140
4330 Volkswagen Sedan $125–140
4331 Humber Super Snipe Sedan Traffic $125–140
4332 Commer Articulated Tanker, Milk Tanker $125–140
4333 International Van, Micro Models $125–140
4334 MGA Sports Car $125–140
4335 Petrol Pump Set, Mobilgas.$125–140
4336 Bedford SB Bus...............$125–140
4337 Ferguson Tractor..............$125–140
4338 Ford Customline Sedan $125–140
4339 Holden FE Sedan.............$125–140
4340 Massey Harris Front End Loader $125–140
4341 Commer Articulated Low Loader $125–140
4342 Commer Articulated Logging Truck............................$125–140
4343 Ford Mainline Utility..........$125–140
4344 Volkswagen Microbus $125–140
4345 Holden FJ Panel Van, Royal Mail NZPO $125–140
4346 Ford O.H.V. V8 Dump Truck, Micro Models $125–140
4347 Ford O.H.V. V8 Truck.......$125–140
4348 International Ambulance, Military $125–140

4349 Ford O.H.V. V8 Truck, Military with tilt..................$125–140
4350 Ford O.H.V. V8 Truck with tilt..................$125–140
4351 International Drink Truck, Coca-Cola..................$125–140
4352 Holden FC Station Wagon .$125–140
4353 Chrysler Royal Sedan.......$125–140
4354 Caterpillar Bulldozer $125–140
—— Holden FE Coupe Utility (Matai/Torro product only)..................$125–140
—— Caterpillar Tractor $125–140

The Third Range, Matai and Torro, New Zealand, 1970s

GB-8 International Delivery Van, Micro Models logo without micrometer ...$125–140
GB-13 Morris Fire Engine, beacon replaces bell..................$125–140
GB-15 Vanguard Estate Car $125–140
GB-16 International Drink Truck....$125–140
GB-23 International Tow Truck.....$125–140
GB-25 Volkswagen Sedan $125–140
G-32 MGA Sports Car $125–140
G-33 Holden FE Special Sedan ..$125–140
G-34 Ford Customline Sedan $125–140
G-35 Ford Mainline Utility..........$125–140
G-38 Holden FE Utility $125–140
G-40 Chrysler Royal $125–140
G-41 Vauxhall Cresta $125–140
G-42 Holden FC Station Wagon ..$125–140

The Fourth Range, Micromodels in plastic, 1982–1983

Holden FJ Panel Van
  v.1 Watsonia, red $40–55
  v.2 Kodak, yellow...................$60–70
  v.3 Corlett Brothers Belmont Bakers, blue..................$45–60
  v.4 Corlett Brothers Bakers, green.$45–60
  v.5 Corlett Brothers "Sunglow" Bread Products, gray...................$45–60

The Fifth Range, Micro Reproductions in white metal, 1980s

1 Holden FX Sedan (GB-9) $90–110
2 Holden FJ Sedan (GB-17) $90–110
3 Holden FX Utility (Pickup) with tow hook (GB-2)..................$90–110
4 Ford Customline Sedan 1956 (G-34) $90–110
5 Holden FJ Panel Van (GB-21) $90–110
6 Holden FC Station Wagon (G-42)..$90–110
7 Ford Mainline Utility (G-35) $90–110
8 Chrysler Royal Sedan (G-40) $90–110
9 Holden FE Sedan (G-33) $90–110
10 Humber Super Snipe (GB-10)...$90–110
11 Holden FC Panel Van (never issued in the original Micro Models range)..$90–110
12 Vauxhall Cresta Sedan 1958 (G-41) $90–110
13 Volkswagen Bus (G-36)..........$90–110
14 Holden FE Coupe Utility with tow hook (G-38)..................$90–110
18 Vauxhall Velox Sedan (GB-1) ..$90–110
19 Vanguard Estate Car (GB-15)...$90–110

20 Volkswagen Sedan (GB-25).....$90–110
21 Bedford SB Suburban Bus (G-31)$90–110

The Sixth & Present Range, 1994–Present [New Zealand value in brackets] US equivalent to right

MM001 International Delivery Van, 1:64, Micro Models "we're back," maroon, no prod #s [$38] $21

MM002 International Delivery Van, 1:64, NZ Model Vehicle Club, Inc., 120 produced [$42] $23

MM003 Holden FJ Panel Van, 1:64, NZ Model Vehicle Club, Inc., 279 produced [$42] $23

MM004 Holden FJ Special Sedan, 1:43, NZ Police, 375 produced [$42].....$23
MM005 Holden FJ Panel Van, 1:43, Australia Mail, 350 produced [$33].....$18
MM006 Holden FX, Taxi, 1:43, 350 produced [$42]..................................$23

MM008 Holden FJ Panel Van, 1:43, New Zealand Transport Department, 375 produced [$42] $23

MM009 International Delivery Van, 1:64, Peter's Ice Cream, 385 produced [$68] ..$37

MM011 Ford Mainline Utility, 1:43, Dept of Civil Aviation, pale mustard, 395 produced [$33] $18

MM012 Holden FX Sedan, 1:43, Victoria Police, 375 produced [$35].......................$19

MM013 Ford Zephyr Mk 1 Sedan, 1:43, NZPO Regional Engineer, gray, 395 produced [$33] $18

MM014 Holden FJ Special Sedan, 1:43, Australia Fire Control NSW, 395 produced [$42]..................................$23
MM015 Jaguar XK120, 1:43, white, no production #s [$42] $23
MM016 Holden FX Sedan, 1:43, cream, 395 produced [$42]......................$23
MM017 Holden FJ Panel Van, 1:64, New Zealand Mail, 395 produced [$42] $23
MM018 Holden FJ Special Sedan, 1:43, Australia Police NT, 395 produced [$42] $23
MM019 Volkswagen Microbus, 1:43, pale blue, no production #s [$36] $20

MM020 Holden FE Utility, 1:43, New South Wales Dept. of Works, 395 produced [$33] $18
MM021 Holden FJ Special Sedan, 1:43, two-tone gray, 395 produced [$42] $23
MM022 Ford Zephyr Mk 1 Sedan, 1:43, Australia Police SA, 395 produced [$33] $18
MM023 Volkswagen Microbus, 1:43, Ambulance, 395 produced [$36]...$20
MM024 Ford Mainline Utility, 1:43, Micro Models, no production #s [$33]......$18
MM025 Bedford SB Bus, 1:55, no production #s [$48]..................................$26
MM026 Holden FX Sedan, 1:43, Australia Police Victoria, 395 produced [$35] $19
MM027 International Delivery Van, 1:64, Micro Models "better than ever," no prod #s [$68] $37
MM028 MGA Roadster, 1:43, no prod #s [$40] $22
MM029 Holden FJ Special Sedan, 1:43, Taxi, 395 produced [$42]............$23

MM402 Holden FJ Special Sedan, 1:43, New South Wales Fire Control, 2000 produced [$33]..................................$18

MM403 Holden FE Utility, 1:43, New South Wales Public Works, yellow, 2000 produced [$33]..................................$18

MM404 Holden FJ Panel Van, 1:43, New Zealand Royal Mail, 2000 produced [$33]..................................$18

MM405 Holden FX Sedan, 1:43, Traffic Patrol, white, 2000 produced [$35]........$19

MM406 Volkswagen Microbus, 1:43, light blue, 950 produced [$36]..........................$20

MM407 Jaguar XK120, 1:43, dark green, 2000 produced [$33] $18

MM408 Ford Mainline Utility, 1:43, Micro Models, maroon, 2000 produced [$32]..$18

MM409 Ford Zephyr Mk 1 Sedan, 1:43, Queensland Police, 2000 produced [$33]..$18

MM501 International Delivery Van, 1:64, Micro Models "better than ever," 2000 produced [$38].......................................$21

MM410 Holden FJ Panel Van, 1:43, Ambulance Q.A.T.B., 2000 produced [$33].......................................$18
MM411 Bedford SB Bus, 1:55, Micro Bus Lines, 2000 produced [$48] $26
MM502 MGA Roadster, 1:43, red, 2000 produced [$32]............................$18

MM503 Holden FX Utility, 1:43, The Press, blue, 2000 produced [$33].........................$18

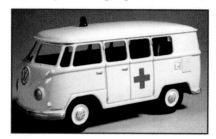

MM504 Volkswagen Microbus Ambulance, 1:43, cream, 1250 produced [$36] $20

MM505 Holden FJ Special Sedan, 1:43, Wellington Taxis, black, 2000 produced [$34] $19

MM506 Holden FE Sedan, 1:43, SA Police, light blue, 875 produced [$33] $18

MM507 Morris Fire Engine, 1:43, 1450 produced [$36]..$20

MM509 Ford OHV F6 Truck, 1:43, NZ Army, 950 produced [$38] $21

MM510 International Delivery Van, 1:64, Anchor Icy Cold Milk, cream, no prod #s [$38] $21

MM511 Holden FE Utility, 1:43, Tasmania Police Force, 875 produced [$33]..........$18

MM512 Holden FX Sedan, 1:43, light green, 950 produced [$32] $18

MM513 MGA Roadster, 1:43, light blue, 850 produced [$32]................................$18

MM514 Ford Customline Sedan, 1:43, Victoria Police, 950 produced [$33].............$18

MM508 Bedford SB Bus, 1:55, Micro Bus Lines
v.1 red, 900 produced [$48]........$26
v.2 blue, 900 produced [$48].......$26
v.3 green, 900 produced [$48]......$26

MM515 Ford Zephyr Mk 1 Sedan, 1:43, NZ Transport Department, black, 850 produced [$33]...............$18

MM516 Holden FC Station Sedan, 1:43, gray, 850 produced [$32] $18

MM517 Holden FX Sedan, 1:43, light green, 2000 produced [$32]........$18

MM518 Volkswagen Microbus, 1:43, Fire Communications, 2000 produced [$36] $20

MM519 Jaguar XK120, 1:43, silver, 2000 produced [$42] $23

MM520 Ford Mainline Utility, 1:43, Newspaper Delivery, 2000 produced [$32] $18

MM521 Ford Zephyr Mk 1 Sedan, 1:43, New Zealand MOT, 2000 produced [$33] $18

MM522 Chrysler Royal Sedan, 1:43, Australia Police, 2000 produced [$33]...$18

MM523 Bedford SB Bus, English Bus, 2000 produced [$48] $26

MM601 Ford OHV V6 Covered Lorry, 1:43, Micro Models "bigger and better," out of prod [$42] $23

MM601 Holden FJ Special Sedan, 1:43, Grey Cabs, Sahara tan, 950 produced [$33] $18

MM602 MGA Roadster, 1:43, dark blue, 2000 produced [$42] $23

MM603 Vickers Viscount Passenger Jet, TAA, 2000 produced [$42] $23

MM602 Jaguar XK120, 1:43, silver, 950 produced [$33]...............$18

MM603 Vanguard Estate Van, 1:43, cream, 950 produced [$32] $18

MM604 Holden FE Sedan, red & white, 950 produced [$32]...............$23

MM604 Volkswagen Microbus, 1:43, Australia Police New Zealand, 2000 produced [$32].....................$18

MM605 Ford Customline Sedan, 1:43, two-tone green, 950 produced [$32].....................$18

MM605 Holden FJ Special Sedan, 1:43, Grey Cabs, light brown, 2000 produced [$42].....................$23

MM606 Holden FX Utility, 1:43, NZAA, yellow, 950 produced [$33] $18

MM607 Holden FC Special Wagon, 1:43, 950 produced [$33].....................$18

MM608 Bedford SB Bus, 1:55, NZ Road Services [$48] $26

MM609 Vauxhall Wyvern Sedan, 1:43, black with silver trim, 1500 produced [$32] $18

MM701 Vauxhall Cresta PA, 1:43, mountain rose, 1500 produced [$40]...........$22

MM701 Vauxhall Velox, 1:43, magenta, no prod #s [$42].....................$23

MM704 Volkswagen Beetle, 1:43, green, no prod #s [$42].....................$23

MM701 Ford Customline, 1:43, 1956 Springbok Tour of New Zealand, 1250 produced [$42]...............$23

MM702 International Breakdown Truck, 1:64, New Zealand AA, yellow, 600 produced [$42]...............$23

MM703 International Breakdown Truck, 1:64, Parks 24 Hr. Towing, red, 600 produced [$42]...............$23

MM801 Volkswagen Beetle, 1:43, maroon, no prod #s [$42] $23

MM802 Brentware Petrol Tanker, 1:43, no prod #s [$48].....................$26

MM803 Petrol Bowser, 1:43, no prod #s [$48] $26

MM804 Ford Mainline Ute, 1:43, 1953 English Tour, no prod #s [$33]........$18

MM804 Holden FJ Panel Van, plastic, 1:43 [$45] $25

MM805 Gold Plated Holden FX Sedan, 1:43, no prod #s [$80].................$44

MM806 Gold Plated Jaguar XK 120, 1:43, no prod #s [$80]...........................$44

Micro Models Promotional Issues

MC001 International Truck, 1:64, Coca Cola [$55].....................$30

MC002 Volkswagen Van, 1:43, Coca Cola [$53].....................$29

MC003 International Bottle Truck, 1:64, Coca Cola [$55].....................$30

MC004 Holden FJ Panel Van, 1:43, plastic, red, Coca Cola, no prod #s [$55].....................$30

MP501 Holden FX Utility, 1:43, MSS Security, cream, no prod #s [$45] $25

MP503 MGA Roadster, 1:43, Canterbury University, yellow, 600 produced [$40] ..$22

MP601 Holden FJ Panel Van, 1:43, "Mega" Toy Swapmeet '96, 400 produced [$40] ..$22

MP602 Holden FJ Panel Van, 1:43, Lea & Perrin Worcestershire Sauce, 850 produced [$35] $19

MP702 Holden FE Utility, 1:43, "Mega" Toy Swapmeet '97, 400 produced [$40] $22

MP703 Holden FJ Special Sedan, 1:43, Sydney Model Auto Club, 250 produced [$40] $22

MC005 Ford Bottle Truck, 1:64, Coca Cola [$55] $30
MC503 Holden FT Panel Van, 1:43, Coca Cola [$55] $30
MP401 Holden FT Utility, 1:43, Security [$45] $25
MP502 Holden FJ Panel Van, 1:43, NZ Royal Mail, red [$40] $22
MP603 Vanguard Estate Van, 1:43, Lea & Perrin Worcestershire Sauce [$35] $19
MP701 Ford Customline Sedan, 1:43, 1956 All Black Springbok [$40] $22
MP801 Holden FC Station Wagon, 1:43, Adelaide Mega Swap Meet '98 [$45] $25
MP802 Holden FJ Panel Van, 1:43, Briggs & Stratton, no prod #s [$45] $25
MP803 Ford Zephyr Mark 1, 1:43, 1950 All Blacks, no prod #s [$45] $25
MP804 Ford Mainline Ute, 1953 All Blacks, no prod #s [$54] $30
MP805 Ford F6 Truck, 1:43, NZ Kiwi Team, no prod #s [$45] $25

Micromodels (see Deoma)

Micro Pet (also see Taiseiya, Cherryca Phenix)

These Japanese models were manufactured by Taiseiya of Tokyo primarily for the Asian market in the 1960s. They are rare in the US since they are long obsolete, relatively unknown and never marketed in the US. Of all the models offered, only a few were American cars; the large majority were Japanese models.

Chevrolet Impala, #9
   v.1 blue and white $150
   v.2 chrome plated $200
Chevrolet Impala Police Car, #10
   v.1 black and white $150
Datsun Bluebird, #2
   v.1 red and gray $125
   v.2 chrome plated $175
Datsun Bluebird Station Wagon, #17
   v.1 blue and white $125
   v.2 yellow and brown $125
   v.3 chrome-plated $150
Delahaye, 1901 .... $125
Ford Falcon, #12
   v.1 red and black $150
   v.2 two-tone green $150
Ford Falcon Police Car, #16
   v.1 black and white $150
Hillman Minx, #15
   v.1 red $125
   v.2 blue and white $125
   v.3 blue and cream $125
Isuzu Bellel 2000 Saloon, #19
   v.1 green and white $125
Mazda Coupe R 360, #7, white and red, or orange and gray $125

Mazda Coupe R 360, #7, chrome plated . $175
Nissan Cedric, #5, blue, pink, or copper and gray $125
Nissan Cedric, #5, chrome plated $175
Nissan Light Truck, #18
   v.1 brown and green $125
   v.2 blue and gray $125
Peugeot, top down, 1896 .... $125
Peugeot, top up, 1896 .... $125
Prince Bus, #14
   v.1 pink, white, and blue
   v.2 red and white $175
   v.3 chrome plated $200
Prince Skyline, #6
   v.1 copper and gray or blue and gray . $125
   v.2 chrome plated $175
Prince Skyway Station Wagon, #11
   v.1 pink and gray $125
   v.2 red, yellow, and white $125
Subaru 360, #1
   v.1 blue and copper $125
Toyota Corona Station Wagon, #8
   v.1 green and gray, or orange and cream $125
   v.2 chrome plated $175

Microtoys (see Deoma)

Midgetoy
1202 Eddy Avenue
Rockford IL 61103
phone: 815-877-7439

The post-war goal of brothers Alvin and Earl Herdklotz was "to produce low-cost diecast vehicles both sturdy and precisely detailed." Their goals mirrored those of the Tootsietoy firm after World War II, and their Midgetoy models are of similar construction, that being generally a single cast pot metal body with no chassis. From 1946 to 1984, Midgetoys were produced in various sizes and available at many discount retail outlets. Thousands, or at least hundreds, of different models were issued. It would be interesting to see a book devoted especially to these proliferous toys. Typical values are from $10 to $15 each.

Around 1985, the Herdlkotz brothers sold the business to a group of investors who did nothing with the factory for several years. Ultimately they bought it back and have been selling off existing stock for the last fifteen years. The machinery has gone into disrepair and current inventory is dwindling as they patiently seek just the right buyer for the company. They don't seem to be in much of a hurry.

A website has been created at www.midgetoy.com to chronicle the company and its distinctive toys.

Army Ambulance, circa 1950s, 3⅞" $14
Army Truck, circa 1950s, 4½" $14
Army Truck & Cannon, circa 1950s, 4½" & 3¼" $29

Camping Trailer, purple, circa 1950s, 2⅜" $4
Convertible, blue, circa 1950s, 5⅜" $19
Corvette, yellow, circa 1950s, 2⅞"............$12
Corvette, green, circa 1970s, 2" $2
El Camino, red, circa 1970s, 3"..................$2
Ford C600 Oil Truck, 1956, 4" $15
Indy-Style Race Car, silver, circa 1950s, 3" ..$15
Jeep, red, circa 1960s $4
MG Sports Car, green, circa 1960s, 2" $2
Military Jeep, circa 1950s, 1¾" $5
Pickup Jeep, blue, circa 1950s, 5¾" $19

Midget Toys

Midget Toys of France, produced for just one year in 1959, are not to be confused with Midgetoys of the United States.

1 Flat Truck, 1:86 ....$45
2 Lumber Semi-Trailer Truck, 1:86 ....$45
3 Quarry Dump Truck, 1:86 ....$45
4 Farm Tractor, 1:86 ....$45
5 Open Semi-Trailer Truck, 1:86 ....$45
6 Dyna-Panhard Convertible, 1:86 ....$45
14 Crane Truck, 1:86 ....$45
Citroën DS19, 1:86 ....$45
Jaguar D-Type, 1:86 ....$45
Transformer Semi-Trailer, 1:86 ....$45
3-Axle Semi-Trailer, 1:86 ....$45
Vanwall Formula 1, 1:86 ....$45
Vespa 400 Mini-Car, 1:86.........................$45
Vespa 400 Mini-Car, 1:43.........................$75

Midwestern Home Products, Inc.

Wilmington, DE 19803

"Generic, crude, yet charming" best describes models manufactured by Midwestern Home Products, Inc., of Wilmington, Delaware. A recently discovered set of three 4" fire engines are cheaply made in China, but possess that ineffable charm that makes them attractive novelty items, although relatively worthless as collectibles. At $1 apiece, their crude castings with sharp edges make them unsuitable for children and are better left in their original blisterpack. Once removed, they are no longer distinguishable as Midwestern brand toys. Two of the three fire engines were found to have a logo embossed into the base that resembles a cluster of pine trees with a leaping deer, the whole of which is surrounded by a double circle, with the cryptic letters "SM" at the bottom of the circle. It was later determined that the symbol is the trademark for Summer Manufacturing, another brand of inexpensive, crude, generic toys from Asia.

8114 Ladder truck $1
8115 Closed-cab pumper/turret...................$1
8116 Open-cab pumper truck.......................$1

Mignon

Mignon is a series of 1:24 scale diecast motorcycles and two go-karts manufactured in Italy for a few years in the early 1960s. Their downfall was unfortunately due to the lack of interest in collecting motorcycle miniatures at the time. Interest is now on the increase, due in part to the rising popularity and number of Harley-Davidson collectibles hitting the market nowadays. Here is a list of Mignon models.

Aermacchi a la Verde 350cc, #112
Aermacchi Chimera 250, #19, 3¼"..$35–40
BMW R-26 250cc, #104, 3¾" $35–40
Gilera Extra Rosso 175, #15, 3¼"...$35–40
Gilera G.T. 175, #17, 3¼"............$35–40
Go Kart "900", 2¾" $35–40
Go Kart Baby, 3"...........................$35–40
Guzzi Falcone 500, #110, 4⅜" $35–40
Guzzi Lodola 175, #11, 3¼" $35–40
Guzzi Zigolo 110, #13, 3¼" $35–40
Harley-Davidson 1200, #102, 3⅝" ..$35–40
Honda CS-92 Sport, #108, 3½".....$35–40
Viberti 3-Wheel Vivi, #21, 3⅝"........$35–40

Mignot, C.B.G.

Lilliput Motor Company, Ltd., offers this informative history of the obscure C.B.G. Mignot brand of quality toys: "Since the company's founding in 1785 by Mr. Lucotte, considered to be the inventor of the 'ronde bosse' (three dimensional) technique of casting toy soldiers and figures, C.B.G. Mignot's manufacturing methods have remained unchanged. They continue to employ the same bronze molds, later sculptured in tempered steel, some of which are more than a century old. The artisans fill the molds with a proprietary alloy consisting of lead, tin, antimony, and other alloys. After air cooling, the molds are carefully removed, the castings are individually de-burred. Then, the separate parts are soldered together. Then, the fully assembled figure gets hand painted and finished. Finally, the groups of figures are put together into the matching diorama boxes, which are wonderful works of art in their own right!"

As pictured in Lilliput's Catalog #16 from September 1997, several sets are available. The Bugatti set depicts a Bugatti Type 35 in the pits at Le Mans, and features a gas pump, driver, and milestone. The Tour de France set features an old Peugeot 203 Convertible with driver and cameraman leading four bicyclists across the finish line.

The Citroën in Jungle set is a fabulous two-tier scene with two Citroën vehicles, explorers, natives, flora, and fauna. The Madagascar Expedition set is even more spectacular, with three tiers. The top tier features a mighty steamer ship with smaller vessels surrounding it. The middle tier features a landing party disembarking from a dinghy to meet some sophisticated-looking natives. The bottom tier features several British sailors encountering more natives. (The sailors don't look very friendly.) All three levels are enhanced by scenic backgrounds of sea and jungle.

Bugatti, LPCBG3, 10" x 5¾" x 5½" $165
Citroën in Jungle, LPCBG1, 12" x 2" x 9" ...$425
Madagascar Expedition, LPCBG8, 18½" x 14½" x 3½"..$1000
Tour de France, LPCBG9, 10" x 5¾" x 5½"..$200

Mikansue

Mikansue models are 1:43 scale white metal kits produced and marketed by Mike and Sue Richardson of England. By the numbers, it would appear that their product line represented nearly a hundred different models. Besides these European cars, Mikansue also represents a line of American automobiles in their Americana series.

Thanks to the contributions of Dario "Dino" Vidovic via e-mail, this list is now much more complete.

Mikansue

2 Austin-Healey Sprite 1958..............$115
8 H.R.G 1500 1948......................$115
12 Wolseley Hornet Swallow 1933....$115
13 Squire 1,5 l supercharged 1935....$115
14 Austin Ruby 7 1935...................$115
16 AC 16/70 supercharged 1936.....$115
18 Healey Elliott saloon 1950...........$115
22 TVR 3 l Coupe 1978..................$115
24 Jowett R4 Jupiter sports 1954........$115
25 Ford 100E Anglia Popular 1954/ 1961...................................$115
26 Triumph Mayflower saloon 1952 ...$115
27 Morris 8 series E saloon 1948.......$115
28 Riley 1,5 l saloon 1964...............$115
29 Morris Mosquito saloon 1943 ....$115
30 Triumph Dolomite roadster 1938....$115
31 Riley Monaco saloon 1934...........$115
32 Rover 100 P4 saloon 1960...........$115
33 Riley 1,5 l RME saloon 1954–55 ..$115
34 Ford Cortina 1600E saloon 1967– 68...................................$115
35 Morris Minor 1000 Traveller break 1965..................................$115
36 Triumph Vitesse 1969 ....$115
37 Morris Minor 1000 pick up 1965 .$115
38 Morris Minor 1000 van 1965.......$115
39 Triumph TR 2 TR3 sports 1954–57 .$115

Mikansue Competition

1 Jaguar Alta 1952.....................$115
4 Dellow 2 seater 1951 ....$115
9 Sigma Le Mans 1975 ....$115
12 Fiat 128 Imola 1976...............$115
15 Allard J2R Le Mans 1953.........$115
17 Brabham BT37 F1 1972..............$115
18 Frazer Nash Le Mans coupe 1953 .$115
19 Aston Martin Spa 1948.............$115
20 ATS F1 1978........................$115
22 Adler Le Mans 1936................$115
23 Martini F1 1978.....................$115
24 Austin-Healey Sprite MK2 rallye......$115
25 Shadow DN 3 F1 1974.............$115
26 Austin-Healey record car 1954 ......$115
31 Arnolt-Climax 1957.................$115
35 Tojeiro Climax LM 1962............$115
38 MG EX-181 record car.............$115

40 Cooper Bristol 1953 ....$115
41 Aero Minor LM 1949/50 ....$115
47 Lotus XI coupe 1957.....................$115
48 Vanwall F1 special 2l 1954.........$115
49 Cosworth 4WD F1 prototype 1969 ..$115
50 Vanwall F1 1961 ....$115
51 Austin-Healey Sprite record car 1959 ....$115
56 Simca 570 ccm sports LM 1939 ...$115
57 OSCA 750 spyder LM 1958........$115
58 Cooper Jaguar sports P. Whitehead 1954 ....$115
59 Vanwall lightweight F1 front engine 1960 ....$115
60 Connaught L-type sports 1949 ....$115
61 MGA LM1960 special coupe $115
62 Lotus XV sports LM 1959 ....$115
63 Jaguar Lister coupe LM 1963 ....$115
64 Healey Westland tourer Mille miglia 1948 ....$115
65 Climax sport LM 1955.................$115
66 ERA G-type F2 1952 Stirling Moss .$115
67 BRM V16 F1 mark 1 1950..........$115
68 Cunningham Ferrari 375 LM 1954..$115
69 MG TC special LM 1949 ....$115
102 March 751 F1 Lavazza..............$115

Americana

5 La Salle saloon 1940 ....$115
7 Plymouth PA4 coupe 1931.............$115
9 Kurtis 500 roadster 1953................$115
10 Austin Nash Metropolitan 1954.....$115
11 Muntz Jet roadster 1954 ....$115
12 Studebaker Starlight coupe 1950 ...$115
13 Chevrolet Styleline 1950...............$115
14 Willys 77 sedan 1938.................$115
15 American Bantam roadster 1938 ...$115
16 Kaiser Henry J sedan 1952 ....$115
17 Studebaker Starlight coupe 1953 ...$115
18 Nash Healey Le Mans coupe 1953 ..$115
19 Kaiser Manhattan sedan 1953 ......$115

Milano

Harvey Goranson reports, "I think this is Milano 43. These are resin hand builts of Ferrari racing cars, typically obscure ones from little known races or also-rans. Very nice. Last list I saw was in a May 1992 issue of TSSK, where the numbers went up to 43 (Coincidence?). The 1897 model you list doesn't fit in with this."

Italy is the assumed home of Milano models.
1897 Gauthier Wehrle $24

Milestone Miniatures

Milestone Miniatures of Cornwall, England, manufactures a variety of precision 1:43 scale models.
Milestone Miniatures Limited
25 West End
Redruth
Cornwall
TR15 2SA
England
phone: +044 01209 218356

fax: (+044) 01209 217983
e-mail: info@modelcars.co.uk
website: www.modelcars.co.uk

Milestone Miniatures — The Milestone Series

1966 Alvis TF21 Coupe, £45 ....$72
1946 Scammell Show Tracs, £167.......$80
1954 Riley Pathfinder, £50 ....$80
1952 Ford Zephyr Convertible, £50.....$80
1935 Ford Model Y Fordor Saloon, £57 .$92
1935 Ford Model Y Tudor Saloon, £57 .$92
1963 Austin A60 Van, £45 ....$72
1960 Austin A60 Pickup, £48.............$77
1927 Austin SS Swallow Saloon, £57...$92
1927 Austin SS Swallow 2 Seat, £57 ...$92
1930 Austin Ulster, £48.....................$77
1964 Humber Super Snipe Series 5, £50 ..$80

Milestone Miniatures — The Jaguar Collecton

1927 Austin Swallow, £57 ....$92
1955 Jaguar Mk 1, maroon or British racing green, £53 ....$85
1959 Jaguar Mk 2 Staffordshire Police, £51 ....$82
1948 Jaguar Mk 5, £51 ....$82
1956 Jaguar Mk 7M, £48 ....$77
1957 Jaguar Mk 8, £54 ....$87
1959 Jaguar Mk 9 Saloon, £54..........$87
1958 Jaguar Mk IX Hearse, £51 ....$82
1961 Jaguar Mk 10, £48 ....$77
1972 Jaguar V12 E Type, white or silver, £50 ....$80
1961 Jaguar E Type Coupe, red, blue, white, or silver, £50.....................$80
1966 Jaguar 420G, two-tone brown and cream, £53 ....$85
1969 Jaguar XJ6, £48 ....$77
1972 Jaguar XJ12, £48 ....$77
1972 Jaguar XJ1 Silverstone Fire Car, bright red, £53 ....$85
1948 Jaguar XK120, £50 ....$80
1958 Jaguar XK150, £50 ....$80
1967 Jaguar S Type, £50 ....$80
1935 Jaguar SS Airline, £53 ....$85
1936 Jaguar SS1, £50 ....$80
1936 Jaguar SS100 Coupe, £51 ....$82
1936 Jaguar SS100 Tourer, £50.........$80
1984 Jaguar XJR5 Quaker State (Le Mans Series), £57 ....$92
1984 Jaguar XJS, £53 ....$85
1996 Jaguar XJR Silverstone Fire Car, £54 ....$87
1996 Jaguar XK8, £50 ....$80
1998 Jaguar XKR, £57 ....$92

Milestone Chequered Flag Series

1936 Jaguar SS 100 Alpine Cup Winner, £57 ....$92
1939 Jaguar SS 100 Shelsley Walsh Twin Rear, £54 ....$87
1950 Jaguar XK 120 Tourist Trophy Winner, £53 ....$85
1953 Jaguar C Type Winner Le Mans, £54 ....$87

1955 Jaguar MK VII M Silverstone Hawthorn, £54 ....$87
1957 Jaguar D Type Winner Le Mans, £57 ....$92

Milestone Jaguar Jubilee Series

1972 Jaguar V12 E Type H/Top, £48 .....$77
1957 Jaguar XK 150S Roadster, £51.....$82
1967 Jaguar XJ 13, £51 ....$82
1994 Jaguar XJR, £50 ....$80
1960 Jaguar Mk 2 Monza Record Car, £51 ....$82
1951 Jaguar C Type Le Mans Winner, £51 ....$82
1968 Jaguar XJ6 Launch Car, £48 ......$77
1947 Jaguar XK120 Jabbeke Record Car, £48 ....$77
1938 Jaguar SS 100 "Old No 8," £50 ....$80
1938 Jaguar 2.5 Litre, £48 ....$77
1937 Jaguar 2.5 Litre Lady Lyons Car, £51 ....$82

Milestone Jaguar World Series

1957 Jaguar Mk 8 Saloon, £54..........$87
1956 Jaguar Mk 7 Monte Carlo Rally Win, £54 ....$87
1927 Austin Swallow Saloon 1927, £57 ....$92
1927 Austin Swallow 2 Seat 1927, £57 ....$92

Milestone Miniatures — The Spirit of Brooklands

1930 Austin Ulster, £48.....................$77
1932 Birkin Bentley, £58 ....$93
1925 Fiat Mephistopheles, £58...........$93
1934 MG K3 Magnette, £48...............$77
1935 Napier-Railton, £58 ....$93
1936 MG NA Bellevue Special, £48 ...$77
1934 Morgan Jap Relay Car, £48 ......$77
1935 Frazer Nash, £48......................$77
1930 Brooklands Riley, £48 ....$77
1919 Sunbeam V12, £58 ....$93
1926 Thomas Leyland Special, £58 ....$93
1921 Chitty Bang Bang, £58 ....$93

Milestone Miniatures — The 43rd Avenue Collection

1965 Plymouth Sport Fury, £53 ....$85
1951 Studebaker Champion Business Coupe, £48 ....$77
1951 Studebaker Commander Business Coupe, £48 ....$77
1947 Cadillac Series 62 Sedan, £57.......$92
1936 Ford 3 Window Coupe, £50......$80
1956 Oldsmobile Super 88 Convertible, £56 ....$80
1959 Chevrolet Nomad Impala Station Wagon, £54 ....$87
1951 Studebaker Panorama Commander, £48 ....$77
1936 Ford Convertible with Dickie (Rumble) Seat, £50 ....$80
1968 Ford Torino Coupe GT, £50 ......$80
1966 Mercury Comet Cyclone, £53.....$85
1959 Dodge Royal Saloon, £57.........$92

Milestone Miniatures Gold Seal Presentation Sets

Milestone Connoisseur Limited Editions:

1930 Austin Ulster, £81	$130
1932 Birkin Bentley, £98	$157
1925 Fiat Mephistopheles, £98	$157
1934 MG K3 Magnette, £98	$157
1935 Napier-Railton, £98	$157
1936 MG NA Bellevue Special, £81	$130
1934 Morgan Jap Relay Car, £81	$130
1935 Frazer Nash, £81	$130
1930 Brooklands Riley, £81	$130
1919 Sunbeam V12, £98	$157
1926 Thomas Leyland Special, £98	$157
1921 Chitty Bang Bang, £98	$157

Milestone Jaguar Legends Collection Gift Sets:

GS1 1927 Austin Swallow Saloon, Green/Green; 1936 SS1 Coupe, Blue/Black, £166	$266
GS2 1938 SS 100 Open Sports, White; 1939 SS100 Coupe, Silver, £166	$266
GS3 1934 SS1 Open Drop Head, Dark Blue; 1935 SS Airline Saloon, Maroon, £166	$266
GS4 1949 Mk 5 Saloon, Silver/Black; 1950 Mk 7 Saloon, Metallic Blue, £166	$266
GS5 1955 Mk 1 Saloon, British Racing Green; 1962 Mk 2 Wire Wheel, Metallic Dark Blue, £166	$266
GS6 1956 Mk 8 Saloon, Gray/Gray; 1961 Mk 10 Saloon, Metallic Blue, £166	$266
GS7 1972 XJC Coupe, Maroon; XJ12 Saloon, Pale Green, £166	$266
GS8 1947 XK 120 Jabbeke Record Car, Cream; 1953 XK120 Bubble Record Car, British Racing Green, £166	$266
GS9 1953 C Type Le Mans Winner, British Racing Green; 1957 D Type Ecurie Ecosse, Flag Blue, £166	$266
GS10 1965 XJ 13 Experimental Car, British Racing Green; 1984 XJR 5 Quaker State Le Mans, White, £166	$266
GS11 1950 XK 120 Drop Head Open, White; 1958 XK150 Coupe, Gold, £166	$266
GS12 1961 XKE Coupe, White; 1996 XK8 Roadster Open, British Racing Green, £166	$266
GS13 1972 XKE V12 Roadster, Black; 1984 XJS Coupe, Metallic Blue, £166	$266

Milestone Models (also see Big River Models)

Milestone Models of South Africa made just two models. They were last known available only from EWA & Miniature Cars USA, Inc., 369 Springfield Ave., P O Box 188, Berkeley Heights, NJ 07922-0188. More recently, Milestone Models is based in Sydney, Australia, and is responsible for a cooperative effort with Big River Models to produce a 1937 Chevrolet Utility (Pickup) in 1997.

1961 Ford Falcon, 1:43	$70
1960 Plymouth Valiant, 1:43	$70

Milton

Milton toys are made in Calcutta, India, from old Corgi, Dinky, Corgi Jr., and other manufacturers' dies. Milton Morgan produced a number of toys under the brand name of Mini Auto Cars, not to be confused with Miniauto-toys from Dugu. The quality is noticeably inferior to the original Corgi Jrs.

Mercedes Fire Ladder Truck, 1:64	$5
201 Volkswagen 1200, 1:90	$20
202 Mercedes-Benz 220 Coupe, 1:90	$18
203 Pontiac Firebird, 1:90	$24
204 BMW 507, 1:90	$16
205 Austin-Healey, 1:90	$16
301 Flat Truck, 1:70	$12
302 Open Truck, 1:70	$12
303 Chevrolet Impala	$32
304 Plymouth Suburban	$36
305 Chevrolet Impala State Patrol	$36
306 Chevrolet Impala Taxi	$36
307 Plymouth Suburban Ambulance	$36
308 Chevrolet Impala Police Car	$36
309 Chevrolet Impala Fire Chief	$32
310 Studebaker Golden Hawk	$45
311 Lumber Truck, 1:70	$12
312 Army Ambulance, 1:70	$12
313 Royal Mail Van, 1:70	$16
314 Articulated Tank Truck, "CALTEX," 1:50	$36
314 Articulated Tank Truck, "MOBILGAS," 1:50	$42
314 Articulated Tank Truck, "BURMAH-SHELL," 1:50	$42
314 Articulated Tank Truck, "ESSO," 1:50	$42
314 Articulated Tank Truck, "INDIAN OIL," 1:50	$42
315 Articulated Refrigeration Truck, 1:50	$36
316 Luxury Coach, 1:50	$54
317 Articulated Lumber Transporter, 1:50	$36
319 Commer Van "MILTON"	$42
320 Commer Ambulance	$42
321 Commer Army Ambulance	$42
322 Commer School Bus	$42
323 Commer Pickup	$42
324 Commer Open Truck	$42
325 Commer Milk Van	$42
327 Jaguar 3.8 Saloon	$42
329 Ford Mustang	$36
330 Foden Tank Truck "CALTEX," 1:50	$8
331 Foden Tank Truck "BURMAH-SHELL," 1:50	$8
332 Commer Fruit Carrier	$45
333 Morris Mini Minor	$50
334 Commer "COCA-COLA" Truck	$60
335 Tractor and Trailer	$42
336 Ford Model T	$24
337 D. D. Bus, "INSIST ON MILTON MINI CARS," 1:50	$52
338 Tipping Truck, 1:50	$24
341 Racing Car	$24
342 Roadster	$24
344 Ladder Truck, 1:70	$12
349 Mini Bus	$24

Minialuxe

Depending on who you ask, Minialuxe are a series of plastic car models begun in France between 1954 and 1959. Their Tacots series represents old-time cars. Here is just a small sampling.

Minialuxe

Peugeot 604 4-Door Sedan, 1:43	$15
Peugeot 504 4-Door Sedan, 1:43	$15
Peugeot 204 4-Door Sedan, 1:43	$15
Renault 17 Coupe, 1:43	$15
Renault 30, 1:43	$15
Simca 1000 Police, 1:43	$15

Tacots Minialuxe

1909 Ford Model T Roadster, top up, 1:43	$15
1911 Ford Model T Roadster, top down, 1:43	$15
1908 Lanchester, 1:43	$15
1913 Muller Sedan, 1:64	$8
1912 Park Royal Landau, 1:43	$15
1906 Peugeot, 1:43	$15

Miniature Auto Emporium

These are 1:43 scale models of exacting detail.

1939 Buick Limo	$185
1959 Cadillac Convertible, top up	$65
1959 Cadillac Fire Car	$65
1961 Chrysler Convertible, top up	$115
1961 Chrysler Convertible, top down	$115
1965 Chevrolet Corvette Convertible, top up	$65
1965 Chevrolet Corvette Convertible, top down	$65

Miniature Pet

As reported by Bob Speerbrecher (see Silver Pet brand), Miniature Pet appears to be a short-lived brand from Japan that may have produced just one model before vanishing from the market. The distinguishing mark on the base is an oval with an "N" inside of it.

Opel 4-Door Sedan, #1	$25–35

Miniature Vehicle Castings Inc. (also known as MVC)

Robert E. Wagner started Miniature Vehicle Castings Inc. in New Jersey in 1985, producing an exquisite series of 1930s and 1940s vehicles in 1:43 scale. Models are made of diecast lead from silicone molds, and represent some of the most beautiful renderings of vintage models on the market. They are produced in small quantities and are very reasonably priced at $21 suggested retail. Current second-market values place them around $40 each.

MVC Series 1, 1985

1937 Ford 2-Door Sedan $30–45
1937 Ford 2-Door Sedan, "New York Fire" $45
1938 Ford Standard Sedan Del $20–40
1934 Olds 2-Door Humpback $20–40
1936 Olds 4-Door Humpback $20–40
1937 Hudson Terraplane 2-Door.....$20–40
1938 Dodge Step Van $20–40
1937 Plymouth 5-Window Coupe...$20–40
1937 Dodge 2-Door Humpback $20–40
1938 Plymouth 2-Door Sedan $20–40
1940 Ford Logging Semi $45
1941 Ford C.O.E. Flatbed Truck $20–40
1941 Ford C.O.E. Dump Truck $20–40
1935 Hudson 2-Door Sedan $20–40
1937 Studebaker 3-Window Coupe.$20–40
1936 Plymouth 4-Door Sedan $20–40
1936 Plymouth 4-Door Taxi $20–40
1935 Pontiac 3-Window Coupe.....$20–40
1940 Dodge 2-Door Sedan $20–40
1939 dodge 2-Door Sedan...........$20–40
1941 Divco Milk Truck "Sunrise Dairy" .$20–40

MVC Series 2, 1993

1934 Dodge 2-Door Sedan $20–40
1935 Pontiac 2-Door Sedan $20–40
1936 Plymouth Pickup...................$20–40
1938 Hudson Coupe $20–40

Other MVC Models

Ford P600 "Coca-Cola" Van $24
Ford P600 "UPS" Van $24

Miniautotoys (see Dugu)

Minic (see Tri-Ang)

Minichamps (see Paul's Model Art)

Minicraft (see Academy Minicraft)

Minimac

Below is a list of known Minimac models from Brazil.
Ford Jeep, "Coca-Cola," 1:43 ....$18
Ford Jeep Fire Brigade Chief, red, 1:43 ....$18
Ford Military Jeep, Army, green, 1:43 ....$18
Ford Jeep Ambulance, Red Cross, white/red, 1:43 ....$18
Ford Jeep, U.N., white/black, 1:43 ....$18
March 762 F.2, "Camel" #12, yellow, 1:25 ..$26
March 762 F.2, "Esso" #1, white/red/blue, 1:25 ....$26
March 762 F.2, "Hollywood" #9, red/white/blue, 1:25 ....$26
March 762 F.2, "Marlboro," Senna, 1:25 ..$45
Scania Refrigerator Semi, "Coca-Cola," 1:50.$48
Scania Semi Van, 1:50.........................$28
Scania 4x2 Truck, "Coca-Cola," 1:50 ....$28
Scania 4x2 Truck, 1:50 ....$22
Huber Road Grader, yellow, 1:87 ....$18
Massey Ferguson 3366 Dozer, yellow, 1:43 ..$28
Hyster H-150F Forklift, 1:43 ....$22
Massey Ferguson 275 Farm Tractor with canopy, red, 1:43 ....$28

Cat D4E Bulldozer, 1:50 ....$28
Dresser A450E Motorgrader, 1:50 ....$48
Galion Road Grader, 1:50......................$48
Komatsu Motorgrader. 1:50....................$48
Case 580H Tractor with Backhoe, 1:43.....$78

Mini Marque 43

All Mini Marque 43 models are 1:43 scale in white metal, hand built in England in very limited quantities.
1932 Packard Dual Cowl Phaeton $129
Clark Gable's 1934 Packard LeBaron Boattail Speedster.......................................$200
1953 Packard Caribbean Convertible $200
2B 1957 Ford Fairlane Convertible, top down...$179
12A 1955 Chevrolet BelAir Sports Coupe .$169
12B 1955 Chevrolet BelAir Nomad $159
18B 1934 Auburn 652Y Convertible Sedan, top down...$159
24A 1954 Cadillac Eldorado Convertible, top down...$198
24B 1954 Cadillac Eldorado Convertible, top up...$198
25C 1929 Duesenberg Model J, top down ..$215
26A 1964 Lincoln Continental Convertible, top down...$179
27B 1958 Chevrolet Corvette, top off (baby blue)...$149
28C 1935 Auburn 851 Boattail Speedster $215
30A 1958 Chevy Sports Coupe with Continental kit $198
30B 1958 Chevrolet Impala Convertible with Continental kit, top down...................$198
31B 1961 Chevrolet Corvette, top off $149
34D 1937 Cord 812 Sportsman Convertible Coupe, top up $169
36A 1959 Lincoln Continental Convertible, top down $189
37A 1962 Chevrolet Corvette, top on.......$149
37B 1962 Chevrolet Corvette, top off (tan or white) $149
37C 1962 Chevrolet Corvette, top on $149
38B 1957 Chevrolet Corvette, top off $149

Mini Metals (see Simba)

Mini Power (see Shinsei)

Mini Racing

Regarding Mini Racing, Harvey Goranson reports: "Now for some history, courtesy of Ma Collection. This operation began in 1976 by Frenchmen Jean-Yves Puillet and Bernard Hue, 65 rue Tolbiac, 75013 Paris. (This address info is 15+ years old.) Their first two models, a Porsche "Pink Pig" from LM71 and a Simca CG Coupe were available as kits or built, but I believe they went kits only early on. The kits number well over 200 today and they are still going. Around 1981 or so they began offering resin kits, and that may be the medium they are

all made in today. My opinion — if there's another kit of the same car available, buy it."

"Those Mini Racing kits I have are with me only because no one else makes, or is likely to make, the vehicle represented. Poor mold line placement, bad proportions, bad decal fit, etc. Sort of a French John Day. Maybe they've improved — I haven't bought one in 15 years or so. I own the 1981 Decadenet Belga you list — never built it because the decals just aren't proportioned right. It DNF'ed (Did Not Finish?) LeMans in the 9th hour."
Decadenet Belga, 1:43.............................$24

Miniroute

Miniroute models are 1:43 scale hand builts made in France.
Peugeot 304 Fire Van Allier.................$40–50
Citroën Jumpy Ambulance $40–50

Mira

Mira of Spain offers detailed scale models currently available from many diecast model dealers. Lately, Mira's 1:18 scale models have dominated their product line, but they were more prominently known in the seventies for their 1:43 scale models. Miras, like most diecast toys, are now made in China.

Mira 1:18 Scale Golden Line

1955 Buick Century Convertible, top down, red, #6134.............................$30–35
1955 Buick Century Convertible, top down, Belfast green, #6185...............$30–35
1955 Buick Century Coupe, red, #6131...$30–35
1955 Buick Century Coupe, Belfast green, #6186.........................$30–35
1955 Buick Century Coupe, metallic green with beige roof, #6283 ....$30–35
1955 Buick Century Coupe, metallic red with beige roof, #6284..............$30–35
1955 Buick Century Coupe, metallic red with black roof, #6285..............$30–35
1955 Buick Century Coupe, beige with black roof, #6286..............$30–35
1955 Buick Century Coupe, black with beige roof, #6287..............$30–35
1955 Buick Century Fire Chief, red, #6119 ....$30–35
1955 Buick Century Sun State Police, black and white, #6118 ....$30–35
1955 Buick Century Taxi, yellow, #6116 ....$30–35
1950 Chevrolet Panel Truck, maroon, #6231 ....$30–35
1950 Chevrolet Panel Truck, forester green, #6232 ....$30–35
1950 Chevrolet Panel Truck, cream medium, #6233 ....$30–35
1950 Chevrolet Panel Truck, mariner blue, #6234 ....$30–35
1950 Chevrolet Panel Military Ambulance, olive drab, #6241 ....$30–35

1950 Chevrolet Suburban Carryall, forester green, #6238 ....$30–35
1950 Chevrolet Suburban Carryall, cream medium, #6239 ....$30–35
1950 Chevrolet Suburban Carryall, mariner blue, #6240 ....$30–35
1950 Chevrolet Suburban Carryall Military Police, olive drab, #6244 ......$30–35
1950 Chevrolet Suburban Boston Fire Department Panel Truck, red, #6242...$30–35
1950 Chevrolet Suburban Police Panel Truck, black with white side doors, #6243 ....$30–35
1950 Chevrolet Suburban School Bus, orange-yellow, #6245 ....$30–35
1950 Chevrolet Military Pickup, olive drab, #6246 ....$30–35
1953 Chevrolet Corvette Convertible, top down, cream, #6153 ....$30–35
1953 Chevrolet Corvette Convertible, top down, black, #6281 ....$30–35

1953 Chevrolet Panel Truck $25

1953 Chevrolet Pickup, metallic green, #6190 ....$30–35
1953 Chevrolet Pickup, burgundy, #6191 ....$30–35
1953 Chevrolet Pickup, black, #6202 ....$30–35
1953 Chevrolet Pickup, red, #6203...$30–35
1953 Chevrolet Pickup, white, #6204 ....$30–35
1953 Chevrolet Pickup Tanker, red with white tank, #6221 ....$30–35

1953 Chevrolet Styleline De Luxe $30

1953 Corvette Coupe, blue..........$25

1953 Chevrolet Pickup Tanker, red with white closed topper, #6223 .....$30–35
1953 Chevrolet Pickup Tanker, blue with white tank, #6270 ....$30–35
1953 Chevrolet Pickup Tanker, blue with white closed topper, #6271 .....$30–35
1954 Chevrolet Corvette Convertible, top down, metallic pennant blue, #6195 ....$30–35
1954 Chevrolet Corvette Convertible, top down, sportsman red, #6198...$30–35
1954 Chevrolet Corvette Convertible, top up, cream with black roof, #6189 ..$30–35
1954 Chevrolet Corvette Convertible, top up, metallic pennant blue with cream roof, #6197 ....$30–35
1954 Chevrolet Corvette Convertible, top up, sportsman red with tan roof, #6200 ....$30–35
1954 Chevrolet Corvette Convertible, top up, black with beige roof, #6282 ....$30–35
1954 Chevrolet Corvette Convertible, top up, harvest gold with black roof, #6299 ....$30–35
1954 Chevrolet Corvette Coupe, cream, #6188 ....$30–35
1954 Chevrolet Corvette Coupe, pennant blue, #6196 ....$30–35
1954 Chevrolet Corvette Coupe, sportsman red, #6199..........$30–35
1954 Chevrolet Corvette Coupe, black, #6280 ....$30–35
1955 Chevrolet Bel Air Convertible..$30–35
1955 Chevrolet Bel Air Hardtop......$30–35
1949 Ford Convertible, top down, blue, #6248 ....$30–35
1949 Ford Convertible, top down, red, #6249 ....$30–35
1949 Ford Convertible, top up, blue with tan roof, #6252..........$30–35
1949 Ford Convertible, top up, red with tan roof, #6253..........$30–35
1949 Ford Coupe, blue, #6250 ....$30–35
1949 Ford Coupe, red, #6251......$30–35
1949 Ford Coupe Fire Department, #6255 ....$30–35
1949 Ford Coupe Police, #6254...$30–35
1956 Ford F-100 Pickup, metallic burgundy, #6156 ....$30–35
1956 Ford F-100 Pickup, red, #6158 ..$30–35
1956 Ford F-100 Pickup, metallic blue, #6159 ....$30–35
1956 Ford F-100 Pickup, metallic dark green, #6183 ....$30–35
1964½ Ford Mustang Convertible, top down, cream, #6114..........$30–35
1964½ Ford Mustang Convertible, top down, red, #6127..........$30–35
1964½ Ford Mustang Convertible, top up, red with white roof, #6142 ......$30–35
1964½ Ford Mustang Convertible, top down, burgundy, #6288 ....$30–35

1964½ Ford Mustang Convertible, top down, Caspian blue, #6289 ....$30–35
1964½ Ford Mustang Convertible, top down, champagne beige, #6290 ....$30–35
1964½ Ford Mustang Convertible, top up, metallic burgundy with tan roof, #6294 ....$30–35
1964½ Ford Mustang Convertible, top up, Caspian blue with tan roof, #6295 ....$30–35
1964½ Ford Mustang Convertible, top up, champagne beige with tan roof, #6296 ....$30–35
1964½ Ford Mustang Coupe, cream, #6113 ....$30–35
1964½ Ford Mustang Coupe, red, #6126 ....$30–35
1964½ Ford Mustang Coupe, burgundy, #6291 ....$30–35
1964½ Ford Mustang Coupe, Caspian blue, #6292 ....$30–35
1964½ Ford Mustang Coupe, champagne beige, #6293 ....$30–35
1965 Ford Mustang Fastback, champagne beige, #6149 ....$30–35
1965 Ford Mustang Fastback, red, #6150 ....$30–35
1965 Ford Mustang Fastback, Caspian blue, #6170 ....$30–35
1998 Ford F-150 Shortbox Flareside Supercab Pick-Up 4x4 XLT, metallic red brighten, #6217..........$30–35
1998 Ford F-150 Shortbox Flareside Supercab Pick-Up 4x4 XLT, red, #6218 ....$30–35
1998 Ford F-150 Shortbox Flareside Supercab Pick-Up 4x4 XLT, Pacific green, #6219 ....$30–35
1950 GMC Panel Truck, permanent red, #6212 ....$30–35
1950 GMC Panel Truck, oakwood brown, #6213 ....$30–35
1950 GMC Panel Truck, Narva green, #6214 ....$30–35
1950 GMC Suburban Carryall, permanent red, #6235..........$30–35
1950 GMC Suburban Carryall, oakwood brown, #6236 ....$30–35
1950 GMC Suburban Carryall, Narva green, #6237 ....$30–35

Mira 1:18 Scale Hobby Class
1989 Ferrari 348 TB, red, #6101..$30–35
1989 Ferrari 348 TB, metallic silver, #6227 ....$30–35
1989 Ferrari 348 TB, pennant blue, #6230 ....$30–35
1989 Ferrari 348 TS, pennant blue, #6231 ....$30–35
1989 Ferrari 348 TS, red, #6105..$30–35
1991 Ferrari Testarossa 512 TR Cabriolet, red, #6145..........$30–35

1991 Ferrari Testarossa 512 TR Cabriolet, metallic silver, #6175 ....$30–35
1991 Ferrari Testarossa 512 TR Cabriolet, pennant blue, #6178 ....$30–35
1991 Ferrari Testarossa 512 TR Coupe, red, #6144 ....$30–35
1991 Ferrari Testarossa 512 TR Coupe, metallic silver, #6174 ....$30–35
1991 Ferrari Testarossa 512 TR Coupe, pennant blue, #6177...................$30–35
1992 Ferrari 348 Spider Cabriolet, pennant blue, #6179 ....$30–35
1992 Ferrari 348 Spider Cabriolet, red, #6181 ....$30–35
1992 Ferrari 348 Spider Cabriolet, top down, metallic silver, #6228 ....$30–35
1992 Ferrari 348 Spider Coupe, red, #6180 ....$30–35
1995 Ferrari F-50 Cabriolet, red, #6205 ....$30–35
1995 Ferrari F-50 Cabriolet, metallic blue, #6209 ....$30–35
1995 Ferrari F-50 Cabriolet, metallic silver, #6226 ....$30–35
1995 Ferrari F-50 Coupe, red, #6201.$30–35
1995 Ferrari F-50 Coupe, pennant blue, #6208 ....$30–35
1995 Ferrari F-50 Coupe, metallic silver, #6229 ....$30–35
Lamborghini Diablo Super Deportivo, red, #6106 ....$30–35
Lamborghini Diablo Super Deportivo, pennant blue, #6107 ....$30–35
Lamborghini Diablo Super Deportivo, metallic silver, #6108.............$30–35

Mira 1:25 Scale
Audi 200 4-Door Sedan $16
Benetton Ford.............$18
BMW Brabham "Olivetti" $18
BMW 323i Coupe $16
BMW 323i 2-Door Sedan $16
Ferrari 348 TB.............$16
Ferrari 348 TB.............$16
Ferrari Spa "Goodyear".............$18
1956 Ford Thunderbird.............$16
Lancia 037 "Martini".............$16
Lotus Ford.............$18
Mercedes-Benz 190E 2.3 Sedan $18
Mercedes-Benz 500 4-Door Sedan.......$16
Mercedes-Benz 540K.............$16
Nissan Jeep.............$16
Porsche 911 "Rothman's Paris-Dakar" $24
Porsche 928.............$16
Renault Espace Ambulance $16
Renault Espace Fire.............$16
Williams Honda.............$18
Williams Renault.............$18

Mira 1:43 Scale
Citroën CX Sedan $15
Mercedes-Benz 450 SE $15
Pegaso Fire.............$18

Mira 1:64 Scale
Caravan Ambulance.............$4

Chrysler 150 4-Door Sedan $4
Ford Fiesta 2-Door Sedan.......................$4
Land Rover Ambulance $4
Mercedes 450 4-Door Sedan $4
Seat 1200 Coupe.............$4
Seat 131E 4-Door Sedan $4
Seat 128 Coupe.............$4

Mitrecraft
Diecast Miniatures offers just one model from Mitrecraft.
Austin A35 4-Door Sedan, 1:43.............$35

MK Models
Only one example of MK Models is known.
Tatra Semi Oil Tanker, 1:120.......................$5

Moboto (or Meboto)
Like so many other obscure brands, only a few models by Moboto (possibly spelled Meboto) of Turkey are offered by Diecast Miniatures.
Lamborghini Marzal, 1:43.........................$11
Lancia Fulvia Coupe, 1:43 ....$11
Mercedes-Benz 250 Sedan, 1:43.............$11

Modelauto/Sun Motor Company, Bugattiana, Rapide, Bijou
Modelauto produces models under the brands of Sun Motor Company, Bugattiana, Rapide, and Bijou. Sun Motor Company is known, among other things for replica firefighting equipment, as so richly illustrated in Toys for Collectors' catalog. Modelauto, of Leeds, England, was started in 1974 by Rod and Val Ward. They also produce *Model Auto Review* 10 times a year and host the Somerville Society for collectors of that prestigious brand of scale models. In addition, they are exclusive UK distributors for a few other exceptional brands — Paradise Garage, Doorkey, Oto, and Scottoy.

Modelauto Sun Motor Company, 1:50 Scale, UK
As of 1/97, n/a = not made. o/s = temporarily out of stock
124 Diamond T M20 British Army, kit price ....(£47) $73 US
    built price...............(£110) $171 US
125 Diamond T M20 US Army, kit price ....(£47) $73 US
    built price ....(£110) $171 US
126 Diamond T ballast Crook & Willington, kit price ....(£47) $73 US
    built price ....(£110) $171 US
127 Diamond T artic tractor Crook & Will., kit price ....(£40) $62 US
    built price ....o/s
128 Diamond T heavy haulage Pickford's, kit price ....o/s
    built price ....(£110) $171 US
129 Diamond T heavy haulage Stoof/Mamut, kit price ....(£47) $73 US
    built price ....(£110) $171 US

130 Diamond T Heavy Haulage Sunters, kit price ....(£47) $73 US
    built price ....(£110) $171 US
131 Diamond T Heavy Haulage Wynns, kit price ....(£47) $ 73 US
    built price ....(£110) $171 US
132 Diamond T Thurston's Fair, kit price ....(£67) $104 US
    built price ....o/s
133 Diamond T M20 Brit. Army Hercules eng., kit price ....(£47) $73 US
    built price ....(£110) $171 US
134 Diamond T tractor STAG (France), kit price ....(£47) $73 US
    built price ....(£110) $171 US
135 Diamond T Recovery (TFL) "Hudson," kit price ....(£47) $73 US
    built price ....o/s
136 Diamond T Recovery (TFL) "Avon," kit price ....(£47) $73 US
    built price ....o/s
137 Diamond T Recovery (TFL) "J&H," kit price ....(£47) $73 US
    built price ....(£120) $186 US
139 Diamond T Brit. Army canvas cab closed, kit price ....(£47) $73 US
    built price ....(£110) $171 US
140 Diamond T British Army artic tractor, kit price ....(£40) $63 US
    built price ....(£95) $148
US141 Diamond T US Army artic tractor, kit price ....(£40) $63 US
    built price ....o/s
143 Diamond T Brit Army canvas cab artic, kit price ....(£40) $63 US
    built price ....(£95) $148 US
144 Diamond T artic tractor, Pickford's, kit price ....(£40) $63 US
    built price ....(£95) $148 US
145 Diamond T artic tractor Stoof Breda, kit price ....(£40) $63 US
    built price ....(£95) $148 US
148 Leyland E Yorks service vehicle, kit price ....(£48) $75 US
    built price ....(£98) $152 US
149 Fairground TRANSKIT for bus or Van, kit price ....(£12) $19 US
    built price ....n/a
150 Daimler CVD6 bus 1949, Exeter, kit price ....(£60) $93 US
    built price ....(£120) $186 US
154 Bedford OY Tanker (Pool, Esso, Caltex), kit price ....(£29) $45 US
    built price ....(£65) $101 US
155 Bedford OY GS lorry (livery varies), kit price ....(£29) $45 US
    built price ....(£65) $101 US
156 Bedford OS Breakdown lorry, kit price ....(£33) $52 US
    built price ....o/s
157 Bedford OS tipper (Marples), kit price ....(£29) $45 US
    built price ....(£65) $101 US

158 Bedford OY cab, transkit for Corgi,
kit price ....(£9) $14 US
built price ....n/a

159 Mann Egerton Breakdown crane transkit,
kit price ....(£9) $14 US
built price ....n/a

160 Ford 7V 1940s Shell airfield tanker,
kit price ....(£45) $70 US
built price ....(£95) $148 US

161 Ford 7V 1940s artic tractor,
kit price ....(£29) $45 US
built price ....o/s

162 Ford 7V 1940s box van LNER,
kit price ....£(33) $52 US
built price ....o/s

163 Ford 7V 1930s Breakdown lorry,
kit price ....(£33) $52 US
built price ....(£75) $117 US

164 Ford 7V wartime tanker "Pool,"
kit price ....(£33) $52 US
built price ....(£75) $117 US

165 Ford 7V 1930s Open Imperial Airways,
kit price ....(£33) $52 US
built price ....(£75) $117 US

166 Ford 7V 1930s tanker Pratts,
kit price ....(£33) $52 US
built price ....(£75) $117 US

167 Ford 7V 1930s box van Ford,
kit price ....(£33) $52 US
built price ....o/s

170 Rotinoff Atlantic large cab Sunters,
kit price ....£(50) $78 US
built price ....(£120) $186 US

171 Rotinoff Atlantic small cab Parnaby,
kit price ....(£50) $78 US
built price ....(£120) $186 US

172 Rotinoff Atlantic small cab Sunter,
kit price ....(£50) $78 US
built price ....(£120) $186 US

173 Rotinoff Atlantic small cab Smith,
kit price ....(£50) $78 US
built price ....(£120) $186 US

175 Bedford OY van BRS, GWR, LMS,
kit price ....(£33) $52 US
built price ....(£117) $75 US

176 Bedford OS Refuse lorry,
kit price ....(£33) $52 US
built price ....o/s

177 Bedford OY tackle wagon, livery varies,
kit price ....(£36) $56 US
built price ....(£79) $125

178 Bedford OS + generator, fairground,
kit price ....(£33) $52 US
built price ....(£75) $117 US

179 Bedford OY plank-side Charringtons,
kit price ....(£33) $52 US
built price ....(£75) $117 US

179 Bedford OY plank-side Cirkus Arena,
kit price ....(£33) $52 US
built price ....(£75) $117 US

180 Scammell Super Constructor Pickford's,
kit price ....(£50) $78 US
built price ....(£120) $186 US

181 Scammell Super Constructor Sunters,
kit price ....(£50) $78 US
built price ....(£120) $186 US

182 Scammell Super Constructor Wynns,
kit price ....(£50) $78 US
built price ....(£120) $186 US

183 Scammell Super Constructor Marples,
kit price ....(£50) $78 US
built price ....(£120) $186 US

185 Bedford O sided lorry LEP,
kit price ....(£33) $52 US
built price ....(£75) $117 US

186 Bedford O tipper Ahearn,
kit price ....(£33) $52 US
built price ....£(75) $117 US

190 Super Pacific Prime Mover Wynn's,
kit price ....(£60) $95 US
built price ....(£120) $186 US

191 Commer Superpoise Van McVities,
kit price ....(£49) $76 US
built price ....(£98) $152 US

191 Commer Superpoise Van, Cadbury,
kit price ....(£49) $76 US
built price ....(£98) $152 US

192 Ford ET6 coachbuilt van Jays or BOAC,
kit price ....£(49) $76 US
built price ....(£98) $152 US

195 Leyland Comet bus Laing or BOAC,
kit price ....(£49) $76 US
built price ....(£98) $152 US

200 Queen Mary artic trailer var. decals,
kit price ....(£55) $86 US
built price ....n/a

201 Bedford OX + Queen Mary artic trailer,
kit price ....n/a
built price ....(£110) $171 US

201 Bedford OX-Queen Mary "Helicopter
Services," kit price ....(£110) $171 US
built price......................................$

202 AOMA Caravan 1920s-30s,
kit price ....(£24) $38
USbuilt price....................(£40) $62 US

203 Rex Caravan 1930s-40s,
kit price ....(£24) $38 US
built price ....(£40) $62 US

204 Sales Trailer Circus, Refreshments, RN,
etc., kit price ....(£27) $42 US
built price ....(£49) $76 US

205 Dyson 85 ton well trailer (specify livery),
kit price ....(£60) $93 US
built price ....(£120) $186 US

206 King 150 ton 6 axle well trailer,
kit price ....(£85) $132 US
built price ....(£145) $225 US

207 King 3 ax artic low load trailer,
kit price ....(£69) $107 US
built price ....(£120) $186 US

209 Bogie bolster trailer 2+2 axle,
kit price ....(£29) $45 US
built price ....(£60) $93 US

210 Bedford OX artic tractor unit,
kit price ....(£29) $45 US
built price ....o/s

211 Single axle artic trailer US style,
kit price ....(£30) $47 US
built price ....(£70) $109 US

212 Single axle artic trailer European style,
kit price ....(£30) $47 US
built price ....(£70) $109 US

213 Single axle artic oval tanker trailer,
kit price ....(£35) $55 US
built price ....o/s

220 Autocar U70 civilian tanker B-A or Skelly, kit price ....(£49) $76 US
built price ....(£98) $152 US

221 Autocar U70 US Navy tanker,
kit price ....(£49) $76 US
built price ....(£98) $152 US

222 Autocar U70 Fire dept tanker,
kit price ....(£49) $76 US
built price ....(£98) $152 US

223 Autocar U70 Avgas tanker,
kit price ....(£49) $76 US
built price ....(£98) $152 US

224 Autocar U70 2 axle open truck,
kit price ....(£33) $52 US
built price ....(£75) $117 US

225 Autocar U70 artic tractor unit NYC,
kit price ....(£29) $45 US
built price ....(£65) $101 US

226 Autocar U70 fire pumper,
kit price ....(£55) $86 US
built price ....o/s

230 Guy Warrior 4x2 artic tractor unit,
kit price ....(£29) $45 US
built price ....(£65) $101 US

231 Guy Invincible 6x4 tractor unit,
kit price ....(£49) $76 US
built price ....(£98) $152 US

232 Guy Invincible 6x4 tipper Wimpey,
kit price ....(£55) $86 US
built price ....(£105) $163 US

235 Guy Invincible 8 wheel flat Wynns,
kit price ....(£55) $86 US
built price ....(£105) $163 US

236 Guy Invincible 4 axle tanker Regent,
kit price ....(£55) $86 US
built price ....(£105) $163 US

242 ERF KV 6x4 tipper Pointer,
kit price ....(£55) $86 US
built price ....(£105) $163 US

245 ERF KV 4 axle flat Gardner 1950s,
kit price ....(£55) $86 US
built price ....(£105) $163 US

246 ERF KV 4 axle tanker Shell-BP,
kit price ....(£55) $86 US
built price ....(£105) $163 US

250 Ford Thames Trader flat lorry,
kit price ....(£33) $52 US
built price ....(£75) $117 US

251 Ford Thames Trader Lubricants tanker,
kit price ....(£37) $58 US
built price ....(£79) $123 US

260 Leyland Octopus flat BRS,
kit price ....(£55) $86 US
built price ....(£105) $163 US

261 Leyland Hippo 6x4 tipper Willment,
kit price ....(£55) $86 US
built price ....(£105) $163 US

161+211 Ford 7v artic flat Pickford's,
kit price ....(£125) $194 US
built price $300

210+213 Bedford OX artic tanker Pickford's,
kit price ....(£125) $194 US
built price $300

210+213 Bedford OX artic tanker Pool,
kit price ....(£125) $194 US
built price $300

Modelauto Bugattiana 1:43 models from UK

BU001 Bugatti T40 Grand Sport 1930,
kit price ....(£30) $47 US
built price ....(£70) $109 US

BU002 Bugatti T40 Sahara, Loiseau 1930,
kit price ....(£35) $55 US
built price ....o/s

BU004 Bugatti T45 16 Cylinder,
kit price ....(£35) $55 US
built price ....(£75) $117 US

BU005 Bugatti T35B Sports 2 seat aero,
kit price ....(£35) $55 US
built price ....(£75) $117 US

BU006 Bugatti T252 Cabriolet,
kit price ....(£35) $55 US
built price ....(£75) $117 US

BU010 Bugatti T57SC Colonel Giles,
kit price ....(£35) $55 US
built price ....(£75) $117 US

BU011 Bugatti T57SC Colonel Giles Rally,
kit price ....(£35) $55 US
built price ....o/s

BU012 Bugatti T57C Shah of Iran,
kit price ....(£35) $55 US
built price ....o/s

Modelauto Rapide 1:43 models from UK

RA002 Jaguar Mark VII red, blue, gray,
green, kit price ....o/s
built price ....(£60) $93 US

RA005 Austin-Healey 100S sports,
kit price ....(£26) $41 US
built price ....(£60) $93 US

RA008 BSA Scout Open sports 1930s,
kit price ....(£27) $42 US
built price ....(£69) $107 US

RA008 BSA Scout Open sports two-tone,
kit price ....(£75) $116 US
built price $250

RA009 Bantam (American Austin) Sports 38,
kit price ....(£28) $44 US
built price ....(£68) $106 US

RA009 Bantam Sports two-tone,
kit price ....(£70) $109 US
built price $225

RA010 BSA Scout Coupe,
kit price ....(£29) $45 US
built price ....(£70) $109 US

RA011 Bantam pickup civil 1939,
kit price ....(£30) $109 US
built price ....(£70) $109 US

RA012 Bantam pickup stakeside 39 NEW,
kit price ....(£34) $53 US
built price ....£76 ($118 US)

RA013 Bantam pickup US Army 1939,
kit price ....(£30) $47 US
built price ....(£70) $109 US

RA014 Bantam pickup Fire dept 1939,
kit price ....(£34) $53 US
built price ....(£76) $118 US

RA015 Bantam avgas tanker 1939,
kit price ....(£30) $47 US
built price ....(£70) $109 US

Modelauto Bijou models, from various countries

1 Vespa parascooter French Army +
bazooka, 1:30, kit price ..(£13) $20 US
built price ....(£19) $30 US

2 Bugatti T52 Baby (by Auto Replicas) 1:43,
kit price ....(£13) $20 US
built price ....(£22) $34 US

3 Austin Pathfinder pedal car (ex Rapide
100) 1:43, kit price ......(£10) $16 US
built price ....(£19) $30 US

6 London E1 tram Model Auto Show 95,
kit price ....n/a
built price ....(£5) $8 US

7 "Inflatable" boat + outboard motor, 1:43
plastic, kit price ....n/a
built price ....(£3) $5 US

ModelCast (also see Chrono A)

ModelCast is a newly emerging company based in San Jose, California. They offer quality diecast models of civilian and military models. Their website at www.isaacnet.com/modelcast describes the various models they offer. Here is their product line as listed on their website. The models they offer are so similar to those offered by Chrono A that I suspect a connection, likely that Chrono A manufactures them for ModelCast.

ModelCast 1:18 Scale

Aston Martin DB5
1001 Aqua Verda Green 1963 .....$15
1002 Peony Red 1963..................$15
1003 Light Ice Blue 1963 ....$15

Lotus Elise
1020 Open Convertible Yellow $15
1021 Open Convertible Blue..........$15
1022 Open Convertible Black $15

ModelCast 1:43 Scale

Hummer
R038 Ambulance with camouflage.....$7
R039 Ambulance Desert Storm $7

Dodge Weapons Carriers
R046 US Army open $7
R047 US Army Closed $7
R048 Liberation de Paris $7

Dodge Command Car
R053 US Army Closed $7
R054 US Army open $7
R055 Command Car D-Day.............$7

Willys Jeep
R001 Closed D-Day 1944 ....$7
R002 Open Liberation de Paris 1944.$7
R003 Open Military Police 1945 ......$7

Model Pet (see Asahi)

Model Planning Co., Ltd. (also see Toyo Kogyo)

Based in Japan, Model Planning Co., Ltd., is the source for Toyo Kogyo models produced in 1:87 scale. For a partial list of models, go to Toyo Kogyo.

Model Power

Model Power, based in Farmingdale, New York, produces over 2,400 O, HO, and N gauge items intended for model railroad layouts, although most are buildings, street lights, layout accessories, and rolling stock. Their series of O scale fire trucks are similar in detail to Ertl's recently introduced models, but are priced somewhat higher ($13 to $15) because of their limited availability, and possess no livery, which leaves the model crying out for customizing.

Perhaps the most interesting part of the Model Power story for diecast toy collectors is that they obtain their diecast models from other manufacturers and repackage them as their own. The fire trucks listed below are all Gaia brand models. The Scania Bus is by Playart. Eidai is also a brand repackaged as Model Power. The package is all that identifies these models as Model Power.

American LaFrance Fire Pumper, 1:87
(Gaia)..$13
American LaFrance Ladder Truck, 1:87
(Gaia)..$15
American LaFrance Snorkel Truck, 1:87
(Gaia)..$15
Scania Bus, "AVIS Courtesy Bus," 1:87 (Playart)..$10

Model Products Corporation (MPC)

Model Products Corporation (MPC) is best known for producing plastic dealer promotional models. A recent find by collector Tom Brown indicates MPC also applied their molds to a series of gravity racers called Dyno-Racers. Original wheels were removed and generic wheels installed in place of them. The models featured a diecast metal base, and were included in a set with race track, apparently a larger-scale version of Hot Wheels. The two models reported by Brown are a yellow plastic Camaro and red plastic Corvette of late sixties or early seventies vintage.

Model Toys (see Doepke)

Models of Yesteryear (see Matchbox)

Moko (also see Matchbox)

Moses Kohnstam established Moko around the turn of the century. Although he died in 1912, his legacy lives on in the British office of Moko, a company renowned for representing toy manufacturers the world over. He contracted such toy companies as Guntermann, Distler, and Fischer, and others to produce made-to-order toys to bear the Moko label.

Early Matchbox toys are marked as "A Moko Lesney Product." Other toy companies relied on Moko for distribution, such as Gama, Tippco, Levy, and Carette.

Most Moko toys are tin windup toys dating around the late 1920s, current valued $1,000 to $1,500.

Montego

The Montego brand is represented by one miniature cruise ship Rotterdam, 12 inches long, offered for $38.

Moose Mountain Toymakers Limited

Parsippany, New Jersey, is headquarters for Moose Mountain Toymakers Limited, manufacturer of two particular playsets first discovered in August 1998 at a local Wal-Mart store. Sets are in the rough form of a bucket, with a strap handle for carrying. Inside are various diecast toys that fit the theme of the set. Each bucket sells for just under $10, and the diecast toys inside are exceptionally well made even though rendered indistinguishably generic when removed from the sets in which they are contained.

Car Wash - Gas - Oil $10
Set includes:
    Ten lightweight diecast cars with opaque black windows, plastic bases, and no interiors
    Car Wash / Gas Station with ramps and accessories
    Peel & Stick Labels for signs, etc.
Dump N' Load $10
Set includes:
    Quarry Truck, Dump Truck, Crane Truck, Scoop Loader, and Bulldozer
    Conveyor Belt, Ramps, Power Shovel with ramps, "rocks," human figures, and accessories
    Peel & Stick Labels for signs, etc.

Morestone

Morris & Stone of Great Britain marketed a line of toys in the 1940s that are more than vaguely similar to Dinky Toys. Most collectors know Morestone by the more familiar Budgie Miniatures, a name adopted in 1959. Herein is listed a representation of the Morestone line.

1 AA Motorcycle and Sidecar	$30
2 RAC Motorcycle and Sidecar	$30
3 AA Land Rover	$30
4 AA Bedford Van	$20
5 Wolseley 6180 Police Car	$25
6 Cooper-Bristol Racing Car	$20
7 Mercedes-Benz Racing Car	$25
8 Volkswagen 1200 Sedan	$35
9 Maudslay Horse Box	$40
10 Karrier GPO Telephones Van	$35
11 Morris Commercial Van	$25
12 Volkswagen Microbus	$40
13 Austin FX3 Taxi	$30
14 Packard Convertible	$40
15 Austin A95 Westminster Countryman	$25
16 Austin-Healey 100	$30
17 Ford Thames 5 cwt. Van	$45
18 Foden Dumper	$25
19 Rover 105R	$25
20 Plymouth Belvedere Convertible	$45

Other Morestone Models

0-6-0 Tank Locomotive	$45
AA Land Rover, 4¼"	$145
AA Land Rover, 3"	$100
AA Motorcycle and Sidecar	$120
Aveling-Barford Road Roller	$45
Bedford Car Transporter	$120
Bedford Dormobile	$160
Breakdown Service Land Rover	$100
Compressor	$50
Daimler Ambulance	$100
Fire Engine, clockwork motor with bell	$90
Fire Escape, large	$90
Fire Escape, smaller	$75
Foden 8-wheel Flat Lorry	$120
Foden 8-wheel Open Lorry	$120
Foden 8-wheel Petrol Tanker	$120
Foden Dumper	$40
Foden Flat Lorry with chains	$120
Horse Drawn Covered Wagon with 4 Horses	$80
Horse Drawn Covered Wagon with 6 Horses	$100
Horse Drawn Gypsy Caravan	$150
Horse Drawn Hansom Cab	$60
Horse Drawn Snack Bar	$100
International Articulated Refrigeration Truck	$60
Klückner Side Tipping Truck	$75
Leyland Double Deck Bus	$120
Military Police Land Rover	$180
Prime Mover with Trailer	$50
RAC Motorcycle and Sidecar	$120
Racing Car	$45
Road Sweeper	$120
Scammell Articulated Tank Truck	$60
Sleigh with Father Xmas	$100
Solo Motorcycle	$75
Stage Coach with 2 horses	$100
Stage Coach with 4 horses	$100
State Landau with 6 horses	$50
Wells Fargo Stage Coach with 2 Galloping Horses	$100
Wells Fargo Stage Coach with 4 horses	$100
Wolseley 6/80 Police Car	$75

Morestone Noddy Character Toys

Big Ears on Bicycle, approx. 2½"	$75
Big Ears on Bicycle, approx. 1¾"	$60
Clown on Bicycle, approx. 2½"	$75
Noddy and His Car, approx. 4"	$75
Noddy and His Car, approx. 2"	$50
Noddy on Bicycle With Trailer	$65
Noddy's Garage Set	$160

Moskovich

Moskovich is a 1:43 scale brand from Russia. The quality is excellent for the price. Doors, hood, and trunk generally open, and detailing is extensive. This list was provided by a foreign dealer known only by his e-mail address: prol@algonet.se. Moskovich is also the brand name of an automotive manufacturer based in Moscow, Russia-based on information provided by collector Werner Legrand of Belgium, so the 1:43 scale models are apparently miniatures of the full-scale Moskovich vehicles.

403 Saloon standard	$12
408 Saloon standard	$8
408 Ambulance	$8
408 Saloon taxi	$8
408 Saloon std + lugg. rack	$8
408 Saloon traffic police	$8
408 Saloon Rally Car	$8
412 Saloon standard	$8
412 Saloon ambulance	$8
412 Saloon taxi	$8
412 Saloon Rally Car	$8
412 Saloon traffic police	$8
412 Saloon standard + luggage rack	$8
426 Estate standard	$8
426 Estate airport service car	$8
426 Estate Rally support	$8
426 Estate standard + luggage rack	$8
427 Estate standard	$8
427 Estate airport service car	$8
427 Estate standard + luggage rack	$8
433 Van books	$9
Pickup standard	$8
IZH 1500 standard	$8
2141 Fastback standard	$9
2141 Fastback ALEKO	$10
2141 Fastback with symbols	$10
2141 Fastback traffic police with beacon	$13

Motor City Classics

Post Office Box 102
[Office: 26 Woodland Road]
Short Hills, NJ 07078-0102 USA
phone: 973-376-4446
fax: 973-376-5444
contact: Ron Gerwin, Sales Manager
e-mail: markets@ix.netcom.com

This collection of diecast models is comprised of 1:18 scale classics from the thirties, forties, fifties, and sixties. This relatively new company was started in 1998 and is based in Short Hills, New Jersey. As with most diecast models, Motor City Classics are manufactured in China.

1939 Chevrolet Woody Station Wagon
  v.1 Italian cream (September 2000) $35
  v.2 Yosemite green (September 2000) .$35
  v.3 Granville gray (September 2000) $35
1948 Chrysler Town & Country Convertible, top down
  v.1 Catalina tan, #5001 ....$35
  v.2 yellow lustre, #5003 ....$35
  v.3 gunmetal gray (July 1999), #5004 ..$35
  v.4 heather green (July 1999), #5007 ...$35
  v.5 military blue (April 2000) $35
1949 Ford Custom 2-Door Woody Station Wagon
  v.1 sea mist green (August 1999), #30001 .$35

v.2 fez red (August 1999), #30002 ....$35

  v.3 Miami cream (August 1999), #30003 ....$35
  v.4 light blue (October 1999), #30004 ....$35
  v.5 "Surf Shop" sea mist green (April 2000).$35
  v.6 "Surf Shop" bayview blue (April 2000).$35
  v.7 "Lifeguard" blazing red (April 2000).....$35
1931 Ford Model A Deluxe Roadster
  v.1 stone brown (August 1999), #20001 ..$35

v.2 Washington blue (August 1999), #20002 ....$35

  v.3 Brewster green (August 1999), #20003 ....$35
  v.4 Bronson yellow (August 1999), #20005 ....$35
  v.5 Riviera blue (May 2000) $35
1931 Ford Model A Pickup Truck
  v.1 Lombard blue (October 2000) $35

v.2 Valley green (October 2000) $35

1957 Studebaker Golden Hawk
  v.1 tiara gold (April 2000) $35
  v.2 arctic white (April 2000) $35
  v.3 woodsmoke gray (April 2000) $35
  v.4 Apache red (April 2000) $35

v. 5 green $35

Motor City USA (also see Design Studio and USA Models)

Motor City USA represents 1:43 scale hand-built models made in the United States by partners Alan Novak and Gene Parrill since 1986. USA Models are somewhat less detailed and less expensive models than their Motor City and Design Studio counterparts.
13400 Saticoy St., No. 12
North Hollywood, CA 91605
phone: 818-503-4835
fax: 818-503-4580

Motor City USA
  MC-1 1949 DeSoto 4-Door Sedan $85
  MC-2 1955 Cadillac 4-Door Sedan $85
  MC-3 1949 Nash Yellow Cab $170
  MC-3 1949 Nash Police Car $175
  MC-5 1955 Chevrolet Nomad Wagon .$85
  MC-6 1955 Chevrolet Convertible, top down $85
  MC-7 1953 Chevrolet 2-Door Hardtop .$235
  MC-8 1953 Chevrolet Convertible $265
  MC-9 1953 Chevrolet Sedan Delivery .$235
  MC-9 1953 Chevrolet Ambulette, body by National $210
  MC-10 1950 Ford Convertible $265
  MC-11 1950 Ford Coupe $235
  MC-12 1950 Ford 2-Door Sedan $165
  MC-13 1950 Ford Wagon $265
  MC-14 1950 Ford 4-Door Sedan Police .$165
  MC-15 1950 Ford Crestliner $265
  MC-22 1948 Chrysler Town & Country Convertible $265
  MC-31 1956 Chevrolet Convertible $265
  MC-34 1951 Lincoln Cosmopolitan Convertible, mint green $180
  MC-40 1954 Buick Skylark $265
  MC-41 1959 Nash Metropolitan $235
  MC-58 Pickup $180
  MC-67 1956 Oldsmobile 98 Convertible, top down $150
  MC-68 1956 Oldsmobile 98 2-Door Hardtop $150
  MC-69 1950 Oldsmobile 88 Convertible, top down, burgundy $180
  MC-70 1950 Oldsmobile 88 Hardtop, black $180

  MC-71 1955 Studebaker President Speedster
    v.1 yellow and olive $180
    v.2 pink and black $180
Design Studio
  DS-3 1949 Hudson Commodore $149
  DS-4 1958 Oldsmobile Convertible $125
  DS-5 1948 Buick Coupe $125
  DS-6 1956 Chevrolet Convertible 2-Door, top down $179
  DS-7 1956 Chevrolet Convertible $145
  DS-9 1940 Ford Convertible, top up $219
  DS-9AMB 1953 Chevrolet Ambulette ...$220
  DS-10 1956 Airstream Trailer $125
  DS-105 1934 Ford Three Window Coupe
    v.1 yellow $80
    v.2 black with flames "California Kid" ..$90
    v.3 red $80
  DS-108 1950 Ford Custom Coupe
    v.1 purple with white accent $150
    v.2 black $150
    v.3 metallic orange with white accent .$150
  DS-109 Custom Convertible, top down, yellow $150
  DS-109 Custom Convertible, top up, red ..$150
  DS-110 1941 Willys Coupe, Pro Street
    v.1 blue $80
    v.2 yellow $80
    v.3 red $80
  DS-111 1936 Ford Three Window Custom Coupe
    v.1 yellow $80
    v.2 black $80
    v.3 wine $80
  DS-113 1937 Ford Cabriolet
    v.1 red $80
    v.2 purple $80
    v.3 yellow $80
  DS-114 1937 Ford "Flat Back" 2-Door Sedan
    v.1 yellow $80
    v.2 red $80
    v.3 turquoise $80
  DS-115 1949 Mercury Custom Coupe
    v.1 orange-red with white accent ...$150
    v.2 wine red with white accent $150
  DS-116 1933 Willys Pro Street Rod, 1:24 scale
    v.1 purple with yellow flames $200
    v.2 red $200
  DS-117 1940 Ford 2-Door Street Rod
    v.1 red $80
    v.2 black $80
  DS-118 1940 Ford 2-Door Coupe $140
  DS-129 Custom Street Rod, yellow $125
  DS-129 Custom Street Rod, red $125
  DS-122KS K.S.Pittman Custom Street Rod, red $125
  DS-131 1951 Ford Custom Woody Wagon $140
  DS-132 Cadillac Custom Coupe $125
  DS-200 1952 Hudson Hornet Stock Car $170
U.S.A. Models
  USA-1 1958 Cadillac Series 75 Limousine, introduced in 1997

v.1 dark metallic blue finish..............$70
v.2 silver with black roof...................$70
USA-2 1955 Chrysler Imperial Hardtop, pink
with white roof $70
USA-3F 1949 Nash Los Angeles Fire Chief's
Car, red..$70
USA-3P 1949 Nash Los Angeles Police Car,
black with white doors.....................$70
USA-3T 1949 Nash Yellow Cab...........$70
USA-4 1951 Chevrolet Bel Air 2-Door
Hardtop, slate green with dark green
roof $70
USA-5 1954 Chevrolet Bel Air 4-Door Sedan
v.1 brown with cream roof $70
v.2 blue with white roof $70
USA-6 1955 Cadillac 62 Convertible, top
down, black $70
USA-7 1955 Cadillac 62 Coupe De Ville,
turquoise with white roof $70
USA-8 1940 Ford 4-Door Sedan
v.1 burgundy....................................$70
v.2 dark green $70
USA-9 1940 Ford 4-Door Yellow Cab ...$70
USA-10 1940 Ford 4-Door Los Angeles
Police Car, black with white doors ...$70
USA-11 1940 Ford 2-Door Sedan, tan ..$70
USA-13 1940 Ford 4-Door Fire Chief's Car,
red..$70
USA-14 Pickup...................................$100
USA-17 1951 Ford Crestliner
v.1 two-tone brown and caramel......$70
v.2 black with cream roof.................$70
v.3 two-tone black and green $70
USA-18 Hudson Convertible $100
USA-21 1951 Chevrolet Bel Air 2-Door Con-
vertible, black..................................$70
USA-22 1955 Chevrolet 210 2-Door Sedan,
light blue $70
USA-25 Convertible............................$75
USA-34 Chrysler Town & Country
Convertible......................................$100

Motormax (see Redbox)

Mountain Service International, Inc. (see Pole Position)

MPC (see Model Products Corporation)

MR
MR Collection Models
Via San Gabriele del Carso 9/A
21047 Saronna (Va) - Italy
phone: 02 9626748
fax: 02 9600787
MR's website at mrc.lrcser.it/mr/
default.html reports that "...M.R. Collection
Models s.n.c. is a small firm specialized and
producing special models of collection cars.
Established in 1988, our firm depends upon a
staff of nine highly specialized people.
"In 1993, after several years of experience,

we began introducing some sets of models. Every
stage of the productive process is made rigorously
by hand: The execution of the prototype, the
assembling, the painting is carried out in the store;
everything is done to ensure high quality products.
Our series constituted of only 499 pieces, are
numbered, equipped with warranty of quality and
assembled by only a highly specialized modelist.
All products are manufactured in a modern factory
with the most up-to-date technology."

What it doesn't say is whether the models
are diecast, resin, or other material.
1951 Alfa Romeo 1900C Sprint Cabriolet,
available in red, dark green, or metallic
gray $199
1954 Alfa Romeo 1900C Sprint Coupe, avail-
able in cream, dark gray, or black.......$199
1971 Ferrari 365 GTC/4, available in red,
metallic blue or yellow $199
1961 Ferrari 400 S.A. Convertible, red $199
1967 Ferrari Dino 206GT, available in red,
metallic gray, or yellow $199
1987 Ferrari F40 Street with Engine..........$199
1994 Ferrari F40 Camp Italiano GT, red...$199
1948 Porsche 356 Speedster, available in silver
or yellow..$199
1996 Porsche 911 Carrera 4S, available in Polar Silver, Midnight Blue, or Guards Red $199
1996 Porsche 911 Carrera Turbo, available in
Speed Yellow, Forest Green, or Arena Red..$199
1996 Porsche 911 GT2, available in Speed Yellow, Guards Red, or Polar Silver $199
1996 Porsche 911 GT2 Evo II, available in Polar
Silver or White..................................$199
1996 Porsche 911 RS, available in Speed Yellow, Midnight Blue, or Polar Silver $199

MRE
Harvey Goranson reports: "MRE — Again,
the info comes from Ma Collection. Begun by
Michel El Koubi in Paris, the first dozen or so
models were conversions of Solido diecasts (MS
series — "Modification Solido"). In 1976 he
brought out a range of white metal models, mostly
Porsche racing cars at first. By 1979 he had
stopped making kits, as he had gotten the racing
bug in 1977, driving a Lola T296. Some of the
built models from 1977 bear the signature of
Dominique Esparcieux (ESDO). They also sold
transkits — I had their 1977 Mirage Renault TK
for Solido 38." Below is listed one documented
representative model.
Simca CG Prototype, 1:43 ....$18
Porsche 936 Le Mans 1977, white with Martini
decals, car # 4....................................$18

MTC
Of the many generic diecast toys, MTC is
just another one. These inexpensive toys are
made in China and marketed by MTC, Inc. of
South San Francisco, California. The line
includes airplanes, cars, and other vehicles.
Their collector value will likely never exceed

their original purchase price of usually less
than $2.

MTECH
Epoch Co., Ltd.
12-3, 1-Chome, Komagata, Taito-Ku
Tokyo 111, Japan
phone: 81-3-3843-8144
fax: 81-3-3841-8150
MTECH is a brand from Japan introduced in
the mid-1990s that offers some fairly nice specimens of popular Japanese cars. Produced in
1:43 scale, MTECH models represent mostly late
model cars, both in street and race/rally versions.
A Japanese-language book just published
in Asia provides detailed photos of some two
or three dozen examples. Determining make
and manufacturer of specific models is difficult,
but several models can be identified among the
mix and are listed below. Other models are not
as easy to identify but appear to be representatives of Lexus, Honda, Mitsubishi, Toyota, Nissan, and Mazda. A departure from the usual is
the representation of the BMW Z3 with right
hand steering and driver. While MTech models
are available in England, they have not yet
been spotted in the U. S. A phone number to
the manufacturer is provided in the book: 03
(3843) 9177.
Upon finally obtaining an MTECH model,
I discovered that Epoch Company Limited,
Japan, is in fact the producer of MTECH models. Thanks to Hiromitsu Higuchi, international
sales & marketing manager for Epoch and
Diecast Toy Collectors Association member,
I've been able to make the connection
between the company and the brand, thus the
address provided.
BMW Z3 Road Star, MC-01-A, red, top up with
right hand drive and driver..............$10–12
BMW Z3 Road Star, MC-01-B, silver, top down
with right hand drive and driver $10–12
City Bus "Pepsi" $10–15
Crane Truck, MC-02, 1997.................$20–24
Daihatsu Midget II, MM-04-A, blue $10–12
Daihatsu Midget II, MM-04-B, yellow.....$10–12
Isuzu Freight Van, MT-07, blue and cream cab,
silver cargo box $15–18
Isuzu Freight Van, MT-07-D, "Art Corporation The
0123"...$17–20
Isuzu Freight Van, MT-07-E, "McDonald's" .$17–20
Isuzu Supermedic, MP-07.....................$17–20
Hino Liesse Limousine Bus, MB-02, 1997.$15–18
Hino Liesse Route Bus, MB-02-A,
"Doraemon" $16–19
Hino Liesse Route Bus, MB-02-C, red, "McDon-
ald's"..$19–22
Hino Liesse Route Bus, MB-03, 1997 ....$15–18
Hino Ranger Auto Carrier Truck, MT-05 .$20–24
Hino Ranger Beverage Truck, MT-01,
"Hino"...$15–18
Hino Ranger Beverage Truck, MT-01-C, "Asahi
Super Dry"......................................$17–20

Hino Ranger Beverage Truck, MT-01-D, "Art Corporation The 0123" $19–22

Hino Ranger Camion, MR-06 ....$20–24

Hino Ranger Car Carrier, "Doraemon Carrier Car," MT-09 ....$15–18

Hino Ranger Cement Mixer Truck, MT-04 ....$20–24

Hino Ranger Dump Truck, MT-02 ....$20–24

Hino Ranger Fire Engine, MP-05 ....$20–24

Hino Ranger Garbage Truck, MT-03 .....$20–24

Hino Ranger Snorkel Fire Truck, "Doraemon Ladder Truck," MP-09 ....$15–18

Hino Ranger Wrecker Truck, MT-06 ......$20–24

Honda Minivan $8–12

Honda CR-V, MS-16-A, silver $8–12

Honda CR-V, MS-16-B, green.................$8–12

Hydraulic Power Shoveler, MC-01, 1997 ....$20–24

Mazda Efini RX-7, MS-03, red $8–12

Mazda Efini RX-7, MS-04, silver $8–12

Mazda Miata, gold, MC-03-A $8–12

Mazda Miata, green, MC-03-B $8–12

Mitsubishi Delica Space Gear Ambulance, MP-01 ....$16–20

Mitsubishi Delica Space Gear, MS-09, green $8–12

Mitsubishi Delica Space Gear, MS-10, black...$8–12

Mitsubishi Delica Space Gear Patrol Car, MP-02 ....$10–12

Mitsubishi Lancer GSR Evol-III, MS-11, yellow-orange...$8–12

Mitsubishi Lancer GSR EvoIII, MS-12, red ..$8–12

Mitsubishi Lancer WRC, MR-05 ....$12–15

Nissan Altima Falken GT-R, MR-04 ....$10–12

Nissan Cedric, MS-13, white $8–12

Nissan Cedric, MS-14, dark blue.............$8–12

Nissan Cedric Patrol Car, MP-03 ....$15–18

Nissan Cedric Patrol Car, MP-10 ....$15–18

Nissan Cedric Taxi, MP-04 ....$10–12

Nissan Endless Advan GT-R, MR-03 ......$10–12

Nissan March Cabriolet with 2 figures, MC-02-A, green $10–12

Nissan March Cabriolet with 2 figures, MC-02-B, red $10–12

Nissan Prince Chiba GT-R, MR-07, blue...$8–12

Nissan Skyline GT-R, MS-07, purple $8–12

Nissan Skyline GT-R, MS-08, silver $8–12

Nissan Skyline GT-R Patrol Car, MP-06 ..$10–12

Subaru Legacy Touring Wagon GT-B.......$8–12

Suzuki Wagon R, MM-01-A, silver $9–12

Suzuki Wagon R, MM-01-C, "Doraemon Pizza Delivery" $11–14

Toyota Blistz Supra, MR-01 ....$10–12

Toyota High Ace, MS-15, silver $8–12

Toyota High Ace, light blue, "Doraemon", MB-01-B...$9–11

Toyota High Ace Kindergarten Bus, fluorescent yellow, MB-01 ....$15–18

Toyota RAV4, MS-05, red......................$8–12

Toyota RAV4, MS-06, blue.....................$8–12

Toyota Supra, MS-01, black...................$8–12

Toyota Supra, MS-02, silver $8–12

Wheel Loader, MC-03 ....$18–22

Muky (also see Hot Wheels)

Muky toys are the Hot Wheels of Argentina, produced from older Hot Wheels dies. Models in the Muky Collection are made in Gualeguay, Argentina, which is in Entre Rios province about 100 miles north of Buenos Aires, but across the Parana River. Thanks to Dr. Craig Campbell, associate professor of geography at Youngstown State University, for the geography lesson.

Custom Corvette $10–12

MVC (see Miniature Vehicle Castings)

Nacoral Intercars

Nacoral is a brand of models from Spain that are of lesser quality than Pilen/Auto Pilen models. While most Nacoral models are 1:43 scale, a few 1:25 scale models were also produced, according to collector John Dean. In addition, Nacoral produced at least one racing motorcycle measuring 14 cm, or about 5½ inches long, according to Werner Legrand of Belgium, making it roughly a 1:12 or 1:10 scale model.

Nacoral 1:43 Scale

1969 Chevrolet Corvette, blue $20

1969 Chevrolet Corvette, red $20

1968 Chevrolet Camaro Europa...........$20

1968 Ford Thunderbird, dark blue.........$20

1968 Ford Thunderbird, orange $20

1968 Ford Thunderbird, red $18

1968 Javelin AMX.............................$20

Ferrari Dino $20

Ford Fiesta $20

Matra Bagheera................................$20

Matra Sport $20

Mercedes 280 Sedan $20

Porsche 917, metallic blue-green, white interior, #3515M $20

Porsche 911S, orange, Bosch, Shell, Monte Carlo, Martini, #3517...................$20

Porsche 911S, red, white interior, Bosch, Shell, Monte Carlo, Martini, #3517...........$20

Porsche 911S Rally — White Car #18, driving lights, skis, Bosch, Shell, Monte Carlo, Martini, #3556...................$20

Scania 10 x 8 Covered Truck, blue & yellow..$20

Nacoral 1:25 Scale

1968 Corvette, red $10

Mercedes C111 ....$10

Rolls Royce Silver Cloud III....................$10

Citroën Maserati..............................$10

Mini $10

Renault 5 ....$10

Fiat 600...$10

Other Nacoral Models

Suzuki 750 Vallelunga GT racing motorcycle, 14cm $15–20

National Products (also see Banthrico)

National Products started at the Chicago World's Fair in 1934 and continued producing promotional models through the forties and fifties. Around 1948, Banthrico purchased the company and issued subsequent models under the National Products Division Banthrico.

1939 Buick Super 4-Door..............$850–1000

1940 Buick Super 4-Door.........$1,000–1,250

1941 Buick Century 4-Door.......$1,000–1,250

1946 Buick Super 4-Door.........$500–650

1947–48 Buick Super 4-Door.........$350–425

1949 Buick Super 4-Door.........$300–350

1950 Buick Super 4-Door.........$350–400

1947 Chevrolet Fleetline 2-Door aero Sedan.................................$325–375

1948 Chevrolet Fleetline 2-Door aero Sedan.................................$350–400

1934 Chrysler Airflow 4-Door $825–875

1946 Chrysler New Yorker 4-Door........$150–175

1947–48 Chrysler New Yorker 4-Door .$150–175

1949 Chrysler New Yorker 4-Door........$300–325

1946–48 DeSoto Custom 4-Door....$375–400

1949 DeSoto Custom 4-Door $300–325

1935 Diamond T Stake Truck $4,000–4,500

1946–48 Dodge Custom 4-Door.................$150–175

1948–50 Dodge Model B Pickup Truck.................................$375–400

1948–50 Dodge Model B Stake Truck.................................$375–400

1949 Dodge Coronet 4-Door $300–325

1948–50 Fargo Pickup Truck..........$450–500

1948–50 Fargo Stake Truck...........$450–500

1936 Federal Tanker $850–1000

1948–50 Ford F-1 Panel Truck $350–375

1948–50 Ford F-1 Pickup Truck.......$325–375

1948–50 Ford F-2 Stake Truck........$500–550

1951 Ford F-1 Panel Truck $425–475

1951 Ford F-1 Pickup Truck $400–450

1951 Ford F-2 Stake Truck $425–475

1952 Ford F-1 Panel Truck $350–375

1952 Ford F-1 Pickup Truck $325–350

1952 Ford F-2 Stake Truck $350–375

1953 Ford F-100 Pickup Truck........$325–350

1934 Graham 4-Door............$1,000–1,250

1948–50 GMC FC Pickup Truck $200–225

1948–50 GMC FF Dump Truck.......$250–275

1954 GMC 100 Pickup Truck.........$275–300

1958 GMC 350 Dump Truck..........$325–350

1934 Hudson Terraplane.............$750–1000

1934–36 International C Panel Truck.................$2,750–3,000

1937–40 International D Panel Truck.................$2,750–3,000

1947 International KB Phone Truck with boom and pole...........................$500–550

1949 Lincoln Cosmopolitan 4-Door.......$375–400

1950 Lincoln Cosmopolitan 4-Door.......$525–600

1940–53 Mack L Tanker $350–375

1949 Mercury 4-Door.......$375–400

1950 Mercury 4-Door.........$450–500

1950 Mercury Pace Car 4-Door $500–575
1949 Nash 600 4-Door, single color $175–200
1949 Nash 600 4-Door, two-tone.......$225–250
1950 Nash Statesman 4-Door, single color $175–200
1950 Nash Statesman 4-Door, two-tone.................................$225–250
1950–52 Nash Rambler Convertible $475–500
1946–48 Plymouth Special Deluxe 4-Door $300–325
1948 Pontiac Streamliner 4-Door......$175–200
1949 Pontiac Chieftain 4-Door.........$275–300
1936 REO 4-Door $900–1,200
1937 REO Tanker.....................$900–1,200
1934 Studebaker, "Replica of Giant World's Fair Studebaker" on trunk.................$350–425
1934 Studebaker President 4-Door.......$375–425
1934 Studebaker T Stake Truck $1,000-1,250
1935 Studebaker President 4-Door, smaller scale $900–1,200
1935 Studebaker President 4-Door, larger scale $3,250–3,750
1936 Studebaker President 4-Door, approx. 4½ inches..............................$475–500
1936 Studebaker President 4-Door, approx. 6½ inches..............................$750–800
1938 Studebaker Commander 4-Door $750–1,000
1947–48 Studebaker Commander 2-Door $250–275
1949 Studebaker Commander 2-Door $250–275
1949–53 Studebaker 2R Pickup Truck..................................$350–375
1949–53 Studebaker 2R Stake Truck..................................$450–475
1936–40 White Stake Truck $525–550
1939–40 White Horse Delivery Van with pop-out engine...............................$550–575
1941 White Stake Truck $550–575
1941–42 White Horse Delivery Van with pop-out engine...............................$575–600
1949–65 White 3000 Stake Truck Cabover with engine $350–400

National Toys

The nation in this case is Italy. The year is 1961. Four 1:45 scale plastic models were produced by this company. No diecast models were ever produced.
Alfa Romeo Giulietta Sprint $45
Fiat 1500 Roadster $45
Fiat 1800 Sedan $45
Vanwall Formula 1 ....$45

Nevco

Box 2355
Atascadero, CA 93423
phone: 805-466-8685
One of the newest companies to appear on the market is Nevco. Their first model is a replica of a classic 1930s streamlined toy car with Art Deco box silkscreened by hand. Their second is a sleek transporter for the first model. "The Special," burgundy and gold, limited edition of 4000 ....$175
The Transporter $275

Nevins International, Ltd.

A pair of 1:43 scale models made by Nevins International, Ltd. were recently offered on specially-marked boxes of Kellogg's Corn Flakes. The two-car set is of the Brooks & Dunn Metal Rodeo Legends Racing cars representing 5:8 scale replicas of early NASCAR racers. While this mail-away promo cost just a dollar, models are already valued at $10–15 for the sealed blisterpack set.

New Clover (also see Clover)

New Clover models are made in Asia by New Clover International Ltd of Hong Kong.
Bobcat X225 Skid Loader, 1:25.................$35
Bobcat 743B Skid Loader, 1:19 ....$25
Bobcat 753 Skid Loader, 1:50 ....$10
Bobcat 753 Skid Loader, 1:25 ....$25
Bobcat 7753 Skid Loader, 1:25 ....$25
1959-1962 Melroe (Bobcat) M-200 Loader, 1:25 (replica of first machine built by Melroe Company).......................................$18
Semi Flatbed with three Bobcat 753 Skid Loaders, 1:50.....................................$55
Kiamaster Ambulance, 1:43.......................$18
Kiamaster Kombi, 1:43 ....$18
Pontiac Firebird Coupe, 1:59 ....$5

New-Ray

New-Ray Toys Inc.
907 S. Alameda St.
Los Angeles, CA 90021
Previously distributed by
Midwestern Home Products, Inc.
1105 Orange St.
Wilmington, DE 19801
New-Ray toys are manufactured in China by New-Ray Toys Co., Ltd. The first examples of New-Ray toys found are approximately 1:43 scale farm tractors with driver and flywheel drive. Tractors are sold separately or with trailers that include detachable containers. Sold in either yellow or orange, the tractors sell for $4 each, while the tractor/trailer combinations sell for $6.
The most popular model found from New-Ray is a neat little Hummer faithfully reproduced in 1:32 scale. The doors open on this top-down version which is labeled on the box as being distributed by Midwestern Home Products, Inc. of Wilmington, Delaware.
Since finding the Hummer, the author has noticed a lot more New-Ray toys, mostly pickup trucks and jeeps of similar construction and quality, showing up at Wal-Mart and other stores. Models for 1999 are marked New-Ray Toys Inc., 907 S. Alameda St., Los Angeles, CA 90021.

Also offered by New-Ray are small (1¼ to 1½ inch long), inexpensive diecast toy cars and motorcycles with pull-back action. Their lack of detail, accuracy, and markings result in little or no collectible value.
In 1998, New Ray issued an assortment of 1:43 scale models dubbed the "Open Top Collections," convertible sports cars in acrylic flip-top display boxes. Mercedes, Mustangs, and Golfs comprise most of the models in the series. Besides being sold individually in fliptop display boxes, they have also been found in window box 4-packs.
A more recent find is of a New Volkswagen Beetle in various colors. Marked with the name Boley, a toy and novelty distributor, and Speedy Wheels on the box, the bottom of the model reveals that it is made by New Ray. Speedy Power and Speedy Wheels were at one time produced by ToyMark.

New Ray 1:32 Scale
Hummer, #45323, 1:32

v.1 red with light gray interior...............$5–6
v.2 blue with white interior.............$6–7
Jeep CJ7, 1:32, red with black roll bar and interior............................$6–7
Jeep Dakar, 1:32, pale bronze, #54203 ....$6–7
Jeep Icon, 1:32, dark gray with silver roll bar, black interior, #54083 ....$6–7
Lamborghini 4 x 4, silver with black interior, 1:32...$6–7
Land Rover Station Wagon, #44323, 1:32

v.1 green with white roof and interior.......................................$5–6
v.2 yellow with black roof and interior $6–7
Mercedes-Benz M-Class, 1:32
v.1 dark blue.............................$6–7

Mustang Shelby GT 350, 1966 ....$5–10

New Ray 1:43 Scale

Alfa Romeo Giulietta Spider 1600CC, 1962, black with cream interior, 1:43 ....$5–6

Alfa Romeo Spider, 1989, white with gray interior, 1:43 ....$4

Alfa Romeo Spider, 1996, red with black interior, 1:43 ....$5–6

Corvette Convertible, 1967, metallic light blue, 1:43 ....$5–6

Corvette Convertible, 1969, bright orange-pink, 1:43 ....$5–6

BMW M3 Convertible, 1988, metallic maroon with butterscotch interior, 1:43 ....$5–6

BMW M3 Convertible, 1995, metallic slate blue-green with butterscotch interior, 1:43 ....$5–6

Buick Century Convertible, 1958, pink, 1:43 ....$5–6

Buick Century Convertible, 1955, metallic light pine green, 1:43 ....$5–6

Ford Mustang Convertible, 1964, black with white interior, 1:43 ....$5–6

Ford Mustang GT Convertible, 1988, green with gray interior, 1:43 ....$5–6

Ford Mustang GT Convertible, 1994, yellow, tan interior, 1:43 ....$5–6

Ford Mustang Mach III Concept Car, red, 1:43 ....$5–6

Jaguar E Type Cabriolet, 1961, green with cream interior, 1:43 ....$5–6

Jaguar XJ-S V12 Convertible, 1988, silver, 1:43 ....$6–7

Jaguar XKE, green, 1:43 ....$6–7

Mercedes 300 SL Roadster, 1957, black with butterscotch interior, 1:43 ....$5–6

Mercedes 280 SL, 1968, red, gray interior, 1:43 ....$5–6

Mercedes 350 SL, 1971, greenish silver with gray interior, 1:43 ....$5–6

Mercedes 600SL, 1992, metallic brass with cream and charcoal interior, 1:43 ..$5–6

MGB, 1967, blue with cream interior, 1:43 ....$5–6

MGF, 1996, red with red and black interior, 1:43 ....$5–6

Volkswagen 1200 Cabriolet, baby blue, 1:43 ....$5–6

Volkswagen Concept One Convertible, yellow with yellow and black interior, 1:43 ....$5–6

Volkswagen Golf Cabriolet, 1993, white, red interior, 1:43 ....$5–6

Volkswagen Golf Cabriolet, 1988, green, 1:43 ....$5–6

New Trax (see Top Gear)

Nicky Toys (also see Dinky)

Nicky Toys began in Calcutta, India, by S. Kumar & Company, also known as Atamco Private Ltd., in 1968 when some older Dinky tooling was obtained from Meccano. Nicky Toys' noticeably poorer castings are the result of old dies that were already worn out by extensive use. The company continued to produce such toys until the 1970s.

Bentley S Coupe $30

Daimler Jaguar 3.4 ....$25

Daimler Jaguar 3.4 Police $45

Dump Truck $50

Howitzer $25

Jaguar D Type $25

Jaguar E Type $25

Jaguar Mk. X $25

Lincoln Continental $45

Mercedes-Benz 220 SE $35

Mercedes-Benz 220 SE Taxi $40

MGB $25

Mighty Antar Tank Transporter $75

Military Ambulance $35

Plymouth Fury Convertible $45

Plymouth Fury Hardtop $45

Standard 20 Mini Atlas Kenebrake Ambulance $25

Standard 20 Mini Atlas Kenebrake Bus $25

Triumph Vitesse $25

Universal Army Jeep $45

Universal Jeep $45

Vanwall $30

Volkswagen 1500 ....$45

Volkswagen 1500 Police $45

Nigam

Resembling crude versions of Mercury models, Nigams were produced in Italy in 1948.

1 Alfa Romeo Grand Prix $125

2 Auto-Union Grand Prix $125

3 Gardner's MG Record Car $125

4 Maserati Grand Prix $125

5 Mercedes-Benz Grand Prix $125

6 E.R.A. Grand Prix $125

N.J. International

Walther's offers a great assortment of N. J. International 1:87 scale (HO gauge) unpainted cast metal kits.

1964 Chevrolet Corvette Sting Ray, 525-102 ....kit, $6

525-114 ....assembled & painted, $9

1965 Ford Shelby GT-350 Mustang,

525-101 ....kit, $6

525-113 ....assembled & painted, $9

Aerial Ladder Fire Truck, 525-106 ....kit, $39

Jeep Gladiator Pickup Truck, 525-112 ....kit, $6

525-115 ....assembled, $9

Mack C Ladder Truck, 525-130 ....kit, $69

Mack C, tractor only, 525-1301 ....kit, $29

Mack MB Tractor Tilt Cab, 525-138 ....kit, $25

Pierce Mid-Ship Pumper, 525-116 ....kit, $35

Pumper Kit with 4-Door Closed Cab, 525-117 ....kit, $37

Snorkel Fire Truck, 525-107 ....kit, $39

UPS Delivery, 525-104 ....kit, $19

Norev

M. Veron started the firm called Norev (Veron spelled backwards) in a suburb of Lyon, France, in 1953. His brother Emile Veron later founded the company that produced Majorettes.

The first Norev models were plastic in 1:43 scale. Later models were made of diecast metal with tinplate or plastic chassis. Norev's product line included 1:72 scale "Mini-Jet" series, the larger "Maxi-Jet" and "Jet-Car" series.

Mini-Jet models are currently valued around $5–8 each. Maxi-Jets are a series of trucks for $12–16, and Jet-Cars are valued between $5 and $30. Norev is now believed to be out of business, and it is reported that Eligor of France has acquired many of Norev's dies.

It has been recently reported that Majorette F of France now owns Norev, which wouldn't be a surprise since M. Veron of Lyon, France, is likely a close relative of Emile Veron, founder of Majorette F, also of Lyon, France.

Norev Plastic Series, 1:43 Scale

Citroën 15CV 6, #3, 1954–1959 ...$12–15

Citroën Ami 6 Break, #2, 1965–1980 ....$12–15

Ford Vedette 54, #2, 1953–1959 ...$30–40

Opel Rekord L-1700, #1, 1965–1969 ....$12–15

Panhard Dyna, #4, 1954–1960 ...$36–48

Panhard PL17 Break, #4, 1965–1971 ....$24–36

Peugeot 201, 1930, #6, 1966–1971 ....$16–24

Peugeot 203, #8, 1955–1958 ...$36–48

Peugeot 204, #5, 1965–1980 ...$6–12

Peugeot J7 Van, #7, 1967–1973 ...$24–32

Renault 16/16TX, #3, 1965–1980 ..$8–12

Renault 4CV, #5, 1955–1957 .....$36–48

Simca Aronde 9, #1, 1953–1956 .$45–55

Simca Aronde 9 Elysee, #5, 1956–1962 ....$32–40

Simca Trianon, #7, 1955–1958 ...$32–40

Simca Versailles, #6, 1955–1959 ..$36–48

Norev Mini-Jet Series, 1:72 Scale

Bertone Trapeze, #412 ....$5–8

Chevrolet Camper Pickup, #460 .....$5–8

Ford Mustang, #424 ....$5–8

Matra Bagheera, #402 ....$5–8

Peugeot 504, #405 ....$5–8
Norev Maxi-Jet Series
Caravan $12–16
DAF Circus Truck $12–16
Volvo Breakdown Truck $12–16
Saviem Drinks Truck $12–16
Norev Jet-Cars
Ford Taunus 12M $20–24
Lancia Stratos $8–12
Matra F1 ....$20–24
Mercedes C-111 ....$12–16
Peugeot 404 Coupe $30–36
Renault 4L $28–32
Volkswagen 1500 ....$28–32

Norscot
Norscot Group, Inc.
10510 North Port Washington Rd.
Mequon, WI 53092

Norscot is a brand of scale model construction equipment first introduced to the market in 1999, although the company has been around since 1970. The resemblance of Norscot diecast replicas to Ertl models, including the package which features a stamped serial number, may not be a coincidence. A connection between the owners of Norscot and Ertl has been suggested but not confirmed. Typical prices range from.

Norscot 1:16 Scale
Two-Ton Tractor $15–46
Norscot 1:25 Scale
GC25K Lift Truck $15–46
Norscot 1:32 Scale
Challenger 95E Agricultural Tractor ..$15–46
226 Skid Steer Loader w/Work Tools .$15–46
Norscot 1:50 Scale
906 Compact Wheel Loader $15–46
5080 Front Shovel $15–46
D11R Track Type Tractor $15–46
980G Forest Machine $15–46
980G Wheel Loader $15–46
545 Grapple Skidder $15–46
924G VersaLink Wheel Loader w/Tools .$15–46
365B L Excavator $15–46
Limited Edition (Gold) D11R $15–46
Track-Type Tractor $15–46
631E Scraper $15–46
D350D Articulated Truck
Norscot 1:64 Scale

D6H Track-Type Tractor $15–46

Challenger 85D Agricultural Tractor...$15–46

950F Wheel Loader $15–46
LEXION 485 Combine $15–46
D6RXL Tractor $15–46
611 Wheel Loader $15–46
12G Motor Grader $15–46
D250D Articulated Truck $15–46
613C Scraper $15–46
Challenger 45 Agricultural Tractor $15–46
Norscot 1:64 Versatile Flotation System
Orthman Grain Cart w/VFS $15–46
Balzer Magnum Tank w/VFS $15–46
Chrome Boom Sprayer w/VFS $15–46
Simonsen Dry Fertilizer Spreader w/VFS ..$15–46
Knight Slinger Spreader w/VFS $15–46
Norscot 1:64 Other
Rome Wing Fold Disk $15–46
Caterpillar GMC Pickup $15–46
Caterpillar Peterbilt Tractor Trailer $15–46
Caterpillar Peterbilt Hauler w/Tractors ...$15–46

Nostalgic
Some Nostalgic models are copies of older Tootsietoys.
202 Ford Model A Canopy Pickup, 1:43 ....$60
203 1930 Ford Roadster, top down, 1:43 ..$60
204 Ford, "Spearmint," white & green, 1:43 ..$60
204 Ford, "Toledo Show," 1:43 ....$60
205 Ford Model A 4-Door Sedan, 1:43 .....$60
219 1931 Ford AA Dump Truck, 1:43 ....$60
220 1937 Cord Coupe, 1:43 ....$60
222 Porsche 356 Coupe, 1:43 ....$65
223 1930 Ford Model A 5-window Coupe,
green & black, 1:43 ....$60
227 1982 Chevrolet Corvette, 1:43 ....$60
229 1932 Ford Coupe Fire Chief, red & black,
1:55 ....$60
230 1975 Chevrolet Corvette, 1:43 ....$60
234 1936 Ford Roadster, 1:43 ....$65
243 1964 Chevrolet Corvette Coupe, 1:43 ...$60
248 1936 Ford Army Ambulance, green,
1:43 ....$65
270 1965 Ford Mustang 2+2, black,
1:43 ....$60
273 1953 Buick Skylark Convertible, top down,
green, 1:43 ....$60
279 1939 Ford Wagon, metallic light blue,
1:43 ....$65

281 1941 Lincoln Continental, 1:43 ....$65
290 1953 Buick Skylark Convertible, top up,
1:43 ....$65
611 1936 Ford Van "UPS," brown & gold,
1:43 ....$60
652 1954 International Soda Truck "Pepsi,"
white/blue/red, 1:55 ....$60
657 1954 International Soda Truck "Coca-
Cola," 1:55 ....$60
6$60 1956 Chevrolet Corvette Roadster, red,
1:43 ....$65
662 1936 Ford Van "UPS," brown & gold,
1:43 ....$65
667 1915 Ford Model T Fire Ladder Truck, red,
1:43 ....$65
668 1915 Ford Model T Van Police, black &
white, 1:43 ....$60
669 1935 Chevy Van "Evening Standard,
1:43 ....$60
673 1934 LaSalle Coupe, 1:43 ....$65
675 1951 Allard J2 Roadster, 1:43 ....$65
677 1930 Ford Model A Pickup, 1:43 ....$60
678 Porsche 356 Roadster, 1:43 ....$65
680 1932 Graham Van "REA," 1:43 ....$60
681 1960 Chevrolet Van "UPS," brown & gold,
1:43 ....$60
682 1934 LaSalle Roadster, 1:43 ....$65
683 Ford AA Chemical Fire Truck, 1:43 ......$65
684 1950 Willys Jeepster, 1:43 ....$65
685 1931 Ahrens-Fox Fire Truck, 1:43 ....$65
686 1932 Seagrave Fire Truck, 1:43 ....$65
687 1950 Divco Van "Borden's," 1:43 ......$65
688 1935 Chevy Van "Coke," 1:43 ....$65
689 1954 Mack B Fire Pumper, 1:43 ....$65
690 1931 Mack AC Fire Hose Truck, 1:43 ..$65
691 1950 Willys Jeepster "Coke," 1:43 .....$65
692 1936 Ford Van, maroon, 1:43 ....$65
696 1935 Chevy Van "Cities Service," 1:43 ..$65
697 1935 Chevy Van "Standard Oil," 1:43 ...$65
698 1935 Chevy Van "Shamrock Oil," 1:43 .$65
699 1935 Chevy Van "Exide," 1:43 ....$65
700 1935 Chevy Van "Conoco," 1:43 .....$65
701 1935 Chevy Van "Tri-Star," 1:43 ....$65
702 1935 Chevy Van "Sunoco," 1:43 ....$65
703 1935 Chevy Van "7-Up," 1:43 ....$65
704 1935 Chevy Van "Goodyear," 1:43 ..$65
705 1935 Chevy Van "UPS," 1:43 ....$65
802 1950 Divco Van "Sealtest," 1:43 ....$65
803 1950 Divco Van "Fire," 1:43 ....$65
806 1950 Divco Van "Coca-Cola," 1:43 ...$65
809 1950 Divco Van "Police," 1:43 ....$65

Novacar
Originally produced by the Portuguese company Minia Portos Juguetes E Brinquedos Lda., Novacar became a division of Majorette of France in 1993. Novacar is a series of small-scale toy vehicles with plastic bodies and metal chassis, except for number 112 F1 Racer, which has a diecast metal body and plastic chassis. Models were most recently available as the new Majorette 100 Series and usually sold in sets of four cars. Some mod-

els from the plastic Novacar series are now being offered in diecast metal as part of the Majorette assortment.

101 Ferrari 308
  v.1 light yellow with red interior $1
  v.2 darker yellow with red interior $1

102 Nissan 300 ZX
  v.1 light blue with red interior, black & gold accents $1
  v.2 darker blue with red interior, black & gold accents $1
  v.3 clear with silver flecks, blue-gray & yellow interior $1
  v.4 clear with silver flecks, purple & white interior $1

103 Chevrolet Corvette
  v.1 white with black "23," green & red accents $1
  v.2 white with red "23," green & red accents $1
  v.3 black with white accents $1
  v.4 black with silver "Corvette" and Chevrolet logo $1
  v.5 clear with red flecks, dark red & white interior $1
  v.6 clear with silver flecks, purple & pink interior $1

104 Ferrari Testarossa
  v.1 red with "Ferrari" & logo on hood $1
  v.2 red with "S RACING" on hood $1

105 Mercedes-Benz 500SL
  v.1 silver with red interior, "500SL" on doors $1
  v.2 silver with red interior, no markings......$1

106 Peugeot 605
  v.1 white with black interior $1
  v.2 white with red interior $1

107 Nissan Pathfinder/Terrano
  v.1 red with black & white Rally markings $1
  v.2 green with black & white Rally markings $1
  v.3 white with black & gold "SHERIFF" markings $1
  v.4 red with "FIRE DEPT." markings...........$1

108 Kenworth Semi Tractor
  v.1 blue with red & white stars & stripes $1

109 Chevrolet Impala Police Car
  v.1 white with blue & gold markings.........$1
  v.2 black with white & gold markings $1

110 Renault Espace Van
  v.1 red with "Espace" on sides in script lettering $1
  v.2 white with blue "Ambulance" markings, orange accents.........................$1
  v.3 yellow with blue & red Rally accents....$1

111 Porsche LeMans GT Racer
  v.1 black with white accents, "TOP DRIVERS" on nose $1
  v.2 clear with yellow flecks, lime green interior $1
  v.3 clear with silver flecks, blue-gray interior..$1

112 F1 Racer
  v.1 yellow with red & black accents, red plastic base $1
  v.2 black with gold & red accents, white plastic base $1

113 Volkswagen Caravelle Van
  v.1 red with black & gold accents $1
  v.2 "Surf" $1

114 Ford Escort GT
  v.1 yellow $1

116 Chevrolet Extended Cab Pickup
  v.1 black with white accents...................$1
  v.2 clear with red flecks, dark red & white interior.........................$1
  v.3 clear with yellow flecks, lime green & pink interior.........................$1

117 Honda Acura NSX
  v.1 red with black interior.....................$1
  v.2 red with white interior....................$1

119 Jeep
  v.1 blue with black top, yellow accents (1995).........................$1

120 Ferrari F40
  v.1 red.........................$1

121 Ford Van
  v.1 purple with flame accents $1

NSG Marketing Corp. (also see Traffic Stoppers and Summer)

There seems to be a connection between NSG and Summer models. NSG Marketing Corporation currently produces a variety of inexpensive toys and sets of crudely cast vehicles in roughly 1:64 scale called Traffic Stoppers. Summer models appear to be larger models of slightly more accurate scale and detail, though still crude compared to other 1:43 scale models.

Traffic Stoppers are virtually unidentifiable out of their package as anything but generic. Even in the package, they are not currently worth much to collectors.

Nutmeg Collectibles

In 1990, Mark Dadio founded Nutmeg Collectibles, a company that established a symbiotic relationship with Matchbox by arranging to produce custom variations of Matchbox number 32 Modified Racer and number 34 Sprint Racer.

Seventeen variations of the Modified Racer were produced by Nutmeg, while 13 variations of the Sprint Racer were produced.

Nutmeg Modified Racer (Matchbox #32 production version introduced in 1988)
  v.1 red body, black interior, chrome exhausts, "Mike 15" $6
  v.2 yellow body, green interior, chrome exhausts, "44 Reggie/Magnum Oils".$6
  v.3 white body, red interior, chrome exhausts, "U2 Jamie" $6
  v.4 white body, black interior, chrome exhausts, "1 Tony/Universal Joint Sales".........................$6

  v.5 red body, red interior, black exhausts, "36" & stripes $6
  v.6 red body, orange-yellow interior, black exhausts, "12" & stripes.........................$6
  v.7 white & blue body, blue interior, black exhausts, "ADAP 15".........................$6
  v.8 white body, translucent blue interior, black exhausts, "41" & stripes.........................$6
  v.9 red body, red interior, chrome exhausts, "38 Jerry Cook".........................$6
  v.10 white body, orange interior, chrome exhausts, "Maynard Troyer".........................$6
  v.11 dark blue body, black interior, chrome exhausts, "3 Ron Bouchard".........$6
  v.12 orange-yellow body, green interior, chrome exhausts, "4 Bugs".........................$6
  v.13 red body, red interior, chrome exhausts, "42 Jamie Tomaino".........................$6
  v.14 orange-yellow body, red interior, chrome exhausts, "4 Satch Wirley".....$6
  v.15 dark blue body, blue interior, chrome exhausts, "3 Doug Heveron" $6
  v.16 black body, black interior, chrome exhausts, "21 George Kent".........................$6
  v.17 dark blue body, black interior, black exhausts, "12".........................$6
  v.18 blue body, black interior, chrome exhausts, "3 Mike McLaughlin".........$8

Nutmeg Sprint Racer (Matchbox #34 production version introduced in 1990)
  v.1 red body, white driver, blue "Williams 5M" $6
  v.2 red body, white driver, white "Williams 5M".........................$85
  v.3 black body, white driver, "TMC 1".....$6
  v.4 white body, red driver, "Schnee 8D".........................$6
  v.5 yellow body, white driver, "Ben Cook & Sons 33x".........................$6
  v.6 blue body, white driver, "Ben Allen 1a" ..$6
  v.7 red body, white driver, "7 Joe Gaerte" ...$6
  v.8 red body, white driver, "4 Gambler" ...$6
  v.9 yellow body, white driver, "17 F&G Classics East" $6
  v.10 yellow body, white driver, "7c Vivarin-D. Blaney".........................$6
  v.11 powder blue body, white driver, "69 Schnee- D. Krietz".........................$6
  v.12 black body, white driver, "49 Doug Wolfgang".........................$6

NuToyz

A division of Parkway International (HK) Ltd.
9/FL., New East Ocean Centre
9 Science Museum Rd.
T.S.T. East, Hong Kong, China

Just Truckin' Metal Trucks are seemingly Hong Kong knock-offs of Remco Tuff Ones. Similarities in packaging and style of manufacturing is so similar that one might conclude that one is manufactured by the other. Construction is a combination of pressed steel and molded plastic.

NZG

NZG Modelle GmbH
Sigmundstr.147
90431 Nürnberg
Germany
phone: 0911/65965-0
fax: 0911/611776
e-mail: info@nzg.de
website: www.nzg.de

Nurnberger Zinkdruckguß, otherwise known as NZG, began in Nurnburg, Germany, in 1968, by producing an assortment of construction vehicles. The company stuck with the heavy equipment theme until 1984, when a series of 1:43 scale Porsches and 1:35 scale Mercedes-Benz models were introduced, along with a few trucks and buses. A large assortment of current models is available from fine toy and model dealers. According to an undated but recent catalog, NZG was for some time distributed by Schuco Toy Co., Inc., New York, likely a division of Schuco of Germany. Latest information indicates NZG is still in business, with new models currently being produced.

126 CAT 627 Scraper, 1:50 ....$48
149 Grove RT 760 Rough Terrain Crane, 1:50 ....$49
160 CAT 245 Excavator, 1:50 ....$45
167 CAT 988B Wheel Loader, 1:50 ....$55
194 Krupp S400 Mining Excavator, 1:50...$75
205 CAT D4E Track Dozer, 1:50.........$30–35
229 Ingersoll-Rand T4W Truck Drill $35–40
231 Demag Paver, 1:50...........................$35
235 Zeppelin 908 Wheel Loader, 1:50.....$19
237 CAT 966F Wheel Loader, 1:50 ....$39
237.06 CAT 966F Wheel Loader, Silver Anniversary Edition, 1:50 ....$49
257 Zeppelin 206 Track Loader, 1:50 ......$42
267 Porsche 911 Targa, 1:43, 1986........$30
285.1L CAT 428 Backhoe, silver anniversary edition, 1:50 ....$31
285.2 CAT 416B Backhoe Loader, 1:50 ...$31
293 Scania City Bus CN112, 1:50...........$42
298 CAT D9N Track Dozer, 1:50 ....$49
299 CAT PR450 Pavement Profilier, 1:50....$45
300 Kramer Tremo Utility Truck, 1:35 ....$19
310F Fiat Ducato Fire Dept. Van, 1:43........$22
311 Volvo Articulated Bus, 1:50.................$52
316 B&T High Rise Forklift, 1:25 ....$35
321.2 Lift Truck "Bulli" $19
327 Porsche 911 Speedster, 1:43 ....$24
332 O&K Grader F 156A, 1:50 ....$42
357 Demag H 485 S Loader, 1:50 ....$169
359 Michigan L150 Wheel Loader, 1:50...$52
359 Volvo VME L150 Wheel Loader with attachments, 1:50 ....$52
361 Mercedes 0404 Touring Bus, 1:43 .....$49
363 Porsche 968 Coupe $24
364 Porsche 968 Cabriolet, 1:43 ....$24
365 Volvo VME BM A25 Dumper, 1:50 ......$37
366 CAT 994 Wheel Loader, 1:50.........$159
367 CAT 325L Excavator, 1:50 ....$42

370 Demag Automatic Remote Control Lift, 1:50...$25
371 Mercedes Unimog, 1:43.....................$29
371.1 Mercedes Unimog, 1:50 ....$29
371.3 Mercedes Unimog UN, 1:50 ....$32
373 Saris Trailer.....................................$15
374 Grove Scissor Lift, 1:50 ....$29
376 CAT 966F Wood Loader, 1:50 ....$45
377 CAT 245 with hydraulic hammer, 1:50...$59
378 CAT 416 Backhoe with Hammer, 1:50 ....$37
378.1 Cat 428 Backhoe with Hammer, 1:50 ..$39
379 Wirtgen Pavement Profiler, 1:50..........$49
380 Grove TM9120 Truck Crane, 1:50...$119
385 Vogele 1800 Paver, 1:50...................$47
386 CAT D7 Dozer WW II, 1:50 ....$129
387 CAT 16G Grader, 1:50 ....$79
389 Kaelble Wheel Loader SJ14B, 1:50 ....$49
390 Porsche 911, 1:43 ....$24
392 Sennebogen 613M Telecrane, 1:50...$42
393 Porsche 911 C2/4 Turbo, 1:43.........$24
Case 850B Angle/tilt dozer, 1:35 ......$40–55
Case 1845 Uni-loader, 1:35..............$40–55

Oddzon

Oddzon is an offspring of the Russ Berrie plush toy company that reportedly produced a few diecast toys along with an eclectic offering of other unusual toys.

Off 43

This unusual brand showed up in a detailed ad in *Model Auto Review* magazine out of Great Britain. They consist of 1:43 scale diecast models made in Italy.

00 Romeo Van, Ola (Italian detergent) $40
00 Romeo Van, Michelin, M Bibendum on roof $40
00 Romeo hiroof ambulance, Italian Red Cross $40
00 Romeo ambulance, military, olive $40
00 Romeo ambulance, Milan, white and green $40
00 Romeo ambulance, Milan, white and blue $40
00 Romeo Van, Fire Vigil del Fuoco...........$40
00 Romeo police Van, Guardia di Finanza, gray..$40
01 Romeo Van, plain red...........................$40
03 Romeo Van Abarth Spark Plugs...........$50
11 Romeo Van Alitalia................................$40
40 Fiat Campagnola, open roof, gray.........$40
40A Fiat Campagnola, open roof, stone......$40
40B Fiat Campagnola, closed roof, Malpensa Airport $45

OGDI Toys of Yesterday

Collecting Toys magazine (Kalmbach Publishing, Waukesha, Wisconsin), featured an article in its August 1995 issue on John Hodges' Toys of Yesterday, toy cars modelled after Dinky toys, but representative of vehicles Meccano planned to produce but didn't.

Hodges felt a loss when Dinky's British based Meccano Ltd. went out of business in 1979. So in his spare time, Hodges attempted to fill the void. His first model, produced in 1980, was so authentic of the Dinky styling that European model journals praised his work and the London Toy Museum purchased one for its collection.

Since then, Hodges has produced a few other models, all reasonably priced and neatly boxed. Below is a list of models offered. For more information, contact John Hodges, Toys of Yesterday, 50 Chiswick Village, London W4 3BY, England.

801 Triumph Dolomite, red, 1980 ....$35
812 Jouett BradFord Van
  v.1 Lyons Tea, green $35
  v.2 Unigate, white $35
  v.3 Esso, red.....................................$35
  v.4 Hovis Bread, yellow $35
  v.5 Walls' Ice Cream, light blue $35
  v.6 Ovaltine, orange...........................$35
823 Jaguar XK150 Coupe, metallic blue $35
834 Ford Consul MKII Saloon, metallic red $35
845 1950 Jouett Javelin Saloon, red $35
856 1948 Ford Prefect, light green.............$35
907 1950s Daimler Conquest Sports Car, metallic burgundy $35
— 1930s Bugatti Roadster, issued 1995 ....$35

Old Cars

Old Cars brand of Turin, Italy, is so named for its first models of antique cars introduced in 1978. Their current line represents anything but old cars, consisting of modern buses, racing transporters, vans, fire trucks, and heavy equipment. Still the name remains, and the company keeps producing so many variations of its basic models that not even the owner of the company could list them all.

252 Fiat EU 175 Forklift, 1:28 ....$19
311 Fiat Military Command Car................$19
520 Iveco Turbodaily Van.........................$23
550 Iveco Ferrari F-1 Maintenance Van $25
560 Fiat-Ferrari Racing Car Transporter, 1959 ....$69
560-3 Fiat-Ferrari Racing Car Transporter with three Brumm Ferrari models, 1959.......$120
601 Fiat-Allis dozer, closed cab, 1:50 ....$49
603 Rossi Wheel Loader, 1:50 ....$45
605 Fiat-Allis Wood Loader, 1:50 ....$49
606 Fiat-Allis Dozer, open cab, 1:50..........$49
608 Fiat-Allis Wheel Loader, 1:50.............$55
609 Fiat-Allis Compactor, 1:50 ....$49
610 Fiat-Allis FE45 Excavator with rubber treads, 1:50 ....$55
690 Iveco Orlandi Touring Bus..................$49
700 Iveco Turbo City Bus $55
702 Fiat 360hp Dump Truck $49
704 Iveco Truck with Flat Bed Trailer, 1:43 ....$49
710 Iveco Padane Touring Bus $55
720 Iveco Padane Two-Tone Touring Bus.....$59

770-2 Iveco Ferrari Transporter, 1980 .$79; with two F-1 Ferrari models......................$113
730 Iveco Orlandi Euroclass Touring Bus $55
900 Fiat-Allis truck and Trailer with Wheel Loader $95
1200 Scania Benneton F-1 Race Car Transporter.....................89
85021 Brown-Moxy Articulated Dump Truck, 1:50 ....$55
85022 Komatsu Articulated Dump Truck, 1:50 ....$59

Omega
One model is known of this brand, thanks to Russell Alameda of San Jose, California.
Opel Sedan, 4-Door, red with pull-back action, 1:43 ....$10

Onyx (see Vitesse)

Oriental Omnibus Company (also see Corgi)
In 1997, Corgi introduced a series of buses based on those seen in the streets of Hong Kong. The series coincides with their Original Omnibus Co. offerings.

Original Omnibus Co. (also see Corgi)
Original Omnibus Co. is a new line from Corgi Collectibles. The series consists of new versions and new models in Corgi's popular line of 1:76 scale diecast buses.
40104 Weymann Trolleybus, BradFord Corporation $50
40205 Leyland Leopard, Ballykissangel $50
40306 Burlingham Seagull Coach, Happiways Tours Ltd................................$50
40307 Burlingham Seagull, N & C $50
40308 Burlingham Seagull Coach, Ribble ..$50
40309 Burlingham Seagull, Seagull Coaches..$50
41501 AEC Breakdown Lorry, MacBraynes ..$50
41801 Leyland Breakdown, Ribble.............$50
42201 Guy Tower Wagon, Birmingham City Transport..............................$50
42504 Bedford OB Coach with quarterlights, Crosville.............................$50
42505 Bedford OB Coach with quarterlights, Malta $50
42506 Bedford OB Coach, Loch Tay Trundler/Vista Coachways $50
Bedford OB, Hants & Dorset with roof quarterlights, 3800 made.........................$50
42705 Van Hool Alizee, OK Travel............$50
42706 Van Hool Alizee, Bakers Dolphin $50
42707 Van Hool Alizee, Citybus (Standard) ..$50
42708 Van Hool Alizee, Bluebird (Bus Company of the Year 1996) $50
42709 Van Hool Alizee, Eavesway Travel (with football club decals) $50
42710 Van Hool Alizee, Railair $50
42711 Van Hool Alizee, Speedlink $50
42713 Van Hool Alizee, Clarkes of London...$50

42714 Van Hool Alizee, Eurolines.............$50
42715 Van Hool Alizee, Shearings 500th....$50
42803 Dennis Dart, Citybus (Standard) $50
42804 Dennis Dart, Stevensons of Uttoxeter .$50
42805 Dennis Dart, Plymouth Citybus $50
42806 Dennis Dart, London Bus Lines..........$50
42807 Dennis Dart, The Bee Line $50
42809 Dennis Dart, VFM Buses $50
42810 Dennis Dart, Orpington Buses..........$50
Dennis Dart, Eastern National Bus.............$50
42901 Optare Delta, Gateshead Supershuttle .$50
42905 Optare Delta, P.M.T. $50
42906 Optare Delta, Crosville.................$50
42907 Optare Delta, Edinburgh Transport ...$50
Optare Delta of Trent Bus, 4000 made.......$50
43001 Leyland Olympian, Wear Buses $50
43005 Leyland Olympian, Stagecoach Scotland $50
43006 Leyland Olympean, North Western Bee Line $50
43101 Leyland Lynx Mk I, City Line.............$50
43102 Leyland Lynx Mk I, Wycombe Bus ...$50
43104 Leyland Lynx Mk II, Nottingham City Transport $50
43105 Leyland Lynx Mk I, Yorkshire Traction (McDonald's) $50
43106 Leyland Lynx Mk I, London United $50
43107 Leyland Lynx Mk II, Stagecoach Transit $50
43108 Leyland Lynx Mk I, Beeline $50
43202 3-Axle Leyland Olympean, Kowloon & Canton Railway Co. $50
43203 3-Axle Leyland Olympian, Kowloon Motor Bus (Handover)..........................$50
43204 3-Axle Leyland Olympian, Citybus (Handover).............................$50
43205 3-Axle Leyland Olympian, Citybus (Standard)..............................$50
43206 3-Axle Leyland Olympean, China Motor Bus (Standard) $50
43301 Plaxton Premiere, Oxford Citylink $50
43302 Plaxton Premiere, Express Shuttle $50
43402 Plaxton Beaver 2, Stagecoach Manchester $50
44901 Bus Station Kit $30
95400 Bus Garage Kit $30

Oto
Oto models are 1:43 diecast reissues of Pilen models from Spain produced for the Netherlands market. The unrelated Holland-Oto brand was previously known as Efsi Toys, a brand still sold in Germany. Thanks to Jan Scholten for the update.
001 Mercedes 250C Coupe ....(£9) $14 US
002 Seat-Fiat 600 Saloon ....(£7) $11 US
003 Mini Cooper ....(£9) $14 US
003M Mini Cooper MC Rally........(£9) $14 US
004 Opel Manta A, 5 colours........(£9) $14 US
005 Citroën SM, 2 colours ....(£9) $14 US
007 Chevrolet Astro Show Car............(£9) $14
US008 Ferrari 512 Show Car........(£8) $12 US
009 Porsche 917 ....(£9) $14 US

010 Porsche Carrera 6 ....(£9) $14 US
011 Vauxhall SRV Show Car.........(£8) $12 US
012 Ferrari P5 Show Car ....(£8) $12 US
013 Stratos Bertone Show Car ....(£8) $12 US
014 Adams Brothers Probe Show Car....................(£8) $12 US
015 VW buggy ....(£7) $11 US
016 Seat-Fiat 850 spyder............(£9) $14 US
017 Seat-Fiat 127, 4 colours ....(£5) $8 US
018 Intermeccanica Indra show Car..(£5) $8 US

Oxford Die-Cast Limited
Started in 1993, Oxford has a rich history of the diecast market with many of its employees originally employed by Corgi and Mettoy. Its first product rolled off the production lines in 1993, and since then it has manufactured in excess of 5,000,000 products. Many of its products can be found used as promotional items on a whole variety of retail items. It also has its own club, Oxford Die-Cast Club, which has grown to 15,000 members.
Chevrolet Open Bed Truck "Tesco Quality Provisions" $10–12
Chevrolet Open Bed Truck with tilt "Radio Times"..............................$10–12
Ford Model T Delivery Truck "Georgia Farm".$10–12
Ford Model T Delivery Truck "Pasco's Dog Food" $10–12
Ford Model T Delivery Truck "Radio Times" $10–12
Ford Model T Delivery Truck "Tesco Gold the Perfect Cup of Tea"......................$10–12
Ford Model T Pickup "Pasco's Dog Food".$10–12
Ford Model T Delivery Truck, "Zeb's Country Store" on sides.......................$15–18
Morris Cowley Bullnose "Radio Times" ...$10–12
Morris Cowley Bullnose "Pasco's Dog Food" $10–12
Morris Cowley Bullnose "St. Dalfour" high fruit content spread......................$10–12
Morris Cowley Bullnose Tesco $10–12
Thornycroft Bus "Pasco's Dog Food".......$10–12
Thornycroft Bus "Tesco Every Little Helps"...$10–12
Thornycroft Bus "Radio Times" $10–12

Papillon Toys
Other than a single model, nothing is known of the Papillon brand of diecast toys.
Milk Float, white three-wheeler, "E Express"...$18–25

Paradise Garage
Paradise Garage represents contemporary 1:43 diecast models made in China for the Australian market. The brand, introduced in 1996 by Zimbler Pty Ltd. of Melbourne, is offered outside of Australia almost exclusively by Modelauto of Leeds, England.
1994 Holden Commodore VS Acclaim, Stratos Blue or Kira Aqua, introduced in 1996 ....$42
1996 Holden Commodore VS Berlina, Velvet Blue or Masai Red, introduced in 1997 .$42

1996 Ford Falcon EF Futura, Reef Green or Cardinal Red, introduced in 1998 .... $42
1998 Ford AU Falcon XR8, white or red, introduced in 1999 .... $42

Paragon Models & Art

1431B S.E. 10th St.
Cape Coral, FL 33990
phone: 941-458-0024

Paragon Models & Art is yet another new arrival in the diecast scale model field. Produced in Spain for the Florida-based company, the first Paragon model appears to be a 1950 Chevy Panel Truck in 1:18 scale.

1950 Chevrolet Panel Truck, cream medium, forester green or mariner blue, 1:18 (no price provided)

Parker White Metal (see Erie)

Past-Time Hobbies (see PTH)

Pathfinder Models

Pathfinder is a series of excellent white metal models from England. Typical subjects are British cars of the fifties. Production of each casting is reportedly limited, so there is a base of avid collectors who snap up most of the new issues. No. 18, introduced maybe a year ago, is a Jowett Jupiter roadster, but they've made Saloons and Estates (sedans and wagons) too.

1 Jensen 541	$75–90
2 Rover 90	$75–90
3 Bristol 401	$75–90
4 Jowett Javelin	$75–90
5 Reliant Scimitar	$75–90
6 Vauxhall Cresta PA	$75–90
7 Wolseley 6/80	$75–90
8 Ford Consul Capri GT	$75–90
9 Daimler Dart SP250 Open	$75–90
10 Jensen CV8	$75–90
11 Standard 10	$75–90
12 Armstrong Siddeley	$75–90
13 Morris Oxford	$75–90
14 Riley 1.5	$75–90
15 Sunbeam Rapier	$75–90
16 Austin HereFord	$75–90
17 Hillman Super Minx	$75–90
18 Jowett Jupiter, open or closed	$75–90
19 Austin Devon	$75–90
20 1954 Morris Oxford Series II	$75–90
21 1952 Humber Hawk	$75–90
22 Morris Minor, open	$75–90
23 Vauxhall Victor FB	$75–90
24 1957 Daimler Conquest	$75–90
25 Morris Eight Series E	$75–90
26 Vauxhall Wyvern	$75–90
27 Triumph 2000 Mk I	$75–90

Paul's Model Art/Minichamps

Paul's Model Art (PMA), was founded by Paul Gunter Lang in Aachen, Germany, where they are currently based. In 1998, Action Performance purchased a controlling interest in Paul's Model Art.

PMA/Minichamps designs and markets diecast scale replicas of motor vehicles, including models of Formula 1 and GT race cars as well as factory production cars. Its products are marketed pursuant to license agreements with some of the world's most popular race car drivers, team owners, and car manufacturers, including exclusive licenses with Michael Schumacher, Jacques Villeneueve, Ferrari, McLaren, and others. Their product line is massive. The extensive list below includes only their street models. Their assortment of race cars would make the list twice as long.

The Max Models name is applied to a large number of Minichamps, but upon examination of one specimen and its box, there is no mention of Paul's Model Art or Minichamps anywhere. What is found on the box is the name Danhausen Modelcar of Aachen, Germany. There has been great confusion as to just what models are legitimate Minichamps and which ones aren't. For simplicity's sake, Max Models are listed below as they were listed in a recent Minichamps catalog.

1:18 Scale Minichamps

1996 BMW Z-3 Roadster, Bond blue . $30–40
1996 BMW Z-3 Roadster, red $30–35
Benetton B194, Schumacher '94 .... $40
Benetton Ford B193 .... $50
BMW R 1200 C Motorbike, canyon red, #182 026200 .... $45
McLaren MP4/8, Senna '93 .... $40
McLaren MP4/8, Hakkinen '93 .... $30

1:24 Scale Minichamps

1970 Volkswagen Karmann Ghia Coupe, red, #241 245000 .... $50
1970 Volkswagen Karmann Ghia Coupe, silver, #241 245001 .... $50
1970 Volkswagen Karmann Ghia Coupe, cream, #241 245003 .... $50

1:43 Scale Minichamps/Max Models

Alfa Romeo 156, silver, #430 120700 . $40
Alfa Romeo German Championship, #8, Larini $35
Alfa Romeo German Championship, #14, Danner $35
1996 Audi A3, metallic dark blue, #430 015100 .... $40
1995 Audi A4, blue, #430 015000 .... $40
1995 Audi A4, silver, #430 015001 ... $40
1995 Audi A4, red, #430 015002 ..... $40
1995 Audi A4, red, #430 015009 ..... $40
1995 Audi A4 Avant, metallic gray, #430 015010 .... $40
1995 Audi A4 Avant, metallic green, #430 015011 .... $40
1997 Audi A6, metallic blue, #430 017100 .... $40
1998 Audi A6 Avant, laser red, #430 017110 .... $40

1994 Audi A8, black, #430 013000 .. $40
1994 Audi A8, metallic cashmere, #430 013001 .... $40
1994 Audi A8, metallic ruby red, #430 013002 .... $40
1994 Audi A8, Isis red, #430 013005 .. $40
1998 Audi TT, yellow, #430 017220 .. $40
1991 Audi V8, metallic titanium, #430 T01000 .... $45
1966–1975 BMW 1600 Saloon, orange, #430 022100 .... $40
1966–1975 BMW 1600 Saloon, yellow, #430 022101 .... $40
1966–1975 BMW 1600 Saloon, light green, #430 022102 .... $40
1966–1975 BMW 1600 Saloon, white, #430 022104 .... $40
BMW 2002 Turbo, white, #430 022200 .... $40
1975–1983 BMW 3-Series, orange, #430 025400 .... $40
1993 BMW 3-Series Cabriolet, metallic green, #430 023330 .... $40
1993 BMW 3-Series Cabriolet, metallic black, #430 023331 .... $40
1993 BMW 3-Series Cabriolet, metallic red, #430 023332 .... $40
1992 BMW 3-Series Coupe, blue, #430 023320 .... $40
1992 BMW 3-Series Coupe, yellow, #430 023321 .... $40
1992 BMW 3-Series Coupe, red, #430 023322 .... $40
1992 BMW 3-Series Saloon, silver, #430 023300 .... $40
1992 BMW 3-Series Saloon, black, #430 023301 .... $40
1992 BMW 3-Series Saloon, red, #430 023302 .... $40
1954–1961 BMW 502 V8 Saloon, white, #430 022400 .... $40
1954–1961 BMW 502 V8 Saloon, black, #430 022401 .... $40
1954–1961 BMW 502 V8 Saloon, dark red, #430 022402 .... $40
1956–1959 BMW 507 Hardtop, red, #430 022530 .... $40
1956–1959 BMW 507 Hardtop, silver, #430 022531 .... $40
1956–1959 BMW 507 Hardtop, creme, #430 022532 .... $40
1956–1959 BMW 507 Cabriolet, top down, red, #430 022507 .... $40
1956–1959 BMW 507 Cabriolet, top down, silver, #430 022508 .... $40
1956–1959 BMW 507 Cabriolet, top down, creme, #430 022509 .... $40
1956–1959 BMW 507 Cabriolet, top up, red, #430 022520 .... $40
1956–1959 BMW 507 Cabriolet, top up, black, #430 022521 .... $40
1956–1959 BMW 507 Cabriolet, top up, green, #430 022522 .... $40

1960–1961 BMW 700 LS Saloon, metallic anthracite, #430 023700 ....$40

1960–1961 BMW 700 LS Saloon, creme, #430 023701 ....$40

1960–1961 BMW 700 LS Saloon, silver, #430 023702 ....$40

1993 BMW E 1, yellow, #430 023000.$40

1993 BMW E 1, metallic blue, #430 023001 ....$40

1993 BMW E 1, red, #430 023002 ..$40

1993 BMW M3 GTR Street, white, #430 023380 ....$40

1993 BMW M3 GTR Street, black, #430 023381 ....$40

1993 BMW M3 GTR Street, red, #430 023382 ....$40

1954–1961 BMW 501-502 Sedan $40

1956–1959 BMW 507 Cabriolet $40

1956–1959 BMW 507 Cabriolet, top up $40

1956–1959 BMW 507 Hardtop $40

1982–1987 BMW 635 CSi, black, #430 025121 ....$40

1960–1961 BMW 700 Sedan $40

1993 BMW E-1 Electromobile..............$40

1994 BMW E-1 Electromobile concept car $40

1992 BMW M-3 Coupe $40

1996 BMW M Roadster, orange, #430 024360 ....$40

1997 BMW Z3 2.8, black, #430 024331 ....$40

BMW Z3 1.9, silver, #430 024341 ....$40

1991 Bugatti EB 110, blue, #430 102110 ....$40

1991 Bugatti EB 110, red, #430 102111 ....$40

1991 Bugatti EB 110, black, #430 102112 ....$40

1993 Bugatti EB 110 Supersport, #430 102115 ....$40

1997 Chevrolet Corvette, metallic blue, #430 142621 ....$40

1993 Dodge Viper GTS, black, #430 144020 ....$40

1993 Dodge Viper GTS, blue, #430 144021 ....$40

1993 Dodge Viper GTS, red, #430 144022 ....$40

1993 Dodge Viper RT/10, yellow, #430 144030 ....$40

1993 Dodge Viper RT/10, blue, #430 144031 ....$40

1993 Dodge Viper RT/10, red, #430 144032 ....$40

1962 Ferrari 250 GTO, red, #430 072000 ....$40

1992 Ferrari 456 GT 2+2, red, #430 072400 ....$40

1992 Ferrari 456 GT 2+2, yellow, #430 072401 ....$40

1992 Ferrari 456 GT 2+2, dark blue, #430 072402 ....$40

1994 Ferrari 512 M, silver, #430 074120 ....$40

1994 Ferrari 512 M, yellow, #430 074121 ....$40

1994 Ferrari 512 M, red, #430 074122 ....$40

1992 Ferrari 512 TR, red, #430 072500 ....$40

1992 Ferrari 512 TR, yellow, #430 072501 ....$40

1992 Ferrari 512 TR, black, #430 072502 ....$40

1996 Ferrari 550 Maranello, yellow, #430 076022 ....$40

1995 Ferrari F130, silver, #430 075150 ....$40

1995 Ferrari F130, yellow, #430 075151 ....$40

1995 Ferrari F130, red, #430 075152 ....$40

1994 Ferrari F355 GTB, yellow, #430 074020 ....$40

1994 Ferrari F355 GTB, black, #430 074021 ....$40

1994 Ferrari F355 GTB, red, #430 074022 ....$40

1994 Ferrari F355 GTS, red, #430 074052 #37 ....$40

1995 Ferrari F355 Spider, top down, red, #430 074032 ....$40

1995 Ferrari F355 Spider Softtop, top up, red, #430 074042 ....$40

1995 Ferrari F50, red, #430 075152 ....$40

1995 Ferrari F50 Spider, yellow, #430 075161 ....$40

1969 Ford Capri, silver, #430 085500 .$40

1970 Ford Capri RS, yellow with black hood, #430 085801 ....$40

1992 Ford Escort RS Cosworth, red, #430 082104 ....$40

1995 Ford Fiesta, blue, #430 085000.$40

Ford Focus Wagon, metallic blue, #430 087010 ....$40

1993 Ford Indy, Newman/Haas/Andretti, 1:43 ....$40

1996 Ford Ka, red, #430 086400 ......$40

1993 Ford Mondeo Wagon, red, #430 082010 ....$40

1993 Ford Mondeo Wagon, metallic green, #430 082011 ....$40

1993 Ford Mondeo Wagon, black, #430 082012 ....$40

Ford Mondeo 4-Door Police, white and green "Polizei," #430 082090 ....$40

1993 Ford Mondeo 4-Door Saloon, red, #430 082000 ....$40

1993 Ford Mondeo 4-Door Saloon, yellow, #430 082001 ....$40

1993 Ford Mondeo 4-Door Saloon, blue, #430 082002 ....$40

1993 Ford Mondeo 5-Door Saloon, red, #430 082070 ....$40

1993 Ford Mondeo 5-Door Saloon, yellow, #430 082071 ....$40

1993 Ford Mondeo 5-Door Saloon, blue, #430 082072 ....$40

1997 Ford Mondeo Wagon, red, #430 086310 ....$40

1997 Ford Mondeo Sedan, silver, #430 086300 ....$40

1994 Ford Mustang Cabriolet, metallic blue, #430 085631 ....$40

1997 Ford Puma, metallic black, #430 086520 ....$40

1995 Ford Scorpio 4-Door Saloon, blue, #430 084000 ....$40

1995 Ford Scorpio 4-Door Saloon, black, #430 084001 ....$40

1995 Ford Scorpio 4-Door Saloon, red, #430 084002 ....$40

1995 Ford Scorpio Wagon, dark gray, 1:43, #430 084010 ....$40

1995 Ford Scorpio Wagon, green, 1:43, #430 084012 ....$40

1960 Ford Taunus, white with red roof, #430 085100 ....$40

1989 Honda CR-X $40

1959–1967 Jaguar Mk II, British racing green, #430 130600 ....$40

1959–1967 Jaguar Mk II, dark red, #430 130602 ....$40

1995 Jaguar XJ12 Saloon, #430 130502 ....$40

1992 Jaguar XJ220, metallic blue, #430 102220 ....$40

1992 Jaguar XJ220, yellow, #430 102221 ....$40

1992 Jaguar XJ220, silver, #430 102222 ....$40

1995 Jaguar XJ6 Saloon, #430 130500 ....$40

1995 Jaguar Sovereign Saloon, #430 130501 ....$40

1993 Jeep Grand Cherokee, black, #430 149660 ....$45

1993 Jeep Grand Cherokee, metallic green, #430 149661 ....$45

1966–1971 Lamborghini Miura, yellow, #430 103000 ....$40

1966–1971 Lamborghini Miura, gold, #430 103001 ....$40

1966–1971 Lamborghini Miura, red, #430 103002 ....$40

1972–1978 Lancia Stratos Street, yellow, #430 125020 ....$40

1972–1978 Lancia Stratos Street, red, #430 125022 ....$40

1968 Lotus Super 7, red, #430 135632 ....$40

1953–1957 Mercedes-Benz 180 Saloon, gray, #430 033100 ....$40

1953–1957 Mercedes-Benz 180 Saloon, black, #430 033101 ....$40

1953–1957 Mercedes-Benz 180 Saloon, red, #430 033102 ....$40

1984–1988 Mercedes-Benz 190 E 2,3-16, metallic blue black, #430 035600 ....$40

1990 Mercedes-Benz 190 E Evolution 1, metallic blue black, #430 B03000 ....$40

1990 Mercedes-Benz 190 E Evolution 1, signal red, #430 R03000 ....$40

1990 Mercedes-Benz 190 E Evolution 1, metallic pearl gray, #430 G03000 $40

Mercedes-Benz 190 E Evolution 2, metallic blue black, #430 B03100.............$40

Mercedes-Benz 190 E Evolution 2, metallic pearl gray, #430 G03100............$40

Mercedes-Benz 190 E Evolution 2, red, #430 R03100 ....$40

1955–1962 Mercedes-Benz 190 SL Cabriolet, white, #430 033130 ....$40

1955–1962 Mercedes-Benz 190 SL Cabriolet, silver, #430 033131 ....$40

1955–1962 Mercedes-Benz 190 SL Cabriolet, red, #430 033132 ....$40

1980–1985 Mercedes-Benz 200 T Wagon, red, #430 032210.........$40

1956–1959 Mercedes-Benz 220 S, black, #430 033000..............................$40

1956–1965 Mercedes-Benz 220 SE Saloon, #430 034000, #430 034001, #430 034002 ....$40

1977–1985 Mercedes-Benz 230 CE Coupe, gold, #430 032220.........$40

1992 Mercedes-Benz 230 CE Coupe, crystal green, #430 003403 ....$40

1992 Mercedes-Benz 230 E, zircon silver, #430 003203 ....$40

1977–1985 Mercedes-Benz 280 CE Coupe, silver, #430 032221 ....$40

1968–1971 Mercedes-Benz 280 SL Cabriolet, silver, #430 032230 ....$40

1968–1971 Mercedes-Benz 280 SL Cabriolet, red, #430 032231 ....$40

1968–1971 Mercedes-Benz 280 SL Cabriolet, dark blue, #430 032232.........$40

1968–1971 Mercedes-Benz 280SL Cabriolet, top down, light blue, #430 032234 ....$40

1968–1971 Mercedes-Benz 280SL Cabriolet, top up, white with black top, #430 032240 ....$40

1968–1971 Mercedes-Benz 280SL Cabriolet, top up, red with white top, #430 032241 ....$40

1968–1971 Mercedes-Benz 280SL Cabriolet, top up, black with white top, #430 032242 ....$40

1968–1971 Mercedes-Benz 280SL Pagode, gold, #430 032250 ....$40

1968–1971 Mercedes-Benz 280SL Pagode, white, #430 032251 ......$40

1968–1971 Mercedes-Benz 280SL Pagode, red, #430 032252 ....$40

1980–1985 Mercedes-Benz 280 TE Wagon, metallic blue, #430 032212 ....$40

1992 Mercedes-Benz 300 CE Coupe, almadin red, #430 003408 ....$40

1992 Mercedes-Benz 300 CE-24 Cabriolet, dark blue, #430 003514...............$40

1992 Mercedes-Benz 300 CE-24 Cabriolet, signal red, #430 003550 ....$40

1992 Mercedes-Benz 300 CE-24 Cabriolet, smoke silver, #430 003551 ....$40

1992 Mercedes-Benz 300 CE-24 Coupe, bornite, #430 003414 ....$40

1992 Mercedes-Benz 300 D, almadin red, #430 003209..............................$40

1951–1958 Mercedes-Benz 300S Cabriolet, top down $40

1951–1958 Mercedes-Benz 300S Cabriolet, top up, black, #430 032320 ....$40

1951–1958 Mercedes-Benz 300S Cabriolet, top up, dark blue, #430 032321 ....$40

1951–1958 Mercedes-Benz 300S Cabriolet, top up, white, #430 032322 ...$40

1951–1958 Mercedes-Benz 300S Cabriolet, top down, black, #430 032330 ....$40

1951–1958 Mercedes-Benz 300S Cabriolet, top down, blue, #430 032331 ....$40

1951–1958 Mercedes-Benz 300S Cabriolet, top down, dark red, #430 032332 ....$40

1951–1958 Mercedes-Benz 300S Coupe, silver, #430 032324 ....$40

Mercedes-Benz 300SL "Caracciola" $40

Mercedes-Benz 300SL Panamerica 1952, 1:43 ....$40

Mercedes-Benz 300SL Spyder $40

1992 Mercedes-Benz 300TD Wagon, metallic blue black, #430 003310 .$40

1971–1980 Mercedes-Benz 350SL Cabriolet, top down, silver, #430 033430 ....$40

1971–1980 Mercedes-Benz 350SL Cabriolet, top down, dark blue, #430 033431 ....$40

1971–1980 Mercedes-Benz 350SL Cabriolet, top down, red, #430 033432 ..$40

1971–1980 Mercedes-Benz 350SL Cabriolet, top down, white, #430 033440 ....$40

1971–1980 Mercedes-Benz 350SL Cabriolet Hardtop, silver, #430 033450 ..$40

1992 Mercedes-Benz 400E Sedan.......$40

1972–1980 Mercedes-Benz 450SLC, silver, #430 033420.............................$40

1972–1980 Mercedes-Benz 450SLC, metallic green, #430 033421 ....$40

1972–1980 Mercedes-Benz 450SLC, gold, #430 033422.............................$40

1992 Mercedes-Benz 500E V8 Saloon, black, #430 003240 ....$40

1992 Mercedes-Benz 500E V8 Saloon, metallic anthracite, #430 003241 ..$40

1992 Mercedes-Benz 600SEC Coupe, black, #430 032600 ....$40

1992 Mercedes-Benz 600SEC Coupe, malachite green, #430 032601 ....$40

1992 Mercedes-Benz 600SEC Coupe, smoke silver, #430 032602 ....$40

1993 Mercedes-Benz C180, Esprit red, #430 032101.............................$40

1993 Mercedes-Benz C220, metallic Classic green, #430 032100 ....$40

1993 Mercedes-Benz C280, Sport silver, #430 032102.............................$40

1993 Mercedes-Benz C36 AMG, metallic blue black, #430 032160 ....$40

1993 Mercedes-Benz C36 AMG, yellow, #430 032161.............................$40

1993 Mercedes-Benz C36 AMG, silver, #430 032162.............................$40

1993 Mercedes-Benz C-Class Sedan (180, 220, 280) $40

1994 Mercedes-Benz C-Class Taxi, white, #430 032195.............................$40

Mercedes-Benz C-Class 1AAF World Championship, #430 032105 ....$45

1994 Mercedes-Benz E-Class 4-Door Sedan, metallic blue black, #430 033500 ....$40

1994 Mercedes-Benz E-Class 4-Door Sedan, metallic blue, #430 033501 ....$40

1994 Mercedes-Benz E-Class 4-Door Sedan, red, #430 033502 ....$40

1994 Mercedes-Benz E-Class 2-Door Coupe, metallic blue-black, #430 033520 .$40

1994 Mercedes-Benz E-Class 2-Door Coupe, metallic blue, #430 033521 ....$40

1994 Mercedes-Benz E-Class 2-Door Coupe, Bornite metallic dark gray, #430 033522 ....$40

1994 Mercedes-Benz E-Class Cabriolet, metallic blue black, #430 033530 .$40

1994 Mercedes-Benz E-Class Cabriolet, metallic blue, #430 033531 ....$40

1994 Mercedes-Benz E-Class Cabriolet, metallic rosewood, #430 033532 .$40

1994 Mercedes-Benz E-Class Taxi Saloon, white, #430 033595 ....$40

1994 Mercedes-Benz E-Class Taxi Wagon, white, #430 033596 ....$40

1994 Mercedes-Benz E-Class Wagon, metallic blue black, #430 033540 ....$40

1994 Mercedes-Benz E-Class Wagon, metallic blue, #430 033541 ....$40

1994 Mercedes-Benz E-Class Wagon, green, #430 033542..............$40

Mercedes-Benz W123 Taxi Saloon, off white, #430 032295 ....$40

Mercedes-Benz W123 Taxi Wagon, off white, #430 032296 ....$40

1975–1985 Mercedes-Benz W123 4-Door Saloon 200D, yellow, #430 032200..............$40

1975–1985 Mercedes-Benz W123 4-Door Saloon 230E, white, #430 032201 ....$40

1975–1985 Mercedes-Benz W123 4-Door Saloon 280E, silver, #430 032202 ..$40

1977–1985 Mercedes-Benz W123 2-Door Coupe 230CE, gold, #430 032220..............$40

1977–1985 Mercedes-Benz W123 2-Door Coupe 230CE, silver, #430 032221..............$40

1977–1985 Mercedes-Benz W123 2-Door Coupe 230CE, metallic blue, #430 032222..............$40

1980–1985 Mercedes-Benz W123 Wagon 200T, red, #430 032210 $40

1980–1985 Mercedes-Benz W123 Wagon 230TE, silver, #430 032211 ....$40

1980–1985 Mercedes-Benz W123 Wagon 280TE, metallic blue, #430 032212.$40

Mercedes-Benz W123 Police Saloon, white and green, #430 032290 ....$40

Mercedes-Benz W123 Police Wagon, white and green, #430 032291 ....$40

1992 Mercedes-Benz W124 Sedan (250D, 300E, 300D) $40

Mercedes-Benz W124 Coupe (230CE, 300CE, 300CE-24) $40

Mercedes-Benz W124 Convertible (300CE-24)..............$40

1962–1969 MGB Cabriolet, black, #430 131030..............$40

1962–1969 MGB Cabriolet, red, #430 131032..............$40

1962–1969 MGB Softtop, cream, #430 131040..............$40

1962–1969 MGB Softtop, British racing green, #430 131041..............$40

1997 Mitsubishi Pajero Long, red, #430 163770..............$45

1991 Mitsubishi Pajero Long, black, #430 163471..............$45

1991 Mitsubishi Pajero Short, metallic blue, #430 163370..............$45

1964–1972 NSU 1000 L, light blue, #430 015200..............$40

1967–1972 NSU TT, Targa orange, #430 015300..............$40

1962–1965 Opel Kadett A Saloon, yellow, #430 043000..............$40

1962–1965 Opel Kadett A Saloon, blue gray, #430 043001 ....$40

1962–1965 Opel Kadett A Saloon, red, #430 043002..............$40

1962–1965 Opel Kadett A Caravan, gray, #430 043010..............$40

1962–1965 Opel Kadett A Caravan, blue, #430 043011..............$40

1962–1965 Opel Kadett A Caravan, white, #430 043012..............$40

1973–1977 Opel Kadett C, red, #430 045601..............$40

1973–1977 Opel Kadett C Coupe, signal green, #430 045620..............$40

1973–1977 Opel Kadett C Caravan, red, #430 045611..............$40

1951–1953 Opel Kapitän 4-Door Saloon, dark red, #430 043300..............$40

1951–1953 Opel Kapitän 4-Door Saloon, black, #430 043301 ....$40

1951–1953 Opel Kapitän 4-Door Saloon, gray, #430 043302 ....$40

Opel Omega 3000 Evolution 4-Door Sedan, metallic black, #430 004001........$40

1958–1960 Opel Rekord P1 2-Door Saloon, green with white roof, #430 043200..............$40

1958–1960 Opel Rekord P1 2-Door Saloon, red with white roof, #430 043204..............$40

1958–1960 Opel Rekord P1 2-Door Saloon, blue with white roof, #430 043206..$40

1958–1960 Opel Rekord P1 Caravan Wagon, yellow with white roof, #430 043210..............$40

1958–1960 Opel Rekord P1 Caravan Wagon, blue with white roof, #430 043211..............$40

1958–1960 Opel Rekord P1 Caravan Wagon, red with white roof, #430 043212..............$40

1958–1960 Opel Rekord P1 Caravan, gray with white roof, #430 043215 ......$40

1995 Peugeot 306 2-Door, red, #430 112502..............$40

1995 Peugeot 306 Cabriolet, red, #430 112532..............$40

1995 Peugeot 306 Cabriolet, metallic black, #430 112531..............$40

1995 Peugeot 306 4-Door, metallic blue, #430 112571..............$40

1995 Peugeot 306 4-Door, metallic gray, #430 112570..............$40

1963–1965 Porsche 356 C Cabriolet, silver, #430 062330 ....$40

1963–1965 Porsche 356 C Cabriolet, creme, #430 062331 ....$40

1963–1965 Porsche 356 C Cabriolet, red, #430 062332..............$40

1963–1964 Porsche 356 C Carrera, black, #430 062361..............$40

1963–1964 Porsche 356 C Carrera, red, #430 062362..............$40

1963–1965 Porsche 356 C Coupe, dark blue, #430 062320..............$40

1963–1965 Porsche 356 C Coupe, silver, #430 062321..............$40

1963–1965 Porsche 356 C Coupe, red, #430 062322..............$40

Porsche 356 Speedster, ivory with red interior, #430 065531..............$40

1997 Peugeot 406 Coupe, metallic red, #430 112620..............$40

1964 Porsche 911, red, #430 067121..$40

1994 Porsche 911 Cabriolet, silver, #430 063030..............$40

1994 Porsche 911 Cabriolet, black, #430 063031..............$40

1994 Porsche 911 Cabriolet, red, #430 063032..............$40

1992 Porsche 911 Carrera 2/4, anthracite, #430 062121..............$40

1992 Porsche 911 Carrera 2/4, metallic violet, #430 062122..............$40

1978–1988 Porsche 911 Coupe, red, #430 062020..............$40

1978–1988 Porsche 911 Coupe, white, #430 062021..............$40

1978–1988 Porsche 911 Coupe, black, #430 062022..............$40

1993 Porsche 911 Coupe, red, #430 063007..............$40

1993 Porsche 911 Coupe, blue, #430 063008..............$40

Porsche 911 GT 3 Street Version, black, #430 986990..............$40

1995 Porsche 911 RS, yellow, #430 065100..............$40

1988 Porsche 911 Speedster, red, #430 066130..............$40

1969–1973 Porsche 914, green, #430 065662..............$40

Porsche 993 Coupe $40

Porsche 993 Cabriolet $40

1993 Porsche Boxster, silver, #430 063130..............$40

Porsche Cup "Cald"..............$34

Porsche Cup, "Land"..............$34

1993 Porsche Cup, #9 ....$34

Porsche Dauer 962 GT Street, yellow, #430 064001..............$40

1964–68 Renault 8 Gordini, blue, #430 113550..............$40

1963–1976 Renault Alpine A 110, metallic blue, #430 113600..............$40

1997 Saab 9-5 Saloon, metallic green, #430 170640..............$40

1995 Saab 900 4-Door, black, #430 170500..............$40

1995 Saab 900 4-Door, aubergine, #430 170501..............$40

1995 Saab 900 Cabriolet, red, #430 170532..............$40

Sauber Mercedes C-9, #61 ....$40

Sauber Mercedes C-11, #1 ....$40

1997 Seat Arosa, red, #430 057100 .$40

1994 Toyota Celica SS II Coupe, black, #430 166620..............$40

1994 Toyota Celica SS II Coupe, red, #430 166622..............$40

1968–1976 Triumph TR 6, British racing green, #430 132751 .... $40

1949 Volkswagen 1200 Beetle "Split Window," black with open sunroof, #430 052000 .... $40

1949 Volkswagen 1200 Beetle "Split Window," gray with solid roof, #430 052001 .... $40

1949 Volkswagen 1200 Beetle "Split Window," blue with closed sunroof, #430 052002 .... $40

1951–1952 Volkswagen 1200 Cabriolet, top down, green, #430 052030 ... $40

1951–1952 Volkswagen 1200 Cabriolet, top down, gray, #430 052031 ..... $40

1951–1952 Volkswagen 1200 Cabriolet, top down, red, #430 052032 .... $40

1951–1952 Volkswagen 1200 Cabriolet, top down, two-tone anthracite and cream, #430 052034 .... $40

1951–1952 Volkswagen 1200 Cabriolet top up, green with brown roof, #430 052042 .... $40

1953–1957 Volkswagen 1200 Beetle, oval window, green gray, #430 052100 .... $40

1953–1957 Volkswagen 1200 Beetle, oval window, pale blue, #430 052101 .... $40

1953–1957 Volkswagen 1200 Beetle, oval window, red, #430 052102 .... $40

1970–1972 Volkswagen 1302 Cabriolet, top down, yellow, #430 055030 .. $40

1970–1972 Volkswagen 1302 Saloon, orange, #430 055000 .... $40

1972–1980 Volkswagen 1303 Cabriolet, top down, black, #430 055130 .... $40

1972–1974 Volkswagen 1303 Saloon, metallic blue, #430 055100 .... $40

Volkswagen Beetle, 1 Millionth, limited edition of 9,999 pieces, gold, #430 052103 .... $75

1994 Volkswagen Concept Car Cabriolet, various colors, #430 054030, #430 054031, #430 054032 .... $40

1994 Volkswagen Concept Car Saloon, various colors, #430 054000, #430 054001, #430 054002 .... $40

1997 Volkswagen Golf, jazz blue, #430 056001 .... $40

1997 Volkswagen Golf, red, #430 056000 .... $40

1949–1950 Volkswagen Hebmueller Cabriolet, top down, two-tone black and red, #430 052130 .... $40

1949–1950 Volkswagen Hebmueller Cabriolet, top down, black, #430 052132 .. $40

1949–1950 Volkswagen Hebmueller Cabriolet, top down, two-tone red and cream, #430 052134 .... $40

1949–1950 Volkswagen Hebmueller Cabriolet, top up, two-tone red and cream, #430 052142 .... $40

1957 Volkswagen Karmann Ghia Cabriolet, top down, light blue, #430 005031 .... $40

1957 Volkswagen Karmann Ghia Cabriolet, top down, metallic blue-gray, #430 051033 .... $40

1957 Volkswagen Karmann Ghia Cabriolet, top up, white with black top, cream, #430 005061 .... $40

1955 Volkswagen Karmann Ghia Coupe, red with white roof, #430 005003 . $40

1955 Volkswagen Karmann Ghia Coupe, yellow with black roof, #430 005004 .... $40

1955 Volkswagen Karmann Ghia Coupe, blue with cream roof, #430 005005 .... $40

1963 Volkswagen Kastenwagen (Delivery Van), blue, #430 052200 .... $40

1963 Volkswagen Kastenwagen (Delivery Van), light gray, #430 052201 ...... $40

1963 Volkswagen Kastenwagen (Delivery Van), light green, #430 052202 .... $40

1998 Volkswagen Lupo, jazz blue, #430 058100 .... $40

1998 Volkswagen New Beetle, red, #430 058001 .... $40

1958–1960 Volkswagen Samba Bus, 25 windows, two-tone gray and blue, #430 052200 .... $45

1958–1960 Volkswagen Samba Bus, 25 windows, two-tone green and light green, #430 052201 .... $45

1958–1960 Volkswagen Samba Bus, 25 windows, two-tone red and cream, #430 052202 .... $45

1994 Volvo 850 Wagon $40

1994 Volvo 850 Saloon, smoke silver, #430 171401 .... $40

1996 Volvo 850 Wagon, red, #430 171411 .... $40

1996 Volvo V40 Wagon, black, #430 171511 .... $40

1958 Wartburg A312 Saloon, two-tone blue and white, #430 015900 .... $40

1958 Wartburg A312 Saloon, two-tone red and white, #430 015901 .... $40

1:64 Scale Models from Paul's Model Art/Microchamps

1993 Ford Indy, Newman/Haas/Andretti, 1:64 .... $8

Paya

Spain is home to the Paya brand of diecast toys, some based on Matchbox models. Paya is better known for producing tin litho windup toys.

Peachstate Muscle Car™ Collectibles Club

P O Box 1537
Winder, GA 30680
phone: 800-536-1637 or 770-307-1042
fax: 770-867-0786

A recent magazine ad states, "Peachstate Muscle Car™ Collectibles Club offers limited edition production quantities of only 2,500 cars per production run of quality diecast sixties and seventies era muscle car replicas. These 1:18 scale beauties are produced exclusively for Peachstate by The Ertl Company and will not be available elsewhere. In addition, each car includes a serialized certificate." Their assortment also includes fifties models.

Peachstate Muscle Car Collectibles Club

1971 Buick GSX, Stratomist blue $38
1955 Chevrolet BelAir, gold $38
1970 Chevrolet Chevelle 454 SS $38
1963 Chevrolet Corvette, saddle tan $38
1970 Chevrolet El Camino, forest green $38
Dodge Daytona, blue $38
Ford Boss 429 Mustang, candy apple red ... $38
1969 Ford Mustang Shelby GT-500 .... $38
1969 Plymouth Road Runner, red $38
1969 Pontiac GTO, black $38
Pontiac Trans Am, black $38
1965 Shelby Cobra, silver $38

P.E.M. (see Precision Engineered Models, also see Hartoy)

Penjoy

PenJoy Company
56 Newcomer Road
Mount Joy, PA 17552-9344
phone: 717-653-7330
fax: 717-653-2662
contact: Phil Wallauer
e-mail: penjoywm@webcom.com
website: www.penjoy.com

Penjoy is one of only two diecast companies whose models are made exclusively in the USA. Below is a sampling of retail issues of Penjoy model trucks with detailed description and price:

ADM TRUCKING INC: Fleet replica of Decatur, IL, based hauler. White sleeper with brown, red, and orange stripes. Retail $40
Club Member price $32

ADMIRAL TRANSPORTATION: Fleet replica of Bellmawr, NJ, based carrier. Green sleeper with green logo on white trailer. Limited edition of 500. Retail $38
Club Member price $29

ALLING & CORY: Fleet replica of major paper distribution company. Blue day cab with large air foil and ferring. Retail $40
Club Member price $30

ANR advance: Fleet replica of Milwaukee based ANR advance Transportation Company rigs hauling general freight throughout North America. Nose of trailer and back doors bear the ANR advance logo. Retail $43
Club Member price $33

BESTWAY TRUCKING INC: Fleet replica of Indiana based common carrier. All white sleeper with Bestway two-color diamond logo on cab doors, rear doors, and trailer nose. Limited edition of 300. Retail $39
Club Member price $29

DIECAST TOY COLLECTORS ASSOCIATION 5TH ANNIVERSARY: Commemorates the November 1998 Fifth Anniversary. 250 planned, only 94 produced.................$45

EMCEA TRANSFER: Fleet replica of Canadian based carrier. White sleeper with red stripes and lettering. Limited edition of 300.
Retail..........................$45
Club Member price........................$34

FOX RIVER FOODS: Reefer Van fleet replica of food service distributor based in Illinois, Indiana, and Wisconsin features four-color graphics on side panels and logos on cab doors and rear doors of trailer. Limited edition; trailer floors imprinted 1 of 400 produced. Retail.................$38
Club Member Price........................$28

GE APPLIANCE: Sleek replica from major manufacturer. White sleeper with GE logo in gray, red accent stripe, and GE slogan "We bring good things to life." Limited edition of 500.
Retail.............................$40
Club Member price...........................$31

KANE FREIGHT LINES INC: Replica of PA based carrier serving the northeast US and all of Canada. "KANE is able" slogan printed on white trailer sides and rear doors in green to match green sleeper. Limited edition of 400.
Retail.............................$42
Club Member price............................$32

KAT, INC: Refrigerated sleeper rig fleet replica of Indiana based food hauler covering 25 states. Tractor is equipped with chrome front wheels just like the real thing. Limited edition; trailer floors imprinted 1 of 1,000 produced.
Retail.............................$45
Club Member price............................$32

KINARD TRUCKING CO: Fleet replica of York, PA, based carrier. Blue sleeper cab and white trailer panels with unique chrome finished roof, floor, and rear doors. Limited edition of 500. Retail $50
Club Member price...........................$39.50

LANDSTAR RANGER: Five scale Mack sleeper boxes painted in black primer are the load on this red flatbed pulled by a white sleeper.
Retail.............................$49.50
Club Member price........................$37.50

LIONS DELIVERY SERVICE LTD: Fleet replica of Ontario, Canada, based carrier. Steel blue cab and large air foil with ferring; white trailer; orange lion-head logo with dark blue printing. Limited edition of 400. Retail.............................$40
Club Member price $31.50

LUKENS STEEL: Flatbed manufactured for Coatesville, PA, based specialty steel manufacturer. Trailer features a unique load of a scaled steel billet and stainless steel coil as produced by Lukens. Limited edition; trailer floors imprinted 1 of 3,000 produced. Retail................$48
Club Member price...**SOLD OUT** $36

MAINES PAPER & FOOD SERVICE INC: Fleet replica of refrigerated sleeper of Conklin, NY, wholesale distributor. White truck with red/black graphics. Limited edition of 500.
Retail.............................$40
Club Member price............................$32

MALONE FREIGHT LINES: From Birmingham, AL, a silver spread-axle flatbed with red sleeper tractor. Ideal for attaching your own loads.
Retail.............................$39
Club Member price $29

MARTIN'S CHIPS: Replica of Thomasville, PA, snack producer. White day cab, small airfoil, and trailer with colorful graphics. Limited edition of 500. Retail $40
Club Member price $32

NCR SYSTEMS MEDIA: Black sleeper cab and white trailer with black/blue graphics produced for NCR Systems with new logo. Limited edition of 300. Retail $45
Club Member price............................$35

NESTLE'S QUIK: Fleet replica of company trucks found operating out of Nestle regional terminals. Duplication of award-winning graphics features four-color process printing on rear doors, and results in one of most colorful trucks produced in 1:64 scale. Retail..........$49.95
Club Member price $42

NM TRANSFER CO. INC: White trailer and day cab with large air foil and ferring duplicates this Wisconsin based carrier. Red/blue logo and graphics. Retail.............................$40
Club Member price $30

PITT-OHIO Express INC: Fleet duplicate of Pittsburgh based carrier. Red day cab with airfoil and white trailer. Limited edition of 5,000.
Retail.............................$38
Club Member price $26.50

PLYMOUTH ROCK: Fleet duplicate of Mass. based carrier. Striking black/yellow graphics on white trailer and yellow day cab with large airfoil and ferrings. First truck produced with detailed printing of all safety placards on trailer nose and rear doors. Retail..........$43
Club Member price $34

R.E.D. INDUSTRIES: The first Penjoy dump truck with a factory produced simulated load. Unusual features include printed clearance lights and warning beacon light. Limited edition of 1,000 imprinted on bottom of truck. Retail $37.50

RICHFIELD YOUTH PARK: White sleeper truck produced as fund raiser for Richfield Youth Park Assoc. Shows full-color baseball field on one side of trailer and soccer field on other side. Very colorful truck. Limited edition of 500. Retail.............................$45

SIMPSON MOTOR TRUCK, INC.: Promotional truck commissioned by a PA Mack dealer. Cream sleeper cab with brown graphics on cream reefer trailer. Limited edition of 400.
Retail.................................$40
Club Member price $30

SPANGLER'S FLOUR MILL: White day cab with small airfoil and blue trailer commemorates historic Mount Joy, PA, flour mill built in 1855. Graphics include near photo quality renditions of old mill, flour bags, etc. Limited edition of 268. Retail.............................$40
Club Member price....**SOLD OUT** $35

STAR OF THE WEST MILLING CO: Fleet replica of Michigan based Midwestern hauler. Yellow day cab and trailer with white/green graphics. Limited edition of 400. Retail...$40
Club Member price $30

TEX-PACK TRUCK LINES: Fleet duplication of Texas based carrier. White day cab with small airfoil; white trailer with red and blue graphics. Limited edition of 250. Retail...$40
Club Member price $31

TRUCK AIR TRANSFER: Fleet duplication produced for 10th Anniversary of southern California contract carrier; all white sleeper with blue logo graphics. Limited edition of 400.
Retail.............................$38
Club Member price $28.50

WEGMANS: Fleet replica of Rochester, NY, based chain of food markets operating in New York and Pennsylvania featuring Wegmans current "pile of vegetables" theme on side panels. Retail.............................$49.95
Club Member price $37

WEIS MARKETS (#1): Fleet replica of Weis Markets based in Sunbury, PA. Brown day cab with large airfoil and ferring; white trailer with brown/yellow logo graphics. Very few in stock. Retail $35
Club Member price.........**SOLD OUT** $29

WEIS MARKETS (#2): Fleet duplication with new corporate graphics released in 1997. White trailer and day cab with small airfoil and red/blue graphics. Limited Edition of 4,000. Retail $42
Club Member price $31.50

WEIS MARKETS 85th ANNIV: Special edition truck to commemorate anniversary; special logo on side panels plus trailer converted to reefer. Limited edition of 7,500. Retail.................$43
Club Member price..**SOLD OUT** $32.50

YELLOW FREIGHT: Fleet replica of carrier recognized throughout North America; distinctive orange cab with white airfoil and trailer, and orange logo. Retail.............................$40
Club Member price $30

YELLOW FREIGHT CALENDAR: Fleet replica except trailer side panels are 1998 calendar with 1999 calendar inside; new year calendar panels available from factory. Great desktop item. Retail.................................$42
Club Member price $32

YUENGLING BREWERY: Fleet duplicate of America's oldest operating brewery located in Pottsville, PA, since 1829. Striking four-color process graphics on side panels and rear doors depict Yuengling eagle logo and lager beer bottles. Limited edition of 5,000. First of a series. Retail.....................$49.50
Club Member price $40

Penny (also see Politoys/Polistil)
Politoys Penny Series

Penny is a brand of very detailed 1:66 scale toys from Politoys/Polistil of Italy. They were produced from 1967 and continued through the early seventies. Models feature opening hoods, narrow "wire" wheels, and hard rubber tires. Thanks to Don Heine for the information.

1 BRM Formula 1, blue, 1967 ....$8–12
2 Lola-Climax Formula 1, yellow, 1967 ...$8–12
3 Lotus-Climax Formula 1, dark green, 1967 ....$8–12
4 Ferrari V6 Formula 1, red, 1967 ......$8–12
5 Brabham-Climaxz Formula 1, silver, 1967 ....$8–12
6 Cooper-Maserati Formula 1, blue, 1967 .$8–12
7 Eagle-Climaz Formula 1, metallic green, 1967 ....$8–12
8 BRM H-16 Formula 1, metallic lime gold, 1967 ....$8–12
9 Ferrari V12 Formula 1, red, 1967........$8–12
10 Honda V12 Formula 1, white, 1967 .$8–12
11 Brabham-Repco Formula 1, dark green, 1968 ....$8–12
12 McLaren-Ford Formula 1, white, 1968...$8–12
13 McLaren-Serenissima Formula 1, red, 1968 ....$8–12
14 Eagle-Weslake Formula 1, metallic blue, 1968 ....$8–12
15 Lotus-BRM H-16 Formula 1, dark green, 1968 ....$8–12
21 Ferrari 250 GT, dark yellow, 1967 ...$8–12
22 Alfa Romeo Giulia Canguro, silver, 1967 ....$8–12
24 Porsche 912, tan, 1968 ....$8–12
25 Alfa Romeo 2600 Sprint Bertone, metallic blue, 1967 ....$8–12
26 Alfa Romeo Giulia SS, metallic dark gray, 1967 ....$8–12
27 Lancia Flavia Zagato Sport, metallic green, 1967 ....$8–12
28 Alfa Romeo Giulia 1300 Junior GT, white, 1968 ....$8–12
29 Maserati 3500 GT, silver, 1967 ....$8–12
30 Fiat 850 Coupe, silver, 1967 ....$8–12
32 Iso Rivolta, metallic burgundy, 1969..............$8–12
34 Mercedes-Benz 230 SL, metallic dark green, 1969 ....$8–12
35 Alfa Romeo 2600 Sprint Bertone, olive green, 1967 ....$8–12
46 Alfa Romeo Giulia 1300 Police, olive green with blue light on top.................$8–12
53 Iso Rivolta and Boat Trailer, metallic dark blue with yellow trailer, 1969 ....$15–18
54 Romeo Minibus, red, 1970 ....$12–15

Pepe

Pepe has produced miniature models of Opels, Volkswagens, Renaults, Fiats, and others, in 1:25 and 1:43 scale. Below is an assortment currently offered.

Pepe 1:25 Scale
15 Opel Fire Pumper Truck $16
16 Opel Tow Truck $16
17 Opel Fire Ladder Truck $16
18 Volkswagen Pickup Plit Window.......$16
26 Volkswagen Beetle Fire Chief $16
32 Renault 5 Police............................$16
33 Renault 5 Ambulance $16
34 Renault 5 Fire..............................$16
35 Renault 5 Taxi.............................$16
37 Austin Mini Ambulance...................$16
45 Cooper F1 Racer $16
46 Lotus F1 Racer $16
48 Fiat 692 Mixer $16
50 Fiat 692 Refrigerator Van $16
51 Fiat 692 Stake Truck $16
52 Jeep CJ2 Army $16

Pepe 1:43 Scale
41 Opel Rekord Ambulance $16
42 Saviem Dump Truck $16
43 1957 Opel Wagon.........................$16

Piccolino

Piccolino models are not to be confused with Shuco Piccolo models. The Piccolino range is an assortment of delicate 1:76 scale white metal models and kits made in Britain by Bellini starting in 1985. According to Crister Skoglund of Sweden, one leaflet distributed at the introduction of the new brand states that the models are going to be produced by Master Models Ltd., Guernsey, C.I., UK.

Their original address was Bellini Models, Ltd., Charwell House, Wilsom Road, Alton, Hants, GU34 TJ, Great Britain.

Upon digging through some old literature, Skoglund found a letter dated February 1992 that says that from now on all orders should be sent to RAE MODELS, Corrie Road, Addlerstone, Surrey KT15 2LP UK.

So it would appear that RAE Models bought the company around January 1992 according to Skoglund's research.

Below is an alphabetical list provided by Skoglund, who writes "...I have listed all Piccolino models in the OO scale I know of. The first column is their catalog number... As you can see, the models are divided into different categories. 'WLS' stands for 'World Land Speed' record cars, 'GP' for 'Grand Prix' Formula One models etc. The 'slash K' (/K) was added to the number to indicate that it is in kit form. The second column doesn't need any explanation. The third stands for price then in UK pounds."

Most prices are retail for unbuilt kits. Ready built models are about double the price. £1 UK is equal to about $1.60 US. Current value is estimated at far right.

Piccolino also produced some 1:24 scale extremely detailed models, according to Bill Cross, another avid collector. No list of those is currently known.

Piccolino 1:76 Scale (Double O Gauge)
GP 48/K, Alfa Romeo 1931 (Monza), original price £5.11
current estimated value $15–20

GP 75/K, Alfa Romeo 512 prototype 1942 original price £5.84
current estimated value $15–20

HSC 92/K, Alfa Romeo 6c 1931, original price £6.11
current estimated value $15–20

GP 36/K, Alfa Romeo Bimotore 1934, original price £6.70
current estimated value $15–20

HSC065/K, Alfa Romeo Disco Volante 1953, original price £6.85
current estimated value $15–20

GP 10/K, Alfa-Romeo 159 1951, original price.....................£5.75
current estimated value $15–20

GP 33/K, Alfa-Romeo P3 1934, original price.....................£4.96
current estimated value $15–20

HSC 99/K, Allard J2X 1950, original price.....................£6.53
current estimated value $15–20

SLC 140, Alvis FWD 1929, original price.....................£13.46
current estimated value $15–20

SLC 125/K, Aquila Italiana 1913, original price.....................£4.70
current estimated value $15–20

HSC 10/K, Aston Martin DB3 S Coupe 1957, original price.....................£7.27
current estimated value $15–20

HSC 53/K, Aston Martin Ulster 1935, original price.....................£4.42
current estimated value $15–20

HSC 14/K, Austin Healy 100 1954, original price.....................£6.20
current estimated value $15–20

SLC 88, Austin Taxi 1934, original price.....................£12.54
current estimated value $15–20

GP 1/K, Auto Union 1936, original price.....................£5.29
current estimated value $15–20

HSC 58/K, Bentley 3 Litre 1927, original price.....................£5.08
current estimated value $15–20

HSC 54/K, Bentley 4 1/2 Litre 1929, original price.....................£6.85
current estimated value $15–20

GP 46/K, Birkin Bentley 192, original price.....................£5.19
current estimated value $15–20

WLS 10/K Bluebird (Arrol Aster) 1929, original price.....................£6.88
current estimated value $15–20

WLS 4/K, Bluebird 1925, original price.....................£6.08
current estimated value $15–20

WLS 15/K, Bluebird 1933, original price.....................£7.49
current estimated value $15–20

WLS 9/F, Bluebird 1935, original price.....................£6.84
current estimated value $15–20

WLS 19/K, Bluebird 1964, original
price....................................£7.49
current estimated value...................$15–20

HSC 69/K, BMW M3 1991, original
price....................................£7.80
current estimated value...................$15–20

GP 66/K, Brabham BT 19 1966, original
price....................................£4.57
current estimated value...................$15–20

GP 80/K, BRM (Original) 1949, original
price....................................£4.38
current estimated value...................$15–20

GP 3/K, BRM P25 1959, original
price....................................£4.29
current estimated value...................$15–20

GP 30/K, BRM P261 High Exhaust 1965, original
price....................................£4.58
current estimated value...................$15–20

GP 8/K, BRM P48 1960, original
price....................................£4.49
current estimated value...................$15–20

GP 56/K, BRM P56 1962, original
price....................................£5.91
current estimated value...................$15–20

WLS 28/K, Budweiser 1979 rocketcar, original
price....................................£7.51
current estimated value...................$15–20

GP082/K, Bugatti 251 1955, original
price....................................£7.29
current estimated value...................$15–20

GP 29/K, Bugatti Type 35 1924, original
price....................................£5.68
current estimated value...................$15–20

SLC 141, Buick Tourer 1924, original
price....................................£13.46
current estimated value...................$15–20

HSC 34/K, Caterham Lotus 7 1981, original
price....................................£3.99
current estimated value...................$15–20

GP 14/K, Connaught A 1952, original
price....................................£3.93
current estimated value...................$15–20

HSC 45, Cooper Bobtail 1955, original
price....................................£4.72
current estimated value...................$15–20

GP 55/K, Cooper Bristol 1953, original
price....................................£4.57
current estimated value...................$15–20

SLC 123, De Dion Buton 1904, original
price....................................£12.49
current estimated value...................$15–20

GP 40/K, Delage 1,5 Litre 1927, original
price....................................£6.08
current estimated value...................$15–20

GP 2/K, ERA B Type 1936, original
price....................................£6.15
current estimated value...................$15–20

GP 51/K, Ferrari 156 Shark Nose 1961, original
price....................................£4.73
current estimated value...................$15–20

HSC 37/K, Ferrari 250 Berlinetta 1960, original
price....................................£6.73
current estimated value...................$15–20

HSC 22/K, Ferrari 250 GTO 1962, original
price....................................£5.27
current estimated value...................$15–20

HSC 24/K, Ferrari 250 Testa Rossa 1959, original
price....................................£6.88
current estimated value...................$15–20

HSC 51/K, Ferrari 330 LMB 1963, original
price....................................£6.26
current estimated value...................$15–20

GT 6/K, Ferrari 330 P4 1967, original
price....................................£4.61
current estimated value...................$15–20

HSC 25/K, Ferrari 330 TR 1962, original
price....................................£5.27
current estimated value...................$15–20

HSC 35/K, Ferrari 365 (Daytona) 1973, original
price....................................£7.27
current estimated value...................$15–20

HSC 9/K, Ferrari 375 MM Le Mans 1954, original
price....................................£7.80
current estimated value...................$15–20

GP 39/K, Ferrari 375 Thinwall 1953, original
price....................................£5.22
current estimated value...................$15–20

GP 11/K, Ferrari 500 1952, original
price....................................£4.36
current estimated value...................$15–20

GT 15/K, Ferrari 512S 1970, original
price....................................£4.82
current estimated value...................$15–20

GT 4/K, Ferrari Dino 206S 1967, original
price....................................£4.33
current estimated value...................$15–20

GP 22/K, Ferrari Dino 246 1959, original
price....................................£5.29
current estimated value...................$15–20

HSC 104/K, Ferrari F40 1987, original
price....................................£5.69
current estimated value...................$15–20

GT 11/K, Ford GT 40 1968, original
price....................................£4.68
current estimated value...................$15–20

HRC 3/K, Ford RS200 1987, original
price....................................£7.91
current estimated value...................$15–20

HSC 66/K, Frazer Nash 1935, original
price....................................£5
current estimated value...................$15–20

HSC 100/K, Frazer Nash 1952, original
price....................................£4.35
current estimated value...................$15–20

WLS 12/K, Golden Arrow 1929, original
price....................................£5.70
current estimated value...................$15–20

WLS 020/K, Golden Rod 1965, original
price....................................£8.75
current estimated value...................$15–20

GP 42/K, Gordini 2 Litre 1952, original
price....................................£6.18
current estimated value...................$15–20

GP 90/K, GP Sunbeam 1923, original
price....................................£7.88
current estimated value...................$15–20

HSC 18/K, Healy Silverstone 1960, original
price....................................£6.50
current estimated value...................$15–20

GT 1/K, Jaguaar XJR8 1987, original
price....................................£9.58
current estimated value...................$15–20

HSC 2/K, Jaguar C Type 1953, original
price....................................£4.97
current estimated value...................$15–20

HSC 55/K, Jaguar SS 100 1939, original
price....................................£4.59
current estimated value...................$15–20

GT 8/K, Jaguar XJR 9 1988 LM winner, original
price....................................£11.14
current estimated value...................$15–20

GT 25/K, Jaguar XJR5 1983, original
price....................................£5.64
current estimated value...................$15–20

HSC 56/K, Jaguar XK 120 1950, original
price....................................£4.63
current estimated value...................$15–20

HSC 109/K, Lagonda M45R 1935, original
price....................................£6.60
current estimated value...................$15–20

GP 18/K, Lancia D50 1955, original
price....................................£4.68
current estimated value...................$15–20

HSC 13/K, Lister Jaguar (Costin) 1959, original
price....................................£5.75
current estimated value...................$15–20

RV 10, London Taxi 1958, original
price....................................£10.79
current estimated value...................$15–20

GP 21/K, Lotus 16 1958, original
price....................................£3.76
current estimated value...................$15–20

GP 52/K, Lotus 18 1960, original price..£4.24
current estimated value...................$15–20

GP 59/K, Lotus 25 1962, original price.......£5
current estimated value...................$15–20

GP 64/K, Lotus 33 1965, original price..£6.99
current estimated value...................$15–20

HSC 44/K, Lotus Elan 1970, original
price....................................£4.56
current estimated value...................$15–20

HSC 73/K, Maserati (Bird Cage) 1961, original
price....................................£6.70
current estimated value...................$15–20

GP 49/K, Maserati 2.9 1934, original
price....................................£6.08
current estimated value...................$15–20

GP 17/K, Maserati 250 F 1957, original
price....................................£4.49
current estimated value...................$15–20

GP058/K, Maserati 48/CTL 1948, original
price....................................£6.27
current estimated value...................$15–20

GT 3/K, McLaren M1C 1965, original
price....................................£4.77
current estimated value...................$15–20

GT 2/K, McLaren M8C 1970, original
price....................................£4.27
current estimated value...................$15–20

HSC 50/K, Mercedes-Benz 300 SL 1952, original price £5.85
current estimated value $15–20

HSC 33/K, Mercedes-Benz 300SLR 1955, original price £6.50
current estimated value $15–20

GP 32/K, Mercedes-Benz W154 1938, original price £5.46
current estimated value $15–20

GP 15/K,, Mercedes- Benz W196 1954, original price £4.88
current estimated value $15–20

HSC 60/K, Mercedes-Benz SSK 1928, original price £7.06
current estimated value $15–20

WLS 33/K, MG EX 120 1931, original price £5.01
current estimated value $15–20

WLS 29/K, MG EX 135 1939, original price £7.38
current estimated value $15–20

WLS 35/K, MG EX127 1933, original price £9.48
current estimated value $15–20

WLS 30/K, MG EX181 1957, original price £7.08
current estimated value $15–20

HSC 101/K, MG K3 (Pointed Tail) 1933, original price £5.52
current estimated value $15–20

HSC 76/K, MG K3 Magnette 1933, original price £4.54
current estimated value $15–20

HSC 102/K, MG M Type (Racing) 1930, original price £6.76
current estimated value $15–20

HSC 90/K, MG M Type 1930, original price £5.39
current estimated value $15–20

HSC 67/K, MG No. 1 (Kimber Special) 1925, original price £5.59
current estimated value $15–20

SLC 130, MG SA 2 Litre 1937, original price £13.18
current estimated value $15–20

HSC 15/K, MG TD 1952, original price £5.63
current estimated value $15–20

HSC 109/K, MG TF 1954, original price £5.76
current estimated value $15–20

WLS 7/K, Napier Bluebird 1927, original price £7.38
current estimated value $15–20

HRC 1/K, Peugeot 205 Turbo 1984, original price £6.44
current estimated value $15–20

GT 16/K, Porsche 917 K 1970, original price £5.57
current estimated value $15–20

GT 24/K, Porsche 956 1983, original price £5.85
current estimated value $15–20

GP 12/K, Porsche F1-804 1962, original price £4
current estimated value $15–20

WLS 16/K, Railton 1938, original price £5.17
current estimated value $15–20

SLC 124, Renault AX 1908, original price £12.49
current estimated value $15–20

SLC 120, Rover 6HP 1906, original price £11.85
current estimated value $15–20

HSC 38/K, Salmson 1926, original price £4.31
current estimated value $15–20

GT 62/K, Spice Pontiac (IMSA) 1986, original price £8.53
current estimated value $15–20

GT 48/K, Spice SE89 1989, original price £11.99
current estimated value $15–20

GT 65/K, Spice Tiga Lamborghini 1986, original price £6.05
current estimated value $15–20

WLS 8/K Sunbeam 1000HP 1927, original price £6.82
current estimated value $15–20

GP 9/K Tabolt Largo 1949, original price £5.62
current estimated value $15–20

HSC091/K Talbot 105 1931, original price £6.91
current estimated value $15–20

WLS 26/K Thrust II 1983, original price £11.42
current estimated value $15–20

WLS 17/K Thunderbolt 1938, original price £7.87
current estimated value $15–20

WLS 11/K Triplex (Stutz Black Hawk) 1928, original price £6.41
current estimated value $15–20

SLC 68 Trojan Achilles 1928, original price £11.85
current estimated value $15–20

GP 5/K Vanwall 1958, original price.....£4.15
current estimated value $15–20

HSC 1/K Vauxhall 30-98 1913, original price £5.21
current estimated value $15–20

Piccolo (see Schuco)

Pilen (see Auto Pilen)

Pioneer

A brand that would likely fall into the "generic" category is Pioneer. The brand was recently discovered by collector Robert Speerbrecher while stationed in Jakarta, Indonesia. Pioneer toys are made in China, and as Mr. Speerbrecher reports, "They have a line of cars that come with a bunch of accessories in them like a small play set on a blister pack. Most sets have one vehicle and a trailer, or two vehicles and some other accessories like picnic tables, trees, ramps in the Off-Road Set, etc. There is a real neat Military Set with a jeep and a tank. Both sets are diecast, plus some army guys and a way-out-of-scale hand grenade.

"The sets come on a large blister pack with printing only on the front. The card and blister pack plastic are pretty thin. The one I bought is a pink Mercedes 500SL Convertible pulling an all plastic trailer with two wind-surfing boards on it. It comes with a table, four chairs, and an umbrella for the table. Pretty neat set really for $1.50.

"The Mercedes is diecast with a plastic base. Really not a bad casting, better than many of the real cheap Chinese ones. As good as the Majorette 500SL but not as good as the Hot Wheels one. The other vehicles were army jeeps, cars, trucks, etc. All are not too bad quality. The military set is real neat."

Later, Speerbrecher added, "Here's some more info. They have at least four sets. One is a Military Set with a green Jeep, a green 4x4 ute [utility or pickup] type vehicle, a couple of army guys, and a hand grenade. The second is the Dive Set with a minivan pulling a trailer, a diver, and a few fish. The third is a Holiday Set with a minivan pulling a boat on a trailer, a few people, and a picnic table. The fourth is a Holiday Set with a Mercedes 500SL pulling a trailer with a windsurf board, a few people, and a table. Really the vehicles are not bad, and the set is a real value at about $1.50, a lot for the money. Especially the Military set with the two diecast vehicles. The cars are all about 1:64 scale. Funny thing is that the people are way out of scale and the hand grenade with the military set is bigger than the vehicles."

Piranha

Piranha white metal models are produced under the auspices of ABC Brianza.

1969 Dodge Daytona Hardtop, 1:43, #PH003 ....$80
1961 Ferrari GTO Prototype, 1:43, #PH004 ....$80

Plan 43X

One of many brands associated with MAFMA, the French model car artisans union, Plan 43X produces prepainted resin kits in 1:43 scale. No model list is known.

Platypus

Platypus Industrie produces hand-built models of incredible detail. Its recent release of a 1:50 scale Euclid R260 Mining Truck is an exquisitely detailed rendering that accurately portrays the massive size of this huge vehicle. More information can be obtained by phoning (in England) +44 1548 844114.

Euclid R260 Mining Truck, 1:50 ..Price unavailable
Tamrock DHA 1000S crawler drill rig,
   1:50....................Price unavailable
Unit Rig Lectra Haul MT-3700 Mining Truck,
   1:50....................Price unavailable

Playart

For about fifteen years, from about 1975 to 1990, Playart of Hong Kong produced a wonderful array of toy vehicles. It is a wonder they are not more popular, but it is likely due to the heavy competition in the U.S. market.

Playart toys have been marketed and packaged under many other names, most notably Sears Roadmates and Model Power, but the models themselves prominently display the Playart logo on the base, making identification easy and unmistakable.

The charm and quality of Playart toys make them worth keeping as collectibles. Their current value is still low, since most collectors are unaware of them. It is uncommon to find very many of them at toy shows or other second-market sources.

According to Dave Weber of Warrington, Pennsylvania, Playart at one time produced a series of models called Charmerz for New York distributor Charles Merzbach, who also packaged and marketed Majorettes in the US in the late sixties. Alex Lakhtman reports that Playart models also were sold in Woolworth's and under the name Peelers. Fastwheels is another name associated with Playart.

American LaFrance Fire Ladder Truck, 1:87 ..$10
American LaFrance Fire Snorkel Truck, 1:87....$8
Austin Mini Cooper S Mk II, red or ochre $10
Bulldozer, red with yellow blade, green cab .$10
Cement Mixer (Ford?), orange/red/gray or
   blue/red/gray $10
Chevrolet Blazer, silver, 1:72, Roadmates
   #7242 ....$4
Chevrolet Blazer Highway Patrol, black & white,
   1:72, Roadmates #7242H...................$4
Chevrolet Camaro Convertible, top up, 1:18..$24
Chevrolet 1967 Camaro, 1:64...................$5
Chevrolet 1977 Camaro Z28, 1:64............$4

Chevrolet Caprice Classic, metallic purple, 1:72, Roadmates #7214................$5

Chevrolet Caprice Fire Chief, 1:72 ....$4
Chevrolet Caprice Police Car, black & white,
   1:72, Roadmates #7232 ....$5
Chevrolet Caprice Yellow Cab Taxi, 1:72, Road-
   mates #7217 ....$5
Combine Harvester, blue, Roadmates #7166.$3

Chevrolet Corvette Stingray, 1:64 ....$6

Container Truck, SeaLand (Ford?), green and
   white......................$10
DeTomaso Pantera, 1:64.....................$3

Dodge Challenger, red with black roof, 1:72, Roadmates #7178................$4

Dodge Omni 024, metallic green, 1:67, Roadmates #7202..................$4

Dodge Paramedic, 1:64 ....$4
Douglas DC-10 "American Airlines"..............$4
Dump Truck (Ford?), apple green cab, metallic
   green-gold dumper $10
Dump Truck (Volvo?), #7185, yellow with orange
   dumper $10
Dump Truck (Volvo?), #7186, yellow with green
   and yellow-orange dumper $10
Farm Tractor with Plow, 1:72.................$5
Fiat X 1/9, 1:64........................$6
Fire Tender ....
Ford Box Truck "Pepsi-Cola," 1:120, Roadmates
   #7260P......................$6
Ford Box Truck "7-Up," 1:120, Roadmates
   #7260U......................$6
Ford Capri, 1:64.....................$6
Ford 1966 Mustang Convertible, lime green or
   red......................$6
Ford 1969 Mustang hardtop Coupe $6
Greyhound Bus, 1:156 (exact copy of Tomica
   Greyhound Bus) $12–15
Helicopter "Air Sea Rescue"...............$6
Helicopter "Coke" $6
Helicopter "Fire" $6
Honda S 800 Convertible, yellow with robin's
   egg blue tonneau cover $10
Honda Z GS, turquoise................$10
Hyster 70 Forklift, 1:64 ....$8
Javelin SST, 1:64......................$6
Jeep CJ U.S. Mail, 1:64 ....$6
Lamborghini Countach LP500S, 1:67, red, Road-
   mates #7246.....................$2

Lamborghini Silhouette, 1:64 ....$6
Lancia Stratos, 1:64, Roadmates #7259 ....$2
London Bus, 1:100 ....$6
Lotus Esprit, 1:64 ....$6
Mazda Pickup Truck, 1:64.................$6
Mazda Pickup Wrecker Truck, orange..........$8
Opel GT, 1:64.......................$4
Rolls Royce Silver Cloud, 1:64 ....$4
Scania Bus "AVIS Courtesy Bus," 1:87 ....$10
Tanker, Shell (Ford?) $10
Toyota Celica, 1:64 ....$4
U.S. Army Jeep, #7852 on sides.............$10
U.S. Jeep (civilian), yellow $10
Volvo 164E Station Wagon, lime green........$5
Volvo 166, 1:64......................$4
Man from U.N.C.L.E. Thrushbuster Car $15

Playart Fastwheels

7100 Batmobile........................$12–16
7101 Plymouth Barracuda $8–10
7102 Porsche Carrera 910 ....$8
7103 Thunderbird
   v.1 purple $8
   v.2 beige........................$8
7104 Opel GT
   v.1 light metallic brown $8
   v.2 white........................$8
7105 Mangusta 5000 Ghia $6-8
7106 Chevrolet Corvette Stingray Mako
   Shark
   v.1 purple $8
   v.2 teal blue $8
7107 Javelin SST $6–8
7108 Lamborghini Miura, dark green $8
7109 Chevy Camaro SS
   v.1 blue.......................$8
   v.2 yellow......................$8
7110 AMX 390, red........................$8
7111 Jensen FF, pink-beige................$8
7112 Alfa Romeo P33, red $8
7113 Alfa Carabo Bertone, green...........$8
7114 Mercedes-Benz C111, dark metallic
   maroon $8
7115 Cadillac Eldorado, brown $8
7116 Mustang Hardtop $8
7117 Toyota, brown $8
7118 Ford Fire Chief Station Wagon, red ..$8
7119 Man From U.N.C.L.E. Car $10–12
7120 Ford Mustang GT $8
7121 Chevrolet Astro-1 ....$8
7122 Toyota 2000 GT, blue $8
7123 Jaguar E Type 2+2, green............$8
7124 VW Bug, red......................$8
7125 Maserati Marzal $8
7126 Cement Mixer, blue, red barrel.......$8
7127 Pickup Truck......................$6–8
7128 Dump Truck, brown-purple cab,
   orange tipper $8
7129 Wrecker Truck $8
7130 Fire Truck.......................$6
7131 Gasoline Truck $6
7132 Ford Police Car, white...............$8
7133 Rolls Royce $6–8
7134 Fiat Dino $6–8

7135 BMW 2002, purple $8
7136 Corvette Stingray $6–8
7137 Datsun 240Z $6–8
7138 Vw Porsche 914 ....$6–8
7139 Honda N360 ....$6–8
7140 Honda S800 ....$6–8
7141 Corona Mark II 1900 Hardtop SL.$6–8
7142 Celica 1600 GT $6–8
7143 Toyota Crown Hardtop SL $6–8
7144 Porsche Targa 911S $6–8
7145 Isuzu 117 Coupe $6–8
7146 Corolla Sprinter SL $6–8
7147 Nissan Sunny 1200 Coupe GX .$6–8
7148 Yamaha Super Discmatic Rotary
   Coupe $6–8
7150 Ford Capri 1600 GT $6–8
7151 Rover 2000 TC $6–8
7152 Honda 2GS, yellow-green $8
7154 Mercedes-Benz 350 SL $6–8
7155 Ford Cortina GXL, light green $8
7156 Hipup Coupe Galant GTO MR ..$6–8
7157 Javelin SST, green $8
7158 Fiat 124 Sport $6–8
7160 Freight Truck (20' Truck) $6–8
7161 Bull Dozer................................$6–8
7162 Double Decker London Bus $6–8
7163 Garbage Collector Truck $6–8
7164 Container Wagon (Open Container
   Truck) $6–8
7165 Diesel Road Roller $6–8
7166 Combine Harvester $6–8
7167 Mercedes Ambulance $6–8
7168 Fire Tender $6–8
7169 Tractor with Angledozer (Bulldozer
   Tractor) $6–8
7170 Zetor Tractor $6–8
7171 Shovel Tractor (Road Tractor With
   Shovel) $6–8
7172 Estate Wagon...........................$6–8
7173 Police Van $6–8
7174 BMW Spicup $6–8
7175 Volvo 164e $6–8
7176 Tractor $6–8
7177 Forklift Truck $6–8
7178 Dodge Challenger Rallye...........$6–8
7179 VW Station Wagon $6–8
7180 Beach Buggy (Dune Buggy) $6–8
7181 Skip Dumper (Earth Dumper)......$6–8
7182 Range Rover $6–8
7183 Fire Engine with Ladder $6–8
7184 Fire Engine with Snorkel $6–8
7185 Scania Tipper Truck $6–8
7186 Scania Dump Truck...................$6–8
7187 Scania Freight Truck with Canvas
   Top $6–8
7188 Scania Open Platform Freight Truck
   With Pipes.............................$6–8
7189 Scania Open Platform Freight Truck
   With Girders...........................$6–8
7190 Brabham Racer $6–8
7191 Shadow Racer $6–8
7192 Lola Racer $6–8
7193 Mclaren Racer $6–8

7194 Lotus Racer $6–8
7195 BRM Racer $6–8
7196 Fiat X1/9 ....$6–8
7197 Citroen CX 2200 ....$6–8
7198 Alfetta GT $6–8
7199 Lotus Elite................................$6–8
7201 Porsche 928 ....$6–8
7202 Dodge Omni 024 ....$6–8
7203 Matra Simca Bagheera $6–8
7205 Mazda RX-7 ....$6–8
7206 Pontiac Firebird $6–8
7207 Camaro Z-28 ....$6–8
7209 Ford Paramedic Van $6–8
7210 Lamborghini 3000 Silhouette $6–8
7211 Renault A110 ....$6–8
7213 Ford Police Tactical Force Van $6–8
7214 Chevrolet Caprice Classic $6–8
7217 Chevrolet Caprice Classic Taxi ...$6–8
7218 Chevrolet Caprice Classic, Fire
   Chief $6–8
7219 Ferrari BB 512 ....$6–8
7220 Pontiac Firebird Trans Am...........$6–8
7222 Jeep.......................................$6–8
7226 Ford Cement Truck....................$6–8
7228 Ford Dump Truck $6–8
7229 Madza Wrecker Truck..............$6–8
7231 Ford Petrol Tanker, Shell............$6–8
7232 Chevrolet Caprice Classic, Police...$6–8
7234 Greyhound City Bus..................$6–8
7236 Corvette Street Machine $6–8
7239 Lancia Fulvia 1600 HF..............$6–8
7241 Audi Quattro............................$6–8
7242 Chevy Blazer $6–8
7242a Chevy Blazer, Police $6–8
7242a Chevy Blazer, Highway Patrol ..$6–8
7243 Lotus Esprit $6–8
7244a U.S. Mail Jeep $6–8
7245 Camaro Z-28 ....$6–8
7246 Lamborghini Countach LP 500S..$6–8
7247a Custom Van, Pirates $6–8
7247b Custom Van, Sea Gulls............$6–8
7247c Custom Van, Stars & Stripes......$6–8
7247d Custom Van, Swirls $6–8
7247e Custom Van, U.S. Mail.............$6–8
7248 De Tomaso Pantera...................$6–8
7249 Mazda Cosmo $6–8
7251 Mazda Pick-up $6–8
7253 Ford Cab With Sleeping Cabin .$6–8
7255 Volvo 343 ....$6–8
7256 Honda Accord $6–8
7258 Volvo 244 ....$6–8
7259 Lancia Stratos..........................$6–8
7260 Ford Freight Truck $6–8

7260p Ford Freight Truck - Pepsi Cola..$6–8

7260u Ford Freight Truck, 7-up............$6–8
7265 Alpine Renault A310 V6...........$6–8
7271 Turbo Mustang........................$6–8
7274 BMW 633 ....$6–8
7275 Opel Senator $6–8

Playing Mantis (see Johnny Lightnings)

Play Power

The Play Power models listed are most likely made in Japan.

Play Power Airplanes

E/T Mk.2 "Patrol of France,"
   red/white/blue, 2¾" $2
McDonnell-Douglas F-16 "USAF Thunderbirds," red/white/blue, 2¾" $2
McDonnell-Douglas F-15 "USAF Bicentenni-
   al," red/white/blue, 2¾" $2
McDonnell-Douglas AV-8A "Red Arrows,"
   red/white/blue, 2¾" $2
McDonnell-Douglas F-18 "USAF Blue Angels,"
   blue/yellow, 2¾ $2

Play Power Vehicles

BMW 2-Door Sedan Police Car, white/yel-
   low/black, 2¾" $2
Chevrolet Pickup Truck "Western Forest Service," bright pink, 3".........................$2
Chevrolet Forest Service Tow Truck, bright
   green/yellow, 3⅓".............................$2
Chevrolet Van Ambulance, white/red/black,
   2⅝"...$2
Hino Snorkel Fire Engine, red/white, 3¼" .$3

Playskool

Playskool has produced many types of preschool toys for decades, but only for a short time in the early eighties did the company market diecast toys in a series of heavy one-piece vehicles driven by Sesame Street characters. The most common one is Oscar the Grouch driving his garbage truck. Each model is larger than the average diecast toy vehicle, about 2 to 2½ inches tall and 3 inches long. Popular at the time but rare now, each model is worth about $6–8.

More recently, Tyco has acquired the Sesame Street license and has issued new models under the Tyco Preschool, Matchbox, and Fisher-Price brands.

Current Playskool preschool diecast models feature Barney the Dinosaur and his friends. Twelve models have been so far documented.

Baby Bop Airplane $2–3
Baby Bop Convertible $2–3
Baby Bop Drum Car $2–3
Baby Bop School Bus $2–3
Barney Cement Mixer $2–3
Barney Convertible $2–3
Barney Dump Truck.................................$2–3
Barney Fire Truck $2–3
Barney Race Car.....................................$2–3
BJ Bulldozer $2–3

BJ Dump Truck..............................$2–3
BJ Fire Truck................................$2–3

Playtoy

According to avid collector John Dean of Federal Heights, Colorado, Belgium is home to this short-lived brand that produced just three models in kit form. Carlo Brianza is known to have assembled such models and sold them under is own ABC Brianza brand. They are presumed to be 1:43 scale models, but might in fact be bigger. Values below are highly speculative and arbitrary guesses.

1953 Buick Skylark.......................$100–150
1957 Cadillac Eldorado................$100–150
Chrysler Town and Country Convertible $100–150

Playtrucks

Two examples of Playtrucks models from Greece are represented below.
Caterpillar Traxcavator, #22, 1:43............$16
Scania 6x4 Cement Truck, #20, 1:43.......$16

PM

Pressomeccanica, or PM, models of Milan, Italy, were produced in the postwar 1940s. Nine models are known to exist. The actual name of the company is even longer — Pressofusione Meccanica.

O.M. Taurus Covered Truck, 1:43.....$75–125
O.M. Taurus Dump Truck, 1:43.........$75–125
O.M. Taurus Fire Truck, 1:43...........$75–125
O.M. Taurus Open Truck, 1:43..........$75–125
O.M. Taurus Street Sweeper, 1:43.....$75–125
O.M. Taurus Tank Truck with Trailer, 1:43.........................$175–200
O.M. Taurus Wrecker, 1:43............$75–125
Lancia Ardea Ambulance, white with red cross decals, 1:40...................$75–125
Lancia Ardea Fire Van, 1:40............$75–125
Lancia Ardea Loudspeaker Van, 1:40..$75–125
Lancia Ardea Van, 1:40.................$75–125
Streamlined Race Car.....................$600–750

Pocher

Pocher 1:8 Scale Models

Pocher (pronounced Po-share) Prestige series 1:8 scale diecast metal car kits are unexcelled in accuracy and detail for their price... if you can afford one. Italian-made Pochers are top of the line in price, scale, quality, and detail. The reason for the high price becomes obvious when you realize these models measure 19 inches long and contain over 2,000 parts! The labor of putting them together even includes having to string the wire wheels so that they are centered and balanced! Each of these sleek statements of status is a streamlined rolling work of art, representing the ultimate automotive icon of its era.

K30 Porsche 911, black, assembled ..$1,000
   unassembled..............................$350
K31 Porsche 911, silver, assembled .$1,200
   unassembled..............................$450

K50 Ferrari Testarossa, yellow, assembled.............................$1,000
   unassembled..............................$300
K55 Pocher Ferrari F-40, red, assembled.............................$1,000
   unassembled..............................$300
K73 1932 Alfa Romeo Spider Touring Gran Sport, assembled.....................$1,200
   unassembled..............................$400
K74 1935 Mercedes-Benz 500K/AK Cabriolet, black, assembled.............$1,000
   unassembled..............................$300
K75 1934 Rolls-Royce Phantom II Torpedo Cabriolet, assembled...............$1,500
   unassembled..............................$500
K76 1933 Bugatti 50T, black & yellow, assembled.............................$1,500
   unassembled..............................$450
K82 Mercedes-Benz 540K Cabriolet Special, white, assembled...........$1,000
   unassembled..............................$300
K83 1933 Rolls-Royce Ambassador, green, assembled.............................$1,500
   unassembled..............................$450
K84 1933 Bugatti 50T, blue & silver, assembled.............................$1,000
   unassembled..............................$300
K86 1932 Bugatti 50T Suprafile, black & red, assembled.....................$1,200
   unassembled..............................$350
K89 Alfa Romeo 8C 2300 Coupe Elegant, assembled.............................$1,500
   unassembled..............................$450
K91 Mercedes-Benz 540K Roadster, assembled $1,200
   unassembled..............................$350
K92 Alfa Romeo, assembled...........$1,200
   unassembled..............................$450
K94 1936 Mercedes-Benz 540K Cabriolet Special, assembled $1,200
   unassembled..............................$450

Pocher 1:43 Scale Models

While the 1:8 scale models may be too expensive, the smaller 1:43 scale Pocher models produced in the 1960s, while rare, may be had for somewhat less.

Fiat 124 ....$125
Fiat 850 ....$125

Pocher Scale Model Engines

KM51 Ferrari Testarossa 12-cylinder engine.$100
KM87 Volvo F16 engine...................$100

Poclain

Poclain is best known as the French heavy equipment manufacturer. Made mainly by Bourbon of France around 1973 and sold as promotional models, Poclain's assortment of plastic miniatures does not qualify as diecast, so they are not listed here, but current estimates put their value around $25 to $35 each.

Pocket Cars (see Tomica)

Pocketoys (see Brimtoy)

Pole Position Collectibles

Pole Position Collectibles are a recent entry into the diecast racing collectibles arena. Resembling Racing Champions, they are made in China for Mountain Service International of Bristol, Virginia. These approximately 1:64 scale models authentically re-create the markings of actual stock cars. The colorful, distinctive blister-pack is designed by Gibson & Lane Graphic Designs, as indicated on the package. Models sell for $1 to $2 each. For more information, you may wish to write or call the manufacturer:
Pole Position Collectibles
Mountain Service International, Inc.
4710 Lee Highway
Bristol, VA 24201
phone: 703-669-4700

Polistil (see Politoys)

Politoys/Polistil (also see Penny Series)

Politoys M of Italy began in 1960 as A.P.S. Politoys, a manufacturer of plastic 1:41 scale models. In 1965, Politoys produced their first series of higher quality diecast vehicles. Because of the similarity of names between Politoys of Italy and Palitoys of Great Britain, the Politoys name was changed to Polistil around 1970.

The Politoys/Polistil product line covers hundreds of models in a variety of scales, from 1:64 scale to 1:18. Reissues and new Polistil models have most recently been produced by McGregor of Mexico.

The Jensen models are particularly interesting, both for their rarity and for the their use of the letters "FF" which stands for "Ferguson Formula," an advanced four-wheel-drive system.

Politoys Plastic Models

3-Ton Army Truck, 4⅛", 1:41, 1960 .....$25
A.B.S. 155mm Mortar, 5¾", 1:41, 1960 .... $25
AMX 13-Ton Tank, 4⅛", 1:41, 1960....$25
Armored Personnel Carrier, 3⅛", 1:41, 1960 ....$25
Panhard Tank, 4⅛", 1:41, 1960 ....$25

Politoys Diecast Models

Bertone Ford Mustang 2+2, #549, 1:43, 1969 ....$55–65

Bertone Corvair, #551, 1:43, 1968.....$45–50

DeTomaso Pantera, 1:43, c. 1972 .$45–50

Ferrari P4, #574, 1:43, 1968..............$45–50

Ford Escort, 1:64 ....$30–45
Ford Lola GT, 1:43, c. 1972.........$45–50
Jensen FF Coupe Vignale, #573, 1:43, silver
   or maroon, with rubber tires.......$55–60
Jensen FF Coupe Vignale, #573, 1:43, sil-
   ver, with speed-type wheels.......$45–50

**Oldsmobile Toronado, #567, 1:43,
1970 ....$65–70**

Opel Diplomat, #521, c. 1972......$55–60
Osi 1200 Coupe, #533, 1:43,
   c. 1972............................$40–45
Samurai, #580, 1:43, 1970 ....$35–40

Poll

Nothing is known of this brand other than a single model of particularly large size.
Gravel Loader, 24" $65

PP Models

PP models are 1:43 scale miniatures from England.
Jaguar SS100 Roadster $40
Morris 1000 4-Door Sedan $40
Morris 1000 Convertible $40
Triumph Spitfire $40
Daimler SP250 Roadster.........................$40
Jensen 541 Coupe $40
1939 Studebaker Coupe $40

Praliné (see Busch/Praliné)

Prämeta

Five Prämeta models were produced in Germany in 1951. Sporting clockwork motors and a transmission with three forward gears, neutral, and reverse, they were made within a 1:30–1:40 scale range, except for the Volkswagen, which was made to a slightly larger scale and reportedly didn't have a windup mechanism. Prämetas are solid cast in several color variations with silver-painted windows, or silver metal with green painted windows.
1947-48 Buick 405 Sedan, 5¾",
   1:40..................................$325
Jaguar XK120 Coupe, 6", 1:30 ....$325
Mercedes-Benz 300 Sedan, 5¾", 1:37 ....$325
Opel Kapitän Sedan, 5¾", 1:33 ....$325
Volkswagen $400

Precision Autos (also see John Day Models)

Precision Autos are reportedly the result of a frustrated Englishman named John Day, who could not find replicas of the models he wanted, so he started making his own. John Day is credited with bringing expensive hand-crafting techniques on models costing thousands of dollars down to merely hundreds of dollars.
Inaltera, 1:43 scale.........................$200–400

Precision Engineered Models (also see Hartoy)

Hartoy's success with American Highway Legends prompted the introduction of Precision Engineered Models, 1:64 scale trucks with trailers. The series has reportedly proven even more successful than the AHL line.

Precision Engineered Models, as extracted from www.hartoy.com, 01/10/99
Van Trailers & Tank Trailers ....$48 each
Flatbed trailers ....$46 each

Kenworth T600
M70505 Stanley $46–48
M70506 Wiley Sanders Truck Lines ...$46–48
M70510 Auto Palace....................$46–48
M70511 Weyerhaeuser................$46–48
M70513 Benton Express................$46–48
M70515 Bekins Van Lines.............$46–48
M70517 Summerford Truck Lines $46–48
M70519 Landstar Ligon.................$46–48
M70520 Danny Hernan Trucking.......$46–48
M70522 Edward Brothers w/Reefer
   Unit $46–48
M70529 Super Service $46–48

Mack CH600
M71500 Hershey's American Dream ...$46–48
M71507 Georgia-Pacific...............$46–48
M71508 Pitt-Ohio Express..............$46–48
M71509 Sweendy Transportation.......$46–48
M71511 Carroll Fulmer $46–48
M71513 Sweeney Transportation II.......$46–48
M71704 Coastal Transport Flatbed .$46–48
M71802 Schwerman Tank Trailer ...$46–48
M71803 CTL Distribution Chemical Tank
   Trailer..................................$46–48
M71903 Kenan Fuel Tank Trailer $46–48

International 9800
M72507 Schneider National II.......$46–48
M72508 Tractor Trailer..................$46–48

Freightliner FLD 120
M73505 Auto Works....................$46–48
M73523 Landstar Ranger $46–48
M73524 Burlington Motor Carriers..$46–48
M73526 Transport Systems $46–48
M73527 Lanstar Inway - Van..........$46–48
M73528 Transport America $46–48
M73531 Dart with Red Tractor $46–48
M73532 Fleetline $46–48
M73533 Deboer..........................$46–48
M73534 National Carriers w/Reefer
   Unit $46–48

M73535 Dart with Blue Tractor......$46–48

Precision Miniatures

Harvey Goranson reports that Precision Miniatures, like Precision Autos, are white metal kits, a built-up range begun by Gene Parrill when he owned Marque Products in the Los Angeles, California, area. The first models were Porsches, then Indy cars, Ferraris, and a Duesenberg were added. I suspect the Indy cars were planned IMRA kits, since these were 1:40 scale. I have a '57 Ferrari Testa Rossa (pontoon fender) from the Targa Florio race, and a '48 Novi Indy racer, plus a kit of an Indy McLaren. The '70s Indy kits were extremely well cast and detailed — not for beginners.

"In 1982 or '83," Mr. Goranson reports, "I went to LA for a weekend because I got a crazy deal on a plane ticket. I visited Marque Products on a day when Gene was doing trial runs casting Hudson Hornets. It was fascinating watching the white metal castings being made. Gene later introduced other '50s American cars in the Precision range, plus the Laser and Mustang you list, then found his niche with the Motor City, Design Studio, and (lately) USA Models ranges."
1964½ Ford Mustang Convertible, red..$75–90
1984 Chrysler Laser............................$75–90
1951 or 1952 Hudson Convertible..$125–140
1951 or 1952 Hudson Coupe $125–140

Pride Lines (also see Manoil)

Pride Lines Ltd. vehicles are diecast in the USA using original sixty-year-old Manoil molds. (See Manoil.) Each highly stylized model is cast from the finest pewter and hand painted to perfection. All vehicles have rubber tires, two-piece metal construction and baked enamel finish. Each model is approximately 4½ inches long. For more details, contact:
Pride Lines Ltd. (Manoil remakes)
651 West Hoffman Ave.
Lindenhurst, NY 11757
phone: 516-225-0033
fax: 516-225-0099

Pride Lines Manoil Reproductions
City Police $50
Coupé $50
Fire Chief $50
Fire Truck $50
Phaeton Convertible $50
Roadster $50
Sedan $50
Sheriff $50
Speedster Sedan $50
Taxi Sedan $50
Taxi Toy Truck $50

Pride Lines Manoil Disney Character Cars
Daisy Duck Roadster, baby blue and yellow .$85
Donald Duck Roadster, red and blue $85
Goofy Wrecker, red $85
Goofy Roadster, orange and black $85

Mickey Mouse Roadster, yellow and purple .$85
Minnie Mouse Roadster, pink and baby blue.$85
Scrooge McDuck, greeen and cream with 24
karat gold-plate trim $100

Process

Diecast Miniatures lists just one model from Process, a United States brand.
1961 Jaguar XKE Roadster, 1:43 ....$5

Profil 24

Profil 24 of France offers 1:24 scale kits, painted or unpainted, and built models. An affiliate of MAFMA, no model list is known.

Progetto K

Progetto K of Italy offers a huge range of currently available 1:43 scale models.

To list this exhaustive selection would consume many pages. Suffice it to say that many models are produced in various liveries, which makes the selection broader. I will attempt to provide a reasonable representation of the product line.
1968 Abarth 1000 Group 5 ....$23

1963 Alfa Romeo Giulia GT $23

1965 Alfa Romeo Giulia GTA....................$23
1967 Alfa Romeo Giulia GTA....................$23
1968 Alfa Romeo Giulia GTA....................$23
1958 Austin-Healey Mk 1 "Frogeye" Convertible,
top down $23
1958 Austin-Healey Mk 1 "Frogeye" Convertible,
top up $23
1952 Ferrari 166 MM $23
1952 Ferrari 225 Coupe $23
1952 Ferrari 225 S $23
1952 Ferrari 250 MM $23
1958 Ferrari TR $23
Fiat 124 Spyder $23
1965 Lancia Fulvia Coupe $23
1966 Lancia Fulvia HF Coupe $23
1959 Maserati T60/61 "Birdcage" $23

Protar

Little is known about Protar of Italy except that they make exquisite motorcycle models. Here is a small sampling.
1991 Ducati, red street or racing version,
1:9.......................................$55
1995 Ducati 916SP5, 1:9.....................$55
1995 Ducati Senna, 1:9......................$50
1996 Ducati Senna, 1:9......................$60
Ducati Superbike Chili, 1:9.................$60
1996 Kawasaki ZX-7R Street, 1:9 ....$55
Moto Guzzi V-850 California, 1:6..........$250

1971 Moto Guzzi V7, 1:9 ....$50
Moto Guzzi Carabinieri, 1:9 ....$50
Moto Guzzi Polizia, 1:9......................$50

Provénce Moulàge

Provénce Moulàge models are precision 1:43 and 1:24 scale resin kits of which a certain number are shipped to dealers as pre-assembled demo models. The majority are sold as kits, unassembled and unpainted. Finishing the model includes sanding and trimming to smooth the surface and remove excess material from windows, wheel wells, and other openings and edges. Prices below are for unfinished models in the original box.

As of February 2001, Provénce Moulàge has merged with Starter Models. Provénce Moulàge will continue offering kits, while Starter will provide finished models.
1950 Buick 2-Door Hardtop $115
1950 Buick Station Wagon.....................$115
1949 Delahaye 173 4.5L LeMans $52
1982 Camaro $52
Facel 2-Door Coupe............................$65
Facel Facellia Coupe...........................$65
1975 Ferrari Daytona Luchard...................$52
1981 Ferrari Pininfarina $52
1946 Ford 2-Door Sedan $115
1946 Ford Station Wagon $115
1957 Jaguar D-Type LeMans....................$52
1960 Jaguar 3.8L Sedan $52
1963 Jaguar 3.8L Sedan $52
1985 Jaguar XJR6 ....$52
Volkswagen 1303 "Beetle" Convertible $90

PTH Models

PTH (Past-Time Hobbies) Models of England produces a stunning assortment of 1:43 scale models new and old. Their latest offering (as of March 1997) is a pair of Dodge Viper GTS models in 1:43 scale, created for their US division. Order direct from PTH:
Past-Time Hobbies, Inc.
9311 Ogden Ave.
Brookfield, IL 60513
phone: 708-485-4544
3 1972 Chevrolet Camaro Z28 Coupe, metallic
orange-yellow or white.......................$129
4 1970 Chevrolet Monte Carlo SS 454, red..$129
5 1982 Chevrolet Corvette, metallic brown-silver,
"Collectors Edition" $139
6 1995 Chevrolet Impala SS, black..........$129
7 1960 Chevrolet Impala Sports Coupe, metallic
orange-brown $129
8 1934 Packard Model 1106 Coupe, deep
blue $149
9 1934 Packard with vinyl roof, metallic
green $149
17C 1958 Ford "Chicago Police"............$129
Dodge Viper GTS Coupe, orange with black
stripes, 1:43, 1997, 50 made...........$145
Dodge Viper GTS Coupe, blue with white
stripes, 1:43, 1997, 50 made..........$150

Qualitoys (See Benbros)

Quarter Mile (see Great American Dreamcars)

Quartzo (also see Vitesse)

Minibri Ltd.
P O Box 283
4471 Maia Codex
Portugal
fax: 351-2-9017464

Quartzo is a brand of the Vitesse Group of Portugal, marketed by Minibri, which focuses on NASCAR models in 1:43 scale. As with most diecast models, Quartzo models are made in China. Models in the Quartzo series can be found within the Vitesse listings.

Quiralu

Now one of the most popular brands on the collector market, Quiralu was at one time a totally obscure French brand of sandcast toys. Their current popularity is due in part to the re-issue of many of the original models as faithful reproductions. That alone wouldn't necessarily make them sell, but the real reason is for the recognition by collectors of the charm and quality of these fine toys. Reproductions can be purchased for a reasonable price, while original models are quickly rising in value.

The original Quiralu brand was introduced in 1933 by a Mr. Quirin of Luxeuil, France. The combination of his name and the primary metal, aluminum, used in the production of these models provides the name derivation.

It wasn't until 1955 that the firm started producing 1:43 scale models. The latest of the original models were introduced in 1959, with production ceasing soon afterward.

Quiralu Originals

1 Simca Trianon, 1955 ....$85
2 Simca Versailles, 1955 ....$85
3 Simca Regence, 1955 ....$85
4 Peugeot 403, single color with no plastic
windows, 1956................................$85
5 Peugeot 403, two-tone, no plastic windows, 1956.....$85
6 Peugeot 403, single color with plastic windows, 1956.....$95
7 Peugeot 403, two-tone with plastic windows, 1956.....$95
8 Mercedes-Benz 300SL, single color, 1956................................$125
9 Mercedes-Benz 300SL, two-tone, 1956................................$125
10 Simca Marly Break Station Wagon, single color, 1957 ....$85
11 Simca Marly Break Station Wagon, two-tone, 1957.....$85
12 Simca Marly Ambulance, 1957.....$120
13 Porsche Carrera, single color, 1957 ..$325
14 Porsche Carrera, two-tone, 1957 ...$325

15 Jaguar XK140, 1957 ....$120
16 Messerschmitt Auto-Scooter, 1958 ....$100
17 Rolls-Royce Silver Cloud, 1958 ......$120
18 Vespa 400 2CV, 1958.................$85
19 BMW Velam Isetta BubbleCar $100
20 Renault Etoile Filante, with decals, 1958 ....$100
21 Renault Etoile Filante, no decals, 1958 ....$95
22 Peugeot D4A Van, red, 1958 ....$350
23 Peugeot D4A Van, yellow or green, 1958 ....$350
24 Peugeot D4A Army Ambulance, 1958 ....$375
25 Berliet GBO Covered Truck, 1959 .$300
26 Berliet GBO Dump Truck, 1959 .....$300
27 Berliet GBO Covered Trailer, 1959.................$125

Quiralu Reproductions
1958 BMW Isetta Velam Bubble Car, #812 ....$40
1960 Citroën ID19 Ambulance.............$40
1960 Citroën ID19 Station Wagon, #815 ....$40
1957 Jaguar XK140 Roadster, #827 ....$40
Mercedes-Benz 300 SL, #814.............$40
1956 Messerschmitt Tiger Auto-Scooter, #810 ....$40
Peugeot 403 Sedan, #816.................$40
Peugeot D4A Military Ambulance $40
Peugeot D4A Van, red, #818.............$40
Peugeot D4A Van, white, #818 ....$40
Peugeot D4A Van, yellow, #818 ....$40
Porsche 356 Coupe, #813.................$40
1956 Renault World Speed Record, #835 ....$40
1957 Rolls-Royce Silver Cloud, #826 ....$40
Simca Marly Station Wagon, #830 .....$40
1958 Vespa 400 Sedan, #811..........$40

R&M
Virtually nothing is known of this obscure brand. More information is appreciated.
Berta Racer, 2" $4
Cheboom Racer, 4" $4

R. W. (see Ziss)

Race Image Collection (also see Corgi, Speedway Collection, Lucky Plan, Dimension 4, Specialty Diecast)
Race Image Collection is a series of 1:43 scale diecast NASCAR models manufactured by Lucky Plan Industries. (See Speedway Collection.)

The distinction, if any, is that the Race Image Collection is an assortment of high-quality low-priced racing models offered in mass-market retail stores such as Wal-Mart. Models sell for about $5 each. The Race Image brand is also connected with Corgi.

Raceway Replicars
Information provided by Russell Alameda indicates at least two models made under this brand.
Ford, #6 Mark Martin, "Valvoline," 1:24, limited edition of 5,000 ....$300
Ford, #28 Davy Allison, "Valvoline," 1:24, limited edition of 5,000 ....$300

Racing Champions
Founded in 1989 by Bob Dods and Boyd Meyer in Glenn Ellyn, Illinois, Racing Champions is a leading producer and marketer of diecast collectibles, available at over 20,000 retail outlets throughout North America, including Wal-Mart, K-Mart, Toys 'R' Us, and Target. The company is best known for its extensive line of officially-licensed diecast replicas from the five most popular racing series, including NASCAR. Racing Champions also markets several lines of non-racing diecast vehicle replicas and, in 1997, launched a new category of adult collectible pewter figures. Additional Racing Champions product information can be found on the World Wide Web at www.RacingChamps.com.

Racing Champions offers an assortment of models that specialize in race car and transporter replicas. Like most modern diecast toys, Racing Champions are manufactured in China and other Asian manufacturing centers. Miniature race car replicas are a collecting specialty in themselves, attracting a specialized group numbering in the thousands of collectors. Racing Champions offers race cars of all types, including NASCAR, NASCAR Craftsman Truck, NHRA, CART, World of Outlaws, and Indy Racing League, in 1:24, 1:43, 1:64, and 1:144 scale. Thousands of models are offered representing every race driver in each category. The product line-up could fill a book. So this book will focus on Racing Champions' offerings with a somewhat broader appeal.

In 1999, Racing Champions purchased the venerable Ertl Company of Dyersville, Iowa.

Racing Champions Mint Editions
The freshest series of diecast models to hit the market in years is Mint Edition from Racing Champions. Introduced in 1996, this series is comprised of classic cars past and present in 1:56 to 1:61 scale. Each model includes a display stand with a diecast emblem representing the hood or fender ornament. Retail price is $5–6. A licensing agreement with *Motor Trend* magazine saw the line converted to Motor Trend Mint Editions in 1998. The series was discontinued after 1999 and replaced by Classified Classics, cars representing those advertised for sale in the classified section of a newspaper or specialty magazine.

1996 Racing Champions Mint Editions
#1 1996 Dodge Viper GTS, blue with white racing stripe $5–6

#2 1950 Chevrolet 3100 Pickup, dark green.................$5–6
#3 1996 Pontiac Firebird, black.........$5–6
#4 1957 Chevrolet Bel Air, red.........$5–6
#5 1968 Ford Mustang, red.........$5–6
#6 1956 Ford Thunderbird, yellow with white roof.................$5–6
#7 1950 Chevrolet 3100 Pickup, dark blue.................$5–6
#8 1996 Pontiac Firebird, metallic purple.................$5–6
#9 1957 Chevrolet Bel Air, turquoise ...$5–6
#10 1968 Ford Mustang, metallic gold.................$5–6
#11 1956 Ford Thunderbird, pale lavender.................$5–6
#12 1996 Dodge Ram, blue.............$5–6
#13 1950 Chevrolet 3100 Pickup, red .$5–6
#14 1996 Pontiac Firebird, white........$5–6
#15 1957 Chevrolet Bel Air, tan $5–6
#16 1956 Ford Thunderbird, gray.......$5–6
#17 1996 Dodge Ram, red $5–6
#18 1964 Chevrolet Impala, blue.......$5–6
#19 1950 Chevrolet 3100 Pickup, brown.................$5–6
#20 1996 Pontiac Firebird, red.........$5–6
#21 1957 Chevrolet Bel Air, yellow $5–6
#22 1996 Dodge Ram, black $5–6
#23 1964 Chevrolet Impala, silver gray.$5–6
#24 1996 Chevrolet Camaro, blue.....$5–6
#25 1957 Chevrolet Bel Air, black......$5–6
#26 1956 Ford Thunderbird, blue with black roof.................$5–6
#27 1996 Dodge Ram, white $5–6
#28 1964 Chevrolet Impala, plum $5–6
#29 1996 Chevrolet Camaro, white $5–6
#30 1997 Ford F-150, red $5–6
#31 1957 Chevrolet Bel Air, bright teal..$5–6
#32 1956 Ford Thunderbird, pink $5–6
#33 1996 Dodge Ram, silver $5–6
#34 1996 Chevrolet Camaro, black ...$5–6
#35 1997 Ford F-150, white $5–6
#36 1963 Chevrolet Corvette, red $5–6
#37 1956 Ford Thunderbird, red $5–6
#38 1964 Chevrolet Impala, white $5–6
#39 1996 Chevrolet Camaro, green...$5–6
#40 1996 Ford F-150, black $5–6
#41 1963 Chevrolet Corvette, white ...$5–6
#42 1969 Pontiac GTO "Judge," orange.................$5–6
#43 1996 Pontiac Firebird, purple $5–6
#44 1968 Ford Mustang, metallic green.................$5–6
#45 1997 Ford F-150, white $5–6
#46 1963 Chevrolet Corvette, metallic dark blue.................$5–6
#47 1969 Pontiac GTO "Judge," school bus yellow.................$5–6
#48 1956 Ford Victoria, light blue.......$5–6
#49 1996 Pontiac Firebird, dark teal ...$5–6
#50 1968 Ford Mustang, mint green...$5–6
#51 1963 Chevrolet Corvette, dark beige.................$5–6

#52 1969 Pontiac GTO "Judge," black $5–6
#53 1956 Ford Victoria, mint green.....$5–6
#54 1970 Plymouth Superbird, red $5–6
#55 1968 Ford Mustang, black..........$5–6
#56 1963 Chevrolet Corvette, silver ...$5–6
#57 1969 Pontiac GTO "Judge," red ..$5–6
#58 1956 Ford Victoria, black $5–6
#59 1970 Plymouth Superbird, blue $5–6
#60 1970 Chevrolet Chevelle SS, dark blue $5–6

1997 Racing Champions Mint Editions
#61 1950 Ford Coupe, maroon $5–6
#62 1997 Ford Mustang, red...........$5–6
#63 1969 Oldsmobile 442, crimson ..$5–6
#64 1932 Ford Coupe, black...........$5–6
#65 1949 Mercury, blue $5–6
#66 1935 Ford Pick Up, black $5–6
#67 1970 Chevrolet Chevelle SS, red .$5–6
#68 1969 Oldsmobile 442, white......$5–6
#69 1932 Ford Coupe, blue............$5–6
#70 1949 Mercury, gray $5–6
#71 1935 Ford Pick Up, red $5–6
#72 1955 Chevrolet Bel Air Convertible, light blue/blue......................$5–6
#73 1997 Ford Mustang, green $5–6
#74 1949 Mercury, black $5–6
#75 1935 Ford Pick Up, gray $5–6
#76 1955 Chevrolet Bel Air Convertible, light green/green....................$5–6
#77 1958 Chevrolet Impala, red $5–6
#78 1997 Chevrolet Corvette, yellow...$5–6
#79 1969 Oldsmobile 442, gold $5–6
#80 1950 Ford Coupe, blue............$5–6
#81 1964.5 Ford Mustang, red $5–6
#82 1970 Chevrolet Chevelle, silver....$5–6
#83 1997 Chevrolet Corvette, white ..$5–6
#84 1959 Cadillac Eldorado, pink $5–6
#85 1949 Mercury, green $5–6
#86 1956 Ford Crown Victoria, black and red $5–6
#87 1997 Chevrolet Corvette or 1964.5 Ford Mustang, black.............$5–6
#88 1959 Cadillac Eldorado, red $5–6
#89 1957 Chevrolet Bel Air, blue $5–6
#90 1968 Plymouth Superbird, orange .$5–6
#91 1969 Pontiac GTO, red $5–6

#92 1959 Cadillac Eldorado, blue..........$5–6

#93 1957 Chevrolet Bel Air, black......$5–6
#94 1968 Plymouth Superbird, red $5–6
#95 1950 Ford Coupe, gray $5–6
#96 1986 Chevrolet El Camino, white ..$5–6
#97 1968 Plymouth, blue $5–6
#98 1950 Ford Coupe, silver $5–6
#99 1986 Chevrolet El Camino, silver .$5–6
#100 1950 Chevrolet 3100, green....$5–6

#101 1968 Chevrolet Camaro, black .$5–6
#102 1958 Ford Edsel, pink $5–6
#103 1957 Chevrolet Bel Air, green ...$5–6
#104 1958 Chevrolet Impala, black ...$5–6
#105 1986 Chevrolet El Camino, black .$5–6
#106 1958 Ford Edsel, light blue........$5–6
#107 1997 Chevrolet Corvette, red $5–6
#108 1997 Plymouth Prowler, purple ..$5–6
#109 1968 Plymouth Superbird, gold..$5–6
#110 1958 Ford Edsel, light blue........$5–6
#111 1997 Plymouth Prowler, yellow ..$5–6
#112 1968 Chevrolet Camaro, red $5–6
#113 1949 Buick Riviera, blue $5–6
#114 1957 Ford Ranchero, light blue ..$5–6
#115 1997 Plymouth Prowler, silver $5–6
#116 1968 Chevrolet Camaro, blue....$5–6
#117 1949 Buick Riviera, yellow $5–6
#118 1958 Chevrolet Impala, brown ..$5–6
#119 1955 Chevrolet Bel Air, black....$5–6
#120 1940 Ford Pick Up, red $5–6
#121 1997 Ford Mustang, orange $5–6
#122 1949 Buick Riviera, dark green ..$5–6
#123 1932 Ford Coupe, gray $5–6
#124 1970 Chevrolet Chevelle SS, black $5–6
#125 1960 Chevrolet Impala, white ...$5–6
#126 1956 Chevrolet Nomad, light green $5–6
#127 1932 Ford Coupe, cream........$5–6
#128 1960 Chevrolet Impala, light blue .$5–6
#129 1956 Chevrolet Nomad, red.....$5–6
#130 1957 Ford Ranchero, black and white.............................$5–6
#131 1997 Plymouth Prowler, red.......$5–6
#132 1978 Pontiac Trans Am, black...$5–6

#133 1949 Mercury, 1:64 ....$5–6

1998 Racing Champions Motor Trend Mint Editions
#133 1948 Ford F-1 Pickup, dark green .$5–6
#134 1965 Ford F-100 Pickup, red $5–6
#135 1955 Chevrolet Bel Air, light green and white $5–6

1959 Chevrolet Impala, red and white..$5–6

#136 1969 Camaro, yellow with black stripes..............................$5–6
#137 1937 Ford Convertible, black $5–6
#138 1970 Plymouth Barracuda, purple .$5–6
#139 1948 Ford F-1 Pickup, red........$5–6

#140 1955 Chevrolet Bel Air, beige ...$5–6
#141 1969 Chevrolet Camaro, black with white stripes $5–6
#142 1937 Ford Convertible, royal blue .$5–6
#143 1970 Plymouth Barracuda, orange.$5–6
#144 1956 Chevrolet Nomad, brown..$5–6
#145 1957 Ford Ranchero, red and white $5–6
#146 1960 Chevrolet Impala, black ...$5–6
#147 1978 Pontiac Trans Am, yellow .$5–6
#148 1940 Ford Pickup, tan $5–6
#149 1965 Ford F-100 Pickup, light blue $5–6
#150 1951 Studebaker, green..........$5–6
#151 1958 Chevrolet Impala, yellow and white $5–6
#152 1978 Pontiac Trans Am, gold ...$5–6
#153 1951 Studebaker, maroon $5–6
#154 1969 Olds 442, blue $5–6
#155 1954 Chevrolet Corvette, blue and green $5–6
#156 1999 Ford F-350 Pickup, tan.....$5–6
#157 1940 Ford Pickup, black $5–6
#158 1970 Chevrolet Chevelle, white with black stripes $5–6
#159 1949 Buick Riviera, light green ..$5–6
#160 1970 Plymouth Superbird, blue ..$5–6
#161 1953 Ford F-100, Pickup, red ...$5–6
#162 1970 Dodge Superbee, white ...$5–6
#163 1969 Chevrolet Camaro, orange with white stripes $5–6
#164 1948 Ford F-1 Pickup, black......$5–6
#165 1999 Ford F-350 Pickup, red ...$5–6
#166 1958 Ford Edsel with top, yellow.$5–6
#167 1970 Dodge Superbee, purple..$5–6
#168 1987 Buick Grand National, black $5–6
#169 1955 Chevrolet Bel Air, white and gray...............................$5–6
#170 1969 Pontiac GTO "Judge," white $5–6
#171 1996 Dodge Viper, silver with white stripes..............................$5–6
#172 1999 Ford F-350 Pickup, black .$5–6
#173 1957 Chevrolet Corvette, red $5–6
#174 1959 Ford F-250 Pickup, black .$5–6
#175 1937 Ford Convertible, tan $5–6
#176 1957 Chevrolet Corvette, black ..$5–6
#177 1953 Ford F-100 Pickup, blue ...$5–6
#178 1959 Ford F-250 Pickup, green .$5–6
#179 1966 Chevrolet Nova, black.....$5–6
#180 1970 Buick GSX, yellow..........$5–6
#181 1987 Buick Grand National, silver $5–6
#182 1951 Studebaker, light green $5–6
#183 1970 Barracuda, lime green $5–6
#184 1957 Corvette, white $5–6
#185 1966 Chevy Nova, red...........$5–6
#186 1970 Buick GSX, white $5–6
#187 1960 Chevy Impala, red $5–6
#188 1953 Ford Pickup, black $5–6
#189 1960 Corvair, dark red $5–6
#190 1968 Firebird, black $5–6

#191 1968 Chevy Camaro, blue.......$5–6
#192 1965 Ford F-100 Pickup, yellow..$5–6
#193 1951 Studebaker, black...........$5–6
#194 1978 Pontiac Trans Am, silver....$5–6
#195 1999 Ford F-350, silver.........$5–6
#196 1970 Dodge Superbee, yellow .$5–6
#197 1960 1960 Chevy Corvair Monza, white...$5–6
#198 1957 Buick Century, red..........$5–6
#199 1971 Buick GSX, black $5–6
#200 1966 Pontiac GTO, teal $5–6
#201 1997 Ford Mustang, yellow $5–6
#202 1953 Ford F-100 Pickup, black .$5–6
#203 1970 Dodge Superbee, 2-tone warm gray..$5–6
#204 1960 Chevy Corvair, gray-green .$5–6
#205 1996 Pontiac Hurst Firebird, red with black top...$5–6
#206 1968 Pontiac Firebird, maroon ..$5–6
#207 1965 Ford Mustang, red with white top...$5–6
#208 1966 Pontiac GTO, black with gold stripe...$5–6
#209 1960 Chevy Corvair, blue $5–6
#210 1970 Dodge Superbee, metallic copper with black roof.......................$5–6

Racing Champions Mint Editon Gift Sets

Five-car sets with a special Racing Champions diecast emblem have been issued starting in September 1996. Retail price $25 per set:

Gift Set #1 (September 1996) includes:
  1996 Dodge Viper GTS, red
  1950 Chevrolet 3100 Pickup, black
  1968 Ford Mustang, blue
  1964 Chevrolet Impala, red
  1953 Chevrolet Corvette, white
Gift Set #2 (October 1996) includes:
  1996 Dodge Viper GTS, white
  1956 Ford Thunderbird, black
  1996 Dodge Ram, green
  1997 Ford F-150, bright teal blue
  1953 Chevrolet Corvette, red
Gift Set #3 (November 1996) includes:
  1963 Chevrolet Corvette, black
  1969 Pontiac GTO "Judge," blue
  1956 Ford Crown Victoria, pink
  1970 Plymouth Superbird, yellow
  1953 Chevrolet Corvette, black
Gift Set #4 (December 1996) includes:
  1950 Ford Coupe, black
  1956 Ford Crown Victoria, red
  1969 Olds 442 W-30, silver
  1964½ Ford Mustang, white
  1970 Plymouth Superbird, orange

Racing Champion Mint Editions "Hot Rods" (Issued October 1996)

#1 1950 Chevrolet 1500, lime green with yellow flames $8–10
#2 1957 Chevrolet Bel Air, black with orange and yellow flames $8–10
#3 1968 Ford Mustang Fastback GT, yellow with green flames......................$8–10

#4 1964 Chevrolet Impala, plum red with silver flames $8–10
#5 1997 Ford F-150, blue back, black front...$8–10
#6 1996 Dodge Ram, black with yellow, green, and pink slashed on the side, oversized tires............................$8–10
#7 1964.5 Ford Mustang, maroon ...$8–10
#8 1970 Plymouth Superbird, mustard yellow with black top $8–10
#13 1957 Chevy Bel Air, black with flames..$8–10

Racing Champions Hot Rod Magazine 3¼" Series

In March 1997 Hot Rod Magazine presents America's hottest street machines, each one produced in quantities of 19,997 and sold for $4 each.

March 1997 Issues
#1 1957 Chevrolet BelAir, red with hood scoop and silver trim, 1:61 scale $6–9
#2 1963 Corvette, fluorescent orange-red with yellow accents, "blown" engine, 1:53 scale.................$6–9
#3 1996 Dodge Ram, white with gold accents $6–9
#4 1969 Oldsmobile 442, metallic deep blue with silver and fuchsia accents, 1:58 scale................$6–9
#5 1964½ Ford Mustang, metallic fuchsia upper to purple to silver lower, 1:56 scale $6–9
#6 1969 GTO, metallic red with orange/white accents, 1:62 scale..........$6–9
April 1997 Issues
#7 1957 Chevrolet BelAir, magenta with hood scoop and silver trim, 1:61 scale $6–9
#8 1996 Dodge Ram, two-tone purple and silver $6–9
#9 1969 Oldsmobile 442, two-tone orange and black..................$6–9
#10 1969 Pontiac GTO, two-tone yellow and blue $6–9
#11 1996 Chevrolet Camaro, two-tone blue and yellow $6–9
#12 1970 Chevrolet Chevelle, two-tone maroon and silver..................$6–9

Racing Champions Hot Rod Magazine 1999

#133 '69 Pontiac GTO, red with gold accents......................................$5–7
#135 '66 Chevy Nova, red with white accents......................................$5–7
#136 '66 Pontiac GTO, maroon with gold and silver accents........................$5–7

Racing Champions Hot Rods 1:144 Scale

1957 Chevy $3
1950 Chevy Pick Up.......................$3
1950 Ford Coupe............................$3
1958 Chevy Impala $3
1964.5 Ford Mustang $3

1970 Plymouth Superbird $3
1996 Dodge Viper.............................$3
1996 Dodge Ram.............................$3
1963 Chevy Corvette $3
1932 Ford $3
1969 Pontiac GTO............................$3

Racing Champions Hot Rods 1:24 Scale

The officially licensed diecast vehicles of Hot Rod Magazine feature exacting detail, a continuing variety of models, custom paint schemes, full interiors, and realistic wheels.

#1 1962 Chevy, purple and metallic orange, August 1998 ....$10
#2 Pro Stock, black w/orange stripes, August 1998..................................$10
#3 1962 Chevy, red, August 1998 ......$10
#4 Pro Stock, metallic red, August 1998..................................$10
#5 1962 Chevy, black with flames, August 1998..................................$10
#6 Pro Stock, silver and purple with pink stripe, August 1998 ....$10
#7 1962 Chevy, magenta and yellow, September 1998 ....$10
#8 1955 Chevy Bel Air, red and white, September 1998 ....$10
#9 1962 Chevy, metallic blue with white scallops, September 1998 ....$10
#10 1955 Chevy Bel Air, dark purple, September 1998 ....$10
#11 1962 Chevy, purple, September 1998..................................$10
#12 1955 Chevy Bel Air, red, orange, blue, and silver, September 1998 ....$10
#13 1962 Chevy, red with flames, October 1998..................................$10
#14 1955 Chevy Bel Air, black with flames, October 1998..................................$10
#15 Pro Street Firebird, two-tone with flames, October 1998..................................$10
#16 1955 Chevy Bel Air, blue, October 1998..................................$10
#17 Pro Street Firebird, metallic pink and silver, October 1998 ....$10
#18 1955 Chevy Bel Air, black and white, October 1998..................................$10
#19 1955 Chevy Bel Air, metallic gray and tan, November 1998 ....$10
#20 1940 Ford Coupe, black with flames, November 1998 ....$10
#21 1955 Chevy Bel Air, metallic pink and silver, November 1998..................$10
#22 1940 Ford Coupe, red, November 1998..................................$10
#23 1940 Ford Coupe, metallic orange and silver, November 1998 ....$10
#24 1940 Ford Coupe, yellow and orange, November 1998 ....$10
#25 1955 Chevy, purple and white, December 1998..................................$10
#26 1940 Ford Coupe, red with flames, December 1998..................................$10

#27 1962 Chevy Bel Air, turquoise and magenta, December 1998............$10

#28 1955 Chevy, metallic green and pearl, December 1998 ....$10

#29 1940 Ford Coupe, dark red, December 1998 ....$10

#30 1962 Chevy Bel Air, white with pink flames, December 1998 ....$10

Racing Champions Police USA, vintage police cars in approximately 1:64 scale, 1998

#1 1956 Ford Victoria, Colorado State Police...................................$5

#2 1949 Mercury, Florida Highway Patrol.$5

#3 1968 Plymouth, Los Angeles Police Department................................$5

#4 1957 Chevrolet Bel Air, Washington State Police...............................$5

#5 1956 Ford Victoria, Alaska State Troopers.....................................$5

#6 1949 Mercury, Missouri Highway Patrol......................................$5

#7 1958 Chevrolet Impala, Michigan State Police...................................$5

#8 1950 Ford Coupe, New York City Police Department................................$5

#9 1957 Chevrolet Bel Air Military Police.$5

#10 1958 Chevrolet Impala, Los Angeles County Sheriff............................$5

#11 1932 Ford, Arizona Highway Patrol.$5

#12 1964 Chevrolet Impala, Iowa Highway Patrol..$5

#13 1968 Plymouth, Kansas Highway Patrol..$5

#14 1950 Ford Coupe, Nevada Highway Patrol..$5

#15 1960 Chevrolet Impala, Arkansas State Police...................................$5

#16 1955 Chevrolet Bel Air, Idaho State Police...................................$5

#17 1932 Ford, New Jersey State Police .$5

#18 1960 Chevrolet Impala, Ohio Highway Patrol..$5

#19 1997 Ford Mustang D.A.R.E. Car....$5

#20 1960 Plymouth, Chicago Police.......$5

#21 1956 Ford Victoria, New Brunswick Safety Patrol...............................$5

#22 1955 Chevrolet Bel Air, Toronto Metro Police...................................$5

#23 1996 Chevrolet Camaro, Royal Canadian Mounted Police $5

#24 1968 Chevrolet Camaro D.A.R.E. Car...$5

#25 1957 Chevrolet Bel Air, Shelton, Connecticut, Police Department...............$5

#26 1999 Ford F-350, Causeway Police Department................................$5

#27 1957 Chevrolet Bel Air, Texas Highway Patrol..$5

#28 1950 Ford Coupe, Georgia State Patrol...$5

#29 1955 Chevrolet Bel Air, Wyoming Highway Patrol...............................$5

#30 1958 Ford Edsel, Milwaukee, Wisconsin, Fire Department.......................$5

#31 1956 Ford Victoria, Sacramento, California, Police..............................$5

#32 1964 Chevrolet Impala, Ankeny, Iowa, Police.............................$5

#33 1957 Chevrolet Bel Air, St. Paul, Minnesota, Police..........................$5

#34 1960 Chevrolet Impala, Pennsylvania State Police...............................$5

#35 1969 Oldsmobile, San Francisco Police...$5

#36 1948 Ford Pickup, Illinois State Police...$5

#37 1970 Barracuda D.A.R.E. Car $5

#38 1950 Ford Coupe, Michigan Police.$5

#39 1955 Chevrolet Bel Air, Indiana State Police...$5

#40 1968 Plymouth, Detroit, Michigan, Police...$5

#41 1996 Chevrolet Camaro, New York State Police...............................$5

#42 1966 Chevrolet Nova, St. Louis Metro Police...$5

#43 1957 Chevrolet Bel Air, Colma, California Fire Department $5

#44 1970 Chevrolet Chevelle, Dallas, Texas Police.............................$5

#45 1949 Mercury, Oklahoma Highway Patrol...$5

#46 1966 Chevrolet Nova, Kansas City, Missouri Police $5

#47 1964 Plymouth Sparta, Mississippi Police...$5

#48 1960 Chevrolet Impala, North Dakota State Patrol...............................$5

#49 1960 Chevrolet Corvair, New Orleans Police...$5

#50 1987 Buick Grand National D.A.R.E. Car...$5

#51 1960 Chevy Camaro, Washington, DC Metro Police..........................$5

#52 1999 Ford F-350, Tuscaloosa County, AL Sheriff............................$5

#53 1958 Chevy Impala, Grinnell, IA Police..$5

#54 1964 Chevy Impala, Vermilion County, IL Sheriff................................

#55 1960 Plymouth, Suffolk County, NY Police...$5

#56 1957 Chevy Bel Air, White Settlement, TX Police.............................$5

#57 1968 Plymouth, NY City Police........$5

#58 1956 Ford Victoria, Harwood Heights, IL Police..............................$5

#59 1996 Chevy Camaro, KS Highway Patrol...$5

#60 1949 Mercury, CA Highway Patrol..$5

#61 1932 Ford Coupe, CA Highway Patrol...$5

#62 1968 Plymouth, Nassau County, NY Police...$5

#63 1987 Buick Grand National, Bernalillo County, NM Police.......................$5

#64 1996 Dodge Viper, Washtenaw County, MI Sheriff................................$5

#65 1956 Chevy Nomad, Ocean County, NJ Sheriff................................$5

#66 1996 Dodge Ram, Honolulu Harbor Police...$5

#67 1949 Buick, Dade County, FL Police.$5

#68 1998 Chevy Corvette D.A.R.E. Car..$5

#69 1950 Ford Coupe, Tennessee Highway Patrol...$5

#70 1957 Chevy Bel Air, Chicago, IL Police...$5

#71 1958 Chevy Impala, Benton County, IN Sheriff................................$5

#72 1986 Chevy El Camino, Reno, NV Police...$5

#73 1996 Chevy Camaro, Utah Highway Patrol...$5

#74 1970 Buick, Lorain County, Ohio Sheriff...$5

#75 1997 Ford F-150, US Border Patrol..$5

#76 1966 Pontiac GTO, Philadelphia, PA Police...$5

#77 1968 Plymouth, VA State Police $5

#78 1950 Ford Coupe, IL State Police.....$5

#79 1955 Chevy Bel Air, Indianapolis, IN Police...$5

#80 1997 Chevrolet Corvette, Florida Highway Patrol $5

#81 1966 Chevrolet, Nova Berkeley, California, Police..............................$5

#82 1959 Ford F-250 Pickup, New Mexico State Police...............................$5

#83 1996 Chevrolet Camaro, Wisconsin State Police...............................$5

#84 1964 Chevy Impala, Frohna, MO Police...$5

#85 1951 Studebaker, South Bend, IN Police...$5

#86 1980 Ford Bronco, Chicago IL Police..$5

#87 1956 Chevy Nomad, Albuquerque, NM Police..............................$5

#88 1950 Ford Coupe, Maryland State Police...$5

#89 1992 Chevy Caprice, WV State Police...$5

#90 1992 Chevy Caprice D.A.R.E. Car..$5

#91 1957 Buick, St. Louis County, MO Police...$5

#92 1996 Chevy Camaro, Chevrolet Special Service $5

#93 1940 Ford Sedan Delivery, Chicago Police...$5

#94 1999 Ford F-350 Pick-Up, Delaware State Police...............................$5

#95 1996 Dodge Ram Pick-Up, Maine State Police...............................$5

#96 1992 Chevy Caprice, Dallas, TX Police...$5

#97 1986 Chevy El Camino, Salt Lake City, UT Police..............................$5

Racing Champions Fire Rescue U.S.A.

New for 1999, this series offers authentic fire & rescue vehicles from 1930s to 1990s.

- #1 '56 Chevy Nomad, Riverside, IL Fire Dept. $5
- #2 '86 Chevy El Camino, St. Louis, MO Fire Dept. $5
- #3 '99 Ford F-350 Pickup, Westchester, IL Fire Dept. $5
- #4 '97 Ford F-150 Tow Truck, Boston, MA Fire Dept. $5
- #5 '50 Ford Coupe, Iron Mountain, MI Fire Dept. $5
- #6 '60 Chevy Corvair, Portland, ME Fire Dept. $5
- #7 '92 Chevy Caprice, Elmwood Park, IL Fire Dept. $5
- #8 1997 Ford F-150 Pickup, Huntington Beach, CA Lifeguard $5
- #9 1980 Ford Bronco, Grand Chute, WI Fire Rescue $5
- #10 1999 Ford F-350, New York City Fire Dept. $5
- #11 1956 Chevy Nomad, Chicago Fire Dept. $5
- #12 1953 Ford F-100, Santa Clara County, CA Central Fire Dist. $5
- #13 1975 Chevy Van, Appleton, WI Fire Dept. $5
- #14 1949 Mercury, Homewood, IL Fire Dept. $5

Racing Champions Hot Country Steel, 1:64 scale cars featuring stars of country music

- #1 LeAnn Rimes 1996 Dodge Viper GTS $10–12
- #2 Hank Williams Jr. 1949 Buick Riviera $6–8
- #3 Alan Jackson 1997 Ford F-150 ......$6–8
- #4 Alan Jackson 1937 Ford Coupe $6–8
- #5 Hank Williams Jr. 1964 Mustang ...$6–8
- #6 Billy Dean 1957 Ranchero............$6–8
- #7 Tim McGraw 1969 Chevy Camaro.$6–8
- #8 Billy Dean 1964 Ford Mustang $6–8
- #9 Alan Jackson 1956 Ford Thunderbird..$6–8
- #10 Hank Williams Jr. 1959 Cadillac Convertible $6–8
- #11 Billy Dean 1966 Chevy Nova $6–8
- #12 Alan Jackson 1940 Ford Truck $6–8
- #13 Hank Williams 1940 Ford Truck...$6–8
- #14 LeAnn Rimes 1941 Willy's Gasser..$6–8
- #15 Hank Williams, Jr. 1941 Willy's Gasser $6–8
- #16 Billy Dean 1996 Plymouth Prowler ..$6–8
- #17 Tim McGraw 1969 Camaro $6–8
- #18 Hank Williams, Jr. 1949 Mercury.$6–8
- #19 Randy Travis 1940 Ford Truck $6–8
- #20 LeAnn Rimes 1963 Corvette........$6–8
- #21 Travis Tritt 1978 Pontiac Trans Am ..$6–8
- #22 Alan Jackson 1940 Ford Truck $6–8

Racing Champions Hot Rockin' Steel, 1:64 scale cars selected by celebrated rock stars. Production limited to 25,000 each.

- Kiss $5
- Ozzie Ozbourne $5
- Sammy Hagar $5
- Stevie Ray Vaughan $5
- The Beach Boys............$5
- The Blues Brothers $5

Racing Champions Dukes of Hazard

- "General Lee"............$6–8
- Boss Hogg's Cadillac............$6–8
- Rosco's Police Car $6–8
- Daisy's Jeep $6–8
- Cooter's Tow Truck............$6–8
- Uncle Jesse's Pickup $6–8
- Enos' Police Car $6–8
- Daisy's Plymouth $6–8
- Sgt. Little's Police Car............$6–8

Racing Champions Stock Rods

"What if your favorite drivers traded in their stock cars to race in a classic hot rod from the past?" That's the unlikely premise in which Racing Champions introduces their line of Stock Rods, "Today's top drivers and team graphics on yesterday's favorite hot rod customized vehicles." Depite this obvious ploy by Racing Champions to sell more models by offering a new series from existing castings, it will probably work. The models are compellingly attractive. Below is listed the complete line-up as of November 1997. Stock Rods retail for $4–5 each.

- #1 Terry Labonte #5 Kellogg's '57 Chevrolet Bel Air $5
- #2 Bill Elliott #94 McDonald's '68 Ford Mustang............$5
- #3 Mark Martin #6 Valvoline '97 Ford Mustang............$5
- #4 Robert Pressley #29 Cartoon Network (Scooby) '63 Chevrolet Corvette $5
- #5 Ted Musgrave #16 Primestar '32 Ford Coupe $5
- #6 Jeff Burton #99 Exide '50 Ford Coupe $5
- #7 Bobby Labonte #18 Interstate Batteries '69 Pontiac GTO $5
- #8 Ricky Craven #25 Hendrick '58 Chevrolet Impala $5
- #9 Darrell Waltrip #17 Western Auto '57 Chevrolet............$5
- #11 Derrike Cope #36 Skittles '96 Firebird $5
- #12 Ricky Rudd #10 Tide '50 Ford $5
- #13 Rick Mast #75 Remington '68 Ford Mustang............$5
- #14 Ricky Craven #25 Hendrick '57 Chevrolet............$5
- #15 Jeff Green #29 Tom & Jerry '64 Impala $5
- #16 Bill Elliott #94 Mac Tonight '56 Ford Victoria............$5
- #17 Mark Martin #6 Valvoline '32 Ford Coupe $5
- #18 Rusty Wallace #2 Penske '64 Ford Mustang............$5

- #19 Ted Musgrave #16 Primestar '64 Ford Mustang............$5
- #20 Jeff Burton #99 Exide '68 Ford Mustang.$5
- #21 Darrell Waltrip #17 Western Auto '58 Chevrolet Impala $5
- #22 Ricky Rudd #10 Tide '32 Ford Coupe............$5
- #23 Rick Mast #75 Remington '56 Ford Victoria............$5
- #24 Steve Grissom #41 Hedrick '86 Chevrolet El Camino SS............$5
- #25 Bill Elliott #94 Mac Tonight '50 Ford Coupe............$5
- #26 Glen Allen #99 Luxaire '49 Buick.....$5
- #27 Dennis Setzer #43 Lance Snacks '57 Chevrolet Convertible $5
- #28 Bill Elliott #94 McDonald's '49 Mercury............$5
- #29 Ricky Craven #2 Raybestos '58 Chevrolet Impala $5
- #30 Sterling Marlin #4 Kodak '53 Chevrolet Corvette $5
- #31 Jeff Green #29 Cartoon Network '57 Chevrolet............$5
- #32 Joe Nemechek #42 Bell South '68 Camaro $5
- #33 Ernie Irvan #28 Texaco – Havoline '57 Ford Ranchero............$5

Racing Champions Eightieth Indianapolis 500 Commemorative

- Dodge Viper GTS Pace Car, blue with white racing stripes, "80th Indianapolis 500, May 26, 1996" $10-15
- Racing Champions Transporters, 1:64 scale, many liveries............$10 each
- Racing Champions Limited Edition Transporters, 1:64 scale, many liveries ....$20 each
- Racing Champions Nascar Stock Cars, 1:64 scale, many liveries............$4 each
- Racing Champions World of Outlaws, 1:24 scale sprint racers, many liveries ....$10 each
- Racing Champions World of Outlaws, 1:64 scale sprint racers, many liveries ....$4 each
- Racing Champions Street Wheels, 1998–1999, inexpensive castings of popular cars accented in wild trim and colors and flashy chrome wheels............$1 each

Racing Collectables Club of America, Inc. (RCCA)

6600 Highlands Parkway, Suite B
Smyrna, GA 30082
phone: 404-333-0305
fax: 404-333-0265

Racing Collectibles, Inc. (RCI) models are issued by the Racing Collectables Club of America, a division of Action Performance. Their first issues were made by Revell in 1:64 scale. Eventually RCCA was able to begin producing their own models.

Revell has continued producing the 1:64 scale NASCAR models under their own name, and Action Performance. Revell was recently purchased by Action Performance.

Racing Collectables, Inc. (RCI) (see Action Performance Companies)

Radar

Radar info comes from Ma Collection, according to Harvey Goranson. He reports that Radar in Portugal made plastic 1:43–1:45 toys of varying quality and made from 1960 to 1970.

BMW Isetta	$12
Citroën 2CV	$12
Double-Deck Bus	$12
Mercedes 300SL Gullwing, 1:43	$12
OSCA racer	$12
Porsche 550 Spyder, 1:43	$12
TramCar with trailer, 1951	$12

Radon (also see Agat)

These are 1:43 scale diecast made in Russia and converted by G+A Models of the Ukraine for Henri Orange of Paris. Most recently, Radon has been reorganized to create the new company of Agat.

Lada Niva Police Ukraine	price unknown

R.A.E.

R.A.E. Models
Unit 2
Service Road Off Corrie Road
Addlestone, Surrey
KT15 2LP Great Britain
phone: 01932 846298
fax: 01932 853292

Established in 1975 primarily to offer a general modelmaking service for industrial product development, R.A.E Models is located South of London, close to Junction 11 on the M25 Motorway.

Bentley Corniche Convertible	$140
Bentley T Series	$140
Jaguar XK120	$79
Jaguar XK150	$99
Lea France Tourer	$100
MG 179 Record Car	$80
MG A	$80
MG B Roadster, 1:20	$129
MG C-Type Tourer, open, 1:43	$129
MG Midget	$90
MG RV8 Convertible, top down, 1:43	$129
MG SA Convertible	$140
MG SA Saloon	$140
MG TVR 3000M, 1:43	$119
Rolls-Royce Corniche Convertible	$140
Rolls-Royce Silver Shadow	$150
Rolls-Royce Silver Shadow II	$150
Triumph TR6, 1:43	$49

Raf

Raf represents 1:43 scale models from Russia.

2203 Minibus standard	$11
2203 Minibus taxi	$11
2203 Minibus traffic police	$11
2203 Minibus ambulance	$11
2203 Minibus fire	$11
2203 Minibus post office	$11
2203 Minibus books	$11
2203 Minibus wth symbols	$11

Ralstoy

The Ralston Toy and Novelty Company, or Ralstoy, was founded in Ralston, Nebraska, in 1939. Combining surviving molds and dies from Best Toy Co. of Manhattan, Kansas, and Kansas Toy Co. of Clifton, Kansas, the former mayor of Ralston, Dr. Felix Despecher, started producing inexpensive slush-mold toys. When Dr. Despecher died and World War II dominated the need for lead and other metals, successor Paul Massey turned to making wooden toys.

When the war was over, the first Ralstoy diecast models were produced. Some, but not all, Ralstoys have the Ralstoy name on them, due to the inheritance of dies from the other companies. Most recent models have been produced as promotional items for moving companies and others.

Open Trailer Truck ....$?

1 1982 Chevrolet Step Van	$18
3 Tanker Truck and Trailer, 7¾"	$45
23 Muzzle Loading Cannon on Wheeled Platform	$25
32 Aircraft	$15
42 Dump Truck, 3⅜"	$35
48 Tractor, 3"	$25
74 Army Tank, 2¼", "US Army"	$25
101 Large Transporter with #74 Tank & #32 Aircraft	$65

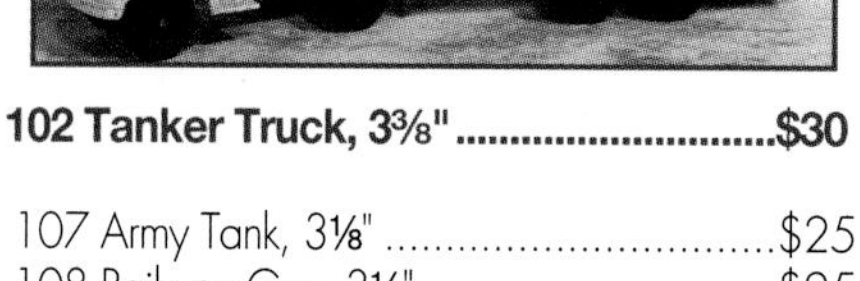

102 Tanker Truck, 3⅜" $30

107 Army Tank, 3⅛"	$25
108 Railway Gun, 3¼"	$25
Oldsmobile Sedan	$150
Phillips 66 Tanker	$75
Safety-Kleen Van	$30–45

Ralstoy Moving Vans, 1:64, 8½"

Allied Van Lines	$30
Atlas Van Lines	$30
Bekins Van Lines	$30
Global Van Lines	$30
Greyhound Van Lines	$30
Lyon Van Lines	$30
Mayflower Moving Van	$30
Neptune Van Lines	$30
20 North American Van Lines	$30
Red Ball Van Lines	$30
Republic Van Lines	$30
Stevens Van Lines	$30
United Van Lines	$30
Wheaton Van Lines	$30

Rami

Les Retrospectives Automobiles Miniature, known variously as R.A.M.I., RAMI, and Rami, are model miniatures representative of actual cars on display at the Musee Francais de l' Automobile (French Automobile Museum) near Lyons, and other museums.

Since 1958, Rami has produced an exceptional assortment of vintage and antique car replicas. Production continued until 1980. No additional models have been offered since.

1 Renault 1907 Taxi De La Marne, 3½", 1958	$50
2 De Dion-bouton 1900 Vis-A-Vis, 2⅛", 1958–1970	$50
2 Motobloc 1902 Tonneau, 2⅝", 1971	$50
3 Lion-Peugeot 1907 Double Phaeton, 2¾", 1958	$50
4 Citroën 1924 5CV Roadster, 2⅞", 1958	$50
5 De Dion 1900 Cab, 2⅛", 1958	$50
6 Bugatti 1928 Type 35, 3⅜", 1959	$50
7 Citroën 1925 B2 Limousine, 3½", 1959	$50
8 Sizaire & Naudin 1906 Racing Car, 2⅞", 1959	$50
9 Rochet-Schneider 1895 Vis-A-Vis, 2¾", 1960	$50
10 Hispano-Suiza 1934 Town Car, 3¾", 1960	$50
11 Gobron-Brillie 1899 Double Phaeton, 2½", 1961	$50
12 Gauthier-Wehrle 1897 Cab, 2⅜", 1961	$50
13 Packard 1912 Landaulet, 3½", 1962	$55
14 Peugeot 1898 Coupe, 3", 1962	$50
15 Ford 1908 Model T, 3¼", 1963	$50
16 Ford 1907 Model R Tourer, 3¼", 1963	$50
17 Panhard & Levassor 1908 La Marquise, 3⅞", 1964	$50
18 Panhard & Levassor 1899 Tonneau Ballon, 3⅛", 1964	$50
19 Hautier 1898 Electric Taxi, 3½", 1964	$55
20 Delaunay-Belleville 1904, 3⅜", 1964	$50
21 Georges Richard 1902 Tonneau, 2⅝", 1964	$50
22 Scotte 1892 Steam Car, 2¾", 1965	$55
23 Renault 1900 Tonneau, 2¾", 1965	$50
24 Lorraine-Dietrich 1911, 3⅝", 1965	$50

25 Panhard & Levassor 1895 Tonneau, 2½",
   1965 ....$50
26 Delahaye 1904 Phaeton, 2⅞", 1965 ....$50
27 Audibert & Lavirotte 1898, 2¾", 1966...$50
28 Leon bollee 1911 Double Berline, 3¾",
   1966 ....$50
29 S.P.A. 1912 Sports Sar, 4", 1966 ....$50
30 Amedee Bollee 1878 La Mancelle, 3⅝",
   1966 ....$50
31 Luc Court 1901 Racing Car, 2¾",
   1967 ....$50
32 Brasier 1908 Landaulet, 3¼", 1967 ......$50
33 Berliet 1910 Limousine, 3¾", 1968 ......$50
34 Mieusset 1903 Runabout, 2⅝", 1968 ...$50
35 De Dion-Bouton 1902 Racing Car, 3¼",
   1968 ....$50
36 Lacroix De La Ville 1898, 3¼", 1968 ....$50
37 Delage 1932 Torpedo, 4⅝", 1968 ......$50
38 Mercedes 1927 SSK, 3⅞", 1969.........$55

Rapide (see Modelauto)

Rapitoy

The most interesting model listed in the Rapitoy of Argentina assortment is a Mercedes van with "Matchbox" livery. It is uncommon for one toymaker to promote another, but this seems to be a rare exception... unless Rapitoy put the Matchbox name on the model to convince the buyer into believing it was a Matchbox toy.

Mercedes Van "Matchbox," 1:43 ....$17
Mercedes Van "Ferrari," 1:43 ....$17
Mercedes Van "Fargopan," 1:43 ....$17
Ford F-100 Pickup, 1:64 ....$4
Dodge Charger Show Car, 1:64 ....$4
Siva Spyder, 1:64 ....$4
Mercedes-Benz 350SL, top up, 1:64 ....$4

Ra-Ro

Of these 1:43 scale models, produced in 1948 from Milan, Italy, four are known. Such models are also identified as Cisitalia, Osca, and Stanguellini models. Obviously, easy identification requires more data.

Alfa Romeo, 3¾" $75
Ferrari, 3⅞" $75
Maserati, 3¾" $75
Veritas, 3¾" $75

Rasant

Frank Wagner first inquired about Rasant of Germany in an e-mail inquiry. The model he found is of a Ford Taunus that looks similar to a 1961 Ford Thunderbird. The base of the model reads "Ford Taunus 17M, RASANT, Made in Germany." The vintage and style of the car raises the question of why the base is not imprinted with "East Germany" or "West Germany" since it was apparently produced in the midst of the Cold War and a divided Germany.

Mr. Wagner later wrote that at the beginning of the 1960s, the German toy company Rasant was founded in Gunzenhausen. They

wanted to produce slot car models like the Faller AMS system. In 1964 they presented their system with models in near HO scale. The system was not accepted by the market. They changed the system in the way that the cars could be driven on any slot car system with 16mm contacts. But that failed again, so they produced their cars as non-slot-cars. In 1969, Rasant had to stop production. Mr. Wagner's Ford Taunus represents one of those last non-slot car models produced.

The wheels are spun metal. The black tires appear to be hard rubber. Several versions of some models include German Fire Chief (feuerwehr), Street Works (strassenwacht), Police (polizei), Post, and Ambulance (Ambulanz). Much of the information on these models was extracted by Frank Wagner from a German-language website at www.screenhouse.de/vincent/slotcar/sub/rasant/rasant01.html.

BMW 2000 ....$15–$35
Cadillac Fleetwood ....$15–$35
Ford Taunus 17M, red, 2½" (65mm) ...$15–$35
Mercedes-Benz 220 SE ....$15–$35
Mercedes-Benz 250 SE ....$15–$35
Opel Diplomat ....$15–$35
Opel Kapitan ....$15–$35

RCCA (see Racing Collectables, Inc.)

RCI (see Racing Collectables, Inc.)

Reader's Digest

Along with various offers from Reader's Digest come special promotional gifts. Several of these gifts are miniature vintage cars, trucks, and airplanes. These are not generally available anywhere else, but Toy Liquidators has obtained a few of these sets for resale. The manufacturer is not indicated, but they are made in China.

Collector's Set of Classic Car Miniatures, $3 per set

Each package includes six boxed vintage 1:87 scale cars, numbered on base, in each set. Outer box has full-color photos of each model around the four sides. Inside is a 5" x 7½" descriptive sheet that provides details of each model. While these models are inexpensively made and lacking in accuracy and detail, they are a charming set nonetheless. Made in Macau, copyright 1989, The Readers Digest Association Inc., Pleasantville, NY 10570.

No. 301 1901 Fiat Modello 8 CV $1
No. 302 1906 Rolls-Royce $1
No. 303 1907 Peugeot $1
No. 304 1910 Ford Model T $1
No. 305 1912 Simplex.........................$1
No. 306 1914 Vauxhall........................$1

Collector's Set of Classic Trucks, $5 per set

A set of four mostly plastic vintage trucks about the size of Matchbox Models of Yesteryear (1:43 scale), packaged in two boxes inside of a larger box, with note included that says "Your FREE Gift... along with our thanks for ordering from Reader's Digest." Made in China.

1910 Water Wagon $1
1912 Model T Ambulance $1
1912 Model T Tanker..........................$1
1918 Delivery Van $1

1939 Ward LaFrance, high speed $1

Collector's Set of Miniature Biplanes, $5 per set

A set of four diecast miniature biplanes, each with 3" wingspan, individually boxed and packaged in a larger box describing each model. A note inside the box says "Your Free Gift ...along with our thanks for ordering Reader's Digest music." Made in China.

1918 British S.E. 5A $1
1918 Curtiss JN-4D Jenny $1
1928 Boeing PT-17 Kaydet $1
1928 Boeing P-12E $1

Real Cars (see Esci)

Real Wheels (see Ja-Ru)

Realtoy

Realtoy International Limited
Wah Fung Industrial Centre
Kwai Fung Rd.
N. T. Hong Kong
China

In just the past few years, Realtoy has made a dramatic appearance in the form of some exceptional playsets. Sets feature from 25 to 75 pieces which include trees, outdoor furniture, human and animal figures as well as a great assortment of attractively decorated vehicles and a big playmat. Interestingly, many models bear a striking resemblance to Matchbox, Hot Wheels, and Majorettes, some even appearing to be outright knockoffs. Sets have been available from Wal-Mart, Toys "R" Us, and other retailers.

Realistic

Realistic toys are cast aluminum vehicles manufactured in Freeport, Illinois, during the late 1940s and early 1950s. Some models used the original molds from Arcade cast-iron toys.

1939 Studebaker President Yellow Cab, 8¼"	$100
Greyhound Bus, Silversides, 8¾"	$100
Trailways Bus, 8¾"	$100

Record

Record models are listed as 1:43 scale vehicles.

1 1952 Chevrolet 2-Door Hardtop	$55
2 1952 Chevrolet Fastback Coupe	$55
3 1952 Chevrolet 4-Door Sedan	$55
4 1952 Chevrolet Convertible	$55
99 Opel Ascona "Bastos"	$55
102 1984 Ferrari GTO	$55
103 Ferrari Testarossa	$55
111 Ferrari 365 GTB	$55

Redbox (also see Zee Toys/Zylmex)

200 Fifth Avenue
New York, NY 10010
Hithercroft Ind Estate, Lesterway
or
WallingFord, Oxon, OX10 9th, U.K.

In 1997, Zyll Enterprise, known for Zylmex and Zee Toys, was purchased by Redbox. Selected Zylmex and Zee Toys are now being reissued with the new Redbox brand on the base and on the box. In July 1997, Redbox started selling the former Zyll 1:24 scale diecast vehicles formerly sold as Z-Wheels. Since then, more Zee Toys have been showing up in multipack and single-pack sets. Here is the current address for Redbox as indicated on package:

Chrysler PT Cruiser, 1:24 .... $10

Mako Shark, 1:18 .... $15

1953 Chevrolet 3100 Wrecker, 1:32 .... $10

1949 Ford $10

GMC pick-up, 3"	$1
Chevy 454SS pick-up, 3"	$1
Chevy Blazer, 3"	$1
GMC Jimmy, 3"	$1
Ford Explorer, 3"	$1
'57 Chevy, 1:24, 3"	$10

Reen Replica

One of the previously unknown brands from Japan, Reen Replica models are likely produced in the early to mid-sixties, according to collector Robert Speerbrecher (see Silver Pet). Models are of moderate detail and of unknown scale but are probably around 1:43 scale.

1937 Nissan 70 Sedan	$20–25
1957 4-Door Sedan, Japanese Car	$20–25

Rei

Rei 1:43 scale models are Schuco models of Germany made in Brazil. Models of other scales are produced for Rei by Matsuda.

Collector Brian Willoughby of Murray, Kentucky, reports that in addition to the 1:43 scale models, Rei also produced several of the former 1:66 scale Schuco models. Willoughby says, "If you are familiar with the original Schuco castings, the [Rei models] were packaged in the same little plastic boxes with the same piece of foam in the bottom to secure the model. All traces of the Schuco name and the wording "Made in Germany" were removed from the models and the boxes (which had the Schuco name molded into the top and "Made in Germany" molded into the bottom). I actually have a small catalog that came with one of the 1:66 REIs I have that lists some of the models. I say "some" due to the fact that I have other REI/Schuco castings that are not illustrated in the brochure."

"Furthermore," continues Willoughby, "Rei also recycled several Siku dies during the 1970s. I don't know what all they re-issued from the former Siku line, though they definitely produced their own rendition of Siku's Ford Capri. There are others, though I don't know exactly which ones."

Alfa Romeo F1 "Parmalat," 1:43	$18
Audi 100 Coupe, 1:66 (REI/Schuco)	$6
Lamborghini Cheetah Fire Chief, 1:43	$18
Lotus F1 "JPS," 1:43	$18
Peterbilt Semi Van "Coca-Cola," 1:43	$18
Peterbilt Semi Van "Transbras," 1:43	$18
Peterbilt Semi Van "Esso," 1:43	$18
Peterbilt Semi Van "Petrobras," 1:43	$18
Peterbilt Semi Van "Mobil," 1:43	$18
Peterbilt Semi Van "Shell," 1:43	$18
Peterbilt Semi Van "Alfa Romeo," 1:43	$18
Peterbilt Semi Van "Ferrari," 1:43	$18
Peterbilt Semi Van "JPS," 1:43	$18
Peterbilt Semi Van "Marlboro," 1:43	$18
Peterbilt Semi Van "Renault," 1:43	$18
Volvo Bus, 1:43	$18
Mercedes-Benz C-111, 1:43	$8–12
Toyota Celica LB2000 GT, 1:64 (REI/Matsuda)	$6

Remco

Since about 1955, Remco has represented a major force in the toy market. Remco "Tuff Ones" are durable diecast and plastic toys most recently associated with Road Champs, Inc. and Jakks Pacific, Inc., according to packaging on models issued with a 1998 copyright. Value remains at or near retail on all but the oldest Remco issues generally made of pressed metal and plastic, often with battery-operated working parts.

Renaissance

Renaissance models are 1:24 scale Ferrari "transkits" and decals, and 1:43 scale hand-made masterpieces, assembled from white metal, resin, plated, photoetched, and machine parts, and produced in genuine Ferrari colors, with production limited to 500 pieces of each model worldwide. The brand represents Ferrari from 1950 to 1996.

R1B Ferrari 250 California Spyder, available in red, blue, dark red, silver, or brown, 1:43	$695
R2 Ferrari 275 GTB/4 Spyder NART, available in red, yellow, black, metallic red, or silver, 1:43	$695
R3 1958 Ferrari 250 Testarossa Le Mans 58, red #14, 1:43	$695

Renwal

Usually associated with plastic toys, Renwal produced a few diecast models that featured crude paint jobs and rough castings. Nevertheless, the rarity of these toys establishes a high value on specimens. Here is a sample listing.

Renwal 3" Series

143 Sedan	$32
145 Fire Truck	$24
146 Hook & Ladder	$24
147 Convertible	$24

144 Coupe $32

148 Gasoline Truck $24

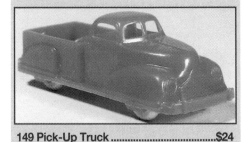

149 Pick-Up Truck $24

150 Racer..................................$48

Other Renwal Models

8001 Ferrari Racer...........................$160
8002 Maserati Racer $160
8003 Pontiac Convertible...................$120
8004 Plymouth Convertible................$120
8005 Chevrolet Sedan $120
8006 Ford Sedan $120
8007 Sedan $72
8008 Gasoline Truck..........................$72
8009 Racer......................................$96
8010 Delivery Truck $72
8011 Pick-up Truck............................$72
8012 Hot Rod $72
8013 Jeep $72
8014 Fire Truck $72
8015 Convertible..............................$72
8020 Futuristic Two-Door Coupe $24
8021 Gasoline Truck..........................$24
8022 Ladder Fire Truck $24
8023 Ford Sunliner Convertible.............$36
8028 Ford Victoria Hardtop $36
8039 Pick-Up Truck $24
8040 Pumper Fire Truck $24
8041 Speed King Racer $48

Renwal 4" Series

Convertible $96
Gasoline Truck $72
Coupe...$72
City Bus...$72

Replex

Replex of France produces scale models of military vehicles, commercial trucks, emergency vehicles, and heavy equipment. Manufacturer's address is: Replex Maquettes de Collection en Metal, Sapois 88120, Vagney, France. Diecast Miniatures offers nearly the entire line of Replex models.

100 Shelter Euromissile, olive drab, 1:50.....$38
101 Renault RVI TRM 2000 Military Transport, 1:43 ....$44
102 AMX 30 Euromissile Tank, 1:50..........$38
103 SPZ Euromissile, 1:50 ....$38
104 Liebherr 981 Shovel, 1:53 ....$54
105 TechnoCar/BalkanCar Forklift, 1:25....$28
106 International Harvester Combine, 1:43 .$48
107 Fenwick Forklift, 1:25 ....$28
108 Sides 2000 Paris Airport, red, 1:43.....$44
109 International Harvester 844 Farm Tractor, 1:43 ....$14
110 Sides 2000 Doubai Airport, yellow, 1:43 ....$44
111 Poclain 1000 Track Excavator, 1:50 ...$64
112 PPM Crane, 1:50 ....$58
113 Poclain 1000 Track Shovel, 1:50........$64
114 1919 Magirus Deutz Bus, 1:43 ....$44
115 Volvo F 614 Cab & Chassis, 1:43 ......$44
116 Sides 2000 Geneva Airport, red, 1:43..$44
118 Magirus Deutz 90/13 Cargo Transport "Panzani," 1:43 ....$44
119 1925 Magirus Deutz Ladder Fire Truck, 1:43 ....$44
120 Mack 200 American Stake Truck, 1:43 ....$42
122 Renault RVI S 170 Tractor and Chassis, 1:43 ....$44
123 Renault RVI S 170 Commercial Transport, 1:43 ....$44
124 Mack 200 Commercial Transport "MIKO," 1:43 ....$44
127 Iveco 90.13 Commercial Transport, 1:43 ....$44
129 DAF FA 1300 Tractor and Chassis, 1:43 ....$44
130 Renault RVI Commercial Transport "Danza," 1:43 ....$44
135 Magirus Tractor and Chassis, 1:43......$44
136 Renault RVI JK90 Fire Service, 1:43 ......$44
140 Renault RVI 95-130 Forest Fire Truck, 1:43 ....$44
141 Renault RVI 75-130 Forest Fire Truck, 1:43 ....$44
142 Renault RVI 85-150 Forest Fire Truck, 1:43 ....$44
143 Renault RVI JN-90 Ladder Fire Truck, 1:43 ....$44
144 Renault RVI SIDES Fire Pumper, 1:43 ....$48
145 Renault RVI JP 13 Fire Ladder Truck, 1:43 ....$48
146 Renault RVI JN 90 Fire Pumper, 1:43....$48
147 Renault RVI JN 90 Fire Equipment Truck, 1:43 ....$44
148 Renault RVI TRM 2000 Water Cannon Fire Truck, 1:43 ....$44
150 Mack 200 Commercial Transport "Michelin," 1:43 ....$44
151 Mack 200 USA Double Cabin Fire Truck, 1:43 ....$48

154 VAB 6x6 Armored Turret, 1:43 ....$58
155 VAB 6x6 Armored Assault Vehicle, 1:43 ....$58
156 VAB 6x6 Armored Troop Transport, 1:43 ....$58
159 DAF FA 1300 Commercial Transport with deflector, "TNT/IPEC," 1:43 ....$44
162 Renault RVI Fire Equipment Truck, 1:43 .$44
163 Renault RVI Fire Auxiliary Truck, 1:43 ....$44
164 Renault RVI Emergency Medical Treatment Vehicle, 1:43 ....$44
165 Renault RVI Fire Auxiliary Truck, 1:43 ....$44
166 Iveco 80-13 AW Dump Truck, 1:43....$42
167 ACMAT 6x6 Semi Tractor/Trailer, 1:50 ....$128
169 RVI Camiva Fire Ladder Truck, 1:48 .....$58
172 Renault Fire Equipment Truck, 1:43 ......$44
174 VAB Panhard Armored Troop Transport, 1:43 ....$44
176 Shelter Generator Load, 1:50 ....$78
177 Shelter Rita SH30 Load to 17, 1:50 ....$34
178 ACMAT 6x6 Flatbed Sand, 1:50........$88
179 ACMAT 6x6 Semi Tractor/Trailer, 1:43 ....$128
186 RVI Premier Security Truck Type 85-200, 1:43 ....$44
187 RVI Military Water Cannon, 1:43........$44
190 VAB 6x6 F.I.N.U.L., white, 1:43 ....$58
191 VAB Armored Police Assault Vehicle, blue, 1:43 ....$44
192 VBL Police Armored Personnel Transport, white, 1:43 ....$44
195 Renault Fire Equipment Truck, 1:43 ......$44
197 Renault RVI S 170 Commercial Transport, "Vittel," 1:43 ....$44
198 Renault RVI 85-150 Civil Protection Truck, 1:43 ....$44
200 ACMAT 6x6 Flatbed, olive drab, 1:43 .$108
201 ACMAT FFM Fire Pumper, 1:50........$108
202 ACMAT 6x6 Troop Transport, 1:50...$118
203 ACMAT TPK 4x4 Troop Transport, 1:50 ....$118
204 Renault RVI Dump Truck, 1:43 ....$44
205 Shelter 650 SH Load to 200, 1:50 .....$28
206 Iveco Magirus TRM 2000 Military Transport, 1:43..............................$44
207 Mercedes 1928AS38 Tar Spreader Semi, 1:50 ....$68
208 Renault R340 Tar Spreader Semi, 1:50..$68
209 VAB 4x4 Armored Troop Transport, 1:43 ....$58
210 RVI-TRM 2000 Covered Transport, green camouflage, 1:43.....................$44
211 VBL-Panhard Armored Troop Transport, green camouflage, 1:43.....................$44
212 Mack 200 Commercial Transport, "Ryder," 1:43 ....$44
216 VAB 4x4 Armored Troop Transport, khaki camouflage, 1:43.....................$44
233 VAB 4x4 Armored Troop Transport, 1:43 ....$44
239 VAB 4x4 Turret T25, 1:43.................$44
240 VAB 4x4 Ambulance, 1:43 ....$44

241 VAB 6x6 Armored Ambulance, 1:43 ...$44
242 VAB 6x6 SATCP Mistral, 1:43 ....$44
243 VAB 4x4 Ambulance, tan with red crescent, 1:43 ....$44
244 Mack 200 Fire Pumper, 1:43 ....$44
245 VAB 4x4 Armored Turret T25, green camouflage, 1:43 ....$44
246 VAB 6x6 Armored Turret T25, green camouflage, 1:43 ....$44
247 VAB 4x4 Armored Turret T25, khaki camouflage, 1:43 ....$44
248 VAB 6x6 Turret T25, 1:43 ....$84
259 VAB 4x4 Armored Assault Vehicle, 1:43 ..$44
260 VAB 4x4 Armored Assault Vehicle, khaki, 1:43 ....$44
261 VAB 4x4 Armored Assault Vehicle, 1:43 ....$44
262 VAB 4x4 Armored Assault Vehicle, 1:43 ....$44
263 VAB 6x6 Armored Troop Transport, 1:43.$44
264 VAB 6x6 Troop Transport, sable camouflage, 1:43 ....$44
265 VAB 6x6 Armored Assault Vehicle, green camouflage, 1:43 ....$44
266 VAB 6x6 Armored Assault Vehicle, sable camouflage, 1:43 ....$44
269 Manitou MLT626RT Bucket Lift, 1:43....$48
274 Yanmar B27 Mini Excavator, 1:30 ......$38
284 Renault 1000 Transport, camouflage, 1:43 ....$84

Repli-Cars (see Bayshore Repli-Cars)

Replicars

Replicars are 1:43 scale models made in England.
1 1934 ERA $60
4 1921 Bugatti Brescia $60
6 1934 MG K3 ....$60
7 1968 Morgan Plus 8 ....$60
13 1951 Ferrari 166M $60
14 1974 Triumph TR6 ....$60
16 1937 Packard Roadster $60
18 1975 Lotus Super 7 ....$60
24 1937 Packard 4-Door Sedan...........$60
24 1937 Packard Tourer $60
24 1937 Packard Town Car $60
28 1954 Sunbeam Alpine Roadster $60
29 1932 Alfa 8C Roadster $60
32 1951 Jaguar C Type $60
35 1932 Alfa Castagna, top up $60
36 1958 Jaguar XK150....................$60
44 1936 Morgan 2-Seater $60
101 1925 Austin Van "Lucas"............$60

Replicast

Replicast Record Models
132 Linaker Street
Southport
Merseyside PR8 5DF
England
phone: 00 44 (0)1704 542233
fax: 00 44 (0)1704 500164
e-mail: info@linaker.u-net.com

website: www.merseyworld.com/replicast

Since 1984, Replicast Record Models has been operated from Merseyside, England, by founder Frank C. Harris. The company offers models of speed record cars and boats in various scales and materials. Most but not all models are available in both kit and built form. The most prolific series is of 1:43 scale white metal land speed record cars. Also available are fiberglass boat kits that can be adapted for radio-control. Values have been converted from British pounds. List is based on information off the Replicast website as of January 7, 2000.

Replicast Land Speed Record Cars, 1:43 Scale

J.S.05 1899 Jeantaud Electric, 94 mm, resin, white metal, photo-etched, kit...........$61
built $218
G.B.10 1902 Electric Torpedo, Baker, 125 mm, resin, built......................$172
J.S.07 1910 Steam Rocket, Stanley, 113 mm, resin, white metal, photo-etched, kit $64
built $221
G.B.11 1914 Benz, L. Hornstead, 110 mm, resin, photo-etched, built $246
D.S.1 1919 Packard, De Palma, 118 mm, resin, kit...........................$66
built $221
G.B.12 1920 Double Duesenberg, T. Milton, 117 mm, resin, built $228
LSR.3 1922 Sunbeam KLG, M. Campbell, 110 mm, white metal, kit...............$99
built $213
LSR.5 1924 Sunbeam Bluebird, M. Campbell, 135 mm, white metal, kit.........$99
built $213
LSR.2 1925 Sunbeam Bluebird, M. Campbell, 135 mm, white metal, kit.........$99
built $213
Pand.21a 1926 BABS, Parry Thomas, 120 mm, white metal, kit $100
built $303
Pand.21b 1927 BABS, Parry Thomas, 135 mm, white metal, kit $87
built $288
W.M.2 1927 Sunbeam 1000 hp, H. Segrave, 170 mm, white metal, kit, ...$80
built $153
Pand.2 1927 Sunbeam Bluebird, M. Campbell, 142 mm, white metal, kit.........$80
built $216
Pand.3 1929 Arrol Aster Bluebird, M. Campbell, 155 mm, white metal, photo-etched, kit $75
built $201
W.M.1 1929 Golden Arrow, H. Segrave, 195 mm, white metal, kit...............$80
built $153
Pand.1 1930 Silver Bullet, Kaye Don, 220 mm, white metal, kit $75
built $201
Pand.17 1931 Stutz Black Hawk, F. Lockhart, 118 mm, white metal, kit.........$49
built $159

Pand.4 1931 Napier Bluebird, M. Campbell, 160 mm, white metal, kit.......$100
built $403
Pand.5 1932 Napier Bluebird, M. Campbell, 160 mm, white metal, kit.......$100
built $403
MOM.7 1935 Bluebird, Sir M. Campbell, 193 mm, resin, white metal, kit.......$61
built $128
MOM.3 1937 Thunderbolt, G. Eyston, 216 mm, resin, white metal, kit.............$72
built $180
G.B.6 1936 Mercedes Benz Class B., R. Caracciola, 140 mm, resin, white metal, kit $44
built $133
G.B.4 1937 Auto Union 'AVUS', B. Rosemeyer, 140 mm, resin, white metal, kit.....$44
built $133
G.B.5 1937 Mercedes Benz 'AVUS', H. Lang, 140 mm, resin, white metal, kit.$44
built $133
G.B.1 1937 Auto Union Class B., B. Rosemeyer, 140 mm, resin, white metal, kit $41
built $128
G.B.2 1938 Mercedes Benz Class B., R. Caracciola, 144 mm, resin, white metal, kit......................................$47
built $138
G.B.3 1938 Auto Union Class B., B. Rosemeyer, 142 mm, resin, white metal, kit $47
built $138
J.S.05a 1938 Railton Special, J. Cobb, 200 mm, resin, kit.......................$61
built $242
MOM.4 1938 Thunderbolt, G. Eyston, 250 mm, resin, white metal, kit.............$72
built $180
Pand.18 1939 Daimler Benz T.80, H. Stuck, 190 mm, resin, kit $75
built $216
J.S.05b 1947 Railton Mobil Special, J. Cobb, 200 mm, resin, kit $61
built $242
M.S.1 1959 Challenger, M. Thompson, 140 mm, resin, kit......................$55
built $131
M.S.2 1960 Challenger, M. Thompson, 140 mm, resin, kit......................$55
built $131
LSR.6 1960 Spirit of Salt Lake, Athol Graham, 150 mm, white metal, kit........$99
built $205
Fad.5 1960 Anteater, Art Arfons, 120 mm, resin,built.....................$221
MOM.5 1960 Bluebird CN7, D.M. Campbell, 210 mm, resin, white metal, kit $72
built $174
MOM.8 1960 Flying Caduseus, Dr. N. Ostich, 200 mm, resin, white metal, kit $80
built $242

MOM.9 1963 Flying Caduseus, Dr. N. Ostich, 200 mm, resin, white metal, kit $80
built $270

J.S.06 1963 Wingfoot Express 1, T. Green, 170 mm, resin, kit $61
built $259

MOM.6 1964 Bluebird CN7, D.M. Campbell, 210 mm, resin, kit..................$72
built $174

J.S.02 1964 Wingfoot Express 1, T. Green, 170 mm, resin, kit $61
built $259

J.S.04 1964 Autolite Special, M. Thompson, 218 mm, resin, kit $61
built $274

Pand.20 1965 Wingfoot Express II, R. Tahoe, 200 mm, white metal, kit ...$100
built $318

J.S.03 1965 Bluebird CMN8, D. Campbell, 178 mm, resin, kit $54
built $201

LSR.4 1965 Goldenrod, Summers Bros., 225 mm, white metal, kit................$82
built $205

J.S.01 1965 Spirit of America "Sonic 1," C. Breedlove, 237 mm, resin, kit..........$61
built $242

MOM.11 1965 Green Monster, A. Arfons, 160 mm, white metal, photo-etched, kit $99
built $401

MOM.10 1970 Blue Flame, G. Gabelich, 270 mm, resin, white metal, kit........$97
built $405

MOM.1 1979 Budwieser Rocket, S. Barrett, 247 mm, resin, white metal, kit........$80
built $288

LSR.1 1983 Thrust II, R. Noble, 195 mm, white metal, kit $99
built $262

Pand.19 1985 Minnesota Special, R. Palm, 168 mm, resin, kit $57
built $174

Fad.6 1991 Speed-O-Motive, Al Teague, 200 mm, resin, built.....................$238

R.S.1 1997 Thrust SSC, R. Noble, 380 mm, resin, white metal, photo-etched, built $572

Replicast 1:43 Scale Boats

Rep.1 1930 Miss England II, H. Segrave, 267 mm, resin, white metal, kit........$79
built $241

Rep.2 1937 Bluebird K3, M. Campbell, 193 mm, resin, white metal, kit........$66
built $203

Rep.3 1938 Bluebird K3, M. Campbell, 180 mm, resin, white metal, kit........$66
built $203

Rep.4 1939 Bluebird K4, M. Campbell, 185 mm, white metal, photo etched, kit $98
built $287

Rep.5 1952 Crusader K6, J. Cobb, 220 mm, resin, kit................................$71
built $211

Rep.6 1955 Bluebird K7, D. Campbell, 190 mm, resin, white metal, kit $69
built $201

Rep.7 1955 Bluebird K7, D. Campbell (Lake Mead), 190 mm, resin, white metal, kit $69
built $201

Rep.8 1964 Bluebird K7, D. Campbell, 190 mm, resin, white metal, kit $69
built $201

Rep.9 1967 Bluebird K7, D. Campbell, 190 mm, resin, white metal, kit $69
built $201

Rep.10 1967 Hustler, Lee Taylor, 220 mm, resin, white metal, kit $74
built $206

Rep.11 1980 US Discovery, Lee Taylor, 290 m, resin, kit ....price to be announced
built ....price to be announced

Rep.12 1953 Laura 3a, Mario Verga, 175 mm, resin, white metal, kitt..price to be announced
built ....price to be announced

Reuhl Products, Inc.
4505 Belt Line Hwy, R3
Madison, Wisconsin
(Now out of business)

What made Ruehl toys of Madison, Wisconsin, unique is that they were sold as diecast construction kits, with the emphasis on developing a child's manual dexterity. They were promoted in 1950 as educational "put-together" toys, requiring no glue or tools.

Caterpillar D-7, T-4000 ....$450
Caterpillar Grader No. 12 ....$1,800
Caterpillar Ripper.....................................$375
Caterpillar Scraper No. 70, 16" plastic, S-4500 ....$650
Cedar Rapids Rock Crusher....................$1,100
Cedar Rapids Paver $150
DW-10 ....$700
Farmall Cub, T-3000, 6¼" $150
Lorain Shovel...$1,425
Massey Harris Combine $375

Revell

Action Performance Companies Inc. markets and distributes products through a variety of channels, including the 100,000-member Racing Collectables Club of America (RCCA), trackside at racing events, mass retail department stores, and a nationwide wholesale network of approximately 5,000 specialty dealers and distributors.

In November 1997, the company announced that it had reached an agreement in principle to purchase the motorsports diecast collectibles business of Revell-Monogram Inc., a unit of Binney & Smith Inc. of Easton, Pennsylva-

nia, for $15 million in cash, and also to form a broad-ranging and long-term strategic alliance with Revell-Monogram. The acquisition includes a 10-year licensing agreement that will provide Action with exclusive use of the trademarked brand names of Revell-Monogram's U.S. motorsports die-cast product lines, "Revell Racing" and "Revell Collection," and existing U.S. distribution channels.

Action will exclusively market and distribute Revell-Monogram's plastic model kits into its trackside distribution channel and assist Revell-Monogram in obtaining motorsports merchandise licenses with drivers and racing teams for plastic model products.

Revell-Monogram, the world leader in plastic model kits, is a business unit of Binney & Smith, maker of Crayola and Liquitex brand products, and a subsidiary of Hallmark Cards Inc. of Kansas City, Missouri. Action Performance is the leader in the design, marketing, and distribution of licensed motorsports merchandise. Its products include a broad range of motorsports-related apparel, souvenirs, die-cast car replica collectibles, and other memorabilia.

While Revell is best known for its plastic model kits, the company started a few years ago producing large scale car replicas that have established a loyal following for their accuracy, detail, and affordability. In addition, it seems that Revell produced a series of diecast Chryslers in approximately 1:64 scale some time in the late sixties or early seventies.

713 1961 Chrysler Windsor Convertible .$25–30
714 1961 Chrysler Imperial Sedan $25–30

Revell Low Riders, 1:64 scale

For 1999, Revell introduced a new series of 1:64 scale diecast models, this time representing low rider custom cars.

#1 1961 Chevrolet Impala "Purple Rose" .$4
#2 1964 Chevrolet Impala "Castillo de Oro"...$4
#3 1971 Buick Riviera "Green's Dragg'n" ..$4
#4 1939 Chevrolet Sedan Delivery "Cherry Bomb"..$4

1959 Chevrolet Impala Sunkissed $4

1995 Honda Civic.....................................$4

259

Revell 1:20 Scale Creative Masters

At least six Creative Masters models were produced around 1987 to 1988, according to Jon Pierce of Winder, Georgia. The only one he specifically mentions is the 427 Cobra as indicated below, which he says is no longer being produced.

427 Cobra $25–40

Revell 1:18 Scale

8500 Ferrari Mythos by Pininfarina $20
8501 Bugatti EB110.........................$20
8503 Bugatti EB110S Sport $20
8654 Mercedes-Benz 500 SL Coupe $20
8659 Ferrari Mythos.........................$20
8660 Porsche 911 Turbo, top down $20
8670 Porsche 911 Turbo, top up..........$20
8671 Mercedes-Benz 500 SL Convertible .$20
8690 BMW 850i Coupe......................$20
8691 1969 Corvette Convertible, metallic blue with open top $20
8692 Acura NSX, red $20
8753 1965 Mustang Convertible, aqua with top down $20
8755 1969 Corvette Convertible, red with open top $20
8757 1969 Mustang Convertible, red with top up..............................$20

Revell 1:12 Scale

8851 1954 Mercedes-Benz 300 SLR.......$120
8853 1962 Ferrari 250 GTO................$120

Revell

While Brumm of Italy produces a series called "Revival," it is not to be confused with Revival models, incidentally also from Italy. They are 1:20 scale models of incredible detail and accuracy. Most of the details are hidden beneath the cowlings. They are available by calling Lilliput of Yerington, Nevada, at 1-800-TIN-TOYS (1-800-846-8697).

1931-32 Alfa Romeo P3 Muletto.............$360
1907 Fiat F-2 130HP......................$350
Auto Union Tipo C Avus....................$625
1938 Mercedes-Benz M163.................$425
1946-51 Alfa Romeo 159..................$360
1952 Ferrari 500 F2.......................$360
1957 Maserati 250........................$360
1961 Ferrari 156 120 Degree $360
1924 Bugatti Type 35 TF..................$400
1932-35 Alfa Romeo P3 TF................$400
1956 Lancia Ferrari D50...................$390
1936-37 Auto Union Tipo C Hillclimb.......$450
1936 Auto Union Tipo C...................$440
1937 Auto Union Tipo C Streamliner $460

Rex/Rextoys

33, Avenue du Rumine
Lausanne, Switzerland

Around 1960, Rex produced a small assortment of diecast models from its original home in Germany. The company eventually moved to its present home in Switzerland. In the meantime, the company had apparently been out of business for some time before the rights were purchased to resume production.

Rex 1:43 Scale Models

1939 Cadillac Coupe de Ville, #2........$35
1939 Cadillac Coupe de Ville, #3........$35
1939 Cadillac 4-Door Sedan, #4.........$35
1939 Cadillac Roadster, #6 ....$35
1939 Cadillac 4-Door Convertible, #12 ...$35
1938–40 Cadillac V-16 2-Door Coupe $30–40
1938–40 Cadillac V-16 Formal Sedan................................$30–40

1938-40 Cadillac V16 Cabriolet Ouvert 6..$30–40

Chrysler Airflow 4-Door Sedan, #21 ......$35
1935 Ford T48 Fordor Sedan, olive & black, #42 ....$25
1935 Ford Van Army Ambulance, #45..$35
Ford Delivery "Bell Telephone," #45.......$35
1935 Ford Woody Wagon, #46...$34 –$35
1935 Ford Woody Wagon, #47.........$35
1935 Ford 4-Door Sedan U.S.Army, #48 .$35
1935 Ford 4-Door Sedan Taxi, #50......$35
1935 Ford 4-Door Sedan Police, #51 ..$35
1935 Ford Coupe, #52 ....$25
1935 Ford Coupe, #53 ....$35
1935 Ford Coupe Fire, #54 ....$35
1935 Ford Coupe Police, #55 ....$35
1935 Ford Coupe, Ghost Patrol, #56....$35
1961 Ford Thunderbird, 4⅝" $75
Mercedes-Benz 300SL Roadster, 4", 1959 ....$65
Opel Kapitän Sedan, 4½", 1959..........$65
1940 Packard Super 8 Sedan, #61......$35
Rolls-Royce Phantom, #33 ....$35

Rex 1:87 Scale (Ho Gauge) Models

Ford Taunus Sedan, 2¹⁄₁₆", 1:87 ....$15
Volkswagen Transporter, 1¾", 1:87.......$15

RHI

Particularly crude little toys seem to be typical of the RHI brand made in Japan.

Camper....................................$1–2
Wrecker $1–2

Rhino

Rhino Toys Manufacturing Ltd.
Unit 11, 4/F,. Harbour Centre, Tower 1, Hunghom, Kowloon, Hong Kong

Rhino toys generally fall into the category of generic toys. The definition of "generic" in this case is any toy that, once taken out of its package, becomes an unmarked and unidentifiable toy.

While they are lightweight with a lot of plastic components, Rhino does however present a few twists that set them apart from other generic toys. Their various farm sets that include tractors, milk tankers, fences, buildings, and farmhands are a good value as a toy. Collectibly speaking, these sets are attractive enough to maintain their original value but not likely to increase past retail price in terms of rising collector value.

Richmond

The previously-unheard-of Richmond firm apparently produced a blue all-metal wrecker with a seal on top saying "another fine Richmond scale model." More information is needed.

Rio

One of the most popular brands of high-quality 1:43 scale model vehicles is Rio of Italy. Begun in 1961 by Reno Tattarletti, Rio is still in business producing excellent models in various scales. Dr. Force's book *Classic Miniature Vehicles Made In Italy* devotes nine pages to detailing the Rio line. This book presents a more brief summary of Rio models.

1 1906 Itala Targa Florio, 1961..........$25–30
2 1906 Itala Peking-Paris, 1961 ....$25–30
3 1919 Fiat 501 Sport, 1961..........$25–30
4 1919 Fiat 501 Tourer, 1961............$25–30
5 1932 Alfa Romeo B-Type, 1962.......$25–30
6 1912 Fiat Model O Tourer, 1962.......$25–30
7 1912 Fiat Model O Spyder, 1962 ...$25–30
8 1924 Isotta-Fraschini Type 8A with cab roof, 1962.....................$30
9 1924 Isotta-Fraschini Type 8A, no cab roof, 1962.....................$30
10 1909 Bianchi Closed Landaulet, 1963.....................$25–30
11 1909 Bianchi Open Landaulet, 1963.....................$25–30
12 1912 Fiat Model O Open Spyder, 1963.....................$25–30
13 1932 Fiat Balilla 2-Door, 1964 ......$25–30
14 1910 Fiat Type 2 Limousine, 1964....$25–30
15 1924 Isotta-Fraschini Type 8A Spyder, 1964.....................$25–30
16 1909 Chalmers-Detroit, 1964........$25–30
17 1909 Mercedes Open Tourer, 1964.....................$25–30
18 1906 Bianchi Coupe De Ville, 1965.....................$25–30
19 1932 Alfa Romeo 6C 1750, 1965.....................$25–30
20 1915 Fiat 18BL Bus, yellow, 1965 ...$25–30
21 1937 Mercedes-Benz Cabriolet, 1966.....................$25–30
22 1937 Mercedes-Benz Cabriolet, 1966.....................$25–30
23 1905 Fiat 60 HP Tourer, top up, 1966.....................$25–30
24 1905 Fiat 60 HP Tourer, top down, 1966.....................$25–30
25 1906 Fiat 24 HP Double Phaeton, 1966.....................$25–30

26 1902 Fiat 12 HP Tourer, 1966.......$25–30

27 1905 Fiat 24 HP Limousine, 1967...$25–30

28 1905 Bianchi Landaulet, 1967.......$25–30

29 1902 Mercedes Simplex, 1967.....$25–30

30 1894 De Dion-Bouton Steam Victoria, 1967...$25–30

31 1901 Fiat 8 HP, 1967.............$25–30

32 1903 Fiat 16-24 HP Tourer, 1967....$25–30

33 1908 Mercedes 70 HP Limousine, 1968...$25–30

34 1907 Renault Type X Double Berline, 1968...$25–30

35 1910 Renault Taxi De La Marne, 1968...$25–30

36 1927 Bugatti Royale, top up, 1968....$25–30

37 1927 Bugatti Royale, top down, 1968...$25–30

38 1908 Fiat 18-24 HP Landaulet, 1969...$25–30

39 1931 Rolls-Royce Phantom II, top up, 1969...$25–30

40 1931 Rolls-Royce Phantom II, top down, 1969...$25–30

41 1929 Lancia Dilambda Torpedo, green, 1969...$25–30

42 1929 Lancia Dilambda Torpedo, red, 1969...$25–30

43 1941 Lincoln Continental, top up, 1969...$25–30

44 1941 Lincoln Continental, top down, 1969...$25–30

45 1934 Deusenberg SJ Phaeton, closed top, 1969...$25–30

46 1934 Deusenberg SJ Phaeton, open top, 1969...$25–30

47 1908 Thomas Flyer New York-Paris, 1970...$25–30

48 1932 Bugatti Type 50 Sport Coupe, 1970...$25–30

49 1921 Fiat V12 Dorsay De Ville, 1971...$25–30

50 1928 Lincoln Sport Phaeton, top up, 1971...$25–30

51 1928 Lincoln Sport Phaeton, top down, 1971...$25–30

52 1923 Renault 40 HP Torpedo, top up, 1971...$25–30

53 1923 Renault 40 HP Torpedo, top down, 1971...$25–$30

54 1927 Bugatti Type 41 Royale, 1972...$25–30

55 1914 Alfa Ricotti, 1973.............$25–30

56 1902 General Grand Prix, 1973....$25–30

57 1923 Fiat 519 S Tourer, top up, 1974...$25–30

58 1923 Fiat 519 S Tourer, top down, 1974...$25–30

59 1923 Fiat 519 S Limousine, 1974...$25–30

60 1899 Le Jamais Contente, 1975.....$25–30

61 1932 Hispano-Suiza Town Car, 1975...$25–30

62 1923 Leyat, 1976.....................$25–30

63 1935 Delahaye 135M, 1976.......$25–30

64 1942 Hitler's Mercedes-Benz 770, 1976...$45

65 1932 Hispano-Suiza Limousine, 1976...$25–30

66 1927 Bugatti Royale Double Berline, 1976...$25–30

67 1929 Isotta-Fraschini, top up, 1976...$25–30

68 1929 Isotta-Fraschini, top down, 1976...$25–30

69 1902 Ford 999, 1980.................$25–30

70 1934 Alfa Romeo B-Type Targa Florio, 1980...$25–30

71 1935 Alfa Romeo B-Type Hill Climb Car, 1980...$25–30

72 1923 Rolls-Royce 20, top up, 1981...$25–30

73 1923 Rolls-Royce 20, top down, 1981...$25–30

74 1929 Bugatti Royale Coupe, 1981...$25–30

75 1905 Fiat PS Limousine, 1981........$25–30

76 1931 Cadillac V16, top up, 1981...$25–30

77 1931 Cadillac V16, top down, 1981...$25–30

78 1938 Bugatti 57C Atlantic Coupe, 1981...$25–30

79 1931 Mercedes-Benz SSKL, 1981....$25–30

80 1927 Mercedes-Benz SSK, 1981...$25–30

81 1914 Alfa Ricotti, 1981.................$25–30

82 1941 Lincoln Continental Coupe, 1985...$25–30

83 1936 Hispano-Suiza, top up, 1985....$25–30

84 1936 Hispano-Suiza, top down, 1985...$25–30

85 1937 Mercedes-Benz 770K Pullman, 1985...$25–30

86 1933 Deusenberg SJ Spider, 1987...$25–30

87 1915 Fiat 18BL Bus, blue, 1986....$25–30

88 1949 Volkswagen, 1988 (see 189-194)...$25–30

89 1930 Isotta-Fraschini Castagna Torpedo, 1988...$25–30

90 1957 Mercedes-Benz 300, 1988....$25–30

91 1953 Volkswagen Beetle, ivory, 1990...$25–30

92 1949 Volkswagen Beetle Cabriolet, top down, 1990...$25–30

93 1949 Volkswagen Beetle Cabriolet, top up, 1990...$25–30

94 Bugatti Royale Torpedo, top up, 1990...$25–30

95 Bugatti Royale Torpedo, top down, 1990...$25–30

96 Bugatti Royale Weymann, 1990.....$25–30

97 1956 Citroën DS19 Sedan............$25–30

98 1956 Citroën Cabriolet, open top...$25–30

99 1958 Citroën ID19 Station Wagon...$25–30

100 1960 Mercedes-Benz 300D Landau...$25–30

100P 1960 Mercedes-Benz 300D Landau with Pope...$35

101 1960 Mercedes-Benz 300D, top up...$25–30

102 1960 Mercedes-Benz 300D, top down...$25–30

103 1939 Volkswagen Beetle Standard Hardtop...$25–30

104 1939 Volkswagen Beetle Sedan with Sunroof...$25–30

105 1939 Volkswagen Beetle Cabriolet, top down...$25–30

106 1939 Volkswagen Beetle Split Window...$25–30

107 1950 Volkswagen Beetle, top down...$25–30

108 1955 Volkswagen One Millionth Beetle...$25–30

109 1959 Citroën DS19 Monte Carlo...$25–30

110 1967 Ferrari 365 GTB4 Daytona, red, 1989...$25–30

111 Citroën ID19 Sedan.................$25–30

116 Citroën ID19 Ambulance.............$25–30

117 1962 Citroën Fire Ambulance.......$25–30

120 1967 Ferrari 365 GTB4 Daytona Spider, 1989...$25–30

121 1967 Ferrari 365 GTB4 Daytona Spider, 1990...$25–30

130 1973 Ferrari 365 GTB4 Le Mans, 1989...$25–30

189 1949 Volkswagen Beetle, black, 1988...**$25–$30**

191 1949 Volkswagen Beetle, red, 1988...$25–30

192 1949 Volkswagen Beetle, green, 1988...$25–30

193 1949 Volkswagen Beetle, cream, 1988...$25–30

194 1949 Volkswagen Beetle, blue, 1988...$25–30

200 1967 Ferrari 365 GTB Daytona, red, 1986...$25–30

201 1967 Ferrari 365 GTB Daytona Spider, black, 1986...$25–30

202 1973 Ferrari 365 GTB Le Mans, 1989...$25–30

A1 1914 Fiat 18BKL Army Truck, 1982...$25–30

A2 1914 Fiat 18BKL Stake Truck, 1982...$25–30

A3 1914 Fiat 18BKL Covered Truck, gray, 1982...$25–30

A4 1914 Fiat 18BKL Open Truck, maroon, 1982...$25–30

CH93 1914 Fiat 18BKL with Santa & present, limited edition, 1993...$35–40

R1 1967 Ferrari 365 GTB Daytona, same as 200 ....$25–30

R2 1967 Ferrari 365 GTB Daytona Spider, same as 201 ....$25–30

R3 1973 Ferrari 365 GTB Daytona Spider, same as 202 ....$25–30

R4 1956 Ford Thunderbird Convertible, pale green, 1990 ....$25–30

R5 1956 Ford Thunderbird Hardtop, lavender, 1990 ....$25–30

R6 1955 Mercedes-Benz 190SL Convertible, white, 1990 ....$25–30

R7 1955 Mercedes-Benz 190SL Convertible, cream, 1990 ....$25–30

R8 1968 Lamborghini Miura S Coupe..$35–40

R9 1968 Lamborghini Miura Roadster, top down $35–40

1000 1938 Bugatti 57C Atlantic Coupe, 1982 ....$25–30

1001 1933 Bugatti Type 50, 1983.....$25–30

1002 1931 Bugatti Type 50 Le Mans, 1985...$25–30

10200 1953 Volkswagen Beetle, charcoal gray, 1989...$25–30

10201 1953 Volkswagen Beetle, maroon, 1989 ....$25–30

10202 1953 Volkswagen Beetle, cream, 1989 ....$25–30

Rivarossi

Although Rivarossi of Italy didn't produce any diecast miniatures, they did produce some interesting plastic Fiat and Mercedes models in 1:43 and 1:87 scales.

Rivarossi's exquisite ship models and detail components were most recently available from Model Expo.

River Series

A dispute ensues among collectors whether D.C.M.T. produced this series or not. Records indicate that diecasting Machine Tools, Ltd. of London, England, likely produced these 1:43 scale castings. Argument to the contrary states that River models are not at all marked with any D.C.M.T. mark, and represent inferior castings prone to metal fatigue, a problem not witnessed on other D.C.M.T. castings. For more details, see the section on D.C.M.T. and the others listed above.

Latest report (*Model Collector* magazine, April 1999) indicates that there may be a connection, not with D.C.M.T, but with another British company Jordan & Lewden Ltd. Evidence comes from a diecast windup key cast with the phrase "River Series." The key has the "JL" (or "LJ"), which is assumed by author Robert Newson to stand for "Jordan & Lewden." This in no way settles the debate, but at least provides some possibilities. It was sometime in the fifties when these mysteries were produced. Each model was produced in a range of colors, and variants include those with and without motors.

An identically named "River Series" was produced in New Zealand, likely with the contribution of dies from Jordan & Lewden to Lincoln Industries Ltd. of Auckland, New Zealand, since models are identical to the British issues except for a difference in color and the lack of "Made in England" on the baseplate.

A third "River Series" was issued in Israel in the early sixties when dies were sold to a company in Israel and produced as Gamda toys.

River Series Cars

Austin A40 Somerset, 98mm............$40–50
    with original box.......................$75–90

1953 Buick Coupe. 108mm $40–50
    with original box.......................$75–90

Daimler Conquest, 100mm.............$40–50
    with original box.......................$75–90

Ford Prefect 100E, 97mm..............$40–50
    with original box.......................$75–90

Standard Vanguard 2-Door Estate Car, 98mm...$40–50
    with original box.......................$75–90

Standard Vanguard Phase II Saloon, 101mm...$40–50
    with original box.......................$75–90

River Series Trucks

Articulated Flat Lorry, 145mm $50–60
    with original box...................$85–100

Articulated Tanker, 151mm $50–60
    with original box...................$85–100

Cable Layer $50–60
    with original box...................$85–100

Car carrier with four miniature cars, 94mm...$50–60
    with original box...................$85–100

Excavator, 114mm $50–60
    with original box...................$85–100

Gully Emptier with movable boom extending over the cab $50–60
    with original box...................$85–100

Horse Transporter...........................$50–60
    with original box...................$85–100

River Transport Lorry with two miniature cars, 101mm $50–60
    with original box...................$85–100

Tipper Lorry, 94mm.......................$50–60
    with original box...................$85–100

Tower Wagon, 94mm $50–60
    with original box...................$85–100

River "Here Comes the Army" Series

Armoured Car, 97mm....................$50–60
    with original box...................$85–100

Army Covered Wagon..................$50–60
    with original box...................$85–100

Army Crane, 94mm $50–60
    with original box...................$85–100

Army Open Wagon, Limber and Field Gun..$50–60
    with original box...................$85–100

Army Tanker, 101mm $50–60
    with original box...................$85–100

Army Articulated Low Loader, 163mm...$50–60
    with original box...................$85–100

Field Gun, 101mm $40–50
    with original box.......................$75–90

Limber, 63mm $35–45
    with original box.......................$55–65

River Series Railway Locomotives

Furness Railway "Old Copperknob," 90mm...$40–50
    with original box.......................$75–90

GNR Stirling No. 1, 110mm $40–50
    with original box.......................$75–90

LNWR 2-4-0 Locomotive, 105mm ...$40–50
    with original box.......................$75–90

Stephenson's Rocket, 48mm..........$40–50
    with original box.......................$75–90

Road Champs

As early as 1980, Road Champs produced various 1:64 scale toy cars with opening doors under the auspices of JRI, Inc., originally based in a suburb of Philadelphia. One of many new arrivals on the diecast market, Road Champs moved to Harrison, West Caldwell, then Union, New Jersey.

Road Champs made its mark in 1993 with its introduction of a nine-car series of 1993 Chevrolet Caprice State Police cars. The ever-expanding series features relatively faithful 1:43 scale reproductions of U.S. and Canadian police cruisers with more Caprice variations. The addition of 1994 Ford Crown Victoria, a 1996 Chevrolet Suburban, and a 1998 Ford Crown Victoria multiply the number of police cars added every year.

Now owned by Jakks Pacific, itself in business since 1995, Road Champs are making an even bigger mark on the diecast toy industry with new models and packaging more focused toward the adult collector.

Before the highly popular state police series, the 1:87 scale "Anteaters" series, named after those curved-nose semi tractors, was the primary item marketed by Road Champs. They remain a popular segment of the Road Champs line-up, now marketed simply as Die Cast Cabs & Trailers.

Offerings of 1:64 scale include Country Tour Buses, a now discontinued series that featured graphics and names of several country music stars; their Fire Rescue Series is still a popular line of models of firefighting equipment, including International and Boardman trucks, and most recently Chevrolet Suburbans; the Deluxe series continues to offer the unusual items such as a Zamboni, International Ramp Wreck Truck, garbage and recycling trucks, an International school bus, and Mercedes stretch limousines.

Buses of 1:87 scale are another currently popular but hard-to-find assortment that includes a classic Greyhound bus and several liveries of city and municipal buses.

The popularity of Road Champs has grown with the expanding police car series, and Road Champs caters to collectors by now producing a great assortment of vintage automobiles in

1:43 scale. For more information, you may contact the company:
Road Champs, Inc.
a subsidiary of JAKKS Pacific, Inc
22761 Pacific Coast Highway, Suite 226
Malibu, CA 90265
phone: 908-206-0666
website: www.roadchamps.com

Road Champs State, U.S. Territories & Canada Provincial Police Vehicles

In 1:43 scale, a perennial favorite with collectors, the Pennsylvania police car issued in 1993 is now reportedly worth $250 according to the back of 1999 Road Champs Police Car packages.

Alabama, 1957 Ford Crown Victoria, 1998 issue $6

Alabama, 1993 Chevrolet Caprice, discontinued, no license plate, closed wheel wells..$20

Alabama, 1993 Chevrolet Caprice, discontinued, 1996 license plate, closed wheel wells..$10

Alabama, 1998 Ford Crown Victoria, 1998 license plate $6

Alaska, 1955 Chevrolet Bel Air, 1998 issue ..$6

Alaska, 1993 Chevrolet Caprice, discontinued, 1996 license plate, closed wheel wells..$10

Alaska, 1998 Ford Crown Victoria, 1998 license plate ....never produced

Arizona, 1957 Ford Crown Victoria, 1998 issue $6

Arizona, 1993 Chevrolet Caprice, discontinued, no license plate..............................$20

Arizona, 1993 Chevrolet Caprice, discontinued, 1996 license plate $10

Arizona, 1993 Chevrolet Caprice, 1997 license plate, open wheel wells..........................$7

Arkansas, 1957 Ford Crown Victoria, 1998 issue $6

Arkansas, 1993 Chevrolet Caprice, discontinued, no license plate, closed wheel wells.........$20

Arkansas, 1993 Chevrolet Caprice, discontinued, 1995 license plate, closed wheel wells..$12

Arkansas, 1993 Chevrolet Caprice, discontinued, 1996 license plate, closed wheel wells..$10

Arkansas, 1998 Ford Crown Victoria, 1998 license plate $7

Arkansas, 1998 Ford Crown Victoria, 1999 license plate $6

California, 1957 Ford Crown Victoria, 1998 issue..$6

California, 1993 Chevrolet Caprice, discontinued, no license plate, closed wheel wells..$20

California, 1993 Chevrolet Caprice, discontinued, 1995 license plate, closed wheel wells..$12

California, 1993 Chevrolet Caprice, discontinued, 1996 license plate, closed wheel wells..$10

California, 1993 Chevrolet Caprice, discontinued, 1996 license plate, open wheel wells..$10

California, 1998 Ford Crown Victoria, 1998.$6

Colorado, 1957 Ford Crown Victoria, 1998 issue..$6

Colorado, 1993 Chevrolet Caprice, discontinued, 1996, closed wheel wells.............$10

Colorado, 1993 Chevrolet Caprice, discontinued, 1997, open wheel wells.................$8

Colorado, 1998 Ford Crown Victoria, 1998 license plate $6

Florida, 1957 Ford Crown Victoria, 1998 issue..$6

Florida, 1994 Ford Crown Victoria, discontinued, no license plate.............................$16

Florida, 1994 Ford Crown Victoria, discontinued, 1996 license plate.........................$10

Florida, 1998 Ford Crown Victoria, 1998 license plate $6

Georgia, 1957 Ford Crown Victoria, 1998 issue..$6

Georgia, 1993 Chevrolet Caprice, discontinued, no license plate, closed wheel wells..$20

Georgia, 1994 Ford Crown Victoria, discontinued, 1996 license plate, open wheel wells..$10

Georgia, 1998 Ford Crown Victoria, 1998 license plate $6

Georgia, 1999 Ford Crown Victoria with matching pin, 1999 license plate $7

Idaho, 1957 Ford Crown Victoria, 1998 issue $6

Idaho, 1993 Chevrolet Caprice, 1996 license plate, closed wheel wells......................$10

Idaho, 1993 Chevrolet Caprice, 1996 license plate, open wheel wells $10

Idaho, 1998 Ford Crown Victoria, 1998 license plate.......................................$6

Illinois, 1957 Ford Crown Victoria, 1998 issue $6

Illinois, 1993 Chevrolet Caprice, discontinued, no license plate, closed wheel wells.......$20

Illinois, 1993 Chevrolet Caprice, discontinued, 1995 license plate, closed wheel wells..$12

Illinois, 1993 Chevrolet Caprice, discontinued, 1996 license plate, closed wheel wells ..$10

Illinois, 1998 Ford Crown Victoria, 1998 license plate.......................................$6

Indiana, 1957 Ford Crown Victoria, 1998 issue $6

Indiana, 1994 Ford Crown Victoria, discontinued, 1996 license plate.......................$10

Indiana, 1998 Ford Crown Victoria, 1998 license plate $6

Iowa, 1957 Ford Crown Victoria, 1998 issue $6

Iowa, 1994 Ford Crown Victoria, 1997 license plate.......................................$8

Iowa, 1998 Ford Crown Victoria, 1998 license plate.......................................$6

Kansas, 1957 Ford Crown Victoria, 1998 issue $6

Kansas, 1994 Ford Crown Victoria, discontinued, 1996 license plate.......................$10

Kansas, 1998 Ford Crown Victoria, 1998 license plate..$6

Kentucky, 1994 Ford Crown Victoria, discontinued, 1996 license plate.......................$10

Kentucky, 1957 Ford Crown Victoria, 1998 issue..$6

Kentucky, 1994 Ford Crown Victoria, discontinued, 1997 license plate.........................$8

Louisiana, 1955 Chevrolet Bel Air, 1998 issue..$6

Lousiana, 1994 Ford Crown Victoria, discontinued, no license plate...........................$15

Lousiana, 1994 Ford Crown Victoria, discontinued, 1995 license plate.......................$12

Lousiana, 1994 Ford Crown Victoria, discontinued, 1996 license plate.......................$10

Louisiana, 1998 Ford Crown Victoria, 1998 license plate $6

Maine, 1993 Chevrolet Caprice, discontinued, 1996 license plate, open wheel wells....$10

Maine, 1998 Ford Crown Victoria, 1998 license plate $6

Maryland, 1957 Ford Crown Victoria, 1998 issue..$6

Maryland, 1993 Chevrolet Caprice, discontinued, no license plate, closed wheel wells.........$20

Maryland, 1993 Chevrolet Caprice, discontinued, 1996 license plate, closed wheel wells..$10

Maryland, 1993 Chevrolet Caprice, discontinued, 1997 license plate, open wheel wells........$8

Maryland, 1998 Ford Crown Victoria, 1998 license plate $6

Massachusetts, 1994 Ford Crown Victoria, discontinued, 1997 license plate................$8

Massachusetts, 1998 Ford Crown Victoria, 1998 license plate $6

Massachusetts, 1999 Ford Crown Victoria with matching pin, 1999 license plate $7

Michigan, 1957 Ford Crown Victoria, 1998 issue..$6

Michigan, 1993 Chevrolet Caprice, discontinued, no license plate, closed wheel wells.........$20

Michigan, 1993 Chevrolet Caprice, discontinued, 1995 license plate, closed wheel wells..$12

Michigan, 1993 Chevrolet Caprice, discontinued, 1996 license plate, closed wheel wells, Dare Logo..$10

Michigan, 1998 Ford Crown Victoria, 1998 license plate $6

Michigan, 1999 Ford Crown Victoria, 1999 license plate, 10,000 limited edition with brass lapel pin $8

Minnesota, 1993 Chevrolet Caprice, discontinued, no license plate, closed wheel wells..$20

Minnesota, 1993 Chevrolet Caprice, discontinued, 1996 license plate, closed wheel wells..$10

Minnesota, 1998 Ford Crown Victoria, 1998 license plate $6

Mississippi, 1994 Ford Crown Victoria, discontinued, 1996 license plate $10

Mississippi, 1994 Ford Crown Victoria, 1997 license plate $8

Mississippi, 1998 Ford Crown Victoria, 1998 license plate $6

Missouri, 1957 Ford Crown Victoria, 1998 issue $6

Missouri, 1994 Ford Crown Victoria, discontinued, no license plate...........................$15

Missouri, 1994 Ford Crown Victoria, discontinued, 1996 license plate $10

Missouri (red), 1998 Ford Crown Victoria, 1998 license plate $6

Missouri (blue), 1998 Ford Crown Victoria, 1998 license plate..................................$6

Montana, 1955 Chevrolet Bel Air, 1998 issue $6

Montana, 1994 Ford Crown Victoria, 1997 license plate $8

Nebraska, 1957 Ford Fairlane, 1998 issue...$8

Nebraska, 1994 Ford Crown Victoria, discontinued, 1996 license plate $10

Nebraska, 1998 Ford Crown Victoria, 1998 license plate $6

Nevada, 1993 Chevrolet Caprice, discontinued, no license plate, closed wheel wells..$20

Nevada, 1993 Chevrolet Caprice, discontinued, 1996 license plate, closed wheel wells..$10

Nevada, 1998 Ford Crown Victoria, 1998 license plate $6

New Jersey, 1957 Ford Crown Victoria, 1998 issue..$6

New Jersey, 1993 Chevrolet Caprice, discontinued, no license plate, closed wheel wells..$20

New Jersey, 1993 Chevrolet Caprice, discontinued, 1996 license plate, closed wheel wells..$10

New Jersey, 1998 Ford Crown Victoria, 1998 license plate $6

New Mexico, 1957 Ford Fairlane, 1998 issue..$8

New Mexico, 1993 Chevrolet Caprice, discontinued, 1995 license plate, closed wheel wells..$12

New Mexico, 1993 Chevrolet Caprice, discontinued, 1996 license plate, open wheel wells..$10

New Mexico, 1998 Ford Crown Victoria, 1998 license plate $6

New York, 1957 Ford Crown Victoria, 1998 issue..$6

New York, 1993 Chevrolet Caprice, discontinued, no license plate, closed wheel wells, light blue...$150

New York, 1993 Chevrolet Caprice, discontinued, no license plate, open wheel wells, light blue..$10

New York, 1993 Chevrolet Caprice, discontinued, no license plate, open wheel wells, dark blue..$10

New York, 1993 Chevrolet Caprice, discontinued, 1996 license plate, closed wheel wells, dark blue $10

New York, 1998 Ford Crown Victoria, 1998 license plate $6

New York, 1998 Chevrolet Camaro, 1999 license plate, 10,000 limited edition with brass lapel pin $9

North Carolina, 1955 Chevrolet Bel Air, 1998 issue $6

North Carolina, 1993 Chevrolet Caprice, discontinued, 1997 license plate.................$8

North Carolina, 1998 Ford Crown Victoria, 1998 license plate $6

North Dakota, 1994 Ford Crown Victoria, 1996 license plate $10

North Dakota, 1998 Ford Crown Victoria, 1998 license plate ....never produced

Ohio, 1955 Chevrolet Bel Air, 1998 issue $6

Ohio, 1993 Chevrolet Caprice, discontinued, no license plate, closed wheel wells, Anniversary $70-100

Ohio, 1993 Chevrolet Caprice, discontinued, 1996 license plate, closed wheel wells, Normal $10

Ohio, 1998 Ford Crown Victoria, 1998 license plate...$6

Oklahoma, 1993 Chevrolet Caprice, discontinued, no license plate, closed wheel wells..$20

Oklahoma, 1993 Chevrolet Caprice, discontinued, 1996 license plate, closed wheel wells..$10

Oklahoma, 1993 Chevrolet Caprice, 1997 license plate, open wheel wells $7

Oklahoma, 1998 Ford Crown Victoria, 1998 license plate ....never produced

Ontario Provincial Police, 1994 Ford Crown Victoria, 1996 license plate $10

Oregon, 1993 Chevrolet Caprice, discontinued, no license plate, closed wheel wells.......$20

Oregon, 1994 Ford Crown Victoria, discontinued, 1996 license plate, open wheel wells..$10

Oregon, 1998 Ford Crown Victoria, 1998 license plate ....never produced

Pennsylvania, 1993 Chevrolet Caprice......$250

Puerto Rico, 1994 Ford Crown Victoria, discontinued, 1997 license plate.........................$8

Quebec Provincial Police, 1993 Chevrolet Caprice, no license plate, closed wheel wells $20

Quebec Provincial Police, 1993 Chevrolet Caprice, 1996 license plate, closed wheel wells...$10

Royal Canadian Mounted Police, 1993 Caprice, discontinued, no license plate, closed wheel wells...$20

Royal Canadian Mounted Police, 1993 Caprice, discontinued, 1995 license plate, closed wheel wells $12

Rhode Island, 1994 Ford Crown Victoria, discontinued, no license plate.........................$16

Rhode Island, 1994 Ford Crown Victoria, discontinued, 1996 license plate....................$10

Rhode Island, 1998 Ford Crown Victoria, 1998 license plate $6

South Carolina, 1993 Chevrolet Caprice, discontinued, no license plate.........................$20

South Carolina, 1993 Chevrolet Caprice, discontinued, 1996 license plate....................$10

South Carolina, 1998 Ford Crown Victoria, 1998 license plate ....never produced

South Dakota, 1994 Ford Crown Victoria, discontinued, 1996 license plate...............$10

South Dakota, 1998 Ford Crown Victoria, 1998 license plate $6

Tennessee, 1957 Ford Fairlane, 1998 issue...$8

Tennessee, 1993 Chevrolet Caprice, discontinued, 1996 license plate......................$10

Tennessee, 1998 Ford Crown Victoria, 1998 license plate $6

Texas, 1957 Ford Crown Victoria, 1998 issue $6

Texas, 1993 Chevrolet Caprice, 1996 license plate, closed wheel wells.....................$10

Texas, 1993 Chevrolet Caprice, 1996 license plate, open wheel wells $10

Texas, 1998 Ford Crown Victoria, 1998 license plate...$6

Utah, 1993 Chevrolet Caprice, discontinued, 1995 license plate, closed wheel wells..$12

Utah, 1993 Chevrolet Caprice, discontinued, 1996 license plate, closed wheel wells..$10

Utah, 1998 Ford Crown Victoria, 1998 license plate ....never produced

Vermont, 1993 Chevrolet Caprice, discontinued, 1996 license plate, closed wheel wells $10

Vermont, 1993 Chevrolet Caprice, 1997 license plate, open wheel wells........................$7

Vermont, 1998 Ford Crown Victoria, 1998 license plate $6

Virginia, 1993 Chevrolet Caprice, discontinued, no license plate.................................$20

Virginia, 1993 Chevrolet Caprice, discontinued, 1996 license plate, closed wheel wells..$10

Virginia, 1998 Ford Crown Victoria, 1998 license plate $6

Washington, 1994 Ford Crown Victoria, 1996 license plate $10

Washington, 1994 Ford Crown Victoria, 1997 license plate $8

Washington, 1998 Ford Crown Victoria, 1998 license plate $6

Washington D.C., 1994 Ford Crown Victoria, discontinued, 1995 license plate...........$12

Washington D.C., 1994 Ford Crown Victoria, discontinued, 1996 license plate...........$10

Washington, DC, 1998 Ford Crown Victoria, 1998 license plate.................................$6

West Virginia, 1955 Chevrolet Bel Air, 1998 issue..$6

West Virginia, 1993 Chevrolet Caprice, discontinued, 1996 license plate $10

West Virginia, 1993 Chevrolet Caprice, 1997 license plate, open wheel wells $8

West Virginia, 1998 Ford Crown Victoria, 1998 license plate $6

Wisconsin, 1955 Chevrolet Bel Air, 1998 issue $6

Wisconsin, 1993 Chevrolet Caprice, discontinued, no license plate, closed wheel wells..$20

Wisconsin, 1993 Chevrolet Caprice, discontinued, 1996 license plate, closed wheel wells $10

Wisconsin, 1998 Ford Crown Victoria, 1998 license plate ....never produced

Wyoming, 1994 Ford Crown Victoria, discontinued, 1996 license plate....................$10

Wyoming, 1994 Ford Crown Victoria, 1997 license plate $8

Wyoming, 1998 Ford Crown Victoria, 1998 license plate ....never produced

Road Champs 1957 Ford Police Cars
Courtesy of Robert Jacaszek.

46101 Alabama $6
46102 Arkansas....................$6
46103 Arizona $6
46104 California $6
46105 Colorado $6
46106 Florida $6
46107 Georgia $6
46108 Iowa $6
46109 Idaho $6
46110 Illinois $6
46111 Indiana $6
46112 Kansas $6
46113 New Jersey $6
46114 New York $6
46115 Texas $6
46116 Kentucky $6
46117 Maryland $6
46118 Tennessee $8
46119 Michigan $6
46120 Missouri $6
46121 Nebraska $8
46122 New Mexico....................$8

Road Champs 1955 Chevrolet Police Cars
Courtesy of Robert Jacaszek.

46201 Ohio....................$6
46202 West Virginia $6
46203 Wisconsin $6
46204 North Carolina $6
46205 Louisiana $6
46206 Alaska....................$6
46207 Montana $6
46208 Oregon $6
46209 South Dakota....................$6

Road Champs Capital City and Municipal Police and Taxis, 1:43 Scale

1997 Anaheim, CA $8
1997 Annapolis, MD $8
1996 Atlanta, GA....................$10
1999 Atlanta, GA, 1999 Ford Crown Victoria, 10,000 limited edition with brass lapel pin .$8

1997 Augusta, ME $8
1998 Austin, TX $6
1997 Baton Rouge, LA $8
1998 Bentonville, AR $6
1998 Bismarck, ND $6
1997 Boise, ID $8
1999 Boston, MA 1999 Ford Crown Victoria, 10,000 limited edition with brass lapel pin....................$6
1996 Branson, MO $10
1997 Charleston, WV $8
1996 Chicago, IL, discontinued $10
1997 Chicago, IL, discontinued $8
1999 Chicago, IL, 1998 Ford Crown Victoria, 10,000 limited edition with brass lapel pin....................$8
1995 Chicago, IL Checker Taxi, 1993 Chevrolet Caprice $15
1997 Columbia, SC $8
1997 Columbus, OH, discontinued $8
1997 Denver, CO, discontinued $8
1997 Des Moines, IA $8
1996 Dyersville, IA, discontinued....................$10
1997 Gettysburg, PA $8
1998 Green Bay, WI....................$6
1997 Hartford, CT $8
1997 Helena, MT, discontinued....................$8
1997 Indianapolis, IN, discontinued $8
1997 Jackson, MS $8
1998 Jefferson City, MS....................$6
1999 Kansas City, MO, 1999 Ford Crown Victoria, 10,000 limited edition with brass lapel pin....................$9
1996 Lancaster, PA....................$10
1996 Las Vegas, NV, 1994 Ford Crown Victoria....................$8
1997 Las Vegas, NV $8
1997 Little Rock, AR....................$8
1997 Lincoln, NE $8
1997 Louisville, KY, discontinued $8
1998 Miami Beach, FL $6
1998 Montgomery, AL $6
1998 Montpelier, VT $6
1997 Montreal, Quebec....................$8
1997 Nashville, TN $8
1997 New Orleans, LA $8
1995 New York City Taxi, 1993 Chevrolet Caprice, boxed....................$9
1996 Niagara Falls Regional PD, Ontario .$10
1997 Niagara Regional Police, 1994 Ford Crown Victoria $8
1997 North Pole, AK, discontinued $8
1998 Oklahoma City, OK $6
1998 Olympia, WA $6
1996 Orlando, FL, discontinued....................$10
1997 Phoenix, AZ, discontinued $8
1997 Port Authority, NY/NJ $8
1997 Providence, RI $8
1997 Richmond, VA, discontinued....................$8
1997 Sacramento, CA $8
1998 St. Paul, MN $8
1997 Salt Lake City, UT $8
1997 Savannah, GA $8

1997 Springfield, IL, discontinued $8
1997 Tallahassee, FL, discontinued....................$8

1997 Topeka, KS....................$8

1997 Trenton, NJ $8
1996 U.S. Park Service....................$8
1996 Vancouver, BC $8

Other Road Champs Police and Fire Vehicles, 1:43 Scale

Bowling Green, KY Fire Chief, Chevy Suburban $6
Hartford, CT Fire Chief, Chevy Suburban ..$6
Lancaster, PA, Dodge Ram with Horse Trailer....................$8
Nassau County, NY PD, Chevy Suburban with Horse Trailer....................$8
Nevada K-9, Chevy Suburban/discontinued $6
New Jersey, Chevy Suburban....................$6
Philadelphia, PA Fire Chief, Chevy Suburban $6
Rhode Island, Chevy Suburban $6
St. Louis, MO Fire Chief, Chevy Suburban $6
Washington, D.C., Chevy Blazer/discontinued $8
West Virginia, Jeep Grand Cherokee $6

Road Champs Vintage Trucks, 1:43 Scale with matching billboard (65400 Series) or without billboard.

Introduced in 1998
64500 Series without matching billboard:
64502 1953 Chevrolet Service Tow Truck $7
64505 1954 Chevrolet Pepsi Panel Van $7
64503 1956 Ford Texaco with Oil Drums....................$7
64504 1959 Chevrolet El Camino....$7
64501 1961 Chevrolet Apache $7
65400 Series with matching billboard:
65401 1961 Chevrolet Apache $9
65402 1953 Chevrolet Service Tow Truck $9
65403 1956 Ford Texaco with Oil Drums....................$9
65404 1959 Chevrolet El Camino....$9
65405 1954 Chevrolet Pepsi Panel Van $9

Road Champs Ford Truck Series, 1:43 Scale, officially licensed by the Ford Motor Company

Ford Explorer
v.1 red and beige, 1994....................$4
v.2 green and beige, 1994....................$4

Ford F100 1956 Pickup
v.1 red, 1994 ....$4
v.2 green, 1994 ....$4
Ford F150 Flareside Pickup
v.1 metallic aqua, 1994.................$4
v.2 dark blue, 1994 ....$4

Road Champs Chevrolet Truck Series, 1:43 Scale

1953 Chevrolet C3100 Pickup
v.1 orange, 1995 ....$4

v.2 green, 1995............................$4

v.3 primer brown, 1995 ....$5

1994 Chevrolet Suburban
v.1 silver and black, 1994.............$4
v.2 red/silver, 1994....................$4
1994 Chevrolet Big Dooley Extended Cab
Pickup, dual rear wheels
v.1 black, 1994.........................$4
v.2 burgundy, 1994 ....$4
1995 Chevrolet S-10 ZR2 with tool box
v.1 black with silver trim, 1995.........$4
v.2 red with black trim, 1995...........$4

v.3 Garden State Parkway Maintenance, yellow body with a silver tool box.............$7

1995 Chevrolet Blazer
v.1 blue with silver trim......................$4
v.2 black with silver trim $4
v.3 teal, 1995 ....$4

Road Champs Jeep Series, 1:43 Scale

1995 Jeep Grand Cherokee Limited
v.1 black $4
v.2 white $4
v.3 silver $4
1995 Jeep YJ
v.1 blue...............................$4
v.2 orange..............................$4

v.3 Sahara green............................$4

Road Champs Fabulous '50s / Classic Collection, 1:43 Scale models with accompanying billboard.

Introduced in 1998 as Fabulous fifties, the series name was changed to Classic Collection for 1999.
1955 Chevrolet Bel Air
v.1 two-tone gray and tan $9
v.2 two-tone white and red...............$9
1959 Chevrolet Impala Convertible
v.1 burnt orange $9
1959 Chevrolet Impala Soft Top.............$9
1959 Chevrolet Impala Hardtop $9
1957 Ford Fairlane Convertible...............$9
1957 Ford Fairlane Convertible with Continental Kit $9
1957 Ford Fairlane Hardtop...................$9
1955 Oldsmobile 98 Starfire Convertible
v.1 two-tone blue and white..............$9
v.2 two-tone orange-red and white $9
1958 Pontiac Bonneville Convertible
v.1 pace car $9
v.2 black $9
1958 Pontiac Bonneville Hardtop $9
1955 Pontiac Safari Station Wagon
v.1 brown and white $9
v.2 blue and white $9

Road Champs Corvette Classics

Chevrolet Corvettes in 1:43 scale with commemorative metal license plate. According to Robert Jacaszek, probably only seven were produced. Others were, as described in Road Champs bulletins, either not produced or have been discontinued.
1953 Corvette Convertible, white, #61501 ....$9-10
1954 Corvette, #61505 ....$9-10
1955 Corvette Soft Top, discontinued 10/98, #61504m, if ever produced $18-20
1955 Corvette Hard Top V-8, red, #61506 ....$9-10
1957 Corvette (actually a 1955 with coves painted on) $9-10
1963 Corvette Split Window............$9-10
1966 Corvette Stingray Hard Top (C-5), discontinued 10/98, 61511, if ever produced..........................$18-20
1967 Corvette L88 Stingray Convertible (C2), discontinued 10/98, 61510, if ever produced.........................$18-20
1975 Corvette ....never produced
1978 25th Anniversary Corvette, silver, #61502 ....$9-10
1978 Corvette Indy Pace Car, black, 61507 ....$9-10
1982 Corvette Collector Edition (C-2) ....never produced
1983 Corvette Collector Edition, discontinued 05/98, #61509, if ever produced $18-20
1984 Corvette Targa Top (C-4), discontinued 05/98, #61513, if ever produced $18-20

1986 Corvette Indy Pace Car discontinued 05/98, #61514, if ever produced $18-20
1988 35th Anniversary Corvette, white, discontinued 05/98, 61515, if ever produced $18-20
1993 40th Anniversary Corvette discontinued 05/98, 61516, if ever produced $18-20
1997 Corvette (C-5), red, 61503 .....$9-10
1998 Corvette (C-5) Convertible, white, 61508 ....$9-10
1998 Corvette (C-5) Indy Pace Car, 61517 ....$9-10

Road Champs Muscle Cars, 1:43 Scale

1959 Chevrolet Camaro Hardtop Z-28....$9
1967 Chevrolet Camaro Hardtop Z-28....$9
1967 Chevrolet Camaro Convertible Pace Car $9
1969 Chevrolet Camaro Convertible Pace Car $9
1969 Dodge Charger Daytona.............$9
1969 Dodge Charger Standard.............$9
1968 Ford Mustang Boss 302 Louver Back.............................$9
1969 Pontiac GTO "The Judge" $9

Road Champions Collectibles Classic Scenes, 1999, 1:43 Scale, packaged in a clear display box with accessories

1953 Chevrolet 3100 Pickup, Chevrolet, green with 6 oil drums in back and accessory engine.............................$9
1953 Chevrolet 3100 Pickup, Texaco, red with gas pump, no payload $9
1953 Chevrolet 3100 Pickup, Texaco, red with gas pump, six oil drums in back ..$9
1953 Chevrolet 3100 Wrecker, Goodyear, silver with 4 accessory tires...............$9
1954 Chevrolet Panel Van, Pepsi-Cola, blue with matching handtruck $9
1959 Chevrolet El Camino, Pepsi-Cola, blue and white with matching vending machine $9
1956 Ford F-100 Pickup, Hershey's, chocolate brown with bottles of Hershey syrup in crate............................$9
1956 Ford F-100 Pickup, Hershey's, chocolate brown with matching vending machine $9
1956 Ford F-100 Pickup, Ford, blue with six oil drums in back and accessory engine $9
1956 Ford F-100 Pickup, Mobilgas, black with gas pump, no payload $9
1956 Ford F-100 Pickup, Mobilgas, black with gas pump, six oil drums in back............................$9
1956 Ford F-100 Wrecker, Mobilgas, black with gas pump $9
1956 Ford F-100 Pickup, Texaco, red with gas pump $9
1956 Ford F-100 Wrecker, Texaco, red with gas pump...........................$9

Road Champions Collectibles Then & Now Sets, 1:43 Scale two-car sets

1953 Chevrolet 3100 Pickup, turquoise, & 1995 Chevrolet S-10 Pickup, navy blue............$12

1953 Chevrolet 3100 Pickup, orange with purple trim, & 1995 Chevrolet S-10 Dually Pickup, red and black with silver and white accents........$9

1953 Chevrolet Corvette, burgundy, & 1998 Chevrolet Corvette, yellow $12

1955 Chevrolet Bel Air, Alaska Territorial Police & 1995 Chevrolet Caprice, Alaska State Trooper.........$12

1955 Chevrolet Bel Air, two-tone metallic light blue and white & 1997 Chevrolet Blazer, metallic olive green............$12

1956 Ford F-100, black, & 1993 Ford Explorer, metallic green gray with white, orange and pink trim.......$9

1957 Ford Fairlane, New York State Police & 1998 Ford Crown Victoria, New York State Police.........$12

1961 Chevrolet Apache 10 Pickup, red, & 1996 Chevrolet S-10 Pickup, blue with white & yellow trim.........$12

1961 Chevrolet Apache 10 Pickup, gold with purple flames, & 1996 Chevrolet S-10 Pickup, white with purple trim $9

1969 Dodge Daytona, white with red tail stripe and spoiler, & 1996 Dodge Ram Pickup, black with red and yellow flame accents $12

1969 Dodge Daytone, red with white tail stripe and spoiler, & 1996 Dodge Ram Pickup, metallic light blue with bright pink accents $9

Road Champions Peterson Cover Cars, 1:43 Scale, packaged in a clear display box with miniature magazine cover depicting the car

1955 Chevrolet Bel Air, *Rod & Custom* magazine, red $8

1955 Chevrolet Bel Air, *Car Craft* magazine, yellow $8

1955 Chevrolet Corvette, *Corvette Fever* magazine, red $8

1969 Chevrolet Camaro, *Chevy High Performance* magazine, silver $8

1970 Chevrolet Chevelle, *Chevy High Performance* magazine, orange $8

Road Champions Collectibles Limited Edition Anniversary Cars, 1:43 Scale, packaged in clear plastic display box

30th Anniversary
  1969 Chevrolet Camaro SS $8
  1969 Dodge Superbee.........$8
  1969 Dodge Daytona $8
  1969 Hurst Oldsmobile 442.....$60–75
  1969 Pontiac GTO $8
  1969 Pontiac Firebird Trans Am.........$8
  1969 Ford Mustang Boss $8
40th Anniversary

1959 El Camino $8
1959 Impala $8
50th Anniversary
  1949 Mercury $8
  1949 Oldsmobile, never made, no casting produced

Road Champs Car & Driver Famous Highway Series

Porsche 959.........$6
Plymouth Prowler.........$6
Dodge Viper $6

Other Road Champs, 1:43 Scale Vintage Cars

1932 Ford Coupe, several variations ...$6–8

1949 Ford Woodie.........$15

1949 Mercury, several variations including two stock and two custom $6–8

1955 Chevy Nomad, purple, Peterson Series I.........$10–12

Road Champs Flip Top, cars with lever on bottom that retracts the convertible top

Capri.........$5
Corvette $5
Mercedes.........$5
Miata.........$5
Saab 900 ....$5
Volkswagen $5

Road Champs Boardman Emergency Vehicles, 1:64 Scale, introduced in 1995

Boardman Tower Unit
  v.1 Boston Fire Department.........$5
  v.2 St. Louis Fire Department $5
  v.3 Washington, D. C. Fire Department .$5
Boardman/International Fire Pumper
  v.1 Boston Fire Department.........$5
  v.2 St. Louis Fire Department $5
  v.3 Washington, D. C. Fire Department .$5
Boardman/International JB-Res-Q
  v.1 Boston Fire Department.........$5
  v.2 St. Louis Fire Department $5
  v.3 Washington, D. C. Fire Department .$5

Road Champs Deluxe Series - 1:64 Scale commercial, municipal, and emergency vehicles

American LaFrance Fire Engine with Movable Boom Crane $4
Delivery Van, Cheetos $4
Delivery Van, Pepsi $4
Delivery Van, United States Postal Service ..$6
Elgin Pelican Street Sweeper.........$6
International Beverage Delivery Truck, Pepsi $4
International Beverage Delivery Truck, Snapple.........$4

International Recycling Truck $4
International School Bus, Golden Rule $4
International School Bus, International $4
International Snow Plow Dump Truck, red with black accents, 1999 issue $4
International Wrecker, blue and white, 1999 issue $4
Jerr-Dan Auto Salvage Transporter, red, white & blue.........$4
Jerr-Dan Auto Salvage Transporter, burgundy & white $4
Mercedes-Benz Airport Stretch Limousine, metallic silver.........$4
Mercedes-Benz Airport Stretch Limousine, white $4
Peterbilt Refuse/Recycling Truck, burgundy.$4
Peterbilt Refuse/Recycling Truck, gray $4
Peterbilt Refuse/Recycling Truck, white $4
Winnebago Chieftain Motor Home, beige .$5
Winnebago Chieftain Motor Home, white ..$4
Winnebago Chieftain Motor Home, "Bug" theme.........$4
Zamboni, blue and white.........$6
Zamboni, flames.........$4

Road Champs Anteaters / Cabs & Trailers, 1:87 Scale semi-trucks and trailers

"Allied Van Lines".........$6
"Bekins Van Lines".........$6
"Cotter & Company True Value Hardware Stores".........$10
"Dole".........$5
"Exxon" Tanker $4
"Frito Lay".........$4
"Goodyear".........$4
"Hershey's Kisses".........$4
"Horseless Carriage Automobile Transportion".........$7
Livestock Truck $4
Low Loader Transporter "Tri State Haulers" .$6
"Mayflower" Moving Van, C.O.E. $6
"Mayflower" Moving Van, conventional....$6
NASA Rocket Transporter.........$4
"Pepsi".........$4
"Pilot" Tanker Truck.........$4
Pipe Truck.........$6
"Reese's Pieces".........$4
Sand Hopper Truck.........$4
"Snapple".........$4

Road Champs Eagle Coach Country Tour Bus Series, 1:64 Scale

Alabama.........$5
Clint Black $5
Billy Ray Cyrus.........$5
Diamond Rio $5
Vince Gill $5
George Jones.........$5
Lorrie Morgan $5
Ricky Skaggs.........$5
Marty Stuart $5
Randy Travis $5
Travis Tritt #1, black upper/tuquiose lower, chrome wheels.........$5

Travis Tritt #2, grayish cream upper/silver-gray lower, "Here's A Quarter," gold wheels $5
Tanya Tucker.................................$5
Hank Williams Jr. #1, gold upper $5
Hank Williams Jr. #2, silver-gray upper $5

Road Champs City and Tour Buses, 1:87 Scale Municipal Transit Buses and one Greyhound

CTA (Chicago Transit Authority) Bus $5
NJT (New Jersey Transit) Bus $5
MCTO (Metropolitan Council) $5
MTA (Metropolitan Transit Authority).........$5
1997 Metro, Houston TX.....................$5
1997 A.C. Transit, Oakland CA $5
Sun Tours Bus $5
DBM Gad About Tour Bus $5
1997 Metro-Houston TX.....................$5
1997 A.C. Transit, Oakland CA $5
Eagle Coach Greyhound $5

Road Champs Flyers / Flying Champs, historic military aircraft, approximately 4" long

AH-64 Apache Helicopter $4
B-17 "Sally Ann" Bomber painted in colors of the 91st Bomb Group, Bassingbourne, England $4
B-25 Mitchell "Panchito" with markings of B-25 owned by National War Plane Museum $4
B-29 Super Fortress $4
B-747 Air Force One Presidential Airplane Limited Edition $6
Douglas C-47, D-Day markings $4
Douglas DC-3 Commercial Jet, 1:200 scale
v.1 Pan Am Airlines $4
v.2 Eastern Airlines $4
v.3 Alaska Airlines..........................$4
F-4U Corsair flown by "Pappy" Boyington, legendary Congressional Medal of Honor winner................................$4
F-111 Aardvark Two-Seat Tactical Fighter-Bomber of the U. S. Air Force $4
F-111 Leopard, flesh color with black leopard spots, 2000 variation $4
F-117A Blackjet Stealth.......................$4
F-14 Tomcat "Jolly Roger" $4
F-16 Falcon Fighter of the U. S. Air Force "Thunderbirds" $4
F-18 Hornet High-Tech Navy Super Fighter..$4
F-18 Wildcat, blue with yellow accents, Blue Angels, U.S. Navy, 2000 variation ...$4
Orbiter Space Shuttle $4
P-38J Lightning...............................$4
P-47 Thunderbolt "Lil Friend" 56th Fighter Group, Halesworth, England............$4
P-51D Mustang $4
SR71 Blackbird $4

Sports Series Trucks

Tennis, white truck with tennis graphics, tennis court on roof, 1:64 ....$4
Touchdown, white truck with football graphics, football field on roof, 1:64 ....$4

Other Road Champs Models

1998 Ford Crown Victoria, Toys 'R' Us Geoffrey, 1998 license plate, 1:43 ....$8
1955 Chevy Taxi, Old Navy, blue and white, 1:43 ....$8
Airport Shuttle Van, 1:64 ....$1
Caterpillar D10N bulldozer, mustard yellow, all plastic, new for 2000, 1:43.........$4
Chevrolet Big Dooley Pickup, black with orange flames bordered in yellow, 2000 variation, 1:43................................$4
Chevrolet Caprice U.S.C.G. Ocean Guard, 2000 variation, 1:43..................$4
Chevrolet S10 ZR2 Pickup, U.S.C.G. Ocean Guard, 2000 variation, 1:43 ....$4
Chevrolet S10 ZR2 Pickup, County Works Road Crew, red, 2000 variation, 1:43.........$4
Chevrolet Step Van, "Mooring's Dairy," white with black cow spots, 2000 variation, 1:64...................................$4
'57 Chevy Bel Air, red with opening doors, 1:64 ....$4
'57 Corvette, white, opening doors, NJ07029 on bottom.....................$4
'68 Corvette, silver with blue accents, "24 fury" on top, opening doors, NJ07028 on bottom................................$4
'82 Corvette, white with flames and "Vette" on top, opening doors, NJ07029 on bottom.................................$4
'85 Corvette, black with red & white "Vette" on hood, opening doors, NJ07029 on bottom $4
Dodge Ram Pickup, fuchsia with yellow, orange and red-orange flames, 2000 variation, 1:43................................$4
Dodge Viper GTS, red with black interior, 2000 variation, 1:43 ....$4
Dump Truck, yellow, Hard Hats series.......$1
Eagle Coach, "HALLOWEEN" graphics, silver lower, black upper, 2000 variation, 1:64.....................................$4
Ferrari, brown with black & gold accents, opening doors and rear engine cover................................$1
Fiero, two-tone green with "Sp" & spoiler on top, opening doors and rear engine cover $1
Firebird, pink, opening doors, "Star cruiser #50" on hood & top, JRI inc. 1982 NJ07029 on bottom.......................$1
Ford Aeromax 120, red cab, white trailer with "HAPPY BIRTHDAY" graphics, 2000 variation, 1:64......................$4
Ford Crown Victoria Fire Chief, red, "052" on roof, white shield, 2000 variation, 1:43 ....$4
Ford Econoline Van, white "U-HAUL" with Nevada graphics, new for 2000, 1:43 ....$4
Ford Explorer, white with bright blue zigzag bordered in black, white interior, 2000 variation, 1:43.............................$4

Ford F150 Pickup, white, "U-HAUL," Idaho graphics on hood, 2000 variation, 1:43 ....$4
Ford Model A, red, doors and rumble seat open, 1:64 ....$6
Jaguar, green with "Slice #51" on top, opening doors, NJ07029 on bottom........$1
Kenworth T600A U-HAUL semi, white with Kansas graphics, 2000 variation, 1:87 ....$4
1998 Plymouth Prowler, purple with black roof, gray bumpers, 2000 variation, 1:43 ....$4
Porsche 911, purple, opening doors, 928 on hood, NJ07C23 on bottom..............$1
Porsche 959, silver with black interior, 2000 variation, 1:43 ....$4
Stake Truck, Farmer Brown, 3" $1
Toyota Pickup with Camper Topper, black, 1:64..$1
Toyota Pickup with Camper Topper, red, 1:64..$1
Toyota Pickup Wrecker, 1:64 ....$1
U-Haul Truck, white with Mississippi graphics, new for 2000................................$4
Volvo Cement Truck, white with green base, new for 2000, 1:64.......................$4

Road Legends (see Yat Ming)

Road Machine

Road Machine is an obscure import from Hong Kong.
Porsche 928, 1:64 ....$4

Roadmaster (also see D.C.M.T., Impy and Lone Star)

Roadmaster, also spelled Road-Master, is part of the brand name given to a line of toy cars made by D.C.M.T. of London, England. The more common name is Impy, short for Lone Star Road-Master Impy Super Cars. For more information, see D.C.M.T. and Lone Star.

Roadmates

Over the years, Sears has offered an assortment of toy vehicles called Roadmates. Individual models in blisterpacks were usually repackaged Playart models, while sets were most often Zee Toys Pacesetters. Since the models themselves are recognized by their brand names, and the Roadmates name was only on the package, they are listed in their respective headings.

Road Rovers (also see Hallmark, LJN)

Hallmark offered several crude but charming diecast toy cars in the seventies called Road Rovers. A connection with LJN has also been reported. Go to Hallmark for list and values.

Road Runners (see MegaMovers)

Road Tough (see Yatming)

Rob Eddie (see Brooklins)

Roberts

One model, a six-wheeler with a bucket loader on the front, has been found with Roberts stamped on the front of the grill. More information is needed.

Roco

Roco models are ready-to-run pre-colored 1:87 scale vehicles made in Austria. Walthers HO catalog lists a huge assortment. While it may be that some Roco models are diecast, they are more likely plastic. The detail and accuracy is, nevertheless, noteworthy of inclusion in this book. When applicable, Walthers catalog number is included with model description. Prices indicated are current catalog prices from Walthers. Here is a sample listing. Many other models are currently available.

Roco Emergency Vehicles

Covered Trailer, 625-1309 ....$3.99
Dodge Red Cross Jeep, Truck & Field Kitchen Trailer, 625-1388 ....$10.49
Dodge Swiss Emergency Truck, 625-1348 ....$9.99
Land Rover KLFA Fire Truck, 625-1359 .$10.49
Land Rover Red Cross, 625-1380 ....$10.49
Land Rover, 625-1381 ....$10.49
Magirus 2312 Fire Ladder Truck, 625-1349 ....$19.99
Magirus D LF 16 Fire Truck, 625-1396 .$15.99
Magirus DLK 23-12 with Turn Ladder, 625-1346 ....$21.49
Magirus TLF Fire Truck, 625-1386 ....$14.99
Magirus TLF 16 Fire Pumper, 625-1366 ....$14.99
MAN THW 5-Ton with Canvas Hood, 625-1302 ....$8.49
MAN THW 5-Ton Equipment Truck, 625-1308 ....$6.49
MAN 5T with Trailer, Red Cross, 625-1339 ....$8.49
MAN 630L 2 A Red Cross Bus & Trailer, 625-1387 ....$11.49
MAN 630 L2A Technical Rescue Service, 625-1372 ....$7.99
Mercedes-Benz DL Ladder, 625-1398 .$19.99
Mercedes-Benz LF8 Fire Truck, 265-1351 ....$10.99
Mercedes-Benz LF 25, 625-1374 ....$17.99
Mercedes-Benz LF8 Fire Truck with Trailer & DKW Portable Motor Pump, 625-1375 ....$14.99
Mercedes-Benz L4500 D122 Ladder Truck, 625-1361 ....$19.99
Mercedes-Benz SRF Repair Truck with Hiab Crane & removable Container, 625-1369 ....$18.99
Mercedes TLFA 4000 Rosenbauer, 625-1379 ....$16.49

Mercedes 1017 Police Truck with Canvas, 625-1383 ....$10.99
Munga DKW Red Cross, 625-1301 ..$5.49
Munga Fire Dept. Radio Car, 625-1300 ....$5.49
Munga Jeep Red Cross, 625-1329 ....$4.49
Opel Blitz TLF 15, 625-1398 ....$12.49
Opel Blitz with Fire Extinguisher Trailer, 625-1337 ....$14.49
Pinzgauer 6x6 Command Car, 625-1386 ....$14.99
Renault DLK 23-12 Fire Ladder Truck, 625-1371 ....$19.99
Steyr 680 TLF Fire Truck, 265-1342 .$13.99
THW Field Kitchen Trailer, 625-1320 ....$3.99
Unimog S with Canvas Hood, Red Cross, 625-1338 ....$7.99
Unimog 1300L Fire Ambulance, 625-1364 ....$8.99
Unimog 4-Wheel Drive Fire Engine, 625-1304 ....$9.49
Volkswagen Ambulance, 625-1355 ...$7.49
Volkswagen Ambulance Van, 625-1377 ....$7.49
Volkswagen Bus and Field Kitchen Unit Truck, 625-1376 ....$18.49
Volkswagen Double Cab Fire fighting Unit, 625-1362 ....$6.49
Volkswagen Minibus with Horse Trailer, 625-1384 ....$17.99
Volkswagen THW, 625-1323 ....$5.49
Volkswagen Type 2 Ambulance, 625-1372 ....$7.99
Volkswagen Type 2 Command Car, 625-1370 ....$7.99
Volkswagen Type 2 DB Railway Police, 625-1382 ....$7.49
Volkswagen 2-Unit Mini Bus Set, 625-1385 ....$18.49
Willys Jeep Fire Dept., 625-1365 ......$6.99

Roco Emergency Helicopters

MBB BO 105 Police, 625-1391 ....$9.49
MBB BO 105 Rescue, 625-1392 ......$9.49
MBB BO 105 Rescue, ADAC, 625-1390 ....$9.49

Roco Construction Vehicles

Construction Set with Site Truck and Two Site Office Trailers, 625-1545 ....$25.99
Magirus D Tipping Semi Trailer, 625-1546 ....$19.99
Magirus Dump Truck, 625-1527 ......$15.49
Magirus 3-Axle Dump Truck with Trailer, 625-1543 ....$22.99
Mercedes-Benz 4500 Tanker, 625-1526 ....No price provided
Mercedes Unimog Road Building Vehicle Set Add-On, 625-1547 ....$49.99
Mercedes Unimog 1300 & Sauer Komet Bus Construction Site Set, 625-1561 ....$19.49
Steyr Construction Vehicle with Accessories, 625-1533 ....$24.99

Steyr 91 Tractor with Flatbed and Power Shovel, 625-1516 ....$37.49
Volvo FL10 with Silo Moving Equipment, 625-1561 ....$23.99

Roco Semi Trucks

Magirus M5 "Schenker," 625-1569 ..$12.49
Magirus Tractor & Trailer "DB/TFG," 625-1524 ....$16.99
Magirus Tractor & Trailer "Danzas," 625-1538 ....$15.49
Mercedes 1838 with "Kieserling" Double Trailers, 625-1571 ....$28.49
Mercedes 1838 with "Kohne & Nagel" Double Trailers, 625-1577 ....$27.49
Mercedes 1838 "Schenker," 625-1576 ....no price provided
Mercedes 1838 with "Sixt" Trailer, 625-1579 ....$28.49
Renault "Kolner Flitzer," 625-1584 ....no price provided
Renault Tractor Trailer "Rouch," 625-1528 ....$14.99
Renault 3-Axle Tractor Trailer "Beck," 625-1567 ....$17.49
Steyr 91 Semi with "Gondrand" 3-Axle Trailer, 625-1557 ....$16.99
Steyr 91 Semi with "Ischler Saltz" Trailer, 625-1520 ....$14.99
Steyr 91 Semi with "Spedition Gartner" Trailer, 625-1514 ....$14.99
Volvo FL10 Truck & Trailer, unmarked, 625-1575 ....no price provided
Volvo FL10 "Kuhlzug" Refrigerator Truck & Trailer, 625-1581 ....$28.49
Volvo FL10 with "La Maxilaterale" Trailer, 625-1430 ....$24.49
Volvo FL10 with Double Trailers, unmarked, 625-1430 ....$24.49
Volvo FL10 with "Kuhne & Nagel" Double Trailers, 625-1570 ....$24.99
Volvo "Laurie Ashley" Freight Truck, 625-1583 ....$11.99

Roco Saurer Buses

Austrian Postal, 625-1600 ....$15.49
"Komet" tour Bus, 625-1602 ....$15.49

Roco Maintenance / Utility Vehicles

Dodge Tow Truck, 625-1712 ....$8.49
MAN 630 with Repair Shop, 625-1410 ....$12.49
Renault G Service, 625-1656 ....$15.49
Unimog 1300 Utility, 625-1503 ......$29.99
Magirus Highway Maintenance, 625-1655 ....$17.49

Many more Roco brand HO gauge models are currently available.

Rolux

Rolux models are lead alloy miniatures made in France in the early 1940s.
Limousine, lead body, aluminum chassis........................$45-60
Army Staff Car, same as limousine with military markings $45-60

ROS (also see Agritec, Ross)

ROS is reportedly a brand of Agritec of Spain, makers of diecast construction and farm equipment. See Agritec for model list.

Ross (also see Agritec, ROS)

Ross, reportedly a division of Agritech of Spain according to collector and dealer Bill Molyneaux, represents a set of high-quality heavy equipment models from Italy. Production of models listed below has been discontinued, and limited quantities are offered through Toys for Collectors while supplies last. A larger assortment is offered by Diecast Miniatures, who chose to spell Ross with one "s." See Agritec for model list.

Rosso

Exoticar at one time offered just one model of these exquisite diecast kits from Rosso.
Ferrari Formula One $369

Rozkvet Mini Models

Collector Neil Edwards reports of an unusual model Skoda 120 made in Czechoslovakia by a company called Rozkvet VDI Mini Models. He paid $1 for it at a flea market. As with most eastern European models, this one is assumed to be produced in 1:43 scale.
Skoda 120, white body, black interior, unpainted base..$15–20

RS Toys

As reported by collector Staffan Kjellin of Sweden, RS Toys were made in Sweden. The company manufactured only three different cars in 1936 and maybe early '37. They were a 1935 De Soto, 1935 Chevrolet, and 1935 Volvo Carioca. Only a few each of these are known to have survived. Replicas have recently been made from the original mould found some years ago by Kaj Wicklander. They are all signed and numbered.
1935 De Soto, 98mm original......$750–1,000
    reproduction $125–200
1935 Chevrolet, 103mm $750–1,000,
    reproduction $125–200
1935 Volvo Carioca, 105mm......$750–1,000
    reproduction $125–200

Ruehl (see Reuhl)

Ruestes

Ruestes models are made in Argentina.
Renault 17 Coupe, 1:43 ....$12
Renault 12 Wagon, 1:43 ....$12

Rullero

Rullero models, like Ruestes, are made in Argentina.
Ike Torino Rally, 10" $22

Russ

Austin Mini, Bump & Go, 2¾" $10

Volkswagen Beetle, Bump & Go, 2¾" $10

Russian models (also see Agat, Gaz, Govroski, Lada, Litan, Lomo, Moskovich, Radon, Saratov, Uaz, Vaz, Volga)

Since the collapse of communism and the beginning of glasnost, Russian exports have started appearing in growing quantities in the US. A wide variety of toys are included in the assortment of goods coming from former Soviet republics. Among them are a large selection of diecast models. Since private corporations have not been widely established, most Russian products are generic. However, most recently, several Russian brand names have emerged such as Radon, Agat, Litan, Saratov, and Lomo, as reported by Alexander Yurcenko in the June 1997 issue of Model Auto Review.

Below is a sampling of Russian models that have recently become a lot more popular.
Cheika Limousine $15
Moskvitch Patrol Car................................$15

Russian Armored Vehicle, crude cast, plastic wheels, thick steel axles $15

Zil Limousine...$15
2 Moskvitch 402 Sedan............................$14
26 Volga GAZ 24 Sedan $14
35 Chaika GAZ 13 Limousine $22
37 Russobalt Tourer.................................$19
38 Lada Niva 4WD $24
40 Moskvitch Pickup $14
49 Russbalt Sedan $19
50 Russbalt Landau $19
56 Chaika GAZ14 Limousine $22
59 Zil Dump Truck $24
64 Volkswagen RAF 977 Van $27
66 Alfa Romeo $14
71 Zis Type 2 Fire Truck $37
77 Zis Type 5 Fire Pumper $37
78 IZ Jupiter Police Motorbike & Side Car, 1:24 ....$24
81 Amo Type 4 Fire Truck.........................$51
83 Zis 5 Ton Truck...................................$24
101 1934 GAZ-Ford AAA Fire Truck ....no price available
108 UAZ 469 4WD Road Police Jeep $24
115 Krupp KMK 4070 4-axle Crane, 1:50 ..$129
116 Krupp KMK 4070 5-axle Crane, 1:50 ..$139
117 Kamaz 4310 Postal Truck...................$29

125 UAZ 452 Military Bus Van.................$29
127 Zis Type 6 3-axle Pumper Fire Truck......$42
506 Zis-8 St. Petersburg City Bus, wood & metal, very limited quantities $139

RW (see Ziss)

Sablon

Sablon toys were made in Belgium starting in 1968. They are fairly accurate representations with opening doors and hoods. After 1970, Nacoral took over the tooling and reissued some of the models under the Nacoral InterCar brand.
BMW 1600 GT $32
    BMW 2000 CS $32
    BMW Glas 3000 V8 ....$32
    Mercedes 6x4 Tank Truck, orange/red/ white, 1:43 ....$25
Mercedes-Benz 200 ....$72
Mercedes-Benz 250 SE $32
Porsche 911 Targa Convertible $42
Porsche 911 Targa Hardtop $42
Porsche 911 Polizei $32
Renault 16 ....$32

Sabra (also see Cragstan, Gamda-Sabra, Gamda-Koor)

Models of 1:43 scale comprise this intriguing series from Sabra of Israel produced in the early seventies first by Cragstan, then by Gamda-Koor, under the Detroit Seniors name.
1964 Chevrolet Chevelle Wagon Fire Chief ..$24
1964 Chevrolet Chevelle Wagon Israeli Ambulance $24
1964 Chevrolet Chevelle Wagon U.S. Ambulance $24
Cadillac Coupe de Ville $48
Chevrolet Corvair....................................$24
Plymouth Barracuda $36
Pontiac GTO...$36

Safar

A single model is known to have been produced in 1947 under the Safar brand of Italy.
Fastback Coupe, 4" $45

Safir

From 1961 to 1978, Safir of France produced a wide variety of 1:43 scale miniature models. Though not very successful, many of their models were copied by Hong Kong firms known for producing cheap unlicensed knock-offs of other manufacturers' products. Safir models are typically valued at $10 to $25 each.
#1 1892 Peugeot Vis-A-Vis $20
#1 1895 Peugeot $20
#2 1898 Peugeot Victoria $20
#3 1899 Peugeot Victoria $20
#4 1896 Peugeot, top down $20
#5 1901 Vis-A-Vis Decauville 5 H.P. $20
#6 1901 Vis-A-Vis Decauville 4½ H.P. $20
#7 1902 Renault Paris-Vienne $20

#8 1911 Ford Model T Roadster "Tin Lizzie" 20 H.P. $20
#9 1924 Citroën Taxi 10 H.P. $20
#10 1900 Renault Coupe 35 H.P. $20
#11 1923 Citroën Fire Truck $20
#12 1923 Citroën Ambulance..................$20
#14 1901 Fiat 8 H.P. $20
#15 1901 Mercedes $20
#16 1899 Renault $20
#17 1898 Panhard $20
#18 1900 Peugeot Coupe.......................$20
#19 1892 Peugeot Toit Bois...................$20
#20 1901 Mercedes 9 H.P. $20
#21 1924 Citroën Taxi, Landau................$20
#22 1924 Citroën Taxi, Top Up $20
#23 1924 Citroën Taxi, Top Down $20
#24 1906 Renault Town Car, Top Up $20
#25 1906 Renault Town Car, Top Down $20
#26 1908 Unic Taxi, Open Cab...............$20
#27 1908 Unic Taxi, Closed Cab.............$20
#30 Lola T70 Temporada $20
#31 Lola T70 Austrian G.P. $20
#32 Lola T70 Paris 1000 KM..................$20
#33 Lola T70 Daytona...........................$20
#34 Lola T70 Nurbringin........................$20
#35 Lola T70 Monza..............................$20
#40 Porsche 917 "Temorada," Buenos Aires, white, Car #28 ....$20
#41 Porsche 917 "Daytona," white w/red stripes, Car #3 ....$20
#42 Porsche 917 "Monza," blue w/Gulf srtipes, Car #7 ....$20
#43 Porsche 917 "Le Mans," white w/stripe, Car #23.........................$20
#44 Porsche 917 "Brands Hatch, "blue w/white stripes, Car #12 ....$20
#45 Porsche 917 "Ecurie Hollandaise," yellow, Car #18.....................$20
#50 Porsche 917L "Le Mans," blue/green stripes, Car #3 ....$20
#51 Porsche 917L "Essais Le Mans," blue, white stripe, Car #3 ....$20
#52 Porsche 917L "Le Mans, 70," white w/red stripes, Car #25............$20
#53 Porsche 917 Hockenheim..................$20
#54 Porsche 917 David Piper..................$20
#55 Porsche 911 Kyalami......................$20
#60 Porsche 917K "Le Mans," 1971 white w/red stripe, Car #22..........$20
#61 Porsche 917K "Ecurie Gulf- John Wyer," blue w/ orange, Car #19 ..$20
#62 Porsche 917K "12 Hour Sebring," silver w/red & blue stripes, Car #3...$20
#63 Porsche 917K "Niburgring," yellow w/green stripes, Car #55 ....$20
#64 Porsche 917L "Le Mans," Ecuri Gulf, John Wyler, blue with orange, Car #18........$20
#65 Porsche 917K "Martini Racing," silver w/blue & red stripes, Car #21 ....$20
#70 Porsche 917 Le Mans $20
#71 Porsche 917 John Wyer....................$20
#72 Porsche 917 Daytona.......................$20
#73 Porsche 917 Nurbraring....................$20

#74 Porsche 917 Gulf Porsche-Wyer $20
#75 Porsche 917 Martini $20
#80 Ferrari 312 T2................................$20
#81 Ligier-Matra JS5.............................$20
#82 Tyrell P34 #4.................................$20
#83 Tyrell P34 #33...............................$20
#101 1910 Gregoire Triple Berline............$20

St. Louis

Six diecast models were produced in 1981 under the St. Louis brand. They are 1:43 scale versions of American cars of the forties and fifties.

Saico

Saico made in China, 1:34 scale and others.

1966 Chevrolet C10, 1:24, D08005 ......$8–10

PT Cruiser, item # DP5019D $5

Sako

Sako models of Argentina are 1:25 scale tin models made in the late 1960s.
1966 Chevrolet Taxi $22
1966 Chevrolet Police Ambulance.............$22
1967 Chevrolet Camaro 2-door Hardtop Rally $22
Porsche 906 Rally.................................$22

Sakura

Sakura models are typical of Japanese diecast manufacturer, offering a mix of 1:43 scale and 5" to 5½" long models for around $20 each.
1 Hino Bus, red, 5".................................$20
1 Honda 360 Pickup, 1:43......................$20
2 Isuzu Fire Pumper, 5½".......................$20
2 Neoplan Double Decker Bus, 5½"..........$20
3 Chevrolet Corvette Coupe, 1:43 ....$20
3 Hino Bus, 1:43.................................$20
3 Suzuki Jeep, 1:36.............................$20
5 Hino Airport Bus $20
6 Hino Bus, 1:43.................................$20
11 Maserati Bora, 1:43..........................$20
13 Lancia Stratos, 1:43.........................$20
105 Nissan R382, 1:64..........................$20
111 Nissan Skyline 4-Door Sedan Fire, 1:43.................................$20
602 Honda Life Police, 1:36 ....$20
609 Nissan Skyline Van, Police, 1:43.........$20
610 Nissan Skyline Van, Fire, 1:43............$20
611 Nissan Skyline Van, Ambulance, 1:43 .$20
4071 Nissan Cedric 4-Door Sedan, Fire, 1:43.................................$20
4085 Nissan School Bus, 5"....................$20
4086 Nissan Kombi, 1:43.......................$20
4088 Nissan Police, 1:43.......................$20

8152 Toyota Land Cruiser, 1:36..............$20
8549 Toyota Mk 2 4-Door Sedan, 1:43.....$20
Toyota Celica Mk 2 Coupe, 1:43.............$20

Salza

Salza models of France have been confused with Cofalu models, except that Salzas are cast aluminum, while Cofalus are plastic. All models are representative of Tour de France support vehicles.
Aspro Ambulance, 4½".............................$40
Jeep with Bicycles, 3½"...........................$40
Gendarmerie Jeep, 3½"............................$40
Press Jeep, 3½".....................................$40
Peugeot 203 Convertible, 5¼"...................$40
Peugeot 404 Sedan, 5¼".........................$40
Peugeot D4A Van, 4"...............................$40
Peugeot D4A Loudspeaker Van, 4".............$40

Sam Toys

Although in business since 1911, Sam Toys of Italy didn't start producing miniature cars until 1958. All Sam Toys are plastic, and currently sell for $10 to $15 each.

Saratov

According to the June 1997 issue of *Model Auto Review*, Saratov remains one of the largest manufacturers of scale models in Russia. A large portion of their current offerings is dominated by Ural models.

Savoye Pewter Toy Company

Back in 1930, "pewter" used to be another name for lead alloy toys. Savoye was based in North Bergen, New Jersey. The last known production year for Savoye was 1936.
Ambulance $35
Army Gun Truck, 3¼" $40
Beer Truck, 4⅜"...................................$80
Bus, 5th Avenue, 4¾".............................$125
Bus, Cross-Country, 3⅜"..........................$40
Bus with Mack Cab, 7½"..........................$45
Convertible $35
Coupe, 3⅜"..$40
Coupe, 3⅜"..$30
Fire Engine, 3¾"...................................$35
Fire Truck, 4¼"....................................$45
Fire Truck, 3¾"....................................$35
Milk Van...$40
Moving Van...$55
Pickup Truck..$40
Police Patrol Van..................................$50
Racer, 4¼"..$30
Roadster, 3½"......................................$40
Roadster, 3⅜"......................................$40
Stake Truck, 4½"..................................$25
Stake Truck, 5¾"..................................$35
Tank Car Set, 10¼"...............................$80
Tow Truck, 4".......................................$40
Tractor, 2¾"..$30
Tractor, 3"..$20

Scale Models (also see Ertl, Scamold)

Ertl is the parent company to the Scale Models brand, some of which are produced in unpainted pewter-like finish. Asheville DieCast of Asheville, North Carolina, is arguably the largest supplier of Ertl, Scale Models, Spec-Cast, Liberty Classics, and others. But Diecast Miniatures offers a considerable selection as well. Below is just a sampling. Like Liberty Classics, Ertl Promotionals, Spec-Cast, and others, Scale Models specialize in producing models with various advertising livery.

Another company, Scale Models, Ltd., is from England and produced accurate replica race cars under the Scamold brand. (See Scamold.)

American Eagle WWII airplane, 10"	$18
Hedge Hopper Helicopter, 10"	$18
Allis WC Tractor, 1:64	$5
Case Steam Engine, 1:64	$7
Dain Commercial Car	$15
Deutz 6275 Tractor, 1:64	$5
Ford 4WD 946 Tractor, 1:64	$7
Hart Parr Tractor, 1:64	$7
1931 International Harvester Tanker "Gilmore Oil Company"	$31
1932 International Harvester Tractor, 1:64	$5
Massey Ferguson 44 Tractor, 1:64	$5
MM Comfort Tractor, 1:64	$5
Oliver 70 Tractor, 1:64	$5
Oliver 770 Tractor, 1:64	$5
Oliver 880 Tractor, 1:64	$5
Rumely Tractor, 1:64	$7
White 185 Tractor, 1:64	$5
White 4270 4WD Tractor, 1:64	$7

Scaleworks

It was in the early months of the year 2000 that this model started appearing in ads and articles in various magazines. Scaleworks is apparently a new diecast model company of which only one model is known, a precision scale model of Craig Breedlove's Spirit of America record car. A removable body panel on the model exposes fully detailed J-79 General Electric jet turbine engine and tube frame, rolling wheels, and tampo printing.

Craig Breedlove's Spirit of America Land Speed Record Jet Car, DPS-SPA99-C, 1:43	$50

Scamold

According to a book on British diecast, Scale Models Ltd of Great Britain manufactured Scamold diecast racing cars from 1939 to 1950. They are extremely accurate 1:35 scale models based on cars that raced at Brooklands race track. Pre-war boxes are marked "Manufactured by Scale Models Ltd, Brooklands Track, Weybridge, Eng." Post-war boxes dropped that designation.

101 ERA Racing Car	$150–200
103 Maserati Racing Car	$150–200
105 Alfa Racing Car	$150–200

Schabak

Schabak models are from Nurnburg, Germany. Started in 1966, Schabak started producing diecast cars after Schuco went out of business. The company has since become associated with Gama, the current owner of the Schuco name. Except where noted all models are produced in 1:43 scale.

1001 VW Jetta, 1979	$20
1002 VW Golf, 1983	$20
1002/3 VW Golf PTT Car, 1984	$20
1003 VW Golf ADAC Car, 1984	$20
1004 VW Golf Tuning, 1984	$20
1008 VW Golf GTI, 1987	$20
1010 VW Jetta, 1984	$20
1011 VW Jetta Police Car	$20
1012 VW Jetta Tuning, 1984	$20
1015 VW Passat, 1988	$20
1016 VW Passat Van, 1988	$20
1018 VW Corrado, 1988	$20
1020 Audi 100 Avant, 1984	$20
1021 Audi 100 Avant Quattro, 1984	$20
1022 Audi 100 Avant DSK Car, 1987	$20
1024 Audi V8, 1989	$20
1025 Audi 80, 1986	$20
1030 Audi 90 Quattro, 1984	$20
1031-A Audi 90 Quattro, 1987	$20
1031-B 1992 Audi 80 Sedan	$17
1035 Audi 80 Quattro, 1987	$20
1036 Audi 80 Quattro Police Car, 1987	$20
1037 Audi 90 Quattro, 1988	$20
1038 Audi 90 Quattro Rally, 1988	$20
1040 VW Caravelle Bus, 1986	$20
1041 VW Caravelle Ambulance, 1986	$20
1042 VW Transporter, 1986	$20
1043 VW Transporter Fire Van, 1986	$20
1045 VW Transporter LUFTHANSA, 1986	$20
1046 VW Caravelle CONDOR, 1986	$20
1047 VW Caravelle Police Bus, green, 1988	$20
1048 VW Caravelle Police Bus, white and green, 1988	$20
1050 1989 Audi Coupe	$16
1080 Ford Sierra Notchback, 1987	$20
1081 Ford Sierrar Police Car, 1988	$20
1086 Ford Fiesta, 1989	$20
1110 1993 Porsche Carrera 2 Convertible	$24
1150 BMW 535i, 1988	$20
1151 BMW 535i Taxi, 1988	$20
1152 BMW 525i Police Car, white with green stripes, 1988	$20
1153 BMW 525i Police Car, white & green, 1988	$20
1154 BMW 525i Fire Department Car, red with white fenders, 1988	$20
1155 BMW 525i Fire Department Car, 1988, white & orange-red, 1988	$20
1156 BMW 525i Doctor's Car, 1988	$20
1158 BMW M5, 1989	$20
1160 BMW Z-1, 1989	$20

Schabak Larger Scale Models

1300 1986 Ford Transit Bus, 1:35, 1987	$30
1301 1986 Ford Transit Van, 1:35, 1987	$30
1500 1985 Ford Scorpio D, 1:25, 1986	$35
1501 1985 Ford Granada, 1:25, 1986	$35
1510 1987 Ford Sierra Notchback, 1:25, 1988	$35
1511 1987 Ford Sierra Notchback, 1:25, 1988	$35
1512 1988 Ford Sierra Cosworth, 1:25, 1989	$35
1513 1988 Ford Sierra Cosworth, 1:25, 1988	$35
1514 Ford Sierra Polizei, 1:25, 1989	$35
1600 BMW Z1 Convertible, 1:25, 1989	$35

Schabak Aircraft of the World Collection

Listed below are Schabak's latest offerings of scale model airplanes. Each model, listed with the Schabak model number and name, is available in various liveries.

Schabak 1:600 Scale Diecast Aircraft Models

901 Boeing 747/200	$4–5
902 McDonnell-Douglas DC-10	$4–5
903 Airbus A 300 B	$4–5
904 McDonnell-Douglas MD-80	$4–5
905 Boeing 737/200	$4–5
906 Boeing 727/200	$4–5
907 Boeing 767/200	$4–5
908 Boeing 757/200	$4–5
909 Lockheed L-1011	$4–5
911 Boeing 747/300	$4–5
920 Concorde	$4–5
921 Boeing 747/400	$4–5
922 McDonnell-Douglac DC-8	$4–5
923 Airbus A 310	$4–5
924 McDonnell-Douglas DC 9-40/MD 87	$4–5
925 Boeing 737/500	$4–5
926 Airbus A 320	$4–5
927 Boeing 767/300	$4–5
929 ATR 42	$4–5
930 Fairchild F-27/F-50	$4–5
931 Fairchild F-28	$4–5
932 Douglas DC-3	$4–5
933 Convair CV 440	$4–5
934 Lockheed L-1049 G	$4–5
935 Boeing 707	$4–5
936 SF 340	$4–5
937 Embraer 120	$4–5
938 McDonnell-Douglas DC-4	$4–5
939 ATR 72	$4–5
940 Fairchild F-100	$4–5
941 Vickers Viscount	$4–5
943 McDonnell-Douglas MD-11	$4–5
945 Boeing 737/500	$4–5
946 BAe 146	$4–5
947 Canadair Jet	$4–5
948 McDonnell-Douglas DC-6	$4–5
950 Tupolev TU 204	$4–5
951 Ilyushin 96	$4–5
952 Ilyushin 62	$4–5
953 Ilyushin 86	$4–5

Schabak 1:500 Scale Diecast Aircraft Models
821 Boeing 747-400 .... $8–11
823 Airbus A 310-300 .... $8–11
825 Boeing 737-300 .... $8–11
827 Boeing 767-300 .... $8–11

Schabak 1:250 Scale Diecast Aircraft Models
850 Boeing 747-400 .... $25
851 Boeing 747-200 .... $25
852 Boeing 747-300 .... $25
1027 Junkers JU 52 .... $7
1028 Douglas DC-3 .... $7
1029 Concorde $12

Schabak 1:250 Scale Tin and Plastic Aircraft Models
1025 Boeing 747/200 .... $13
1026 Boeing 747 F $13
Schabak 880/881, 4½" Plastic Baby-Jet .... $5 each

Schuco (also see Spiel-Nutz)
Schuco GmbH & Co.
Werkstr. 1
90765 Fürth, Germany
phone: ++49 911 97 65 04
fax ++49 911 97 65 415
website: www.schuco.de

Schuco has been around for a long time, beginning in 1912 as a distinctive brand of clockwork tin toys. Now that the original Schuco company has gone out of business, Gama has purchased the company and is now producing remakes of many of the original models as well as new models, now marketed in the US by Lil-liput Motor Company of Yerington, Nevada.

The Piccolo series in particular, never having attracted much attention when they were introduced in 1957, are now rising in value. These small 1:90 scale models, usually about an inch long, are described by Dr. Edward Force as "rather uninspiring little blobs." The charisma of these tiny models is what attracts collectors today.

Schuco's main entry into the diecast market happened in the late fifties with the introduction of precision scale models in 1:43 and 1:66 scale. Now, the Schuco brand celebrates a revival with new 1:18 scale models added to the growing assortment.

Presented below is an extensive list of Schucos, both diecast and otherwise. Replicas are now being made from the original machining and are listed just below the original version.

Schuco 1:18 Scale Series
0012 BMW 327 Cabriolet, 1996 ..... $270
0021 BMW 327 Coupé, 1996 .... $290
0032 Mercedes-Benz 170V Delivery Van, 1996 .... $280
0034 Mercedes-Benz 170V Mail Van, 1996 .... $300
0041 Mercedes-Benz 170V Truck with Tarp, 1997 .... $290

Schuco 100 Series
101 Micro Racer 101, 3½", 1950s Porsche style $175
102 Micro Racer 102, 3½", 1950s Indy style $175
104 Micro Racer 104, 3½", 1950s Indy style $175

Schuco 1:43 Scale 600 Series
610 Audi 80 LS, 1972 .... $25
611 Audi 80 GL, 1972 .... $25
612 Mercedes-Benz 350 SE, 1972 ..... $25
613 BMW Turbo, 1973 .... $25
614 Volkswagen Passat TS, silver, 1973 .. $25
615 Volkswagen Passat TS, red, orange-red or yellow-green, 1973 .... $25
616 Mercedes-Benz 350 SE Police Car, 1973 .... $25
617 BMW 520, 1973 .... $25
618 Mercedes-Benz 450 SE, 1973 ..... $25
619 Volkswagen Passat Variant, 1974 .. $25
620 Volkswagen Scirocco, 1974 .... $25
621 Volkswagen Golf, 1974 .... $25
622 Audi 50, 1974 .... $25
623 Volkswagen Polo, 1975 .... $25
624 Volkswagen Golf Rally, 1975 .... $25
625 BMW 525, 1973 .... $25
626 BMW 316, 1975 .... $25
627 BMW 320, 1975 .... $25
628 Porsche 924, 1975 .... $25
629 BMW 630 CS, 1976 .... $25
630 VW Passat Variant ADAC Car, 1975 .... $25
631 VW Passat Variant Fire Chief, 1975 .$25
632 VW Scirocco Racing Service Car, 1975 .... $25
633-A Mercedes-Benz 350 SE Taxi, 1975 .... $25
633-B Mercedes-Benz 350 SE Doctor's Car, 1976 .... $25
634 Audi 80 Police Car, 1974 .... $25
635 BMW 520 Police Car, 1976 .... $25
636 BMW 320 Rally Car, 1976 .... $25
637 BMW 535 Doctor's Car, 1976 .... $25
638 VW Golf Mail Car, 1976 .... $25
639 Audi 100, 1976 .... $25

Schuco Piccolo Series 1:90 Scale one-piece diecast toys
Collector Crister Skoglund of Sweden at one time offered several original Schuco Piccolo models on his Internet site at www.torget.se/users/z/zzzzz at $90 without the box $150 in original box. This indicates that values are rising considerably on these tiny metal blobs. Reissues from the 1990s are now available and listed below along with the originals.

265 Volkswagen Beetle Herbie, 1997 Limited Edition $35
266 Volkswagen Beetle ADAC, 1997 Limited Edition $35
281 Porsche 356A, 1996 .... $25
301 Magirus Tow Truck, 1996 .... $37
321 Volkswagen Bully Van, 1996 .... $25

322 Volkswagen Bully Van, "Shell," 1996 Limited Edition $35
331 Austin Mini, 1996 .... $25
351 DKW 3=6, 1997 .... $25
391 Mercedes-Benz 300SL, 1997 .... $25
401 Volkswagen Cabriolet, 1997 .... $25
701 Ferrari Grand Prix Car, 2", 1958 .... $75–90
   in original box $150
702 Mercedes-Benz Grand Prix F1, 2", streamlined, 1958 .... $75–90
   in original box $150
702 Replica Mercedes Streamliner, 1995 .$25
703 Mercedes-Benz Grand Prix, 2", 1958 .... $75–90
   in original box $150
703 Mercedes 2.5L F1 single seater in silver with red no 4, 1958 .... $90
703 Replica Mercedes 2.5L F1, 1995 ..$25
704 1936 Mercedes-Benz Grand Prix, 2", 1958 .... $75–90
   in original box $150
704 Replica Mercedes '36 GP, 1995 ..$25
705 Midget Racer, 2", 1958 .... $75–90
   in original box $150
706 Maserati Grand Prix, 2", 1958 ..$75–90
   in original box $150
707 BMW 507 Convertible, 2", 1958 ================= $75–90
   in original box $150
708 Porsche Spyder, 2", 1958 ...... $75–90
   in original box $150
708 Replica Porsche Spyder, 1996 .... $25
709-A Austin-Healey 100 Six, 2", 1958 .... $75–90
   in original box $150
709-B Mercedes-Benz 300 SL, 2", 1958 .... $75–90
   in original box $150
710 Firebird II Experimental Car, 2", 1958 .... $75–90
   in original box $150
711 FX Atmos Experimental Car, 2", 1958 .... $75–90
   in original box $150
712 Volkswagen, 2", 1958 .... $75–90
   in original box $150
712 Replica Volkswagen, 1996 .... $25
712 Volkswagen Polizei, 1996 Limited Edition $35
712 Volkswagen Fire, 1996 Limited Edition $35
713 Mercedes-Benz 190 SL, 2", 1958 .... $75-90
   in original box $150
713 Replica Mercedes-Benz 190 SL, 1996 .... $25
714 MGA Coupe, 2", 1958 .... $75–90
   in original box $150
715 VW Karmann-Ghia, 2", 1958 .$75–90
   in original box $150
716 NSU-Fiat Spyder, 2", 1958 ..... $75–90
   in original box $150

717 Mercedes-Benz 220 Coupe, 2",
1958 ....$75–90
  in original box..................$150
718 Volvo PV 544, 2", 1958........$75–90
  in original box..................$150
719 Citroën DS 19, 2", 1958.......$75–90
  in original box..................$150
720 Volkswagen Police/Fire Chief, 2",
1958 ....$75–90
  in original box..................$150
722 Camping Trailer, 2", 1958......$75–90
  in original box..................$150
723 VW Karmann-Ghia & Trailer, 3½",
1958 ....$65
724 Mercedes-Benz 220 S, 2¼",
1960 ....$75–90
  in original box..................$150
724 Replica Mercedes-Benz 220 S,
1996 ....$25
725 Ford Hot Rod, 1¾", 1964 ....$75–90
  in original box..................$150
740 Mercedes-Benz Bus, 3", 1960 .$75–90
  in original box..................$150
741 Mercedes-Benz Delivery Van, 2",
1960 ....$75–90
  in original box..................$150
742 Mercedes-Benz Low Loader, 4",
1960 ....$85–100
  in original box..................$160
742 Replica Mercedes Tractor with Lowboy,
1996 ....$40
743 Mercedes-Benz Refrigerator Van, 5½",
1960 ....$85–100
  in original box..................$160
744 Mercedes-Benz Tanker Semi, 4",
1960 ....$85–100
  in original box..................$160
745 Magirus Ladder Truck, 4",
1960 ....$85–100
  in original box..................$160
745 Replica Magirus Deutz Fire Truck,
1996 ....$40
746 Krupp Open Truck, 3¾",
1960 ....$85–100
  in original box..................$160
747 Magirus Wrecker, 3", 1960..$85–100
  in original box..................$160
748 Krupp Dump Truck, 3¼",
1960 ....$85–100
  in original box..................$160
749 Krupp Flat Truck, 4", 1960 ....$85–100
  in original box..................$160
750 Krupp Quarry Dump Truck, 3¼",
1960 ....$85–100
  in original box..................$160
751 Krupp Lumber Truck, 6",
1962 ....$85–100
  in original box..................$160
752 Deutz Farm Tractor, 1¾, 1962..$85–100
  in original box..................$160
753 Deutz Caterpillar Tractor, 2",
1962 ....$85–100
  in original box..................$160

754 Deutz Bulldozer, 2¼", 1962..$85–100
  in original box..................$160
755 Mercedes-Benz Searchlight Truck, 1¾",
1962 ....$85–100
  in original box..................$160
756 Mercedes-Benz Fire Van, 1⅞",
1962 ....$85–100
  in original box..................$160
757 Tipping Trailer, 3", 1962 ......$85–100
  in original box..................$160
758 Faun Street Sweeper, 2¼",
1962 ....$85–100
  in original box..................$160
759 Conveyor belt, 4½", 1962 ....$85–100
  in original box..................$160
760 Demag Power Shovel, 3⅛",
1962 ....$75–90
  in original box..................$150
761 Krupp Car Transporter, 8", 1962.$75–90
  in original box..................$150
762 Liebherr Tower Crane, 6¼" high,
1962 ....$90
763 Krupp Tank Truck, 3¼", 1962 .$85–100
  in original box..................$160
764 Boat and Trailer, 2", 1962 ....$85–100
  in original box..................$160
765 Fork Lift truck, 2¾", 1962 ......$85–100
  in original box..................$160
766 VW Karmann-Ghia and Boat Trailer,
3½", 1962.........................$85–100
  in original box..................$160
767 Krupp Bucket Truck, 3⅛",
1962 ....$85–100
  in original box..................$160
768 Hopper Trailer, 2¾", 1962 ...$85–100
  in original box..................$160
769 Krupp Crane Truck, 4"...........$85–100
  in original box..................$160
770 Krupp Cherry Picker, 3½" $85–100
  in original box..................$160
771 Dingler Road Roller, 1½" $85–100
  in original box..................$160
772 Krupp Cement Mixer, 3⅝".....$85–100
  in original box..................$160
773 Henschel Covered Semi, 4½" ..$75–90
  in original box..................$150
774 Faun Quarry Dump Truck, 3⅝" ..$85–100
  in original box..................$160
775 Coles Crane Truck and Trailer..$85–100
  in original box..................$160
776 MAN Doubledeck Bus, 3" $85–100
  in original box..................$160
777 Linhoff Road Paver, 5" $85–100
  in original box..................$160
778 Krupp Cement carrier, 5½" $85–100
  in original box..................$160
799 Coles Hydraulic Crane............$75–90
  in original box..................$150

Schuco Airplanes
779 Junkers F-13 ....$40
780 Thunderjet $40
781 Magister 170-R....................$40
782 Super Sabre $40

783 Douglas F4D-1....................$40
784 Junkers JU-52 ....$40
785 Boeing 737 ....$40
786 Boeing 727 ....$50
787 Boeing 707 ....$50
788 Boeing 747 ....$50
789 Concorde $50
790 Douglas DC8 ....$50
791 Douglas DC9 ....$40
792 Douglas DC10 ....$50
793 Boeing 747 ....$50
794 Lear Jet..........................$50
795 Airbus A300B $50
796 Boeing 747 Freighter..............$50
797 Ilyushin IL-62 ....$50

Schuco 800 Series
805 Mercedes-Benz 200, 2¾", 1971...$10
806 Mercedes-Benz 200 Police Car, 2¾",
1971 ....$10
807 Ford Taunus 20M, 2¾", 1971 ....$10
808 BMW 1600, 2¾", 1971 ....$10
809 BMW 2002, 2½", 1971 ....$10
810 Ford Escort 1300 GT, 2⅜", 1971 .$10
811 Opel Commodore GS, 2¾", 1971 .$10
812 Volkswagen 411, 2¾", 1971 ....$10
813 Porsche 911S, 2½", 1971 ....$10
814 Opel GT 1900, 2⅜", 1971 ....$10
815 BMW 2800 CS, 2¾", 1971........$10
816 Ford Capri 1700 GT, 2½", 1971 .$10
817 Audi 100 LS, 2¾", 1971 ....$10
818 Volkswagen 1300, 2½", 1971 .....$10
819 Opel Admiral 2800 E, 3", 1971...$10
820 Mercedes-Benz 250 CE, 2¾",
1971 ....$10
821 Audi 100 Coupe, 2¾", 1971 ....$10
822 Opel Commodore GS Rally, 2¾",
1971 ....$10
823 Mercedes-benz 200 Taxi, 2¾",
1971 ....$10
824 Volkswagen 411 Fire Chief, 2¾",
1971 ....$10
825 Porsche 911S Police Car, 2⅜",
1971 ....$10
826 VW Porsche 914 S, 2⅜", 1971....$10
827 VW Porsche 914-6, 2⅜", 1971....$10
828 Mercedes-Benz C-111, 2¾", 1971 .$10
829 BMW 2500, 2¾", 1972 ....$10
830 BMW 2800, 2¾", 1972 ....$10
831 Volkswagen K70, 2¾", 1972 ....$10
832 Volkswagen 1302 S, 2½", 1972 ..$10
833 Volkswagen ADAC Service Car, 2½",
1972 ....$10
834 Ford Capri 1700 GT Rally, 2⅝",
1972 ....$10
835 Porsche 911 S Racing Car, 2⅜",
1972 ....$10
836 VW Porsche 914-6 Racing Car, 2⅜",
1972 ....$10
837 Ford Taunus GT Coupe, 2⅜",
1972 ....$10
838 Ford Taunus GXL Coupe, 2⅜",
1972 ....$10
839 Opel Manta SR, 2⅜", 1972 ....$10

840 Ferrari Formula Two, 2½", 1972....$10
841 BMW Formula Two, 2½", 1972....$10
842 Matra Ford Formula One, 2½", 1972 ....$10
843 Porsche 917, 2½", 1972 ....$15
844 Mercedes-Benz 350 SL Convertible, 3", 1972 ....$10
845 BMW 200 tii, 2½", 1972 ....$10
846 Opel Ascona Voyage, 2½", 1972.$10
847 Brabham Ford Formula One, 2½", 1972 ....$10
848 Opel GT-J, 2½", 1972 ....$10
849 Opel Manta SR, 2½", 1972 ....$10
850 Renault 16, 2½", 1972 ....$10
851 Ford Escort Rally, 2⅜", 1972 ......$10
852 Audi 100 GL, 2¾", 1972 ....$10
853 Renault 17, 2½", 1972 ....$10
854 Porsche 917, 2½", 1972 ....$15
855 Audi 80 LS, 2½", 1973 ....$10
856 Opel Rekord II, 2¾", 1973 ....$10
857 Opel Commodore, 2¾", 1973 .....$10
858 Ford Consul, 2¾", 1973 ....$10
859 Ford Granada, 2¾", 1973 ....$10
860 Renault 16 TS, 2½", 1973 ....$10
861 Renault 17 TS, 2½", 1973 ....$10
862 Audi 80 GL, 2½", 1973 ....$10
863 Tyrell Ford Formula One, 2½", 1973 .$10
864 BMW Turbo Turbo, 2½", 1973 .....$10
865 BMW Turbo, 2½", 1973 ....$10
866 Mercedes-Benz 350 SE, 3", 1973.$10
867 Volkswagen Passat, 2½", 1973 .....$10
868 Mercedes-Benz 450 SE Police Car, 3", 1974 ....$10
869 VW Porsche 914 Race Control Car, 2⅜", 1974 ....$10
870 Lotus Ford 72 Formula One, 2½", 1974 ....$10
871 Renault 5, 2⅛", 1974 ....$10
872 Volkswagen Passat TS, 2½", 1974 ..$10
873 Mercedes-Benz 450 SE, 3", 1974 ..$10
874 Ford Capri II, 2½", 1974 ....$10
875 BMW 3.0 CSL, 2¾", 1974..........$10
876 Audi 80 Fire Chief, 2½", 1974 .....$10
877 Ford Capri RS, 2½", 1974 ....$10
878 Matra Simca Bagheera, 2½" $10
879 Volkswagen Scirocco, 2⅜", 1974..$10
880 Volkswagen Golf, 2¼", 1974 ....$10
881 Ford Escort, 2⅜, 1975 ....$10
882 Volkswagen Golf Mail Car, 2¼", 1975 ....$10
888 Ford Escort Rally, 2⅜", 1975.........$10
889 Volkswagen Police Bus, 2⅝", 1975..$10
890 Ford Transit Fire Van, 2⅝", 1975 ...$10

Schuco 900 Series
900 Mercedes-Benz Bus, 3", 1972 ....$20
901 Bussing Open Truck, 3¾", 1972....$20
902 Bussing Dump Truck, 3", 1972 ......$20
903 Bussing Flat Truck, 3⅞", 1972 ......$20
904 Bussing Quarry Dump Truck, 2¾", 1972 ....$20
905 Bussing Covered Semi-Trailer Truck, 4½", 1972 ....$20
906 Bussing Cement Carrier, 5⅜", 1972.$20

907 Demag Power Shovel, 3⅜", 1972 .$20
908 Faun Quarry Dump Truck, 3⅝", 1972 ....$20
909 Magirus-Deutz 232D Dump Truck, 3⅞", 1973 ....$20
910 Volkswagen Kombi, 2⅝", 1973.....$20
911 Volkswagen Transporter, 2⅝", 1973..$20
912 Ford Transit Van, 2⅝", 1974 ....$20
913 Ford Transit Bus, 2⅝", 1974..........$20
914 Volkswagen Ambulance, 2⅝", 1974 ....$20
915 Volkswagen Mail truck, 2⅝", 1974..$20
916 Mercedes-Benz 0303 Bus, 7", 1975 ....$45
917 Magirus-Deutz 232D Quarry Dumper, 4", 1975 ....$20
919 Volkswagen LT35 Pickup, 3¼", 1976 ....$20

Schuco 1000 Series/Micro Racers
1001 MirakoCar, 4½", 1950s............$150
1001/1 MirakoCar Polizei, 4¾" $150
1007 Motodrill Clown, 5", composition head, 1950s $750
1010 Mystery Car, 5½", 1950s, non-fall action $175
1010 Replica Wonder Auto Mystery Car $100
1010 Replica Wonder Auto Mystery Car, Tu-Tone Blue $120
1011 Dalli, 6½", 1950s, tin Car, plastic driver $150
1034 Rally 1034, 4", 1950s $100
1035 Go Kart 1035, 4", 1950s ..$180
1036 Hot Rod 1036, 4½" 1950s..$180
1036/1 Mercer 1036/1, 4", 1950s $180
1038 Mercedes-Benz 220S $180
1038 Replica Mercedes-Benz 220S..$50
1039 Volkswagen Polizei, 4", 1950s $180
1039 Replica Volkswagen Fire Chief .$55
1040 Micro Racer, 4", 1950s $180
1041 USA Midget, 4", 1950s $180
1041 Replica USA Midget $50
1042 USA Midget, 4", 1950s $180
1042 Replica USA Midget $50
1043 Mercedes Formula Racer 2.5L, 4", 1950s $180
1043 Replica Mercedes Formula Racer 2.5L $50
1044 Mercedes-Benz 190SL, 4", 1950s $200
1044 Replica Mercedes-Benz 190SL..$50
1045 '57 Ford Custom 300, 4", 1950s $180
1045 Replica '57 Ford Custom 300 .$50
1045 Replica '57 Ford Custom 300 Police Car $55
1046 1958 Volkswagen, 4", 1950s $175
1046 Replica 1958 Volkswagen $50
1047 Porsche 356, 4", 1950s.....$200
1047 Replica Porsche 356............$50

1048 Alfa Romeo 1048, 4", 1950s $175
1049 Stake Truck 1049, 4", 1950s $175
1050 Studio Racer 1050 with tools, 5½", 1950s....................$225
1050 Replica Studio Racer 1050 1936 Grand Prix Mercedes $80
1070 Grand Prix Racer, 6", 1950s $150
1070 Replica Ferrari Classic Grand Prix Racer, red....................$100
1070 Replica Chrome Ferrari Grand Prix Racer $125
1071 Lotus Formula One Racer .$100–125
1072 Radio Car with Garage Set, new limited edition, lithographed garage with #5000 Radio Car $350
1075 1024S Grand Prix Racing Edition 1997 Replica of 1075 with replica of #1070 Ferrari Racer, 1912 produced worldwide $275
1111 Fex, 6", 1950s $100
1225 Mercer Auto, 7½", 1950s...$175
1220 Replica Studio II Auto Union Type C $90
1222 Replica Auto Union Studio II Kit....................$130
1250 Jaguar, 5½", 1940s $300

Schuco Oldtimers
1228 1901 Opel Doctor-Wagen with opening top, 1990s reproduction $180
1230 1911 Renault 6CV/Voiturette, 1990s reproduction $180
1235 1913 Mercer Type 35J, 1990s reproduction $180
1237 1917 Ford Model T, 1990s reproduction $180
1238 1901 Opel Doctor-Wagen, 1990s reproduction $160
1239 1902 Mercedes Simplex, 1990s reproduction $160

Schuco 2000/4000 Series, 1:43 Scale
2000 Anno 2000, 5½", 1940s.........$150
2002 Akustico 2002, 5½", 1940s $150
2002 Replica Akustico with working horn....................$150
2002 Replica Akustico with opening hood and Fritz....................$260
2002 Replica Akustico Tutone, special limited edition $180
2008 Magico, 5½", 1950s.............$100
2012 Replica BMW 501, white, 1996..$55
2014 BMW 501, 1950s $180
2014 Replica BMW 501, dark blue, 1996 ....$55
2015 BMW 502, gray, 1996 ....$45
2016 BMW 502, ivory, 1996 ....$45
2017 BMW 502, maroon, 1996 ....$45
2040 BMW 501 Fire Chief, 1995 ......$60
2041 BMW 502 Taxi, 1996...........$45
2042 BMW 502 Police, 1996........$45

2043 BMW 502 Fire Chief, 1996 ......$45
2052 Goliath Tempo Pritsche, gray, 1995 .$60
2053 Goliath Tempo Pritsche, red & gray, 1995 ....$60
2062 Tempo Van, gray, 1996............$55
2064 Tempo Van, ivory & green 1996 .$55
2063 Goliath Tempo Van, 1995..........$60
2070 Goggomobil, yellow, 1996........$40
2071 Goggomobil, green, 1996..........$40
2072 Goggomobil, red, 1996 ....$40
2073 Goggomobil Tu-Tone green & white, 1996 ....$45
2074 Goggomobil Tu-Tone red & white, 1996 ....$45
2075 Goggomobil Fire Chief, 1996.....$45
2080 Lloyd 600, red, 1995 ....$45
2081 Lloyd 600, blue, 1995 ....$45
2083 Lloyd 600 Race-Car, 1996........$45
2084 Lloyd 600, green, 1996............$40
2091 BMW Isetta (open top), green, 1995 ....$45
2092 BMW Isetta (open top), yellow, 1995 ....$45
2093 BMW Isetta (open top), red, 1995 ....$45
2095 Mercedes 190SL, 8", 1950s $275
2100 Isetta Police, 1996................$40
2102 Isetta "Lufthansa," 1996..........$40
2105 Isetta Racer #13, 1996............$40
2107 Isetta "Der Stern," 1997 ....$40
2120 Tempo Tarp, green, 1996 ....$55
2121 Tempo Tarp, red, 1996............$55
2135 Tempo "Deutsche Bundespost," 1996 limited edition of 2,000..................$60
2136 Tempo "Shell," 1996 limited edition of 2,000 ....$60
2140 Tempo "Trix-Express," 1996 limited edition of 2,000 ....$60
2151 BMW Dixi Sedan, maroon, 1995.$45
2152 BMW Dixi Sedan, green, 1995 ..$45
2153 BMW Dixi Sedan, ivory, 1995 ...$45
2161 BMW 2000, blue, 1995............$45
2162 BMW 2000, maroon, 1995......$45
2163 BMW 2000, white, 1995 ....$45
2164 BMW 2000 Taxi, 1995............$45
2165 BMW 2000 Police, 1996..........$45
2171 BMW 507, green, 1995............$45
2172 BMW 507, black, 1995............$45
2173 BMW 507, silver, 1995............$45
2181 BMW 328, black, 1996............$45
2182 BMW 328, silver, 1996............$45
2191 BMW 3.0, blue, 1996..............$45
2192 BMW 3.0, red, 1996 ....$45
2201 Lloyd Alex TS, blue & white, 1996.$45
2202 Lloyd Alex TS, gray & white, 1996.$45
2203 Lloyd Alex TS, green & white, 1996 ....$45
2210 Tempo "Dunlop," 1996 limited edition of 2,000....................$60
2211 Tempo "Persil," 1996 limited edition of 2,000 ....$60
2212 Tempo Fire Truck, 1996 limited edition of 2,000 ....$60

2221 BMW 2002, blue, 1996............$45
2222 BMW 2002, yellow, 1996........$45
2223 BMW 2002, silver, 1996..........$45
2231 BMW 335 Limo, maroon & black, 1996 ....$45
2232 BMW 335 Limo, ivory & brown, 1996 ....$45
2233 BMW 335 Limo, light green & green, 1996 ....$45
2241 BMW 503 V-8, ivory, 1996.......$45
2242 BMW 503 V-8, gray, 1996.......$45
2243 BMW 503 V-8, red, 1996........$45
2251 Mercedes 170 V Van, maroon & black, 1996 ....$45
2252 Mercedes 170 V Van, black, 1996 ....$45
2253 Mercedes 170 V Van "Deutsche Reichspost," 1996 ....$50
2254 Mercedes 170 V Box "Maggi," 1996 limited edition of 2,000..................$60
2255 Mercedes 170 V Box "Deutsche Bundespost," 1996 limited edition of 2,000 ....$60
2261 Mercedes 170 V Pickup, blue, 1996 ....$45
2262 Mercedes 170 V Pickup, ivory, 1996 ....$45
2271 DKW 3=6, black, 1996............$45
2272 DKW 3=6, green, 1996............$45
2273 DKW 3=6, ivory, 1996............$45
2281 NSU 1000TTS, silver, 1996.......$45
2282 NSU 1000TTS, white, 1996 ......$45
2283 NSU 1000TTS, red, 1996.........$45
2291 BMW Dixi Cabriolet, black, 1996 ....$45
2292 BMW Dixi Cabriolet, red & white, 1996 ....$45
2293 BMW Dixi Cabriolet, yellow & black, 1996 ....$45
2301 Isetta (closed roof), maroon, 1996..$45
2302 Isetta (closed roof), light blue, 1996 ....$45
2303 Isetta (closed roof), black, 1996 ...$45
2371 DKW 3=6 Cabriolet, maroon, 1996 ....$45
2372 DKW 3=6 Cabriolet, gray, 1996 .$45
2373 DKW 3=6 Cabriolet, dark blue, 1996 ....$45
2411 Isetta Delivery, beige, 1997 ....$45
2412 Isetta Delivery, green, 1997 ....$45
2421 BMW 328 Soft Top, red, 1996 ....$45
2422 BMW 328 Soft Top, white, 1996 ....$45
2423 BMW 328 Soft Top, green, 1996 ....$45
4002 BMW 316i, metallic green, 1996..$50
4003 BMW 316i, metallic black, 1996..$50
4011 BMW 318ti, yellow, 1996 ....$50
4012 BMW 318ti, metallic red, 1996 .$50
4013 BMW 318ti, metallic blue, 1996..$50
4081 BMW 328i Touring, red, 1996 ..$50
4082 BMW 328i Touring, silver, 1996..$50

4083 BMW 328i Touring, metallic green, 1996 ....$50
4111 Porsche Turbo, red, 1996 ....$55
4112 Porsche Turbo, metallic black, 1996 ....$55
4113 Porsche Turbo, yellow, 1996.......$55
4141 BMW Z3, red, 1996 ....$50
4142 BMW Z3, black, 1996 ....$50
4143 BMW Z3, green, 1996 ....$50
4151 Porsche Carrera, light blue, 1996 $55
4152 Porsche Carrera, metallic blue, 1996 ....$55
4153 Porsche Carrera, silver, 1996......$55
4221 Porsche Boxter Open, blue, 1996..$50
4222 Porsche Boxter Open, yellow, 1996 ....$50
4223 Porsche Boxter Open, red, 1996 .$50
4231 Porsche Boxter Hard Top, metallic green, 1996 ....$50
4233 Porsche Boxter Hard Top, metallic gray, 1996 ....$50
4241 Porsche Boxter Soft Top, white, 1996 ....$50
4242 Porsche Boxter Soft Top, orange, 1996 ....$50
4243 Porsche Boxter Soft Top, metallic black, 1996 ....$50
4251 BMW Z3 Soft Top, silver, 1996..$50
4252 BMW Z3 Soft Top, yellow, 1996 .$50
4253 BMW Z3 Soft Top, blue, 1996...$50
4281 Mercedes-Benz V 230, silver, 1996 ....$45
4282 Mercedes-Benz V 230, metallic black, 1996 ....$45
4283 Mercedes-Benz V 230, red, 1996 ....$45
4321 Porsche Carrera S, red, 1996 .....$50
4322 Porsche Carrera S, dark metallic blue, 1996 ....$50

Schuco 3000 Series

3000 Telesteering 3000 Limo, 4", 1950s $80
3010 Varianto 3010, playset with two 4½" tin cars, 1950s $180
3010 Varianto 3010 Super, service station with two 4½" tin cars, 1950s........$325
3010/30 Varianto Box 3010/30, tin garage and 3041 Limo, 4½", 1950s....................$200
3041 Varianto 3041 Limo, 4", 1950s $150
3042 Lasto, 4½", 1950s $100
3044 Varianto Bus 3044, 4", 1950s..$100
3054 Gas Station, 8", 1950s $100
3064 Varianto 3064, 8" plastic, 1950s..$50
3112 Varianto Electro 3112, 4" truck, 1950s $100
3112u Varianto Electro 3112u, 4½" truck, 1950s $100
3118 Station Car 3118, 4½", 1950s.$100

Schuco 4000 Series of Clockwork Toys

4000 Girato Mercedes, plastic body with diecast grille and bumpers, 9.44" 1960 ....$400

4000 Replica Girato Mercedes, plastic body with diecast grille and bumpers, 9.44", 1996 ....$250
4001 Examico 4001, 6", 1950s $225
4001 Replica Examico $165
4001 Replica Examico with opening hood $195
4001 Replica Chrome Examico $175
4012 Radio 4012, 6", musical car, 1950s $375

Schuco 5000 Series

5000 Replica Radio Auto with music box $300
5311 Buick, 9" $375
5311 Elektro Ingenico, 8½", remote control, 1950s $400
5505 Cadillac DeVille Convertible, 11", 1960s plastic $150
5700 Synchromatic 5700, resembles Packard Hawk, 11", 1950s $1000

Other Schuco Models

1928 Mercedes SSK, 8", 1950s $175
Magico Car and Garage, 6", 1950s ..$225
Monkey Car, 6", 1930s, orange/black, smiling monkey $2,500
Scientific Forklift $125

Other Schuco Series / Brands

Schuco toys are sold in various markets under different names. Lilliput, Nutz, Oldtimer, Paya, and Rei are all trademark brands from Schuco. Rei in particular is a brand name of Schuco models sold in Brazil.

Schwung

Schwung is a brand name of 1:32 scale tin toys made in Germany.
Opel Rekord 4-door Sedan $16
Opel Fire Chief $24
Opel Police $24
Opel Ambulance $24
Skoda Dump Truck $24
Tatra 815 Van $16

Schylling

P O Box 667
Ipswich, MA 01938
toll free: 800-541-2929
fax: 978-356-5959

Schylling once produced only tin toys. Now they have expanded into a wholesale toy distributor. Besides their own assortment of tinplate toys and ornaments, they now offer an array of intriguing toys from other manufacturers, including diecast toys from Kintoy / Kinsmart, Superior / Sunnyside, and others.

SCM

Colin Jesmer wrote via e-mail that he has an SCM model diecast car, and he wondered how old it is and if it is worth any money. "The car is not built," he wrote. "The car is a 1:64 scale put-together model with a marking on the top of the inside that says 'E1 S C M.' It may

be a Ford Thunderbird. There is an address on one of the pieces which is 'P.O. Box 74 R.S. PA. 16673'."

Based on the zip code, the complete address is "P O Box 74, Roaring Spring, Pennsylvania 16673." The closest match I could find currently for such a business is SCM Metal Products Incorporated, 101 Bridge St, Johnstown, PA 15902, phone 814-533-7800. Upon calling, I found that SCM is now OMG Americas. On a recommendation from OMG's receptionist, I contacted Russ Kelly in purchasing. Mr. Kelly has been with SCM since 1973, but he knows of no diecast toys of any kind ever produced by the company, adding that their manufacturing is in "powder castings," and that they don't do any die-casting. The mystery continues.

Scorchers (Hot Wheels)

Hot Wheels Scorchers were introduced in 1979 and consist of plastic bodies and spring activated motors. They are mentioned here separately because they are so distinctly different from Hot Wheels, and are highly collectible. Prices listed are highly speculative since I've found no reputable source for values.

Twelve original Scorchers were issued in 1979

#2544 Zappin' Z-28 ....$15–20
#2589 Blackbird $15–20
#2640 White Thunder $15–20
#2641 Magnum XE $15–20
#2642 Good Looker $15–20
#2643 El Camino Real $15–20
#2645 Cool Capri $15–20
#2892 Magnum Fever $15–20
#2893 Vandemonium $15–20
#2894 Chevy Light $15–20
#2895 Cookin' Camaro $15–20
#2896 Capri Turbo $15–20

1981 saw the expansion of the series with six additional models

#1505 Time Bender $15–20
#1593 Turbo 928 ....$15–20
#1594 Firebrand $15–20
#1595 Sundrifter $15–20
#1596 Britework $15–20
#1597 Blue Fever $15–20

Scottoys

Scottoys are white metal Italian reproductions of obsolete Mercury models. Each 1:48 to 1:66 scale model is offered in two or three color choices, and are available from Modelauto of Leeds, England, and from Lilliput Motor Company of Yerington, Nevada.
SC01 Fiat 600 Saloon $40
SC02 Fiat 600 Multipla two tone $46
SC03 Alfa Romeo Giulietta $46
SC04 Alfa Romeo 1900 Saloon $46
SC05 Fiat 1100 Saloon $46
SC06 Cadillac Eldorado $56

SC07 Innocenti 950 ....$46
SC08 Alfa Romeo Giulietta Sprint $46
SC09 Fiat Nuova 500 ....$46
SC10 Lancia Appia 3a $46
SC10T Lancia Appia 3a Taxi $48
SC11 Autobianchi Bianchina $46
SC17 Lambretta scooter 1:30 ....$25
SC17G Vespa scooter, gold, limited edition of 250 ....$30
SC18 Vespa scooter 1:30 ....$30
SC18 Vespa scooter 1:30 KIT $20
SC19 Lancia Appia 1a $46
SC19 Lancia Appia 1a Taxi $48

Septoy

Gasquy models were first issued as Septoys, produced in Belgium. Septoys are simple castings with minimal or no interior.
1939 Plymouth...$75

Shackleton

Collector Bill Cross reports regarding Shackleton, "I believe these are the Foden truck (lorry, in my native language!) models made by Abbey-Corinthian Games of London in the 1950s. I have an advertisement in front of me, in a 1958 issue of *Meccano Magazine*. These were magnificent diecast and pressed steel models of 1950s Foden trucks. Actually, there were three models in the range: a 3-axle Foden flatbed, a matching 4-wheel Dyson flatbed trailer, and a 3-axle dump. The trucks were powered by a wind-up motor in the cab, driving the rear wheels through a driveshaft and scale differential. ...Operating Ackerman steering as well. Some parts, I remember from ownership as a (very lucky) child, were very fragile — springs broke very easily. The models came completely apart with nuts and bolts. The cab and bed were diecast. Frame parts, fenders, etc. were pressed steel. Weak parts were 'Chinese Cheese Metal.' I remember that the flatbeds came in yellow, the dump truck I think in red/green. In good condition, these now bring several hundred pounds [£500 British = approx. $800 US as of 02-99]. Original price in 1958 was 65 shillings, about $22 I think, at the 1958 exchange rate."

Shinsei

Shinsei models of Japan are highly accurate scale models last known to be available from Jeff Bray Jr.'s Diecast Miniatures and Toys for Collectors. Shinsei also made tin litho battery-operated toy cars and other items. Listed below are known models and current values.
61 Kenworth SKYWAY, 1:99 ....$12
62 Kenworth Car Transporter, 1:99 ....$12
402 Gulf Mirage, 1:43 ....$18
407 BMW 3.5 CSL Coupe, 1:43 ....$16
421 Lamborghini Countach, 1:50 ....$8
452 Chevrolet Corvette Stingray, 1:56 ....$8
601 CAT 922C Wheel Loader, 1:75 ....$45

605 KATO NK 800 Hydraulic Crane, 1:61 .$75
614 Komatsu PC 650 Excavator, 1:50 ....$75
615 Komatsu WA 350 Wheel Loader, 1:50 ....$50
617 Komatsu D 475 Dozer with Ripper, 1:48 ....$75
618 Hitachi EX 200 Excavator, 1:48 ....$50
619 Hitachi LX 70 Wheel Loader $45
620 Hitachi EX 1800 Mining Excavator, 1:60 ....$90
625 Fuso TOKYO OSAKA, 1:43 ....$25
658 Komatsu HD 785 Heavy Dump Truck, 1:45 ....$85
675 TMC 860 Wheel Loader, 1:50 ....$45
921 Komatsu PC 200 Shovel $75
950 CAT 325 Hydraulic Excavator, 1:50 ...$85
4101 Aerial Ladder Fire Engine, 1:64 ....$30
4102 Mechanical Truck Crane, 1:64 ....$30
4103 Bucket Wheel Excavator, 1:64 ....$30
4104 Snorkel Fire Engine, 1:64 ....$15
4105 T911 Aerial Work Vehicle, 1:64 .....$35
4106 K201 Aerial Work Vehicle, 1:64 .....$35
4107 Bucket Crawler Crane, 1:64 ....$25
4108 Chemical Fire Engine, 1:64 ....$15
4109 Snorkel Chemical Fire Engine, 1:64 ...$15
4110 Dump Truck, 1:64 ....$15
4111 Tractor Shovel, 1:64 ....$15
4112 Hydraulic Excavator, 1:64 ....$20
4113 Bulldozer, 1:64 ....$15
4114 Dozer Shovel, 1:64 ....$15
4121 Asphalt Finisher, 1:64 ....$25
4122 Lift Truck, 1:64 ....$20
4123 Lift Truck with Roll Clamp, 1:64 ....$20
4124 Crane Truck, 1:64 ....$35
4125 Hydraulic Motor Scraper, 1:64 ....$25
4126 Hydraulic Motor Grader, 1:64 ....$15
4127 Pile Driver, 1:64 ....$20
4128 Macadam Roller, 1:64 ....$25
4129 Loader Shovel, 1:64 ....$25
4130 Hydraulic Crawler Crane, 1:64 ....$30
4131 Earth Drill, 1:64 ....$20
4132 Tractor Multi Ripper, 1:64 ....$20
4136 Amphibious Bulldozer, 1:64 ....$20
4137 Heavy Vehicle carrier, 1:64 ....$25
4215 GMC Dump Truck, 1:43 ....$20
4216 GMC Cement Mixer, 1:43 ....$20
4217 GMC Oil Tanker SHELL, 1:43 ....$20
4218 GMC Refrigerator Van, 1:43 ....$20
4219 GMC U. S. Trucking, 1:43 ....$20
4220 GMC Garbage Collector, 1:43 ....$20
4233 GMC Street Sweeper, 1:43 ....$20
4234 GMC Conrete Pump Truck, 1:43 ....$20
4235 GMC Crane Auger, 1:43 ....$20
4315 Mercedes-Benz Dump Truck, 1:43 .....$20
4316 Mercedes-Benz Cement Mixer, 1:43 .$20
4317 Mercedes-Benz Oil Tanker, 1:43 ....$20
4318 Mercedes-Benz Refrigerator Van, 1:43 ....$20
4319 Mercedes-Benz Van Truck, 1:43 ....$20
4320 Mercedes-Benz Garbage Collector, 1:43 ....$20
4333 Mercedes-Benz Street Sweeper, 1:43 ....$20

4334 Mercedes-Benz Concrete Pump Truck, 1:43 ....$20
4335 Mercedes-Benz Crane Auger, 1:43 ...$20
4412 Lancia Stratos, 1:43 ....$18
4422 Lamborghini Jota, 1:64 ....$6

Sibur

These are older hand-built diecast models from France.
GMC 6X6 Army Open Truck, 1:43 ....$35
GMC 6X6 Army Closed Truck, 1:43 ....$35
GMC Army Bookmobile, 1:43 ....$35
GMC Truck Paris-Dakar, 1:50 ....$35

Sieperwerke (see Siku)

Siku

Siku is a division of Sieperwerke, a venerable German company established in 1921 by Richard Sieper. The name "Siku" is an acronym formed from the first two letters of the Sieper name combined with the first two letters of "kunststoff," the German word describing synthetic material or plastic.

From 1949 to 1963, Siku toys were made of plastic, but in 1963, as Matchbox started marketing their products in Germany, the first Siku diecast models were produced to attempt to keep up with the increasing competition. Models of 1:55 scale currently marketed in the US are packaged as Siku "Super Series" models. While the predominant scale for Siku is 1:55, they are also produced in 1:64 scale and in the 1:32 scale Farm Series. List below includes model number, description, production years, and current relative value.

201 Fiat 1800, 1963–1968 ....$25
202 BMW 1500, 1962–1968 ....$40
203 Ford 12M, 1963 ....$35
204 Opel Kadett, 1963–1966 ....$40
206 Ford 17M Turnier, 1963–1968 ....$35
209 Cadillac Fleetwood, 1963–1968 .$35–45
211 Volkswagen Bus, 1963–1964 ....$40
212 Volkswagen Bus Polizei (Police) Loudspeaker Van, 1963–1970 ....$30
218 Porsche Standard T Diesel Tractor, 1963–1972 ....$25
220 Tempo Matador Bus, 1963–1969 ......$35
221 Mercedes-Benz 300SL, 1963–1969 ..$35
222 Ford F500 LKW (US Truck), 1963–1972 ..$30
223 Opel Rekord (1963), 1964–1966 .....$40
224 DKW F12, 1964–1966 ....$50
225 Farm Trailer, 1964–1968 ....$15
226 Opel Caravan 1500 (1963), 1964–1966 ....$30
228 Jeep with Trailer, 1964–1972 ....$35
229 Mercedes-Benz 230SL, 1964–1968 ..$30
230 Volkswagen 1200 "Beetle," 1964–1969 ....$30
231 Volkswagen 1200 with antenna on roof, 1964–1968 ....$45
232 Ford 17M, 1964–1966 ....$30
233 Mercedes-Benz Binz Ambulance, 1964–1970 ....$35

234 Porsche 901, 1964–1969 ....$35
234 Porsche 911 Targa, 1970–1974 ......$30
235 Porsche 901 Polizei, 1964–1970 .....$25
235 Ford Capri Polizei, 1971–1974 ....$25
237 Ford TSF Service Van with ladder on roof, 1964–1971 ....$25
238 Fiat 40 CA Bulldozer with loader on front, 1964–1972 ....$20
239 Fiat CA40 Bulldozer with blade, 1964–1972 ....$20
241 Roller Trailer, 1964–1968 ....$15
242 Hay Rake, 1964–1965 ....$30
244 Fiat 1800 Taxi, 1964–1968 ....$25
244 Mercedes 250 SE Taxi, 1968–1971 ..$30
244 Mercedes 250/8 Taxi, 1972–1974 ..$20
245 Oldsmobile 98 Holiday Sports Coupe, 1964–1969 ....$30
246 Ford M12 with trailer, 1964–1966 .....$40
246 Ford 15M, 1967–1968 ....$35
247 Volkswagen 1500 Variant, 1965–1968 .$25
248 Volkswagen Karmann Ghia 1500, 1965–1969 ....$35
249 Faun K10/26AP Dump Truck, 1965–1973 ....$20
250 Mercedes-Benz 190, 1965–1969 ....$20
250 Mercedes-Benz 250, 1970–1974 ....$15
251 Ford Transit Double Cab Pickup Van, 1965–1969 ....$15
252 Opel Kapitän (1964), 1965–1970 ....$30
253 Mercedes-Benz 600 Pullman Limousine, 1965–1972 ....$40
254 Diesel Tractor with Dump Trailer, 1966–1973 ....$40
255 Buick Wildcat Sport Coupe, 1965–1971 ....$30
256 Mercedes-Benz 250SE, 1966–1969 ..$35
257 Ford F500 Wrecker, 1965–1973 .....$35
257 Hanomag Henschel Wrecker, 1974 ..$40
258 Liebherr Mobile Crane, 1965–1972 ..$15
259 Cargo Trailer, 1966–1972 ....$15
260 Klaus Autodumper, 1966–1973 ......$25
261 Mercedes-Benz Metz DL30H Fire Ladder Truck, 1966–1974 ....$50
262 Pontiac Bonneville Convertible, 1966–1971 ....$70
263 Log Trailer, 1966–1968 ....$25
264 Tempo Matador Camping Van with Kayak, 1966–1971 ....$50
264 Ford Transit Camping Van with Kayak, 1972–1974 ....$35
265 Cadillac Fleetwood 75, 1966–1971 ..$40
266 BMW 2000CS, 1967–1974 ....$25
267 Oldsmobile Toronado, 1967–1974 ...$20
268 Ford Transit Kombi Van, 1967–1974 ..$20
269 Ferrari Berlinetta 275 GTB, 1967–1974 ....$25
270 Zettelmeyer Europ L2000 Front End Loader, 1967–1974 ....$20
271 Opel Rekord Coupe, 1967–1974 ......$35
272 Opel Rekord Caravan with skis and louge, 1967–1972 ....$50
273 Ford Taunus 15M, 1967–1969 ....$25
274 Magirus Garbage Truck, 1967–1974 ..$50

275 Magirus Auto Transporter, 1967–1973 ..$35

276 Ford OSI 20M TS, 1968–1972 ....$30

277 Pontiac GTO Convertible, 1967–1972 .$50
278 Side Dumping Trailer, 1967–1969 .....$25
279 Opel Kapitän (252, 1964) w/Westfalia Travel Trailer, 1968–1971 ....$55
279 Ford 20M (288) with Westfalia Travel Tariler, 1972–1974 ....$60
280 Euclid S-7/E 915R "ATHEY" Earth Mover, 1968–1972....................................$35
281 Magirus Deutz M250 D22 FK 6x4 Dump Truck, 1968–1979 ....$35
282 Chevrolet Corvette Sting Ray, 1968–1974..$20
283 Ford 20M, 1968–1974 ....$35
284 Ford 17M Station Wagon, 1968–1970 .$40
285 Porsche Carrera 906, 1968–1974.....$20
286 Opel Olympia, 1968–1969 ....$60
287 Hanomag Robust 900 Farm Tractor, 1969–1974.................................$15
288 Henschel-Sattelzug F201S-2A "ARAL" Semi Tanker, 1968–1974 ....$45
289 Magirus Transporter, 1968–1972......$45
290 Citroën DS21, 1968–1974 ....$45
291 Magirus Cement Truck, 1969–1974 ..$35–50
292 Mercedes-Benz Binz Ambulance Van, 1969–1974.................................$20
293 Mercedes Crane Truck, 1969–1974...$30
294 Jaguar E 2+2, 1968–1974 ....$25
295 Maserati Mistral, 1968–1974 ....$25
296 Ford GT40, 1969–1974 ....$25
297 Oldsmobile Toronado with Boat and Trailer, 1969–1974................................$35
298 Lincoln Continental Mark III, 1969–1972 .$30
299 Zettelmeyer Europ S12 Road Roller, 1969–1974.................................$15
300 VW 411, 1969 ....$55
301 Fiat 850 Sport Coupe, 1969–1972 ...$25
302 Mercedes-Benz 280SL, 1969–1974 ..$20
303 Hanomag Robust 900 Farm Tractor with Trailer, 1969–1973.........................$25
304 Opel GT1900, 1970–1974 ....$25
305 Mercedes-Benz Postal Truck "Deutsche Bundespost," 1970–1974.....................$20
306 Mercedes-Benz Europ 1200L Binz Ambulance, 1970–1974 ....$20
307 Hanomag Henschel Garage Transporter, 1971–1974.................................$40
308 Audi 100LS, 1970–1974 ....$20
309 Mercedes-Benz 250, 1970–1974 .....$20
310 Ford Capri 1700GT, 1970–1974 ....$20
311 Volkswagen 1300 Beetle, 1970–1974.................................$20
312 Volkswagen-Porsche 914/6, 1970–1974.................................$20

313 Ford 17M Station Wagon "ADAC," 1970–1974..................................$25
314 Ford F500 Pickup (222) with Dump Trailer (225), 1970–1972 ....$45
315 Ford F500 Pickup (222) with Side Dumping Trailer (278) $55
316 Toyota 2000GT, 1971–1973 ....$20
317 Lamborghini Espada 400GT, 1971–1974.................................$20
318 Hanomag-Henschel Container Transporter, 1971–1974.................................$25
319 Mercedes LP608 ADAC Auto Salvage Truck, 1971–1974 ....$20
320 VW Bus Postal Van, DEUTSCHE BUNDESPOST, 1970–1972 ....$30
320 Volkswagen Vanagon Postal Van, DBP PEILWAGEN, 1973–74 ....$25
321 Alfa Romeo Montreal, 1971–1974.....$20
322 Citroën SM, 1971–1974 ....$20
323 Ford Taunus Transit Highway Construction Truck, 1971–1974 ....$30
324 Ford Transit Polizei (Police) Emergency Van, 1971–1974.................................$20
325 Menck Power Crane Shovel, 1971–1974 ....$25
326 Michigan 180 Wheel Dozer with Plow, 1971–1974.................................$35
328 Pontiac GTO "The Judge," 1972–1974 ..$40
329 Hanomag Robust 900 with Trailer, 1972–1973.................................$45
330 Ford T5 Mustang Mach 1, 1972–1974 ..$20
331 MAN Racing Fuel Tanker "Renndienst," 1971–1974.................................$40
332 Metz Airport Fire Tender, 1972–1974 .$25
333 Lamborghini 400GT Espada with Building Transporter Trailer, 1972–1974 ....$45
334 Ford Transit School Bus Van "SCHULBUS," 1972–1974..................................$20
335 Mercedes LP608D Street Maintenance Truck, 1972–1974 ....$40
336 Mercedes LP608D Silo Transporter, 1972–1974.................................$40
337 Faun Snow Plow Sand Truck, 1972–1974 ....$35
338 Hanomag Henschel Covered Truck, 1972–1974.................................$10
339 Mercedes Water Service Van, 1972–1974.................................$25
341 BMW Polizei (Police) Loudspeaker Car, 1997–1974.................................$20
342 Ford 17M Fire Command Station Wagon, 1973–1974.................................$30
343 Hanomag Henschel ADAC Vehicle Safety Check Truck, 1973–1974 ....$35
344 Lamborghini Fire Hunter, 1973–1974 ..$30
345 Volkswagen Vanagon Bus with Radar in front compartment, 1973–1974 ....$25
346 Volkswagen-Porsche 914/6 "Rennpolizei," 1973–1974.................................$25
347 Magirus Sand Truck, 1973–1974 ......$25
348 MAN Container Truck, 1973–1974 ...$30
349 MAN Lumber Truck with Crane, 1973–1974.................................$30

350 Hanomag Henschel Pipe Laying Truck, 1973–1974.................................$35
351 Maserati Boomerang, 1974.............$15
352 Magirus Transporter with Tractors, 1973–1974.................................$95
353 Audi 100 "Arzt-Notfall-Einsatz," 1973–1974.................................$25
354 Hanomag Henschel Covered Truck and Trailer, 1973–1974 ....$25
355 Hanomag Henschel ARAL Service Station Transporter, 1974..............................$40
356 Volkswagen Vanagon Ambulance "Malteser Hilfsdienst," 1974 ....$25
357 Mercedes Fire Command Truck, 1974.$20
360 Hanomag Henschel Tank Truck, 1974.$35
361 Mercedes Unimog Hydraulic DBP Truck, 1974.................................$35
362 Magirus Skip Truck, 1974 ....$30
0801 Excavator, 1992– $5–10
0802 Front Loader, 1992– $5–10
0803 Scraper, 1992– $5–10
0804 Mercedes-Benz G-Wagon Police Van, 1992.................................$5–10
0805 Mercedes-Benz G-Wagon Ambulance, 1992– $5–10
0806 Coach, 1992– $5–10
0807 Police Helicopter, 1992– $5–10
0808 Tipper Truck, 1992– $5–10
0811 Refuse Truck, 1992– $5–10
0813 Cement Mixer, 1992– $5–10
0814 Dumper Truck, 1992– $5–10
0815 Livestock Transporter, 1992– $5–10
0817 Space Shuttle, 1992– $5–10
0820 Volkswagen Delivery Van, 1992–.$5–10
0821 Unimog Snow Plow, 1992– $5–10
0822 Tipper Truck, 1992– $5–10
0823 Bulldozer, 1992– $5–10
0824 Volkswagen School Bus, white.......$5–10
0825 Volkswagen Caravelle, 1992–......$5–10
0826 Airport Fire Engine, 1992– $5–10
0828 Recycling Transporter, 1992–.......$5–10
0831 ADAC Helicopter, 1992– $5–10
0832 Fire Rescue Helicopter, 1992– $5–10
0833 Volkswagen Police Van, 1992– $5–10
0834 Volkswagen Fire Rescue Bus, 1992–.$5–10
0835 Rescue Van Ambulance, 1992– $5–10
0836 Morgan Plus 8, 1992– $5–10
0837 Porsche 911 Convertible, 1992–..$5–10
0838 Peugeot 205 Convertible, 1992–..$5–10

0839 Volkswagen Beetle Convertible, 1992–.................................$5–10

0840 Iveco Pickup, 1992–...................$5–10
0841 Audi 80 Convertible, 1992– $5–10

0842 Volkswagen Golf Convertible, 1994– $5–10
0843 Deutz DX 85 Tractor, 1995–............$4–6
0844 Wrecker Truck, 1996–..................$4–6
0845 Ford Fiesta, 1997–.......................$4–6

0846 BMW Z-3, 1997– $4–6

0847 Massey-Ferguson Tractor, 1997–.....$4–6
0848 Dump Truck, 1997–.......................$4–6
0849 Porsche Boxster, 1998– $4–6
0850 BMW Z3 Hardtop, 1998–............$4–6
0851 Mercedes-Benz SLK, 1998–...........$4–6
0852 Vespa Scooter, 1998 ....$4–6
1010 Porsche 911 Targa, 1975–1987 .$8–12
1010 Volkswagen Golf, 1993–...............$4–8
1011 BMW 2000CS, 1975–1981 ...$9–12
1011 Mercedes-Benz 500 SEL Convertible, 1993– $4–10
1012 Ferrari Berlinetta, 1975–1981 ....$15
1012 Mercedes-Benz 500 SEL Hardtop, 1993–.................................$4–10
1013 Porsche Carrera 906, 1975–1982 .$6–10
1013 Skip Truck, 1994–......................$4–10
1014 Citroën DS21, 1975–1980...........$15
1014 Scania Wreck Truck, 1994–.........$4–10
1015 Jaguar E 2+2, 1975–1982 ....$12
1015 Fire Engine.................................$4–10
1016 Ford GT 40, 1975–1981 ....$12
1016 Container Transporter Truck, "Sea Land," 1993–.................................$4–10
1017 Mercedes 280 SL, 1975–1984.......$12
1017 Mercedes Racing Truck, 1993– $4–10
1018 Opel GT 1900, 1975–1978 ....$20
1018 Iveco Racing Truck, 1994–...........$4–10
1019 Audi 100 LS, 1975–1982 ....$12
1019 Simon Snorkel, 1994–.................$4–10
1020 Mercedes-Benz 250, 1975–1984 ..$12
1020 Boeing 737, 1994– $5–10
1021 Ford Capri, 1975–1978 ....$16
1021 Airbus 320, 1993–....................$5–10
1022 Volkswagen 1300 Beetle, 1975–1986 ....$15
1022 Iveco Camping Car, 1993–.........$5–10
1023 Volkswagen Porsche 914/6, 1975–1980.................................$16
1023 Unimog with Crane, 1993– $5–10
1024 Lamborghini Espada 400 GT, 1975–1981.................................$12
1024 Deutz Combine, 1993–...............$5–10
1025 Alfa Romeo Montreal, 1975–1981...$12
1025 Volkswagen Golf Driving School, 1994–.................................$5–10
1026 Citroën SM, 1975–1981...........$15
1026 Unimog with Awning, 1994–.......$5–10
1027 Ford T5 Mustang Mach 1, 1975–1976.................................$15

127 Opel Frontera Sport, 1994– $5–10

1028 Ford Granada Station Wagon, 1975–1984.................................$6–10
1028 BMW 320i, 1994–....................$5–10
1029 Volkswagen Passat Variant, 1975–1984 ....$8–12
1029 Mercedes-Benz C-Class, 1994–....$5–10
1030 Volkswagen Pickup Van, 1975–1989 ....$4–10
1030 Tanker Citerne, 1994–.................$5–10
1031 Volkswagen Bus, 1975–1976......$7–10
1031 Mini Cooper, 1977–....................$4–6
1032 Volkswagen 181 "Thing," 1976–1984 ....$10
1032 Citroën 2CV, 1985–.....................$12
1033 Volkswagen Golf, 1977–.............$4–6
1034 Maserati Boomerang, 1978–1983...$10
1034 Water Cannon, 1994– $4–6
1035 BMW 633 CSi, 1978–1989.....$5–10
1036 Range Rover, 1978–1986 ....$4–8
1036 Opel Astra Caravan Estate Car, 1995– $4–6
1037 Porsche 928, 1979–...................$6–10
1038 Renault 5, 1979–1988 ....$5–10
1038 Tractor with Front End Loader, 1996–.$4–6
1039 Volkswagen Golf Cabriolet, 1980–.$4–10
1040 Opel Senator, 1981–1988.........$4–10

1041 Audi 200 5T, 1982–1988...............$5–10

1042 Mercedes-Benz 500 SE, 1982– ...$4–10
1043 Peugeot 505 STI, 1982–1988.....$5–10
1044 Mercedes-Benz 280 GE, 1982– ..$4–10
1045 Porsche Turbo 917/10, 1976–....$6–10
1046 McLaren, 1976–1986 ....$7–10
1046 Volkswagen Sharan, 1996– $4–6
1047 Opel Kadett SR, 1982–1989......$5–10
1047 BMW R1100RS Motorbike, 1996– $4–6
1048 Ford Escort GL, 1982–1989 ....$4–6

1052 BMW 730i, 1996–............................$4–6

1048 Mercedes-Benz E230, 1996– ...$4–6
1049 Volkswagen Golf Pick Up, 1983–.$4–12
1050 Sign Pack, 1976–.....................$5–10
1051 Camaro Z28, 1983–..................$4–10
1052 Mercedes-Benz 500 SEC, 1983–.$4–10
1053 Jeep CJ-5, 1983–.......................$4–10
1054 Mercedes-Benz 190E, 1984–1988 .$4–10
1054 Opel Omega Caravan Estate Car, 1996–.................................$4–6
1055 Chevrolet Corvette, 1984–..........$4–10
1056 Ford Sierra 2.3 Ghia, 1984–....$4–10
1057 Audi 100 AVant, 1984–1988 ..$6–10
1057 Ford Mondeo, 1996–.................$4–6
1058 Jeep CJ-7, 1985–......................$4–10
1059 Porsche 911 Turbo, 1985–......$4–10
1060 Ferrari GTO, 1985–...................$4–10
1061 Nissan 300ZX, 1985–...............$4–10
1061 Volkswagen Passat Variant Station Wagon, 1996–.........................$4–6
1062 Morgan Plus 8, 1986–..............$4–10
1063 Mercedes-Benz 300E, 1986– ...$4–10
1064 Mercedes-Benz 300TE Station Wagon, 1986–.................................$4–10
1065 Volvo 760 GLE, 1986–1989......$4–10
1066 Saab 9000, 1987–...................$4–10

1067 Porsche 911 Cabriolet, 1987– $4–10

1068 Porsche 959, 1987–...................$6–10
1069 Jaguar XJ6, 1988–....................$4–10
1070 BMW 735iL, 1988–...................$4–10
1071 Peugeot 205 Cabriolet, 1988–.....$4–10
1072 Suzuki SJ413, 1988–.................$4–10
1073 Mercedes-Benz 300SL, 1988–......$4–10
1074 Mercedes SSK, 1988–.................$4–10
1076 Volkswagen Passat Variant, 1989–.................................$4–10
1075 Ferrari F40, 1989–....................$4–10
1077 Volkswagen Beetle 1303 LS Convertible, 1989–.................................$4–10
1078 Volkswagen Beetle 1303 LS, 1990–.................................$4–10
1079 Audi A6 AVant, 1994–................$4–6
1084 Volvo V 40, 1997–....................$4–6
1085 Post Van, 1997–.......................$4–6
1086 Audi A 4, 1997–.......................$4–6
1087 Citroën Xantia, 1997–................$4–6
1088 Mercedes E 290 T Station Wagon, 1997–.................................$4–6
1089 Citroën 2 CV, 1998–..................$4–6
1090 VW Golf IV, 1998–....................$4–6
1091 Tipper Truck, 1998–..................$4–6
1092 Audi A 6, 1998–.......................$4–6
1310 Ford Sierra Taxi, 1985–............$4–10
1310 Mercedes-Benz 300TE Taxi, 1993.................................$5–10

1311 Mercedes-Benz 190 Polizei, 1985–1988 ....$8–10
1311 Mercedes-Benz 300, 1989– $4–10
1312 Volkswagen Bus with radar, 1975.$4–10
1312 Volkswagen Golf ADAC with antenna, 1985–1986 ....$7–10
1312 Volkswagen Golf ADAC withno antenna, 1987– $4–10
1313 Audi 100 Arzt-Notfall-Einsatzwagen, 1975 ....$8–10
1313 ADAC Pick-Up-Service, 1994– $5–8
1314 Volkswagen Bus Bundespost-Peilwagen, 1975–1980 ....$7–10
1314 Volkswagen Transporter, 1981–....$4–10
1315 Volkswagen Bus Highway Service Truck, 1975–1988 ....$5–10
1316 Ford Capri Highway Emergency Car, 1975–1978 ....$6–10
1316 Porsche 911 Targa Highway Emergency Car, 1978–1988................................$6–10
1316 Porsche 911 Turbo Highway Emergency Car, 1989– $4–10
1317 Mercedes-Benz 250 Taxi, 1975–1984 ....$15
1318 Mercedes-Benz 250 Polizei, 1975–1984 ....$15
1319 Ford Transit with Boat, 1975–1982..$4–10
1320 Ford Transit School Bus, 1975–1982.$4–10
1320 Opel Omega ADAC Road Patrol Car, 1997– $4–6
1321 BMW 2000CS Polizei Loudspeaker Car, 1975–1977 ....$6–10
1321 Volkswagen Passat Variant Polizei Loudspeaker, 1978–1989 ....$5–10
1321 Volkswagen Passat Polizei Loudspeaker Car, 1990 ....$4–10
1322 Ford Granada with Boat, 1975–1984..$20
1322 LKW Road Maintenance Lorry, 1997– $6–8
1323 Volkswagen Porsche Rennpolizei, 1975–1978 ....$6–10
1323 ADAC Breakdown Service, 1997–..$6–8
1324 Volkswagen 1300 ADAC, 1975–1984................................$18
1324 ADAC Car Club Motorbike, 1997–.$4–6
1325 Covered Trailer, 1976–1979 ....$10
1325 Police Motorbike, 1997– $46
1326 Hydraulic Crane, 1997– $46
1327 Ford Mustang Mach 1, 1976–1978.$6–10
1328 McLaren, 1976–1981 ....$6–10
1329 Porsche Turbo 917/10, 1976–1981.$6–10
1330 Maserati Boomerang, 1975–1977...$6–10
1331 Volkswagen Bus, 1976–1980.....$6–10
1331 Volkswagen Transporter, many variations, 1981– $4–20
1332 Volkswagen 181 Military, 1976–1979 ....$20
1333 Volkswagen 181 with Raft, 1977–1982 ....$20
1334 Volkswagen LT 28, 1977–..........$4–10
1335 Volkswagen 181 Fire Command Vehicle, 1977–1982 ....$25
1336 Lamborghini Fire Truck, 1978........$8–10
1337 Volkswagen Golf DBP, 1979–1984 .$6–10

1338 Range Rover Emergency Vehicle, 1979–1989 ....$5–10
1339 Porsche 928 Emergency Doctor, 1979–1994 ....$4–10
1339 Emergency Doctor, 1995– $5–7
1340 Matra Simca Rancho, 1979–1988 ....$4–10
1341 Range Rover, 1979–1986..........$4–10
1342 Volkswagen Passat ADAC, 1979–1986 ....$20
1343 Volkswagen Transporter Service Van, 1982– $6–10
1344 Mercedes G Fire Command Wagon, 1983– $4–10
1345 Porsche 911 Rallye, 1986–..........$4–10
1346 Mercedes G Police Command Wagon, 1986– $4–10
1347 Volkswagen Covered Pickup Van, 1990– $4–10
1349 Mercedes 190E Fire Command Car, 1993– $4–10
1350 Volkswagen EuroVan Police Team Van, white & green, 1994–......................$5–10
1351 Volkswagen EuroVan Police, green, 1994 ....$4–10
1352 BMW Police Patrol Car $5–10
1353 Doubledecker Coach, 1994–.......$5–10
1354 Opel Frontera with Boat, 1996–......$5–8
1355 Taxi, 1996– $5–7
1356 Police Car with Loudspeaker, 1996–...$5–7
1357 Formula 1 Racing Car, red, 1998–...$5–7
1358 Formula 1 Racing Car, blue, 1998–...$5–7
1510 Unimog with Builder's Hut, 1994–.$9–12
1511 Mercedes Recycling Lorry with Trailer, 1994– $9–12
1512 Pipe Transporter with Trailer, 1996– .$8–10
1513 Deutz DX 85 Tractor with Trailer, 1996– $8–10
1514 Tipper Truck, 1996–.....................$8–10
1515 Deutz DX 85 Tractor with Vacuum Tanker, 1996– $8–10
1516 Tipper Truck and Trailer, 1997– $8–10
1517 Unimog with Motor Boat, 1997– ..$8–10
1518 Skip Lorry with Trailer, 1998–..........$4–6
1610 Low Loader with Helicopter, 1996– $10–12
1611 Hanomag, 1975– $10–12
1611 Low Loader with Excavator, 1996– $10–12
1612 Zettelmeyer Europ S12, 1975–1983 ....$10–12
1612 Low Loader with Space Shuttle, 1996– $10–12
1613 Mercedes-Benz Europ 1200 Binz Ambulance, 1975–1980 ....$15–18
1613 Mercedes-Benz 200 Ambulance, 1981–1988 ....$10–12
1613 Low Loader with Boat, 1996–.....$10–12
1614 Ford 17M ADAC, 1975............$12–15
1614 VW Passat ADAC, 1976–1981.$10–12
1614 Low Loader with Rocket, 1998–..$10–12
1615 Ford Transit Polizei Loudspeaker Car, 1975–1978 ....$16–18

1615 Ford Transit Polizei Loudspeaker Car, 1979–1983..............................$16–18
1615 Tram $8–10
1616 Hanomag Henschel Covered Truck, 1975–1982 ....$10–12
1617 Ford Granada Fire Command Wagon, 1975–1982 ....$12–15
1618 Lamborghini Fire Car, 1975–1977...$10–12
1619 VW Bus Ambulance, 1975–1978 .$10–12
1620 Mercedes-Benz Unimog, 1975–1983 ....$10–12
1620 Mercedes-Benz Unimog, 1984–.$10–12
1621 VW Bus Military Ambulance, 1976–1979 ....$18–20
1622 Mercedes Wrecker, 1978–1989.$10–12
1623 VW Medi-Mobil, 1979–1989 ...$10–12
1624 Mercedes Bus "TOURIST BUS," 1980–1986 ....$10–12
1625 MAN-VW Express Truck, 1983–.$10–12
1626 Range Rover with Sailboard, 1982–1987 ....$18–20
1627 Mercedes Polizei Wagon, 1983–.$10–12
1628 Mercedes 208 Schulbus, 1983–1988 ....$10–12
1629 Linde Forklift, 1986– $10–12
1630 Mercedes-Benz 260E Binz Ambulance, 1989– $10–12
1716 Unimog, 1993–..........................$12–14
1717 Linde Forklift Truck, 1993– $12–14
1719 Boeing 767-200, 1993– $12–14
1720 Lockheed Tristar L-1011, 1993–..$12–14
1721 Piggy Back Forklift, 1997–..........$12–14
1910 Hanomag Henschel Wrecker, 1975–1978 ....$15–18
1911 Ambulance "NOTARZT," 1975–1984 ....$18–20
1911 Ambulance "UNFALL-NOTFALL," 1985–1986 ....$15–18
1912 Mercedes Postwagen, 1975–1987 .$15–18
1913 Tractor with Trailer, 1975– $15–18
1914 Ford Granada with Motorboat and Trailer, 1975–1984 ....$20–22
1915 Oldsmobile Toronado and Caravan, 1975–1979 ....$30–33
1916 Hanomag Henschel LKW, 1975–1981 ....$20–22
1917 Hanomag Henschel with Horse Trailer, 1975 ....$15–18
1917 Range Rover with Horse Trailer, 1980–1988 ....$15–18
1917 Mercedes 280 GE with Horse Trailer, 1989– $15–18
1918 Mercedes Bus with Trailer "AIRPORT SERVICE," 1981–1983 ....$15–18
1918 Mercedes Bus with Trailer, 1983–1985 ....$15–18
1918 Mercedes Bus with Trailer "HOLIDAY INN," 1986–1988 ....$15–18
1919 MAN-VW Covered Truck with Trailer, 1982– $15–18
1920 Mercedes 809 Binz Ambulance, 1987– $15–18
1921 Mercedes 809 Police Bus, 1987–.$15–18

1922 Mercedes 809 Postwagen, 1987– ..$15–18
1923 Mercedes 280 GE with Fire Boat and Trailer, 1989–................$15–18
1924 Wheel Loader, 1990 ....$15–18
1925 Renault Tractor with Front End Loader, 1993–...............................$15–18
1926 Boeing 747-400, 1993– $15–18
1927 Airbus A340-200, 1993–.........$15–18
1928 Mercedes-Benz Binz Ambulance, 1993–...............................$15–18
1929 Mercedes Sprinter Post, 1997–....$15–18
1930 Mercedes Sprinter Bus, 1997–....$15–18
1931 Binz Ambulance, 1998–...........$15–18
1950 Disc Harrow, 1993–................$15–18
1951 Five-Bottom Plow, 1993–.........$15–18
1952 Amazone Seed Drill, 1993–.......$15–18
1953 Deutz Rotary Mower, 1993–......$15–18
1955 Crop Sprayer, 1993–...............$15–18
1956 Reversible Farm Plow, 1993–......$15–18
1957 Harrow, 1993–......................$15–18
1958 Roller Harrow, 1994–.............$15–18
1959 Trailer with Awning, 1994–.......$15–18
1960 Silage Block Cutter, 1996– $15–18
2010 Range Rover with Horse Box, 1993–...............................$18–20
2010 Opel Frontera with Horse Box, 1996–...............................$18–20
2011 Mercedes-Benz Binz Rescue Van, 1993–...............................$18–20
2015 Mercedes-Benz Binz Red Cross Recovery Van, 1993–................$18–20
2016 Police Mini Bus, 1996– $18–20
2017 Mercedes with Refuse Containers, 1997–...............................$18–20
2210 Michigan Grader-Tractor, 1975– 1977...............................$21–24
2211 Mercedes ADAC, 1975–1981 ..$21–24
2212 Faun Snow Plow Truck, 1975– 1981...............................$21–24
2212 Unimog Snow Plow, 1982–1983 .$21–24
2212 Unimog Snow Plow, 1984–.......$21–24
2213 Mercedes Water Truck, 1975– 1980...............................$21–24
2214 Mercedes Truck, 1975–1978 ....$21–24
2215 Unimog with Sign Trailer, 1975– 1983...............................$21–24
2215 Unimog with Sign Trailer, 1984– 1989...............................$21–24
2216 Ford Granada with Boat and Trailer, 1975–1979....................$30–32
2217 Siku Racing Team, 1978–.........$21–24
2217 Porsche Racing Team, 1985–1986 .$21–24
2218 Unimog Red Cross Truck, 1978– 1985...............................$21–24
2219 Mercedes Bucket Truck, 1978– 1982...............................$30–32
2220 Mercedes Wrecker with Auto Salvage Trailer, 1979–1988..................$21–24
2221 Mercedes ADAC with Auto Transport Trailer and Car, 1983–.............$21–24
2222 Police Helicopter, 1986 ....$21–24
2223 Unimog with Tandem Trailer, 1988–...............................$21–24

2224 Fire Rescue Helicopter, 1990–....$21–24
2225 Loader, 1990–.......................$21–24
2226 Renault Tractor with Trailer, 1990–...............................$21–24
2227 Massey Ferguson Tractor with Hay Trailer, 1990–.......................$21–24
2228 ADAC Helicopter, 1993–.........$21–24
2230 Unimog with Road Work Signs, 1996–...............................$21–24
2231 Opel Frontera with Motorcycle and Trailer $21–24
2232 Unimog with Dumper Truck, 1997–..$21–24
2252 Vacuum Tanker Trailer, 1993– $21–24
2254 Deutz Hay Rake, 1993–...........$21–24
2257 Livestock Trailer, 1993–............$21–24
2258 Hose Drum Irrigator, 1994–.......$21–24
2259 Trailer with Farm Produce, 1994–...$21–24
2260 Corn Seed Drill, 1994– $21–24
2261 Seed Drill, 1996– $21–24
2262 Claas Baler, 1996– $21–24
2263 Cambridge Roller, 1997– $21–24
2264 Champion Rotary Cropper, 1997–..$21–24
2265 Rotary Mowers, 1998–............$21–24
2266 Round Baler, 1998–................$21–24
2408 Peterbilt with Grove Low Loader Trailer, 1992–...............................$21–24
2510 Zettelmeyer Loader, 1975–.........$24–27
2511 Magirus, 1975–1977..............$24–27
2511 Mercedes 2232, 1978–1982...$24–27
2512 Magirus Concrete Truck, 1975– 1977...............................$24–27
2513 Mercedes Street Sign Truck, 1975– 1980...............................$24–27
2513 Volvo F7 Street Sign Truck, 1981– 1985...............................$24–27
2513 Volvo FL6 Street Sign Truck, 1986– 1988...............................$24–27
2513 Mercedes Street Sign Truck, 1989–...............................$24–27
2514 Magirus Dump Truck, 1975.......$24–27
2514 Volvo, 1976–1986 ....$24–27
2515 Unimog BP, 1975–1977..........$24–27
2516 Mercedes Silo Transporter, 1975–...............................$24–27
2517 Volvo Covered Cargo Truck, 1976– 1983...............................$24–27
2517 Ford Covered Cargo Truck, 1984– 1985...............................$24–27
2517 Mercedes Covered Cargo Truck, 1986–1988............................$24–27
2518 VW LT 28 Camper with Travel Trailer, 1980–1989............................$24–27
2518 Jeep CJ-7 with Travel Trailer, 1990–..$24–27
2519 Unimog with Site Trailer, 1980– 1983...............................$25–28
2519 Unimog with Site Trailer "HEITKAMP," 1984–1989............................$24–27
2520 Ford Flatbed Truck with Winch and Camper Pickup, 1984–.............$24–27
2520 ADAC Breakdown Truck with Car, 1993–...............................$24–27
2521 White Old Timer Truck, 1985– 1987...............................$24–27

2522 Unimog U1500 with Linde Forklift Truck, 1985–...............................$24–27
2523 Mercedes-Benz Freight Truck with handtruck and pallets, 1986– 1989...............................$24–27
2524 Mercedes Tanker, 1986–...........$24–27
2525 Jeep CJ-5 with Sport Boat, 1988– 1989...............................$24–27
2525 Mercedes GE with Sport Boat, 1990–...............................$24–27
2526 Wrecker with Trailer, 1988–......$24–27
2527 Mercedes Highway Sand Truck with Snow Plow, 1989–.........................$24–27
2528 Kässbohrer Track Groomer, 1989–...............................$24–27
2529 Liebherr Bulldozer, 1989– $24–27
2531 Polizei Helicopter, 1993–1995 ..$24–27
2531 Opel Frontera with Motor Bike Trailer, 1996–...............................$24–27
2532 Range Rover with Travel Trailer, 1993–...............................$24–27
2532 Opel Frontera with Boat and Caravan, 1996–...............................$24–27
2533 Unimog with Builder's Hut, 1993–.$24–27
2534 ADAC Recovery Van, 1996–......$24–27
2535 Red Cross Helicopter, 1993– $24–27
2536 Camping Car, 1996–...............$24–27
2537 Unimog with Hydraulic Loader, 1996–...............................$24–27
2551 Farm Trailer, 1993–................$24–27
2552 Farm Dump Trailer, 1993–.........$24–27
2553 Manure Spreader, 1993–..........$24–27
2555 Hay Elevator with hay bales, 1993–...............................$24–27
2556 Deutz-Fahr Round Baler, 1993–...$24–27
2558 Farm Animals, 1 horse, 1 cow, 1 pig, 1 sheep, 1 goat, 1993–.............$24–27
2559 Horse Box Trailer with horse, 1993–...............................$24–27
2560 Claas Whirl Rake, 1994–..........$24–27
2561 Land Rover Defender Pickup, 1998–...............................$24–27
2562 Land Rover Defender Softtop, 1998–...............................$24–27
2610 MAN Road Maintenance Lorry with traffic signs, 1993–.......................$27–30
2612 VW 1303 cabriolet, blue, opening doors, 1:43, limited edition, 1993–.....$27–30
2613 VW 1303 cabriolet, white, opening doors, 1:43, limited edition, 1993–.....$27–30
2614 Helicopter with Floats, orange with blue pontoons, "Katastrophenschutz," 1993–...............................$27–30
2615 Unimog Excavator, 1993– $27–30
2616 Mercedes Tipper Lorry, 1993–....$27–30
2617 Mercedes Hazardous Waste Truck, 1994–...............................$27–30
2618 Lorry with Awning, 1994–.........$27–30
2650 Tipping Loader Trailer, 1994–......$27–30
2651 Seed Drill, 1997– $27–30
2652 New Holland 5635 Tractor, 1997–...............................$27–30
2653 New Holland L75, 1997– $27–30

2654 Massey Ferguson 4270 Tractor, 1998– $27–30
2810 MAN ARAL Tanker, 1975–1977 ..$30–32
2811 MAN Container Truck, 1975 .....$30–32
2812 MAN Lumber Truck, 1975–1978 .$30–32
2813 Magirus Skip Truck, 1975 ....$30–32
2814 Volvo Crane Truck with Boat, 1975–1983 ....$30–32
2815 Mercedes Fire Truck, 1975–1977 .$30–32
2816 Mercedes Crane Truck, 1975–1978 ....$30–32
2817 Volvo Cement Truck, 1977–1984 ..$30–32
2818 Rear Digger Tractor with Front End Loader, 1977–1985 ....$30–32
2819 Mercedes Extending Ladder Fire Truck, 1978– $30–32
2820 Unimog Side-Mount Scoop with Pipe Trailer, 1978–1981 ....$35–36
2820 Mercedes-Benz Garbage Truck, 1984– $30–32
2821 White Old Timer "Coca-Cola" Truck, 1986–1987 ....$30–32
2821 White Old Timer "Sinalco" Truck, 1987 ....$30–32
2822 Unimog with Site Office Trailer, 1987–1988 ....$30–32
2823 Fire Boat Transporter, 1987–1988 .$30–32
2823 Police Boat Transporter, 1989– ..$30–32
2824 Mercedes Street Cleaning Truck, 1988– $30–32
2825 Volvo Payload Hauler, 1989– $30–32
2826 Mercedes SkipTruck, 1989– $30–32
2827 Unimog Winter Service with Snowblower, Snowplow & Hopper/Spreader, 1993– $30–32
2850 Deutz-Fahr Agrostar 6.61 Turbo Tractor, 1993– $30–32
2851 Fendt-Farmer 308/310 LS Tractor, 1993– $30–32
2853 Massey Ferguson MF284 with Transporter Box, 1993– $30–32
2855 Ford TW35 Tractor, 1993– $30–32
2856 Renault TX145-14 Tractor, 1993– .$30–32
2859 Beet Trailer, 1993– $30–32
2860 White Old-Timer Beverage Delivery Truck, 1988– $30–32
2860 Round Bale Trailer, 1993– $30–32
2861 Fiat 180-90 Turbo DT Tractor, 1993– $30–32
2862 Deutz Baler, 1993– $30–32
2863 Deutz-Fahr AgroXtra Tractor, 1993– $30–32
2864 Steyr 9094 Tractor, 1993– $30–32
2865 Deutz-Fahr Fun-Trac Tractor, 1993– .$30–32
2866 Claas Tipping Trailer, 1993– $30–32
2867 Renault Ceres 95X Tractor, 1994– .$30–32
2868 Massey Ferguson 9400 Tractor, 1996– $30–32
2869 Slurry Tanker, 1998– $30–32
2910 Panzer Leopard A3 Tank, 1976–1979 ....$33–36
2911 Panzer Gepard, 1976–1979 .....$33–36
2912 Panzer Leopard A1, 1977–1979 .$33–36

2913 Foam Unit with Light Trailer, 1979–1984 ....$33–36
2914 Faun Crane Truck, 1979– $33–36
2915 MAN Tree Transporter, 1980–1982 ....$45–48
2916 Volvo Refrigerated Truck, 1981–1984 ....$33–36
2917 Mack Heavy Wrecker, 1981–1989 ....$33–36
2918 Ford Cargo Beverage Truck, 1983–1986 ....$33–36
2919 Mercedes-Benz Dump Trailer Truck, 1984– $33–36
2920 Mercedes Recycling Transporter, 1986– $33–36
2921 Mercedes Snorkel Fire Truck with Snorkel Trailer, 1986–1989 ....$33–36
2922 Mercedes Cement Mixer, 1989–...$33–36
2923 Mercedes Dump Truck, 1989–...$33–36
2924 Faun 3-Axle Ladder Truck, 1993–...$33–36
2926 Mercedes Refuse Truck, 1992–...$33–36
2927 Fire Brigade Team Bus, 1993– ..$33–36
2928 Police Information Bus, 1994–.....$33–36
2929 Unimog with Grass Cutter, 1994–.$33–36
2930 Overhead Maintenance Lorry, 1993– $33–36
2931 Faun Refuse Truck, 1997– $33–36
2932 Faun Gully Emptier, 1997–.........$33–36
2933 LKW Truck with Piggy Back Forklift, 1997– $33–36
2934 O&K Heavy Duty Tipper Truck, 1997– $33–36
2935 Roller, 1998– $33–36
2951 Mercedes-Benz MB Trac 800 Tractor w/Tipping Hopper, 1993– $33–36
2956 Deutz AgroXtra Tractor with Twin Rear Wheels, 1993– $33–36
2957 Fendt Xylon 524, 1994– $33–36
2958 Deutz-Fahr Agrotron 6.05 tt, 1994–...$33–36
2959 Steyr Tractor with Twin Wheels Fron and Rear, 1997– $33–36
2960 Massey Ferguson 9240 with Twin Rear Wheels, 1997– $33–36
2961 Fendt Farmer Favorit 926, 1997– $33–36
2962 Steyr 9145 Tractor, 1998– $33–36
2963 Case CS150 Tractor, 1998– $33–36
2964 Bergmann Manure Spreader, 1998–.$33–36
3153 Unimog, green, 1993– $35–39
3155 Forester Trailer, 1993– $35–39
3156 Deutz-Fahr Agroxtra Tractor with Front Mower, 1994– $35–39
3110 Hanomag Henschel ARAL Tanker, 1975–1977 ....$35–39
3110 Mercedes ARAL Tanker, 1978–1979 ....$35–39
3110 Mercedes ESSO Tanker, 1980–1983 ....$35–39
3111 Hanomag Henschel Container Transporter, 1975–1977 ....$35–39
3111 Volvo Container Transporter, 1978–1985 ....$35–39
3112 Mercedes Auto Transporter, 1975– .$35–39

3114 Menck Loader, 1975–1977 .....$40–42
3115 Volvo Cargo Truck and Trailer, 1978–1985 ....$39–42
3115 Volvo FL10 Hollis Transport and Trailer, 1986 ....$35–39
3115 Renault Turbo Hollis Transport and Trailer, 1987–1988 ....$39–42
3115 Renault Turbo BMX Transport and Trailer, 1989– $35–39
3116 Volvo 7 Covered Transport, 1982–1984 ....$35–39
3117 Mack Semi-Freighter, 1982–1986 ..$35–39
3117 Renault Turbo Semi-Freighter, 1986–1988 ....$35–39
3118 TOPAS Tanker, 1989 ....$35–39
3119 Man Semi-Tanker, 1989– $35–39
3120 Zettelmeyer Wheel Loader, 1990–..$35–39
3121 Bus, Red upper, white lower, scenery on sides, "erdgas," 1993– $35–39
3121 Bus, "EuropaBus," 1993– $35–39
3122 Forklift Truck, 1993– $35–39
3123 Wheel Loader with Accessory Plow, 1993– $35–39
3125 Mercedes-Benz Roll-Off Skip Loader, 1993– $35–39
3128 Roll-Off Skip Loader, 1994–.....$35–39
3129 Motor Home with Accessories, 1998 ....$35–39
3155 Forest Trailer, 1994– $35–39
3156 Tractor with Front Mower, 1994–...$35–39
3157 Tractor with Silage Block Cutter, 1996– $35–39
3410 Hanomag Henschel Garage Transporter, 1975–1977 ....$45–48
3410 Mercedes Garage Transporter, 1978–1981 ....$45–48
3411 Faun Airport Foam Tender, 1975–1985 ....$45–48
3412 Mercedes Covered Transport, 1975–1983 ....$45–48
3413 Power Shovel, 1978– $45–48
3414 Volvo F7 Double Freighter, 1979–1980 ....$45–48
3415 MAN Loader Truck with Loader Crane, 1980–1985 ....$50–55
3415 Volvo FL6 Loader Truck with Loader Crane, 1986 ....$45–48
3415 White Loader Truck with Loader Crane, 1987 ....$45–48
3416 Volvo Tanker Semi, 1982–1986 .$45–48
3417 Man "AIR FRANCE" Bus, 1982–1987 ....$45–48
3418 Kenworth "BP" Tanker Semi, 1986–1989 ....$45–48
3419 Mercedes Auto Transporter, 1986–..$45–48
3420 Kenworth Sand Transporter, 1987–1988 ....$45–48
3421 Mercedes Double Freighter, 1987–1988 ....$45–48
3421 Iveco Double Freighter, 1989–....$45–48
3422 TOPAS Tanker, 1989– $45–48
3424 Iveco Double Container Truck, 1993– $45–48

3425 DAF Garage Transporter, 1993–....$45–48

3426 Mercedes-Benz 500SEL, blue, doors open, 1:43, limited edition $45–48

3427 Mercedes-Benz 500SEL, gold, doors open, 1:43, limited edition $45–48

3428 Mercedes Truck with hydraulic boom platform, 1993– $45–48

3429 Mercedes-Benz Ziegler Water Cannon w/working pump, 1993–.........$45–48

3430 ADAC Automobile Club Testing Service, 1993– $45–48

3431 Cement Mixer, 1994– $45–48

3432 Wrecker Truck, 1994– $45–48

3433 Mercedes-Benz Ladder Fire Engine, 1996– $45–48

3434 Four Wheel Loader, 1998– $45–48

3435 Bulldozer, 1998– $45–48

3450 Fendt Farmer 308 LS Tractor with Front Loader, 1993– $45–48

3451 Mercedes-Benz MB Trac 800 Tractor with Snow Plow, 1993– $45–48

3453 Massey Ferguson Front End Loader, 1993– $45–48

3454 Claas Automatic Hay Loader, 1993– $45–48

3455 Claas Teleskoplader Ranger 911 T, 1994– $45–48

3456 Fendt Xylon with Rope Winder, 1994– $45–48

3457 Deutz Fahr Agrostar with Scraper and Toolbox, 1997– $45–48

3510 Hydraulic Excavator, 1993– $45–48

3511 Mercedes Shell Tanker, 1993– ...$45–48

3512 Mercedes Fire Equipment Truck w/ hydraulic boom & small boat..........$45–48

3512L Ford Fire Dept. Truck with fire boat, limited edition $50–55

3513 Rosenbauer Airport Crash Truck, limited edition, 1993– $45–48

3514 Track Type Lattice Boom Clamshell Excavator, 1993– $45–48

3515 Mercedes Covered Lorry with Twin Axle Trailer, Eurotrans, 1994– $45–48

3515 Mercedes Covered Lorry with Twin Axle Trailer, JumboCargo, 1994– $45–48

3515 Mercedes Covered Lorry with Twin Axle Trailer, Container Service, 1998 ....$45–48

3516 Recycling Skip Truck with Skip Trailer, 1994– $45–48

3517 Articulated Bus, 1996– $45–48

3518 Caterpillar Shovel, 1996– $45–48

3550 Deutz-Fahr DX6.31 Turbo Forestry Tractor, 1993– $45–48

3551 Fendt Xylon Front End Loader, 1996– $45–48

3552 Fendt Xylon with Crop Sprayer, 1998– $45–48

3710 Hanomag Henschel ADAC Vehicle Safety Test Veh., 1975–1978 ....$50–55

3710 Mercedes ADAC Vehicle Safety Test Vehicle, 1979–1981 ....$45–48

3711 Hanomag Henschel Pipe Loader Truck, 1975–1978 ....$45–48

3711 Volvo Pipe Loader truck, 1979–1982 ....$45–48

3712 Hanomag Henschel ARAL Gas Station Transporter, 1975–1977 ....$45–48

3712 Volvo ARAL Gas Station Transporter, 1978–1985 ....$45–48

3713 Mercedes Parking Lot Transporter, 1977–1984 ....$50–55

3714 Volvo Double Freighter, 1979–1983 ....$50–55

3714 Mercedes Double Freighter, 1984–1985 ....$50–55

3715 MAN Building Transporter and Trailer, 1980–1986 ....$45–48

3716 MAN Transporter with Wheel Loader, 1982–1986 ....$45–48

3717 Mack Heavy Wrecker and MAN Truck, 1982–1984 ....$45–48

3718 Mercedes "BP" Double Tanker, 1983–1985 ....$45–48

3719 Ford Low Loader Helicopter Transporter, 1985– $45–48

3720 MAN Bus, 1987–1992 ....$45–48

3720 Mercedes Snorkel Truck with working water pump, 1992– $45–48

3721 White Horse Transporter, 1987–1988 ....$50–55

3721 Mercedes Tractor, 12 Meter Trailer, SIKU-TRANSPORT, 1993–...............$45–48

3722 MAN Circus Transporter with two Cage Trailers, 1987– $45–48

3722 Rosenbauer Airport Crash Truck w/working water pump, 1993– $45–48

3723 Rethmann Recycling Transporter, 1988–1992 ....$45–48

3723 Faun Telescoping Crane Truck, 1994– $45–48

3724 Low Loarder with Garage, 1997- $45–48

3725 Container Grabber with Container, 1998– $45–48

3750 Massey Ferguson MF 284 Tractor with Farm Trailer, 1993– $45–48

3751 Deutz-Fahr Agrostar DX6.61 Turbo Tractor with Tandem-Axle Trailer, 1993–.....$45–48

3752 Deutz-Fahr Tractor with Vacuum Tanker, 1993– $45–48

3755 Renault Tractor with Rear Digger, 1993– $45–48

3756 Deutz Fahr Agrostar with Rear Digger, 1997– $45–48

3780 Ladder Truck with flashing lights and siren, 1992– $45–48

3812 DAF Loader Truck and Trailer with Beams, 1989– $55–60

3813 Iveco Recycling Truck with Trailer, 1993– $55–60

3814 Mercedes-Benz Double Decker Touring Coach, 1993– $55–60

3815 Large Volume Lorry "M. Schneider Hamburg - Paris - Amsterdam," 1996–....$55–60

3816 Lorry with Trailer, Lufthansa Cargo, 1998– $55–60

3854 Claas Jaguar 695 Combine, 1993– $55–60

3855 Claas Jaguar 695 Forage Harvester, 1994– $55–60

3856 Potato Digger, 1994–.............$55–60

3857 Fendt Xylon Forestry Tractor, 1998–.$55–60

3880 Pumper with working water pump and flashing lights, 1992– $55–60

3910 Shell Gas Station Transporter, 1987–1989 ....$62–66

3911 Scania Low Loader with Wheel Loader and Power Shovel, 1990– $62–66

3913 Liebherr Fast Erecting Tower Crane, 1992– $62–66

3915 Wood Transporter with Colored Pencils, 1996– $62–66

3953 Fendt Xylon Front-Loader with Rear Digger, 1997– $62–66

4010 Faun Hydraulic Crane, 1975–....$70–75

4011 Giant Boom Crane Transporter, 1978– $70–75

4012 Low Loader with Payloader, 1980– $70–75

4013 Mack Low Loader with Power Shovel, 1981–1988 ....$70–75

4014 Peterbilt Sloop Transporter with Boat, 1983–1988 ....$70–75

4015 Volvo Fire Watch Tower Transporter, 1985–1989 ....$70–75

4016 Peterbilt Space Shuttle Transporter, 1988– $70–75

4017 Mercedes Auto Transporter with five cars, 1993– $70–75

4018 DAF Low Loader with Gas Station, 1994– $70–75

4019 MAN Low Loader with Car Wash Station, 1994– $70–75

4051 Deutz-Fahr Top Liner Combine Harvester, 1993– $70–75

4052 Deutz-Fahr M36.10 Corn Combine Harvester, 1993–..............................$70–75

4053 FMG 280 Forester with Logs and Crane, 1993– $70–75

4054 Fendt with Forester Trailer, 1996– .$70–75

4110 Grove Hydraulic Truck Crane, 1992– $70–75

4111 Mercedes Lorry with Low Loader Trailer and Excavator, 1993– $70–75

4112 Tower Construction Crane, 1993– ..$70–75

4150 Claas Lexion 480, 1997–.........$70–75

4210 Mobile Tower Construction Crane, 1992– $70–75

4310 Lattice Mast Crane, 1997–.......$70–75

4810 Latticed Mast Crane, 1998–........$70–75

7015 Pallets for 1717 ....$5–10

7016 5x2 Containers for 2920 ....$5–10

7017 Recycle Containers for 3813........$5–10

7050 Milk Cans for 2853 ....$5–10

7051 Silage Blocks for 1960 ....$5–10

7052 Front Cutter for 3855 ....$5–10

7053 Front Cutter for 4052 ....$5–10

7054 Front Cutter for 3854 ....$5–10

7056 Round Bales for 2556 ....$5–10

7057 Front Cutter for 4051 .... $5–10
7062 Rectangular Hay Bales for 2862....$5–10

Siku Junior Plastic Toys

    2583 Side Tipping Trailer............... $24–27
    2881 Massey-Ferguson 6150 .... $28–30
    2882 Claas Tipping Trailer............ $28–30
    2982 Fendt Farmer Favorit 926 ..... $32–35
    3781 Tractor with Side Tipping Trailer $48–50
    3881 Tractor with Claas Tipping Trailer $54–60

Silhouette

Silhouette models of France are offered as 1:43 scale kits.
1011 1982 Rondeau M382 .... $14
1014 1982 Dumont Fuji $14

Silver Pet

Robert Speerbrecher, a collector stationed at the US embassy in Jakarta, Indonesia, reports of a new book written in Japanese that lists several brands of diecast from Japan not previously reported. Silver Pet is among them, likely a company that existed for a short time in the sixties. Models feature crude castings with stamped tin or thin pressed steel base. All the models are silver. "Pet" is a common name for many toys produced in Japan, including brands such as Micropet, Diapet, and Miniature Pet. The appearance of silver Pet models is of stylized cars of the late fifties.

Simba

Simba Toys GmbH & Co
Werkstraße 1
90765 Fürth-Stadeln, Germany
phone: 0911/976501
fax: 0911/9765120
e-mail: simbatoys@simbatoys.de
website: www.simbatoys.de
Simba España
S. A. Edificio Euro 3
Frederic Mompou
No. 5 6º 1a
08960 Sant Just Desvern
C.I.F. A-59.129.551
Barcelona, Spain
Simba Toys Hungaria Kft
H-1033 Budapest, Hungary
Dovzce Simba Toys Praha
Simba Toys Polska Sp. z o.o.
00-975 Warszawa ul. Pulawska 14, Poland

The Germany-based Simba produces, among other toys, a line of quality diecast models manufactured in China and dubbed "Mini Metals." One package identifies one of their models only as a "Concept Car." A local toy store reports that the model was recalled when Volkswagen protested the US marketing of the toy that is obviously an unlicensed knockoff model of their New Beetle.

Similarly, their Jeep Grand Cherokee is marked only as a "Family Car." I wonder if Daimler / Chrysler will catch up with that one and demand it also be recalled.

The "spinning top" logo and accompanying text on the base reveals that the toy is produced in China by "Tins Toys."

In addition, R. C. Johnston of White Rock, British Columbia, reports of a pair of diecast miniatures produced by Comet Miniatures of England in 1988, also dubbed "Mini Metals" (one "l"), to commemorate the popular TV series *Voyage to the Bottom of the Sea*.

"Concept Car" 1998 VW Beetle Convertible, baby blue with silver fenders, 1:36 ...... $4–6
"Concept Car" 1998 VW Beetle Convertible, lime green with white fenders, 1:36 ..... $4–6
"Concept Car" 1998 VW Beetle Hardtop, red with black roof, 1:36 .... $4–6
"Concept Car" 1998 VW Beetle Hardtop, yellow with black roof, 1:36 .... $4–6
Mercedes-Benz CLK GTR, 1:43 .... $4–6
Mercedes A-Class $4–6
Ford Ka $4–6
"Family Car" Jeep Grand Cherokee $4–6

Singfund

On November 1, 1998, collector Robert Speerbrecher reported, "Found a new diecast brand… maybe. It's a company out of China called Singfund Industries Ltd. They make several single-carded and sets of fire trucks and emergency vehicles. I've seen two different 1:64 scale hook and ladder fire trucks on individual blisterpacks and two different sets with several fire and rescue vehicles of mixed scale. Thing is, they tend to be only 30–40% diecast. Usually just the cab of the vehicle and, on some, part of the trailer. They are cheap stuff like many China toys. Maybe better than the really crude ones but not as good as Yatming for example."

Sizzlers

The distinction of these rechargeable battery-powered race cars is that they represent the first commercial application of nickel-cadmium rechargeable batteries, back in the early 1970s. Originally produced by Mattel, Sizzlers became a brand owned, but never used, by the Estes Model Rocket Company.

In 1996, Playing Mantis obtained licensing from Estes to produce a new line of Sizzlers under the Johnny Lightning brand originally owned by Topper in the early 1970s. New models retail for around $10. Original Sizzlers are valued from $30–120.

After losing the license to produce Sizzlers, Mattel attempted to compensate by producing X-V Racers, a line currently available, and touting "From the original makers of Sizzlers" on the package, demonstrating an attempt to capitalize on the name they regrettably gave up.

Mike Grove is the undisputed Sizzlers expert and has written a book on them. Contact him at the address below.
Mike Grove
Sizzlers Hotline
1047 E 5th St
Fremont NE 68025
phone: 402-727-9505
e-mail: Sizzler@aol.com

Sky

Sky is an obscure brand of 1:43 scale models known to be offered only from Jeff Bray Jr.'s Diecast Miniatures of Amston, Connecticut.
501 1950 Mercury Coupe $148
509 1937 Packard 4-Door Sedan $148
510 1937 Packard 4-Door Sedan Fire Chief $178
5041 1950 Mercury Indy Pace Car...... $168
5089 1961 Ford Thunderbird Indy Pace Car $168

Skyline

Tin Wizard Modelcars
and Skyline Models
c/o Thomas Wolter Modelltechnik
Talstrasse 170
D-69198 Schriesheim, Germany
phone: 06203/68680
fax: 06203/68329
e-mail: THWOLTER@aol.com
website: www.tinwizard.de
or www.toynet.de/tinwizard

Handmade 1:43 and 1:24 scale white metal models with plated parts comprise this series from Schriesheim, Germany. Also see Tin Wizard Models.

Skyline Models 1:43 Scale

    5010 Ford Mercury Coupe, 1950, kit...$50
    5012 Ford Mercury Coupe, 1950, beige white, ready made $125
    5014 Ford Mercury Coupe, 1950, blue, ready made.............................. $125
    5015 Ford Mercury Coupe, 1950, green, ready made.............................. $125
    5020 Ford Mercury "N.Y.Firechief," 1950, kit.. $50
    5021 Ford Mercury "N.Y.Firechief," 1950, red, ready made $130
    5030 Ford Mercury Convertible, 1950, kit.. $50
    5031 Ford Mercury Convertible, 1950, white, ready made $125
    5032 Ford Mercury Convertible, 1950, red, ready made.............................. $125
    5033 Ford Mercury Convertible, 1950, black, ready made $125
    5040 Ford Mercury Indianapolis Pace Car, 1961, kit $50
    5041 Ford Mercury Indianapolis Pace Car, 1961, yellow, ready made $130
    5050 Ford Thunderbird Hardtop, 1963, kit.. $50

5051 Ford Thunderbird Hardtop, 1963, white, ready made $125

5053 Ford Thunderbird Hardtop, 1963, red, ready made...........................$125

5054 Ford Thunderbird Hardtop, 1963, pink, ready made $125

5080 Ford Thunderbird Indianapolis Pace Car, 1961, kit $50

5089 Ford Thunderbird Indianapolis Pace Car, 1961, metallic gold, ready made...$130

5090 Packard 4-Door Sedan, 1937, kit ..$50

5091 Packard 4-Door Sedan, 1937, white, ready made...........................$125

5093 Packard 4-Door Sedan, 1937, bordeaux red, ready made...............$125

5094 Packard 4-Door Sedan, 1937, blue, ready made...........................$125

5100 Packard 4-Door Sedan Feuerwehr CH, 1937, ready made $50

5103 Packard 4-Door Sedan Feuerwehr CH, 1937, red, ready made.........$130

5150 Nash Statesman, 1950, kit $50

5151 Nash Statesman, 1950, blue, ready made...$125

5152 Nash Statesman, 1950, red, ready made...$125

5153 Nash Statesman, 1950, blue, ready made...$125

5160 Nash Statesman "Taxi," 1950, kit ..$50

5161 Nash Statesman "Taxi," 1950, yellow, ready made...........................$130

6201 Cadillac Convertible Series 62, 1955, ready made........................$125

6211 Cadillac Eldorado Indianapolis Pace Car, 1960, ready made $155

6212 Cadillac Eldorado Convertible, top down, 1960, ready made $155

6213 Cadillac Eldorado Convertible, top up, 1960, ready made $155

6214 Cadillac Eldorado Convertible, top up, 1960, ready made $155

6221 Chevrolet Corvette Indianapolis Pace Car, 1978, ready made.............$185

Slik-Toys (see Lansing Slik-Toys)

SM

An obscure Hong Kong based company known only as SM produces inexpensive but nevertheless attractive miniature cars and trucks usually sold in budget sets. Price of individual vehicles is generally between 25 and 50 cents each when purchased as part of the set.

Small Wheels and Western Models

As EWA & Miniature Cars USA puts it, "Western Models were one of the first companies in the world to make high quality hand-built metal models. The company was founded in the early 1970s just southeast of London, England, and moved in the mid '80s to Taunton in the southwest of England. They now

have a range of about 70 quality 1:43rd scale models of European and American, race and street cars, old and new, plus some interesting record cars. A few new models are introduced annually and some withdrawn, which makes the models very collectible.

"Small Wheels is another name used by Western for some of their models. All are made in the Western factory to the same high standards."

Small Wheels 1:43 Scale

1 Jaguar XK140 ....$98

2 Ferrari 275 GTB $108

3 Rolls Royce SC2 Convertible, top up .$108

3 Rolls Royce SC2 Convertible, top down .$108

4 Jaguar Mk 2, blue with disc hubs $88

4 Jaguar Mk 2, red with wire wheels ...$108

5 1952 Bentley R Continental $98

8 Saab 96 ....$98

9 Saab 96 Rally....................................$98

10 1967 Mustang GT $98

12 1957 DeSoto Firesweep 4-Door Sedan ....$98 -119

12 1957 DeSoto Firesweep Sedan, kit ..$48

12T 1957 DeSoto 4-Door Sedan Taxi ...$98

13 1953 Corvette Roadster, kit $48

14 1958 Chrysler Windsor 2-Door Hardtop $98

15 1948 Hudson Commodore 4-Door Sedan...............................$98–109

15P 1948 Hudson Commodore Police $109–119

17 1958 Ford Custom Taxi $124

Small Wheels 1:24 Scale

Jaguar XK150 ....$328

Ferrari Lusso $308

Jaguar Mark 2 ViCarage....................$348

Jaguar XJ13, kit $148

Smart Toys

Smart Toys Ltd.
Rm. 822, Peninsular Ctr.
67 Mody Rd.
Kowloon, Hong Kong, China

Collector Robert Speerbrecher first discovered Smart Toys on a trip to Bangkok in December 1998. Smart Toys are China-produced commercial and construction vehicles. Sold in multipacks in Bangkok and labeled as "for display — not a toy," they showed up in March 1999 at a liquidator store in Redmond, Oregon, in individual flip-top display boxes for $1 each. They are labeled as HO gauge 1:87 scale and are barely discernable as Smart Toys except for an embossed brand name on the base of the box. Speerbrecher questions whether the quality is good enough to be called a collectible, but they do possess charm and operating parts that make them excellent little toys, and great additions to HO gauge dioramas and train layouts.

Bulldozer, yellow, with Stop sign and man with shovel $2–4

Cement Mixer, yellow, with Do Not Enter sign...$2–4

Power Shovel, orange, with sign................$2–4

Road Roller, burgundy, with Stop sign and flag man...$2–4

Tractor, burgundy, with two signs and woman carrying a milk can $2–4

Tractor with Grabber, green, with One Way sign and construction worker holding a rake...$2–4

Unimog, burgundy cab, with One Way sign and construction worker carrying a bucket $2–4

Unimog, yellow cab, with One Way sign and construction worker carrying a bucket...$2–4

Wheel Loader with dumping Cargo platform, green, with One Way sign $2–4

More recently found is a set of eight HO gauge semi-tractor trailers. If it weren't for the diecast upper cab portion of the tractor, these couldn't be called diecast at all since the rest of the model is plastic. Quality is still excellent for their $2 price tag. Two types of tractors are used for these models — a cab-over-engine (COE) and a conventional. Each is packaged in a sturdy, clear fliptop box similar to the construction toys but with a longer package to accommodate the 7" trucks.

Fire Chief from Boley, 1:87.....................$2–4

Hanjin, bright blue box trailer with white COE tractor $2–4

Hapag-Lloyd, orange box trailer with yellow conventional tractor $2–4

Hyundai, bright orange box trailer with white conventional tractor $2–4

K-Line, red box trailer with white COE tractor $2–4

Kuhne & Nagel, dark blue box trailer with light blue accent stripe and matching dark blue COE tractor $2–4

Maersk, silver-grey box trailer with dark gray COE tractor $2–4

Mitsui O.S.K. Lines, pale gray box trailer with dark gray COE tractor......................$2–4

OOCL, pale gray box trailer with yellow conventional tractor $2–4

Pickup from Boley, 1:87.....................$2–4

VW Beetle from Boley, 1:87 ....$2–4

Smer

Smer models are made in Czechoslovakia.
Ford Model T Roadster, kit, 1:32 ....$14

Smith Family Toys

Collector Henri Mueller discovered this unusual brand of semi-tractors of unknown scale. The package offers the brand name "John Smith" as well as "Smith Family Toys" accompanying an illustration of four models as listed below:

California Hauler Conventional Sleeper Cab, yellow with red and black trim.....................$4
Highway Express Conventional Sleeper Cab, black with red, blue and white accents.....$4
Long Haul Conventional Sleeper Cab, red with yellow and black trim..............................$4
Pacer Cabover, red with yellow accents.........$4

Smith-Miller

Smith-Miller toys are sturdy cast-metal and aluminum replicas of trucks of the era around 1945 when they were introduced in Santa Monica, California. The Smith-Miller firm later became Miller-Ironson before fading into oblivion in 1954. So popular were these "Smitty" trucks to collector/enthusiast Fred Thompson that he purchased the defunct company lock, stock, and barrel in 1979.

Under Thompson's vision, Smith-Miller still produces quality reproductions of these classic toys, along with new models and replacement parts for older ones.

Smitty toys remain a testament to the quality of the era, even though Smitty Toys were considered expensive for their time, from $7 to $28 each. What's perhaps most intriguing about the new models produced since 1979 is that they retail for around the same price as the old ones are currently worth on the second market. All models listed below have been issued in the last twenty years.

#201-L Lumber Truck with 60 Boards, 6-wheel, 14" long $700
#202-M Material Truck with 3 Barrels, 3 cases, 18 boards, 4-wheel, 14" long $900
#203-H Heinz Grocery Truck, 6-wheel, 14" long..............................$475
#204-A Arden Milk Truck with 12 Milk Cans, 4-wheel, 14" long..............................$325
#205-P Oil Truck with 4 drums, 6-wheel, 14" long..............................$450

#206-C Coca-Cola Truck with 16 Coca-Cola Cases, 4-wheel, 14" long $900
#208-B Bekins Vanliner, 14-wheel, 23½" long.............................$325
#209-T Timber Giant with 3 Logs, 14-wheel, 23½" long $325
#210-S Stake Truck, 14-wheel, 23½" long.............................$500
#211-L Sunkist Special, 14-wheel, 23½" long.............................$375
#212-R Red Ball, 14-wheel, 23½" long $375
#301-W GMC Wrecker, 4-wheel $250
#302-M GMC Materials Truck with 4 Barrels, 3 Timbers..............................$400
#303-R GMC Rack Truck, 6-wheel $350
#304-K GMC Kraft Foods, 4-wheel $600
#305-T GMC Triton Oil with 3 Drums $350
#306-C GMC Coca-Cola, 16 Coca-Cola Cases, 4-wheel..............................$900
#307-L GMC REdwood Logger Tractor-Trailer with 3 Logs $1100
#308-V GMC Lyon Van Lines Tractor-Trailer, 14-wheel..............................$650
#309-S GMC Super Cargo Tractor-Trailer with 10 Barrels, 14-wheel..............................$400
#310-H GMC Hi-Way Freighter Tractor-Trailer, 14-wheel..............................$300
#311-E GMC Silver Streak Express Tractor-Trailer, 14-wheel..............................$550
#312-P GMC Pacific Intermountain Express "P.I.E." Tractor-Trailer..............................$600
#401 Tow Truck, 4-wheel, 15" long $250
#401-W GMC Wrecker, 6-wheel $450
#402 Dump Truck, 11½" long $350
#402-M GMC Material Truck with 4 barrels, 2 timbers..............................$400
#403 Scoop Dump, 14" long $250
#403-R GMC Rack Truck, 6-wheel $250
#404 Lumber Truck, 19" long..................$750
#404-B GMC Bank of America with Lock and Key, 4-wheel..............................$400
#404-T Lumber Trailer, 17" long $300
#405 Silver Streak Tractor, 6-wheel, 28" long $350
#405-T GMC Triton Oil with 3 Drums, 6-wheel..............................$375
#406 Bekins Van, 6-wheel Tractor and 4-wheel Trailer..............................$650
#406-L GMC Lumber Tractor-Trailer with 8 Timbers, 14-wheel $425
#407 Searchlight Truck Hollywood Filmad, 18½" long $300
#407-V GMC Lyon Van Tractor-Trailer, 10-wheel..............................$650
#408 Blue Diamond Dump Truck, 10-wheel, 18½" long $1700
#408-H GMC Machinery Hauler, 13-wheel..............................$1700
#409 Pacific Intermountain Express "P.I.E." 6-wheel Tractor and 8-wheel Cast Aluminum Trailer, 29" long $900
#409-G GMC Mobilgas Tanker with 2 Hoses, 14-wheel $500

#410 Aerial Ladder Semi, 6-wheel Tractor and 4-wheel Trailer, "SMFD," 36" long $800
#410-F GMC Transcontinental Tractor-Trailer, 14-wheel..............................$375
#411-E GMC Silver Streak Tractor-Trailer, 14-wheel..............................$475
#412-P GMC P.I.E., 14-wheel..............$625
Chevrolet Bekins Van, plain tires, hubcaps, 14-wheel..............................$525
Chevrolet Coca-Cola, plain tires, 4-wheel..$850
Chevrolet Flatbed Tractor-Trailer, unpainted wood trailer, plain tires, hubcaps, 14-wheel..............................$350
Chevrolet Milk Truck, 1945-46, plain tires, hubcaps, 4-wheel..............................$400
Ford Bekins Van, 1944, plain tires, hubs...$400
Ford Coca-Cola with Wood Soda Cases, 1944, 4-wheel..............................$900
Mack "B" Associated Truck Lines, 14-wheel..............................$500
Mack "B" Jr. Fire Truck with Warning Light, Battery-Operated, 4-wheel $950
Mack "B" Orange Dump, 10-wheel.......$1800
Mack "B" P.I.E., 18-wheel $850

SMTS (Scale Model Technical Services)

SMTS is an English company, making white metal models for US Model Mint (at one time), Conquest, and Madison, as well as their own ranges. Voiturette is a related brand from SMTS. Latest addition to the SMTS line is Goldvarg of Argentina. (See Goldvarg.)

1 Arrows A6 Barclay, 1:43 ....$98
1 Arrows A6 GPI, 1:43.........................$78
2 Ferrari 216C3, 1:43 ....$78
3 Toleman TG184, 1:43 ....$117
4 1957 Lotus Elite, 1:43 ....$98
5 Aston Martin DB4 GT Zagato, 1:43 ....$98
6 1965 Lotus 33 GP, 1:43 ....$117
7 1930 Bentley Speed 6 LeMans, 1:43 ...$118
8 Lotus Europa, 1:43 ....$98
8 Lotus Europa GLTL, 1:43 ....$88
9 Eagle Weslake Racer, 1:43 ....$117
10 1965 Lotus 38 Indy Racer, 1:43 ....$98
11 1968 Lotus 56 Indy, 1:43 ....$98
12 1968 Lotus 56B F1, 1:43 ....$84
13 1970 Ferrari 312B, 1:43 ....$138
14 1967 STP Paxton Turbine Indy, 1:43 ...$117
15 Lotus Europa Special Twincam, 1:43 ...$117
16 Lotus Seven, 1:43 ....$108
17 March 701, 1:43 ....$134
18 1957 Lotus Seven, 1:43 ....$108
22 1967 Brabham BT26 Racer, 1:43 ....$138
25 Bugatti 35 Racer, 1:43 ....$108
26 BRM P56, 1:43 ....$108
33 1963 Aston Martin Project 215, 1:43 ...$98
34 Lotus 30 Racer, 1:43 ....$98
35 Lotus 40 Racer, 1:43 ....$98
41 Lola T90 Racer, 1:43 ....$118-128
44 1963 Aston Martin P214 Racer, 1:43...$98
2059 1959 Watson Roadster, 1:43........$117
2060 1960 Watson Roadster, 1:43........$117

2061 1961 Watson Roadster, 1:43........$117
2062 1962 Watson Roadster, 1:43........$128
2063 1963 Watson Roadster, 1:43........$117
2064 1964 Watson Roadster, 1:43........$128
Don Garlits Swamp Rat 1 Dragster,
1:43.................$100-120

Solido

Oulins 28260
Anet, France
phone : +33 (0) 2 37 65 81 00
fax : +33 (0) 2 37 64 51 31
website: www.solido.fr

The venerable Solido firm of Nanterre, France, was formed in 1932 by Ferdinand de Vazeilles. While this book presents a survey of the wide range of high-quality models produced by Solido, a more detailed study is presented by Dr. Edward Force, renowned author and collector of a wide variety of diecast toys (see bibliography).

In 1980, Majorette purchased the Solido company, and continues the tradition of producing quality miniature replica vehicles. The brand survives today under the auspices of Groupe Ideal Loisirs, the French toy conglomerate.

Presented below is a sampling of the huge assortment of models produced.

40 Peugeot 604, 1:43 ....$15
Renault Express Van, 1:43 ....$12

Solido Nostalgia 1:43 Scale, 1994 reissues of popular Solido models of the sixties

1101 1956 Ferrari 500 TRC, 1994
reissue.................$20
1102 1959 Cooper F2, 1994 reissue..$20
1103 1962 Lola Climax V8 F1, 1994
reissue.................$20
1104 1956 Maserati 250, 1994
reissue.................$20
1105 1960 Lotus F1, 1994 reissue $20
1106 1955 Porsche Spyder, 1994
reissue.................$20
1107 1959 Panhard DB, 1995 reissue.$20
1108 1962 Ferrari 2.5 l, 1995 reissue ..$20
1109 1961 Fiat Abarth, 1996 reissue ..$20
1110 1965 Alpine F3, 1996 reissue....$20

Solido 1/12th 1:12 Scale Models

1201 1958 Chevrolet Corvette Convertible,
red, 1994..............$120
1202 1958 Chevrolet Corvette Hardtop,
turquoise, 1995...........$120

Solido 1200 Series

Models in this 1988–89 series are Portugal-produced reissues of the 1300 Cougar series. Each model is produced in at least two color variations.

1201 Citroën Visa, 1:43, same as
1302 ....$15-25
1202 Fiat Ritmo / Strada, 1:43, same as
1303 ....$15-25
1203 Renault Fuego, 1:43, same as
1308 ....$15-25
1204 Porsche 934, 1:43, same as
1323 ....$15-25

1205 Lancia Rally, 1:43, same as
1327 ....$15-25
1206 Ford Sierra XR4, 1:43, same as
1340 ....$15-25
1207 Ford Escort RS Turbo, 1:43, same as
1315 ....$15-25
1208 Renault 5 Maxi Turbo, 1:43, same as
1321 ....$15-25
1209 BMW M1, 1:43, same as
1329.................$15-25
1210 Citroën 2CV, 1:43, same as
1301 ....$15-25
1211 Renault Super 5, 1:43, same as
1353 ....$15-25
1212 Volkswagen Golf GTI, 1:43, same
as 1314 ....$15-25
1213 Renault 4 Van, 1:43, same as
1325 ....$15-25
1214 Porsche 935, 1:43, same as
1332 ....$15-25
1215 Audi Quattro, 1:43, same as
1328 ....$15-25
1216 Nissan Prairie, 1:43, same as
1341 ....$15-25
1217 BMW 530, 1:43, same as
1304 ....$15-25

Solido Cougar (1980–1982)

Recently submitted by collector Henri Mueller is evidence of this series of six Cougar brand models in the form of a simple bubble card. If not for the partially visible Solido logo at the bottom of the card, it would be easy to think this was a distinct brand of diecast toys.

Dr. Edward Force, in his book devoted to Solido toys, says that 1300 Series Cougar models were also marketed by Dinky Toys.

1301 Citroën 2 CV, 1:43, 1980–
1982 ....$20-30
1302 Citroën Visa, 1:43 1980–
1982 ....$20-30
1303 Fiat Ritmo-Strada, 1:43, 1980–
1982 ....$20-30
1304 BMW 530, 1:43, 1980–
1982 ....$20-30
1305 Alfa Romeo Alfetta GTV, 1:43,
1980–1982 ....$20-30
1306 Peugeot 504 Berline, 1:43, 1980–
1982 ....$20-30
1307 Talbot Tagora, 1:43, 1980–
1982 ....$20-30
1308 Renault Fuego, issued later as
1203 ....$20-30
1309 Renault 14, 1:43, 1981–
1982 ....$20-30
1310 Alfa Romeo Alfasud, 1:43, 1981–
1982 ....$20-30
1311 Car carrier.............not issued
1312 Peugeot 505 ....not issued
1313 Ford Fiesta, 1:43, 1981–
1982 ....$20-30
1314 Volkswagen Golf, 1:43, 1981–
1982 ....$20-30

1315 Ford Escort.............not issued
1316 Peugeot 104 ZS, 1:43,
1981–1982 ....$20-30
1317 Renault 5, 1:43, 1981–
1982 ....$20-30
1318 Renault 18.............not issued
1319 Talbot Horizon ....not issued
1320 Peugeot 305 ....not issued

Solido 1300 Series (1982–1987)

After April 1982, the Cougar series that had also been sold by Dinky Toys was renamed simply as the Solido 1300 Series. The Dinky name was at that time purchased by Universal, then owner of the Matchbox brand as well. The Dinky Collection by Matchbox was inaugurated that same year.

1301 Citroën 2VC6, 1:43, 1982–
1987 ....$20-30
1302 Citroën Visa, 1:43, 1982–
1987 ....$20-30
1303 Fiat Ritmo, 1:43, 1982–1987 ....$20-30
1304 BMW 530, 1:43, 1982–
1986 ....$20-30
1305 Alfa Romeo Alfetta GTV, 1:43,
1982–1986 ....$20-30
1306 Peugeot 504, 1:43, 1982–
1985 ....$20-30
1307 Talbot Tagora, 1:43, 1982–
1985 ....$20-30
1308 Renault Fuego, 1:43, 1982–
1987 ....$20-30
1309 Renault 14, 1:43, 1982–
1985 ....$20-30
1310 Alfa Romeo Alfasud, 1:43,
1982–1987 ....$20-30
1311 Peugeot 504, 1:43, 1981 toy show
prototype ..... (pre-production only) $75-90
1312 Peugeot 505, 1:43, 1982–
1987 ....$20-30
1313 Ford Fiesta, 1:43, 1982–
1985 ....$20-30
1314 Volkswagen Golf, 1:43, 1982–
1984 ....$20-30
1315 Ford Escort GL, 1:43, 1982–
1986 ....$20-30
1316 Peugeot 104 ZS, 1:43, 1982–
1985 ....$20-30
1317 Renault 5 TL, 1:43, 1982–
1983 ....$20-30
1318 Renault 18, 1:43, 1982–
1987 ....$20-30
1319 Talbot Horizon, 1:43, 1982–
1985 ....$20-30
1320 Peugeot 305, 1:43, 1982–
1985 ....$20-30
1321 Renault 5 Turbo, 1:43, 1982–
1985 ....$20-30
1322 Fire Jeep, 1:43, 1982–
1985 ....$20-30
1323 Porsche 934 Turbo, 1:43,
1983–1987 ....$20-30
1324 Porsche 924, 1:43, 1983–
1985 ....$20-30

1325 Renault 4L Van, 1:43, 1983–1987 ....$20–30

1326 Matra Rancho (see 2004)

1327 Lancia Rally, 1:43, 1983–1987 ....$20–30

1328 Audi Quattro, 1:43, 1983–1987 ....$20–30

1329 BMW M1, 1:43, 1983–1986 ....$20–30

1330 Renault 4L Van, 1:43, 1983–1986 ....$20–30

1331 Jeep Rally, 1:43, 1984–1987 ....$20–30

1332 Porsche 935 Turbo, 1:43, 1984–1987 ....$20–30

1333 Alpine Renault A442B, 1:43, 1984–1986 ....$20–30

1334 Porsche 936, 1:43, 1984–1986 ....$20–30

1335 Peugeot 504 V6, 1:43, 1984–1985 ....$20–30

1336 Porsche 928, 1:43, 1984–1987 ....$20–30

1337 Mercedes-Benz 190, 1:43, 1984–1987 ....$20–30

1338 Chevrolet Camaro, 1:43, 1984–1987 ....$20–30

1339 Renault 25, 1:43, 1985–1987 ....$20–30

1340 Ford Sierra XR4i, 1:43, 1985–1987 ....$20–30

1341 Nissan Prairie, 1:43, 1985–1987 ....$20–30

1342 Visa 4x4 Tele-Union, A2, 1:43, 1982–1987 ....$20–30

1343 Visa 4x4 Tele-Union, RTL, 1:43, 1982–1987 ....$20–30

1344 Visa 4x4 Tele-Union, Monte Carlo, 1:43, 1982–1987 ....$20–30

1345 Visa 4x4 Tele-Union, SSR, 1:43, 1982–1987 ....$20–30

1346 Visa 4x4 Tele-Union, Canada, 1:43, 1982–1987 ....$20–30

1347 Peugeot 205 Turbo 16 ....not issued

1348 Porsche 944, 1:43, 1986–1987 ....$20–30

1349 Peugeot 205 GTI, 1:43, 1986–1987 ....$20–30

1350 Ford Escort RS Turbo, 1:43, 1986–1987 ....$20–30

1351 Peugeot 205 GTI, 1:43, 1986–1987 ....$20–30

1352 Mercedes-Benz 190, 1:43, 1986–1987 ....$20–30

1353 Renault Maxi 5 Turbo, 1:43, 1986–1987 ....$20–30

1354 Alfa Romeo Alfetta GTV, 1:43, 1987 ....$20–30

1355 BMW M1, 1:43, 1987 ......$20–30

1356 Porsche 959 Coupe (planned for 1987 but not issued)

1357 Renault Super 5, 1:43, 1987 ....$20–30

1358 Volkswagen Golf GTI, 1:43, 1987 ....$20–30

1359 Citroën 2CV6, 1:43, 1987....$20–30

1365 Citroën CX 2400 Ambulance, 1:43, 1987 ....$20–30

Solido Hi-Fi / To Day 1:43 Scale late model cars

1501 Jaguar XJ 12 ....$15–20

1502 1984 Porsche 944 ....$15–20

1503 Alpine Renault A 310 ....$15–20

1504 Renault 25, 1:43, 1988–1989 ....$15–20

1505 Porsche 928S..................$15–20

1506 Mercedes-Benz 190..............$15–20

1507 1983 Chevrolet Camaro Z 28..................$15–20

1508 1984 Peugeot 205 GTI........$15–20

1509 Chevrolet Camaro Racing, 1:43, 1988–1989 ....$25–30

1510 1986 Mercedes-Benz 190 2.3/16S $15–20

1511 1987 Rolls Royce Corniche ...$15–20

1512 1987 Bentley Continental......$15–20

1513 1984 Chevrolet Corvette Hardtop $15–20

1514 1984 Chevrolet Corvette Convertible $15–20

1515 Ferrari Berlinetta Boxer..........$15–20

1516 1989 Peugeot 605..............$15-20

1517 1989 Mercedes-Benz SL Convertible $15–20

1518 1989 Mercedes-Benz SL Coupe Hard Top $15–20

1519 1990 Renault Clio $15–20

1520 1991 Renault Clio 16 S $15–20

1521 1990 BMW Series 3...........$15–20

1522 1991 Renault Espace $15–20

1523 1991 Citroën ZX Aura..........$15–20

1524 1991 Citroën ZX Volcane $15–20

1525 1989 Porsche 928 GT........$15–20

1526 1991 Renault Clio 16S "Coupe"..................$15–20

1527 1990 Lamborghini Diablo $15–20

1528 1992 Renault Twingo, 1994....$15–20

1529 1993 BMW Series 3 Convertible, 1994 ....$15–20

1530 1992 Renault Twingo, 1994....$15–20

1531 1993 Renault Clio "Williams," 1994 ....$15–20

1532 1993 Renault Twingo Open Top, 1994 ....$15–20

1533 1995 Renault 19 Convertible, 1995 ....$15–20

1534 1991 Renault Espace Fire Van, 1996 ....$15–20

1535 1993 Mercedes 500 SEL, 1996 ....$15–20

1536 1995 Mini British Open, 1996 ....$15–20

1537 1995 Mini Cabriolet, 1996 ...$15–20

Solido Yesterday

1801 1970 Maserati Indy $15–20

1802 1976 Ferrari BB..................$15–20

1803 1970 Alpine A110.............$15–20

1804 1973 Alpine A110 Monte-Carlo $15–20

1805 1968 Opel GT 1900 ....$15–20

1806 1978 Jaguar XJ 12 ....$15–20

1807 1970 Citroën SM..............$15–20

1808 1973 Porsche Carrera $15–20

1809 1978 Lancia Stratos $15–20

1810 1972 Ferrari 365 GTB4.....$15–20

1811 1972 Ferrari 365 GTB4.......$15–20

1812 1979 BMW M1..............$15–20

1813 1968 Chevrolet Corvette, 1994 ....$15–20

1814 1972 Alpine A310, 1994 ...$15–20

1816 1968 Alfa Romeo Carabo, 1994 reissue $15–20

1817 1978 Range Rover, 1995 new ...$20–25

1818 1978 Peugeot 504 Coupe, 1995 reissue $20–25

1819 1979 Citroën 2CV open roof, 1995 reissue $20–25

1820 1979 Citroën 2CV, 1995 reissue $20–25

1821 1969 Mini Cooper, green, 1996 ....$20–25

1822 1969 Mini Cooper, red, 1996 ....$20–25

Solido Racing 1:43 Scale race-related vehicles

1903 1952 Citroën 15 CV Monte-Carlo $20

1904 1973 Alpine A 110 Monte-Carlo .$20

1906 1978 Lancia Stratos $20

1908 1985 Renault 5 Maxi Turbo $20

1909 1965 AC Cobra 427...............$20

1910 1968 Chevrolet Corvette $20

1911 1980 Iveco TransAfrica $20

1912 1986 Mercedes Unimog Rallye ...$20

1913 1977 Fiat 131 Racing, 1994 reissue $20

1914 1980 Land Rover, 1994 reissue ..$20

1915 1977 Toyota Celica, 1994 reissue $20

1916 1983 Audi Quattro, 1994 reissue ..$20

1917 1975 Peugeot Safari, 1994 reissue $20

1918 1993 Renault Clio Rallye $20

1919 1954 Renault 4CV Rallye, 1994 .$20

1920 1973 Porsche Carrera...............$20

1921 1962 Triumph Spitfire Mk 1, 1994 ....$20

1922 1965 Ford Mustang, 1994 ....$20

1923 1983 Lancia Rally, 1995 variation $20

1924 1978 Peugeot 504 Coupe Rallye, 1995 reissue $20

1925 1979 Porsche 935, 1995 reissue ..$20

1926 1962 Renault Dauphine "1093," 1995 ....$20

1927 1984 Range Rover Rallye, 1995 .$20

1928 1967 Ford Mk IV, 1996 ....$20

1929 1968 Alpine 3 L, 1996 reissue ...$20

1930 1968 Mini Cooper, 1996 ....$20

Solido

Solido Tonergam I

2101 Saviem First Aid	$20
2106 Fire Engine	$20
2117 Jeep with Hose Reel	$20
2118 Citroën C35 with Ladder	$20
2121 Marmon Tanker	$20
2122 Renault Express with Trailer	$20

2123 Dodge Tanker $20

2124 Marmon Recovery Truck	$20
2125 Mercedes Unimog	$20
2126 Peugeot J9 Ambulance, red	$20
2127 Mercedes Unimog Forest Fire	$20
2128 Dodge WC 54	$20
2129 Iveco Covered Truck	$20
2130 Mercedes Express Emergency Van and Trailer	$20
2131 Mercedes Unimog Ambulance	$20
2132 Mercedes Tender	$20
2133 Mercedes Ambulance	$20
2134 Mercedes Unimog Breakdown Tow Truck	$20
2135 Peugeot J9 Ambulance, yellow	$20
2136 Dodge WC 51, 1994 new	$20
2137 Renault Trafic, 1994 new	$20
2138 Renault Trafic Ambulance, 1994 new	$20
2139 Dodge WC 56 Hose and Ladder, 1995 variation	$20
2140 Dodge WC 51 Tanker, 1995 variation	$20
2141 Renault Trafic Bus, 1995 variation	$20
2142 Renault Express with Trailer, 1996 variation	$20
2143 Dodge Tow Truck, 1996 variation	$20
2144 Renault Trafic with Ladder, 1996 variation	$20
2145 Renaul Trafic Civil Security, 1996 variation	$20
2146 Mercedes Unimog Forest Fire Tender, 1996 variation	$20
2147 Dodge 4x4 with Protective Cover, 1996 variation	$20

Solido Tonergam II

3102 Fire Department Crane	$20
3106 Mack Fire Engine	$20
3107 Berliet Jet Spray Truck	$20
3110 GMC Fire Engine Recovery Truck	$20
3111 Mercedes Ladder Truck	$20
3112 Berliet Hoist	$20
3113 GMC Road Maintenance Truck	$20
3114 Mercedes Jet Spray Truck	$20
3115 GMC Tanker	$20
3116 GMC Tanker	$20

3117 GMC Tow Truck	$20
3118 Iveco Tanker	$20
3119 Sides 2000 Mark 3 Paris	$20
3121 GMC Covered Truck	$20
3122 Mercedes Van with Zodiac Raft	$20
3123 Sides 2000 Mark 3 Strasbourg	$20
3124 Volvo Front End Loader, 1994 reissue	$20
3125 Acmat VLRA Forest Fire Tender, 1994	$20
3126 Acmat VLRA Tanker, 1994 new	$20
3127 Dodge WC 56 with Inflatable Raft and Trailer, 1995 variation	$20
3128 Dodge WC 51 with Trailer, 1995 variation	$20
3129 Renault Trafic with Inflatable Raft and Trailer, 1995 variation	$20
3130 Peugeot 19 Express and Trailer, 1995 variation	$20
3131 Mercedes with Foam Cannon, 1996 reissue	$20
3132 GMC with Protective Cover, 1996 reissue	$20
3133 Jeep with Ladder and Trailer, 1996 variation	$20
3134 Land Rover and Trailer, 1996 variation	$20

Solido Tonergam III

3501 DAF Covered Truck "DANZA"	$25
3507 DAF Double Covered Truck, "IPONE"	$25
3508 MACK Freighter "TEAM HUSQVARNA"	$25
3509 Renault Fire Tanker Semi, red	$25
3510 Mercedes Semi Trailer	
v.1 "BRIDGESTONE"	$25
v.2 "ANDROS Fruits"	$25
3511 Mack R 600 Fire Engine	$25
3512 Mercedes Fire Brigade Tanker	$25
3513 Mack R600 Fire Brigade Tanker	$25
3514 Mack R600 Fire Truck Semi	$25
3515 Renault Field Casualty Vehicle	$25
3516 Mercedes Training Simulator	$25

Solido Tonergam IV

3601 Kassbohrer Track Rammer	$20
3602 Kassbohrer Expedition Rammer	$20
3603 Kassbohrer Rammer and Sand Spreader	$20
3606 Mercedes Snow Plow	$20
3607 Fire Department Track Rammer	$20

Solido Helicopters

3814 Alouette III "SECURITE' CIVILE"	$15
3815 Gazelle Missile Launcher	$15
3822 Gazelle Civile	$15
3823 Alouette III Police	$15
3824 Puma AS 332 Military	$15
3825 Puma AS 332 Civil	$15
3826 Alouette III "ADP"	$15
3827 Gazelle Gendarmerie	$15
3828 Cougar AS 532	$15
3829 Gazelle HOT	$15
3830 Agusta A 109 K2	$15
3831 Agusta A 109 CM	$15

Solido l'age d'or 1:43 Scale vintage cars

4002 1938 Jaguar SS 100	$20
4003 1937 Talbot T 23	$20
4004 1930 Mercedes SSKL	$20
4032 1939 Citroën 15 CV	$20
4035 1931 Duesenberg J Spider	$20
4036 1930 Bugatti Royale	$20
4047 1937 Packard Sedan	$20
4048 1937 Delahaye 135 M	$20
4051 1938 Delage Coupe De Ville	$20
4055 1930 Cord L 29	$20
4057 1931 Cadillac V16 452.A Police Car	$20
4059 1925 Renault 40 CV Berline	$20
4065 1931 Cadillac Van	$20
4070 1931 Cadillac Fire Chief Van	$20
4071 1939 Rolls Royce Coupe	$20
4077 1939 Rolls Royce Convertible	$20
4080 1930 Cord L 29 Spider	$20
4085 1931 Cadillac 452A	$20
4086 1938 Mercedes 540K Convertible	$20
4088 1939 Bugatti Atalante	$20
4097 1934 Renault Reinastella	$20
4099 1937 Packard Convertible	$20
4109 1939 Bugatti Atalante Convertible	$20
4115 1939 Citroën 15 CV	$20
4149 1926 Renault 40 CV Landaulet	$20
4156 1935 Duesenberg Model J	$20
4159 1936 Ford V8 Berline	$20
4160 1939 Alfa Romeo 2500 Sport Convertible, top down	$20
4161 1939 Alfa Romeo 2500 Sport Convertible, top up	$20
4162 1926 Hispano Suiza Torpedo Convertible, top down	$20
4163 1936 Ford V8 Taxi	$15
4165 1923 Renault 40 CV Presidentielle, top down	$20
4166 1939 Ctroen Traction Fire Brigade	$20

Solido Buses

4401 Renault Paris Bus	$20
4402 London Bus	$20
4404 Country English Bus	$20
4417 Open Top Bus	$20
4422 1930 Citroën C4F Tanker	$20
4427 1940 Dodge Stake Truck "Pepsi"	$20
4428 1940 Dodge Fire Department Recovery Truck	$20
4429 1930 Citroën C4F Van	$20
4430 1940 Dodge Pickup "Sunlight"	$20
4431 1936 Ford Van "New York Times"	$20
4432 1936 Ford Fire Department Tow Truck	$20
4433 1936 Ford V8 Pickup "Kodak"	$20
4434 1936 Ford V8 Fire Department Tanker	$20
4435 1936 Ford V8 Coal Truck, 1995 variation	$20
4436 1936 Ford V8 Pickup "MIKO," 1995 variation	$20

Solido sixties

4500 1957 Cadillac Eldorado Biarritz Convertible	$20
4502 1954 Mercedes 300 SL	$20
4505 1961 Ford Thunderbird	$20
4506 1963 Ferrari 250 GTO	$20
4508 1950 Chevrolet	$20
4511 1950 Buick Super Convertible, top up	$20
4512 1950 Buick Super, top down	$20
4513 1946 Chrysler Windsor	$20
4514 1946 Chrysler Windsor Taxi	$20
4515 1962 Facel Vega Hard Top	$20
4516 1962 Facel Vega Convertible, top down	$20
4517 1963 Ford Thunderbird Grand Sport	$20
4518 1950 Chevrolet Fire Car	$20
4519 1952 Citroën 15 CV	$20
4520 1957 Cadillac Eldorado Seville	$20
4521 1957 Studebaker Silver Hawk	$20
4522 1957 Studebaker Silver Hawk Hard Top	$20
4523 1950 Buick Super Hard Top	$20

4524 1948 Tucker Torpedo $20

4526 1952 Citroën 15 CV Monte Carlo	$20
4529 1950 Chevrolet Checker Cab Taxi	$20
4530 1946 Chrysler Police	$20
4531 1964 Ford GT40	$20
4532 1964 Ford GT40 Le Mans	$20
4533 1965 AC Cobra	$20
4534 1966 VW Van	$20
4535 1966 VW Van Fire Brigade	$20
4536 1952 Citroën 15 CV Taxi	$20
4537 1954 Renault 4 CV, 1994	$20
4538 1954 Renault 4 CV Open Top, 1994	$20
4539 1962 Triumph Spitfire Mk 1, 1994	$20
4540 1964½ Ford Mustang, 1994	$20
4541 1961 Renault Dauphine Berline, 1995	$20
4542 1961 Renault Dauphine Open Roof, 1995	$20
4543 1966 Volkswagen Van, "Michelin," 1996	$20
4544 1964 Renault 4 L Berline, 1996	$20
4545 Renault 4 L (open), 1996	$20

Solido 50th Anniversary of Liberation of France and North-Western Europe 1944–1994

4494/11 US Jeep	$35
4494/12 Dodge 4x4 WC 54	$35
4494/13 Dodge 4x4 WC 56 Command Car	$35
4494/21 US Jeep and Trailer	$35
4494/22 Dodge 6x6 WC 63	$35
4494/23 GMC	$35
4494/31 US Jeep SAS & Trailer	$35
4494/32 GMC "Le Roi"	$35
4494/33 GMC "Tourelle"	$35
4494/34 Dodge 4x4 WC 51	$35
4494/35 Dodge 4x4 WC 56 Command Car	$35
4494/36 Dodge 6x6 WC 63	$35
4494/37 Dodge Pickup	$35
4494/38 Packard Sedan HQ	$35
4494/39 Citroën Traction FF1	$35
4494/41 Half-Track US M3	$35
4494/42 Sherman M4A3	$35
4494/43 Destroyer M10	$35

Solido Military

6001 GMC Compressor Truck	$20
6002 GMC Lot 7 Recovery Truck	$20
6003 Cadillac HQ	$20
6004 Dodge WC54 "Signal Corps"	$20
6005 Kaiser Jeep M 34	$20
6006 Packard HQ	$20
6007 VAB 4X4	$20
6025 Panhard AML 90	$20
6027 V.A.B. 4X4	$20
6032 GMC	$20
6033 Chevrolet HQ	$20
6034 Jeep and Trailer	$20
6036 GMC Covered Truck	$20
6037 Jeep Auto-Union and Trailer	$20
6038 Mercedes Unimog	$20
6039 Land Rover and Trailer	$20
6041 Jeep and Zodiac Inflatable Raft with Trailer	$20
6042 Chrysler Windsor HQ	$20
6043 Dodge WC 54 Ambulance	$20
6046 Mercedes Unimog Ambulance	$20
6047 GMC Turret Truck	$20
6048 US Jeep with Trailer	$20
6049 US Jeep with accessories	$20
6053 Sherman Tank	$20
6055 Leopard Tank	$20
6058 AMX 13/105 Tank	$20
6060 AMX 30 Tank	$20
6063 Tigre Tank	$20
6064 Jagdpanther Tank	$20
6065 Patton M47 Tank	$20
6067 General Lee Tank	$20
6068 Destroyer M10	$20
6069 Half-Track Recovery Vehicle	$20
6070 Kaiser - Jeep Crane Truck	$20
6071 General Grant Tank	$20
6074 Somua S35 Tank	$20
6075 PT 76 Tank	$20
6076 AMX 10 Tank	$20
6077 Sherman Bulldozer Tank	$20
6078 Sherman Egyptian Tank	$20
6079 AMX 30 B2 Tank	$20
6101 GMC Covered Truck, 1995 reissue	$20
6102 Renault Traction Gaz FFI, 1995 reissue	$20
6103 Dodge WC 51 4X4, 1995 reissue	$20
6104 Combat Car M20, 1995 reissue	$20
6105 US Jeep and Trailer, 1995 reissue	$20
6106 GMC Truck with accessories, 1995 variation	$20
6107 Dodge 6x6	$20
6108 Desert Jeep with Trailer	$20
6109 GMC with accessories	$20
6110 Dodge Cammand Car	$20
6111 Dodge 4x4	$20
6112 Jeep Ambulance	$20
6113 Jeep and Trailer	$20
6114 Dodge Signal Corp	$20
6115 GMC Compressor	$20
6116 Packard HQ	$20
6117 Dodge Command Car	$20
6118 GMC Lot 7	$20
6201 Sherman M4A3 Tank, 1995 reissue	$20
6202 Destroyer Tank, 1995 reissue	$20
6203 US Half-Track Radio M3, 1995 reissue	$20
6204 Tigre Tank, 1995 reissue	$20
6205 Renault R35 Tank, 1995 reissue	$20
6206 Jagdpanther Tank, 1995 reissue	$20
6207 PZ IV	$20
6208 Half Track Hanomag	$20
6209 Priest M7 B1	$20
6210 Sherman M4 A3	$20
6211 General Grant	$20
6212 Tigre	$20
9423 1944 GMC Troop Transporter	$20

Solido Transports

7006 Car Transporter	$20
7013 Special Convoy Transport	$20

Solido Prestige 1:18 Scale vintage models

8001 1930 Bugatti Royale Type 41, 11"	$35
8002 1936 Ford Pickup, 9½"	$30
8005 1936 Ford Fire Department Tanker, 9½"	$30
8006 1961 Rolls Royce Silver Cloud II, 10½"	$32
8007 1961 Bentley S2, 10½"	$32
8008 1934 Ford Roadster Convertible, top down, 9½"	$30
8009 1934 Ford Roadster Convertible, top up, 9½"	$30
8010 1934 Ford Pickup Covered Delivery "Perrier," 9½"	$30
8011 1955 Cadillac Eldorado Convertible, top down	$30
8012 1955 Cadillac Eldorado Convertible, top up	$30
8014 1949 Volkswagen Beetle Convertible, top down	$30
8015 1949 Volkswagen Beetle Convertible, top up	$30
8016 1949 Volkswagen Beetle Berline Hardtop	$30

8017 1969 Ferrari 365 GTS Convertible, top down \$30
8018 1969 Ferrari 365 GTS Convertible, top up..................\$30
8021 1964 Mini Cooper S, blue with white fenders..................\$30
8022 1964 Mini Cooper S \$30
8023 1964 Mini Cooper S Rallye \$30
8024 1936 Ford Pickup "MICHELIN" ...\$30
8026 1936 Ford Pickup Fire Truck, 1994 ....\$30
8027 1936 Ford Tanker, 1994 ....\$30
8028 1966 Citroën 2 CV, closed roof, 1994 ....\$30
8029 1966 Citroën 2CV, open roof, red, 1994 ....\$30
8029 1966 Citroën 2CV, open roof, gray \$30
8030 1966 Citroën 2CV, open roof, red & white, 1994 ....\$30
8031 1966 Volkswagen Van, red & white, 1994 ....\$30
8032 1966 Volkswagen Van, purple, "PEACE AND LOVE," "FLOWER POWERED," 1994..................\$30
8033 1963 Citroën DS 19 Berline, white with black roof, 10⅜", 1995 ....\$30
8034 1963 Citroën DS 19 Rallye, blue with white roof, "233" on doors, 10⅜", 1996 ....\$30
8035 1963 Citroën DS 19 Presidentielle, black, 10⅜", 1996 ....\$30
8036 1966 Citroën 2 CV Raid, gray with map on sides, spare on hood..........\$30
8037 1936 Ford Wreck Truck, 9½"......\$30
8038 1958 Volkswageon Beetle Rallye, 9½", 1996..................\$30
8039 1936 Ford Custom Roadster, 9½"..\$30
8040 1966 Citroën 2 CV Charleston, 8⅞" \$30
8041 1966 Volkswagen Van, yellow and blue, "Michelin," 8⅞", 1996 ....\$30
8042 1960 Fiat 500, white, 7½", 1996 ....\$30
8043 1960 Fiat 500 (open), red, 7½", 1996 ....\$30
8044 1965 Fiat 500 Racing, red with "29" and white racing stripe, 7½", 1996..................\$30
8045 1957 Chevrolet Bel Air Convertible with Continental Kit, baby blue, 11", 1996 ....\$30

8063 1946 Chevrolet Pickup, 1:18 ....\$30

1955 Ford Pickup, 9½", 1996 ....\$30
8067 1934 Ford Panel Truck "Ford Parts," 9½" \$30

Solido Custom 1:18 scale customized vehicles
8302 1949 VW Beetle Convertible, top down \$30
8303 1936 Ford Pickup..................\$30
8304 1949 VW Beetle Berline hardtop.\$30
8305 1964 Mini Cooper S \$30
8306 1958 VW Beetle Berline............\$30

Solido MIniatures/ACTUA 1:18 Scale modern models
8501 1989 Citroën XM..................\$30
8502 1989 Peugeot 605 ....\$30
8503 1991 Citroën ZX Rallye Raid \$30
8504 1992 Renault..................\$30

Solido Coca-Cola Promotionals
9503 1936 Ford Pickup, 1:18.............\$35
9504 1934 Ford Roadster, 1:18..........\$35
9505 1949 VW Beetle, 1:18 ....\$35
9506 1949 VW Beetle Berline, 1:18 ...\$35
9507 1955 Cadillac Eldorado Convertible, top down, 1:18 ....\$35
9508 1966 VW Van, red upper, white lower body, 8⅞", 1:18..................\$35
9509 1966 Citroën 2CV, red, top open, 8⅞", 1:43..................\$20
9510 1936 Ford Roadster, red with navy fenders, 9½", 1:18, 1996 ....\$35
9511 1958 Volkswagen Beetle, white with blue top, red fenders, 9½", 1:18, 1996 ....\$35
9601 1931 Cadillac Delivery Van, 1:43..\$20
9603 1940 Dodge Covered Pickup, yellow with blue cover, 1:43, 1996 ....\$20
9605 1940 Dodge Platform Truck, yellow with blue platform, 1:43, 1996 ......\$20
9606 1930 Citroën C4F Delivery Van, 1:43 ....\$20
9607 1950 Chevrolet, 1:43 ....\$20
9608 1946 Chrysler Windsor, 1:43 ....\$20
9609 1940 Dodge Platform Truck, 1:43.\$20
9610 1957 Cadillac Eldorado, 1:43 ...\$20
9611 1936 Ford V8, 1:43 ....\$20
9612 1936 Ford V8 Platform Truck, red with brown platform, 1:43 ....\$20
9613 1966 VW Van, 1:43 ....\$20
9614 1991 Renault Espace, red, 1:43 .\$20
9615 1964½ Ford Mustang, 1:43, 1995 ....\$20
9616 1994 Renault Trafic, red, 1:50, 1995 ....\$20
9617 1936 Ford Pickup with Cover, black, 1:43, 1996 ....\$20
9618 1966 Volkswagen Van, red upper, white lower body, 1:43, 1996.......\$20
9701 English Bus, 1:50..................\$20

Solido Signature Series Limited Edition Vehicles featuring Celebrity Signatures, introduced in 1994
9801 1955 Cadillac Eldorado, red, "James Dean," 1:18..................\$50

9802 1934 Ford Roadster, black, "Humphrey Bogart," 1:18 ....\$50
9803 1961 Rolls Royce, silver with black hood, "Orson Welles," 1:18 ....\$50
9804 1955 Cadillac Eldorado, white, "Marilyn Monroe," 1:18 ....\$50
9901 1950 Buick Super, black, "James Dean," 1:43..................\$25
9902 1937 Packard Sedan, silver with black fenders, "Humphrey Bogart," 1:43 ....\$25
9903 1939 Rolls Royce, pale yellow with black fenders, "Orson Welles," 1:43.\$25
9904 1950 Buick Super, pink, "Marilyn Monroe," 1:43..................\$25

Solido Pepsi-Cola Licensed Models
99019 1934 Ford Panel Truck "Milk Delivery," 9½"..................\$15–25
99020 1934 Ford Sedan "Checker Cab," 9½"..................\$15–25
99021 1936 Ford Pick-Up Truck, 9½"..................\$15–25
99022 1946 Chevrolet Pick-Up Truck, 9⅝"..................\$15–25
99052 1936 Ford Platform Truck, 9½"..................\$15–25
99053 1936 Ford Pick-Up Truck, 9½" ..\$15–25
99054 1934 Ford Roadster, 9½"........\$15–25
99055 1936 Ford Delivery Truck, 9½" ...\$15–25
99056 1936 Ford Pick-Up Truck, 1:43 ..\$15–25
99057 19326 Ford Panel Truck, 1:43..\$15–25
99058 1930 Citroën C4F Truck, 1:43 ..\$15–25
99059 1936 Ford V8 Platform Truck, 1:43 ....\$15–25

Somerville
Somerville 1:43 scale high-quality hand-built models are made in Great Britain. Most models are issued in more than one color variation. The Somerville Society is a now-defunct organization devoted to the appreciation of these fine models. For more information on this club and available models, contact:
The Somerville Society
c/o Rod Ward, Modelauto
120 Gledhow Valley Road
Leeds LS17 6LX England
phone: +44 (0)113 268 6685
fax: +44 (0)1977 681991
e-mail: hotline@modelauto.co.uk
website: www.modelauto.co.uk
100 Taxi..................\$89
102 Mercedes-Benz 260D..................\$89
103 1937 Ford Popular E190 Sedan.........\$89
105 Mercury 300 SL..................\$89
106 Standard Flying 12 Sedan..................\$99
107 Fordson Van, "India Tyres" \$89
109 Fordson Van, "Castrol" \$89
110 Fordson Van, "Turf" \$89
111 Fordson Van, "Somerville" \$89
112 Fordson Van with fish design \$89
113 Fordson Van, "L...East" \$89
114 Fordson Van, Butcher \$89

117 1949 Ford Anglia A494CV, top up or
   down $89
118 Fordson Van with tractor design $69
119 Saab 92 ....$89
120 Sunbeam Talbot $89
121 1947 Volvo PV444 ....$89
122 1985 Saab 9000 Turbo..............$89–99
123 Saab 95 Estate $99
124 Volvo Amazon $109
125 Saab 97 Sonett $89
126 Volvo Jakob $99
127 1987 Saab 9000 CD $89
128 Volvo 544 Station Wagon $89
129 1937 Riley Kestrel $99
130 Saab 900 Cabriolet $89
132 1992 Saab 9000 CS..............$99–119
133 Hillman Minx Convertible, top down ..$119
134 Rover P2 14 Sports............................$109
136 Volvo Amazon 123 GT..........................$89
137 1953 Sunbeam Alpine $109
138 1953 Volvo Valbo 445 Cabriolet $109
139 Saab 9000 CS Police $109
140 Volvo 210 Van $99
141 Sunbeam Talbot 90 Drophead............$99
143 Austin Allegro $99
144 Saab 93A $99

South Eastern Finecast

Dave Ellis
South Eastern Finecast
Glenn House, Hartfield Road, Forest Row
Sussex RH18 5DZ Great Britain
phone: 01342 824711
fax: 01342 822270

South Eastern Finecast produces white metal 1:24 and 1:43 scale model kits, according to various Internet sources. Until Paul Carpenter e-mailed me in March 2000 asking me why I didn't list them, I had never heard of them before. The company apparently also makes etched brass locomotive kits for hobbyists.

Spa Croft Models

98 High Street, Tibshelf
Derbyshire DE55 5NU
England
phone & fax: +01773 872780
Contact Mike Coupe
e-mail: SpaCroft@aol.com
website: www.spacroftmodels.bizland.com

As reported by company representative Mike Coupe, Spa Croft Models is a small but growing manufacturer of fine quality white metal models of British cars. Models are of a quality similar to Crossway, Kenna, and Somerville. Spa Croft Models was established in 1995.

Spa Croft Models does not have any distributors in the US although their products have been sold in the States. They are sold in the UK mainly through Modelauto, Wheels, JM Toys, Crossway, B&L Models, and Peregrine Models, as well as on Spa Croft's own website.

SPC1 Morris Isis Series II Damask red & gray or
   gray & turquoise..................(£69) $115 US
SPC2 FC Vauxhall VX 4/90, white with red
   side flash or Fawn with black side
   flash...............................(£69) $115 US
SPC3 Austin A70 Hampshire, gray green or dark
   blue ....(£89) $145 US
SPC4 Standard Vanguard Phase I, pale metallic
   green or pale bronze...........(£69) $115 US
SPC5 Austin A70 Hampshire Countryman
   (Woody Wagon), elfin green or
   cream...............................(£89) $145 US
Phase III Standard Vanguard.......(£89) $145 US
Hillman Minx Californian ....(£89) $145 US
Series III Morris Oxford ....(£89) $145 US

Spec-Cast

428 6th Ave. NW
Dyersville, Iowa 52040
phone: 319-875-8706
fax: 319-875-8056
website: www.speccast.com

The SpecCast website tells the story the best: "SpecCast was founded in 1974 in Rockford, Illinois, for the purpose of producing diecast belt buckles. While under the original management, the product line expanded slightly to include desk and trophy-type items. During the first three years in business, SpecCast employed up to ten people.

"The late '70s and early '80s brought gradual improvements and expansions of process and product to SpecCast. The practice of investing greater amounts of time at the front-end of a project (by creating precision molds which require little re-work) increased sales and profits. Some of the bigger customers at the time were IH, Northrup King, and John Deere. The product line included belt buckles, lapel pins, key chains, statues, and replicas.

"In 1986 the current owner of SpecCast, Dave Bell, purchased the business. Within a year, the company was moved from Rockford to Dyersville. Dave Bell's thirteen years of employment within the diecast collectible industry provided a broad and valuable base of experience for developing all areas of SpecCast.

"The company is focused on diversifying products within existing product lines. SpecCast now releases collectible cars, trucks, tractor trailers, planes, and blimps. The three market areas currently include ag-related, retail, and custom imprint for promotional and specialty items. Licensing has been obtained from such companies as Pepsi-Cola, Hershey's, Planters, Nabisco, John Deere, and Harley Davidson — to name a few.

"SpecCast is also a leader in several up and coming product lines. Many new and exciting products outside of our traditional diecast and pewter offerings were introduced in the past few years. Some of these new products include poly-resin replicas, plush tractors

with sound, and puzzles. As time goes on, look for many more new and exciting products from SpecCast.

"Recently, SpecCast has been expanding in the Internet and technology area. The company offers its retail products available through a secure e-commerce site, www.toycollectorclub.com. An electronic newsletter is also available for subscription (at no charge) on the Toy Collector Club website at www.toycollectorclub.com.

"The company employed only a handful when Dave took the wheel; today approximately sixty employees report to work each day."

Specialty Diecast (see Dimension 4)

Speed Wheels

Speed Wheels are of a quality almost comparable to Hot Wheels, at least the Series V models that sold for about 70 cents each. Lesser quality cars are available for 40 cents but are not worth collecting, according to Russell Alameda. The parent company and accompanying information is still under research.

Speedway Collection (see Specialty Diecast)

Speedy Power (also see Toymark and Speedy Racer)

Speedy Power is a recently discovered brand of 1:32 scale diecast toys from Toymark Co., Ltd. They retail for $3.99 each. Features include opening doors and pullback action. Recent evidence indicates the brand has been purchased and is now marketed by New-Ray.
1997 BMW Z-3 Convertible, metallic teal $5
1997 BMW Z-3 Convertible, red $5
Land Rover...$5
Jeep..$5

Speedy Racer (see Speedy Power and Toymark)

Spiel-Nutz

Collector Bob Yates reports, "After the decline of the original Schuco Micro Racers series and before they became the Micro Racers (Lilliput) of today, there were some released under this name. I have a Spiel-Nutz Micro Racer 1043 as marked on the key and the rubber nose piece (where Schuco used to put their name). My understanding is that the die maker for Schuco received the Micro Racer series dies from Schuco as severance when they folded in 1975. His name was Nutz and he made some of these under his name. It looks exactly like the the original Schuco Mercedes Micro Racer 1043."

Spot-On (also see Tri-Ang Minic)

Spot-On is a brand of 1:43 scale models from Belfast, Northern Ireland, according to collector Brian Willoughby. Introduced in 1959, Spot-On was a division of Great Britain's Tri-Ang brand, established by the Line Brothers in 1935. Quality is excellent, and popularity of these models in Europe and rarity in the U.S. keeps values high.

100 Ford Zodiac	$125
100SL Ford Zodiac with lights	$150
101 Armstrong Siddeley Sapphire 236	$150
102 Bentley 4-Door Sports Saloon	$200
103 Rolls-Royce Silver Wraith	$275
104 MGA Sports Car	$200
105 Austin-Healey 100-Six Sports Car	$200
106A/0 Austin Prime mover with flat float, no sides	$125
106A/0C Austin prime Mover with MGA Sports Car in Crate "BMC"	$400
106A/1 Austin Prime mover and flat float with sides	$300
106A/1C Austin Prime Mover and flat float with sides and crate load	$375
107 Jaguar XK-SS	$200
108 Triumph TR3A	$200
109/2 ERF 68G with flat float	$225
109/2B ERF 68G with brick load	$275
109/2P ERF 68G with flat float and wood planks	$300
109/3 ERF 68G flat float with sides	$250
109/3B ERF 68G flat floatwith sides and barrel load	$300
110/2 AEC Mammoth Major 8 with flat float	$300
110/2B AEC Mammoth Major 8 with flat float and brick load "London Brick Co."	$300
110/3 AEC Mammoth Major 8 with flat float and sides "British Road Services"	$325
110/3D AEC Mammoth Major 8 flat float with sides and oil drum load	$300
110/4 AEC Mammoth Major 8 Shell BP Tanker	$750
111A/1 Ford Thames Trader with sides "British Railways"	$275
111A/1S Ford Thames Trader with sides and sack load	$275
111A/0T Ford Thames Trader with log load	$275
111A/0G Ford Thames Trader with garage load	$375
112 Jensen 541	$225
113 Aston Martin DB3	$200
114 Jaguar 3.4 Mk I	$175
115 Bristol 406	$175
116 Caterpillar D9 Bulldozer	$675
117 Jones Mobile Crane	$325
118 BMW Isetta Bubble Car	$125
119 Meadows Friskysport	$125
120 Fiat Multipla	$125
122 United Dairies Milk Float	$150
131 Goggomobil Super	$125
135 Sailing Dinghy and Trailer	$60
136 Sailing Dinghy	$30
137 Massey Harris Tractor	$600
145 AEC Routemaster Bus	$725

154 Austin A40	$125
155 Austin FX4 Taxi Cab	$125
156 Mulliner Luxury Coach	$400
157 Rover 3-Litre	$200
157SL Rover 3-Litre, with lights	$225
158A/2 Bedford 10-ton tanker, "Shell BP"	$775
161 Long wheelbase Land Rover	$125
165 Vauxhall Cresta PA	$225
166 Renault Floride Convertible	$125
183 Humber Super Snipe Estate	$200
184 Austin A60 with roof rack and skis	$125
185 Fiat 500	$150
191/1 Sunbeam Alpine Convertible	$200
191/2 Sunbeam Alpine Hard top	$200
193 NSU Prinz	$150
195 Volkswagen 1200 Rally	$125
207 Wadham Ambulance	$500
210/1 Morris Mini Van, "Royal Mail"	$175
210/2 Morris Mini Van, "Post Office Telephones"	$175
211 Austin Seven Mini	$175
213 Ford Anglia	$125
215 Daimler Dart SP250	$225
216 Volvo 122S	$175
217 Jaguar E Type	$225
218 Jaguar Mk 10	$175
219 Austin-Healey Sprite	$175
229 Lambretta Scooter	$175
256 Jaguar 3.4 Mk I Police Car, white and black	$250
258 Land Rover RAC	$200
259 Ford Consul Classic	$150
260 Royal Rolls-Royce Phantom V	$425
261 Volvo P1800	$125
262 Morris 1100	$125
263 Bentley Supercharged 4.5 Liter	$125
264 Tourist Caravan	$75
265 Bedford "Tonibell" Ice CreamVan	$175
266 Bullnose Morris Cowley	$100
267 MG 1100	$125
270 Ford Zephyr 6	$150
271 Express Dairies Milk Float	$150
273 Commer Security Van	$250
274 Morris 1100 with canoe	$100
276 Jaguar S Type	$200
278 Mercedes-Benz 230SL	$125
279 1935 MG PB Midget	$125
280 Vauxhall Cresta PB	$125
281 MG Midget Mk II	$175
286 Austin 1800	$100
287 Hillman Minx	$100
289 Morris Minor 1000	$200
306 Humber Super Snipe with luggage rack	$200
307 Volkswagen Beetle 1200	$275
308 Land Rover and Trailer	$175
309 Police "Z" Car	$175
315 Commer Window Cleaners Van	$200
316 Fire Dept, Land Rover	$175
401 Volkswagen Variant with skis	$500
402 Crash Service Land Rover	$125
403 Hillman Minx and dinghy	$125

404 Morris Mini Van	$425
405 Vauxhall Cresta PB "BEA"	$125
407 Mercedes-Benz 230SL	$125
410 Austin 1800 with row boat	$125
415 RAF Land Rover	$150
417 Bedford Military Field Kitchen	$150
419 Land Rover and Missile carrier	$300

Stahlberg (or Stallberg)

Several classy models have been produced by Stahlberg of Finland. These are generally sold as plastic dealer promotional models.

Mercedes 300 Wagon, 1:25	$25
Saab Lancia 600 4-Door Sedan, 1:25	$25
Volvo 245 GL Wagon, 1:25	$25

Starter

Starter is the brand name of 1:43 scale resin-cast models produced in France. As of February 2001, Provénce Mouláge has merged with Starter Models. Provénce Mouláge will continue offering kits, while Starter will provide finished models. No model list is available.

Streamlux

Streamlux toys are a short-lived series of small (approximately 1:80) scale diecast models from Streamlux Pty Ltd. of Australia that began in the 1950s and had disappeared by 1960 only to reappear in 1977 in kit form. In addition to the smaller models, one larger model — a Holden FE Sedan in 1:36 scale — was produced in 1957. Streamlux dies were purchased by Underwood Engineering in 1964, the castings improved and sold as Fun Ho! Midgets. Streamlux models are marked with the Streamlux brand on the base.

Airport Bus, One-and-a-Half Deck	$50–60
Austin Open Back Truck, 2"	$65–70
Austin Petrol Tanker, 2"	$65–70
Austin Tip Truck, 2"	$80–90
Commer Coach, 2⅛"	$65–70
Holden FE Special Sedan, 2⅛"	
v.1 coppered body, chrome base	$65–70
v.2 coppered body, red painted base	$65–70
Massey Ferguson 35 Tractor, unpainted, 1⅝"	$65–70
Mercedes-Benz W196 Racer, 2"	$65–70
Volkswagen Combi Bus, 2⅛"	$65–70
Volkswagen Sedan, 1⅝"	$65–70

Strombecker (see Tootsietoys)

Stylish Cars

Stylish Cars are superb hand-built models, of which one is available from Diecast Miniatures.

1933 Duesenberg SJ Speedster, 1:43	$338

Summer

Summer models of Hong Kong are reported to be approximately 1:60 scale issues from

NSG Marketing. Other NSG toys are offered as Traffic Stoppers. Both brands represent somewhat crude versions of popular car models. Both brands fall under the category of generic toys for the lack of identifying marks. Most Summer models are relatively unremarkable, cheaply made, and considered fairly worthless. The company is a recent (circa 1990s) outgrowth of the explosion of crude diecast toys coming out of Hong Kong.

Jaguar XJ $1
Mercedes-Benz 500K $1

Sun Motor Company (see Model-auto)

Sun Star

Sun Star America Inc.
2415 Radley Court #2
Hayward, CA 94545
phone: 510-670-0882
fax: 510-670-0883
e-mail: uscic@aol.com

Sun Star America Inc., based in Hayward, California, is a new producer of 1:18 and 1:43 scale diecast cars made in China. Models below are available in an assortment of colors and livery.

Sun Star 1:18 Scale Models

1953 Chevrolet Bel Air $40

1963 Aston Martin DB5....................$40
1965 Chevrolet C-10 Styleside Pickup ...$40

1963 Chevrolet Corvair............................$40

1957 Ford Fairlane Skyliner with retractable hardtop $40

1964 Ford Galaxie 500..............................$40

1965 Ford F-100 Pickup $40

1967 Mercury Cougar $40

1999 Lincoln Limousine $40
2000 Lincoln Limousine $40
1998 London Taxi Cab $40
1977 Mercedes-Benz 350 SL convertible, top down $40
1977 Mercedes-Benz 350 SL convertible, top up $40
Mercedes-Benz E320 ....$40
1998 Mitsubishi Pajero Long.................$40
1998 Porsche 996 Carrera....................$40
Porsche GT3 ....$40
Volkswagen Open Convertible $40

Sun Star 1:43 Scale Models

1958 Buick Special...............................$25
1950 Cadillac Eldorado $25
1953 Cadillac Eldorado $25
1955 Chevrolet BelAir Convertible, top down..............................$25
1959 Chevrolet Impala $25
1968 Chevrolet Corvette Convertible, top down..............................$25
1969 Chevrolet Corvette Convertible, top down..............................$25
1947 Chrysler Town & Country.............$25
Dodge WC51 Weapons Carrier..........$25
Dodge WC52 Weapons Carrier..........$25
Dodge WC56 Command Car, closed ..$25
Dodge WC56 Command Car, open $25
Dodge WC57 Command Car, open $25
Hummer Ambulance $25
Hummer Command Car, closed $25
Hummer Pickup $25
Hummer Prototype $25
Jeep Willys, closed $25
Jeep Willys, open $25
Volkswagen Kubelwagen (Thing), open ..$25
Volkswagen Kubelwagen (Thing), closed.$25
Volkswagen Cabrio Military Police $25
Volkswagen Schwimmwagen, open.......$25
Volkswagen Schwimmwagen, closed $25
Opel Blitz Troop Carrier........................$25
Opel Blitz Canvas Covered $25
Opel Blitz Canvas Covered Wehrmacht.$25
Land Rover...$25

Sunnyside

Sunnyside Ltd.
21/F, Blk K
Shield Industrial Centre
84-92 Chai Wan Kok Street
Tsuen Wan
N. T. Hong Kong, SAR
phone: 852-2492-0276 (7 lines)
852-2493-2366 (8 lines)
fax: 852-2416-7401
e-mail: sunny@sunnyside.com.hk
website: www.sunnyside.com.hk

Since 1979, Sunnyside Ltd. has produced quality diecast models previously considered generic due to the usual lack of identifying marks. But upon closer inspection, they are found to bear the "Flying S" logo and a model number designation starting with "SS-". The 1:43 scale models are comparatively accurate replicas for their $3 or less price tag. Other models include 1:32 and 1:24 scale models. Such models have also been sold under the K-mart MegaMovers brand among others. Models often feature pullback-action motors.

BMW 325i Convertible $6
BMW 325 M3 2-Door Sedan $6
BMW 635 CSi....................................$6
BMW 728 4-Door Sedan $6
BMW Z1 Roadster $6
Bugatti T44 Coupe $6
Bugatti T57 Coupe $6
1950 Buick Super Convertible, top down $6
1951 Cadillac Roadster $6
1953 Cadillac Convertible, top up $6
1955 Chevrolet 3100 Stepside Pickup Truck, 1:24 ....$8-10
Chevrolet Astro Van..............................$6
Chevrolet Astro "FireVan" $6
Chevrolet Astro Van "Superman" $6
1955 Chevrolet Bel Air Nomad, 1:24 ....$8–10
1995 Chevrolet C/K Pickup Truck, 1:24 ....$8–10
Chevrolet Suburban, 1:24.................$8–10
1970 Chevrolet El Camino SS 454, 1:24 ..$8–10
1964 Chevrolet Impala Hardtop, 1:24 ...$8–10
1955 Chevrolet Nomad, 1:25 ....$6
1957 Chevrolet Bel Air 2-Door Hardtop, 1:25..............................$9
Chevrolet Blazer Tow Truck Fire..............$6
Chevrolet Blazer Tow Truck Police $6
Chevrolet Blazer Ambulance....................$6
Chevrolet Blazer Police $6
1957 Chevrolet Corvette Hardtop.............$6
1957 Chevrolet Corvette Roadster $6
Hayashi Dome-O Exotic Car.....................$6
Excalibur Roadster................................$6
Ferrari F40, 1:24 ....$6–8
Ferrari 288 GTO Coupe $6
Ferrari Testarossa, 1:40 ....$6
Ferrari Testarossa, 1:25 ....$9
Ford 3100 4WD Tractor $6
1932 Ford Coupe $6
Ford Escort Convertible $6

1940 Ford Woody Wagon, 1:38 ....$6

Ford E100 Ambulance Van	$6
Ford E100 Police Van	$6
1998 Ford F-150 4x4 Offroad Pickup Truck	$8–10
1964½ Ford Mustang Convertible, 1:24	$6–8
Ford Shelby Cobra 427 S/C Convertible, 1:24	$6–8
1955 Ford Thunderbird Hardtop, 1:24	$6–8
1955 Ford Thunderbird Convertible, 1:24	$6–8
1959 Ford Galaxie Convertible	$6
1952 GMC Wrecker, 1:34, issued 1999, opening doors and tool compartments	
v.1 red	$13
v.2 maroon	$13
v.3 black	$13
Jeep CJ5	$6
Jeep CJ5 Ambulance	$6
Jeep CJ2 Army Jeep with top	$6
Jeep Army Rocket Launcher	$6
Jeep Army Machine Gun	$6
Jeep Army Radar	$6
John Deere 3130 Tractor	$6
International Harvester 4WD Tractor	$6
Lamborghini Diablo, 1:24	$6–8
Lincoln Town Car Stretch Limousine, 1:24	
v.1 black	$15–20
v.2 white	$15–20
v.3 silver	$15–20
v.4 gold	$15–20
v.5 gray	$15–20
London Bus, dark green with cream upper window section, "Country Matches," "24 Berkshire"	$6
Mercedes-Benz 190E "Fire Dept."	$6
Mercedes-Benz 500SEL Convertible, top down	$6
Mercedes-Benz 500SEL Convertible, top up	$6
1991 Mercedes-Benz 500SL Convertible, top down	$6
Mercedes-Benz 540K Roadster	$6
Mercedes-Benz 540K Coupe	$6
1984 Mercedes-Benz 500SL Roadster	$6
Mercedes-Benz 560SEC Coupe	$6
Mercedes-Benz 207 Police	$6
Mercedes-Benz 207 Fire	$6
Michelotti Laser	$6
Nissan HD Fire Pumper Truck	$6
Nissan HD Fire Ladder Truck	$6
Nissan HD Fire Snorkel Truck	$6
Nissan HD Fire Aerial Ladder Truck	$6
Opel Omega 4-Door Sedan	$6
Pontiac Firebird Trans Am T-Top "Sunbeam Bread" #42 Race Car, yellow	$15
1986 Porsche 911 Roadster	$6
1989 Porsche 911 Roadster	$6
Porsche 959 Coupe	$6
1931 Rolls Royce Phantom II	$6
1947 Talbot Convertible, top up	$6
Volkswagen 1303 Beetle	$6
Volkswagen Beetle	$6
Volkswagen Beetle Convertible	$6
Volkswagen Golf Cabriolet	$6
Volkswagen LT Police Van	$6
Volkswagen LT Fire Van	$6

Sunshine Toys

Many Sunshine models were previously assumed to be Superior brand, confusing them with Sunnyside models. Both feature a large assortment of pull-back action toys, but Sunshine models lack the "Flying S" logo and are designated by a single "S" in front of the model number rather than the double "SS" that marks them as Sunnyside Superior models. Sunshine Toys are generally considered inexpensive generic toys.

Super Champion (see Champion)

Supercar Collectibles

Supercar Collectibles, Ltd.
Jim Thoren
7311 75th Circle North
Minneapolis, MN 55428
phone: 612-425-6020
fax: 612-425-3357

Supercar Collectibles represent a new offering of 1:18 scale diecast models most likely made in China.

Bill Jenkins' 1969 Camaro SS/C drag car	$40–50
1969 Baldwin-Motion 427 Camaro	$40–50

Superior (also see Sunnyside)

Sunnyside Ltd.
21/F, Blk K
Shield Industrial Centre
84-92 Chai Wan Kok Street
Tsuen Wan
N. T. Hong Kong, SAR
phone: 852-2492-0276 (7 lines)
852-2493-2366 (8 lines)
fax: 852-2416-7401
e-mail: sunny@sunnyside.com.hk
website: www.sunnyside.com.hk

It was originally thought that Superior was the brand name assigned to certain Sunnyside models. Recently a Sunnyside representative wrote to indicate that "Superior" is only a descriptive term, not a brand name. Please see the Superior listing under the section on Sunnyside models.

SVP

In 1948, the S. V. Paraboni company of Italy, SVP, produced just one model, presumed to be a 1:43 scale model with a clockwork motor and steering.

Fiat-Farina Coupe, 4½"	$60

Swan Hill

Pleasanton, California, was home to the Swan Hill toy company, manufacturer of a heavy cast aluminum replica of a lumber hauler that stands about 8½ inches high and measures about 8½ inches long.

Cari-Car Lumber Hauler	$60–90

Tai Cheong Toys

Tai Cheong Toys are classic examples of what diecast collectors usually refer to as "generic junk." The only distinguishing mark on these toys is the designation "TC" on the base followed by a number. Value will likely remain near the retail price of three for 99 cents. The package is also nondistinct except for a circular logo formed by a curved "T" and a sideways "C" in the lower left corner of the three-pack blister card. Some logos are imprinted with "Tai Cheong," others are not.

Taiseiya (also see Cherryca Phenix, Micro Pet)

Taiseiya of Japan is best known for producing Cherryca Phenix models, exceptional 1:43 scale diecast cars, some with battery-operated lights, under the "Micropet" brand in the early sixties. Taiseiya was later purchased by Yonezawa, known for Diapet diecast models. A few models were apparently marketed under the Taiseiya brand.

1912 Chevrolet Phaeton, pewter-like	$165–180
1932 Datsun	$165–180

Takara

Takara is a Japanese company of which little is known. Among their products are some toys made for Tonka called Turbo Tricksters. See Tonka for more information.

Tak-A-Toy (also see Welly)

Tak-A-Toy is an inexpensive brand of toys that, like so many other inexpensive toys, is usually rendered an unmarked generic toy once removed from package. Interestingly, at least one particular model is found to be an exception to this rule. One Audi Quattro in white with red, light blue, and black rally markings was found to be made by Welly and holds the distinctive Welly name on the base along with the number 8368. It was purchased for 89 cents from a local grocery store in November 1996. Welly toys are slightly better made than most in the budget genre of diecast toys and are usually marked with the brand name on the bottom. Tak-A-Toy is a division of Larami Corp., Philadelphia, PA 19107.

Tamiya

Tamiya is best known for quality plastic car kits and radio-controlled models. Recently Tamiya has begun producing a few large scale diecast models.

Tbilisi

Collector Lemiere Bruno of France reports that Tbilisi is the alternate name of the town of Tiflis in the Russian province of Georgia. It is there that a small toy factory installed obsolete Norev casting equipment around 1980. In the USSR, no brand names were applied apart from those intended for export, hence the town name. "Poor finish for the domestic market as far as I remember," comments

Bruno. "A couple of other Norevs were remanufactured there."

Robert Jacaszek adds: "Tbilisi is the name of Georgia capital. Up to the nineties, Georgia was part of the Soviet Union. (The name Tifilis was used up to 1936.) Plastic models with this name were manufactured in the seventies. In Poland, where I am living, in the late seventies were available three models. These models were in 1:43 scale. These models were quite good (for the times). I had seen only photo of French Dinky Panhard 24 Coupe, but I think that these models were copies of French Dinky models. At the same time in Poland was available the first Soviet diecast model — Moskvitch in 1:43 scale. The name Tbilisi was only on plastic models. Only car name, scale, and 'Made in USSR' were on diecast models."

1927 Panhard, hard plastic body, black, 3½"	$8–10
Panhard 24 Coupe, white	$8–10
Renault Dauphine, white	$8–10

TD

1950 Caterpillar Bulldozer, tin, made in USA, 8"	$20

Team Caliber

Another recent arrival on the diecast scene is Team Caliber, a brand of 1:24 scale models largely comprised of race cars.

John Andretti #43 STP Winston Cup Pontiac Grand Prix	$20
Bob Evans #1 Monte Carlo	$20
Terry Labonte #5 K-Sentials Monte Carlo	$20
Terry and Justin Labonte #44 Slim Jim NASCAR Busch Series Monte Carlo	$20
Mark Martin #6 Valvoline / Cummins Winston Cup Ford Taurus	$20
Jeremy Mayfield #12 Mobil 1 25th Anniversary Winston Cup Ford Taurus	$20
Dick Trickle #5 Schneider Busch Monte Carlo	$20

Techno Giodi (see Giodi)

Tekno / Chico (also see Dalia)

Tekno toys are especially nice 1:43 scale models made in Denmark. Chico toys are the Colombian division of Tekno. Dalia of Spain established a working relationship with Tekno to produce a special line of models separate from the main Tekno line.

The Tekno line of tinplate toys was started in Denmark in 1920. The company survived through several economic and political crises, not least of which was World War II, until 1974 when the company finally folded and was purchased by Dutch importer Van Min. Thanks to Jan Scholten for the update.

Tekno of Holland survives today, having celebrated the 25th anniversary of its revival in 1999, as announced in a recent issue of

Diecast Collector, a British monthly magazine.

439 Volvo Timber Transporter........$100–125

442 Scooter Solo	$75–90
444 Scooter Delivery	$75–90
709 Milling Machine	$30–45
713 Wet Grinder	$45–60
736 Beer Truck "Tuborg" (with 20 cases)	$45–60
761 Motorcycle	$75–90
762 Motorcycle/Side Car	$75–90
763 Motorcycle/Side Car	$75–90
764 Motorcyle/Side Car	$75–90
770 Truck (lorry)	$45–60
773 Animal Truck	$45–60
775 Trailer	$30–45
785 Hawker Hunter Jet	$45–60
802 Alfa Romeo	$45–60
804 M.G.	$45–60
808 Triumph Sports Car	$45–60
809 1956 Ford Thunderbird Roadster	$32
953 Army Truck/anti-aircraft	$75–90
Beer Trailer (Carlsberg)	$30–45
Chevrolet Monza GT	$35
Delivery Truck (barrels, 9 sacks & trolley)	$30–45
Deutz Van Police	$32
Ford Cable Truck	$20
1953 Ford Taunus Van	$35
Kul & Koks (Coal & Coke) Truck	$30–45
Mercedes-Benz Tow Truck	$18
M.I.G. 15	$30–45
Scania CR-76 Bus	$35
Volkswagen 1500 Sedan	$100
Volvo F10 "SPETRA"	$32
Volvo Truck	$18
Volvo Cement Truck	$14
Volvo 2-axle Truck	$4
Volvo 2-axle Trailer	$4

Tenariv

Tenariv represents 1:43 scale resin kits of 1960–1970 Formula One race cars. Tenariv is one of many brands connected with MAFMA, the French automotive model artisans union. No model list is known.

TfC (see Toys for Collectors)

Thomas Toys

The fact that Thomas Toys are plastic eliminates them from the category to which this book is devoted. But the history and style of Thomas Toys

deserves at least some mention. Most well known for its Art Deco "Flash Gordon" style cars, Thomas Toys present a distinctive and highly collectible assortment of models. Based in Newark, New Jersey, Islyn Thomas created some of the most distinctive plastic toy cars of their era or any era. for the collector of toy cars not necessarily diecast, Thomas is one brand worth searching out. Their values are still low, only $15 to $45 apiece.

#138 Airline Limousine $10

Timpo Toys

Timpo is a shortened version of Toy Importers Ltd. The brand was started in 1939 when World War II restricted imports to Great Britain, and the company began producing their own toys. While a few models were produced in 1940–1941, major production of the Timpo line was started in 1946. Timpo toys ceased production in 1951–1952 due to war restrictions on the use of zinc. Some Timpo dies were eventually sold to Benbros. Timpo Toys are identified by the name cast somewhere on the toy.

AEC Monarch Brewery Lorry, 5⅛", 1950, reissued by Benbros	$80–100
Alvis 14 Police Car, loudspeakers on roof, wire aerial, 4⅛", 1947	$35–45
Alvis 14 Saloon, 4¼", 1947	$25–35
American Star Racer, 4", 1946	$20–25
Armstrong Siddeley Hurricane, 4⅛", 1947	$25–35
Articulated Box Van, 5⅞", 1947, reissued by Benbros	
v.1 green, blue, or red trailer with "Timpo Toys" decals	$40–50
v.2 black with "Pickfords" decals	$40–50
v.3 orange with "United Dairies" decals	$55–65
v.4 light blue and cream, "Wall's Ice Cream" decals	$55–65
v.5 dark blue and cream, "Lyons Tea" decals	$55–65
v.6 pale yellow, "Bishop & Sons" decals	$55–65
v.7 pale yellow, "John H. Lunn Ltd." decals	$55–65
Articulated Low Loader, 6⅞", 1947, reissued by Benbros	$15–25
Articulated Petrol Tanker, 5⅞", 1947, reissued by Benbros	$25–35
Austin 16 Saloon, black with Timpo toys underneath (later reissued by Betal), 3⅝"	$50–$70
Buick Saloon, composition wheels, 3⅞", 1947	$15–25

Forward Control Box Van, 3¾", 1949, reissued by Benbros..............................$55–65

Forward Control Luton Van, 3⅞", 1947
  v.1 no decals..................................$25–35
  v.2 "Smith's Crisps"....................$55–65
  v.3 "W.D. & H.O. Wills".............$55–65

Forward Control Tipper Lorry, 4", 1947 .$25–35

Lincoln Convertible, 4½", 1947...........$25–35

London Taxi, cast in two halves, 3¾", 1947...$35–45

MG Midget, composition wheels, 3¼", 1946..$25–35

MG Record Car, hollow cast lead, 3⅞", 1940..$35–45

MG Record Car, zinc diecast, 3¾", 1946...$20–$25

Normal Control Box Van, with or without motor, 4⅛", 1949, reissued by Benbros
  v.1 "Eveready"..............................$40–50
  v.2 "Golden Shred".....................$55–65

Normal Control Petrol Tanker, 4⅝", 1949, reissued by Benbros..................$55–65

Packard Saloon with no base, 4½", 1946..$15–25

Packard Saloon with aluminum base and friction motor, 4½", 1948..........$15–25

Pick-Up Truck, separate body and chassis, 3¾", 1940 (later reissued with name blocked out)...$50–60

Pick-Up Truck with 8 cast barrels, 4⅛", 1947..$25–35

Speed of the Wind Record Car, 3⅞", 1946..$25–35

Streamlined Fire Engine with aluminum ladders, no base, 4⅛", 1947.............$40–50

Streamlined Fire Engine with aluminum ladders, aluminum base and friction motor, 4⅛", 1949................................$40–50

Streamlined Saloon, separate body and chassis, 3⅞", 1940.........................$50–60

Timpo Saloon, similar to a Morris 8, 3⅝", 1946..$20–25

Utility Van, 4" (early casting) or 4⅛" (later casting) without motor 1947, with friction motor 1948
  v.1 no decals, no motor................$25–35
  v.2 "Tyresoles Service," no motor $50–65
  v.3 "His Master's Voice," with or without motor....................................$50–65
  v.4 green, with or without motor....$50–65

Tin Wizard (also see Skyline Models and Zaugg)

Tin Wizard Modelcars
and Skyline Models
c/o Thomas Wolter Modelltechnik
Talstrasse 170
D-69198 Schriesheim, Germany
phone: 06203/68680
fax: 06203/68329
e-mail: THWOLTER@aol.com
website: www.tinwizard.de
or www.toynet.de/tinwizard

Handmade 1:43 and 1:24 scale white metal models and kits with plated parts comprise this series from Schriesheim, Germany. Also see Skyline Models. Some Tin Wizard models are reissues of Zaugg models of Switzerland.

Tin Wizard Scale 1:43

1160 Volvo 242 GT (1978), kit $50
1161 Volvo 242 GT (1978), metallic silver, ready made....................................$125
1170 Volvo 244 DL (1975), kit $50
1171 Volvo 244 DL (1975), green, ready made..$115
1172 Volvo 244 DL (1975), yellow, ready made..$115
1173 Volvo 244 DL (1975), metallic gold, ready made....................................$115
1179 Volvo 244 GL "TAXI" (1975), ready made..$120
1180 Volvo 245 DL Kombi (1975), kit ..$50
1181 Volvo 245 DL Kombi (1975), red, ready made....................................$120
1182 Volvo 245 DL Kombi (1975), white, ready made....................................$120
1183 Volvo 245 DL Kombi (1975), metallic blue, ready made.............................$120
1200 Volvo ES 1800 Kombi (1971), kit ..$50
1201 Volvo ES 1800 Kombi (1971), white, ready made....................................$120
1202 Volvo ES 1800 Kombi (1971), metallic gold, ready made $120
1203 Volvo ES 1800 Kombi (1971), metallic blue, ready made $120
1130A Volvo PV 444A (1944) Standard, kit..$40
1131A Volvo PV 444A (1944) Standard, black, ready made $90
1131AS Volvo PV 444A (1944) Spezial, black, ready made.............$95
1132AS Volvo PV 444A (1944) Spezial, gray, ready made $95
1130B Volvo PV 444B (1950) Standard, kit..$40
1131B Volvo PV 444A (1944) Standard, black, ready made $90
1131BS Volvo PV 444A (1944) Spezial, black, ready made $95
1132BS Volvo PV 444A (1944) Spezial, gray, ready made $95
1130D Volvo PV 444D (1952) Standard, kit..$40
1131D Volvo PV 444D (1952) Standard, black, ready made $90
1133DS Volvo PV 444D (1952) Spezial red, ready made $95
1130H Volvo PV 444H (1954) Standard, kit..$40
1131H Volvo PV 444D (1952) Standard black, ready made $90
1132HS Volvo PV 444D (1952) Spezial, gray, ready made $95
1130K Volvo PV 444K (1955) Standard, kit..$45

1131K Volvo PV 444D (1952) Standard, black, ready made $90
1134KS Volvo PV 444D (1952) Spezial, blue, ready made........................$95
1135KS Volvo PV 444D (1952) Spezial California, white, ready made.......$105
1130L Volvo PV 444L (1957) Standard, kit..$45
1131L Volvo PV 444L (1957) Standard black, ready made $90
1135LS Volvo PV 444L (1957) Spezial California, white, ready made...........$105
1136LS Volvo PV 444L (1957) Spezial red, ready made........................$95
1140 Volvo PV 445 Cabriolet "Valbo," kit..$45
1141 Volvo PV 445 Cabriolet "Valbo," black, ready made $105
1142 Volvo PV 445 Cabriolet "Valbo," gold beige, ready made...................$105
1143 Volvo PV 445 Cabriolet "Valbo," red, ready made........................$105
1150A Volvo PV 544 A (1958) Standard, kit..$45
1151A Volvo PV 544 A (1958) Standard, black (1958), ready made.............$90
1154AS Volvo PV 544 A (1958) Spezial A, blue (1958), ready made...............$95
1157AS Volvo PV 544 A (1958) Spezial A, green (1958), ready made.............$95
1156BS Volvo PV 544 A (1958) Spezial B "Sport," red (1960), ready made.....$95
1155BS Volvo PV 544 A (1958) Spezial California, white (1960), ready made.....$105
1152CS Volvo PV 544 A (1958) Spezial D "B18," gray (1961), ready made....$95
1155DS Volvo PV 544 A (1958) Spezial D "B18," white (1962), ready made...$95
1156DS Volvo PV 544 A (1958) Spezial D "Sport," red (1962), ready made.....$95
1151GS Volvo PV 544 A (1958) Spezial G "Sport," black (1965), ready made..$95
1150S Volvo PV 544 A (1958) Umrüstsatz PV 544 spezial, kit $15
1130S Volvo PV 544 A (1958) Umrüstsatz PV 444 spezial, kit $15
1190 Saab Sonett I Roadster (1955), kit ..$50
1191 Saab Sonett I Roadster (1955), red, ready made................................$115
1192 Saab Sonett I Roadster (1955), white, ready made............................$115
1193 Saab Sonett I Roadster (1955), blue, ready made................................$115
1199 Saab Sonett I Roadster Mille Miglia, ready made................................$125
1110 Saab Sonett III (1970), kit...........$50
1111 Saab Sonett III (1970), emerald green, ready made..........................$120
1112 Saab Sonett III (1970), red, ready made..$120
1113 Saab Sonett III (1974), kit...........$50
1118 Saab Sonett III (1970), yellow, ready made..$120

1119 Saab Sonett III (1970), red, ready made................$120
1630 Glas 1700 GT Coupe (1965), kit .$40
1631 Glas 1700 GT Coupe (1965), blue, ready made................$85
1632 Glas 1700 GT Coupe (1965), gray, ready made................$85
1633 Glas 1700 GT Coupe (1965), green, ready made................$85
1650 DKW F12 Cabriolet (1965), kit ...$40
1651 DKW F12 Cabriolet (1965), green, ready made................$75
1652 DKW F12 Cabriolet (1965), beige white, ready made................$75
1653 DKW F12 Cabriolet (1965), green, ready made................$75
1120 Opel Manta A (1970), kit..........$40
1121 Opel Manta A (1970), red, ready made................$85
1122 Opel Manta A (1970), yellow, ready made................$85
1123 Opel Manta A (1970), black, ready made................$85
1350 Ferrari 410 Superamerica (1959), kit................$55
1351 Ferrari 410 Superamerica (1959), red, ready made................$140
1352 Ferrari 410 Superamerica (1959), white, ready made................$140
1353 Ferrari 410 Superamerica (1959), blue, ready made................$140
3100 Opel Super 6 Cabriolet, kit.........$50
3101 Opel Super 6 Cabriolet, red, ready made................$120
3102 Opel Super 6 Cabriolet, blue, ready made................$120
3103 Opel Super 6 Cabriolet, green, ready made................$120
3120 Opel Kapitän Cabriolet (1951), kit.$50
3121 Opel Kapitän Cabriolet (1951), bordeaux red, ready made................$120
3122 Opel Kapitän Cabriolet (1951), white, ready made................$120
3123 Opel Kapitän Cabriolet (1951), gray, ready made................$120
4011 Ferrari 340 Mexico (1953) Road Car, red, ready made................$120
4014 Ferrari 340 Mexico (1953) Racing Car, yellow, ready made............$120
4021 Porsche 550A 1500 RS "Le Mans" (1956), silver, ready made..........$120
4053 Maserati Mexico, ready made...$155
4061 Jaguar E Kombi "Harold and Maude," black, ready made.....................$155

Tin Wizard Scale 1:24

8010 VW "Hebmüller" Cabriolet (1949), kit................$120
8011 VW "Hebmüller" Cabriolet (1949), black and red, ready made.........$200
8012 VW "Hebmüller" Cabriolet (1949), brown-beige, ready made..........$200
8013 VW "Hebmüller" Cabriolet (1949), red-beige, ready made................$200

8050 Opel GT Coupe, kit $85
8051 Opel GT Coupe, black, ready made................$160
8052 Opel GT Coupe, yellow, ready made................$160
8053 Opel GT Coupe, metallic blue, ready made................$160
8060 Opel GT "Aero," kit.................$85
8061 Opel GT "Aero," blue, ready made................$160
8062 Opel GT "Aero," metallic blue, ready made................$160
8070 Opel GT "Cabriolet," kit.............$85
8071 Opel GT "Aero," red, ready made................$160
8080 Alfa Romeo Giulia Super 1,3 1,6 (1964–1971), kit................$85
8081 Alfa Romeo Giulia Super 1,3 1,6 (1964–1971), white, ready made $160
8082 Alfa Romeo Giulia Super 1,3 1,6 (1964–1971), green, ready made$160
8083 Alfa Romeo Giulia Super 1,3 1,6 (1964–1971), red, ready made ...$160

Tin Wizard Scale 1:18

Z1010 Heinkel Tourist 103A, kit $50
Z1011 Heinkel Tourist 103A, black, ready made................$90
Z1012 Heinkel Tourist 103A, red, ready made................$90
Z1013 Heinkel Tourist 103A, turquoise, ready made................$90
Z1014 Heinkel Tourist 103A, blue, ready made................$90
Z2020 Norton Commando 750, kit......$75
Z1021 Norton Commando 750, green, ready made................$145
Z1030 Boom Trike, kit $100
Z1031 Boom Trike, black, ready made .$195
Z1040 Rassler Trike, kit $100
Z1041 Rassler Trike, black, ready made..$195
Z1050 Donkervoort, kit $115
Z1051 Donkervoort, yellow, ready made .$200
Z1052 Donkervoort, black, ready made..$200
Z1053 Donkervoort, red, ready made .$200
Z1054 Donkervoort, green, ready made .$200
Z1060 Lomax, ready made $105
Z1061 Lomax, green, kit...................$170

Tins Toys (also see Simba)

Simba offers an assortment of Volkswagen Concept 1 vehicles which bear a "spinning top" logo with the phrase "Tins Toys" across it. Go to Simba for details.

Tintoys

While Tintoys are a punctuation mark in the novel of diecast toys, the few lightweight models produced under this brand name, while lacking in detail, are interestingly accurate miniatures of the two cars discovered by the author. Their value won't likely rise, but they are noteworthy nonetheless.

Cadillac Seville, 1:69 ....$0.75
Toyota Celica 2000GT Liftback, 1:63 .....$0.75

Tip Top Toy Co.

Slush mold (lead cast) vehicles dominate the Tip Top Toy Company's line of toys produced in San Francisco in the 1920s and 1930s.

Airflow, larger	$40
Airflow, smaller	$30
Bus, 3⅜"	$40
Coupe, 3³⁄₁₆"	$35
1923 Dodge Coupe, 3⅛"	$30
Gasoline Tanker, 3½"	$35
1935 Hupmobile, 3¼"	$50
Parcel Delivery Panel Truck, 2⅛"	$30
Pickup Truck with Tailgate, 3³⁄₁₆"	$40
Small Coupe, 2⅛"	$25
Small Tanker, 2¹¹⁄₁₆"	$20
Stake Truck, 5⁵⁄₁₆"	$55
1935 Studebaker Sedan, 2⁹⁄₁₆"	$45
Tow Truck, 3⁵⁄₁₆"	$35

Togi

Collector Robert Speerbrecher comments, "Togi is one of my favorite makers. They are an Italian firm that makes diecast 1:23 scale Alfa Romeos. The company uses them to make factory promos, and I think they make some that are not promos. I have yet to see a Togi that's not an Alfa Romeo. They are generally very expensive compared to the Polistil from the same country. As far as I know they are still in business."

Alfa Romeo Sprint Speciale $60–75
Alfa Romeo 159...............................$60–75

Tomica

Tomy started the Tomica line of diecast toy vehicles in 1970. Until around 1980, the Japanese gems known as Tomica Pocket Cars from Tomy were widely distributed in the US, even available in grocery stores. But because their high quality and accurate scale meant that they cost a little more than Hot Wheels and Matchbox, they were unable to compete with the lower-priced and better-known brands. The normal price for Pocket Cars was around $1.25 to $1.75 each. Now they sell from private importers for $4–15 each. Their current value reflects the growing interest from collectors who discovered these terrific little toys too late to save them from disappearing from the US market.

Another reason for a lack of popularity was their focus on Japanese vehicles such as Mazda, Hino, Mitsubishi, and Fuso. Now, models of Japanese vehicles are more desirable just because they are Japanese.

Tomica's F series provided models of cars foreign to Japan, such as Cadillac, Rolls Royce, Porsche, and others. It was that assortment that helped Tomica establish itself worldwide.

New models are still being produced but are not generally available in the US, as the Tomica series retreated to European and Asian markets where Pocket Cars still hold a better market share.

The numbering system for Pocket Cars is not particularly consistent, so the preferred method of listing them is alphabetically by description. Most models are well marked on the base, and are heavier than usual for their size, due to more metal and less plastic. It is known that the "F" represents a vehicle foreign to Japan, while lack of designation indicates a domestic Japanese vehicle.

Other companies, in an attempt to capture some of the Pocket Car market, produced cheap copies of many of these models. A major difference is that these generic knock-offs had plastic bases and other components, and lighter-weight metal parts, and are generally unmarked. The generic versions are considered essentially worthless to collectors, except as an oddity. Models are listed alphabetically, with model number, copyright date and scale when available, and current value. The premier source for current and older Tomicas is Bob Blum, 8 Leto Road, Albany, NY 12203, phone: 518-456-0608.

Alpine Renault Sports Racer, 191-F48 ....$5

American Cement Truck, Peterbilt, 219-F63, c1978, 1:98 ....$5

American LaFrance Ladder Chief, 160-F33/187-F33, c1978, 1:143 ....$8
American Wrecker, Peterbilt, F63, c1978, 1:98 ....$5
Amusement Park Shuttle Bus, 49, 1:130 ....$5
Asahi Event Truck (similar to Coca Cola truck), 109, 1998 ....$4
Auto Transporter, 137-14 ....$12
Baja Jeep 4 Wheeler $6
Big Rig Cement Mixer, Peterbilt, 219-F63, c1978, 1:98 ....$5
Big Rig Dump Truck, Peterbilt, 205-F63, c1978, 1:98 ....$5
Big Rig Tow Truck, Peterbilt, 171-F63, c1978, 1:98 ....$5
BLMC Mini Cooper S Mark III, F8, c1979, 1:50 ....$8
BMW 3.5 CSL, 167-F30 ....$5
BMW 320i, 239-F43, 1:62 ....$5
Box Van, 35/36/37 ....$6
Bugatti Royale Coupe DeVille 1927, 186-F46, c1978, 1:80 ....$6
Bulldozer, 247-106 ....$8
Bus, 79, 1:130 ....$6
Cadillac Ambulance, F-2 ....$12
Cadillac Seville 1981, 233-F45, 1:69 ....$6

Cadillac Superior Ambulance, 181-F60, c1976, 1:77 ....$10
Cadillac Fleetwood Brougham, 86-F2, c1976, 1:77 ....$6
Cadillac Fleetwood Brougham, 211-F2, c1976, 1:77 ....$6
Camper Pickup, Chevrolet Truck, 214-F44, 1:77 ....$6
Canter Garbage Truck $4
Cargo Container, 100, 1:47 ....$8
Cargo Container Truck, Fuso, 7/67-90,-91, 1:127 ....$9
Cedric 280E $4
Celica LB 2000 GT, 33, 1:63 ....$5
Chemical Fire Engine, Datsun UD Condor, 145-94, 1:90 ....$12
Chevy Van, F22, c1977, 1:78 ....$5
Chevy Van, Custom, 216F23 ....$5
Chevy Van Ambulance, 143-F22, c1977, 1:78 ....$6
Chevy Van Sheriff, F22, c1977, 1:78 ....$6

Citroën "H" Truck, 97, 1:71 ....$5–10

Continental Mark IV, Ford Lincoln, 114-F4, c1976, 1:77 ....$5
Corvette, 144-F21 ....$5
Crane Picrover Mobile, 65-33, 1:96 ....$6
Custom Chevy Van, 216F23 ....$5
Custom Stepside Pickup, 212-F44 ....$6
Daihatsu Midget, 62, 1:50 ....$5
Datsun 200SX, 235-6 ....$5
Datsun 260Z, 47-58 ....$5
Datsun 280Z Rally, 210-58 ....$5
Datsun UD Condor Chemical Fire Engine, 145-94, 1:90 ....$12
Datsun R382 Racer, 25-22 ....$5
Datsun Silvia $4
Datsun Station Wagon, 138-47 ....$6
Datsun Tipper Truck, 136-56 ....$6
Datsun Touring Car 1932, 03-60, c1974, 1:49 ....$6
DeTomaso Pantera, 193-F55, silver $5
DeTomaso Pantera, F64, blue $5
Dodge Coronet Custom Police Car, 105/178-F8, c1976, 1:74 ....$7
Dodge Fire Chief, 163-F10 ....$6
Dodge Taxi, 139-F18 ....$6
Dyna Vac, 18, 1:68 ....$5
Elf Backhoe, 152-64 ....$8
Elf Rally Renault, 238-F58 ....$6
Emergency Van, Chevy, 207-F22, c1977, 1:78 ....$6
Ferrari 308 GTB, F35, 1:60 ....$5

Dynapac CC21, 1:62 ....$5

Ferrari F-1 ....$5

Ferrari 312 Formula 1 Racer, 209-59 ....$5
Ferrari Dino 308 GTB, 155-F35, c1977, 1:60 ....$5
Fiat X1/9, 165-F28 ....$5
Firebird Turbo, 243-F42 ....$5
Ford Livestock Truck, F62, 1:95 ....$6
Ford Lotus Europa "John Player Special," 161-F36/164-F25 ....$6
Ford Model T Convertible Coupe 1915, 112/248-F11, c1977, 1:60 ....$8
Ford Model T Delivery Van 1915, 134-F11/F13, c1977, 1:60 ....$8
Ford Model T Touring Car 1915, 125/246-F12/F11, c1977, 11:60 ....$8
Ford P-34 Tyrell Formula 1 Racer, 168-F32, c1977, 1:52 ....$6
Ford Fritos Truck, 236-F62, 1:95 ....$6

Furukawa Wheel Loader, 36-63 ....$6

Fuso Truck Crane, 66 ....$5

Fuji Subaru, 21, 1:50, depending on variations..$4–20

Fuso Truck Series Freight Truck, 77-7/90/91, 1:127...............................$5

Fuso Truck Series Pepsi Truck, 77-7/90/91, 1:127...............................$5

Fuso Truck Series Tanker, 77-7/90/91, 1:127...............................$5

Gran Porsche, 197-F3........................$5

Greyhound Bus "Americruiser," 222-F49, c1979, 1:156..................................$25

Hato School Bus................................$4

Hato City Bus...................................$4

Heavy Crane, 141-66..........................$6

Hino Aerial Ladder Fire Truck, 1:125..........$

Hino Big Rig Semi-Trailer, 89-24.................$10

Hino Cement Mixer, 29-52/-53/-54, 1:102..$6

Hino Dozer carrier, 56, 1:102....................$7

Hino Gasoline Truck, 29-52/-53/-54, 1:102.$6

Hino Grandview Bus, 1, 1:154...............$5–12

Hino Truck, 29-52/-53/-54, 1:102..............$6

Hitachi DH321 Dump Truck, 35-59, 1:117...$6

Honda Accord, 142-78.............................$5

Honda Acura NSX, black & red, 78, 1:59...$5

Honda Beat, 72, 1:50...............................$5

Honda Civic GL/CVCC, 241-83, c1974, 1:57..$8

Honda Motorcycle, 42, 1:34.....................$8

Honda NSX Patrol Car, 1:59..................$5

Hovercraft, Mitsui Zosen, 93, 1:210.............$8

IMSA Turbo Toyota Celica, 217-65, c1979, 1:62...$5

Isuzu Bonnet Police Bus, 6, 1:110..............$15

Isuzu Elf, 1:67.....................................$8

Isuzu Hipac Van, 27, 1:70.........................$6

Isuzu Red Cross Van................................$4

Isuzu Road Construction Truck, 1:78......$5

Jaguar XJ-S, 199-F68, c1978, 1:67.............$6

Jr. Hiway Bus, 101, 1:145.........................$8

Komatsu Bulldozer-Shovel, 66-106.............$8

Komatsu D65A Bulldozer, 1:87.................$5

Komatsu D375A Bulldozer, 1:135.............$5

Komatsu Fork Lift, 34-48..........................$8

Komatsu Steam Shovel, 49-09....................$12

Kubota Farm Tractor, 61-92, 1:42...............$8

LaFrance Ladder Chief, 160-F33/187-F33, c1978, 1:143......................................$8

Lamborghini Countach, 162-F37/170-F50....$5

Lancia Stratos HF Racer, 153/159-F27.......$5

Lancia Stratos Turbo Racer, 223-F66, c1987, 1:62...$5

Lincoln Continental Mark IV, 114-F4, c1976, 1:77...$5

Lion Bus, 26...$5

London Bus, F15, c1977, 1:130 ....$10

Lotus Elite, F47, c1978, 1:63.....................$6

Lotus Esprit Special, 220-24......................$5

Lotus Europa John Player Special, 161-F36/164-F25...$6

Maserati Merak SS, 177-F45, c1978, 1:62.$6

Mazda 787B, 1:64...............................$7

Mazda Bongo Friendee, 1:64....................$5

Mazda Familia 1500XG, 4, 1:59...............$6

Mazda GT Racer, 158-80.........................$5

Mazda RX-500, 17-34.............................$5

Mazda Savannah RX-7, 203/245-50, c1979, 1:60...$5

Mazda Savannah GT, 80, 1:59...................$7

Mechanical Sweeper, 1:66.....................$6

Mitsubishi Airport Towing Tractor, 95, 1:110.$8

Mitsubishi Fuso Container Truck, 74, 1:102...$5

Mitsubishi Jeep J58................................$4

Misubishi Fuso Amusement Park Shuttle Bus, 1:130 ....$6

Mitsubishi Fuso Refrigerated Truck, 1:102 ....$5

Mitsubishi Jeep Bigfoot $6

Mitsubishi Pajero Jr., 1:56 ....$6

Mitsubishi Minica Toppo, 71, 1:56 ....$5
McLaren M26 Ford Formula 1, 224/169-F39 ...$5
Mercedes-Benz 300SL Gullwing, 1956, 221-F19 ....$6
Mercedes-Benz 450SEL, 111/176-F7, c1976, 1:67 ....$5
Mercedes Unimog, 184-F41, c1978, 1:70 ..$6
Mini Cooper, DJ015, 1:64 ....$5
Mitsubishi Big Rig Truck, Fuso, 62-07 ....$6
Mitsubishi Canter Garbage Truck, 47, 1:72 ...$6
Mitsubishi Car Transporter, 14, 1998 ....$4
Mitsubishi Fuso Racing Transporter, 93, 1:102 ..$6
Mitsubishi McDonalds Truck, 65, 1998 ....$4
Mitsubishi Rosa School Bus, 60, 1:84 ....$5
Mitsui Zosen Hovercraft, 93, 1:210 ....$8
Mobile Picrover Crane, 65-33, 1:96 ....$6

Morgan Plus 8, 140-F26, c1977, 1:57 ....$6
Moving Van, 117-20 ....$8
Mustang II Ghia, 156/188-F38 ....$6
Newspaper Truck, 118-107 ....$15
Nissan Bluebird SSS Coupe, 1 ....$7–20
Nissan Caball Utility Truck, 54/87/88, 1:68 ..$6
Nissan Caravan, 3, 1:66 ....$5

Nissan Condor Crane Truck with pipes, 80, 1:104 ....$5

Nissan Diesel Aerial Ladder Fire Truck, 1:120 ....$5

Nissan Diesel Dump Truck, 1:102 ....$8

Nissan Diesel Moving Van, 16, 1:102 ....$6
Nissan Diesel Tanker, 16, 1:102 ....$6
Nissan Fairlady 280Z-T, 15, c1979, 1:61 ....$6

Nissan Fairlady Z 300ZX, 1:59 ....$6

Nissan Skyline GT-R, 1:60 ....$6

Nissan Skyline Racing, 1:60 ....$6

Nissan Paramedic Ambulance, 51, 1:78 ....$5
Nissan Pulsar $4
Nissan Silvia $4
Off Road Cruiser, 226-2 ....$5

Off Road Dump Truck, 1:119 ....$7

Ohara Snow Tiger SM30, 84, 1:73 ....$12
Packard Coupe Roadster 1937, 179-F52, 1978, 1:72 ....$8
Pajero, 30, 1:62 ....$5
Panda Truck, 76, 1:102 ....$10
Pepsi Soft Drink Truck, 198-76 ....$8
Peterbilt Wrecker, F63, c1978, 1:98 ....$5
Picrover Mobile Crane, 65-33, 1:96 ....$6
Pizza Scooter, 82 ....$5
Police Bike, 4, 1:34 ....$5
Police Bus, Isuzu Bonnet Bus, 6, 1:110 ....$15
Police Car, Dodge Coronet Custom, 178-F8/9/10/18 ....$7
Police Van Special Weapons Team 2, Toyota Type HQ15V, 185-67, c1978, 1:81 ..$8–10
Pontiac Firebird Trans Am, 201-F42 ....$6
Porsche 356, 89, 1:59 ....$5
Porsche 911S, 106-F3/F17, c1976, 1:61 ...$6
Porsche 928, 204-F53 ....$5
Porsche, Gran Porsche, 197-F3 ....$5
Porsche Sports Racer, 237-F43 ....$5
Porsche Turbo 935, 183-F31 ....$5
Power Company Service Truck, Nissan Caball, 75-54/87/88, 1:68 ....$6
Propane Truck, 115-42 ....$6

Range Rover, 1:64 ....$7

Renault Elf Rally, 238-F58 ....$6
Rural School Bus, 109-F5, 1:108, c1976 .....$6

Rolls Royce Phantom VI, 110-F6, c1976, 1:78 ....$6

Sakai Tire Roller, 103-65, 1:90.....................$8
School Bus, 91-01...................................$8
School Bus, Rural, 109-F5, 1:108, c1976 ....$6
Screamin' Sports Car, 180-71.....................$5
Sheriff's Van, Chevrolet Chevy Van, 242-F22,
    c1977, 1:78 ....$6
Sightseeing Bus, 130-41 ....$10
Silvia 240 SX, 6, 1:59.........................$5–12
Snow Tiger, Ohara SM30, 147-84,1:73 ...$12
Soarer Lexus Coupe, 5, 1:63 ....$5
Special Weapons Team Police Van, Toyota Type
    HQ15V, 185-67, c1978, 1:81 ......$8–10
Squirt Fire Engine, 41-03 ....$6
Steam Shovel, Komatsu, 49/192-9 ....$12
Street Sweeper, light yellow, 113, 1:66 ....$5
Subaru Milk Truck, 96, 1:130...................$5
Subaru Sambar POST Van, 31, 1:52.........$9
Subaru Post Van, 67, 1998 ....$4
Super Bug Volkswagen, 195-F20, 1:60......$10
Suzuki Carry Stake Truck, 39, 1:55.............$6
Suzuki Wagon R (Micro MPV), 71, 1998......$4
Swim School Bus, 83, 1:145.....................$5
Tadano Rough Terrain Crane, 218-2, c1979,
    1:96 ....$5
Taxi, Toyota Crown, 4/27/32/110, 1:65 ..$8

Terex 72-81 Leader, 1:137 ....$5

Texaco Gas Truck, 234-F62 ....$6
Texaco Tanker, Fuso, 77-7/90/91, 1:127...$5
Telephone Truck, Nissan Caball, 244-
    54/87/88, 1:68 ....$6
Toyota 2000-GT, 22-05, c1974, 1:60......$10
Toyota Ambulance, 46-40 ....$6
Toyota Caribe (Tercel)...............................$4
Toyota Celica Supra Racer, 65 ....$5
Toyota Celica Supra LB 2000GT, 215-33,
    c1978, 1:63 ....$6
Toyota Corolla Levin, 78, 1:61..................$6
Toyota Crown Taxi, 4/27/32/110, 1:65...$8
Toyota Ex-7, 04-31 ....$6
Toyota Fork Lift, 182-12...........................$8
Toyota Hiace Auto Wrecker, 38/50,
    1:68 ....$8
Toyota Hiace Airport Stairway Truck, 38/50,
    1:68 ....$10

Toyota Dyna Vacuum Car, 1:68 ....$6

Toyota Fork Lift FD200, 182-12, 1:120 ......$8
Toyota Hiace Loudspeaker Vending Truck,
    38/50, 1:68 ....$15

Toyota Hilux Bigfoot $5

Toyota Hilux Surf, 84, 1:65 ....$5
Toyota Land Cruiser, 83-02.......................$8
Toyota MR2 ....$4
Toyota Previa, red & gray, 99, 1:64 ....$5
Toyota Prius (Hybrid Vehicle), 86, 1998 ....$4

Toyota Quick Delivery Van, 1:72 ....$5

Toyota RAV4, 1:57 ....$6

Toyota Spacio (Mini MPV), 16, 1998 ....$4
Toyota Towing Tractor, 96, 1:50, with Cargo
    container, 100, 1:47 & box Van,
    35/36/37 ....$25

Toyota Supra, 1:60 ....$6

Toyota Type HQ15V Special Weapons Team
    Police Van, 185-67, c1978, 1:81....$8–10
Toyota Utility Truck, 128-38.......................$6
Toyota Wrecker, 129-39...........................$5
Turbo Firebird, 243-F42 ....$5
Turbo Porsche 935, 240-F31 ....$5
Tyrell P34 Formula 1 Ford, 168-F32, c1977,
    1:52 ....$6
UD Condor Chemical Fire Engine, Datsun, 145-
    94, 1:90...$12
Utility Truck Nissan Caball, 244-54/87/88,
    1:68 ....$6
Utility Truck Toyota, 1280-38 ....$6
Vette Racer, 175-F21 ....$5
VW Beetle, gold, 100, 1:60 ....$7

Volkswagen 1200LSE, 1:60 ....$7

Volkswagen Convertible, 146/225-F20,
    c1977, 1:60 ....$10
Volkswagen Rabbit/Golf GLE, 232-F5, 1:56 .$6
Volkswagen Microbus, 166-F29 ....$18
Wheel Loader, 206-63 ....$8
Winnebago Chieftain Motor Home, 92-F1,
    c1976, 1:97 ....$12

Tomica Dandy

These are 1:43 scale models whose detail, packaging, and accessories set them apart from most other models in their price range. Here is a small sampling of Tomica Dandy models.

Datsun Silvia Coupe.............................$18
Fiat 131 Abarth $18
Hino Fire Ladder Truck, 2.......................$18
London Double Decker Bus......................$45
Mercedes 560 SEL, G-8 ....$30
Nissan Caravan Police, 1........................$18
Nissan Cedric 4-Door Sedan Police Car.$18
Nissan Condor Fire Truck.........................$18
Nissan Skyline.......................................$18
Nissan Van Ambulance, 12.....................$18
Regent III RT London Transport Bus, F19...$45
Toyota Landcruiser $18
1970 Toyota Mk2 2-Door Hardtop, 11.$20
VW Bug, DJ011 ....$22
VW Police, "METRO," DE006 ....$22
VW Van, "NGK," DT002 ....$24

Tomy (also see Tomica)

Besides producing the popular Tomica Pocket Cars, Tomy is a prominent manufacturer of many other toys. Based in Japan, Tomy has been a major force in the toy industry for many years. A few diecast specialty toys have been produced under the Tomy name. The one listed below is of particular note for the standard Tomica-style wheels and the quality of diecasting synonymous with Tomica.

Mickey Mouse Fire Engine, red with yellow plastic trim, gray wheels with gold hubs, 2⅝" $8–12

Tonka

Most Tonka toys are manufactured of stamped or pressed steel and do not qualify as diecast. But this brand from Mound, Minnesota, has a rich heritage that deserves mention. Vintage Tonka trucks of the fifties are often selling for $100 to $400 each, and restored vehicles are also rising in value, to $50 and more. There is currently only one known book on Tonka trucks, covering 1947 to 1963.

Tonka Turbo Tricksters are produced for Tonka by Takara Co., Inc. of Macau. They are plastic toys with centrifugal flywheel motors that assist in making the cars do wild acrobatic tricks.

Tonka is now owned by Hasbro. Besides the usual large pressed steel toys, miniature Tonka toys have also shown up as kid's meal premiums at McDonald's.

An arrangement with Maisto in 1998 has resulted in four 3½ inch long diecast and plastic Maisto versions of several classic Tonka toys. The series was so popular that in 1999, Maisto expanded the assortment to 50 models. See Maisto for a list.

Tonka sets for 2000 include some mostly plastic but well-constructed sets of toy trucks and accessories originally manufactured by Kentoy of Hong Kong and marketed by Manley ToyQuest.

Tonkin

Tonkins are ready built 1:53 scale 1988 Ford twin trailer truck models available from Jeff Bray Jr.'s Diecast Miniatures for just under $50 each.

Tootsietoys

Tootsietoys were first introduced by Dowst Manufacturing after Charles Dowst saw a demonstration of the diecasting process at the 1893 Columbian Exposition (otherwise known as the Chicago World's Fair). He envisioned many applications of the process and started making the first diecast buttons. In 1914, he introduced the first Tootsie Toy, named after his brother's granddaughter Toots. (Later the name was changed to Tootsietoy.)

The Tootsietoy legacy can be divided into two eras — pre-war and post-war. The reason for this is that before World War II, Dowst concentrated on producing realistic replicas of popular vehicles of the era. The focus after the war shifted to producing less expensive toys that were more Affordable and therefore more accessible to children.

Serious collectors prefer pre-war Tootsietoys because of their greater detail and realism. Today's assortment of Tootsietoys runs the full gamut of styles, from crude generic toys to accurate miniature models, but the focus is still on affordability. While this book presents a survey of models, a more detailed study can be found in David Richter's *Collector's Guide to Tootsietoys*, $16.95 from Collector Books.

In 1964, with the purchase of the Strombecker Corporation, one of the oldest companies in the US, Dowst's Tootsietoys became Strombecker's Tootsietoys.

Early Tootsietoy Models

4482 Bleriot Aeroplane, 1910, 2⅝" ...$200
4491 Bleriot Aeroplane, 1910, 2" $90
4528 Limousine, 1911, 1⅞" $45
4570 1914 Model T Ford Convertible, 1914, 3" $90
4610 1914 Model T Ford Pickup, 1916, 3" $90
4626 Passenger Train Set, 1925 ....$90
4627 Freight Train Set, 1925 ....$90
4629 1921 Yellow Cab, 1923, 2¾" ...$90
4630 1924 Federal Delivery Van, laundry; grocery, milk or delivery, 1924 ....$90
4630 Delivery Van, Special Issue: Watt & Shand, 1924 ....$400
4630 Delivery Van, Special Issue: Adam, Meldrum & Anderson Co., 1924 ....$400
4630 Delivery Van, Special Issue: Bamberger, 1924 ....$400
4630 Delivery Van, Special Issue: Pomeroy's, 1924 ....$400
4630 Delivery Van, Special Issue: U. S. Mail, 1924 ....$600
4636 1924 Buick Series 50 Coupe, 1924, 3" $90
4638 1921 Mack AC Stake Truck, 1925, 3¼" $90
4639 1921 Mack AC Coal Truck, 1925, 3¼" $90
4640 1921 Mack AC Tank Truck, 1925, 3¼" $90
4641 1924 Buick Touring Car, 1925, 3" $90
4650 Bi-Wing Seaplane, 1926 ....$50
4651 1926 Fageol Bus Safety Coach, 1927, 3½" $50
4675 Wings Seaplane, 1929, 3¾" $65
Cadillac Coupe $30
Graham Sedan $360
Tractor $20

Postwar Tootsietoys

#234 3" Box Truck (1942–1947), mint .$25
    near mint $20
#235 3" Oil Tanker (1947–1954), mint..$25
    near mint $20

6" Ford Oil Tanker, Texaco (1949–1952), mint $55
    near mint $45
6" Ford Oil Tanker, Shell (1949–1952), mint $65
    near mint $55
4" 1949 Ford F6 Oil Tanker, solid color (1950–1969), mint $25
    near mint $20
4" 1949 Ford F6 Oil Tanker, 2-tone w/silver tank (1950–1969), mint $20
    near mint $15
6" International KII Oil Tanker, Sinclair (1949–1955), mint $55
    near mint $45
6" International KII Oil Tanker, Standard (1949–1955), mint $55
    near mint $45
6" International KII Oil Tanker, Shell (1949–1955), mint $65
    near mint $55
6" International KII Oil Tanker, Texaco (1949–1955), mint $65
    near mint $55

Mack AC "Wrigley's" Delivery Truck $90

Mack L-Line Oil Tanker w/tank trailer, "Tootsietoy" decal (1954–1959), mint $90
    near mint $80
1955 Mack B-Line Oil Tanker, "Mobil" decal (1960–1965, 1967–1969), mint..$70
    near mint $60
1955 Mack B-Line Oil Tanker, "Tootsietoy" decal (1960–1965, 1967–1969), mint................................$85
    near mint $75
RC 180 Oil Tanker (1962), mint $55
    near mint $45

Contemporary Tootsietoys

Today's Tootsietoys represent a broad range of models, often with generous amounts of plastic incorporated into the design. The most popular line of Tootsietoys is their series called "Hard Body." Below is an assortment of models that fall under this category.

Tootsietoy Hard Body 1:43 Scale
    Corvette $3–4
    Ferrari F40 ....$3–4
    Firebird $3–4
    Mercedes-Benz Convertible $3–4
    Mercedes-Benz Coupe $3–4
    Porsche Targa $3–4
Tootsietoy Hard Body 1:64 Scale
    Corvette $1

Ferrari F40 ....$1
Flareside Pickup, Universal Air Lines.....$1
Jaguar XKE $1
Tootsietoy Hard Body 1:32 Scale
  1997 Ford F-150, fuchsia $4–5
  1996 Chevy Tahoe, black or red...$4–5

1940 Ford Coupe $4–5

1959 Chevy El Camino Custom..............$4–5

1959 Chevy El Camino Lowrider $4–5

Top Gear Trax
Top Gear
Locked Bag 5300
Parramatta, New South Wales
2124 Australia

It is truly remarkable that Top Gear models, begun in 1986, has remained so obscure outside of Australia until now. Their 1:43 scale renditions of Australia's own Holden automobiles are terrific. Holdens new and old, stock and street, station wagons and pickups... all are showcased by Top Gear in their latest brochure, provided by Bob Robinson of New South Wales, Australia. For more information, write to Top Gear at the address above.

Listed below are the known Top Gear models, with approximate collector value in US dollars.

1951 Holden Ute, woodsman green.....$36–40
1951 Holden Ute, Navajo beige $36–40
Chrysler Valiant Charger RT $45
1966 Ford Falcon 4-Door Sedan $55
1966 Ford XC Cobra Coupe....................$55
1974 Ford Falcon GT (Mustang GT) $36–40
1953 Holden Van $36–40
1963 Holden Station Wagon $36–40
Holden Monaco HK Coupe.......................$45
Sixties EH Holden Sedan, maroon and white $36–40

Sixties EH Holden Sedan, blue and white $36–40
TRG1 Australia's Hottest Ever Production Cars! Limited Edition Gift Boxed Set........$95–120 includes: Ford GTHO Phase 3 Falcon, wild violet, Holden GTS Monaro Coupe, silver mink; Valiant R/T Charger, Hemi orange
TR3C HK Monaro Racing, Palmer/ West..$50–60
TR5D EH Holden Premier Sedan, valley mist.$45–55
TR6 sixties EH Holden Wagon, gray and white $36–40
TR6C sixties EH Holden Wagon, Sorrel tan and white $32–36
TR8A Torana GTR XU-1, white $36–40
TR8B Torana GTR XU-1, lime green $32–36
TR8C Torana GTR XU-1, "Strike Me Pink".$32–36
TRS10 Bathurst Twin Set Ford Dealer Team Falcons, drivers Alan Moffat and Colin Bond, with video $60–75
TR10 Falcon XC Cobra $32–36
TR10B Brabham XC Falcon GT, with Bathurst '77 racing decals..................$36–40
TR11 Holden Charger, metallic green $32–36
TR11B Holden Charger Highway Patrol, white with roof-mounted lights and sirens ...$36–40
TRG15 Golden Holden 48-215 (FJ) commemorating Holden's 50th Anniversary (1948-1998) $45–55

50th Anniversary Holden FX Sedan........$15

50th Anniversary Holden FX Ute.............$15

50th Anniverary Holden FX Sedan and Ute $36

TR12 HZ Holden NRMA Road Service Van, blue and white...................................$36–40

TR13C Silvertop Taxi $45–55
TR13E Yellow Cab Taxi.....................$45–55
TR13F B & W Taxi.............................$45–55
TR14B Holden Torana SL/R 5000 Channel 7/Ron Hodgson with full racing decals $36–40
TRS14 LX Series Holden Torana SL/R 5000 and SS Hatchback, gift boxed twin pack $60–75
TR15 Holden 48-215 (FX) Sedan, black..................................$36–40
TR15B Holden 48-215 (FX) Sedan, powder blue..................................$36–40
TR16 1986 VL Holden Commodore, chardonnay $36–40
TR16B 1986 VL Holden Commodore, Pacific blue..................................$36–40
TR17C 1971 HQ Monaro Kingswood Sedan, mustard..............................$36–40
TR18C 1971 HQ Monaro 80337 Coupe, Purr Pull $36–40
TRS19 HT Monaro "Bathurst 69" Twin Set, Brock / Bond $80–100
TR20B 1960 FB Holden Standard Sedan, buckskin $36–40
TR20C 1960 FB Holden Standard Sedan, pyramid coral $36–40
TR21 1960 EK Holden Standard Sedan, Wedgwood blue $36–40
TR21B 1960 EK Holden Standard Sedan, glade green $36–40
TR22 1977 HZ Holden Sandman Ute, Deauville blue..................................$36–40
TR22B 1977 HZ Holden Sandman Ute, Mandarin red $36–40
TR23 1977 HZ Holden Sandman Van, yellow..................................$36–40
TR23B 1977 HZ Holden Sandman Van, white..................................$36–40
TR24B 1968 XT Ford Falcon V8 GT, silver with burgundy stripes $36–40
TR24C 1968 XT Ford Falcon GT Sedan, cruise blue..................................$36–40
TR27 1961 XK Ford Falcon Van, wattle bark tan $36–40
TR29 1961 XK Ford Falcon Utility, Merino white..................................$36–40
TR29B 1961 XK Ford Falcon Utility, Botany green..................................$36–40
TR30 1960 XK Ford Falcon Wagon, torch red $36–40
TD02 display cabinet holds up to 24 Top Gear Trax models, 15" high, 12" wide, 3" deep $80–90

Top Marques
Top Marques are 1:43 scale models made in England.
1951 Mercedes 170 ....$125

Top Model Collection
Top Model Collection SRL
Via Cupa Terracina n. 33
80125 Naples, Italy

phone: 0039 81 2422508
fax: 0039 81 624947
e-mail: topmodel@iol.it
website: members.tripod.com/topmodel
collection

The Top Model Collection is an assortment of 1:43 scale vintage European racing models made in Naples, Italy.

December 1998 – January 1999 Releases

TMC 135 Ferrari 121 LM Le Mans 1955, red, N.3; drivers: Maglioli-Hill $35

TMC 136 Ferrari 121 LM Le Mans 1955, red, N.4; drivers: Castellotti - Marzotto $35

TMC 137 Ferrari 121 LM Le Mans 1955, red, N.5; drivers: Trintignan - Shell ...$35

TMC 138 Ferrari 121 LM, red, street version $35

TMC 140 Ferrari 340 MM Le Mans 1953, blue, N.16; drivers: Chinetti - Cole ..$35

TMC 141 Ferrari 340 MM 1953, red, street version $35

March – April 1999

TMC 142 Ferrari 166S Allemano Coupe 1°Mille Miglia 1948, N.16, red, drivers: Biondetti....................................$35

TMC 143 Ferrari 166S Allemano Coupe Intereurop Cup 1949, N.12, silver, drivers: Biondetti....................................$35

TMC 144 Ferrari 166S Allemano Super-Cortemaggiore 1949, N.6, red, drivers: Biondetti....................................$35

TMC 145 Ferrari 166S Allemano Coupe 1948, red, street version $35

TMC 146 Alfa Romeo 412 Vignale Milli Miglia 1951, silver, N.427; drivers: Bonetto $35

TMC 147 Alfa Romeo 412 Vignale 1951, red, street version....................$35

TMC 148 Talbot Lago T26 GS Carrera Panam. 1954, blue, N.6; drivers: Rosier $35

May – June 1999

TMC 149 Ferrari 625 LM 3° Le Mans 1956, red, N.12; drivers: Trintignan - Gendebien....................................$35

TMC 150 Ferrari 625 LM Le Mans 1956, red, N.10; drivers: Simon - Hill........$35

TMC 151 Ferrari 625 LM Le Mans 1956, red, N.11; drivers: De Portago - Hamilton....................................$35

TMC 152 Ferrari 625 LM 1956, red, street version $35

TMC 154 BMW 328 Circuito Piacenza 1947, silver, N.132; drivers: Rovelli ...$35

TMC 155 BMW 328 1947, silver, street version $35

TMC 156 Ferrari 340 Vignale 1° Mille Miglia 1953, red, N.547; drivers: Marzotto ....$ 35

July – August 1999

TMC 157 Ferrari 335 MM Le Mans 1957, red, N.6; drivers: Hill - Collins $35

TMC 158 Ferrari 335 MM Le Mans 1947, red, N.7; drivers: Hawthorn - Musso ..$35

TMC 159 Ferrari 335 MM Mille Miglia 1947, red, N.531; drivers: De Portego $35

TMC 160 Ferrari 335 MM 1947, red, street version $35

TMC 162 Maserati 6C Sport GP Piacenza 1947, red, N.146; drivers: Angiolini....................................$35

TMC 163 Maserati 6C Sport Sassi Superga 1947, red, N.130; drivers: Angiolini....................................$35

TMC 164 Maserati 6C Sport 1947, red, street version $35

September – December 1999

TMC 165 Ferrari 315S Le Mans 1957, red, N.8; drivers: Evans - Severi $35

TMC 166 Ferrari 315S 1° Mille Miglia 1957, red, N.535; drivers: Taruffi...$35

TMC 167 Ferrari 315S 1957, red, street version $35

TMC 169 Aston Martin DBR1 3° Le Mans 1960, green, N.7; drivers: Border - Reivers $35

TMC 170 Aston Martin DBR1 1960, metal green, street version $35

TMC 171 Maserati 6C Sport GP Piacenza 1947, silver, N.164; drivers: Barbieri....................................$35

TMC 172 Maserati 6C Sport 1947, red, street version $35

TMC 139 Ferrari 121 LM 1955, yellow, street version $35

TMC 153 Ferrari 625 LM 1956, yellow, street version $35

TMC 161 Ferrari 335 MM 1957, yellow, street version $35

TMC 168 Ferrari 315 S 1957, yellow, street version $35

TMC 148/B Talbot Lago T26GS Carrera Panam. 1954, blue, N.6; drivers: Rosier, silted version $35

TMC 173 Ferrari 225 S GP Monsanto, 1953, black, N.28......................$35

Topper Toys (also see Johnny Lightnings)

Here is a brief chronology of the Topper Toy company, original manufacturer of Johnny Lightnings. For more information, refer to the section on Johnny Lightnings.

1953 Orensteins marketed Toys thru Supermarkets
1966 De Luxe Topper Corp. incorporation (Delaware)
1968 Name Change to Topper Corp
1969 Johnny Lightning line begins (Feb/Mar)
1970 Public offering of Stock
1970 FTC accuses Topper of False Advertising (Mattel is listed too)
1971 Second Public Offering
1972 SEC suspends trading of Topper stock
1972 Orenstein resigns as president
1973 Topper files chapter 11 bankruptcy
1973 Topper loses right to produce Sesame street toys...End of the Road (Dec)
(Sources: Topper Fed from S-1, Wall Street Journal, FTC lawsuit copy, courtesy of Donal Wells)

Toy Collector Club of America (see First Gear)

ToyMark (also see Speedy Power, Speedy Racer)

Recently discovered is Speedy Power brand diecast toys from Toymark Co., Ltd. Models found represent a 1:32 scale 1997 BMW Z-3 Convertible in two color schemes, purchased for $2.99 each ($3.99 suggested retail price). Features include opening doors and pullback action. Model listing are under the Speedy Power section. Most recent evidence indicates, ToyMark, Speedy Power, Speedy Wheels, and Boley have all been purchased by New-Ray.

Toyo Kogyo

Produced by Model Planning Co., Ltd., the Histories Collection from Toyo Kogyo of Japan represents 1:87 scale diecast models. A partial list is provided thanks to Werner Legrand of Belgium.

Toyo Kogyo Histories Collection

1966 Mazda Carol
v.1 white with blue roof, #20011.$12–18
v.2 white with red roof, #20012..$12–18
v.3 light blue with white roof, #20013 ....$12–18
v.4 light gray with white roof, #20014 ....$12–18

Toys of Yesterday (see OGDI)

Toys for Collectors

As if their incredible assortment of diecast models isn't enough, Toys for Collectors (TfC) has introduced its own range of scale models, in response to many requests from collectors. As stated in their Auto Miniatures catalog issue XVI, "Our objective is a small range of models with limited production runs to provide the serious collector with the alternatives not available elsewhere. The models are made of pewter, resin, or both, and production is shared in-house and overseas. Because of the effort and the time it takes to produce these miniatures, not all of them can be available at all times."

TfC began as a mail-order source for diecast precision models from a large variety of manufacturers, and has become one of only a few premiere diecast mail-order businesses in the US.

TfC's current catalog features beautiful full-color photos of models from Siku, Gama, Cursor, Conrad, and others, many of which are featured in this book.

Many of these TfC 1:43 scale models are already sold out and quickly rising in collector value.

Through the courtesy of Toys for Collectors, illustrations are provided from the pages of their Auto Miniatures Catalog, Issue XVI ($6 from TFC, P O Box 1406, Attleboro Falls MA 02763).

TFC — The American Collection from catalog pages 4 & 5

1 1970 Oldsmobile 4-4-2 Hardtop Coupe, metallic mint green $120
1a 1970 Oldsmobile 4-4-2 Hardtop Coupe, red with white roof $120
2 1970 Oldsmobile 4-4-2 W-30 Coupe, gold $144
2a 1970 Oldsmobile 4-4-2 W-30 Coupe, yellow..$144
3 1970 Oldsmobile 4-4-2 W-30 Convertible, yellow..................................$144
4 1970 Oldsmobile 4-4-2 W-30 Convertible, white "INDY OFFICIAL PACE Car"...........................$150
5 1961 Ford Thunderbird, gold "INDY OFFICIAL PACE Car".....................$160
6 1933 Chrysler Imperial, white "INDY OFFICIAL PACE Car"....................$150
7 1958 Oldsmobile Super 88 Holiday Coupe, white with red roof $148
7a 1958 Oldsmobile Super 88 Holiday Coupe, black with red roof $148
8 1933 Chrysler Imperial Custom Eight Convertible, beige with red running board & fenders.....................................$148
9 1970 Oldsmobile Cutlass S Holiday Coupe, metallic silver with black roof $124
10 1944 Mack Delivery Van, "Columbia Electric".....................................$130
11 1944 Mack Delivery Van, "Fram Filters"...$130
12 1968 Mercury Cougar XR-7 Coupe, metallic red...............................$130
12 1968 Mercury Cougar XR-7 Coupe, metallic blue $130
12 1968 Mercury Cougar XR-7 Coupe, pale yellow............................$130
13 1968 Mercury Cougar 7.0 Litre GT-E, bright orange-red.....................$164
13 1968 Mercury Cougar 7.0 Litre GT-E, metallic dark green $164
14 1939 Mack Service Truck, "NBC Engineering Department" $130
15 1972 Oldsmobile Hurst Indy Pace Car $150
16 1973 Cadillac Eldorado Indy Pace Car $150
17 1973 Cadillac Eldorado Convertible, black with red interior $130
18 1950 Mack L Type Oil Tanker "Riley" $120
19 1984 Cadillac Seville $130
20 1984 Cadillac Seville Elegante......$140
21 1941 Mack Service Van "Brewster Glass" $130

Traffic Stoppers

Originally, NSG Marketing Corporation of Passaic, New Jersey, marketed these cheaply made metal and plastic toys that retail for 50 cents to $1 apiece and offer generic representations of various trucks. Collectible value on such models is nonexistent, but they provide an interesting contrast to the accuracy and detail of other models. Once removed from the package, these models are rendered unidentifiable, as no markings exist as to make and manufacturer anywhere on the model, which defines it as a generic.

Most recently, these toys have been marketed by Rhino Toys Manufacturing Ltd., Hunghom, Kowloon, Hong Kong. See "generic" listing for photos of these and other such models.

Trax (see Top Gear)

Tri-Ang

George Lines, founder in 1870 of the original Lines Company of England, was joined by brother Joseph, who later purchased George's share. In turn, three of Joseph's sons formed a company called Lines Bros., Ltd. TriAng is named for the company logo formed by three lines, representing the three Lines brothers.

Besides diecast toys, Tri-ang products included prams, bicycles, pedal cars, stamped steel truck, wooden toys, doll houses, and many other toys.

Tri-Ang Minic models are heavy steel clockwork toys introduced in 1935 with 14 models. The line quickly expanded, resulting in a large assortment of toys. A numbering system was established around 1938 or 1939. Many of the toys had working lights, presumably powered by a small battery.

1M Ford Saloon, 1936 ....$120
1MCF Ford Saloon, Camouflaged, 1940 .$120
2M Ford Light Van, 1936......................$120
3M Ford Royal Mail Van, 1936...............$120
4M Sports Saloon, 1935 ....$120
5M Limousine, 1935 ....$120
6M Cabriolet, 1935 ....$175
7M Town Coupe, 1935.........................$125
8M Open Touring Car, 1935..................$125
9M Streamline Saloon, 1935 ....$125
10M Delivery Lorry, 1935 ....$175
11M Tractor, 1935.................................$50
12M Learner's Car, 1936.......................$125
13M Racing Car, 1936 ....$125
14M Streamline Sports, 1935.................$125
15M Petrol Tank Lorry Oil Tanker, 1936....$150
15MCF Petrol Tank Lorry, Camouflaged, 1940..$120
16M Caravan House Trailer, 1937..........$200
17M Vauxhall Tourer, 1937 ....$150
18M Vauxhall Town Coupe, 1937 ....$125
19M Vauxhall Cabriolet, 1937...............$175
19MCF Vauxhall Cabriolet, Camouflaged, 1940..$125

20M Light Tank, 1935............................$125
20MCF Light Tank, 1940......................$125
21M Transport Van, 1935 ....$125
21MCF Transport Van, 1940...............$125
22M Carter Paterson Van, 1936..............$175
23M Tip Lorry (Dump Truck)..................$150
24M Luton Transport Van, 1936 ....$175
24MCF Luton Transport Van, Camouflaged, 1940..$150
25M Delivery Lorry with cases, 1936........$125
26M Tractor and Trailer with cases, 1936.$150
29M Traffic Control Police Car, 1938.......$125
30M Mechanical Horse and Pantechnicon, 1935..$175
31M Mechanical Horse and Fuel Oil Tanker, 1936..$175
32M Dust Cart Refuse Truck, 1936..........$125
33M Steam Roller, 1935 ....$90
34M Tourer with Passengers, 1937.........$125
35M Rolls Royce Tourer, 1937 ....$125
36M Daimler Tourer, 1937.....................$125
37M Bentley Tourer, 1938.....................$125
38M Caravan Set Limousine and House Trailer, 1937..$200
39M Taxi, 1937 ....$125
40M Mechanical Horse and Trailer, 1936..$150
41ME Caravan, 1937..........................$150
42M Rolls Royce Sedanca, 1937 ....$125
43M Daimler Sedanca, 1937.................$125
44M Traction Engine, 1938...................$125
45M Bentley Sunshine Saloon, 1938........$125
46M Daimler Sunshine Saloon, 1938.......$125
47M Rolls Royce Sunshine Saloon, 1938 ..$125
48M Breakdown Lorry Wrecker, 1936.....$200
48MCF Breakdown Lorry Wrecker, Camouflaged, 1940..$150
49ME Searchlight Lorry, 1936................$125
49MECF Searchlight Lorry, Camouflaged, 1940..$125
50ME Rolls Royce Sedanca, 1936..........$125
51ME Daimler Sedanca, 1937 ....$125
52M Single Deck Bus, red, 1936.............$125
53M Single Deck Bus, green, 1936..........$125
54M Traction Engine and Trailer, 1939 ....$150
55ME Bentley Tourer, 1938...................$125
56ME Rolls Royce Sunshine Saloon..........$125
57ME Bentley Sunshine Saloon, 1938......$125
58ME Daimler Sunshine Saloon, 1938.....$125
59ME Caravan Set, tourer with passengers and Caravan with electric light, 1937........$200
60M Double Deck Bus, red, 1935...........$375
61M Double Deck Bus, green, 1935.......$225
62ME Fire Engine, 1936.......................$225
63M No. 1 Presentation Set, 1937.........$225
64M No. 2 Presentation Set, 1937.........$225
65M Construction Set, 1936.................$225
66M Six Wheel Army Lorry, 1939 ....$150
66MCF Six Wheel Army Lorry, Camouflaged, 1940..$150
67M Farm Lorry, 1939 ....$175
68M Timber Lorry, 1939.......................$175
69M Canvas Tilt Lorry, 1939.................$150

69MCF Canvas Tilt Lorry, Camouflaged, 1940......................................$150
70M Coal Lorry, 1939..............never produced
71M Mechanical Horse and Milk Trailer, 1939......................................$175
72M Mechanical Horse and Lorry with Barrels, 1939......................................$250
73M Cable Lorry, 1939..........never produced
74M Log Lorry, 1939.................never produced
75M Ambulance, 1939..........never produced
76M Balloon Barrage Wagon and Trailer, Camouflage, 1940......................$200
77M Double Deck Trolley Bus, 1939......................never produced
78M Pool Tanker, 1940......................$125
79M Mechanical Horse and Pool Tanker, 1940................................$175
M704 S. S. United States luxury cruise ship ..$40

Trident

Trident models of Austria, imported by Walthers and Diecast Miniatures, are a 1:87 scale line of modern military vehicles that are "perfect for flat car loads, war games, or collecting. Many of the U.S. prototypes can be converted as 'military surplus' vehicles for civilian use on your layout. The HO scale kits consist of detailed metal castings (unless noted)."

Trident Soviet Main Battle Tanks & Self-Propelled Guns

2S1 "Gvozdika" 122mm Howitzer ..$26.99
2S3 "Akatsiya" 152mm Howitzer.....$29.99
T-62 with 115mm Gun $26.99
T-62A with 115mm Gun $26.99
T-64 with 125mm Gun $28.99
T-72 M1 with 125mm Gun.............$28.99
T-80 ERA with 125mm Gun & Reactive Armor $29.99

Trident Engineering Vehicles

DOK-L Engineering Tractor/End Loader..................................$38.99

Trident Soviet Airborne Assault Weapons

ASU-57 with 57mm Gun.................$18.49
ASU-85 with 85mm Gun.................$24.99
BMD-2 Airborne Combat Vehicle......$24.99

Trident Soviet Armored Personnel Carriers

BMP-1 Armored with 73mm Gun $24.99
BMP-2 with 30mm Gun $28.99
BRDM-2 Reconaissance Vehicle........$25.99
BRDM-26 Armored Command Vehicle...................................$25.99
BRM-1 Reconnaissance Vehicle with 73mm Gun $24.99
BTR-60PA Armored.........................$28.99
BTR-60PB Armored.........................$28.99
BTR-70 Armored............................$28.99
BTR-80 Armored............................$30.49
MT-LBW Troop Transporter/Artillery Tractor..................................$24.99
PTS-M Amphibious Armored.............$40.99

Trident Light Trucks

Chevrolet Blazer $11

1987 Chevrolet Suburban USAF Fire Truck......................................$12
Chevrolet Truck Ambulance $12
Chevrolet K-10 Blazer Sheriff................$12
Chevrolet K-10 Blazer Park Police $12

Troféu

c/o Replicar
P O Box 371
4501-912 Espinho, Portugal
fax: 351-22 734 4920

Troféu of Portugal represents a collection of 1:43 scale diecast models mostly of European rally cars. Just a few models are decorated in numerous colors and markings to form a large assortment. Base models include the following:

Alpine Renault A 110
Fiat 131 Abarth
Ford Escort Mk I
Ford Escort Mk II
Ford Sierra Cosworth
Joest Porsche WSC
Mitsubishi Galant VR4
Porsche 936/78
Porsche LMP1/98
Saab 96
Subaru Impreza
Toyota Celica GT 4

I recently e-mailed Vitesse to ask about the connection with Troféu. Paulo Matinha of Vitesse Group wrote back to explain that, in the past, Vitesse shared their sales and distribution with Troféu along with their supply of know-how in diecast. With the change of factory plant to China, Vitesse was forced to stop their cooperation. Troféu remains today as one of the premiere European producers of quality 1:43 scale diecast models.

Alpine Renault A 110
v.1 1600S Monte Carlo 1972, #807 ....$30–45
v.2 1800S le Monte Carlo 1973, #810 ....$30–45
v.3 1800S le TAP Rally 1973, #811 .$30–45
v.4 1800S Safari 1974, #812 ......$30–45
v.5 1800S Nicolas 1973, #813 ...$30–45
v.6 Defense Monte Carlo 1973, #814 ....$30–45
Fiat 131 Abarth
v.1 "Muleto" (Test Car), red.............$30–45
v.2 Le Mans..................................$30–45
Ford Sierra Cosworth
v.1 Portugal Crash 1988, #116 .....$30–45
v.2 Ireland McRae 1989, #118 .....$30–45
Ford Escort Mk I
v.1 RS 1600 Broadspeed Fitzpatrick, 1974, #526 ....$30–45
v.2 1600 TC Silverstone Stewart 1970, #527 ....$30–45
Ford Escort Mk II
v.3 1100 Popular 1978, #1001 ...$30–45
v.4 1300 Ghia 1978, #1002.......$30–45
v.5 1600 Sport 1978, #1003.......$30–45
v.6 1600 Harrier 1978, #1004 ....$30–45

v.7 Mexico 1979, #1005.............$30–45
v.8 1800RS 1979, #1006 ....$30–45
Porsche 936
v.1 Martini Le Mans 5 Ickx/PesCarolo 1978, #1201 ....$30–45
v.2 Martini Le Mans Wollek 1979, #1202 ....$30–45
v.3 Essex Le Mans Ickx/Redman 1979, #1203 ....$30–45
v.4 Essex Le Mans Wollek 1979, #1204 ....$30–45
v.5 Jules Le Mans Ickx/Bell 1981, #1205 ....$30–45
v.6 Jules Le Mans Mass/Schuppan 1981, #1206 ....$30–45
Porsche LMP1/98
v.1 Carbon Paul RiCard 1998, #1301 ....$30–45
v.2 Le Mans test Alboreto 1998, #1302 ....$30–45
v.3 Le Mans Alboreto/Johanson 1998, #1303 ....$30–45
v.4 Le Mans Raphanel/Weaver 1998, #1304 ....$30–45
v.5 Le Mans Road Atlanta Alboreto 1998, #1305 ....$30–45
Porsche WSC95
v.1 Joest Donington Johansson 1997, #905 ....$30–45
Saab 96
v.1 Roadcar Standard 1960...........$30–45
v.2 1st Monte Carlo 1962 ....$30–45
v.3 2nd East African Safari 1964 ....$30–45
Subaru Impreza 4x4 Turbo
v.1 RAC Duckworth 1998, #623....$30–45
v.2 Police 1997, #624 ....$30–45
Subaru Impreza WRC
v.1 555 Safari McRae 1997, #1103.$30–45
v.2 Portugal C. McRae 1998, #1105.$30–45
v.3 Monte Carlo Kremer 1997, #1106 ....$30–45
v.4 Russia Uspenskiy 1998, #1107 ...$30–45
v.5 Q8 San Remo Dallavill 1998, #1108 ....$30–45
v.6 RAC De Mevius 1998, #1109 ....$30–45
Toyota Celica GT4
v.1 Castrol Safari Duncan 1996, #714.$30–45

Tron

Particularly classy are these 1:43 scale models reportedly produced by Angelo or PaoloTron of Italy, both apparently designers of models for a variety of other companies as well.

1949 Oldsmobile 88 Indy Pace Car $169
1947 Cadillac Series 62 Convertible........$179
1968 Corvette Tour de France Coupe.......$149

Tru-Scale

Carter Machine Company, founded in the 1940s by Joseph Carter, produced mostly International and John Deere tractors and farm implements. The company is best known for its assortment of pressed steel 1950s vintage International trucks, of which there were many variations.

True Dimensions

According to collector Dick Browne, True Dimensions was based in Minnesota. Browne reports, "I have a 1:43 white metal Kaiser-Darrin made by them. They made only 435, which was the exact production of the real car. They used only actual colors. Some of the models were top-up, some top-down, and some half-top. Mine is a pale green half-top. I wrote to them but didn't receive a reply. I imagine they are out of business."

Tucker Box (also see Lincoln)

According to an article in *Diecast Collector* magazine by author Robert Newson (Issue 18, April 1999,) five models comprise the Tucker Box Series from Australia, an assortment consisting of fairly crude toys measuring about 2 inches long. Introduced in 1957 according to best information, Tucker Box toys were an Australian attempt to capitalize on the popularity of Matchbox toys from England.

A year later, the five original castings were incorporated into the Lincoln Matchbox Series of New Zealand. The name was changed to Motorway Mini Series under threat of trademark infringement by Lesney Products Company, the legitimate owner of the Matchbox brand until 1982.

The Tucker Box Series

Austin Petrol Tanker, 2¼"	$25 – 40
Fire Engine and ladder, 2"	$25 – 40
Sand Truck / Pickup, 2¼"	$25–40
Land Rover, 1¾"	$25–40
Massey Harris Tractor, 1⅝"	$25–40

The Lincoln Matchbox Series

Dump Truck, 2"	$20–35
Land Liner Coach, 2¼"	$20–35
Breakdown Truck, 2⅛"	$20–35
Jaguar XK120 Roadster, 2⅛"	$20–35
Racing Car, 2"	$20–35
Ambulance, 2⅞"	$20–35
Pantechnicon, 2¹⁄₁₆"	$20–35

Tuff Ones (see Remco)

Turtle Creek Scale Models, Inc.

2420 East Ridge Rd.
Beloit, WI 53511
phone: 608-365-0579

Just recently introduced to the 1:16 scale market are two late-model trucks from the new Turtle Creek Scale Models, Inc., of Beloit, Wisconsin. Seeing a niche for such a high-end model to accompany 1:16 scale tractor and farm equipment models, Gene Arner, who has worked for General Motors in their Kodiak/Topkick plant for 30 years, has

reproduced this truck in two versions, a stake truck and a milk truck. The distinction of these new models is accuracy, detail, and workmanship. Made of spincast metal, trucks retail for $500 each, with a production limit of just 400 each, with a ratio of three Topkicks to one Kodiak, the same ratio in which the real ones are produced at GM.

GMC Topkick Stake Bed Truck, 1:16, 300 produced	$500
GMC Kodiak Stake Bed Truck, 1:16, 100 produced	$700–800
GMC Topkick Milk Truck, 1:16, 300 produced	$500
GMC Kodiak Milk Truck, 1:16, 100 produced	$700–800

Uaz

UAZ represents 1:43 scale models from Russia.

469 jeep military covered	$16
469 jeep military open	$16
469 jeep military police	$16
469 jeep fire	$16
469 jeep UN	$16
469 jeep Russian traffic police	$16
469 jeep traffic police with horn	$16
469 jeep with heavy-duty bumper	$16
469 jeep baggy	$16
452 D lorry standard	$12

Unique Industries, Inc.

Unique Industries produces a variety of inexpensive party favors. Among the assortment are some four-car sets of simple diecast vehicles. They are considered generic, and are rendered so once removed from the colorful blisterpack. Even though the cars are stylized "chubby" designs, the eight models are barely identifiable as a Porsche racer, Morris Mini, pickup truck, Volkswagen Beetle, Ferrari, sports car, compact car and van. Value will likely remain low on these models made in China, but they are charming yet inexpensive additions to a collection of toys.

Unique Industries, Inc.

Philadelphia, PA 19148

Unique Party Favors

Etobicoke, Ontario
M9W 5T6 Canada

Unique Industries

Schrijnwererstraat 2
2984 BC Ridderkerk
Rotterdam Port Area
The Netherlands

Universal (also see Matchbox)

David Yeh is, or at least in 1982 was, the C.E.O of Universal Holdings of Hong Kong.

Among his 1980s acquisitions were such brands as Kidco, Champ of the Road, Kresge, and Matchbox which he held until selling the brand to Tyco in 1992. Lock-Ups and Burnin' Key Cars were briefly incorporated into the Matchbox line-up during that time.

Universal Hobbies Ltd., Inc. (also see Eagle's Race)

In 1999, Great Planes/Hobbico became the exclusive licensed distributor for Universal Hobbies and its Eagle's Race brand of diecast models in 1:43 and 1:18 scale. See Eagle's Race for a list of models and prices.

U.S.A. Models (also see Motor City and Design Studios)

USA Models are less detailed and much less expensive models than their Motor City and Design Studios counterparts, but still represent some fabulous models not commonly reproduced in miniature. The first release (USA-1) is a 1958 Cadillac Series 75 Limousine, in dark metallic blue finish, introduced in 1997, retails for $79.

USA 1 1958 Cadillac Limousine, blue	$79
USA 1A 1958 Cadillac Limousine, silver with black roof	$85
USA 2F 1955 Chrysler Imperial, dark gray	$85
USA 3 1949 Nash Ambassador, maroon	$79
USA 3P 1949 Nash Ambassador Los Angeles Police, black and white	$85
USA 3T 1949 Nash Ambassador Yellow Cab, yellow	$85
USA 4 1951 Chevrolet Bel Air 2-Door, two-tone green	$85
USA 5 1954 Chevrolet Bel Air 4-Door, brown and beige	$85
USA 8 1950 Ford Custom Coupe, burgundy	$85
USA 9 1949 Mercury 2-Door Custom, burgundy	$85
USA 10 1941 Willys Coupe Street Rod, red	$79
USA 11 1940 Ford 2-Door Sedan	$95

U.S. Model Mint (also see SMTS)

P O Box 505
Granger, IN 46530

U.S. Model Mint models are white metal scale models in 1:43 scale similar to Brooklins, Durham and others. They are distinguished by their beautiful representations of U.S. manufactured cars.

While the U.S. headquarters are in Granger, Indiana, U.S. Model Mint cars are made by SMTS of England.

US-1 1956 Chevrolet Bel Air Hardtop, two-tone cream and black	$100
US-2 1950 Ford F-1 Pickup, red	$100
US-3 1956 Chevrolet Bel Air Convertible, top down, two-tone turquoise and white	$100
US-4 1956 Chevrolet Bel Air Convertible, top up, two-tone red and white	$100

US-5 1949 Willys Overland Jeepster, top down, cream with black interior......................$100
US-6 1949 Willys Overland Jeepster, top up, green with black top $100
US-7 1949 Jeepster Station Wagon, burgundy with wood paneling $100
US-8 1949 Willys Panel Delivery, red, "Drewry's Beer" $100
US-10 1950 Ford Telephone Truck, dark green, "Bell Systems" $100
US-12 1949 Willys Panel Delivery, yellow, "Sterling Beer" $100
US-13 1954 Studebaker Conestoga Station Wagon, baby blue $100
US-16 1969 Plymouth GTX, 1:43 ....$100

UT

Gateway Global of Europe GmbH
Postfach 485
D-52005
Aachen, Germany or
Gateway Global Limited
3/F, 8 Yip Cheong Street
On Lok Tsuen, Fanling
New Territories, Hong Kong
Gateway Global USA, Inc. or
10485 NW 28th St
Miami, FL 33172-2152

Unique Toys (HK) Limited of China, otherwise known as UT, is the manufacturer of exceptional scale models. In 1999, UT was purchased by Gateway Global and incorporated into their product line along with their new Gate and AutoArt brands.

UT 1:18 Scale Models

Benetton B193, Patrese '93 ....$30–35
BMW E36 3-Series Cabriolet, black with cream interior, #20456 ....$30–35
BMW E36 3-Series Coupe, yellow, #20451 ....$30–35
BMW E36 3-Series Coupe, silver, #20452 ....$30–35
BMW E36 3-Series 318is Saloon, red, #20461 ....$30–35
BMW E36 3-Series 318is Saloon, white, #20462 ....$30–35
BMW E46 3-Series Saloon, red, #20511 ....$30–35
BMW E46 3-Series Saloon, silver, #20512 ....$30–35
BMW E36 M3 Convertible, violet, #20471 ....$30–35
BMW E36 M3 Convertible, blue, #20472 ....$30–35
BMW E36 M3 Convertible, yellow, #20473 ....$30–35
BMW E36 M3 Coupe, blue, 20467 .$30–35
BMW E36 M3 Coupe, black, #20468 ....$30–35
BMW E36 M3 Coupe, yellow, #20466 ....$30–35
BMW E36 M3 GTR, black, #20481 .$30–35
BMW E36 M3 GTR, white, #20482 .$30–35

BMW E36 M3 Saloon, white, #20476 ....$30–35
BMW E46 3-Series 4-Door Sedan, #20511 ....$30–35
BMW E46 3-Series 328i Saloon 6-cylinder, silver, #20512 ....$30–35
BMW Z3 Coupe, black with dark gray/black interior, #20422 ....$30–35
BMW Z3 Coupe 2.8, metallic silver, #20421 ....$30–35
BMW Z3 M Coupe, black with red/black interior, #20432 ....$30–35
BMW Z3 M Coupe, blue with black/gray interior, #20431 ....$30–35
BMW Z3 M Roadster, metallic blue with black/gray interior, #20412 ....$30–35
BMW Z3 M Roadster, red with red/gray interior $30–35
1996 BMW Z3 Roadster, James Bond metallic light blue with gray interior, #20400 ....$30–35
1996 BMW Z3 Roadster, red with gray/black interior, #20401 ....$30–35
1996 BMW Z3 Roadster 2.8, silver, #20402 ....$30–35
1996 BMW Z3 Roadster, baby blue, #20403 ....$30–35
1995 Chevrolet Caprice Brea Police, black and white, #21022 ....$30–35
1995 Chevrolet Caprice Brossard, Quebec, Canada Police, white, #21023 .$30–35
1995 Chevrolet Caprice Cheyenne Police, white, #21025 ....$30–35
1995 Chevrolet Caprice Chicago Police, white, #21020 ....$30–35
1995 Chevrolet Caprice Glendale Police, black and white, #21026 ....$30–35
1995 Chevrolet Caprice Miami Police, #21024 ....$30–35
1995 Chevrolet Caprice Metro - Dade Miami Police, white, #21025 ..$30–35
1995 Chevrolet Caprice New York Police, blue and white, #21021 ....$30–35
1995 Chevrolet Caprice New York City Taxi, yellow, #21011 ....$30–35
1995 Chevrolet Caprice New York City Taxi, yellow, #21012 ....$30–35
1995 Chevrolet Caprice Sebring Police, white, #21029 ....$30–35
1995 Chevrolet Caprice Watkins Glen Police, white, #21028 ....$30–35
1978 Chevrolet Corvette Pace Car, black upper, gray lower body, #21070 ....$30–35

1978 Chevrolet Corvette Coupe, yellow $30–35

1978 Chevrolet Corvette Coupe, black, #21071 ....$30–35
1978 Chevrolet Corvette Coupe, red $30–35
1978 Chevrolet Corvette Coupe, silver, #21072 ....$30–35
1998 Chevrolet Corvette Convertible, black, #21007 ....$30–35
1998 Chevrolet Corvette Convertible, metallic lavender gray, #21010 ....$30–35
1998 Chevrolet Corvette Convertible, red, #21006 ....$30–35
1998 Chevrolet Corvette Convertible, silver, #21008 ....$30–35
1998 Chevrolet Corvette Convertible, white, #21009 ....$30–35
1998 Chevrolet Corvette Coupe, red, #21001 ....$30–35
1998 Chevrolet Corvette Coupe, black, #21002 ....$30–35
1998 Chevrolet Corvette Coupe, silver with black roof, #21003 ....$30–35
1998 Chevrolet Corvette Coupe, blue, #21004 ....$30–35
1998 Chevrolet Corvette Coupe, silver, #21005 ....$30–35
1999 Chevrolet Corvette Hardtop, black, #21042 ....$30–35
1999 Chevrolet Corvette Hardtop, red, #21041 ....$30–35
1999 Chevrolet Corvette Hardtop, silver, #21043 ....$30–35
Chevrolet Corvette Mako Shark, blue upper to silver lower body, #21061 ...$30–35
1996 Chevrolet Impala SS, black, #21031 ....$30–35
1996 Chevrolet Impala SS, metallic blue, #21032 ....$30–35
1996 Ferrari 550 Maranello, red, #22121 ....$30–35
1996 Ferrari 550 Maranello, silver, #22122 ....$30–35
1994 Ferrari F355 Berlinetta Coupe, red, #22101 ....$30–35
1994 Ferrari F355 Berlinetta Coupe, yellow, #22102 ....$30–35
1994 Ferrari F355 Berlinetta Coupe, black, #22103 ....$30–35
1994 Ferrari F355 GTS, red, #22111 ....$30–35
1994 Ferrari F355 GTS, yellow, #22112 ....$30–35
1994 Ferrari F355 Spider, red, #22106 ....$30–35
1992 Ford Escort RS Cosworth, black, #22704 ....$30–35
1992 Ford Escort RS Cosworth, red, #22701 ....$30–35
1992 Ford Escort RS Cosworth, navy blue, #22702 ....$30–35
1992 Ford Escort RS Cosworth, white, #22703 ....$30–35

1997 Ford Escort WRC, silver, #22706 ....$30–35
Ford Expedition Eddie Bauer, black, #22710 ....$30–35
Ford Expedition Eddie Bauer, metallic red, #22711 ....$30–35
Ford Expedition Eddie Bauer, white, #22712 ....$30–35
Ford Expedition XLT, metallic teal blue, #22717 ....$30–35
Ford Expedition XLT, silver, #22716 .$30–35
1996 McLaren F1 GTR Road Car, pale orange, #26006 ....$30–35
1997 McLaren F1 GTR Road Car, black, #26011 ....$30–35
McLaren F1 Road Car, silver, #26001 .$30–35
Mercedes-Benz C 36 AMG, black, #36102 ....$30–35
Mercedes-Benz C 36 AMG, silver, #26101 ....$30–35
Mercedes-Benz C 36 AMG Safety Car, silver, #26106 ....$30–35
Mercedes-Benz SLK AMG, blue, #26153 ....$30–35
Mercedes-Benz SLK AMG, red, #26154 ....$30–35
Mercedes-Benz SLK AMG, silver, #26151 ....$30–35
Mercedes-Benz SLK AMG, yellow, #26152 ....$30–35
1996 Porsche 911 GT1 Street, metallic bright blue, #27842 ....$30–35
1996 Porsche 911 GT1 Street, silver, #27846 ....$30–35
1996 Porsche 911 GT1 Street, white, #27841 ....$30–35
Porsche 911 GT2, red, #27833 ....$30–35
Porsche 911 GT2, silver, #27831 ..$30–35
Porsche 911 GT2, yellow, #27832 ..$30–35
Porsche 911 Turbo, black, #27812 ..$30–35
Porsche 911 Turbo, light burgundy, #27811 ....$30–35
Porsche 911 Turbo, silver, #27813 .$30–35
Porsche 911 Turbo S, pale yellow, #27836 ....$30–35
Porsche 993 Cabriolet, black, #27806 ....$30–35
Porsche 993 Cabriolet, burgundy, #27808 ....$30–35
Porsche 993 Cabriolet, silver, #27807 ....$30–35
Porsche 993 Carrera S, burgundy, #27827 ....$30–35
Porsche 993 Carrera S, metallic purple, #27828 ....$30–35
Porsche 993 Carrera S, silver, #27826 ....$30–35
Porsche 993 Coupe, light blue, #27801 ....$30–35
Porsche 993 Coupe, silver with black interior, #27802 ....$30–35
Porsche 993 Coupe, silver with tan interior, #27803 ....$30–35

Porsche 993 RS, bright blue, #27818 ..$30–35
Porsche 993 RS, red, #27816 ....$30–35
Porsche 993 RS, white, #27817 ....$30–35
Porsche 993 Targa, red, #27821 ...$30–35
Porsche 996 Cabriolet, metallic dark blue, #27907 ....$30–35
Porsche 996 Cabriolet, yellow, #27906 ....$30–35
Porsche 996 Coupe, black, #27902 .$30–35
Porsche 996 Coupe, metallic green, #27901 ....$30–35
Porsche Boxster, black, #27853 .....$30–35
Porsche Boxster, red, #27851 ....$30–35
Porsche Boxster, silver, #27852 ......$30–35
Sauber C12, Wendinger '93 ....$30–35
Sauber C12, Frentzen '93 ....$30–35
Sauber C12, Lehto '93 ....$30–35
1999 VW New Beetle $30–35
Williams FW15, Hill '93 ....$30–35
Williams FW15, Prost '93 ....$30–35

Vanguard (see Lledo)

Vanbo (also Vanke)

Manufacturers in China are realizing the growing popularity of quality diecast toys and models, and they are capitalizing on the trend. One of the newest such companies, begun in 1995, is ShenzhenVanke Fine Products Manufacture Company of Shenzhen, in the Peoples Republic of China. According to literature provided by Tom Hammel, editor of *Collecting Toys* magazine, Vanke produces a varied assortment of presentation pieces, model vehicles, and ornaments under the brand name Vanbo. Besides fine quality diecast cars and trucks, Vanke also produces fine award plaques, trophies, medals, sundials, desk sets, silver plates, clocks, globes, even presentation daggers, as well as other unusual items, all cast metal. Vanke even produced a model of Leonardo DaVinci's Flying Machine.

Vanbo car and truck models range from 1:12 to 1:87 scale. The RE series is designated exclusively for OEM and ODM sales (original manufacturer and dealerships only). The Mercedes-Benz 500K and Black Prince, model numbers 97002 and 97003 respectively, appear to be the two popular models that were recently issued by CMC of Germany. Both models won Vanke the "Best Model Medals of 1995 and 1996" by Mercedes GmbH.

No prices were included in the Vanke literature, so I've made an educated estimate for current values.

Benz First Automobile, 97001, 1:10, 1997 issue $175–225
BMW Motorcycle, 96010, 1:12, 1996 issue $35–45
Datong Tipping Lorry, 95050, 1:43, 1995 issue $20–25
Jiefang (Liberation) Army Truck, 95030, 1:43, 1995 issue $20–25

Jiefang (Liberation) Cannon Truck, 95035, 1:43, 1995 issue $20–25
Jiefang (Liberation) Tip Truck, 95020, 1:43, 1995 issue $20–25
Jiefang (Liberation) Tower Truck, 96088, 1:43, 1996 issue $20–25
Hongqi (Red Flag) Car CA7220, 96121, 1:24, 1996 issue $20–25
Hongqi (Red Flag) Car CA7220, sterling silver on stand, 95010, 1:87, 1995 issue..............................$90–120
Mercedes-Benz 500K, 97002, 1:24, 1997 issue $125–150
Mercedes-Benz Black Prince, 97003, 1:24, 1997 issue $125–150
Santana 2000, gold on stand, 95011, 1:87, 1995 issue $250–300
Fire Truck, 96046, 1:43, 1996 issue ...$20–25
Tanker Truck, 95045, 1:43, 1995 issue .$20–25

Vanbo RE Series
Bugatti Royale Coupe Napoleon, RE003, 1:18 ....$90–120
Cadillac circa 1910, RE005, 1:24.$75–90
Hispano-Suiza Open Boattail Roadster circa 1925, RE004, 1:24 ....$75–90
Mercedes-Benz 770K circa 1920, RE002, 1:24 ....$75–90
Rolls-Royce Silver Ghost circa 1915, RE001, 1:24 ....$75–90

Vanke (see Vanbo)

Vaz (see Lada)

Verem

Verem of France is a producer of high-quality low-cost models in 1:43 scale. Many models from Solido have been used to create Verem models. It is reported that Verems are higher quality than their Solido counterparts, comparable to the detailing done on Matchbox models by White Rose Collectibles. Cofradis is another company that uses modified Solido models.

6 Citroën Fire Van.......................$18
7 Citroën Fire Ambulance $18
10 Citroën Fire Ladder.................$18
91 Citroën 11BL Circus................$18
92 Citroën C4 Circus Van $18
93 Citroën C4 Circus Truck...........$18
94 Renault Reina Circus $18
101 Citroën C4 Fire Van $18
102 Citroën C4 Fire Ladder Truck.....$18
104 Citroën C4 Fire Van $18
301 1928 Mercedes Convertible, top up....$18
305 Delahaye Convertible, top down $18
307 1931 Cadillac Harlem Hearse, white ..$18
310 Rolls Royce Silver Cloud, gold $18
312 Panhard 24BT...........................$18
402 Citroën SM...............................$18
404 Maserati Indy Coupe $18
407 1966 Oldsmobile Toronado..............$18
408 Ferrari Daytona, red....................$18

409 Ferrari Daytona, yellow.....................$18
411 Ferrari Berlinetta Boxer, red $18
412 Porsche Carrera, white $18
413 Porsche 914, yellow $18
501 Peugeot 604, gold $18
506 1984 Chevrolet Camaro, yellow........$18
508 Porsche 928, black $18
605 Alfa Romeo GTZ, green $18
606 Lola T280, yellow $18
607 Porsche Carrera, white $18
608 1973 Porsche Can Am, white............$18
611 1974 "Gulf" Mirage, blue..................$18
650 Alpine A110, red.............................$18
651 Lancia Stratos, black $18
701 Alpin A110, blue $18
704 Lancia Stratos, blue $18
950 4-Piece "Pinder Circus" Set..............$54

VF-Modelautomobile Germany

VF Modellautomobile
P O Box 100 618
D-52306 Düren, Germany

"VF" are the initials of Volker G. Feldkamp, proprietor of VF-Modelautomobile. The German company produces handmade white metal sedans, convertibles, stretch limousines, hearses and ambulances. Cadillac, Lincoln, Rolls Royce, and Bentley, as well as DeLorean, Kaiser, Oldsmobile, Ford Thunderbird, Buick, Mercedes, all of the James Bond cars, and more, are all replicated in 1:43 scale and presented in wood-and-acrylic dustproof showcases, personalized for your collection or as an award. Each model is produced in quantities of no more than 100.

VF-Modelautomobile Germany models are distributed exclusively in the U.S.A. by
Sinclair's Mini-auto
P O Box 8403
Erie, PA 16505
phone & fax: 814-838-2274
1971 Cadillac Eldorado Convertible, 5 colors available, VF-AMC0001 ....$199
1960 Cadillac Fleetwood 75 Limousine, black with red interior or metallic dark red with black interior, VF-0005 ....$279
1959 Cadillac Hearse, Hess & Eisenhardt Coachwork, black with red interior, VF-CC0004...$259
1996 Cadillac Catera Sedan ...Price unavailable

Victoria (see Vitesse)

Victory Models

P O Box 156,
Clarksburg, NJ 08510
e-mail: raypazjr@aol.com
fax: 732 446 9297

Ray Paz Jr. writes: "I want to bring to your attention a company that has been manufacturing 1:43rd scale models vehicles since 1992. The models are cast in resin and are hand-built limited production." The following cars have been produced:

1941 Cadillac, 3 different body styles $125–150
1941 Chrysler Windsor Highlander Convertible, 2 versions $125–150
1949 Diamond T 201 pickup and tow truck $125–150
1947 GMC Coach 36 passenger bus $125–150
1938 Buick Special 4 door sedan & business coupe $125–150

Viking

There are actually three toy companies named Viking.

Viking Modell of Germany

Viking Modell, alternately marked Viking Model, was a German manufacturer of crude pot metal ships. Some are imprinted with "German Made," others "Made in Germany." Most are replicas of pre-WWII ships. They might have a connection with Wiking, based on a similar logo.

Viking of Ohio

One example is known from this company, a 27 inch long dump truck, presumably made of pressed steel. Vintage is unknown but presumed to be from the fifties or late forties.
Dump Truck, 27" $1,200

Viking Toys of Sweden

A third toy manufacturer with the name Viking was recently discovered as a producer of distinctive plastic toys. Two examples were discovered, both simple designs intended for the preschool set.
Front End Loader, green and red, 5" $5
Fire Ladder Truck, red and yellow, 5" $5

Vilmer

Thanks to an article by Karl Schnelle dated February 10, 1995 entitled "Vilmer Kvalitet," a short history of Vilmers is extracted below.

Production of Vilmer diecast model cars of Denmark started in 1955 or 1956 and lasted until 1966. The first models produced were Dodge trucks. These trucks were based on the same molds used for the Tekno Dodge series of the 1950s (Tekno of Denmark #948-958). Similar to the Tekno philosophy, the same cab and chassis were attached to every type body imaginable, all roughly 112 mm long.

There are three small differences between the Teknos and the Vilmers that help the collector easily tell which is which. The obvious difference is that the Tekno baseplate was changed to read Vilmer in the script style font used on all their models and boxes. Also, the Vilmer versions use a spare tire and wheel on top of the cab to control the steering; Tekno usually employ a spotlight for this purpose. The military Vilmer Dodges may use a tire, machine gun, or spotlight while the military Tekno use a machine gun. Finally, the Tekno versions appear to have an extra brace across the chassis under the rear wheels.

As companions to the 112 mm Dodges, a smaller range was also made. All the small Dodge trucks (military and civilian) are 98 mm and have a spare tire on the roof to control steering the front wheels. The spare wheel has a script "Vilmer" across the center while the four actual wheels have five cast lug nuts instead.

All the wheels are metal except for the military version which has olive drab plastic wheels of the same design. At least one version has no steering. These smaller Dodges are slightly bigger than the small Tekno Dodge trucks. The small Vilmer appear to be scaled-down versions of the larger Dodge, as opposed to a copy of the small Teknos. Both the small and large have "Vilmer Made in Denmark" on the baseplate under the cab. A tin-plate grill is attached using three tabs to the front of both size Dodges. They also both use two white plastic headlights.

In 1957, Vilmer introduced a limited number of automobile models. The Vilmer VV196R was said to be a copy of the Marklin version.

From 1957 to 1960, the series of Chevrolet 6400 trucks were produced which use many of the same bodies as the larger Dodge models and use a spare wheel or a machine gun for steering the front wheels.

After 1960, both Volvo and Mercedes-Benz trucks were made. Some of the best castings exist on these chassis. Not surprisingly the Vilmer versions were cruder than the Tekno castings but did include opening doors and hood on the Volvo and an opening hood on the Mercedes. Both the Volvo and Mercedes have the following components: plastic grill, clear plastic headlights, plastic wheels, plastic tail pipe and rear transmission, and front and rear suspension.

The Ford Thames Trader was introduced in 1964. Only four different models have been identified, which seems to make the Ford much rarer than the other models. The Ford had "Thames Trader" cast into the front of the cab above the grill. The grill was made up of a wide plastic insert with two clear headlights. All other models had only "Vilmer" and "Made in Denmark" somewhere on the base.

Because of the competition from Tekno, Vilmer ceased production in 1966. It appears that the Mercedes truck molds went to Metosul in Portugal and then on to Chico in Columbia. The baseplates were changed by both companies to update the manufacturer's name and country of origin. Chico also obtained the Volvo and Thames Trader molds at some point.

Mr. Schnelle cites the following as references and sources for the information he has compiled: Bertrand du Chambon, Frits Monsted, Bjorn Schultz, James Greenfield, and Richard Lay; Clive Chick (1989), "Made in Denmark, Part Three"; Horst Macalka (1990), "Catalog Corner"; Karl Schnelle (1990),

"Vilmer & Airports"; anonymous (1957, 1964), "Legetojs-Tidende," Danish toy wholesalers magazine, various pages.

While Mr. Schnelle's original article included many details not mentioned here, he did not offer values, current or otherwise. So an educated guess of $45–60 for each model is provided based on the quality and rarity of this series. Some models are likely worth as much as $90–100 or more, depending on collector interest, availability, quality, and condition.

339 Baggage Cart, blue, yellow driver, suitcase.....................................$45–60
340 Dodge stake (timber) truck, 98 mm .$45–60
341 Dodge flatbed, 98 mm................$45–60
342 Dodge cattle truck, 98 mm...........$45–60
345 Dodge wooden barrel truck, 98 mm..$45–60
346 Dodge towtruck, 98 mm..............$45–60
347 Dodge flatbed w/ tailboard, 98 mm...................................$45–60
348 Dodge dropside truck, 98 mm.......$45–60
34x Dodge gas truck, 98 mm $45–60
34x Dodge Carlsberg high sided truck (with cover), 98 mm......................$45–60
350 Dodge cement truck, 1 round tank 1957, 98 mm...............................$45–60
444 Volvo PV 444, 1957 ....$45–60
Mercedes 220, 1957 ....$45–60
Mercedes W196R, 1957 ....$45–60
Opel Record, 1960 ....$45–60
Opel Record station wagon, 1960 ......$45–60
Lambretta scooter, yellow $45–60
454 Chevrolet military tanker..............$45–60
455 Chevrolet 3 rocket truck, 1957-60 .$45–60
456 Dodge military crane truck, 1955-56.$45–60
457 Chevrolet 4 canon truck, 1957-60.$45–60
457 Dodge 2 canon truck, with man, 1955-6.............................$45–60
458 Dodge military spot light truck, with man $45–60
Dodge spot light truck, with man..........$45–60
458 Chevrolet military spot light truck, with man, 1957 ....$45–60
459 Dodge radar truck, with man, 1957..$45–60
460 Chevrolet ten rocket launcher, 1957-60.................................$45–60
461 Chevrolet single canon truck, 1957.................................$45–60
462 Chevrolet single rocket truck, 1957.................................$45–60
463 Dodge military dropside truck, 1957.................................$45–60
463 Chevrolet military dropside truck.....$45–60
464 Dodge military tarp covered truck, 1957.................................$45–60
465 Chevrolet red cross covered truck...$45–60
467 Chevrolet dropside truck, milk containers..............................$45–60
468 Chevrolet covered truck $45–60
469 Dodge crane truck (wrecker).........$45–60
469 Chevrolet crane truck (wrecker).....$45–60
Dodge ladder truck.......................$45–60
470 Chevrolet spot light truck $45–60

471 Chevrolet open truck $45–60
472E Chevrolet gas tanker, ESSO $45–60
472S Chevrolet gas tanker, SHELL $45–60
474 Chevrolet dump truck w/ shovel $45–60
475 Renault 4 CV, 1957 ....$45–60
476 Chevrolet cement truck, 2 round tanks.$45–60
477 Chevrolet cement mixer with chute on back................................$45–60
540 Dodge military stake (timber) truck, 98 mm.................................$45–60
541 Dodge military flatbed, 98 mm......$45–60
542 Dodge military cattle truck, 98 mm $45–60
545 Dodge military wooden barrel truck, 98 mm.................................$45–60
546 Dodge military towtruck, 98 mm $45–60
547 Dodge military flatbed w/ tailboard, 98 mm.................................$45–60
548 Dodge military dropside, 98 mm ...$45–60
572 Chevrolet gas truck, military $45–60
575 Massey Ferguson tractor, 1965.....$45–60
576 trailer for tractor $45–60
578 Ford tractor $45–60
580 Austin Champ (open), military or blue.................................$45–60
Austin Champ (open), military with single gun in rear $45–60
620 Bedford cattle transport, 1965.......$45–60
621 Bedford cattle truck (3-axle) and trailer................................$45–60
624 Bedford flat truck for milk $45–60
624 Bedford dropside truck w/ MEJERIET milk tank.................................$45–60
625 Bedford flat truck for milk with trailer ..$45–60
654 Bedford military gas tanker $45–60
656 Bedford military tow truck (crane)....$45–60
657 Bedford military 4 canon truck $45–60
Bedford military twin 40mm guns $45–60
658 Bedford military searchlight............$45–60
660 Bedford ten rocket launcher $45–60
Bedford multi-rocket launcher (3 axle).....$45–60
661 Bedford single canon truck $45–60
662 Bedford single missile truck $45–60
663 Bedford military dropside truck $45–60
Bedford military dropside truck (3-axle)...$45–60
664 Bedford military covered truck $45–60
665 Bedford red cross covered truck $45–60
668 Bedford covered truck................$45–60
669 Bedford tow truck.....................$45–60
670 Bedford spot light truck................$45–60
671 Bedford open truck....................$45–60
672 Bedford gas tanker, ESSO BENZIN SMOREOLIE (red).....................$45–60
672 Bedford gas tanker, SHELL $45–60
677 Bedford cement mixer, with chute...$45–60
710 Merecedes Benz dump truck $45–60
720 Ford Thames bucket truck $45–60
725 Ford Thames truck with magnet, 1964.................................$45–60
725 Ford Thames crane FALCK, 1964..$45–60
730 Ford Thames cable truck $45–60
850 Mercedes-Benz tipping truck, 1965 .$45–60
851 Mercedes-Benz milk truck, 1965....$45–60

852 Mercedes-Benz tarp covered truck, 1964.................................$45–60
853 Mercedes-Benz Red Cross covered truck, 1965.................................$45–60
854 Mercedes-Benz military tarp covered, 1965.................................$45–60
855 Mercedes-Benz refuse truck FODERBUS or plain, 1964 ....$45–60
856 Mercedes-Benz dump truck w/ front shovel, 1965.................................$45–60
857 Mercedes-Benz ladder truck, 1965..$45–60
862 Mercedes-Benz cattle truck, 1965..$45–60
Mercedes-Benz SWISSAIR $45–60
Mercedes-Benz FALCK tow truck $45–60
2651 Volvo milk truck, 1966 ....$45–60
2652 Volvo tarp covered truck (military), 1966.................................$45–60
2655 Volvo cattle truck, 1966 ....$45–60
2722 Volvo tow truck FALCK w/crane, tow bar, 1966.................................$45–60
2723 Volvo tipping truck, 1966..........$45–60
2724 Volvo 98 mm ladder truck, FALCK, 1966.................................$45–60
2820 Volvo cement tipper, 1966........$45–60
Volvo 98 mm covered truck, plain or KLM $45–60
Volvo 98 mm dropside, plain, BEA or ESSO.................................$45–60
Volvo 98 mm milk truck....................$45–60
Volvo 98 mm stake truck $45–60
Volvo 98 mm military.......................$45–60
Volvo 98 mm dump truck with shovel $45–60
Volvo 98 mm dumping cement truck, CRO BRETON.................................$45–60
Volvo 98 mm covered, Red Cross, white.................................$45–60
Volvo flatbed, small crane and tire bar, FALCK.................................$45–60
Volvo (I) covered truck ASG, SABENA or plain.................................$45–60
Volvo (I) flatbed with chains and trailer...$45–60
Volvo (I) flatbed, lowering sides, plain or DSB.................................$45–60
Volvo (I) flatbed and trailer, ramps, chocks .$45–60
Volvo (I) tanker and trailer, SHELL, ESSO, BP.................................$45–60

Vintage Casting

Located in New Jersey, Vintage Casting manufactures slushmold reproductions of Barclay and other toys from the 40s and 50s.

1940 Buick Special $15

Vitesse (also Vitesse, City, Onyx, Quartzo, Skid, 2Wheels, Victoria)

Vitesse Group
Cinerius Ltd.
P O Box 106
4471 Maia Codex Portugal
fax: 351-2-9017464
e-mail: vitesse.group@mail.telepac.pt
website: www.vitessegroup.com

Vitesse is a popular brand of 1:43 scale models from Portugal. Victoria models are military models produced by Vitesse. See Victoria listing for more information. Other specialty offerings from Vitesse include Quartzo race cars and Onyx, an assortment of mostly Formula One race cars. New series for 1999 include Skid rally cars and 2Wheels motorcycles. The Millennium Collection is the year 2000 addition to the vast Vitesse empire.

Vitesse Millennium Collection 2000

1899 Opel Lutzman $25
1910 Ford T....................................$25
1920 Austin Seven.........................$25
1934 Citroën Traction $25
1939 Volkswagen $25
1945 Jeep Willys...........................$25
1948 Citroën 2CV $25
1952 Ferrari 500 F2.......................$25
1953 Cadillac Eldorado....................$25
1955 Jaguar D-Type $25
1956 Morgan 4/4..........................$25
1956 Citroën DS19.........................$25
1959 Austin 850............................$25
1963 Aston Martin DB5...................$25
1964 Porsche 911..........................$25
1968 Mercedes 600........................$25
1970 Range Rover..........................$25
1972 Lotus 72...............................$25
1977 Lancia Stratos........................$25
1980 Alfa Romeo Spider $25
1989 Trabant................................$25
1990 Lamborghini Countach $25
1991 Hummer................................$25
1999 VW New Beetle.......................$25

The Vitesse Collection

02 1959 Volkswagen 1200 with Sunroof $25
03 Volkswagen Karmann Convertible, top down......................................$25
05 Volkswagen Van Fire Department......$28
10 1956 Ford Fairlane Victoria.............$25
12 1967 Porsche 911R.......................$25
14 Triumph TR3A, open top.................$25
15 1963 Austin-Healey 3000, open top .$25
17 Ferrari Dino.................................$25
20 1947 Chrysler Town & Country........$25

23 1958 Buick Special Convertible $25

25 1959 Nash Metropolitan Hardtop Coupe $25
31 1960 Steyr-Puch 650T Scooter $25
32 Nash Metropolitan 1959 Convertible, open top $25
33 1965 Mercedes-Benz 600 Pullman ..$28

36 1969 Chevrolet Corvette Convertible, open top $25
38 1958 Buick Roadmaster 2-Door Coupe $25
40 1953 Cadillac 4 Carrera Panamerican.$28
44 Corvette Le Mans $25
50 1953 Cadillac Eldorado with Continental Kit $25
56 1956 Ford Fairlane Purple Hog, NASCAR $28
57 1956 Triumph TR3 open Convertible ..$25
59 Volkswagen 1200, U. S. Dollar $25
62 1971 Chevrolet Corvette Spyder "Daytona" $25
63 Mercedes-Benz 600 Landaulet........$28
81 Mercedes-Benz 600 with Pope $28
111 Chevrolet Corvette LeMans $25
140 Ferrari Spyder California...............$25
250 White Tanker "Texaco" $50
280 Cadillac Eldorado, open top.........$25
282 Cadillac Coupe $25
284 Cadillac Fire Department $25
286 Cadillac Eisenhower $25
370 1947 Chrysler Windsor Sedan......$25
373 Chrysler Fire Department..............$25
378 Chrysler Parks Department............$25
390 1959 Chevrolet Impala Convertible, open top $25
391 1959 Chevrolet Impala Convertible, closed top $25
392 1959 Chevrolet Impala Hardtop....$25
393 Chevrolet Jr. Johnson $25
394 Chevrolet Impala #7 Jim Reed, NASCAR $28
405 Volkswagen Hebmueller with Sunroof .$25
421 DeSoto Taxi...............................$25
433 Mack "Ryder" Truck $50
434 Mack Fire Pumper, white $50
450 1950 Buick Special Convertible, open top $25
451 1950 Buick Special Convertible, closed top $25
460 1956 Ford Fairlane Convertible, open top $25
550 Volkswagen Bulli Van...................$25
555 Volkswagen Bulli "Nestle's" Van $25
560 Volkswagen Kombi.....................$25
600 1977 Ferrari 508 GTB................$25
680 Messerschmitt KR 200..................$25
681 Messerschmitt KR 200 Kabrio-Limousine, open top $25

684 Messerschmitt KR 200 Tiger, open top $25

683 Messerschmitt KR 200 Tiger, closed top $25
690 1956 Citroën DS 19 Salon De Paris $25
730 Porsche Carrera Roadcar $25
V98001 Lotus Seven S2 1960 Open Convertible, British racing green............$25
V98002 Citroën 2CV 1960 with Snow Plough $25
V98003 Opel Kadett "B" Coupe 1966, light gray $25
V98004 Opel Kadett "B" Coupe 1966, light blue $25
V98005 Opel Kadett "B" Coupe 1966, dark blue $25
V98006 Opel Kadett "B" Coupe 1966, dark red $25
V98007 Mercedes ML320 1998, imperial red $25
V98008 Renault Laguna Break "F1 Medical Car" $25
V98009 Renault Megane Coupe "F1 Safety Car" $25
V98010 Renault Spider "F1 PACE Car" $25
V98011 Renault Espace "F1 STAFF Car" $25
V98012 Toyota Picnic 1997, dark blue $25
V98013 Toyota RAV4 1996, metallic red $25
V98014 Toyota RAV4 1996, metallic blue $25
V98015 Toyota RAV4 1996, light metallic green $25
V98016 Toyota RAV4 1996, light silver gray $25
V98017 Toyota Corolla WRC D. Auriol Finland Rally 1997 ....$25
V98018 Toyota Corolla WRC Grundholm Finland Rally 1997 ....$25
V98019 Porsche 911GT2 "JUMBO" Le Mans 1997 ....$25
V98020 Porsche 911GT2 "NAVISION" Le Mans 1997 ....$25
V98021 Porsche 911GT2 "FAT TURBO" Le Mans 1997 ....$25
V98022 Porsche 911GT2 "CHEREAU" Le Mans 1997 ....$25
V98023 Porsche 911GT2 "PHILIPPE CHARRIOL" Le Mans 1997 ....$25
V98024 Porsche 911GT2 "KONRAD" Le Mans 1997 ....$25
V98025 Porsche 911GT2 "LLOYD'S" Le Mans 1997 ....$25
V98026 Porsche 911GT2 "STADLER" Le Mans 1997 ....$25
V98027 Porsche 911GT2 "TAISAN" Japan GT Championship 1997.............$25
V98028 Peugeot 306 Maxi Spain 1997 J. Azcona - J. Billmer.....................$25
V98029 Aston Martin DB5 1963, metallic silver gray.................................$25

V98030 Renault 5TL Sedan 1972 orange $25

V98031 Opel GT 1900 Coupe 1960 orange $25

V98032 Renault Megane Open Convertible 1997, yellow $25

V98033 Renault Spider with front windscreen 1997, yellow $25

V98034 Mitsubishi Lancer Evo. IV Roadcar 1997, white $25

V98035 Mitsubishi Lancer Evo. IV Roadcar 1997, silver gray $25

V98036 Mitsubishi Lancer Evo. IV Roadcar 1997 Rallyart $25

V98037 Chevrolet Corvette '97 closed Coupe, light pewter metal $25

V98038 Peugeot 306 Maxi "PANIZZI" Tour de Corse 1997 .... $25

V98039 Peugeot 306 Maxi "DELECOUR" Tour de Corse 1997 .... $25

V98040 Fiat Cinquencento Rally "TARGET" A. Maselli Europa Cup 1997 ... $25

V98041 Ford Escort WRC "Sainz" winner Acropolis Rally 1997 .... $25

V98042 Mini "STUDIO 2"1990 .... $25

V98043 Renault 4 Jogging Open Convertible 1981 .... $25

V98044 Opel Kadett "B" Fastback Rally 1900 1967, red & matt black $25

V98045 Lancia Strato"ALITALIA" Munari winner Rally MONTECARLO 1976 ... $25

V98046 Chevrolet Nomad 1957, red & ivory $25

V98047 Lotus Elise 1997 Open Convertible, yellow $25

V98048 Citro Berlingo Multispace 1997 Vert Innsbruck $25

V98049 Peugeot Partner Week End, red $25

V98050 Mercedes S600L Pullman 1997, dark metallic gray $25

V98051 Toyota Corolla Liftback 1997, Night Shadow $25

V98052 Toyota Corolla Hatchback 1997 Cool Water $25

V98053 Mitsubishi Lancer Evo. IV T. Makkinen winner Catalunya Rally 1997 ... $25

V98054 Ford Escort WRC "TOTTA" F. Peres Rally de Portugal 1997 .... $25

V98055 Lotus Seven S2 1500 1960 Open Convertible w/doors, red & aluminium ... $25

V98056 Citroën 2CV "MARCATELO" 1976 .... $25

V98057 Peugeot 404 Injection 1972, metallic silver $25

V98058 Fiat Spider 2000 Open Convertible 1979, metallic red $25

V98059 Honda S800 closed Convertible 1965, ivory $25

V98060 Jaguar XK8 closed Convertible, carnival red $25

V98061 Renault Kangoo Saloon Vert Fidji $25

V98062 Renault Kangoo Express Van Rouge Vif $25

V98063 Toyota Corolla WRC Sainz winner Rally MONTECARLO 1998 .... $25

V98064 Mitsubishi Carisma GT Burns Rally de Portugal 1997 .... $25

V98065 Ford Escort WRC Kankkunen Finland Rally 1997 .... $25

V98066 Morgan +8 1968 Open Convertible, indigo blue $25

V98067 Jaguar MkII British Saloon Car Graham Hill 1963 .... $25

V98068 Citroën Traction 7A 1934, beige maintenon & black $25

V98069 Porsche 904GTS 1964, silver gray $25

V98070 Opel ASCONA 400 "BASTOS" G. Colsoul-A. Lopes Rally MONTECARLO 1982 ... $25

V98071 Lancia 037 Rally Pioneer Andruet Tour de France 84 .... $25

V98072 Chevrolet Bel Air Coupe 1955, India ivory & black $25

V98073 Renault Master 1998, "Blanc Glacier" white $25

V98074 Renault CLIO 1998, metallic red $25

V98075 Mitsubishi Lancer Evo. G. Trelles Tap Rally de Portugal 1998 ... $25

V98076 Ford Escort "BELGACOM" De Mevius Portugal Rally 1997 .... $25

V98077 Peugeot 306 Maxi "SG" A. Lopes Rally Tap-Portugal 1998 ...... $25

V98078 Renault Megane Maxi "YACCO" 98 B. Rousselot Rally Lyon-Charboon ... $25

V98079 Aston Martin DB5 1963, peony red $25

V98080 Renault 5TS 1975 with Open Roof, red $25

V98081 Opel Kadett "B" Rally 1100 1966, yellow & matt black $25

V98082 Lancia StratoS MARLBORO Munari winner Sanremo Rally 1974 ... $25

V98083 Lotus Elise closed Convertible 1997, Lotus racing green $25

V98084 Citroën Berlingo Van "Citroën ASSISTANCE" $25

V98085 Renault Spider "TESSITURA FABRI" A. Belicchi Eurocup 1998 .. $25

V98086 Chevrolet Corvette '98 Open Convertible, red $25

V98087 Citroën XSARA Rally P. Bugalski Catalunya Rally 1998 ...... $25

V98088 Toyota Corolla WRC "MARLBORO" F. Loix Portugal 1998 .... $25

V98089 Mitsubishi Lancer Evo. IV Winfield T. Makinen Australia Rally 97 ... $25

Vitesse Classic Cars

VCC99001 Aston Martin DB4GT Zagato "180L" Kerguen LM 61 .... $25

VCC99002 Lotus Seven S3 1600 68 Open Convertible, aluminum & green ... $25

VCC99003 Mini Beaubourg $25

VCC99004 Renault "VOITURETTE" 1898, red $25

VCC99005 Citroën 2CV 1948, silver gray (the first 2cv !) $25

VCC99006 Porsche 904GTS n°34 Buchet-Ligier LeMans 1964 .... $25

VCC99007 Alfa Romeo Spider Duetto 66 Closed Cabriolet, yellow ... $25

VCC99009 Honda S600 Open Convertible 1966, red $25

VCC99010 Mini Moke "CAGIVA" 1997 Open Convertible, red $25

VCC99011 Morgan +8 1968 Closed Convertible, Connaught green $25

VCC99012 Aston Martin DB5 "Paris-Pekin" 1998 .... $25

VCC99013 Renault 5 Alpine 1976, metallic gray $25

VCC99014 Citroën Traction 7S 1934, gris perle & black $25

VCC99015 Volkswagen KdF Saloon 1938, dull blue (the first VW !) . $25

VCC99016 Fiat 500 1957, open blue celeste (the first Fiat 500!) . $25

VCC99017 Chevrolet Bel Air 1955 Open Convertible, coral red $25

VCC99018 Morris 1100 1962, ivory white $25

VCC99019 Austin-Healey 3000 59 Open Convertible, black & Colorado red ... $25

VCC99020 Mini Cooper 1990, red & white $25

VCC99021 Citroën DS19 1956 Aubergine, Dark Red (the first Citroën DS !) ... $25

VCC99022 Renault 4 "SIXTIES" 1985, bleu vif $25

VCC99023 Opel Kadett "B" Coupe Rallye 1900 67, metal gray & black ... $25

VCC99024 Alfa Romeo 2000 Veloce 1971 Open Convertible, red $25

VCC99025 Lancia StratoS "TORINO CAR SHOW" 1971, red $25

VCC99026 Aston Martin Zagato "181L" 1961, dark blue $25

VCC99027 Lotus Seven S3 1600 1968 Convertible with doors, yellow ... $25

VCC99028 TRIUMPH TR3A 1957 Open Convertible, British racing green ... $25

VCC99029 Citroën Traction 11B 1953, black $25

VCC99030 Citroën 2CV "BAMBOO" 1982, green $25

VCC99031 Porsche 904GTS n°31 Schiller-Koch LeMans 1964 ...... $25

VCC99032 Fiat 124 Spider 2000 "50th ANNIVERSARY" 81, champagne ... $25

VCC99033 Nash Metropolitan 59 Open Convertible, white & red .. $25

VCC99034 Austin Van Den Plas 1300 1963, dark metal brown $25

VCC99035 Mini Moke "AUSTRALIAN" 1968 closed, blue............$25

VCC99036 Renault 5 "AUTOMATIC" 1978, red.............$25

VCC99037 Messerschmitt KR200 1960, ivory & red.............$25

VCC99038 Porsche 911 Carrera RS 1992, indische rot.............$25

VCC99039 Ferrari 365GT4 BB 1973, red.............$25

VCC99040 Honda S600 1964 closed Convertible, silver gray.............$25

VCC99041 Mini Neon 1991, Nordic blue.............$25

VCC99042 Jaguar MkII 3.4 1959, dove gray.............$25

VCC99043 Aston Martin Zagato 182R Fiarman-Consten LM61.............$25

VCC99044 Renault 5 TURBO 1978, metallic blue.............$25

VCC99045 Citroën Traction 7C 1934, rouge bordeaux.............$25

VCC99046 Opel GT/J 1972, orange $25

VCC99047 Alfa Romeo Spider Duetto 1966 w/ hard top ivory white $25

VCC99048 Chevrolet Nomad 1957 "CHE GUEVARA," ivory & dusk plum $25

Vitesse Modern Cars

VMC99001 Lotus Elise Open Convertible, silver $25

VMC99002 Renault Spider Pare Brise "SALON DE PARIS 98," metgray.............$25

VMC99003 Porsche 911GT2 1998, Roadcar, indische rot.............$25

VMC99004 Chevrolet Corvette "PACE CAR INDIANAPOLIS" 1998.............$25

VMC99005 Mitsubishi Space Star 1998, firenze gold.............$25

VMC99006 Citroën Berlingo 5-PLACES, Calendula metallic.............$25

VMC99007 Renault Laguna II Sedan 1998, noir nacré.............$25

VMC99008 Porsche 996 Carrera 4 Coupe 1998, Artic silver gray.............$25

VMC99010 Toyota Land Cruiser Short, dark blue & silver.............$25

VMC99011 Renault Kangoo "PAMPA" 1998, metallic greeen.............$25

VMC99012 Renault Espace, white.......$25

VMC99013 Mercedes M320 4x4, dark metal blue.............$25

VMC99014 Mitsubishi Pajero Evolution Short, light metal gray.............$25

VMC99015 Jaguar XK8 Open Convertible, titanium.............$25

VMC99016 Peugeot Partner Combi Space, gris quartz.............$25

VMC99017 Porsche 996 Open Convertible 1998 Zenith, metallic blue.............$25

VMC99018 Chevrolet Corvette Coupe w/ Open Roof, red.............$25

VMC99019 Mitsubishi Lancer Evo.VI 1999, white.............$25

VMC99020 Renault Clio 1998, vert epicéa.............$25

VMC99021 Renault Laguna Break with Mistral Surfboard, white.............$25

VMC99022 Porsche 996 Carrera 3.4 1998, black.............$25

VMC99023 Toyota Land Cruiser long wheelbase, green & silver.............$25

VMC99024 Citroën Berlingo Multispace Open Roof, leu Balmoral $25

VMC99025 Mercedes S600L, brilliant silver.............$25

VMC99026 Mitsubishi Spacester 1998, Scandinavia blue.............$25

Vitesse City

The City collection is the latest offering from Vitesse, featuring commercial and street vehicles based on the Volkswagen 1200, Bulli and Combi, and others.

CT001 Volkswagen 1200 "Mexico City Taxi".............$25

CT003 Volkswagen 1200 "Rio De Janeiro Taxi $25

CV001B 1955 Volkswagen Bulli, turquoise and white $25

CV001C 1955 Volkswagen Bulli, red and white $25

CV002A 1955 Volkswagen Combi, red and black $25

CV002C 1955 Volkswagen Combi, yellow and white.............$25

City Classic Commercials

CCC99001 Renault 4 F4 Van "PTT" (French Post).............$25

CCC99002 Morris LD150 Evening Standard $25

CCC99003 Renault Estafette "Aspro" Tour De France $25

CCC99004 Volkswagen Bulli "LUFTHANSA" $25

City Modern Commercials

CMC99001 Peugeot Partner Electrique "LA POSTE" $25

CMC99002 Renault Kangoo DHL $25

CMC99003 Citroën Berlingo.............$25

CMC99004 Renault Master.............$25

CITY TAXIS OF THE WORLD

CPC99001 Renault 5 Police De Paris.............$25

CPC99002 Chevrolet Nomad "STATE HIGHWAY PATROL" $25

CPC99003 Renault Laguna Politie Amsterdam $25

CPC99004 Opel GT Polizei $25

CPC99005 Morris LD150 Metropolitan Police Control.............$25

City Police Cars

CTW99001 Mercedes 170V "Taxibal" Berlin 1952.............$25

CTW99002 Mercedes 220SE Taxi Singapore $25

CTW99003 Chrysler Windsor Taxi Cuba.............$25

CTW99004 Renault Scenic Taxi Paris ...$25

CTW99005 Volkswagen Beetle "British Car Hire" Berlin 1947.............$25

City Lorries

CL001A Opel Blitz 3.5 ton Cargo HIGH CANVAS COVERED TRUCK blue....$25

CL001B Opel Blitz 3.5 ton Cargo LOW CANVAS COVERED TRUCK, dark green & black.............$25

CL001C Opel Blitz 3.5 ton Open TRANSPORT TRUCK black.............$25

City Police Cars

CP001 Volkswagen Bulli Polizei $25

CP002 Renault Estafette French Police.....$25

CP003 Jaguar MkII Police $25

CP004 Chrysler Windsor New York Police USA $25

CP005 Mercedes 220SE Polizei $25

CP006 Peugeot 404 French Police.......$25

CP007 Renault Estafette "GENDARMERIE".$25

City Fire Brigade Cars

CS001 Jeep Willys Fire Brigade "Pompiers De Rethel" $25

CS002 Jeep WILYS Fire Brigade "Pompiers Aeroport De Paris" $25

CS003 Renault Estafette "Pompiers Sdis Doubs" $25

CS004 Renault Estafette Ambulance "Pompiers De Limoges" $25

CS005 Mercedes 220SE "DORTMUND BERUFSFEUERWEHR".............$25

CS006 Volkswagen Kubelwagen "FRANKFURT FEUERWEHR" $25

CS007 Renault 4L "Pompiers De Paris" ...$25

CS008 Jeep Amphibian Fire Brigade "Pompiers D' ANGERS" $25

CS009 Renault Prairie Pompier "LES TROIS EPIS".............$25

CS010 Opel Blitz 3.5 ton "DUSSELDORF FEURWEHR" $25

City Taxis of the World

CT007 Mercedes 220SE Taxi $25

CT008 Renault COLORALE Taxi "SAHARA DESERT" $25

CT009 Chrysler WINSOR "DOLMUS" Taxi ISTAMBUL $25

CT010 Mercedes 220SE Taxi CAIRO ...$25

CT011A Mercedes 220SE Taxi MADRID..$25

CT011B Mercedes 220SE Taxi BARCELONA.............$25

CT012A Peugeot 404 Taxi "G7" Paris ..$25

CT012B Peugeot 404 Taxi PARISIEN $25

CT013 Peugeot 404 Taxi CASABLANCA..$25

CT014 Peugeot 404 Taxi BUENOS AIRES.$25

CT015 Mercedes 220SE Taxi COPENHAGEN.............$25

CT016 Peugeot 404 Taxi SAIGON $25

CT017 Peugeot 404 Taxi NAIROBI $25

CT018 Mercedes 220SE Taxi ATHENS $25

CT019 Peugeot 404 Taxi HONG KONG $25

City Commercial Vans

CV017 Volkswagen Bulli DEUTSCHE BUNDESPOST $25

CV018 Volkswagen Bulli POSTES SUISSES $25

CV019 Renault Estafette PTT (French Post) ..$25

CV020 Renault Estafette POSTES BELGES $25

CV021 Morris LD150 ROYAL MAIL $25

CV022 Morris LD150 POST OFFICE TELEPHONES $25

CV023 Volkswagen Bulli "CARLSBERG" .$25

CV024 Volkswagen Bulli "PAULANER" ...$25

CV025 Renault Estafette "KRONENBOURG" $25

CV026 Renault Estafette "HOEGAARDEN" $25

CV027 Morris LD150 "WHITBREAD" $25

CV028 Morris LD150 "McEWAN'S" $25

CV029 Renault Estafette MICHELIN $25

CV030 Renault Estafette Firestone $25

Vitesse Onyx

Onyx is a line of race cars offered by Vitesse of Portugal. All Onyx models are currently available.

Onyx Le Mans

XLM99001 NISSAN R390 GT1 "CLARION" nº30 5th LE MANS 1998 ....$25

XLM99002 NISSAN R390 GT1 "ZEXEL" nº31 6th LE MANS 1998 ....$25

XLM99003 NISSAN R390 GT1 "CALSONIC" nº32 3rd LE MANS 98 ....$25

XLM99004 NISSAN R390 GT1 "JOMO NUMBER" 10th LM 1998 ....$25

XLM99005 Toyota GT-ONE "ESSO" nº27 9th LE MANS 1998 ....$25

XLM99006 Toyota GT-ONE "ZENT" nº 28 LE MANS 1998 ....$25

XLM99007 Toyota GT-ONE "VENTURE SAFENET" LE MANS 1998 ....$25

XLM99008 Porsche GT1 98 "MOBIL" nº25 2nd LE MANS 1998 ....$25

XLM99009 Porsche GT1 98 "MOBIL" nº26 winner LE MANS 1998 ....$25

XLM99010 Porsche GT1 98 ZAKSPEED "JEVER" green SILVERSTONE 98 ......$25

XLM99011 Porsche GT1 98 ZAKSPEED "JEVER" (white) SILVERSONE 98 ......$25

XLM99012 Porsche GT1 98 "MOBIL" TEST VERSIONS (Carbon brown) $25

XLM99013 Porsche GT1 98 Roadcar white $25

XLM99014 NISSAN R390 GT1 Roadcar metallic blue..........................$25

XLM99015 Toyota GT-ONE Roadcar red $25

Onyx Touring Cars

XTC99001 VOLVO S40 RYDELL-RICHARDS winner BATHURST 1000 1998 ......$25

XTC99002 NISSAN PRIMERA "NISMO" KASIKAM ASIAN CHAMPIONSHIP 98 ....$25

XTC99003 Honda ACCORD "CHRISTY'S" M.PIGOLO ITALIAN 98 ....$25

XTC99004 VAUXHALL VECTRA "MASTERFIT" BATHURST 98 ....$25

XTC99005 Renault Laguna NESCAFE FUJITSU PLATO BTCC 1999 ....$25

XTC99006 Renault Laguna NESCAFE FUJITSU BOUILLON BTCC 1999 ....$25

XTC99007 VOLVO S40 R.RYDELL BTCC 1999 ....$25

XTC99008 VOLVO S40 V. RADERMECKER BTCC 1999 ....$25

XTC99010 NISSAN PRIMERA L.AIELLO BTCC 1999 ....$25

XTC99011 NISSAN PRIMERA D.LESLIE BTCC 1999 ....$25

XTC99012 VAUXHALL VECTRA Y.MULLER BTCC 1999 ....$25

XTC99013 VAUXHALL VECTRA J.CLELAND BTCC 1999 ....$25

XTC99014 HOLDEN VECTRA MURPHYINGALL BATHURST 1000 1998 .....$25

Onyx Club

XCL99001 Porsche 911GT2 "FRENCH FLAG" JARRIER French Champ 98 ....$25

XCL99002 Porsche 911GT2 "FINA BASTOS" 24h. ZOLDER 98 ....$25

XCL99003 Renault Spider "GAULOISES" SERVIA Spider Eurocup 98 ....$25

XCL99004 Renault Spider "SWAN" J.PLATO winner British Spider 97 ....$25

XCL99005 Renault Spider "TESSITURA" A.Belicchi Eurocup Champ 98 ....$25

XCL99006 Renault Megane CUP CAMPANI Italian Champion 98 ....$25

XCL99007 Renault Megane CUP MAGALHAES Portugal Champion 98..........$25

XCL99008 Renault Megane CUP "MAGIC" KANBER French Champ 98 ....$25

XCL99009 Renault CLIO SPORT 24v RoadCar Salon De Paris 98 ....$25

XCL99010 Renault CLIO SPORT 24v CUP PRESENTATION Yellow $25

XCL99011 Porsche 996 SUPERCUP "WALKER MONROE" HUISMAN 1st 98 ...$25

XCL99012 Porsche 996 PIRELLI SUPERCUP "VOSS" S.ORTELLI 1998 ....$25

XCL99013 Porsche 996 PIRELLI SUPERCUP "UPS" M.BASSENG 1998.............$25

XCL99014 Renault Megane Coupe BREITEX ICKX 24H. SPA 98 ....$25

Onyx Formula

XFC99001 Dallara F398 F3 "FINA" D.SAELENS FRENCH F3 Champion 99 ....$25

XFC99002 Dallara F398 F3 "TOBI" P.DUMBRECK winner MACAU GP 98 ....$25

XFC99003 Dallara F398 F3 "KWIK FIT" HABERFELD British F3 Champ 98 ....$25

XFC99004 Dallara F398 F3 "AROHIPEL" LEINDERS German F3 Champ 98 ...$25

XFC99005 Dallara F398 F3 "PINK" CREVELS ITALIAN F3 CHAMPION 98 .....$25

XFC99006 Dallara F398 F3 "MANITOU" O.TERRIEN 98 ....$25

Onyx Touring Cars

XT033 Peugeot 406 "TOTAL" P.WATTS BTCC 1996 ....$25

XT034 Peugeot 406 "TOTAL" T. HARVEY BTCC 1996 ....$25

XT035 Peugeot 406 "HASSERODER" L. AIELLO STW CUP 1996 ....$25

XT036 Peugeot 406 "HASSERODER" H. HEGER STW CUP 1996 ....$25

XT037 Peugeot 406 E. BACHELART BELGIAN PROCAR 1996 ....$25

XT038 Peugeot 406 FACTORY TEST CAR1996 ....$25

XT041 Honda Accord D. LESLIE BTCC 1996 ....$25

XT042 Honda Accord J. KAYE BTCC 1996 ....$25

XT043 Honda Accord "HART" P. CUNNINGHAM North American Touring Car Championship 1997 ....$25

XT044 Honda Accord "LABATT BLUE" N. CROMPTON North American Touring Car Championship 1997.............$25

XT045 Honda Accord "STELLA ARTOIS" T. TASSIN Belgian ProCar 1997 ....$25

XT046 Renault Laguna WILLIAMS A. MENU BTCC CHAMPION 1997 ....$25

XT047 Renault Laguna WILLIAMS J. PLATO BTCC 1997 ....$25

XT048 Peugeot 406 "ESSO ULTRON" T. HARVEY BTCC 1997 ....$25

XT049 Peugeot 406 "ESSO ULTRON" J. WATTS BTCC 1997 ....$25

XT050 Peugeot 406 "HASSERODER" L. AIELLO STW CUP CHAMPION 1997 ....$25

XT051 Peugeot 406 "HASSERODER" J. Van OMMEN STW CUP 1997 ....$25

XT052 Peugeot 406 V. RADERMACKER BELGIAN PROCAR 1997 ....$25

XT053 Honda Accord J. THOMPSON BTCC1997 ....$25

XT054 Honda Accord G. TARQUINI BTCC 1997 ....$25

XT055 Honda Accord "DHL" H. HEGER STW CUP 1997 ....$25

XT057 Nissan Primera "VODAPHONE" D. LESLIE BTCC 1997 ....$25

XT058 Nissan Primera "VODAPHONE" A. REID BTCC 1997 ....$25

XT059 Nissan Primera "CASTROL-KAGERRTL" STW CUP 1997 ....$25

XT061 Vauxhall Vectra J. CLELAND BTCC 1997 ....$25

XT062 Vauxhall Vectra D. WARWICK BTCC 1997 ....$25

XT063 Opel Vectra "PAULANER" M. REUTER STW CUP 1997 ....$25

XT064 Opel Vectra "PAULANER" A. BURGSTALLER STW CUP 1997 ....$25

XT065 Opel Vectra "PROMARKT" K. THIIM STW CUP 1997.................$25

XT066 Opel Vectra "PROMARKT" U. ALZEN STW CUP 1997.................$25

XT067 Volvo S40 R. RYDELL BTC 1997.$25

XT068 Volvo S40 K. BURT 1997.........$25

XT070 Peugeot 406 "TOTAL2 L. BROOKES BTCC 1997.........................$25

XT082 Vauxhall Vectra J. CLELAND BTCC 1997.................................$25

XT083 Vauxhall Vectra D. WARWICK BTCC 1997.................................$25

XT084 Renault Laguna "ANZ" BATHURST AUSTRALIA 1997.....................$25

XT085 Opel Vectra "EMMA" BATHURST AUSTRALIA 1997.....................$25

XT086 Opel Vectra "QUANTAS" P. BROOKS BATHURST AUSTRALIA 1997.................................$25

XT087 Renault Laguna "NESCAFE" A. MENU BTCC 1997.....................$25

XT088 Renault Laguna "NESCAFE" J. PLATO BTCC 1997.........................$25

XT089 Peugeot 406 "ESSO ULTRON" T. HARVEY BTCC 1998.................$25

XT090 Peugeot 406 "ESSO ULTRON" P. RADISH BTCC 1998.................$25

XT091 Peugeot 406 "HASSERODER" L. AIELLO STW CUP 1998.................$25

XT092 Peugeot 406 "HASSERODER" J. Van OMMEN STW CUP 1998.............$25

XT093 Vauxhall Vectra "MASTERFIT" D. WARWICK BTCC 1998.............$25

XT094 Vauxhall Vectra "MASTERFIT" J. CLELAND BTCC 1998.............$25

XT099 Nissan Primera "VODAPHONE" D. LESLIE BTCC 1998.................$25

XT100 Nissan Primera "VODAPHONE" A. REID BTCC 1998.....................$25

XT101 Nissan Primera "ROSBERG TEAM" M. KRUMM STW 1998.................$25

XT102 Nissan Primera "ROSBERG TEAM" R. ASCH STW 1998.....................$25

XT103 Honda Accord "KALIBER" J. THOMPSON BTCC 1998.................$25

XT104 Honda Accord "KALIBER" P. KOX BTCC 1998.........................$25

XT105 Honda Accord "JAS" G. TARQUINI STW CUP 1998.....................$25

XT106 Honda Accord "JAS" T. KRISTENSEN STW CUP 1998.....................$25

XT107 Honda Accord "HARIBO" R. COLCIAGO ITALIA 1997.................$25

XT109 Alfa Romeo 156 "TV SPIELFILM" S. MODENA STW CUP 1998..........$25

XT110 Alfa Romeo 156 "TV SPIELFILM" N. LARINI STW CUP 1998.............$25

XT113 Volvo S40 R. RYDELL BTCC 1998.................................$25

XT114 Volvo S40 G. MORBIDELLI BTCC 1998.................................$25

XT121 Renault Laguna "D. C. COOK" T. RUSTAD BTCC 1998.................$25

XT122 Nissan Primera "100+ALLOW WHEELS" M. NEAL BTCC 1998....$25

XT123 Alfa Romeo 156 "SELENIA" N. LARINI BTCC 1998.....................$25

XT124 Alfa Romeo 156 "SELENIA" F. GIOVINARDI BTCC 1998.................$25

XT125 Vauxhall Vectra "CONTROLLED" M. LEMMER BTCC 1998.................$25

XT126 Honda Accord "CASTROL GRUNDIG" R. MOEN BTCC 1998.................$25

XT127 Honda Accord "ROCK-IT CARGO" R. GRAVETT BTCC 1998.................$25

XT128 Volvo S40 "Volvo SWEDEN" J. NILSON, Swedish Touring Car Champ. 1998.................................$25

XT129 Peugeot 406 "EFSA" C. BUENO, South American Touring cars Championship 1998.........................$25

XT130 Chevrolet Vectra "INI" A. GUERRA, South American Touring cars Championship 1998.........................$25

Vitesse Quartzo

Chevrolet Lumina, #14 Terry LeBonte "Kelloggs"...............................$25

Chevrolet Lumina, #41 Joe Nemechek, "Meineke"............................$25

1956 Ford Fairlane, NY Police Radar Unit.................................$50

Ford, #27 Bill Elliott, "McDonald's"........$25

Pontiac Grand Prix, #40 Frankie Kerr, "Dirt Devil"...............................$25

Vitesse Quartzo — Classic Le Mans

QLM99001 Porsche 962C LONG "ROTHMANS" winner Le Mans 86...........$25

QLM99002 Porsche 962C LONG "FORTUNA" 2nd Le Mans 86.................$25

QLM99003 Peugeot 905 n°5 BALDI-ALLIOT-JABOUILLE Le Mans 1991.............$25

QLM99004 Peugeot 905 n°6 ROSBERG-DALMAS-RAPHANEL LM91...........$25

QLM99005 Porsche 956 SHORT "DANONE" 4th Le Mans 1985......$25

QLM99006 Porsche 962C SHORT "ALPHA" 3rd Le Mans 1990.................$25

QLM99007 Porsche 962C LONG ROTHMANS winner Le Mans 1987........$25

QLM99008 Porsche 962C LONG "PRIMAGAZ" 2nd Le Mans 1987...$25

QLM99009 Peugeot 905 n°1winner Le Mans1992.........................$25

QLM99010 Peugeot 905 n°2 BALDI-ALLIOT-JABOUILLE 3rd LM 1992.................$25

QLM99011 Porsche 962C SHORT "RIZLA" Le Mans 1990.....................$25

QLM99012 Porsche 962C SHORT "FUJI GOLF" Le Mans 1990.................$25

Quartzo — Classic Formula 1

QFC99001 Brabham Repco BT24 J.RINDT MONACO GP 1968.................$25

QFC99002 Brabham Repco BT24 J.BRABHAM BELGIAN GP 1967.............$25

QFC99003 Ferrari 156 W.VON TRIPS winner British GP 1961.....................$25

QFC99004 Ferrari 156 P.HILL winner BELGIAN GP 1961.....................$25

QFC99005 Lotus 72E "JPS"R.PETERSON SWEDISH GP 1975.................$25

QFC99006 Lotus 72E "JPS"J.ICKX BELGIAN GP 1975.........................$25

QFC99007 Cooper Climax T51 O.GENDEBIEN BELGIAN GP 1960.............$25

QFC99008 Cooper Climax T51 T.BROOKS MONACO GP 1960.................$25

QFC99009 Honda RA272 R.GINTHER FRENCH GP 1965.....................$25

QFC99010 Honda RA272 R.BUCKNUM FRENCH GP 1965.....................$25

QFC99011 Lotus 25 J.CLARK winner British GP 1963.........................$25

QFC99012 Lotus 25 T.TAYLOR MONACO GP 1963.................................$25

QFC99013 Ferrari 625 M.HAWTHORN ITALIAN GP 1954.....................$25

QFC99014 Ferrari 625 G.FARINA ARGENTINA GP 1950.................$25

QFC99015 March 701 H.PESCAROLO SOUTH AFRICA GP 1971.............$25

QFC99016 March 701 H.HAHNE GERMAN GP 1970.........................$25

QFC99017 Ferrari 312 J.SURTEES winner BELGIAN GP 1966.................$25

QFC99018 Ferrari 312 M.PARKES FRENCH GP 1966.....................$25

QFC99019 Ferrari 375 A.ASCARI winner GERMAN GP 1951.................$25

QFC99020 Ferrari 375 L.ROSIER winner ALBI GP 1951.........................$25

QFC99021 Lotus 78 JPS R.PETERSON USA WEST GP 1978.....................$25

QFC99022 Matra MS80 J.STEWART MONACO GP 1969.................$25

QFC99023 Tyrrell 001 P.REVSON USA WATKINS GLEN GP 1971..........$25

QFC99024 Tyrrell P34 SIX-WHEELS R.PETERSON BELGIAN GP 1977.................................$25

QFC99025 Cooper Ferrari T51 G.MUNARON British GP 1960.....$25

QFC99026 Cooper Ferrari T51 G.CABIANCA ITALIAN GP 1960.................$25

QFC99027 Ferrari 312T2 N.LAUDA winner DUTCH GP 1977.....................$25

QFC99028 Ferrari 312T2 G.VILLENEUVE CANADIAN GP 1977.................$25

QFC99029 Lotus Ford 49B D.ATWOOD MONACO GP 1969.................$25

QFC99030 Renault RS01 J-P.JABOUILLE MONACO GP 1978.................$25

QFC99031 Ferrari 312T3 J.SCHECKTER BRAZILIAN GP 1979.................$25

QFC99032 Ferrari 312T3 G.VILLENEUVE BRAZILIAN GP 1979.................$25

QFC99033 March 711 "MOTUL" H.PESCAROLO British GP 1971.....$25

QFC99034 March 711 "STP" R.PETERSON ITALIAN GP 1971.....................$25

QFC99035 Ferrari 246 DINO L.MUSSO ARGENTINA GP 1958 .... $25

QFC99036 Ferrari 246 DINO P.COLLINS winner British GP 1958 .... $25

Quartzo — The World Champions Collection

QWC99008 Ferrari 500F2 ALBERTO ASCARI World Champion 1952 .... $25

QWC99009 Brabham Repco BT24 Dennis HULME World Champion 67 .... $25

QWC99010 Lotus Ford 72C+B145 Jochen RINDT World Champion 1970 .... $25

QWC99011 Ferrari 156 Phil HILL World Champion 1961 .... $25

QWC99012 WILLIAMS Renault FW14B N.MANSELL World Champion 92 .... $25

Quartzo — Classic Formula 1

Q4001 Lotus 49 JIM CLARK 1st DUTCH GP 1967 .... $25

Q4002 Lotus 49 GRAHAM HILL DUTCH GP 1967 .... $25

Q4009 Lotus 49B "GOLD LEAF" MARIO ANDRETTI USA GP 68 .... $25

Q4011 Lotus 49B "GOLD LEAF" J. RINDT SOUTH AFRICA GP 69 .... $25

Q4013 Lotus 49B "ROB WALKER" JO SIFFERT S. AFRICA GP 69 .... $25

Q4017 MATRAMS80 J. STEWART MONACO GP 69 .... $25

Q4019 Lotus 72 "GOLD LEAF" J. RINDT winner GERMAN GP 1970 .... $25

Q4020 Lotus 72 "GOLD LEAF" J. MILES GERMAN GP 1970 .... $25

Q4021 Lotus 72 "BROOK BOND OXO" G. HILL Canadian GP 1970 .... $25

Q4022 Lotus 72D "JPS" E. FITTIPALDI British GP 72 .... $25

Q4024 Lotus 72D "LUCKY STRIKE" D. CHARLTON British GP 1972 .... $25

Q4025 Lotus 72D "JPS" R. PETERSON winner ITALIAN GP 1972 .... $25

Q4026 Lotus 72D "JPS"E. FITTIPALDI ITALIAN GP 1972 .... $25

Q4027 Tyrrell P34 6-WHEELS SPANISH GP 76 P. DEPAILLER $25

Q4032 Ferrari 312T ITALIAN GP75 winner C. REGAZZONI $25

Q4033 Renault RE30B winner BRAZILIAN GP 1982 Alain PROST $25

Q4035 Tyrrell 001 "BLADE NOSE" USA GP 70 J. STEWART.......................... $25

Q4036 Tyrrell 001 "BLADE NOSE" MONACO GP 71 winner J. STEWART $25

Q4037 Tyrrell 002 "BLADE NOSE" MONACO GP 71 F. CEVERT $25

Q4040 Tyrrell P34 6-WHEELS "CITY BANK" MONACO GP 77 R. PETERSON...$25

Q4041 Tyrrell P34 6-WHEELS "CITY BANK" MONACO GP 77 P. DEPAILLER $25

Q4042 Brabham Repco BT24 J. BRABHAM 1st CANADIAN GP 1967 .... $25

Q4043 Brabham Repco BT24 D. HULME 1st GERMAN GP 1967 .... $25

Q4044 Lotus 72 "GOLD LEAF" E. FITTIPALDI British GP 1971 .... $25

Q4045 Lotus 72 "GOLD LEAF" R. WISELL GERMAN GP 1971 .... $25

Q4046 Tyrrell 003 "BUFF NOSE" British GP 71 winner J. STEWART $25

Q4047 Tyrrell 002 "BUFF NOSE" USA GP 71 winner F. CEVERT...................... $25

Q4048 Renault RS01 RS01/01 British GP 1977 J-P. JABOUILLE $25

Q4049 Renault RS01 RS01/01 DUTCH GP 1977 J-P. JABOUILLE $25

Q4050 Renault RS01 RS01/02 USA GP 1978 J-P. JABOUILLE $25

Q4051 Renault RS01 RS01/02 ARGENTINA GP 1979 R. ARNOUX $25

Q4061 Renault RS11 J-P. JABOUILLE 1st FRENCH GP 1979 .... $25

Q4062 Renault RS12 R. ARNOUX USA GP 1979 .... $25

Q4065 Tyrrell 004 "BUFF NOSE" FRENCH GP 72 P. DEPAILLER...................... $25

Q4066 Tyrrell 004 "LUCKY STRIKE" SOUTH AFRICAN GP 73 E. KEIZAN $25

Q4068 Ferrari 312T2 BELGIAN GP 1976 C. REGAZZONI $25

Q4069 Lotus 72E R. PETERSON MONACO GP 1974 .... $25

Q4070 Lotus 72E J.ICKX 74 GERMAN GP 1974 .... $25

Q4083 Ferrari 312T2 N. LAUDA 1st DUTCH GP 1977 .... $25

Q4084 Ferrari 312T2 C.REUTEMANN 1st BAZILIAN GP 1977 .... $25

Q4085 Ferrari 312T2 78 C. REUTEMANN 1st BRAZILIAN GP 1978................ $25

Q4086 Ferrari 312T2 78 G. VILLENEUVE CANADIAN GP 1979 .... $25

Q4087 Lotus 78 winner USA GP 1977 M. ANDRETTI $25

Q4088 Lotus 78 winner BELGIUM GP 1977 G. NILSSON.............................. $25

Q4091 Lotus 78 "IMPERIAL" G. NILSSON JAPANESE GP 1977 .... $25

Q4092 Lotus 78 H. REBAQUE GERMAN GP 1978 .... $25

Q4093 Honda RA272 winner MEXICAN GP 1965 R. GINTHER $25

Q4094 Honda RA272 MEXICAN GP 1965 R.BUCKNUM....................... $25

Q4095 Ferrari 312T3 C. REUTEMANN 1st British GP 1978 .... $25

Q4096 Ferrari 312T3 G. VILLENEUVE 1st CANADIAN GP 1978 .... $25

Q4097 Ferrari 312T3 G. VILLENEUVE USA-WEST GP 1978 .... $25

Q4098 Ferrari 312T3 C.REUTEMANN MONACO GP 1978 .... $25

Q4099 Cooper Climax T51 winner British GP 1959 J.BRABHAM.................. $25

Q4100 Cooper Climax T51 "WALKER TEAM" S. MOSS 1st ITALIAN GP 1959 .... $25

Q4101 Cooper Climax T51 winner USA GP 1959 B.McLAREN $25

Q4102 March 701 "STP" FRENCH GP 1970 C. AMON.......................... $25

Q4103 March 701 "STP" GERMAN GP 1970 J. SIFFERT............................ $25

Q4104 March 701 "STP" SPANISH GP 1970 M. ANDRETTI.......................... $25

Q4105 March 701 "ELF" winner SPANISH GP 1970 J. STEWART................. $25

Q4106 March 701 "ELF" J. SERVOZ-GAVIN SPANISH GP 1970 .... $25

Q4107 March 701 R. PETERSON SPANISH GP 1970......................... $25

Q4108 Porsche 804 D. GURNEY winner FRENCH GP 1962 .... $25

Q4109 Porsche 804 BONNIER FRENCH GP 1962 .... $25

Q4115 Ferrari 375 A. ASCARI 1st SPANISH GP 1950 .... $25

Q4116 Ferrari 375 D. SERAFINI ITALIAN GP 1950 .... $25

Q4117 Ferrari 375 A. ASCARI 1st ITALIAN GP 1951 .... $25

Q4118 Ferrari 375 L. VILLORESI ITALIAN GP 1951 .... $25

Q4119 Ferrari 375 P. TARUFFI SWISS GP 1951 .... $25

Q4120 March 711 R. PETERSON SOUTH AFRICAN GP 1951 .... $25

Q4121 March 711 A. SOLER ROIG FRENCH GP 1971 .... $25

Q4122 March 711 N. LAUDA AUSTRIAN GP 1971 (first N. LAUDA F1 race)... $25

Q4124 Ferrari 500F2 winner SWISS GP 1952 P. TARUFFI $25

Q4125 Ferrari 500F2 winner EUROPE GP 1952 A. ASCARI........................... $25

Q4128 Ferrari 500F2 winner GERMAN GP 1953 G. FARINA............................ $25

Q4129 Ferrari 500F2 winner FRENCH GP 1953 M. HAWTHORN $25

Q4130 Cooper Climax T51 M. TRINTIGNANT MONACO GP 1959......... $25

Q4131 Cooper Climax T51 R. SALVADORI GERMAN GP 1959 .... $25

Q4139 Lotus 25 CLARK J. CLARK 1st British GP 1963........................... $25

Q4140 Lotus 25 T. TAYLOR MONACO GP 1963 .... $25

Q4151 Lotus 33 J. CLARK 1st British GP 1965 .... $25

Q4152 Lotus 33 M. SPENCE British GP 1965 .... $25

Q4153 Ferrari 156 P. HILL ITALIAN GP 1961 .... $25

Q4154 Ferrari 156 W. VN TRIPS ITALIAN GP 1961 .... $25

Q4155 Ferrari 156 G. BAGHETI ITALIAN GP 1961 .... $25

Q4156 Ferrari 156 R. GINTHER ITALIAN GP 1961 .... $25

Q4157 Ferrari 625 A. ASCARI ITALIAN GP 1954 ....$25

Q4158 Ferrari 625 M. TRINTIGNANT winner MONACO GP 1955 ....$25

Q4159 Ferrari 126CK G. VILLENEUVE 1st SPANISH GP 1981 ....$25

Q4160 Ferrari 126CK D. PIRONI MONACO GP 1981 ....$25

Q4161 Renault RE20/24 R. ARNOUX MONACO GP 1980 ....$25

Q4162 Renault RE20/22 J-P. JABOUILLE ARGENTINA GP 1980 ....$25

Q4163 Ferrari 500F2 R. FISHER SWISS GP 1952 ....$25

Q4164 Ferrari 500F2 L. ROSIER British GP 1953 ....$25

Q4165 Ferrari 156 P. HILL MONACO GP 1962 ....$25

Q4166 Ferrari 156 W. MAIRESSE MONACO GP 1962 ....$25

Q4167 Ferrari 312T3 G. VILLENEUVE ITALIAN GP 1978 ....$25

Q4168 Ferrari 312T3 C. REUTEMANN 1st USA (EAST) GP 1978 ....$25

Q4169 Ferrari 375 F. GONZALES ITALIAN GP 1951 ....$25

Q4170 Ferrari 500F2 J. SWATERS 1st AVUS GP 1953 ....$25

Vitesse Skid

According to the Vitesse website at www.vitessegroup.com, SKID is a completely new brand launched in 1999, fully dedicated to reproducing Rallye and Rallye RAID cars.

Skid Rally Classic

SKC99001 Fiat Cinquecento Rallye "NILO DEL AQUILA" 93 J.ALESI .$25

SKC99002 Lancia Stratos "OLIO Fiat" F.TABATON SANREMO 80 .....$25

SKC99003 Porsche 904GTS "BUCHETLINGE" Tour De France 64 ....$25

SKC99004 Peugeot 404 "NOWICKICLIFF" winner SAFARI 1968 ......$25

SKC99005 Opel Ascona "DENIM" ARKENTIS-JAVERIS SAN MARINO 82 ....$25

SKC99006 Fiat 124 Abarth "MIKKOLATODT" MONTECARLO 1975 ...$25

SKC99007 Opel Kadett Fastback 1900 M-C.BEAUMONT TdC 69 ....$25

SKC99008 Mini Cooper "British MOTOR HERITAGE" MONTECARLO 97 ....$25

SKC99009 Renault 5 Turbo "GITANES" SABY-TILBER TdC 1980...........$25

SKC99010 Lancia StratoS "L'AUTOMOBILE" DARNICHE winner TdC 81...$25

Skid Montecarlo Series

SMC007 Lancia Delta Integral 16v "Auriol-OCCELLI" winner 92 ....$25

SMC008 Porsche 911S WALDEGAARD-HELMER winner 1969 .$25

SMC009 Opel Ascona 400 ROTHMANS ROHRL winner 1982.....$25

Skid Special Edition "World Champion"

SKW99001 Mitsubishi Lancer Evo.V T.Makkinen WORLD CHAMPION 98 ....$25

Skid Rally Modern

SKM99001 Peugeot 206WRC PRESENTATION 1998, silver gray $25

SKM99002 Toyota Corolla WRC "TEIN" MALAYSIA Rally 98 ....$25

SKM99003 Mitsubishi Lancer Evo.V R.Burns winner Rally GB 98.......$25

SKM99004 Ford Escort WRC "GAZ PROM" NIKONENKO ACROPOLIS 98......$25

SKM99005 Renault Megane Maxi "Renault BELGIQUE" PRINCEN 98 ....$25

SKM99006 Peugeot 306 Maxi "SWITZERLAND" Rallye DU VALAIS 98 ....$25

SKM99007 Seat Cordoba WRC ROVENPERA FINLAND Rally 1998 ....$25

SKM99008 Toyota Corolla WRC "ASG" M.GRONHOLM FINLAND 98 ...$25

SKM99009 Mitsubishi Lancer Evo.V "Winfield" Makkinen AUST.98 ..$25

SKM99010 Citroën XSARA KIT Car "PRIMAGAZ"TROPHEE ANDROS 99 ....$25

SKM99011 Mitsubishi Carisma Evo.IV "SONY" KUZAS Portugal 98 ....$25

SKM99012 Peugeot 206 WRC "ESSO" SALON De Paris 1998 ....$25

SKM99013 Toyota Corolla WRC "MOBIL 1" ZIVAS ACROPOLIS 98...........$25

SKM99014 Renault Megane Maxi "TURKEY" N.AVCI 1998 ....$25

SKM99015 Mitsubishi L200 GALP SOUSA GRANADA-DAKAR 1999.............$25

SKM99016 Mitsubishi L200 SMULEVICI GRANADA-DAKAR 1999.........$25

SKM99017 Ford Escort WRC "TEXACO" PAPADIMITROU ACROP.97 ....$25

SKM99018 Seat Cordoba WRC M.DUEZ Rallye SANREMO 1998 ....$25

SKM99019 Ford Focus WRC MARTINI C.McRAE MONTECARLO 1999..$25

SKM99020 Toyota Corolla WRC "SHELL" HAGSTROM DEFA Rally 98 ....$25

SKM99021 Ford Escort WRC "VALVOLINE" KIRKOS ACROPOLIS 98 ..$25

SKM99022 Citroën XSARA KIT Car J.PURAS Spain Rally 98 ....$25

SKM99023 Mitsubishi Pajero EVO "PIAA" FONTENAY DAKAR 99 .$25

SKM99024 Mitsubishi Pajero EVO "MITSU OIL" SHINUZOKA DAKAR 99 ....$25

SKM99025 Mitsubishi Pajero EVO "PLAYSTATION" KLEINSCHMIDT 99 ....$25

SKM99026 Peugeot 206WRC G.PANIZZI TOUR De CORSE 1999 ....$25

SKM99027 Toyota Corolla WRC C.Sainz Rallye MONTECARLO 99 ....$25

SKM99028 Mitsubishi Lancer Evo.V T.Makkinen 1ST MONTECARLO 99 ....$25

SKM99029 Ford Escort WRC "TOSHIBA" A.SCHWARZ GB Rally 1998.......$25

SKM99030 Renault Megane Maxi "LEBANON" J.NASARALLAH 98 .$25

SKM99031 Mitsubishi Pajero EVO "ATAC" STRUGO DAKAR 99....$25

SKM99032 Mitsubishi Pajero EVO "GECO SPORT" QUANDT DAKAR 99 ......$25

SKM99033 Mitsubishi Pajero EVO "INVESCO" CASSEGRAIN DAKAR 99 ....$25

SKM99034 Seat Cordoba P.LIATI Rallye MONTECARLO 99 ....$25

SKM99035 Ford Focus WRC S.JEAN-JOSEPH MONTECARLO 1999.$25

SKM99036 Toyota Corolla WRC D.Auriol MONTECARLO 1999 .$25

SKM99037 Mitsubishi Lancer Evo.V F.Loix MONTECARLO 1999 ....$25

SKM99038 Citroën XSARA KIT Car P.Bugalski TOUR De CORSE 99..............$25

SKM99039 Mitsubishi Pajero EVO 'FPEE' ALPHAND DAKAR 99 ....$25

SKM99040 Mitsubishi Pajero EVO "PICOBELLO" BOXOEH DAKAR 99 ....$25

SKM99053 Toyota Land Cruiser LONG "JVC" WAMBERGUE DAKAR 98 ..$25

Vitesse Victoria

This list of Victoria models has been provided thanks to Alex Antonov of Herndon, Virginia. Victoria is a series of models produced by Vitesse of Portugal. Models are made in China. All models are 1:43 scale and sell for $22–26 US.

R001 Jeep, 1944 Willys closed khaki D-Day version $22–26

R002 Jeep, 1944 Willys open khaki Liberation of Paris.............................$22–26

R003 Jeep, 1945 Willys open khaki Military Police.................................$22–26

R004 Hummer 94 United Nations UN white 2 door covered top.................$24–28

R005 Hummer, 1994 U.S. Army Desert Storm Open All Purpose, brown.$32–36

R006 Hummer, 1994 U.S. Army green 2 door open back All Purpose $22–26

R007 Hummer, 1994 U.S. Army camouflage 4 door All Purpose $22–26

R008 VW, 1945 Beetle Kubelwagen Afrika Korps Open............................$22–26

R009 VW, 1945 Beetle Kubelwagen Wehrmcht Open $22–26

R010 VW, 1945 Beetle Kubelwagen clsd Hitler Yugend $22–26

R011 Mercedes 170V Afrika Korps ..$22–26

R012 Mercedes 170V cabriolimosine Wehrmacht parade $22–26

R013 VW, 1945 Beetle Type82 Wehrmacht $22–26

R014 VW Beetle 82E Afghan Beetle Army tan Coupe $22–26

R015 VW, 1944 Beetle Type92 Wehrmacht charcoal burner $22–26

R016 VW, 1944 Beetle Type92 2dr black tire on Roof $22–26

R017 Jeep, Willys Armoured Car General LeClerc $22–26

R018 Hummer Command Car GulfWar Desert Storm MP $22–26

R019 Opel Blitz 3.5 Ton Troop carrier $22–26

R020 Opel Blitz 3.5 Ton Canvas Covered Truck Afrika Korps $22–26

R021 Opel Blitz 3.5 Ton Canvas Covered Truck..................$22–26

R022 VW Kubelwagen Factory Test Car $22–26

R023 Jeep, 1978 Willys UN Lebanon, white with figures $22–26

R024 Hummer Pickup US camouflag Desert Storm $22–26

R025 Opel Blitz 3.5 Ton Radio HQ Wehrmacht $22–26

R026 Opel Blitz 3.5 Ton Ambulance Afrika Korps $22–26

R027 unknown $22–26

R028 Jeep, US Army, Normandy 1944 Ambulance with figures...........$22–26

R029 Mercedes 170V Wehrmacht with Camouflage $22–26

R030 Hummer open pick-up US NAVY .$22–26

R031 VW Kubelwagen Closed Normandy 1944 with Camouflage $22–26

R032 Jeep GPA Amphibian, U.S. Army..........................$22–26

R033 Jeep GPA Amphibian, U.S. Army, camouflage $22–26

R034 Jeep GPA Amphibian, British ..$22–26

R035 VW Schwimmwagen, open, gray $22–26

R036 VW Schwimmwagen, Afrika Korps $22–26

R037 VW Schwimmwagen, Wehrmacht, top up $22–26

R038 Hummer Ambulance U.S. Army Camouflage $22–26

R039 Hummer Ambulance U.S. Army Desert Storm $22–26

R040 Renault Prairie Command Car French Army $22–26

R041 Renault Prairie Ambulance French Army....................$22–26

R042 Citroën U23 French Army Troop carrier $22–26

R043 Citroën U23 FFI with Camouflage....................$22–26

R044 Citroën U23 Troop Carrier Wehrmacht....................$22–26

R045 VW Cabrio Hebmuller Military Police, no doors..................$22–26

R046 Dodge WC51 Weapons carrier U.S. Army, open..................$22–26

R047 Dodge WC51 Weapons carrier U.S. Army, closed..................$22–26

R048 Dodge 1944 WC52 Weapons carrier Liberation of Paris $22–26

R049 VW Cabrio Hebmuller Military Police, doors $22–26

R050 Chevy, 1944 8A Canvas Truck British Army Normandy..................$22–26

R051 Chevy, 1944 8A Canvas Truck Canadian Army D-Day 1944..........$22–26

R052 Chevy, 1944 8A Troop carrier Truck U.S. Army $22–26

R053 Dodge WC56 Command Car U.S. Army, closed..................$22–26

R054 Dodge WC56 Command Car U.S. Army, open..................$22–26

R055 Dodge 1944 WC56 Command Car U.S. Army D-Day 1944..........$22–26

R056 GMC CCKW353 6x6 Canvas Covered Truck U.S. Army $22–26

R057 GMC CCKW353 6x6 Troop Carrier Truck D-Day 1944..................$22–26

R058 GMC CCKW353 6x6 Canvas Covered Truck U.S Army $22–26

Vitesse — 2-Wheels Series

2-Wheels Racing Bikes

TWR99001 Honda NSR 500 "REPSOL" 1998 M.DOOHAN (world champ 98)..............................$25

TWR99002 Honda NSR 500 "REPSOL" 1998 T.OKADA 1998 ....$25

TWR99003 Honda NSR 500 "REPSOL" 1998 A. CRIVILLE $25

TWR99004 Honda NSR/V2 500 "REPSOL" 1998 S.GIBERNAU $25

TWR99005 Honda NSR 500 "KANEMOTO" 1998 M. BIAGGI $25

TWR99006 Honda NSR 500 "MOVISTAR-PONS" 1998 C.CHECA ...$25

TWR99007 Honda NSR 500 "MOVISTAR-PONS" 1998 J.KOCINSKI .$25

TWR99008 Honda NSR 500 "GRESINO" 1998 A.BARROS ..$25

TWR99009 Honda NSR/V2 500 "SHELL" 1998 J.BORJA.............$25

TWR99010 Honda NSR/V2 500 "SHELL" 1998 G.McCOY........$25

TWR99011 Honda NSR/V2 500 "DEE CEE JEANS" 1998 J.V.D.GOORBERGH $25

TWR99012 Honda NSR/V2 500 "TECMAS ELF" 1998 S.GIMBERT $25

TWR99013 Honda NSR/V2 500 "TEAM MILLAR" 1998 S.SMART $25

TWR99014 Yamaha YZR 500 1998 "TEAM RAINEY" N.ABE $25

TWR99015 Yamaha YZR 500 1998 "TEAM RAINEY" J-M.BAYLE $25

TWR99016 Yamaha YZR 500 1998 "TEAM RAINEY" K.NANBA..............$25

TWR99017 Yamaha YZR 500 1998 "RED BULL" S.CRAFAR.............$25

TWR99018 Yamaha YZR 500 1998 "RED BULL" R.LACONI..............$25

TWR99019 Yamaha YZR 500 1998 "Yamaha RACING" HAGA Japanese GP..............................$25

TWR99020 Honda NSR/V2 5001998 "SHELL" F.TEIXEIRA Spanish GP..............................$25

TWR99021 Yamaha YZR 500 1998 "TEAM RAINEY" CADALORA French GP..............................$25

TWR99022 Honda NSR 500 1998 "MOVISTAR-PONS" LAVILLA German GP..............................$25

TWR99042 Ducati 916 "Ducati" C.FOGARTY SUPERBIKE world cham 98..............................$25

TWR99043 Ducati 916 "Ducati ADVF" T.CORSER SUPERBIKE 98........$25

TWR99044 Ducati 916 "REMUS RACING TEAM" MEKLAU SUPERBIKE 98................$25

TWR99023 Aprilia RSV 250 1998 "Aprilia TEAM" L.CAPIROSSI world camp $25

TWR99024 Aprilia RSV 250 1998 "Aprilia TEAM" T.HARADA........$25

TWR99025 Aprilia RSV 250 1998 "Aprilia TEAM" M.LUCCHI $25

TWR99026 Aprilia RSV 250 1998 "NASTRO AZZURO" V.ROSSI...$25

TWR99027 Aprilia RSV 250 1998 "DOCSHOP RACING" J.FUCHS..............................$25

2-Wheels Street Bikes

TWS99001 Honda NSR V2 RACING TEST BIKE $25

TWS99002 Ducati 996 BIPOSTO, yellow $25

TWS99003 Ducati 996SPS, red....$25

TWS99004 Ducati 748SPS 99, yellow $25

2-Wheels Street Bikes (The Vespa Story Collection)

TWC99001 Vespa "98" 1946, green $25

TWC99002 Vespa 125 1948, light metal gray $25

TWC99003 Vespa 125 1951, light green $25

TWC99004 Vespa 150GS 1955, silver gray $25

TWC99005 Vespa 150GL 1963, off white $25

TWC99006 Vespa 125 1966, light beige $25

Vivid Imaginations (Tyco Canada)

The Vivid Imaginations brand from Tyco Canada surfaced recently with the introduction of an assortment of models based on Gerry Anderson's popular action adventure *Captain Scarlet and the Mysterons*. Several models have been produced based on this children's marionette-based TV series that debuted in 1966. The resurgence in popularity of Captain Scarlet has been bolstered by the reintroduction of another Gerry Anderson TV show called *Thunderbirds*, first broadcast in 1965. Models are available in sets or sold individually. Also offered by Vivid Imaginations are 12" tall action figures.

Captain Scarlet and the Mysterons models and sets

Spectrum Command Team Set includes:
Spectrum Jet Liner.......................$8–10
Angel Interceptor (2 each)...........$8–10

Spectrum Pursuit Vehicle $20–25

Captain Scarlet's Spectrum Car $8–10

Spectrum Cloudbase H.Q. playset $90–110

Voiturette (see SMTS)

Volga

Besides being the name of Russia's most famous river, Volga is also a brand of Russian cars that also go by the name Gaz, to the best of my knowledge. These diecast replicas of this Russian standard automobile are exceptional quality for the price.
Volga 2401 Saloon fire chief $9
Volga 2401 Saloon road safety service $9
Volga 2402 Estate standard..........................$9
Volga 2402 Estate ambulance $12
Volga 2402 Estate airport "follow me".........$12
Volga 2402 Estate closed door $8
Volga 3102 Saloon Rally Car $12
Volga 3102 Saloon fire chief $12
Volga 3102 Saloon with symbols $12
Volga 3102 Saloon happy new year..........$12
Volga Gaz A Tourer, open.......................$12

Volga Gaz 66 Truck $16
Volga Gaz 66 Tanker United Nations $20
Volga Gaz 66 Airlines..............................$20

Walker Model Service

Walthers HO Gauge Catalog features over three pages of 1:87 scale Walker Model Service kits consisting of unpainted cast white metal and styrene, wire and wood details. Models represented are of vintage trucks for $15 to 56 each.

Walldorf

Walldorf is a manufacturer of 1:43 scale white metal kits from the town of Walldorf, Germany, not far from Frankfurt.
1949 Buick Roadmaster $60–90
1977 Cadillac Sedan DeVille $60–90

Welly

Welly Diecast Factory Limited
Flat H.I.
18/F Shield Industrial Centre
84-92 Chai Wan Kok Street
Tsuen Wan, Hong Kong
phone: +852 2416 5487
fax: +852 2412 0042
e-mail: welly@wellydiecast.com.hk

Though marketed as generic low-cost toys, Welly of Hong Kong remains one of the more viable producers of quality 1:64 scale toys and toy sets. While incorporating less metal and more plastic in their design than most, Welly toys still display the kind of charm and durability that are the marks of a well-made toy. Real value on these "sleepers" of diecast toys may not be realized for years, maybe decades, but they are nonetheless worthy of being called "collectible." All Welly toys are made in China.
Lamborghini Countach $1
Porsche 935 Turbo Whale Tail $1
Oil Tanker...$1
Dome-O $2
Country Tractor 18-piece set includes #9132 farm tractor with horse box, livestock wagon, harrow, cultivator, six fence sections, and assorted plastic livestock $6

Western Models (also see Small Wheels)

According to EWA & Model Miniatures USA Inc., "Western Models were one of the first companies in the world to make high quality hand-built metal models. The company was founded in the early 1970s just southeast of London, England, and moved in the mid '80s to Taunton in the southwest of England. They now have a range of about 70 quality 1:43 scale models of European and American, race and street cars, old and new, plus some interesting record cars. A few new models are introduced annually and some withdrawn, which makes the models very collectible.

"Small Wheels is another name used by Western for some of their models. All are made in the Western factory to the same high standards."

Western Models

W1H 1966 Pontiac GTO 2-Door Hardtop, silver with a black top...................$135
WM6 1933 Chrysler Imperial $105
WM9 1933 Rolls Royce Powered Campbell Bluebird Record Car $125
WM13 1953 Chevrolet Corvette $160
WM15 1951 Hudson Police $180
WM15 1929 Golden Arrow Record Car $125
WM17F 1958 Ford Fairlane 300 Fire Chief $180
WM18 1957 Desoto Police $185
WM20 1942 Hudson Sedan $180
WM23 1927 Sunbeam 1000HP Record Car $140
WM24 1935 Duesenberg SJ Special, top down.............................$105
WM25 1939 Napier Railton Record Car $125
WM28 1933 Cadillac V16 4-Door Convertible, top up.......................$125
WM28X 1933 Cadillac V16 4-Door Convertible, top down....................$105
WM29 1931 Bugatti Royale 41 Esders..............................$125
WM30 1938 Thunderbolt Record Car $145
WM32 1930 Bentley 6.5L Barnato ...$105
WM35 1938 Alfa Romeo 8C 2900B Spyder...............................$105
WMS37 1933 Chrysler Imperial LeBaron, top up.............................$135
WMS37X 1933 Chrysler Imperial Lebaron Phaeton, top down $115
WM38 MG EX 135 Gardner..........$105
WM39 1938 Bugatti T57 Corsica TRR.............................$105
WM40 1948 Daimler Straight 8 DE36 ....$105
WM41 1949 Jaguar MK V 4-Door Sedan...............................$105
WM41X 1949 Jaguar MK V 2-Door Convertible.............................$105
WM41Z 1949 Jaguar MK V Sedan with landau roof...........................$105
WM42 1935 Rolls Royce Powered Campbell Record Car....................$145
WMS43 1936 Jaguar SS1 Tourer.....$160
WMS44 1957 Chevrolet BelAir Hardtop...............................$160
WMS44X 1957 Chevrolet BelAir Convertible, top down $160
WM45 1951 Jaguar XK120 FHC.....$105
WMS46 1959 Ford Galaxie Skyliner Hardtop with Continental Kit...............$160

WMS46X 1959 Ford Galaxie Skyliner Convertible, top down with Continental Kit $160

WMS46Z 1959 Ford Galaxie Skyliner Convertible, top down without Continental Kit $160

WM48 1964 Rolls Royce Silver Cloud III, righthand drive $75

WM48C 1964 Rolls Royce Silver Cloud III, lefthand drive $105

WMS49 1964 Bentley S III Saloon $160

WMS50 1958 Plymouth Fury, beige with gold trim......................................$160

WMS51 1958 Plymouth Belvedere Hardtop "Christine" $160

WMS51X 1958 Plymouth Belvedere Convertible, top down......................$160

WM53 1959 Ford Ranchero, Mackechnie..$105

WM53X 1959 Ford Ranchero, Mentone Co. $105

WM54 1949 Alfa Romeo Villa D'Este..$105

WMS55X 1974 Checker Police Car, white $160

WM55 1974 Checker Cab NY $185

WMS56 1959 Buick Electra Hardtop ...$160

WMS56X 1959 Buick Electra Convertible, top down $160

WMS56P 1959 Buick Electra Convertible Indy Pace Car.............................$195

WM57 1952 Rolls Royce Silver Dawn, righthand drive $125

WM57L 1952 Rolls Royce Silver Dawn, lefthand drive $125

WM58 1953 Benntley R Type Sedan, righthand drive $105

WM58L 1953 Benntley R Type Sedan, lefthand drive $125

WMS59 1959 Buick Invicta, top up ...$160

WMS60 1959 DeSoto Adventurer Hardtop.......................................$160

WMS60X 1959 DeSoto Adventurer Convertible, top down $160

WMS61 1960 Cadillac Eldorado Seville $160

WMS61X 1960 Cadillac Eldorado Biarritz, top down.................................$160

WMS62X 1947 Alfa Romeo Frecia D'Oro, open roof $145

WMS63 1959 Chrysler Saratoga Hardtop.......................................$160

WMS64 1957 Dodge Custom Royal Lancer Hardtop.................................$160

WMS64X 1957 Dodge Custom Royal Lancer Convertible, open top.........$160

WMS65 1958 Plymouth Plaza Business Coupe.......................................$160

WM65P 1958 Plymouth Police $185

WMS66 1957 Pontiac Bonneville Convertible, top up $160

WMS66X 1957 Pontiac Bonneville Convertible, top down $160

WMS67 1941 Buick Century Model 66S Sedanet $195

WMS67P 1941 Buick Century California Highway Patrol $200

WMS68 1949 Cadillac Coupe DeVille $175

WMS68X 1949 Cadillac Coupe DeVille Convertible, top down...................$175

WMS69 1972 Buick Riviera..............$160

WM70 1960 Dodge Polara 2-Door Hardtop.......................................$185

WM74 1955 Lincoln Capri Coupe $185

WM74X 1955 Lincoln Capri Convertible.....................................$185

WP104 Lotus Esprit $150

WP104X Lotus Esprit.........................$150

WP107X 1957 Ferrari 246 GT Dino, open top $145

WP110X 1982 Ferrari 308 GTS........$145

WP112 1985 Chevrolet Camaro IROC-Z $145

WP113 1984 Ferrari Testarossa........$160

WP115 1987 Jaguar XJS V-12 Coupe.......................................$145

WP118 1978 Pontiac Firebird TransAm.......................................$145

WP120 1990 Jaguar XJRS Coupe $145

WP125 1992 Dodge Viper..............$160

WP125P 1992 Dodge Viper Indy Pace Car $130

Western Models 1:200 Scale Airliners

WMBU1 Boeing KC-97L Stratotanker, Ohio Air Guard $265

WMCA2 Douglas DC-7C, Pan Am Seven Sears $250

WMCA3 Lockheed Super Constellation, Trans World Airlines.....................$260

WMCA4 Douglas DC-6B, American Airlines $235

WMCA5 Convair 440 Metropolitan, Swissair or National Airlines $230

WMCA6 Boeing Stratocruiser, American Overseas Airlines.........................$250

WMCA9 Lockheed L-188 Electra, Western Airlines $245

WMCA10 Douglas DC-3, British European Airways or American Airlines.........$230

WMCA11 Ilyushin IL-18, Aeroflot........$245

Wheeler

Hong Kong is home base for these relatively generic small-scale diecast toy cars.

1975 AMC Pacer $5

1968 Cadillac Eldorado $5

1963 Chevrolet Corvette Stingray $5

White Rose Collectibles

Since 1989, White Rose Collectibles has offered specialty limited edition collectibles. Hundreds of models and variations exist. White Rose began by offering licensed promo versions of Matchbox models.

One White Rose model marketed with hundreds of different markings is Matchbox's #38 Model A Van. Of the 400+ variations of this Matchbox model, many such variations are due to White Rose's marketing of a wide variety of baseball and football team vans using the Matchbox Model A.

New White Rose models, don't indicate the original manufacturer, but state on the box only that they are distributed by White Rose Collectibles and made in China.

For 1999, White Rose has expanded its promotional offerings to include the following:

Baseball Pick-Up Trucks, approx 2¾ inches long, each includes a Fleer baseball Card, 30 different models $12

Baseball Transporters, 1:80 scale semi-truck/trailers $12

TeamMates, double trailer transporters $12

Miniature Zamboni, representing all 3 Hockey Leagues $12

NHL Motorcoaches with sound...............$12

Police Patrol Collection, 1949 Fords in 10 state trooper liveries.............................$12

For more information, write to:

White Rose Collectibles
P O Box 2941
York, PA 17405

Or visit their website at www.whterose.com, or e-mail White Rose at info@whterose.com.

Matchbox Collector's Choice, 1994 From White Rose Collectibles

Twenty-four assorted models from the Matchbox 1-75 Series have been selected to form the 1994 Collector's Choice Series of models with better-than-usual detailing and color variations. They currently retail for $10 each, but can be purchased for considerably less. The 1995 series originally promised, but never delivered, 48 new variations. See Matchbox section for photos.

#1 '57 Chevy....................................$4-8
#2 Ambulance $4-8
#3 Flareside Pickup Truck $4-8
#4 Bulldozer $4-8
#5 Model "A" Hot Rod $4-8
#6 '62 Corvette $4-8
#7 Corvette "T" Top $4-8
#8 Jaguar XK 120.............................$4-8
#9 Lamborghini Countach...................$4-8
#10 Ford LTD Police Car....................$4-8
#11 Ford Bronco II $4-8
#12 GMC Wrecker $4-8
#13 Grand Prix Racing Car.................$4-8
#14 '87 Corvette $4-8
#15 Model "T" Ford $4-8
#16 Chevrolet Lumina $4-8
#17 Highway Maintenance Truck........$4-8
#18 Jeep Eagle 4x4 ....$4-8
#19 Extending Ladder Fire Engine $4-8
#20 School Bus $4-8
#21 Camaro Z-28 ....$4-8
#22 Ferrari Testarossa $4-8
#23 Porsche 944 Turbo $4-8
#24 Ferrari F40 ....$4-8

White Rose International Hockey League (IHL) Zamboni 1997

Originally priced at $14.99, these were available at Toy Liquidators in Troutdale, Oregon, at 2 for $5 in April 1998.

IHLW97-01 Chicago Wolves	$3-15
IHLW97-02 Cincinnati Cyclones	$3-15
IHLW97-03 Cleveland Lumberjacks	$3-15
IHLW97-04 Utah Grizzlies	$3-15
IHLW97-05 Detroit Vipers	$3-15
IHLW97-06 Fort Wayne Komets	$3-15
IHLW97-07 Grand Rapids Griffins	$3-15
IHLW97-08 Houston Aeros	$3-15
IHLW97-09 Indianapolis Ice	$3-15
IHLW97-10 Michigan K-Wings	$3-15
IHLW97-11 Kansas City Blades	$3-15
IHLW97-12 Las Vegas Thunder	$3-15
IHLW97-13 Long Beach Ice Dogs	$3-15
IHLW97-14 Manitoba Moose	$3-15
IHLW97-15 Milwaukee Admirals	$3-15
IHLW97-16 Orlando Solar Bears	$3-15
IHLW97-17 Phoenix Roadrunners	$3-15
IHLW97-18 Quebec Les Rafales	$3-15
IHLW97-19 San Antonio Dragons	$3-15

Wiking

Wiking is now owned by Sieper Werke GmbH, parent company to Siku toys. Wikings are highly accurate, all plastic 1:87 scale models made in Germany.

Williams, A. C. (see A. C. Williams)

Winross

Since the 1960s, Winross of Palmyra and Rochester, New York, has offered quality 1:64 scale toy trucks manufactured exclusively in the U.S. Their literature states that their purpose is "to provide the private collector with the finest scale models hand crafted in the USA today, at factory direct prices. Each model featured on the Collector Series has been used in a unique promotion by the company it represents, and has been approved for private sale through this catalog. Winross by Mail is the catalog division of the Winross Company, Inc. These models are not available for retail nor intended for resale. Purchase is limited to six of any one model unless otherwise specified."

For collectors of Winross trucks, the Winross Collectors Club of America, Inc., publishes "The Winross Model Collector," a monthly newsletter intended to "share and preserve the common interest of dedication to the collection and preservation of 1:64 scale Winross Trucks." Winross stopped production late in the year 2000 and is now operating under new ownership.

Winross 119 Set March 1995 (order from Winross by mail, shipping and handling is extra)

119-1 Molson Breweries	$38
119-2 Tyson Foods	$37
119-3 Central Freight	$37
119-4 Dr. Pepper	$39
119-5 Valvoline	$37
119-6 Praxair, Inc.	$35
119-7 Sharkey Transportation	$36
119-8 International #7	$46
119-9 Own the Set	$280

Winross 120 Set, April 1995 (order from Winross by mail, shipping and handling is extra)

120-1 Slice Delivery	$35
120-2 Walgreens Freighter	$36
120-3 Pyroil Tanker	$37
120-4 Unisource Freighter	$35
120-5 General Chemical Corporation Freighter	$35
120-6 Snap-On Tools Freighter	$37
120-7 Silver Eagle Company Double Freighter	$42
120-8 Batesville Casket Company Double Freighter	$46

Other Winross Models

Agway	$20
Air Products Pup '88	$38
Alliance Racing '92	$80
American Home Foods	$40
American Road Line	$45
ANR Double '91	$45
AP For the Long Haul	$45
Apache Transport	$65
Atlantic Tanker '91	$55
Auto Palace	$48
Burlington Northern	$45
Burlington Northern Double	$65
Campbell's Tanker V-8	$85
Campbell's Tomato Soup	$60
Carolina Double Freighter	$55
Carolina Mack	$60
Carrier Systems Container	$60
Chevron	$35
Crete '94	$50
Diamond Spring Water Van	$40
Drydene Tanker	$60
Earnhardt Racing	$110
Eastman Chemical	$30
Ethyl Van, silver	$30
Exxon '86 Tanker	$65
Ford Historical #9	$26
Forex Halon Tanker	$35
Gerhart Racing	$265
GP Trucking	$65
Graves Double Freighter	$60
Gully Transportation	$55
HBI Service	$45
Hemway '75	$85
Hershey Tanker	$23
HTL '94	$45
Interstate '83	$185
JLG Crane	$40
John Zern	$35
Keebler	$55

KLM Nationwide	$60
Kodak 100 Years	$38
Kodak Gold Plus	$23
Kohl Bros., Inc.	$35
Leasway Aeromax	$45
Leasway White 7000	$45
Lebanon Valley Bank	$20
Lend Lease	$40
Lincoln Highway Garage	$150
May Trucking	$60
May Trucking Double	$125
Matlack Tanker	$240
McLean Double	$125
McLean 50th Anniversary	$100
MDR Cartage	$48
MDR Cartage White 7000	$45
MFX '83	$160
Midland Ross	$45
Mohawk Carpet	$40
Morton Salt	$55
Mrs. Paul's	$60
Mrs. Paul's Tanker	$60
MS Carriers	$50
Mt. Olive Pickle '91	$35
National Truck Driving Championships 1994 Tanker	$55
New Penn 50 Years	$85
North Penn	$215
Nussbaum Double Freighter	$65
Old DoMinion	$41
Old DoMinion Double Freighter	$60
Old DoMinion Anniversary Double Freighter	$65
PIE '88	$65
PIE Nationwide	$55
PIE Nationwide Double Freighter	$65
Pitt-Ohio	$55
Penfield Trucking	$37
Polaroid	$38
Preston 60th Anniversary	$50
Preston White 9000 Double Freighter	$70
Preston New Graphics Double Freighter	$55
Reeses Tanker	$120
Rite Aid	$26
Roadway '72	$85
Roadway '82	$65
Roadway White 9000	$65
Roadway	$55
Roadway Gray Trailers Double Freighter	$65
Roadway Double Freighter	$55
Rollins Rent Lease	$45
Seltzer Bologna Van	$38
Shell	$55
Sico Tanker '83	$95
Smith Transfer '72	$85
Smith Transfer ARA Double	$95
Southeastern Express	$60
Spinnaker '90	$38
Spinnaker	$45
St. Johnsbury	$45
Stauffers of Kissel Hill	$35
Sunflower '94	$45
Super Bowl 25	$65

Super Bowl 26.........................$55
Super Bowl 27.........................$60
T. Labonte Racing '92 ....$40
Tenn Ohio................................$42
Terminal Freight $50
Time DC '72 ....$130
TNT Reddaway Triple 75th..............$55
TNT Redstar Express Double Freighter $75
Trans America '74 ....$65
Travel Port................................$38
USA Eastern L/S Double.................$60
Watkins 1994 Double Freighter $65
Weaver Chicken 50th Anniversary........$55
Wheel Horse.............................$55
White House Apples....................$45
Wilbur Chocolate Tanker................$60
Wilbur Chocolate Van $50
Wilson '72 ....$140
Winross, Rochester Chapter $60
Wisk.....................................$40
Wooster Motor Freight $55
Wyler's Soft Drink Mixes................$65
Yeager Supply $40
Yellow Freight '82 ....$48
Yellow Double Freighter.................$45
Zembo Temple '92 ....$30

World Zechin (see Grip Zechin)

Xonex

What distinguished this brand from Japan is one 1:24 scale model Mercedes Limousine designed after the one owned by Emperor Hirohito. The most popular offerings from Xonex are a series of miniature scale model bicycles and 1:3 scale pedal cars.
1935 Mercedes-Benz 770 Limousine, Emperor Hirohito, black & red $135

Yat Ming

Yat Ming Industrial Factory Ltd.
3/F., William Enterprises Industrial Building
23-25 Ng Fong Street, San Po Kong
Kowloon, Hong Kong

Perhaps one of the most underrated toy companies, Yat Ming (also spelled Yatming), has produced some exceptional toys and precision models considering their original selling price is relatively low. Listed below is an assortment of models with current values. Older 1:64 scale models were released as "Fastwheel." New models are issued under the brand name of "Road Tough." Newer models are marketed under the "Road Legends" brand.

Yat Ming Road Legends (previously Road Tough) 1:18 Scale

92018 1957 Chevrolet Corvette
   v.1 red with white trim $25–30
   v.2 black with red trim, 1999 ....$25–30
92019 1957 Chevrolet Corvette Gasser, pink or black, 1998 ....$25–30
92028 1990 BMW 850i Sport Coupe $25–30

92058 1964 Shelby Cobra 427S/C
   v.1 blue with white racing stripe .$25–30
   v.2 silver with black racing stripe, 1999 ....$25–30
92068 1955 Ford Thunderbird
   v.1 yellow..........................$25–30
   v.2 pink, 1999 ....$25–30
92078 1976 Volkswagen Beetle
   v.1 yellow..........................$25–30
   v.2 red, 1999 ....$25–30
92079 1976 Volkswagen Beetle Special Edition
   v.1 orange with purple rear fenders, Flower Power decorations, 1998.........................$25–30
   v.2 white with pink rear fenders, Flower Power decorations, 1999 ...$25–30
92088 1957 Chevrolet BelAir Nomad Wagon..............................$25–30
92098 1992 Toyota Land Cruiser

v.1 metallic green, 1998.....................$25–30

   v.2 metallic blue, 1999 ....$25–30
92106 1957 Chevrolet BelAir Fire Chief, red and white $25–30
92107 1957 Chevrolet BelAir Police Chief, black and white.....................$25–30
92108 1957 Chevrolet BelAir Convertible, top down, pastel green or light blue $25–30
92118 1959 Chevrolet Impala Convertible, top up, metallic blue or black, 1997....$25–30
92119 1959 Chevrolet Impala Convertible, top down, metallic blue or black..$25–30
92128 1956 Chevrolet BelAir Convertible, top down
   v.1 red, 1998......................$25–30
   v.2 turquoise, 1998 ....$25–30
   v.3 orange, 1999 ....$25–30
   v.4 lime green, 1999.............$25–30
92129 1956 Chevrolet BelAir Hardtop, red or turquoise $25-30
92138 1955 Ford Crown Victoria Hardtop
   v.1 surf green and white, 1997 .$25–30
   v.2 pink and white, 1998........$25–30
   v.3 yellow and black, 1999 .....$25–30
92139 1955 Ford Crown Victoria Mild Custom, burgundy or black, 1998 ...$25-30
92148 1953 Ford F-100 Pickup
   v.1 metallic blue, 1998 ....$25–30
   v.2 cream, 1998...................$25–30
   v.3 burgundy, 1999 ....$25–30
92149 1953 Ford F-100 Pickup Mild Custom, bright yellow or starlight purple, 1998 ....$25–30

92157 1958 Cadillac Eldorado Biarritz Police Chief, black and white, 1999 ....$25–30
92158 1958 Cadillac Eldorado Biarritz Convertible, bronze or blue, 1998 ....$25–30
92168 1968 Mustang Shelby GT-500KR, copper green or cream, 1998 ..$25–30
92178 1969 Plymouth Barracuda
   v.1 mango yellow, 1998 ....$25–30
   v.2 green, 1999 ....$25–30
92188 1967 Chevrolet Camaro Z-28
   v.1 cream with orange stripes, 1998.................................$25–30
   v.2 black with burnt orange stripes, 1999.................................$25–30
92198 1966 Volkswagen Karmann-Ghia, green or orange, 1998...........$25–30
92208 1957 Ford Ranchero, red and white or black and red, 1998 ....$25–30
92209 1957 Ford Courier Sedan Delivery, dark green or burgundy with black roof, 1998 ....$25–30
92218 1948 Ford F-1 Pickup, red or dark green, 1998 ....$25–30
92228 1953 Ford F-100 Wrecker, blue and white with red boom, 1998 ......$25–30
92229 1948 Ford F-1 Ice Cream Truck, white, 1999 ....$25–30
92238 1937 Ford Convertible, top down, bright green, 1998...................$25–30
92239 1937 Ford Convertible, top up, bright blue, 1998.....................$25–30
92248 1932 Ford 3-Window Coupe, black or red, 1998 ....$25–30
92249 1932 Ford Roadster Street Rod, yellow or blue, 1999...................$25–30
92257 1934 Ford Pickup Wrecker, brown or gray, 1998 ....$25–30
92258 1934 Ford Pickup Stake Truck, red or beige, 1998 ....$25–30
92259 1934 Ford Pickup Pro Street, yellow or orange, 1998....................$25–30
92268 1948 Tucker Torpedo, blue or cream, 1999 ....$25–30
92278 1941 Willys Coupe Hot Rod, purple or black, 1999 ....$25–30
92288 1940 BMW 328 with removable top, cream or red, 1999 ....$25–30
92298 1958 Edsel Citation Convertible, pink, 1999............................$25–30
92299 1958 Edsel Citation Hardtop, black, 1999 ....$25–30
92307 1949 Cadillac Coupe Deville Convertible 50th Anniversary Special Real Leather Edition, black, 1999 .....$45–60
92308 1949 Cadillac Coupe Deville Convertible, teal blue, 1999 ....$25–30
92309 1949 Cadillac Coupe Deville Hardtop, beige with bronze roof, 1999 ....$25–30
1957 Chevrolet BelAir Nomad Station Wagon, metallic orange or teal.$25–30

Chevrolet Corvette ZR-1 ....$25–30
1955 Ford Thunderbird $25–30
1964 Shelby Cobra 427 S/C $25–30

Yat Ming 1:24 Collection

93019 1957 Chevrolet Corvette, red or
baby blue..............................$8–12
93029 1990 BMW 850i, dark green or
burgundy..............................$8–12
93079 1967 Volkswagen Beetle, red or
cream....................................$8–12
93089 1957 Chevrolet Nomad, teal or
orange...................................$8–12
93099 Range Rover, dark green or
silver.....................................$8–12
93128 1999 Land Rover Freelander, purple,
1999......................................$8–12
93129 1999 Land Rover Freelander,
1999......................................$8–12

Yat Ming 1:43 Collection

94201 1957 Chevrolet Bel Air, light blue or yellow..**$5–8**

94202 1955 Ford Crown Victoria, two-tone white and light blue or yellow and black...**$5–8**

94203 1957 Chevrolet Bel Air Nomad, teal or orange..**$5–8**

94204 1953 Ford F-100 Pickup, red or cream...**$5–8**

94205 1995 Ford F-150 Pickup, light blue
or black................................$5–8

94206 Volkswagen Karmann Ghia, cream or orange..**$5–8**

94209 1957 Chevrolet Corvette, red on
white or white on red...................$5–8
94210 1967 Volkswagen Beetle Convertible, pink or bright blue $5–8
94211 1978 Volkswagen Rabbit Convertible, red or yellow......................$5–8
94212 1948 Ford F-1 Pickup, blue or dark
green $5–8
94214 1968 Shelby Mustang GT 500-KR,
yellow or cream.........................$5–8
94216 1967 Chevrolet Camaro Z-28,
cream or red.............................$5–8
94217 1998 Ford F-150 Pickup, teal or tore-
ador red...................................$5–8
94218 1971 Plymouth GTX, silver or fluorescent green $5–8

Yat Ming Fastwheel (1001-1024) 1:64 Scale

1001 Lamborghini Miura $3
1002 Chevrolet Racer............................$3
1003 Chevrolet Concept Car $3
1004 Lamborghini Marzal.......................$3
1005 Adams Probe 16 ....$3
1006 Toyota 2000 GT $3
1007 Nissan Laurel 200 SGX $3
1008 Ford Thunderbird $3
1009 Volkswagen $3
1010 Jaguar E 4.2................................$3
1011 Mercedes-Benz 350 SL $3
1012 Mercedes-Benz 450 SEL $3
1013 Maserati Bora $3
1014 Saab Sonnet $3
1015 Ford Station Wagon $3
1016 Porsche Targa $3
1017 BMW $3
1018 Opel Admiral $3
1019 Porsche Audi $3
1020 Porsche 910.................................$3
1021 Hairy $3
1022 Chevron.......................................$3
1023 Porsche 917.................................$3
1024 Boss Mustang $3

Other Yat Ming 1:64 Scale Models

1062 Datsun 280 Z-T............................$1
1086 1983 Camaro, MASK....................$2
1087 Mercedes-Benz 500SEC...............$1
1088 BMW 635CSI................................$1
1400 Kenworth Truck with Trailer, 14".....$3
8201 Kenworth Truck with Trailer, "Sea
Land" $3
8202 Kenworth Truck with Tanker Trailer,
"Exxon" $3
8203 Kenworth Truck with Gravel Dump
Trailer.......................................$3

8204 Kenworth Truck with Auto Transporter
Trailer.......................................$3

Other Yat Ming Models

8503 Duesenberg Model J, 1:43.......$5–7
8504 Rolls Royce Convertible, 1:43 ....$5–7
Bucket Truck $4–6

Yat Ming 1:48 Scale Airplane Collection, Diecast metal with display stand, New for 1999

99018 P-51D Mustang
v.1 silver gray with red and black trim,
"Buckeye Blitz VI" $20–30
v.2 silver gray with yellow and maroon
trim, "Flying Dutchman" $20–30
99028 F4U Bird Cage Corsair
v.1 blue "301" "M" $20–30
v.2 green "19" "WF" $20–30
99038 F6F-5N Night Hellcat
v.1 blue "92" $20–30
v.2 two-tone blue camouflage....$20–30
99048 P-47D Thunderbolt
v.1 silver gray "Sleep Walker" ...$20–30
v.2 silver gray "Lt. D. G. Pyler" ..$20–30

Yat Ming 1:10 Scale Motorcycles

97010 Honda Goldwing, pearl beige or
candy red................................$25–30

Yat Ming 1:12 Scale Motorcycles

95012 BMW R100.RS, silver or metallic
blue $20–25
95013 BMW R100.RS Police, black and
white $20–25
95022 Honda NR, red $20–25
95032 Yamaha XV1100 Virago, burgundy
or black...................................$20–25

Yat Ming 1:18 Scale Motorcycles

98001 Yamaha YZF-R1 ....$5–8
98002 Honda Magna $5–8
98003 Yamaha YZ250F $5–8
98004 Yamaha YZ400F $5–8
98005 Yamaha VXZ650......................$5–8
98006 Yamaha (Classic) $5–8
98007 Yamaha (Solitaire) $5–8
98008 Honda CBR1100XX.................$5–8

Yatming (see Yat Ming)

Yaxon (also see Forma and Giodi)

Yaxon of Italy inherited the Forma line of models in 1978. All models are currently being produced under the Giodi brand name.

001 Irrigation Hose Reel Trailer, 1:43, 1980.$8
002 Conveyor Belt, 1:32, 1980..................$8
003 Six-Bottom Plow, 1:43, 1980 ....$8
004 Hay Turner, 1:43, 1980.....................$8
005 Pig Cage, 1:43, 1981.......................$8
006 Livestock Trailer, 1:43, 1981..............$8
007 Sheep Trailer, 1:43, 1981..................$8
008 Manure Loader, 1:43, 1981................$8
009 Milk Can Rack, 1:43, 1981................$8
010 Hand Manure Spreader Cart, 1:43, 1981.$8
011 Rotary Hay Tender, 1:43, 1981...........$8
012 Hay Rake, 1:43, 1981.......................$8
013 Two-Wheel Farm Trailer, 1:43 ....$8

014 Manure Spreader Trailer, 1:43............$8
015 Tank Trailer, 1:43.............................$8
016 Tipping Four-Wheel Trailer, 1:43.........$8
017 Hay Loader, 1:43.............................$8
030 International 955 Tractor, 1:43, 1982.$20
033 Volvo BM Tractor, 1:43, 1984..........$20
035 Leyland 802 tractor, 1:43, 1984.......$20
040 Fendt 308 LS Tractor, 1:43, 1982......$20
045 Ford 8210 Tractor, 1:43, 1984.........$20
050 Renault 4514 Tractor, 1:43, 1981.....$20
055 Fiat 780 tractor, 1:43, 1978............$20
056 Fiat 880 Tractor, 1:43, 1978...........$20
059 Steyr 8160 Tractor, 1:43, 1980........$20
060 Landini 12500 Tractor, 1:43, 1980...$20
067 Massey-Ferguson 1134 Tractor, 1:43,
    1980..$20
069 Ford Tractor, 1:43, 1980................$20
070 Two-Wheel Farm Trailer, 1:43, 1978..$20
071 Manure Spreader Trailer, 1:43, 1978.$20
072 Tank Trailer, 1:43, 1978.................$20
080 Roller Trailer, 1:43, 1980...............$20
081 Four-Wheel Open Trailer, 1:43, 1978.$20
082 Hay Loader Tariler, 1:43, 1978........$20
085 Same Galaxy Tractor, 1:43, 1982.....$20
086 Lamborghini Tractor, 1:43, 1982......$20
090 Fiat 880DT Tractor, 1:32, 1983........$20
091 Round Press, 1983.........................$20
092 Tank Trailer, 1983..........................$20
100 Renault TX Tractor, 1:32, 1985........$20
106 Same Tractor with Front Loader, 1:32,
    1980..$20
110 Volvo BM Tractor, 1:32, 1984..........$20
118 Steyr Six-Wheel Tractor, 1:32, 1980...$20
120 New Holland Hay Baler, 1:32,
    1985..$20
121 Tank Trailer, 1:32, 1985.................$20
122 Four-Wheel Tipping Trailer, 1:32.......$20
138 Massey-Ferguson Six-Wheel Tractor,
    1980..$20
300 Semi-Trailer Truck, 1:43, 1978.........$40
301 Overhead Service Truck, 1:43, 1978..$40
302 Garbage Truck, 1:43, 1978.............$40
303 Flat Semi-Trailer Truck with Lumber, 1:43,
    1978..$40
304 Open Truck and Trailer, 1:43, 1978...$40
305 Covered Semi-Trailer Truck, 1:43,
    1978..$40
306 Container Semi-Trailer Truck, 1:43,
    1980..$40
308 Semi-Trailer Tank Truck, 1:43, 1980...$40
310 Quarry Dump Truck, 1:43, 1980.......$40
311 Open Truck with Shovel, 1:43, 1978..$40
312 Open Truck with trailer, 1:43, 1980...$40
313 Cable Drum Truck, 1:43, 1980.........$40
317 Container Truck, 1:43, 1978.............$40
320 Circus Cage Truck, 1:43, 1980.........$40
321 Circus Cage Truck and Trailer, 1:43....$40
400 Padane Z3 Bus, 1:43, 1980.............$40
401 American Freight Semi......................$40
402 American Covered Semi....................$40
403 American Tanker Semi......................$40
501 Landini Tractor with Front Loader, 1:43,
    1981..$20

502 Landini Tractor with Loader & Backhoe,
    1:43, 1981......................................$20
503 Landini Tractor with Snowplow, 1:43,
    1981..$20
504 Landini Tractor with Plow and Backhoe,
    1:43, 1981......................................$20
600 New Holland Combine, 1:32, 1982..$20
610 Fiat Laverda Combine, 1:43, 1984....$20
700 Ferrari 312 T2 Formula 1, 1:43, 1978...$20
701 Alfa Romeo 1980 Formula 1, 1:43,
    1978..$20
703 McLaren M26 Formula 1, 1:43, 1978...$20
704 Lotus JPS3 Formula 1, 1:43, 1978......$20
705 Wolf WR1 Formula 1, 1:43, 1978....$20
706 Ferrari 312 T3 Formula 1, 1:43, 1979.$20
707 Brabham BT46 Formula 1, 1:43,
    1979..$20
708 Ligier JS 11 Formula 1, 1:43, 1979....$20
709 Ferrari 312 T4 Formula 1, 1:43, 1980...$20
710 Alfa Romeo 179 Formula 1, 1:43,
    1980..$20
711 Alfa Romeo 179 Formula 1, 1:43,
    1980..$20
712 Renault RE20, 1:43, 1981...............$20
713 Williams FW-07 Formula 1, 1:43,
    1981..$20
714 Brabham-Alfa Romeo BT46, 1:43......$20
800 BMW M1 Marlboro, 1:43, 1981......$20
801 BMW M1 Denim, 1:43, 1981.........$20
802 Porsche 935 Martini, 1:43, 1981......$20
803 Porsche 935 Eminence, 1:43, 1981...$20
804 Lancia Beta, 1:43, 1981.................$20
805 Lancia Beta, 1:43, 1981.................$20
806 Ferrari 512 BB Pozzi, 1:43, 1981......$20
807 Ferrari 512 BB Jolly Club, 1:43, 1981...$20
808 BMW M1 BASF, 1:43, 1981..........$20
809 Porsche 935 Vaillant, 1981..............$20
810 Lancia Beta Martini, 1:43, 1982........$20
811 Ferrari 512 BB Yaxon, 1:43, 1981....$20
812 Porsche 935 Vaillant, 1:43................$20

Yidalux

Diecast Miniatures list just one 1:18 scale Yidalux model from Argentina.

Renault Trafic Fire Van, 1:18......................$28

Yoder

Although the highly accurate 1:16 scale tractor models made by the Yoder family of New Paris, Indiana, are made of ABS plastic, they deserve a special place in a book devoted to diecast toys and scale models. They definitely fall into the latter category of scale models with the painstaking attention to detail given by the Yoders. The first Yoder models were produced in 1982. In 1996, the family sold their line of precision tractor molds to Spec-Cast, due to the increasing difficulty in obtaining licensing for the various brands of tractors produced and the rising cost of producing new molds. The original price for a Yoder tractor was $65 to $75. The first issues from 1982 have now been seen offered for $200. Presented below is the complete line of Yoder tractors produced from 1982 to 1996, including production quantity. Price in parentheses indicate the original retail price.

1982

#1 550 Oliver, square grill, 1,000 made
    ($55)...$150–200
#2 550 Oliver, slot grill, 1,000 made
    ($55)...$150–200
#3 550 Cockshutt, square grill, 1,000 made
    ($55)...$150–200

1985

#4 Super 55 Oliver, green wheels, 875
    made ($65).................................$175–225
#5 Super 55 Oliver, red wheels, 125 made
    ($65)...$250–300
#6 Case 800, original mold run, 175 made
    ($250).......................................$375–400

1986

#7 Case 400, Lafayette show tractor, 2,218
    made ($44)...................................$75–125
#8 Case 400, shelf model, 1,000 made
    ($57.50)....................................$100–125
#9 Case 700, Beaver Falls show, 1,008
    made ($44)...................................$75–100
#10 Case 700, shelf model, 1,000 made
    ($60)...$100–125

1987

#11 John Deere 730 NF, Lafayette show
    tractor, 1,000 made ($44).......$65–80

1988

#12 John Deere 730 NF, red, 225 made
    ($200).......................................$275–300
#13 John Deere 730 WF, red, 225 made
    ($200).......................................$225–275
#14 John Deere 730 WF, Lafayette show
    tractor, 4,800 made ($65).......$70–80
#15 Allis Chalmers D-14, original mold run,
    225 made ($120)..............$150–175
#16 Allis Chalmers D-15, Beaver Falls show,
    1,200 made ($54).................$75–90
#17 John Deere 730 WF, industrial yellow,
    1,200 made ($65).................$80–95

1989

#18 Case 700, black, 225 made
    ($200).......................................$260–275
#19 Case 400, black, 225 made
    ($200).......................................$260–275
#20 Case 400, orange, 300 made
    ($85)...$100–125
#21 John Deere 720 WF, electric start
    diesel, Beaver Falls show, 1,200 made
    ($65)...$75–90
#22 John Deere 720 WF, Gospel Echoes
    Team benefit sale, with emblem, 1 auctioned...$260
#23 John Deere 720 NF, Gospel Echoes
    Team benefit sale, with emblem, 1 auctioned...$260
#24 John Deere 720 NF, electric start diesel,
    3,010 made ($69).................$70–75

1990

#25 International Harvester Super MTA NF,
    gas, 5,100 made ($69).........$70–75

#26 International Harvester Super MTA NF, gas, Gospel Echoes benefit sale, with emblem, 1 auctioned $65
#27 John Deere 720 NF Pony Start, diesel, 1,250 made ($69) $75–90
#28 John Deere 720 WF Pony Start, diesel, 1,185 ($69) $75–90

1991
#29 International Harvester Super MTA WF, gas, 1954 made ($65) $70–75
#30 International Harvester Super MTA WF, gas, white, 225 made ($200) $225–250
#31 International Harvester Super MTA NF, gas, white, 225 made ($200) $225–250
#32 International Harvester Super MTA NF, gas with duals, Michiana Toy Club show tractor, 630 made ($65) $70–75

1992
#33 International Harvester Super MTA NF, diesel, 670 made ($65) $70–75
#34 International Harvester Super MTN WF, diesel, 530 made ($65) $70–75
#35 International Harvester Super MTA NF, diesel with duals, Gospel Echoes benefit sale, with emblem, 1 auctioned $100
#36 International Harvester Super MTA WF, diesel with duals, Gospel Echoes benefit sale, with emblem, 1 auctioned $100
#37 John Deere 720 Standard, electric start, 750 made ($69) $75–100
#38 John Deere 720 Standard, Pony Motor start, 1,110 made ($69) $70–90

1993
#39 John Deere 720 Standard, electric start, Gospel Echoes benefit sale, with emblem, 1 auctioned $100
#40 John Deere 720 Standard, Pony Motor start, Gospel Echoes benefit sale, with emblem, 1 auctioned $100
#41 John Deere 730 Standard Moline, show tractor, 1,280 made ($69) $70–75
#42 John Deere 720 Standard, adjustable front axle, electric start, still available $100
#43 John Deere 720 Standard, adjustable front axle, Pony Motor start, still available................................$100

1994
#44 John Deere 730 Standard, industrial, yellow, 1,000 made ($69) $70–75
#45 John Deere 730 Standard, adjustable front Axle, 3 point, no front weights, numbered signed, dated, 25 made ($85)....................$125–150
#46 John Deere 730 Standard, Industrial, fixed axle, no 3 point or weights, regular hitch, numbered, signed, dated, 25 made ($85)......................$125–150
#47 John Deere 730 Standard, Industrial, fixed axle, Nebraska Highway Dept., orange, 500 made ($125)................$150–175

1995
#48 John Deere 730 Standard, Industrial, electric start, still available $100

1996
#49 John Deere 720 Standard, Industrial, electric start, still available $100
#50 John Deere 720 Standard, Industrial, Pony Motor start, still available.......$100

Yorkshire

The Yorkshire Company
650 Roosevelt Road
Glen Ellyn, IL 60138

The Yorkshire Company is a relatively obscure brand from Glen Ellyn, Illinois, that around 1985–1989 produced several Bell System trucks. All of these models have the Bell System logo on the doors of the trucks and have 1984, 1985, or 1986 copyright dates on the boxes.

An advertisement from an October 1988 issue of *Antique Toy World* indicates that six different models were available directly from the manufacturer for $21.95 plus shipping and handling, $28.95 for model on marble base with pen. A name plate was available for $3 more.

Additional information indicates that another model was produced for the U. S. Postal Service in 1990. It was discontinued after the first issue, according to collector Lou Harmin, after the U. S. Congress told the U. S. Post Office that they were not in the business of selling toys and t-shirts. That policy has since changed, and new U.S.P.S. marketing has ensued in the form of stationery, keychains, and a host of other items but no more diecast models. Best information suggests the company is no longer in business.

Yorkshire Bell System Trucks

1st Edition 1931 Model A Ford Telephone Lineman / Installer Truck, issued 1984, 1:25 ....$80–100
2nd Edition 1950 Dodge Power Wagon Hydraulic Pole Digger / Derrick, issued 1985, 1:25 ....$80–100
3rd Edition 1931 Model A Ford Line Installation Utility Truck, issued 1985, 1:25 ....$80–100
4th Edition 1927 Model TT Ford Cherry Picker-Construction Truck, issued 1986, 1:25 ....$80–100
5th Edition 1927 Model TT Ford Pick Up Truck, issued 1987, 1:25 ......$80–100
6th Edition 1917 Model TT Ford Wagon, black canvas roll-up side curtains, issued 1988, 1:25..........................$80–100

Other Yorkshire Trucks

8th Edition 1917 Model TT Ford Moving Van, white, 1989, 1:25 ....$80–100
1929 Model A Ford U.S. Postal Truck, 1990, 1:25.......................$100–120

Yot

Yot has produced generic toys made in Taiwan. One Yot model is known.
VW Beetle 1200 Sedan, 1:60 ....$15

Zaugg (also see Tin Wizard)

Zaugg miniatures are older high quality 1:43 scale hand-built models from Switzerland. They were occasionally sold as Empire models, according to collector Andreas Rutishauser. He reports that production was later taken over by Tin Wizard of Germany who reused the dies and made models under the Tin Wizard brand name. Many were issued as fire brigade, taxi, pace car, and other versions as well as the basic model.

1955 Cadillac Convertible..............$140–160
1951 Chevrolet Wagon $140–160
Citroën 2CV Sahara $175–200
Commer Circus Van $45–60
1970 Dodge Challenger................$125–150
1959 Ford Edsel Pacer, resin with metal chassis..............................$75–100
1963 Ford Thunderbird, resin with metal chassis..............................$75–100
1950 Mercury $125–150
1968 Mercury Cyclone GT Coupe...$150–175
1949 Nash Statesman....................$150–175
Volvo 122 Amazon $100–125

Zax

In 1948, the Zax company of Bergamo, Italy, manufactured an assortment of 1:87 and 1:43 scale models.

Racing Car, 1:43.............................$60
Speed Record Car, 1:43...................$60
Roadster, 1:43...............................$60
Fastback Coupe, 1:43......................$60
Racing Car, 1:87.............................$24
Speed Record Car, 1:87...................$24
Roadster, 1:87...............................$24
Sedan, 1:87..................................$24
Fiat 1400 ....$24
Fiat 1400 Taxi $24
Fiat 1400 Police Car $24

Zebra Toys (see Benbros)

Zee Toys/Zylmex (also see Redbox)

Zylmex and Zee Toys are interchangeable brand names of Zyll Enterprise Ltd. Like most, these lightweight diecast and plastic toys are manufactured in China. Their quality varies and collector value remains comparatively low. However, some unusual models have been produced in past years. Besides a large array of models of different sizes and scales, two product lines stand out, both roughly 1:64 scale, dubbed "Pacesetters" and "Dynawheels." Pacesetters are the better quality of the two, usually sporting metal chassis, opening doors and other parts, while Dynawheels are generally lighter, with plastic chassis and no opening parts.

Many other series exist, most notably Ridge Riders series of approximately 1:24 scale motorcycles, and Dyna-Flites military airplane toys. Other manufacturers that have carried the

Zee Toys brand name include Edocar, a Dutch licensee, and Intex Recreation. Sets of Zee Toys Pacesetters were also issued through Sears as Roadmates.

Zyll Enterprise Ltd. went out of business in March 1996, and all the dies and trademarks were sold to a Hong Kong firm in 1997. The Zee Toys connection with Intex Corporation is that, up until 1993, Intex was the sole importer of Zee Toys to the US. Now, Zyll products are being sold under the Redbox brand.

D69 Morgan Plus 8, 3" $2–4

P301 Citroën $4–6

P302 Datsun Fairlady (240Z) $2–4

P303 Toyota GT2000 ....$2–4
P304 Mazda GT $2–4
P305 Honda 600 ....$2–4
P306 Mazda GT Police $2–4
P307 Bulldozer $2–4
P308 Front Loader $2–4
P309 Cement Mixer $2–4
P310 Dump Truck $2–4
P311 Crane Truck $2–4
P312 Fire Engine (ladder) $2–4
P313 Tipper Truck $2–4
P314 Hydraulic Excavator $2–4
P315 Fork Lift Truck $2–4
P316 Fire Engine (snorkel) $2–4
P317 Track-type Loader $2–4
P318 Hydraulic Excavator $2–4
P319 '70s Datsun Pick-up $2–4
P320 '70s Dodge Van $2–4
P321 McLaren Indy Car $2–4
P322 Crown School Bus, "32 VALLEY DISTRICT SCHOOLS" $25
P323 '70s Chevelle Hardtop $2–4
P324 Pinto $2–4
P325 '32 Ford Roadster $3
P326 GMC Motorhome $5–7
P327 Skyline 2000GT $2–4
P328 Corolla 30 1400 GSL $2–4
P329 Corona 2000GT $2–4
P330 Celica LB 2000GT $2–4
P331 Benz $2–4
P332 '70s VW Bus $3–5
P333 Toyota Van $2–4
P334 Double Decker Bus $2–4

P335 (English) Ford Van $2–4
P336 Oil Tank Truck $2–4
P337 Fire Engine (pumper) $2–4
P338 Early '70s Chevy Pick-up $2–4
339 Monza Hatchback $2–4
P340 McLaren M8-A $2–4
P341 Super Van (from movie) $2–4
P342 Wheaties Custom Dodge Van $12–15
P343 Van Killer Custom Dodge Van $2–4
P344 Straight Arrow Custom Dodge Van ...$2–4
P345 '70s Plymouth Police $2–4
P345 Plymouth Satellite Taxi $4–6
P346 Chevy Ambulance Van $2–4
P347 U.S. Mail Truck $5–7
P348 '70s Ford Country Squire Wagon $5–8
P349 Farm Tractor $2–4
P350 Jeep $2–4
P351 Mustang II Cobra Street Racer $2–4
P352 Mercedes-Benz 450 SL $2–4
P353 Fun Trucking Ford Courier Pick-up $2–4
P354 '30s Benz $2–4
P355 '57 Chevy Bel Air $2–4
P356 '56 Ford Thunderbird $3–5
P357 Kandy Van Custom Dodge Van $2–4
P358 Ford Pinto Mini Van $2–4
P359 Chevy Blazer $2–4
P360 '70s Dodge Pick-up Camper $2–4
P361 '35 Chevy $2–4
P362 Firebird Trans Am T-Top $2–4

P363 Lincoln Continental Mark IV $3–5

P364 '63 Chevrolet Corvette $2–4

P365 '57 Chevrolet Corvette $2–4

P366 Big Rig Tow Truck $2–4
P367 Camaro Z28 T-Top $2–4
P368 Jeep $2–4
P369 Ford Bronco 4X4 ....$2–4
P370 Mercedes-Benz 300 SL $2–4
P371 '70s Chevy Corvette $2–4
P372 '70s Mazda RX-7 ....$2–4
P373 '70s Camaro Z-28 Hwy. Patrol $2–4

P374 DeLorean $2–4

P375 '85 Corvette $2–4
P376 Porsche 928 ....$2–4
P377 Scraper $2–4
P378 unknown
P379 Loader $2–4
P380 unknown
P381 '80s Camaro Z28 Convertible $2–4
P382 '80s Pontiac Firebird $2–4
P383 Firebird Funny Car $2–4
P384 unknown
P385 Racing Rig $2–4
P386 unknown
P387 unknown
P388 unknown
P389 unknown
P390 '80s T-Bird Stock Car $2–4
P391 '69 Pontiac GTO $2–4

P392 Mustang Fastback Pro/Street $2–4

P393 Charger Funny Car $2–4
P394 '80s Mustang $2–4
P396 Pontiac Fiero $2–4
P399 '80s Camaro Pro/Stock $2–4
P397 '70 Hemi 'Cuda $2–4
3005 '69 'Vette $2–4
P3201 Class 8 Wrecker $2–4
P3202 Sand Buggy $2–4
P3203 unknown
P3204 Sprint Car $2–4
P3205 Beretta Pro/Stock $2–4
P3206 Custom '80s Nissan Pick-up $2–4
P3207 Olds Aerotech $2–4
P3208 Olds Funny Car $2–4
P3209 unknown
P3210 unknown
P3211 Nissan GTP $2–4
P3212 Mazda Miata $2–4
P3213 Flip Car II (Manta Ray/Space Raycer) $2–4
P3214 Flip Car I (Indy Champ/Max 2000) .$2–4
P3215 Flip Car III (Bonneville Blaster/DD Coupe) $2–4
P3216 Flip Car IV (Retro Rod/Formula Fusion) .$2–4
Ferrari Testarossa $2–4
Ferrari 308 GTB $2–4
Ford Sierra XR4i $2–4
Mercedes-Benz 500 SEC.....................$2–4
Mercedes-Benz 500 SL, #13 Edocar $3–5

Porsche 928, Intex Recreation Corp...........$2–4
Porsche 959 ....$2–4
VW Golf GTI...$2–4

Zee Toys Z Wheels Pacesetters Specials

This 1:24 scale model has been discovered in the clearance rack at Shopko. It is likely a product of test marketing, as only one specimen has been found so far.

Chevrolet Corvette ZR-1 ....$10

Zee Toys Dyna-Flites/Airplanes

A111 MIG-27 Jet Fighter......................$3
A115 DC-10 American Airlines, 1:600 ...$3
A118 Phantom II F-4E USAF...................$3
A118 Phantom II F-4C Camouflage $3
A127 SR-71 Blackbird $3
A129 Saab AJ-37 Viggen Jet Fighter $3
A130 A-4E Skyhawk USN $3
A144 F-16 USAF....................................$3
A145 F-15 Eagle USAF $3
A150 Grumman X-29A $3
A152 EF-111 Military Jet Fighter $3
A153 MIG-29 Fulcrum Jet Fighter...........$3
A202 DC-10 AMERICAN, 1:500 ....$3
A208 Bell Jet Ranger.............................$3
A212 F-20 Tigershark $3
F-18 Hornet $3
Gee Bee $12
OH-6A Cayuse Police Helicopter $3

Other Zee Toys:

Bell 21 Racing Motorcycle $3
California Hauler Tractor Trailer, "Consolidated Freightways"................................$4
GT Bicycle...$3
Honda Racing Motorcycle $3
Kawasaki 250 KDX Motorcycle $3
Kawasaki Mach 3 Motorcycle $3
Kawasaki Ninja $3
Mack Refrigerated Container Truck, "STP" .$3
Mack Freighter, "Flying Tiger" $4
Maico 490 Motorcycle...........................$3
Mercedes 540K Coupe $3
Mongoose Bicycle $3
Peterbilt 2-Boom Wrecker.....................$5
Sprint Racer $4
Suzuki RM125 Motorcycle......................$3
Porsche 911 Speedster, Intex, 1:18.......$21
1989 Mercedes-Benz 500SL RDS, 1:18 ..$21

Zil

Zil models represent some of the best 1:43 models to come out of Russia. Price is low for these exceptional models.

115 Limousine "Brezhnev" $12
115 Limousine "wedding Car" $16
115 Limousine "Parade" $16
4505 Truck...$21
MMZ-555 Tank Truck $21
MMZ-4502 Tipper $21

Zinoki

There seem to be hundreds of inexpensive diecast and plastic toy brands coming out of China. Out of the package, the majority are rendered unidentifiable and hence generic. Zinoki is one of those. Two playsets have been found, a construction set and an emergency set. Each set sells for about $9–12 and contains over a dozen cheaply made mostly plastic toys consisting of just enough metal components to define them as diecast.

Ziss

Ziss models, also known as R.W. Ziss, were produced throughout the 1960s and early 1970s from Dusseldorf, Germany, until the death of Mr. Wittek, proprietor of the Mini-Auto company of Lintorf, on the outskirts of Dusseldorf.

14 1905 Mercedes Grand Prix, 1:43, 1972 ....$25
15 1908 Ford Model T, 1:43 ....$25
16 1907 Ford Model T Roadster, 1:43, 1966 ....$25
17 1919 Ford Model T Torpedo, 1:43, 1966 ....$25
20 1908 Opel Doktorwagen, 1:43, 1963.$25

21 1901 Mercedes Simplex, 1:43, 1963..$25

22 1908 Opel Stadt-Coupe, 1:43, 1963 ..$25
23 1910 Benz Limousine, 1:43, 1964.......$25

27 1904 N.A.G. Phaeton, 1:43, 1964.......$25

30 1906 Adler Limousine, 1:43, 1964 ......$25
31 1905 Mercedes Roadster, 1:43, 1966.$25
38 1904 N.A.G. Touren Sport, 1:43, 1966..$25
39 1906 Adler Phaeton, 1:43, 1966 ....$25
40 1905 Mercedes Coupe, 1:43, 1966 ...$25
43 1909 Opel Torpedo, 1:43, 1966 ....$25
44 1909 Ford Ranch Car, 1:43, 1966......$25
50 1910 Benz Landaulet, 1:43, 1966.......$25
52 1924 Hanomag Kommissbrot, 1:43, 1967 ....$25
53 1924 Hanomag Coupe, 1:43, 1967...$25
57 1927 BMW Dixi, 1:40, 1968 ....$25
60 1913 Audi Alpensieger, 1:43, 1969....$25
62 1916 Chevrolet Phaeton, 1:43, 1969...$25

65 1914 NSU Phaeton, 1:43, 1971........$25
66 1932 Fiat Balilla, 1:43, 1972 ....$25
289 Krupp Hydraulic Hammer, 1:50, 1972 .$35
290 Fiat Scraper, 1:24, 1972 ....$35
291 O & K Fork Lift, 1:50, 1972 ....$35
292 Clark Fork Lift, 1:50, 1972 ....$35
293 Hyster 40 Fork Lift, 1:39, 1971 ....$35
294 Fiat 600 Farm Tractor, 1:43, 1971 .....$65
295 O & K RH6 Excavator, 1971 ....$65
296 O & K MH6 Excavator, 1971 ....$65
297 Deutz Farm Tractor, 1968 ....$65
298 Hanomag Matador Open Truck, 1968 .$45
299 Three Musketeers Jeep, 1968 ....$65
300 Army Jeep, 1968 ....$50
301 Mercedes-Benz 600, 1:43, 1966 ......$50
302 1926 Henschel Open Truck, 1:43, 1967 ....$50
303 1926 Henschel ARAL Tank Truck, 1:43, 1967 ....$50
304 1925 MAN Open Truck, 1:43, 1967..$50
305 1925 MAN BP Tank Truck, 1:43, 1968 ....$50
306 1925 MAN Bus, 1:43, 1969 ....$65
310 1971 Opel Rekord Sedan, 1:43, 1971 ....$40
311 1971 Opel Commodore Coupe, 1:43, 1971 ....$40
312 1975 Opel Manta, 1:43, 1975 ....$50
400 Ford Transit Van, 1:43, 1968 ....$50
401 Ford Transit Van with side windows, 1:43, 1968 ....$50
410 Hanomag Dump Truck, 1:43, 1968...$45
411 Hanomag Open Semi-Trailer Truck, 1:43, 1968 ....$40
412 Hanomag Open Truck, 1:43, 1970 ...$45
413 Hanomag Container Semi-Trailer Truck, 1:43, 1970 ....$50
414 Hanomag ESSO Tank Truck, 1:43, 1971 ....$50
415 Hanomag Cement Truck, 1:43, 1971.$50
420 1969 Volkswagen Van, 1:43, 1970 ..$50
421 1969 Volkswagen Transporter, 1:43, 1970 ....$50
422 1969 Volkswagen Pickup Truck, 1:43, 1970 ....$50
430 Mercedes-Benz 1313 Dump Truck, 1:60, 1971 ....$50
999 1913 Audi, top down, 1:43 ....$20

Zowees (see Hot Wheels)

Zschopau

Zschopau models are plastic scale models, probably made in Germany circa 1960s to 1970s, based on the models offered.

Ferrari 275 Coupe, 1:30 ....$18
Wartburg 1000 4-Door Sedan, 1:32 ....$14
Wartburg 1000 Wagon, 1:32 ....$14
Skoda S110R Coupe, 1:32 ....$14
Skoda 6x4 Dump Truck, 1:32 ....$18

American Toy Emergency Vehicle (ATEV) Club
Jeff Hawkins, President
11415 Colfax Road
Glen Allen, Virginia 23060
phone: 804-262-8934
For details, send e-mail: atevclub@hotmail.com
website: www.atevclub.org
publication: ATEV Siren
frequency: bi-monthly

Bay Area Matchbox® Collectors Association (BAMCA)
P.O. Box 1534
San Jose, California 95109-1534
website: www.bamca.org/
Contact Chris Potter for further information and details on next meet by sending SASE (self-addressed stamped envelope)

Blues City Hot Wheels® Club
c/o David Conley
4807 Walden Glen
Memphis, Tennessee 38128
phone: 901-386-6077
e-mail: CanyonRdr@aol.com

British Diecast Model Collectors Association
P.O. Box 11
Norwich NR7 0SP England
phone: 01603 505210 / 701929 / 507917
fax: 01603 507355
from overseas: 44-1-603 505210 / fax: 44-1-603 507355
e-mail: bdmca@swapmeet.freeserve.co.uk
website: www.swapmeet.freeserve.co.uk
Annual subscriptions:
UK: £17.50
Europe: £20.00
Overseas: £22.50
(all prices in UK Pounds and include VAT) payable by cheque/credit card/postal orders made payable to BDMCA. Overseas applicants please use Eurocheques or Sterling cheques drawn on a UK bank or pay by credit card. Please allow up to 28 days for your membership acknowledgement to reach you.

Brooklin Collectors' Club
The Brooklin Collectors' Club was formed over ten years ago to share and enjoy the collecting of Brooklin Models. We offer both advice and information from past models to the latest releases with four magazines a year and a yearly club model available only to club members. If you are interested in any of the Brooklin ranges, the Brooklin Collectors' Club invites you to join them. For further information contact:
John Scrivens
Brooklin Collectors' Club
47 Byron Avenue East
Sutton
Surrey SM1 3RB
England
email: brooklincollclub@currantbun.com

Central Indiana Hotwheels Club
Anderson, Indiana
contact: Scooter
e-mail: xscooter@netdirect.net

Central California Hotwheel Club
Roseville, California 95661
Ron & Sandy Davis
phone: (916) 782-7598
e-mail: DAVISR@ns.net

Chesapeake Miniature Vehicle Collectors Club
c/o Win Hurley
709 Murdock Rd.
Baltimore, Maryland 21212

Club Hot Wheels® of Bakersfield
Bakersfield, California
contact: Scott Hamblin
phone: 805-396-8801
e-mail: schamblin@earthlink.com
website: www.greeks.net/hotwheels

Cruisin' Connection
c/o Helen Jeong
2548 E. Worman Ave.,
Suite 413
West Covina, California 91791

Die Cast Car Collectors Club (D4C)
c/o Jay Olins
Diecast Club
P O Box 670226
Los Angeles, California 90067-1126
phone: 213-500-4355
Diecast Car Collectors Homebase: www.diecast.org
Jay Olins, chairman
e-mail: jay@diecast.org
George Dills, associate editor
e-mail: gdill@concentric.net
publication: Precision Die Cast Car Collector Newsletter
frequency: bi-monthly
cost: $20 including a bi-monthly newsletter and membership directory

Dinky Toy® Club of America
c/o Jerry Fralick
P O Box 11
Highland, Maryland 20777
phone: 301-854-2217
website: www.erols.com/dinkytoy/
cost: $20/yr.
publication: newsletter
frequency: quarterly

Durham Classics® Collectors Club
24 Montrose Crescent
Unionville, Ontario
L3R 7Z7 Canada

Emergency Vehicle Collectors Club
Box 14616
Minneapolis, Minnesota 55414

Gateway Hot Wheelers Club
Collinsville, Illinois
contact: Mike Blaylock
phone: 618-345-4971 (after 7:00 pm CST, please!)
e-mail: ghwcMike@aol.com
website: www.siue.edu/~dbrown/gatewayhw.html
Meets bi-monthly

Heartland Hot Wheelers Club
Omaha, Nebraska
website: www.radiks.net/hotwheels
e-mail: hotwheels@probe.net
Neal Hendrickson, president, e-mail: bearman85@aol.com
Jeff Farrar, secretary, e-mail: jfarr@radiks.net
Bob Norton, member, e-mail: rgn57@radiks.net
Terry Tramp, member, e-mail: tramp@alaska.net

High Desert Diecast Car Collectors Club
c/o J. Chris Root
1894 NE Taylor Ct.
Bend, Oregon 97701
phone: 541-382-5936
Meets on third Saturday of every month (except in June, July, and August) from 1 to 3pm at Round Table Pizza, N. 3rd in Bend. Call or write for details.

Hot Wheels® Cincinnati Collector's Club
Cincinnati, Ohio
website: members.aol.com/hwcinti/home.html
For more information, e-mail Jay Yaeger at Jayaeger@aol.com or Dave Wynn at Davehtwhel@aol.com

Hot Wheels® Newsletter Club
c/o Michael Thomas Strauss
26 Madera Ave.
San Carlos, California 94070
phone: 415-591-6482
e-mail: hwnewsltr@aol.com
publication: Hot Wheels Newsletter
frequency: quarterly with monthly updates
cost: $20 for 6 issues

Illinois Matchbox® Collectors Club
c/o Bob Neumann
PO Box 1582
Bridgeview, Illinois 60455
phone: 630-257-0579
residence: Lemont, Illinois

International Miniature Aircraft Collectors Society
G. R. Webster
P O Box 845
Greenwich, Connecticut 06836-0845
phone: 203-629-5270
publication: The Plane News
e-mail: grwebster@aol.com
frequency: Quarterly
focus: diecast, ID, travel agency, and desk model airplanes

International Toy Collectors Association - ITCA
804 West Anthony Drive
Champaign, Illinois 61822
217-351-1845

cost: $129 per year (US), scheduled to increase to $149 per year
benefits: Full color catalogs (minimum of 4) for all ITCA 1000 lot. Vintage Toy Auctions for 1 year, monthly ITCA newsletter, exclusive access to ITCA Junkyard of spare parts, discounts, a lot more. Call for details.

Johnny Lightning® Newsflash™
c/o Tom Lowe, President and Founder
Playing Mantis
P O Box 3688
South Bend, Indiana 46619-3688
phone: 800-626-8478 (800-MANTIS-8)
e-mail: PlayingM@aol.com
website: www.johnnylightning.com/index1.html
publication: Johnny Lightning Newsflash
frequency: Quarterly
cost: $14.95/yr
shipping address:
3600 McGill Street, Suite 300
South Bend, Indiana 46628

Kansas City Hot Wheels® Club
Kansas City, Kansas
President: Jim Gerber
Vice President: Steve Reddell
e-mail: exokie@aol.com
website: members.aol.com/exokie/club1.htm

Kentucky Hot Wheels® Association
international e-mail: khwa@altavista.net
continental U.S. e-mail: khwa@usa.net
local e-mail: jcb@wwd.net
website: www.wwd.net/user/jcb/index.htm

Limited Edition Club
c/o Artworks International
11 Cherry Tree Drive
Sunnybrow, Crook, Co. Durham
DL15 OXG, England
phone & fax:+441388 745926
e-mail: aviationart@artworksinternational.freeserve.co.uk
website: www.F1-Art.com
contact: Dave Williams
Primarily for those who collect our 1:20 and 1:18 models but is open to any diecast collector, especially those who are into racing cars.

Lledo Collectors Club
c/o RDP Publications
P O Box 1946
Halesowen
West Midlands B62 8TP
Great Britain

Madison Area Diecast Club
Madison, Wisconsin
Keefe Bartz: Batrz@itis.com
Terry F. Nadosy: Madisonwheels@mail.execpc.com

Matchbox® Collectors Club
c/o Everett Marshall
P O Box 977
Newfield, New Jersey 08344
frequency: Bi-monthly

Matchbox® International Collectors Association (MICA) of North America

c/o Stewart Orr and Kevin McGimpsey
P O Box 28072
Waterloo, Ontario
N2L 6J8 Canada
frequency: bi-monthly

Matchbox® International Collectors Association (MICA) UK & Europe

c/o Maureen Quayle
13A Lower Bridge St.
Chester CH1 1RS
England
phone: 0124 434 6297
publication: magazine
frequency: bi-monthly
Founded in 1985

Matchbox® Northwest Collectors Club

Tom Larson
Seattle, Washington
e-mail: matchbxtom@aol.com
website: members.aol.com/matchbxtom/mbclub.html

Matchbox® USA

c/o Charles Mack
62 Saw Mill Rd.
Durham, Connecticut 06422
e-mail: MTCHBOXUSA@aol.com
publication: Matchbox USA
frequency: monthly

Michiana Farm Toy Collectors Club

1701 Berkey Avenue
Goshen, Indiana 46526

Middle Tennessee Hot Wheelers

Hermitage, Tennessee
Club meets the 2nd Sunday of each month at 1:00 P.M. in the back basement of the Hermitage Church of Christ just off of Lebanon Rd. and Old Hickory Blvd., Hermitage, TN
phone: 791-7665
e-mail: illtownTN@webtv.net
contact: George B Ottley III

Milezone's Hot Wheels® Internet Club

Glendale, Arizona
Benefits:
1. 10% discount on all items sold at Milezone's
2. Bi-monthly club newsletter
3. Great trades among members
4. Placing items on the auction at no charge
5. The club car is only $5.00 (non-members pay $9.95)
6. One of the fastest growing clubs for Hot Wheels
7. More benefits as the club grows
$10 yearly fee to:
Milezone's Hot Wheels (check payable to Russ Burke)
7102 N. 43rd Ave #457
Glendale AZ 85301
e-mail: milezone@milezone.com
website: milezone.com/hwclubs.html

Mohawk Valley Hot Wheelers

Meetings are held the 2nd Wednesday of every month at:
173 Riverside Dr.
Utica, New York
For more information
e-mail: MPaulFam@aol.com (president)
GMC50@aol.com (vice president)
MZarnock@aol.com (secretary)

Mo-Kan Hot Wheelers Club

P.O. Box 892
Belton, Missouri 64012
contact: Bernie
e-mail: exokie@aol.com
website: members.aol.com/exokie/club1.htm

Motor City Hot Wheelers Club

c/o Steve and Anna Cinnamon
PO Box 55
Belleville, Michigan 48112-0055
official membership newsletter: The Informer (quarterly)
e-mail: cinman@provide.net
website: www.geocities.com/MotorCity/Speedway/8300/main.html

NAMAC (Nederlandse Algemene Miniatuur Auto Club)

P.O. Box 16004
2301 GA Leiden
Netherlands
phone: *31-715224004
fax: *31-848821387
e-mail: g.bom@home.nl
website: www.namac.nl
publication: Auto In Miniatuur (bimonthly)
swapmeet: Euretco, Meidoornkade, Houten (near Utrecht), bimonthly
Annual membership (2001):
Netherlands Dfl. 55,00
Europe Dfl. 73,00
overseas Dfl. 88,00
registration fee: Dfl. 7,50
admission swapmeet: Dfl. 7,50
Payment has to be made free of bankcharges or must be raised by Dfl. 20,00. Members receive 6x Auto In Miniatuur and also have 6x free entrance to the swapmeet.

New Jersey Diecast Collectors Club

Meets on the second Wednesday of every month at 8 pm at
Bethlehem Lutheran Church
155 Linwood Ave
Ridgewood, New Jersey
Frank Koeller, president
e-mail: njdcc@webtv.net for details or visit
homepages.msn.com/hobbyct/yaustephen

Nor Cal Hot Wheels® Collectors Club

David Lopez, president
395 E. Campbell Avenue
Campbell, California 95008
phone: 408-629-9928 eves until 10pm Pacific
e-mail: dmlopez@jps.net
Meets approx. every 6–8 weeks in various locations around the Silicon Valley and south of San Francisco. Dues are only $5 per year to cover copier costs and stamps to mail out flyers.

North Dallas Hot Wheels® Limited

801 E. Plano Parkway
Plano, Texas 75074
West side entrance, 2nd floor, first door on the left
Meets 1:00pm to 3:00/3:30pm, first Saturday of each month
e-mail: skaw@gte.net
website: members.tripod.com/ndhwl/

Ohio Matchbox® Collectors Club

Cleveland, Ohio
No cost to attend and no obligation to join the club
For details, contact Chuck
e-mail: cwwcpa@aol.com

The Penjoy Company Collectors Club

The Penjoy Company
56 Newcomer Road
Mount Joy, Pennsylvania 17552-9344
phone: 717-653-7330
fax: 717-653-2662
e-mail: penjoywm@webcom.com
website: www.penjoy.com/
new membership: $40.00; includes membership truck and four quarterly
  newsletters
renewal membership: $40.00; includes above membership truck and
  four quarterly news letters
renewal membership: $12.00; four quarterly newsletters only

Pennsylvania Matchbox® Collectors Club

c/o Mike Apnel
Kiddie Kar Kollectibles
1161 Perry
Reading, Pennsylvania 19604
frequency: monthly

Pikes Peak Hot Wheelers

Colorado Springs, Colorado
contact: Jeff Gibbs
e-mail: agibbs6848@aol.com
website: members.aol.com/agibbs6848/page2/index.htm

River Valley Hot Wheels® Collectors Association

Fort Smith, Arkansas
president: Wayne Bryson
publication: The Redliner by Sean Boyd
frequency: monthly
contact Kelly Dooley
e-mail: KrazeKelly@aol.com

Rocky Mountain Hot Wheelers Club

Denver, Colorado
contact: Lee Atherton
e-mail: CLNJAth@aol.com

Sacramento Hot Wheels® Collectors Club

Sacramento, California
Bradley Panida - club secretary / treasurer / web editor
e-mail: hotwhls@ns.net
website: www.ns.net/~psc/club

San Francisco Bay Brooklin Club

"Limited Editions" is the official newsletter of the San Francisco Bay Brook-
lin Club, produced five times each year, and including an annual list-
ing of all Brooklin models that have been made. Dues for one year
membership are $25.00 for collectors in the United States, £30.00
(US) (International Money Order/US Bank Cheque) for collectors in
Canada and overseas. Send inquiries/membership dues to:
Roger Mateo
San Francisco Bay Brooklin Club
PO Box 61018
Palo Alto, CA 94306
phone & fax: 650-591-9580
Members in the UK may send their dues of £19.00 to:
Roger Perrie
San Francisco Bay Brooklin Club
62 Morris Street
Swindon
Wiltshire
SN2 2HU
phone: + 44 (0) 1793 521652

SIKU® Collectors Club

Bluecherstrasse 10
42329 Wuppertal
Germany
e-mail: siku-club@geocities.com
website in English: www.geocities.com/MotorCity/Downs/2515/
  siku-eng.htm
website in German: www.geocities.com/MotorCity/Downs/2515/
  siku-deu.htm

Space City Hot Wheels® Collectors

Houston, Texas
club president: Chuck Gronemeyer
e-mail: chazz63@msn.com
website: www.spacecityhw.com/
contact: Paul Maner via
e-mail: paul@spacecityhw.com

West Michigan Hot Wheelers Club

c/o Michael Karp
2444 Marquette Ave.
Muskegon, Michigan 49442
website: www.waygroovy.com/redhots/html/wmhc.htm

Wheels of Fire — A Hot Wheels® Club of Arizona

Meets the fourth Saturday of most months at
Glendale Adult Day Health Care Center
6010 W. Northern Ave.
Glendale, Arizona
Established June 1996
membership: $20 per year plus $2 per adult for each meeting attended-
  Jim Sutton, chairman of the board & webpage administrator
For more information, contact:
Wheels Of Fire — A Hot Wheels Club of Arizona
P.O. Box 86431
Phoenix, Arizona 85080-6431
e-mail: JSutton666@aol.com
website: www.azneighbors.com/466
or call Valerie Griffin at (623) 848-1521

Winross® Collectors Club of America, Inc.
P.O. Box 444
Mount Joy, PA 17552-0444
phone & fax: 717-653-7327
e-mail: winrossclub@altavista.net
website: www.free-host.com/winrossclub/wcca.html

Winross® Collectors Club of Rochester, New York
P O Box 60728
Rochester NY 14606-0728

Zee Toys® Collectors Club
Contact Zed via e-mail: zeetoys@hotmail.com
website: www.geocities.com/MotorCity/4882/index.html
no membership fee, no printed newsletter

BIBLIOGRAPHY

Butler, Steve. *Promotionals 1934–1983 Dealership Vehicles in Miniature.* L-W Book Sales.

Charlie, Mack. *The Encyclopedia of Matchbox Toys, 2nd Edition.* Collector Books, August 1999.

DeSalle, Don & Barb. *Smith-Miller & Doepke Trucks, The DeSalle Collection.* L-W Book Sales, 1997.

DeSalle, *Tonka Trucks 1947–1963.* L-W Book Sales.

Force, Edward. *Classic Toy Vehicles Made in France.* Schiffer.

——. *Classic Toy Vehicles Made in Germany.* Schiffer.

——. *Classic Toy Vehicles Made in Italy.* Schiffer.

——. *Corgi Toys.* Schiffer, 1991.

——. *Dinky Toys.* Schiffer, 1996.

——. *Lledo Toys.* Schiffer, 1996.

——. *Matchbox & Lledo, 1982–1988.* Schiffer.

——. *Solido Toys, 1930–1992.* Schiffer.

Grove, Mike. *Sizzlers.*

Hutchison, Ken and Johnson, Greg. *The Golden Age of Automotive Toys 1925–1941.* Collector Books.

Johnson, Dana. *Collector's Guide to Diecast Toys and Scale Models, 2nd Edition.* Collector Books, 1998.

——. *Majorette Toys of France, 2000 Edition.*

——. *Matchbox Toys 1947 to 1998, 3rd Edition.* Collector Books.

——. *Micro Models Historical Survey and Collectors Guide.*

——. *Schuco Toys of Germany.* 1996.

——. *Siku Toys of Germany.* 1996.

——. *Tomica, Japan's Most Popular Diecast Toys.*

Kelly, Douglas R. *Diecast Price Guide.* Krause.

Mack, Charlie. *Lesney's Matchbox, The Regular Wheels Years 1947–1968.* Schiffer.

——. *Lesney's Matchbox, The Superfast Years 1968–1982.* Schiffer.

——. *Matchbox Toys, The Tyco Years 1993–1994.* Schiffer.

——. *Matchbox Toys, The Universal Years 1983–1992.* Schiffer.

Manocchi, Vincent & Wagner. Rob. *Toy Tractors.* Motorbooks International, 1996.

Manzke. *The Unauthorized Encyclopedia of Corgi Toys.* Schiffer Publishing, 1997.

O'Brien, Richard. *Collecting Toy Cars & Trucks, Second Edition.* Krause Publishing, 1997.

Pennington, Carter. *Johnny Lightnings, Topper's Original Series.* 1994.

Resch. *A World of Bus Toys & Models.* Schiffer, 1999.

Richter, David. *Tootsietoys.* Collector Books, 1996.

Schiffer. *Matchbox Toys, 1947–1982* (with 1998 updated value guide by Charlie Mack). Schiffer.

Schroeder's Collectible Toys Antique to Modern, 1999 Edition.

Tomart's Price Guide to Hot Wheels, 4th Edition. Strauss, 1968–2000.